About the Authors

William N. Lanen

Courtesy of William Lanen

William (Bill) Lanen is the KPMG Professor of Accounting Emeritus at the **University of Michigan**. He was previously on the faculty of the **Wharton School** at the **University of Pennsylvania**. He received his AB from the **University of California–Berkeley**, his MS from **Purdue University**, and his PhD from the **Wharton School**. He has taught cost accounting to undergraduates, MBA students, and executives, including in global programs in Europe, South America, Australia, Africa, and Asia. Bill has also served as the director of the Office of Action-Based Learning at the Ross School of the University of Michigan. His research focuses primarily on performance evaluation and reward systems.

Shannon W. Anderson

Courtesy of Shannon Anderson

Shannon Anderson is the Michael and Joelle Hurlston Presidential Chair and professor of management at the **University of California–Davis**. Previously she taught at **Rice University**, the **University of Melbourne**, and the **University of Michigan**. She received her PhD from **Harvard University** and a BSE from **Princeton University**. Shannon has taught undergraduate, masters, and doctoral students a variety of courses on cost accounting, cost management, and management control. Her research focuses on the design and implementation of performance measurement and cost control systems.

Michael W. Maher

Courtesy of Michael Maher

Michael Maher is a professor of management at the **University of California–Davis**. He previously taught at the **University of Michigan** and was a visiting professor at the **University of Chicago**. He received his MBA and PhD from the **University of Washington** and his BBA from **Gonzaga University** and was awarded a CPA by the State of Washington. He has published more than a dozen books, including several textbooks that have appeared in numerous editions. He has taught at all levels from undergraduate to MBA to PhD and executives. His research focuses on cost analysis in service organizations, corporate governance, and white-collar crime. In 2015, he received a Lifetime Achievement Award for his research and teaching in managerial accounting from the AICPA and the AAA.

Dedication

To my wife, Donna, and my children, Cathy and Tom, for encouragement, support, patience, and general good cheer throughout the years and to my colleagues in accounting around the world for their insights into both teaching and practice.

Bill

I dedicate this book to extraordinary public school teachers who shaped my early development, to the staff and students of The Summer Science Program of 1980, who changed my aspirations, and to my first and most influential teachers, Max and Nina Weems. I am grateful to my partner, Randy Anderson, and to my sons, Evan and David Anderson, for decades of teamwork, support, and fun.

Shannon

I dedicate this book to my wife, Kathleen; our children and their significant others; and our eight beautiful grandchildren.

Michael

Fundamentals of Cost Accounting

7e

William N. Lanen
University of Michigan

Shannon W. Anderson
University of California at Davis

Michael W. Maher
University of California at Davis

FUNDAMENTALS OF COST ACCOUNTING, SEVENTH EDITION

Published by McGraw Hill LLC, 1325 Avenue of the Americas, New York, NY 10019.
Copyright ©2023 by McGraw Hill LLC. All rights reserved. Printed in the United States of America.
Previous editions ©2020, 2017, and 2014. No part of this publication may be reproduced or distributed
in any form or by any means, or stored in a database or retrieval system, without the prior written
consent of McGraw Hill LLC, including, but not limited to, in any network or other electronic storage or
transmission, or broadcast for distance learning.

Some ancillaries, including electronic and print components, may not be available to customers outside
the United States.

This book is printed on acid-free paper.

1 2 3 4 5 6 7 8 9 LWI 26 25 24 23 22

ISBN 978-1-264-10084-2 (bound edition)
MHID 1-264-10084-1 (bound edition)
ISBN 978-1-264-46493-7 (loose-leaf edition)
MHID 1-264-46493-2 (loose-leaf edition)

Director: *Rebecca Olson*
Portfolio Manager: *Danielle McLimore*
Product Development Manager: *Michele Janicek*
Product Developer: *Kristina Dehlin*
Marketing Manager: *Lauren Schur*
Senior Content Project Managers: *Sherry Kane/Bruce Gin*
Buyer: *Rachel Hirschfield*
Designer: *Beth Blech*
Lead Content Licensing Specialist: *Melissa Homer*
Cover Image: *Matt Anderson Photography/Getty Images*
Compositor: *Straive*

All credits appearing on page or at the end of the book are considered to be an extension of the
copyright page.

Library of Congress Cataloging-in-Publication Data

Names: Lanen, William N., author. | Anderson, Shannon W., author. | Maher,
  Michael, 1946- author.
Title: Fundamentals of cost accounting / William N. Lanen, University of
  Michigan, Shannon W. Anderson, University of California at Davis,
  Michael W. Maher, University of California at Davis.
Description: 7e [edition]. | New York, NY : McGrawHill Education, [2023] |
  Includes index.
Identifiers: LCCN 2021045972 | ISBN 9781264100842 (hardcover; alk. paper)
Subjects: LCSH: Cost accounting.
Classification: LCC HF5686.C8 M224 2023 | DDC 657/.42—dc23
LC record available at https://lccn.loc.gov/2021045972

The Internet addresses listed in the text were accurate at the time of publication. The inclusion of a
website does not indicate an endorsement by the authors or McGraw Hill LLC, and McGraw Hill LLC
does not guarantee the accuracy of the information presented at these sites.

Step into the Real World

The updates and features in *Fundamentals of Cost Accounting* 7e prepare students for application beyond the classroom.

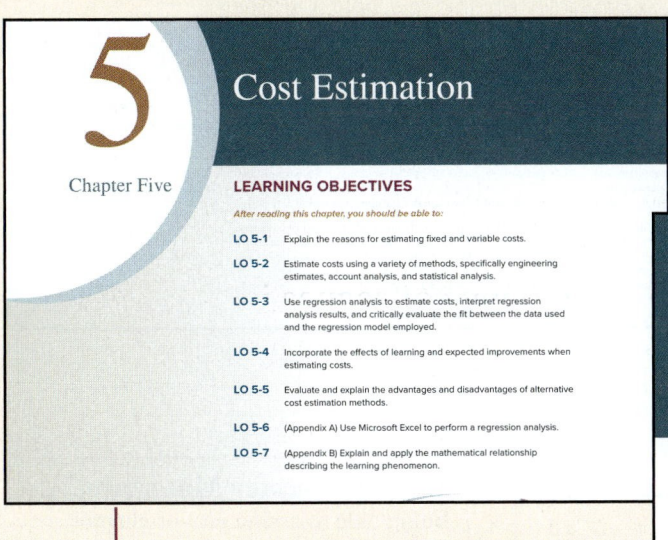

Chapter Opening Vignettes

Do your students sometimes wonder how this course connects with their future? Each chapter opens with *The Decision,* a vignette in which a decision maker needs cost accounting information to make a better decision. This sets the stage for the rest of the chapter and encourages students to think of concepts in a business context.

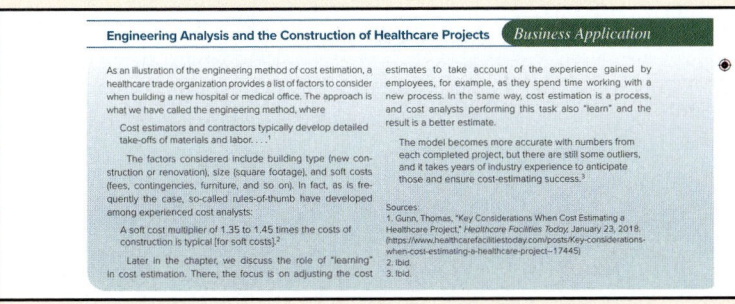

Business Application

Do your students need help connecting theory to application? The *Business Application* examples tie in to *The Decision* chapter-opening vignettes and are drawn from contemporary news reports and the authors' own experiences. They illustrate how to apply cost accounting methods and tools.

"[This text] helps students connect theory to real business application."

—Hyunpyo Kim
Shippensburg University

Key Takeaways

Do your students understand the key concepts covered in the chapter? All chapters end with a Key Takeaways feature that summarizes the primary concepts and tools in the chapter.

Key Takeaways

1. Decision making requires an understanding of cost behavior, that is, which costs are fixed and which are variable. We can use a variety of methods to determine this, including
   a. Engineering estimates, where costs are estimated from detailed specification about the inputs required.
   b. Account analysis, where cost behavior is inferred by looking at past account information.
   c. Statistical analysis, where costs are estimated by analyzing past cost data and related activity.
2. Regression analysis is a statistical method to estimate costs using past data on costs and activities to identify relationships and provide a predictive model. Regression analysis uses all information and not just select data points. It also provides statistics that can be used to assess how well the model fits the data. There are potential problems

that can arise with regression that a cost analyst needs to consider, including
   a. Nonlinear relationships, where variable costs are not proportional to activity.
   b. Influential observations (outliers) that can distort the relation because of unusual events such as labor strikes, weather disasters, or supply disruptions.
   c. Changes in the underlying process caused, for example, by a change in the production process or input mix.
   A scatter diagram of the data used in the model can be used to screen for these problems.
3. The learning phenomenon is the systematic relationship with a process and the time taken to complete the process, whether producing a product or providing a service. Failure to incorporate learning in the cost estimates when learning exists risks overstating the costs of future production.

SUMMARY

Accurate cost estimation is important to most organizations for decision-making purposes. Although no estimation method is completely accurate, some are better than others. The usefulness of a cost estimation method depends to a great extent on the user's knowledge of the business and the costs being analyzed.

The following summarizes the key ideas tied to the chapter's learning objectives:

LO 5-1 Explain the reasons for estimating fixed and variable costs. The behavior of costs, not the accounting classification, is the important distinction for decision making. Cost estimation focuses on identifying (estimating) the fixed and variable components of costs.

LO 5-2 Estimate costs using a variety of methods, specifically engineering estimates, account analysis, and statistical analysis. Cost estimates can be developed by identifying all activities and resources required to make a product or provide a service.

(LO 5-1, 2)   **5-28. Methods of Estimating Costs: Engineering Estimates**

Ferdinand Construction (FC) manages the design and construction of hospitals. Ferdinand has developed several formulas that it uses to quote jobs. These include costs of basic construction but exclude equipment and furniture. These estimates are also dependent on the purpose of the hospital (teaching hospitals are more costly to build) and location (downtown hospitals are more costly to build). Both of these are based on the building costs. The estimated costs also depend on whether the hospital has few or many stories (high-rise buildings are more expensive). The following are the cost estimates for one region in the Northeast:

End-of-Chapter Material

Being able to assign end-of-chapter material with confidence is important. The authors have tested the end-of-chapter material over time to ensure quality and consistency with the chapter content. In the seventh edition, the authors have updated virtually all exercises and problems and have added several new items.

This icon denotes questions that present ethical issues in accounting.

"This book is well written and relatable."

—John Fortune
Indiana University

What's New in the Seventh Edition?

We remain committed in the seventh edition to the same goal we have had for the previous six editions—to offer a cost accounting text that lets the student see the development of cost accounting tools and techniques as a natural response to decision making. We continue to emphasize the intuition behind concepts and work to minimize the need to "memorize." We believe that students who develop this intuition will, first, develop an appreciation of what cost accounting is about and, second, have an easier time understanding new developments that arise during their careers. Each chapter clearly establishes learning objectives, highlights numerous real-world examples, and identifies where ethical issues arise and how to think about these issues. We include examples throughout the text that illustrate how data visualization tools can be used to either illustrate the concepts or support decision making. Each chapter includes at least two end-of-chapter items that require using data analytic and data visualization tools and are based on the examples in the text.

We present the material from the perspective of both the preparer and the user of the information. We do this so that both accounting majors and those students planning other careers will appreciate the issues in preparing and using the information. The opening vignettes tie to one of the *Business Application* features in the chapter to highlight the relevance of cost accounting to today's business problems. All chapters end with *Key Takeaways* that summarize the core concepts of the chapter.

The end-of-chapter material has increased by about 10 percent overall. In addition, names and data for virtually all existing exercises and problems are changed from previous editions. We have also added video walkthroughs in Connect for select end-of-chapter material.

Finally, we have retained the clear writing style that is frequently cited as a strength of the text.

Chapter-Specific Changes

1 Cost Accounting: Information for Decision Making

- New section on "Critical Thinking and Data Analytics."
- Illustration of data visualization using Microsoft Excel, Tableau, and Microsoft PowerBI.
- One new *Business Application.*
- Updated discussion and examples on Trends in Cost Accounting.
- Two new exercises.
- Two new problems.

2 Cost Concepts and Behavior

- One new and one updated *Business Application.*
- Two new exercises.
- Four new problems.

3 Fundamentals of Cost-Volume-Profit Analysis

- One new and one updated *Business Application.*
- New section on "Data Analytics and CVP Analysis."
- Five new exercises.
- Three new problems.

4 Fundamentals of Cost Analysis for Decision Making

- Two new *Business Applications.*
- Seven new exercises.
- Five new problems.

5 Cost Estimation

- Three new *Business Applications.*
- Revised discussion of the learning effect.
- Ten new exercises.

6 Fundamentals of Product and Service Costing

- One new *Business Application*.
- Eleven new exercises.
- Two new problems.

7 Job Costing

- New section on "Choosing the Time Period for Computing the Predetermined Overhead Rate" using graphs to illustrate the effect of different choices.
- One new *Business Application*.
- One new exercise.
- Six new problems.

8 Process Costing

- Four new exercises.
- Two new problems.

9 Activity-Based Costing

- Data visualizations illustrating the effect of alternative costing methods.
- Two new *Business Applications*.
- Four new exercises.
- Three new problems.

10 Fundamentals of Cost Management

- Five new *Business Applications*.
- Eight new exercises.
- Two new problems.

11 Service Department and Joint Cost Allocation

- New visualizations illustrating the effect of alternative costing methods.
- One new *Business Application*.
- Two new exercises.
- Two new problems.

12 Fundamentals of Management Control Systems

- Data visualizations illustrating the effect of alternative allocation methods.
- Three new *Business Applications*.
- Two new exercises.
- Four new problems.

13 Planning and Budgeting

- New appendix on zero-based budgeting.
- Three new *Business Applications*.
- Two new exercises.
- Two new problems.

14 Business Unit Performance Measurement

- Data visualizations to illustrate the sensitivity of EVA results to the assumed cost-of-capital.
- Three new *Business Applications*.
- Four new exercises.
- Two new problems.

15 Transfer Pricing

- Material previously in an appendix moved into text.
- Data visualizations to illustrate the choice of the appropriate transfer price.
- One new and one updated *Business Application*.
- One new exercise.
- Two new problems.

16 Fundamentals of Variance Analysis

- Data visualizations to illustrate the relative importance of different variances.
- One new *Business Application*.
- Two new exercises.
- Two new problems.

17 Additional Topics in Variance Analysis

- New section on "Monitoring Variances with Charts."
- One new and one updated *Business Application*.
- Three new exercises.
- Three new problems.

18 Performance Measurement to Support Business Strategy

- New section on "Using the Balanced Scorecard to Monitor Performance," with data visualizations.
- Two new *Business Applications*.
- Three new exercises.
- Three new problems.

Appendix Capital Investment Decisions: An Overview

- New example for illustrating the principles of capital investment analysis.
- Additional discount rates added to present value tables.
- Revised exercises and problems.

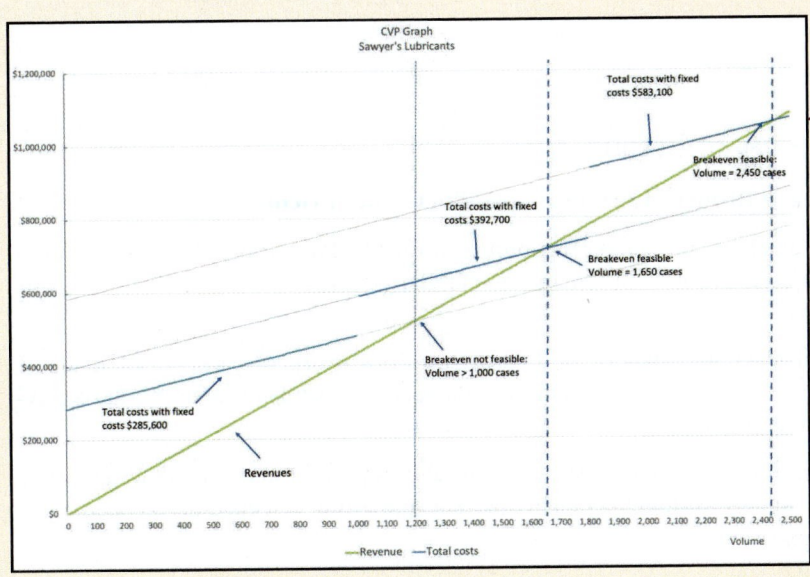

New! Data Visualizations Based on Chapter Concepts

Throughout the text, students are introduced to how data visualizations can be used to communicate the results of their analyses to decision makers. End-of-chapter material allows the students to develop their own visualizations based on their analysis of the problem.

New! Integrated Excel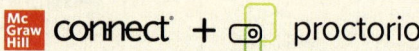

Integrated Excel assignments pair the power of Microsoft Excel with the power of Connect. A seamless integration of Excel within Connect, Integrated Excel questions allow students to work in live, auto-graded Excel spreadsheets—no additional logins, no need to upload or download files. Instructors can choose to grade by formula or solution value, and students receive instant cell-level feedback via integrated Check My Work functionality.

New! Guided Examples

The Guided Example, or "Hint," videos in Connect provide a narrated, step-by-step walkthrough of exercises that are similar to those being assigned, providing reinforcement when students need it most. These short presentations can be turned on or off by instructors.

Proctorio

McGraw Hill connect + proctorio

Remote Proctoring & Browser-Locking Capabilities

Remote proctoring and browser-locking capabilities, hosted by Proctorio within Connect, provide control of the assessment environment by enabling security options and verifying the identity of the student.

Seamlessly integrated within Connect, these services allow instructors to control students' assessment experience by restricting browser activity, recording students' activity, and verifying students are doing their own work.

Instant and detailed reporting gives instructors an at-a-glance view of potential academic integrity concerns, thereby avoiding personal bias and supporting evidence-based claims.

ReadAnywhere

Read or study when it's convenient for you with McGraw Hill's free ReadAnywhere app. Available for iOS or Android smartphones or tablets, ReadAnywhere gives users access to McGraw Hill tools including the eBook and SmartBook 2.0 or Adaptive Learning Assignments in Connect. Take notes, highlight, and complete assignments offline—all of your work will sync when you open the app with WiFi access. Log in with your McGraw Hill Connect username and password to start learning—anytime, anywhere!

New! OLC-Aligned Courses

Implementing High-Quality Online Instruction and Assessment through Preconfigured Courseware

In consultation with the Online Learning Consortium (OLC) and our certified Faculty Consultants, McGraw Hill has created preconfigured courseware using OLC's quality scorecard to align with best practices in online course delivery. This turnkey courseware contains a combination of formative assessments, summative assessments, homework, and application activities, and can easily be customized to meet an individual's needs and course outcomes. For more information, visit www.mheducation.com/highered/olc.

Tegrity: Lectures 24/7

Tegrity in Connect is a tool that makes class time available 24/7 by automatically capturing every lecture. With a simple one-click start-and-stop process, you capture all computer screens and corresponding audio in a format that is easy to search, frame by frame. Students can replay any part of any class with easy-to-use, browser-based viewing on a PC, Mac, iPod, or other mobile device.

Educators know that the more students can see, hear, and experience class resources, the better they learn. In fact, studies prove it. Tegrity's unique search feature helps students efficiently find what they need, when they need it, across an entire semester of class recordings. Help turn your students' study time into learning moments immediately supported by your lecture. With Tegrity, you also increase intent listening and class participation by easing students' concerns about note-taking. Using Tegrity in Connect will make it more likely you will see students' faces, not the tops of their heads.

Test Builder in Connect

Available within Connect, Test Builder is a cloud-based tool that enables instructors to format tests that can be printed, administered within a Learning Management System, or exported as a Word document of the test bank. Test Builder offers a modern, streamlined interface for easy content configuration that matches course needs, without requiring a download.

Test Builder allows you to
- access all test bank content from a particular title.
- easily pinpoint the most relevant content through robust filtering options.
- manipulate the order of questions or scramble questions and/or answers.
- pin questions to a specific location within a test.
- determine your preferred treatment of algorithmic questions.
- choose the layout and spacing.
- add instructions and configure default settings.

Test Builder provides a secure interface for better protection of content and allows for just-in-time updates to flow directly into assessments.

Writing Assignment

Available within Connect and Connect Master, the Writing Assignment tool delivers a learning experience to help students improve their written communication skills and conceptual understanding. As an instructor, you can assign, monitor, grade, and provide feedback on writing more efficiently and effectively.

Create
Your Book, Your Way

McGraw Hill's Content Collections Powered by Create® is a self-service website that enables instructors to create custom course materials—print and eBooks—by drawing upon McGraw Hill's comprehensive, cross-disciplinary content. Choose what you want from our high-quality textbooks, articles, and cases. Combine it with your own content quickly and easily, and tap into other rights-secured, third-party content such as readings, cases, and articles. Content can be arranged in a way that makes the most sense for your course, and you can include the course name and information as well. Choose the best format for your course: color print, black-and-white print, or eBook. The eBook can be included in your Connect course and is available on the free ReadAnywhere app for smartphone or tablet access as well. When you are finished customizing, you will receive a free digital copy to review in just minutes! Visit McGraw Hill Create®—www.mcgrawhillcreate.com—today and begin building!

Instructors: Student Success Starts with You

Tools to enhance your unique voice

Want to build your own course? No problem. Prefer to use an OLC-aligned, prebuilt course? Easy. Want to make changes throughout the semester? Sure. And you'll save time with Connect's auto-grading too.

65%
Less Time Grading

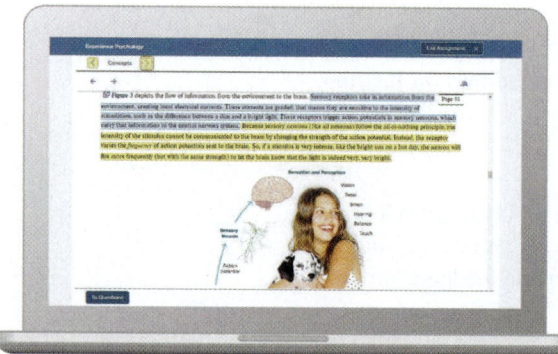

Laptop: McGraw Hill; Woman/dog: George Doyle/Getty Images

Study made personal

Incorporate adaptive study resources like SmartBook® 2.0 into your course and help your students be better prepared in less time. Learn more about the powerful personalized learning experience available in SmartBook 2.0 at **www.mheducation.com/highered/connect/smartbook**

Affordable solutions, added value

Make technology work for you with LMS integration for single sign-on access, mobile access to the digital textbook, and reports to quickly show you how each of your students is doing. And with our Inclusive Access program you can provide all these tools at a discount to your students. Ask your McGraw Hill representative for more information.

Padlock: Jobalou/Getty Images

Solutions for your challenges

A product isn't a solution. Real solutions are affordable, reliable, and come with training and ongoing support when you need it and how you want it. Visit **www.supportateverystep.com** for videos and resources both you and your students can use throughout the semester.

Checkmark: Jobalou/Getty Images

SUPPORT AT every step

Students: Get Learning That Fits You

Effective tools for efficient studying

Connect is designed to help you be more productive with simple, flexible, intuitive tools that maximize your study time and meet your individual learning needs. Get learning that works for you with Connect.

Study anytime, anywhere

Download the free ReadAnywhere app and access your online eBook, SmartBook 2.0, or Adaptive Learning Assignments when it's convenient, even if you're offline. And since the app automatically syncs with your Connect account, all of your work is available every time you open it. Find out more at **www.mheducation.com/readanywhere**

> *"I really liked this app—it made it easy to study when you don't have your text-book in front of you."*
>
> - Jordan Cunningham,
> Eastern Washington University

Calendar: owattaphotos/Getty Images

Everything you need in one place

Your Connect course has everything you need—whether reading on your digital eBook or completing assignments for class, Connect makes it easy to get your work done.

Learning for everyone

McGraw Hill works directly with Accessibility Services Departments and faculty to meet the learning needs of all students. Please contact your Accessibility Services Office and ask them to email accessibility@mheducation.com, or visit **www.mheducation.com/about/accessibility** for more information.

Top: Jenner Images/Getty Images. Left: Hero Images/Getty Images, Right: Hero Images/Getty Images

Acknowledgments

A special thank you

To the following individuals who helped develop and critique the ancillary package: Patti Lopez for accuracy checking the manuscript, solutions manual, Connect, and SmartBook; Mark Sears for accuracy checking Connect; Stacie Hughes for updating the test bank and SmartBook; William Lyle for accuracy checking the test bank, and preparing the instructor's manual and PowerPoint slides; Crystal Cleary for accuracy checking the PowerPoint slides; and Eric Weinstein for accuracy checking the Guided Example videos.

We are grateful for the outstanding support of McGraw Hill. In particular, we would like to thank Rebecca Olson, Senior Portfolio Director; Danielle McLimore, Associate Portfolio Manager; Michele Janicek, Product Development Manager; Kristina Dehlin and Destiny Hadley, Product Developers; Kevin Moran, Associate Director of Digital Content; Xin Lin, Lead Project Manager; Sarah Sacco, Product Coordinator; Lauren Schur, Executive Marketing Manager; Natalie King, Director of Marketing; Sherry Kane and Bruce Gin, Content Project Managers; Rachel Hirschfield, Buyer; Melissa Homer, Content Licensing Specialist; and Laurie Entringer, Designer.

We also want to recognize the valuable input of all those dedicated instructors who helped guide our editorial and pedagogical decisions for the seventh edition:

John Fortune, *Indiana University–Southeast*

Hyunpyo Kim, *Shippensburg University*

Chuo-Hsuan (Jason) Lee, *SUNY Plattsburgh*

Tota Panggabean, *PhD, California State University–Sacramento*

Stephanie Anne Rowe, *Sacramento City College*

Ronald Rubenfield, *Robert Morris University*

Susan T. Sadowski, *University of Maryland Global Campus*

Liang Song, *University of Massachusetts–Dartmouth*

Tracy L. Stant, *Indian River State College*

Inna Voytsekhivska, *Western Michigan University*

We are equally grateful to the reviewers over the past six editions who have helped inform the development of this text, and whose ideas have aided thousands of students.

Brief Contents

INTRODUCTION AND OVERVIEW

One   Cost Accounting: Information for Decision Making   2

Two   Cost Concepts and Behavior   44

COST ANALYSIS AND ESTIMATION

Three   Fundamentals of Cost-Volume-Profit Analysis   96

Four   Fundamentals of Cost Analysis for Decision Making   134

Five   Cost Estimation   190

COST MANAGEMENT SYSTEMS

Six   Fundamentals of Product and Service Costing   244

Seven   Job Costing   280

Eight   Process Costing   334

Nine   Activity-Based Costing   384

Ten   Fundamentals of Cost Management   446

Eleven   Service Department and Joint Cost Allocation   494

MANAGEMENT CONTROL SYSTEMS

Twelve   Fundamentals of Management Control Systems   546

Thirteen   Planning and Budgeting   590

Fourteen   Business Unit Performance Measurement   644

Fifteen   Transfer Pricing   688

Sixteen   Fundamentals of Variance Analysis   730

Seventeen   Additional Topics in Variance Analysis   784

Eighteen   Performance Measurement to Support Business Strategy   828

Appendix   Capital Investment Decisions: An Overview   A-1

Glossary   G-1

Index   IND-1

Contents

Step into the Real World v

1

Cost Accounting: Information for Decision Making 2

  Business Application: *Understanding Costs in a Small Business* 3

Value Creation in Organizations 3

  Why Start with Value Creation? 3

  Value Chain 4

  Supply Chain and Distribution Chain 5

  Business Application: *Choosing Where to Operate in the Supply Chain* 5

  Using Cost Information to Increase Value 5

  Accounting and the Value Chain 6

Accounting Systems 6

  Financial Accounting 6

  Cost Accounting 6

  Cost Accounting, GAAP, and IFRS 7

  Customers of Cost Accounting 7

Key Financial Players in the Organization 8

Our Framework for Assessing Cost Accounting Systems 9

  The Manager's Job Is to Make Decisions 9

  Decision Making Requires Information 9

  Finding and Eliminating Activities That Don't Add Value 9

  Identifying Strategic Opportunities Using Cost Analysis 10

  Owners Use Cost Information to Evaluate Managers 10

Cost Data for Managerial Decisions 11

  Costs for Decision Making 11

  Business Application: *Reducing Costs by Making Small Changes* 12

  Costs for Control and Evaluation 12

  Different Data for Different Decisions 14

Trends in Cost Accounting and Business Decisions 15

  Cost Accounting in the Value Chain 15

  Creating Value in the Organization 15

  Enterprise Resource Planning 15

  Critical Thinking and Data Analytics 16

  Applying the Framework 18

Choices: Ethical Issues for Accountants 21

  What Makes Ethics So Important? 21

  IMA Code of Ethics 21

  The Sarbanes-Oxley Act of 2002 and Ethics 22

  Business Application: *Accounting Decisions at Tesco: Choices and Consequences* 23

Cost Accounting and Other Business Disciplines 23

  Key Takeaways 23

Summary 24

Key Terms 24

Review Questions 24

Critical Analysis and Discussion Questions 25

Exercises 26

Problems 31

Integrative Cases 40

Solutions to Self-Study Questions 42

2

Cost Concepts and Behavior   44

What Is a Cost?   46

Cost versus Expenses   46

Presentation of Costs in Financial Statements   47

Service Organizations   47

Retail and Wholesale Companies   47

Business Application: *Components of Cost of Goods Sold for a Retailer*   49

Manufacturing Companies   50

Direct and Indirect Manufacturing (Product) Costs   50

Prime Costs and Conversion Costs   51

Nonmanufacturing (Period) Costs   51

Cost Allocation   52

Direct versus Indirect Costs   53

Business Application: *Indirect Costs and Allocating Costs to Contracts*   53

Details of Manufacturing Cost Flows   54

How Costs Flow through the Statements   55

Income Statements   55

Cost of Goods Manufactured and Sold   56

Direct Materials   56

Work in Process   56

Finished Goods Inventory   57

Cost of Goods Manufactured and Sold Statement   57

Cost Behavior   58

Fixed versus Variable Costs   58

Components of Product Costs   60

Unit Fixed Costs Can Be Misleading for Decision Making   61

Business Application: *The Importance of Gross Margin*   64

How to Make Cost Information More Useful for Managers   65

Gross Margin versus Contribution Margin Income Statements   65

Developing Financial Statements for Decision Making   66

Key Takeaways   67

Summary   67

Key Terms   69

Review Questions   69

Critical Analysis and Discussion Questions   69

Exercises   70

Problems   81

Integrative Case   92

Solutions to Self-Study Questions   93

3

Fundamentals of Cost–Volume–Profit Analysis   96

Cost–Volume–Profit Analysis   97

Business Application: *How "Big Oil" Uses Break-Even Analysis*   97

Profit Equation   98

CVP Example   99

Graphic Presentation   102

Profit–Volume Model   103

Use of CVP to Analyze the Effect of Different Cost Structures   104

Business Application: *Operating Leverage as a Framework to Describe a Business Model*   105

Margin of Safety   105

CVP Analysis with Spreadsheets   106

Extensions of the CVP Model   107

Income Taxes   107

Multiproduct CVP Analysis   108

Alternative Cost Structures   109

Assumptions and Limitations of CVP Analysis   110

Data Analytics and CVP Analysis   110

Key Takeaways   111

Summary   111

Key Terms   112

Review Questions   112

Critical Analysis and Discussion Questions   113

Exercises   113

Problems   120

Integrative Case   130

Solutions to Self-Study Questions   132

4

Fundamentals of Cost Analysis for Decision Making   134

Business Application: *Outsourcing and the Effect of Corporate Culture*   135

Differential Analysis   136

Differential Costs versus Total Costs   137

Differential Analysis and Pricing Decisions   137

Short-Run versus Long-Run Pricing Decisions   138

Short-Run Pricing Decisions: Special Orders   138

Long-Run Pricing Decisions   140

Long-Run versus Short-Run Pricing: Is There a Difference?   141

Cost Analysis for Pricing   141

Legal Issues Relating to Costs and Sales Prices   142

Predatory Pricing   142

Dumping   143

Price Discrimination   143

Peak-Load Pricing   143

Price-Fixing   144

Use of Differential Analysis for Production Decisions   144

Make-It or Buy-It Decisions   144

Make-or-Buy Decisions Involving Differential Fixed Costs   145

Opportunity Costs of Making   148

Business Application: *Insourcing*   150

Decision to Add or Drop a Product Line or Close a Business Unit   150

Product Choice Decisions   152

The Theory of Constraints   156

Key Takeaways   158

Summary   158

Key Terms   158

Review Questions   159

Critical Analysis and Discussion Questions   159

Exercises   160

Problems   168

Integrative Cases   185

Solutions to Self-Study Questions   187

5

Cost Estimation   190

Why Estimate Costs?   191

Business Application: *Data Analytics for Managing Operations and Forecasting Revenue*   191

Basic Cost Behavior Patterns   191

What Methods Are Used to Estimate Cost Behavior?   192

Engineering Method   192

Business Application: *Engineering Analysis and the Construction of Healthcare Projects*   193

Account Analysis Method   193

Statistical Cost Estimation   195

Multiple Regression   200

Practical Implementation Problems   201

Learning Phenomenon   204

Business Application: *The Importance of Learning and Reduced Costs*   204

Applications   206

How Is an Estimation Method Chosen?   206

Data Problems   207

Effect of Different Methods on Cost Estimates   208

Key Takeaways   209

Summary   209

Key Terms   210

Appendix A: Regression Analysis Using Microsoft Excel®   210

Appendix B: Learning Curves   215

Review Questions   216

Critical Analysis and Discussion Questions   217

Exercises   218

Problems   228

Integrative Cases   240

Solutions to Self-Study Questions   242

6

Fundamentals of Product and Service Costing   244

Cost Management Systems   245

Reasons to Calculate Product or Service Costs   245

Business Application: *Who's Responsible for These Costs?*   246

Cost Allocation and Product Costing 247

Cost Flow Diagram 247

Fundamental Themes Underlying the Design of Cost Systems for Managerial Purposes 248

Costing in a Single-Product, Continuous Process Industry 248

Basic Cost Flow Model 248

Costing with No Work-in-Process Inventories 249

Costing with Ending Work-in-Process Inventories 249

Costing in a Multiple-Product, Discrete Process Industry 250

Predetermined Overhead Rates 252

Product Costing of Multiple Products 252

Choice of the Allocation Base for Predetermined Overhead Rate 253

Choosing among Possible Allocation Bases 254

Multiple Allocation Bases and Two-Stage Systems 255

Choice of Allocation Bases 255

Different Companies, Different Production and Costing Systems 256

Operations Costing: An Illustration 258

Key Takeaways 259

Summary 260

Key Terms 260

Review Questions 261

Critical Analysis and Discussion Questions 261

Exercises 261

Problems 270

Integrative Cases 274

Solutions to Self-Study Questions 277

7

Job Costing 280

Defining a Job 281

Using Accounting Records in a Job Shop 282

Computing the Cost of a Job 282

Production Process at Gupta Designs 282

Records of Costs at Gupta Designs 282

How Manufacturing Overhead Costs Are Recorded at Gupta Designs 286

The Job Cost Sheet 288

Over- and Underapplied Overhead 289

An Alternative Method of Recording and Applying Manufacturing Overhead 290

Multiple Allocation Bases: The Two-Stage Approach 296

Summary of Steps in a Job Costing System 296

Using Job Costing in Service Organizations 296

Ethical Issues and Job Costing 298

Misstating the Stage of Completion 299

Charging Costs to the Wrong Jobs 299

Business Application: *Cost Allocation and Government Contracts* 299

Misrepresenting the Cost of Jobs 299

Managing Projects 301

Business Application: *Fraudulent Reporting of Project Completion to Improve Financial Performance* 301

Key Takeaways 302

Summary 303

Key Terms 304

Review Questions 304

Critical Analysis and Discussion Questions 304

Exercises 305

Problems 315

Integrative Cases 330

Solutions to Self-Study Questions 333

8

Process Costing 334

Determining Equivalent Units 335

Using Product Costing in a Process Industry 337

Step 1: Measure the Physical Flow of Resources 337

Step 2: Compute the Equivalent Units of Production 337

Business Application: *Overstating Equivalent Units to Commit Fraud* 338

Step 3: Identify the Product Costs for Which to Account 339

Required: An Assumption about Costs and the Work-in-Process Inventory 339

Step 4: Compute the Costs per Equivalent Unit: Weighted Average   340

Step 5: Assign Product Cost to Batches of Work: Weighted-Average Process Costing   341

Reporting This Information to Managers: The Production Cost Report   341

Sections 1 and 2: Managing the Physical Flow of Units   343

Sections 3, 4, and 5: Managing Costs   343

Assigning Costs Using First-In, First-Out (FIFO) Process Costing   343

Step 1: Measure the Physical Flow of Resources   344

Step 2: Compute the Equivalent Units of Production   344

Step 3: Identify the Product Costs for Which to Account   346

Step 4: Compute the Costs per Equivalent Unit: FIFO   346

Step 5: Assign Product Cost to Batches of Work: FIFO   347

How This Looks in T-Accounts   347

Determining Which Is Better: FIFO or Weighted Average?   348

Computing Product Costs: Summary of the Steps   348

Using Costs Transferred in from Prior Departments   349

Who Is Responsible for Costs Transferred in from Prior Departments?   350

Choosing between Job and Process Costing   352

Operations Costing   352

Product Costing in Operations   353

Operations Costing Illustration   353

Comparing Job, Process, and Operations Costing   355

Key Takeaways   356

Summary   356

Key Terms   357

Review Questions   357

Critical Analysis and Discussion Questions   358

Exercises   358

Problems   367

Integrative Cases   378

Solutions to Self-Study Questions   379

9

Activity-Based Costing   384

Reported Product Costs and Decision Making   385

Dropping a Product   385

The Death Spiral   387

Business Application: *The Death Spiral*   388

Two-Stage Cost Allocation   388

Two-Stage Cost Allocation and the Choice of Cost Drivers   390

Plantwide versus Department-Specific Rates   392

Choice of Cost Allocation Methods: A Cost-Benefit Decision   393

Activity-Based Costing   394

Developing Activity-Based Costs   394

Cost Hierarchies   396

Activity-Based Costing Illustrated   397

Step 1: Identify the Activities   397

Step 2: Identify the Cost Drivers   398

Step 3: Compute the Cost Driver Rates   398

Step 4: Assign Costs Using Activity-Based Costing   398

Unit Costs Compared   399

Cost Flows through Accounts   401

Choice of Activity Bases in Modern Production Settings   403

Business Application: *ABC in Health Care*   404

Activity-Based Costing in Administration   404

Who Uses ABC?   405

Time-Driven Activity-Based Costing   406

Developing Time-Driven Activity-Based Costs   406

Business Application: *What Are a Hospital's Costs?*   408

Extensions of TDABC   408

Key Takeaways   409

Summary   409

Key Terms   410

Review Questions   410
Critical Analysis and Discussion Questions   411
Exercises   411
Problems   424
Integrative Cases   437
Solutions to Self-Study Questions   443

10
Fundamentals of Cost Management   446

Using Activity-Based Cost Management to Add Value   447

Business Application: *Responding to a Sudden Drop in Resources*   448

Using Activity-Based Cost Information to Improve Processes   448

Using Activity-Based Cost Management in a Service Setting   449

Lean Manufacturing and Activity-Based Cost Management   449

Business Application: *The Costs of Lean Production*   450

Using Cost Hierarchies   451

Managing the Cost of Customers and Suppliers   451

Business Application: *Customer Profitability—Revenue and Cost Effects*   452

Using Activity-Based Costing to Determine the Cost of Customers and Suppliers   452

Determining Why the Cost of Customers Matters   455

Using Cost of Customer Information to Manage Costs   455

Business Application: *Managing the Customer Portfolio for Profit*   456

Determining the Cost of Suppliers   456

Capturing the Cost Savings   457

Managing the Cost of Capacity   458

Using and Supplying Resources   458

Computing the Cost of Unused Capacity   460

Assigning the Cost of Unused Capacity   462

Seasonal Demand and the Cost of Unused Capacity   462

Business Application: *Managing Excess Capacity Resources—The Case of Employees*   464

Managing the Cost of Quality   465

How Can We Limit Conflict between Traditional Managerial Accounting Systems and Total Quality Management?   465

What Is Quality?   466

What Is the Cost of Quality?   466

Trade-Offs, Quality Control, and Failure Costs   467

Business Application: *Technology, Data Analysis, Customer Profitability, and Cost of Quality*   469

Key Takeaways   470

Summary   471
Key Terms   472
Review Questions   472
Critical Analysis and Discussion Questions   472
Exercises   473
Problems   484
Integrative Cases   492
Solutions to Self-Study Questions   493

11
Service Department and Joint Cost Allocation   494

Service Department Cost Allocation   495

Methods of Allocating Service Department Costs   497

Allocation Bases   497

Direct Method   498

Step Method   500

Reciprocal Method   503

Comparison of Direct, Step, and Reciprocal Methods   506

The Reciprocal Method and Decision Making   507

Business Application: *The Risks of Outsourcing a Service Center*   509

Allocation of Joint Costs   510

Joint Costing Defined   510

Reasons for Allocating Joint Costs   510

Joint Cost Allocation Methods   511

Net Realizable Value Method   511

Physical Quantities Method   514

Evaluation of Joint Cost Methods   514

Deciding Whether to Sell Goods Now or Process Them Further 515

   Business Application: *Different Demands for Different Parts* 516

Deciding What to Do with By-Products 516

   Key Takeaways 517

Summary 518

Key Terms 519

Appendix: Calculation of the Reciprocal Method Using Computer Spreadsheets 519

Review Questions 521

Critical Analysis and Discussion Questions 522

Exercises 522

Problems 529

Integrative Case 540

Solutions to Self-Study Questions 541

12

Fundamentals of Management Control Systems 546

Why a Management Control System? 547

   Alignment of Managerial and Organizational Interests 547

   Evolution of the Control Problem: An Example 548

Decentralized Organizations 548

   Why Decentralize the Organization? 548

   Advantages of Decentralization 549

   Disadvantages of Decentralization 549

   Business Application: *Centralizing as a Cost-Cutting Approach* 550

Framework for Evaluating Management Control Systems 551

   Organizational Environment and Strategy 551

   Results of the Management Control System 551

   Elements of a Management Control System 552

   Balancing the Elements 552

Delegated Decision Authority: Responsibility Accounting 553

   Cost Centers 553

   Revenue Centers 554

   Profit Centers 554

   Investment Centers 554

   Responsibility Centers and Organization Structure 555

Measuring Performance 555

   Two Basic Questions 556

   Cost Centers 556

   Revenue Centers 557

   Profit Centers 557

   Investment Centers 557

Evaluating Performance 558

   Relative Performance versus Absolute Performance Standards 558

   Evaluating Managers' Performance versus Economic Performance of the Responsibility Center 558

   Relative Performance Evaluations in Organizations 559

Compensation Systems 559

   Business Application: *Beware of the "Kink"* 560

Illustration: Corporate Cost Allocation 560

   Business Application: *Why Allocate Corporate Costs?* 561

   Incentive Problems with Allocated Costs 562

   Effective Corporate Cost Allocation System 562

Do Performance Evaluation Systems Create Incentives to Commit Fraud? 564

   Business Application: *Performance Incentives and Accounting Manipulation* 565

Internal Controls to Protect Assets and Provide Quality Information 566

   Business Application: *When the Internal Control System Fails* 567

   Internal Auditing 567

   Key Takeaways 567

Summary 568

Key Terms 569

Review Questions 569

Critical Analysis and Discussion Questions 570

Exercises 571

Problems 576

Integrative Cases 584

Solutions to Self-Study Questions 587

13

Planning and Budgeting   590

How Strategic Planning Increases Competitiveness   591

Overall Plan   592

Organization Goals   592

Strategic Long-Range Profit Plan   592

Master Budget (Tactical Short-Range Profit Plan): Tying the Strategic Plan to the Operating Plan   592

Business Application: *Planning and Budgeting in a Time of Great Uncertainty*   593

Human Element in Budgeting   594

Value of Employee Participation   594

Developing the Master Budget   595

Where to Start?   595

Sales Forecasting   595

Business Application: *Using AI to Enhance Sales Predictions*   597

Comprehensive Illustration   598

Forecasting Production   598

Forecasting Production Costs   599

Direct Labor   600

Overhead   600

Completing the Budgeted Cost of Goods Sold   601

Revising the Initial Budget   602

Marketing and Administrative Budget   602

Pulling It Together into the Income Statement   603

Key Relationships: The Sales Cycle   604

Using Cash Flow Budgets to Estimate Cash Needs   605

Multiperiod Cash Flows   605

Planning for the Assets and Liabilities on the Budgeted Balance Sheets   607

Big Picture: How It All Fits Together   608

Budgeting in Retail and Wholesale Organizations   609

Budgeting in Service Organizations   610

Ethical Problems in Budgeting   610

Business Application: *"Budgeting in Government Agencies"*   611

Budgeting under Uncertainty   611

Key Takeaways   614

Summary   614

Key Terms   615

Appendix: Zero-Based Budgeting   615

Business Application: *Current Experiences with Zero-Based Budgeting*   619

Review Questions   619

Critical Analysis and Discussion Questions   619

Exercises   620

Problems   630

Integrative Cases   639

Solutions to Self-Study Questions   641

14

Business Unit Performance Measurement   644

Divisional Performance Measurement   645

Business Application: *What Performance Measure(s) Do Companies Use?*   646

Accounting Income   646

Computing Divisional Income   646

Advantages and Disadvantages of Divisional Income   647

Some Simple Financial Ratios   647

Return on Investment   648

Performance Measures for Control: A Short Detour   649

Limitations of ROI   650

Business Application: *Performance Measurement at Walmart*   653

Residual Income Measures   653

Limitations of Residual Income   654

Economic Value Added (EVA)   655

Business Application: *EVA as a Performance Measure*   657

Limitations of EVA   657

Divisional Performance Measurement: A Summary   660

Measuring the Investment Base   660

Gross Book Value versus Net Book Value   661

Historical Cost versus Current Cost   661

Beginning, Ending, or Average Balance   663

Other Issues in Divisional Performance Measurement   664

Key Takeaways   664

Summary   664

Key Terms   665

Review Questions   665

Critical Analysis and Discussion Questions   665

Exercises   666

Problems   672

Integrative Cases   680

Solutions to Self-Study Questions   686

15

Transfer Pricing   688

What Is Transfer Pricing and Why Is It Important?   689

Business Application: *Pricing Intellectual Property in Multinational Tech Companies*   691

Determining the Optimal Transfer Price   691

The Setting   691

Determining Whether a Transfer Price Is Optimal   692

Case 1: A Perfect Intermediate Market for Milk   693

Case 2: No Intermediate Market   694

Optimal Transfer Price: A General Principle   698

Other Market Conditions   698

Applying the General Principle   699

How to Help Managers Achieve Their Goals While Achieving the Organization's Goals   700

Top-Management Intervention in Transfer Pricing   700

Centrally Established Transfer Price Policies   701

Establishing a Market Price Policy   701

Establishing a Cost-Based Policy   701

Alternative Cost Measures   702

Remedying Motivational Problems of Transfer Pricing Policies   703

Negotiating the Transfer Price   704

Imperfect Markets   704

Global Practices   705

Multinational Transfer Pricing   705

Business Application: *Tax Considerations in Transfer Pricing*   707

Segment Reporting   707

Business Application: *Transfer Pricing at Weyerhaeuser*   708

Key Takeaways   708

Summary   709

Key Terms   709

Review Questions   709

Critical Analysis and Discussion Questions   710

Exercises   710

Problems   716

Integrative Cases   725

Solutions to Self-Study Questions   728

16

Fundamentals of Variance Analysis   730

Using Budgets for Performance Evaluation   731

Profit Variance   732

Business Application: *When a Favorable Variance Might Not Mean "Good" News*   733

Why Are Actual and Budgeted Results Different?   734

Flexible Budgeting   734

Comparing Budgets and Results   735

Sales Activity Variance   735

Profit Variance Analysis as a Key Tool for Managers   737

Sales Price Variance   737

Variable Production Cost Variances   737

Fixed Production Cost Variance   737

Marketing and Administrative Variances   737

Visualizing Profit Variances   739

Performance Measurement and Control in a Cost Center   740

Variable Production Costs   740

Variable Cost Variance Analysis   741

General Model   741

Direct Materials   743

Direct Labor   745

Variable Production Overhead   747

Variable Cost Variances Summarized in Graphic Form   748

Fixed Cost Variances   749

Fixed Cost Variances with Variable Costing   749

Visualizing Cost Variances   750

Absorption Costing: The Production Volume Variance   750

Summary of Overhead Variances   753

Key Points   754

Business Application: *Does Standard Costing Lead to Overproduction?*   754

Key Takeaways   754

Summary   755

Key Terms   756

Appendix: Recording Costs in a Standard Cost System   756

Review Questions   760

Critical Analysis and Discussion Questions   760

Exercises   761

Problems   769

Integrative Cases   778

Solutions to Self-Study Questions   782

17

Additional Topics in Variance Analysis   784

Profit Variance Analysis When Units Produced Do Not Equal Units Sold   785

Reconciling Variable Costing Budgets and Full Absorption Income Statements   786

Materials Purchases Do Not Equal Materials Used   788

Market Share Variance and Industry Volume Variance   790

Sales Activity Variances with Multiple Products   792

Evaluating Product Mix   792

Evaluating Sales Mix and Sales Quantity   792

Business Application: *Sales Mix and Financial Reporting*   794

Production Mix and Yield Variances   794

Mix and Yield Variances in Manufacturing   794

Variance Analysis in Nonmanufacturing Settings   797

Using the Profit Variance Analysis in Service and Merchandise Organizations   797

Efficiency Measures   797

Mix and Yield Variances in Service Organizations   798

Business Application: *Changes in Bank Distribution Channels—A Mix Variance Interpretation*   799

Keeping an Eye on Variances and Standards   799

How Many Variances to Calculate   799

When to Investigate Variances   800

Updating Standards   801

Monitoring Variances with Charts   801

Key Takeaways   804

Summary   805

Key Terms   805

Review Questions   805

Critical Analysis and Discussion Questions   806

Exercises   806

Problems   812

Integrative Case   822

Solutions to Self-Study Questions   825

18

Performance Measurement to Support Business Strategy   828

Strategy and Performance   829

The Foundation of a Successful Business Strategy   830

Porter Framework   830

Business Application: *A New Strategy for an Old Business*   831

Beyond the Accounting Numbers   832

Responsibilities According to Level of Organization   833

Business Model   833

Multiple Measures or a Single Measure of Performance?   834

Balanced Scorecard   835

Continuous Improvement and Benchmarking   838

Performance Measurement for Control   843

Some Common Nonfinancial Performance Measures   843

Customer Satisfaction Performance Measures   843

Functional Performance Measures   844

Productivity   845

Nonfinancial Performance and Activity-Based Management   848

Objective and Subjective Performance Measures   849

Business Application: *The Risks of Focusing on Efficiency*   849

Employee Involvement   850

Difficulties in Implementing Nonfinancial Performance Measurement Systems   851

Fixation on Financial Measures   851

Reliability of Nonfinancial Measures   851

Lack of Correlation between Nonfinancial Measures and Financial Results   851

Key Takeaways   852

Summary   852

Key Terms   853

Review Questions   853

Critical Analysis and Discussion Questions   853

Exercises   854

Problems   859

Integrative Case   869

Solutions to Self-Study Questions   870

Appendix

Capital Investment Decisions: An Overview   A-1

Glossary   G-1

Index   IND-1

Fundamentals of
Cost Accounting

7e

1

Chapter One

Cost Accounting: Information for Decision Making

LEARNING OBJECTIVES

After reading this chapter, you should be able to:

LO 1-1   Describe the way managers use accounting information to create value in organizations.

LO 1-2   Distinguish between the uses and users of cost accounting and financial accounting information.

LO 1-3   Explain how cost accounting information is used for decision making and performance evaluation in organizations.

LO 1-4   Identify current trends in cost accounting, including data analytics and data visualization.

LO 1-5   Understand ethical issues faced by accountants and ways to deal with ethical problems that you face in your career.

The Decision

" *I opened this bakery shortly after I graduated from a local culinary school. I have always enjoyed baking, and owning my own bakery will allow me to experiment a bit. So far, the financial returns from the store have been sufficient for me to survive, but I am not sure if they will be enough for me to continue.*

I took some courses at the local community college last year hoping to learn some business skills that will help me really take control and increase the store's value. One thing I need to do is develop a better understanding of my costs. This semester I'm taking a cost accounting class. I know a little bit about the subject, but I know there is a lot more to learn. I'm curious, though, how this class will help me. I need to decide whether to expand the business or fold. If I expand the business, I need some help on managing my costs and remaining profitable.

I need to decide soon whether to expand or to close down and maybe go to work as a pastry chef in one of the local restaurants. "

Adam Mercer is the owner and founder of The AM Bakery, which he opened three years ago. The bakery has been marginally profitable, but Adam knows he must make a decision soon. Should he expand the business and work on making it financially viable, or should he abandon it and look for a job baking for someone else?

Adam wants to add value in his business. Like all managers, he wants the business to succeed financially. Like you, he is now studying cost accounting as one of the disciplines that he will use to do this. Adam knows that the world is a fast-changing place. He wants to learn not only what is current but also a way to think about problems that he can apply throughout his career. To do this, he knows that he must develop an intuition about the subject. He does not want to just learn a few facts that he is sure to soon forget. After developing this intuition, he can evaluate the merits of new cost accounting methods that he encounters throughout his career.

In this chapter, we give an overview of cost accounting and illustrate a number of the business situations we will study to put the topic in perspective. The examples we use and the description of how they apply to larger organizations (or to not-for-profit organizations or government agencies) are discussed in more detail in individual chapters. The examples also illustrate how the discipline of cost accounting can make a person a more valuable part of any organization.

Understanding Costs in a Small Business · *Business Application*

Opening a small business is always risky. Based on information from the U.S. Bureau of Labor Statistics, about one-half of all new businesses fail within the first five years, and this rate has been relatively constant over the past 20 years. Understanding the costs and other financial issues is a large part of the problem: ". . . over half of businesses discontinue operations because of lack of profits or financial funding."

Source: Speights, Keith, "What Percentage of Businesses Fail in Their First Year?" *USA Today*, May 21, 2017.

Value Creation in Organizations

Why Start with Value Creation?

We start our discussion with the concepts of value creation and the value chain because in cost accounting our goal is to assist managers in achieving the maximum value for their organizations. Measuring the effects of decisions on the value of the organization is one of the fundamental services of cost accounting. As providers of information (accountants) or as the users of information (managers), we have to understand how the information can and will be used to increase value. We can then come back to questions about how to design accounting systems that accomplish this goal.

LO 1-1
Describe the way managers use accounting information to create value in organizations.

Value Chain

value chain

Set of activities that transforms raw resources into the goods and services that end users purchase and consume.

The **value chain** is the set of activities that transforms raw resources into the goods and services end users (households, for example) purchase and consume. It also includes the treatment or disposal of any waste generated by the end users. As an example, the value chain for gasoline stretches from the search and drilling for oil, through refining the oil into gasoline, to the distribution of gasoline to retail outlets such as convenience stores, and, finally, to the treatment of the emissions produced by automobiles or the waste oil recycled at a service station.

In much of our discussion about cost accounting, we will be concerned with the part of the value chain that comprises the activities of a single organization (a firm, for example). However, an important objective of modern cost accounting is to ensure that the entire value chain is as efficient as possible. It is necessary for the firm to coordinate with vendors and suppliers and with distributors and customers to achieve this objective. In the gasoline example, ExxonMobil must work with suppliers of drilling equipment to ensure the equipment is available when needed. It also needs to work with owners of its On the Run franchises to ensure that gasoline is delivered to the stations as needed.

The cost accounting system provides much of the information necessary for this coordination. Therefore, at times we will also consider where in the value chain it is most efficient to perform an activity.

value-added activities

Those activities that customers perceive as adding utility to the goods or services they purchase.

The **value-added activities** that the firms in the chain perform are those that customers perceive as adding utility to the goods or services they purchase. The value chain comprises activities from research and development (R&D) through the production process to customer service. Managers evaluate these activities to determine how they contribute to the final product's service, quality, and cost.

Exhibit 1.1 identifies the individual components of the value chain and provides examples of the activities in each component, along with some of the costs associated with these activities. Although the list of value chain components in Exhibit 1.1 suggests a sequential process, many of the components overlap. For example, the R&D and design processes might take place simultaneously. Feedback from production workers

Exhibit 1.1   The Value Chain Components, Example Activities, and Example Costs

Component	Example Activities	Example Costs
• Research and development (R&D)	• The creation and development of ideas related to new products, services, or processes.	• Research personnel • Patent applications • Laboratory facilities
• Design	• The detailed development and engineering of products, services, or processes.	• Design center • Engineering facilities used to develop and test prototypes
• Purchasing	• The acquisition of goods and services needed to produce a good or service.	• Purchasing department personnel • Vendor certification
• Production	• The collection and assembly of resources to produce a product or deliver a service.	• Machines and equipment • Factory personnel
• Marketing and sales	• The process of informing potential customers about the attributes of products or services that leads to their sale.	• Advertising • Focus group travel • Product placement
• Distribution	• The process for delivering products or services to customers.	• Trucks • Fuel • Website creation, hosting, and maintenance
• Customer service	• The support activities provided to customers for a product or service.	• Call center personnel • Returns processing • Warranty repairs

on existing products might be incorporated in the development of new models of a product. Companies such as Apple solicit "feature requests" from customers for new versions of software.

Most organizations operate under the assumption that each of the value chain components adds value to the product or service. Before product ideas are formulated, no value exists. Once an idea is established, however, value is created. When research and development of the product begins, value increases. As the product reaches the design phase, value continues to increase. Each component adds value to the product or service.

You may have noticed that administrative functions are not included as part of the value chain. They are included instead in every business function of the value chain. For example, human resource management is involved in hiring employees for all business value chain functions. Accounting personnel and other managers use cost information from each business function to evaluate employee and departmental performance. Many administrative areas cover each value chain business function.

Supply Chain and Distribution Chain

Firms buy resources from suppliers (other companies, employees, and so on). These suppliers form the **supply chain** for the firm. Firms also sell their products to distributors and customers. This is the **distribution chain** of the firm. At times in our discussion, we will consider the companies and individuals supplying to or buying from a firm and the effect of the firm's decisions on these suppliers and customers. We can think of these suppliers and customers as being on the firm's *boundaries.* Thus, the supply chain and distribution chain are the parts of the value chain outside the firm.

The value chain is important because it creates the value for which the customer is willing to pay. The customer is not particularly concerned with how work is divided among firms producing the product or providing the service. Therefore, one decision firms must make is where in the value chain a value-added component is performed most cost effectively. Suppose, for example, that some inventory is necessary to provide timely delivery to the customer. Managers need accounting systems that will allow them to determine whether the firm or its supplier can hold the inventory at the lower cost.

supply chain
Set of firms and individuals that sells goods and services to the firm.

distribution chain
Set of firms and individuals that buys and distributes goods and services from the firm.

Choosing Where to Operate in the Supply Chain   *Business Application*

Customers are concerned with the total experience (including cost, delivery time, and so on) of producing and supplying a product or service. They are usually not concerned about which firm in the supply chain incurred the cost for or delivered the product or service. Therefore, companies think about not only reducing their own costs but also reducing costs and improving performance in the entire chain. Sometimes, a company might choose to have other firms produce parts used in its final product or deliver the service (outsourcing). Other times, the same company might decide to to do this work internally (in-sourcing).

For example, Amazon has recently begun to develop its own delivery and logistics service instead of relying on UPS or the Post Office. Why? Cost is one reason. Another is control over the process. "Amazon's move into airplanes, hubs, and delivery vans is a way to provide a better customer experience."

Source: Hyken, Shep, "Look Out FedEx and UPS -- Is Amazon Going to Disrupt the Shipping Industry?" Forbes.com, January 17, 2019. (https://www.forbes.com/sites/shephyken/2019/01/17/look-out-fedex-and-ups-is-amazon-going-to-disrupt-the-shipping-industry/#70b034c17621)

Using Cost Information to Increase Value

How can cost information add value to the organization? The answer to this question depends on whether the information provided improves managers' decisions. Suppose a production process is selected based on cost information indicating that the process would be less costly than all other options. Clearly, the information adds value to the process and its products. The measurement and reporting of costs is a valuable activity. Suppose cost information is received too late to help managers make a decision. Such information would not add value.

Accounting and the Value Chain

If you have taken a financial accounting course, you focused, for the most part, on preparing and interpreting financial statements for the firm as a whole. You were probably not concerned with what stage in the value chain produced profits. In cost accounting, as we will see, we need to understand how the individual stages contribute to value and how to work with other managers to improve performance. Although financial accounting and cost accounting are related, there are important differences.

Accounting Systems

LO 1-2

Distinguish between the uses and users of cost accounting and financial accounting information.

All accounting systems are designed to provide information to decision makers. However, it is convenient to classify accounting systems based on the primary user of the information. Investors (or potential investors), creditors, government agencies, tax authorities, and so on, are outside the organization. Managers are *inside* the organization. The classification of accounting systems into financial and cost (or managerial) systems captures this distinction between decision makers.

Financial Accounting

financial accounting
Field of accounting that reports financial position and income according to accounting rules.

Financial accounting information is designed for decision makers who are not directly involved in the daily management of the firm. These users of the information are often external to the firm. The information, at least for firms that are publicly traded, is public and typically available on the company's website. The managers in the company are keenly interested in the information contained in the financial accounting reports generated. However, the information is not sufficient for making operational decisions.

Individuals making decisions using financial accounting data are often interested in comparing firms, deciding whether, for example, to invest in Bank of America or Wells Fargo. An important characteristic of financial accounting data is that it be *comparable* across firms. That is, it is important that when an investor looks at, say, revenue for Bank of America, it represents the same thing that revenue for Wells Fargo does. As a result, financial accounting systems are characterized by a set of rules that define how transactions will be treated.

Cost Accounting

cost accounting
Field of accounting that measures, records, and reports information about costs.

Cost accounting information is designed for managers. Because the managers are making decisions only for their own organization, there is no need for the information to be comparable to similar information in other organizations. Instead, the important criterion is that the information be relevant for the decisions that managers operating in a particular business environment with a particular strategy make. Cost accounting information is commonly used in developing financial accounting information, but we are concerned primarily with its use by managers to make decisions.

This book is about accounting for costs; it is for those who currently (or will) use or prepare cost information. The book's perspective is that managers (you) add value to the organization by the decisions they (you) make. From a different perspective, accountants (you) add value by providing good information to managers making the decision. The better the decisions, the better the performance of your organization—whether it is a manufacturing firm, bank, not-for-profit hospital, government agency, school club, or, yes, even a business school. We have already identified some of the decisions managers make and will discuss many of the current trends in cost accounting. We do this to highlight the theme we follow throughout: The cost accounting system is not designed in a vacuum. It is the result of the decisions managers in an organization make and the business environment in which they make them.

Exhibit 1.2   Comparison of Financial and Cost Accounting

	Financial Accounting	Cost Accounting
• Users of the information (decision makers)	• External (investors, creditors, and so on)	• Internal (managers)
• Important criteria	• Comparability, decision relevance (for investors)	• Decision relevance (for managers), timeliness
• Who establishes or defines the system?	• External standard-setting group (FASB in the United States)	• Managers
• How to determine accounting treatment	• Standards (rules)	• Relevance for decision making

Exhibit 1.2 summarizes some of the major differences between financial and cost accounting.

Cost Accounting, GAAP, and IFRS

The primary purpose of financial accounting is to provide investors (for example, shareholders) or creditors (for example, banks) information regarding company and management performance. The financial data prepared for this purpose are governed by **generally accepted accounting principles (GAAP)** in the United States and **international financial reporting standards (IFRS)** in many other countries. GAAP and IFRS provide consistency in the accounting data used for reporting purposes from one company to the next. This means that the cost accounting information used to compute cost of goods sold, inventory values, and other financial accounting information used for external reporting must be prepared in accordance with GAAP or IFRS. Although GAAP and IFRS are converging, differences remain. For the reasons discussed in the next paragraph, these differences are not important for our discussion, but you should remain aware of them.

In contrast to cost data for financial reporting to shareholders, cost data for managerial use (that is, within the organization) need not comply with GAAP or IFRS. Management is free to set its own definitions for cost information. Indeed, the accounting data used for external reporting are often entirely inappropriate for managerial decision making. For example, managerial decisions deal with the future, so estimates of future costs are more valuable for decision making than are the historical and current costs that are reported externally. Unless we state otherwise, we assume that the cost information is being developed for internal use by managers and does not have to comply with GAAP or IFRS.

This does not mean there is no "right" or "wrong" way to account for costs. It does mean that the best, or correct, accounting for costs is the method that provides relevant information to decision makers so that they can make the best decision.

generally accepted accounting principles (GAAP)
Rules, standards, and conventions that guide the preparation of financial accounting statements for firms registered in the United States.

international financial reporting standards (IFRS)
Rules, standards, and conventions that guide the preparation of the financial accounting statements in many other countries.

Customers of Cost Accounting

To management, customers are the most important participants in a business. Without customers, the organization loses its ability and its reason to exist; customers provide the organization's focus. There are fewer and fewer markets in which managers can assume that they face little or no competition for the customer's patronage.

Cost information itself is a product with its own customers. The customers are managers. At the production level, where products are assembled or services are performed, information is needed to control and improve operations. This information is provided frequently and is used to track the efficiency of the activities being performed. For example, if the average defect rate is 1 percent in a manufacturing process and data from the cost accounting system indicate a defect rate of 2 percent on the previous day, shop-floor employees would use this information to identify what caused the defect rate to increase and to correct the problem.

At the middle management level, where managers supervise work and make operating decisions, cost information is used to identify problems by highlighting when some aspect of operations is different from expectations. At the executive level, financial information is used to assess the company's overall performance. This information is more strategic in nature and typically is provided on a monthly, quarterly, or annual basis. Cost accountants must work with the users (or customers) of cost accounting information to provide the best possible information for managerial purposes.

Many proponents of improvements in business have been highly critical of cost accounting practices in companies. Many of the criticisms—which we discuss throughout the book—are warranted. The problem, however, is more with the misuse of cost accounting information, not the information itself. The most serious problems with accounting systems appear to occur when managers attempt to use accounting information that was developed for external reporting for decision making. Making decisions often requires different information from that provided in financial statements to shareholders. It is important that companies realize that different uses of accounting information require different types of accounting information.

Key Financial Players in the Organization

All managers in the organization, not just financial professionals, use cost accounting information. Because our focus is on cost accounting and decision making, we will often be viewing a decision from an operational manager's perspective. For example, we might look at a pricing decision or a sourcing decision that a marketing or production manager has to make.

As a financial or operational manager in an organization, you will work closely with many financial professionals. See Exhibit 1.3 for a list of the typical financial titles in organizations and examples of their activities. If you work in the accounting or finance

Exhibit 1.3   Key Financial Managers in an Organization

Title	Major Responsibilities and Primary Duties	Example Activities
• Chief financial officer (CFO)	• Manages entire finance and accounting function	• Signs off on financial statements • Determines policy on debt versus equity financing
• Treasurer	• Manages liquid assets • Conducts business with banks and other financial institutions • Oversees public issues of stock and debt	• Determines where to invest cash balances • Obtains lines of credit
• Controller	• Plans and designs information and incentive systems	• Determines cost accounting policies • Maintains the accounting records
• Internal auditor	• Ensures compliance with laws, regulations, and company policies and procedures • Provides consulting and auditing services within the firm	• Ensures that procurement rules are followed • Recommends policies and procedures to reduce inventory losses
• Cost accountant	• Records, measures, estimates, and analyzes costs • Works with financial and operational manager to provide relevant information for decisions	• Evaluates costs of products and processes • Recommends cost-effective methods to distribute products

function in an organization, you are likely to have one of these jobs. If you are an auditor or consultant, you will work with many of these financial managers. If you work in marketing, operations, or management, these financial managers will be on one of many teams working with you.

Whatever your job, you will work in cross-functional teams of people from many areas such as engineering, production, marketing, finance, and accounting. Consider a project to identify a new design for an airplane. Cross-functional teams add value to decision making by

* Bringing a variety of expertise and perspectives to the problem.
* Ensuring that the product is appropriate for its customer base (requiring interaction between engineering and marketing).
* Giving production a chance to formulate an efficient production process (requiring interaction between engineering and production).
* Obtaining financing for the project (requiring interaction among all groups, including finance and accounting).
* Determining whether the project is economically feasible (requiring interaction among all functions).

Our Framework for Assessing Cost Accounting Systems

Individuals form organizations to achieve some common goal. Although the focus in this book is on economic organizations, such as the firm, most of what we discuss applies equally well to social, religious, or political organizations. The ability of organizations to remain viable and achieve their goals, whether profit, community well-being, or political influence, depends on the decisions made by managers of the organization.

Throughout the text, we emphasize that it is individuals (people) who make decisions. This theme and the following framework give us a common basis we can use to assess alternative accounting systems:

* Decisions determine the performance of the organization.
* Managers use information from the accounting system to make decisions.
* Owners evaluate organizational and managerial performance with accounting information.

The Manager's Job Is to Make Decisions

Why do organizations employ people? What do they do to add value? For *line employees,* those directly involved in production or who interact with customers, the answer to this question is clear. They produce the product or service and deal with the customer. The job of managers, however, is more difficult to describe because it tends to be varied and ambiguous. The common theme among all managerial jobs, however, is decision making. Managers are paid to make decisions.

LO 1-3

Explain how cost accounting information is used for decision making and performance evaluation in organizations.

Decision Making Requires Information

Accounting systems are important because they are a primary source of information for managers. We describe here some common decisions that managers make. Many, if not most, decisions require information that is likely to come from the accounting system. Our concern with the accounting system is whether it is providing the "best" information to managers. The decisions managers make will be only as good as the information they have.

Finding and Eliminating Activities That Don't Add Value

How do managers use cost information to make decisions that increase value? In their quest to improve the production process, companies seek to identify and eliminate

nonvalue-added activities
Activities that do not add value to the good or service.

nonvalue-added activities, which often result from the current product or process design. If a poor facility layout exists and work-in-process inventory must be moved during the production process, the company is likely to be performing nonvalue-added activities.

Why do managers want to eliminate nonvalue-added activities? An important concept in cost accounting is that *activities cause costs.* Moving inventory is a nonvalue-added activity that causes costs (for example, wages for employees and costs of equipment to move the goods). Reworking defective units is another common example of a nonvalue-added activity. In general, if activities that do not add value to the company can be eliminated, then costs associated with them will also be eliminated. At the same time, the value to the customer is not affected, leading to an overall increase in value to the organization.

A well-designed cost accounting system also can identify nonvalue-added activities that cross boundaries in the value chain. For example, many companies such as Alaska Airlines, Hyatt Hotels, and National Car Rental allow customers to purchase tickets and reserve rooms and cars directly using the company website. This change has eliminated the need for as many dedicated telephone agents. Not only does this save clerical costs, but it reduces the chances of costly errors in the details of the reservation.

cost-benefit analysis
Process of comparing benefits (often measured in savings or increased profits) with costs associated with a proposed change within an organization.

A major activity of managers is evaluating proposed changes in the organization. Ideas often sound reasonable, but if their benefits (typically measured in savings or increased profits) do not outweigh the costs, management will likely decide against them. The concept of considering both the costs and benefits of a proposal is **cost-benefit analysis.** Managers should perform cost-benefit analyses to assess whether proposed changes in an organization are worthwhile. The concept of cost-benefit analysis applies equally to deciding whether to implement a new cost accounting system. The benefits from an improved cost accounting system come from better decision making. If the benefits do not exceed the cost of implementing and maintaining the new system, managers will not implement it.

Identifying Strategic Opportunities Using Cost Analysis

Using the value chain and other information about the costs of activities, companies can identify strategic advantages in the marketplace. For example, if a company can eliminate nonvalue-added activities, it can reduce costs without reducing the value of the product to customers. By reducing costs, the company can lower the price it charges customers, giving it a cost advantage over competitors. Or the company can use the resources saved from eliminating nonvalue-added activities to provide better service to customers.

Alternatively, a company can identify activities that customers value and which the company can provide at lower cost. Many logistics companies, such as Owens & Minor, a healthcare services provider, offer their customers consulting services and inventory management.

The idea here is simple. Look for activities that do or do not add value. If your company can save money by eliminating those that do not, then do so. You will save your company money. Implement those activities that do. In both cases, you will make the organization more competitive.

Owners Use Cost Information to Evaluate Managers

We have seen that it is important that managers make good decisions if they are to increase organizational value, but how will we know if they make good decisions? If managers own the organization, it is their money and resources that are at risk. We can assume that they will make decisions that are in their own interest. In other words, the interest of the organization and the owner-manager can be assumed to be the same, or *aligned.* However, most large organizations, especially businesses, are not owned by the managers but by a large number of shareholders. Most of these shareholders are not involved in managing the business. Therefore, there is a second role of the accounting system in addition to aiding managerial decision making. It is to provide information, perhaps indirectly through financial reports, to the owners of the organization about the performance of the organization and the manager.

Cost Data for Managerial Decisions

This book covers many topics on the use of cost data for managers. The following sections provide examples of these topics.

Costs for Decision Making

One of the most difficult tasks in calculating the financial consequences of alternatives is estimating how costs (or revenues or assets) among the alternatives will differ. For example, The AM Bakery has been making and selling a variety of baked goods through a small store. One of Adam's customers, who works at a local office park, suggests to Adam that he expand his operation and sell the bakery offering at the morning and afternoon break times at the office park using a food truck. The key is to determine which would be more profitable—remain the same size or expand operations by adding a new distribution channel.

Now Adam has the difficult task of estimating how revenues and costs will change if he expands into this new distribution channel. He uses his work experience and knowledge of the company's costs to estimate cost changes. He identifies **cost drivers,** which are factors that cause costs. For example, to make scones requires labor. Therefore, the number of scones made is a cost driver that causes, or drives, labor costs. To estimate the effect of adding a food truck channel, Adam estimates how much additional product he would have to make. Based on that estimate, he determines the additional costs and revenues to the company that selling additional merchandise will generate.

cost drivers
Factors that cause, or "drive," costs.

Do we "know" how this decision will affect the firm? We do not, of course. These are *estimates* that require making many assumptions and forecasts, some of which may not be realized. This is what makes this type of analysis both fun and challenging. In business, nobody knows for certain what will happen in the future. In making decisions, however, managers constantly must try to predict future events. Cost accounting has more to do with estimating future costs than recording past costs. For decision making, information about the past is a means to an end; it helps you predict what will happen in the future.

To complete the example, assume that Adam estimates that his revenues would increase by 50 percent; ingredients and labor would increase by 45 percent; and utilities would increase 20 percent. Rent per month would not change. Adam knows that he will need a strong marketing campaign to create awareness, so he plans to triple his marketing budget. The new channel would require a lease for a truck at $900 per month, and he would incur truck operating expenses of $150 per month. Adam enters the data into a spreadsheet to estimate how profits would change if he were to add the new channel. See Columns 1 and 2 of Exhibit 1.4 for the present and estimated costs, revenues, and profits for the business. The costs shown in Column 3 are the differences between those in Columns 1 and 2.

We refer to the costs and revenues that appear in Column 3 as **differential costs** and **differential revenues.** These are the costs and revenues, respectively, that change in response to a particular course of action. The costs in Column 3 of Exhibit 1.4 are differential costs because they differ if Adam decides to sell bakery goods off the food truck.

differential costs
With two or more alternatives, costs that differ among or between alternatives.

differential revenues
Revenues that change in response to a particular course of action.

The analysis shows a $1,790 increase in operating profits if Adam adds this new selling option. Based on this analysis, Adam decides to expand his bakery business. Note that only differential costs and revenues affect the decision. For example, rent does not change, so it is irrelevant to the decision.

In Chapters 2 through 11, we discuss methods to estimate and analyze costs, as well as how accounting systems record and report cost information.

Exhibit 1.4

Differential Costs,
Revenes, and Profits

	A	B	C	D	E	F	G	H	I
1			THE AM BAKERY						
2			Projected Income Statement						
3			For a Representative Week						
4									
5			(1)			(2)			(3)
6						Alternative			
7			Status Quo:			Original Bakery			
8			Original Bakery			Plus Food			
9			Sales Only			Truck Sales			Difference
10	Sales revenue		$11,200			$16,800	(a)		$5,600
11	Costs								
12	Ingredients (Flour, butter, and so on)		$2,700			$3,915	(b)		$1,215
13	Labor		3,100			4,495	(b)		1,395
14	Utilities		500			600	(c)		100
15	Rent		900			900	(d)		0
16	Marketing		25			75	(e)		50
17	Truck lease		0			900	(f)		900
18	Truck operating costs		0			150	(f)		150
19	Total costs		$7,225			$11,035			$3,810
20	Operating profits		$3,975			$5,765			$1,790
21									
22	(a) 50 percent higher than status quo.								
23	(b) 45 percent higher than status quo.								
24	(c) 20 percent higher than status quo.								
25	(d) No additional rent required.								
26	(e) 300 percent higher than status quo.								
27	(f) New costs for food trucks only.								

Business Application   **Reducing Costs by Making Small Changes**

It is not just small businesses that think about costs. With increased energy and labor costs and strong competition pressuring prices, even large companies look for any edge they can find. For example, United Airlines found that by reducing the weight of the paper used to print its in-flight magazine and safety cards found in the seat back pockets, it is saving "170,000 gallons of fuel each year, or $290,000 in annual fuel costs." Previously it had dropped the sale of duty-free items sold on board. The reduced weight resulted in fuel savings of $2.3 million. Of course, these changes are advantageous only if they do not materially affect the customer experience on the flight.

Source: Martin, Hugo, "United Airlines Saves 170,000 Gallons of Fuel by Using Lighter Paper on Inflight Magazine," *Los Angeles Times*, January 22, 2018.

Costs for Control and Evaluation

An organization of any but the smallest size divides responsibility for specific functions among its employees. These functions are grouped into organizational units. The units, which may be called *departments, divisions, segments,* or *subsidiaries,* specify the reporting relations within the firm. These relations are often shown on an organization chart. The organizational units can be based on products, geography, or business function. We use the general term **responsibility center** to refer to these units. The manager assigned to lead the unit is accountable for, that is, has responsibility for, the unit's operations and resources.

responsibility center
Specific unit of an organization assigned to a manager who is held accountable for its operations and resources.

For example, the chief of internal medicine is responsible for the operations of a particular part of a hospital. The president of GM North America is responsible for most of the company's operations in North America. The president of a company is responsible for the entire company.

Consider The AM Bakery. When he first opened the store, Adam managed the entire operation himself. As the enterprise became more successful, he added a new distribution channel using food trucks. He then hired two managers: Ed Walsh to manage the original retail store and Ady Joss to manage the food truck channel. Adam, as president, oversaw the entire operation. See the top part of Exhibit 1.5 for the company's organization chart.

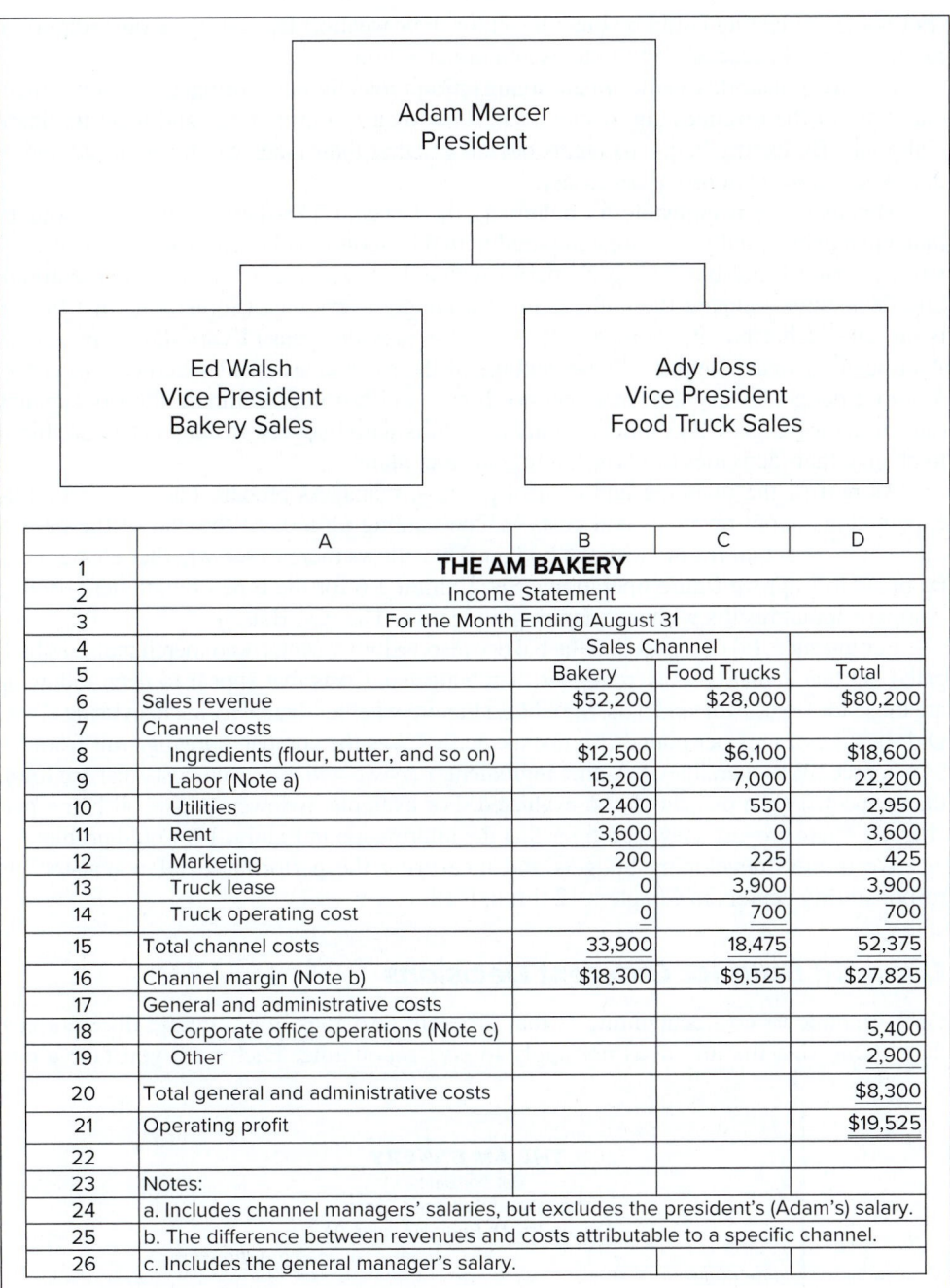

Exhibit 1.5

Responsibility Centers, Revenues, and Costs

	A	B	C	D
1	**THE AM BAKERY**			
2	Income Statement			
3	For the Month Ending August 31			
4		Sales Channel		
5		Bakery	Food Trucks	Total
6	Sales revenue	$52,200	$28,000	$80,200
7	Channel costs			
8	Ingredients (flour, butter, and so on)	$12,500	$6,100	$18,600
9	Labor (Note a)	15,200	7,000	22,200
10	Utilities	2,400	550	2,950
11	Rent	3,600	0	3,600
12	Marketing	200	225	425
13	Truck lease	0	3,900	3,900
14	Truck operating cost	0	700	700
15	Total channel costs	33,900	18,475	52,375
16	Channel margin (Note b)	$18,300	$9,525	$27,825
17	General and administrative costs			
18	Corporate office operations (Note c)			5,400
19	Other			2,900
20	Total general and administrative costs			$8,300
21	Operating profit			$19,525
22				
23	Notes:			
24	a. Includes channel managers' salaries, but excludes the president's (Adam's) salary.			
25	b. The difference between revenues and costs attributable to a specific channel.			
26	c. Includes the general manager's salary.			

Exhibit 1.5 also includes the company income statement, along with the statements for the two centers. Each manager is responsible for the revenues and costs of his or her center. The Total column is for the entire company. Note that the costs at the bottom of the income statement are not assigned to the centers; they are the costs of running the company. These costs are not the particular responsibility of either Ed or Ady. Consider the other (administrative) costs. Adam, not Ed or Ady, is responsible for designing the administrative systems (e.g., accounting and payroll), so Adam manages this cost as part of his responsibility to run the entire organization. Ed and Ady, on the other hand, focus on managing ingredient and labor costs (other than their own salaries) and responsibility center revenues.

Budgeting   You have probably had to budget—for college, a vacation, or living expenses. Even the wealthiest people budget to make the best use of their resources.

budget
Financial plan of the revenues and resources needed to carry out activities and meet financial goals.

(For some, budgeting could be one reason for their wealth.) Budgeting is very important to the financial success of individuals and organizations.

Each responsibility center in an organization typically has a **budget** that is its financial plan for the revenues and resources needed to carry out its tasks and meet its financial goals. Budgeting helps managers decide whether their goals can be achieved and, if not, what modifications are necessary.

Managers are responsible for achieving the targets set in the budget. The resources that a manager actually uses are compared with the amount budgeted to assess the responsibility center's and the manager's performance. For example, managers in an automobile dealership compare the daily sales to a budget every day. (Sometimes that budget is the sales achieved on a comparable day in the previous year.) Every day, managers of American Airlines compare the percentage of their airplanes' seats filled (the *load factor*) to a budget. Every day, managers of hotels and hospitals compare their occupancy rates to their budgets. By comparing actual results with budgets, managers can do things to change their activities or revise their goals and plans.

As part of the planning and control process, managers prepare budgets containing expectations about revenues and costs for the coming period. At the end of the period, they compare actual results with the budget. This allows them to see whether changes can be made to improve future operations. See Exhibit 1.6 for the type of statement used to compare actual results with the planning budget for The AM Bakery.

For instance, Ed observes that the bakery responsibility center sold merchandise as budgeted but that actual costs were higher than budgeted. Costs that appear to need follow-up are those for flour, fruit, and nuts. Should Ed inquire whether there was waste in using flour? Did the cost of nuts per pound rise unexpectedly? Was the company buying fruit from the best source? Was there theft of some ingredients? As we will see, even costs that are lower than expected (like oil) should be evaluated. For example, is lower-quality oil being purchased? These are just a few questions that the information in Exhibit 1.6 would prompt.

We discuss developing budgets and measuring the performance of managers and responsibility centers in Chapters 12 through 18.

Different Data for Different Decisions

One principle of cost accounting is that different decisions often require different cost data. "One size fits all" does *not* apply to cost accounting. Each time you face a cost

Exhibit 1.6

Budget versus Actual Data

	A	B	C	D
1		\[\] THE AM BAKERY		
2		Bakery Sales		
3		Actual and Budgeted Costs		
4		For the Month Ending August 31		
5		Actual	Budgeted	Difference
6	Ingredients			
7	Flour	$ 3,900	$ 3,700	$ 200
8	Butter	3,500	3,400	100
9	Oil	1,700	1,800	(100)
10	Fruit	1,300	1,000	300
11	Nuts	900	800	100
12	Chocolate	800	800	-
13	Other	400	300	100
14	Total ingredients	$ 12,500	$ 11,800	$ 700
15	Labor			
16	Channel manager	4,500	4,500	-
17	Other	10,700	10,900	(200)
18	Utilities	2,400	2,300	100
19	Rent	3,600	3,600	-
20	Marketing	200	100	100
21	Total bakery costs	$ 33,900	$ 33,200	$ 700
22				
23	Revenues	$ 52,200	$ 52,200	-
24				

information problem in your career, you should first learn how the data will be used. Are the data needed to value inventories in financial reports to shareholders? Are they for managers' use in evaluating performance? Are the data to be used for decision making? The answers to these questions will guide your selection of the most appropriate accounting data.

Self-Study Questions

1. Suppose that the ingredients, labor, and utilities for The AM Bakery (Exhibit 1.4) were differential and increased proportionately with sales revenue. Adam plans to increase marketing costs to $60 per week with the new channel. Rent would not change. The truck expenses would be as given in Exhibit 1.4 with the new channel. What would have been the impact on profits of adding the new distribution channel?

2. For what decisions would estimated cost information be useful if you were a hospital administrator? The director of a museum? The marketing vice president of a bank?

The solutions to these questions are at the end of the chapter.

Trends in Cost Accounting and Business Decisions

Cost accounting continues to experience dramatic changes. Developments in information technology (IT) have nearly eliminated manual bookkeeping. Emphasis on cost control is increasing in banks, hospitals, manufacturing industries (from computers to automobiles), airlines, school districts, and many other organizations that have traditionally not focused on it. Cost accounting has become a necessity in virtually every organization, including fast-food outlets, professional organizations, and government agencies.

> **LO 1-4**
> Identify current trends in cost accounting, including data analytics and data visualization.

Cost Accounting in the Value Chain

One reason for this rapid change is that managers at each stage of the value chain require information on the performance of products, services, suppliers, customers, and employees. Managers of the activities and cost accountants must work together at each stage to make decisions that increase firm value. Because these processes themselves have undergone great change in recent years, cost accountants and cost accounting methods must continuously adapt to changes in all business areas.

Exhibit 1.7 summarizes how cost accounting methods have developed with various management practices. Together, the management practices and cost accounting methods support business decision makers in their daily activities. Some examples of these methods and practices are also identified in Exhibit 1.7

Creating Value in the Organization

These trends in the way organizations do business create exciting times in cost accounting and excellent future opportunities for you to make important contributions to organizations. Keep in mind that these new methods are not ends in themselves. They are tools to help you add value to organizations and their employees, customers, shareholders, and communities.

Enterprise Resource Planning

We have seen how cost accounting is used throughout the value chain. It is important that the information be consistent in all components of the chain.

As the cost of information technology falls and the value of information increases, managers have adopted **enterprise resource planning (ERP)** systems. ERP systems are

enterprise resource planning (ERP)
Information technology that links the various systems of the enterprise into a single comprehensive information system.

Exhibit 1.7   Cost Accounting Methods Used in the Value Chain

Stage in the Value Chain	Cost Accounting Method/ Management Practice	Example(s)
Research and development (R&D)	Life-cycle costing	Catepillar, Inc.: Provides a life-cycle costing template for customers to use when considering equipment purchases.
Design	Activity-based costing (ABC)	IKEA: Designing flat-pack products to reduce storage and transportation costs.
Purchasing	Performance measures	Raytheon Technologies: Supplier metrics.
	Benchmarking	Sainsbury (UK): Web portal for suppliers to monitor their performance.
Production	Just-in-time (JIT)	Starbucks: Redesign flow to reduce bottlenecks in service times.
	Lean accounting	University of Utah Health Systems: Using detailed cost information to understand cost of services.
Marketing	Customer relationship management (CRM)	Harrah's: Using customer profitability measures to determine complimentary services (comps).
	Cost of customer	Alaska Airlines: Determine breakpoints in status levels to optimize benefits offered.
Distribution	Outsourcing	UPS & FedEx: Providing consulting services to customers about optimal distribution practices.
	Differential costing	Sysco: Consulting to restaurants on menu design in addition to supplying ingredients.
Customer Service	Total quality management (TQM)	Hyundai: Determining optimal warranty policies for new cars.]

integrated information systems that link various activities in an organization. Typical systems include modules for production, purchasing, human resources, finance, and sales. By integrating these systems, managers hope to avoid lost orders, duplication of effort, and costly studies to determine the current state of the enterprise.

Because all of the company's systems are integrated, the potential for ERP to provide information on costs of products and services is large. Implementation problems and the scale of the task in large firms (enterprises) have kept many companies from realizing that potential so far. However, with the increased emphasis on internal control from the Sarbanes-Oxley Act (discussed later in the chapter), ERP systems will become even more valuable.

Critical Thinking and Data Analytics

critical thinking
A systematic process used to analyze a business issue or decision.

The development of ERP systems and the reduced costs of information processing have also generated a discussion about how more general frameworks could be applied to these business issues and assist managers making decisions. These frameworks may be referred to by different names, but a common one is **critical thinking.** For our purposes, critical thinking is a systematic process used to analyze a business issue or decision. It includes answering the following questions:

1. What are the relevant questions (what decisions do I need to make)?
2. What are the data relevant to the analysis and where do I find them?
3. What are the appropriate tools for analyzing data?
4. How can I effectively and persuasively communicate the results of my analysis?

1. What are the relevant questions (what decisions do I need to make)?
Determining the relevant question to ask seems an obvious and often easy first step in an analysis. It is often neither. It is common for analysts to focus too quickly on a particular problem or issue and work on solving that. But if the problem is actually a symptom of something else, then the solution might not solve the underlying problem.

For example, it might seem that in a service business with financial difficulties, the relevant question is, "How can I reduce costs?" The solution could be to reduce customer representatives that handle customer questions. This could lead to loss of sales because unhappy customers have to wait to have their questions answered. A different question might be, "How can I more effectively use the customer representatives to increase sales?" Although this might seem obvious when both questions are listed together, it is easy to focus on costs when facing declining profits.

2. What are the data relevant to the analysis and where do I find them?
Perhaps the most difficult step in the analysis is identifying and finding the data relevant to the decision. Data include both quantitative data, such as sales revenue, and qualitative data, such as employee satisfaction. Recently, the term *big data* has been used to describe information for analyzing business decisions. **Big data** has many definitions, but for our purposes, it refers to data (information) that may be defined by the sheer amount of data (individual clicks on a website), the speed at which the data are generated and made available (real-time aircraft movements), or the variety of data available (customer purchasing behavior). Our focus in this text is primarily on generating information for decision making. When we do analyze the data, we want to consider the following:

big data
The volume and speed with which information is generated and made available.

- Do the data measure the concepts appropriately for the questions we are considering? A common theme in the text is that information generated to answer one question (product costs for pricing, for example) might not be appropriate for other decisions (which products to drop).

- Are the data likely to be available? One important difference between financial accounting and cost accounting is that most cost accounting data are considered proprietary. That means that if you want to benchmark your organization's costs with a competitor, those costs are unlikely to be readily available.

- Are the data comparable? Do data that use similar terms represent the same thing? As you know from financial accounting, firms may calculate depreciation expense in different ways. You want to consider whether these data are appropriate for your analysis.

3. What are the appropriate tools for analyzing data?
Data analytics is the systematic evaluation of information to address a decision problem. The analysis should use methods appropriate for the data and provide useful information for the decision-making problem. There are various tools that can be used for this including spreadsheets (Microsoft Excel, Apple Numbers, Google Sheets, and so on), statistical software (SAS, SPSS, Stata, R, and so on), or other analysis software (Mathematica, MATLAB, and so on). This text is not about data analytics in this sense, however. We focus on computing numbers and measures that are useful for business decisions. For the most part, we do not consider explicitly the inherent uncertainty associated with the environment in which business decisions are made. The information generated by the cost accounting system is

data analytics
Systematic evaluation of information to address a decision problem.

often used in data analytics, and by understanding the basics of both cost accounting and data analytics, you will be in a better position to provide useful information.

4. How can I effectively and persuasively communicate the results of my analysis?   Once the analysis has been completed and a tentative decision reached, it is important to be able to communicate the decision and the analysis to the decision maker. In one sense, this can be done by providing a transcript of your work. This includes the approaches you followed, the data you used, the analysis techniques employed, and so on. **Data visualization** refers to how the results of the analysis are summarized and presented to decision makers. Although the visualization might be textual (consisting of words and numbers), we generally think of data visualization in terms of graphical presentations.

At one extreme, the analyst could present a listing of the data collected. This would be an accurate representation, but generally not effective. The decision maker is looking to the analyst to summarize the data in a way that explains what the analyst is recommending. The result is often a graph of some sort that highlights results of the analysis.

There are many data visualization tools that can be used to summarize the results of the analysis. These include spreadsheet software, such as Microsoft Excel, as well as more specialized software such as Tableau and Microsoft Power BI. This text is not about data visualization, although there will be exhibits that highlight various results and you can consider whether there are different ways to present the results that would be more or less effective.

data visualization
How the results of the data analysis are summarized and presented.

Applying the Framework

We can illustrate the concepts of critical thinking, data analytics, and data visualization with an example. Understand that this example is simplified because we want to highlight the different elements of the critical thinking framework, not the analysis technique.

The AM Bakery has grown to 30 stores organized in six districts with four to six stores in a district. Adam Mercer, the owner of The AM Bakery, must decide which district manager to promote to oversee corporate operations. Although he will take many things into consideration, an important factor will be district profitability. He asked Emily Cho, a local consultant, to determine the most profitable district.

The decision to be made is clear (who is the best manager) and the question for Emily is to identify the most profitable district. She collects monthly financial information on the 30 stores for the previous calendar year and decides that she will use district profits to answer the question. (Problem 1-55 asks you to think about measures you would use to answer the question.) The data she has collected are summarized in Exhibit 1.8.

Emily is preparing a presentation for Adam, and her first thought is to show him the table in Exhibit 1.8. Thinking about that, she decides she should highlight

Exhibit 1.8

Annual Financial Results by District

	A	B	C
1		THE AM BAKERY	
2		Annual Revenue and Profit by District	
3			
4	**District**	**Annual Revenue**	**Annual Profit**
5	District 1	$ 3,926,503	$ 1,050,686
6	District 2	3,749,256	1,165,390
7	District 3	5,568,574	1,769,757
8	District 4	3,690,913	1,217,799
9	District 5	6,159,927	2,212,114
10	District 6	4,927,492	2,056,521
11		$ 28,022,665	$ 9,472,267
12			

her conclusion, so Adam can focus on her conclusion. Her new visual is shown in Exhibit 1.9

The graphic shown in Exhibit 1.9 does not provide more (or less) information, but it highlights the data the analyst wants to present. This is an example of data visualization. Emily decides to experiment with other visualizations, as shown in Exhibit 1.10.

	A	B	C
1		THE AM BAKERY	
2		Annual Revenue and Profit by District	
3			
4	District	Annual Revenue	Annual Profit
5	District 1	$ 3,926,503	$ 1,050,686
6	District 2	3,749,256	1,165,390
7	District 3	5,568,574	1,769,757
8	District 4	3,690,913	1.217.799
9	District 5	6,159,927	2,212,114
10	District 6	4,927,492	2,056,521
11		$ 28,022,665	$ 9,472,267

Exhibit 1.9

Annual Financial Results by District: Highlighted Results

Panel A: Heat Map Created Using Microsoft Excel

Exhibit 1.10

Annual Financial Results by District: Alternative Visualizations

	A	B	C
1		THE AM BAKERY	
2		Annual Revenue and Profit by District	
3			
4	District	Annual Revenue	Annual Profit
5	District 1	$ 3,926,503	$ 1,050,686
6	District 2	3,749,256	1,165,390
7	District 3	5,568,574	1,769,757
8	District 4	3,690,913	1,217,799
9	District 5	6,159,927	2,212,114
10	District 6	4,927,492	2,056,521
11		$ 28,022,665	$ 9,472,267

Panel B: Bar Chart Created Using Microsoft Power BI

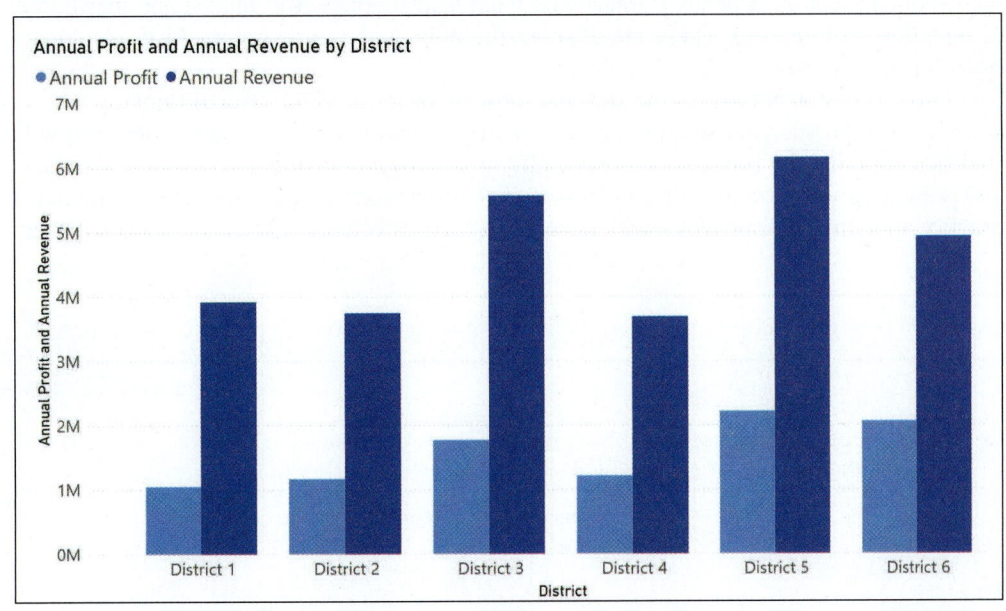

(Continued)

Exhibit 1.10
(*Continued*)

Panel C: Scatter Plot Created Using Tableau
Tableau Software

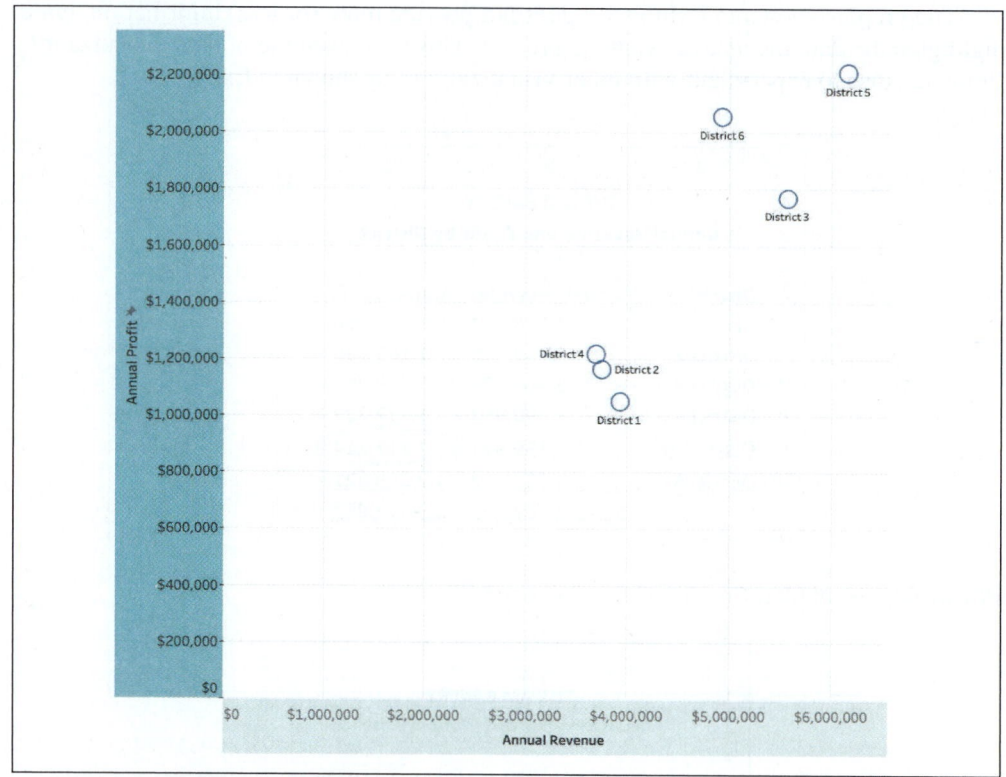

Exhibit 1.10 Panel A presents a heat map prepared using Microsoft Excel with values color-coded to highlight high (green) and low (red) results. Exhibit 1.10 Panel B presents a bar chart prepared using Microsoft Power BI to indicate graphically the difference in profits among districts. Finally, Exhibit 1.10 Panel C presents a scatter plot prepared using Tableau of profits and revenues to highlight the relation among districts and between revenue and profits.

Although the graphics in Exhibit 1.10 were prepared using different software applications, any of these graphics could have been prepared in any of the applications. The choice of application depends primarily on what is available to the analyst and the source of data that will be used. These are also not the only, and maybe not the best, visualizations for this decision.

This discussion introduces the idea and some of the terms of the critical-thinking framework. As you pursue your studies and your career, you will be able to learn more. You will find that applying the framework—especially in identifying the question, finding the data, and presenting visualizations that are persuasive—is as much an art as a science. Continued practice applying the framework will make you a more effective analyst and decision maker.

Self-Study Question

3. Consider the Business Application "Choosing Where to Operate in the Supply Chain," earlier in the chapter. At a very general level, how would you answer the four questions in the critical thinking framework?

    The solution to this question is at the end of the chapter.

Choices: Ethical Issues for Accountants

We have discussed decisions that you will make in using or preparing cost accounting information. Now, we alert you to ethical issues that you will have to face. The sooner you are aware of these issues, the better you will be able to deal with them in your career. The design of cost systems is ultimately about the assignment of costs to various activities, products, projects, corporate units, and people. How that is done affects prices, reimbursement, and pay. As you know from current events, the design of the cost accounting system has the potential to be misused to defraud customers, employees, or shareholders. As a user or preparer of cost information, you need to be aware of the implications of the way in which information is used. Most important, you need to be aware of when the system has the potential for abuse.

LO 1-5
Understand ethical issues faced by accountants and ways to deal with ethical problems that you face in your career.

What Makes Ethics So Important?

Accountants report information that can have a substantial impact on the careers of managers. Managers are generally held accountable for achieving financial performance targets. Failure to achieve them can have serious negative consequences for the managers, including losing their jobs. If a division or company is having trouble achieving financial performance targets, accountants may find themselves under pressure by management to make accounting choices that will improve performance reports.

As a professional accountant, manager, or business owner, you will face ethical situations on an everyday basis. Your personal ethical choices can affect not only your own self-image but also others' perception of you. Ultimately, the ethical decisions you make directly influence the type of life you are likely to lead. You should confront ethical dilemmas bearing in mind the type of life that you want to lead.

In an attempt to influence the accounting profession, many of its professional organizations such as the Institute of Management Accountants (IMA), Institute of Internal Auditors (IIA), and the American Institute of Certified Public Accountants (AICPA) have developed codes of ethics to which their members are expected to adhere. Similarly, businesses such as Johnson & Johnson generally use these codes as a public statement of their commitment to certain business practices with respect to their customers and as a guide for their employees.

Throughout this book, we include discussions of ethical issues. Our aim is to make you aware of potential problems that you and your colleagues will face in your careers. Many accountants, managers, and business owners have found themselves in serious trouble because they did many small things, none of which appeared seriously wrong, only to find that these small things added up to big trouble. If you know the warning signs of potential ethical problems, you will have a chance to protect yourself and set the proper moral tone for your company and your profession at the same time.

IMA Code of Ethics

The IMA Code of Ethics discusses the steps cost accountants should take when faced with an ethical conflict. Essentially, these steps are

- DISCUSS the conflict with your immediate superior or, if the conflict involves your superior, the next level in authority. This might require contacting the board of directors or an appropriate committee of the board, such as the audit committee or the executive committee;
- CLARIFY the relevant issues and concepts by discussions with a disinterested party or by contacting an appropriate and confidential ethics hotline;
- CONSULT your attorney about your rights and obligations.

Unethical behavior often leads to illegal activities as managers attempt to improve reported results. See the Business Application item on revenue and expense recognition for an example and the text in this section for some approaches to handling ethical problems.
Photodisc/Getty Images

The IMA code of conduct is available on its website at

https://www.imanet.org/-/media/b6fbeeb74d964e6c9fe654c48456e61f.ash

In its "Statement of Ethical Professional Practice," the IMA states that management (and cost) accountants have a responsibility to maintain the highest levels of ethical conduct. They also have a responsibility to maintain professional competency, refrain from disclosing confidential information, and maintain integrity and objectivity in their work. These standards recommend that accountants faced with ethical conflicts follow the established policies that deal with them. If the policies do not resolve the conflict, accountants should consider discussing the matter with superiors, potentially as high as the audit committee of the board of directors. In extreme cases, the accountant could have no alternative but to resign.

The Sarbanes-Oxley Act of 2002 and Ethics

When the public perception of widespread ethical problems in business exists, the result is often legislation making certain conduct not only unethical but also illegal. In the late 1990s and early 2000s, the investing and consuming public became aware of several practices, including manipulation of accounting results, designed to increase the compensation of managers at several firms. These practices came to light with the failure of many of these businesses when the "tech bubble" burst in early 2000.

The U.S. Congress passed legislation in 2002 that was intended to address some of the more serious problems of corporate governance. The legislation, termed the *Sarbanes-Oxley Act of 2002,* has many provisions and affects both companies and accounting firms. For our purposes, some of the important provisions concern those in Title III and Title IV that deal with corporate responsibility and enhanced financial disclosure, respectively. The CEO and CFO are responsible for signing financial statements and stipulating that the financial statements do not omit material information. The requirement that these officers sign the company's financial statements makes it clear that the "buck stops" with the CEO and CFO and that they are personally responsible for the financial statements. They cannot legitimately claim that lower-level managers or employees misled them about the financial statements, as was stated by defendant executives in many fraud trials in the past. Top executives take this sign-off very seriously, especially knowing that misrepresentation of their company's financial reports could mean substantial prison time. They must further disclose that they have evaluated the company's internal controls and that they have notified the company's auditors and the audit committee of the board of any fraud that involves management.

Section 404 of Title IV requires managers to attest to the adequacy of their internal controls. Good internal controls assure that financial records accurately and fairly reflect transactions and that expenditures are in accordance with the authorization of company management and directors. Further, good internal controls help protect against the unauthorized purchase, use, or sale of company assets.

An example of an internal control is the requirement that two people, not just one, sign checks. Requiring two people to sign checks reduces the probability that someone will divert the company's cash to personal use.

Sarbanes-Oxley is important for managers who design cost information systems. Whether the cost information is used for pricing decisions or performance evaluation, the manager must be aware of the potential that the resulting information could be misleading or support fraudulent activity. Compliance with Sarbanes-Oxley does not, however, mean that the manager has met all of his or her ethical responsibilities. Sarbanes-Oxley is a law; ethics is based on behavior. The IMA guidelines suggest you answer the following questions when faced with an ethical dilemma:

- Will my actions be fair and just to all parties affected?
- Would I be pleased to have my closest friends learn of my actions?

Consider the *Business Application* discussion of accounting choices. You as the manager or cost accountant need to be aware of the powerful incentives created by performance

An accounting scandal at British retailer Tesco in 2014 led to fraud charges being filed against three former employees. At the time of the fraud, Tesco suspended eight managers thought to be involved in a scheme to book revenues early and delay reporting of expenses. Such a practice would lead to overstating profits and making company performance look better than it actually was.

Although criminal charges have been filed, the company did not believe that the managers benefited personally. Some managers resigned before the scandal broke feeling ". . . 'compromised' as a financial professional." Others were "too scared to speak out because they're worried about losing their jobs and paying their mortgages."

Tesco paid a fine of $162 million and compensation to shareholders as a result of the activities.

Sources: Jolly, David, and Chad Bray, "3 Former Tesco Executives Charged with Fraud over Accounting Scandal," *New York Times,* September 9, 2016; "Tesco Agrees to Pay $162 Million Fine over Accounting Scandal," *Fortune,* March 28, 2017; Colson, Thomas, "'The Current Environment Has Broken Me': Tesco Accounting Scandal 'Compromised' Staff and Sparked Resignations," *Business Insider,* October 3, 2017.

measurement and compensation systems and how those incentives could lead to unethical (or even illegal) conduct. For example, imagine the pressure you would feel to remain silent about unfavorable accounting implications of actions that your boss (the CEO) wanted to take. You would probably find it difficult to tell your boss about these implications, especially when he or she would stand to benefit personally from the actions.

4. What are the three essential steps a cost accountant should take when faced with an ethical conflict?

The solution to this question is at the end of the chapter.

Cost Accounting and Other Business Disciplines

Finally, keep in mind that cost accounting does not exist in a vacuum. The boundary between what is cost accounting and what belongs in another discipline is often blurred. This is natural because in the "real world," problems are generally multidisciplinary. Production managers use cost accounting data to make scheduling and inventory decisions requiring concepts from operations. We will look to some concepts from organizational behavior because changes in the cost accounting system must be implemented by individuals in the organization who will react in different ways. Marketing issues arise when we use cost accounting data to evaluate pricing decisions. Throughout the book, we will venture into these other disciplines as a matter of course.

Key Takeaways

1. Cost accounting identifies where value is being added (or lost) throughout the value chain.
2. The critical thinking framework includes
   a. Defining the question.
   b. Identifying the data
   c. Applying data analytics.
   d. Presenting effective data visualizations.
3. Cost accountants are often confronted with ethical issues. Professional guidelines provide advice on how to deal these issues.

SUMMARY

This chapter discusses the use of cost accounting in its two primary managerial uses: decision making and performance evaluation. The following list summarizes key ideas tied to the chapter's learning objectives. For example, LO 1-1 refers to the first learning objective in the chapter.

LO 1-1 Describe the way managers use accounting information to create value in organizations. Managers make decisions to increase the value of the organization using information from the accounting system. Cost information helps identify value-increasing alternatives and activities that do not add value to the product or service.

LO 1-2 Distinguish between the uses and users of cost accounting and financial accounting information. Financial accounting information provides information to users (decision makers) who are not involved in the operations and strategy of the firm. These users are often external to the firm. While cost accounting information is often used in the financial accounting system, its primary role is to aid managers inside the firm in making operational and strategic decisions.

LO 1-3 Explain how cost accounting information is used for decision making and performance evaluation in organizations. Cost accounting information can be used for decision making by assessing differential costs associated with alternative courses of action. Accounting information also can be used to evaluate performance by comparing budget amounts to actual results.

LO 1-4 Identify current trends in cost accounting, including data analytics and data visualization. Cost accounting changes with changes in information technology and the adoption of new operational techniques. A critical thinking framework is increasingly important for analyzing business decisions.

LO 1-5 Understand ethical issues faced by accountants and ways to deal with ethical problems that you face in your career. Ethical standards exist for management accountants. These standards are related to competence, confidentiality, integrity, and objectivity.

KEY TERMS

big data, *17*
budget, *14*
cost accounting, *6*
cost-benefit analysis, *10*
cost drivers, *11*
critical thinking, *16*
data analytics, *17*
data visualization, *18*
differential costs, *11*
differential revenues, *11*
distribution chain, *5*

enterprise resource planning (ERP), *15*
financial accounting, *6*
generally accepted accounting principles
   (GAAP), *7*
international financial reporting standards
   (IFRS), *7*
nonvalue-added activities, *10*
responsibility center, *12*
supply chain, *5*
value-added activities, *4*
value chain, *4*

REVIEW QUESTIONS

1-1. Explain why it is important to consider the concepts of value and value creation in a textbook about cost accounting.

1-2. Explain the differences between financial accounting and cost accounting. Why are these differences important?

1-3. Place the letter of the appropriate accounting cost in Column 2 in the blank next to each decision category in Column 1.

Column 1	Column 2
_____ Providing cost information for financial reporting	A. Costs for performance evaluation
_____ Identifying the best store in a chain	B. Costs for inventory valuation
_____ Determining which plant to use for production	C. Costs for decision making

1-4. Distinguish among the value chain, the supply chain, and the distribution chain.

1-5. Who are the customers of cost accounting?

1-6. How can cost accounting information, together with a classification of activities into those that are value-added and those that are nonvalue-added, help managers improve an organization's performance?

1-7. Identify three key financial managers in an organization and their major responsibilities.

1-8. What are the four questions of the critical thinking framework?

1-9. Does the passage of Sarbanes-Oxley mean that codes of ethics are no longer necessary?

CRITICAL ANALYSIS AND DISCUSSION QUESTIONS

1-10. Explain how cost accounting supports value creation in the organization.

1-11. As the owner of a wholesale firm that only sells to retailers, should you be interested in the efficiency of your customers (the retailers)? Why?

1-12. You are considering lending a car to a friend so she can drive to Aspen. What costs would you ask her to reimburse? How would your answer change, if at all, if you decided to go along? Identify the possible options and explain your choices.

1-13. How does cost accounting help determine an organization's strategy? What problems might arise from a faulty cost accounting system?

1-14. Would you support a proposal to develop a set of "generally accepted" accounting standards for measuring executive performance that would be used to determine compensation? Why or why not?

1-15. How would cost accounting information help managers in a not-for-profit organization? Is it as important as in a publicly traded, for-profit firm?

1-16. Goodyear Tire and Rubber Company manufactures a well-known automotive tire. They are produced in Goodyear plants and sold to consumers in many outlets including auto parts retail chains such as Pep Boys. Both Goodyear and Pep Boys need to calculate the cost of a tire for, among other things, determining the cost of goods sold and inventory balances for financial statements. What are some important differences in determining the cost of tires for the two companies?

1-17. Hostess Brands makes a variety of baked goods just like The AM Bakery. In what ways are the cost accounting issues the same? In what ways are they different?

1-18. What potential conflicts might arise between marketing managers and the controller's staff? How might these potential conflicts be resolved with a minimum of interference from the chief executive officer?

1-19. Refer to the Business Application discussion of supply chain costs. A colleague says, "We don't have to worry about other firms in the supply chain. If every firm in the chain minimizes its own cost, we can minimize the total cost and give the customer the best value." Do you agree?

1-20. Refer to the Business Application discussion of accounting choices. In the case of Tesco, managers made choices about the timing of revenues and expenses that led to fraud charges. In order to avoid that, perhaps accountants should always assume the worst-case outcome. Then they will not be accused of misleading investors. What do you think about this approach?

1-21. Why does a cost accountant need to be familiar with new developments in information technology?

1-22. Will studying cost accounting increase the chances that The AM Bakery will succeed? How? Will it guarantee success? Explain.

1-23. Many companies, especially in the travel industry (airlines, hotels, and so on), have so-called loyalty programs offering members benefits that depend on the frequency of purchases, miles traveled, or amount of money spent, among other measures. One example is an upgrade to a better seat or to a better room for the same price as a regular seat or regular room. Such upgrades are generally based on availability, meaning the hotel or airline does not believe it will sell the room or seat. What, if anything, does such an upgrade cost the hotel or airline? Would these costs show up in the accounting records? Explain.

EXERCISES      All applicable Exercises are included in Connect.

(LO 1-1)   **1-24. Value Chain and Classification of Costs**

Pfizer Inc., a pharmaceutical firm, incurs many types of costs in its operations.

Required

For each cost in the following table, identify the stage in the value chain where this cost is incurred.

Cost	Stage in the Value Chain
____ Salaries for employees to develop most efficient dropper to administer drug	1. Customer service
____ Cost of chemicals to make the drug	2. Design
____ Cost to visit doctors to explain the value of the drug	3. Research and development
____ Expenses to deliver products to customers	4. Marketing
____ Laboratory experiments to evaluate drug effectiveness	5. Production
____ Employee costs to work with hospitals to ensure adequate supplies	6. Distribution

(LO 1-1)   **1-25. Value Chain and Classification of Costs**

Tesla, Inc., incurs many types of costs in its automobile operations.

Required

For each cost in the following table, identify the stage in the value chain where this cost is incurred.

Cost	Stage in the Value Chain
____ Engineering cost to develop optimal batteries	1. Production
____ Costs for employees to develop grill logo	2. Customer service
____ Costs to assemble cars	3. Design
____ Costs to attend the Detroit Auto Show	4. Marketing
____ Costs to ship cars to sales centers for customer delivery	5. Distribution
____ Call center to handle maintenance calls from customers with problems on the road	6. Research and development

(LO 1-1)   **1-26. Supply Chain and Supply Chain Costs**

Marquette Company manufactures and sells kits that homeowners can buy and assemble into office and home furniture.

Marquette and one of its customers, Goulburn Furnishings, have a dispute about inventory. Goulburn orders 100,000 units annually of one of the desk models sold by Marquette. Because demand fluctuates, Goulburn wants Marquette to keep a six-week inventory for unexpected demand. Marquette operates with a zero-inventory policy as a way of remaining competitive, though it has never been able to completely avoid holding inventory.

After an analysis of costs, you determine that inventory storage costs per kit are $25 at Marquette and $10 at Goulburn.

Required

How do you suggest the two companies settle their dispute?

(LO 1-2)   **1-27. Accounting Systems**

Five Below is a discount retailer.

Required

For each of the following decisions, indicate whether the decision maker would be more likely to get information from the financial (F) or cost (C) accounting system of Five Below (in addition, perhaps, to other information).

a.   A retailing competitor wants to compare her company's financial performance to Five Below.

b.   A labor organization representing workers at Five Below stores is deciding whether Five Below is profitable enough to negotiate for pay raises.

c.   An advertising manager at Five Below is deciding what media to use for commercials based on the profitability of different demographic groups.

d.   A marketing manager at Five Below is trying to determine whether to enter a new geographic location.

e.   An investor is deciding whether to purchase stock in Five Below.

1-28. Accounting Systems (LO 1-2)

John Deere Company manufactures farm equipment. Managers at assembly plants must make many decisions, and for this, they use cost accounting information.

Required

For each of the following managers, identify a decision that they might make for which cost accounting data would be useful:

a. Quality supervisor

b. Purchasing manager

c. Personnel manager

d. Maintenance supervisor

e. Plant manager

1-29. Cost Data for Managerial Purposes (LO 1-3)

As an analyst at Delta Air Lines, you are asked to help the operations staff. Operations has identified a new method of loading baggage that is expected to result in a 30 percent reduction in labor time but no changes in any other costs. The current labor cost to load bags is $2 per bag. Other costs are $1 per bag.

Required

a. What differential costs should the operations staff consider for the decision to use the new method next year? What would be the cost savings per bag using it?

b. Describe how management would use the information in requirement (*a*) and any other appropriate information to proceed with the contemplated use of the new baggage loading method.

1-30. Cost Data for Managerial Purposes (LO 1-3)

Lessing Toy and Hobby (LTH) is a chain of hobby and craft stores in the Southeast. LTH operates multiple stores and is organized into two divisions: Northern and Southern. Individual stores are placed in one or the other division based on geography. Recent demographic changes in the Northern Division area have led to declining foot traffic and sales in the LTH stores. Senior corporate executives have been asking whether the chain should close those stores and focus on the stores in the Southern Division. The most recent income statement for the Northern Division follows.

LESSING TOY & HOBBY
Northern Division
For the Year Ending January 31
($000)

Sales revenue	$12,040
Costs	
Cost of goods sold	$ 6,020
Advertising	490
Administrative salaries	810
Sales commissions	1,624
Rent and occupancy expense	2,058
Allocated corporate support	1,330
Total costs	$12,332
Net loss before tax benefit	$ (292)
Tax benefit at 25%	(73)
Net loss	$ (219)

The CEO has asked for your thoughts on the decision to close the Northern Division stores. If the Northern Division is eliminated and the stores closed, neither total corporate support costs nor operations or costs of the Southern Division stores are expected to change.

Required

What revenues and costs are probably differential for the decision to close the Northern Division stores? What will be the effect on LTH's income if the Northern Division stores are closed? Is there any other information you would like to have before making your recommendation?

(LO 1-3)   **1-31. Cost Data for Managerial Purposes**

Swain Athletic Gear (SAG) operates six retail outlets in a large Midwest city. One is in center city on Cornwall Street and the others are scattered around the perimeter of the city. Management at SAG is concerned about declining sales and profitability of the Cornwell store and believes that outlet has been a drag on profits in recent years. The most recent income statement for the Cornwall store follows.

SWAIN ATHLETIC GEAR
Cornwall Street Store Income Statement
For the Year Ending February 28

Sales revenue.................................	$12,300,000
Costs	
Cost of goods sold	$ 5,289,000
Advertising.................................	1,421,000
Store administrative salaries	975,000
Sales commissions	1,056,000
Leases and utilities..........................	2,100,000
Allocated corporate support	1,622,000
Total costs	$12,463,000
Net loss before tax benefit.....................	$ (163,000)
Tax benefit at 25%	(40,750)
Net loss.....................................	$ (122,250)

The CFO at SAG has asked for your advice on closing the Cornwall Street store. If the Cornwall Street store is closed, neither total corporate support costs nor operations or costs of the other stores are expected to change.

Required

What revenues and costs are probably differential for the decision to close the Cornwall Street store? What will be the effect on SAG's income if the Cornwall Street store is closed? Is there any other information you would like to have before making your recommendation?

(LO 1-3)   **1-32. Cost Data for Managerial Purposes**

One of the major activities of the City Art Museum (CAM) is a Neighborhood Outreach Program, which was developed both as a public service and to market the museum and its other programs. One of the Outreach offerings, which is popular with both city and suburban residents, is the weekly Evening Lecture Series. The Series provides lectures on local art and history in various locations throughout the greater metropolitan area.

CITY ART MUSEUM
Neighborhood Outreach: Evening Lecture Series
For the Year Ending June 30

Sales revenue.................................	$386,000
Costs	
Advertising.................................	$ 15,000
Lecturer fees and expenses	195,000
Operating costs (staff)........................	26,000
Space rental	12,000
Food and beverage expenses..................	25,000
Allocated museum overhead	143,000
Total costs	$416,000
Net loss.....................................	($ 30,000)

A new museum director has been hired with the goal to make the museum more self-sustaining and less reliant on donations and government grants. One of the director's first actions was to ask the museum staff to put together detailed financial information on the individual activities. The result, shown in the accompanying table, indicates that the series operates at a loss.

The director is considering canceling the program if the loss cannot be eliminated. After discussions with various staff, the director concludes that raising the fees for attending the lectures is not possible given current economic conditions in the area. The director has asked you for your recommendation.

If the Series is cancelled, the total museum overhead is not expected to change. However, the other costs, which are directly related to the program (lecturer fees, space rental, and so on) would be saved. Dropping the Series will not affect the costs or operations of any of the other Outreach programs.

Required
What revenues and costs are probably differential for the decision to drop the Evening Lecture Series? What will be the net effect on the museum's contribution (profit) if the Series is cancelled? Is there any other information you would like before making your recommendation for the director?

1-33. Cost Data for Managerial Purposes   (LO 1-3)

Refer to the information in Exercise 1-32. The museum director is considering a proposal by the head of the Neighborhood Outreach Program to keep the Evening Lecture Series but expand it by offering a Weekend Lecture Series as well. The Weekend Series would be offered in a single location downtown near the museum itself.

The program head estimates that the attendance of the combined Series (Evening and Weekend) would be double that of the current Evening Series. The revenue of the combined Series would be 90 percent higher because of some price discounts that would be offered. Because the Weekend Series would be new, a more intensive advertising campaign would be required. The director estimates that advertising costs for the combined Series would be 150 percent higher than their current level. Lecturer fees and expenses will increase by only 75 percent because of the larger rooms used on the weekend. Staff operating costs will increase by 25 percent. Rental costs for the Weekend Series will be $12,000 annually. Total food and beverage costs will increase by 60 percent with the new Series. The larger program will require an increase in museum overhead of $8,000. Allocated museum overhead for the combined Series will be $35,000 annually.

Required
a.   Given these estimates, what will the contribution of the expanded lecture series be?

b.   Are there other factors the director should consider before making a decision?

1-34. Cost Data for Managerial Purposes—Budgeting   (LO 1-3)

Refer to Exhibit 1.6, which shows budgeted versus actual costs. Assume that The AM Bakery is preparing a budget for the month ending October 31. Management prepares the budget by starting with the *actual* results for August 31 that appear in Exhibit 1.6. Next, management considers what the differences in costs will be between August and October.

Management expects revenue in October to be 20 percent more than in August, and it expects all ingredient costs (e.g., flour, butter, and so on) to be 20 percent higher in October than in August. Management expects "other" labor costs to be 25 percent higher in October than in August, partly because more labor will be required in October and partly because employees will receive a pay raise. The manager will receive a pay raise that will increase his salary from $4,500 in August to $5,000 in October. Rent, utilities, and marketing costs are not expected to change.

Required
Prepare a budget for The AM Bakery for October.

1-35. Cost Data for Managerial Purposes—Budgeting   (LO 1-3)

Refer to the information in Exercise 1-30. The managers of Lessing Toy & Hobby (LTH) have decided to keep the stores in the Northern Division open, in spite of the dwindling demand in the area. They want to forecast what the income will be in the coming year, using the income statement in Exercise 1-30 as the base. The cost analyst at LTH estimates sales in the coming year will only be 85 percent of the current year sales. Cost of goods sold is estimated to be 90 percent of the current year. The managers have decided to increase advertising next year by 10 percent above the current year, but will cut administrative salaries in the Northern Division by 30 percent. They also expect to lower rent and occupancy costs by 15 percent. Allocated corporate overhead, based on information from the CFO, is expected to be $1.2 million.

Required

Prepare an income statement for the coming year for the Northern Division based on the estimates provided by the cost analyst and other managers at LTH.

(LO 1-4)   **1-36. Trends in Cost Accounting**

Required

For each cost accounting development listed as follows, identify one value chain component where it might be used and describe how it could be used in that component.

a.   Activity-based costing

b.   Benchmarking

c.   Cost of quality

d.   Customer relationship management

e.   Lean accounting

(LO 1-4)   **1-37. Critical Thinking in Cost Accounting**

Refer to the opening vignette of Adam Mercer and The AM Bakery. Adam has hired you to help him make the decisions he needs to make.

Required

Answer the four questions in the critical thinking framework identified in the chapter that will guide your analysis.

(LO 1-4)   **1-38. Data Visualization in Cost Accounting**

Refer to Exhibit 1.10 (Panel A), which is a heat map based on the profitability of the six districts for The AM Bakery. A new intern tells you that a better heat map is the one shown here, ". . . because the high numbers are all green and the low numbers are all red."

Required

a.   Can you identify the most profitable district from the intern's heat map?

b.   Do you think the intern's heat map is as effective at communicating the results of the analysis compared to the heat map in Exhibit 1.10? Explain.

	A	B	C
1		**THE AM BAKERY**	
2	**Annual Revenue and Profit by District**		
3			
4	**District**	**Annual Reve**	**Annual Profit**
5	District 1	$3,926,503	$1,050,686
6	District 2	3,749,256	1,165,390
7	District 3	5,568,574	1,769,757
8	District 4	3,690,913	1,217,799
9	District 5	6,159,927	2,212,114
10	District 6	4,927,492	2,056,521
11		28,022,665	9,472,267

(LO 1-5)   **1-39. Ethics and Channel Stuffing**

Continental Condiments is a large food products firm in Pennsylvania. Its sales staff has a strong incentive plan tied to meeting quarterly budgets. On June 25, the divisional controller learns that some of the sales staff asked customers to take delivery of sizable quantities of products before June 30. The customers were told they could return the products after July 1 if they determined the items were not needed. (This is referred to as "channel stuffing.") The sales staff also offered to reimburse the customers for any storage costs incurred.

Required

a.   From the viewpoint of the IMA's "Statement of Ethical Professional Practice," what are the controller's responsibilities?

b.   What steps should the controller take to resolve this problem?

(CMA adapted)

(LO 1-5)   **1-40. Ethics and Cost Analysis**

Refer to the information in Exercise 1-33. The cost analyst working in the CFO's office at the City Art Museum learns that the space to be rented for the Weekend Lecture Series is owned by a company in which the museum director is a principal investor. After some research, the analyst also identifies another comparable site, which rents for $8,000 per year.

Required

a.   From the viewpoint of the IMA's "Statement of Ethical Professional Practice," what are the analyst's responsibilities?

b.   What steps should the analyst take to resolve this problem?

1-41. Cost Data for Managerial Purposes

(LO 1-3)

Haverhill Electronics (HE) has offered to supply the county government with one model of its security screening device at "cost plus 20 percent." HE operates a manufacturing plant that can produce 22,000 devices per year, but it normally produces 20,000. The costs to produce 20,000 devices follow.

	Total Cost	Cost per Device
Production costs:		
Materials	$ 1,000,000	$ 50
Labor	2,000,000	100
Supplies and other costs that will vary with production	600,000	30
Indirect cost that will not vary with production	600,000	30
Variable marketing costs	400,000	20
Administrative costs (will not vary with production)	1,200,000	60
Totals	$5,800,000	$290

Based on these data, company management expects to receive $348 (= $290 × 120 percent) per device for those sold on this contract. After completing 200 devices, the company sent a bill (invoice) to the government for $69,600 (= 200 devices × $348 per device).

The president of the company received a call from a county auditor, who stated that the per device cost should be as follows.

Materials	$ 50
Labor	100
Supplies and other costs that will vary with production	30
	$180

Therefore, the price per device should be $216 (= $180 × 120 percent). The county government ignored marketing costs because the contract bypassed the usual selling channels.

Required

What price would you recommend? Why? (*Note:* You need not limit yourself to the costs selected by the company or by the government auditor.)

1-42. Cost Data for Managerial Purposes

(LO 1-3)

Durham Parts (DP) makes a variety of products. It is organized in two divisions, Eastern and Western. The managers for each division are paid, in part, based on the financial performance of their divisions. The Western Division normally sells to outside customers but, on occasion, also sells to the Eastern Division. When it does, corporate policy states that the price must be cost plus 25 percent to ensure a "fair" return to the selling division. Western received an order from Eastern for 1,200 units. Western's planned output for the year had been 4,800 units before Eastern's order. Western's capacity is 6,000 units per year. The costs for producing those 4,800 units follow.

	Total	Per Unit
Materials	$240,000	$ 50
Direct labor	115,200	24
Other costs varying with output	76,800	16
Fixed costs (do not vary with output)	288,000	60
Total costs	$720,000	$150

Required

a.   If you are the manager of the Western Division, what unit cost would you ask the Eastern Division to pay? Show calculations.

b.   If you are the manager of the Eastern Division, what unit cost would you argue you should pay? Show calculations.

c.   What unit cost would you recommend for a sale of units from the Western Division to the Eastern Division? Explain briefly.

(LO 1-3)   **1-43. Cost Data for Managerial Purposes**

Bates Courier Services provides delivery services in and around Butte City. Its profits have been declining, and management is planning to add an express service that is expected to increase revenue by $62,500 per year. The total cost to lease the necessary additional package delivery vehicles from the local dealer is $10,000 per year. The present manager will continue to supervise all services at no increase in salary. Due to expansion, however, the labor costs and utilities would increase by 50 percent. Rent and other costs will increase by 20 percent. The income statement assuming no expansion follows.

	A	B
1	**BATES COURIER SERVICES**	
2	**Annual Income Statement before Expansion**	
3		
4	Sales revenue............................	$ 190,000
5	Costs	
6	Vehicle leases	$ 75,000
7	Labor.......................................	60,000
8	Utilities.....................................	10,000
9	Rent...	20,000
10	Other costs.............................	10,000
11	Manager's salary......................	30,000
12	Total costs.................................	$ 205,000
13	Operating profit (loss)..................	$ (15,000)

Required

a.   Prepare a report of the differential costs and revenues if the express service is added. (*Hint:* Use the format of Exhibit 1.4.)

b.   Should management start the express service?

c.   Are there factors beyond the differential costs and revenues that management should consider?

(LO 1-3)   **1-44. Cost Data for Managerial Purposes**

Kendall & Floyd provides landscaping services in Eastvale. Sara Kendall, the owner, is concerned about the recent losses the company has incurred and is considering dropping its yard cleanup services, which she feels are marginal to the company's business. She estimates that doing so will result in lost revenues of $125,000 per year (including the lost tree business from customers who use the company for both services). The present manager will continue to supervise the tree services with no reduction in salary. Without the lawn business, Sara estimates that the company will save 20 percent of the equipment leases, labor, and other costs. She also expects to save 15 percent on rent and utilities. The income statement before dropping the yard cleanup service follows.

Required

a.   Prepare a report of the differential costs and revenues if the yard cleanup service is discontinued. (*Hint:* Use the format of Exhibit 1.4.)

b.   Should Sara discontinue the lawn service?

c.   Are there factors other than the differential costs and revenues that Sara should consider?

	A	B
1	**KENDALL & FLOYD**	
2	**Annual Income Statement**	
3	**(Before Dropping Yard Cleanup Services)**	
4		
5	Sales revenue.............................	$ 684,000
6	Costs	
7	Equipment leases	$ 270,000
8	Labor.......................................	216,000
9	Utilities....................................	36,000
10	Rent...	72,000
11	Other costs..............................	36,000
12	Manager's salary.......................	90,000
13	Total costs................................	$ 720,000
14	Operating profit (loss).................	$ (36,000)
15		

1-45. Cost Data for Managerial Purposes

(LO 1-3)

B-You is a consulting firm that works with managers to improve their interpersonal skills. Recently, a representative of a high-tech research firm approached B-You's owner with an offer to contract for one year with B-You to improve the interpersonal skills of a newly hired manager. B-You reported the following costs and revenues during the past year (before the proposed contract).

	A	B
1	**B-YOU**	
2	**Annual Income Statement**	
3		
4	Sales revenue...........................	$ 550,000
5	Costs	
6	Labor.......................................	260,000
7	Equipment lease......................	40,000
8	Rent..	35,000
9	Supplies.................................	27,000
10	Officers' salaries......................	160,000
11	Other costs.............................	17,000
12	Total costs...............................	$ 539,000
13	Operating profit (loss).................	$ 11,000
14		

If B-You decides to take the contract to help the manager, it will hire a full-time consultant at $85,000. The equipment lease will increase by 20 percent. Supplies will increase by an estimated 10 percent and other costs by 15 percent. The existing building has space for the new consultant. No new offices will be necessary for this work.

Required

a. What are the differential costs that would be incurred as a result of taking the contract?

b. If the contract will pay $100,000, should B-You accept it?

c. What considerations, other than costs, do you think are necessary before making this decision?

1-46. Cost Data for Managerial Purposes

(LO 1-3)

Forman's Services is a small accounting firm that offers payroll and bookkeeping services to small businesses and individuals. A local merchant has approached Will Forman, the owner, about taking over his payroll disbursements but is concerned about the fees Forman's normally charges. The costs and revenues at Forman's Services follow.

	A	B
	FORMAN'S SERVICES	
1		
2	**Annual Income Statement**	
3		
4	Sales revenue.....................	$ 1,080,000
5	Costs	
6	Labor.............................	715,500
7	Equipment lease.................	75,600
8	Rent...............................	64,800
9	Supplies...........................	48,600
10	Owner's salary..................	112,500
11	Other costs.......................	34,200
12	Total costs.........................	$ 1,051,200
13	Operating profit (loss).............	$ 28,800
14		
15		

If Forman's gets the merchant's business, it will incur an additional $30,000 in labor costs. Will also estimates that he will have to increase equipment leases by about 10 percent, supplies by 15 percent, and other costs by 5 percent. There will be no additional rent.

Required

a. What are the differential costs that would be incurred as a result of adding this new client?

b. Will would normally charge about $50,000 in fees for the services the store would require. How much could he offer to charge and still not lose money on this client?

c. What considerations, other than costs, are necessary before making this decision?

(LO 1-3)   **1-47. Cost Data for Managerial Purposes**

Langholm Bistro is a popular restaurant in a small, coastal village. Brian Langholm, who opened the restaurant five years ago, has seen it grow steadily. Currently, Langholm's is only open for dinner, but many of the regular customers have been asking Brian to consider opening for lunch as well. Brian has been talking to his accountant about the financial impact of the expanded services on the overall business. He knew that the bistro did not make much money and he was concerned that the new business might be too risky. The accountant asked Brian for his best estimates of the impact of the new business on revenues and costs. He had been thinking about this for some time and estimated that revenues would grow by about 25 percent. Food costs would increase by about 40 percent and labor costs by about 25 percent. Rent on the bistro would not change, but utilities would increase by about 20 percent. Other costs would increase by 10 percent. The salary Brian pays himself as manager of the bistro would not change. A few days later, Brian's accountant stops by with the following estimated income statement assuming Brian adds the lunch business.

	A	B
1	**Langholm Bistro**	
2	**Annual Income Statement**	
3	**(Assuming Both Lunch and Dinner Services)**	
4		
5	Sales revenue	$ 676,000
6	Costs	
7	Food costs	$ 196,000
8	Labor	270,000
9	Rent	36,000
10	Utilities	52,500
11	Other costs	39,050
12	Manager's salary	60,000
13	Total costs	$ 653,550
14	Operating profit (loss)	$ 22,450
15		

Required

a. Based on the financial impact, should Brian open the bistro for lunch? Explain.

b. Are there other factors he should consider? Explain briefly.

1-48. Cost Data for Managerial Purposes   (LO 1-3)

Holborn Appliance Shop is a small business located on the coast. It specializes in appliance repair and is known in the area for fast, reliable, and friendly service. Katie Holborn, the owner and primary repair specialist, has been working with appliances since she learned about them helping her father in his shop. After teaching a class on appliance repair at the local technical college, Katie thinks she might be able to develop a training business to complement the shop's repair work. Katie has put together some estimates on the impact of a training program on revenues and costs. She estimates that revenues would grow by about 30 percent. Parts costs (mostly for demonstration machines) would increase by about 10 percent and labor costs by about 50 percent. The rent, which is based on revenue, would also increase by about 30 percent. Utilities would increase by about 30 percent and insurance costs by 18 percent. Other costs would increase by 20 percent. Using her spreadsheet skills, Katie puts together the following estimated annual income statement assuming she offers both repair and training services.

	A	B
1	**Holborn Appliance Shop**	
2	**Annual Income Statement**	
3	**(Assuming Both Repair and Training Services)**	
4		
5	Sales revenue	$ 474,500
6	Costs	
7	Parts	$ 110,000
8	Labor	180,000
9	Rent	52,000
10	Utilities	39,000
11	Insurance	4,130
12	Other costs	21,600
13	Total costs	$ 406,730
14	Operating profit (loss)	$ 67,770
15		

Required

a. Based on the financial impact, should Katie add training to her current repair business? Explain.

b. Are there other factors she should consider? Explain briefly.

1-49. Cost Data for Managerial Purposes—Budgeting   (LO 1-3)

Refer to Exhibit 1.6. Assume that The AM Bakery is preparing a budget for the month ending November 30. Management prepares the budget by starting with the *actual* results for August that appear in Exhibit 1.6. Then, management considers what the differences in costs will be between August and November.

Management expects revenue in November to be 30 percent higher than in August, and it expects all ingredient costs (e.g., flour, butter, and so on) to be 25 percent higher in November than in August. Management expects "other" labor costs to be 30 percent higher in November than in August, partly because more labor will be required in November and partly because employees will get a pay raise. The manager will get a pay raise that will increase his salary from $4,500 in August to $5,000 in November. Rent, utilities, and marketing costs are not expected to change.

Now, fast-forward to early December and assume the following actual results occurred in November.

	A	B
1	**THE AM BAKERY**	
2	Bakery Sales	
3	Actual Costs	
4	For the Month Ending November 30	
5		Actual
6	Ingredients	
7	Flour	$ 4,950
8	Butter	4,600
9	Oil	2,030
10	Fruit	1,550
11	Nuts	1,200
12	Chocolate	1,030
13	Other	460
14	Total ingredients	$ 15,820
15	Labor	
16	Channel manager	$ 5,000
17	Other	14,120
18	Utilities	2,400
19	Rent	3,600
20	Marketing	200
21	Total bakery costs	$ 41,140
22		
23	Revenues	$ 68,000

Required

a. Prepare a statement like the one in Exhibit 1.6 that compares the budgeted and actual costs for November.

b. Suppose that you have limited time to determine why actual costs are not the same as budgeted costs. Which three cost items would you investigate to see why actual and budgeted costs are different? Why would you choose those three costs?

(LO 1-3)   **1-50. Cost Data for Managerial Purposes—Budgeting**

Refer to Exhibit 1.6, which shows budgeted versus actual costs. Assume that The AM Bakery is preparing a budget for the month ending December 31. Management prepares the budget for the month ending December 31 by starting with the *actual* results for August that appear in Exhibit 1.6. Then, management considers what the differences in costs will be between August and December.

Management expects revenue to be 100 percent greater in December than in August because of the holiday season. Management expects that all food costs (e.g., flour, butter, and so on) will be 120 percent higher in December than in August because of the increase in sales and because prices for ingredients are generally higher in the high-demand holiday months. Management expects "other" labor costs to be 130 percent higher in December than in August, partly because more labor will be required in December and partly because employees will get a pay raise. The manager will get a pay raise that will increase his salary from $4,500 in August to $5,000 in December. Utilities will be 15 percent higher in December than in August. Rent and marketing will be the same in December as in August.

Now, move ahead to January of the following year and assume the following actual results occurred in December.

Required

a. Prepare a statement like the one in Exhibit 1.6 that compares the budgeted and actual costs.

b. Suppose that you have limited time to determine why actual costs are not the same as budgeted costs. Which three cost items would you investigate to see why actual and budgeted costs are different? Why would you choose those three costs?

	A	B
1	**THE AM BAKERY**	
2	Bakery Sales	
3	Actual Costs	
4	For the Month Ending December 31	
5		Actual
6	Ingredients	
7	Flour	$ 8,465
8	Butter	7,680
9	Oil	3,800
10	Fruit	3,125
11	Nuts	2,200
12	Chocolate	1,600
13	Other	850
14	Total ingredients	$ 27,720
15	Labor	
16	Channel manager	$ 5,000
17	Other	24,400
18	Utilities	3,125
19	Rent	3,600
20	Marketing	210
21	Total bakery costs	$ 64,055
22		
23	Revenues	$ 103,200

1-51. Cost Data for Managerial Purposes—Budgeting   (LO 1-3)

Luce Original Baking Supplies (LOBS) sells equipment to homes and small businesses for baking. There are two distribution channels. Customers can shop and purchase at a retail outlet located near the company warehouse. Alternatively, they can order online and have it delivered.

The company founder and president has been disappointed in the retail profitability and is considering offering only the online option. The most recent income statement for the Retail Channel follows.

	A	B	C	D
1	**LUCE ORIGINAL BAKING SUPPLIES**			
2	Retail Distribution Channel Income Statement			
3	For the Year Ending October 31			
4				
5	Sales revenue			$19,100,000
6				
7	Costs			
8		Cost of goods sold		$11,222,000
9		Advertising		2,895,000
10		Retail store staff costs		1,013,000
11		Sales commissions		500,000
12		Retail store lease expenses		1,640,000
13		Allocated corporate costs		1,954,000
14	Total costs			$19,224,000
15	Net loss before tax benefit			($124,000)
16	Tax benefit at 25%			(31,000)
17	Net loss			($93,000)
18				

Closing the retail outlet will not affect total corporate costs. The marketing manager at LOBS estimates that the company will lose 40 percent of the current retail sales. This estimate assumes that some retail customers will switch to the online service while others will shop elsewhere. The marketing manager also plans to cut advertising currently assigned to retail by 25 percent. The remaining amount will be added to the online marketing campaign.

The operations manager estimates that cost of goods will also fall by 40 percent of the current cost of the retail operation. Sixty percent of current retail staff costs will be saved. The remaining 40 percent will be added to warehouse staffing costs. No sales commissions are paid for sales through the online channel. The retail outlet building and property are currently leased on an annual basis and the lease can be cancelled without penalty at any time. Shipping costs in the online channel will increase by $200,000 because of the additional online sales.

Required

a. What revenues and costs are probably differential for the decision to discontinue the Retail Channel at LOBS?

b. What will be the effect on LOBS income if the Retail Channel is closed?

c. Is there any other information you would like to have before making your recommendation?

(LO 1-3)   **1-52. Cost Data for Managerial Purposes—Finding Unknowns**

Whitcomb Foods is a small company in Oregon that packages and sells organic juices. Recently, a sales rep from one of the company's suppliers suggested that Whitcomb could increase its profitability by 50 percent if it introduced a second line of products, packaged dried fruit for snacks. The rep offered to do the analysis and show the company the assumptions made.

When Whitcomb's management opened the spreadsheet sent by the sales rep, they noticed that there were several blank cells. In the meantime, the sales rep had taken a job with a competitor and told the managers at Whitcomb that "I can no longer advise you." Although they were not sure they should rely on the analysis, they asked you to see if you could reconstruct the sales rep's analysis. They had been considering this new business already and wanted to see if their analysis was close to that of an outside observer. The incomplete spreadsheet follows.

	A	B	C	D	E
1		**WHITCOMB FOODS**			
2		**Projected Annual Income Statement**			
3		Status Quo: Single Product	% Increase (Decrease)	Alternative: Two Products	Difference
4	Sales..........................	$ (d)	30%	$ 195,000	(e)
5					
6	Costs.........................				
7	Material...................	30,000	40%	42,000	12,000
8	Labor......................	(k)	20%	(m)	(o)
9	Rent........................	(l)	0%	(n)	(p)
10	Depreciation.............	6,000	25%	7,500	1,500
11	Utilities...................	3,000	25%	(h)	(i)
12	Other.......................	10,500	(j)	15,750	5,250
13	Total costs..............	$ 114,000		(g)	(f)
14	Operating profit........	$ 36,000	(a)	(b)	$ (c)
15					

Required

Complete the spreadsheet by filling in the blank cells.

(LO 1-3)   **1-53. Cost Data for Managerial Purposes—Finding Unknowns**

Clifton Instruments is a small components maker located in Kansas. The company specializes in aircraft instruments and focuses its production around a single family of products. Recently, one of the new members of the company's board of directors suggested the company could increase its profitability by adding a second product line with an increase in the rent the company currently pays on its manufacturing facility of only 10 percent.

The board member had to resign because of a conflict of interest before presenting the analysis. An incomplete spreadsheet, following, was all that was available.

	A	B	C	D	E
1		**CLIFTON INSTRUMENTS**			
2		Projected Income Statement			
3		For One Year			
4		($000)			
5					
6		Status Quo:	% Increase	Alternative:	
7		Single Product	(Decrease)	Two Products	Difference
8	Sales revenue	(a)	(b)	(c)	$ 20,000
9					
10	Costs				
11	Material	24,000	22%	(d)	(e)
12	Labor	(f)	(g)	16,640	3,840
13	Rent	3,200	(h)	(i)	(j)
14	Depreciation	8,000	15%	9,200	1,200
15	Utilities	(k)	30%	16,640	(l)
16	Other	4,800	(m)	(n)	1,200
17	Total costs	$ 65,600		(o)	(p)
18	Operating profit	(q)		$ 18,720	(r)
19					

Required
Complete the spreadsheet by filling in the blank cells.

Hint: The letters do not necessarily indicate the order you should follow.

1-54. Cost Data for Managerial Purposes—Finding Unknowns   (LO 1-3)
Henderson Designs provides basic interior design services in a small town in the Rocky Mountain area. Lately, the growth in the business has slowed considerably and the managers have been looking at new services that might improve their prospects. The sales manager has suggested that adding some landscape design services would be a nice complement to their existing offerings. The manager put the analysis together and then suddenly quit.

You have been asked to reconstruct the analysis. The last known spreadsheet with the analysis is shown as follows. You recall that, in the last meeting, the sales manager estimated that Henderson would probably have to hire some additional employees to do the extra work. The analysis included an estimate that the new service would add about $108,000 to the annual labor costs.

	A	B	C	D	E
1		**HENDERSON DESIGNS**			
2		Projected Income Statement For the Year			
3					
4		Status Quo:	% Increase	Alternative	
5		Current Services	(Decrease)	Enhanced Services	Difference
6	Sales revenue	(a)	(b)	$ 2,250,000	(c)
7					
8	Costs				
9	Equipment lease	500,000	10%	550,000	50,000
10	Labor	(d)	(e)	468,000	(f)
11	Rent	(g)	20%	75,000	(h)
12	Depreciation	100,000	5%	(i)	(j)
13	Utilities	275,000	(k)	(l)	(m)
14	Other	100,000	(n)	(o)	(p)
15	Total costs	(q)		(r)	(s)
16	Operating profit	$ 477,500		(t)	$ 119,500
17					

Required
Complete the spreadsheet by filling in the cells. If you do not have sufficient information to determine the value in the cell, enter a "?".

Hint: The letters do not necessarily indicate the order you should follow.

1-55. Critical Thinking in Cost Accounting: Data Analysis   (LO 1-4)
Emily Cho, the consultant for The AM Bakery shows you the following table with district profitability and asks for a report on which district is most profitable, along with a brief explanation.

	A	B	C	D
1		THE AM BAKERY		
2		Annual Revenue and Profit by District		
3				
4	**District**	**Number of Stores**	**Annual Revenue**	**Annual Profit**
5	District 1	5	$3,926,503	$1,050,686
6	District 2	4	3,749,256	1,165,390
7	District 3	6	5,568,574	1,769,757
8	District 4	5	3,690,913	1,217,799
9	District 5	6	6,159,927	2,212,114
10	District 6	4	4,927,492	2,056,521
11	Total	30	28,022,665	9,472,267
12				

Required

Write a short report with your conclusions. Be sure to provide your reasoning.

   Hint: There is not necessarily a right or wrong answer here. Emily is more interested in your analysis.

(LO 1-4)   **1-56. Critical Thinking in Cost Accounting: Data Visualization**

Refer to the information in Problem 1-55. Prepare a report to communicate your findings. Emily tells you that Adam Mercer, the president, prefers graphics that help him understand the analysis.

Required

Prepare appropriate graphics to communicate the conclusions in your report.

   Note: You should not feel limited to the graphics or the software discussed in the text.

(LO 1-5)   **1-57. Responsibility for Ethical Action**

Dewi Hartono is an assistant controller at Giant Engineering, which contracts with the Defense Department to build and maintain roads on military bases. Dewi recently determined that the company was including the direct costs of work for private clients in overhead costs, some of which are charged to the government. She also discovered that several members of management appeared to be involved in altering accounting invoices to accomplish this. She was unable to determine, however, whether her superior, the controller, was involved. Dewi considered three possible courses of action: She could discuss the matter with the controller, anonymously release the information to the local newspaper, or discuss the situation with an outside member of the board of directors whom she knows personally.

Required

a.   Does Dewi have an ethical responsibility to take a course of action?

b.   Of the three possible courses of action, which are appropriate and which are inappropriate?

(CMA adapted)

INTEGRATIVE CASES

(LO 1-5)   **1-58. Identifying Unethical Actions**

The managers of Whitcomb Foods (Problem 1-52) decide they will hire a management accountant to help them analyze the decision to expand their product line. They solicit bids from various accountants in the city and receive three proposals. In describing their qualifications for the job, the three state the following:

   Accountant A: "I have recently advised the symphony on how to raise money and therefore I know the local area well."

   Accountant B: "I have advised several small firms on expansion plans."

   Accountant C: "I have advised Patrician Juices [Whitcomb's main competitor] and can share its experiences and insights with you."

All of the proposals have the same price.

Required

a.   As the accounting manager of Whitcomb Foods, prepare a memo recommending which accountant you would prefer to retain. Be sure to include your reasons.

b.   Which, if any, of the accountants making a proposal are violating the IMA's code of ethics? What is (are) the violation(s)?

1-59. Cost Data for Managerial Purposes—Finding Unknowns   (LO 1-3)

Miller Cereals is a small milling company that makes a single brand of cereal. Recently, a business school intern recommended that the company introduce a second cereal in order to "diversify the product portfolio." Currently, the company shows an operating profit that is 20 percent of sales. With the single product, other costs were twice the cost of rent.

The intern estimated that the incremental profit of the new cereal would only be 2.5 percent of the incremental revenue, but it would still add to total profit. On his last day, the intern told Miller's marketing manager that his analysis was on the company laptop in a spreadsheet with the file name NewProduct.xlsx (see below). The intern then left for a 12-month walkabout in the outback of Australia and cannot be reached.

When the marketing manager opened the file, it was corrupted and could not be opened. She then found an early (incomplete) copy on the company's backup server. The marketing manager then called a cost management accountant in the controller's office and asked for help in reconstructing the analysis indicated in the accompanying incomplete spreadsheet.

Required

As the management accountant, fill in the blank cells.

1-60. Identifying Unethical Actions   (LO 1-5)

Before Miller Cereals can introduce the new cereal, the board of directors has to give their approval. The marketing manager really wants to introduce the new product and believes (honestly) that it will be profitable and an important next step in the firm's evolution. However, the marketing manager knows that with the forecasted profit, the board will not approve its introduction.

MILLER CEREALS
Projected Income Statement
for One Year

	Status Quo: Single Product	% Increase (Decrease)	Alternative: Two Products	Difference
Sales revenue	$ (a)	40%	$ (b)	$60,000
Costs				
Material	40,000	(j)	60,000	(k)
Labor	(l)	20%	60,000	(m)
Rent	(q)	50%	(s)	(u)
Depreciation	8,000	(n)	8,000	—
Utilities	(o)	(p)	5,000	1,000
Other	(r)		(t)	(v)
Total costs	(g)		(i)	(h)
Operating profit	(c)	(f)	(e)	$ (d)

The marketing manager asks the management accountant what can be done. Based on that request, the accountant reviewed the numbers generated by the intern and thinks the numbers are reasonable. However, the accountant tells the marketing manager that "other" costs consist of many different things, so it would be difficult to question a lower number. The marketing manager suggests that the management accountant lower the estimated other costs by an amount sufficient to get board approval.

Required

Is the management accountant violating the IMA's code of ethics? If so, what is (are) the violation(s)?

1-61. Responsibility for Unethical Action   (LO 1-5)

The following story is true except that all names have been changed and the time period has been compressed.

Charles Austin graduated from a prestigious business school and took a job in a public accounting firm in Atlanta. A client hired him after five years of normal progress through the ranks of the accounting firm. This client was a rapidly growing, publicly held company that produced software for the healthcare industry. Charles started as assistant controller. The company promoted him to controller after four years. This was a timely promotion. Charles had learned a lot and was prepared to be controller.

Within a few months of his promotion to controller, the company's chief financial officer abruptly quit. Upon submitting her resignation, she walked into Charles's office and said, "I have given Holmes (the company president) my letter of resignation. I'll be out of my office in less than an hour. You will be the new chief financial officer, and you will report directly to Holmes. Here is my card with my personal cell phone number. Call me if you need any advice or if I can help you in any way."

Charles was in over his head in his new job. His experience had not prepared him for the range of responsibilities required of the company's chief financial officer. Holmes, the company president, was no help. He gave Charles only one piece of advice: "You have lots of freedom to run the finance department however you want. There is just one rule: Don't ever cross me. If you do, you'll never work again in this city." Charles believed his boss could follow through on that threat because he was so well-connected in the Atlanta business community.

The end of the company's fiscal year came shortly after Charles's promotion to chief financial officer. After reviewing some preliminary financial amounts, Holmes stormed into Charles's office and made it clear that the results were not to his liking. He instructed Charles to "find more sales." Charles was shocked, but he did as he was told. He identified some ongoing software installation work that should not have been recorded as revenue until the customer signed off on the job. Charles recorded the work done as of year-end as revenue, even though the customer had not signed off on the job. He sent an invoice to the customer for the amount of the improper revenue, then called her to say that the invoice was an accounting error and she should ignore it.

The next year, Charles's work life was better, but his personal life was not. He went through a costly divorce that resulted in limited time spent with his two small children. Now he was particularly concerned about not crossing his boss because of the threat that he would never work in Atlanta if he did. He could not bear to look for a new job that would take him away from his children. Further, it would be difficult to find a job anywhere that came close to paying the salary and benefits of his current job. With high alimony and child support payments, Charles would feel a dire financial strain if he had to take a cut in pay.

The company struggled financially during the year. Clearly, the company would not generate the level of revenues and income that Holmes wanted. As expected, he again instructed Charles to find some way to dress up the income statement. It did not matter to Holmes whether what Charles did was legal or not.

Charles had exhausted all legitimate ways of reducing costs and increasing revenues. He faced an ethical dilemma. He could resign and look for a new job, or he could illegitimately record nonexistent sales. He now understood why the former chief financial officer had resigned so abruptly. He wished that he could talk to her, but she was traveling in Australia and could not be contacted. The board of directors would be no help because they would take the president's side in a dispute.

After considering his personal circumstances, Charles decided to record the illegitimate sales as the president had instructed. Charles knew that what he did was wrong. He believed that if the fraud was discovered, Holmes, not he, would be in trouble. After all, Charles rationalized, he was just following orders.

Required

a.   Can you justify what Charles did?

b.   What could Charles have done to avoid the ethical dilemma that he faced? Assume that the company president would have made it impossible for Charles to work in Atlanta in a comparable job.

c.   What if the Securities and Exchange Commission discovered this fraud? Would Charles's boss get in trouble? Would Charles?

(Copyright © Michael W. Maher, 2020)

SOLUTIONS TO SELF-STUDY QUESTIONS

1.   The ingredients, labor, and utilities costs in Exhibit 1.4 would increase 50 percent, as shown in the spreadsheet that follows. Total costs would increase from $7,225 in the status quo to $11,460. Profits would increase from $3,375 in the status quo to $5,340 (= $16,800 revenues − $11,460 costs). Adam's profits increase compared to the status quo but not as much as in Exhibit 1.4 because some of the costs there do not increase proportionately with sales revenue.

	A	B	C	D	E	F	G	H	I
1			**THE AM BAKERY**						
2			Projected Income Statement						
3			For a Representative Week						
4									
5			(1)			(2)			(3)
6						Alternative:			
7			Status Quo:			Original Bakery			
8			Original Bakery			Plus Food			
9			Sales Only			Truck Sales			Difference
10	Sales revenue		$11,200			$16,800	(a)		$5,600
11	Costs								
12	Ingredients (flour, butter, and so on)		$2,700			$4,050	(a)		$1,350
13	Labor		3,100			4,650	(a)		1,550
14	Utilities		500			750	(a)		250
15	Rent		900			900	(b)		0
16	Marketing		25			60	(c)		35
17	Truck lease		0			900	(c)		900
18	Truck operating costs		0			150	(c)		150
19	Total costs		$7,225			$11,460			$4,235
20	Operating profits		$3,975			$5,340			$1,365
21									
22	(a) 50 percent higher than status quo.								
23	(b) No additional rent required.								
24	(c) Given								
25									

2. Examples of questions for which cost accounting information would be useful include the following:
   - For a hospital administrator:
     - Where should I purchase supplies?
     - What services cost more than the reimbursements we receive from insurers?
     - Should we invest in a new CAT scanner?
   - For a museum director:
     - What ticket prices should we charge?
     - Should we expand the hours of the museum café?
     - Are opening galas profitable?
   - For a bank's marketing vice president:
     - Where should I spend my advertising dollars?
     - If we lower the rate on checking accounts, how much will we lose when customers switch?
     - What fees should we set for online banking?
3. The answers to the four questions will certainly vary but might include the following:
   - The relevant question is whether it is better to control delivery to the customer or outsource it to a logistics supplier (UPS, for example).
   - The data relevant to the analysis include costs (internal and payments to suppliers), delivery performance (delays, and so on), and customer experience (satisfaction, for example).
   - The appropriate tools for analysis include cost analysis of the alternatives as well as statistical analysis of performance.
   - The visualization of the analysis results would consist of charts and graphs highlighting the effects of the alternatives and perhaps a scatter graph showing the trade-off between costs and delivery performance.
4. The three steps are to discuss, clarify, and consult. Specifically:
   - DISCUSS the conflict with your immediate superior or the person at the next level in authority.
   - CLARIFY the relevant issues and concepts by discussions with a disinterested party. You might need to contact an appropriate and confidential ethics "hotline."
   - CONSULT your attorney about your rights and obligations.

2

Chapter Two

Cost Concepts and Behavior

LEARNING OBJECTIVES

After reading this chapter, you should be able to:

LO 2-1 Explain the basic concept of "cost."

LO 2-2 Explain how costs are presented in financial statements.

LO 2-3 Explain the process of cost allocation.

LO 2-4 Understand how material, labor, and overhead costs are added to a product at each stage of the production process.

LO 2-5 Define basic cost behaviors, including fixed, variable, semivariable, and step costs.

LO 2-6 Identify the components of a product's costs.

LO 2-7 Understand the distinction between financial and contribution margin income statements.

❝ When I graduated in engineering several years ago, I knew I wanted to go to work in manufacturing. I started here at Three Rivers Fabrication in the design department, but have also worked in R&D and manufacturing. Now I have moved into management as the plant manager at our Peoria plant.

As an engineer, I just assumed that the cost information provided by finance was correct. Now I am seeing the details and having a difficult time understanding what all the cost terms mean. There seem to be many terms for the same thing. Unfortunately, none of them help me with the decisions I have to make. For example, we are always getting requests for quotes on products and I am not sure whether we are too high when we don't get the business or too low when we do.

I am meeting later this week with Angela Berroa, our plant comptroller. I need to review our financials with the area manager next week and I want to show that I am ready for this job. **❞**

Ingrid Jensen is the new plant manager at the Peoria plant of Three Rivers Fabrication. The plant makes parts for heavy equipment manufacturers selling in both the agricultural and construction markets. She has been promoted into this position based on her success in managing several important projects on some of the company's newest products. She is expected to ensure that Peoria maintains a comparative advantage in cost without losing its reputation for quality and innovation. She is hoping to learn more about the basics of costs and the terminology that cost accountants use so she can manage more effectively.

Cost accounting systems provide information to help managers make better decisions. Managers who use cost accounting information to make decisions need to understand the cost terms used in their organizations. Because cost accounting systems are tailored to the needs of individual companies, several terms are used in practice to describe the same or similar cost concepts, depending on the use or the audience. Therefore, before we discuss the design of cost systems to aid decision making, we introduce a set of terms that we will use throughout the book. These terms are important to the discussion because they form the "language" we use in the book. These terms are common, but they are not universal, so you need to be aware that a company you work for may use different terms for some of the concepts we discuss here.

In addition, managers need to understand how financial statements are prepared because this will be the primary form in which the information is available. The effects of the decisions made by managers are shown publicly in the firm's published financial statements.

Although these statements allow investors to evaluate the firm, they are not useful for managing the business. Most of you are familiar with traditional financial statements, either from earlier course work in accounting, your own investment analysis, or access to publicly available financial statements. Therefore, we start by linking the fundamental concepts of cost accounting to financial statements.

We discussed the differences between cost and financial accounting in Chapter 1. Although the two systems serve different purposes, they are not unrelated. The financial statements prepared by the firm for external reporting use information from the cost accounting system. Fundamentally, the cost accounting system records the use of economic resources by the organization. We illustrate how resources are used and costs are added to a product or service in different types of industries and how the use (cost) of these resources is reported in the financial statements. We explain the types of costs that managers use in making decisions. Finally, we present several diagrams that will help you track the different components of a product's cost.

Exhibit 2.16 in the chapter summary highlights the most important cost concepts in this chapter; refer to it often as you review for exams or need a quick reference.

What Is a Cost?

cost
Sacrifice of resources.

A **cost** is a sacrifice of resources. Every day, we buy many different things: clothing, food, books, music, perhaps an automobile, and so on. When we buy one thing, we give up (sacrifice) the ability to use these resources (typically cash or a line of credit) to buy something else. The price of each item measures the sacrifice we must make to acquire it. Whether we pay cash or use another asset, whether we pay now or later (by using a credit card), the cost of the item acquired is represented by what we forgo as a result.

Cost versus Expenses

expense
Cost that is charged against revenue in an accounting period.

It is important to distinguish cost from expense. An **expense** is a cost charged against revenue in an accounting period; hence, expenses are deducted from revenue in that accounting period. We incur costs whenever we give up (sacrifice) resources, regardless of whether we account for it as an asset or an expense. We may even incur costs that the financial accounting system never records as an asset or expense. An example is lost sales. If the cost is recorded as an asset (for example, prepaid rent for an office building), it becomes an expense when the asset has been consumed (i.e., the building has been used for a period of time after making the prepayment). In this book, we use the term *expense* only when referring to external financial reports.

The focus of cost accounting is on costs, not expenses. Generally accepted accounting principles (GAAP) and regulations such as the income tax laws specify when costs are to be treated as expenses. Although the terms *cost* and *expense* are sometimes used as synonyms in practice, we use *cost* in this book for all managerial purposes.

outlay cost
Past, present, or future cash outflow.

The two major categories of costs are *outlay costs* and *opportunity costs*. An **outlay cost** is a past, present, or future cash outflow. Consider the cost of a college education—the cash outflows for tuition, books, and fees are outlay costs. Cash is not all that college students sacrifice; they also sacrifice their time to get a college education. This sacrifice of time is an opportunity cost. **Opportunity cost** is the forgone benefit that could have been realized from the best forgone alternative use of a resource.[1] For example, many students give up jobs to take the time to earn a college degree. The forgone income is part of the cost of getting a college degree and is the forgone benefit that could be realized from an alternative use of a scarce resource—time. These are other examples of opportunity costs:

opportunity cost
Forgone benefit from the best (forgone) alternative course of action.

- The opportunity cost of funds that you invest in a bank certificate of deposit is the forgone interest you could have earned on another security, assuming that both securities are equal in risk and liquidity.

- The opportunity cost of spending spring break in Florida is the forgone income from a temporary job; the opportunity cost of taking a temporary job during spring break is the forgone pleasure of a trip to Florida.

- The opportunity cost of time spent working on one question on an examination is the forgone benefit of time spent working on another question.

Of course, no one can ever know all of the possible opportunities available at any moment. Hence, some opportunity costs are undoubtedly not considered. Accounting systems typically record outlay costs but not opportunity costs. As a result, it is easy for managers to overlook or ignore opportunity costs in making decisions. A well-designed cost accounting system presents all relevant information to managers, including opportunity costs that they may otherwise ignore in decision making.

---

[1] In some definitions, the *outlay* cost is also an opportunity cost because you forgo the use of the cash that could be used to purchase other goods and services. In this text, we reserve the use of the term *opportunity costs* to those costs that are not outlay costs.

Presentation of Costs in Financial Statements

LO 2-2

Explain how costs are presented in financial statements.

We are concerned with information for use by managers. Therefore, when we present or discuss financial statements, we assume that the statements are prepared for internal management use, not for external reporting. We also focus on **operating profit,** the excess of operating revenues over the operating costs incurred to generate those revenues. This figure differs from net income, which is operating profit adjusted for interest, income taxes, extraordinary items, and other adjustments required to comply with GAAP or other regulations such as tax laws.

operating profit
Excess of operating revenues over the operating costs necessary to generate those revenues.

It is important to remember that information from the cost accounting system is just a means to an end; the final products are managerial decisions and actions (and the change in firm value) that result from the information generated by the system. We are not seeking the "most accurate" information. We are looking for the best information, understanding how the information is used in decision making, and recognizing the cost of preparing and using the information. The following sections present some examples of how cost information appears in financial statements prepared for managers. These are basic statements on which we build. As we proceed through the book, we show you how to improve these basic statements and the data they contain to make them more informative.

A generic income statement for a firm, a division, a product, or any unit is shown in Exhibit 2.1. It summarizes the revenues (sales) of the unit and subtracts the costs of the unit. The costs include the cost of the goods or service the activity sells. Although the basic form of the income statement is the same regardless of the product or service an organization sells, the details, especially with respect to costs, vary depending on how the organization acquires the resources used to produce the product or service.

In the sections that follow, we illustrate three types of income statements where the organization sells (1) a service, (2) a product that it acquires from another organization (a retailer), or (3) a product that it builds using materials from other organizations (a manufacturer). It is important to remember, however, that most firms are made up of activities that combine features of all three types of activities. Even in a manufacturing firm, you might find income statements for a unit, such as repair services, that look like those of a service business. Similarly, many service firms, such as those in financial services, have important transactions and billing functions that use repeatable, discrete processes, not unlike many manufacturing processes.

Revenue	XXX
Costs.	YYY
Operating profit .	ZZZ

Exhibit 2.1

Generic Income Statement

Service Organizations

A service company provides customers with an intangible product. For example, consulting firms provide advice and analyses. Traditionally, labor costs were the most significant cost category for most service organizations. However, as information services become increasingly important, this is changing. Some service firms provide information, and for these companies information technology can represent the major cost. Other firms provide information analysis, and for these firms labor costs will likely remain the most important single cost.

The costs associated with RPE Associates, a compensation consulting firm, are shown in the income statement in Exhibit 2.2. The line item cost of services sold includes the costs of *billable hours,* which are the hours billed to clients plus the cost of other items billed to clients (for example, charges for performing an information search or printing reports). Costs that are not part of services billable to clients are included in the marketing and administrative costs. At RPE, many managers report costs both in the cost of services sold (working with a client) and in marketing and administrative costs (developing project proposals for new business). The distinction is based on the nature of the work, not who performs the task.

Retail and Wholesale Companies

When you buy food, clothes, or a book, you are buying from a retail (or maybe a wholesale) firm. Retail and wholesale firms sell but do not make a tangible product. The income

Exhibit 2.2

Income Statement for a
Service Company

RPE ASSOCIATES
Income Statement
For the Year Ending December 31, Year 2
($000)

Sales revenue	$32,000
Cost of services sold.	23,500
Gross margin	$ 8,500
Marketing and administrative costs	4,300
Operating profit	$ 4,200

statement for these companies includes revenue and cost items as does that for service companies, but for retailers and wholesalers, it has an added category of cost information (called *cost of goods sold*) to track the cost of the tangible goods they buy and sell.

Southwest Office Products is a retail company that sells office supplies, such as paper products and computer accessories. The company's income statement and cost of goods sold statement are shown in Exhibit 2.3. The cost of goods sold statement shows how the cost of goods sold was computed. Exhibit 2.3 shows the following information for Southwest:

- It had a $300,000 beginning inventory on January 1. This represents the cost of the paper, writing supplies, toner cartridges, and other salable items on hand at the beginning of the year.
- The company purchased $1,830,000 of goods during the year and had transportation-in costs of $90,000. Therefore, its total cost of goods purchased was $1,920,000 (= $1,830,000 for the purchases + $90,000 for the transportation-in costs).
- Based on the information so far, Southwest had a $2,220,000 cost of items available for sale (= $1,920,000 total cost of goods purchased + $300,000 from beginning inventory). The $2,220,000 is the cost of the goods that the company *could* have sold, in other words, the cost of goods *available* for sale.

At the end of the year, the company still had on hand inventory costing $445,000. Therefore, Southwest sold items costing $1,775,000 (= $2,220,000 − $445,000).

Exhibit 2.3

Income Statement
and Cost of Goods
Sold Statement for a
Merchandise Company

SOUTHWEST OFFICE PRODUCTS
Income Statement
For the Year Ended December 31, Year 2
($000)

Sales revenue		$3,225
Cost of goods sold (see following statement)		1,775
Gross margin		$1,450
Marketing and administrative costs		825
Operating profit		$ 625

Cost of Goods Sold Statement
For the Year Ended December 31, Year 2
($000)

Beginning inventory		$ 300
Cost of goods purchased		
Merchandise cost	$1,830	
Transportation-in costs	90	
Total cost of goods purchased		1,920
Cost of goods available for sale		$2,220
Less cost of goods in ending inventory		445
Cost of goods sold		$1,775

The income statement summarizes Southwest's operating performance with the following information:

- Sales revenue for the year was $3,225,000.
- The cost of goods sold amount, $1,775,000, came from the cost of goods sold statement. Therefore, the gross margin (the difference between sales revenue and cost of goods sold) is $1,450,000 (= $3,225,000 sales revenue − $1,775,000 cost of goods sold). If you were Southwest's manager, you would know that, on average, every $1 of sales gave you about $0.45 (= $1,450,000 ÷ $3,225,000) to cover marketing and administrative costs and earn a profit.
- The income statement also shows that marketing and administrative costs were $825,000, and operating profits were $625,000 (= $1,450,000 gross margin − $825,000 marketing and administrative costs).

The term **cost of goods sold** includes only the actual costs of the goods that were sold. It does not include the costs required to sell them such as the salaries of salespeople, which are marketing costs, or the salaries of top executives, which are administrative costs.

cost of goods sold
Expense assigned to products sold during a period.

Compare the income statement for Southwest Office Products with that for the service company, RPE Associates (Exhibit 2.2). Like other retail and wholesale organizations, Southwest has an entire category of amounts that do not appear in a service company's income statement. This category appears in the cost of goods sold statement, which accounts for the inventories, purchases, and sales of tangible goods. By contrast, the service company does not "purchase" anything to be held in inventory until sold. Service companies are generally most interested in measuring the cost of providing services while retail and wholesale firms focus on two items: The gross margin reflects the ability to price the products, while the marketing and administrative costs reflect relative efficiency in operating the business itself.

Components of Cost of Goods Sold for a Retailer   *Business Application*

As discussed in the text, the cost of goods sold for a retailer is based on the cost of items purchased from a wholesaler or manufacturer. What does that include? The following note from the financial statements for Target Corporation shows that there is managerial discretion on classifying costs into cost of goods sold or selling expense. For example, labor costs in distribution centers are considered part of cost of goods sold and labor costs for store employees are included in selling, general, and administrative expenses.

When comparing costs and performance across firms using financial statement information, the note at the bottom of the table is important: Different firms classify similar costs in different ways.

Source: Target Corporation 2019 Annual Report, p. 41.

3. Cost of Sales and Selling, General and Administrative Expenses

The following table illustrates the primary items classified in each major expense category:

Cost of Sales	Selling, General and Administrative Expenses
Total cost of products sold including • Freight expenses associated with moving merchandise from our vendors to and between our distribution centers and our retail stores • Vendor income that is not reimbursement of specific, incremental, and identifiable costs Inventory shrink Markdowns Outbound shipping and handling expenses associated with sales to our guests Payment term cash discounts Distribution center costs, including compensation and benefits costs and depreciation Compensation and benefit costs associated with shipment of merchandise from stores Import costs	Compensation and benefit costs for stores and headquarters, except ship from store costs classified as cost of sales Occupancy and operating costs of retail and headquarters facilities Advertising, offset by vendor income that is a reimbursement of specific, incremental, and identifiable costs Pre-opening and exit costs of stores and other facilities Credit cards servicing expenses Costs associated with accepting 3rd party bank issued payment cards Litigation and defense costs and related insurance recovery Other administrative costs

Note: The classification of these expenses varies across the retail industry.

Manufacturing Companies

You are probably acquainted with the term *cost of goods sold* from a financial accounting course. It is likely that most, if not all, of the examples you encountered in studying financial accounting were retail firms. The reason is that in financial accounting the focus is on preparing and presenting the statements. In a retail firm, the unit cost of an item sold is known because it was purchased from a third party. A manufacturing company has a more complex income statement than do service or retail/wholesale companies. Whereas the retailer/wholesaler *purchases* goods for sale, the manufacturer *makes* them. For decision making, it is not enough for the manufacturer to know how much it paid for a good; it must also know the different costs associated with making it.

Financial reporting distinguishes costs in a manufacturing firm based on when the costs are recognized as expenses on the financial statements. **Product costs** are those costs assigned to units of production and recognized (expensed) when the product is sold. Product (manufacturing) costs follow the product through inventory. **Period costs** (nonmanufacturing costs) include all other costs and are expensed as they are incurred. Although we are not directly concerned with financial statement preparation in this book, the cost accounting system must be able to provide cost information for the financial reporting system.

Before we present example statements for a manufacturing firm, we need to define some additional terms.

product costs
Costs assigned to the manufacture of products and recognized for financial reporting when sold.

period costs
Costs recognized for financial reporting when incurred.

Direct and Indirect Manufacturing (Product) Costs

Product costs consists of two types—direct and indirect costs. **Direct manufacturing costs** are those product costs that can be identified with units (or batches of units) at relatively low cost. **Indirect manufacturing costs** are all other product costs. The glass in a light bulb is a direct cost of the bulb. The depreciation on the light bulb manufacturing plant is an indirect cost.

Direct costs are classified further into direct materials cost and direct labor cost. The manufacturer purchases materials (for example, unassembled parts), hires workers to convert the materials to a finished good, and then offers the product for sale. Thus, there are three major categories of product costs:

direct manufacturing costs
Product costs that can be feasibly identified with units of production.

indirect manufacturing costs
All product costs except direct costs.

1. **Direct materials** that can be feasibly identified directly, at relatively low cost, with the product. (To the manufacturer, purchased parts, including transportation-in, are included in direct materials.) Direct materials are often called *raw materials*. Materials that cannot be identified with a specific product (for example, paper for plant reports, lubricating oil for machines) are included in category 3.
2. **Direct labor** of workers who can be identified directly, at reasonable cost, with the product. These workers transform the materials into a finished product.
3. All other costs of transforming the materials into a finished product, often referred to in total as **manufacturing overhead.** Some examples of manufacturing overhead follow.

direct materials
Materials that can be identified directly with the product at reasonable cost.

direct labor
Labor that can be identified directly with the product at reasonable cost.

manufacturing overhead
All production costs except direct labor and direct materials.

*   *Indirect labor,* the cost of workers who do not work directly on the product yet are required so that the factory can operate, such as supervisors, maintenance workers, and inventory storekeepers.
*   *Indirect materials,* such as lubricants for the machinery, polishing and cleaning materials, repair parts, and light bulbs, which are not a part of the finished product but are necessary to manufacture it.
*   *Other manufacturing costs,* such as depreciation of the factory building and equipment, taxes on the factory assets, insurance on the factory building and equipment, heat, light, power, and similar expenses incurred to keep the factory operating.

Although we use *manufacturing overhead* in this book, common synonyms used in practice are *factory burden, factory overhead, burden, factory expense,* and the unmodified word, *overhead.*

Prime Costs and Conversion Costs

You are likely to encounter the following two categories of costs in manufacturing companies: prime costs and conversion costs. **Prime costs** are the direct costs, namely, direct materials and direct labor. In some companies, managers give prime costs much attention because they represent 80 to 90 percent of total manufacturing costs.

In other cases, managers give most of their attention to **conversion costs,** which are the costs to convert direct materials into the final product. These are the costs for direct labor and manufacturing overhead. Managers who focus on conversion costs use a controllability argument: "We can manage conversion costs. Direct materials costs are mostly outside our control."

Generally, companies with relatively low manufacturing overhead focus on managing prime costs. Companies that have high direct labor and/or manufacturing overhead tend to be more concerned about conversion costs. In practice, you have to determine the cost information that decision makers need to manage effectively. It is not only the relative magnitude of costs that matters in determining which costs to monitor. The important issue is identifying the most important costs over which the firm has control. For example, in some processing firms, the largest costs are the direct materials costs. However, because those materials are commodities with prices set in well-functioning markets, it may be infeasible to exercise much control over those costs other than monitoring usage.

Exhibit 2.4 summarizes the relation between conversion costs and the three elements of manufactured product cost: direct materials, direct labor, and manufacturing overhead.

Nonmanufacturing (Period) Costs

Nonmanufacturing costs have two elements: marketing costs and administrative costs. **Marketing costs** are the costs required to obtain customer orders and provide customers with finished products. These include advertising, sales commissions, shipping costs, and marketing departments' building occupancy costs. **Administrative costs** are the costs

prime costs
Sum of direct materials and direct labor.

conversion costs
Sum of direct labor and manufacturing overhead.

marketing costs
Costs required to obtain customer orders and provide customers with finished products, including advertising, sales commissions, and shipping costs.

administrative costs
Costs required to manage the organization and provide staff support, including executive salaries, costs of data processing, and legal costs.

Exhibit 2.4   Components of Manufactured Product Cost

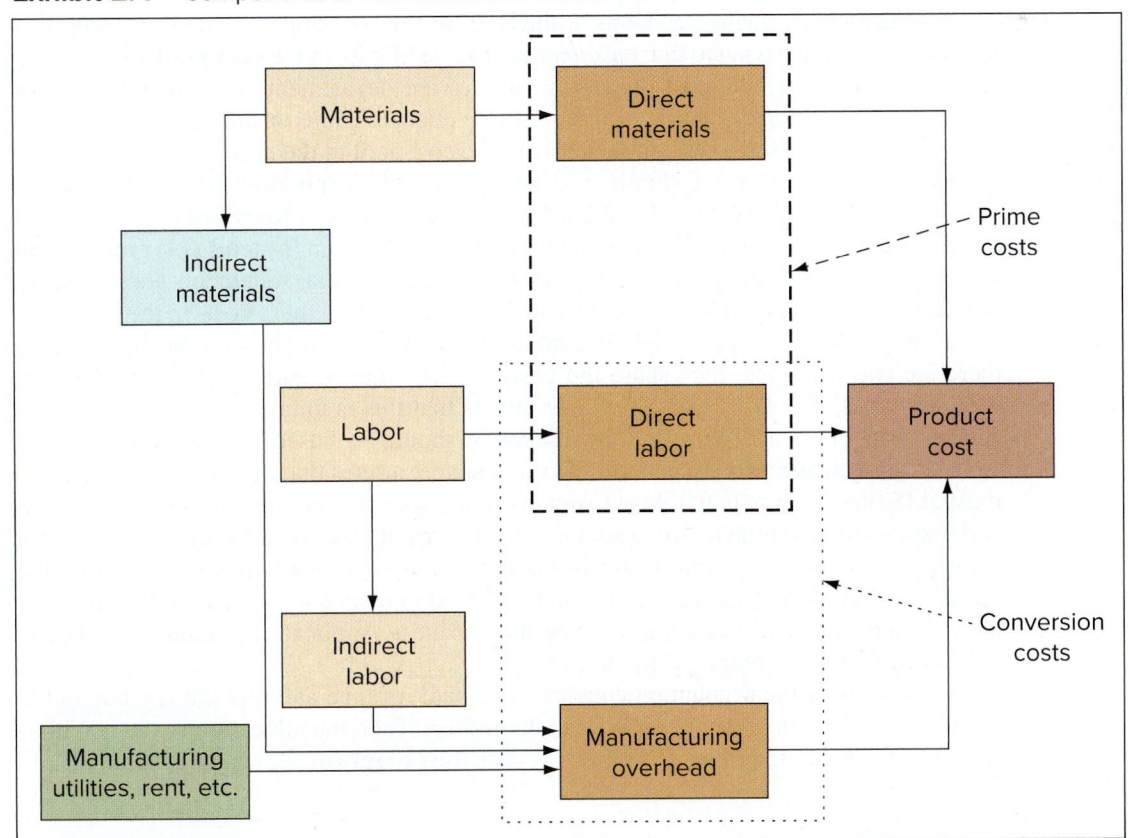

required to manage the organization and provide staff support, including executive and clerical salaries; costs for legal, financial, data processing, and accounting services; and building space for administrative personnel.

Nonmanufacturing costs are expensed periodically (often in the period they are incurred) for financial accounting purposes. For managerial purposes, however, managers often want to see nonmanufacturing costs assigned to products. This is particularly true for commissions and advertising related to a specific product. For example, managers at consumer products companies such as Procter & Gamble and Anheuser-Busch want the cost of advertising a specific product, which can be substantial, to be assigned to that product. For most of our purposes, this distinction between manufacturing and nonmanufacturing costs is artificial because we are interested in the costs that products and services impose on the firm, not in the financial accounting treatment of these costs.

Sometimes distinguishing between manufacturing costs and nonmanufacturing costs is difficult. For example, are the salaries of accountants who handle factory payrolls manufacturing or nonmanufacturing costs? What about the rent for offices for the manufacturing vice president? There are no clear-cut classifications for some of these costs, so companies usually set their own guidelines and follow them consistently.

Cost Allocation

cost allocation
Process of assigning indirect costs to products, services, people, business units, etc.

cost object
Any end to which a cost is assigned; examples include a product, a department, or a product line.

cost pool
Collection of costs to be assigned to the cost objects.

cost allocation rule
Method used to assign costs in the cost pool to the cost objects.

cost flow diagram
Diagram or flowchart illustrating the cost allocation process.

Many costs result from several departments sharing facilities (buildings, equipment) or services (data processing, maintenance staff). If you share an apartment with someone, the rent is a cost to the people sharing the apartment. If we want to assign costs to each individual, some method must be devised for assigning a share of the costs to each user. This process of assigning costs is called **cost allocation.**

We discuss implications of allocating costs throughout this book. However, cost allocation is a process that is familiar to most people, even those who do not study cost accounting. First, we need some definitions. A **cost object** is any end to which a cost is assigned, for example, a unit of product or service, a department, or a customer.

Managers make many decisions at the level of the cost object. Should we drop this *product?* How can we make this *customer* profitable? Costs in the **cost pool** are the costs we want to assign to the cost objects. Examples are department costs, rental costs, or travel costs a consultant incurs to visit multiple clients. The **cost allocation rule** is the method or process used to assign the costs in the cost pool to the cost object.

Consider the following simple example. Rockford Corporation has two divisions: East Coast (EC) and West Coast (WC). Computing services at Rockford are centralized and provided to the two divisions by the corporate Information Systems (IS) group. Total systems costs for the quarter are $1 million. Divisional financial statements are being prepared, and the accountant has asked for your help in allocating these costs to the divisions.

How would you suggest the accountant proceed? You might suggest that because there are two divisions, they share the costs equally, that is, each is charged $500,000 for IS services. The West Coast manager argues that this is unfair because WC is much smaller than EC. She argues that the allocation should be based on a measure of divisional size, such as revenues. The East Coast manager argues that this is not right because most of IS time is spent in the West Coast division, where the equipment is more complex and requires more maintenance. There is often no "right" way to solve this dilemma (but there may be some ways that result in poor decisions). As we will see throughout the book, the allocation of indirect costs can often lead to disputes both within the firm and between the firm and its customers. See the Business Application "Indirect Costs and Allocating Costs to Contracts" for an example.

Let's suppose the accountant chooses divisional revenue and that the revenue in EC is $80 million and the revenue in WC is $20 million. Then the allocation to the two divisions can be illustrated in the flowchart, or **cost flow diagram,** shown in Exhibit 2.5.

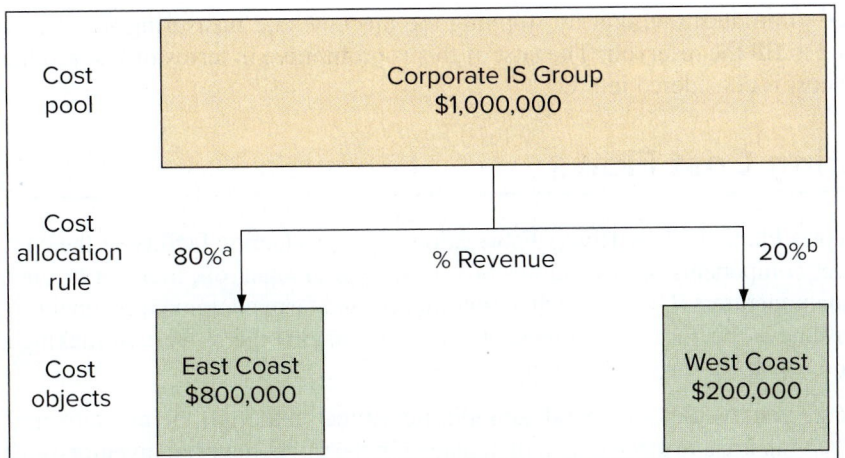

Exhibit 2.5   Cost Flow Diagram

a 80% = $80 million revenue ÷ ($80 million + $20 million)

b 20% = $20 million revenue ÷ ($80 million + $20 million)

Because the East Coast division earns 80 percent (= $80 million of the total $100 million in revenues), it is assigned, or allocated, 80 percent of the IS costs, or $800,000 (= 80% of $1,000,000). Similarly, the West Coast division is assigned $200,000 (= 20% of $1,000,000). Many of the cost allocation methods we discuss are more complex than this simple example, but the fundamental approach is the same: (1) identify the cost objects, (2) determine the cost pools, and (3) select a cost allocation rule. We will make extensive use of cost flow diagrams such as the one in Exhibit 2.5 because they can help us understand (1) how a cost system works and (2) the likely effects on the reported costs of different cost objects from changes in the cost allocation rule.

Direct versus Indirect Costs

Any cost that can be unambiguously related to a cost object is a **direct cost** of that cost object. Those that cannot be unambiguously related to a cost object are **indirect costs.** We have already seen one use of this distinction in our discussion of manufacturing costs. Accountants use the terms *direct cost* and *indirect cost* much as a nonaccountant might expect. One difficulty is that a cost may be direct to one cost object and indirect to another. For example, the salary of a supervisor in a manufacturing department is a direct cost of the department but an indirect cost of the individual items the department produces. So when someone refers to a cost as either direct or indirect, you should immediately ask, direct or indirect with respect to what cost object? Units produced? A department? A division? (When we use *direct* and *indirect* to describe labor and materials, the cost object is the unit being produced.)

Whether a cost is considered direct or indirect also depends on the costs of linking it to the cost object. For example, it is possible to measure the amount of lubricating

direct cost
Any cost that can be directly (unambiguously) related to a cost object at reasonable cost.

indirect cost
Any cost that *cannot* be directly related to a cost object.

Indirect Costs and Allocating Costs to Contracts   *Business Application*

Many contracts, especially when selling to government agencies, specify prices based on the "cost" of the service or product. As we see in this section, when there are indirect costs, the calculated cost depends on how the indirect costs are allocated. When a company has multiple clients, it is possible that the choice of allocation method affects the prices (and profits) although the total costs have not changed. There is an incentive to allocate costs in a way to increase the company's profits. Depending on the terms of the contract, there can be

both ethical and legal considerations in how indirect costs are allocated.

For example, the U.S. government is "conducting a civil and criminal investigation into Booz Allen Hamilton's cost accounting and indirect cost charging practices." When the news was released, Booz Allen Hamilton stock lost 12 percent of its value.

Source: Armental, Maria, "Justice Department Probing Booz Allen's Accounting, Billing Practices with U.S." *Wall Street Journal,* June 15, 2017.

oil used to produce one unit by stopping the machine and measuring the amount of oil required to fill the reservoir. The cost of this is prohibitive in terms of lost production, so the oil cost is considered indirect.

Details of Manufacturing Cost Flows

The Peoria Plant of Three Rivers Fabrication is the production facility of the company. It produces components such as pumps of various types (water, oil, fuel) for original equipment manufacturers (OEMs), such as automobile and farm equipment companies. Even if you have never been in a machine shop, you can imagine the process of making a pump. It would consist of three basic steps:

- First, you would see metal and plastic (direct material) being delivered to the receiving area, inspected, and then placed in the direct material inventory area (store) of the shop.

- Next, when it was time to produce pumps, the metal and plastic would be transported to an assembly line. It would be fed to large machines (presses, lathes, and so on) that would turn the unformed metal and plastic into the finished pump. While the metal is in this part of the factory, it is neither direct material nor a pump; it is **work in process.**

- Finally, the pump is complete, and it is moved out to a separate area in the factory with other completed products. These pumps are **finished goods** and ready for sale.

work in process
Product in the production process but not yet complete.

finished goods
Product fully completed, but not yet sold.

Just as the manufacturing plant at Three Rivers has direct material, work-in-process, and finished goods inventories, the cost accounting system at Three Rivers has three major categories of inventory accounts—one category for each of these three stages: Direct Materials Inventory, Work-in-Process Inventory, and Finished Goods Inventory. Our goal with the cost accounting system is simple: By tracing the physical flows with cost flows through the inventory accounts, we can represent the use of resources in the plant to produce the finished pumps.

Each inventory account is likely to have a beginning inventory amount, additions (debits) and withdrawals (credits) during the period, and an ending inventory based on what is still on hand at the end of the period. Those costs added (debited) to inventory accounts are called **inventoriable costs.**

inventoriable costs
Costs added to inventory accounts.

To show how this works, Exhibit 2.6 illustrates a simplified version of the actual production process at the Peoria Plant. It shows the stages of production from receipt of materials through manufacturing to shipment to the finished goods warehouse.

The Peoria Plant receives raw metal (steel, brass, etc.) at its Direct Materials Receiving Department. The people in this department are responsible for checking each order to be sure that it meets quality specifications and that the goods received are what were ordered.

If Three Rivers uses just-in-time (JIT) inventory methods, people in direct materials receiving send the components—metals, plastics—to the machining line immediately.

If Three Rivers does not use JIT, people in this department send the components to a materials warehouse until it is needed for production. Any product that has been purchased but not yet transferred to manufacturing departments will be part of Direct Materials Inventory on the balance sheet at the end of the accounting period.

Exhibit 2.6   Production Process at the Peoria Plant

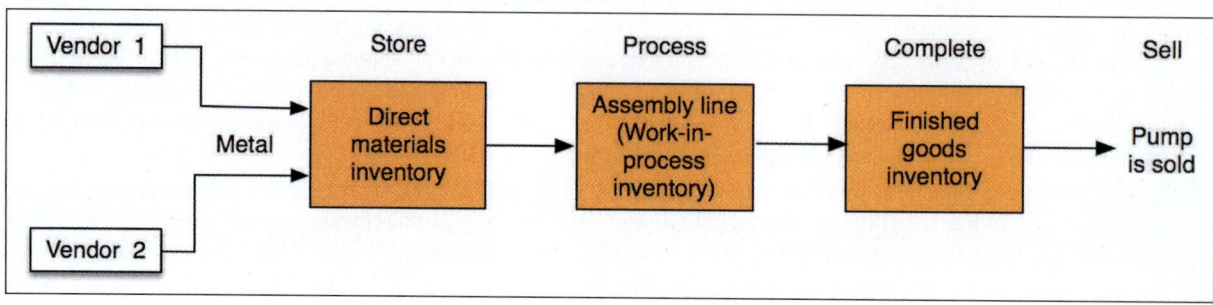

When the production process begins, the metal moves along the machining line as it is transformed (rods added to the pumps, individual bowls cut, and so on). Any pumps that are not complete—that is, those still on the machining line at the end of an accounting period—are part of Work-in-Process Inventory on the balance sheet.

After the completed pumps are inspected, they are moved to a holding area awaiting shipment to customers around the country. The cost of any product that is finished but not yet sold to customers is included in Finished Goods Inventory at the end of an accounting period.

How Costs Flow through the Statements

Income Statements

Now that we understand the physical flow of the product through the process, we can use a numerical example to show how to report revenues and expenses at Three Rivers Fabrication. The result is a typical income statement for a manufacturing company (see Exhibit 2.7). The income statement shows that Three Rivers generated sales revenue of $40,900,000, had cost of goods sold of $26,200,000, and incurred marketing and administrative costs of $7,700,000 for the year, thereby generating an operating profit of $7,000,000.

THREE RIVERS FABRICATION
Income Statement
For the Year Ending December 31, Year 2
($000)

Sales revenue	$40,900
Cost of goods sold (see Exhibit 2.8)	26,200
Gross margin	$14,700
Less marketing and administrative costs	7,700
Operating profit before taxes	$ 7,000

Exhibit 2.7

Income Statement for a Manufacturing Firm

THREE RIVERS FABRICATION
Cost of Goods Manufactured and Sold Statement
For the Year Ending December 31, Year 2
($000)

Beginning work-in-process inventory, January 1			$ 540
Manufacturing costs during the year:			
Direct materials:			
Beginning inventory, January 1	$ 190		
Add purchases.	11,254		
Direct materials available.	$11,444		
Less ending inventory, Dec. 31	144		
Direct material put into production		$11,300	
Direct labor.		2,440	
Manufacturing overhead		13,560	
Total manufacturing costs incurred			27,300
Total work-in-process during the year			$27,840
Less ending work-in-process inventory, December 31			620
Cost of goods manufactured.			$27,220
Beginning finished goods inventory, January 1			840
Finished goods available for sale.			$28,060
Less ending finished goods inventory, December 31			1,860
Cost of goods sold			$26,200

Exhibit 2.8

Cost of Goods Manufactured and Sold Statement for a Manufacturing Firm

Cost of Goods Manufactured and Sold

We now demonstrate how to derive the cost of goods manufactured and sold amount on the income statement from the company's activities. The resulting statement is the cost of goods manufactured and sold statement, which appears in Exhibit 2.8. You will be able to see how these items appear in the cost of goods manufactured and sold statement if you track each amount from the following example in Exhibit 2.8.

Direct Materials

Assume the following for the company:

- Direct materials inventory on hand January 1 totaled $190,000.
- Materials purchased during the year cost $11,254,000.
- Ending inventory on December 31 was $144,000.
- Therefore, the cost of direct materials put into production during the year was $11,300,000, computed as follows (in thousands of dollars).

Beginning direct materials inventory, January 1	$ 190
Add purchases during the year	11,254
Direct materials available during the year	$11,444
Less ending direct materials inventory, December 31	144
Cost of direct materials put into production	$11,300

Work in Process

Consider the following:

- The Work-in-Process Inventory account had a beginning balance of $540,000 on January 1, as shown in Exhibit 2.8.
- Exhibit 2.8 shows that costs incurred during the year totaled $11,300,000 in direct materials (as shown in the preceding direct materials inventory schedule), $2,440,000 in direct labor costs, and $13,560,000 in manufacturing overhead. The sum of materials, labor, and manufacturing overhead costs incurred, $27,300,000, is the total manufacturing costs incurred during the year. Managers in production and operations give careful attention to these costs. Companies that want to be competitive in setting prices must manage these costs diligently.
- From here on the process can seem complicated, but it's not really so difficult if you realize that accountants are just adding and subtracting inventory values. In other words, just as materials, in different forms, are moving from one inventory in the plant to another, the costs in the cost accounting system are moving from one inventory account to another. Adding the $540,000 beginning work-in-process inventory to the $27,300,000 total manufacturing costs gives $27,840,000, the total cost of work in process during the year. This is a measure of the resources that have gone into production. Some of these costs were in the work-in-process inventory on hand at the beginning of the period (that is, the $540,000 in beginning inventory), but most have been incurred this year (that is, the $27,300,000 total manufacturing costs).
- At year-end, the work-in-process inventory has a $620,000 cost, which is subtracted to arrive at the cost of goods manufactured during the year: $27,220,000 (= $27,840,000 – $620,000), which represents the cost of pumps and other products finished during the year. Production departments usually have a goal for goods completed each period. Managers would compare the cost of goods manufactured to that goal to see whether the production departments were successful in meeting it.

Finished Goods Inventory

The work finished during the period is transferred from the production department to the finished goods storage area or is shipped to customers. If goods are shipped to customers directly from the production line, no finished goods inventory exists. Three Rivers has a finished goods inventory, however, because some of the products are common across manufacturers and so it keeps some of them on hand to expedite orders. Here's how the amounts appear on the financial statements:

- Exhibit 2.8 shows that Three Rivers had $840,000 of finished goods inventory on hand at the beginning of the year (January 1). From the discussion about work in process, we know that Three Rivers completed $27,220,000 worth of product, which was transferred to finished goods inventory. Therefore, Three Rivers had $28,060,000 finished goods inventory available for sale, in total.
- Of the $28,060,000 available, Three Rivers had $1,860,000 finished goods still on hand at the end of the year. This means that the cost of goods sold was $26,200,000 (= $28,060,000 available − $1,860,000 in ending inventory).

Cost of Goods Manufactured and Sold Statement

As part of its internal reporting system, Three Rivers prepares a cost of goods manufactured and sold statement (Exhibit 2.8). Such statements are for managerial use; you will rarely see one published in external financial statements. Exhibit 2.8 incorporates and summarizes information from the preceding discussion.

Manufacturing companies typically prepare a cost of goods manufactured and sold statement to summarize and report manufacturing costs such as those discussed for Three Rivers Fabrication, most often for managers' use. Some companies have experimented with preparing these statements for production workers and supervisors, who in some cases have found them effective communication devices once these people learn how to read them. For example, managers at Three Rivers use the cost of goods manufactured and sold statement to communicate the size of manufacturing overhead and inventories to stimulate creative ideas for reducing these items.

The cost of goods manufactured and sold statement in Exhibit 2.8 has three building blocks. The first reports the cost of direct materials. Next is the work-in-process account with its beginning balance, costs added during the period, ending balance, and cost of

1. A review of accounts showed the following for Pacific Parts for last year.

Administrative costs	$1,216,000
Depreciation, manufacturing	412,000
Direct labor	1,928,000
Direct materials purchases	1,252,000
Direct materials inventory, January 1	408,000
Direct materials inventory, December 31	324,000
Finished goods inventory, January 1	640,000
Finished goods inventory, December 31	588,000
Heat, light, and power—plant	348,000
Marketing costs	1,088,000
Miscellaneous manufacturing costs	48,000

(continued)

Plant maintenance and repairs	$ 296,000
Sales revenue	8,144,000
Supervisory and indirect labor	508,000
Supplies and indirect materials	56,000
Work-in-process inventory, January 1	540,000
Work-in-process inventory, December 31	568,000

Prepare an income statement with a supporting cost of goods manufactured and sold statement. Refer to Exhibits 2.7 and 2.8.

2. Using the data from question 1, place dollar amounts in each box in Exhibit 2.4.

The solutions to these questions are at the end of this chapter.

goods manufactured. Third, the statement reports the beginning and ending finished goods inventory and cost of goods sold.

These financial statements are presented in a standard format that you will find used by many companies and on the CPA and CMA examinations. Please be aware that we discuss many variations in this book, but many more exist in practice. For example, some companies prepare separate statements of cost of goods sold and cost of goods manufactured. It is important that financial statements effectively present the information that best suits the needs of your customers or information users (for example, managers of your company or your clients). For managerial purposes, it is important that the format of financial statements be tailored to what users want (or to what you want if you are the user of financial information).

Cost Behavior

LO 2-5

Define basic cost behaviors, including fixed, variable, semivariable, and step costs.

The financial statements of Three Rivers Fabrication report what happened, but they fail to show why. For that, we need to understand how costs behave and how managers analyze costs to arrive at their decisions. Managerial decisions lead to the activities that the firm undertakes, and these activities create (or destroy) the value in an organization. Information from the cost accounting system is a key ingredient in making these decisions.

Cost behavior deals with the way costs respond to changes in activity levels. Throughout this book, we refer to the idea of a cost driver. As defined in Chapter 1, a cost driver is a factor that causes, or "drives," costs. For example, the cost driver for the cost of lumber for the activity of building a house could be the number of board feet of lumber used or the size of the house in square feet. The cost driver for direct labor costs could be the number of labor-hours worked.

Managers need to know how costs behave to make informed decisions about products, to plan, and to evaluate performance. We classify the behavior of costs as being in one of four basic categories: fixed, variable, semivariable, and step costs, as discussed next.

Fixed versus Variable Costs

fixed costs
Costs that are unchanged as volume changes within the relevant range of activity.

variable costs
Costs that change in direct proportion with a change in volume within the relevant range of activity.

Suppose that management contemplates a change in the volume of a company's activity. The following are some questions different managers might ask:

- *An operations manager at Home Depot:* How much will our costs decrease if we close stores one hour earlier?
- *A manager at the U.S. Postal Service:* How much will our costs decrease if we eliminate Saturday deliveries?
- *A business school dean:* How much will costs increase if we reduce average class size by 10 students because we increase the number of classes offered?

For the U.S. Postal Service, the cost of Post Office Buildings is fixed. The cost of fuel is variable per mile or per kWh.
Allkindza/iStock/Getty Images

To answer questions such as these, we need to know which costs are **fixed costs** that remain unchanged as the volume of activity changes and which are **variable costs** that change in direct proportion to the change in volume of activity.

If the activity is producing units, variable manufacturing costs typically include direct materials, certain manufacturing overhead (for example, indirect materials, materials-handling labor, energy costs), and direct labor in some cases (such as temporary workers). Certain nonmanufacturing costs such as distribution costs and sales commissions are typically variable. Much of manufacturing overhead and many nonmanufacturing costs are typically fixed costs.

Although labor has traditionally been considered a variable cost, today the production process at many firms is capital intensive, and the amount of labor required is not sensitive to the amount produced. In a setting in which a fixed amount of labor is needed only to keep machines operating, labor is probably best considered to be a fixed cost.

In merchandising, variable costs include the cost of the product and some marketing and administrative costs. All of a merchant's product costs are variable. In manufacturing, a portion of the product cost is fixed. In service organizations, variable costs typically include certain types of labor (such as temporary employees), supplies, and copying and printing costs. Exhibit 2.9 depicts (a) variable cost behavior and (b) fixed cost behavior. Note in the graph that volume is on the horizontal axis, and total costs (measured in dollars) are on the vertical axis. Item (a) shows that total variable costs increase in direct proportion to changes in volume. Thus, if volume doubles, total variable costs also double. Item (b) shows that fixed costs are at a particular level and do not increase as volume increases.

The identification of a cost as fixed or variable is valid only within a certain range of activity. For example, the manager of a restaurant in a shopping mall increased the capacity from 150 to 250 seats, requiring an increase in rent costs, utilities, and many other costs. Although these costs are usually thought of as fixed, they change when activity moves beyond a certain range. This range within which the total fixed costs and unit variable costs do not change is called the **relevant range.**

Five aspects of cost behavior complicate the task of classifying costs into fixed and variable categories. First, not all costs are strictly fixed or variable. For example, electric utility costs may be based on a fixed minimum monthly charge plus a variable cost for each kilowatt-hour. Such a **semivariable cost** has both fixed and variable components. Semivariable costs, also called *mixed costs,* are depicted in Exhibit 2.9(c).

Second, some costs increase with volume in "steps." **Step costs,** also called *semifixed costs,* increase in steps as shown in Exhibit 2.9(d). For example, one supervisor might be needed for up to four firefighters in a fire station, two supervisors for five to eight, and so forth as the number of firefighters increases. The supervisors' salaries represent a step cost.

Third, as previously indicated, the cost relations are valid only within a relevant range of activity. In particular, costs that are fixed over a small range of activity are likely to increase over a larger range of activity.

Fourth, although we have defined four types of cost behavior here, these are idealized abstractions and do not account for random distortions, unique events, and other "real world" phenomena. The actual cost behavior in any organization is unlikely to fit any of the four patterns shown in Exhibit 2.9 exactly. Using appropriate data analytic methods, some of which we discuss later in Chapter 5, cost analysts in these organizations can evaluate how closely various costs appear to be variable, fixed, and so on.

Finally, the classification of costs as fixed or variable depends on the measure of activity used. For example, at Three Rivers, part of the production cost is setting up the machines to run a specific part. Plant engineers have to calibrate the machine for each production run, but each run can produce up to 4,000 parts. If production volume is the activity measure, then the plant engineer costs are a step cost. However, if the number of production runs is the activity measure, then the plant engineer costs are variable; they spend the same amount of time for each run.

Understanding cost behavior is an important part of using cost accounting information wisely for decisions. Consider a recent example at Three Rivers. Calumet Tractors,

relevant range
Activity levels within which a given total fixed cost or unit variable cost will be unchanged.

semivariable cost
Cost that has both fixed and variable components; also called *mixed cost.*

step cost
Cost that increases with volume in steps; also called *semifixed cost.*

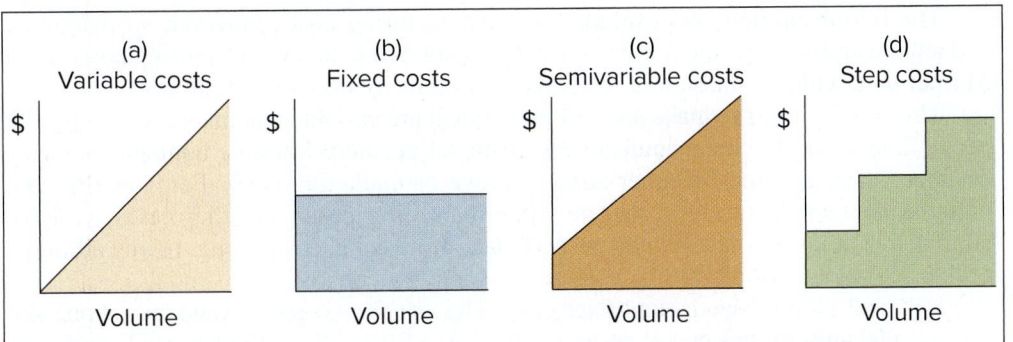

Exhibit 2.9 Four Cost Behavior Patterns

Exhibit 2.10   Cost Data for Price Quotation

	A	B	C	D
1	Cost Item	Amount		Notes
2	Develop production specifications for CT-24SF	$ 2,000		This is a one-time expenditure for drawings.
3	Direct materials (metal)	10.00		This is the cost per pump.
4	Direct labor	2.00		This is the cost per pump.
5	Set up machinery	1,000		Up to 5,000 pumps can be produced in a single production run.
6	Inspect pumps: Equipment	500		A new measuring device is required.
7	Labor	0.25		Per pump.
8				

a longtime customer of Three Rivers, has requested a price quotation from Three Rivers for a modified version of a common water pump. The modified pump is the CT-24SF. Calumet wants the quotation to cover a volume of CT-24SF pumps from 4,000 to 7,500 because it is not sure of its final requirement.

Angela Berroa, the plant controller, has prepared the preliminary cost data in Exhibit 2.10 for Mark Mays, the Three Rivers sales representative for Calumet. The cost for developing production specifications is fixed. It does not depend on the volume of pumps actually produced. The direct materials and the direct labor costs are variable. They increase proportionately with volume.

The cost for setting up the machinery is neither fixed nor variable with respect to volume. The setup costs are semifixed—they are incurred to set up the initial production run, and then they are not affected by production until 5,000 pumps have been produced. To produce more than 5,000 pumps, another fixed amount must be spent. The inspection costs are semivariable. The new measuring device is a fixed cost and the $0.25 per part is variable.

Components of Product Costs

LO 2-6

Identify the components of a product's cost.

full cost

Sum of all costs of manufacturing and selling a unit or product (includes both fixed and variable costs).

full absorption cost

All variable and fixed manufacturing costs; used to compute a product's inventory value under GAAP.

We have now seen that various concepts of costs exist. Some are determined by the rules of financial accounting. Some are more useful for managerial decision making. In this section, we develop several diagrams to explain various cost concepts and identify the differences.

Starting with Exhibit 2.11, assume that Three Rivers Fabrication estimates the cost to produce a specialized tractor pump during year 3. The **full cost** to manufacture and sell one pump is estimated to be $40, as shown on the left side of Exhibit 2.11. The unit cost of manufacturing the pump is $29, also shown on the left side of the exhibit. (One unit is one pump.) This full cost of manufacturing the one unit is known as the **full absorption cost.** It is the amount of inventoriable cost for external financial reporting according to GAAP. The full absorption cost "fully absorbs" the variable and fixed costs of manufacturing a product.

The full absorption cost excludes nonmanufacturing costs, however, so marketing and administrative costs are not inventoriable costs. These nonmanufacturing costs equal $11 per unit, which is the sum of the two blocks at the bottom of Exhibit 2.11.

The variable costs to make and sell the product are variable manufacturing costs, $23 per unit, and variable nonmanufacturing costs, $4 per unit. Variable nonmanufacturing costs could, in general, be either administrative or marketing costs. For Three Rivers, variable nonmanufacturing costs are primarily selling costs. In other cases, variable administrative costs could include costs of data processing, accounting, or any administrative activity that is affected by volume.

Exhibit 2.11 also includes unit fixed costs. The unit fixed costs are valid only at one volume—2,000 units (of this pump) per year—for Three Rivers. By definition, total fixed costs

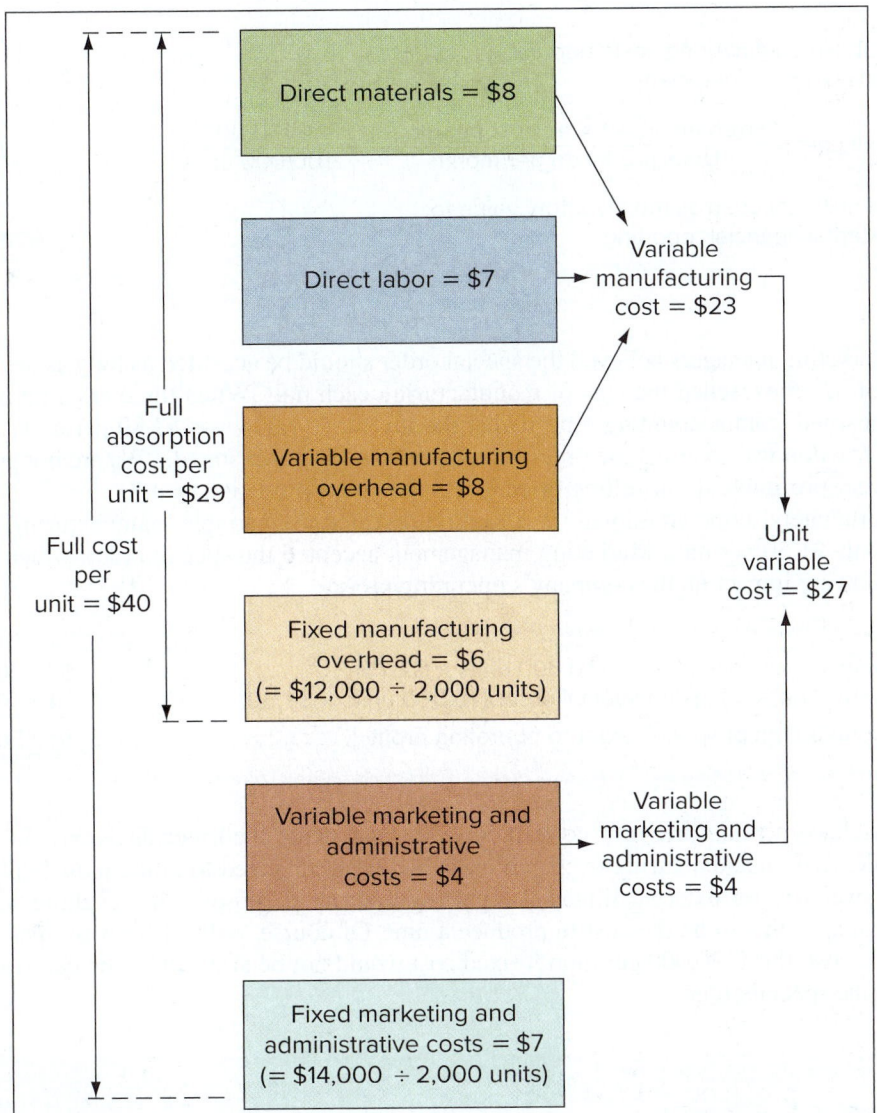

Exhibit 2.11
Product Cost
Components—Three
Rivers Fabrication

do not change as volume changes (within the relevant range, of course). Therefore, a change in volume results in a change in the unit fixed cost, as demonstrated by Self-Study Question 3.

Unit Fixed Costs Can Be Misleading for Decision Making

When analyzing costs for decisions, you should use unit fixed costs very carefully. Many managers fail to realize that they are valid at only one volume. When fixed costs are allocated to each unit, accounting records often make the costs appear as though they are variable. For example, allocating some of factory rent to each unit of product results in including rent as part of the "unit cost" even though the total rent does not change with the manufacture of another unit of product. Cost data that include allocated common costs therefore may be misleading if used incorrectly. The following example demonstrates the problem.

One of the parts Three Rivers sells has a unit manufacturing cost of $2.80 ($1.50 per unit variable manufacturing cost + $1.30 per unit fixed manufacturing cost), computed as shown on the next page (each part is one unit).

Three Rivers received a special order for 10,000 parts at $2.75 each. These units could be produced with currently idle capacity. Marketing, administrative, and the total fixed manufacturing costs of $130,000 would not be affected by accepting the order, nor would accepting this special order affect the regular market for this part.

Variable manufacturing costs per unit....................................	$1.50
Fixed manufacturing costs:	

$$\text{Unit cost} = \frac{\text{Fixed manufacturing cost per month}}{\text{Units produced per month}} = \frac{\$130,000}{100,000 \text{ units}} = \underline{1.30}$$

Total unit cost used as the inventory value for external financial reporting	$2.80

Marketing managers believed the special order should be accepted as long as the unit price of $2.75 exceeded the cost of manufacturing each unit. When the marketing managers learned from accounting reports that the inventory value was $2.80 per unit, their initial reaction was to reject the order because, as one manager stated, "We are not going to be very profitable if our selling price is less than our production cost!"

Fortunately, some additional investigation revealed the variable manufacturing cost to be only $1.50 per unit. Marketing management accepted the special order, which had the following impact on the company's operating profit.

Revenue from special order (10,000 units × $2.75)	$27,500
Variable costs of making special order (10,000 units × $1.50)...........	15,000
Contribution of special order to operating profit	$12,500

It is easy to interpret unit costs incorrectly and make incorrect decisions. In this example, fixed manufacturing overhead costs had been allocated to units, most likely to value inventory for external financial reporting and tax purposes. The resulting $2.80 unit cost appeared to be the cost to produce a unit. Of course, only $1.50 was a per unit variable cost; the $130,000 per month fixed cost would not be affected by the decision to accept the special order.

Self-Study Question

3. Refer to the Three Rivers example in Exhibit 2.11 that is based on a volume of 2,000 units per year. Assume the same total fixed costs and unit variable costs but a volume of only 1,600 units. What are the fixed manufacturing costs per unit and the fixed marketing and administrative costs per unit?

The solution to this question is at the end of this chapter.

gross margin
Revenue – Cost of goods sold on income statements. Per unit, the gross margin equals Sales price – Full absorption cost per unit.

Exhibits 2.12 and 2.13 are designed to clarify definitions of gross margin, contribution margin, and operating profit. You may recall from your study of financial accounting statements that the **gross margin** appears on external financial statements as the difference between revenue and cost of goods sold. We refer to this format as a *traditional income statement*. Cost of goods sold is the full absorption cost per unit times the number of units sold. Exhibit 2.12 presents the gross margin per unit for the pumps that Three Rivers produces and sells for $45 each.

Recall from Exhibit 2.11 that each pump is estimated to have a $29 full absorption cost. Therefore, the gross margin per unit is $16 (= $45 − $29). The operating profit per unit is the difference between the sales price and the full cost of making and selling the product. For Three Rivers, Exhibit 2.12 shows the operating profit per unit to be $5 (= $45 sales price − $40 full cost).

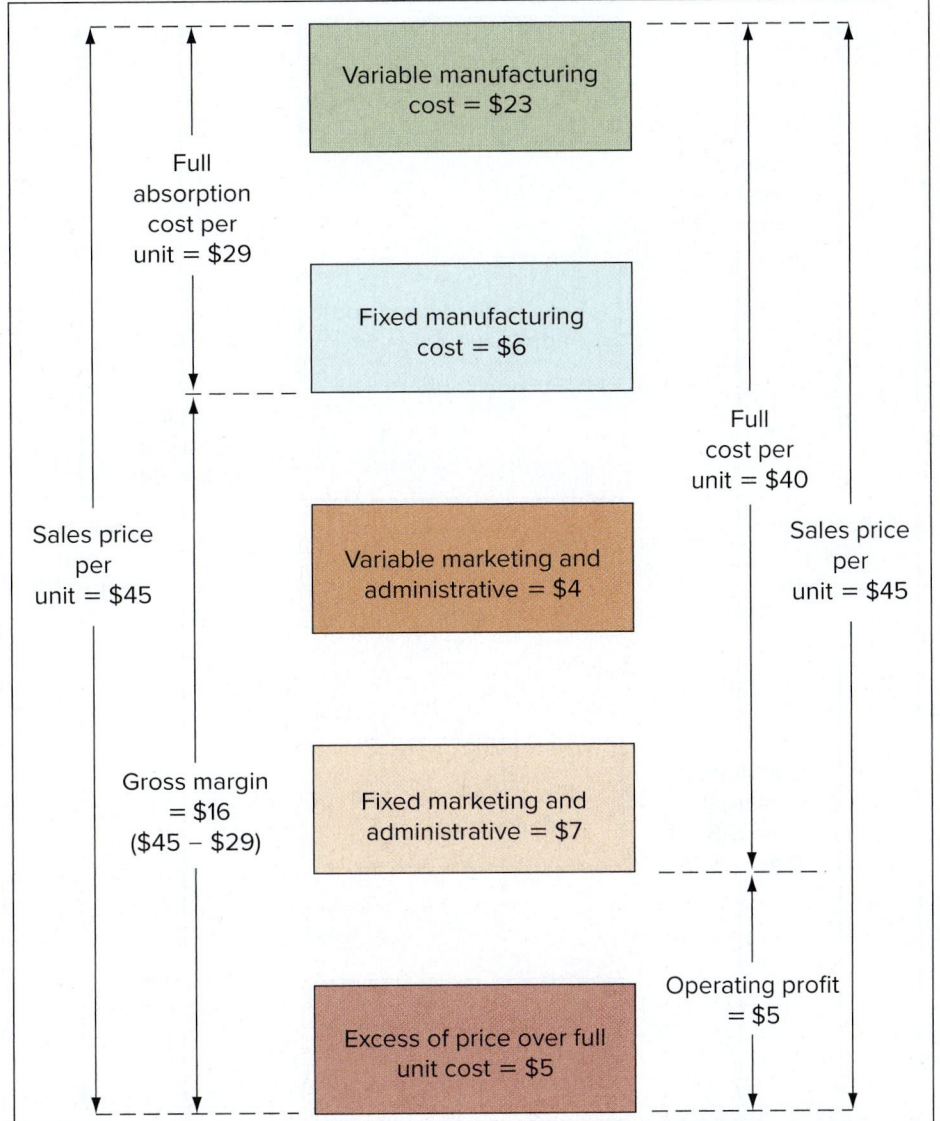

Exhibit 2.12
Gross Margin per Unit—
Three Rivers Fabrication

Exhibit 2.13 also shows the contribution margin per unit. On a per unit basis, the **contribution margin** is the difference between the sales price and the variable cost per unit. Think of the contribution margin as the amount available to cover fixed costs and earn a profit.

The contribution margin is important information for managers because it allows them to assess the profitability of products before factoring in fixed costs (which tend to be more difficult to change in the short run). For example, a coffee shop sells both drip coffee and espresso drinks. A cup of drip coffee sells for $1.50 and a cappuccino sells for $2.50. Which product contributes more per unit to profits? Answer: We don't know until we know the contribution margin per unit for each product. Suppose that the variable cost per cup is $0.25 for drip coffee and $1.50 for cappuccino. Then the contribution margins (per unit) are as follows:

- Drip coffee, $1.25 (= $1.50 sales price − $0.25 variable cost).
- Cappuccino, $1.00 (= $2.50 sales price − $1.50 variable cost).
- Although the cappuccino sells for more, the drip coffee provides a higher contribution per unit toward covering fixed costs and earning a profit.

contribution margin
Sales price − Variable costs per unit.

Exhibit 2.13

Contribution Margin
per Unit—Three Rivers
Fabrication

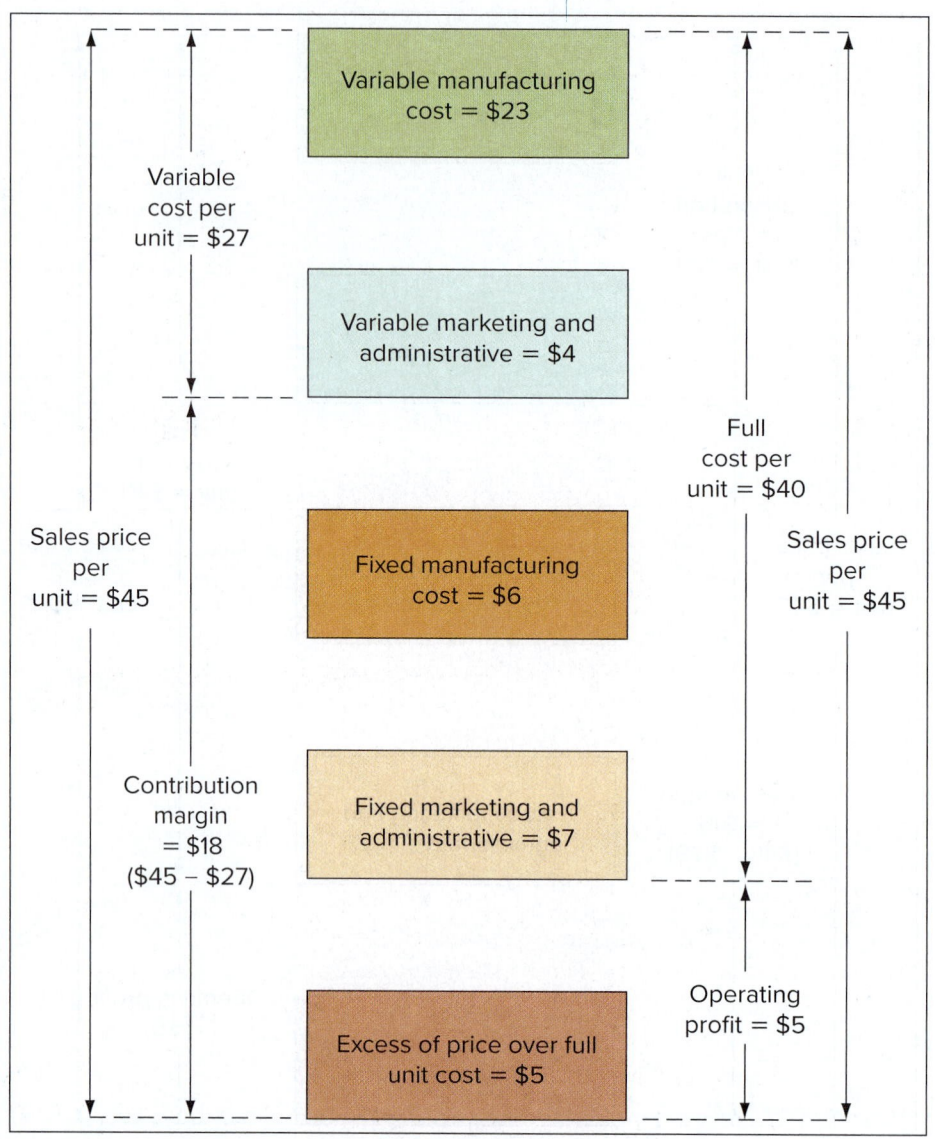

The Importance of Gross Margin

As we have seen, costs incurred may be classified in different ways for financial reports. This classification can matter for decision makers using the financial information to assess the performance of the organization, even though, however classified, the cost is ultimately used in computing income in some period. Investors and other stakeholders in an organization use the gross margin, the difference between revenues and cost of goods or services sold, to assess how efficiently the organization is using resources. For example,

Investors watch Apple's gross margin, a measure of how efficiently it turns sales into profit, because a contraction could foreshadow the end of Apple's dominance in the smartphone era.

This is not only true of for-profit firms. The Mayo Clinic, a not-for-profit organization with over $13 billion in annual revenues, uses gross margin as a measure of financial performance. In a stable economic environment, the classification of costs into

cost of goods or inventory causes little distortion in a comparison of gross margins over time. However, when there is a major disruption, as the Clinic experienced during the COVID-19 crisis, financial managers were forced to reconsider this classification.

Previously, the hospital system had recognized gear as inventory if it was stored in a warehouse; if the gear were kept at a clinical facility or on a hospital floor, it would be recognized as an expense. Faced with the pandemic, the clinic had no choice but to keep the gear close to its medical staff.

One role of a financial executive is to communicate performance in a manner that portrays the underlying economics of the business. When those economics change, the calculations often change to reflect new conditions.

Sources: Mickle, Tripp, "Jobs, Cook, Ive—Blevins? The Rise of Apple's Cost Cutter," *Wall Street Journal,* January 23, 2020; Maurer, Mark, "Inventory or Expense: Coronavirus Pushes Mayo Clinic to Revisit Its Accounting Practices," *Wall Street Journal,* May 11, 2020.

Refer to the Three Rivers examples in Exhibits 2.12 and 2.13.

4. Assume that the variable marketing and administrative cost falls to $3 per unit; all other cost numbers remain the same. What are the new gross margin, contribution margin, and operating profit amounts?

5. Assume that the fixed manufacturing cost dropped from $12,000 to $10,000 in total, or from $6 to $5 per unit. All other unit cost numbers remain the same as in Exhibits 2.12 and 2.13. What are the new gross margin, contribution margin, and operating profit amounts?

The solutions to these questions are at the end of the chapter.

How to Make Cost Information More Useful for Managers

As discussed earlier, cost accountants divide costs into product or period categories. In general, product costs are more easily attributed to products; period costs are more easily attributed to time intervals. Once product costs are defined, all other costs are assumed to be period costs. It is important to note, however, that the determination of product costs varies, depending on the approach used. Three common approaches are outlined here:

LO 2-7
Understand the distinction between financial and contribution margin income statements.

- *Full absorption costing (traditional income statement).* Under this approach required by GAAP, all fixed and variable manufacturing costs are product costs. All other costs are period costs.
- *Variable costing (contribution margin income statement).* Using this approach, only variable manufacturing costs are product costs. All other costs are period costs.
- *Managerial costing.* This approach assumes that management determines which costs are associated with the product and should be considered product costs. Management asks whether adding a product will incur new costs. Any new costs are considered *product costs.* For example, management could decide that promotional campaigns associated with a new product are product costs. Under the other two approaches, promotional costs would be period costs. Clearly, the managerial costing approach to defining product costs is subjective and depends on management's use of cost information.

Gross Margin versus Contribution Margin Income Statements

A traditional income statement using full absorption costing (the first approach in the list) and a contribution margin income statement using variable costing (the second approach) for a special order of pumps are shown in Exhibit 2.14. The data come from Exhibits 2.12 and 2.13, but unit costs are multiplied by 2,000 pumps to give total amounts for year 3. Operating profit is the same for each approach because total units produced equal total

Exhibit 2.14 Gross Margin versus Contribution Margin Income Statements

Gross Margin Income Statement		Contribution Margin Income Statement	
Sales revenue	$90,000	Sales revenue	$90,000
Variable manufacturing costs	46,000	Variable manufacturing costs	46,000
Fixed manufacturing costs	12,000	Variable marketing and	
		administrative costs	8,000
Gross margin	$32,000	Contribution margin	$36,000
Variable marketing and			
administrative costs	8,000		
Fixed marketing and		Fixed manufacturing costs	12,000
administrative costs	14,000	Fixed marketing and	
		administrative costs	14,000
Operating profit	$10,000	Operating profit	$10,000

units sold, but note the difference in product costs on each statement. We do not provide an income statement example for the third approach (managerial costing) because the treatment of product costs using this approach varies from one company to the next.

Product costs for units not yet sold are assigned to inventory and carried in the accounts as assets. When the goods are sold, the costs flow from inventory to the income statement. At that time, these previously inventoried costs become expenses.

Developing Financial Statements for Decision Making

While the gross margin and contribution margin statements illustrated in Exhibit 2.14 are common, there is no reason to restrict managers to these statements. The goal of the cost accounting system is to provide managers with information useful for decision making. In designing the cost accounting system, we determine the information that managers use in making decisions and then provide it to them in ways that support their work.

For example, many firms are concerned with ensuring that the activities they undertake add value to their product or service. If this is important to managers for making decisions, we can develop financial statements that classify costs into value-added or nonvalue-added categories. By classifying activities as value added or nonvalue added, managers are better able to reduce or eliminate nonvalue-added activities and therefore reduce costs.

Suppose that Ingrid Jensen, the plant manager of Three Rivers, wants to know which costs add value in the case of the special order. The controller reviews production activities and related costs in detail for the order and prepares the value income statement shown in Exhibit 2.15. The data come from Exhibit 2.14. However, costs are shown in greater detail and separated into nonvalue-added and value-added categories. For example, variable marketing and administrative costs of $8,000 from Exhibit 2.14 are shown as two line items under variable marketing and administrative costs in Exhibit 2.15:

Exhibit 2.15   Value Income Statement

THREE RIVERS FABRICATION
Value Income Statement Special Order
For the Year Ending December 31, Year 3

	Nonvalue-Added Activities	Value-Added Activities	Total
Sales revenue.		$90,000	$90,000
Variable manufacturing costs			
Materials used in production		15,000	15,000
Materials waste	$ 1,000		1,000
Labor used in production		11,500	11,500
Labor used to rework products.	2,500		2,500
Manufacturing overhead used in production		15,500	15,500
Manufacturing overhead used to rework products	500		500
Variable marketing and administrative costs			
Marketing and administrative services used to sell products		6,000	6,000
Marketing and administrative services used to process			
returned products	2,000		2,000
Contribution margin.	$(6,000)	$42,000	$36,000
Fixed manufacturing			
Fixed manufacturing costs used in production.		10,500	10,500
Salaries of employees reworking products.	1,500		1,500
Fixed marketing and administrative costs			
Marketing and administrative services used to sell products		13,500	13,500
Marketing and administrative services used to process			
returned products	500		500
Operating profit (loss)	$(8,000)	$18,000	$10,000

marketing and administrative services used to sell products totaling $6,000 and market-ing and administrative services used to process returned products totaling $2,000. The value income statement outlines costs linked to three segments of the value chain: pro-duction, marketing, and distribution. Remember that the primary idea of the value chain is that value is added to the product in each business function. The goal is to maximize value-added activities and minimize nonvalue-added activities.

The controller identifies nonvalue-added activities associated with two areas—materials waste and reworked products. *Materials waste* refers to material that was thrown away because of incorrect cuts or defective material. *Reworked products* consist of prod-ucts that have been manufactured incorrectly (for example, incorrect pump size or num-ber of teeth) and have to be fixed (or reworked). Costs to rework products are generally incurred by the production, marketing, and administration departments. Marketing gets involved because failure detection sometimes does not occur until the customer returns the goods. Thus, nonvalue-added activities are not limited to production.

Assume that the company sold 2,000 units in year 3, and the controller uses the per unit costs outlined in Exhibit 2.13. The controller's value income statement shows total nonvalue-added activities to be $8,000. This amount is only 10 percent of total costs but is 80 percent of operating profit. Clearly, reducing nonvalue-added activities could sig-nificantly increase profits.

Reducing nonvalue-added activities is not a simple task. For example, how should the production process be changed to reduce materials waste? Should higher-quality materials be purchased, resulting in higher direct materials costs? Or should production personnel be trained and evaluated based on materials wasted? However, providing the information highlights the problem and the potential effect that changes could have on firm performance. Depending on the business and strategic environment of the firm, we could construct financial statements around activities related to quality, environmental compliance, or new product development.

Key Takeaways

1. A cost is the sacrifice of resources. It is measured by what you forgo by choosing one alternative over another.
2. Cost allocation is fundamental to cost accounting. It is the process used to assign (allocate) cost pools to cost objects (products, services, business units, and so on) about which we make decisions.
3. Cost behavior or how costs change relative to an activ-ity or other factor is important for decision making and cost accounting. The accounting treatment of costs into product or period cost is important for product costing for financial reporting. Reported costs from financial report-ing might not be appropriate for decision making.

SUMMARY

The term *cost* is ambiguous when used alone; it has meaning only in a specific context. The adjec-tives used to modify *cost* constitute that context. Exhibit 2.16 summarizes definitions of the word. It is important to consider how the use of these terms in cost accounting differs from common usage. For example, in common usage, a variable cost may vary with anything (geography, tem-perature, and so forth). In cost accounting, variable cost depends solely on volume.

The following summarizes key ideas tied to the chapter's learning objectives:

LO 2-1 Explain the basic concept of "cost." A *cost* is a sacrifice of resources, and an *expense* is a cost charged against revenue in an accounting period, typically for external reporting purposes.

LO 2-2 Explain how costs are presented in financial statements. Cost of goods sold in a merchandising organization simply includes the costs of purchase and incoming trans-portation of the goods. Cost of goods sold for manufacturing organizations is much more complicated and includes direct materials (raw materials), direct labor, and

Exhibit 2.16

Summary of Cost Terms
and Definitions

Nature of Cost	
Cost	A *sacrifice* of resources.
Opportunity cost	The forgone benefit from the best (forgone) alternative course of action.
Outlay cost	A past, present, or future cash outflow.
Expense	A cost that is charged against revenue in an accounting period.

Cost Concepts for Cost Accounting Systems	
Product cost	Cost that can be attributed to a product.
Period cost	Cost that can be attributed to time intervals.
Full absorption cost	All variable and fixed manufacturing costs; used to compute a product's inventory value under GAAP.
Direct cost	Cost that can be directly (unambiguously and at low cost) related to a cost object.
Indirect cost	Cost that *cannot* be directly related to a cost object.

Cost Concepts for Describing Cost Behavior	
Variable cost	Cost that changes in direct proportion with a change in volume within the relevant range of activity.
Fixed cost	Cost that is unchanged as volume changes within the relevant range of activity.

manufacturing overhead. Cost of goods (i.e., services) sold in a service organization primarily includes labor and overhead.

LO 2-3 Explain the process of cost allocation. Cost allocation is required to assign, or allocate, costs recorded in various accounts (the cost pools) to the cost objects (product, department, customer) of interest. An allocation rule specifies how this is done because there is generally no economically feasible way of associating the costs directly with the cost objects.

LO 2-4 Understand how materials, labor, and overhead costs are added to a product at each stage of the production process. Manufacturing organizations have three stages of production: direct materials, work in process, and finished goods. All items not sold at the end of the period are included in inventory as an asset on the balance sheet. All finished goods sold at the end of the period are included as cost of goods sold in the income statement.

LO 2-5 Define basic cost behaviors, including fixed, variable, semivariable, and step costs. Cost behavior can be classified in one of four ways: fixed, variable, semivariable, or step costs.

LO 2-6 Identify the components of a product's costs.

- Variable cost per unit.
- Full absorption cost per unit, which is the inventoriable amount under GAAP.
- Full cost per unit of making and selling the product.
- Gross margin, which equals sales price minus full absorption cost.
- Contribution margin, which equals sales price minus variable cost.
- Profit margin, which equals sales price minus full cost.

LO 2-7 Understand the distinction between financial and contribution margin income statements. The traditional income statement format is used primarily for external reporting purposes, and the contribution margin income statement format is used more for internal decision-making and performance evaluation purposes. A third alternative is the value approach, which categorizes costs into value- and nonvalue-added activities.

KEY TERMS

administrative costs, *51*	full cost, *60*
contribution margin, *63*	gross margin, *62*
conversion costs, *51*	indirect cost, *53*
cost, *46*	indirect manufacturing costs, *50*
cost allocation, *52*	inventoriable costs, *54*
cost allocation rule, *52*	manufacturing overhead, *50*
cost flow diagram, *52*	marketing costs, *51*
cost object, *52*	operating profit, *47*
cost of goods sold, *49*	opportunity cost, *46*
cost pool, *52*	outlay cost, *46*
direct cost, *53*	period costs, *50*
direct labor, *50*	prime costs, *51*
direct manufacturing costs, *50*	product costs, *50*
direct materials, *50*	relevant range, *59*
expense, *46*	semivariable cost, *59*
finished goods, *54*	step cost, *59*
fixed costs, *58*	variable costs, *58*
full absorption cost, *60*	work in process, *54*

REVIEW QUESTIONS

2-1. What is the difference in meaning between the terms *cost* and *expense?*

2-2. What is the difference between *product* costs and *period* costs?

2-3. What is the difference between *outlay* cost and *opportunity* cost?

2-4. Provide a business example illustrating opportunity costs.

2-5. Is "cost-of-goods sold" an expense?

2-6. Is "cost-of-goods" a product cost or a period cost?

2-7. What are the similarities between the Direct Materials Inventory account of the manufacturer and the Merchandise Inventory account of the merchandiser? Are there any differences between the two accounts? If so, what are they?

2-8. Does a retailer typically have a Work-in-Process account? Explain.

2-9. What are the three categories of product cost in a manufacturing operation? Describe each element briefly.

2-10. What is the difference between *gross margin* and *contribution margin?*

2-11. To a manager making a decision, which is likely more important: *gross margin* or *contribution margin?* Why?

2-12. What do the terms *step costs* and *semivariable costs* mean?

2-13. What do the terms *variable costs* and *fixed costs* mean?

2-14. How does a value income statement differ from a gross margin income statement? From a contribution margin income statement?

2-15. Why is a value income statement useful to managers?

CRITICAL ANALYSIS AND DISCUSSION QUESTIONS

2-16. "Materials and labor are always direct costs, and supply costs are always indirect." What is your opinion of this statement?

2-17. The cost per seat-mile for a major U.S. airline is 14.1¢. Therefore, to estimate the cost of flying a passenger from Detroit to Los Angeles, we should multiply 1,980 miles by 14.1¢. Do you agree? Explain.

2-18. In evaluating product profitability, we can ignore marketing costs because they are not considered product costs. Do you agree?

2-19. You and two friends drive your car to Texas for spring break. A third friend asks if you can drop her off in Oklahoma. How would you allocate the cost of the trip among the four of you?

2-20. The friend in question 2-19 decides that she does not want to go to Oklahoma after all. How will the costs of your trip change? Was your choice of allocation in question 2-19 incorrect? Why?

2-21. Consider a digital music service such as those provided by Amazon or Apple. What are some of the major cost categories? Are they mostly fixed or mostly variable?

2-22. Consider the Business Application "Components of Cost of Goods Sold for a Retailer." During the COVID-19 pandemic, Target continued operations at its retail stores, after taking steps to ensure the health and safety of its employees and customers. These steps included additional cleaning protocols, additional fixtures for social distancing, and so on. The costs of these additional steps were incurred in both the distribution centers and the retail stores. According to Target policies as stated in the Business Application, how will these costs be treated in the financial statements: as a period or product cost? Do you agree with this treatment for these costs?

2-23 Consider again the Business Application "Components of Cost of Goods Sold for a Retailer." Some of the costs associated with opening during the COVID-19 pandemic were outlay costs and some were opportunity costs. Give one example of each for a retail store.

2-24. Pick a unit of a hospital (for example, intensive care or maternity). Name one example of a direct materials cost, one example of a direct labor cost, and one example of an indirect cost.

2-25. The dean of Midstate University Business School is trying to understand the costs of the school's two degree programs: Bachelor's (BBA) and Master's (MBA). The dean asks you for recommendations on how to allocate the costs of the following services, which are used by students in both programs: cafeteria, library, and career placement. How would you respond?

2-26. Currently, generally accepted accounting principles (GAAP) in the United States require firms to expense research and development (R&D) costs as period costs. Therefore, when the resulting product is sold, R&D costs are not part of reported product costs. Does this mean that R&D costs are irrelevant for decision making?

2-27. If value income statements are useful for decision making, why are value income statements not used in financial reporting?

EXERCISES      All applicable Exercises are included in Connect.

(LO 2-1, 5) **2-28. Basic Concepts**

For each of the following statements, indicate whether it is true, false, or uncertain. Explain why. Give examples in your answer.

a. A cost is something used up to produce revenues in a particular accounting period.

b. Variable costs are direct costs; only fixed costs are indirect costs.

c. The cost of direct materials is fixed per unit but variable in total.

(LO2-1) **2-29. Basic Concepts**

For each of the following statements, indicate whether it is true, false, or uncertain. Explain why. Give examples in your answer.

a. Cost accountants should be concerned with both product and period costs.

b. Opportunity costs tend to be easier to identify and measure than outlay costs.

c. Cost accountants should only be concerned with outlay costs, not opportunity costs.

(LO 2-1, 5) **2-30. Basic Concepts**

For each of the following costs incurred in a manufacturing firm, indicate whether the costs are most likely fixed (F) or variable (V) and whether they are most likely period costs (P) or product costs (M) under full absorption costing.

a. Administrative support for sales supervisors.

b. Assembly line workers' wages.

c. Cafeteria costs for the factory.

d. Controller's office rental.

e. Depreciation on the building for administrative staff offices.

f. Energy to run machines producing units of output in the factory.

g. Overtime pay for assembly workers.

h. Salaries of top executives in the company.

i. Sales commissions for sales personnel.

j. Transportation-in costs on materials purchased.

2-31. Basic Concepts   (LO 2-1, 2)

For each of the following costs incurred in the manufacture of steel components, indicate whether the costs are prime costs (P), conversion costs (C), or both (B).

a. Transportation-in costs for steel.

b. Lease payments on the factory.

c. Steel used in making the components.

d. Maintenance on the manufacturing machines.

e. Machine operator wages.

2-32. Basic Concepts   (LO 2-1, 2, 5)

Place the number of the appropriate definition in the blank next to each concept.

Concept	Definition
_____ Cost	1. Sacrifice of resources.
_____ Direct cost	2. Cost that *cannot* be directly related to a cost object.
_____ Expense	3. Cost that varies with the volume of activity.
_____ Fixed cost	4. Cost used to compute inventory value according to GAAP.
_____ Full absorption cost	5. Cost charged against revenue in a particular accounting period.
_____ Indirect cost	6. Cost that can be directly related to a cost object.
_____ Opportunity cost	7. Past, present, or near-future cash flow.
_____ Outlay cost	8. Lost benefit from the best forgone alternative.
_____ Period cost	9. Cost that can more easily be attributed to time intervals.
_____ Product cost	10. Cost that does not vary with the volume of activity.
_____ Variable cost	11. Cost that is part of inventory.

2-33. Basic Concepts: Multiple Choice   (LO 2-1, 6)

Gregorie Tool & Die reports the following information for the quarter:

Sales price	$ 55
Fixed costs (for the quarter)	
Selling and administration	75,000
Production	175,000
Variable cost (per unit)	
Materials	15
Labor	12
Plant supervision	3
Selling and administrative	5
Number of units (for the quarter)	25,000 units

Required

Select the answer for each of the following costs.

a. Variable cost per unit.

   1. $30

   2. $35

   3. $42

   4. $45

b. Variable production cost per unit.

   1. $30

   2. $35

   3. $42

   4. $45

c. Full cost per unit.

   1. $10

   2. $35

   3. $42

   4. $45

d.   Full absorption cost per unit.
1. $30
2. $35
3. $37
4. $45

e.   Prime cost per unit.
1. $12
2. $15
3. $27
4. $30

f.   Conversion cost per unit.
1. $12
2. $22
3. $30
4. $37

g.   Contribution margin per unit.
1. $10
2. $20
3. $22
4. $25

h.   Gross margin per unit.
1. $10
2. $18
3. $20
4. $25

(LO 2-1, 6)   **2-34. Basic Concepts: Multiple Choice**
The following information is available for Alcoy Partners for the year just ended:

Sales price	$	34
Fixed costs (for the year)		
Selling and administrative		420,000
Production		560,000
Variable cost (per unit)		
Materials		9
Labor		3
Plant supervision		6
Selling and administrative		3
Number of units (for the year)		140,000 units

Required
Select the answer for each of the following costs.

a.   Variable cost per unit.
1. $12
2. $18
3. $21
4. $25

b.   Variable production cost per unit.
1. $12
2. $18
3. $21
4. $25

c.   Full cost per unit.
1. $12
2. $21
3. $28
4. $34

d. Full absorption cost per unit.
    1. $18
    2. $21
    3. $22
    4. $28

e. Prime cost per unit.
    1. $9
    2. $12
    3. $18
    4. $21

f. Conversion cost per unit.
    1. $7
    2. $9
    3. $12
    4. $13

g. Contribution margin per unit.
    1. $6
    2. $12
    3. $13
    4. $16

h. Gross margin per unit.
    1. $6
    2. $12
    3. $13
    4. $16

2-35. Basic Concepts
(LO 2-1, 5)

For each of the following costs incurred in a manufacturing firm, indicate whether the costs are fixed (F) or variable (V) and whether they are period costs (P) or product costs (M) under full absorption costing.

a. Straight-line depreciation on corporate headquarters.
b. Plant manager's salary.
c. Property taxes on land on which factory is located.
d. Factory supplies for cleaning assembly machines.
e. Freight costs for shipping products to customers.

2-36. Basic Concepts
(LO 2-1, 2, 6)

Elmo Security Consultants (ESC) offers a standardized review of data security for small business owners. The following data apply to the provision of these reviews:

Sales price per unit (1 unit = 1 test plus feedback to client)	$ 500
Fixed costs (per month):	
Selling and administration	50,000
Production overhead (e.g., rent of facilities)	70,000
Variable costs (per test):	
Labor for oversight and feedback	250
Outsourced security analysis	40
Materials used in testing	10
Review overhead	20
Selling and administration (e.g., scheduling and billing)	30
Number of reviews per month	2,500 reviews

Required
Give the amount for each of the following (one unit = one review):

a. Variable review (production) cost per unit.
b. Variable total cost per unit.
c. Full cost per unit.

> d. Full absorption cost per unit.
> e. Prime cost per unit.
> f. Conversion cost per unit.
> g. Contribution margin per unit.
> h. Gross margin per unit.
> i. Suppose the number of units decreases to 2,000 reviews per month, which is within the relevant range. Which parts of (*a*) through (*h*) will change? For each amount that will change, give the new amount for a volume of 2,000 tests.

(LO 2-1, 2, 6)   **2-37. Basic Concepts**

Lillibridge & Friends, Inc. provides you with the following data for its single product:

Sales price per unit... $	50
Fixed costs (per quarter):	
Selling, general, and administrative (SG&A)	1,500,000
Manufacturing overhead...	4,500,000
Variable costs (per unit):	
Direct labor	8
Direct materials...	11
Manufacturing overhead...	9
SG&A	5
Number of units produced per quarter	500,000 units

Required

Give the amounts for each of the following:

> a. Prime cost per unit.
> b. Contribution margin per unit.
> c. Gross margin per unit.
> d. Conversion cost per unit.
> e. Variable cost per unit.
> f. Full absorption cost per unit.
> g. Variable production cost per unit.
> h. Full cost per unit.
> i. Suppose the number of units increases to 600,000 units per quarter, which is within the relevant range. Which of amounts (*a*) through (*h*) will change? For each that will change, give the new amount for a volume of 600,000 units.

(LO 2-3)   **2-38. Cost Allocation—Ethical Issues**

In one of its divisions, an aircraft components manufacturer produces experimental navigational equipment for spacecraft and for private transportation companies. Although the products are essentially identical, they carry different product numbers. The XNS-12 model is sold to a government agency on a cost-reimbursed basis. In other words, the price charged to the government is equal to the computed cost plus a fixed fee. The JEF-3 model is sold to the private transportation companies on a competitive basis. The product development cost, common to both models, must be allocated to the two products in order to determine the cost for setting the price of the XNS-12.

Required

> a. How would you recommend the product development cost be allocated between the two products?
> b. What incentives do managers have to allocate product development costs? Why?

(LO 2-3)   **2-39. Cost Allocation—Ethical Issues**

A local coffee shop has two major product lines—drinks and pastries. If the manager allocates common costs on any objective basis discussed in this chapter, the drinks are profitable, but the pastries are not. The manager is concerned that the supervisor at corporate headquarters will drop the pastries. The manager is concerned because a relative, who is struggling to make a go of a new business, supplies pastries to the coffee shop. The manager, therefore, decides to allocate all common costs to the drinks because "Drinks can afford to absorb these costs until we get the pastries line on its feet." After assigning all common costs to drinks, both the drinks and pastries product lines appear to be marginally profitable. Consequently, corporate headquarters decides to continue the pastries line.

Required

a.   How would you recommend the manager allocate the common costs between drinks and pastries?

b.   You are the assistant manager and have been working with the manager on the allocation problem. What should you do?

2-40. Prepare Statements for a Manufacturing Company

(LO 2-2, 4)

The following balances appear on the accounts of Greusel Fabrication:

	March 1 (Beginning)	March 31 (Ending)
Direct materials inventory	$36,000	$41,000
Work-in-process inventory	62,000	66,200
Finished goods inventory..................	42,500	38,200

Direct materials used during the month amount to $525,000 and the cost of goods sold for the month was $1,436,000.

Required

Find the following by completing a cost of goods sold statement.

a.   Cost of direct materials purchased during March.

b.   Cost of goods manufactured for March.

c.   Total manufacturing costs incurred for March.

2-41. Prepare Statements for a Manufacturing Company

(LO 2-2, 4)

The following balances (in thousands of dollars) are from the accounts of Birwood Furniture:

	January 1 (Beginning) ($000)	December 31 (Ending) ($000)
Direct materials inventory	$ 712	$ 784
Work-in-process inventory	1,154	1,330
Finished goods inventory..................	139	264

Direct materials used during the year amount to $1,096,000 and the cost of goods sold for the year was $1,278,000.

Required

Find the following by completing a cost of goods sold statement.

a.   Cost of direct materials purchased during the year.

b.   Cost of goods manufactured during the year.

c.   Total manufacturing costs incurred during the year.

2-42. Prepare Statements for a Service Company

(LO 2-2)

Harbor Island Investments (HII) is a discount brokerage firm offering clients investment advice, trading services, and a variety of mutual funds for investment. HII has collected the following information for November:

	A	B	C
1	Employee compensation	$880,000	
2	Employee training programs	467,500	
3	Fees paid to execute trades	2,200,000	
4	Lease and facility costs	192,500	
5	Marketing	99,000	
6	Revenues (Advisory fees)	1,650,000	
7	Revenues (Brokerage commissions)	3,300,000	
8	Sales commissions to brokers	275,000	
9	Supervisors' salaries	330,000	
10			
11			

Required

Prepare an income statement for November for HII.

(LO 2-2)   **2-43. Prepare Statements for a Service Company**

Tuscola Counseling Services is a small firm that advises job seekers on both employment and education alternatives. Robert Gibson, the founder and president, has collected the following information for the year just ended:

	A	B	C
1	Employee training	$8,300	
2	Marketing	70,000	
3	Rent and facilities costs	28,000	
4	Revenue (client fees)	264,000	
5	Supplies	51,000	
6	Travel	39,700	
7	Wages and salaries	81,000	
8			

Required

Prepare an income statement for the year just ended for Tuscola Counseling Services.

(LO 2-2)   **2-44. Prepare Statements for a Service Company**

The following data are available for Gray Services for the month just ended:

Gross margin	$ 635,000
Operating profit	240,000
Revenues	1,640,000

Required

Find the following by completing a cost of services sold statement.

 a. Marketing and administrative costs.

 b. Cost of services sold.

(LO 2-2)   **2-45. Prepare Statements for a Service Company**

Sheffield Advisors offers financial counseling services to self-employed business owners. Sheffield's operating profits average 22 percent of revenues and its marketing and administrative costs average 30 percent of the cost of services sold. Sheffield Advisors expects revenues to be $840,000 for October.

Required

Prepare an income statement for October for Sheffield Advisors assuming the revenue expectations are met.

(LO 2-2, 4)   **2-46. Prepare Statements for a Manufacturing Company**

The following balances are from the accounts of Santa Maria Parts:

	July 1 (Beginning)	September 30 (Ending)
Direct materials inventory	$76,800	$94,400
Work-in-process inventory	69,600	37,200
Finished goods inventory	78,000	72,000

Direct materials purchased during the quarter amount to $480,000, and the cost of goods sold for the quarter was $1,740,000.

Required

Reconstruct a cost of goods sold statement and fill in the following missing data.

 a. Cost of direct materials used during the quarter.

 b. Cost of goods manufactured during the quarter.

 c. Total manufacturing costs incurred during the quarter.

2-47. Basic Concepts (LO 2-1, 2)

The following data refer to the month of May for Bonita Components. Fill in the blanks.

Direct materials inventory, May 1	a. _____
Direct materials inventory, May 31	$ 3,900
Work-in-process inventory, May 1.......................	4,000
Work-in-process inventory, May 31	5,200
Finished goods inventory, May 1	2,800
Finished goods inventory, May 31	500
Purchases of direct materials	25,000
Cost of goods manufactured during the month...........	87,000
Total manufacturing costs	b. _____
Cost of goods sold	85,000
Gross margin	c. _____
Direct labor...	d. _____
Direct materials used	22,000
Manufacturing overhead	20,500
Sales revenue..	108,000

2-48. Basic Concepts (LO 2-1, 2)

The following data refer to the most recent fiscal year for Sterritt Company. Amounts are in thousands of dollars.

	A	B
1		($000)
2	Cost of goods manufactured for the year	$2,800
3	Cost of goods sold	3,250
4	Direct labor	1,170
5	Direct materials inventory, July 1	205
6	Direct materials inventory, June 30	213
7	Direct material purchases	565
8	Finished goods inventory, July 1	490
9	Finished goods inventory, June 30	314
10	Manufacturing overhead	680
11	Sales revenue	5,050
12	Work-in-process inventory, June 30	51
13		

Required

Find the following amounts.

a. Direct materials used for the year.

b. Gross margin for the year.

c. Total manufacturing costs for the year.

d. Work-in-process inventory, July 1.

2-49. Prepare Statements for a Retailing Company (LO 2-2)

The cost accountant for Sunset Fashions has compiled the following information for last quarter's operations:

Administrative costs	$ 208,000
Merchandise inventory, April 1	49,000
Merchandise inventory, June 30........................	39,500
Merchandise purchases................................	1,730,000
Miscellaneous store costs	21,000
Sales commissions	132,000
Sales revenue..	2,970,000
Store lease	47,000
Utilities...	55,500
Transportation-in costs...............................	122,000
Wages and benefits	710,000

Required
Prepare an income statement with a supporting cost of goods sold statement.

(LO 2-2)   **2-50. Prepare Statements for a Retailing Company**
Norwood Stationary has provided the following information (in thousands of dollars) for October.

	A	B
1		($000)
2	Administrative costs	$16.3
3	Commissions	58.0
4	Marketing	10.8
5	Merchandise inventory, Oct. 1	16.2
6	Merchandise inventory, Oct. 31	20.1
7	Merchandise purchases	291.3
8	Rent and utilities	23.5
9	Sales revenue	526.7
10	Support for local youth activities	4.2
11	Transportation-in costs	9.8
12	Wages and salaries	13.4
13		

Required
Prepare an income statement for October with a supporting cost of goods sold statement.

(LO 2-5)   **2-51. Cost Behavior and Forecasting**
Trumball Catering served 4,000 meals last month. Trumball recorded the following costs with those meals:

Variable costs:	
Ingredients used.	$10,200
Direct labor.	22,500
Indirect materials and supplies.	9,300
Utilities	3,600
Truck fuel and other variable costs	6,200
Fixed costs:	
Managers' salaries	28,700
Rent.	14,200
Depreciation on trucks and equipment (straight-line, time basis).	7,600
Miscellaneous fixed costs	3,500

Required
Unit variable costs and total fixed costs are expected to remain unchanged next month. Calculate the unit cost and the total cost if 4,800 meals are served next quarter.

(LO 2-5)   **2-52. Cost Behavior and Forecasting**
Otsego Industries manufactured 300,000 units of product last year and identified the following costs associated with the manufacturing activity:

Required
Unit variable costs and total fixed costs are expected to remain unchanged in the following year. However, management expects a slowdown in sales, because of the economy in the following year. Calculate the unit cost and the total cost if 255,000 units are produced next year.

	A	B
1		($000)
2	Variable costs:	
3	Direct materials used	$6,120.0
4	Direct labor	4,060.0
5	Indirect materials and supplies	1,420.0
6	Power to run plant equipment	1,300.0
7		
8	Fixed costs:	
9	Supervisory salaries	$560.0
10	Plant utilities (other than for plant equipment)	851.7
11	Depreciation on plant and equipment	1,335.0
12	Property taxes on building	568.3
13		

2-53. Cost Behavior and Forecasting   (LO 2-5)
Refer to the original data (based on 4,000 meals catered) in Exercise 2-51.

Variable costs:	
Ingredients used.	$10,200
Direct labor.	22,500
Indirect materials and supplies.	9,300
Utilities	3,600
Depreciation on trucks and equipment (straight-line, unit basis)	6,200
Fixed costs:	
Managers' salaries	$28,700
Rent.	14,200
Depreciation on equipment (straight-line, time basis)	7,600
Other fixed costs.	3,500

Trumball expects to serve 30 percent more meals in the next month. Unit variable costs are expected to remain unchanged. The controller at Trumball knows that if the business caters over 5,000 meals in a month, the company must hire an additional manager (part-time) at a cost of $3,195 for the month. Miscellaneous fixed costs are expected to increase by 15 percent.

Required
Calculate the unit cost and the total cost if expectations for costs and volume are met next month.

2-54. Components of Full Costs   (LO 2-6)
Acacia Manufacturing has compiled the following information from the accounting system for the one product it sells:

Sales price	$45 per unit
Fixed costs (for the month)	
Marketing and administrative	$23,100
Manufacturing overhead	$8,400
Variable costs (per unit)	
Marketing and administrative	$2
Direct materials	$13
Manufacturing overhead	$3
Direct labor.	$9
Units produced and sold (for the month)	21,000

Required
Determine each of the following unit costs:
a. Variable manufacturing cost.
b. Variable cost.
c. Full absorption cost.
d. Full cost.

2-55. Components of Full Costs   (LO 2-6)
Refer to Exercise 2-54.

Required
Compute:
a. Product costs per unit.
b. Period costs for the period.

2-56. Components of Full Costs   (LO 2-6)
The controller at Wesson Company's manufacturing plant has provided you with the following information for the first quarter's operations:

Direct materials	$96 per unit
Fixed manufacturing overhead costs	$2,340,000
Sales price	$325 per unit
Variable manufacturing overhead	$37 per unit
Direct labor.	$54 per unit
Fixed marketing and administrative costs.	$270,000
Units produced and sold during the quarter	45,000
Variable marketing and administrative costs	$4 per unit

Required
Determine each of the following unit costs:

a.   Variable cost.
b.   Variable manufacturing cost.
c.   Full absorption cost.
d.   Full cost.
e.   Profit margin.
f.   Gross margin.
g.   Contribution margin.

(LO 2-7)   **2-57. Gross Margin and Contribution Margin Income Statements**
Accounting records for The Ralston Company show the following for the most recent fiscal year:

Units produced and sold	59,500
Total revenues and costs	
Sales revenue	$369,600
Direct materials costs.	95,200
Direct labor costs	47,600
Variable manufacturing overhead	23,800
Fixed manufacturing overhead.	61,600
Variable marketing and administrative costs	19,500
Fixed marketing and administrative costs	46,700

Required
Prepare:

a.   A gross margin income statement.
b.   A contribution margin income statement.

(LO 2-7)   **2-58. Gross Margin and Contribution Margin Income Statements**
Refer to Exercise 2-56.

Required
Prepare:

a.   A gross margin income statement.
b.   A contribution margin income statement.

(LO 2-7)   **2-59. Gross Margin and Contribution Margin Income Statements**
Tracey Packaged Snax reports the following information for November:

Units produced and sold	320,000
Per unit revenue and costs:	
Sales revenue	$3.10
Direct materials costs.	1.00
Direct labor costs	0.25
Variable manufacturing overhead	0.15
Fixed manufacturing overhead (at 320,000 units)	0.90
Variable marketing and administrative costs	0.10
Fixed marketing and administrative costs (at 320,000 units) .	0.50

Required

Prepare:

a.   A gross margin income statement.

b.   A contribution margin income statement.

2-60. Value Income Statement

(LO 2-7)

Coastal Bistro has the following information for July, when several new employees were added to the waitstaff:

Sales revenue	$125,000
Cost of food served[a]	45,000
Employee wages and salaries[b]	32,000
Manager salaries[c]	14,000
Building costs (rent, utilities, etc.)[d]	18,000

[a] 10 percent of this cost was for food that was not used by the expiration date, and 12 percent was for food that was incorrectly prepared because of errors in orders taken.

[b] 13 percent of this cost was for kitchen staff time spent fixing dishes to replace meals prepared incorrectly because of errors in the original orders taken.

[c] 15 percent of this cost was time taken to address customer complaints about incorrect orders.

[d] 70 percent of the building was used.

Required

a.   Using the traditional income statement format, prepare a value income statement.

b.   What value would there be for managers at Coastal Bistro from preparing the same information in August and the following months?

2-61. Value Income Statement

(LO 2-7)

Baubee Meal Delivery Service (BMDS) provides restaurant to customer meal deliveries for food establishments in a suburban neighborhood. The company provides you with the following information for the third quarter of operations:

	A	B	C	D
1				
2	Sales revenue	$ 210,000		
3	Variable costs of operations, excluding labor costs (note a)	52,000		
4	Employee wages and salaries (note b)	63,000		
5	Manager salaries (note c)	15,000		
6	Fixed cost of delivery vans (note d)	14,000		
7	Building costs (rent, utilities, etc.) (note e)	9,200		
8	IT costs including support (note f)	30,000		
9				
10	Notes:			
11	a. 10 percent of this cost was wasted due to poor directions given to delivery van drivers.			
12	b. 10 percent of this cost was for time spent by delivery van drivers because of poor directions.			
13	c. 15 percent of this cost was time taken to address customer complaints.			
14	d. The vans have 30 percent unused capacity.			
15	e. The building has 20 percent unused capacity.			
16	f. The IT system has 40 percent unused capacity.			
17				

Required

a.   Using the traditional income statement format, prepare a value income statement.

b.   What value would there be to the managers at BMDS from preparing the same information in the following quarters?

PROBLEMS

2-62. Cost Concepts

(LO 2-2, 6)

The accountant at Roland Industries provides you with the following information for the first quarter:

	A	B
133	fx	
	A	B
1	Direct labor costs	$202,000
2	Direct materials inventory, January 1	20,700
3	Direct materials inventory, March 31	17,100
4	Direct materials purchased during the quarter	271,500
5	Finished goods inventory, January 1	61,000
6	Finished goods inventory, March 31	80,400
7	Manufacturing overhead for the quarter	293,000
8	Work-in-process inventory, January 1	11,700
9	Work-in-process inventory, March 31	8,900
10		

Required

Compute for the first quarter:

a.   Total prime costs.

b.   Total conversion costs.

c.   Total manufacturing costs.

d.   Cost of goods manufactured.

e.   Cost of goods sold.

(LO 2-2, 6)   **2-63. Cost Concepts**

The controller at Bethune Chemicals asks for your help in sorting out some cost information. You receive the following sheet for the most recent year:

	A	B
	A	B
1	Cost of goods manufactured	$846,000
2	Cost of goods sold	667,400
3	Direct labor costs	184,000
4	Direct materials inventory, December 31	46,000
5	Direct materials purchased	263,200
6	Finished goods inventory, December 31	230,400
7	Prime costs for the year	460,600
8	Total manufacturing costs	854,400
9	Work-in-process inventory, January 1	20,200
10		

Required

Compute:

a.   Direct materials used.

b.   Direct materials inventory, January 1.

c.   Conversion costs.

d.   Work-in-process inventory, December 31.

e.   Manufacturing overhead.

f.   Finished goods inventory, January 1.

(LO 2-2, 6)   **2-64. Cost Concepts**

Loretto Audio produced and sold 750 units of the company's signature (and only) product in November. You have collected the following information from the accounting records:

Sales price (per unit).	$ 695
Manufacturing costs:	
Fixed overhead (for the month)	62,250
Direct labor (per unit)	44
Direct materials (per unit).	137
Variable overhead (per unit)	86
Marketing and administrative costs:	
Fixed costs (for the month)	83,250
Variable costs (per unit)	17

Required

a. Compute:
   1. Variable manufacturing cost per unit.
   2. Full cost per unit.
   3. Variable cost per unit.
   4. Full absorption cost per unit.
   5. Prime cost per unit.
   6. Conversion cost per unit.
   7. Profit margin per unit.
   8. Contribution margin per unit.
   9. Gross margin per unit.

b. If the number of units produced increases from 750 to 900, which is within the relevant range, cost per unit will decrease (you can check this by redoing requirement [a] above). Therefore, we should recommend that Loretto Audio increase its production to reduce its costs. Do you agree? Explain.

2-65. Prepare Statements for a Manufacturing Company   (LO 2-2, 4)

East Ferry Tool & Die, a manufacturer of parts for agricultural equipment, provides the following financial information for the most recent fiscal year (all costs are in thousands of dollars):

	A	B
1		($000)
2	Inventories:	
3	As of January 1:	
4	Direct materials	$47
5	Work-in-process	56
6	Finished goods	624
7	As of December 31:	
8	Direct materials	54
9	Work-in-process	49
10	Finished goods	643
11		
12	Other amounts (for the year):	
13	Administrative costs	1,540
14	Direct labor	3,546
15	Direct material purchases	4,674
16	Indirect plant labor	1,558
17	Indirect plant supplies	652
18	Machine depreciation	3,951
19	Marketing costs	984
20	Plant depreciation	1,235
21	Plant supervision	956
22	Plant utilities	633
23	Property taxes on plant and equipment	281
24	Sales revenue	20,234
25		

Required

Prepare an income statement with a supporting cost of goods sold statement.

2-66. Prepare Statements for a Manufacturing Company   (LO 2-2, 4)

Mount Elliott Fixtures produces a variety of hardware products, primarily for the home construction and remodeling business. The cost accountant provides you with the following data for the year (in $000):

	A	B	C
1	Inventory information:		
2		January 1	December 31
3	Direct materials	$ 154	$ 172
4	Work in process	210	184
5	Finished goods	2,918	3,265
6			
7	Other information:	For the Year	
8	Administrative costs	$ 6,891	
9	Depreciation (Corporate building)	654	
10	Depreciation (Factory)	8,002	
11	Depreciation (Factory machines)	14,112	
12	Direct labor	20,137	
13	Direct materials purchased	14,030	
14	Indirect labor (Factory)	4,981	
15	Indirect materials (Factory)	1,421	
16	Property taxes (Corporate building)	142	
17	Property taxes (Factory)	528	
18	Selling costs	3,211	
19	Sales revenue	70,897	
20	Utilities (Factory)	1,499	
21			

Required

Prepare the income statement with a supporting cost of goods sold statement.

(LO 2-2, 4)   **2-67. Prepare Statements for a Manufacturing Company**

Alwar Brothers is a small, family-owned business that produces animal feed for dairy farms. The administrative offices and manufacturing plant of Alwar share the same building. Financial records provided by the company for the most recent fiscal year show the following (all amounts in thousands of dollars):

	A	B	C
1		($000)	
2	Sales revenue	$7,985.0	
3	Direct materials purchases	2,058.0	
4	Administrative costs	976.0	
5	Utilities (Note A)	810.0	
6	Indirect factory labor	566.0	
7	Marketing costs	532.0	
8	Direct labor	511.0	
9	Depreciation (Note B)	480.0	
10	Property taxes (Note C)	470.0	
11	Factory supplies	415.0	
12	Factory supervision	311.0	
13	Finished goods inventory, December 31	46.0	
14	Finished goods inventory, January 1	41.0	
15	Work-in-process inventory, January 1	16.1	
16	Work-in-process inventory, December 31	14.2	
17	Direct materials inventory, December 31	13.1	
18	Direct materials inventory, January 1	10.2	
19			
20			
21	Notes:		
22	A. 80% of this amount is for the factory.		
23	B. 85% of this amount is for the factory.		
24	C. 60% of this amount is for the factory.		
25			
26			

Required

Prepare an income statement with a supporting cost of goods sold statement.

(LO 2-3)   **2-68. Cost Allocation with Cost Flow Diagram**

Merton Electronics operates two retail outlets in Port Wren, one downtown and the other in Docklands. The stores share the use of a corporate staff responsible for functions such as personnel,

IT, marketing, purchasing, and so on. The cost of the corporate activities for last year was $162,000. The following are the operating results for the two stores for the year:

	Downtown	Docklands
Sales revenue	$720,000	$900,000
Number of computers sold	45	30

Required

a.   Allocate the cost of the corporate activities to the two stores based on
   1. Number of employees.
   2. Store revenue.
b.   Draw a cost flow diagram to illustrate your answer to requirement (*a*), part (2).

2-69. Cost Allocation with Cost Flow Diagram   (LO 2-3)

Algonac Moldings produces a product made from a metal alloy. Two suppliers, Liebold Metal and Cecil Distributors, supply the alloy. Neither supplier can meet Algonac's typical demand because of capacity constraints. The material from Liebold is less expensive to buy but more difficult to use, resulting in greater waste. The metal alloy is highly toxic and any waste requires costly handling to avoid environmental accidents. Last year the cost of handling the waste totaled $1,200,000. Additional data from last year's operations are shown as follows:

	Liebold Metals	Cecil Distributors
Amount of material purchased (tons).	64.8	115.2
Amount of waste (tons)	9.0	11.0
Cost of purchases.	$1,488,000	$3,312,000

Required

a.   Allocate the cost of the waste handling to the two suppliers based on
   1. Amount of material purchased.
   2. Amount of waste.
   3. Cost of material purchased.
b.   Draw a cost flow diagram to illustrate your answer to requirement (*a*), part (1).

2-70. Cost Allocation with Cost Flow Diagram   (LO 2-3)

The Norfolk School of Commerce (NSC) operates a Career Counseling Center (CCC) to advise students and help with job placement. The CCC is available for both undergraduate and graduate

	A	B	C	D
1	Costs driven by enrollment:			
2	Center management	$ 980,000		
3	Company visits and support	1,277,200		
4		$ 2,257,200		
5				
6	Costs driven by usage:			
7	Center staff	$ 765,000		
8	Facility maintenance	495,000		
9	IT support	171,000		
10	Utilities and supplies	351,000		
11		$ 1,782,000		
12	Total CCC costs	$ 4,039,200		
13				
14				
15	Data on enrollment and usage:	Undergraduate	Graduate	
16	Enrollment (students)	825	275	
17	Usage (hours)	9,450	17,550	
18				

degree students. The CFO at NSC wants better cost information about the noninstructional activities of the School to be able to advise the dean on managing costs. The CFO asks the head of the CCC to recommend an allocation of the annual cost of the Center to the two degree programs.

The CCC head, who has headed the Center for 10 years, believes that two factors explain most of the costs—enrollment (number of students) and usage (number of hours using the center for both counseling and interviews). Using information from a previous analysis, the Center budget was separated as shown on the previous page.

Required

a.   Allocate the cost of the library to the two programs (undergraduate and graduate).

b.   Draw a cost flow diagram to illustrate your answer to requirement (*a*).

(LO 2-3)   **2-71. Cost Allocation and Pricing**

Woodrow Economic Advisors (WEA) is a for-profit consulting firm that offers economic analyses and policy recommendations. WEA is organized into two divisions: the Commercial Division and the Defense Division. Commercial clients are charged a fixed fee negotiated at the beginning of the engagement. The Defense Division has only two clients: the U.S. Department of Defense and the National Aeronautics and Space Administration (NASA). Defense Division business is charged based on the total costs (direct and indirect) of an engagement plus a 15 percent fee (profit).

During the planning process for the following year, the controller at WEA has estimated costs for the two divisions.

	Commercial	Defense	Total
Direct costs	$1,470,000	$3,430,000	$4,900,000
Direct contract hours worked	1,760	6,240	8,000

The controller expects indirect costs to total $6,370,000 next year. Revenues from Corporate clients next year are expected to be $3 million.

Required

a.   Suppose WEA chooses to allocate indirect costs based on direct costs.
   1. What costs would be allocated to the two units (Commercial and Defense)?
   2. What total revenue would they expect to collect next year?

b.   Suppose WEA chooses to allocate indirect costs based on direct contract hours worked.
   1. What costs would be allocated to the two units (Commercial and Defense)?
   2. What total revenue would they expect to collect next year?

(LO 2-3)   **2-72. Cost Allocation and Pricing**

Refer to the information in Problem 2-71. Consider the Business Application "Indirect Costs and Allocating Costs to Contracts."

Required

a.   How should Woodrow Economic Advisors (WEA) allocate indirect costs to units? Why?

b.   What ethical issues arise for the controller at WEA related to cost allocation?

(LO 2-1, 5, 6)   **2-73. Basic Cost Behaviors**

Salvay Company is a small manufacturer that produces and sells one product for use in medical instruments. Demand is erratic and can vary widely from year to year. The financial managers at Salvay are planning for the coming year and have asked for your help in forecasting unit costs and gross margin.

Stacy Choo, the cost accountant at Salvay, provides you with information about the components of manufacturing costs along with specifying the behavior of the components. This information is summarized in the memo on the next page.

Stacy also tells you that the company has a zero-inventory policy and all projections are made under that assumption. Finally, she points out that capacity constraints require assuming a second shift for the year if annual production volume exceeds 600,000 units.

The marketing manager tells you that the best estimate of the price of the product is $20 per unit. His best guess is that demand could be as low as 500,000 units or as high as 750,000 units.

Salvay Company Memo:

To: Jorge Alcala, Controller
From: Stacy Choo, Cost Accountant

Date: November 3.

Subject: Cost Information Projections

As you requested, the following table summarizes our best estimates for manufacturing costs for the upcoming fiscal year. These estimates are valid for any reasonable range of production.

Cost Category	Cost Behavior	Cost Information
Direct costs:		
Materials	Semivariable	If production volume is below 550,000 units, we can source all our materials from Bourke Supplies at $3.00 per unit. This is a negotiated price. For any production greater than this, we will have to pay the going market price of $4.80 per unit.
Labor	Variable	$4.50 per unit.
Overhead:		
Indirect plant labor	Variable	$2.25 per unit.
Indirect plant supplies	Variable	$1.25 per unit.
Machine depreciation	Fixed	$218,000 per year.
Plant depreciation	Fixed	$102,000 per year.
Plant maintenance	Step	$105,000 per shift.
Plant supervision	Step	$280,000 per shift.
Plant utilities	Step	$210,000 for production up to 800,000 units; $350,000 (total) if production is over 800,000 units.
Property taxes on plant	Fixed	$65,000 per year.

Required

Compute the cost per unit and the gross margin per unit assuming output and sales of

a.   500,000 units.

b.   750,000 units.

2-74. Basic Cost Behaviors; Visualization   (LO 2-5)

Refer to the information in Problem 2-73. Stacey Choo would like you to prepare a presentation for the CFO and Controller at Salvay discussing the estimated gross margins. They are especially interested in the effect of the individual cost items on the gross margins. Stacey also mentions that both managers like to see visual support for any conclusions.

Required

Prepare a presentation explaining your results from Problem 2-73. Be sure to include some visuals to support your discussion.

2-75. Basic Cost Behaviors   (LO 2-1, 5, 6)

Cheyenne Contractors makes fixtures for aircraft fueling and hydraulic systems. As a supplier to the aircraft industry, the annual volumes can vary greatly depending on both civilian and military activity. Managers at Cheyenne have developed certain procedures as a part of their risk-management strategy. One of those procedures is to forecast financial results based on the possible range of production and sales for the year.

As the company's senior cost analyst, it is your responsibility to provide these forecasts. As a first step, you have collected the following information about the individual cost components:

	A	B	C
1	**Cost Category**	**Cost**	**Cost Information**
2	Direct costs:		
3–4	Materials	Variable	$52 per unit.
5	Labor	Variable	$25 per unit.
6			
7	Overhead:		
8–9	Indirect plant labor	Variable	$60 per unit.
10–11	Indirect plant supplies	Variable	$14 per unit.
12–13	Machine leases	Step	$698,000 per year if production is below 35,000 units; otherwise, total lease costs are $1,233,000.
14–15	Overtime	Semivariable	$0 for any production up to 30,000 units; $15 per unit for any additional production.
16–17	Plant depreciation	Fixed	$122,000 per year.
18–19	Plant maintenance	Step	$210,000 per shift.
20–21	Plant supervision	Step	$200,000 per shift. There is also a shift differential of $50,000, additional compensation for supervisors on a second shift.
22–23	Plant utilities	Fixed	$190,000 per year.
24	Miscellaneous overhead	Fixed	$105,000 per year.
25			

Cheyenne Contractors produces to order, and for the purpose of this assignment, you can assume it has no inventories. Capacity constraints require a second shift for any production over 35,000 units. Cheyenne uses an average revenue of $312 per unit for forecasting purposes.

Required
Compute the cost per unit and the gross margin per unit assuming output and sales of
a. 25,000 units.
b. 45,000 units.

(LO 2-5)   2-76. Basic Cost Behaviors; Visualization
Refer to the information in Problem 2-75. The CEO has asked for a briefing on the projections before the next analyst call. You have also been asked to provide some accompanying visuals to help clarify any remarks.

Required
Prepare a presentation explaining your results from Problem 2-75. Be sure to include some visuals to support your discussion.

(LO 2-1, 6)   2-77. Find the Unknown Information
Gates Manufacturing reports based on an October 31 fiscal year. As a part of your interview for a cost analyst position, the interviewer provides you with the information on the following page.

Required
Find the following:
a. Cost of goods manufactured.
b. Total manufacturing costs.
c. Direct materials used.
d. Sales revenue.
e. Increase (decrease) in direct materials inventory.

Direct materials purchases	$96,000
Work-in-process inventory, November 1	53,000
Finished goods inventory, November 1	30,800
Finished goods inventory, October 31	31,800
Manufacturing overhead	57,600
Cost of goods sold	221,000
Direct labor	30,400
Increase in work-in-process inventory	28,000
Average sales price per unit	20
Gross margin percentage	35%

2-78. Find the Unknown Information

(LO 2-1, 6)

Paul & Paul, Inc. is a manufacturing firm. The following selected pieces of information are from July operations:

	A	B
1		
2	Average selling price per unit	$ 64
3	Cost of goods sold	$ 2,083,200
4	Decrease in direct materials inventory	$ 1,512
5	Direct labor	$ 946,400
6	Gross margin percentage (based on sales)	30%
7	Increase in finished goods inventory	$ 57,575
8	Manufacturing overhead	$ 787,500
9	Total manufacturing costs	$ 2,143,120
10		

Required

Find the following:

a.   Cost of goods manufactured.

b.   Direct materials used.

c.   Direct materials purchases.

d.   Units sold.

e.   Increase (decrease) in work-in-process inventory.

2-79. Cost Allocation and Regulated Prices

(LO 2-3)

Alpine Township contracts with Dragoon Environmental Services (DES) to provide solid waste collection to households and businesses. Until recently, DES had an exclusive franchise to provide this service in Alpine, which meant that other waste collection firms could not operate legally in the township. The price per pound of waste collected was regulated at 20 percent above the average total cost of collection.

Cost data for the most recent year of operations for DES are as follows:

Administrative cost	$ 480,000
Operating costs—trucks	1,536,000
Other collection costs	384,000

Data on customers for the most recent year are as follows:

	Households	Businesses
Number of customers	11,520	2,880
Waste collected (tons)	4,000	12,000

The Township Board of Alpine is considering allowing other private waste haulers to collect waste from businesses but not from households. Service to businesses from other waste collection firms would not be subject to price regulation. Based on information from neighboring cities, the price that other private waste collection firms will charge is estimated to be $0.05 per pound (= $100 per ton).

DES's CEO has approached the board with a proposal to change the way costs are allocated to households and businesses, which will result in different rates for households and businesses. The CEO proposes that administrative costs and truck operating costs be allocated based on the number of customers and the other collection costs be allocated based on pounds collected. The total costs allocated to households would then be divided by the estimated number of pounds collected from households to determine the cost of collection. The rate would then be 20 percent above the cost. The rate for businesses would be determined using the same calculation.

Required

a. Based on cost data from the most recent year, what is the price per pound charged by DES for waste collection under the current system (the same rate for both types of customers)?

b. Based on cost and waste data from the most recent year, what would be the price per pound charged to households and to businesses by DES for waste collection if the CEO's proposal were accepted?

c. As a staff member to one of the board members, would you support the proposal to change the way costs are allocated? Explain.

(LO 2-1, 2, 6)   **2-80. Reconstruct Financial Statements**

Melville Manufacturing produces metal components for automotive suppliers. Financial records for September show the following:

	A	B
1	Administrative salaries	$ 525,000
2	Depreciation on the administrative building	228,400
3	Depreciation on the manufacturing plant	350,000
4	Direct labor	938,500
5	Direct materials inventory, September 1	213,840
6	Direct materials inventory, September 30	247,000
7	Direct materials purchased during the month	1,791,200
8	Distribution costs	131,400
9	Finished goods inventory, September 1	328,400
10	Finished goods inventory, September 30	273,900
11	Indirect manufacturing labor	108,400
12	Insurance (on manufacturing plant)	10,640
13	Legal fees	99,260
14	Maintenance (on the manufacturing plant)	43,080
15	Manufacturing plant utilities	156,820
16	Marketing costs	149,850
17	Other manufacturing plant costs	126,176
18	Sales revenue	4,530,984
19	Taxes (on manufacturing plant and property)	43,120
20	Work-in-process inventory, September 1	80,650
21	Work-in-process inventory, September 30	79,340
22		
23		

Required

Prepare a cost of goods manufactured and sold statement and an income statement.

(LO 2-1, 6)   **2-81. Reconstruct Financial Statements**

Omira Cycle Parts manufactures components for motorcycles and off-road vehicles. The company's administrative and manufacturing operations share the company's only building. Eighty percent of the building is used for manufacturing, and the remainder is used for administrative activities. Indirect labor is 8 percent of direct labor.

As the cost analyst at Omira, you have gathered the information on the following page for the year ended December 31.

Required

Prepare a cost of goods manufactured and sold statement and an income statement.

	A	B
1	Administrative salaries	$ 960,000
2	Attorney fees to settle zoning dispute	114,800
3	Building depreciation (manufacturing portion only)	907,200
4	Cost of goods manufactured	13,883,800
5	Direct materials inventory, December 31	1,240,000
6	Direct materials purchased during the year	5,040,000
7	Direct materials used	5,349,400
8	Distribution costs	22,400
9	Finished goods inventory, January 1	1,120,000
10	Finished goods inventory, December 31	1,260,000
11	Insurance (on plant machinery)	266,000
12	Maintenance (on plant machinery)	169,400
13	Marketing costs	518,000
14	Other plant costs	410,800
15	Plant utilities	520,800
16	Sales revenue	22,750,000
17	Taxes on manufacturing property	194,000
18	Total (direct and indirect) labor	6,048,000
19	Work-in-process inventory, January 1	362,600
20	Work-in-process inventory, December 31	344,400
21		

2-82. Reconstruct Financial Statements   (LO 2-1, 6)

Kessler Brothers produces products for farms and ranches. The administrative and manufacturing operations occupy the same 240,000-square-foot building. The manufacturing plant uses 180,000 square feet. Depreciation is assigned based on building use. Indirect labor represents 15 percent of the total manufacturing plant labor.

The financial information for the year just ended is shown as follows:

	A	B
1	(Thousands of Dollars)	
2		
3	Administrative costs	$ 480
4	Total building depreciation	1,200
5	Direct materials inventory, January 1	45
6	Direct materials inventory, December 31	60
7	Direct materials purchased during the year	4,710
8	Finished goods inventory, December 31	240
9	Indirect labor	540
10	Maintenance on plant machinery	420
11	Marketing costs	360
12	Operating profit	2,880
13	Other plant overhead	249
14	Plant supervision and administration	465
15	Plant supplies and indirect materials	201
16	Sales revenue	15,000
17	Taxes on manufacturing property	351
18	Work-in-process inventory, January 1	240
19	Work-in-process inventory, December 31	330
20		

Required
Prepare a cost of goods manufactured and sold statement and an income statement.

2-83. Finding Unknowns   (LO 2-2)

Conner's Fixtures produces and sells a single product, a specialized plumbing fixture. The business began operations on January 1 this year, and its costs incurred during the year include the following:

Variable costs (based on units produced):
    Direct materials cost. . . . . $ 24,000
    Direct manufacturing labor costs 108,000
    Indirect manufacturing costs. 21,600
    Administration and marketing. 13,500
Fixed costs:
    Administration and marketing costs 72,000
    Indirect manufacturing costs. 24,000

At the end of the first year (December 31), direct materials inventory consisted of 7,500 pounds of material. Production in that year was 10,000 fixtures. All prices and unit variable costs remained constant during the year. Sales revenue for year 1 was $293,250. Finished goods inventory was $24,420 on December 31. Each finished fixture requires 3.20 pounds of material.

Required
Compute the following:

a. Direct materials inventory cost, December 31.
b. Finished goods ending inventory in units (fixtures) on December 31.
c. Selling price per unit.
d. Operating profit for year 1.

(LO 2-2)   **2-84. Finding Unknowns**

Guilford Boards started operations on March 3. There were no direct materials in inventory as of March 2. Data for the month of March include the following:

Direct labor cost per unit[a]	$ 50
Direct labor-hours worked, March	
Direct labor wage rate per direct labor-hour	$ 20
Direct materials cost per unit[a]	$ 40
Direct materials cost per pound of direct material	$ 8
Direct materials inventory (cost), March 31	$ 1,600
Direct materials inventory (pounds), March 31	
Finished goods inventory (cost), March 31	$ 8,640
Finished goods inventory (units), March 31	
Manufacturing overhead cost per unit[a]	$ 126
Operating profit, March	$ 9,545
Production (units), March	
Sales revenue, March	$45,425
Sales (units), March	
Sales price per unit	
Selling, general, and administrative costs per unit[b]	$ 96

[a] Unit cost based on units produced in March.
[b] Unit cost based on units sold in March.

Required
Complete the table.

INTEGRATIVE CASE

(LO 2-2)   **2-85. Analyze the Impact of a Decision on Income Statements**

You were appointed the manager of Storage Solutions Section (S3) at Milbank Technologies, a manufacturer of mobile computing parts and accessories, late last year. S3 manufactures a drive assembly for the company's most popular product. Your bonus is determined as a percentage of your division's operating profits before taxes.

One of your first major investment decisions was to invest $2 million in automated testing equipment for device testing. The equipment was installed and in operation on January 1 of this year.

This morning, the assistant manager of the division told you about an offer by Joliet Systems. Joliet wants to rent to S3 a new testing machine that could be installed on December 31 (only two weeks from now) for an annual rental charge of $460,000. The new equipment would enable you to increase your division's annual revenue by 7 percent. This new, more efficient machine would also decrease fixed cash expenditures by 6 percent.

Without the new machine, operating revenues and costs for the year are estimated to be as follows. Sales revenue and fixed and variable operating costs are all cash.

Sales revenue	$3,200,000
Variable operating costs.	400,000
Fixed operating costs	1,500,000
Equipment depreciation.	300,000
Other depreciation	250,000

If you rent the new testing equipment, S3 will have to write off the cost of the automated testing equipment this year because it has no salvage value. Equipment depreciation shown in the income statement is for this automated testing equipment. Equipment losses are included in the bonus and operating profit computation.

Because the new machine will be installed on a company holiday, there will be no effect on operations from the changeover. Ignore any possible tax effects. Assume that the data given in your expected income statement are the actual amounts for this year and next year if the current equipment is kept.

Required

a.   Assume the new testing equipment is rented and installed on December 31. What will be the impact on this year's divisional operating profit?

b.   Assume the new testing equipment is rented and installed on December 31. What will be the impact on next year's divisional operating profit?

c.   Would you rent the new equipment? Why or why not?

SOLUTIONS TO SELF-STUDY QUESTIONS

1.

PACIFIC PARTS
Income Statement

Sales revenue	$8,144,000
Cost of goods sold (see following statement)	4,956,000
Gross margin	$3,188,000
Less	
Marketing costs.	1,088,000
Administrative costs	1,216,000
Operating profit.	$ 884,000

PACIFIC PARTS
Statement of Cost of Goods Manufactured and Sold

Beginning work-in-process inventory, January 1			$ 540,000
Manufacturing costs during the year			
Direct materials			
Beginning inventory, January 1	$ 408,000		
Add purchases	1,252,000		
Direct materials available	$1,660,000		
Less ending inventory, December 31	324,000		
Direct materials put into production		$1,336,000	
Direct labor.		1,928,000	
Manufacturing overhead			
Supervisory and indirect labor	$ 508,000		
Supplies and indirect materials	56,000		
Heat, light, and power—plant	348,000		

PACIFIC PARTS
Statement of Cost of Goods Manufactured and Sold—Continued

Plant maintenance and repairs..........	$ 296,000	
Depreciation—manufacturing...........	412,000	
Miscellaneous manufacturing costs......	48,000	
Total manufacturing overhead	$1,668,000	
Total manufacturing costs incurred during the year		$4,932,000
Total cost of work-in-process during the year		$5,472,000
Less ending work-in-process inventory, December 31		568,000
Cost of goods manufactured during the year		$4,904,000
Beginning finished goods inventory, January 1.......................		640,000
Finished goods inventory available for sale..........................		$5,544,000
Less ending finished goods inventory, December 31		588,000
Cost of goods manufactured and sold		$4,956,000

2.

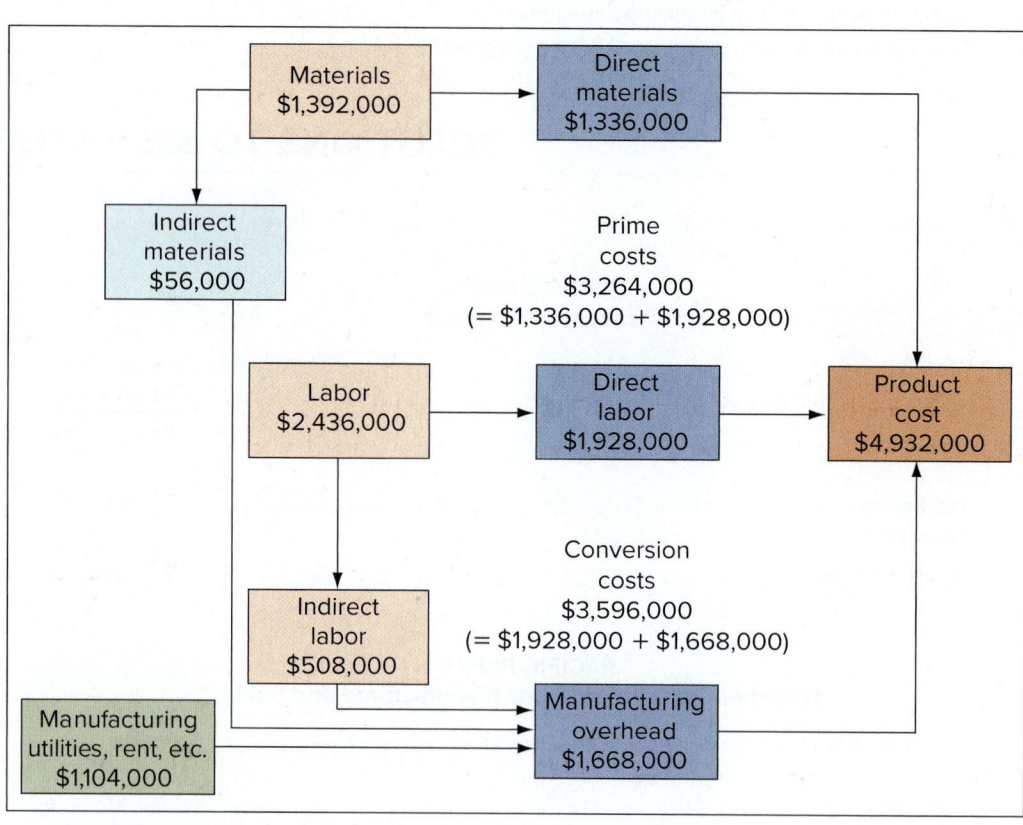

3. Fixed manufacturing = $7.50 (= $12,000 ÷ 1,600)
    Fixed marketing and administration = $8.75 (= $14,000 ÷ 1,600)
4. Gross margin = Sales price − Full absorption cost
       = Sales price − (Variable manufacturing + Fixed manufacturing)
       = $45 − ($23 + $6) = $16
    Contribution margin = Sales price − Variable costs
       = Sales price − (Variable manufacturing + Variable marketing and administrative)
       = $45 − ($23 + $3) = $19

Operating profit = Sales price − Full cost to make and sell product

   = Sales price − (Variable manufacturing + Fixed manufacturing + Variable marketing and administrative + Fixed marketing and administrative)

   = $45 − ($23 + $6 + $3 + $7)

   = $6

(*Note:* The gross margin does not change from Exhibit 2.12 because marketing and administrative costs are subtracted after gross margin.)

5.   Gross margin = $45 − ($23 + $5) = $17

Contribution margin = $45 − ($23 + $4) = $18

Operating profit = $45 − ($23 + $5 + $4 + $7) = $6

(*Note:* The contribution margin does not change from Exhibit 2.13; however, the gross margin changes from Exhibit 2.12.)

3

Chapter Three

Fundamentals of Cost–Volume–Profit Analysis

LEARNING OBJECTIVES

After reading this chapter, you should be able to:

LO 3-1   Use cost–volume–profit (CVP) analysis to evaluate data and decisions.

LO 3-2   Understand the effect of cost structure on decisions.

LO 3-3   Use Microsoft Excel to perform CVP analysis.

LO 3-4   Incorporate taxes, multiple products, and alternative cost structures into the CVP analysis.

LO 3-5   Understand the assumptions and limitations of CVP analysis.

The Decision

> *Several years ago, I started my own travel business leading small groups on three-day excursions into the high desert. Now, I am so busy running my business that I am only able to lead a few of these trips each year. I am also spending more time planning new services and thinking about my costs and the price I can charge. I know that my costs vary with the number of trips I offer. I am looking for a way to analyze my business in a more systematic way. I recently read that even large firms look at something called cost–volume–profit analysis to understand their operations. [See the Business Application on* "How 'Big Oil' Uses Break-Even Analysis."] *I know that my firm is not an oil firm and it certainly is not big, but I wonder if it is something I could use to understand the financial side of my business better.*

Daniela Flores is the owner of Desert Adventures, a travel services provider based in Santa Fe. Desert Adventures offers travelers a small-group desert experience. Daniela wants to expand the types of trips she offers, but first she wants to determine how to analyze the financial impact of her current offerings.

Our theme in this book is that the cost accounting system serves managers by providing them with information that supports good decision making. In this chapter and the next, we develop two common tools that managers can use to analyze situations and make decisions that will increase the value of the firm. We begin in this chapter by developing the relations among the costs, volumes, and profits of the firm. In the next chapter, we use these relations to make pricing and production decisions that increase profit.

cost–volume–profit (CVP) analysis
Study of the relationships among revenues, costs, and volume and their effect on profit.

Cost–Volume–Profit Analysis

Managers are concerned about the impact of their decisions on profit. The decisions they make are about volume, pricing, or incurring a cost. Therefore, managers require an understanding of the relationships among revenues, costs, volume, and profit. The cost accounting function supplies the data and analysis, called **cost–volume–profit (CVP) analysis,** that support these managers.

LO 3-1
Use cost–volume–profit (CVP) analysis to evaluate data and decisions.

How "Big Oil" Uses Break-Even Analysis | *Business Application*

Even large companies use cost–volume–profit analysis to analyze changing environments. For example, big oil firms use CVP or break-even analysis to look at the impact of changing oil extraction processes on their operations. The focus is not always on calculating break-even volumes. Prices for a commodity such as oil are set in the market and there is little the firm can do to influence those. Further, production in this business is difficult to control, given the high costs of changing production levels. This leaves operating expenses as the primary means a company has to influence its break-even price and profit. For example:

> . . . BP said spending cuts allowed the company to break even at $47 a barrel in the first half.

In other words, CVP can provide a target for managing costs when prices are determined in the global oil market and production is set.

> The companies also consider break-even levels for individual projects in addition to the entire firm.

> Shell has said it is looking at new projects that can be profitable even if oil is at less than $40 a barrel.

In addition to its use as a managerial tool, CVP analysis provides a simple measure to report to investors. It allows investors to make comparisons across firms and evaluate potential firms to earn returns:

> Once obscure and little noted, the break-even number has become an obsession for investors in oil giants such as Exxon Mobil Corp.

The COVID pandemic of 2020 illustrates how the break-even price of oil can help investors and managers anticipate the effect of large changes in demand.

> Second-quarter [2020] earnings are likely to be brutal across the U.S. oil patch because global oil demand fell by some 18% during the period. . . .
> U.S. benchmark oil prices averaged about $29 a barrel during the second quarter, compared with around $46 a barrel during the first quarter.

Sources: Kent, Sarah, "Big Oil's Suddenly Popular Measure for Success: Break-Even Oil Price," *The Wall Street Journal,* October 26, 2017; Elliott, Rebecca, "Exxon Warns Production, Refining Losses to Hurt Earnings," *The Wall Street Journal,* July 2, 2020.

Profit Equation

profit equation
Operating profit equals total revenue less total costs.

The key relation for CVP analysis is the **profit equation.** Every organization's financial operations can be stated as a simple relation among total revenues (*TR*), total costs (*TC*), and operating profit:

$$\text{Operating profit} = \text{Total revenues} - \text{Total costs}$$
$$\text{Profit} = \quad TR \quad - \quad TC$$

(For not-for-profit and government organizations, the "profit" may go by different names such as "surplus" or "contribution to fund," but the analysis is the same.) Both total revenues and total costs are likely to be affected by changes in the amount of output.[1] We rewrite the profit equation to explicitly include volume, allowing us to analyze the relationships among volume, costs, and profit. Total revenue (*TR*) equals average selling price per unit (*P*) times the units of output (*X*):

$$\text{Total revenue} = \text{Price} \times \text{Units of output produced and sold}$$
$$TR = PX$$

In our profit equation, total costs (*TC*) may be divided into a fixed component that does not vary with changes in output levels and a variable component that does vary. The fixed component is made up of total fixed costs (*F*) per period; the variable component is the product of the average variable cost per unit (*V*) multiplied by the quantity of output (*X*). Therefore, the cost function is

$$\text{Total costs} = (\text{Variable costs per unit} \times \text{Units of output}) + \text{Fixed costs}$$
$$TC = VX + F$$

Substituting the expanded expressions in the profit equation yields a form more useful for analyzing decisions:

$$\text{Profit} = \text{Total revenue} - \text{Total costs}$$
$$= TR - TC$$
$$TC = VX + F$$

Therefore,

$$\text{Profit} = PX - (VX + F)$$

Collecting terms gives

$$\text{Profit} = (\text{Price} - \text{Variable costs}) \times \text{Units of output} - \text{Fixed costs}$$
$$= (P - V)X - F$$

unit contribution margin
Difference between revenues per unit (price) and variable costs per unit.

total contribution margin
Difference between revenues and total variable costs.

We defined *contribution margin* in Chapter 2 as the difference between the sales price and the variable cost per unit. We will refer to this as the **unit contribution margin** to distinguish it from the difference between the total revenues and total variable cost, the **total contribution margin.** In other words, the total contribution margin is the unit contribution margin multiplied by the number of units: (Price − Variable costs) × Units of output, or (*P* − *V*)*X*. It is the amount that units sold contribute toward (1) covering fixed costs and (2) providing operating profits. Sometimes we use the contribution margin, in total, as in the preceding equation. Other times, we use the contribution margin per unit, which is

$$\text{Price} - \text{Variable cost per unit}$$
$$P - V$$

---

[1] We adopt the simplifying assumption that production volume equals sales volume so that changes in inventory can be ignored in this chapter.

Recall from Chapter 2 that an important distinction for decision making is whether costs are fixed or variable. That is, for decision making, we are concerned about *cost behavior* not the *financial accounting treatment,* which classifies costs as either manufacturing or administrative. Thus, *V* is the sum of variable manufacturing costs per unit and variable marketing and administrative costs per unit; *F* is the sum of total fixed manufacturing costs and fixed marketing and administrative costs for the period; and *X* refers to the number of units produced and sold during the period.

CVP Example

When Daniela started Desert Adventures, she offered one excursion (trip) only, a three-day tour for six people. She charged an average price of $4,000. The average variable cost of each trip was $1,200, computed as follows:

Cost of trip (meals, supplies, and guides).....................	$ 900
Other costs (sales and support)	300
Average variable cost per trip	$1,200

The fixed costs to operate the business for a typical year were $134,400.

Last year, Desert Adventures operated 55 trips. The operating profit can be determined from the company's income statement for the year, as shown in Exhibit 3.1.

As a manager, Daniela might want to know how many units (trips) she needs to sell in order to achieve a specified profit. Assume, for example, that Daniela is hoping for sales to improve next year, when new backpacking trails are open. Given the data price = $4,000, variable cost per unit = $1,200 (therefore, contribution margin per unit = $2,800), and fixed costs = $134,400, the manager asks two questions: What volume is required to break even (earn zero profits)? What volume is required to make a $70,000 operating profit? Although we could use the income statement and guess at the answer to these questions, it is easier to set up an equation that summarizes the cost–volume–profit relation.

Recall that last year, Desert Adventures operated 55 trips. Using the profit equation, the results for March, therefore, were

$$\text{Profit} = \text{Contribution margin} - \text{Fixed costs}$$
$$= (P - V)X - F$$
$$= (\$4,000 - \$1,200) \times 55 \text{ trips} - \$134,400$$
$$= \$19,600$$

which is equal to the operating profit shown on the income statement in Exhibit 3.1. To simplify the equation, we use the term *profit* in the equation to mean the same thing as *operating profit* on income statements.

Exhibit 3.1
Income Statement

DESERT ADVENTURES Income Statement For the Year Ended December 31		
Sales (55 trips at $4,000)......................................		$220,000
Less		
Variable trip costs (55 trips × $900)....................	$49,500	
Other variable costs (55 trips × $300)..................	16,500	66,000
Contribution margin		$154,000
Less fixed costs...		134,400
Operating profit...		$ 19,600

Finding Break-Even and Target Volumes

We can use the profit equation to answer Daniela's questions about volumes needed to break even or achieve a target profit by developing the formulas discussed here. We start with the answer to the first question, which we call *finding a break-even volume.* Managers might want to know the break-even volume expressed either in units or in sales dollars. If the company makes many products, it is often much easier to think of volume in terms of sales dollars; if we are dealing with only one product, it's easier to work with units as the measure of volume.

break-even point
Volume level at which profits equal zero.

Break-Even Volume in Units   We can use the profit equation to find the **break-even point** expressed in units:

$$\text{Profit} = 0 = (P - V)X - F$$
$$\text{If Profit} = 0, \text{then } X = \frac{F}{(P - V)}$$

$$\text{Break-even volume (in units)} = \frac{\text{Fixed costs}}{\text{Unit contribution margin}}$$
$$= \frac{\$134,400}{\$2,800}$$
$$= 48 \text{ trips}$$

To show this is correct, if Desert Adventures operates 48 trips during the year, its operating profit is

$$\text{Profit} = TR - TC$$
$$= PX - VX - F$$
$$= (\$4,000 \times 48 \text{ trips}) - (\$1,200 \times 48 \text{ trips}) - \$134,400$$
$$= \$0$$

contribution margin ratio
Contribution margin as a percentage of sales revenue.

Break-Even Volume in Sales Dollars   To find the break-even volume in terms of sales dollars, we first define a new term, **contribution margin ratio.** The contribution margin ratio is the contribution margin as a percentage of sales revenue. For example, for Desert Adventures, the contribution margin ratio can be computed as follows:

$$\text{Contribution margin ratio} = \frac{\text{Unit contribution margin}}{\text{Sales price per unit}}$$
$$= \frac{\$2,800}{\$4,000}$$
$$= .70 \text{ (or } 70\%)$$

Using the contribution margin ratio, the formula to find the break-even volume is[2]

$$\text{Break-even volume sales dollars} = \frac{\text{Fixed costs}}{\text{Contribution margin ratio}}$$

---

[2] We can derive the break-even point for sales dollars from the original formula for units:

$$X = \frac{F}{P - V}$$

The modified formula for dollars multiplies both sides of the equation by P:

$$PX = \frac{F \times P}{P - V}$$

Because multiplying the numerator by P is the same as dividing the denominator by P, we obtain:

$$PX = \frac{F}{(P - V)/P}$$

The term $(P - V)/P$ is the contribution margin ratio.

For Desert Adventures, the break-even volume expressed in sales dollars is

$$\text{Break-even sales dollars} = \frac{\$134,400}{.70}$$
$$= \$192,000$$

Note that $192,000 of sales dollars translates into 48 trips at a price of $4,000 each. We get the same result whether expressed in units (48 trips) or dollars (sales of 48 trips generates revenue of $192,000).

Target Volume in Units   To find the target volume, we use the profit equation with the target profit specified. The formula to find the target volume in units is

$$\text{Target volume (units)} = \frac{\text{Fixed costs} + \text{Target profit}}{\text{Contribution margin per unit}}$$

Using the data from Desert Adventures, we find the volume that provides an operating profit of $70,000 as follows:

$$\text{Target volume} = \frac{\text{Fixed costs} + \text{Target profit}}{\text{Contribution margin per unit}}$$
$$= \frac{\$134,400 + \$70,000}{\$2,800}$$
$$= 73 \text{ trips}$$

Desert Adventures must sell 73 trips during the year to achieve the target profit of $70,000. Each additional trip sold increases operating profits by $2,800.

Target Volume in Sales Dollars   To find the target volume in sales dollars, we use the contribution margin ratio instead of the contribution margin per unit. The formula to find the target volume follows:

$$\text{Target volume (sales dollars)} = \frac{\text{Fixed costs} + \text{Target profit}}{\text{Contribution margin ratio}}$$

For Desert Adventures the target volume expressed in sales dollars is

$$\text{Target volume (sales dollars)} = \frac{\$134,400 + \$70,000}{.70} = \$292,000$$

Note that sales dollars of $292,000 translates into 73 trips at $4,000 each. We get the same target volume whether expressed in units (73 trips) or dollars (sales of 73 trips generates revenue of $292,000).

Exhibit 3.2 summarizes the four formulas for finding break-even and target volumes.

Break-even Volume

$$\text{Break-even volume (units)} = \frac{\text{Fixed costs}}{\text{Unit contribution margin}}$$

$$\text{Break-even volume (sales dollars)} = \frac{\text{Fixed costs}}{\text{Contribution margin ratio}}$$

Target Volume

$$\text{Target volume (units)} = \frac{\text{Fixed costs} + \text{Target profit}}{\text{Unit contribution margin}}$$

$$\text{Target volume (sales dollars)} = \frac{\text{Fixed costs} + \text{Target profit}}{\text{Contribution margin ratio}}$$

Exhibit 3.2

Summary of Break-Even and Target Volume Formulas

Exhibit 3.3

CVP Graph—Desert
Adventures

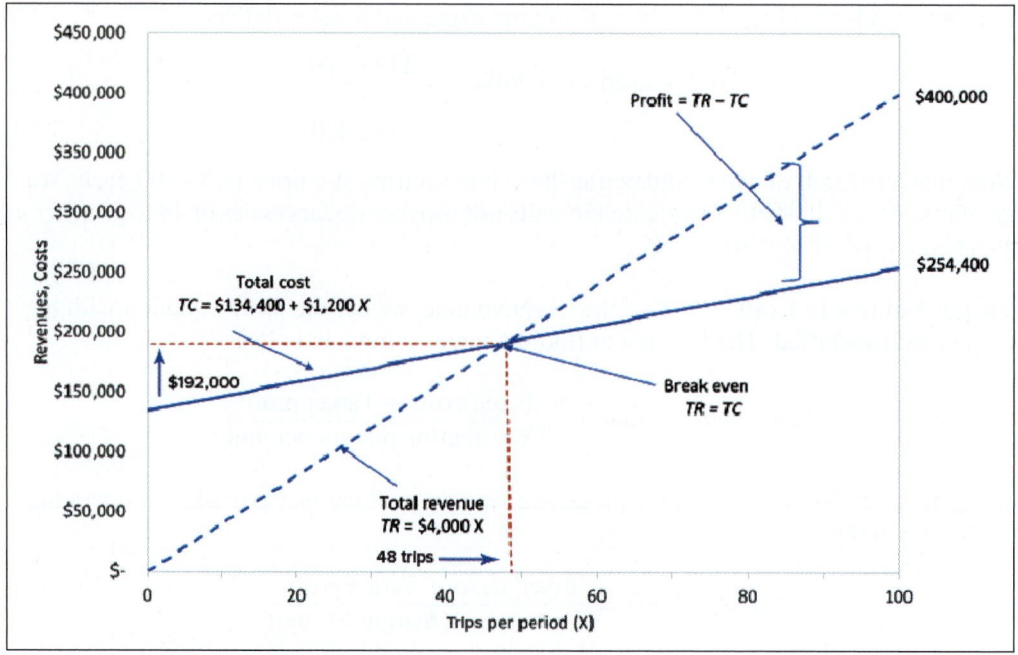

Graphic Presentation

The graph shown in Exhibit 3.3 for Desert Adventures is a helpful aid in presenting cost–volume–profit relationships. We plot dollars on the vertical axis (revenue dollars or cost dollars, for example). We plot volume on the horizontal axis (number of trips sold per month or sales dollars, for example). The total revenue (TR) line relates total revenue to volume (for example, if Desert Adventures sells 100 trips in a month, its total revenue would be $400,000, according to the graph). The slope of TR is the price per unit, P (for example, $4,000 per trip for Desert Adventures).

The total cost (TC) line shows the total cost for each volume. For example, the total cost for a volume of 100 trips is $254,400 (= [100 × $1,200] + $134,400). The intercept of the total cost line is the fixed cost for the period, F, and the slope is the variable cost per unit, V.

The break-even point is the volume at which $TR = TC$ (that is, where the TR and TC lines intersect). Volumes lower than breakeven result in an operating loss because $TR < TC$; volumes higher than breakeven result in an operating profit because $TR > TC$. For Desert Adventures, 48 trips is the break-even volume.

Self-Study Question

1. The following information for Jennifer's Framing Supply is given for March:

Sales	$360,000
Fixed manufacturing costs	35,000
Fixed marketing and administrative costs	25,000
Total fixed costs.	60,000
Total variable costs.	240,000
Unit price	90
Unit variable manufacturing cost	55
Unit variable marketing cost.	5

Compute the following:

a. Monthly operating profit when sales total $360,000 (as here).

b. Break-even number in units.

c. Number of units sold that would produce an operating profit of $120,000.

d. Sales dollars required to earn an operating profit of $20,000.

e. Number of units sold in March.

f. Number of units sold that would produce an operating profit of 20 percent of sales dollars.

The solution to this question is at the end of the chapter.

The amount of operating profit or loss can be read from the graph by measuring the vertical distance between *TR* and *TC*. For example, the vertical distance between *TR* and *TC* when $X = 100$ indicates Profit = $145,600 (= $400,000 − $254,400).

Profit–Volume Model

Instead of considering revenues and costs separately, we can analyze the relation between profit and volume directly. This approach to CVP analysis is called **profit–volume analysis.** A graphic comparison of profit–volume and CVP relationships is shown in Exhibit 3.4. The cost and revenue lines are collapsed into a single profit line in the profit–volume graph. Note that the slope of the profit–volume line equals the unit contribution margin. The intercept equals the loss at zero volume, which equals fixed costs. The vertical axis shows the amount of operating profit or loss.

profit–volume analysis
Version of cost-volume–profit analysis using a single profit line.

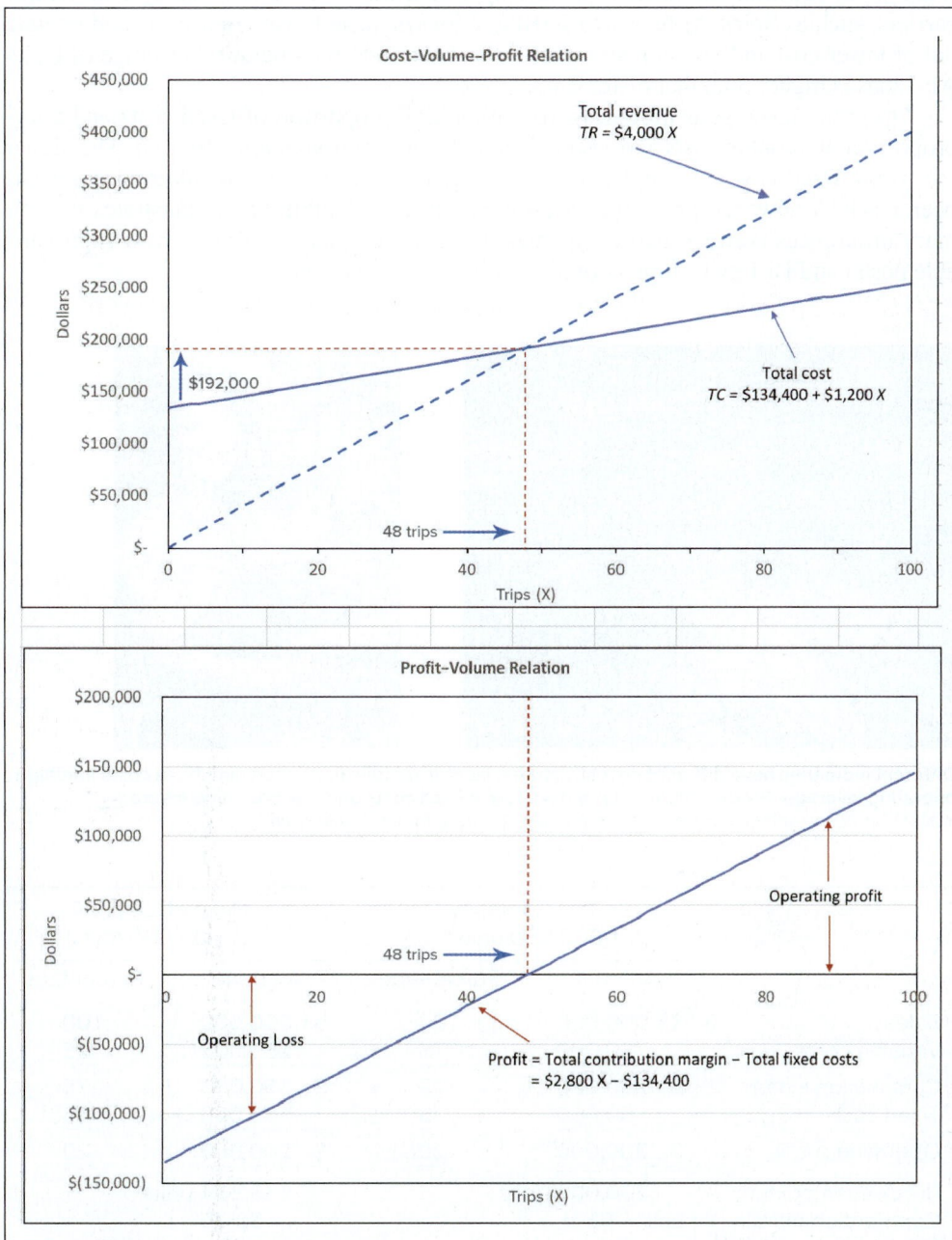

Exhibit 3.4

Comparison of CVP Graph and Profit–Volume Graph—Desert Adventures

Use of CVP to Analyze the Effect of Different Cost Structures

LO 3-2
Understand the effect
of cost structure on
decisions.

cost structure
Proportion of fixed and variable
costs to total costs of an
organization.

operating leverage
Extent to which an
organization's cost structure
is made up of fixed costs. It
is calculated as contribution
margin divided by operating
profit.

An organization's **cost structure** is the proportion of fixed and variable costs to total costs. Cost structures differ widely among industries and among firms within an industry. Electric utilities such as Southern California Edison or Public Service of New Mexico have a large investment in equipment, which results in a cost structure with high fixed costs. In contrast, grocery retailers such as Albertsons or Safeway have a cost structure with a higher proportion of variable costs. The utility is capital intensive; the grocery store is labor intensive.

An organization's cost structure has a significant effect on the sensitivity of its profits to changes in volume. **Operating leverage** describes the extent to which an organization's cost structure is made up of fixed costs. Operating leverage is calculated as contribution margin divided by operating profit. Operating leverage can vary within an industry as well as between industries. The airline industry in the United States, for example, consists of so-called legacy carriers, such as Delta Air Lines and United Airlines, which have high fixed labor, pension, and other costs and operate using a hub and spoke system. Newer carriers, such as Spirit Airlines and JetBlue Airways, have lower labor costs and operate out of lower-cost and less-congested airports. Therefore, the operating leverage of Delta Air Lines is higher than that of Jet Blue.

Operating leverage is high in firms with a high proportion of fixed costs and a low proportion of variable costs and results in a high contribution margin per unit. The higher the firm's fixed costs, the higher the break-even point. Once the break-even point has been reached, however, profit increases at a high rate. Exhibit 3.5 demonstrates the primary differences between two companies, Lo-Lev Company (with relatively high variable costs) and Hi-Lev Company (with relatively high fixed costs).

Different industries have different cost structures. Electric utilities (left) have high fixed costs and high operating leverage. Grocery stores (right) have lower fixed costs and low operating leverage.
(left): ©Stockbyte/Getty Images (right): ©Andersen Ross/Digital Vision/Getty Images

Exhibit 3.5
Comparison of Cost
Structures

	Lo-Lev Company (1,000,000 units)		Hi-Lev Company (1,000,000 units)	
	Amount	Percentage	Amount	Percentage
Sales................	$1,000,000	100	$1,000,000	100
Variable costs	750,000	75	250,000	25
Contribution margin ..	$ 250,000	25	$ 750,000	75
Fixed costs..........	50,000	5	550,000	55
Operating profit......	$ 200,000	20	$ 200,000	20
Break-even point	200,000 units		733,334 units	
Contribution margin per unit	$0.25		$0.75	

Operating Leverage as a Framework to Describe a Business Model | *Business Application*

CVP analysis can be useful in managing a business, as the Business Application "Break-Even Analysis Used by 'Big Oil'" illustrates. It, along with related concepts such as "operating leverage," can also be useful in explaining the economics of the business to shareholders and others.

For example, Grubhub is a food delivery service. Similar firms, such as DoorDash in the United States and Deliveroo in the United Kingdom, act as a logistics business. They deliver a package (food or meals) to customers at their homes or offices. Traditional logistics companies such as UPS or FedEx exploit the scale of their operations to earn profits, although the margin between price and variable cost is relatively small. However, as the managers of Grubhub explain in a letter to shareholders, there is a significant difference between their business and those of large logistics companies that currently prevents Grubhub from enjoying the same benefits of scale:

Extremely large delivery/logistics companies can generate slim margins, but only because of the hub and spoke efficiencies they gain at substantial scale. The point-to-point nature of our business mostly eliminates that aspect of operating leverage.

They go on to explain that they added restaurants that did not offer their own delivery service to use the Grubhub platform.

It was not because, as some might think, more volume would reduce delivery costs, but that it would add volume:

Delivery/logistics is valuable to us because it increases potential restaurant inventory and order volume, not because it improves per order economics.

Complicating the attempts of companies such as Grubhub and DoorDash to profit from more volume is the resistance of restaurants and grocery stores to the delivery fees charged. An approach some restaurants have taken in an attempt to reduce the fees paid to the shared delivery services is to focus on pickup services for customers.

Restaurants such as Pizza Hut and Chili's have expanded upon pickup service that spares them the cost of delivery at lower prices for customers.

As a result of this pressure on fees and the variable expenses of delivery, margins for the delivery services are small. If competition from pickup services reduces volume, the prospects for profitability are not good.

Sources: Grubhub Corporation, Letter to Shareholders, October 28, 2019, page 4 (https://s2.q4cdn.com/772508021/files/doc_financials/2019/q3/October-2019-Shareholder-Letter.pdf); Haddon, Heather, and Jaewon Kang, "Pickup Gains Ground Over Delivery," *The Wall Street Journal,* June 25, 2020.

Note that although these firms have the same sales revenue and operating profit, they have different cost structures. Lo-Lev Company's cost structure is dominated by variable costs with a lower contribution margin ratio of .25. Every dollar of sales contributes $0.25 toward fixed costs and profit. Hi-Lev Company's cost structure is dominated by fixed costs with a higher contribution margin of .75. Every dollar of sales contributes $0.75 toward fixed costs and profit.

Suppose that both companies experience a 10 percent increase in sales. Lo-Lev Company's profit increases by $25,000 ($0.25 × $100,000), and Hi-Lev Company's profit increases by $75,000 ($0.75 × $100,000). Of course, if sales decline, the fall in Hi-Lev's profits is much greater than the fall in Lo-Lev's profits. In general, companies with lower fixed costs have the ability to be more flexible to changes in market demands than do companies with higher fixed costs and are better able to survive tough times.

Margin of Safety

The **margin of safety** is the excess of projected (or actual) sales over the break-even sales level. This tells managers the margin between current sales and the break-even point. In a sense, margin of safety indicates the risk of losing money that a company faces, that is, the amount by which sales can fall before the company is in the loss area. The margin of safety formula is

margin of safety
The excess of projected or actual sales over the break-even volume.

$$\text{Sales volume} - \text{Break-even sales volume} = \text{Margin of safety}$$

If Desert Adventures sells 55 trips and its break-even volume is 48 trips, then its margin of safety is

$$\text{Sales} - \text{Break-even volume} = 55 - 48$$
$$= 7 \text{ trips}$$

Sales volume could drop by 7 trips before the company incurs a loss, all other things held constant. In practice, the margin of safety may also be expressed in sales dollars or as a percentage of current sales.

margin of safety percentage
The excess of projected or actual sales over the break-even volume expressed as a percentage of the actual volume.

The excess of the projected or actual sales volume over the break-even volume expressed as a percentage of actual sales volume is the **margin of safety percentage.** If Desert Adventures sells 55 trips and the break-even volume is 48 trips, the margin of safety percentage is 13 percent ($= 7 \div 55$). This means that volume can fall by 13 percent, a relatively large amount, before Desert Adventures finds itself operating at a loss.

CVP Analysis with Spreadsheets

LO 3-3
Use Microsoft Excel to perform CVP analysis.

It is important to be able to do CVP analysis and understand the relations, so it is useful to work examples and do problems by hand at first. However, a spreadsheet program such as Microsoft Excel® is ideally suited to doing CVP routinely. Exhibit 3.6 shows a Microsoft Excel worksheet for Desert Adventures. The basic data (price per unit, variable cost per unit, and total fixed costs) for Desert Adventures are entered. The profit equation (or formula) is shown in the formula bar of the spreadsheet.

Exhibit 3.6

Screenshot of Spreadsheet Program for CVP Analysis—Desert Adventures

	B7			fx	=B8*(B3–B4)–B5
	A		**B**		**C**
1	Desert Adventures				
2					
3	Price		$ 4,000		
4	Variable cost		$ 1,200		
5	Fixed cost		$ 134,400		
6					
7	Profit		$ (22,400)		
8	Volume		40		
9					

Once the data are entered, an analysis tool such as Goal Seek can be used to find the volume associated with a given desired profit level. In the left-side screenshot of Exhibit 3.7, the problem is set up as follows:[3]

1. With the spreadsheet open, choose the "Data" tab and select "What-If Analysis" from the ribbon. Then select "Goal Seek" from the drop-down box.
2. In the "Set cell:" edit field, enter the cell address for the target profit calculation (B7). The formula in cell B7 is: = B8*(B3-B4)-B5.
3. In the "To value:" edit field, enter the target profit (in this example, the target profit is zero because we are looking for the break-even point).
4. In the "By changing cell:" edit field, enter the cell address of the volume variable (B8). (The 40 volume in cell B8 in Exhibit 3.6 is only a placeholder; any number will suffice.)
5. Click "OK" and the program will find the break-even volume, as shown in the right-side screenshot of Exhibit 3.7.

Although this spreadsheet is extremely simple, it can easily be edited to analyze alternative scenarios, so-called what-if analyses. For example, we could ask, "Given that I expect to sell 50 trips, what price do I need to charge to break even?" In this case, we would change Step 4 to enter the cell for Price (B3) and find the answer ($3,888).

---

[3] The exact dialog boxes might differ slightly depending on the version of Excel being used. The basic process is the same.

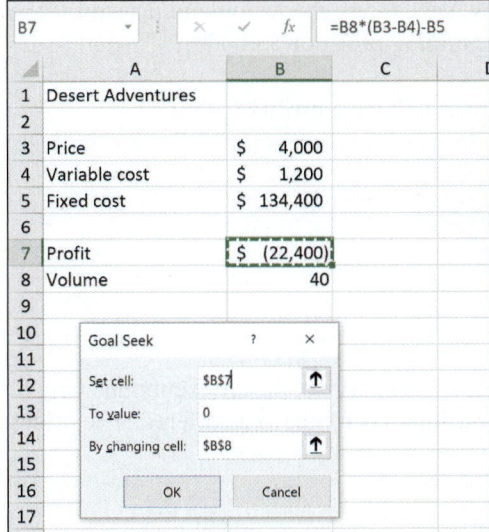

Exhibit 3.7
Screenshot of
Spreadsheet Analysis
Tool—Goal Seek

Extensions of the CVP Model

The basic CVP model that we have developed can also be extended to answer other questions or modified to incorporate complications. For example, we can use the model to determine the fixed costs required to achieve a certain profit for a given volume. We can incorporate the effects of income taxes by modifying the profit equation to include taxes. Making some simplifying assumptions, we can extend the analysis to firms that make multiple products. Finally, we can incorporate more complicated cost structures (for example, step fixed costs) by incorporating these complications in the profit equation. We illustrate these extensions here.

LO 3-4

Incorporate taxes, multiple products, and alternative cost structures into the CVP analysis.

Income Taxes

Assuming that operating profits before taxes and taxable income are the same, income taxes may be incorporated into the basic model as follows:

$$\text{After-tax profit} = [(P - V)X - F] \times (1 - t)$$

where t is the tax rate.

Rearranging, we can find the target volume as follows:

$$\text{Target volume (units)} = \frac{\text{Fixed costs} + [\text{Target profit}/(1 - t)]}{\text{Unit contribution margin}}$$

Notice that taxes affect the analysis by changing the target profit. That is, to determine the volume required to earn a target after-tax income, you first determine the required before-tax operating income (= target after-tax income ÷ [1 − tax rate]) and then solve for the target volume using the required before-tax income as before.

For example, suppose that the owner of Desert Adventures wants to find the number of trips required to generate after-tax operating profits of $25,200. Recall that $P = $4,000, $V = $1,200, the contribution margin per unit = $2,800, and $F = $134,400. We assume the tax rate $t = .25$; that is, Desert Adventures pays an average tax of 25 percent tax on income. To find the target volume, first determine the required before-tax income, which is $33,600 (= $25,200 ÷ [1 − .25]). Now, we can use the formula to determine the volume required to earn a target (before-tax) operating profit of $33,600:

$$\text{Target volume (units)} = \frac{\text{Fixed costs} + [\text{Target profit}/(1 - t)]}{\text{Unit contribution margin}}$$

$$= \frac{\$134,400 + \$33,600}{\$2,800}$$

$$= 60 \text{ trips}$$

Multiproduct CVP Analysis

When Desert Adventures started, it provided only one service, desert excursions (trips). After a short time, a second service, day-long rafting experience, was offered. The prices and costs of the two follow:

	Excursions	Rafting
Selling price	$4,000	$500
Variable cost	1,200	100
Contribution margin	$2,800	$400

When these two services were offered, monthly fixed costs totaled $144,000.

Without some assumptions, there is an infinite number of combinations of the two services that would achieve a given level of profit. To simplify matters, managers often assume a particular product mix and compute break-even or target volumes using either of two methods, a fixed product mix or weighted-average contribution margin, both of which give the same result.

Fixed Product Mix   Using the fixed product mix method, managers define a package or bundle of products in the typical product mix and then compute the break-even or target volume for the package. For example, suppose that the owner of Desert Adventures is willing to assume that the excursions and rafting experiences will sell in a 25:75 ratio; that is, of every 100 "units" of service sold, 25 will be desert excursions and 75 will be rafting experiences. Defining X as a package of 25 desert excursions and 75 rafting experiences, the contribution margin from this package is

Desert excursions . . . . 25 × $2,800	$70,000
Rafting experiences. . . . . 75 × $400	30,000
Contribution margin	$100,000

Now the break-even point is computed as follows:

$$X = \text{Fixed costs} \div \text{Contribution margin}$$

$$= \$144,000 \div \$100,000$$

$$= 1.44 \text{ packages}$$

where X refers to the break-even number of packages. This means that the sale of 1.44 packages of 25 desert excursions and 75 rafting experiences per package, totaling 36 (= 1.44 × 25) desert excursions and 108 (= 1.44 × 75) rafting experiences, is required to break even.

Weighted-Average Contribution Margin   The weighted-average contribution margin also requires an assumed product mix, which we continue to assume is 25 percent desert excursions and 75 percent rafting experiences. The problem can be solved by using a weighted-average contribution margin per unit. When a company assumes a constant product mix, the contribution margin is the weighted-average contribution margin of all of its products. For Desert Adventures, the weighted-average contribution margin per unit can be computed by multiplying each product's proportion by its contribution margin per unit:

$$(.25 \times \$2,800) + (.75 \times \$400) = \$1,000$$

The multiple-product breakeven for Desert Adventures can be determined from the break-even formula:

$$X = \$144,000 \div \$1,000$$
$$= 144 \text{ units of service}$$

where X refers to the break-even number. The product mix assumption means that Desert Adventures must sell 36 (= .25 × 144) desert excursions and 108 (= .75 × 144) rafting experiences to break even.

Find Breakeven in Sales Dollars   To find the breakeven in sales dollars, divide the fixed costs by the weighted-average contribution margin percentage. The weighted-average contribution margin percentage is the ratio of the weighted-average contribution margin (which is $1,000 in our example) divided by the weighted-average revenue.

To find the weighted-average revenue, multiply the proportion of sales (25 percent desert excursions and 75 percent rafting experiences) by the sales prices per unit. Desert excursions sell for $4,000 per unit and rafting experiences sell for $500 per unit. Therefore, the weighted-average revenue can be found as follows:

$$(.25 \times \$4,000) \text{ for excursions} + (.75 \times \$500) \text{ for experiences} = \$1,375$$

Now, the weighted-average contribution margin percent is found as follows:

$1,000 weighted-average contribution margin ÷ $1,375 weighted-average revenue = 72.7273%

The break-even sales amount in dollars (rounded) is

$144,000 fixed costs ÷ .727273 weighted-average contribution margin percentage = $198,000

(You can verify that $198,000 = $1,375 × 144 units.)

Alternative Cost Structures

The cost structures we have considered so far have been relatively simple. We have separated costs into fixed and variable and we have assumed that the variable cost per unit is the same for all levels of volume. In Chapter 2, we defined other cost behavior patterns, including semivariable costs and step costs.

We illustrate how more complicated cost structures can be analyzed by assuming that the fixed costs of Desert Adventures include the rental of equipment for transportation and that the capacity of this equipment is limited. Suppose, for example, that the fixed costs of $134,400 (from Exhibit 3.1) are sufficient for annual volumes less than or equal to 40 trips. For every additional 40 trips, additional equipment, renting annually for $19,600, is required. Now what is the break-even volume for Desert Adventures?

We know from our analysis earlier in the chapter that for a fixed cost of $134,400, the break-even point is 48 trips. But 48 trips cannot be provided without the additional equipment. At a volume of 48, Desert Adventure's profit will be

$$\text{Profit} = (\$4,000 - \$1,200) \times 48 - (\$134,400 + \$19,600) = (\$19,600)$$

which is less than breakeven.

If we are going to have to sell more than 48 trips to break even, we are going to have to rent the additional equipment. Therefore, to break even, our annual fixed costs will be (at least) $154,000 (= $134,400 + $19,600). At this level of fixed costs, the break-even point is

$$\text{Break-even volume} = \frac{\text{Fixed costs}}{\text{Unit contribution margin}}$$

$$= \frac{\$154,000}{\$2,800}$$

$$= 55 \text{ trips}$$

which is less than 80 trips. Therefore, Desert Adventures can break even at a volume of 55 trips. If we had found that the new break-even point was greater than 80 trips, we would have repeated the analysis, adding another $19,600 for additional equipment.

Assumptions and Limitations of CVP Analysis

LO 3-5

Understand the assumptions and limitations of CVP analysis.

As with all methods of analysis, CVP analysis relies on certain assumptions, and these assumptions might limit the applicability of the results for decision making. It is important to understand, however, that the limitations are due to the assumptions that the cost analyst makes; that is, they are not inherent limitations to the method of CVP analysis itself.

For example, many people point to the assumptions of constant unit variable cost and constant unit prices for all levels of volume as important limitations of CVP analysis. As we saw in the previous section, however, these assumptions are simplifying assumptions that are made by the analyst. If we know that unit prices are lower for higher volumes, we can incorporate that relation into the CVP analysis. The result will be a more complicated relation among costs, volumes, and profits than we have worked with here, and the break-even and target volume formulas will not be as simple as those we have derived. But with analysis tools such as Microsoft Excel, we can model the more complicated relations and find the break-even point (or points) if they exist.

The lesson from this is that CVP analysis is a tool that the manager can use to help with decisions. The more important the decision, the more the manager will want to ensure that the assumptions made are applicable. In addition, if the decisions are sensitive to the assumptions made (for example, that prices do not depend on volume), the manager should be cautious about depending on CVP analysis without considering alternative assumptions.

Data Analytics and CVP Analysis

We often imagine large data sets, sophisticated statistical analysis methods, and enterprise-level software graphics packages when we think of data analytics and data visualization. However, CVP analysis represents a data analytic structure that can help managers understand the economics of their business, plan operations, and make decisions. We introduced CVP analysis with revenue and cost equations expressed as proportional to volumes and including some fixed costs.

We also saw, however, that we are not limited to these relatively simple relations. We can analyze settings with multiple products. We can incorporate complications such as income taxes. In Chapter 5, we will discuss techniques for estimating the relation between volume and cost and allow for the possibility that it is not proportional.

Although it is beyond the scope of the book, we could also expand the CVP analysis developed here to incorporate uncertainty about prices and costs. Using simulation analysis, we could look at various scenarios to assess prospects for profitability. For example, we could look at the possible range of prices assuming different economic conditions along with the likelihood of those conditions occurring. This would allow us to use CVP analysis to assess the probability that a specified target income would be achieved.

In the end, CVP analysis is like all data analysis tools. Used appropriately and with an understanding of the assumptions and limitations, it allows managers to understand better the effect of their decisions on profitability. However, if it is applied where the assumptions do not hold or where the data are poor, the results may give an impression of precision that is not warranted.

Key Takeaways

1. CVP analysis can be used to evaluate the relationships among costs, volume, and profit. It is based on the following equation:

$$\text{Profit} = \text{Revenues} - \text{Costs}$$

or

$$\text{Profit} = PX - VX - F$$

where P is price per unit; V is variable cost per unit; and F is fixed costs.

2. The cost structure of a firm measures the relative mix of variable and fixed costs that make up the firm's total cost. It is summarized in the measure "operating leverage," which is measured as

$$\text{Operating leverage} = \text{Contribution margin} \div \text{Operating profit}.$$

3. CVP analysis can be extended to consider firms with multiple products, income taxes, and other modifications to the profit formula shown above. As with any analysis tool, its value depends on how well the underlying assumptions fit the situation and on the reliability of the data.

Self-Study Questions

2. High Desert Campgrounds (HDC) rents spaces for recreational vehicles (RVs) by the day. HDC charges $15 per day for a space. The variable costs (including cleaning, maintenance, and supplies) are $7 per day. The fixed costs of HDC are $60,000 per year. HDC is subject to a tax rate of 35 percent on its income. If a "unit" is one space rented for one day, how many units does HDC have to rent annually to earn $48,750 after taxes?

3. Suppose HDC rents spaces for both RVs and tent camping. The price and cost characteristics for each are as follows (one unit is a tent or RV space rented for one day).

	Price per Unit	Variable Cost per Unit	Units Rented per Year
Tent space......	$ 6	$3	6,000
RV space.......	15	7	9,000

The fixed costs of HDC are $60,000 annually. Assuming the mix of tent and RV spaces is the same as the current mix, how many tent spaces and how many RV spaces must be rented annually for HDC to break even?

The solutions to these questions are at the end of the chapter.

SUMMARY

The cost-analysis approach to decision making is used when the decisions affect costs and revenues and, hence, profit. In this chapter, we considered the cost–volume–profit (CVP) analysis framework for cost analysis.

The following summarizes key ideas tied to the chapter's learning objectives.

LO 3-1 Use cost–volume–profit (CVP) analysis to evaluate data and decisions. CVP analysis is both a management tool for determining the impact of selling prices, costs, and volume on profits and a conceptual tool, or way of thinking, about managing a company. It helps management focus on the objective of obtaining the best possible combination of prices, volume, variable costs, and fixed costs. CVP analysis examines the impact of prices, costs, and volume on operating profits, as summarized in the profit equation

$$\text{Profit} = PX - (VX + F)$$

where

P = Average unit selling price

V = Average unit variable costs

X = Quantity of output

F = Total fixed costs

Management can use CVP analysis to plan future projects and to help in determining a project's feasibility. By altering different variables within the equation (e.g., selling price or amount of output), managers are able to perform a what-if analysis (often referred to as *sensitivity analysis*).

LO 3-2 Understand the effect of cost structure on decisions. An organization's cost structure is the proportion of fixed and variable costs to total costs. Operating leverage is high in firms with a high proportion of fixed costs, a small proportion of variable costs, and the resulting high contribution margin per unit. The higher the firm's leverage, the higher the degree of the profit's sensitivity to volume.

LO 3-3 Use Microsoft Excel to perform CVP analysis. A spreadsheet program such as Microsoft Excel can be used to perform most CVP analyses. For example, the Goal Seek function of Excel is designed to find values of variables such as volume by setting other variables (for example, profit) equal to a selected target value (such as zero).

LO 3-4 Incorporate taxes, multiple products, and alternative cost structures into the CVP analysis. More complicated relationships among costs, volumes, and profits can be analyzed. With income taxes, the target profit, which is *after* income taxes, has to be converted to a target profit *before* income taxes. With multiple products, an assumption about product mix allows the application of CVP analysis by treating the multiple products as if they are a "basket" of goods. More complicated cost structures, such as step fixed costs, can be analyzed by considering costs at different volumes.

LO 3-5 Understand the assumptions and limitations of CVP analysis. All analysis methods require assumptions that limit the applicability of the results. The cost analyst must understand which assumptions are most important for the decision being made and consider how sensitive the decision is to the assumptions before relying on CVP analysis alone to make a decision.

KEY TERMS

break-even point, *100*	operating leverage, *104*
contribution margin ratio, *100*	profit equation, *98*
cost structure, *104*	profit–volume analysis, *103*
cost–volume–profit (CVP) analysis, *97*	total contribution margin, *98*
margin of safety, *105*	unit contribution margin, *98*
margin of safety percentage, *106*	

REVIEW QUESTIONS

3-1.   Write out the profit equation and describe each term.

3-2.   What are the components of total costs in the profit equation?

3-3.   How does the total contribution margin differ from the gross margin that is often shown on companies' financial statements?

3-4.   Compare cost–volume–profit (CVP) analysis with profit–volume analysis. How do they differ?

3-5.   Fixed costs are often defined as "fixed over the short run." Does this mean that they are not fixed over the long run? Why or why not?

3-6.   What is operating leverage? Why is knowledge of a firm's operating leverage important to its managers?

3-7.   What is the margin of safety? Why is this important for managers to know?

3-8.   What is the function in Microsoft Excel that you can use for CVP analysis?

3-9.   Write out the equation for the target volume (in units) profit equation when the income tax rate is *t*.

3-10.   How do income taxes affect the break-even equation? Why?

3-11.   Why is it common to assume a fixed sales mix before finding the break-even volume with multiple products?

3-12.   What are some important assumptions commonly made in CVP analysis? Do these assumptions impose serious limitations on the analysis? Why or why not?

CRITICAL ANALYSIS AND DISCUSSION QUESTIONS

3-13. Why might the operating profit calculated by CVP analysis differ from the net income reported in financial statements for external reporting?

3-14. Why does the accountant use a linear representation of cost and revenue behavior in CVP analysis? How is this justified?

3-15. The typical cost–volume–profit graph assumes that profits increase continually as volume increases. What are some of the factors that might prevent the increasing profits that are indicated when linear CVP analysis is employed?

3-16. "The assumptions of CVP analysis are so simplistic that no firm would make a decision based on CVP alone. Therefore, there is no reason to learn CVP analysis." Comment.

3-17. "I am going to work for a hospital that is a not-for-profit organization. Because there are no profits, I will not be able to apply any CVP analysis in my work." Do you agree with this statement? Why or why not?

3-18. Consider a class in a business school where volume is measured by the number of students in the class. Would you say the operating leverage is high or low? Why?

3-19. A manager of a retailing firm says that he can lower his operating leverage by renting his stores rather than buying. Would you recommend this? Explain.

3-20. The chapter describes how to incorporate income taxes into CVP analysis. Why are other taxes not discussed? Is CVP analysis unable to analyze other taxes, such as property taxes, carbon taxes, sales taxes, and so on? Explain.

3-21. An online news report stated that a fall in airline fuel prices brought down the load factors necessary for one particular airline to break even from 78 percent to 63 percent. What important assumptions and limitations should be considered when using this piece of information? (The load factor is the percentage of available seats on a flight that are occupied.)

3-22. A technology company called Luxe allows customers, through its app, to have valets who will meet the customer, take their car, and park it. Curtis Lee, the founder, was quoted as saying about a leased parking space, "If we turn it over X amount of times, per-unit it becomes cheaper." What does he mean when he says it becomes cheaper? Does the price Luxe pays go down the more it is used? Would you advise Luxe to use the per-unit lease cost when deciding which parking space to use for a car? Explain.

3-23. Consider the Business Application "Operating Leverage as a Framework to Describe a Business Model." From the description of the company in the text (and perhaps based on your experience), would you say food delivery services have high or low operating leverage? Explain.

3-24. Consider the Business Application "Break-Even Analysis Used by Big Oil." In a part of the article not quoted in the text, one definition of the break-even measure that some firms use is "the oil price that a company needs to generate enough cash so it can cover its capital spending and dividend payments." In what ways is this measure of break-even different from the way the concept is described in the text? In what ways is this similar?

All applicable Exercises are included in Connect.

EXERCISES

3-25. Profit Equation Components

(LO 3-1)

Identify each of the following profit equation components on the following graph.

a.   The total cost line.

b.   The total revenue line.

c.   The total variable costs area.

d.   Variable cost per unit.

e.   The fixed costs area.

f.   The break-even point.

g.   The profit area (range of volumes leading to profit).

h.   The loss area (range of volumes leading to loss).

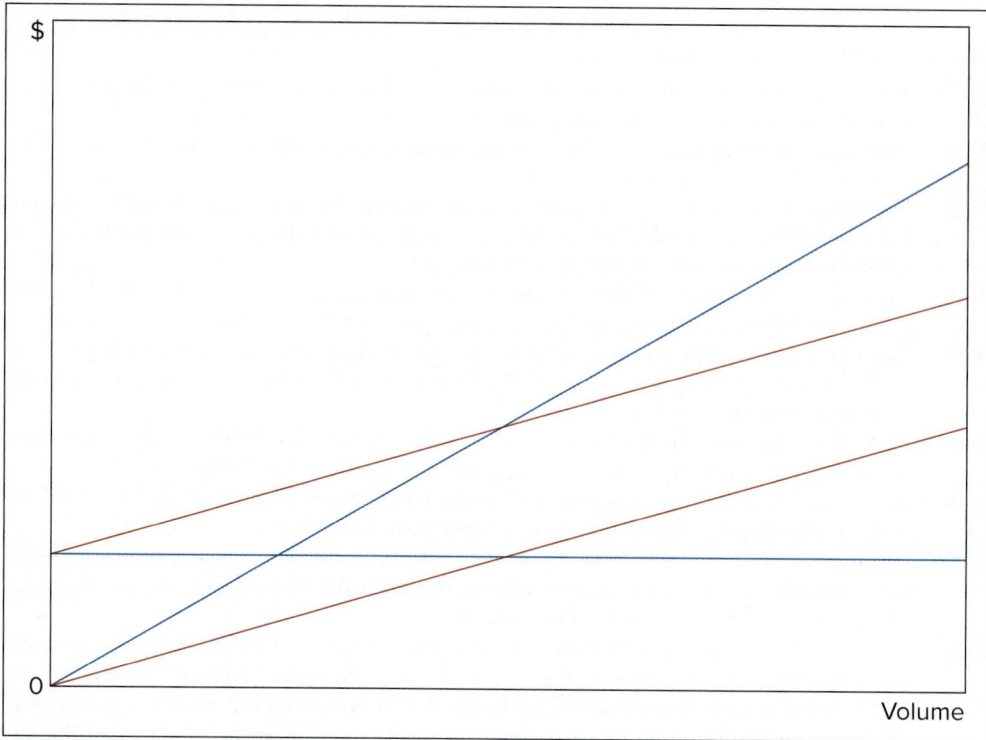

(LO 3-1)   **3-26. Profit Equation Components**
Identify the letter of each profit equation component on the graph that follows.

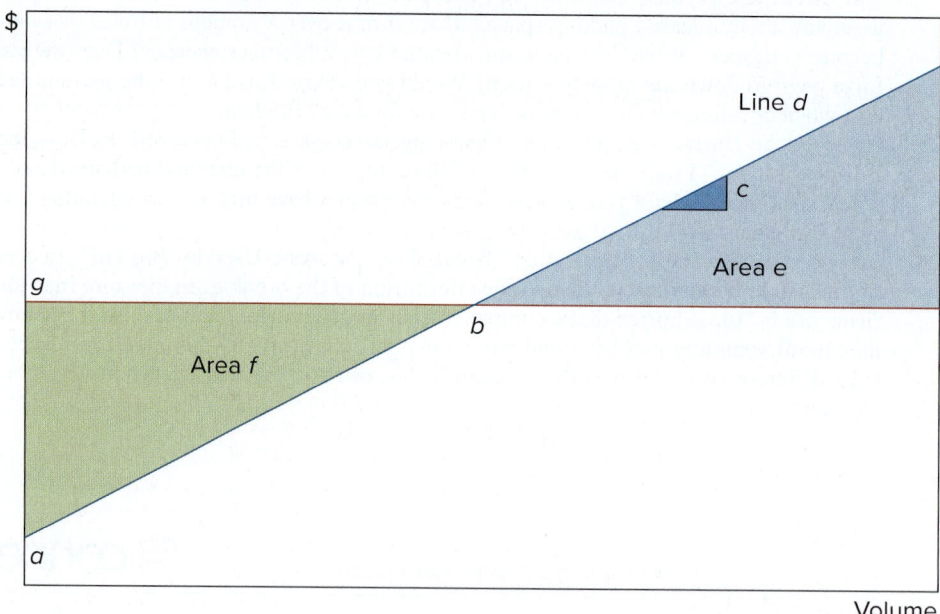

(LO 3-1)   **3-27. Basic Decision Analysis Using CVP**
Belleterre Tiles makes tiles for flooring and other applications. The CFO of the company provides you with the following information for the period October through December, the company's third quarter:

Belleterre Tile Revenues and Costs Third Quarter	
Total quantity sold	125,000 tiles
Total revenues	$437,500
Total variable costs	343,750
Total fixed costs	90,000

Required

a.   What is the average selling price per tile?

b.   What is the average variable cost per tile?

c.   What is the average contribution margin per tile?

d.   What is the current operating profit for a quarter?

e.   What is the break-even point?

f.   The CFO tells you that the company owners have said that unless the quarterly operating profit exceeds $15,000, they will liquidate the company. How many tiles would have to be sold in a quarter for Belleterre Tiles to earn $15,000 in quarterly operating profit?

3-28. Basic Decision Analysis Using CVP   (LO 3-1)

Waterman's WaterWorld Tourist Park has collected the following data for operations for the year:

Total revenues	$2,000,000
Total fixed costs	$ 546,875
Total variable costs	$ 1,125,000
Total tickets sold	50,000

Required

a.   What is the average selling price for a ticket?

b.   What is the average variable cost per ticket?

c.   What is the average contribution margin per ticket?

d.   What is the break-even point?

e.   Waterman's management has decided that unless the operation can earn at least $140,000 in operating profits, they will close it down. What number of tickets must be sold for Waterman's to make a $140,000 operating profit for the year on ticket sales?

3-29. Basic CVP Analysis   (LO 3-1)

The manager of Gratiot Flooring estimates operating costs for the year will include $540,000 in fixed costs.

Required

a.   Find the break-even point in sales dollars with a contribution margin ratio of 30 percent.

b.   Find the break-even point in sales dollars with a contribution margin ratio of 27 percent.

c.   Find the sales dollars required to generate a profit of $58,000 for the year assuming a contribution margin ratio of 23 percent.

3-30. CVP Analysis—Ethical Issues   (LO 3-1)

Mark Ting desperately wants his proposed new product, DNA-diamond, to be accepted by top management. DNA-diamond is a piece of jewelry that contains the DNA of a partner, spouse, or other loved one. Top management will not approve this product in view of its high break-even point.

Mark knows that if he can reduce the fixed costs in his proposal, then the break-even point will be reduced to a level that top management finds acceptable. Working with a friend in the company's finance department, Mark finds ways to credibly misstate the estimated fixed costs of producing DNA-diamonds below those that any objective person would estimate.

Mark knows that if the product is successful (and he is certain that it will be), then top management will not find out about the understatement of fixed costs. Mark believes that this product, once it is successful, will benefit the shareholders and employees of the company.

Required

Are Mark's actions ethical? Explain.

3-31. Basic Decision Analysis Using CVP   (LO 3-1)

Grove Audio is considering the introduction of a new model of wireless speakers with the following price and cost characteristics.

Sales price	$ 430 per unit
Variable costs	190 per unit
Fixed costs	624,000 per year

Required

a.   What number must Grove Audio sell annually to break even?

b.   What number must Grove Audio sell to make an operating profit of $180,000 for the year?

(LO 3-1)   **3-32. Basic Decision Analysis Using CVP**

Refer to the data for Grove Audio in Exercise 3-31. Assume that the projected number of units sold for the year is 3,750. Consider requirements (*b*), (*c*), and (*d*) independently of each other.

Required

a.   What will the operating profit be?

b.   What is the impact on operating profit if the sales price decreases by 20 percent? Increases by 10 percent?

c.   What is the impact on operating profit if variable costs per unit decrease by 10 percent? Increase by 20 percent?

d.   Suppose that fixed costs for the year are 20 percent lower than projected, and variable costs per unit are 10 percent higher than projected. What impact will these cost changes have on operating profit for the year? Will profit go up? Down? By how much?

(LO 3-1)   **3-33. Basic Decision Analysis Using CVP**

Charlevoix Cases makes mobile phone cases. The company has collected the following price and cost characteristics:

Sales price.	$ 12.00 per case
Variable costs	5.50 per case
Fixed costs	390,000 per year

Required

a.   How many cases must Charlevoix sell annually to break even?

b.   How many cases must Charlevoix sell annually to make an operating profit of $46,280?

(LO 3-1)   **3-34. Basic Decision Analysis Using CVP**

Refer to the data for Charlevoix Cases in Exercise 3-33. Assume that the company plans to sell 75,000 units annually. Consider requirements (*b*), (*c*), and (*d*) independently of each other.

Required

a.   What will be the operating profit?

b.   What is the impact on operating profit if the sales price decreases by 20 percent? Increases by 10 percent?

c.   What is the impact on operating profit if variable costs per unit decrease by 20 percent? Increase by 10 percent?

d.   Suppose that fixed costs for the year are 20 percent lower than projected and variable costs per unit are 20 percent higher than projected. What impact will these cost changes have on operating profit for the year? Will profit go up? Down? By how much?

(LO 3-1)   **3-35. Basic CVP Analysis**

Stahelin Valves produces a single component, a valve. The valve sells for $23 per unit. Fixed costs are $1,585,000 annually. Production and sales of 405,000 units annually result in profit before taxes of $1,250,000.

Required

What is the unit variable cost?

(LO 3-2)   **3-36. Analysis of Cost Structure**

The cost structure of Dennis's Retail Mart is dominated by variable costs with a contribution margin ratio of .30 and fixed costs of $60,000. Every dollar of sales contributes 30 cents toward fixed costs and profit. The cost structure of a competitor, Oakfield Convenience Store, is dominated by fixed costs with a higher contribution margin ratio of .70 and fixed costs of $540,000. Every dollar of sales contributes 70 cents toward fixed costs and profit. Both companies have sales of $1,200,000 for the year.

Required

a.   Compare the two companies' cost structures using the format shown in Exhibit 3.5.

b.   Suppose that both companies experience a 20 percent increase in sales volume. By how much would each company's profits increase?

3-37. Analysis of Cost Structure   (LO 3-2)
Couzen's Company's cost structure is dominated by variable costs with a contribution margin ratio of .25 and fixed costs of $450,000. Every dollar of sales contributes 25 cents toward fixed costs and profit. The cost structure of a competitor, Jones & Family, is dominated by fixed costs with a higher contribution margin ratio of .75 and fixed costs of $2,325,000. Every dollar of sales contributes 75 cents toward fixed costs and profit. Both companies have sales of $3,750,000 annually.

Required

a.   Compare the two companies' cost structures using the format shown in Exhibit 3.5.

b.   Suppose that both companies experience a 12 percent decrease in sales volume. By how much would each company's profits decrease?

3-38. CVP and Analysis of Cost Structure   (LO 3-1, 2)
Bewick Company and Stout, Inc. both earn annual operating profits of $40 million on revenues of $150 million. Bewick Company has an operating leverage of 2.4 and Stout, Inc. has an operating leverage of 1.5.

Required

Calculate the break-even points in sales dollars for

a.   Bewick Company.

b.   Stout, Inc.

3-39. CVP and Analysis of Cost Structure   (LO 3-1, 2)
Grandville Fittings earns a quarterly operating profit of $1,500,000 and has an operating leverage of 1.8. Wheeler Works, Inc. earns a quarterly operating profit of $660,000 and has an operating leverage of 3.0. Quarterly revenues total $4,500,000 for Grandville Fittings and $2,400,000 for Wheeler Works, Inc.

Required

Calculate the break-even points in sales dollars for

a.   Grandville Fittings.

b.   Wheeler Works, Inc.

3-40. CVP and Margin of Safety   (LO 3-1, 2)
Northampton City Tours (NCT) offers personalized historical and architectural tours in a large mid-western city and the local suburbs. NCT charges $350 per trip to or from the airport. The variable cost for a tour totals $42 for fuel, driver, and so on. The monthly fixed cost for NCT is $13,860.

Required

a.   How many tours must NCT sell every month to break even?

b.   NCT's owners believe that 50 tours is a reasonable forecast of the average monthly demand. What is the margin of safety in terms of the number of tours?

3-41. CVP and Margin of Safety   (LO 3-1, 2)
Golden Gate Novelties (GGN) sells souvenir key chains at the local airport. GGN charges $12 per chain. The variable cost for a chain, including the wholesale cost of the chain, packaging, the commission paid to the airport operator, and so on, is $10.40. The annual fixed cost for GGN is $15,000.

Required

a.   How many cases must Golden Gate Novelties sell every year to break even?

b.   The owner of GGN believes that the company can sell 12,500 chains a year. What is the margin of safety in terms of the number of chains?

3-42. CVP and Margin of Safety Percentage   (LO 3-1, 2)
Braile Gear Works sells a single gear for a price of $55 per unit. The variable costs are $23 per gear and annual fixed costs are $448,000.

Required

a. What is the break-even level of annual sales for Braile Gear Works?

b. The cost analyst tells you that, based on the price and cost information of the gear and the marketing department's sales projection for next year, the margin of safety percentage is 30 percent. How many units does marketing expect to sell next year?

(LO 3-1, 2) **3-43. CVP and Margin of Safety Percentage**

Annchester Car Service offers limousine service to the local airport. The cost of a trip (one-way) is $95 and the variable costs of a trip are $42, which covers fuel, variable car maintenance, labor, and so on. Fixed costs for the quarter are $24,380.

Required

a. What is the quarterly break-even level for Annchester Car Service?

b. Based on the owner's forecast for the following quarter and using the price and cost information on the airport trips given above, the margin of safety percentage is 42.5 percent. How many airport trips does the owner plan to sell next quarter?

(LO 3-3) **3-44. Using Microsoft Excel to Perform CVP Analysis**

Refer to the data for Grove Audio in Exercise 3-31.

Required

Using the Goal Seek function in Microsoft Excel:

a. What number must Grove Audio sell to break even?

b. What number must Grove Audio sell to make an operating profit of $180,000 per year?

(LO 3-3) **3-45. Using Microsoft Excel to Perform CVP Analysis**

Refer to the data for Charlevoix Cases in Exercise 3-33.

Required

Using the Goal Seek function in Microsoft Excel:

a. What number must Charlevoix Cases sell to break even?

b. What number must Charlevoix Cases sell to make an operating profit of $46,280 annually?

(LO 3-4) **3-46. CVP with Income Taxes**

Cruse Cleaning offers residential and small office cleaning services. An average cleaning service has the following price and costs.

Sales price............	$ 125 per service
Variable costs..........	87 per service
Fixed costs	108,680 per year

Cruse Cleaning is subject to an income tax rate of 22 percent.

a. How many cleaning services must Cruse Cleaning sell in a year to break even?

b. How many cleaning services must Cruse Cleaning sell in a year to earn an annual operating profit of $29,640 after taxes?

(LO 3-4) **3-47. CVP with Income Taxes**

Preston Products produces a disinfecting liquid. The liquid is sold in one gallon containers and has the following price and cost characteristics.

Sales price............	$ 36 per gallon
Variable costs..........	12 per gallon
Fixed costs	504,000 per month

Preston Products is subject to an income tax rate of 21 percent.

Required

a. How many gallons must Preston Products sell every month to break even?

b. How many gallons must Preston Products sell to earn a monthly operating profit of $75,840 after taxes?

3-48. CVP with Income Taxes   (LO 3-4)

Gardendale Associates offers landscape consultations, where they provide design advice and plans to residential customers. A single consultation is priced at $750. The variable costs of a consultation total $330, consisting mostly of labor and supplies. Annual fixed costs are $102,900. Gardendale Associates is subject to an income tax rate of 24 percent.

Required

a. What total revenue does Gardendale have to generate from selling consultations to break even?

b. What total revenue does Gardendale have to generate from selling consultations to earn an annual operating profit of $106,400 after taxes?

3-49. Using Microsoft Excel to Perform CVP Analysis with Income Taxes   (LO 3-3, 4)

Rochester Street Taco Shop (RSTS) sells a variety of tacos to go all at a price of $4.50 each. The variable cost of an RSTS taco averages $2.40. RSTS incurs monthly fixed costs of $7,350. RSTS is subject to a 20 percent tax rate.

Required

Using the Goal Seek function in Microsoft Excel, how many tacos must RSTS sell to earn a monthly operating profit after taxes of $6,720?

3-50. Using Microsoft Excel to Perform CVP Analysis with Income Taxes   (LO 3-3, 4)

Refer to the data for Rochester Street Taco Shop in Exercise 3-49.

Required

Suppose RSTS expects to sell 7,000 tacos next month, but the fixed costs are uncertain. Using the Goal Seek function in Microsoft Excel, what must be the fixed costs for RSTS to earn a monthly operating profit after taxes of $6,720?

3-51. Multiproduct CVP Analysis   (LO 3-4)

Georgeland Cycles makes and sells two models of electric bicycles. The Commuter (a folding model) sells for $2,500 and the Tour-X (a fat-tire trail model) sells for $4,500. Unit variable costs for the Commuter are $1,750 and for the Tour-X, $3,200. Annual fixed costs at Georgeland are $454,000. The marketing manager estimates that the annual mix of sales is 30 percent Commuter model and 70 percent Touring model.

Required

a. How many of each model ebike must Georgeland Cycles sell every year to break even?

b. How many of each model ebike must Georgeland Cycles sell every year to earn operating profits of $102,150 *before* taxes?

3-52. Multiproduct CVP Analysis   (LO 3-4)

Grixdale Tax Services prepares taxes for individuals. Grixdale offers a simplified pricing model with two alternatives for taxpayers: Standard Deduction (Standard) or Itemized Deductions (Itemized). Price and variable costs for the two services are listed below.

	Standard	Itemized
Sales price (per return)	$50	$250
Variable costs (per return)	10	30

The annual fixed costs at Grixdale are $262,500. Based on experience, the owner estimates that standard deduction returns represent 25 percent of the the firm's business.

Required

How many Standard Deduction and Itemized Deduction returns must be filed annually to break even?

3-53. Multiproduct CVP Analysis

Pierson Pet Products produces two models of dog beds: Basic and Custom. Price, cost, and expected sales volume data for the two models are as follows:

	Basic	Custom
Selling price per bed.............	$19	$54
Variable cost per bed	$12	$33
Expected sales (beds)...........	36,000	24,000

Required

The total fixed costs for the company are $396,900.

a.   What is the anticipated level of profits for the expected sales volumes?

b.   Assuming that the expected product mix applies regardless of total sales, compute the break-even volume.

c.   If the product sales mix were to change to three Basic beds for each Custom bed, what would be the new break-even volume?

PROBLEMS

 **connect** All applicable Problems are included in Connect.

3-54. CVP Analysis and Price Changes

Littlefield Partners produce a part sold to agricultural equipment suppliers. For the last year (Year 1), the price, costs, and volume of the part were as follows:

Unit price.............	$60
Unit variable costs	$40
Annual fixed costs	$3,200,000
Sales volume...........	230,000 units

Managers at Littlefield believe that next year (Year 2), conditions in the industry will result in lower prices, both for the part they sell and the materials they purchase. Their best estimates at this time are that the selling price will decline by 10 percent while the unit variable cost will decline by 5 percent taking account of changes in both materials and labor. They believe that fixed costs will remain the same.

Required

a.   What was the break-even volume in number of units last year (Year 1)?

b.   Assume that the managers' estimates are correct for Year 2. How many units would have to be sold in Year 2 to earn the same operating profits as earned in Year 1?

c.   Assume that the managers' estimates on price and unit variable costs are correct for Year 2, but they are uncertain about fixed costs. By how much would fixed costs have to change (in amount and as a percentage of current fixed costs) if the break-even level was to remain the same in Year 2 as in Year 1?

3-55. CVP Analysis and Price Changes

Chalmers Corporation operates in multiple areas of the globe, and relatively large price changes are common. Presently, the company sells 105,600 units for $50 per unit. The variable production costs are $20, and fixed costs amount to $2,079,000. Production engineers have advised management that they expect unit labor costs to rise by 10 percent and unit materials costs to rise by 15 percent in the coming year. Of the $20 variable costs, 25 percent are from labor and 50 percent are from materials. Variable overhead costs are expected to increase by 20 percent. Sales prices cannot increase more than 12 percent. It is also expected that fixed costs will rise by 10 percent as a result of increased taxes and other miscellaneous fixed charges.

     The company wishes to maintain the same level of profit in real dollar terms. It is expected that to accomplish this objective, profits must increase by 8 percent during the year.

Required

a. Compute the volume in units and the dollar sales level necessary to maintain the present profit level, assuming that the maximum price increase is implemented.

b. Compute the volume of sales and the dollar sales level necessary to provide the 8 percent increase in profits, assuming that the maximum price increase is implemented.

c. If the volume of sales were to remain at 105,600 units, what price increase would be required to attain the 8 percent increase in profits?

3-56. CVP Analysis and Price Changes   (LO 3-1)

Yacama Shades supplies sun-blocking shades to home remodeling supply stores such as Home Depot and Lowes as well as discounters such as Walmart. The CFO is worried about inflation and the effect on Yacama Shades' financial results. The variable production costs are $150, and fixed costs amount to $2 million. Production engineers have advised management that they expect unit labor costs to rise by 20 percent and unit materials costs to rise by 15 percent in the coming year. Of the $150 variable costs, 50 percent are from labor and 20 percent are from materials. Variable overhead costs are expected to increase by 10 percent. Sales prices cannot increase more than 6 percent. It is also expected that fixed costs will rise by 12.5 percent as a result of increased taxes and other miscellaneous fixed charges.

Presently, the company sells 25,000 units for $400 per unit.

The company wishes to maintain the same level of profit in real dollar terms. It is expected that to accomplish this objective, profits must increase by 10 percent during the year.

Required

a. Compute the volume in units and the dollar sales level necessary to maintain the present profit level, assuming that the maximum price increase is implemented.

b. Compute the volume of sales and the dollar sales level necessary to provide the 10 percent increase in profits, assuming that the maximum price increase is implemented.

c. If the volume of sales were to remain at 25,000 units, what price change would be required to attain the 10 percent increase in profits?

3-57. CVP Analysis—Missing Data   (LO 3-1)

Chandler Packaged Treats (CPT) sells a specialty pet food to pet stores. CPT management prides itself on its scientific management methods. Applying those methods, the controller estimates the following monthly costs based on 6,000 units (produced and sold):

	Total Annual Costs (6,000 units)
Direct material	$ 108,000
Direct labor.	50,000
Manufacturing overhead	112,000
Selling, general, and administrative.	90,000
Total.	$360,000

Required

a. Compute CPT's unit selling price that will yield a profit of $120,000, given sales of 6,000 units.

b. What dollar sales does CPT need to achieve to generate a 15 percent profit on sales, assuming variable costs per unit are 55 percent of the selling price per unit and fixed costs are $158,100.

c. Management believes that a selling price of $85 per unit is reasonable given current market conditions. How many units must CPT sell to generate the revenues (dollar sales) determined in requirement (b)?

3-58. CVP Analysis—Missing Data   (LO 3-1)

Clarendon Instruments produces a patented testing device, which it sells for $3,000 per unit. As a financial analyst that reports on the company, you learn that there is a good chance that the variable cost per unit will increase by 20 percent because of shortages in the materials market. The CFO at Clarendon mentions that if the variable cost does increase, the break-even level of sales will increase by 50 percent, but it should not threaten the company's ability to pay dividends or make debt payments. You are interested in checking this.

Required
Compute the current variable cost per unit and the variable cost per unit should the increase occur.

(LO 3-1)   **3-59. CVP Analysis with Subsidies**

Lappin Community Transit (LCT) is a not-for-profit mostly volunteer organization that provides transportation to seniors. As a not-for-profit, it refers to an excess of revenues over costs as a "surplus" and an excess of costs over revenues as a "deficit." LCT prices a round-trip ticket to downtown at $2.25 per trip. The variable costs of a ride are $4.00. The fixed costs of LCT, primarily for its paid staff and van leases, are $75,000 annually. The town of Lappin provides LCT with a flat subsidy, partially funded by downtown merchants, of $120,000 annually plus a per-trip subsidy of $0.25.

Required
a.   What is the break-even point for LCT in terms of number of round-trip tickets sold?
b.   The director of LCT expects 21,000 riders this year and asks you if it will operate at a surplus or deficit. What is your answer?

(LO 3-1)   **3-60. CVP Analysis with Subsidies—Data Visualization**

Refer to the information in Problem 3-59 for Lappin Community Transit (LCT). The director of LCT recently attended a seminar on financial analysis for nonfinancial managers, which covered CVP among other topics.

The director is interested in growing LCT and believes that by adding riders from a new planned community just outside the city, LCT can increase ridership to 35,000 round trips annually. The current price and cost structure would remain the same because the new demand will be covered by existing excess capacity on the vans. Although he asked the city for additional subsidies, he was told no new subsidies would be available.

Required
a.   The director wants to know if LCT will continue to generate a surplus with this expansion. Write a brief response to the director and explain why or why not.
b.   The director is not quite convinced by your response and asks if you could provide some visual explanations that he can use in his discussion with the governing board of LCT. Prepare a response to this additional request.

(LO 3-1)   **3-61. CVP Analysis—Sensitivity Analysis (spreadsheet recommended)**

Conrad Coding Institute (CCI) offers online courses in coding. One of CCI's most popular courses is the introductory course that teaches basic coding skills. CCI prices this course aggressively because of the potential for creating demand for the more advanced (and more profitable) courses. The introductory coding course has the following price and cost characteristics:

Tuition.	$ 65 per student
Variable costs (instruction, support, and so on)	40 per student
Fixed costs (advertising, salaries, and so on)	180,000 per year

Required
a.   What enrollment will enable CCI to break even?
b.   How many students will enable CCI to make an operating profit of $30,000 from the introductory coding course for the year?
c.   Assume that the projected enrollment for the year is 7,500 students for each of the following (considered independently):

1. What will be the operating profit (for 7,500 students)?
2. What would be the operating profit if the tuition per student (that is, sales price) decreased by 20 percent? Increased by 10 percent?
3. What would be the operating profit if variable costs per student decreased by 20 percent? Increased by 10 percent?
4. Suppose that fixed costs for the year are 15 percent lower than projected, whereas variable costs per student are 15 percent higher than projected. What would be the operating profit for the introductory coding course for the year?

3-62. CVP, Operating Leverage, and Margin of Safety Percentage

(LO 3-1, 2, 4)

Miami Training Support (MTS) produces materials for companies to use for training new hires as well as advanced training for employees who have been promoted to new positions. Most of the material has been created and produced by Miami employees. There is some unique content, however, and that material differentiates the company from competitors. MTS includes this content in all its courses. This content was created and produced by one of the founders of MTS, who is about to leave the company. As a part of the compensation agreement to be signed, MTS may continue to use the unique content but must pay the founder (the original creator) a royalty. Many of the details have been decided, but some specific issues need to be resolved. MTS is looking to you for advice on how to structure the agreement.

Specifically, MTS is considering two options for paying the royalty. The first is course based, where MTS will pay the founder $1,000 for each of the courses sold. The second is a flat, annual fee of $168,000 for the use of the material in any of its course. The royalty agreement will run one year and the royalty option chosen cannot be changed during the agreement. All other royalty terms are the same.

MTS charges $5,000 for a training course. The variable costs for a course (excluding any royalty) is $800. Annual fixed costs (excluding any royalties) are $470,400.

Required

a. What is the annual breakeven in terms of courses sold level assuming:
   1. The course-based royalty agreement?
   2. The flat-rate royalty agreement?
b. At what annual volume would the operating profit be the same regardless of the royalty option chosen?
c. Suppose MTS is unsure of the pricing and costs for its courses (other than the costs of the royalty payments under the two options). At what annual volume would the operating profit be the same regardless of the royalty option chosen? If you do not have enough information to answer the question, list the additional information you would need to get from MTS.
d. Assume an annual volume of 300 courses. What is the operating leverage assuming
   1. The course-based royalty agreement?
   2. The flat-rate royalty agreement?
e. Assume an annual volume of 300 courses. What is the margin of safety assuming
   1. The course-based royalty agreement?
   2. The flat-rate royalty agreement?

3-63. CVP, Operating Leverage, and Margin of Safety

(LO 3-1, 2, 4)

Maryland Manufacturing (M2) produces a part using an expensive proprietary machine that can only be leased. The leasing company offers two contracts. The first (unit-rate lease) is one where M2 would pay $20 per unit produced, regardless of the number of units. The second lease option (flat-rate lease) is one where M2 would pay $432,000 annually, regardless of the number produced. The lease will run one year and the lease option chosen cannot be changed during the lease. All other lease terms are the same.

M2 sells the part for $200 per unit and unit variable costs (excluding any machine lease costs) are $100. Annual fixed costs (excluding any machine lease costs) are $1,440,000.

Required

a. What is the annual break-even level assuming
   1. The unit-rate lease?
   2. The flat-rate lease?
b. At what annual volume would the operating profit be the same regardless of the royalty option chosen?

c. Suppose M2 is unsure of the pricing and costs for the part (other than the costs of the lease under the two payment options). At what annual volume would the operating profit be the same regardless of the lease payment option chosen? If you do not have enough information to answer the question, list the additional information you would need to get from M2.

d. Assume an annual volume of 30,000 parts. What is the operating leverage assuming
    1. The unit-rate lease?
    2. The flat-rate lease?

e. Assume an annual volume of 30,000 parts. What is the margin of safety assuming
    1. The unit-rate lease?
    2. The flat-rate lease?

(LO 3-2, 4)   **3-64. Extensions of the CVP Model—Semifixed (Step) Costs**

Southfield Stylers, with three chairs, offers a no-frills hair style service at a single price. The price of $25 and the variable cost of $5 per customer remain constant regardless of volume. The owner can handle additional volume by hiring on-call stylists to staff the two additional chairs if demand is sufficient. Southfield pays the on-call stylists for one full week regardless of actual demand that week. Southfield has three choices every week, as follows:

	Weekly Volume Range (Number of Customers)	Total Fixed Costs
1 chair	0–100	$2,300
2 chairs	101–200	3,600
3 chairs	201–300	5,400

Required

a. Calculate the break-even point(s).

b. If Southfield Stylers had sufficient demand to keep all chairs busy, should it operate with one, two, or three chairs? Support your answer.

(LO 3-2, 4)   **3-65. Extensions of the CVP Model—Semifixed (Step) Costs**

Sawyer's Lubricants produces a specialty oil for machine lubrication. The production facility can operate one shift, two shifts, or three shifts. The shift decision is made on a weekly basis because of labor agreements. Each shift is eight hours long, five days per week. The factory is closed on weekends. The sales price of $432 per case and the variable cost of $194 per case remain constant regardless of volume. Sawyer's Lubricants can increase volume by opening and staffing additional shifts. The company has the following three choices:

	Weekly Volume Range (Number of Cases)	Total Fixed Costs per Week
1 shift	0–1,000	$285,600
2 shifts	1,001–1,800	392,700
3 shifts	1,801–2,500	583,100

Required

a. Calculate the break-even point(s).

b. If Sawyer's Lubricants can sell all the oil it can produce, should it operate at one, two, or three shifts? Support your answer.

(LO 3-4)   **3-66. Extensions of the CVP Model—Semifixed (Step) Costs—Visualization**

Refer to the information and data in Problem 3-65 (Sawyer's Lubricants). The CFO would like to discuss the results of your analysis in Problem 3-65 with the rest of the management team. The corporate culture at Sawyer's encourages visual presentations of analyses and recommendations when possible.

Required
Prepare a short discussion with visual support of your findings in Problem 3-65 on the break-even levels and your recommendations on the number of shifts to operate in the production facility at Sawyer's Lubricants.

3-67. Extensions of the CVP Model—Taxes   (LO 3-4)
Ford Legal Services (FLS) is considering adding a new line of simplified wills and estate plans to its current family law practice. This new service will target individuals who are currently not clients and whose legal needs are modest but who prefer to have their wills and estate plans personally drafted. FLS estimates the following prices and costs for the new service.

Client fee	$ 1,200
Variable cost per client	$ 750
Fixed costs per year associated with this product	$ 51,750
Income tax rate	22%

Required
a. Compute Ford Legal Service's break-even point in clients per year for this new service.
b. How many clients must Ford Legal Services have to attract to earn $87,750 per year after taxes for this new service?

3-68. Extensions of the CVP Model—Taxes   (LO 3-4)
Muncey Fishing Charters consists of one boat with a capacity of 15 passengers, not including the crew. Muncey offers only one charter package: a one-half day fishing trip off the coast. Because of weather, crew availability, and so on, Muncey operates an average of 20 days a month and only makes one trip on the day it operates. Price and cost information for Muncey follows:

Selling price per passenger-trip	$ 325
Variable cost per passenger-trip	$ 75
Fixed costs per month	$65,000
Income tax rate	24%

A passenger-trip is considered to be one passenger per trip.

Required
a. Compute Muncey's break-even point in number of passenger-trips per month.
b. How many passenger-trips per month must Muncey sell to earn $6,650 after taxes?
c. The owner of Muncey decides it is not worth staying in business unless it can earn at least $10,000 per month after taxes. Is this feasible? Explain.

3-69. Extensions of the CVP Model—Taxes   (LO 3-4)
Dobel Devices manufactures an electronic lock used in dockless bicycles and scooters. The product's price and cost characteristics are as follows:

Selling price per unit	$ 46
Variable cost per unit	27
Fixed cost per year	317,000

Required
The company must sell 23,000 units annually in order to earn $93,000 in profits after taxes. What is Dobel Devices's tax rate?

3-70. Extensions of the CVP Model—Taxes   (LO 3-4)
Roxford Plastics manufactures and sells model airplane kits for hobbyists for a price of $14. The fixed costs amount to $170,000 per year, of which $105,000 is manufacturing related. At an annual

sales volume of 35,000 kits, Roxford earns $71,225 after taxes. Roxford has an income tax rate of 23 percent.

Required
What is the variable cost per unit for a kit?

(LO 3-4)   **3-71. Extensions of the CVP Analysis—Taxes**

Davis Devices makes an electronic bathroom scale that can connect to a smartphone and automatically record various measurements for tracking progress. Davis has experienced reasonable growth in the three years it has been selling the scale, where advertising was often by word of mouth and reviews left on online e-commerce sites. The chief marketing officer (CMO) at Davis believes that a formal advertising campaign will be necessary to continue the current growth trend. To prepare for the campaign, the company's cost analyst has prepared and presented the following financial data for the current year, year 1:

Variable costs:	
Direct labor (per unit)........................	$ 15
Direct materials (per unit).....................	7
Variable overhead (per unit)....................	3
Total variable costs (per unit)..................	$ 25
Fixed costs (annual):	
Manufacturing...............................	$ 92,600
Selling	75,000
Administrative...............................	160,000
Total fixed costs (annual).....................	$ 327,600
Selling price (per unit).........................	$ 60.00
Expected sales revenues, year 1 (35,000 units)......	$2,100,000

Davis has an income tax rate of 22 percent.

The CMO has set the sales target for year 2 at a level of $2,400,000 (or 40,000 units). The CMO believes that market conditions prevent any possible increase in price.

Required

a. What is the projected after-tax operating profit for year 1?

b. What is the break-even point in units for year 1?

c. The CMO believes that attaining the sales target (40,000 units) will require additional selling expenses of $52,500 for advertising in year 2, with all other costs remaining constant. What will be the after-tax operating profit for year 2 if the firm spends the additional $52,500?

d. What will be the break-even point in sales dollars for year 2 if the firm spends the additional $52,500 for advertising?

e. If the firm spends the additional $52,500 for advertising in year 2, what is the sales level in dollars required to equal the year 1 after-tax operating profit?

f. At a sales level of 40,000 units, what is the maximum amount the firm can spend on advertising to earn an after-tax operating profit of $717,522?

(CMA adapted)

(LO 3-4)   **3-72. Extensions of the CVP Model—Multiple Products**

Woodland Wearables produces two models of a smart watch, the Basic and the Flash. The watches have the following characteristics:

	Basic	Flash
Selling price per watch.................	$250	$450
Variable cost per watch	$170	$210
Expected sales (watches) per year......	15,000	5,000

The total fixed costs per year for the company are $1,440,000.

Required

a.   What is the anticipated level of profits for the expected sales volumes?

b.   Assuming that the product mix is the same at the break-even point, compute the break-even point.

c.   If the product sales mix were to change to nine Basic watches for each Flash watch, what would be the new break-even volume for Woodland Wearables?

3-73. Extensions of the CVP Model—Multiple Products   (LO 3-4)

Rossiter Fittings produces two models of pipe fittings for underwater lines. The two models (RF-12 and RF-25) have the following characteristics, as developed by a product cost analyst:

	RF-12	RF-25
Selling price per unit	$327	$472
Variable cost per unit.	$247	$312
Expected units sold per year	3,285	11,315

The total fixed costs per year for the company are $1,056,480.

Required

a.   What is the anticipated level of profits for the expected sales volumes?

b.   Assuming that the product mix is the same at the break-even point, compute the break-even point.

c.   The head of marketing agrees with the data provided by the cost analyst but believes that the sales of the RF-12 model will be double in units from what the cost analyst predicts. The head of marketing agrees that the total unit volume is likely to be as predicted by the cost analyst. What would be the break-even point of sales using the assumptions of the head of marketing?

3-74. Extensions of the CVP Model—Multiple Products   (LO 3-2, 4)

Orion Languages, Inc. (OLI) offers conversational instruction in several languages. Customers can choose from three approaches: Group, Individual, or Intense. Group customers meet as a part of a class at scheduled times. Individual customers receive one-on-one instruction over the same time frame as a group class, but at times most convenient for them. Intense customers receive focused, individual instruction over two weeks; this approach is often chosen by executives who are relocating to offices located in countries where a new (to the executive) language is spoken. The courses have the following characteristics:

	Group	Individual	Intense
Price charged per customer	$300	$2,500	$5,000
Variable cost per customer	$ 50	$1,500	$3,250
Expected customers per year	600	200	200

The total fixed costs per year for the company are $490,000.

Required

a.   What is the anticipated level of profits for the expected sales volumes?

b.   Assuming that the product mix is the same at the break-even point, compute the break-even point.

c.   As a result of recently changed economic conditions, the marketing director at OLI expects many fewer customers for the Intense offering and also a shift from Group classes to Individual instruction. The current thinking at OLI is that there will be the same total number of customers, but the mix will change to about 5 Group, 4 Individual, and 1 Intense customer for every 10 customers that sign up for a course. Assuming that this revised product mix is the same at the break-even point, compute the break-even point under these new expectations.

d.   Consider the two product mixes [in the original data and in the revised information in requirement (c) above]. Assume that the total number of customers remains as estimated originally. Which mix of customers is more profitable? Explain why.

(LO 3-4)   **3-75. Extensions of CVP Analysis—Multiple Products (finding missing data)**
Philadelphia Sunglasses sells two models of glasses at its single retail location—The Shore and The Poconos. The Shore model sells for $180 a pair and The Poconos model sells for $400 a pair. The variable cost of The Shore model is $120 and that of The Poconos model is $250. Annual fixed costs at Philadelphia Sunglasses are $594,750. The break-even point at the current sales mix is 6,500 total pairs.

Required

How many pairs of sunglasses of each model are sold at the break-even level? In other words, what is the assumed sales mix?

(LO 3-4)   **3-76. Extensions of the CVP Basic Model—Multiple Products and Taxes**
Franklin Prepared Foods (FPF) sells three varieties of microwaveable meals with the following prices and costs:

	Selling Price per Case	Variable Cost per Case	Fixed Cost per Month
Meat.............	$30.20	$23.20	–
Fish..............	44.00	32.00	–
Vegetarian........	50.00	45.60	–
Entire firm	–	–	$29,700

The sales mix (in cases) is 50 percent Meat, 35 percent Fish, and 15 percent Vegetarian.

Required

a.   At what sales revenue per month does the company break even?

b.   FPF is subject to a 21 percent tax rate on income. At what sales revenue per month will the company earn $17,380 after taxes assuming the same sales mix?

(LO 3-2, 4)   **3-77. Extensions of the CVP Model—Multiple Products and Taxes**
Maxwell Professional Coaching (MPC) offers three coaching services for individuals at different career stages. Its prices and costs follow:

	Price per Unit	Variable Cost per Unit	Units Sold per Year
Entry................	$ 240	$ 140	2,200
Management	940	540	800
Executive............	4,800	3,020	200

Variable costs include the labor costs of the coaches who work as contract employees. Fixed costs of $700,000 per year include marketing, information technology, and other costs of administration. A basic "unit" is a scheduled block of coaching and feedback sessions. The number of sessions in a block, the length of the sessions, and the experience of the coach vary across the services. The Entry service is designed for someone about to enter the job market, often about to leave college or be discharged from the military. The Management service is designed for those with some work experience who are about to take on managerial and supervisory duties. The Executive service is designed for those about to enter the top level of management at their organization.

Maxwell Professional Coaching is subject to a 23 percent tax rate.

Required

a.   Given this information, how much will MPC earn each year after taxes?

b.   Assuming the given sales mix is the same at the break-even point, at what sales revenue does MPC break even?

c.   At what sales revenue will MPC earn $277,200 per year after taxes assuming the given sales mix?

    d. MPC is considering becoming more specialized in Management and Executive services, or, as the marketing manager puts it, "our best clients." The marketing group has put together a plan that would result in the following changes. The number of Management clients would increase to 1,000 per year and the number of Executive clients would increase to 400 per year. At the same time, the number of Entry clients would drop to 600 per year. After additional study, the MPC believes this would require an increase in fixed costs to $950,000 per year (up from the $700,000 in fixed costs above). Considering this new information and if MPC's managers seek to maximize the company's after-tax earnings, would this change be a good idea? Explain.

    e. Do you agree with the marketing manager that the Management and Executive service users are MPC's "best customers"? Explain

3-78. Extensions of the CVP Model—Multiple Products and Taxes

(LO 3-2, 4)

Elliott Trophies makes three types of awards for organizations to give employees or team members. The following are its prices and costs:

	Price per Unit	Variable Cost per Unit	Units Sold per Year
Sport.................	$ 24	$ 16	36,000
Employee.............	80	60	9,000
Celebrity	656	516	3,000

Fixed costs of $432,000 per year include building and equipment costs, marketing costs, and the costs of administration. Elliott Trophies is subject to a 21 percent tax rate on income.

Required

    a. Given this information, how much will Elliott Trophies earn each year after taxes?

    b. Assuming the given sales mix is the same at the break-even point, at what sales revenue does Elliott Trophies break even?

    c. Assuming the given sales mix, at what sales revenue will the company earn $276,500 per year after taxes?

    d. Elliott Trophies is concerned about the future of the Celebrity trophy market, given recent cost-cutting by companies, and is considering becoming more specialized in the Sport and Employee markets. If Elliott Trophies drops the Celebrity model, fixed costs will fall to $402,000 per year. If it follows through with this plan, Elliott Trophies expects that the relative sales mix between the Sport and Employee models will remain the same. That is, for every 36,000 units of the Sport model sold, Elliott Trophies would expect to sell 9,000 units of the Employee model. How many units of the Sport and Employee models would Elliott Trophies have to sell to achieve the same after-tax income they currently earn with the three models?

3-79. Extensions of the CVP Model—Taxes with Graduated Rates

(LO 3-4)

Barlum Motors produces and sells a small engine used in lawn tractors. Each engine is priced at $850 and the variable cost for each engine is $725. The annual fixed cost is $1,687,500.

    Barlum Motors operates in a jurisdiction with a graduated tax structure and pays a rate of 18 percent on annual taxable income up to and including $500,000 and a rate of 25 percent on annual income above $500,000.

Required

    a. How many units must Barlum Motors sell to break even?

    b. Barlum Motors has an after-tax profit target for the year of $920,000. How many units must Barlum Motors sell in order to make the $920,000 requirement?

3-80. CVP Analysis with Increasing Unit Variable Costs—Visualization

(LO 3-1, 5)

As discussed in the text, you can analyze CVP relations even when prices and unit variable costs are not constant for all volumes. Sometimes the analysis is more complicated, but as long as you can express the relation among costs, volumes, and profits, you can use the ideas of CVP analysis in this chapter to answer some basic questions, such as finding the break-even point (or points).

For example, Kentucky Tools produces a specialty grinder that uses material that often is in short supply and sometimes is rationed. The more of the material used, the higher the price per unit the supplier charges. After doing some analysis, you determine that the best way to describe the (total) variable cost of production, *TVC*, is

$$TVC = 0.05\,x^2$$

where x is the number of units produced and sold. That is, if 50 units are sold, the total variable costs are $125 (= 0.05 × 50 × 50), for a unit variable cost of $2.50 ($125/50 units). If 100 units are sold, the total variable costs are $500 (= 0.05 × 100 × 100), for a unit variable cost of $5 (= $500/100 units).

For our purposes, the price of the grinder is a constant $74 per unit (the selling price does not depend on the number of units Kentucky Tools sells). Monthly fixed costs are $17,255.

Required

a.   What is (are) the break-even level (levels) in units for Kentucky Tools?

b.   Prepare a CVP graph to provide a visual explanation of your results.

INTEGRATIVE CASE

(LO 3-1, 2, 3, 4, 5)   **3-81. Financial Modeling**

Three entrepreneurs were looking to start a new brewpub near Sacramento, California, called Roseville Brewing Company (RBC). Brewpubs provide two products to customers—food from the restaurant segment and freshly brewed beer from the beer production segment. Both segments are typically in the same building, which allows customers to see the beer-brewing process.

After months of research, the owners created a financial model that showed the following projections for the first year of operations:

Sales	
Beer sales.	$ 781,200
Food sales	1,074,150
Other sales.	97,650
Total sales.	$1,953,000
Less cost of sales	525,358
Gross margin	$1,427,642
Less marketing and administrative expenses	1,125,430
Operating profit.	$ 302,212

In the process of pursuing capital through private investors and financial institutions, RBC was approached with several questions. The following represents a sample of the more common questions asked:

· What is the break-even point?

· What sales dollars will be required to make $200,000? To make $500,000?

· Is the product mix reasonable? (Beer tends to have a higher contribution margin ratio than food, and therefore product mix assumptions are critical to profit projections.)

· What happens to operating profit if the product mix shifts?

· How will changes in price affect operating profit?

· How much does a pint of beer cost to produce?

It became clear to the owners of RBC that the initial financial model was not adequate for answering these types of questions. After further research, RBC created another financial model that provided the following information for the first year of operations:

Sales

Beer sales (40% of total sales).....................	$ 781,200	
Food sales (55% of total sales)	1,074,150	
Other sales (5% of total sales)	97,650	
Total sales		$1,953,000

Variable Costs

Beer (15% of beer sales)	$ 117,180	
Food (35% of food sales)	375,953	
Other (33% of other sales)	32,225	
Wages of employees (25% of sales)................	488,250	
Supplies (1% of sales)............................	19,530	
Utilities (3% of sales)	58,590	
Other: credit card, misc. (2% of sales)..............	39,060	
Total variable costs		1,130,788
Contribution margin..............................		$ 822,212

Fixed Costs

Salaries: manager, chef, brewer	$ 140,000	
Maintenance.....................................	30,000	
Advertising	20,000	
Other: cleaning, menus, misc......................	40,000	
Insurance and accounting	40,000	
Property taxes...................................	24,000	
Depreciation	94,000	
Debt service (interest on debt)	132,000	
Total fixed costs		520,000
Operating profit		$ 302,212

Required

a.   What were potential investors and financial institutions concerned with when asking the questions listed in the case?

b.   Why was the first financial model prepared by RBC inappropriate for answering most of the questions asked by investors and bankers? Be specific.

c.   If you were deciding whether to invest in RBC, how would you quickly check the reasonableness of RBC's projected operating profit?

d.   Why is it difficult to answer the question: How much does a pint of beer cost to produce?

e.   Perform a sensitivity analysis by answering the following questions:
  1.   What is the break-even point in sales dollars for RBC?
  2.   What is the margin of safety for RBC?
  3.   Why can't RBC find the break-even point in units?
  4.   What sales dollars would be required to achieve an operating profit of $200,000? $500,000? What assumptions are made in this calculation?

(©Kurt Heisinger, 2023)

SOLUTIONS TO SELF-STUDY QUESTIONS

1. *a.* Operating profit:

$$\text{Profit} = PX - VX - F$$
$$= \$360,000 - \$240,000 - \$60,000$$
$$= \$60,000$$

   b. Break-even point:

$$X = \frac{F}{P - V}$$
$$\$60,000 \div (\$90 - \$55 - \$5) = \$60,000 \div \$30 = 2{,}000 \text{ units}$$

   c. Target volume in units: Profit = $120,000

$$X = \frac{F + \text{Target profit}}{P - V}$$
$$= (\$60,000 + \$120,000) \div \$30 = 6{,}000 \text{ units}$$

   d. Target volume in sales dollars: Profit = $20,000

$$\text{Contribution margin ratio} = \$30 \div \$90 = .333 \text{ (rounded)}$$
$$PX = \frac{F + \text{Target profit}}{\text{Contribution margin ratio}}$$
$$= (\$60,000 + \$20,000) \div .333 = \$240,000$$

   e. Number of units sold in March

$$X = \$360,000 \div \$90 = 4{,}000 \text{ units}$$

   f. Number of units sold to produce an operating profit of 20 percent of sales

$$PX - VX - F = 20\% \, PX$$
$$\$90X - \$60X - (20\%)(\$90)X = \$60,000$$
$$(\$90 - \$60 - \$18)X = \$60,000$$
$$X = \$60,000 \div \$12 = 5{,}000 \text{ units}$$

2.
$$\text{After-tax profits} = [(P - V)X - F](1 - t)$$
$$\$48,750 = [(\$15 - \$7)X - \$60,000](1 - .35)$$
$$\$48,750 = (\$8X - \$60,000)(.65)$$
$$(\$48,750 \div .65) = \$8X - \$60,000$$
$$\$75,000 + \$60,000 = \$8X$$
$$\$8X = \$135,000$$
$$X = \$135,000 \div \$8$$
$$X = 16{,}875 \text{ units}$$

3. Based on the current mix of tent spaces and RV spaces, the sales mix at HDC is 40 percent
    (= 6,000 ÷ 15,000) tent spaces and 60 percent (= 9,000 ÷ 15,000) RV spaces. The weighted-
    average contribution margin for HDC is

$$.40 \times (\$6 - \$3) + .60 \times (\$15 - \$7) = \$6$$

The multiple-product break-even point can be determined by the break-even formula:

$$X = \text{Fixed costs} \div \text{Weighted-average contribution margin per unit}$$
$$= \$60,000 \div \$6 = 10,000 \text{ units}$$

At the current sales mix, this would be 4,000 tent spaces (40 percent of 10,000 units) and
6,000 RV spaces (60 percent of 10,000 units).

4

Chapter Four

Fundamentals of Cost Analysis for Decision Making

LEARNING OBJECTIVES

After reading this chapter, you should be able to:

LO 4-1 Use differential analysis to analyze decisions.

LO 4-2 Use differential analysis to make pricing decisions.

LO 4-3 Apply several approaches for establishing prices based on costs for long-run pricing decisions.

LO 4-4 Use differential analysis to make production decisions.

LO 4-5 Understand and apply the theory of constraints.

❝ The CVP (cost–volume–profit) analysis that I learned in Chapter 3 was really helpful in understanding my business when I first started, and I still use it for quick assessments when I am considering new ideas. But as Desert Adventures has expanded beyond excursions and rafting trips and into a wide range of desert experiences, I find myself making decisions about pricing and operations routinely. I would like to have a structured way to analyze some of the common decisions I face almost daily about pricing and operations.❞

Desert Adventures, the travel business introduced in Chapter 3, has grown and expanded. Daniela Flores, the owner and founder of Desert Adventures, has added a second location in the neighboring state. Some common decisions that she must make include

- How much business is required to be profitable?
- How should I price tours for special groups?
- Should I drop one or more of the services?

- What is the right product mix, especially between more luxurious tours designed for adults and tours directed toward families?
- Should we do everything, or should we outsource some things like transportation or food to another firm?

❝ I am particularly concerned about suggestions that we outsource some of the activities, such as transportation or food, to third parties. I know that we have to consider what the financial analysis tells us, but one of the characteristics that defined us and let us achieve the success we have had is that we control the customers' experience. I read a recent article where some employees at Honda Motors were concerned that outsourcing some engineering activities changed the 'soul' of the company (see the Business Application: Outsourcing and the Effect of Corporate Culture). I know they are much larger and technologically more advanced than we are, but I don't want that to happen at Desert Adventures. Once we outsource, we lose that control.❞

What do all of these decisions have in common? They all require an understanding of (1) the effect of the decision on the organization's revenues and costs and (2) the business and competitive environment. In this chapter, we will build on the CVP analysis of Chapter 3 by considering some common business decisions managers face. We will focus on the use of *differential analysis,* which compares alternative actions with the status quo to make decisions.

Our purpose in this chapter is simple. By understanding the types of decisions managers make and how they think about the issues, you will be ready in later chapters to ensure that the cost accounting systems you design will be useful for managers. As a manager who makes the decisions, you will have a better understanding of the strengths and weaknesses of the cost accounting data you will use.

Outsourcing and the Effect of Corporate Culture — *Business Application*

Daniella is concerned that growth and success might threaten the nature of Desert Adventures if she decides to outsource some of the operations. Although we focus primarily on the financial benefits and costs of outsourcing in the chapter, it is important to keep in mind the nonfinancial effects as well. One of these is culture of the company. An example where outsourcing has had an effect is Honda, which has had a long reputation for refusing "to depend on anyone else."[1]

Like many automotive companies, Honda is developing semi-autonomous electric vehicles. Such vehicles require sophisticated sensing technology. Honda turned to its engineering team to develop the technology. It was not successful,

and ultimately the company purchased the technology from Bosch, a German supplier.

Such outsourcing is causing concern at the company, especially among some of the longer-term employees. In the words of a former employee in R&D, developing its own products is "Honda's soul."[2]

Honda is not the only automotive company to outsource some of the technology development for its new vehicles. Two factors drive this: first, the rapid changes in computer technology, which is increasingly important in today's vehicles, and second, the costs associated with the investment in new technologies that strain firms' development budgets. As a result,

To trim costs, most [automotive companies] are leaning on megasuppliers such as Bosch, Continental AG and Denso Corp., as well as smaller companies with cutting-edge technology such as Intel Corp. subsidiary Mobileye.[3]

The result of all of this is that the business environment and rapidly changing technology is leading Honda to reconsider its own corporate identity.

Sources:

1. McLain, Sean "Honda Took Pride in Doing Everything Itself. The Cost of Technology Made That Impossible," *The Wall Street Journal,* August 5, 2018.

2. Ibid.

3. Ibid.

Differential Analysis

LO 4-1

Use differential analysis to analyze decisions.

differential analysis

Process of estimating revenues and costs of alternative actions available to decision makers and of comparing these estimates to the status quo.

short run

Period of time over which capacity will be unchanged, usually one year.

differential costs

With two or more alternatives, costs that differ among or between alternatives.

sunk cost

Cost incurred in the past that cannot be changed by present or future decisions.

We start by describing the general approach of differential analysis and identifying decision situations in which it is appropriate. We then illustrate its use with two general applications, pricing and production decisions.

Every decision that a manager makes requires comparing one or more proposed alternatives with the status quo. (If there is only one alternative and the status quo is unacceptable, there really is no decision to make.) The task is to determine how costs in particular and profits in general will be affected if one alternative is chosen over another. This process is called **differential analysis.** Although decision makers are usually interested in all differences between alternatives, including financial and nonfinancial ones, we focus on financial decisions involving costs and revenues.

Differential analysis is used for both short-run decisions, such as the ones we discuss in this chapter, and long-run decisions, such as those discussed in the Appendix to the book. Generally, when the term **short run** is applied to decision horizons over which capacity will be unchanged, one year is used for convenience.

One important distinction between short-run and long-run decisions is whether the timing of cash receipts and cash disbursements is important; that is, whether the time value of money is a significant factor. Short-run decisions affect cash flow for such a short period of time that the time value of money is immaterial and hence ignored. Thus, the amount of cash flows is important for short-run analysis, but the timing of the flows is assumed to be unimportant. If an action affects cash flows over a longer period of time (usually more than one year), the time value of money is considered, as discussed in the Appendix to this book.

Decisions by companies to enter markets in Asia involve long-run differential analysis. Decisions by automobile companies to offer incentives and rebates to boost sales are generally made as if they are short run. (Companies often discover, however, that these decisions have long-run pricing implications.)

Differential costs change in response to alternative courses of action. Both variable costs and fixed costs may be differential costs. Variable costs are differential when a decision involves possible changes in volume. For example, a decision to close a plant reduces variable costs and usually some fixed costs. All of the affected costs are termed *differential.* On the other hand, if a machine replacement does not affect either the volume of output or the variable cost per unit, variable costs are not differential.

An important category of costs to identify when making decisions includes costs that were incurred in the past and cannot be changed regardless of the decision made. These costs are called **sunk costs** and are not relevant for the decision. By definition, they cannot be differential because they will be the same for all decisions. Examples of sunk costs include material and equipment already purchased, for which there are no markets for used or preowned goods.

As the examples in this chapter are presented, you will find that differential analysis requires examining the facts for each option relevant to the decision to determine which costs will be affected. Differential and variable costs have independent meanings and applications and should not be considered interchangeable.

Differential Costs versus Total Costs

Although we are focusing on differential costs, the information presented to management can show the detailed costs that are included for making a decision, or it can show just the differences between alternatives, as in the following right-hand column (in thousands).

	Status Quo	Alternative	Difference
Sales revenue	$750	$900	$150
Variable costs.	(250)	(300)	(50)
Contribution margin	500	600	100
Fixed costs	(350)	(350)	–0–
Operating profit.	$150	$250	$100

The first two columns show the total operating profit under the status quo and the alternative. This part of the presentation is referred to as the *total format*. The third column shows only the differences; this presentation is called the *differential format*. An advantage of the total format is that, first, all the information is available so it is easy to derive the differential format if desired. Second, the total format provides information to managers about the total resources required if one alternative is chosen. The advantage of the differential format is that it highlights the differences between alternatives.

Differential Analysis and Pricing Decisions

The differential approach is useful for many decisions that managers make about pricing because it provides information about the likely impact of these decisions on profit. We learn in economics that prices are determined by supply and demand. Why do we study pricing decisions in cost accounting? Managers make pricing decisions in part to determine whether they wish to participate in the market, that is, whether to make their products and services available. This is where the supply curve that you studied in economics comes from. Thus, we do not say that managers (or firms) set the price; we say that they decide at what price they would be willing to enter the market. They also decide how much to sell based on the price.

LO 4-2
Use differential analysis to make pricing decisions.

The Full-Cost Fallacy in Setting Prices In making pricing decisions, it is tempting to consider all costs incurred by the firm, divide them by total volume, and consider the resulting number a minimum price. The terms **full cost** or *full product cost* describe a product's cost that includes both (1) the variable costs of producing and selling the product and (2) a share of the organization's fixed costs. Sometimes decision makers use these full costs, mistakenly thinking that they are variable costs, and fall victim to the full-cost fallacy.

full cost
Sum of all costs of manufacturing and selling a unit or product (includes both fixed and variable costs).

For example, during the first year of business, an employee of Desert Adventures claimed that accepting a **special order** from an alumni group for a custom tour would be a mistake, even though the group was willing to pay $3,000. "Because our variable costs are $1,200 per tour and our fixed costs are $134,400 per year, our total costs for the year without the special tour are $206,400 for 60 tours [= $134,400 + (60 tours × $1,200)]. That is $3,440 per tour ($206,400 ÷ 60), which is more than the $3,000 offered by the customer. We'd be losing $440!"

special order
Order that will not affect other sales and is usually a short-run occurrence.

By considering fixed costs in the analysis, the employee might be including irrelevant information. If the fixed costs will be incurred whether the special order is accepted or rejected, these costs should not bear on the decision. Instead, the employee should focus on the variable costs of $1,200 per tour in deciding whether to accept the special order from the customer.

This is a common mistake in short-run decisions. All costs must be covered in the long run or the company will fail. In the short run, it will be profitable to accept the order because the price of $3,000 exceeds variable costs of $1,200, assuming that this price does not affect other business at the company. Full product costs serve a wide variety of important purposes, but they are generally not relevant to the type of short-run operating decision described in this example.

Short-Run versus Long-Run Pricing Decisions

The time horizon of the decision is critical in computing the relevant costs in a pricing decision. The two ends of the time-horizon spectrum are as follows:

$$\underset{\text{Years: 0}}{\underbrace{\overset{\text{Short-run pricing decisions}}{\underset{\text{Shorter than 1 year}}{\longrightarrow}}}} 1 \underbrace{\overset{\text{Long-run pricing decisions}}{\underset{\text{Longer than 1 year}}{\longrightarrow}}}$$

Short-run decisions include (1) pricing for a one-time-only special order with no long-term implications and (2) adjusting product mix and volume in a competitive market. The time horizon is typically one year or less. Long-run decisions include pricing a main product in a large market in which there is considerable leeway to set prices. Managers often use a time horizon of longer than a year for these long-run decisions.

For example, a college's order for shipping athletic equipment to a football bowl site involves a short-run pricing decision by FedEx. Determining prices for a new ground package delivery service is, however, a long-run pricing decision.

Short-Run Pricing Decisions: Special Orders

The differential approach particularly helps in making decisions regarding special orders where the order will not affect other sales and is not expected to recur. Determining which costs are relevant depends on the decision being considered. A framework for decision making, based on a company that receives a special order, is diagrammed in Exhibit 4.1. Each alternative is stated as a branch of a decision tree and then the value of each alternative is determined. Finally, the alternative with the highest value is chosen.

Desert Adventures now offers self-guided tours in addition to the traditional guided tours it started with. At the current levels of activity, the self-guided tours do not affect the company's ability to offer the guided tours. A local museum director asks Desert Adventures about offering discounted self-guided tours to museum members who donate above a certain level during the next monthly fund drive. The museum expects that five members will want to do this. Desert Adventures has idle capacity adequate for these additional five tours, which will not affect the demand for other self-guided tours for the month. The museum director asks Daniela to offer the members a special price of $700 for the tours, a discount off the regular price of $900.

Exhibit 4.1
Framework for Decision Making

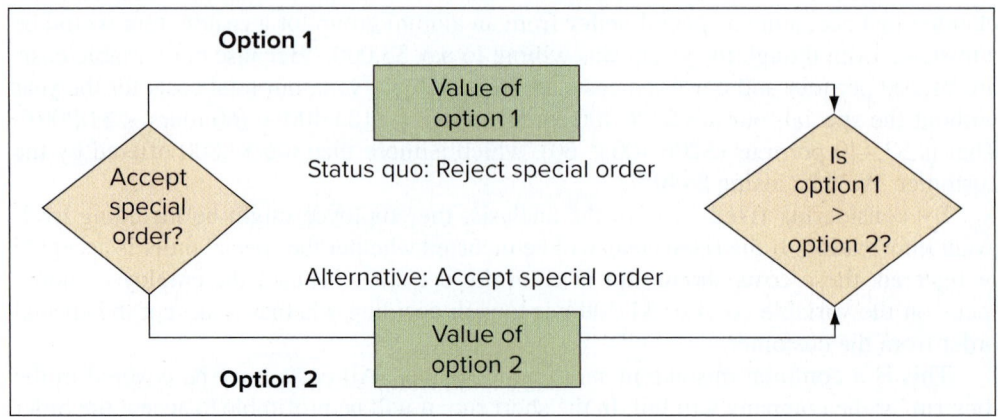

In deciding whether to accept the special order, Daniela estimates the following operating data for the month in question.

	A	B
1	Sales (20 tours at $900)	$ 18,000
2	Variable costs including food, labor, and so on (20 tours at $300)	6,000
3	Total contribution margin	$ 12,000
4	Fixed costs (insurance, depreciation, and other costs assigned to self-guided tours)	5,400
5	Operating profit	$ 6,600
6		

To make the decision, Daniela identifies the alternatives, determines the value of each alternative to the company, and selects the alternative with the highest value to the company.

The values of the alternatives are shown in Exhibit 4.2. The best economic decision is to accept the museum's offer because the company will gain $2,000 from it. Fixed costs are not affected by the decision because they are not differential in this situation. Therefore, they are not relevant.

The differential approach to pricing works well for special orders, but some criticize its use for pricing a firm's regular products. Critics suggest that following the differential approach in the short run leads to underpricing in the long run because the contribution to covering fixed costs and generating profits will be inadequate.

A second criticism of the differential approach is that it may be difficult to sell a product to a customer at a reduced price on a particular day when capacity utilization happens to be low if that customer might return on another day when capacity utilization happens to be high. For example, many analysts worry that the U.S. auto industry's cycle of discounting cars will be difficult to break, even after capacity is cut to be more in line with demand. We see similar behavior in the airline industry, where customers

M31		A		B	C	D	
1				Status Quo	Alternative		
2				Reject Special Order	Accept Special Order	Difference	
3	Comparison of Totals						
4	Sales revenue			$ 18,000	$ 21,500	$ 3,500	
5	Variable costs			6,000	7,500	1,500	
6	Total contribution			$ 12,000	$ 14,000	$ 2,000	
7	Fixed costs			5,400	5,400	-	
8	Operating profit			$ 6,600	$ 8,600	$ 2,000	
9	Alternative presentation: Differential Analysis						
10	Differential sales revenue, 5 tours at $700				$ 3,500		
11	Less differential costs, 5 tours at $300				1,500		
12	Differential operating profit (before taxes)				$ 2,000		
13							

Exhibit 4.2
Analysis of Special Order—Desert Adventures

strategically withhold purchases until the last minute, expecting carriers to discount fares. The root of the problem is that pricing is dynamic, not just a static optimization of profits during the period of low demand.

Others respond to these criticisms in two ways. First, the differential approach does lead to correct short-run pricing decisions. Once the firm has set plant capacity and incurred fixed costs, the fixed costs become irrelevant to the short-run pricing decision. Clearly, airlines understand this with their discount fares. The firm must attempt to set a price that at least equals the differential, or variable, costs.

Second, in both the short and long runs, the differential approach indicates only the minimum acceptable price. The firm always can charge a higher amount, depending on its customers and competitors. Some of these issues are pursued in this chapter's questions and exercises.

The Desert Adventures example also illustrates a limitation in using financial analyses for many business decisions. There are several benefits that are difficult to quantify and are, therefore, excluded from the analysis. By offering this discount to the museum, Daniela is encouraging an interest in adventure travel and contributing to the development of charitable giving in the community. These are factors that Daniela can and should consider before deciding whether to accept the offer.

Self-Study Question

1. Live Oak Products has an annual plant capacity to produce 50,000 units. Its predicted operations for the year follow:

Sales revenue (40,000 units at $20 each). . . .	$ 800,000
Manufacturing costs	
Variable.	$8 per unit
Fixed	$ 200,000
Selling and administrative costs.	
Variable (commissions on sales).	$2 per unit
Fixed	$ 40,000

Should the company accept a special order for 4,000 units at a selling price of $15 each, which is subject to half the usual sales commission rate per unit? Assume no effect on fixed costs or regular sales at regular prices. What is the effect of the decision on the company's operating profit?

The solution to this question is at the end of the chapter.

Long-Run Pricing Decisions

LO 4-3

Apply several approaches for establishing prices based on costs for long-run pricing decisions.

Most firms rely on full-cost information reports when setting prices. *Full cost* is the total cost to produce and sell a unit; it includes all costs incurred by the activities that make up the value chain. Typically, the accounting department provides cost reports to the marketing department, which then adds appropriate markups to determine benchmark or target prices for all products the firm normally sells. This approach is often called *cost-plus*.

Using full costs for pricing decisions can be justified in three circumstances:

1. When a firm enters into a long-term contractual relationship to supply a product, most costs depend on the production decisions under the long-term contract. Therefore, full costs are relevant for the long-term pricing decision.
2. Many contracts for developing and producing customized products and those entered into with governmental agencies specify prices as full costs plus a markup. Prices set in regulated industries such as electric utilities also are based on full costs.
3. Firms initially can set prices based on full costs and then make short-term adjustments to reflect market conditions. Accordingly, they adjust the prices of the product downward to acquire additional business. Conversely, when demand for their products is high, firms recognize the greater likelihood that the existing capacity of resources is inadequate to satisfy all of the demand. Accordingly, they adjust the prices upward based on the higher incremental costs when capacity is fully utilized.

Long-Run versus Short-Run Pricing: Is There a Difference?

When used in pricing decisions, the differential costs required to sell and/or produce a product provide a floor. In the short run, differential costs may be very low, as when selling one additional seat on an already scheduled airline flight or allowing one more student into an already scheduled college course.

In the long run, however, differential costs are much higher than in the short run. For an airline, long-run differential costs include the costs to buy and maintain the aircraft and to pay crew salaries, landing fees, and so forth. In the long run, these costs must be covered. To simplify this type of analysis, the full product costs to make and/or sell a product are often used to estimate long-run differential costs. Hence, a common saying in business is: I can drop my prices to just cover variable costs in the short run, but in the long run, my prices have to cover full product costs.

Cost Analysis for Pricing

To this point, we have discussed differential analysis and its usefulness for short-run and long-run pricing decisions. Several other approaches are used, however, to establish prices based on costs. In addition to the cost-plus or full-cost approach described earlier, two approaches—life-cycle product costing and pricing and target costing from target pricing—are discussed here. In general, these approaches are especially useful in making long-run pricing decisions.

Life-Cycle Product Costing and Pricing

product life cycle
Time from initial research and development to the time that support to the customer ends.

The **product life cycle** covers the time from initial research and development to the time at which support to the customer is withdrawn. For pharmaceuticals, this time span may be several years. For some electronic goods, it may be less than one year.

Managers estimate the revenues and costs for each product from its initial research and development to its final customer support. Life-cycle costing tracks costs attributable to each product from start to finish. The term *cradle-to-grave costing* conveys the sense of capturing all life-cycle costs associated with a product.

Life-cycle costs provide important information for pricing. For some companies, such as Merck and Pfizer in pharmaceuticals and Boeing and Airbus in aircraft, the development period is relatively long, and many costs are incurred prior to manufacturing.

A product life-cycle budget highlights for managers the importance of setting prices that will cover costs in all value-chain categories, not just in the production through customer service categories. To be profitable, companies must generate enough revenue to cover costs incurred in all categories of the value chain.

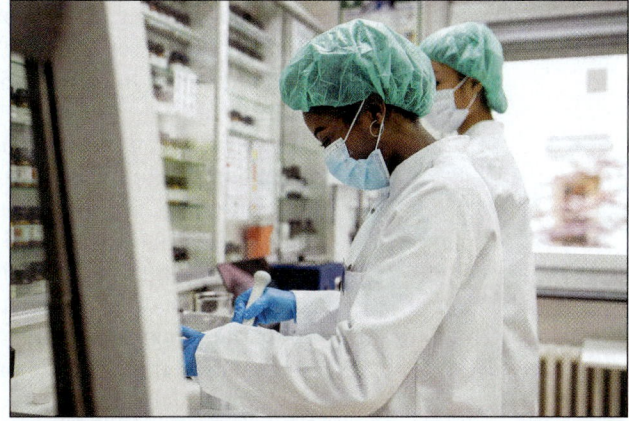

The life-cycle costs for pharmaceuticals include many costs incurred prior to production and distribution. Luis Alvarez/DigitalVision/Getty Images

Life-cycle costing is becoming increasingly important as environmental regulations that require firms to "take back" and dispose of the product at the end of the life cycle are adopted. These regulations give literal meaning to the phrase "cradle-to-grave." The costs of recycling used products are especially important for certain companies—for example, refrigerator manufacturers, such as Whirlpool and Haier (GE Appliances), and producers of toner cartridges for printers, such as HP and Epson. These firms need to consider these additional costs at the end of the useful life of the product in making pricing decisions.

In some jurisdictions, so-called "Take-Back" laws make the costs of recycling and disposal of products the

Life-cycle costing includes the cost of taking back used products. Ermingut/iStock/Getty Images Plus/Getty Images

responsibility of the manufacturer. This, in turn, can affect product design as manufacturers trade off the cost of manufacture and disposal. For example, some materials may be easier to work with in manufacturing the product but are more difficult to dispose of or recycle.

target price
Price based on customers' perceived value for the product and the price that competitors charge.

target cost
Equals the target price minus desired profit margin.

Target Costing from Target Pricing
Simply stated, target costing is the concept of "price-based costing" instead of "cost-based pricing." A **target price** is the estimated price for a product or service that potential customers will be willing to pay. A **target cost** is the estimated long-run cost of a product or service whose sale enables the company to achieve targeted profit. We derive the target cost by subtracting the target profit from the target price. For instance, assume that Dell can sell a tablet for $300 and wants profits of at least $30; this means that Dell needs to find a way to limit costs to $270. Target costing is widely used by companies including Mercedes Benz and Toyota in the automobile industry, IKEA in the home furnishings industry, and McDonald's and The Cheesecake Factory in the restaurant industry.

Legal Issues Relating to Costs and Sales Prices

Predatory Pricing

predatory pricing
Practice of setting price below cost with the intent to drive competitors out of business.

Laws in many countries, including the United States, require managers to take costs into account when they set sales prices. For example, managers will face charges of predatory pricing if they set prices below costs. **Predatory pricing** is the practice of setting the selling price of a product at a low price with the intent of driving competitors out of the market or creating a barrier to entry for new competitors. For the practice to be predatory, managers must set the price below cost and intend to harm competition. In many countries, including the United States, predatory pricing is anticompetitive and illegal under antitrust laws.

At first, you might wonder what is wrong with setting prices low and intending to harm competition. It sounds like free enterprise, and setting prices low is normally good for consumers. The legal problem arises when prices are set sufficiently low to drive competitors out of the market or keep competitors out of the market. With little competition left in the market, the company that has set predatory prices is able to act like a monopolist and then raise prices. From the consumers' point of view, they benefit in the short run when the "predators" set prices low, but these same consumers suffer in the long run when they face monopoly prices.

One usually finds evidence of predatory pricing when larger companies drive out smaller companies. For example, a small airline recently added several routes to compete with one of the large, international airlines. In response, the large airline dropped its prices below those of the small airline. The small airline went bankrupt and stopped flying those routes. The large airline then raised its prices.

To qualify as predatory pricing, the "predator" must drop its prices below costs. In theory, pricing below marginal costs is irrational because the marginal revenue from each unit sold is less than the marginal cost. Why would a manager set prices below marginal cost, thereby incurring a loss on each unit sold? Regulators argue that managers who set prices below marginal costs are likely to do so to drive out competition so they can later raise prices to recoup the losses. If you combine the act of setting prices below costs with intent to harm competition, then you have predatory pricing.

In theory, setting prices below marginal costs is one of the tests for predatory pricing. In practice, however, marginal costs are difficult to measure. Therefore, courts have generally used average variable costs as the floor below which prices should not be set.[1]

---

[1] For an authoritative work on antitrust law, see P. E. Areeda and H. Hovenkamp, *Antitrust Law: An Analysis of Antitrust Principles and Their Application* (Wolters Kluwer, 2018).

Dumping

Dumping occurs when a company exports its product to consumers in another country at an export price that is below the domestic price. The harm to consumers is similar to that imposed by predatory pricing. For example, suppose an electronics company in a foreign country sells its products in the United States at a price below what it charges in its domestic market. Eventually, U.S. electronics companies will be unable to compete and will go out of business. Now the foreign company has an opportunity to raise its prices *above* what consumers in the United States paid prior to the foreign company's practice of dumping. Consumers may appear to have a good deal when foreign companies dump their products at a discount, but these same consumers would suffer if the U.S. companies no longer existed. Market prices would no longer be competitive.

Many industries, such as airlines, steel, and navigational electronics equipment, provide goods and services that are important to the U.S. national defense. The U.S. federal government considers it important to keep at least the capability to produce such goods and services in the United States.

Policymakers disagree on the merits of prohibiting dumping. On the one hand, protection of domestic industry has national security benefits and it benefits the employees of those protected industries. On the other hand, dumping is simply a practice of free trade and free markets. Restrictions that create oligopoly power generally hurt consumers. Managers in many industries have sought protection against dumping, including producers of semiconductors, shoes, automobiles, textiles, computers, and lumber. The remedies to domestic producers are usually tariffs on the dumped products that bring their prices up to the level of prices charged by domestic companies.

While we have used the United States to demonstrate how dumping works, many countries must deal with dumping. For example, the European Union (EU) recently considered whether Chinese manufacturers of e-bikes were "dumping" their products in the EU.

dumping
Exporting a product to another country at a price below domestic price.

Price Discrimination

Price discrimination is the practice of selling identical goods or services to different customers at different prices. Price discrimination requires market segmentation. For example, a movie theater may sell tickets to the same movie at the same time to students for $7 and nonstudents for $14. In this case, student status segments the market.

Airlines use price discrimination when they sell tickets to different customers at different prices for the same flight. Customers who stay at a destination over Saturday night are sometimes charged a lower fare than customers who fly the same flights but do not stay over Saturday night. The airlines' idea is to segment customers into a group that is more price sensitive and a group that is less price sensitive. Business travelers are usually less price sensitive than pleasure travelers and generally do not stay over Saturday night at their destinations. Managers of movie theaters segment the market of movie goers into a price-sensitive segment—students—and a less price-sensitive segment—nonstudents.

Price discrimination benefits companies because it enables them to sell products to customers who might not otherwise purchase them. For example, if an airline has empty seats, it would rather sell those seats at a discount than not at all.

Certain types of price discrimination are illegal. For example, price discrimination on the basis of race, religion, disability, or gender is illegal. Some companies take advantage of people who have been struck by tragedies, such as tornadoes, hurricanes, or personal disasters. Even if not illegal, discriminating against victims of natural or personal disasters is often considered to be unethical.

price discrimination
Practice of selling identical goods to different customers at different prices.

Peak-Load Pricing

Peak-load pricing is the practice of setting prices highest when the quantity demanded for the product approaches the physical capacity to produce it. Many companies, such as electric utilities and travel providers, engage in peak-load pricing when facing high

peak-load pricing
Practice of setting prices highest when the quantity demanded for the product approaches capacity.

demand levels. For example, in warm-weather geographic locations, peak loads for electricity occur in the late afternoon hours when the temperature is highest. For providers of travel services, the peak loads are often during the high seasons and local special events. Prices are highest per unit of service at those times and lower at other times. Hence, you can get lower rates for travel and electricity services at off-peak times.

Price-Fixing

price-fixing
Agreement among business competitors to set prices at a particular level.

Price-fixing is the agreement among business competitors to set prices at a particular level. Generally, the idea is to "fix" prices at a level higher than equilibrium prices in competitive markets. The Organization for Petroleum Exporting Countries (OPEC) provides us with a daily reminder of the effects of price-fixing. OPEC sets prices for its members that are likely above equilibrium prices in a competitive market for oil.

Price-fixing is a particular legal and ethical problem because it is not universally illegal. In many developing countries, price-fixing is not illegal. Companies with business units in both developed and developing countries face different sets of rules depending on where managers are doing business. OPEC, for example, operates legally in setting oil prices because its activities are not illegal in its member countries.

Managers must be particularly alert to price-fixing because the activities that law enforcement officials regard as illegal include even informal or unspoken agreements to fix prices. This appears to be the case in previous allegations of price-fixing in the market for dynamic random access memory (DRAM) chips. Companies from Germany, South Korea, and Japan were charged with price-fixing in their U.S. operations.

Use of Differential Analysis for Production Decisions

LO 4-4

Use differential analysis to make production decisions.

We now apply our cost analysis concepts to production and operating decisions. The following are typical production and operating questions that managers often ask:

- Should we make the product (or provide the service) internally or buy it from an outside source (called *outsourcing*)?
- Should we add to or drop parts of our operations?
- Which products (services) should we continue to produce and which should we drop?

This chapter provides several approaches to addressing these questions. As you go through each, ask yourself what costs and revenues will differ as a result of the choices made and which course of action would be the most profitable for the company.

Make-It or Buy-It Decisions

make-or-buy decision
Decision concerning whether to make needed goods internally or purchase them from outside sources.

A **make-or-buy decision** is any decision by a company to acquire goods or services internally or externally. A restaurant that uses its own ingredients in preparing meals "makes"; one that serves meals from frozen entrees "buys." A steel company that mines its own iron ore and processes it into pig iron makes; one that purchases ore for further processing buys.

The make-or-buy decision is often part of a company's long-run strategy. Some companies choose to integrate vertically (own the firms in the supply chain) to control the activities that lead to the final product; others prefer to rely on outsiders for some inputs and specialize in only certain steps of the total manufacturing process. Aside from strategic issues, the make-or-buy decision is ultimately a question of which firm in the value chain can produce the product or service at the lowest cost.

Whether to rely on outsiders for a substantial amount of materials depends on both differential cost comparisons and other factors that are not easily quantified, such as suppliers' dependability and quality control. Although make-or-buy decisions sometimes appear to be simple one-time choices, frequently they are part of a more strategic analysis in which top management makes a policy decision to move the company toward more or less vertical integration.

We present the make or buy decision here as a binary, either-or, choice because we want to illustrate the use of differential analysis in evaluating the two alternatives. However, firms often choose a middle path. Recall that in the Business Application "Outsourcing and the Effect of Corporate Culture," managers at Honda were concerned about the effect on company culture that may result from outsourcing technology development. Another approach to managing the cost of technological development has been taken by Toyota Motor Corporation. With ownership stakes in other automotive firms including Mazda and Suburu, the firms collaborate to develop new technology, lowering the cost to any one company. Renault, Mitsubishi, and Fiat Chrysler have formed a similar alliance, again with the goal, at least in part, to manage costs.[2]

Make-or-Buy Decisions Involving Differential Fixed Costs

After several years in the business, Desert Adventures has grown significantly and offers a broad range of excursions, tours, and other experiences. At the same time, it continues to provide the small-group tour that was the initial service offering. The current cost of the six-person desert excursion trip follows:

	Per Tour	150 Tours
Costs that can be directly assigned to the service:		
Labor..	$300	$ 45,000
Food and food preparation...........................	400	60,000
Supplies and other variable costs	300	45,000
Direct fixed costs.....................................		48,000
Common costs allocated to this service		24,000
Total costs..		$222,000

This year's expected volume is 150 tours, so the full cost of operating one of these tours is $1,480 (= $222,000 ÷ 150 tours).

Desert Adventures has received an offer from a local tour operator to organize and lead these tours for a cost (to Desert Adventures) of $1,400. Desert Adventures would continue to collect the tour price of $4,000 from the customer and market this tour along with its other services.

The accounting department prepared this differential cost analysis for management:

- Differential costs are labor, food and food preparation, and supplies, and definitely will be saved by outsourcing the provision of desert tours.

- The direct fixed cost is the cost of leasing the building where the tours are staged. The building is also where equipment for the tour is stored and maintained. Although the building cost is fixed for levels of any tour activity up to 200 tours, we can eliminate it if we stop leading these tours and outsource them instead. Thus, although the building cost is a fixed cost of leading these tours, it is a differential cost if we eliminate the service.

- No other costs are affected.

---

[2] McLain, Sean "Honda Took Pride in Doing Everything Itself. The Cost of Technology Made That Impossible," *The Wall Street Journal,* August 5, 2018.

Exhibit 4.3
Make-or-Buy
Analysis—Desert
Adventures

	Status Quo: Operate Tours	Alternative: Outsource Tours	Difference
150 Tours			
Labor....................	$ 45,000	$ –0–[a]	$ 45,000 lower
Food and food prep........	60,000	–0–	60,000 lower
Supplies and other costs....	45,000	210,000[b]	165,000 higher
Direct fixed costs..........	48,000	–0–	48,000 lower
Common costs............	24,000[c]	24,000[c]	–0–
Total costs...............	$222,000	$234,000	$ 12,000 higher

Differential costs *increase* by $12,000, so reject alternative to outsource.

	Status Quo: Operate Tours	Alternative: Outsource Tours	Difference
100 Tours			
Labor....................	$ 30,000[d]	–0–[e]	$ 30,000 lower
Food and food prep........	40,000[d]	–0–	40,000 lower
Supplies and other costs....	30,000[d]	140,000[f]	110,000 higher
Direct fixed costs..........	48,000	–0–	48,000 lower
Common costs............	24,000[c]	24,000[c]	–0–
Total costs...............	$172,000	$164,000	$ 8,000 lower

Differential costs *decrease* by $8,000, so accept alternative to *outsource*.

[a] If tours are outsourced, no Desert Adventures labor is required for leading the tours.
[b] Pay outside supplier $210,000 (= 150 tours × $1,400) to operate tours.
[c] These common costs remain unchanged for these volumes. Because they do not change, they could be omitted from the analysis.
[d] Total variable costs reduced by 1/3 because volume was reduced by 1/3 (= [150 tours – 100 tours]/150 tours).
[e] If tours are outsourced, no Desert Adventures labor is required for leading the tours.
[f] Pay outside supplier $140,000 (= 100 tours × $1,400) to operate tours.

The accounting department also prepared cost analyses at volume levels of 100 and 150 tours per year (see Exhibit 4.3). At a volume of 150 tours, it is less costly for Desert Adventures to operate the tours, but if the volume drops to 100 tours, Desert Adventures would save money by outsourcing the tour operation.

This decision is sensitive to volume. To see why, consider only the costs affected by the make-or-buy decision: food, labor, supplies and other variable costs, and fixed overhead. By setting the costs to make equal to the costs to buy, we find that a unique volume exists at which Desert Adventures is indifferent (in terms of costs):

Make				Buy
Direct Fixed Overhead	+	Variable Operating Costs	=	Cost to Outsource Tours
$48,000	+	$1,000X	=	$1,400X

where X equals the number of tours operated.
Solve for X :

$$\$48,000 + \$1,000X = \$1,400X$$
$$\$48,000 = \$400X$$
$$\$48,000 \div \$400 = X$$
$$X = 120$$

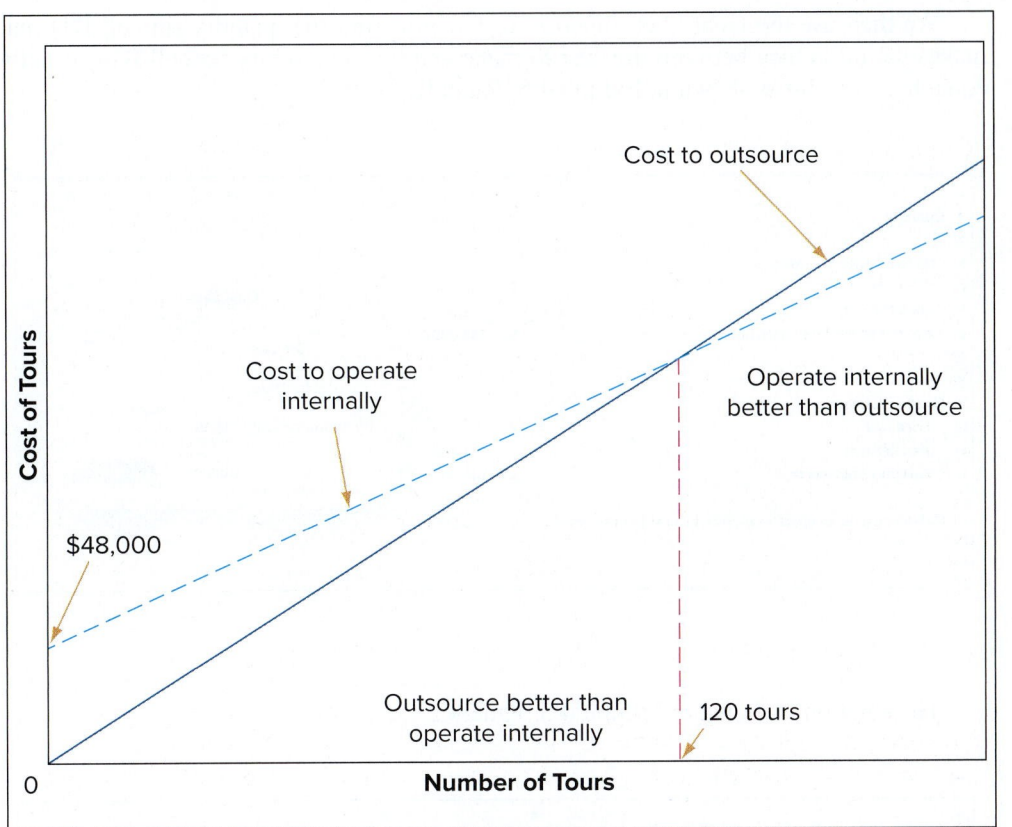

Exhibit 4.4
Graphical Analysis of Make-or-Buy Analysis—Desert Adventures

Exhibit 4.4 shows the result graphically. At a volume higher than 120 tours, the preferred alternative is to operate the tours internally; at a volume less than 120 tours, the preferred alternative is to pay the local tour operator to operate the tour (i.e., outsource).

We can also find the volume where the cost to operate the tours internally is the same as the cost to outsource by using the Goal Seek formula in Microsoft Excel®. The method is the same one we used to solve for the break-even point in Chapter 3. We want to find the point at which the difference between the cost to operate internally and the cost to outsource is equal to zero. Exhibit 4.5, Panel A, shows how the spreadsheet is set up.

	A	B
1	Quantity	100
2		
3	Cost to operate internally	
4	Fixed cost	$ 48,000
5	Variable cost	1,000
6	Total cost to operate internally	$ 148,000
7		
8		
9	Cost to outsource	
10	Fixed cost	$ –
11	Variable cost	1,400
12	Total cost to outsource	$ 140,000
13		
14	Difference (cost to operate internally – cost to outsource)	$ 8,000
15		

Exhibit 4.5, Panel A
Using Excel to Find the Quantity Where the Cost to Operate Internally Equals the Cost to Outsource

We then use the Goal Seek function in Excel to find the quantity (in cell B1) that makes the difference between the cost to make and the cost to buy (in cell B14) exactly equal to zero. This is shown in Exhibit 4.5, Panel B.

Exhibit 4.5, Panel B
Setting Up the Goal Seek Solution

	A	B	C	D	E	F	G
1	Quantity	100					
2							
3	Cost to operate internally						
4	Fixed cost	$ 48,000					
5	Variable cost	1,000			Goal Seek		
6	Total cost to operate internally	$ 148,000					
7				Set cell: B14			
8							
9	Cost to outsource			To value: 0			
10	Fixed cost	$ -					
11	Variable cost	1,400		By changing cell: B1			
12	Total cost to outsource	$ 140,000					
13				Cancel OK			
14	Difference (cost to operate internally – cost to outsource)	$ 8,000					
15							
16							
17							

The solution is shown in Exhibit 4.5, Panel C.

Exhibit 4.5, Panel C
The Goal Seek Solution

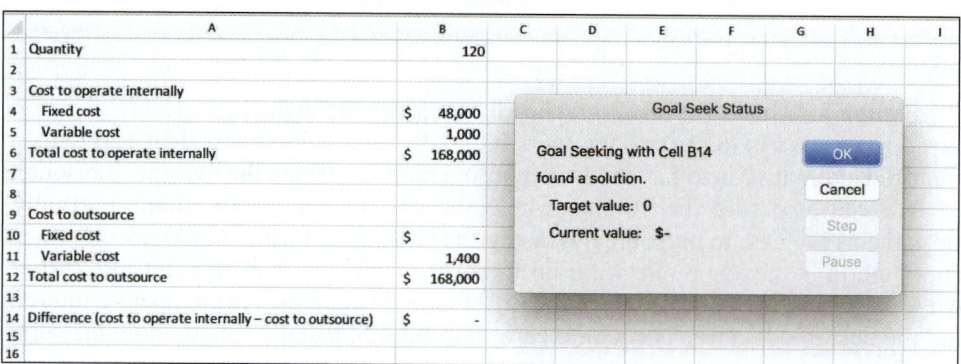

	A	B	C	D	E	F	G	H	I
1	Quantity	120							
2									
3	Cost to operate internally								
4	Fixed cost	$ 48,000			Goal Seek Status				
5	Variable cost	1,000							
6	Total cost to operate internally	$ 168,000		Goal Seeking with Cell B14			OK		
7				found a solution.					
8							Cancel		
9	Cost to outsource			Target value: 0					
10	Fixed cost	$ -		Current value: $-			Step		
11	Variable cost	1,400							
12	Total cost to outsource	$ 168,000					Pause		
13									
14	Difference (cost to operate internally – cost to outsource)	$ -							
15									
16									

Note the importance of separating fixed and variable costs for this analysis. Although determining differential costs usually requires a special analysis, the work can be made simpler if the accounting system routinely separates costs into fixed and variable components. The previous analysis would not have been possible for Desert Adventures had overhead costs not been separated into fixed and variable components.

Opportunity Costs of Making

Suppose that Desert Adventures' volume is projected to be 150 trips. If it is expected to be more than 120 trips, the preceding analysis indicates that Desert Adventures should continue to operate them. However, that analysis has not considered the opportunity cost of using the facilities to offer other services. Recall that opportunity costs are the forgone returns from not employing a resource in its best alternative use. Theoretically, determining opportunity cost requires considering every possible use of the resource in question.

Panel A

	Status Quo: Operate Desert Trips	Alternative: Outsource Desert Trips; Use Facilities for Aerial Service	Difference
Method 1			
Total cost of 150 trips.........	$222,000	$234,000	$12,000 higher
Opportunity cost of using facilities for desert trips	40,000	–0–	40,000 lower
Total costs, including opportunity costs	$262,000	$234,000	$28,000 lower

Differential costs decrease by $28,000, so accept the alternative.

Panel B

	Status Quo: Operate Desert Trips	Alternative: Outsource Desert Trips; Use Facilities for Aerial Service	Difference
Method 2			
Total cost of 150 trips	$222,000	$234,000	$12,000 higher
Opportunity cost of using facilities for desert trips	–0–	(40,000)	40,000 lower
Total costs, including opportunity costs	$222,000	$194,000	$28,000 lower

Differential costs decrease by $28,000, so accept the alternative.

If Desert Adventures has no alternative beneficial use for its facilities, the opportunity cost is zero, in which case the previous analysis would stand.

Suppose, however, that the building used to store and maintain equipment could be used for aerial excursions of the local canyons. This new service would provide a $40,000 differential contribution. If the aerial service is the best alternative use of the facility, the opportunity cost of using the facility to store and maintain equipment for desert trips is $40,000. In that case, Desert Adventures would be better off outsourcing the desert trips and using the facilities to offer the aerial service, as shown by the two alternative analyses of the problem in Exhibit 4.6.

Determining opportunity cost is typically very difficult and involves considerable subjectivity. Opportunity costs are not routinely reported with other accounting cost data because they are not the result of completed transactions. Some opportunity costs, such as the alternative use of plant facilities as just described, can be estimated in monetary terms; others, like the loss of control over production, might not be so readily quantified. When a benefit is forgone, it is not possible to determine whether the opportunity cost estimate is realistic.

The fact that they are difficult to estimate or subject to considerable uncertainty does not mean opportunity costs should be ignored (as they often are). Opportunity costs can represent a substantial part of the cost of an alternative, and the financial analyst has to be aware of the forgone opportunities when preparing the analysis.

Business Application   Insourcing

We have focused the analyses in this section on the question of whether the firm should continue to perform certain activities in the production of its product (or service) or if it should hire an outside organization (outsource). The analysis is the same if the decision is whether to start performing certain activities, currently done by other organizations, back in the firm itself. This is often referred to as "insourcing."

For many years, firms outsourced much of their information technology (IT) activities to firms, especially to those located in countries with relatively low cost but highly skilled IT workers. Some of the risks of doing so were discovered during the COVID pandemic of 2020:

> The shutdown in India and other outsourcing hotspots such as the Philippines has been a challenge for companies in Europe and North America that depend on these businesses to manage internal systems or run call centres.[1]

However, even before 2020, many firms found benefits in bringing much of their IT development back in-house. The retailing industry provides one such example, where firms are working rapidly to develop online shopping portals for their customers to compete with large online retail firms.

The idea is to be more hands-on in tailoring technology to their customers and employees—and to do it quickly—as they compete with the likes of Amazon.com Inc. in an increasingly digital retail landscape.[2]

The question, as always, is what technologies should be developed within the firm and what can be left to specialty IT providers. This will depend on a variety of factors, including cost, turnaround time, reliability, and knowledge of the customer and the firm. According to the chief information officer at Lowe's:

> "Wherever you have secret sauce that you want to put your fingerprints on, for your customer experience or for your own associates, . . . I've always believed that you should build your own technology."[3]

Sources:

1. B. Parkin, "India Coronavirus Shutdown Hits Outsourcing Groups," *Financial Times,* March 29, 2020.

2. J. Council, "Target and Lowe's Tech Execs Credit Talent, Culture for Insourcing Success," *The Wall Street Journal,* January 13, 2020.

3. Ibid.

Self-Study Question

2. EZ Stor, Inc., produces hard disk drives of various sizes for use in computer and electronic equipment. Costs for one product, EZ-5, follow for the normal volume of 5,000 per month:

Unit manufacturing costs		
Variable materials	$30	
Variable labor.	5	
Variable overhead.	5	
Fixed overhead	50	
Total unit manufacturing costs		$ 90
Unit nonmanufacturing costs		
Variable.	$10	
Fixed	20	
Total unit nonmanufacturing costs		30
Total unit costs.		$120

A proposal is received from an outside supplier who will test, produce, and ship 1,000 units per month directly to EZ Stor's customers as orders are received from EZ's salesforce. EZ Stor's fixed and variable nonmanufacturing costs would be unaffected, but its variable manufacturing costs would be cut by 20 percent per unit for those 1,000 units shipped by the contractor. EZ Stor's plant would operate at 80 percent of its normal level, and total fixed manufacturing costs per month would be cut by 10 percent. Should the proposal be accepted for a payment to the contractor of $38 per unit? (Revenue information is not needed to answer this question.)

The solution to this question is at the end of the chapter.

Decision to Add or Drop a Product Line or Close a Business Unit

Managers often must decide whether to add or drop a product line or close a business unit. Product lines that were formerly profitable may be losing market share to newer products. For example, DVD production may be having difficulty competing with new

	Total	Desert	Rafting	Aerial
Sales revenue	$910,000	$140,000	$350,000	$420,000
Cost of sales (all variable)	377,000	62,000	150,000	165,000
Contribution margin	$533,000	$ 78,000	$200,000	$255,000
Less fixed costs:				
Rent.	150,000	29,000	36,000	85,000
Salaries.	209,000	45,000	62,000	102,000
Marketing and administrative . . .	48,000	12,000	15,000	21,000
Operating profit (loss).	$126,000	$ (8,000)	$ 87,000	$ 47,000

Exhibit 4.7

Annual Product Line Income Statement— Desert Adventures

video-streaming technology. As a result, companies are forced to rethink their approach to the market.

Today, Desert Adventures sells three types of experiences: desert excursions (desert), rafting trips (rafting), and aerial excursions (aerial). Daniela Flores, the owner, is deciding whether to drop the desert trips because the volume of those trips has declined. Exhibit 4.7 shows the financial statements prepared by Desert Adventures' accountant.

Although the economics of dropping the desert trips appeared favorable, the manager asked the accountant to investigate which costs were differential (that is, avoidable in this case) if the desert trips were dropped. The accountant reported the following:

- All variable costs of sales for that line could be avoided.
- All salaries presently charged to desert trips, $45,000, could be avoided.
- None of the rent could be avoided.
- Marketing and administrative costs of $8,000 could be avoided.

The accountant prepared the differential cost and revenue analysis shown in Exhibit 4.8 and observed the following:

- Assuming that the sales of the other product lines would be unaffected, sales would decrease by $140,000 from dropping the desert trips.
- Variable cost of sales of $62,000 would be saved by dropping the product line.
- Fixed costs of $53,000 ($45,000 in salaries and $8,000 in marketing and administrative expenses) would be saved.
- In total, the lost revenue of $140,000 exceeds the total differential cost saving by $25,000. Thus, the net income for Desert Adventures for the year would have been $25,000 lower if desert tours had been dropped.

The discrepancy between what is shown on the product line financial statements and the differential analysis stems from the assumptions about differential cost. The financial

	Status Quo: Keep Desert Trips	Alternative: Drop Desert Trips	Difference
Sales revenue	$910,000	$770,000	$140,000 decrease
Cost of sales (all variable)	377,000	315,000	62,000 decrease
Contribution margin	$533,000	$455,000	$ 78,000 decrease
Less fixed costs:			
Rent	150,000	150,000	–0–
Salaries	209,000	164,000	45,000 decrease
Marketing and administrative	48,000	40,000	8,000 decrease
Operating profit (loss)	$126,000	$101,000	$ 25,000 decrease

Exhibit 4.8

Differential Analysis—Desert Adventures

statement presented in Exhibit 4.7 was designed to calculate department profits, not to identify the differential costs for this decision. Thus, managers relying on operating profit calculated after all cost allocations, including some that are not differential to this decision, would incorrectly conclude that the product line should be dropped. Financial statements prepared in accordance with generally accepted accounting principles do not routinely provide differential cost information. Differential cost estimates depend on unique information that usually requires separate analysis.

The financial statement that was prepared on a contribution margin basis clearly reveals the revenues and variable costs that are differential to this decision. A separate analysis was required, however, to determine which fixed costs were differential. It is possible, of course, to prepare reports that reflect each product's contribution to companywide costs and profits. This product margin would include product revenues less all direct costs of the product and would exclude allocated costs.

Nonfinancial Considerations of Closing a Business Unit

Dropping a product line in some companies is equivalent to closing a business unit. For example, many auto assembly plants are used for specific models, and if those models are dropped, managers will consider closing the plant. In the analysis of Desert Adventures' product line decision, we focused primarily on the financial aspects of the decision. When a business unit is closed, important nonfinancial impacts need to be considered. Plant closures, for example, have serious effects for the employees and communities involved. When General Motors eliminated production of the Chevrolet Cruze model in the United States and closed the manufacturing plant, Youngstown, Ohio, suffered thousands of job cuts. These nonfinancial considerations are often so important that they outweigh the financial issues.

As production processes become more flexible, companies can change the product mix at lower cost. Monty Rakusen/Digital Vision/Punchstock/Getty Images

Product Choice Decisions

Another common managerial decision is determining what products or services to offer. This choice directly affects costs. Many companies are capable of producing a large variety of goods and services but may be limited in the short run by available capacity. For instance, Desert Adventures may have to decide whether to use its limited space to continue to sell desert trips or expand its sale of aerial excursions. In another case, staffing issues may cause a hospital to decide between adding a new intensive care unit and expanding its obstetrics ward.

We usually think of product choices as short-run decisions because we have adopted the definition that in the short run, capacity is fixed, but in the long run, it can be changed. In the long run, the constraints on available capacity can be overcome by capacity addition, but in the short run, capacity limitations require choices.

For example, Desert Adventures offers its clients framed photos of their experience. They offer two types of frames—wood or metal—which they purchase from a local supplier, Southwestern Frames. For now, assume that Southwestern Frames can sell all the frames it produces. Its cost and revenue information is presented in Exhibit 4.9.

Southwestern can sell 15,000 metal frames or 15,000 wooden frames, or any combination totaling 15,000, to break even. The contribution margin of each product is the same, so the profit-volume relationship is the same regardless of the mix of products produced and sold.

	A	B	C	D	E	F	G	H	I
1			Metal Frames			Wood Frames			
2	Price		$ 50			$ 80			
3	Less variable costs per unit								
4	Material		8			22			
5	Labor		8			24			
6	Overhead		4			4			
7	Contribution margin per unit		$ 30			$ 30			
8									
9	Fixed costs							Total	
10	Manufacturing							$ 300,000	
11	Marketing and administrative							150,000	
12								$ 450,000	
13									
14									

Exhibit 4.9

Revenue and Cost Information—Southwestern Frames

Southwestern's objective is to maximize the contribution from its sale of frames, but which should it produce—metal or wood? Without knowing either Southwestern's maximum production capacity or the amount of that capacity used to produce one product or the other, we might say that it doesn't matter because both products are equally profitable. But because capacity is limited, that answer is incorrect if Southwestern uses its capacity at a different rate for each product.

Suppose that Southwestern's capacity is limited to 20,000 machine-hours per month. This limitation is known as a **constraint.** Further assume that machines may be used to produce either two metal frames or one wooden frame per machine-hour.

With a constrained resource, the important measure of profitability is the **contribution margin per unit of scarce resource** used, not the contribution margin per unit of product. In this case, metal frames are more profitable than wooden frames because metal frames contribute $60 per machine-hour (= $30 per metal frame × 2 metal frames per hour), but wooden frames contribute only $30 per machine-hour

constraints
Activities, resources, or policies that limit or bound the attainment of an objective.

contribution margin per unit of scarce resource
Contribution margin per unit of a particular input with limited availability.

	A	B	C	D	E	F	G	H
1			Metal Frames			Wood Frames		
2	Price		$ 50			$ 80		
3	Less variable costs per unit							
4	Material		8			22		
5	Labor		8			24		
6	Overhead		4			4		
7	Contribution margin per unit		$ 30			$ 30		
8								
9	Fixed costs							Total
10	Manufacturing							$ 300,000
11	Marketing and administrative							150,000
12								$ 450,000
13								
14	Machine hours per unit		0.5			1.0		
15	Machine hours used		7,500			12,500		20,000
16	Machine hours available							20,000
17								
18	Quantity		15,000			12,500		
19								
20	Profit		$ 375,000					
21								

Exhibit 4.10

Screenshot of the Data for Metal and Wooden Frames

(= $30 per wooden frame × 1 wooden frame per machine-hour). The hours required to produce one frame times the contribution per hour equals the contribution per frame.

For the month, Southwestern could produce 40,000 metal frames (= 2 per hour × 20,000 hours) or 20,000 wooden frames (= 1 per hour × 20,000 hours). If it produces only metal frames, Southwestern's operating profit would be $750,000 (= 40,000 metal frames × a contribution of $30 each − fixed costs of $450,000). If only wooden frames are produced, Southwestern's operating profit would be only $150,000 (= 20,000 wooden frames × a contribution margin of $30 each − $450,000). By concentrating on the product that yields the higher contribution per unit of scarce resource, Southwestern can maximize its profit.

We can also use Microsoft Excel's Solver function to find the optimal product mix when there are constraining resources, such as a limited number of machine-hours. Exhibit 4.10 shows the data for Southwestern's decision regarding the production of wooden and metal frames. The data on machine-hours and the profit calculation are added to the basic product data in Exhibit 4.9.

Before we use Solver to find the optimum product mix, we need to ensure that the Solver Add-In is installed in Excel. Click on the "Data" tab. If "Solver" appears as an option, it is installed and you do not need to do anything. If Solver is not installed, choose File ⇒ Options ⇒ Add-ins ⇒ Manage Excel options ⇒ Go. Click on "Add-ins." Select "Solver Add-in" in the section "Inactive Application Add-ins." Select "Go." A dialog box will open, as shown in Exhibit 4.11. Check the "Solver Add-in" box and click "OK." You will be guided through the process required to add the Solver module.

With Solver installed, we can use it to find the optimum product mix. The spreadsheet in Panel A of Exhibit 4.12 shows the setup for the problem. Click on the "Data" tab and then select "Solver" from the menu bar, and the dialog box shown in Panel A of Exhibit 4.12 will open. In the edit box "Set Objective," enter the cell address for the profit formula. In the next line, click the radio button "Max," signifying you want to maximize profit. In the edit box "By Changing Variable Cells," enter the cell addresses of the quantities for the two products. In the edit box "Subject to the Constraints," enter the constraints on the problem.

Exhibit 4.11

Installing the Solver Module

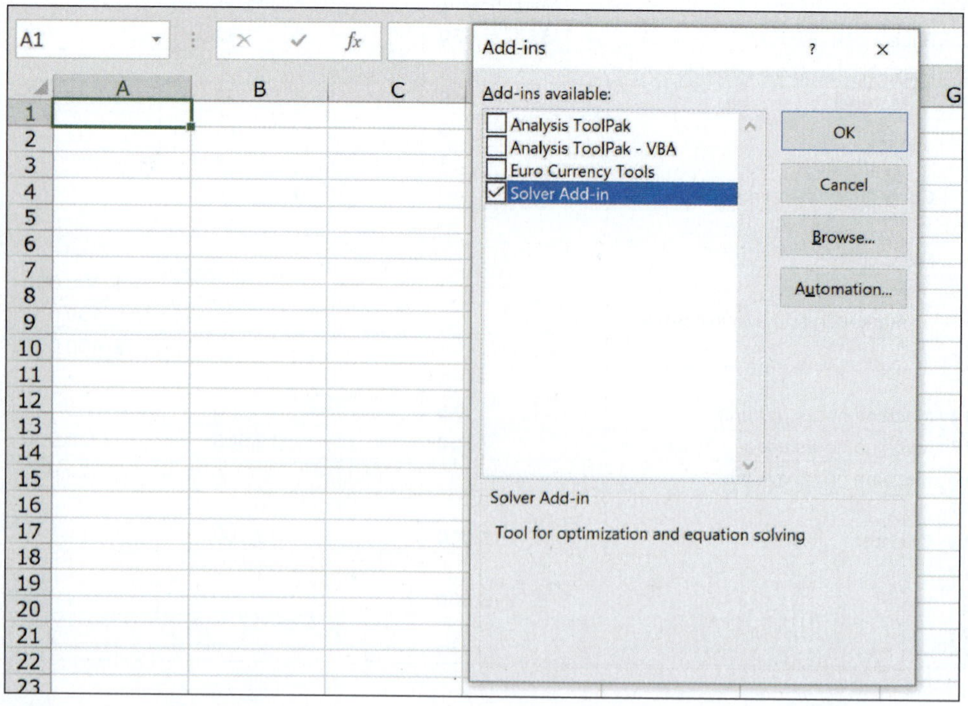

Exhibit 4.12   The Solver Solution to the Optimum Product Mix

Panel A

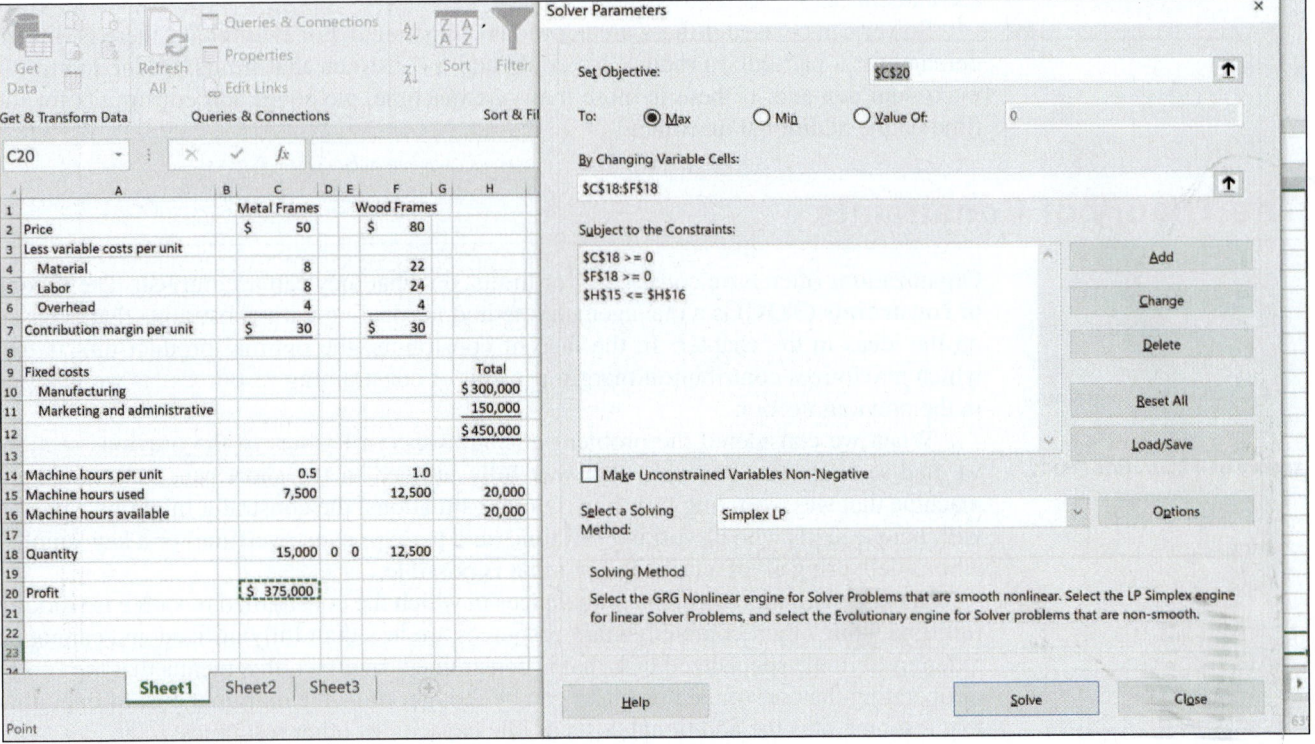

Panel B

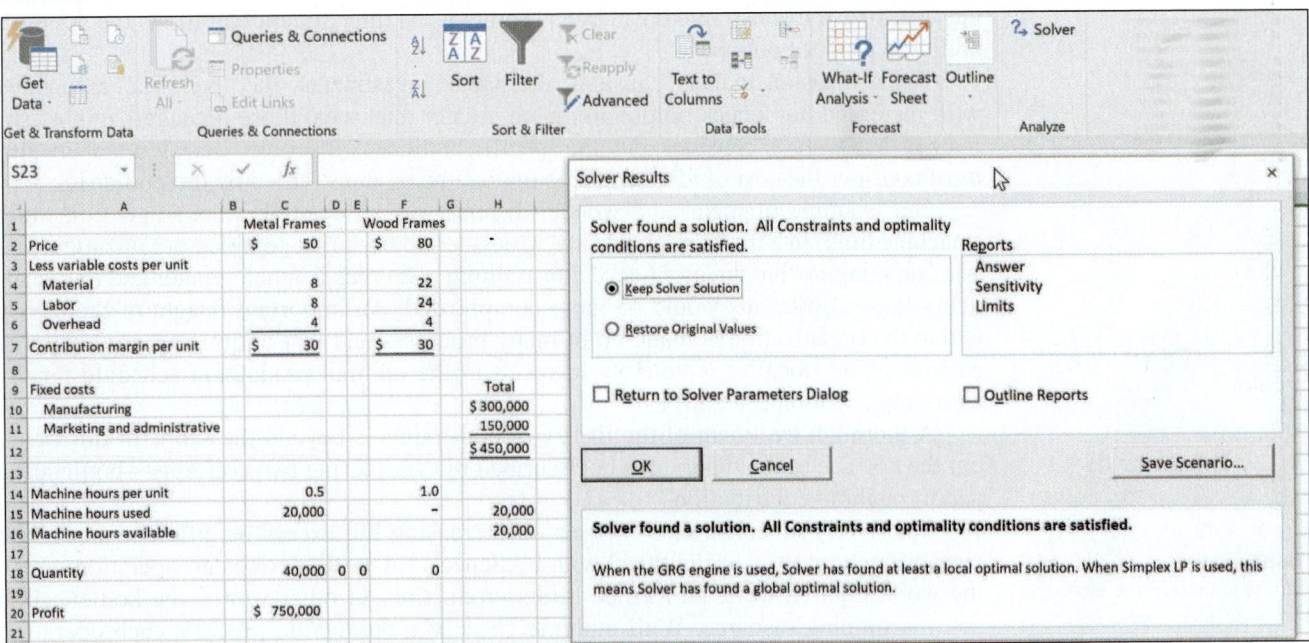

For Southwestern's decision problem of metal versus wooden frames, there are three constraints. The first two require that the amount produced be greater than or equal to zero. The third constraint states that the total machine-hours required for the selected production quantities be less than or equal to the total machine-hours available (20,000). Click "Solve."

The results are shown in Panel B of Exhibit 4.12. The optimum solution is to produce 40,000 metal frames and no wooden frames, which is exactly what our earlier analysis recommended.

Solver can be used if there are additional constraints. For example, if there is limited demand for a particular product, we could add a constraint that limits production to the maximum demand. If there is more than one machine, we could add constraints for the time on the additional machines.

The Theory of Constraints

LO 4-5

Understand and apply the theory of constraints.

theory of constraints (TOC)
Focuses on revenue and cost management when faced with bottlenecks.

Organizations often have constraints, or limits, on what they can accomplish. The **theory of constraints (TOC)** is a management method for dealing with constraints that is based on the ideas in the chapter: In the face of constraints, the optimal product mix is that which maximizes contribution margin per unit of constraining resources, as we just saw in the previous section.

When we considered the problem of Southwestern Frames in the previous section, we had to adapt to a resource that was fully utilized in the short run, for example, a machine that was operating full time. In other situations, the constraint might be a person with unique skills who is working full time (and perhaps even overtime) or a key supplier who is delivering all of a critical input that is possible.

These constraints can create imbalances in which the constrained resource is working full time while other, complementary resources are less than fully utilized and cannot be redeployed in the specialized task that is constrained. In effect, this means that the "cost" of operating the constrained resource can be thought of as the marginal cost of operating that resource plus the additional costs of idle capacity of other resources.

In the theory of constraints, we learn that maximizing the output of the constrained resource is the best route to increased marginal revenues. Even if one could increase the output of other processes, it would not matter (and would produce no incremental revenue) because the constrained resource is acting as an impediment that limits the system's ability to produce output.

When decision makers consider alternative investments, the "benefits" associated with increased bottleneck output are much greater than what those managers might estimate if they were to consider only the specific bottleneck resource. Decision makers also must consider the cost of idle resources that are being constrained by the bottleneck.

Our example of metal and wooden frames was an example of a single constraint (machine time) in a medium-sized firm. Consider now a large, complex organization, and you can imagine that the number of constraining resources is much greater and that managing these constraints would be more complicated. An important insight of the theory is that the organization is made up of many processes and that optimizing production at each machine (locally) is unlikely to result in the optimal production schedule for the entire organization (globally).

A thorough treatment of the theory of constraints is beyond the scope of this book, but the essence of the theory can be described by considering two concepts—bottlenecks and throughput contribution.[3]

bottleneck
Operation where the work required limits production.

The theory of constraints focuses on increasing the excess of differential revenue over differential costs when faced with bottlenecks. A **bottleneck** is an operation where the work required to be performed limits production. In other words, the bottleneck is the constraining resource. With multiple parts of a production process, each operation depends on the preceding operations. One operation cannot be started until the previous one has completed its work.

---

[3] For a more complete treatment of the theory of constraints, see E. M. Goldratt and J. Cox, *The Goal* (North River Press, 1992). For the role of the cost accountant in the theory of constraints, see Institute of Management Accountants, *Statements on Management Accounting,* "Theory of Constraints (TOC) Management System Fundamentals" (IMA, 1999).

For example, Southwestern Frames has a single machine used to produce two products (metal and wooden frames). At peak times, when both types of frames are being produced, it is likely that one of the products will have to wait for the machine. The machine is the bottleneck in the system.

The theory of constraints focuses on such bottlenecks. It encourages managers to find ways to increase profits by relaxing constraints and increasing throughput. At Southwestern, this means finding ways to process frames at peak times.

The theory of constraints focuses on three factors:

1. *The rate of throughput contribution.* **Throughput contribution** equals sales dollars minus direct materials costs and other variable costs such as energy and piecework labor.
2. *Minimizing investments.* Investments are inventories, equipment, buildings, and other assets used to generate throughput contribution.
3. *Minimizing other operating costs.* Other operating costs are all operating costs other than direct materials and other variable costs. Other operating costs are incurred to earn throughput contribution; they include most salaries and wages, rent, utilities, and depreciation.

throughput contribution
Sales dollars minus direct materials costs and variables such as energy and piecework labor.

The objective of the theory of constraints is to maximize throughput contribution given investments and operating costs. The theory of constraints assumes a short-run time horizon and few variable costs. In most versions of the theory, only materials, purchased parts, piecework labor, and energy to run machines are considered variable. Most direct labor and overhead costs are assumed fixed. This is consistent with the ideas that the shorter the time period, the more costs are fixed and that the theory of constraints focuses on the short run. Generally, this assumption about cost behavior seems reasonable, but it is important to remember that the approach is ultimately to maximize the contribution margin (the difference between price and all variable costs) per unit of the constraining resource.

Self-Study Question

3. On-the-Move, Inc., manufactures two types of roof racks for automobiles: BikeRac and KayakRac. Data concerning selling prices and costs for each unit follow:

	BikeRac	KayakRac
Selling price	$100	$80
Materials (variable)	26	23
Direct labor (variable)	5	4
Overhead (90% fixed)	50	40
Gross margin	$ 19	$13
Marketing costs (variable)	4	4
Administrative costs (fixed)	10	8
Profit	$ 5	$ 1

Management decided that at least 5,000 BikeRacs and at least 2,000 KayakRacs must be manufactured and sold each month.

The company's production facilities are limited by machine capacity in the Assembly Department. Each BikeRac requires 6 minutes and each KayakRac requires 3 minutes in

the Assembly Department. A total of 650 hours (39,000 minutes) is available per month in the Assembly Department; there are no other relevant constraints on production.

a. What is the contribution per unit for BikeRacs? For KayakRacs?

b. At the required monthly levels of production (5,000 BikeRacs and 2,000 KayakRacs), how many minutes are used in the Assembly Department?

c. Suppose there is unlimited demand for BikeRacs and KayakRacs at current prices. What production schedule (number of BikeRacs and number of KayakRacs) should On-the-Move adopt to maximize profit while meeting its constraint to produce and sell at least 5,000 BikeRacs and 2,000 KayakRacs?

d. Suppose demand is limited to 2,500 units of KayakRacs. What production schedule should On-the-Move adopt to maximize profit while meeting its constraint on the minimum levels for the two products?

The solution to this question is at the end of the chapter.

Key Takeaways

1. Differential analysis is a method of decision making that considers the revenues and costs of competing alternatives and how they differ among alternatives. The alternatives are compared to a benchmark, which is often the status quo.
2. Costs are a basis of pricing, even in cases where the price is determined in a market. For short-term decisions (those with less than a one-year time horizon), the relevant costs are the differential (often variable) costs. Full unit costs are often inappropriate for short-term decisions because they include fixed costs that will not change based on the decision. For long-term decisions, costs that are fixed in the short term might become relevant if they can be avoided or modified depending on the alternative.
3. Costs are a basis of production decisions. One example of production decisions where cost issues arise is whether to undertake an activity inside the firm (insourcing) or to hire another firm to perform the activity (outsourcing). A second is what products should be produced. In a setting where the capacity to perform some activity is constrained, the contribution margin of the constrained resource is the appropriate measure to consider when choosing among products.

SUMMARY

Differential cost analysis is an approach to decision making when the decisions affect costs and revenues, and, hence, profit.

The following summarizes key ideas tied to the chapter's learning objectives.

LO 4-1 Use differential analysis to analyze decisions. Decision makers use differential analysis, which compares alternative actions with the status quo, to select a specific course of action given several different alternatives.

LO 4-2 Use differential analysis to make pricing decisions. Differential analysis is particularly helpful in making short-run pricing decisions, an example of which is a special order. Once each alternative is presented with related revenues and costs, the alternative with the highest value is chosen.

LO 4-3 Apply several approaches for establishing prices based on costs for long-run pricing decisions. For long-term pricing decisions, differential analysis is less useful because most costs are differential in the long term. Other methods for long-term pricing decisions include life-cycle costing and target costing.

LO 4-4 Use differential analysis to make production decisions. Make-or-buy decisions are based on differential analysis in conjunction with nonquantitative factors such as dependability of suppliers and the quality of purchased materials. Companies often reduce the size of their operations by outsourcing their products (that is, by having an outside contractor produce them). In the short run, if the differential revenue from the sale of a product exceeds the differential costs required to provide it, the product generates profits, and the firm should continue production. For product mix decisions, a problem arises when limited amounts of resources are being fully utilized and must be assigned to multiple products. The objective of product mix decisions is to maximize the contribution margin per unit of scarce resource used. For example, if the scarce resource is the limited number of hours a machine can operate per month and the machine can make either of two products, the objective is to maximize the contribution per hour (or other unit of time) that each of the two products makes and then produce the product with the higher contribution margin per hour of machine-time used.

LO 4-5 Understand and apply the theory of constraints. The theory of constraints focuses on revenue and cost management when dealing with bottlenecks. The objective is to increase throughput contribution—sales dollars minus variable costs—to find ways to increase production at bottlenecks.

KEY TERMS

bottleneck, *156*
constraint, *153*
contribution margin per unit of scarce
   resource, *153*

differential analysis, *136*
differential costs, *136*
dumping, *143*
full cost, *137*

make-or-buy decision, *144*

peak-load pricing, *143*

predatory pricing, *142*

price discrimination, *143*

price-fixing, *144*

product life cycle, *141*

short run, *136*

special order, *137*

sunk cost, *136*

target cost, *142*

target price, *142*

theory of constraints (TOC), *156*

throughput contribution, *157*

REVIEW QUESTIONS

4-1. Fixed costs are often defined as "fixed over the short run." Does this mean that they are not fixed over the long run? Why or why not?

4-2. What is the difference between a sunk cost and a differential cost? Can a sunk cost ever be a differential cost?

4-3. What is the difference between short-run and long-run decisions? Give one example of each.

4-4. What costs are included in the full cost of a product? Is a product's full cost always the appropriate cost for decision makers to use?

4-5. What is a special order? What costs should be considered for a special order?

4-6. What are life-cycle product costing and pricing?

4-7. When is cost-plus pricing most likely to be used?

4-8. What do the terms *target cost* and *target price* mean? Explain how they are developed.

4-9. What are predatory pricing, dumping, and price discrimination? What role would a cost accountant play in determining whether dumping or price discrimination has occurred?

4-10. If we want to maximize profit, why do we use unit contribution margins in our analysis instead of unit gross margins?

4-11. Why are production constraints important in determining the optimal product mix?

4-12. What are some nonfinancial factors in decisions to drop a product line?

4-13. On what three main factors does the theory of constraints focus?

4-14. According to the theory of constraints, what are the ways to increase profit?

CRITICAL ANALYSIS AND DISCUSSION QUESTIONS

4-15. Consider the Business Application item "Outsourcing and the Effect of Corporate Culture." Would the impact on company culture show up in a differential cost analysis? If so, how? If not, should we ignore it?

4-16. As a marketing manager for an airline, would you sell a seat to a passenger who walked up to the gate at the last minute at the variable (marginal) cost? Why or why not? Do the costs from the accounting system include all relevant costs for the decision?

4-17. A company has several units of old-model telephones that it is selling for $10 per unit. The units cost $25 to produce. Is the company engaging in predatory pricing? Explain.

4-18. One of your acquaintances notes, "This whole subject of differential costing is easy; variable costs are the only costs that are relevant." How would you respond?

4-19. A manager in your organization just received a special order at a price that is "below cost." The manager points to the document and says, "These are the kinds of orders that will get you in trouble. Every sale must bear its share of the full costs of running the business. If we sell below our full cost, we'll be out of business in no time." What do you think of this remark?

4-20. Many airline frequent-flier programs upgrade elite (high-volume) flyers one, three, or five days in advance from economy to first class. What are the differential costs of doing this? What are the opportunity costs? What are the opportunity costs of not doing this?

4-21. Skywest Airlines is a regional airline operating in the Western U.S. Several large airlines (Alaska Airlines, for example) outsource some lower-volume routes to Skywest. Skywest flies planes painted with the Alaska colors and logo and uses the Alaska-branded interiors. Passengers buy their tickets from Alaska, which provides more convenience, especially for connecting flights. In making the decision to outsource flights to Skywest, what are some nonfinancial issues Alaska should consider?

4-22. If you are considering driving to a weekend resort for a quick break from school, what are the differential costs of operating your car for that drive? If you are considering buying a second car, what are the differential costs of that decision? Are they the same? Why or why not?

4-23. Management notes that the contribution from one product is higher than the contribution from a second product. Hence, it concludes that the company should concentrate on production of the first product. Under what, if any, conditions will this approach result in maximum profits?

4-24. Under what circumstances would fixed costs be relevant when management is making decisions in a multiproduct setting?

4-25. In the theory of constraints, what are ways to improve performance at the bottleneck?

EXERCISES

All applicable Exercises are included in Connect.

(LO 4-1, 2) **4-26. Special Orders**

Rowe Tool and Die (RTD) produces metal fittings as a supplier to various manufacturing firms in the area. The following is the forecasted income statement for the next quarter, which is the typical planning horizon used at RTD. RTD expects to sell 45,000 units during the quarter. RTD carries no inventories.

	Amount	Per Unit
Sales revenue	$1,170,000	$26.00
Costs of fittings produced	900,000	20.00
Gross profit.	$ 270,000	$ 6.00
Administrative costs	207,000	4.60
Operating profit.	$ 63,000	$ 1.40

Fixed costs included in this income statement are $292,500 for depreciation on plant and machinery and miscellaneous factory operations and $94,500 for administrative costs. RTD has received a request for 10,000 fittings to be produced in the next quarter from Endicott Manufacturing. Endicott has never purchased from RTD, although it has been a local company for many years. Endicott has offered to pay $20 per unit. RTD can easily produce the 10,000 units with its existing capacity. Production of the 10,000 units will incur all variable manufacturing costs but no fixed manufacturing costs. No administrative costs will be incurred because of the order.

Required

a. What impact would accepting this special order have on operating profit?

b. Should RTD accept the order?

(CPA adapted)

(LO 4-1, 2) **4-27. Special Orders**

Nardin Outfitters has the capacity to produce 12,000 of its special arctic tents per year. The company is currently producing and selling 5,000 tents per year at a selling price of $900 per tent. The cost of producing and selling one tent follows:

Variable manufacturing costs	$440
Fixed manufacturing costs.	90
Variable selling and administrative costs	80
Fixed selling and administrative costs.	50
Total costs.	$660

The company has received a special order for 500 tents at a price of $600 per tent from Chipman Outdoor Center. It will not have to pay any sales commission on the special order, so the variable selling and administrative costs would be only $45 per tent. The special order would have no effect on total fixed costs. The company has rejected the offer based on the following computations:

Selling price per tent	$600
Variable manufacturing costs	440
Fixed manufacturing costs	90
Variable selling and administrative costs	45
Fixed selling and administrative costs	50
Net profit (loss) per tent	$ (25)

Required

a. What is the impact on profit for the year if Nardin Outfitters accepts the special order? Show computations.

b. Do you agree with the decision to reject the special order? Explain.

4-28. Pricing Decisions and Special Orders   (LO 4-1, 2)

Parkview Fish Tacos sells tacos for $4.50 each. The cost of each taco follows:

Materials (food)	$1.35
Labor	0.55
Variable overhead	0.25
Fixed overhead ($7,200 per month, 4,500 tacos per month)	1.60
Total costs per taco	$3.75

One of Parkview's regular customers asked the company to fill a special order of tacos at a selling price of $3.50 each for a youth basketball tournament at the local school. Parkview has capacity to fill it without affecting total fixed costs for the month. Parkview's general manager (and owner and cook) was concerned about selling the tacos below the cost of $3.75 and has asked for your advice.

Required

a. Prepare a schedule to show the impact on Parkview's profits of providing 300 tacos in addition to the regular production and sales of 4,500 tacos per month.

b. Based solely on the data given, what is the lowest price per taco at which the special order can be filled without reducing Parkview's profits?

c. What other factors might the general manager want to consider in setting a price for the special order?

4-29. Pricing Decisions and Special Orders   (LO 4-1, 2)

Dwight Furniture makes desks specially designed for small spaces, such as studio apartments and extended-stay hotels. Each desk sells for $110 (without chair). The cost of each desk follows:

Materials	$36
Labor	41
Variable overhead	6
Fixed overhead ($208,000 per month, 13,000 units per month)	16
Total costs per unit	$99

The local university is building a new dorm and asked Dwight for a special price of $90 per desk for an order of 900 desks. Dwight's can fill the order using existing capacity without affecting total fixed costs for the month. However, because the sale would be to a state agency, Dwight would have to file specified compliance documents with the state purchasing office. Dwight's manager estimates that the time and expenses incurred by this filing will amount to $7,200 and are independent of the number of desks ordered. Dwight's manager is unsure whether to accept this order and wants your advice.

Required

a. Prepare a schedule to show the impact of providing the special order of 900 desks on Dwight's profits in addition to the regular production and sales of 13,000 desks per month.

b. Based solely on the data given, what is the lowest price per unit at which the desks could be sold to the university without reducing Dwight's profits?

c. What other factors might Dwight's manager want to consider in setting a price for the special order?

(LO 4-1, 2) **4-30. Special Order**

Alpena Corporation manufactures smartphone and tablet cases. The following is the cost of each unit.

Materials..	$ 7.20
Labor..	2.80
Variable overhead...	0.80
Fixed overhead ($1,800,000 per year; 150,000 units per year)......	12.00
Total..	$22.80

Decatur Devices has approached Alpena with an offer to buy 3,000 cases at a price of $17.50 each for its new specialty tablet designed for healthcare workers. The regular price of an Alpena case is $25. Alpena has the capacity to produce 180,000 units without increasing its fixed overhead. Decatur Devices requires that each case use its branding, which requires a more expensive embossing step. This will result in an additional $2.70-per-case labor cost. The material cost of the Decatur case will be the same as for the current models. The Decatur order will also require a one-time rental of embossing equipment for $7,200.

Required

a. Prepare a schedule to show the impact of filling the Decatur Devices order on Alpena's profits for the year.

b. Would you recommend that Alpena accept the order?

c. Considering only profit, determine the minimum quantity of cases in the special order that would make it profitable, assuming capacity is available.

(LO 4-1, 2) **4-31. Special Order**

Schweizer Products produces smart thermostats for home heating, ventilation, and air-conditioning (HVAC) systems and markets them to vendors who sell them under their own label. The cost of one of its thermostats follows.

Materials..	$27.00
Labor..	18.00
Variable overhead...	7.50
Fixed overhead ($405,000 per year; 45,000 units per year).........	9.00
Total..	$61.50

French Road DIY Stores, a chain of home improvement stores, has asked Schweizer to supply it with 3,000 thermostats for a special promotion French Road is planning at one of its larger outlets. French Road has offered to pay Schweizer a unit price of $60 per thermostat. The regular selling price is $90. The special order would require some modification to the basic model. These modifications would add $4.00 per unit in material cost, $2.00 per unit in labor cost, and $0.50 in variable overhead cost. Although Schweizer has the capacity to produce the 3,000 units without affecting its regular production of 45,000 units, a one-time rental of special testing equipment to meet French Road's requirements would be needed. The equipment rental would be $9,000 and would allow Schweizer to test up to 6,000 units.

Required

a.   Prepare a schedule to show the impact of filling the French Road order on Schweizer's profits for the year.

b.   Would you recommend that Schweizer accept the order?

c.   Considering only profit, determine the minimum quantity of thermostats in the special order that would make it profitable.

4-32. Special Orders and Capacity Constraints   (LO 4-1, 2)

Refer to the data for Rowe Tool and Die (RTD) in Exercise 4-26. Suppose RTD's capacity is limited to 50,000 units per quarter. Endicott will not accept any quantity other than the 10,000 units in the order.

Required

a.   What impact would accepting this special order have on operating profit?

b.   Should RTD accept the order?

4-33. Special Orders and Capacity Constraints   (LO 4-1, 2)

Refer to the data for Nardin Outfitters in Exercise 4-27. Suppose Nardin's capacity is limited to 5,300 per year. Chipman Outdoor Center will not accept any quantity other than the 500 tents in the order.

Required

a.   What is the impact on profit for the year if Nardin Outfitters accepts the special order? Show computations.

b.   Should Nardin accept the special order given the capacity constraint?

4-34. Target Costing and Pricing   (LO 4-3)

Whitmore Glassware makes a variety of drinking glasses and mugs. The company's designers have discovered a market for a 16-ounce mug with college logos. Market research indicates that a mug like this would sell well in the market priced at $26. Whitmore only introduces a product if it can earn an operating profit of 30 percent of costs.

Required

What is the highest acceptable manufacturing cost for which Whitmore would be willing to produce the mugs?

4-35. Target Costing and Pricing   (LO 4-3)

Riverdale Partners wants to introduce a new line of fragrances. Market research indicates that a potential fragrance would sell well in the market priced at $268.80 each. Riverdale requires an operating profit of 28 percent of costs.

Required

What is the highest acceptable manufacturing cost for which Riverdale would be willing to produce the fragrance?

4-36. Target Costing and Purchasing Decisions   (LO 4-3)

Mather, Inc. makes and sells enclosures for external hard drives. Mather management believes that a new model of enclosure made out of a hard plastic would sell well at a price of $17.00. Labor costs are estimated at $5.30 per unit and overhead costs would be $1.20 per unit. The major uncertainty is the price of the plastic. Mather is considering several vendors and is preparing for negotiations. Mather management insists on an estimated return on selling price of 24 percent.

Required

What is the most Mather can pay for the plastic per unit (per enclosure) and meet its profitability goal?

4-37. Target Costing   (LO 4-3)

Short Bakers makes baked goods for catered events and for sale at local grocery stores. The owner of Short Bakers believes that a new type of breakfast pastry would sell well for a price of $9 per dozen. Short estimates unit materials costs to be $4.25 for the pastry, and overhead costs would average $.55 per dozen. The local wage rate for direct labor is $18 per hour. Short has a goal of earning an operating profit of 20 percent of production costs for each of its products.

Required
What direct labor-hour input (hours per dozen) could Short Bakers allow for the new pastry and still achieve its profit goal?

(LO 4-4) **4-38. Make-or-Buy Decisions**
Coram Audio makes wireless headphones. Each pair of headphones comes with a travel case. Since its founding, Coram has manufactured its own travel cases. Recently, Holmur Travel Gear (HTG), a local outfitter that manufactures and sells backpacks, tent cases, and so on, contacted Coram and proposed that it produce the headphone travel cases. Based on management experience, Coram's cost per travel case is as follows (based on annual production of 40,000 units).

Direct materials	$10.00
Direct labor	21.20
Variable overhead	6.40
Fixed overhead	4.70
Total	$42.30

HTG has offered to sell the case to Coram for $39 each. The total order would amount to 40,000 travel cases per year. Coram's management decides that it will make the switch to HTG cases if Coram can save at least $12,000 per year. Accepting the offer would eliminate annual fixed overhead of $76,000.

Required
Should Coram continue to make the travel cases or buy them from HTG? Prepare a schedule that shows the differential costs per travel case.

(LO 4-4) **4-39. Make-or-Buy Decisions**
Harbortown Marine Products (HMP) manufactures and sells various fixtures for boat cabins. One fixture uses a specialized fitting that is not used in any other HMP product. The management of HMP has considered outsourcing the fitting for several years but has never identified a suitable supplier. HMP has collected the following data on the cost of the fitting:

Materials	$ 6.40
Labor	4.80
Manufacturing overhead	14.40
Total	$25.60

Rivard Fittings, a local auto supplier, contacts HMP and tells it that because of the loss of one of Rivard's customers, there is enough capacity to produce up to 5,000 units of the fitting monthly. Rivard has offered to sell HMP any quantity (up to 5,000 units monthly) at a price of $20 per fitting.

If Rivard supplies all of the 3,000 fittings currently produced by HMP, HMP will avoid all of the variable overhead associated with the fitting and one-third of the fixed overhead. Management estimates that variable overhead for the fitting is $4.80 per unit.

Required
Should HMP continue to make the fittings or buy them from Rivard Fittings? Prepare a schedule that shows the differential costs.

(LO 4-4) **4-40. Make or Buy with Uncertain Costs**
Refer to the facts in Exercise 4-39. Harbortown management is concerned about future changes in material prices arising from volatility in the commodities market.

Required
At what unit costs for materials would HMP be just indifferent between making and buying the 3,000 units of the fitting if all other costs remain as predicted in Exercise 4-39?

4-41. Make or Buy—Insourcing

(LO 4-4)

Lantz Family Restaurant operates in a suburb of a major city. Recently, the managers at Lantz have noticed an increase in the use of delivery apps such as Grubhub and DoorDash by their customers. The average fee paid by Lantz for this service currently is $6 per delivery. The managers are considering starting their own delivery service that they estimate would attract about 75 percent of the current deliveries. (Not all customers will switch, even though the service would be free, because of the convenience of the app, habit, and other factors.)

Estimates by the financial consultant to Lantz are that the cost of the service, if provided by Lantz, would be $2.30 per delivery and an incremental $1,350 per month fixed costs. In an average month, 480 orders Lantz receives are to be delivered.

Required

Should Lantz Family Restaurant provide its own delivery service or continue to rely on other firms? Prepare a schedule that shows the differential costs.

4-42. Make or Buy—Insourcing

(LO 4-4)

Rathbone Industries produces and sells an instrument used in hospital monitoring systems. The instrument uses a specialized sensor that Rathbone currently purchases from Norfolk Electronix. Norfolk charges Rathbone $94 per sensor for the 12,000 sensors Rathbone requires annually.

Some manufacturing capacity recently opened up at Rathbone, and engineers at the company believe that it would be possible for Rathbone to produce the sensor internally. Unit cost estimates to make the sensors are shown here:

Direct materials	$37
Direct labor	42
Manufacturing overhead	20
Total unit cost	$99

Of the $20-per-unit overhead cost, $8 is for variable overhead specifically used by the sensor. The remaining $12 unit cost is fixed overhead that remains from the previously used capacity. Forty percent of the fixed overhead can be avoided if the sensor is produced outside the firm by Norfolk Electronix.

Required

a. Should Rathbone Industries make the sensor (insource) or continue to purchase it from Norfolk Electronix (outsource)? Why?

b. What nonfinancial factors would you recommend managers at Rathbone consider before making their decision?

4-43. Make or Buy—Capacity Constraints

(LO 4-4)

Refer to the information in Exercise 4-42. A new customer has approached Rathbone Industries and asked if it could make an instrument for the customer's medical testing equipment. If it chose to take on this work, Rathbone would not be able to make the sensor currently purchased from Norfolk Electronix. The potential new customer will not allow Rathbone to outsource the production of its instrument.

Negotiations are continuing, but the companies agree that if Rathbone will make the instrument, the quantity to be delivered will be 24,000 units annually. Rathbone estimates that the annual incremental cost will be $678,000.

Required

The new customer has proposed a price of $31 per unit for the instrument. At this price, would you change your recommendation made in Exercise 4-42 concerning outsourcing the sensor to Norfolk Electronix? Explain.

4-44. Dropping Product Lines

(LO 4-4)

Lamothe Kitchen and Bath makes products for the home, which it sells through major retailers and remodeling (do-it-yourself, or DIY) outlets. One product that has had varying success is a ceiling fan for the kitchen. The fan comes in three sizes (36-inch, 44-inch, and 54-inch), which are designed for various kitchen sizes and cooling requirements. The chief financial officer (CFO) at

Lamothe has been looking at the segmented income statement for the fan and is concerned about the results for the 36-inch model.

	36 Inch	44 Inch	54 Inch
Revenues	$357,000	$557,600	$335,400
Variable costs.	223,600	277,680	155,500
Fixed costs allocated to products.	139,230	217,464	130,806
Operating profit (loss).	$ (5,830)	$ 62,456	$ 49,094

If the 36-inch model is dropped, the revenue associated with it would be lost and the related variable costs saved. In addition, the company's total fixed costs would be reduced by 25 percent.

Required
Should Lamothe Kitchen and Bath drop the 36-inch model product line? Prepare a differential cost schedule like the one in Exhibit 4.8 to support your recommendation.

(LO 4-4)   **4-45. Dropping Product Lines**
Gilbert Canned Produce (GCP) packs and sells three varieties of canned produce: green beans, sweet peas, and tomatoes. The company is currently operating at 82 percent of capacity. Worried about the company's performance, the chief marketing officer is considering dropping the canned sweet peas. If sweet peas are dropped, the revenue associated with it would be lost and the related variable costs saved. In addition, the company's total fixed costs would be reduced by 15 percent.
Segmented income statements appear as follows:

	Green Beans	Sweet Peas	Tomatoes
Sales	$81,500	$107,000	$128,000
Variable costs.	57,200	100,300	104,300
Contribution margin	$24,300	$ 6,700	$ 23,700
Fixed costs allocated to each product line	9,780	12,840	15,360
Operating profit (loss).	$14,520	$ (6,140)	$ 8,340

Required
Prepare a differential cost schedule like the one in Exhibit 4.8 to indicate whether Gilbert Canned Produce should drop the sweet pea product line.

(LO 4-4)   **4-46. Dropping Product Lines**
ASA Tours operates a network of offices around the globe specializing in local tours given by local residents and academics. Depending on the year, it operates at between 60 and 70 percent of capacity, which consists of locals who meet the criteria required by ASA. ASA operates three types of tours. Web-based tours consist of live stream broadcasts with a limit of 15 participants. Group tours consist of small groups of no more than eight people. Finally, there are individual tours, which are personalized tours for no more than six people.
Segmented income statements for a typical month appear as follows:

Routes	Web-Based	Group	Individual
Sales	$102,800	$270,600	$176,600
Variable costs.	21,100	214,300	99,300
Fixed costs allocated to tours	32,896	86,592	56,512
Operating profit (loss).	$ 48,804	$ (30,292)	$ 20,788

ASA is considering dropping the group tours. If these tours are dropped, the revenue associated with the tours would be lost and the related variable costs saved. In addition, the company's total fixed costs would be reduced by 35 percent.

Required

a.   Prepare a differential cost schedule like the one in Exhibit 4.8 to indicate whether ASA Tours should drop the group tours.

b.   Are there other factors you would recommend ASA Tours consider before making the decision?

4-47. Theory of Constraints
(LO 4-5)

Wing Sporting Goods (WSG) is a small company that makes two models of a metal baseball bat—Sport and Collegiate. Both models are produced on a single machine. The price and costs of the two models are

	Sport	Collegiate
Price per unit	$190	$375
Variable cost per unit	$70	$137
Machine minutes per unit	6	14

The one machine that is used to produce both models has a capacity of 29,400 machine-minutes per quarter. Fixed manufacturing costs per quarter are $350,000.

Required

a.   Suppose that the maximum unit sales in a quarter that WSG can achieve is 6,000 units of each product. How many units of each model should WSG produce in a quarter?

b.   Suppose that the maximum unit sales in a quarter that WSG can achieve is 4,200 units of each product. How many units of each model should WSG produce in a quarter?

4-48. Theory of Constraints
(LO 4-5)

Brandon Technology makes two models of a specialized sensor for the aerospace industry. The difference in the two models relates to the required accuracy of the sensor. The Standard model is used for most normal operations while the High-Performance model is used for high-altitude and specialized missions. Before shipment, the two models are passed through a machine that, among other things, certifies the accuracy of the sensor. The company only has one testing machine. The price and costs of the two sensor models are shown here:

	Standard	High-Performance
Price per sensor	$ 52	$ 96
Variable cost per sensor	$ 34	$ 41
Testing hours per sensor	0.04	0.11

The testing machine used for both models has a capacity of 8,250 hours annually. Fixed manufacturing costs are $2,400,000 annually.

Required

a.   Suppose that the maximum annual unit sales that are possible for Brandon Technology are 250,000 units of the Standard model and 80,000 of the High-Performance model. How many units of each sensor model should Brandon Technology produce annually?

b.   Suppose that the maximum annual unit sales that are possible for Brandon Technology are 150,000 units of the Standard model and 50,000 of the High-Performance model. How many units of each sensor model should Brandon Technology produce annually?

(LO 4-5) **4-49. Theory of Constraints**

Leach Finishing makes various metal fittings for the construction industry. Three of the fittings, models X-12, X-24, and X-30, require grinding on a patented machine of which Leach has only one. The cost-of-production information for the three products follows:

	X-12	X-24	X-30
Price per fitting	$27	$43	$62
Variable cost per fitting	$12	$19	$36
Units per hour of grinding	18.0	12.5	10.0

The testing machine used for both models has a capacity of 2,750 hours annually. Fixed manufacturing costs are $480,000 annually.

Required

a. Suppose that Leach Finishing can sell at most 54,400 units of any one fitting. How many units of each fitting model should Leach Finishing produce annually?

b. Suppose that Leach Finishing can sell at most 14,400 units of any one fitting. How many units of each fitting should Leach Finishing produce annually?

PROBLEMS  All applicable Problems are included in Connect.

(LO 4-1, 2) **4-50. Special Order**

Oakland Precision Products (OPP) manufactures and sells a variety of scales for the kitchen and office. OPP sells primarily to kitchenware stores, discount stores, and so on. Two of the scales it produces for kitchen use are the Cook and Baker. The Cook is a basic food scale. The Baker has a greater capacity and special features that facilitate adjusting baking recipes for more or fewer people. The following information is available:

Costs per unit	Cook	Baker
Direct materials	$ 1.60	$14.40
Direct labor.............................	0.80	3.20
Variable overhead........................	0.60	2.40
Fixed overhead	8.00	15.00
Total cost per unit	$11.00	$35.00
Price.....................................	$15.00	$45.00
Units sold	230,000	120,000

The average wage rate is $32 per hour. Variable overhead varies with the quantity of direct labor-hours. The plant has a capacity of 20,000 direct labor-hours, but current production uses only 17,750 direct labor-hours.

Required

a. A nationwide kitchenware chain has offered to buy 30,000 Cook models and 15,000 Baker models if the prices are lowered to $10 and $35, respectively, per unit. If OPP accepts the offer, how many direct labor-hours will be required to produce the additional scales? How much will the profit increase (or decrease) if OPP accepts this proposal? Prices on regular sales will remain the same.

b. Suppose that the kitchenware chain has offered instead to buy 50,000 Cook models at $10 per unit and 30,000 Baker models at $35. This customer will purchase the models only in an all-or-nothing deal. That is, OPP must provide all 50,000 units of the Cook model and 30,000 units of the Baker model or nothing at all. In view of its capacity constraints, OPP will reduce sales to regular customers as needed to fill the special order. How much will the profits change if the order is accepted? Assume that the company cannot increase its production capacity to meet the extra demand, if required.

c. Answer the question in requirement (*b*) assuming instead that the plant can work overtime. Direct labor costs for the overtime production increase to $45 per hour. Variable overhead costs for overtime production are $6 per hour more than for normal production.

4-51. Special Orders

(LO 4-1, 2)

Miles Audio produces and sells car audio systems. It specializes in receivers and currently offers two models. The Growler is a high quality but affordable unit that the company produces for sale in auto parts and electronics stores. The Maniac is sold almost solely to individuals and high-end car stereo installers. The Maniac is only produced to order. In other words, the Maniac is not kept in inventory and is only produced when a customer orders one. Based on estimates of next quarter's business, the financial staff at Miles has produced the following forecasted income statement.

	Growler	Maniac	Total
Number of systems....................	2,400	450	2,850
Sales revenue	$480,000	$405,000	$885,000
Materials............................	$ 91,200	$ 69,750	$160,950
Labor...............................	108,000	101,250	209,250
Materials inspection	54,720	41,850	96,570
Factory lease	33,150	17,850	51,000
Utilities	14,690	7,910	22,600
Miscellaneous factory costs	27,300	14,700	42,000
Sales and administration			142,130
Total costs.........................			$724,500
Operating profit....................			$160,500

Firm orders have already been placed with Miles for the 450 Maniac systems reflected in the forecasted quarterly income statement. Materials inspection varies with material cost. The labor wage rate at Miles (excluding variable overhead) is $30 per hour. The factory lease, utilities, and miscellaneous factory costs are allocated to the product lines based on the amount of floor space occupied. Sales and administration costs are not allocated to the two product lines.

Lanoo Custom Systems, a custom car audio shop, has called Miles and asked about placing an order for the upcoming quarter for 100 units of the Maniac. Miles Audio is already scheduled to work at capacity in the next quarter and would have to give up some other business to fulfill this order. Miles is committed to the orders for the Maniac it already has accepted but can reduce the number of Growler systems produced in the next quarter to 1,900. Miles would not be able to make up the losses from the reduced Growler sales as the market is quite competitive and customers for this relatively standard system will buy another product. Miles also is expecting to be operating at close to full capacity for the foreseeable future, which is another reason the lost Growler systems could not be replaced later. The customer is willing to pay a premium price of $940 for the special order. The factory lease, utilities, miscellaneous factory costs, and sales and administration would not be affected by the special order.

Required

a. Should Miles accept the offer from Lanoo Custom Systems? Explain.
b. What is the minimum price Miles should accept to take the special order from Lanoo Custom Systems?
c. What are the other factors, if any, besides price that Miles should consider?

4-52. Pricing Decisions

(LO 4-2)

Frederick's Motivational Workshops (FMW) offers hands-on workshops by noted experts on various business and life-skill topics, such as sales techniques, negotiation, and leadership. FMW works exclusively with corporate clients, so that the participants in any one workshop are all from the same organization. Halleck Industries has contacted FMW about offering one or more workshops on change management to be hosted on the FMW campus. Halleck is considering three alternatives. The first would be a single workshop for 10 senior leaders. The second would be for 5 workshops for 90 functional area managers (18 managers per workshop).The third would be 10 workshops for 150 fast-track managers in the operations and human resources areas. At this time,

Halleck plans to only select one, if any, of the three alternatives based on the proposed price from FMW. The financial staff at FMW has put together the estimated differential cost related to the three alternatives:

Initial costs to design workshop	
(independent of the number of workshops)...................	$ 5,400
Materials and other costs per participant	
(notes, meals, events, and so on)...........................	200
Differential Direct Labor Costs:	
One workshop...	$12,000
Five workshops..	36,000
Ten workshops...	50,000

In addition to the preceding differential costs, FMW allocates fixed general and administrative costs to workshops such as these on a direct-labor-cost basis, at a rate of 125 percent of direct labor costs (excluding design costs). For example, if direct labor costs are $100, FMW would also charge the job $125 for general and administrative costs. FMW prices workshops at cost plus a 25 percent fee with a 10 percent surcharge on total costs (not including the fee) if only one workshop is given. Cost equals the design costs plus materials costs plus differential labor costs plus allocated fixed costs for the purpose of setting the price to quote prospective customers. FMW is not limited by any labor or other capacity constraint.

Required

a. Assume FMW's bid equals the total cost, including fixed costs allocated to the job, plus the 25 percent markup on cost (along with any appropriate surcharge). What should FMW bid for each of the alternatives being considered by Halleck Industries?

b. Compute the differential cost (including design costs) and the contribution to profit for each of the three alternatives.

c. The human resources director at Halleck is looking over the bids and tells FMW that the bids for the one- and five-workshop alternatives are acceptable, but the bid for the 10 workshops is simply too high. Instead, Halleck says it will accept the 10-workshop proposal if the bid is 80 percent of FMW's proposed bid. The sales director at FMW is concerned about deviating from company practice. Considering only the financial impact and not current bidding practice, should FMW lower the bid as requested by Halleck Industries? Explain.

(LO 4-2)   **4-53. Pricing Decisions**

Pierson Landscape Architects (PLA) develops and sells plans for various types of gardens and outdoor spaces. Customers buy the plans and then install the garden, the water feature, or other installation by themselves or by hiring a contractor who will take the plans and complete the job. The cost of producing one typical set of plans is

Average Cost per Plan:	
Labor, including architects and landscapers	$ 537
Variable overhead, including supplies.........................	213
Fixed production costs (equipment and so on)	344
Fixed marketing and administrative costs....................	496
Total cost per set of plans	$1,590

The fixed costs allocated to each plan are based on the assumption that the studio produces 2,500 sets of plans annually.

Required

Treat each question independently. Unless stated otherwise, PLA charges $2,000 per set of plans.

a. How many sets of plans must PLA produce annually to earn zero profits (break even)?

b. Market research estimates that a price increase to $2,250 per set of plans would decrease annual volume to 2,000 sets of plans. The financial analyst at PLA estimates that the variable cost per set of plans and the total fixed costs would remain unchanged if PLA produced and sold 2,000 sets of plans at the new price. How would a price increase affect profits?

c. PLA is currently operating at the normal volume of 2,500 sets of plans annually. Blaine's Home Station, a chain of home and garden stores, has asked PLA for a set of 500 plans exclusively for sale through Blaine's. Capacity at PLA is limited to 2,800 sets of plans annually, and because of the shortage of qualified individuals, PLA will not be able to increase capacity and provide the appropriate training in time to meet the extra demand. However, the plans for Blaine's could be produced at a total variable cost (labor plus overhead) of only $600 because some of the plans would have common features. Blaine's has asked PLA for a special price of $1,200 because of the size of the order and the reduced variable costs. Total fixed costs will be the same whether or not PLA accepts the special order. Would you suggest PLA accept the special order? Explain.

d. Refer to the situation presented in requirement (c). PLA and Blaine's are still negotiating on price for the special order. What is the lowest price that PLA could charge and be no worse off for taking this order?

4-54. Comprehensive Differential Costing Problem   (LO 4-1, 2, 4)

Medbury Communications Systems (MCS) produces mobile radios for arctic and other harsh environments. The costs to manufacture and market the radios at the company's normal quarterly volume of 12,000 units are shown in the following table:

Unit manufacturing costs		
Materials (variable)	$ 80	
Labor (variable)	120	
Overhead (variable portion)	40	
Overhead (fixed portion)	96	
Total unit manufacturing costs		$336
Unit marketing costs		
Variable	$ 40	
Fixed	112	
Total unit marketing costs		152
Total unit costs		$488

Required

Assume that no connection exists among the situations described in each question below unless otherwise stated. Each is independent. Also assume a regular selling price of $600 per unit unless otherwise stated. Ignore income taxes and other costs that are not mentioned in the accompanying table or in the question itself.

a. Market research estimates that quarterly volume could be increased to 14,000 units, which is well within production capacity limitations if the price were cut from $600 to $525 per unit. Assuming that the cost behavior patterns implied by the data in the table are correct, would you recommend taking this action? What would be the impact on quarterly sales, costs, and income?

b. On April 1, the federal government offers MCS a contract to supply 2,000 radios to military bases for a June 30 delivery. Because of an unusually large number of rush orders from its regular customers, MCS plans to produce 16,000 units during the second quarter, which for MCS runs from April 1 through June 30. This level of production will use all available capacity for the quarter. If it accepts the government order, MCS would lose to a competitor 2,000 units normally sold to regular customers. The government contract would reimburse its "share of quarterly manufacturing costs" plus pay a $90,000 fixed fee (profit). (No variable marketing costs would be incurred on the government's units.) What impact would accepting the government contract have on second quarter income? (*Hint: Part of the question is to figure out the meaning of "share of quarterly manufacturing costs."*)

c. MCS has an opportunity to enter a highly competitive foreign market. An attraction of the foreign market is that its demand is greatest when the domestic market's demand is quite low; thus, idle production facilities could be used without affecting domestic business. An order for 4,000 radios is being sought at a below-normal price to enter this market. For this order, shipping costs will total $64 per unit; total (marketing) costs to obtain the contract will be $6,400. No other variable marketing costs would be required on this order, and it would not affect domestic business. What is the minimum unit price that MCS should consider for this order of 4,000 radios?

d. An inventory of 500 units of an obsolete model of the radio remains in the stockroom. These must be sold through regular channels (thus incurring variable marketing costs) at reduced prices or the inventory will soon be valueless. What is the minimum acceptable selling price for these units?

e. A proposal is received from an outside contractor who will make and ship 4,000 radios per quarter directly to MCS's customers as orders are received from MCS's sales representatives. The fixed marketing cost at MCS would be unaffected, but its variable marketing costs would be cut by 20 percent for these 4,000 units produced by the contractor. MCS's plant would operate at two-thirds of its normal level, and total fixed manufacturing costs would be cut by 40 percent. What in-house unit cost should be used to compare with the quotation received from the supplier? Should the proposal be accepted for a price (that is, payment to the outside contractor) of $390 per unit?

f. Assume the same facts as in requirement (e) except that the idle facilities would be used to produce 3,200 modified radios per month for use in high-security operations. These modified radios could be sold for $720 each, while the costs of production would be $440 per unit variable manufacturing expense. Variable marketing costs would be $80 per unit. Fixed marketing and manufacturing costs would be unchanged whether the original 12,000 regular radios were manufactured or the mix of 8,000 regular radios plus 3,200 modified radios were produced. Should MCS accept the proposal from the outside contractor at a price of $390 per unit?

(LO 4-4)   **4-55. Make or Buy**

Spinnaker Museum of Sailing (SMS) is a popular tourist site in a coastal town. The museum boasts a large collection of both current sailing exhibits and historical displays focused on ocean exploration and maritime adventures. SMS, like many museums, is a not-for-profit organization, but it charges for admission and operates a highly rated book shop on-site.

The museum has several operating divisions. One of them, the Visitor Division, is responsible for activities related to visits from the public, such as collecting admission fees, providing coat and bag check service, operating the book store, and so on. The museum's financial director has provided the forecasted cost of the Visitor Division for the upcoming year, beginning July 1. SMS expects 250,000 visitors in the next fiscal year.

Labor (variable)	$2,200,000
Miscellaneous (variable)	1,125,000
Supervision (fixed)	560,000
Miscellaneous (fixed)	595,000

The average admission fee is $30 per visitor, and the average visitor spends 2.5 hours in the museum.

The museum director has received a proposal from Gitre Operations to provide staff and some other services for the Visitor Division. Gitre has proposed a fee of $15 per visitor. If SMS accepts the proposal from Gitre, SMS would avoid all labor cost and 60 percent of the variable miscellaneous costs. The museum would also save 70 percent of the supervision costs and 40 percent of the miscellaneous fixed costs.

Required

a. Do you recommend that SMS accept the proposal from Gitre to provide staff and other services to the Visitor Division? Show calculations.

b. The marketing director informs the museum director that based on the latest economic conditions, the museum now is forecasting only 150,000 visitors for the upcoming fiscal year. Do you want to change the recommendation you made in requirement (a)? Show calculations.

c. At what forecasted attendance level will SMS be indifferent between staffing the Visitor Division internally and accepting the proposal from Gitre Operations? Show calculations.

d. The museum director is confident that the museum will attract 250,000 visitors next year. The Board of Directors at SMS is encouraging the director to negotiate a lower fee with Gitre

Operations. With 250,000 visitors, what fee would make SMS indifferent between staffing the Visitor Division internally and accepting the proposal from Gitre Operations? Show calculations.

4-56. Make or Buy—Visualization

Refer to the information in Problem 4-55 requirement *(c)* for Spinnaker Museum of Sailing. The museum director continues to be a bit uncertain about the attendance for the upcoming fiscal year and would like a graphical representation of the analysis done to arrive at the decision whether to staff internally or outsource to Gitre Operations.

(LO 4-4)

Required

Prepare a visualization of the analysis you used to arrive at the decision on outsourcing.

4-57. Make or Buy—Insourcing

(LO 4-4)

Platt Instruments produces and sells medical devices for both home and professional use. One line of products that has been consistently profitable for Platt is its range of sphygmomanometers (blood pressure monitors). Platt sells professional models to hospitals and doctors' offices. Platt also sells a simpler model for personal use. The professional models sell for an average of $160 per unit, and the personal models sell for an average of $50 unit.

For the last few years, Platt has focused on manufacturing the professional model and has outsourced the production, but not distribution, of its personal use models. Platt has contracted with Westmoreland Products, which produces a wide range of electronic products, to produce the monitor. The contract can be cancelled by either party with 30 days' notice. The arrangement has worked well, and there have been no significant problems with delivery or quality of the outsourced monitors. Platt pays a flat $25 for each monitor Westmoreland supplies. In addition to the Westmoreland fee, Platt incurs a shipping and handling cost (variable overhead cost) of $1 per unit on the monitors it buys from Westmoreland. In addition, monthly (overhead) fixed costs of shipping, packaging, and handling amounting to $60,000 are incurred for the personal monitor products. Current and expected demand for personal monitors is 7,500 units per month.

Managers at Platt are considering bringing the personal monitors back inside Platt where they would both produce and distribute the units. The financial and manufacturing staff have put together some estimates of costs if the monitors were to be produced internally. Based on their analysis, direct materials cost would be $8 per unit and direct labor costs would be $4 per unit. These costs are both variable. Under the outsourcing arrangement with Westmoreland, Platt pays neither any material nor labor cost.

Estimating the overhead costs that Platt would incur if it produced the monitors internally was a bit more difficult, but the staff analysts at Platt estimated that by using Westmoreland, Platt is saving 75 percent on the variable overhead costs (shipping and handling) and 60 percent on fixed overhead costs associated with the personal monitor.

Required

a.   Given the current demand of 7,500 units of the personal monitor, should Platt Instruments end its contract with Westmoreland Products and start producing the personal monitors internally?

b.   The chief marketing officer (CMO) has done some research on consumers' interests in health and believes that demand for the personal monitor could be 10,000 units monthly. Would the answer you made in requirement *(a)* change?

c.   At what monthly quantity will Platt be indifferent between producing the personal monitor internally and continuing with the current contract with Westmoreland Products?

d.   The CMO is confident in the monthly forecast of 10,000 monitors. Suppose the board of directors at Platt is not convinced that producing the monitors internally is a good idea. At what price per unit for an outsourced monitor paid to Westmoreland would Platt be indifferent between producing the personal monitor internally and continuing with the current contract with Westmoreland Products?

4-58. Make or Buy—Visualization

(LO 4-4)

Refer to the information in Problem 4-57 requirement *(c)* for Platt Instruments. The CMO would like a visual representation of the analysis done to arrive at the decision whether to staff internally or outsource to Westmoreland Products. The company can then more easily discuss the implications of demand changes and outsourcing and insourcing decisions.

Required

Prepare a visualization of the analysis that will help the CMO and other managers at Platt analyze and make the outsourcing/insourcing decision.

(LO 4-4)   **4-59. Make or Buy**

Florida Kitchens produces high-end cooking ranges. The costs to manufacture and market the ranges at the company's volume of 3,000 units per quarter are shown in the following table:

Unit manufacturing costs		
Variable costs	$1,440	
Fixed overhead	720	
Total unit manufacturing costs		$2,160
Unit nonmanufacturing costs		
Variable	$ 360	
Fixed	840	
Total unit nonmanufacturing costs		1,200
Total unit costs		$3,360

The company has the capacity to produce 3,000 units per quarter and always operates at full capacity. The ranges sell for $4,000 per unit.

Required

a.   Florida Kitchens receives a proposal from an outside contractor, Burns Electric, who will manufacture 1,200 of the 3,000 ranges per quarter and ship them directly to Florida's customers as orders are received from the sales office at Florida. Florida would provide the materials for the ranges, but Burns would assemble, box, and ship the ranges. The variable manufacturing costs would be reduced by 40 percent for the 1,200 ranges assembled by Burns. Florida's fixed nonmanufacturing costs would be unaffected, but its variable nonmanufacturing costs would be cut by 60 percent for these 1,200 units produced by Burns. The Florida plant would operate at 60 percent of its normal level, and total fixed manufacturing costs would be cut by 20 percent. What in-house unit cost should be compared with the quotation received from Burns Electric? Should the proposal be accepted for a price (that is, payment to the contractor) of $840 per unit?

b.   Assume the same facts as in requirement (a) but assume that the idle facilities would be used to produce 320 specialty ranges per quarter. These ranges could be sold for $18,000 each, while the costs of production would be $12,650 per unit variable manufacturing cost. Variable marketing costs would be $400 per unit. Fixed nonmanufacturing and manufacturing costs would be unchanged whether the original 3,000 regular ranges were manufactured or the mix of 1,800 regular ranges plus 320 specialty ranges was produced. Considering this opportunity to use the freed-up space, what is the maximum purchase price per unit that Florida Kitchens should be willing to pay Burns Electric to assemble regular ranges? Should the Burns proposal of $840 per unit be accepted?

(LO 4-3)   **4-60. Target Costing**

King Bathroom Fixtures (KBF) makes faucets, basins, and so on primarily for home use and sold through major retail chains. The design team at KBF has been working on a unique design to provide reasonable pressure while still conserving water. The market is quite competitive, and KBF analysts believe that the fixture could sell for a unit price of $36.40.

The cost accounting team at KBF has estimated the following manufacturing costs for the new design.

Direct materials	$19.75
Direct labor	5.90
Manufacturing overhead	8.85
Total	$34.50

An operating profit of 12 percent of manufacturing costs is required for all new products at KBF without the explicit consent of the top executive team. At KBF, operating margin is defined as revenues less manufacturing costs, all divided by manufacturing costs.

Required

a. Suppose KBF uses cost-plus pricing, setting the price equal to manufacturing costs plus 12 percent of manufacturing costs. What price should it charge for the fixture?

b. Suppose KBF uses target costing. What is the highest acceptable manufacturing cost at which KBF would be willing to produce the fixture?

c. If you were in charge of the decision to produce the fixture or not, would you produce it? Explain your answer.

4-61. Target Costing   (LO 4-3)

Nagle Devices produces medical instruments, primarily for hospital and medical office use. A new design for its best-selling hospital thermometer has the marketing team considering possibly entering the home market. This would be new for Nagle because it would be selling to large chain retailers and online resellers rather than directly to the user.

Management at Nagle Devices requires an operating profit of 30 percent of manufacturing costs. After doing some market research in this new market, the marketing team has determined that the new thermometer could sell for no more than $46.80.

The manufacturing department at Nagle estimates the following manufacturing costs for the new thermometer:

Direct materials	$21.20
Direct labor	8.70
Manufacturing overhead	7.10
Total	$37.00

Required

a. Suppose Nagle Devices uses cost-plus pricing, setting the price to manufacturing costs plus 30 percent of manufacturing costs. What price should it charge for the thermometer?

b. Suppose Nagle Devices uses target costing. What is the highest acceptable manufacturing cost at which Nagle Devices would be willing to produce the thermometer?

c. If you were in charge of the decision whether to produce the thermometer or not, would you? What are some of the factors you would consider?

4-62. Target Costing   (LO 4-3)

Mcquade Equipment is considering a new product for the road construction industry. The analyst has collected some information about the product design, summarized as follows:

Prime cost per unit	$5,600
Conversion cost per unit	2,800
Direct labor cost per unit	1,200

The marketing group at Mcquade believes this product can be a success if sold at a price of $8,250 per unit. Mcquade desires an operating profit (as a percentage of costs) of 25 percent on products of this type.

Required

a. Will Mcquade achieve its target operating profit based on these product characteristics?

b. A product engineer suggests that they are still uncertain about the direct material costs. By how much would direct material cost have to fall or by how much could they increase direct material cost per unit such that the desired operating profit would be met exactly?

(LO 4-3)   **4-63. Target Costing**

Lakeside Accessories manufactures computer backpacks, messenger bags, and other items for carrying electronics, documents, and so on. In developing a new bag for the newest release of laptops, the design group has estimated the following unit costs:

Fabric.	$26
Leather	$7
Direct labor hours — Sewing.	1.4
Direct labor hours — Assembly.	1.0

Direct labor at Lakeside Accessories earns $25 per hour for sewing and $20 per hour for assembly. Overhead is estimated for new products at 40 percent of direct labor cost. Lakeside has a target operating profit of 21 percent (as a percentage of costs) on this type of product. The marketing team has estimated that a price of $125 is expected for the bag.

Required

a.   Will Lakeside Accessories achieve the target operating profit for this product?

b.   The product manager, who is the company's main advocate for this new design, tells you that he plans to have all the labor (sewing and assembly) done by the assembly labor because "it is not all that difficult." Under the new plan for producing the bags, will Lakeside Accessories achieve the target operating profit for this bag?

(LO 4-3)   **4-64. Target Costing and Ethical Issues**

Refer to the details in Problem 4-63.

Required

What are the issues, ethical and otherwise, that arise with the product manager's suggestion?

(LO 4-4)   **4-65. Decision Whether to Add or Drop**

Hazlett & Family is organized into two geographic markets: Northern and Southern. The company makes an off-road vehicle for recreation and agricultural use. The vehicle is sold in three models, depending on the power and options. The three models, from least expensive to most expensive, are the H-L, H-LX, and H-LXS. The company's financial staff has prepared the following forecasted income statement for the upcoming fiscal year (in thousands of dollars):

	Total	Northern	Southern
Sales revenue	$58,500	$45,000	$13,500
Cost of goods sold	45,450	34,875	10,575
Gross margin	$13,050	$10,125	$ 2,925
Marketing costs	$ 4,725	$ 2,700	$ 2,025
Administrative costs	2,340	1,800	540
Total marketing and administrative	$ 7,065	$ 4,500	$ 2,565
Operating profits	$ 5,985	$ 5,625	$ 360

Management has expressed special concern with the Southern market because of the extremely poor return on sales. This market was entered a year ago because it seemed like the best opportunity for growth. Hazlett & Family knew that it would take some time to build profitability in the market, but there has been no noticeable change in the low returns over time.

The financial staff has also prepared product-line information to help the managers of the company decide whether to leave the Southern market.

	Products		
	H-L	H-LX	H-LXS
Sales revenue	$22,500	$18,000	$18,000
Variable manufacturing costs as a percentage of sales revenue	50%	75%	65%
Variable marketing costs as a percentage of sales revenue	5	2	3

Sales revenue by market and product are as follows (in thousands of dollars):

	Northern	Southern
H-L.......................	$18,000	$4,500
H-LX.....................	13,500	4,500
H-LXS	13,500	4,500

Marketing costs that are not listed as variable are fixed for the period and separable by market. Fixed marketing costs assigned to the Southern market would be saved if that market were eliminated. Eliminating the Southern market will not affect administrative costs or fixed manufacturing costs.

Required

a. Assuming there are no alternative uses for Hazlett & Family's present capacity, would you recommend dropping the Southern market?

b. Prepare the forecasted annual income statement showing contribution margins by products. Do not allocate fixed costs to products.

c. It is believed that a new model can be ready for sale next year if Hazlett decides to go ahead with continued research. The new product would replace H-LX and can be produced by simply converting equipment presently used in producing the H-LX model. This conversion will increase fixed costs by $450,000 annually. What must be the minimum annual contribution margin for the new model to make the changeover financially feasible?

(CMA adapted)

4-66. Decision Whether to Add or Drop (LO 4-4)

Greenview Dairies produces a line of organic yogurts for sale at supermarkets and specialty markets in the Southeast. Economic conditions and changing tastes have resulted in slowing demand growth. After recently expanding capacity, the company is now operating at 65 percent of the new capacity. The company is considering dropping one of the yogurt flavors, mixed berry, in hopes of improving profitability. If the mixed berry variety is dropped, the revenue associated with it will be lost and the related variable costs saved. The production manager estimates that the fixed costs will also be reduced by 30 percent.

The following quarterly product line income statements (in thousands of dollars) are available:

Product	Vanilla	Peach	Mixed Berry
Sales	$21,190	$33,280	$27,820
Variable costs..................................	14,300	26,065	25,090
Contribution margin	$ 6,890	$ 7,215	$ 2,730
Fixed costs allocated to each product line.........	3,055	4,615	3,900
Operating profit (loss).........................	$ 3,835	$ 2,600	$ (1,170)

Required

a. Prepare a schedule like the one in Exhibit 4.8 to indicate whether Greenview Dairies should drop the mixed berry line.

b. One of the sales reps for Greenview heard about the possibility of dropping the mixed berry line and warned the marketing manager that it was a mistake to consider the three products independently. Based on experience from stocking local grocery shelves, he knows that when customers stop seeing a particular flavor, they sometimes switch to a competitor, even for flavors Greenview might still sell. The financial staff sent a request to marketing asking for estimates of possible losses on the sales of other products. The marketing group responded that perhaps 5 percent of vanilla sales and 10 percent of peach sales would be lost if the mixed berry flavor is dropped. Would this new information change your recommendation in requirement (a)?

(LO 4-4) **4-67. Decision Whether to Close a Store**

Sparta Fashions owns four clothing stores, where it sells a wide range of women's fashions, from casual attire to formal wear. In addition, it rents formal wear and gowns for special occasions. At the end of last year, the financial statements showed that although Sparta Fashions as a whole was comfortably profitable, the Downtown store had shown a substantial loss. The following is the income statement for the Downtown store store for year just ended:

Sparta Fashions
Downtown Store
Store-Level Income Statement

Sales		$1,072,500
Cost of goods sold		924,000
Gross margin		$ 148,500
Costs:		
Salaries, wages, and commissions[a]	$84,150	
Lease[b]	26,565	
State taxes[c]	4,125	
Insurance on inventory.	30,360	
Depreciation[d]	12,375	
Administration and general office[e]	33,000	
Interest for inventory carrying costs[f]	7,425	
Total costs.		198,000
Loss		$ (49,500)

[a] These costs would be saved if the store were closed.

[b] The lease is cancellable and would be saved if the store were closed.

[c] Assessed annually on the basis of average inventory on hand each month.

[d] 12 percent of cost of departmental equipment. The equipment has no salvage value, and Sparta Fashions would incur no costs in scrapping it.

[e] Allocated on the basis of store sales as a fraction of total company sales. Management estimates that 15 percent of these costs allocated to the Downtown store could be saved if the store were closed.

[f] Based on average inventory quantity multiplied by the company's borrowing rate for three-month loans.

The Downtown store is the only one in the chain that shows an annual loss, and members of the board believe it should be closed. Both the corporate operations and finance staff agree that closing the Downtown store will not negatively impact sales at the other stores.

Required

What would you recommend Sparta Fashions do about the Downtown store? Should it be closed? Why?

(LO 4-4) **4-68. Closing a Plant**

Wexford Manufacturing and Mining (WMM) operates several factories in three western states: Arizona, Montana, and Utah. WMM's home office is located in Idaho. All three factories produce the same product, and Wexford's management believes it can operate more efficiently by closing one of the three factories. The financial staff at Wexford has put together an estimate (in thousands of dollars) of operations for the upcoming fiscal year:

	(Thousand of Dollars)			
	Total	Arizona	Montana	Utah
Sales revenue	$44,000	$22,000	$8,000	$14,000
Fixed costs				
Plant.	$11,000	$ 5,600	$2,600	$ 2,800
General administration.	3,500	2,100	300	1,100
Variable costs.	14,500	6,650	3,600	4,250
Allocated corporate costs	5,000	2,250	1,000	1,750
Total.	$34,000	$16,600	$7,500	$ 9,900
Operating profit.	$10,000	$ 5,400	$ 500	$ 4,100

The sales price per unit is $250.

Looking at the financial statement, the results in the Montana factory seem troubling. WMM management has decided, as a result, to sell that factory's machinery and equipment and stop manufacturing by the end of this year. WMM expects that the proceeds from the sale of these assets would equal all termination costs. WMM, however, would like to continue serving most of its customers in that area if it is economically feasible and is considering one of the following three alternatives:

- Expand the operations of the Utah factory by using space presently idle. This move would result in the following changes in that factory's operations:

Increase over Utah's factory's current operations	
Sales revenue	55%
Fixed costs	
Factory	30
Administration	10

Under this proposal, variable costs would be $100 per unit sold.
- Enter into a long-term contract with a competitor that will serve that area's customers. This competitor would pay WMM a royalty of $60 per unit based on an estimate of 30,000 units being sold.
- Close the Montana factory and not expand the operations of the Utah factory.

Total allocated corporate costs of $5,000,000 will remain the same if the Utah factory is expanded (the first alternative above). If a competitor is used to serve the Montana market (the second alternative above), 65 percent of the corporate cost allocated to the Montana factory will be saved. If the Montana factory is closed and the Utah factory's operations are not expanded (the third alternative above), 80 percent of the corporate cost allocated to the Montana factory will be saved.

Required

To assist the management of WMM, prepare a schedule computing WMM's estimated operating profit from each of the following options:

a. Expansion of the Utah factory.

b. Negotiation of the long-term contract on a royalty basis.

c. Shutdown of the Montana operations with no expansion at other locations.

(CPA adapted)

4-69. Expanding Surgical Units in a Hospital   (LO 4-4)

Parkway Health System (PHS) has two divisions that are part of PHS but are located in separate buildings. The Extended Care Division performs typical hospital service including emergency care, surgeries, and surgical recovery. The Out-Patient Care Division performs surgeries where the patients are not required to stay overnight. When possible and assuming good medical practice warrants it, surgical patients are scheduled for the Out-Patient Care Division in an effort to manage costs. The Out-Patient Care Division routes surgical patients through three areas of the Division: (1) Surgery; (2) Tier I Post-Op, where patients rest until they are stabilized; and (3) Tier II Post-Op, where patients are stabilized but not yet ready to leave the facility. Daily capacities and activity levels are as follows:

	Surgery	Tier I Post-Op	Tier II Post-Op
Daily capacity (surgeries)...........	55	40	70
Daily activity (surgeries)............	40	40	40

The hospital receives an average of $1,200 per surgery, regardless of which division performs the surgery. (The surgeon's fee and the anesthesiologist's fee are billed separately.) The variable cost per surgery is $400 in the Out-Patient Care Division. There is sufficient demand for surgeries that the hospital could perform 65 surgeries per day. Surgeries not performed by the Out-Patient Care Division are sent to the Extended Care Division for operations. The variable cost per surgery in the Extended Care Division is $750, while the hospital still receives $1,200 per surgery.

PHS administrators are considering three alternatives to reduce the number of outpatients that have to be seen by the Extended Care Division:

1. Continue performing 40 surgeries per day in the Out-Patient Care Division and send the other 25 patients per day to the Extended Care Division.
2. Remodel the Out-Patient Care Division's Tier I and Tier II Post-Op rooms so that some of the Tier II space could be used for Tier I. This would cost $2,800 per day and enable the Out-Patient Care Division to perform 55 surgeries per day. They would then send 10 patients to the Extended Care Division's operating rooms.
3. Expand the facilities of the Out-Patient Care Division's surgery center at a differential cost of $6,000 per day so that it could perform 65 surgeries per day, and service 65 patients per day in Tier I Post-Op. That would mean the hospital would service 65 patients per day in Tier II Post-Op.

Required
Which of these alternatives should Parkway Health System choose? Explain your recommendation.

(LO 4-5)   **4-70. Theory of Constraints**
Refer to the information in Problem 4-69 for Parkway Health System. Regardless of your recommendation, the PHS administrators did not change operations (they chose the first alternative described in Problem 4-69). For this problem, assume that the expansion alternatives in Problem 4-69 are no longer possible.

During a meeting with the PHS administrators, a contractor working on an addition to the Extended Care Division's building says that his firm could remodel either the Tier I or Tier II Post-Op areas so that the capacity in those areas would increase by 10 patients per day. The contractor cannot give a price quote without a more detailed look at the areas but could provide one in a week.

Required
What is the maximum PHS would be willing to pay per day to extend the Tier I Post-Op area? The Tier II Post-Op area? Explain.

(LO 4-5)   **4-71. Theory of Constraints**
Ontario Audio makes a popular satellite radio receiver for over-the-road trucks and other professional uses. The two major parts of the radio are the electronics (receiver, speaker, and so on) and the metal case housing the radio. The electronics are manufactured at the Santa Rosa Plant, which sends the resulting kits to the company's Borman Plant. The case is manufactured at the Borman Plant and the electronics kit and completed case are assembled, also at the Borman Plant. Monthly capacities and production levels are as follows:

	Santa Rosa Plant (Electronics)	Borman Plant (Cases)
Monthly capacity	1,350	1,050
Monthly production.	1,050	1,050

Ontario Audio does not sell electronic kits or cases separately. The company could sell as many as 1,350 radios per month. The radios (electronics kit assembled and enclosed in the case) sell for $125 per radio and have a variable cost of $62 each.

Required

a.   Is there a bottleneck at Ontario Radio? If so, where is it?

b.   The Borman Plant manager tells managers at Ontario Audio that the plant could increase capacity by 300 cases (and radios) per week by producing cases in the evening after the normal shift. Producing in the evening would not affect the sales price or quantity. Variable cost per unit would increase by $20 for those produced in the evening because of the shift differential (overtime pay) for labor. Fixed costs would also increase by $11,000 per month. Should Ontario Audio produce cases (and radios) in the evening?

c.   Independent of the situation in requirement (b), Ontario Audio could add additional equipment and workers in the Borman Plant, which would increase its capacity by 300 cases (and radios) per month. This would not affect the sales price or variable cost per unit but would increase fixed costs by $21,000 per month. Should the company add the additional equipment and workers to the Borman Plant?

4-72. Theory of Constraints   (LO 4-5)

Senator Pet Foods makes a variety of canned and dried food for pets. The Center Street Manufacturing Campus is the site of the original Senator plant and is used solely for the production of its original variety of canned food for dogs. The production of the food requires roughly five steps: grinding, mixing, canning, cooking, and packaging. Grinding and mixing take place in the North Building on the campus. The raw, mixed food is then transported to the South Building, also on the campus, where it is canned, cooked, and packaged in cases of 12 cans. The cases are shipped daily and are never kept in inventory.

Weekly capacities and production levels (in cases) in the two buildings are as follows.

	North Bldg.	South Bldg.
Capacity (weekly)	10,000	15,000
Production (weekly)	10,000	10,000

The company could sell 12,000 cases weekly. The cases sell for $12 each and have a variable cost of $6 each. Fixed costs are $61,000 per week.

Required

a.   Is there a bottleneck at Senator Pet Foods' Center Street Campus? If so, where is it?

b.   The plant manager reports that capacity could be increased by 3,000 cases weekly in the North Building by producing on the weekend. Producing on the weekend would not affect the sales price. Variable cost per unit would increase by $1.50 for those cases produced on the weekend because of the premium paid to labor. Fixed costs would also increase by $7,800 per week. Should the Center Street Manufacturing Campus produce pet food on the weekend?

c.   The managers at the Center Street Manufacturing Campus are also studying increasing capacity in the North Building by adding additional personnel to clean and prepare the mixer between batches. This would increase its capacity in the North Building by 2,500 cases weekly. This would not affect sales price. Variable cost would increase by $0.75 per case for *all* units produced. Fixed costs will increase by $4,600 per week. Should the Center Street Campus expand the North Building's capacity by adding these additional workers? Consider this alternative independently of the situation in requirement (b).

(LO 4-4)   **4-73. Optimum Product Mix**

Williams Gear makes and sells three types of computer laptop sleeves: leather, fabric, and plastic. Management is trying to determine the most profitable mix. Sales prices, demand, and use of manufacturing inputs follow:

	Leather	Fabric	Plastic
Sales price	$160	$70	$40
Maximum quarterly demand (sleeves).	2,500	12,500	20,000
Input requirements per unit			
Direct material quantity per sleeve (ounces)	16	6	10
Direct material price per ounce of material	$4.25	$6.00	$2.20
Direct labor quantity per sleeve (hours)	0.9	0.4	0.3
Direct labor price per hour	$35	$35	$35

Other Costs	
Variable costs	
Factory overhead	$5 per direct labor-hour
Marketing	6% of sales price
Quarterly fixed costs	
Manufacturing	$70,000
Marketing	$15,000
Administration	$60,000

Williams has two production limits: (1) the demand for the individual sleeves (see maximum quarterly demand) and (2) 10,000 direct labor-hours per quarter caused by the physical layout of the production area.

Required

a.   How much operating profit could Williams earn if it were able to satisfy the annual demand?

b.   Which of the three product lines makes the most profitable use of the constrained resource, direct labor?

c.   Given the information in the problem so far, what product mix do you recommend?

d.   How much operating profit should your recommended product mix generate?

e.   Suppose that the company could expand its labor capacity by leasing a new stitching machine that will free up 2,160 direct labor-hours per quarter. What is the maximum quarterly lease payment that Williams Gear would be willing to pay?

f.   Refer to the facts in requirement (e). Suppose the company selling the stitching machine is not quite sure without further analysis how many direct labor-hours the new machine would free up. Regardless of the number of new hours, what is the maximum quarterly lease payment Williams Gear would be willing to pay?

(LO 4-4)   **4-74. Optimum Product Mix**

Conservatory Lumber sells rough and finished lumber for building products. At one of the company mills in the Northwest, it processes only one type of wood into two products: rough-cut lumber (sold for further processing) and dimensional lumber (for paneling and so on). The company has one particular cutting machine on which it can produce either of two types of lumber: rough-cut or dimensional. Sales demand for both products is such that the machine could operate at full capacity on either of the products. Regardless of what is produced, demand is such that Conservatory Lumber can sell all the output it produces at current prices. One unit of rough-cut lumber requires 0.6 hour of machine time, and one unit of the dimensional lumber requires four hours of machine time. Each "unit" consists of 1,000 board-feet.

Following are the costs per unit for the lumber:

	Per Unit (1,000 board-feet is a unit)	
	Rough-Cut	Dimensional
Selling price	$3,000	$7,000
Costs		
Materials	$1,200	$1,400
Labor	1,200	2,000
Cutting machine depreciation[a]	15	100
Other depreciation (fixed)[b]	35	200
Other factory costs (allocated)[b]	400	400
Total cost per unit	$2,850	$4,100
Gross margin per unit	$ 150	$2,900

[a] This item is a variable cost because it is based on machine usage.
[b] This item is a fixed cost because it is unaffected by the usage of the machine.

All other costs are the same regardless of the production mix, so you may ignore them.

Required

a. Should Conservatory Lumber produce rough-cut or dimensional lumber, or both?

b. Suppose the machine usage time for the dimensional lumber is unknown. What machine usage (units per hour) for dimensional lumber would make Conservatory Lumber indifferent to what production mix was chosen?

4-75. Optimum Product Mix—Excel Solver   (LO 4-4)
Talbot Industries manufactures two models of wireless headset: TI-12 and TI-28. Each model requires time on a single machine. The machine has a monthly capacity of 540 hours. Total market demand for the two models is limited to 2,000 units of TI-12 and 1,000 units of TI-28 monthly. Talbot is currently producing and selling 1,500 TI-12 models and 780 TI-28 models each month. Cost and machine-usage data for the two models are shown in the following spreadsheet, which analysts at Talbot use for production planning purposes:

	A	B	C	D	E	F	G	H	I
1			TI-12			TI-28			
2	Price		$80			$290			
3	Less variable costs per unit								
4	Material		23			90			
5	Labor		29			64			
6	Overhead		8			20			
7	Contribution margin per unit		$20			$116			
8									
9	Fixed costs							Total	
10	Manufacturing							$34,000	
11	Marketing and administrative							$31,000	
12								$65,000	
13	Machine hours per unit		0.1			0.5			
14									
15									
16	Machine hours used							540	
17	Machine hours available							540	
18									
19	Quantity produced		1,500			780			
20	Maximum demand		2,000			1,000			
21	Profit							$55,480	
22									
23									

Required

a. What is the optimal production schedule for Talbot Industries? In other words, how many TI-12s and TI-28s should the company produce each month to maximize monthly profit?

b. If Talbot Industries produces at the level found in requirement (*a*), how much will monthly profit increase over the current production schedule?

(LO 4-4) ## 4-76. Optimum Product Mix—Excel Solver

Pierson Products manufactures furniture, primarily for institutional use, such as for furniture rental companies, college dorm rooms, and budget hotel and motel chains. The company's Verne Valley plant manufactures one of the desk products. The desk comes in two models. The Basic desk is essentially a small table with a center drawer. The Professional desk has a keyboard tray and drawers on the side.

The production process at Pierson Products starts in the Cutting Department, where wood is cut and the desk is prepared for assembly (holes drilled, and so on). From the Cutting Department, the desk goes to the Assembly Department, where it is painted, inspected, and packaged for shipment. The process in each department uses a single machine. There are 30,000 machine-minutes available in the Cutting Department in a month and 40,000 machine-minutes in the Assembly Department each month. The monthly demand is limited to 6,000 Basic desks and 4,000 Professional desks. The current production plan is to manufacture 4,000 of each desk model monthly. Cost and machine-usage data for the two products follow:

	A	B	C	D E	F	G	H	I
			Basic		Professional		Total	
1								
2	Price		$ 70.00		$ 120.00			
3	Less variable costs per unit							
4	Material		28.00		54.00			
5	Labor		15.00		20.00			
6	Overhead		9.00		12.00			
7	Contribution margin per unit		$ 18.00		$ 34.00		$208,000	
8								
9	Monthly fixed costs							
10	Manufacturing						$53,000	
11	Marketing and administrative						39,000	
12	Total monthly fixed costs						$92,000	
14	Cutting machine minutes per unit		2.4		5.0			
15	Assembly machine minutes per unit		1.5		2.5			
16	Cutting machine minutes used						29,600	
17	Cutting machine minutes available						30,000	
18	Assembly machine minutes used						16,000	
19	Assembly machine minutes available						40,000	
21	Quantity produced		4,000		4,000			
22	Maximum demand		6,000		4,000			
23	Profit						$116,000	
24								

Required

a. What is the optimal production schedule for Pierson Products? In other words, how many Basic desks and how many Professional desks should the company produce monthly to maximize profit?

b. If Pierson Products produces at the level found in requirement (*a*), how much will monthly profit increase over the current production schedule?

(LO 4-4, 5) ## 4-77. Theory of Constraints

Oxley, Inc. manufactures three products (Alpha, Beta, and Gamma) utilizing, in one of the processes, a single machine for all products. Data on the individual products follow:

	Alpha	Beta	Gamma
Price per unit	$350	$1,416	$704
Variable cost per unit	$182	$840	$434
Machine minutes per unit	12	48	30
Maximum demand per period (units).	25,000	1,600	12,500

The single machine used for all three products has a maximum capacity of 480,000 minutes per period.

Required

a.   How many units of each product should be produced each period?

b.   Oxley has received a proposal from one of its vendors that the vendor could increase the capacity on the machine. What is the maximum Oxley would be willing to pay the vendor for an increase of 1,200 machine minutes?

c.   Suppose the maximum capacity on the machine was 300,000 minutes (instead of 480,000 minutes). What is the maximum Oxley would be willing to pay for an increase of 1,200 machine minutes?

d.   At what capacity (in machine minutes) would the machine no longer be a bottleneck?

4-78. Theory of Constraints   (LO 4-5)
Refer to the information in Problem 4-77.

Required

a.   A local engineering firm claims it can revise the production process such that the Gamma product only requires 20 machine minutes on the shared machine. How much would Oxley be willing to pay per period for the new process?

b.   Suppose, instead, that the local engineering firm can revise the production process such that Beta only requires 40 machine minutes on the shared machine. (Gamma requires 30 machine minutes as in Problem 4-77.) How much would Oxley be willing to pay per period for the new process?

INTEGRATIVE CASES

4-79. CVP, Make vs. Buy, and Data Visualization   (LO 4-4)
Refer to the information in Problem 4-55 requirements (c) and (d) and Problem 4-56 for Spinnaker Museum of Sailing. The museum board was very happy with the visualization the museum director used to explain the decision about outsourcing staffing to Gitre Operations. However, they are not sure how much certainty there is about the attendance forecast. They ask about the possibility of getting another visualization of the analysis, but this time they do not want to specify either the attendance level or the outsourcing fee per visitor. Instead, they would like a visual tool that will let them see, for a given outsourcing fee, the attendance level that would make the museum indifferent between staffing internally and outsourcing staffing to Gitre. They would like the tool to also be able, for a given attendance level, to let them see the outsourcing fee that would make the museum indifferent between the two staffing alternatives.

Required
Prepare a visual representation that the board of directors can use to accomplish their goal.

4-80. The Effect of Cost Structure on Predatory Pricing   (LO 4-1, 2)
To win a predatory pricing case, law enforcement officials traditionally have had to prove that a company has sold products or services for less than their average variable cost. Companies with relatively high fixed costs and low variable costs are less likely to be accused of predatory pricing than are companies with high variable costs and low fixed costs. A court case in which the U.S. Department of Justice alleged that American Airlines had committed predatory pricing against smaller airlines demonstrates this point.

The airline industry has relatively high fixed costs and low variable costs, at least in the short run. If one defines a "unit" as a passenger flying an already scheduled flight, the additional cost of a passenger is small—charges for credit cards, a small amount of fuel because of extra weight, a beverage or two, and not much else. If one defines a "unit" as a flight, then more costs are variable—flight crew costs, fuel, and the cost of baggage handling, for example. Even if the unit is a flight, a large portion of the total costs is fixed.

American Airlines had dropped its fares when smaller airlines scheduled competing flights from the Dallas–Fort Worth airport to Kansas City, Wichita, and other cities, arguing that this was simply business competition in the marketplace. The judge in the case acknowledged that American had been a tough competitor but ruled that American had priced its tickets *above* their average variable cost. Therefore, he ruled that the case against American should be dropped.

Required

a. Why is the relation between price and variable cost an issue in predatory pricing?

b. Identify companies or industries in which variable costs are relatively low compared to fixed costs, thus making predatory pricing hard to prove.

c. Identify companies in which variable costs are relatively high compared to fixed costs.

(LO 4-1, 4)   **4-81. Make versus Buy (Including Discounted Cash Flows)**

Liquid Chemical Company manufactures and sells a range of high-grade products. Many of these products require careful packaging. The company has a special patented lining made that it uses in specially designed packing containers. The lining uses a special material known as GHL. The firm operates a department that maintains and repairs its packing containers to keep them in good condition and that builds new ones to replace units that are damaged beyond repair.

Walsh, the general manager, has for some time suspected that the firm might save money and get equally good service by buying its containers from an outside source. After careful inquiries, he has approached a firm specializing in container production, Packages, Inc., and asked for a quotation. At the same time, he asked Dyer, his chief accountant, to let him have an up-to-date statement of the costs of operating the container department.

Within a few days, the quotation from Packages, Inc. arrived. The firm proposed to supply all the new containers required—at that time, running at the rate of 3,000 per year—for $1,250,000 a year, the contract to run for a guaranteed term of five years and thereafter renewable from year to year. If the number of containers required increased, the contract price would increase proportionally. Packages, Inc., also proposed to perform all maintenance and repair work on existing packaging containers for a sum of $375,000 a year, on the same contract terms.

Walsh compared these figures with Dyer's cost figures, which covered a year's operations of the container department of Liquid Chemical Company and appear in Exhibit 4.13.

Walsh concluded that he should immediately close the packing container department and sign the contracts offered by Packages, Inc. He felt an obligation, however, to give the manager of the department, Duffy, an opportunity to question his decision before acting. Walsh told Duffy that Duffy's own position was not in jeopardy. Even if Walsh closed his department, another managerial position was becoming vacant to which Duffy could move without any loss of pay or prospects. The manager Duffy would replace also earned $80,000 per year. Moreover, Walsh knew that he was paying $85,000 per year in rent for a warehouse a couple of miles away that was used for other corporate purposes. If he closed Duffy's department, he'd have all the warehouse space he needed without renting additional space.

Duffy gave Walsh a number of considerations to think about before he closed the department: "For instance," he said, "what will you do with the machinery? It cost $1,200,000 four years ago, but you'd be lucky if you'd get $200,000 for it now, even though it's good for another five years. And then there's the stock of GHL (a special chemical) we bought a year ago. That cost us $1,000,000, and at the rate we're using it now, it'll last another four years. We used up only about one-fifth of it last year. Dyer's figure of $700,000 for materials includes $200,000 for GHL. But it'll be tricky stuff to handle if we don't use it up. We bought it for $5,000 a ton, and you couldn't

Exhibit 4.13

Liquid Chemical Company: Container Department

Materials..		$ 700,000
Labor		
Supervisor		50,000
Workers..		450,000
Department overhead		
Manager's salary..................................	$ 80,000	
Rent on Container Department.....................	45,000	
Depreciation on machinery........................	150,000	
Maintenance of machinery	36,000	
Other expenses....................................	157,500	
		468,500
		$1,668,500
Proportion of general administrative overhead..........		225,000
Total cost of department for the year		$1,893,500

buy it today for less than $6,000. But you'd get only $4,000 a ton if you sold it, after you'd covered all the handling expenses."

Walsh also worried about the workers if he closed the department. "I don't think we can find room for any of them elsewhere in the firm. However, I believe Packages would take all but Hines and Walters. Hines and Walters have been with us since they left school 40 years ago. I'd feel bound to give them a supplemental pension—$15,000 a year each for five years, say. Also, I'd figure a total severance pay of $20,000 for the other employees, paid in a lump sum at the time we sign the contract with Packages."

Duffy showed some relief at this. "But I still don't like Dyer's figures," he said. "What about this $225,000 for general administrative overhead? You surely don't expect to sack anyone in the general office if it's closed, do you?" Walsh agreed.

"Well, I think we've thrashed this out pretty well," said Walsh, "but I've been turning over in my mind the possibility of perhaps keeping on the maintenance work ourselves. What are your views on that, Duffy?"

"I don't know," said Duffy, "but it's worth looking into. We wouldn't need any machinery for that, and I could hand the supervision over to the current supervisor, who earns $50,000 per year. You'd need only about one-fifth of the workers, but you could keep on the oldest and save the pension costs. You'd still have the $20,000 severance pay, I suppose. You wouldn't save any space, so I suppose the rent would be the same. I don't think the other expenses would be more than $65,000 a year."

"What about materials?" asked Walsh.

"We use 10 percent of the total on maintenance," Duffy replied.

"Well, I've told Packages that I'd give them my decision within a week," said Walsh. "I'll let you know what I decide to do before I write to them."

Assume the company has a cost of capital of 10 percent per year and uses an income tax rate of 40 percent for decisions such as these. Liquid Chemical would pay taxes on any gain or loss on the sale of machinery or the GHL at 40 percent. (Depreciation for book and tax purposes is straight-line over eight years.) The tax basis of the machinery is $600,000. Also assume the company had a five-year time horizon for this project and that any GHL needed for year 5 would be purchased during year 5.

Required

a. What are the four alternatives available to Liquid Chemical?

b. What action should Walsh take? Support your conclusion with a net present value analysis of all the mutually exclusive alternatives. Be sure to consider factors not explicitly discussed in the case that you think should have a bearing on Walsh's decision.

c. What, if any, additional information do you think Walsh needs to make a sound decision? Why?

SOLUTIONS TO SELF-STUDY QUESTIONS

1. The special order should be accepted after the following analysis of alternatives:

	Status Quo (do not accept offer)	Alternative (accept offer)	Difference
Sales revenue	$ 800,000	$ 860,000	$ 60,000
Variable cost	(400,000)	(436,000)	(36,000)
Contribution	$ 400,000	$ 424,000	$ 24,000
Fixed costs	240,000	240,000	–0–
Operating profit	$ 160,000	$ 184,000	$ 24,000

Alternative approach:

Special order sales (4,000 × $15)		$60,000
Less variable costs		
Manufacturing (4,000 × $8)	$32,000	
Sales commissions (4,000 × $1)	4,000	36,000
Addition to profit		$24,000

2. Using the outside supplier at a cost of $38 per unit will decrease profit by $5,000 (= $33,000 increase in profit as shown in the following table − $38,000 paid to the supplier).

	Status Quo (do not accept offer)	Alternative (accept offer)	Difference
Variable cost (ignoring payment to supplier).....	$250,000	$242,000[a]	$ 8,000 lower
Fixed costs...............	350,000	325,000[b]	25,000 lower
Costs....................	$600,000	$567,000	$33,000 lower

[a] $242,000 = (1,000 × $42) + (4,000 units × $50)
[b] $325,000 = (0.90 × $250,000 manufacturing fixed costs) + ($100,000 nonmanufacturing fixed costs)

3. *a.* Contribution margins per unit:

	BikeRac	KayakRac
Selling price.....................	$100	$80
Variable costs....................	40	35
Contribution margin per unit.....	$ 60	$45

Note: Variable costs are materials, direct labor, the variable portion of overhead, and variable marketing costs.

b. Minutes at required minimum production:

$$= (5,000 × 6) + (2,000 × 3) = 36,000 \text{ minutes}$$

c. The contribution margin per unit of the constraining resource (time in the Assembly Department) is

	BikeRac	KayakRac
Contribution per unit......................	$60	$45
Time in Assembly Department (minutes)	÷ 6	÷ 3
Contribution margin per minute.............	$10	$15

Because KayakRacs contribute more per minute, On-the-Move should use the additional time in the Assembly Department to produce KayakRacs. The optimal production schedule for the firm requires it to produce 5,000 BikeRacs and 2,000 KayakRacs (the minimum). It should then produce an additional 1,000 KayakRacs with the extra time [= (39,000 minutes − 36,000 minutes) ÷ 3 minutes per KayakRac]. The total contribution margin is $435,000 (= 5,000 × $60 + 3,000 × $45). If On-the-Move used the extra time to produce another 500 BikeRacs (= 3,000 minutes ÷ 6 minutes per BikeRac) instead, the total contribution margin would be only $420,000 (= 5,500 × $60 + 2,000 × $45).

d. If demand is limited to 2,500 KayakRacs, On-the-Move should produce 5,250 BikeRacs and 2,500 KayakRacs. Using the analysis from requirement (*b*), On-the-Move will produce the minimum demand of 5,000 BikeRacs and 2,000 KayakRacs using 36,000 minutes of assembly time. This leaves 3,000 minutes (= 39,000 minutes − 36,000 minutes). From requirement (*c*), we know that the company should next produce KayakRacs, so it should produce the additional 500 units to the maximum demand of 2,500 KayakRacs. This requires an additional 1,500 minutes (500 KayakRacs × 3 minutes per KayakRac). With the remaining 1,500 minutes (3,000 minutes − 1,500 minutes), On-the-Move can produce 250 BikeRacs (1,500 minutes ÷ 6 minutes per BikeRac).

5

Chapter Five

Cost Estimation

LEARNING OBJECTIVES

After reading this chapter, you should be able to:

LO 5-1 Explain the reasons for estimating fixed and variable costs.

LO 5-2 Estimate costs using a variety of methods, specifically engineering estimates, account analysis, and statistical analysis.

LO 5-3 Use regression analysis to estimate costs, interpret regression analysis results, and critically evaluate the fit between the data used and the regression model employed.

LO 5-4 Incorporate the effects of learning and expected improvements when estimating costs.

LO 5-5 Evaluate and explain the advantages and disadvantages of alternative cost estimation methods.

LO 5-6 (Appendix A) Use Microsoft Excel to perform a regression analysis.

LO 5-7 (Appendix B) Explain and apply the mathematical relationship describing the learning phenomenon.

> ❝ *I've read several books on cost analysis and worked through decision analysis problems in some of the college classes I am taking in the evening. I own my own business and I realize that there is one important thing that we always take for granted in doing those problems. We are always given the data. Now I know that doing the analysis once you have the data is the easier part. But once I have the data, there are still questions I want to answer. How are the costs determined? How do I know if they are fixed or variable?* ❞

Joseph Kim owns JK Renovations, a network of home renovation centers located throughout the West. Joseph is thinking about opening a new center and has asked you to help him make a decision. He especially wants your help estimating the costs to use in the analysis.

Why Estimate Costs?

When managers make decisions, they need to compare the costs (and benefits) among alternative actions. Therefore, managers need to estimate the costs associated with each alternative. We saw in Chapter 4 that good decisions require good information about costs; the better these estimates, the better the decisions managers will make. In this chapter, we discuss how to estimate the cost data required for decision making. Cost estimates can be an important element in helping managers make decisions that add value to the company.

Joseph Kim recognizes the importance of data and analysis for managing a business and is looking for ways to estimate costs more accurately. Although we focus on cost estimation in this chapter, analytic techniques and data are used for estimation in many facets of a business. Their use is also not limited to new businesses or businesses in high technology industries, as the Business Application "Data Analytics for Managing Operations and Forecasting Revenue" shows.

LO 5-1
Explain the reasons for estimating fixed and variable costs.

Data Analytics for Managing Operations and Forecasting Revenue   *Business Application*

Norfolk Southern Corporation, the operator of the Norfolk Southern Railway, has found itself with a large trove of data thanks to rail safety legislation that required sensors to monitor train operations. The data from those sensors, while helping to improve safety, is being used by the company in other ways. It is

> . . . also giving rise to applications that can help operations run smoothly and even help Ms. [Cynthia] Earhart [Norfolk Southern Corporation Chief Financial Officer] decide where to spend the hundreds of millions of dollars allocated annually for track maintenance, for example.[1]

Another area where the company is employing these analytic tools and in a way that mirrors the cost estimation process here is revenue forecasting. The statistical techniques the railroad uses are like those we discuss later in the chapter, although they differ in the data and methods used.

The revenue-forecasting system, a mix of new technologies and processes, was developed internally and uses macroeconomic data to be more predictive.

Previously, the process of revenue forecasting was a more "bottom-up" process that focused on individual customer's needs. . . .[2]

Combining a robust revenue-forecasting model with a well-formulated cost estimation model can provide an organization with good information for decision making and planning.

Sources:
1. Minaya, Ezequiel "Norfolk Southern Uses Analytics to Keep Trains on Track," *The Wall Street Journal,* April 27, 2018.
2. Ibid.

Basic Cost Behavior Patterns

The most important characteristic of costs for decision making is how they behave, that is, how they vary with activity. Therefore, the basic idea in cost estimation is to estimate the relation between costs and the variables affecting them, the cost drivers. We focus on the relation between costs and one important variable that affects them—activity level. Activities can be measured by volume (e.g., units of output, machine-hours, pages typed, miles driven), by complexity (e.g., number of different products, number of components in a product), or by any other cost driver.

You already know the key terms for describing cost behavior: *variable costs* and *fixed costs*. You also know that variable costs change proportionately with activity levels, but fixed costs do not. Building on that, the formula that we use to estimate costs is the familiar cost equation:

$$TC = F + VX$$

where *TC* refers to total costs, *F* refers to fixed costs that do not vary with activity levels, *V* refers to variable costs per unit of activity, and *X* refers to the volume of the activity.

In practice, we usually have data about the total costs incurred at each of the various activity levels, but we do not have a breakdown of costs into fixed and variable components because accounting records typically accumulate costs by account, not by behavior. What we need to do is to use the information from the accounts to estimate cost behavior.

What Methods Are Used to Estimate Cost Behavior?

LO 5-2
Estimate costs using a variety of methods, specifically engineering estimates, account analysis, and statistical analysis.

We will study three general methods to estimate the relation between cost behavior and activity levels that are commonly used in practice:

- Engineering estimates.
- Account analysis.
- Statistical methods, such as regression analysis.

Results are likely to differ from method to method. Consequently, it is a good idea to use more than one method so that results can be compared. Large differences in cost estimates suggest it is worthwhile to conduct additional analysis. If the estimates are similar, you may have more confidence in them. In practice, operating managers frequently apply their own best judgment as a final step in the estimation process. They often modify the estimate submitted by the controller's staff because they have more knowledge of the process and, more important, they bear ultimate responsibility for all cost estimates. These methods, therefore, should be seen as ways to help management arrive at the best estimates possible. Their weaknesses as well as their strengths require attention.

Engineering Method

How might you begin to help Joseph estimate the cost of a new renovation center? One approach is to start with a detailed step-by-step analysis of what needs to be done, that is, the activities the staff would conduct to operate the center. Probably the first thing you would want to know is the size of the center. Because this is a service firm, the size can be easily represented by the time it takes employees to provide renovation services (labor-hours). Joseph estimates that the new center will average about 960 labor-hours monthly.

Once you determine the size of the center, you can turn to the other necessary activities. Examples might be renting the office where the administrative work will take place, using lights and other utilities, providing support, or using supplies such as gloves and screws. You would then estimate the times or costs for each of these activities. The times required for each step requiring labor (billing support, for example) would be multiplied by an estimated wage rate. Other costs, such as licensing fees and so on, would be estimated from local market information. The estimate you just made is an **engineering estimate.**

engineering estimate
Cost estimate based on measurement and pricing of the work involved in a task.

In practice, labor time estimates might come from a time and motion study. Engineering estimates of the supplies required for typical renovation projects can be obtained from the experience of builders. Other costs are estimated similarly; for example, the size and cost of the building needed to house the center can be estimated based on area rental costs and space requirements.

One advantage to the engineering approach is that it can detail each step required to perform an operation. This permits comparison with other centers in which similar operations are performed and enables the company to review its productivity and identify specific strengths and weaknesses. Another advantage to this approach is that it does not require data from prior activities in the organization. Hence, it can be used to estimate costs for totally new activities.

A company that uses engineering estimates often can identify where "slack" exists in its operations. For example, if an engineering estimate indicates that 1,000 square feet of floor space is sufficient for housing the administrative support, but the company has been renting 2,000 square feet in other centers, the company might find it beneficial to rearrange the plan to make floor space available for other uses or look for smaller rental space.

An engineering estimate is based on detailed plans and is frequently used for large projects or new products.
Chris Sattlberger/Photodisc/Getty Images

A difficulty with the engineering approach is that it can be quite expensive to use because it analyzes each activity involved in the business. Another consideration is that engineering estimates are often based on optimal conditions. Therefore, when evaluating performance, bidding on a contract, planning expected costs, or estimating costs for any other purpose, it is important to recognize that the actual work conditions will be less than optimal.

One way to reduce the problem of optimistic estimates is to include allowances for contingencies as described in the Business Application "Engineering Analysis and the Construction of Healthcare Projects."

Engineering Analysis and the Construction of Healthcare Projects   *Business Application*

As an illustration of the engineering method of cost estimation, a healthcare trade organization provides a list of factors to consider when building a new hospital or medical office. The approach is what we have called the engineering method, where

> Cost estimators and contractors typically develop detailed take-offs of materials and labor. . . .[1]

The factors considered include building type (new construction or renovation), size (square footage), and soft costs (fees, contingencies, furniture, and so on). In fact, as is frequently the case, so-called rules-of-thumb have developed among experienced cost analysts:

> A soft cost multiplier of 1.35 to 1.45 times the costs of construction is typical [for soft costs].[2]

Later in the chapter, we discuss the role of "learning" in cost estimation. There, the focus is on adjusting the cost estimates to take account of the experience gained by employees, for example, as they spend time working with a new process. In the same way, cost estimation is a process, and cost analysts performing this task also "learn" and the result is a better estimate.

> The model becomes more accurate with numbers from each completed project, but there are still some outliers, and it takes years of industry experience to anticipate those and ensure cost-estimating success.[3]

Sources:
1. Gunn, Thomas, "Key Considerations When Cost Estimating a Healthcare Project," *Healthcare Facilities Today*, January 23, 2018. (https://www.healthcarefacilitiestoday.com/posts/Key-considerations-when-cost-estimating-a-healthcare-project--17445)
2. Ibid.
3. Ibid.

Account Analysis Method

One approach to estimating costs that includes the realities of downtime, missed work, machine repair, and the other factors that can cause engineering estimates to underestimate costs is to look at results from existing activities. Accountants often use the **account analysis** approach to estimate costs. This method calls for a review of each cost account used to record the costs that are of interest, and the identification of each as fixed or variable, depending on the relation between the cost and some activity.

Identifying the relation between the activity and the cost is the key step in account analysis. For example, in estimating the production costs for a specified number of units within the range of present manufacturing capacity, direct materials and direct labor costs

account analysis
Cost estimation method that calls for a review of each account making up the total cost being analyzed.

Exhibit 5.1

Cost Estimation Using
Account Analysis—JK
Renovations

	A	B	C	D	E
1	Account	Total	Variable	Fixed	
2	Office rent	$ 13,875	$ 6,875	$ 7,000	
3	Utilities	1,217	482	735	
4	Administrative support	12,130	930	11,200	
5	Supplies	11,230	10,880	350	
6	Licenses and permits	2,805	1,580	1,225	
7	Other	2,531	1,285	1,246	
8	Totals	$ 43,788	$ 22,032	$ 21,756	
9					

are generally considered variable, and building occupancy costs are generally considered fixed. The identification depends on the accountant's judgment and experience.

Exhibit 5.1 shows a typical schedule of estimated overhead costs per month for operating an average JK center, where the average center operates at 720 labor-hours.

Following this approach, each major class of overhead costs is itemized and then divided into its estimated variable and fixed components. JK typically signs a rental contract that includes a share of the revenue as part of the rent, so a portion is variable. The other costs are also mixed, having some fixed and variable elements. The fixed and variable components of each cost item can be determined on the basis of the experience and judgment of accounting or other personnel. Additionally, other cost estimation methods discussed later in this chapter might be used to divide mixed costs into fixed and variable components.

The total cost for the coming period is the sum of the estimated total variable and total fixed costs. For JK, assume that accounting personnel have relied on the judgment of a number of people in the company and have estimated fixed costs at $21,756 and the total variable costs at $22,032 for 720 labor-hours, as shown in Exhibit 5.1.

Because the variable costs are directly related to the expected activity, we can state the variable overhead per renovation-hour as $30.60 (= $22,032 ÷ 720 labor-hours) and the general cost equation as

$$TC = F + VX$$

Overhead costs = $21,756 per month + ($30.60 per hour × Number of hours)

For 720 labor-hours

Overhead costs = $21,756 per month + ($30.60 per hour × 720 hours)

= $21,756 + $22,032

= $43,788

Recall that the proposed center was expected to operate at an average of 960 labor-hours. To estimate overhead costs for the new center, we substitute that figure for the 720 labor-hours in the previous equation, resulting in

Overhead costs = $21,756 per month + ($30.60 per hour × 960 hours)

= $21,756 + $29,376

= $51,132

This is simpler than reestimating all overhead cost elements listed in Exhibit 5.1 for the different activity levels that management might wish to consider. Moreover, management's attention is drawn to the variable cost amount as the cost that changes with each change in volume.

Account analysis is a useful way to estimate costs. It uses the experience and judgment of managers and accountants who are familiar with company operations and the way costs react to changes in activity levels. Account analysis relies heavily on personal judgment, however. This may be an advantage or disadvantage, depending on the bias of the person making the estimate. Decisions based on cost estimates often have major economic consequences for the people making them. Thus, these individuals might not be entirely objective. More objective results are often used in conjunction with account analysis to obtain the advantages of multiple methods.

1. Brown's Baskets makes decorative baskets for sale at local craft shops. Mary Brown, the owner and founder, has collected the following information on costs based on two years of operations and has asked you to help her analyze the behavior of her overhead costs. Mary summarized monthly data as two-year totals.

Direct labor-hours.	12,000
Direct labor costs	$180,000
Machine-hours.	14,400
Units produced	20,000

Indirect materials.	$ 27,200
Indirect labor	44,300
Lease.	56,000
Utilities (heat, light, etc.)	19,200
Power to run machines	18,500
Insurance	16,400
Maintenance	14,500
Depreciation.	9,000
Total overhead.	$205,100

After visiting the workshop and discussing operations with Mary, you determine that three costs—indirect materials, indirect labor, and the power to run the machines—are variable. All other costs are fixed.

Prepare three analyses of overhead costs that, using the account analysis method, calculate the monthly average fixed costs and the variable rate per (1) direct labor-hour, (2) machine-hour, and (3) unit of output.

The solution to this question is at the end of the chapter.

Statistical Cost Estimation

Engineering estimates and account analysis are valuable approaches to estimating costs, but they have important limitations. Engineering estimates may omit inefficiencies, such as downtime for unscheduled maintenance, absenteeism, and other miscellaneous random events that affect all firms. Account analysis is often based on last period's costs alone and is subject to managers focusing on specific issues of the previous period even though these might be unusual and infrequent. One approach to dealing with both random and unusual events is to use several periods of operation or several locations as the basis for estimating cost relations. We can do this by applying statistical theory, which allows for random events to be separated from the underlying relation between costs and activities.

Our discussion of statistical methods centers on practical applications rather than underlying statistical theory. We describe the estimation of costs and cost behavior with both single and multiple cost drivers, as well as some important implementation issues.

Relevant Range of Activity   When using statistical approaches to cost estimation, we need to ensure that the activity levels of the past are relevant for the activity levels estimated. Extrapolations beyond the upper and lower bounds of past observations are highly subjective. Suppose, for example, that the highest activity level observed at any center is 1,200 labor-hours per month and we wish to predict the cost of a center with 1,600 labor-hours per month. An estimate may be highly inaccurate simply because the past data do not reflect cost behavior with output of more than 1,200 labor-hours.

The level of activity for which a cost estimate may be valid is the **relevant range.** It should include only those activity levels for which the assumed cost relations used in the estimate are considered to hold. Thus, when past data are used, the relevant range for the projection is usually between the upper and lower limits of past activity levels for which data are available.

Although the use of past data for future cost estimation has limitations, it works quite well in many cases. Past data are often adequate representations of future cost relations, even if the forecasted level of activity is somewhat outside the relevant range. Moreover, reliance on past data is relatively inexpensive; it could be the only readily available, cost-effective basis for estimating costs. Past data do show the associations that held in prior periods and at least can be a meaningful starting point for estimating costs as long as their limitations are recognized.

relevant range
Activity levels within which a given total fixed cost or unit variable cost will be unchanged.

scattergraph
Graph that plots costs against activity levels.

Scattergraphs and High-Low Estimates

When you begin a statistical analysis of costs and activities, it is helpful to begin by graphing the costs against activities using a **scattergraph.** This visualization of the data provides a quick indication of the fixed–variable relation of costs and activities and can indicate whether the relation seems to change at certain activity levels. To prepare the graph, we first obtain the relevant data. For example, if estimates of manufacturing overhead are to be based on machine-hours, we must first obtain data about past manufacturing overhead and related machine-hours.

Number of Observations

The number of observations to include depends on the availability of the data, the variability within the data, the relative costs and benefits of obtaining reliable data, and the length of time the current process has been in operation. A common rule of thumb is to use three years of monthly data if the physical processes have not changed significantly within that time. If the company's operations have changed significantly, however, data that predate the change may be misleading because you will be estimating the relation for two different processes. If cost and activity levels are highly stable, a shorter time period could be adequate.

Data for the past 15 months were collected for a representative center of JK Renovations to estimate variable and fixed overhead. These data are presented and plotted in Exhibit 5.2. Once all data points were plotted, a line was drawn to fit them as closely as possible and was extended to the vertical axis on the scattergraph.

The slope of the line represents the estimated variable costs per unit, and the intercept with the vertical axis represents an estimate of the fixed costs. The slope is referred to as the *variable cost per unit* because it represents the change in costs that occurs as a result of changes in activity. The intercept is referred to as the *fixed cost* because it represents the costs incurred at a zero activity level given the existing capacity if the relation plotted is valid from the data points back to the origin. Note that there are no observations of cost behavior around the zero activity level in this example, so the data do not indicate the costs that would be incurred if the activity level were zero. Rather, they provide an estimating equation useful within the relevant range.

Preparing an estimate on the basis of a scattergraph is subject to a high level of error, especially if the points are scattered widely. Determining the best fit is often a matter of "eyeball judgment." Consequently, scattergraphs are usually not used as the sole basis for cost estimates but to illustrate the relations between costs and activity and to point out any past data items that might be significantly out of line.

High-Low Cost Estimation

A simple approach to estimating the relation between cost and activity is to choose two points on the scattergraph and use these two points to determine the line representing the cost–activity relation. Typically, the highest and the lowest activity points are chosen, hence the name **high-low cost estimation.** Activity can be defined in terms of units of production, hours of work, or any other measure that makes sense for the problem at hand.

high-low cost estimation
Method to estimate costs based on two cost observations, usually at the highest and lowest activity levels.

The slope of the total cost line, which estimates the increase in variable costs associated with an increase of one unit of activity, can be estimated using the following equation:

$$\text{Variable cost per unit } (V) = \frac{\text{Cost at highest activity level} - \text{Cost at lowest activity level}}{\text{Highest activity level} - \text{Lowest activity level}}$$

The intercept is estimated by taking the total cost at either activity level and subtracting the estimated variable cost:

Fixed cost = Total cost at highest activity level − (Variable cost × Highest activity level)

or

Fixed cost = Total cost at lowest activity level − (Variable cost × Lowest activity level)

Based on the data for JK Renovations in Exhibit 5.2, the highest activity level is 1,136 labor-hours (*LH*). At this activity level, total overhead costs are $55,581.

	A	B	C	D
1	**Month**	**Overhead Costs**	**Labor-hours**	**Materials Costs**
2	1	$38,910	496	$2,130
3	2	$35,797	496	$2,904
4	3	$59,921	960	$7,000
5	4	$43,319	568	$3,136
6	5	$35,612	400	$3,088
7	6	$41,737	760	$2,444
8	7	$55,581	1,136	$5,972
9	8	$41,645	688	$3,682
10	9	$44,844	896	$3,308
11	10	$56,508	1,088	$4,200
12	11	$43,428	680	$2,490
13	12	$55,852	824	$5,400
14	13	$44,881	768	$4,400
15	14	$58,050	808	$6,220
16	15	$30,297	424	$1,504

Exhibit 5.2 Data and Scattergraph for Cost Estimation—JK Renovations

The lowest activity level is 400 hours, with overhead costs of $35,612. Substituting these data in the equation for variable costs yields the following:

$$\text{Variable cost per } RH\ (V) = \frac{\$55,581 - \$35,612}{1,136\ LH - 400\ LH}$$

$$= \frac{\$19,969}{736\ LH}$$

$$= \$27.13 \text{ per } LH$$

To obtain the fixed-cost estimate, either the highest or lowest activity level and costs can be used. Assuming that the highest activity level is used

$$\text{Fixed cost} = \$55,581 - \$27.13 \times 1,136\ LH$$

$$= \$55,581 - \$30,820$$

$$= \$24,761$$

An estimate for the costs at any given activity level can be computed using this equation:

$$TC = F + VX$$
$$\text{Total costs} = \$24,761 + (\$27.13 \times \text{Specified } LH)$$

For the 960 labor-hours, the estimate of overhead cost is

$$\text{Total costs} = \$24{,}761 + (\$27.13 \times 960 \ LH)$$
$$= \$24{,}761 + \$26{,}045$$
$$= \$50{,}806$$

Although the high-low method is easy to apply, use it carefully to ensure that the two points chosen to prepare the estimates represent cost and activity relations over the range of activity for which the prediction is made. This is one reason to prepare the scattergraph. The highest and lowest points could represent unusual circumstances. When this happens, you should choose the highest and lowest points that appear representative.

Statistical Cost Estimation Using Regression Analysis

regression

Statistical procedure to determine the relation between variables.

The scattergraph can be used graphically to illustrate cost–activity relations based on past experience and provides a useful visual display of the cost–volume relation. However, because it offers only a rough approximation of the relation, we recommend using the scattergraph in conjunction with other cost estimation methods, especially those that rely on statistical approaches. Although the high-low method allows computation of estimates of the fixed and variable costs, it ignores most of the information available to the analyst.

With computational tools included in many calculators or in spreadsheets such as Microsoft Excel®, the additional cost of using all the data instead of two points is quite small. **Regression** techniques are designed to generate a line that best fits a set of data points. Because the regression procedure uses all the data points, the resulting estimates have a broader base than those based on a few select points (such as the highest and lowest activity levels). In addition, regression techniques generate information that helps a manager determine how well the estimated regression equation describes the relations between costs and activities. Regression analysis also permits the inclusion of more than one predictor, a feature that can be useful when more than one factor affects costs. For example, variable overhead can be a function of both direct labor-hours and the amount of direct material processed. We leave the description of the computational details and theory to computer and statistics courses; we will focus on the use and interpretation of regression estimates. We describe the steps required to obtain regression estimates using Microsoft Excel in Appendix A to this chapter.

independent variable

X term, or predictor, on the right-hand side of a regression equation.

dependent variable

Y term or the left-hand side of a regression equation.

Obtaining Regression Estimates

The most important step in obtaining regression estimates for cost estimation is to establish the existence of a logical relation between activities and the cost to be estimated. These activities are referred to as *predictors, X terms,* **independent variables,** or the *right-hand side (RHS)* of a regression equation. The cost to be estimated can be called the **dependent variable,** the *Y term,* or the *left-hand side (LHS)* of the regression equation.

Although regression programs accept any data for the *Y* and *X* terms, entering numbers that have no logical relation can result in misleading estimates. The accountant or cost analyst has the important responsibility of ensuring that the activities are logically related to costs.

Assume, for example, that a logical relation exists between labor-hours and overhead costs for JK Renovations. A cost analyst starts by estimating the parameters (labor-hours) to use in a simple regression (one with a single predictor) to estimate overhead costs. The analyst enters data on labor-hours as *X,* or the independent variable. Data on overhead costs are entered as *Y,* or the dependent variable. The computer output giving the estimated relation between labor-hours and overhead for this situation is shown in Exhibit 5.3. (The scattergraph for this regression is shown in Exhibit 5.2, along with the data.)

The computer output is interpreted as follows:

$$\text{Total overhead} = \$20{,}378 + (\$34.64 \text{ per } LH \times \text{Number of } LH)$$

For cost estimation purposes, when you read the output of a regression program, understand that the intercept term, $20,378, is an *estimate* of fixed costs. Of course, it should be used with caution because the intercept at zero activity is outside the relevant

Exhibit 5.3

Regression Results
for the Overhead
Cost Estimation—JK
Renovations

	A	B	C	D	E	F	G	H	I
1	SUMMARY OUTPUT								
2									
3	*Regression Statistics*								
4	Multiple R	0.856171411							
5	R Square	0.733029485							
6	Adjusted R Square	0.712493291							
7	Standard Error	4963.789683							
8	Observations	15							
9									
10	ANOVA								
11		*df*	*SS*	*MS*	*F*	*Significance F*			
12	Regression	1	879484602.1	879484602	35.694516	4.635E-05			
13	Residual	13	320309704.3	24639208					
14	Total	14	1199794306						
15									
16		*Coefficients*	*Standard Error*	*t Stat*	*P-value*	*Lower 95%*	*Upper 95%*	*Lower 95.0%*	*Upper 95.0%*
17	Intercept	20378.27078	4437.27384	4.5925204	0.0005045	10792.123	29964.42	10792.1235	29964.4181
18	Labor-hours	34.63500166	5.797149024	5.9744888	4.635E-05	22.111023	47.15898	22.1110226	47.1589807
19									

range of observations. The coefficient of the *X* term (in this example, \$34.64 per labor-hour) is an estimate of the variable cost per labor-hour. This is the slope of the cost line. The coefficients are often labeled *b* or given the variable name (labor-hours) on the program output. Thus, the cost estimation equation based on this regression result is

$$\text{Total costs} = \text{Intercept} + (b \times LH)$$

Substituting 960 *LH* into the equation yields

$$\text{Total costs} = \$20{,}378 + (\$34.64 \text{ per } LH \times 960 \ LH)$$
$$= \$20{,}378 + \$33{,}254$$
$$= \$53{,}632$$

This estimate of cost behavior is shown graphically in Exhibit 5.4.

Correlation Coefficients

In addition to the cost-estimating equation, the regression program provides other useful statistics. The **correlation coefficient** (*R*, referred to as Multiple *R* in Exhibit 5.3) measures the proximity of the data points to the regression line. The closer *R* is to 1.0, the closer the data points are to the regression line. Conversely, the closer *R* is to zero, the poorer the fit of the regression line.

The square of *R* is called *R-squared* (R^2) or the **coefficient of determination.** R^2 is interpreted as the proportion of the variation in *Y* explained by the right-hand side of the regression equation, that is, by the *X* predictors.

correlation coefficient
Measure of the linear relation
between two or more
variables, such as cost and
some measure of activity.

coefficient of determination
Square of the correlation
coefficient, interpreted as the
proportion of the variation
in the dependent variable
explained by the independent
variable(s).

Exhibit 5.4

Graphical Representation
of Overhead Cost
Estimation—JK
Renovations

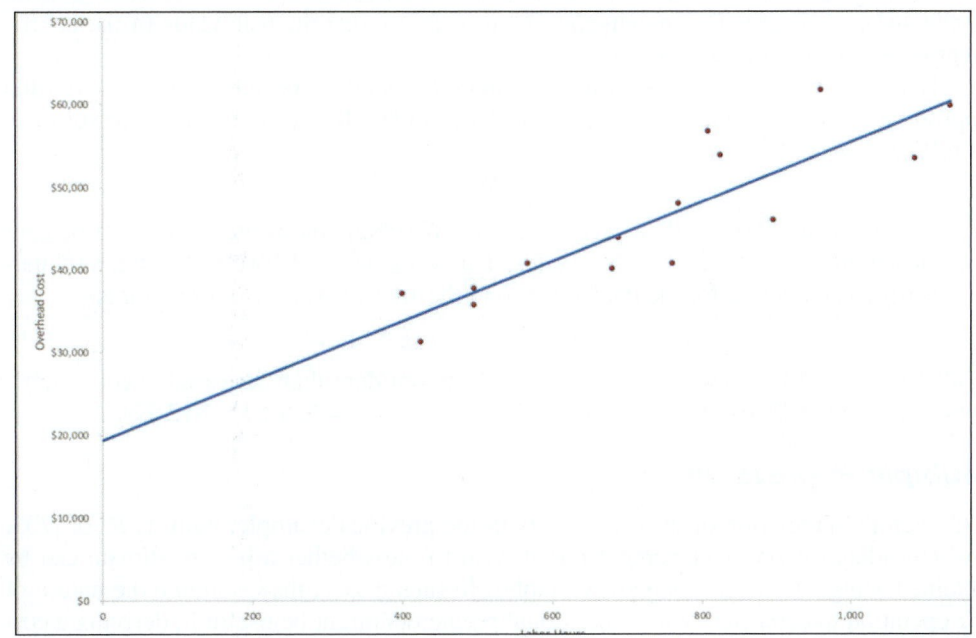

For JK Renovations, the correlation coefficient and R^2 are the following (see the regression results in Exhibit 5.3):

> Correlation coefficient (R) 856
> R^2 733

Because the R^2 is .733, it can be said that 73.3 percent of the changes in overhead costs can be explained by changes in labor-hours. For data drawn from accounting records, an R^2 of .733 is considered a good fit of the regression equation to the data.

The most commonly used regression technique is called *ordinary least squares regression (OLS)*. With this technique, the regression line is computed so that the sum of the squares of the vertical distances from each point to the regression line is minimized. Thus, as a consideration, it is important to beware of including data points that vary significantly from the usual. Because the regression program seeks to minimize squared differences, the inclusion of these extreme points, or "outliers," can significantly affect the results. Consequently, organizations often exclude data for periods of unusual occurrences such as strikes, extreme weather conditions, and shutdowns for equipment retooling. Plotting data on a scattergraph often reveals such outliers so they can be identified and omitted. We discuss the effects of outliers later in this section.

Confidence in the Coefficients   In many cases, it can be desirable to determine whether the estimated coefficient on the independent variable is significantly different from zero. For example, when determining fixed and variable costs, if the estimated coefficient is significantly different from zero, we can conclude that the cost is not totally fixed. The **t-statistic** is used to test the significance of the coefficient.

t-statistic

t is the value of the estimated coefficient, *b,* divided by its standard error.

The *t*-statistic is computed as the value of the estimated coefficient, *b,* divided by its estimated standard error (SE_b). For the data used in the JK Renovations regression, which is shown in Exhibit 5.3, the *t*-statistic is

$$t = b \div SE_b$$
$$= 34.6350 \div 5.79715$$
$$= 5.9745$$

As a general rule of thumb, a *t*-statistic greater than 2.0 is considered significant. The significance level of the *t*-statistic is called the *p*-value and is shown in Exhibit 5.3. For the JK Renovations data, the *p*-value for the estimated coefficient on labor-hours is 0.0000463 (4.63E-05). This means that the probability that the true value of the coefficient is zero, given the data, is virtually zero.

To construct a 95 percent confidence interval around *b,* we add or subtract to *b* the appropriate *t*-value for the 95 percent confidence interval times the standard error of *b,* as follows:

$$b \pm t \times SE_b$$

For the JK Renovations data, $SE_b = 5.79715$. We obtain the value of *t* for a 95 percent confidence interval from probability tables. This value is $t = 2.160$. Therefore, a 95 percent confidence interval for the coefficient *b* in the JK Renovations regression is

$$b \pm 2.160 \times 5.79715 = b \pm 12.5218$$

With *b* equal to $34.64, we would be 95 percent confident that the variable cost coefficient is between $47.16 (= $34.64 + $12.52) and $22.12 (= $34.64 − $12.52).

Multiple Regression

Although the prediction of overhead costs in the previous example, with its R^2 of .733, was considered good, management might wish to see whether a better estimate can be obtained using additional predictor variables. In such a case, they examine the nature of the operation to determine which additional predictors might be useful in deriving a cost estimation equation.

Assume that JK Renovations has determined that materials cost as well as labor-hours can affect overhead. The results of using both labor-hours (X_1) and materials cost (X_2) as predictors of overhead, Y, were obtained using a spreadsheet-based regression analysis. The output from the analysis using labor-hours and materials cost yields the prediction equation

$$\text{Overhead costs} = \text{Intercept} + b_1 \times LH + b_2 \times \text{Materials cost}$$
$$= \$19{,}894 + \$17.84\ LH + 3.32\ \text{Materials cost}$$

The statistics supplied with the output (rounded off) are

> Correlation coefficient (R) .... .951
>
> R^2 .... .904
>
> Adjusted R^2 .... .888

The **adjusted R-squared (R^2)** is the correlation coefficient squared and adjusted for the number of independent variables used to make the estimate. This adjustment to R^2 recognizes that as the number of independent variables increases, R^2 (unadjusted) increases. Statisticians believe that adjusted R^2 is a better measure of the association between X and Y than the unadjusted R^2 value when more than one X predictor is used.

adjusted R-squared (R^2) Correlation coefficient squared and adjusted for the number of independent variables used to make the estimate.

The correlation coefficient for this equation is .951, and the adjusted R^2 is .888. This is an improvement over the results obtained when the regression equation included only labor-hours. Improved results can be expected because some overhead costs may be related to materials cost (for example, administrative support) but not to labor-hours.

Preparing a cost estimate using this multiple regression equation requires not only the estimated labor-hours for the new center but also the estimated materials cost. The additional data requirements for multiple regression models can limit their usefulness in many applications. Of course, in planning for the new center's activity, JK Renovations probably has already estimated materials cost and labor-hours, and in such a situation the added costs of obtaining data could be quite low.

Joseph estimates that in addition to 960 labor-hours at the new center, materials cost will be \$5,200. Using the estimated equation, he estimates the total overhead costs as

$$\text{Total costs} = \$19{,}894 + (\$17.84\ LH \times 960\ LH) + (3.32 \times \$5{,}200)$$
$$= \$19{,}894 + \$17{,}126 + \$17{,}264$$
$$= \$54{,}284$$

Although our focus in this chapter is on cost estimation, we could also use the regression results to test whether a particular factor is related to cost. In other words, we could test whether the factor is a cost driver. For example, in the analysis on the previous page, we could examine the t-statistics for each of the coefficients to determine if they are both significant. (In Appendix A, where we discuss the use of Excel for estimating the regression, we see that they are both significant.) If the analysis showed, for example, that materials cost was not significant, we would conclude that labor-hours is the better cost driver.

Practical Implementation Problems

Advances in easy-to-use computer software, especially spreadsheet software, have greatly simplified regression analysis and made it available to more people. Consequently, regression methods have been increasingly used (and misused). In particular, analysts can be tempted to enter many variables into a regression model without careful thought of their validity. The results can be misleading and potentially disastrous.

Some of the more common problems with using regression estimates include (1) attempting to fit a linear equation to nonlinear data; (2) failing to exclude nonrepresentative observations (called "outliers"); (3) including predictors with apparent, but spurious, relations to the dependent variable; and (4) using data that do not fit the assumptions of regression analysis.

Exhibit 5.5

The Effect of Nonlinear Relations

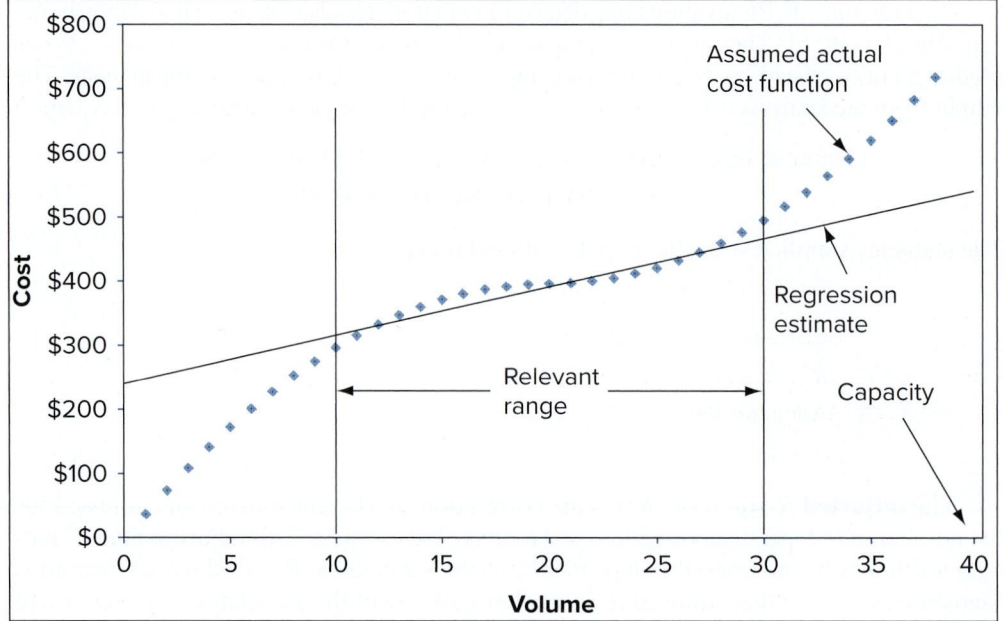

Effect of Nonlinear Relations   The effect of attempting to fit a linear model to nonlinear data is likely to occur when the firm is operating near its capacity limits. Close to maximum capacity, costs increase more rapidly than activity because of overtime premiums paid to employees, increased maintenance and repair costs for equipment, and similar factors. The linear cost estimate understates the slope of the cost line in the ranges close to capacity. This situation is shown in Exhibit 5.5.

One way to overcome the problem is to define a relevant range of activity (for example, from 25 percent to 75 percent capacity), and use the range for one set of cost-estimating regression equations. A different equation could be derived for the levels between 81 and 100 percent capacity. Another approach is to model the nonlinearity explicitly by including the squared value of an independent variable as well as the variable itself. However, this approach does not provide a constant unit variable cost estimate; the estimate is different at each level of activity.

Effect of Outliers   Because regression minimizes the sum of the squared deviations from the regression line, observations that lie a significant distance away from the line could have an overwhelming effect on the regression estimates. Exhibit 5.6 shows a case in which most of the data points lie close to a straight line, but because of the effect of one significant outlier, the computed regression line is a substantial distance from most of the points.

This type of problem can easily arise in accounting settings. Suppose that a year's worth of supplies was purchased and expensed entirely (but not used) within a single month or a large adjustment was made for under-accrued payroll taxes. The accounting records in such cases are clearly abnormal with respect to the activity measure.

An inspection of the scattergraph can often reveal this problem. When an outlier appears in the data set, scrutiny of the output from the regression analysis will rarely identify it. Instead, a plot of the regression line on the data points is usually needed. If multiple predictors are used, an outlier will be even more difficult to find. The best way to avoid this problem is to examine the data in advance and eliminate highly unusual observations before running the regression.

Effect of Spurious Relations   It is sometimes tempting to include many variables in the regression and let the program "find" relations among the variables. This can lead, however, to spurious relations. For example, a relation between variable 1 and variable 2 could appear to exist, when, in fact, variable 3, which was left out of the analysis, explains the situation. An obvious example is estimation of a regression to explain direct

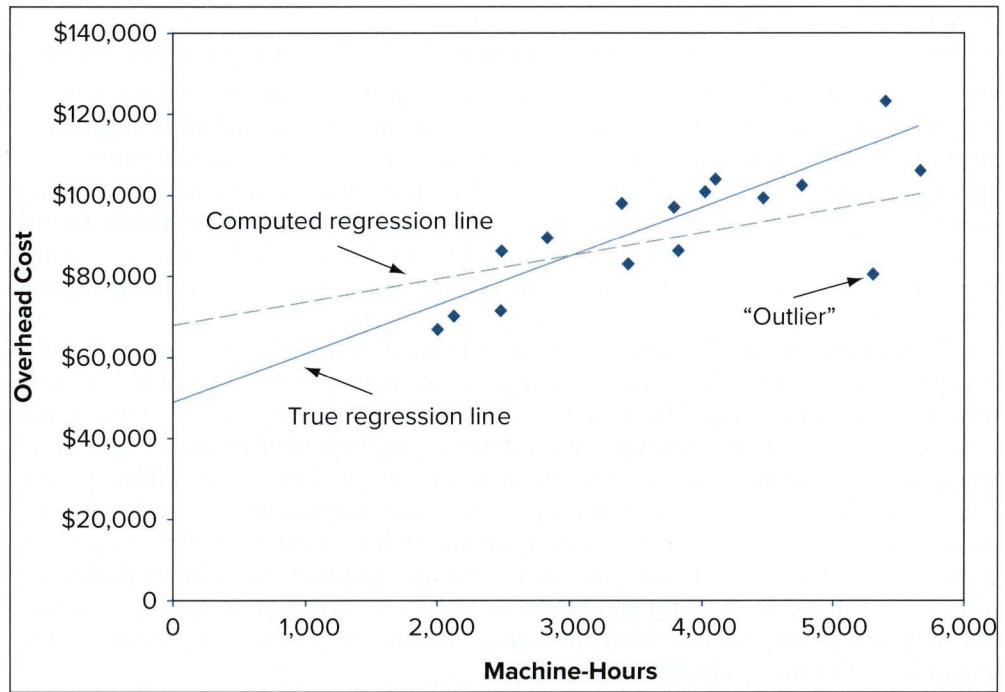

Exhibit 5.6
The Effect of Outliers
on the Computed
Regression

materials cost by using, say, direct labor costs as the independent variable. The association will typically be quite high, but both are driven by output.

Effect of Using Data That Do Not Fit the Assumptions of Regression Analysis

Regression analysis is a powerful tool for analyzing and estimating costs, but it relies on several important assumptions. If the assumptions are not satisfied, the results of the regression will not be reliable. Two important assumptions that are often *not* satisfied in estimating costs are that (1) the process for which costs are being estimated remains constant over time and (2) the errors in estimating the costs are independent of the cost drivers.

Businesses today change processes frequently as part of continuous improvement efforts. Regression analysis assumes, however, that the process remains the same. This situation leaves the cost analyst with two choices. The analyst can restrict the data to a short period and thereby assume the process has remained the same. However, the estimates will not be as reliable because there are relatively few observations. Alternatively, the analyst can use a longer period. As long as the process has not changed, the estimates will be more reliable (because they are based on more information), but the analyst risks using estimates that might not be meaningful if the process has changed.

These trade-offs indicate that using regression analysis for estimating costs requires care in the selection and use of the data. It is not enough to rely on a spreadsheet program to generate the results; the analyst must be assured that the data being used are appropriate for regression analysis.

Regression Must Be Used with Caution

A regression estimate is only an estimate. Computerized statistical techniques sometimes have an aura of truth about them. In fact, a regression estimate can be little better than an informal estimate based on plotted data. Regression has advantages, however. It is objective, provides a number of statistics not available from other methods, and could be the only feasible method when more than one predictor is used.

We recommend that users of regression (1) fully understand the method and its limitations; (2) specify the model, that is, the hypothesized relation between costs and cost predictors; (3) know the characteristics of the data being used; and (4) examine a plot of the data.

Learning Phenomenon

LO 5-4

Incorporate the effects of learning and expected improvements when estimating costs.

learning phenomenon
Systematic relationship between the amount of experience in performing a task and the time required to perform it.

You might recall the first time that you used a spreadsheet program on a computer. While you might have been slow at first, your speed improved as you gained more experience. In the same way, companies find that experience—or learning—affects labor costs. Specifically, the more experience that workers have performing a task, the less time they spend on it. As we discussed in the previous section, cost estimation methods assume that the process for which costs are being estimated has not changed. If, because of learning, for example, the process has changed, we need to incorporate that change in our estimation methods.

The **learning phenomenon** refers to the systematic relationship between the amount of experience in performing a task and the time required to perform it. This can occur when companies introduce new production methods, make new products (either goods or services), or hire new employees. For example, the effect of learning on the cost of aerospace components is well known. Manufacturers of products for the industry, such as Lockheed Martin and Raytheon Technologies, recognize the effect of learning on the production cost of a new product by writing contracts that establish a lower cost for consecutive units produced. For example, the second unit produced has a lower production cost than the first unit, the third unit produced has a lower production cost than the second unit, and so on. Another example is described in the Business Application "The Importance of Learning and Reduced Costs."

Business Application ▸ The Importance of Learning and Reduced Costs

The results from the learning curve can have an important effect on the success or failure of a company relying on new technology. At the beginning of 2018, Tesla Motors was in the process of launching the Model 3, an electric car targeted for a mass market. However, with high costs and other start-up problems, the company was struggling to meet production goals and was suffering cash flow problems, with a $1.7 billion cash outflow. The company, however, was able to increase production from "a few hundred" sedans a week to over 4,000. At the same time, the company had a cash inflow of $774 million in the third quarter of 2018.[1]

Although there were several factors in this reversal of fortunes, an important one was the investment Tesla made in battery technology. This investment benefited Tesla in two ways. First, as battery output increases, the average cost declines because fixed costs are averaged over more units. The second benefit comes when the variable cost per unit of production declines as workers become more experienced and learn to operate more efficiently.

A key to Tesla's success thus far has been its heavy investment in batteries. Lithium-ion battery production follows a well-documented learning curve: Whenever global production capacity doubles, prices decline by about 18 percent, according to data from Bloomberg New Energy Finance.[2]

The reduction in battery costs led to a significant reduction in production costs.

In a rare disclosure of Tesla's battery prices, [Tesla CEO Elon] Musk said in June that his company's costs for battery cells—the small cylindrical components of its battery packs—had dropped to $110 per kilowatt hour (kWh) and would reach $100 per kWh by the end of 2018. That compares with an average price of about $127 per kWh industrywide, according to data compiled by BNEF.[3]

The effect of lower battery prices on the battery pack, a major cost component in the manufacturing cost of the car, is a significant competitive advantage.

Tesla is on track for pack prices of $100 per kWh in 2020, according to Musk. If accurate, that could put Tesla about three years ahead of its competitors.[4]

Sources:
1. Randall, Tom "Tesla's Life after Hell: 7 Charts Show Musk on Firmer Footing," *Bloomberg*, January 7, 2019, (https://www.bloomberg.com/news/features/2019-01-07/tesla-s-life-after-hell-7-charts-show-musk-on-firmer-footing).
2. Ibid.
3. Ibid.
4. Ibid.

The following example and Exhibit 5.7 show the effect of learning on costs. Assume that the company's engineers have found a systematic relation between the time required to produce units and the volume of units produced. These engineers estimate that the time required to produce the second unit is 80 percent of the time required to produce the first unit. Further, the time to produce the fourth unit is 80 percent of the time to produce the

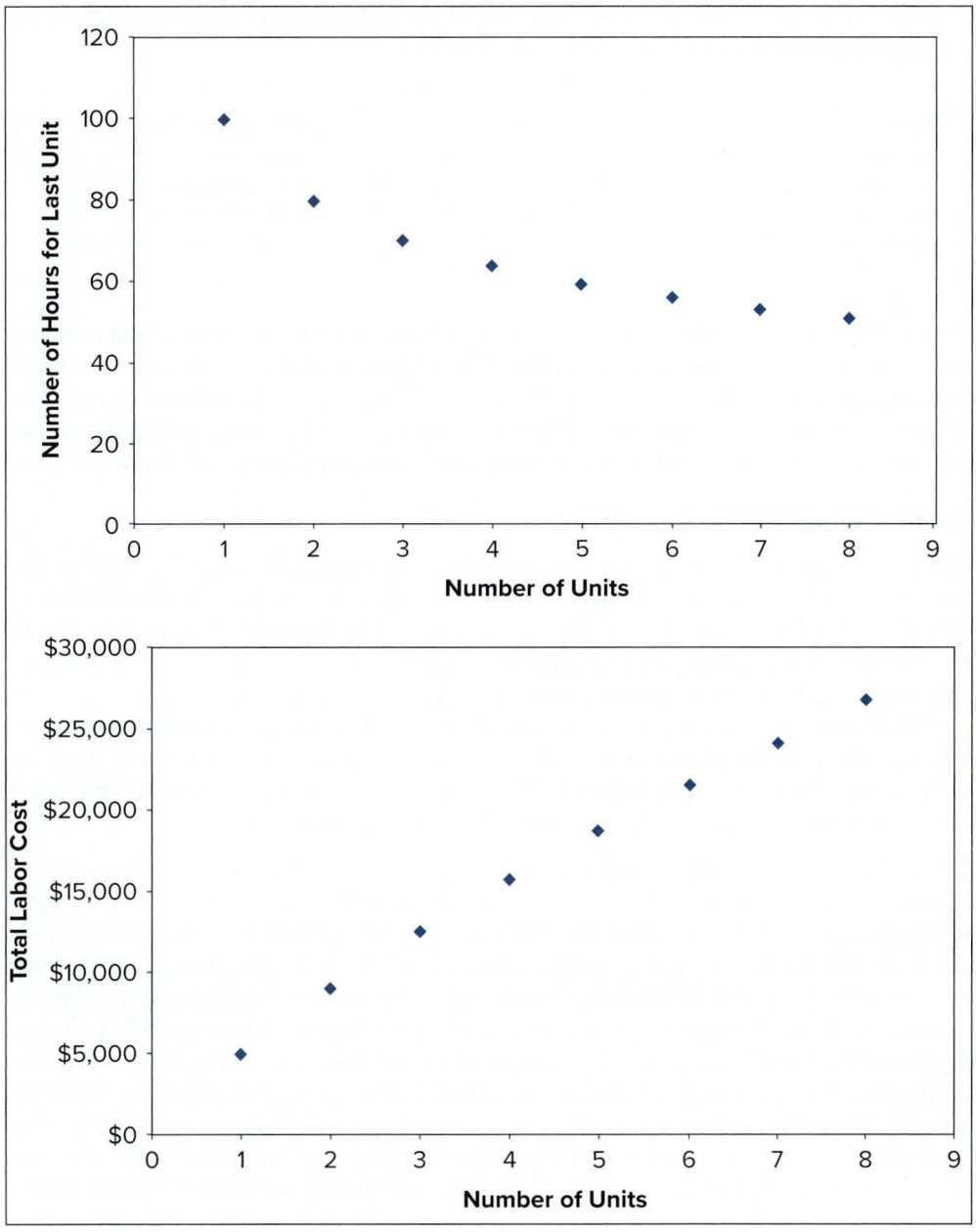

Exhibit 5.7
The Effect of Learning on
Hours and Costs

second unit, and so forth. (What is the time to produce the eighth unit? Answer: 80 per-cent of the time to produce the fourth unit.)

This is called an 80 percent learning curve.[1] If the time to produce the fourth unit was 70 percent of the time to produce the second unit, then the relationship would be called a 70 percent learning curve. If the time to produce the fourth unit was 90 percent of the time to produce the second unit, then the relationship would be called a 90 percent learn-ing curve. You get the idea.

Now assume that the first unit takes workers 100 hours to produce. Then, given an 80 percent learning curve, the second unit will require 80 hours to produce (= 80 percent × 100 hours). The fourth unit will require 64 hours (= 80 percent × 80 hours), and so forth,

---

[1] The approach that we demonstrate is the incremental unit-time learning model. Another approach is the cumulative average-time learning model. For a discussion of this latter model, see Ronald W. Hilton, Michael W. Maher, and Frank Selto, *Cost Management,* 4th ed. (Burr Ridge, IL: McGraw-Hill/Irwin, 2008), chapter 11.

as shown in the table that follows. Appendix B presents the mathematical formula for deriving the learning curve and extends this example:

Unit		Time to Produce
First unit	100 hours	(assumed)
Second unit	80 hours	(= 80 percent × 100 hours)
Fourth unit	64 hours	(= 80 percent × 80 hours)
Eighth unit.	51.2 hours	(= 80 percent × 64 hours)

Exhibit 5.7 shows the relation between volume and the number of labor-hours required to produce the last unit in Panel A. The relation between volume and total labor costs appears in Panel B. Assume the labor cost is $50 per hour. Note that the labor cost per unit for the first unit is $5,000 but that the cost drops to $2,560 per unit for the eighth unit, a substantial decrease due to the learning phenomenon ($2,560 = 51.2 hours × $50).

Applications

The learning phenomenon means that variable costs tend to decrease per unit as the volume of activity increases. Thus, a linear cost estimate, such as the one shown in Exhibit 5.4, will overstate the variable cost per unit. The learning phenomenon affects most professional activities such as consulting, legal, medical, and engineering work, as well as any overhead costs, such as supervision, that are related to labor time.

When estimating costs, decision makers should consider the potential impact of learning. The learning phenomenon can affect costs used in cost management, decision making, and performance evaluation. Failing to recognize learning effects can have some unexpected consequences, as shown in the following examples.

Decision Making   Assume that a supplier to the National Weather Service (NWS), such as Lockheed Martin or Raytheon, is considering producing a new device for monitoring space weather from spacecraft. NWS has indicated it will pay $600,000 per unit for the device. Engineers and cost management analysts at Raytheon estimate the cost to produce the first unit of the device to be $800,000. At first, Raytheon decides not to produce the device because the unit cost exceeds the unit price. However, NWS assures Raytheon that it will order at least eight units of the device. After considering the learning phenomenon for the device, Raytheon realizes that the average cost per unit will drop below $550,000 for eight units. For four units, producing the device is unprofitable. For eight units, however, it is profitable because the learning phenomenon reduces the time and costs for units 5 through 8 sufficiently to bring the average cost down to $535,000.

Performance Evaluation   Elite State University (not its real name) developed labor time and cost expectations for clerical activities that were subject to the learning phenomenon. For example, employees were expected to answer an inquiry about the status of an application to the university's law school in one minute. Management observed that time spent on these activities was systematically greater than expected. Upon investigating the problem, management found high personnel turnover, which meant that the activities were often being performed by inexperienced people. As a result, the university never experienced the expected benefits of learning. After changing personnel practices to reduce turnover, the university had more experienced people in jobs. These experienced people performed the activities faster than less experienced people, and the time spent on activities now met expectations.

How Is an Estimation Method Chosen?

Each of the methods discussed has advantages and disadvantages. Probably the most informative estimate of cost behavior results from using several methods discussed because each has the potential to provide information that the others do not.

We have discussed a variety of cost estimation methods ranging from the simple account analysis method to sophisticated techniques involving regression analysis. Which of these methods is best? In general, the more sophisticated methods yield more accurate cost estimates than the simpler methods do. However, even a sophisticated method yields only an imperfect estimate of an unknown cost behavior pattern.

All cost estimation methods make assumptions to simplify the analysis. The two most common assumptions follow:

1. *Cost behavior depends on just one cost driver.* (Multiple regression is an exception.) In reality, however, costs can be affected by a host of factors, including the weather and the mood of the employees.
2. *Cost behavior patterns are linear within the relevant range.* We know that costs actually follow curvilinear, step, semivariable, and other patterns.

You must consider on a case-by-case basis whether these assumptions are reasonable. You must also decide when it is important to use a more sophisticated, and more costly, cost estimation method and when it is acceptable to use a simpler approach. As with all management accounting methods, you must evaluate the costs and benefits of various cost estimation techniques.

LO 5-5
Evaluate and explain the advantages and disadvantages of alternative cost estimation methods.

Data Problems

If a company's operations have followed a particular pattern in the past and that pattern is expected to continue in the future, using the relation between past costs and activity to estimate future costs can be useful. Of course, if the relation changes, it could be necessary to adjust the estimated costs accordingly or explicitly consider the changes when developing the estimates.

Analysts must be careful when predicting future costs from historical data. In many cases, the cost–activity relation changes. Technological innovation, increased use of automation, more mechanized processes, and similar changes have made the past cost–activity relations inappropriate for prediction purposes in many organizations. For example, switching to a just-in-time inventory system will alter the relation between materials-handling costs and volume because the intermediate storage step is eliminated.

In other cases, the costs change so dramatically that old cost data are worthless predictors of future costs. Because of the high variation in costs, companies using precious metals or relying on labor in developing countries have found that past cost data are not very helpful in predicting future costs. Although accountants can adjust the data, the resulting cost estimates tend to lose their objectivity as the number of adjustments increases.

No matter what method is used to estimate costs, the results are only as good as the data used. Collecting appropriate data is complicated by the following problems:

Cost analysts must ensure that data used to estimate costs do not come from periods that are unusual. Strikes, natural disasters, or other events lead to abnormally low volumes that could distort estimated costs.
Aaron Roeth Photography

- *Missing data.* Misplaced source documents or failure to record a transaction can result in missing data.
- *Outliers.* Extreme observations of cost–activity relations can unduly affect cost estimates. For example, a tornado recently affected operations in Oklahoma businesses, resulting in unusually low volume.
- *Allocated and discretionary costs.* Fixed costs are often allocated on a volume basis, resulting in costs that could appear variable. Discretionary costs also can be budgeted so that they appear variable (e.g., advertising expense budgeted as a percentage of revenue).
- *Inflation.* During periods of inflation, historical cost data do not accurately reflect future cost estimates. Even if inflation remains low in one country, firms with international operations must consider the effects of subsidiary operations when making cost estimates.
- *Mismatched time periods.* The time period for the dependent and independent variables may not match (e.g., running a machine in February and receiving [recording] the energy bill in March).

Effect of Different Methods on Cost Estimates

Each cost estimation method can yield a different estimate of the costs that are likely to result from a particular management decision. This underscores the advantages of using two or more methods to arrive at a final estimate. The different manufacturing overhead estimates that resulted from the use of four different estimation methods for JK Renovations are summarized in Exhibit 5.8.

The numbers in Exhibit 5.8 are close, but there are differences. It is impossible to state which method is best, so management could find that having all four estimates gives the best indication of the likely range within which actual costs will fall. Moreover, by observing the range of cost estimates, management is better able to determine whether more cost data need to be gathered. If decisions are the same for all four cost estimates, management can conclude that additional information gathering is not warranted.

Exhibit 5.8

Summary of Cost Estimates—JK Renovations

Method	Total Estimated Cost[a]	Estimated Fixed Cost	Estimated Variable Cost
Account analysis	$51,132	$21,756	$30.60 per labor-hour
High-low	50,806	24,761	27.13 per labor-hour
Simple regression (LH)[a] . . .	53,632	20,378	34.64 per labor-hour
Multiple regression (LH and materials cost)[b].	54,284	19,894	17.84 per labor-hour + 332% of materials cost

[a] For 960 labor-hours.

[b] For 960 labor-hours and $5,200 in materials cost.

Self-Study Question

2. The following computer output presents the results of two simple regressions for the Brown's Baskets overhead costs using (1) direct labor-hours and (2) units of output (baskets) as the independent variables. Each regression has 24 data points, one data point per month for two years. Which activity base, units of output or labor-hours, do you believe best explains variation in overhead costs?

The solution to this question is at the end of the chapter.

	A	B	C	D	E	F	G
1	SUMMARY OUTPUT						
2							
3	*Regression Statistics*						
4	Multiple R	0.73161563					
5	R Square	0.53526143					
6	Adjusted R Square	0.51413695					
7	Standard Error	942.922704					
8	Observations	24					
9							
10	ANOVA						
11		*df*	*SS*	*MS*	*F*	*Significance F*	
12	Regression	1	22528490.87	22528490.9	25.33844	4.85539E-05	
13	Residual	22	19560270.97	889103.225			
14	Total	23	42088761.84				
15							
16		*Coefficients*	*Standard Error*	*t Stat*	*P-value*	*Lower 95%*	*Upper 95%*
17	Intercept	4705.95547	826.1235525	5.696430583	9.94E-06	2992.678242	6419.23269
18	Labor-Hours	8.08808907	1.606778337	5.033730468	4.86E-05	4.75583117	11.420347
19							

(Continued)

	A	B	C	D	E	F	G
1	SUMMARY OUTPUT						
2							
3	*Regression Statistics*						
4	Multiple R	0.881023603					
5	R Square	0.77620259					
6	Adjusted R Square	0.76602998					
7	Standard Error	590.8985221					
8	Observations	24					
9							
10	ANOVA						
11		*df*	*SS*	*MS*	*F*	*Significance F*	
12	Regression	1	26642104	26642104	76.30319	1.33090E-08	
13	Residual	22	7681543.39	349161.063			
14	Total	23	34323647.39				
15							
16		*Coefficients*	*Standard Error*	*t Stat*	*P-value*	*Lower 95%*	*Upper 95%*
17	Intercept	4338.878836	519.189015	8.357031275	2.84E-08	3262.14556	5415.61211
18	Baskets	5.293345397	0.60598082	8.735169864	1.33E-08	4.03661675	6.55007405
19							

Key Takeaways

1. Decision making requires an understanding of cost behavior, that is, which costs are fixed and which are variable. We can use a variety of methods to determine this, including

   a. Engineering estimates, where costs are estimated from detailed specification about the inputs required.

   b. Account analysis, where cost behavior is inferred by looking at past account information.

   c. Statistical analysis, where costs are estimated by analyzing past cost data and related activity.

2. Regression analysis is a statistical method to estimate costs using past data on costs and activities to identify relationships and provide a predictive model. Regression analysis uses all information and not just select data points. It also provides statistics that can be used to assess how well the model fits the data. There are potential problems that can arise with regression that a cost analyst needs to consider, including

   a. Nonlinear relationships, where variable costs are not proportional to activity.

   b. Influential observations (outliers) that can distort the relation because of unusual events such as labor strikes, weather disasters, or supply disruptions.

   c. Changes in the underlying process caused, for example, by a change in the production process or input mix.

   A scatter diagram of the data used in the model can be used to screen for these problems.

3. The learning phenomenon is the systematic relationship with a process and the time taken to complete the process, whether producing a product or providing a service. Failure to incorporate learning in the cost estimates when learning exists risks overstating the costs of future production.

SUMMARY

Accurate cost estimation is important to most organizations for decision-making purposes. Although no estimation method is completely accurate, some are better than others. The usefulness of a cost estimation method depends to a great extent on the user's knowledge of the business and the costs being analyzed.

The following summarizes the key ideas tied to the chapter's learning objectives:

LO 5-1 Explain the reasons for estimating fixed and variable costs. The behavior of costs, not the accounting classification, is the important distinction for decision making. Cost estimation focuses on identifying (estimating) the fixed and variable components of costs.

LO 5-2 Estimate costs using a variety of methods, specifically engineering estimates, account analysis, and statistical analysis. Cost estimates can be developed by identifying all activities and resources required to make a product or provide a service.

An engineering cost estimate applies unit costs to the estimate of the physical resources required to accomplish a task.

An account analysis determines cost behavior by considering the reasons for the underlying expenditures.

A statistical analysis of data allows estimates of costs to be based on many periods of operation. Statistical analyses allow data to be visualized using scattergraphs. High-low analysis is one approach using two observations to estimate the slope (an estimate of the unit variable cost) and the intercept (an estimate of the fixed cost).

LO 5-3 Use regression analysis to estimate costs, interpret regression analysis results, and critically evaluate the fit between the data used and the regression model employed. *Regression analysis* uses all data and can be accomplished easily with a spreadsheet program. Using regression analysis avoids the problem of selecting observations in the high-low method that might not be representative.

Using regression analysis requires care because the estimates depend on certain assumptions. At a minimum, you should look at a scattergraph to determine whether the relation appears to be representative for your data. You should also check the coefficient of determination (R^2) to determine how closely the estimates fit the observed data. Regression methods rely on certain assumptions. For example, the relation between cost and output is assumed to be linear, the observations are representative, and there have been no special circumstances, such as strikes or weather disasters. Finally, it is important to guard against spurious relations that are masked by a good statistical fit.

LO 5-4 Incorporate the effects of learning and expected improvements when estimating costs. Many of the cost estimation methods discussed in this chapter assume that the same relation holds over time. However, especially for new products, learning can take place, making it possible for the same hours of work to produce more output, use less of the required materials, or lead to other improvement efficiencies. The learning curve approach allows the cost analyst to make this learning explicit in estimating cost.

LO 5-5 Evaluate and explain the advantages and disadvantages of alternative cost estimation methods. Each method has its advantages and disadvantages. Using two, three, or four of the methods together can indicate whether you should be confident of the estimates (if all the methods give similar results) or invest in more analysis.

LO 5-6 (Appendix A) Use Microsoft Excel to perform a regression analysis. Microsoft Excel or many other statistical software programs can be used to perform a regression analysis.

LO 5-7 (Appendix B) Explain and apply the mathematical relationship describing the learning phenomenon. The learning phenomenon can be expressed mathematically. This mathematical relationship can be applied to estimate costs for all levels of production.

KEY TERMS

account analysis, *193*	independent variable, *198*
adjusted *R*-squared (R^2), *201*	learning phenomenon, *204*
coefficient of determination, *199*	regression, *198*
correlation coefficient, *199*	relevant range, *195*
dependent variable, *198*	scattergraph, *196*
engineering estimate, *192*	*t*-statistic, *200*
high-low cost estimation, *196*	

APPENDIX A: REGRESSION ANALYSIS USING MICROSOFT EXCEL®

LO 5-6

Use Microsoft Excel to perform a regression analysis.

Using Microsoft Excel to Estimate Regression Coefficients

There are many statistical packages that you can use to estimate a regression equation such as that for JK Renovations. In this appendix, we describe how to estimate the coefficients using Microsoft Excel®. The following steps and screenshots are based on Version 2102 of Excel (part of Microsoft 365), but any recent versions of Excel for Windows or for Mac OS are similar.

Step 1: *Ensure you have the Analysis ToolPak installed.*

To use Excel for regression analysis, you must have the Analysis ToolPak installed. Open Excel and click on the Data tab (circled in red in Exhibit 5.9).

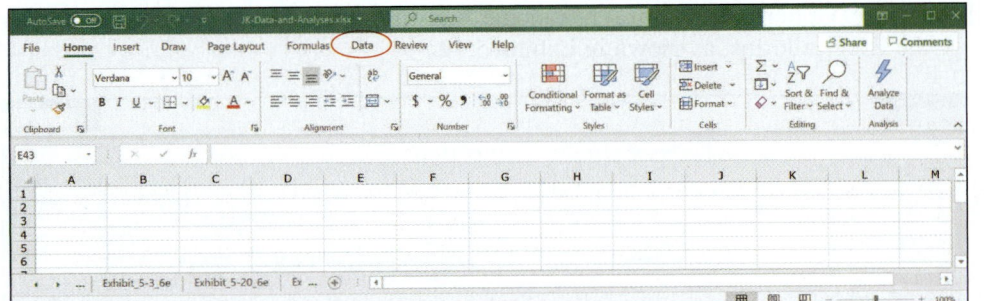

Exhibit 5.9
The Opening Screen

If the Analysis ToolPak is installed, there will be a box on the right labeled "Analysis" with a button labeled "Data Analysis." This is shown in Exhibit 5.10.

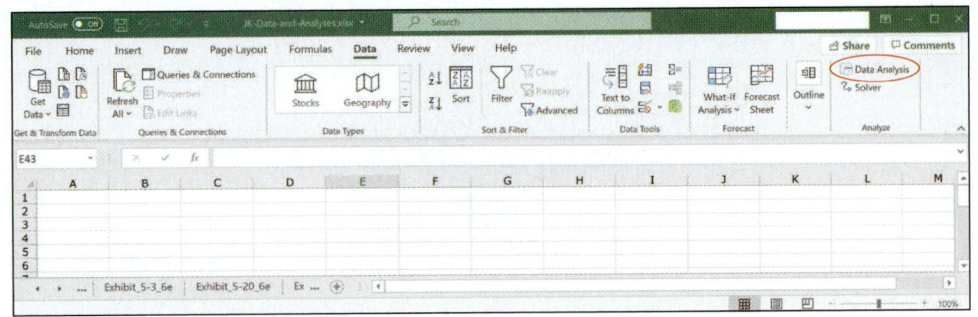

Exhibit 5.10
The Data Analysis Button under the Data Tab

If you see the Data Analysis button, proceed to step 2; otherwise, follow these steps to install the Analysis ToolPak.

Select File and then Options and click on Excel Options, as shown in Exhibit 5.11.

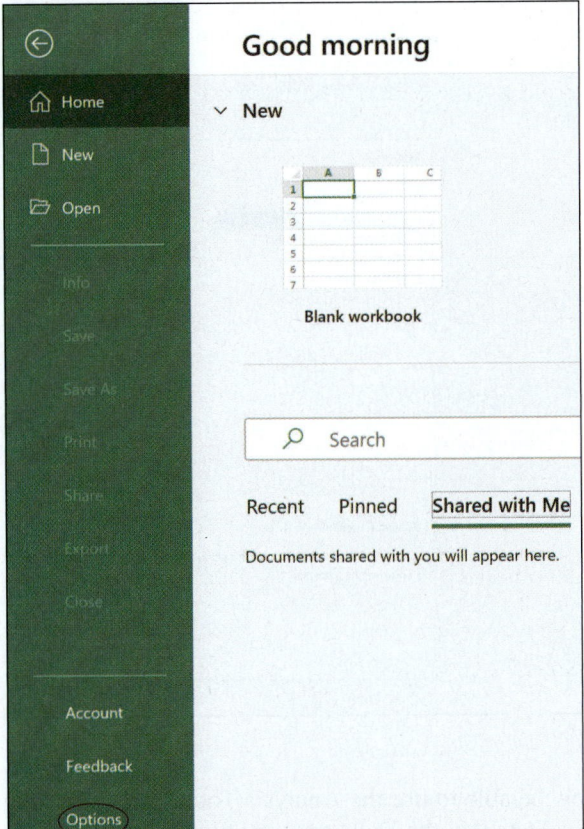

Exhibit 5.11
Installing the Analysis ToolPak—Excel Options

In the Excel Options dialog box, click on the Add-Ins button and then click "Go" to manage the Excel Add-Ins, as shown in Exhibit 5.12.

Exhibit 5.12

Managing the Excel Add-ins

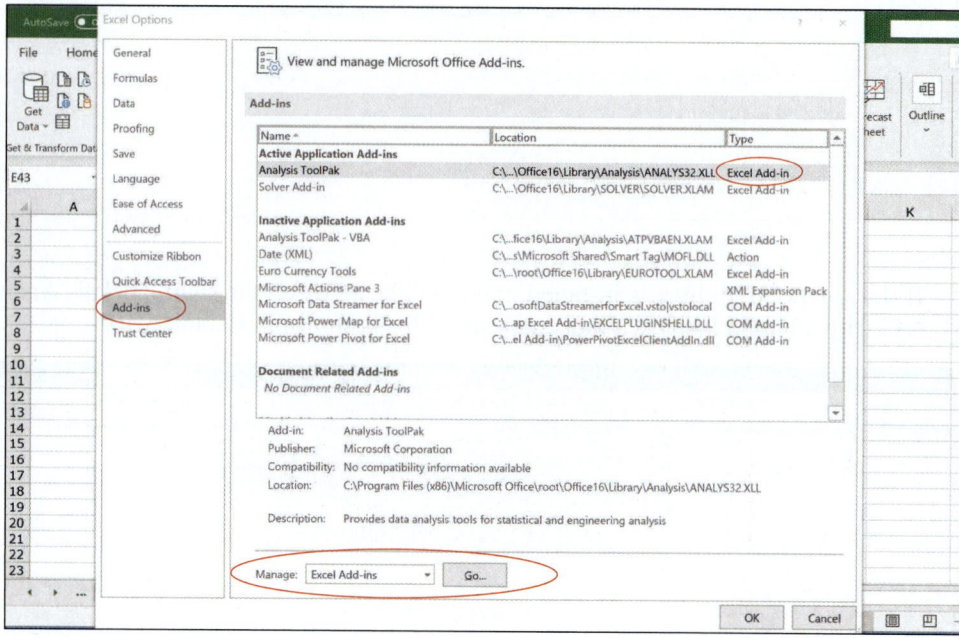

In the Add-ins dialog box, select the Analysis ToolPak and click "Ok," as shown in Exhibit 5.13.

Exhibit 5.13

Installing the Analysis ToolPak

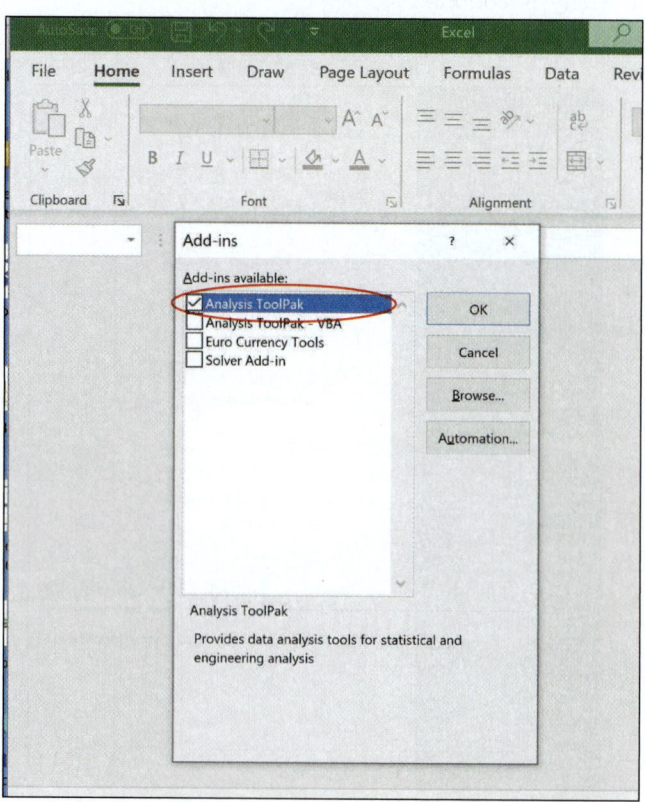

You should now be able to use the Analysis ToolPak for your regression analysis. If you click on the Data tab, the Data Analysis button should be available on the right, as shown in Exhibit 5.14.

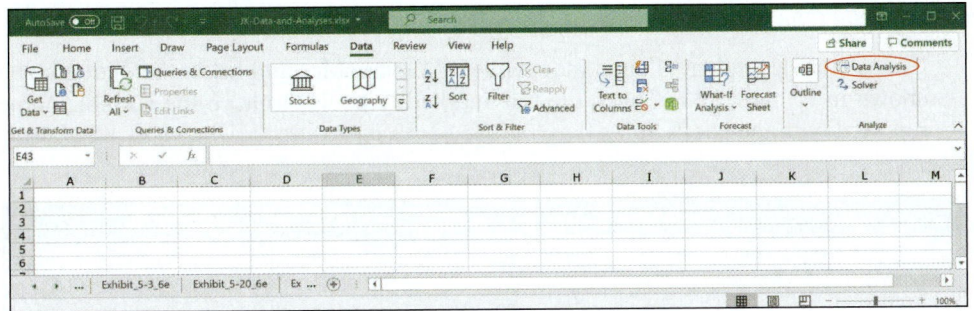

Exhibit 5.14

Checking for the Data
Analysis Button

Step 2: *Enter the data for the Dependent and Independent Variables.*

Next, enter the data to be used in the analysis. Exhibit 5.15 shows the data for the JK
Renovations example used in the chapter.

	A	B	C	D
1	Month	Overhead Costs	Labor-hours	Materials Costs
2	1	$38,910	496	$2,130
3	2	$35,797	496	$2,904
4	3	$59,921	960	$7,000
5	4	$43,319	568	$3,136
6	5	$35,612	400	$3,088
7	6	$41,737	760	$2,444
8	7	$55,581	1,136	$5,972
9	8	$41,645	688	$3,682
10	9	$44,844	896	$3,308
11	10	$56,508	1,088	$4,200
12	11	$43,428	680	$2,490
13	12	$55,852	824	$5,400
14	13	$44,881	768	$4,400
15	14	$58,050	808	$6,220
16	15	$30,297	424	$1,504
17				

Exhibit 5.15

Entering the Data for the
Regression Analysis

Step 3: *Select the data to use in the regression.*

Next, choose the Data tab and select Data Analysis and Regression, as shown in
Exhibit 5.16. Click "OK."

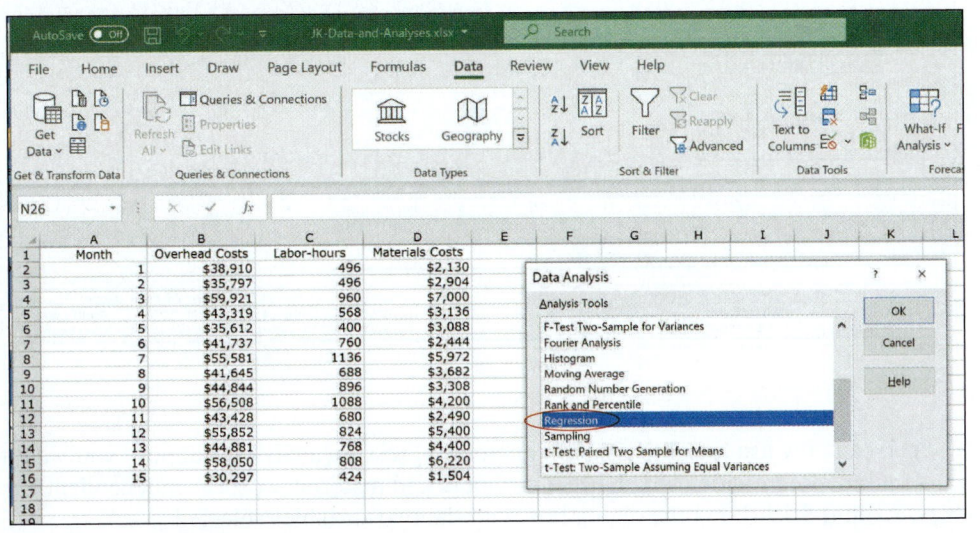

Exhibit 5.16

Selecting the Data
Analysis Option and
Choosing Regression
Analysis

Step 4: *Select the data to use in the regression.*

Choose the dependent (*Y*) and independent (*X*) variables and fill in the dialog box as shown in Exhibit 5.17. Check the box marked "Labels" to have the variable names reported with the coefficients.

Exhibit 5.17

Choosing the Variables to Be Included in the Regression Analysis

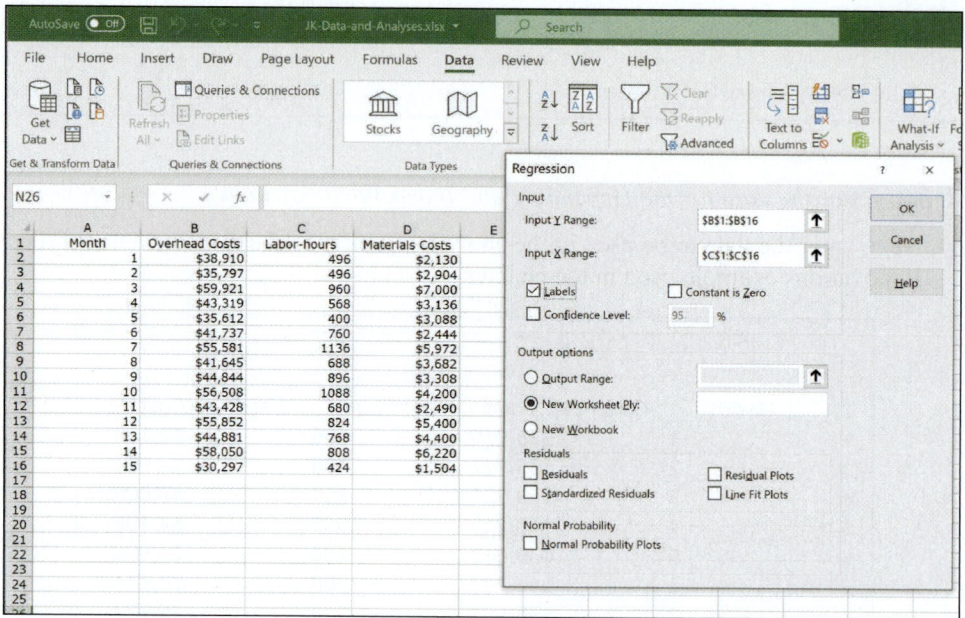

Step 5: *Run the regression.*

Select "OK" in the dialog box. The result is shown in Exhibit 5.18, which is identical to Exhibit 5.3 (except for rounding differences).

Exhibit 5.18

The Regression Results

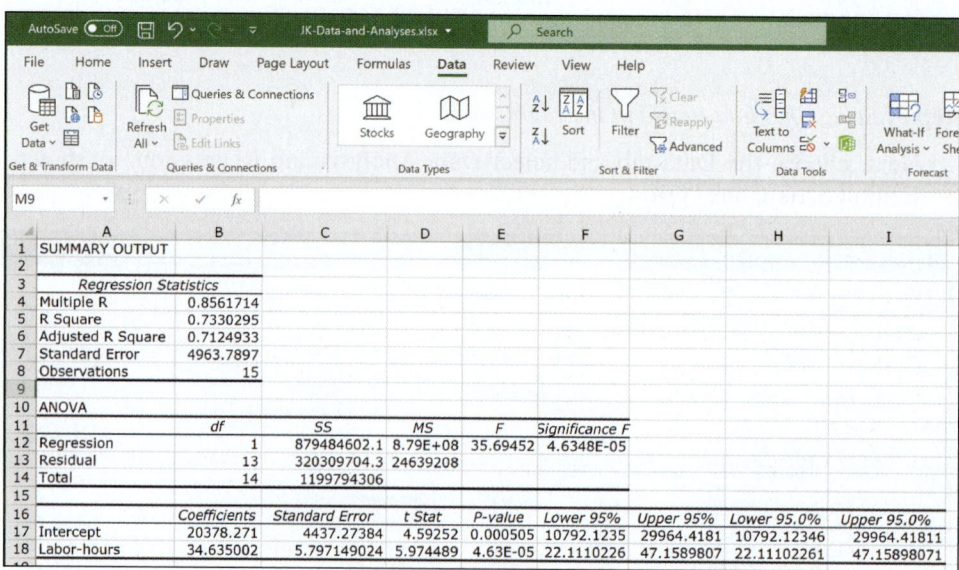

You can now use Excel to perform another regression analysis. Suppose you want to run a multiple regression using both labor-hours and materials costs as independent variables. Exhibit 5.19 shows the dialog box with the two variables selected.

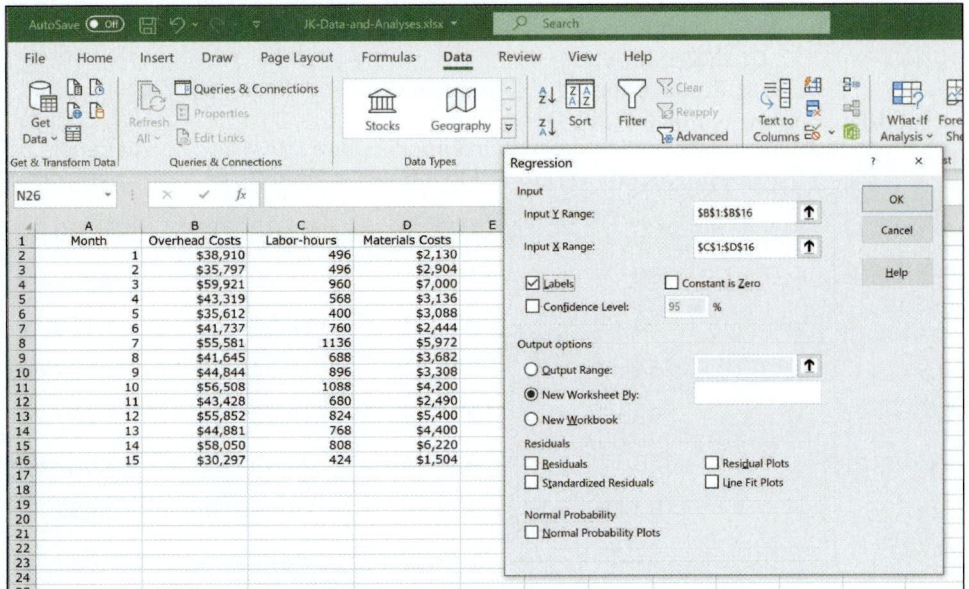

Exhibit 5.19

Performing a Multiple Regression

Exhibit 5.20 shows the results for the multiple regression.

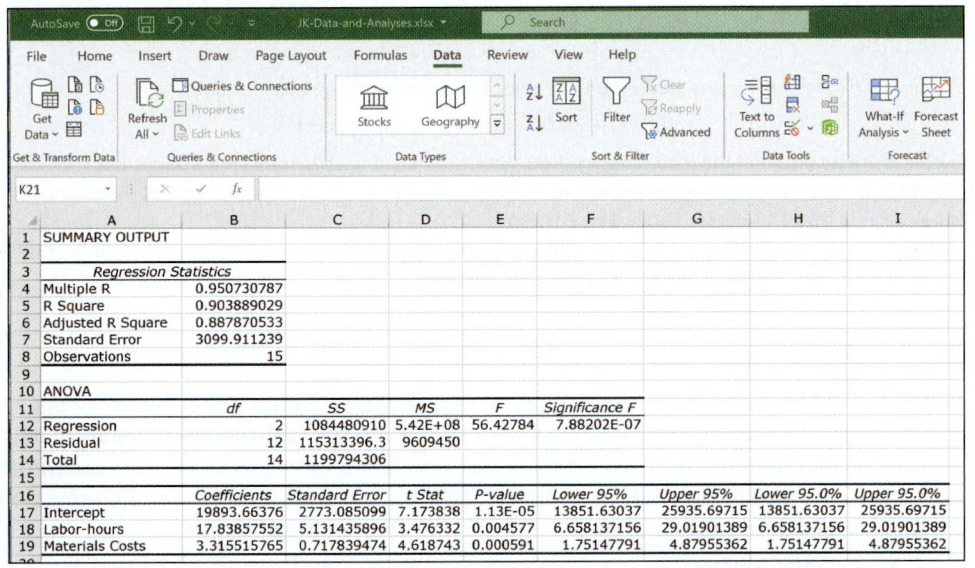

Exhibit 5.20

Multiple Regression Results

APPENDIX B: LEARNING CURVES

Engineers have found the following mathematical relationship for the learning phenomenon:

$$Y = aX^b$$

where

LO 5-7

Explain and apply the mathematical relationship describing the learning phenomenon.

Y = Number of labor-hours per unit required for the last single unit produced,
a = Number of labor-hours required to produce the first unit,
X = Cumulative number of units produced, and
b = Index of learning equal to the natural logarithm (ln) of the learning rate divided by the ln of 2.

For example, for an 80 percent cumulative learning rate,

$$b = ln(.80)/ln(2) = -0.2231 \div 0.6931 = -0.3219$$

Exhibit 5.21

Learning Curve Time and Costs

Unit Produced (X)	Labor Time Required to Produce the Xth Unit (i.e., the last single unit produced)[1] (Y)	Cumulative Total Time in Labor-Hours[2]	Total Cost[3]	Average Cost per Unit[4]
1	100	100	$ 5,000.00	$5,000.00
2	80	180	9,000.00	4,500.00
3	70.21	250.21	12,510.50	4,170.17
4	64	314.21	15,710.50	3,927.63
5	59.56	373.77	18,688.50	3,737.70
6	56.17	429.94	21,497.00	3,582.83
7	53.45	483.39	24,169.50	3,452.79
8	51.2	534.59	26,729.50	3,341.19

[1]Going down the column, the labor time for each unit comes from the formula, $Y = aX^b$. For example, the labor time to produce the third unit is found as follows: $Y = 100$ hours to produce the first unit times 3 (because this is the third unit produced), to the exponent -0.3219, which is the learning rate coefficient for an 80 percent learning rate.

So,

$$Y = 100 \times 3^{-0.3219} = 70.21 \text{ hours}$$

[2] This is the sum of the hours worked on the units. For example, three units requires

$$100.00 + 80.00 + 70.21 = 250.21 \text{ hours}$$

[3] This is the total cost of the labor time worked, which is the cumulative total time in labor-hours times the $50 per hour labor cost given in the text on page 206. For example, the total cost of producing three units = 250.21 hours × $50 = $12,510.50.

[4] This is the average cost per unit, which is the total cost of the units produced divided by the number of units produced. For example, the average cost per unit of producing three units = $12,510.50 ÷ 3 = $4,170.17.

Exhibit 5.21 shows the time per unit required to produce up to eight units for an 80 percent learning curve. Assuming the labor cost is $50 per hour, the table shows the marginal and average cost per unit and the total costs of the cumulative units produced. If you compare this table to the discussion in the text around Exhibit 5.7, then you will see that this table and the discussion in the text coincide at one, two, four, and eight units.

These calculations can also be easily done online with free resources such as Wolfram Alpha (https://www.wolframalpha.com) or Good Calculators (https://goodcalculators .com/learning-curve-calculator/.) If you use the Good Calculator tool, be sure to select Crawford's model to reflect the unit cost calculations in the appendix.

REVIEW QUESTIONS

5-1.   Why is cost estimation important for managerial decision making?

5-2.   What are the common methods of cost estimation?

5-3.   Which method of cost estimation is *not* usually based primarily on company accounting records? Explain.

5-4.   Under what conditions is the engineering estimates technique preferred to other estimation techniques?

5-5.   If one wishes to prepare a cost estimate using regression analysis and enters data into a program to compute regression estimates, what problems might be encountered?

5-6.   When using cost estimation methods based on past data, what are the trade-offs between gathering more data and gathering less?

5-7. What is the difference between simple and multiple regression?

5-8. What is the difference between R^2 and adjusted R^2?

5-9. Why are accurate cost estimates important?

5-10. What are three practical implementation problems when using regression analysis to estimate costs?

5-11. Why is it important to incorporate learning into cost estimates? Is learning only important in manufacturing?

5-12. What are some complications that can arise when collecting data for cost estimation?

CRITICAL ANALYSIS AND DISCUSSION QUESTIONS

5-13. Why might an experienced executive prefer account analysis to statistical cost estimation methods?

5-14. When preparing cost estimates for account analysis purposes, should the costs be extracted from the historical accounting records?

5-15. How can one compensate for the effects of price instability when preparing cost estimates using high-low or regression techniques?

5-16. Some people claim that the scattergraph and the regression methods go hand in hand. Why?

5-17. When using past data to predict a cost that has fixed and variable components, it is possible to have an equation with a negative intercept. Does this mean that at a zero production level, the company will make money on its fixed costs? Explain.

5-18. A decision maker is interested in obtaining a cost estimate based on a regression equation. There are no problems with changes in prices, costs, technology, or relationships between activity and cost. Only one variable is to be used. What are some questions an analyst should consider if a regression is prepared for this purpose?

5-19. Consider the Business Application item "Data Analytics for Managing Operations and Forecasting Revenue." How would using analytic techniques, including regression analysis, be similar for forecasting revenue and estimating costs? How would it differ?

5-20. A friend comes to you with the following problem. "I provided my boss with a cost equation using regression analysis. He was unhappy with the results. He told me to do more work and not return until I had a lower cost estimate for one of the variables—the number of machine-hours. My initial analysis covered the last 36 months (36 observations). By dropping four months in which the relation between costs and machine-hours was very high, I was able to get a lower cost estimate for machine-hours. My boss was happy with my new results. Do you think that what I did was unethical?" How would you respond?

5-21. You are in the middle of performing a cost study and are using statistical regression analysis to make some cost estimates. As you proceed, you realize that there could be errors in the accounting records. For example, maintenance costs were recorded as zero in December. However, you know that maintenance was performed in December. You find that maintenance costs were about double the normal monthly amount in the next month, January. You suspect that maintenance costs were not recorded in December, the last month of the year, so the department's costs would appear to be below budget. The apparent error could affect regression analysis because you are using both December and January in your analysis. Should you report your concerns about the way maintenance costs have been recorded? If so, to whom would you report your concerns?

5-22. Give at least three applications of the learning phenomenon that were not mentioned in the text.

5-23. Are learning curves likely to affect materials costs per unit? Explain.

5-24. McDonald's, the fast-food restaurant, is known for high employee turnover, high quality, and low costs. Using your knowledge of the learning phenomenon, how does McDonald's get high quality and low costs when it has so much employee turnover?

5-25. A manager asks you for a cost estimate to open a new retail outlet and says, "I want you to use statistical analysis, so it will be based on real data and therefore objective." How might you respond?

5-26. Consider a bank that offers both online and branch access for customers. Based on the estimated costs of service through the two channels, the bank has decided it should motivate customers to use online services in place of branch services. After several months, it has persuaded over 50 percent of its customers to use the online service for most of their business. However, with the latest profit report, it appears that the bank is actually making lower profits than before. Why might that be?

EXERCISES    All applicable Exercises are included in Connect.

(LO 5-1, 2)   **5-27. Methods of Estimating Costs: Engineering Estimates**

Collingwood Contractors (CC) designs and builds new model homes for individual customers. CC has developed a reputation in the market for relatively upscale, unique designs with high-end finishings. CC has developed several formulas, which it uses to estimate costs and provide price quotes for prospective buyers. These include costs for materials, labor, and other resources. Although multiple configurations are possible for any house, CC uses three levels (or tiers) to represent increasing levels of luxury in terms of materials used. In addition, the customer can choose among three levels of increasingly sophisticated appliances and other house equipment. Finally, there is cost to bring utilities (electricity, water, and so on) to the house if required. Of course, these estimates are dependent on the region of the country and whether the lot is located in a city or in a suburb or rural area. If the building site is in a city, a premium is added based on the building and equipment costs. The following are the cost estimates for one region in the Northwest:

Design and administrative costs.	$35,000
Building costs per square foot (Tier I)	110
Building costs per square foot (Tier II).	180
Building costs per square foot (Tier III)	235
Equipment (appliances, and so on)—Ruby	18,000
Equipment (appliances, and so on)—Sapphire.	27,000
Equipment (appliances, and so on)—Emerald	36,000
Utilities required? If yes	39,000
City premium (applied to building and equipment costs).	15%

Required

a.   A customer has expressed interest in having CC build a Tier III, 4,500-square-foot home. The building site is a city lot, and the customer wants the Sapphire-level equipment. Based on the engineering estimates above, what will such a house cost to build? No additional utilities access is required.

b.   Another customer has expressed interest in having CC build a smaller, Tier I home, but with Emerald-level equipment. This home will be on a vacant lot in the country and requires utilities access to be added. The customer has chosen a 2,200-square-foot design. Based on the engineering estimates above, what will such a house cost to build?

(LO 5-1, 2)   **5-28. Methods of Estimating Costs: Engineering Estimates**

Ferdinand Construction (FC) manages the design and construction of hospitals. Ferdinand has developed several formulas that it uses to quote jobs. These include costs of basic construction but exclude equipment and furniture. These estimates are also dependent on the purpose of the hospital (teaching hospitals are more costly to build) and location (downtown hospitals are more costly to build). Both of these are based on the building costs. The estimated costs also depend on whether the hospital has few or many stories (high-rise buildings are more expensive). The following are the cost estimates for one region in the Northeast:

Design costs.	$15,000,000
Building costs—per square foot (low-rise).	300
Building costs—per square foot (high-rise).	360
Downtown premium	60%
Teaching hospital premium	20%

Required

A local university medical school has asked Ferdinand Construction to provide a quote on a high-rise teaching hospital located in the city center downtown. The university estimates the hospital will be 300,000 square feet in total. Based on the engineering estimates above, what will such a hospital cost to build?

5-29. Methods of Estimating Costs: Engineering Estimates   (LO 5-1, 2)
Refer to the information in Exercise 5-28.

Required
A rural county government has requested an estimate to build a 200,000-square-foot hospital in a small city (though the largest in the county). It will be a single-story building and not affiliated with any teaching institution. Based on the engineering estimates given in Exercise 5-28, what will such a hospital cost to build?

5-30. Methods of Estimating Costs: Engineering Estimates   (LO 5-1, 2)
Dickerson Consultants offers logistics advice for large retail firms. Dickerson classifies its consultants into three categories, based on their experience and skills. The three levels are partner, senior, and associate. Dickerson quotes prices for prospective clients based on standardized hourly billing rates for the consultants. It then adds an estimate for travel, supplies, and so on (referred to as *out-of-pocket costs*). Finally, it applies a percentage to the total of consultant time and out-of-pocket cost to cover general and administrative (G&A) expense. The estimates for each of these elements are shown as follows:

Partner cost (per hour)	$1,000
Senior cost (per hour).	750
Associate cost (per hour).	425
G&A factor	35%

Required
Grand Fashions, a national clothing chain, has requested a quote from Dickerson for an analysis of the current Grand Fashions supply chain. The financial staff at Dickerson and the managing partner for the clothing sector estimate that the work will require 25 partner hours, 300 senior hours, and 700 associate hours. Based on similar jobs, they estimate out-of-pocket costs to be $135,000. What is the estimated cost of the proposed consulting project, based on these estimates?

5-31. Methods of Estimating Costs: Account Analysis   (LO 5-1, 2)
Summit Corporation manufactures machines for the apparel industry. The production manager and cost analyst reviewed the accounts for the previous quarter and have provided an estimated breakdown of the fixed and variable portions of manufacturing overhead:

	Fixed	Variable	Total
Administration and supervision	$ 30,450	$ 9,500	$ 39,950
Engineering and indirect labor	5,700	58,900	64,600
Indirect supplies	7,600	26,600	34,200
Facilities cost	133,000	11,400	144,400
Repair and maintenance	57,900	76,000	133,900
Total.	$234,650	$182,400	$417,050

Direct materials for the quarter amounted to $351,500. Direct labor for the quarter was $712,500. During the quarter, 9,500 units were produced.

Required
a. No changes are expected in these cost relations next quarter. The firm has budgeted production of 12,350 units. Provide an estimate for total production cost for next quarter.
b. Determine the cost per unit of production for the previous quarter and the estimated cost per unit next quarter.

5-32. Methods of Estimating Costs: Account Analysis   (LO 5-1, 2)
Hemlock Nutritional Supplements (HNS) provides you with the following accounting records on manufacturing cost for the most recent month:

Direct materials	$126,000
Direct labor.	105,000
Variable overhead.	92,400

Production was 60,000 units (cases). Fixed manufacturing overhead was $144,000.

For the coming year, costs are expected to increase as follows: direct materials costs by 30 percent, excluding any effect of volume changes; direct labor by 6 percent; and fixed manufacturing overhead by 13.5 percent. Variable manufacturing overhead per unit is expected to remain the same.

Required

a.   Prepare a cost estimate for a volume level of 48,000 units of product in the upcoming month.

b.   Determine the costs per unit for the most recent month and for the upcoming month.

(LO 5-1, 2)   **5-33. Methods of Estimating Costs: Account Analysis**

Hughes Payroll and Clerical Services (HPCS) provides payroll, bookkeeping, and other services to small businesses. HPCS financial records show the following costs for last quarter (QTR 1):

Supplies	$ 14,000
Employee costs.	1,015,000
Total administration.	455,000

HPCS recorded 4,375 billable hours in QTR 1, and fixed administrative cost was $245,000.

Assuming no change in billable hours in the next quarter (QTR 2), supplies costs are expected to increase by 5 percent. Direct labor costs are expected to increase by 12 percent. Variable administration per billable hour is expected to remain the same, but fixed administration cost is expected to decrease by 7 percent.

Required

a.   HPCS expects to bill 5,425 hours next quarter. What are the estimated direct materials, direct labor, variable overhead, and fixed overhead costs for next quarter (QTR 2)?

b.   Determine the total costs per billable hour for QTR 1 and QTR 2.

(LO 5-1, 2)   **5-34. Methods of Estimating Costs: High-Low**

Kirby Fasteners supplies the electronics industry with accessories for cases, disc enclosures, and so on. Below are the costs and volumes for the past six months at its Plant #6:

	A	B
1	Kirby Fasteners	
2		
3	Plant #6	
4	January-June Results	
5		
6	Volume (Units)	Total Cost
7	10,400	$ 189,990
8	9,340	180,795
9	12,670	215,400
10	13,200	228,080
11	11,200	207,555
12	10,980	204,212
13		

Required

a.   Use the high-low method to estimate the monthly fixed cost of production and the variable cost of production per unit.

b.   Kirby analysts forecast a production level of 11,400 units in July. Based on the results from requirement (a), what would be the estimated production costs in July?

5-35. Methods of Estimating Costs: High-Low, Ethical Issues

(LO 5-1, 2)

Witherell Musum of Technology (WMT) provides the following data on the costs of maintenance and the number of visitors for the last four quarters:

Number of Visitors per Quarter	Quarterly Staffing Costs
12,775	$404,750
15,656	461,400
14,049	425,750
16,625	464,810

Required

a. Use the high-low method to estimate the fixed cost of quarterly staffing and the staffing cost per visitor.

b. The museum expects a record 22,500 visitors next quarter because several new conventions have been scheduled. What would be the estimated staffing costs?

c. The director of the museum is considering contracting with an outside firm for most staffing. The director is especially concerned with the fixed costs of staffing. The museum director tells you, the cost analyst, that 16,625 visitors is an outlier and should not be used in the analysis. Assume that this will lower estimated fixed costs. Is it ethical to treat this observation as an outlier?

5-36. Methods of Estimating Costs: High-Low

(LO 5-1, 2)

Fiske Corporation manufactures a popular regional brand of kitchen utensils. The design and variety have been fairly constant over the last three years. The managers at Fiske are planning for some changes in the product line next year, but first they want to understand better the relation between activity and factory costs as experienced with the current products. Discussions with the plant supervisor suggest that overhead seems to vary with labor-hours, machine-hours, or both. The following data were collected from the last three years of operations:

	A	B	C	D
1	Quarter	Machine-Hours	Labor-Hours	Factory Costs
2	1	18,850	14,905	$ 3,388,671
3	2	18,590	15,477	3,425,136
4	3	17,480	16,720	3,617,144
5	4	19,240	15,983	3,573,240
6	5	21,280	17,501	3,812,284
7	6	19,630	17,369	3,777,312
8	7	19,240	15,290	3,531,726
9	8	18,850	14,366	3,369,102
10	9	18,460	15,994	3,512,487
11	10	20,670	16,995	3,730,734
12	11	17,550	14,278	3,324,915
13	12	18,460	17,644	3,723,786
14				

Required

a. Use the high-low method to estimate the fixed and variable portions of factory costs based on labor-hours.

b. Managers expect the plant to operate at 16,000 labor-hours next quarter. Assuming the relationship remains the same with the new product line, what are the estimated quarterly factory costs?

5-37. Methods of Estimating Costs: High-Low

(LO 5-1, 2)

Refer to the information in Exercise 5-36 for Fiske Corporation.

Required

a. Use the high-low method to estimate the fixed and variable portions of factory costs based on machine-hours.

b. Managers expect the plant to operate at 21,000 machine-hours next quarter. Assuming the relationship remains the same with the new product line, what are the estimated quarterly factory costs?

(LO 5-1, 2)   **5-38. Methods of Estimating Costs: Data Visualization**
Refer to the information in Exercise 5-36 for Fiske Corporation.

Required
Prepare a scattergraph based on the factory cost and labor-hour data for Fiske Corporation in Exercise 5-36.

(LO 5-1, 2)   **5-39. Methods of Estimating Costs: Data Visualization**
Refer to the information in Exercise 5-36 for Fiske Corporation.

Required
Prepare a scattergraph based on the factory cost and machine-hour data in Exercise 5-36.

(LO 5-1, 3)   **5-40. Methods of Estimating Costs: Simple Regression**
Results from a regression of factory costs on labor-hours using the data of Fiske Corporation (Exercise 5-36) are as follows:

> Equation:
>   Overhead = $1,401,352 + ($134.90 × Labor-hours)
> Statistical data
>   Correlation coefficient 963
> R^2 928

Required
Managers expect the plant to operate at 16,000 labor-hours next quarter. Assuming the relationship remains the same with the new product line and using the results from this regression, what are the estimated quarterly factory costs?

(LO 5-1, 3)   **5-41. Methods of Estimating Costs: Simple Regression**
Results from a regression of factory costs on machine-hours using the data of Fiske Corporation (Exercise 5-36) are as follows:

> Equation:
>   Overhead = $1,770,363 + ($94.36 × Machine-hours)
> Statistical data
>   Correlation coefficient 625
> R^2 391

Required
Managers expect the plant to operate at 21,000 machine-hours next quarter. Assuming the relationship remains the same with the new product line and using the results from this regression, what are the estimated quarterly factory costs?

(LO 5-1, 3)   **5-42. Methods of Estimating Costs: Multiple Regression**
Results from a multiple regression of factory costs on labor-hours and machine-hours using the data of Fiske Corporation (Exercise 5-36) are as follows:

> Equation:
>   Overhead = $993,339 + ($33.79 × Machine-hours) +
>   ($120.26 × Labor-hours)
> Statistical data
>   Correlation coefficient 984
> R^2 967
>   Adjusted R^2 960

Required
Managers expect the plant to operate at 16,000 labor-hours and 21,000 machine-hours next quarter. Assuming the relationship remains the same with the new product line and using the results from this regression, what are the estimated quarterly factory costs?

5-43. Interpretation of Cost Estimation Results: Data Analysis and Visualization   (LO 5-1, 3)

Refer to the data and results from Exercises 5-36 through 5-42 for Fiske Corporation. Managers at Fiske Corporation are unsure which estimate of factory costs should be used next quarter and have asked you for a recommendation.

Required

Based on the results of the high-low estimation and the regression analyses completed in Exercises 5-36 through 5-42, prepare a short memo recommending the estimate of factory cost you would recommend. Include any visualizations of the data that are appropriate for supporting your recommendation.

5-44. Methods of Estimating Costs: High-Low   (LO 5-1, 2)

Waveney DIY Centers (WDC) operates a few dozen stores in the eastern United States. The stores are popular with home remodelers, contractors, and do-it-yourself customers. The managers at Waveney are interested in understanding what drives costs as well as getting better cost estimates when planning new stores. The area manager for the Southeast Region is interested in new data analysis approaches to management and offered to run a test using data from the 14 stores in the region.

The initial thoughts of the managers and the financial analysts in the region were that two primary factors drove store costs: store area (square footage) and revenue. The following data were collected from the most recent year of operations (revenues and costs in thousands of dollars):

	A	B	C	D
1		**Revenues**	**Area**	**Costs**
2	**Store**	**($000)**	**(Square Feet)**	**($000)**
3	SE-01	$ 20,545	69,147	$ 15,799
4	SE-02	15,482	51,417	12,495
5	SE-03	25,721	83,331	19,210
6	SE-04	19,389	67,374	15,079
7	SE-05	19,666	58,509	15,112
8	SE-06	17,756	67,374	14,099
9	SE-07	24,505	95,748	18,691
10	SE-08	12,701	46,098	10,747
11	SE-09	23,081	78,012	17,453
12	SE-10	15,830	62,055	12,864
13	SE-11	20,358	65,601	15,633
14	SE-12	17,120	72,693	13,797
15	SE-13	13,674	62,055	11,570
16	SE-14	22,904	74,466	17,294
17				

Required

a. Use the high-low method to estimate the fixed and variable portions of store costs based on store revenues.

b. The managers in the region are interested in opening a new store with expected revenues of $19 million. Assuming the data and cost estimates from the current stores are appropriate for the new store (SE-15), what are the estimated store costs for store SE-15?

c. Managers are also considering a "mega-store" with revenues of $30 million. Based on the results from the high-low analysis in requirement (*a*), what are the estimated store costs for the mega store?

d. Are you more or less confident in the estimate obtained in requirement (*c*) relative to the estimate in requirement (*b*), or are you equally confident in both? Explain.

5-45. Methods of Estimating Costs: High-Low   (LO 5-1, 2)

Refer to the information in Exercise 5-44 for Waveney DIY Centers.

Required

a. Use the high-low method to estimate the fixed and variable portions of store costs based on store area.

b. The managers in the region are interested in opening a new store with expected area of 50,000 square feet. Assuming the data and cost estimates from the current stores are appropriate for the new store (SE-16), what are the estimated store costs for store SE-16?

    c.   Managers are also considering a concept store focused on downtown home and condo own-ers. These stores would have a much smaller area and carry a narrower range of products. The managers envision such stores being an average of 35,000 square feet. Based on the results from the high-low analysis in requirement (*a*), what are the estimated store costs for the aver-age concept store?

    d.   Are you more or less confident in the estimate obtained in requirement (*c*) relative to the esti-mate in requirement (*b*), or are you equally confident in both? Explain.

(LO 5-1, 2)   **5-46. Methods of Estimating Costs: Data Visualization**
Refer to the information in Exercise 5-44.

Required
Prepare a scattergraph based on the store cost and revenue data for Waveney DIY Centers in Exercise 5-44.

(LO 5-1, 2)   **5-47. Methods of Estimating Costs: Data Visualization**
Refer to the information in Exercise 5-44.

Required
Prepare a scattergraph based on the store cost and store area data for Waveney DIY Centers in Exercise 5-44.

(LO 5-1, 3)   **5-48. Methods of Estimating Costs: Simple Regression**
Results from a regression of store costs on revenues using the data of Waveney DIY Centers (Exercise 5-44) are as follows.

> Equation:
>   Store costs = $2,591.22 + (64.6% × Revenue)
> Statistical data
>   Correlation coefficient 999
> R^2 998

Required
The managers in the region are interested in opening a new store with expected revenues of $19 million. Assuming the data and cost estimates from the current stores are appropriate for the new store (SE-17), what are the estimated store costs for store SE-17 using the results from this regression?

(LO 5-1, 3)   **5-49. Methods of Estimating Costs: Simple Regression**
Results from a regression of store costs on store area using the data of Waveney DIY Centers (Exercise 5-44) are as follows:

> Equation:
>   Store costs = $3,025.02 + ($0.176 × Area)
> Statistical data
>   Correlation coefficient 863
> R^2 745

Required
The managers in the region are interested in opening a new store with expected area of 50,000 square feet. Assuming the data and cost estimates from the current stores are appropriate for the new store (SE-18), what are the estimated store costs for store SE-18 using the results from this regression?

(LO 5-1, 3)   **5-50. Methods of Estimating Costs: Multiple Regression**
Results from a multiple regression of store costs on revenues and area using the data of Waveney DIY Centers (Exercise 5-44) are as follows:

Equation:
    Store cost = $2,298.88 + (60.0% × Revenues)
            + ($0.017 × Area)
Statistical data
    Correlation coefficient 999
    Adjusted R^2 999

Required
The managers in the region are interested in opening a new store with expected revenues of $19 million and expected area of 50,000 square feet. Assuming the data and cost estimates from the current stores are appropriate for the new store (SE-19), what are the estimated store costs for store SE-19 using the results from this regression?

5-51. Interpretation of Cost Estimation Results: Data Analysis and Visualization   (LO 5-3)
Refer to the data and results from Exercises 5-44 through 5-50 for Waveney DIY Centers. Managers at Waveney are unsure which estimate of store costs should be used when planning new stores and have asked you for a recommendation.

Required
Based on the results of the high-low estimation and the regression analyses completed in Exercises 5-44 through 5-50, prepare a short memo recommending the estimate of store cost you would recommend. Include any visualizations of the data that are appropriate for supporting your recommendation.

5-52. Interpretation of Regression Results: Multiple Choice   (LO 5-3)
Talon Services offers standardized job counseling services. The company is planning a new service line targeted to active seniors who are retiring and looking forward to a new career. The service will sell for a flat $960 per client and will consist of a standardized offering. The service will consist of a total of 8 hours with a counseling specialist and a battery of tests to assess interests and aptitudes. Counseling specialists, who are contract employees, are paid $32 per hour. The testing is estimated to cost $120 per client.

Administrative costs for the new service have not been estimated, but the company has collected information on counseling hours and administrative costs for other services over the past 15 months. The following is a summary of a simple regression of administrative costs on counseling hours:

Simple Regression Analysis Results
Dependent variable—Administrative costs (monthly)
Independent variable—Counseling hours (monthly)
Computed values
    Intercept $75,000
    Coefficient on independent variable . . . . $ 18.40
    Coefficient of correlation 0.835
    R^2 . . . .   0.697

Required
a. What percentage of the variation in administrative costs is explained by the independent variable?
    1. 83.5%   4. 48.6%
    2. 69.7%   5. Some other amount
    3. 92.1%
b. What is the total administrative cost for an estimated activity level of 5,400 counseling hours?
    1. $99,360   4. $174,360
    2. $75,000   5. Some other amount
    3. $24,360

c.   What is the total estimated variable cost per client (assuming that counseling costs are variable costs)?

1. $523.20   4. $147.20
2. $403.20   5. Some other amount
3. $267.20

d.   What is the expected contribution margin per client to be earned?

1. $704.00   4. $436.80
2. $556.80   5. Some other amount
3. $584.00

e.   What is the estimating equation for total cost based on number of clients implied by these results?

1. Total cost = $75,000 + ($436.80 × Number of clients)
2. Total cost = $75,000 + ($403.20 × Number of clients)
3. Total cost = $75,000 + ($50.40 × Number of counseling-hours)
4. Some other equation

(CMA adapted)

(LO 5-3)   **5-53. Interpretation of Regression Results**

Belfast Export-Import Partners has a large staff of buyers and sales personnel who travel extensively on company business. The CFO is trying to manage travel costs for the sales staff and has collected monthly information from the past 24 months on sales dollars (the dependent variable) and travel costs (the independent variable). The regression results indicated the following relation:

$$\text{Sales dollars} = \$802{,}360 - (23.78 \times \text{Travel costs})$$
$$\text{Correlation coefficient} = -.652$$

These results seemed to imply that travel costs were reducing sales. The CFO concluded that there must be a problem in the way the data were collected.

Required

Help the CFO. What might cause the negative relationship between travel costs and sales?

(LO 5-1, 2, 3)   **5-54. Methods of Cost Estimation: Account Analysis and Simple Regression Analysis**

Point Products produces field hockey balls, which are packaged in cases. The balls are produced in a single plant. Because of the nature of the production process at Point Products, overhead includes all labor costs. Data on production output (in cases) and total overhead costs (in thousands of dollars) from the past 15 months follow:

	A	B	C
1	**Month**	**Cases**	**Costs**
2	1	4,426	$ 461.4
3	2	3,291	239.4
4	3	5,334	558.1
5	4	4,313	433.8
6	5	3,745	347.6
7	6	4,313	321.3
8	7	6,129	542.9
9	8	2,951	153.4
10	9	4,994	488.8
11	10	3,972	275.9
12	11	4,199	437.9
13	12	4,653	302.3
14	13	3,972	195.8
15	14	4,767	502.5
16	15	3,178	238.8

Using the data given, the cost analyst at Point Products ran a regression analysis of overhead costs on number of cases, with the following results:

Dependent variable:	Monthly overhead costs
Independent variable:	Production output (cases)
Computed values:	
Intercept:........................	−199.7
Coefficient on cases:	0.132
R^2	0.715

At the same time, the cost analyst, working with the plant manager, started an account analysis of the individual overhead accounts. They estimated a fixed cost per month of $22,600 and a variable cost per case of $80.

Required

a. Based on the results of the regression analysis, what are the estimated fixed costs per month and variable cost per case at Point Products?
b. Based on the results of the regression analysis, what would be the estimated overhead costs for a month in which 5,000 cases were produced?
c. Based on the results of the account analysis, what would be the estimated overhead costs for a month in which 5,000 cases were produced?

5-55. Interpretation of Cost Estimation Results: Data Analysis and Visualization   (LO 5-5)
Refer to the information for Point Products in Exercise 5-54. The managers at Point Products are uncertain what to do with these costs estimation results. Specifically, they are uncertain which, if either, method (account analysis or regression analysis) they should use or whether it may depend on the information they want for making their decisions. They ask you for your recommendations.

Required
Write a memo with your recommendation about when or how to use these analyses. Be sure to state your reasons and provide any visual information that would help explain your reasoning.

5-56. Interpretation of Regression Results: Simple Regression   (LO 5-3)
Clarion Clinics operates a chain of 24-hour walk-in clinics. The administrator is trying to understand the variation in Clarion's costs across the different clinics. The chief medical officer believes that the number of walk-in clients is the best measure to explain an individual clinic's costs. The cost analyst collected data from the past year from Clarion's 27 clinics. The data collected were clinic cost (labor, supplies, and so on) along with the number of walk-in clients visiting each of the clinics. The following output was generated from a regression analysis of clinic cost on walk-in clients:

Equation	
Intercept........................	$126,250
Coefficient on clients	$ 76
Statistical data	
Correlation coefficient	0.527
R^2	0.278

Required
a. Use the regression output to write the cost equation for clinic costs.
b. Based on the cost equation, compute the estimated costs for a clinic with 15,000 walk-in clients in a year.
c. The director of surgery has asked you for advice on whether he should rely on the estimate. What will you say?

5-57. Learning Curves   (LO 5-4)
Shrewsbury Technologies, which manufactures high-technology instruments for spacecraft, is considering the sale of a navigational unit to a private company that wishes to launch its own

communications satellite. The company plans to purchase 8 units, although it would also consider buying 16 units. Shrewsbury has started a chart relating labor time required to units produced:

Units Produced (X)	Time Required to Produce the Xth Unit
1	5,000 hours
2	4,500 hours
4	4,050 hours
8	?
16	?

Required

a. Complete the chart by filling in the labor time required to produce 8 and 16 units.

b. Assume that labor time costs $140 per hour. Compare the cost of producing the 1st unit to the cost of producing the 16th unit. What is the percentage of the cost of the 16th unit to the cost of the 1st unit?

(LO 5-4)   5-58. Learning Curves

Winkleman Associates requires prospective recruits to take an examination that includes both computational and essay questions. It employs contract workers to grade the exams. Hiring of Winkleman recruits takes place four times per year, and a different exam is used each time. The contract workers are paid $25 per hour to grade the exams.

The last worker to grade exams graded 16 complete exams. A Winkleman analyst, who is interested in learning curves, estimated that the worker exhibited an 80 percent learning rate. The worker was paid $204.80 for the last exam (the 16th) that was graded.

Required

a. Based on the estimated rate of learning, how long did it take the worker to grade the first exam?

b. What is the percentage of the cost of the 16th exam to the cost of the 1st exam?

(LO 5-4)   5-59. Learning Curves

Fountain Precision Products (FPP) manufactures high-technology measurement systems. The systems are both complex and unique in the sense that only a handful are sold, usually to a single customer's specification. The last unit of model FPP-28X sold was the eighth produced. The labor cost for that unit was $6,360.56 and required 127.2112 hours of labor. The second unit, produced required 172.0000 hours of labor.

Required

a. Assuming that learning has been consistent for this product, what is the rate of learning?

b. Assuming that the hourly labor rate has remained the same, what was the labor cost to produce the fourth unit?

(LO 5-4, 7)   5-60. Learning Curves (Appendix B)

Refer to the example in Appendix B. The numbers in Exhibit 5.21 for the fifth, sixth, and seventh units were given.

Required

Using the formula $Y = aX^b$ and the data given in the problem, verify the labor time required and the cost amounts for the fifth, sixth, and seventh units. ("Verify" means that you should check the accuracy of the amounts given in Exhibit 5.21.)

PROBLEMS    **connect**   All applicable Problems are included in Connect.

(LO 5-1, 2)   5-61. Account Analysis

The Customer Support Department at Wadsworth Supply is analyzing the costs of its services. A cost analyst has collected monthly data on the three main functions of the department and the total costs for the last year, which follow.

Month	Special Reports Completed	Customer Accounts Maintained	Transactions Processed	Customer Support Costs ($000)
1.........	31	2,795	85,140	$ 1,276
2.........	17	2,636	65,240	1,378
3.........	53	2,597	71,540	1,280
4.........	37	1,831	49,580	1,226
5.........	29	1,948	50,230	1,232
6.........	41	1,840	44,710	1,016
7.........	35	1,126	28,770	1,020
8.........	56	1,057	25,640	1,086
9.........	20	1,289	30,240	1,010
10.........	26	2,545	67,870	1,296
11.........	12	1,831	51,110	1,160
12.........	43	1,905	49,930	1,152
Totals......	400	23,400	620,000	$14,132

The cost analyst also has identified the Customer Support Department costs for each of the three main functions. Any costs not assigned to one of the functions is considered general administration cost. The costs for the last year follow.

Total cost of special reports	$5,040
Total cost of maintaining customer accounts.............	3,510
Total cost of processing transactions	1,922

Required

a.   What is the cost per unit for (1) special reports completed, (2) customer accounts maintained, and (3) transactions processed?

b.   Assuming the following level of cost-driver volumes for a month, what are the accounting department's estimated costs of doing business using the account analysis approach?

- 40 special reports

- 2,500 customer accounts maintained

- 55,000 transactions processed

5-62. Account Analysis: Working Backwards and the High-Low Method   (LO 5-1, 2)

Belden Frozen Foods packages a variety of frozen meals and vegetables. In its Saratoga Street plant, the company packages frozen corn only. The cost analyst at the Saratoga plant has conducted an analysis of the plant overhead cost accounts. Partial information from the analysis, based on the month studied, is shown here:

Account	Fixed Portion	Variable Portion
Indirect labor	$43,360	$53,440
Supervision....................	16,960	18,240
Maintenance	??	32,320
Depreciation..................	52,960	??

From this information, the cost analyst used the account analysis method to derive a cost estimation equation of the form

Total cost = Monthly fixed cost + (Variable cost per case × Number of cases)

Using the newly derived equation, the cost analyst estimated overhead costs for the following two months:

	Production (cases)	Estimated Overhead Cost
Month 1................	80,000	$291,840
Month 2................	100,000	317,440

In the month the study was conducted, the plant produced 89,000 cases.

Required

a.   What is the estimated variable overhead cost per case?

b.   What is the estimated monthly fixed overhead cost?

c.   What was the fixed maintenance cost in the month the study was conducted?

d.   What was the variable depreciation cost in the month the study was conducted?

(LO 5-1, 3)   **5-63. Regressions from Published Data: Data Analysis and Visualization**
Obtain 13 years of data from the published financial statements of a company. You will be able to find the data on the Internet. Also, Moody's, Standard & Poor's, and Value Line are good sources of financial data. Using the first 12 years of data, perform a regression analysis in which the dependent variable is cost of goods sold and the independent variable is revenue (some companies call it *sales* or *sales revenue*).

Required

a.   Use the results from the regression on the first 12 years of data to estimate the cost of goods sold for year 13. How far off was your estimate of cost of goods sold for year 13?

b.   Prepare a report that describes your work and discusses reasons why your estimate of cost of goods sold is different from the actual cost of goods sold for year 13. Be sure to include any visual supporting material in your report.

(LO 5-1, 3)   **5-64. Regressions from Public Data: Data Analysis and Visualization**
Using the same data source as in Problem 5-63, collect a total of 20 years of data.

Required

a.   Using the latest 10 years of data, perform a regression analysis in which the dependent variable is cost of goods sold and the independent variable is revenue. What is the estimated coefficient on the output (sales) variable?

b.   Using all 20 years of data, perform a regression analysis in which the dependent variable is cost of goods sold and the independent variable is revenue. What is the estimated coefficient on the output (sales) variable?

c.   Which estimate would you use to estimate costs for next year for the company? Why? Be sure to include any visual supporting material in your analysis.

(LO 5-1, 2)   **5-65. High-Low Method, Data Visualization**
Fordson Bank operates a branch in a relatively small rural community. Fordson has a strong customer service focus and knows that branch visits can be important in fostering a reputation for good customer service. However, as Internet banking increases in popularity, the financial staff at Fordson question whether the costs of the branch are worth it.

As part of looking at the question, a financial analyst has collected monthly data on the number of customer visits to the branch and the operating cost of the branch over the last fiscal year. The data follow:

	A	B	C
1	Month	Customer Visits	Branch Cost
2	1	962	$ 69,600
3	2	1,378	86,250
4	3	1,170	73,750
5	4	1,014	66,875
6	5	1,586	96,120
7	6	1,222	76,250
8	7	1,144	73,750
9	8	1,248	77,500
10	9	1,430	87,500
11	10	1,040	68,125
12	11	1,092	70,625
13	12	1,066	68,750
14			

Required

a.   Estimate the monthly fixed costs and the unit variable cost per customer visit using the high-low estimation method.

b.   Draw a scattergraph relating branch costs to the number of customer visits.

c.   Considering your scattergraph, how much confidence do you have in your estimate from requirement (*a*)?

5-66. High-Low Method, Data Visualization   (LO 5-1, 2)

Willis Cosmetics produces a variety of cosmetics and hair care products. One popular shampoo is produced at the company's Genoa Street Plant (GSP). The financial staff are in the process of revising the estimates for overhead and are looking at different approaches. After much discussion, the staff selected direct labor costs as the best cost driver to explain overhead cost.

  The staff have collected monthly data on direct labor and overhead costs at GSP for the most recent fiscal year. The data follow:

	A	B	C
1	Month	Direct Labor Cost	Overhead Costs
2	1	$ 232,200	$ 122,500
3	2	292,250	271,250
4	3	248,500	152,500
5	4	215,900	97,500
6	5	264,600	187,500
7	6	259,750	175,000
8	7	243,500	137,500
9	8	336,000	463,850
10	9	303,600	312,500
11	10	220,750	105,000
12	11	204,500	82,500
13	12	227,250	113,750
14			

Required

a.   Estimate the monthly fixed costs and the unit variable cost per direct labor cost using the high-low estimation method.

b.   Draw a scattergraph relating overhead costs to the number of direct labor costs.

c.   Considering your scattergraph, how much confidence do you have in your estimate from requirement (*a*)?

5-67. High-Low Method, Data Visualization, Issues with Data   (LO 5-1, 2, 5)

Mendota Foods sells a variety of food products around the world. The company engages directly with individuals with an interest in cooking by offering ideas and recipes in various staff blogs and podcasts. The management team at Mendota believes this drives brand loyalty and allows Mendota to charge a premium for its products.

  One initiative that Mendota has been running for the last three years is a call center with staff who can provide help and answer questions about cooking in general and Mendota products in particular. The chief financial officer is interested in learning more about the costs of this initiative and how they vary with the demands placed on the center. To help answer the question, the financial staff have collected call center volume (number of calls) and call center cost for the last 12 months. The data follow:

	A	B	C
1	Month	Number of Calls	Call Center Costs
2	1	60,750	$ 287,710
3	2	67,150	268,095
4	3	60,250	238,500
5	4	62,000	244,515
6	5	45,250	182,700
7	6	74,150	280,690
8	7	52,100	252,710
9	8	65,600	282,795
10	9	77,500	314,925
11	10	45,250	153,675
12	11	66,700	292,410
13	12	69,900	271,885
14			

Required

a. Prepare a scattergraph relating call center costs to call center volume.

b. Using the high-low method, estimate call center costs for a month when call center volume is expected to be 62,250 calls.

(LO 5-1, 3)   **5-68. Interpretation of Regression Results: Simple Regression Using a Spreadsheet**

Goulburn, Inc. produces parts for heavy equipment used in mining and construction. The plant that produces one part common to many vehicles is highly automated, so all labor is considered part of factory overhead. The plant manager, who has just been promoted, would like to understand how overhead costs fluctuate in order to improve planning and budgets. After discussions with both financial and operations members of the plant staff, there is general agreement that the best cost driver for overhead is machine-hours.

Monthly data were collected from the most recent two years on machine-hours and overhead. More months of data were available, but a process change had taken place about 30 months earlier, so the staff believed any data from before that time would be misleading. The data are shown in the following table:

	A	B	C
1	Month	Machine-Hours	Factory Overhead
2	1	39,300	$ 527,100
3	2	37,300	416,500
4	3	30,100	365,800
5	4	42,400	498,200
6	5	50,600	590,700
7	6	45,500	503,400
8	7	42,400	476,900
9	8	62,100	702,400
10	9	36,300	425,300
11	10	53,700	661,000
12	11	52,700	616,700
13	12	36,300	490,500
14	13	59,900	693,000
15	14	58,900	654,700
16	15	45,500	580,000
17	16	39,300	527,900
18	17	55,800	683,400
19	18	50,600	613,700
20	19	60,900	669,500
21	20	49,600	619,100
22	21	53,700	672,100
23	22	29,100	445,000
24	23	59,900	692,400
25	24	58,900	718,500
26			

Required

a. Use the high-low estimation method to estimate the overhead cost behavior (fixed and variable components of cost) for the Goulburn plant.

b. Prepare a scattergraph showing the overhead costs plotted against the machine-hours.

c. Use a spreadsheet program to compute regression coefficients to describe the overhead cost equation.

d. Use the results of your regression analysis to develop an estimate of overhead costs assuming 48,000 machine-hours will be worked next month.

5-69. Estimation Methods—Simple Regression, Data Analysis and Visualization   (LO 5-1, 3)

Bradford Fabric Shops is a chain of retail stores offering fabrics, accessories, and machines for sewing, knitting, and so on. The company's 13 retail stores are managed by employees, most of whom started working on the sales floor and rose through the ranks. The chief financial officer (CFO) would like to understand how the operating costs of the stores (not including the cost of the goods sold) vary across stores. While there are differences among the stores in terms of location, size, and clientele, these differences are not thought to be too great.

The CFO has asked you to prepare an analysis of store operating cost and, after discussion with the CFO and the store managers, the financial staff have provided information on store operating costs and customer visits for each of the stores for the past year. (All online sales are the responsibility of a different unit and not any of the stores.) The information collected follows:

	A	B	C
1	Store	Store Visits	Store Costs
2	1	28,575	$ 208,000
3	2	30,450	221,100
4	3	39,150	280,270
5	4	28,125	205,300
6	5	31,575	224,300
7	6	36,825	262,900
8	7	31,275	232,400
9	8	37,650	267,800
10	9	38,625	283,000
11	10	29,925	218,500
12	11	31,950	296,200
13	12	38,250	269,000
14	13	36,450	266,600
15			

Required

Prepare an analysis providing the CFO and others at Bradford with information about how store operating costs are related to store visits. Be sure to include any visual information that you used in the analysis.

5-70. Interpretation of Regression Results: Multiple Choice   (LO 5-2, 3, 6)

Jordan's Gym is located in a popular vacation spot with much higher demand in the summer than in the winter. The gym has both annual memberships and individual visit prices, which makes it a popular alternative for seasonal visitors. The owner of the gym is interested in developing a budget for the coming year and would like to predict the operating costs of the gym. The accountant for the gym has compiled data on gym operating costs and gym visits, which the accountant believes is the best predictor of operating costs. The data are presented in the accompanying table, and a simple regression analysis follows.

	A	B	C
1	Month	Gym Visits	Operating Costs
2	January	828	$ 11,270
3	February	840	17,640
4	March	3,736	25,170
5	April	3,360	29,530
6	May	4,398	35,250
7	June	4,499	29,910
8	July	4,628	31,220
9	August	4,612	33,440
10	September	3,574	28,610
11	October	3,772	26,190
12	November	1,411	23,260
13	December	1,059	17,490
14			

	A	B	C	D	E	F	G
1	SUMMARY OUTPUT						
2							
3	*Regression Statistics*						
4	Multiple R	0.91424491					
5	R Square	0.83584376					
6	Adjusted R Square	0.81942813					
7	Standard Error	3057.51245					
8	Observations	12					
9							
10	ANOVA						
11		*df*	*SS*	*MS*	*F*	*Significance F*	
12	Regression	1	475996943.1	475996943	50.9176	3.1582E-05	
13	Residual	10	93483823.59	9348382.4			
14	Total	11	569480766.7				
15							
16		*Coefficients*	*Standard Error*	*t Stat*	*P-value*	*Lower 95%*	*Upper 95%*
17	Intercept	12824.3478	2014.800228	6.3650717	8.2E-05	8335.09318	17313.6025
18	Gym Visits	4.22386976	0.591938612	7.1356551	3.2E-05	2.90494834	5.54279118
19							

Required

a. In the standard regression equation $y = a + bx$, the letter b is best described as the
    1. Independent variable.   4. Correlation coefficient.
    2. Variable cost coefficient.   5. Constant coefficient.
    3. Dependent variable.

b. In the standard regression equation $y = a + bx$, the letter y is best described as the
    1. Independent variable.   4. Correlation coefficient.
    2. Variable cost coefficient.   5. Constant coefficient.
    3. Dependent variable.

c. In the standard regression equation $y = a + bx$, the letter x is best described as the
    1. Independent variable.   4. Correlation coefficient.
    2. Variable cost coefficient.   5. Constant coefficient.
    3. Dependent variable.

d. If the accountant uses the high-low method to estimate costs, the cost equation for gym operating costs is
    1. Cost = $5,708 + ($6.72 × Gym visits).   4. Cost = $6,923 + ($5.25 × Gym visits).
    2. Cost = $6,923.   5. Some other equation.
    3. Cost = $5.25 × Gym visits.

e. Based on the results of the accountant's high-low method, the estimate of gym operating costs in a month with 3,500 gym visits would be
    1. $10,375.   4. $28,500.
    2. $6,923.   5. Some other amount.
    3. $10,423.

f. The correlation coefficient (rounded) for the regression equation for operating costs is
    1. 0.819.   4. 0.956.
    2. 0.836.   5. Some other amount.
    3. 0.914.

g. The percentage of the total variance (rounded) that can be explained by the regression is
    1. 81.9.   4. 95.6.
    2. 83.6.   5. Some other amount.
    3. 91.4.

(LO 5-3, 5)   **5-71. Cost Estimation—Data Analysis and Visualization**
The Hereford Plant produces a single part used in airplane hydraulic systems. The plant manager has asked the plant controller to determine the monthly volume that would result in the plant meeting its monthly operating profit goal. Operating profits at the plant are calculated as revenue less direct costs (material and labor) less overhead (both fixed and variable). The monthly profit goal is $78,000 before taxes. The plant sells the part for $205 per unit. Direct costs are $102 per unit.

Using the high-low approach, an analyst in the controller's office has estimated overhead costs at $24,440 per month for fixed overhead costs and $80 per unit for variable overhead costs. One of the other cost analysts decided to run a simple regression and, based on that, reported that "a better cost estimation equation was"

$$\text{Monthly overhead} = \$65,420 + \$72 \text{ per unit}$$

The analyst reported that the R^2 was about 66% and that the estimated coefficient for the intercept was "not significant." The data the controller's office used for both analyses follow:

	A	B	C
	Month	Units Produced	Overhead Costs
1	Month	Units Produced	Overhead Costs
2	1	4,150	$ 356,440
3	2	4,490	375,160
4	3	4,660	380,570
5	4	5,700	480,240
6	5	4,610	394,280
7	6	5,430	446,150
8	7	4,210	352,860
9	8	5,550	454,450
10	9	4,710	502,620
11	10	4,410	370,790
12	11	5,770	486,040
13	12	5,640	456,450

The company controller is surprised that the cost estimates are so different and would like to reconcile this before reporting back to the plant manager.

Required

a.   Analyze the data and recommend a cost estimation equation based on the data provided. Be sure to include any visual support for your analysis.

b.   Based on your analysis, provide an estimate to the controller of the volume (in units) that will generate $78,000 per month in operating profits before taxes.

5-72. Interpretation of Regression Results   (LO 5-3)

Aurora Town Museum is a small town historical and cultural museum specializing in artifacts from early settlers and local residents. The town council is interested in understanding the costs of the museum given the other demands on the limited funds. After collecting data from the past year and talking to some of the museum volunteers, the town treasurer decides that costs are driven primarily by attendance (customer visits) at the museum. A regression analysis was completed with the following results:

Average monthly visits......................	326
Average monthly museum costs	$ 3,086
Regression results:	
Intercept.....................................	$ 2,070
b coefficient...............................	$ 3.12
R^2	0.7853

Required

a.   In a regression equation expressed as $y = a + bx$, how is the letter y in the regression equation best described?

b.   How is the letter x in the regression equation best described?

c.   How is the letter b in the regression equation best described?

d.   What is the percentage of the total variance that can be explained by the regression equation?

e.   Based on the data derived from the regression analysis, what are the estimated costs for 600 visits in a month?

(CMA adapted)

(LO 5-3, 6)   **5-73. Cost Estimation: Simple Regression**

The Cary Plant produces a part for agricultural equipment. The plant produces to demand rather than maintaining significant inventories, so there can be significant fluctuation in monthly output. One of the significant cost items is maintenance and repair (M&R) costs. M&R consists of both routine and unscheduled costs. The plant manager is trying to understand what effect production volume has on M&R costs and is getting conflicting information from the machine operators (who believe that higher output is related to higher M&R costs) and the financial staff (who say that their analyses do not show this). Data on monthly output (in machine-hours) and monthly M&R costs for the most recent two fiscal years follow:

	A	B	C
1	Month	Machine-Hours	M&R Cost
2	October	223,560	$ 56,510
3	November	235,980	59,320
4	December	397,440	24,150
5	January	310,500	34,230
6	February	385,020	36,340
7	March	558,900	9,140
8	April	273,240	36,580
9	May	360,180	43,380
10	June	285,660	53,230
11	July	298,080	52,290
12	August	322,920	30,250
13	September	186,300	55,570
14	October	211,140	48,070
15	November	322,920	29,780
16	December	372,600	42,670
17	January	385,020	38,220
18	February	447,120	15,940
19	March	633,420	230
20	April	335,340	41,740
21	May	298,080	35,870
22	June	422,280	22,040
23	July	447,120	28,140
24	August	360,180	28,140
25	September	285,660	42,910
26			

Required

a. Ignoring the data, would you predict that, in general, there is a positive relation between revenues and maintenance and repair costs? Why?

b. Estimate a linear regression with maintenance and repair (M&R) cost as the dependent variable and production (measured in machine-hours) as the independent variable. Does the result support your prediction in requirement (*a*)? What are some factors that may explain the result?

(LO 5-1, 3)   **5-74. High-Low Method, Data Visualization**

Genesee Fishing Tours (GFT) offers small group fishing expeditions off the local coast. The managers of the company are considering expanding the business to another city and want to put together a financial plan. As a part of that effort, the financial staff are analyzing the operating costs of GFT. They believe that a good predictor of operating cost is the number of clients that use the service. As a part of their analysis, they have collected 30 months of data on operating costs and number of clients, which follow:

	A	B	C
1	Month	Clients	Operating Cost
2	1	458	$ 36,980
3	2	741	42,790
4	3	608	41,810
5	4	526	38,500
6	5	648	41,860
7	6	436	35,850
8	7	391	34,400
9	8	713	40,310
10	9	831	42,010
11	10	565	39,240
12	11	714	44,220
13	12	652	39,980
14	13	665	41,760
15	14	548	39,680
16	15	453	38,890
17	16	371	36,030
18	17	565	50,640
19	18	613	55,770
20	19	484	44,160
21	20	518	48,570
22	21	476	45,590
23	22	481	44,680
24	23	584	53,490
25	24	602	53,820
26	25	779	65,490
27	26	649	58,830
28	27	612	54,460
29	28	527	48,060
30	29	509	46,290
31	30	547	51,590
32			

Required

a.   Estimate the operating costs assuming 700 clients for the month using the high-low method.

b.   Draw a scattergraph relating operating costs to the number of clients.

c.   Based on the scattergraph, how confident are you in your estimate of operating costs?

d.   Considering only the high-low method, what adjustments would you suggest that would give you more confidence in the estimate. (Note: You do not have to actually calculate a new estimate.)

5-75. Cost Estimation Using Simple Regression Using Spreadsheet   (LO 5-3, 6)
Refer to the information in Problem 5-74.

Required

a.   Estimate the labor costs assuming 700 clients for the month using the results of a simple regression based on the 30 months of available data.

b.   How confident are you in the estimate using the regression results? Why?

c.   You learn that starting in month 16, Genesee Fishing Tours started using a different, more personalized protocol for interacting with clients. Estimate the operating cost assuming 700 clients, using the results of a simple regression based on the data for months 16 through 30 only.

d.   How confident are you in the estimate using the regression results? Why?

(LO 5-3, 5, 6)   **5-76. Cost Estimation: Simple and Multiple Regression Using a Spreadsheet (Appendix A)**
Recall the analysis for Mendota Foods in Problem 5-67. During a discussion of those results, one of the cost analysts suggests that length of the calls (total hours) is probably a better driver of call center costs. The managers asked the analyst to collect the information and report on how it should be used. The combined data follow:

	A		B
1	Administrative salaries	$	525,000
2	Depreciation on the administrative building		228,400
3	Depreciation on the manufacturing plant		350,000
4	Direct labor		938,500
5	Direct materials inventory, September 1		213,840
6	Direct materials inventory, September 30		247,000
7	Direct materials purchased during the month		1,791,200
8	Distribution costs		131,400
9	Finished goods inventory, September 1		328,400
10	Finished goods inventory, September 30		273,900
11	Indirect manufacturing labor		108,400
12	Insurance (on manufacturing plant)		10,640
13	Legal fees		99,260
14	Maintenance (on the manufacturing plant)		43,080
15	Manufacturing plant utilities		156,820
16	Marketing costs		149,850
17	Other manufacturing plant costs		126,176
18	Sales revenue		4,530,984
19	Taxes (on manufacturing plant and property)		43,120
20	Work-in-process inventory, September 1		80,650
21	Work-in-process inventory, September 30		79,340
22			

Required

a.   Use the high-low method to estimate the fixed and variable portions of call center costs based on call center time (hours).

b.   Use the results of your high-low analysis to estimate the call center cost for a month with 16,000 hours of call center time.

c.   Prepare a scattergraph between call center costs and hours.

d.   Prepare an estimate of the cost for a month with 16,000 hours of call center time using the results from a simple regression of call center cost on call center time (hours).

e.   Prepare an estimate of the call center cost in a month of 62,250 calls and 16,000 hours of call center time (hours) using the results of a multiple regression of call center costs on call center calls and call center time (hours).

f.   Comment on the results of the regression analyses in parts (*d*) and (*e*). (*Hint:* Consider how the managers of Mendota Foods might staff their call centers and what this might mean for the data being used in the multiple regression analysis.)

(LO 5-3, 5, 6)   **5-77. Methods of Cost Analysis: Account Analysis, High-Low Method, Simple and Multiple Regression, Data Analysis and Visualization**
Prest Metal Products manufactures and sells various products. The products are manufactured at one of a few plants (depending on the product) and then shipped to a distribution center for eventual delivery to customers. The Auburn Distribution Center (ADC) of Prest Metal Products handles a subset of Prest Products. The products handled by the ADC are fairly similar in size and weight and differ primarily in features that do not affect handling or packaging.

When the sales staff at Prest receive an order, they send it to the appropriate distribution center to fill (collect units and package for shipping) and ship the units to the customer. A single order may consist of one (although unusual) or more units. Regardless of the number of units in the order, the ADC has to follow certain steps to process the order, such as verifying the customer's address and credit information, reviewing the order for errors, and so on. The ADC is also responsible for following up on any complaints from the customer about problems with the order.

The ADC expects to distribute 250,000 units of products next month. As a part of the normal planning process at the ADC, the center controller has classified next month's expected operating costs (excluding costs of the distributed product) as fixed or variable (with respect to units shipped) as follows:

	A	B	C
1	Account	Operating Costs	Behavior
2	Administration	$ 36,000	$32,000 fixed
3	Center labor	261,000	$141,500 fixed
4	Center lease	125,000	$100,000 fixed
5	Depreciation on equipment	122,200	$112,000 fixed
6	Miscellaneous	124,600	$54,000 fixed
7	Order processing	176,000	$38,000 fixed
8	Supervision	73,500	$50,000 fixed
9	Supplies (including packing materials)	198,500	All variable
10	Utilities	83,200	$60,000 fixed
11	Total	$ 1,200,000	
12			

The center manager has asked the financial staff for more information about center costs and whether there is a better way to estimate them rather than having the controller go through the monthly account analysis. The center manager assigned the controller's staff to recommend improvements to the current process.

Historically, all the financial and operation performance measures at the ADC have been based on the number of units shipped. However, in preparing the analysis, one of the analysts on the controller's staff collected information from the last 12 months on orders processed as well as units shipped and ADC operating costs. These follow here:

	A	B	C	D
1	Month	Units	Orders	Center Cost
2	1	232,970	8,990	$ 990,030
3	2	244,450	16,300	1,223,470
4	3	241,750	13,030	1,063,400
5	4	256,610	15,210	1,203,840
6	5	252,560	16,770	1,220,720
7	6	266,740	13,430	1,220,330
8	7	247,830	16,030	1,156,060
9	8	278,220	12,680	1,215,190
10	9	268,760	8,710	1,135,390
11	10	284,300	12,090	1,162,750
12	11	281,600	13,100	1,181,670
13	12	291,770	11,290	1,219,350
14				

The controller and other managers at the ADC agree that operations and costs last year were representative for the center.

Required

a. Prepare an estimate of operating costs based on the controller's analysis of accounts assuming that 275,000 units will be shipped in a future month .

b. Use the high-low method based on units shipped and center costs to prepare an estimate of operating costs assuming that 275,000 units will be shipped in a future month.

c. Prepare an estimate of operating costs assuming that 275,000 units will be shipped in a future month by using the results of a simple regression of operating costs on units shipped.

d. Prepare an estimate of operating costs assuming that 275,000 units, based on 13,000 orders, will be shipped in a future month by using the results of a multiple regression of operating costs on units shipped and orders processed.

e. Make a recommendation to the center manager and controller about the most appropriate estimate given the circumstances.

5-78. Learning Curves (Appendix B)   (LO 5-4, 7)

Refer to the example in Appendix B. Gale Technologies is proposing to build a new component for sale to a private space exploration company. Engineers at the company expect a learning rate of 85 percent. The first unit is expected to take 200 labor hours. Labor at Gale is paid $60 per hour. The 85 percent learning rate coefficient is −0.23447 (rounded); that is $b = -0.23447$ in the formula $Y = aX^b$.

Required

Using the formula, $Y = aX^b$ and the example in Appendix B, recompute the labor time and costs for the first eight units with the new learning rate, hours for the first unit, and the hourly labor cost, using the format of Exhibit 5.21.

(LO 5-4, 7)   **5-79. Learning Curves (Appendix B)**

Sunnyside Systems, Inc. is in an industry with rapidly evolving technology. With every change in production processes, Sunnyside has to build new design and measurement monitors. Sunnyside uses five of these monitors for production. Engineers at the company are in the process of designing and planning production of the next generation of monitors. They estimate that the first monitor will require 60 hours to build. Labor cost at Sunnyside is $75 per hour. The engineering team estimates that based on similar types of monitors, a learning rate of 90 percent is reasonable.

Fairview Associates, one of the outside contractors at Sunnyside, hears of the plans for the new monitors and proposes to Sunnyside that it (Fairview) build the monitors. It would charge Sunnyside $4,200 for each monitor, for up to 10 monitors. Materials and overhead would be provided by Sunnyside, and the monitors would be built at the Sunnyside plant, so labor is the only cost that would differ.

Required

a.   Assume that Sunnyside could experience labor-cost improvements on the monitor production consistent with a 90 percent learning curve. Should Sunnyside build the five monitors or purchase the five monitors from Fairview? Explain your answer. (Note that the 90 percent learning rate coefficient is −0.1520.)

b.   Suppose that Sunnyside is uncertain of how many monitors it will require. How would this change your recommendation in requirement (a)?

(CMA adapted)

INTEGRATIVE CASES

(LO 5-1, 3, 5, 6)   **5-80. Cost Estimation, CVP Analysis, and Decision Making**

Luke Corporation produces a variety of products, each within its own division. Last year, the managers at Luke developed and began marketing a new chewing gum, Bubbs, to sell in vending machines. The product, which sells for $5.25 per case, has not had the market success that managers expected, and the company is considering dropping Bubbs.

The product-line income statement for the past 12 months follows:

Revenue		$14,682,150
Costs		
Manufacturing costs	$14,440,395	
Allocated corporate costs (@5%)	734,108	15,174,503
Product-line margin		$ (492,353)
Allowance for tax (@20%)		98,470
Product-line profit (loss)		$ (393,883)

All products at Luke receive an allocation of corporate overhead costs, which is computed as 5 percent of product revenue. The 5 percent rate is computed based on the most recent year's corporate cost as a percentage of revenue. Data on corporate costs and revenues for the past two years follow:

	Corporate Revenue	Corporate Overhead Costs
Most recent year	$106,750,000	$5,337,500
Previous year	76,200,000	4,221,000

Roy O. Andre, the product manager for Bubbs, is concerned about whether the product will be dropped by the company and has employed you as a financial consultant to help with some analysis. In addition to the information given, Andre provides you with the following data on product costs for Bubbs:

Month	Cases	Production Costs
1.............	207,000	$1,139,828
2.............	217,200	1,161,328
3.............	214,800	1,169,981
4.............	228,000	1,185,523
5.............	224,400	1,187,827
6.............	237,000	1,208,673
7.............	220,200	1,183,699
8.............	247,200	1,226,774
9.............	238,800	1,225,226
10............	252,600	1,237,325
11............	250,200	1,241,760
12............	259,200	1,272,451

Required

a. Bunk Stores has requested a quote for a special order of Bubbs. This order would not be subject to any corporate allocation (and would not affect corporate costs). What is the minimum price Andre can offer Bunk without reducing profit any further?

b. How many cases of Bubbs does Luke have to sell in order to break even on the product?

c. Suppose Luke has a requirement that all products have to earn 5 percent of sales (after tax and corporate allocations) or they will be dropped. How many cases of Bubbs does Andre need to sell to avoid seeing Bubbs dropped?

d. Assume all costs and prices will be the same in the next year. If Luke drops Bubbs, how much will Luke's profits increase or decrease? Assume that fixed production costs can be avoided if Bubbs is dropped.

5-81. CVP, Outsourcing, Cost Estimation, CVP Analysis: Data Analysis and Visualization (LO 5-1, 2, 3, 5, 6)

Pilgrim Fitness makes various devices for personal fitness tracking. One of its well-established products is a low-cost band, the PF-24, meant to compete with more sophisticated smart watches and other expensive devices. The PF-24 has been on the market for 18 months, and the managers at Pilgrim Fitness believe it has at least another 24 months before it becomes obsolete at any price.

Recently, Pilgrim Fitness was approached by Banneker Ltd., an international electronics company. Banneker proposed that it produce the PF-24 for Pilgrim Fitness. Banneker would be responsible for the total production effort, from purchasing materials to shipping the finished devices to various Pilgrim warehouses around the country. Because Pilgrim leases the manufacturing facility where the PF-24 is made and because that facility has no other use for Pilgrim, it could avoid all manufacturing costs of the PF-24, both direct costs and all overhead, if it purchased the PF-24 from Banneker. Banneker has stated that it would be willing to sell the PF-24 to Pilgrim for $15 per unit, for up to 200,000 units per month.

The special studies team in the controller's office at Pilgrim has been charged with making a recommendation to senior management regarding the Banneker proposal. Engineers at the manufacturing facility report that the direct costs (materials and labor) for the PF-24 amount to $5 per unit. After some internal discussion with the operations team at the manufacturing facility, the special studies team agreed that data from the last 12 months of manufacturing would be representative of the overhead cost for the PF-24. The data the team collected follow:

	A	B	C
1	Month	Units	Overhead Costs
2	1	143,400	$ 1,406,740
3	2	104,700	1,211,050
4	3	140,500	1,563,480
5	4	151,700	1,549,450
6	5	179,300	1,643,730
7	6	104,200	975,340
8	7	154,300	1,585,970
9	8	161,700	1,500,740
10	9	139,400	1,377,960
11	10	120,500	1,445,970
12	11	155,300	1,469,520
13	12	171,500	1,529,880
14			

Required

Prepare a report for the senior management at Pilgrim Fitness recommending a decision on the Banneker proposal. Be sure to include a discussion of the analysis that led to your recommendation along with any visual materials you have to help support your conclusions.

SOLUTIONS TO SELF-STUDY QUESTIONS

1.

Indirect materials..........................	$27,200
Indirect labor	44,300
Power to run machines	18,500
Total variable costs.....................	$90,000

Lease..................................	$ 56,000
Utilities (heat, light, etc.)...................	19,200
Insurance	16,400
Maintenance	14,500
Depreciation............................	9,000
Total fixed costs.......................	$115,100

Average monthly fixed costs = $115,100 ÷ 24   = $4,796
Variable cost per DLH = $90,000 ÷ 12,000 = $ 7.50
Variable cost per machine-hour = $90,000 ÷ 14,400 = $ 6.25
Variable cost per unit produced = $90,000 ÷ 20,000 = $ 4.50

2. Based on the statistical results, overhead costs appear more closely related to output measured in baskets than to labor-hours. The coefficient of determination (R^2) is .54 for labor-hours and .78 for baskets. This suggests that 54 percent of the variation in overhead costs is "explained" by labor-hours, but 78 percent is "explained" by output. In addition, the t-statistic on the coefficient for baskets is greater (8.735) than that on labor-hours (5.034). Both of these results suggest that the model using baskets is better for explaining overheard costs. However, we would not want to make the determination based on statistical results alone. We should ensure that there are good reasons that overhead costs are related to output.

6

Chapter Six

Fundamentals of Product and Service Costing

LEARNING OBJECTIVES

After reading this chapter, you should be able to:

LO 6-1 Describe how a product costing system works and apply these principles to a variety of business environments.

LO 6-2 Allocate overhead to products and services in a manner that provides useful information for decision making.

LO 6-3 Allocate costs using a two-stage allocation system.

LO 6-4 Describe the three basic types of product costing systems (job, process, and operations), calculate product costs using these systems, and identify the business environments for which each system is the best fit.

❝ I have been working with two other managers in a breakout session at this executive education course on financial management. We are trying to decide on the best pricing strategy. We started by looking at the costs. However, we soon discovered that the businesses we manage are very different, so we all approached the costing in a different way. We are all familiar with the basic cost categories of materials, labor, overhead, and selling costs, but how we add those up for a product and even what costs to include has us wondering which of the three ways we use in our companies is best. In fact, we started to question whether it was even important to calculate product costs to establish a price. **❞**

Huma Khan, the production manager at Sandia Custom Furniture, a manufacturer of furniture for executive offices and luxury homes, was talking during a break at a local college. The other two people in her group were Cathy Miller, owner of Miller Paints, and Alec Thornton, the marketing manager at Bayou Workspaces.

This chapter provides an overview of alternative cost systems for product and service costing. Details and extensions to the basic models described here are presented in the following three chapters. The fundamental approach and the problems that arise from using cost data generated by these basic costing systems can be illustrated by the examples in this chapter. We follow two principles in our discussion: The cost system should be oriented to the needs of the decision makers (that is, the users of the information), and the cost system should be designed so that its benefits exceed its costs.

Our goal in this chapter is to provide the intuition behind costing systems, not the procedural details. In the three chapters that follow, we take a more in-depth look at three costing systems: job costing, process costing, and activity-based costing. If this is your first introduction to costing systems, we want you to appreciate that, although these costing systems may differ in the ways that costs are accumulated, they are alike in the basic flow of costs from accounts to products. If you have seen this material before, we want you to step back from the details and think about costing systems as a natural result of managers developing costs to help make decisions.

Cost Management Systems

The objective of the **cost management system** is to provide information about the costs of the goods and services sold by the firm and the processes used to produce the goods and services. While financial accounting requires that product cost information be accumulated in particular ways for external reporting, the focus in this book is on cost management systems that aid managers who require information to make decisions.

A well-designed cost management system accumulates and reports costs that are relevant to the decisions that managers make. These include the costs associated with the processes the organization uses to meet customer needs, serve the customers, and comply with regulatory and tax authorities. A major role of the cost management system is to report the costs of producing or providing the organization's products or services. In what follows, we often use the term *cost system* as an abbreviation for the cost management system.

LO 6-1
Describe how a product costing system works and apply these principles to a variety of business environments.

cost management system
System to provide information about the costs of processes, products, and services used and produced by an organization.

Reasons to Calculate Product or Service Costs

A firm's financial statements summarize the cost of the services or products it sells and the total profit that they generate. What is the purpose of calculating the individual product cost?[1] From your financial accounting course, you know that one reason is to compute the inventory values and cost of goods sold for the financial statements. The accountant has to have the costs of the individual products by which to multiply the number of units of inventory to get the inventory values (and, as a result, the cost of goods sold). More important, however, is that the accountant needs to provide the individual product costs to the various product managers so they can make decisions regarding pricing, production, promotion, and so on.

In Chapter 4, you saw examples of many of the kinds of decisions managers make that use information about product costs. Perhaps the most common decision is determining the price at which to sell the product (or whether the firm wants to offer it, given the market price). This is very common for industries in which companies submit bids in response to a request. One basis for the bid is the cost of producing the item. Other decisions that use cost information include adding or dropping a product, whether to outsource selected products or services, and how to price alternative sales channels (online vs. in-store, for example).

An example of the use of product costing in pricing in a company whose rates (prices) are based the company's cost is discussed in the Business Application "Who's Responsible for These Costs?"

Business Application   Who's Responsible for These Costs?

One setting in which product costs are tied explicitly to prices is that of regulated utilities (providers of electricity, natural gas, and so on). In this setting, regulators

> . . . approve retail electricity rates and establish the profits that utilities can earn based on the companies' investment in transmission lines, power plants and other equipment.[1]

The costs included in these rates are not limited to the fuel, labor, and other resources needed to generate electricity on a daily basis. Additional costs, such as those for capital equipment, safety systems, and other infrastructure, are included in rate schedules by applying a rate of return on the capital invested.

Under this approach, two cost issues arise. First, is the cost paid by the utility "reasonable"? In other words, because the utility is allowed to pass costs along to the consumer, the regulator wants to ensure that the utility company is operating efficiently and exercising good judgment in paying for the resources.

A second issue, and one to which we will return later in the book, is what costs, reasonable or not, should be passed along to the consumer. In 2019, one utility, Pacific Gas & Electric Company (PG&E) in California, asked state regulators

> . . . for permission to raise electricity rates to pay for safety improvements and to offset the financial risk of more wildfires.[2]

The issue arises because, in California, utilities can be held responsible for damages caused by utility structures regardless of negligence. As a result of significant damages done after a series of wildfires, PG&E faced what it estimated to be $30 billion in claims. The purpose of seeking rate relief from the regulators was to pass the cost of safety upgrades onto the consumer to mitigate future damages. However, as one observer remarked,

> "Does PG&E have any other assets that it can use to offset at least part of the liabilities associated with wildfires?" . . . "I don't think it's proper to assign that cost entirely to the ratepayer."[3]

A well-designed cost management system can help an organization's managers address two questions:

1. What are the costs that should be considered in pricing various products (electricity and natural gas in the case of PG&E or different models of tents in the case of North Face)?

2. Who is responsible for the cost? Should the cost be included (implicitly or explicitly) in the price, or should the organization bear the cost because it is for its benefit or due to its errors and does not reflect expected resource usage?

Answering these two questions represents the theme of cost management.

Sources:
1. Ivan Penn, "Blamed for Wildfires, PG&E Seeks Higher Electricity Rates," *The New York Times*, April 23, 2019.
2. Ibid.
3. Ibid.

---

[1] In this chapter, we use the term *product* to include both tangible products and intangible products (services). We use the term *service* when we discuss issues associated with costing services specifically.

Cost Allocation and Product Costing

When we introduced cost allocation and product costing in Chapter 1, we said that for a retail firm, the calculation of the product costs was straightforward: It was the cost paid to the wholesaler plus any cost to transport the product to the retailer. It is not quite so simple for a manufacturing or service firm that buys different resources (materials, labor, supplies, etc.) and combines them into two or more finished products. For these firms, the cost management system must in some way allocate the costs of the resources to the finished products.

We know that, by definition, costs that are common to two or more cost objects are likely to be allocated to those cost objects on a somewhat arbitrary basis. This arbitrariness has led critics of cost allocation to claim that cost allocations can result in misleading information and poor decisions.

The goal of a well-designed cost management system is to balance the potential distortion in reported product costs with the cost of conducting a special study every time a manager needs to make a decision. In other words, it is always possible to conduct a special study to determine the "right" product cost when making a bid. Depending on the frequency of bidding, the amount of revenue the average bid represents, and the other tasks facing managers, the firm could decide that the product costs reported routinely from the cost system, even though they are known to be not quite "right," are "good enough" for making the decision. Our goal in designing the cost management system is to ensure that we make the best trade-off between the cost of bad decisions and the cost of developing the information.

Cost Flow Diagram

The cost flow diagram is helpful as you study product costing by providing a graphical representation of the product costing process. Exhibit 6.1 illustrates the basic cost flow diagram that we will use throughout the next several chapters as you study product costing. Recall from the discussion in Chapter 2 that the cost flow diagram illustrates how costs from the cost pools "flow" or are assigned and allocated to the cost object. In this case, the cost object, the item we are costing, is the product.

In Exhibit 6.1, Haft Company produces two products—alpha and beta. Haft uses three types of resources to make them: direct materials, direct labor, and overhead. In the costing process, direct material and direct labor costs can be assigned "directly" to the two products. Overhead costs are allocated on the basis of direct labor costs.

Exhibit 6.1   Basic Cost Flow Diagram: Product Costing—Haft Company

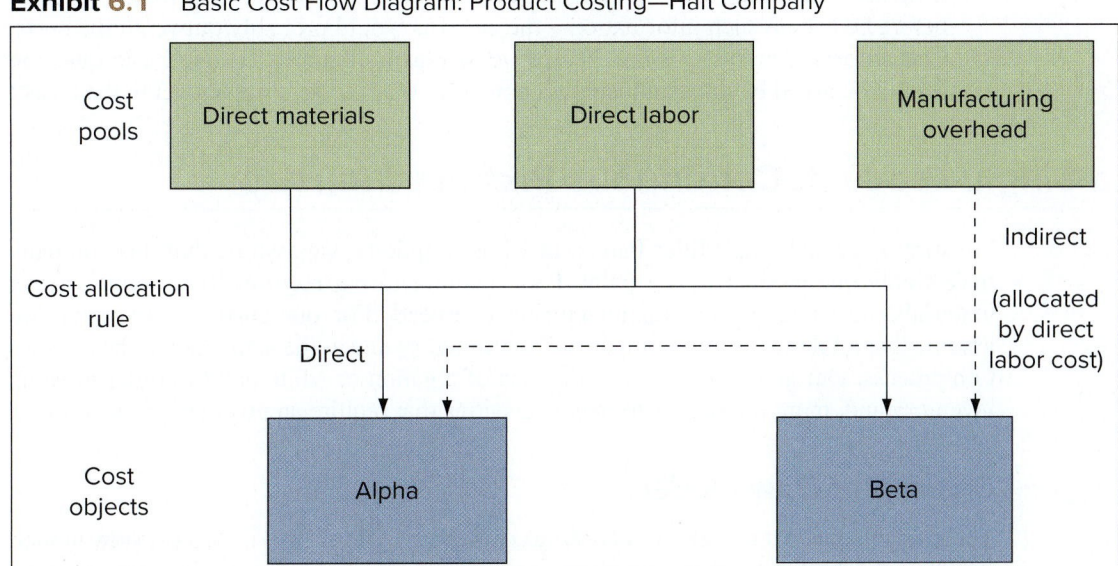

The cost flow diagram in Exhibit 6.1 shows that the direct materials and direct labor are "assigned" directly; that is, we can observe the link between the resource and the product in an unambiguous way. We can then allocate overhead to the two products based on the amount of direct labor in the two products. As the direct labor in one product (e.g., alpha) goes up, that product will be allocated more of the overhead resources.

Fundamental Themes Underlying the Design of Cost Systems for Managerial Purposes

As we continue through this text, we will notice key themes that are critical to designing a cost system for managerial purposes. Before undertaking the design of a new one, we must first ask several important questions. How will managers use the information the system is designed to provide? What type of decisions will be made using the cost information? Will the benefits of improved decision making outweigh the costs of implementing the new cost system? These are valid and important questions to ask. The following three points relate to designing a new cost system for managerial purposes:

- *Cost systems should have a decision focus.* Cost systems must meet the needs of the decision makers, who are the customers (or users) of cost accounting. Alec Thornton, the marketing manager at Bayou Office Workspaces, routinely makes decisions about pricing concessions to customers. He needs to know which customers are most profitable. If the cost system is not designed to provide these data, it will not meet the manager's needs. Clearly, it is important to design the cost system so that the cost data provided by the cost system facilitate the decision making of the user.

- *Different cost information is used for different purposes.* What works for one purpose will not necessarily work for another purpose. For example, financial reporting requires the use of cost information from the past. Managerial decision makers, however, require information about the future. Cost information is often used to assess departmental profitability; other information is used to review customer profitability. As we can see, the cost information must provide the appropriate data for its intended purpose.

- *Cost information for managerial purposes must meet the cost-benefit test.* Cost information can always be improved. However, the benefits of improvements (i.e., better decision making) must outweigh the costs of making the improvements. For example, if Alec Thornton uses customer profitability analyses for informational purposes only and they do not provide him any additional information needed to make better decisions, the costs of preparing this information could outweigh the benefits. However, if he uses this information to decide where to focus his marketing efforts—whereas before he had no such information—the benefits would probably outweigh the costs. Cost information systems can be very costly to implement, so one basic question should be asked before establishing a new one: Will the benefits outweigh the costs?

Costing in a Single-Product, Continuous Process Industry

We start by considering Miller Paints, Inc. For simplicity, we assume that this company makes only one product, white paint. Paint manufacturing requires three inputs: direct materials, direct labor, and manufacturing overhead. For our current discussion, we assume that all three resources are added continuously and at the same rate in the production process. Our goal is to arrive at the cost of a gallon of white paint in order to value inventory and, more important, to make decisions that require an estimate of this cost.

Basic Cost Flow Model

The fundamental framework for recording costs in any type of firm is the cost flow model, which is the basic inventory equation. You have applied this model in your previous accounting classes; we repeat it here because it is so important and helpful in assigning costs to products. The model is

$$\underset{BB}{\underset{\text{balance}}{\text{Beginning}}} + \underset{TI}{\underset{\text{in}}{\text{Transfers}}} - \underset{TO}{\underset{\text{out}}{\text{Transfers}}} = \underset{EB}{\underset{\text{balance}}{\text{Ending}}}$$

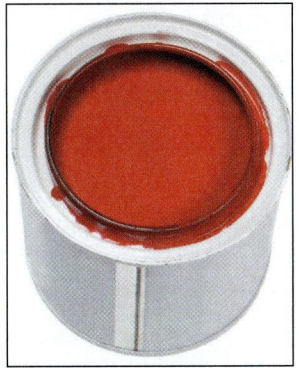

Paints are produced in a continuous process.
Stockbyte/SuperStock

Costing with No Work-in-Process Inventories

This inventory equation applies to both physical units (the paint itself) and the costs associated with the paint. We can now apply the equation to determine the cost of the paint. Miller Paints begins production on April 1, year 2. It starts and completes production of 100,000 gallons of paint in April and has no ending work-in-process inventory. From our inventory equation, we know that Miller produces 100,000 gallons of paint in April. Miller's costs of the resources used in April consist of the following:

Materials............................	$ 400,000
Labor...............................	100,000
Manufacturing overhead	500,000
Total.............................	$1,000,000

For April, Miller has incurred costs of $1,000,000 to produce 100,000 gallons of paint. Because 1 gallon of paint is assumed to be like every other gallon, we assign a cost of $10 (= $1,000,000 ÷ 100,000 gallons) to each gallon of paint produced. This is the cost that the cost accounting system reports for paint.

Costing with Ending Work-in-Process Inventories

While this example seems simple (even simplistic, perhaps), it conveys the basic approach to product costing. Let's add one new element. Production for Miller Paints for May, year 2, follows:

	Gallons
Beginning inventory.....................................	–0–
Started in May	
Total...	110,000
Ending work-in-process inventory (50% complete)	20,000
Transferred out.......................................	90,000

Costs incurred in May, year 2, were

Materials..............................	$390,000
Labor.................................	100,000
Manufacturing overhead	500,000
Total..............................	$990,000

There is a new element here. How much did Miller Paints produce in May? It transferred 90,000 gallons to finished goods, but some paint still remains in work in process. Therefore, Miller did more than 90,000 gallons' worth of work in May. On the other hand, a gallon of paint in the ending work-in-process inventory is not the same as a completed

Exhibit 6.2

Cost Flow Diagram:
Product Costing—Miller
Paints

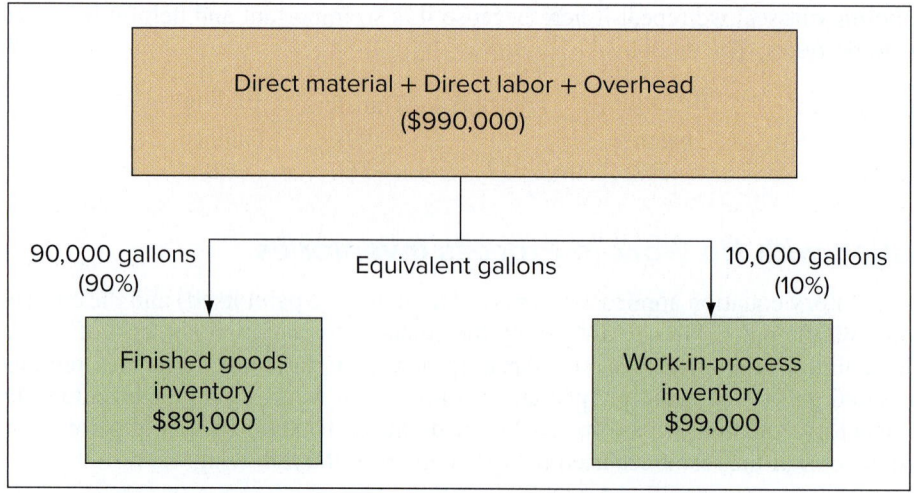

gallon of paint because it requires additional resources to complete. If it did not require additional resources to complete, it would have been transferred out.

In the summary of the physical flow, Miller's accountant estimates that, on average, the paint still in process is 50 percent complete. Because paint production is a continuous process, some paint is almost complete, but some has just started. Therefore, we say that the paint in process is the same as or "equivalent" to 10,000 gallons of finished paint (= 50% × 20,000 gallons). Therefore, the amount of work done at Miller in May is equivalent to 100,000 gallons of completed paint. This is made up of the 90,000 gallons transferred to finished goods plus the 10,000 *equivalent* gallons of paint in the ending work-in-process inventory.

Now we can compute the cost of paint for May. Miller incurred $990,000 of cost and produced 100,000 equivalent gallons, so the paint cost $9.90 per gallon (= $990,000 ÷ 100,000 gallons). Because 90,000 gallons were transferred out, we assign $891,000 (= 90,000 gallons × $9.90) to the units transferred out and $99,000 (= 10,000 equivalent gallons × $9.90) to the ending work-in-process inventory. We have allocated the $990,000 incurred to the two cost objects (transferred out and work in process). In Chapter 8, we extend the discussion to a case with beginning work-in-process inventory. The cost flow diagram in Exhibit 6.2 illustrates the costing process used at Miller Paints and the results for May, year 2.

Self-Study Questions

1. Lawrence Chemicals manufactures industrial solvents. On November 1, it has no work-in-process inventory. It starts production of 13,000 barrels of solvent in November and completes 8,000 barrels. The costs of the resources used by Lawrence in November consist of the following:

Materials...........................	$223,000
Conversion costs (labor and overhead)	272,000
Total............................	$495,000

The production supervisor estimates that the ending work in process is 60 percent complete. Compute the cost of solvent transferred to finished goods and the amount in work-in-process ending inventory as of November 30.

2. Draw the cost flow diagram for Lawrence Chemicals for November.

The solutions to these questions are at the end of the chapter.

Costing in a Multiple-Product, Discrete Process Industry

The costing system developed for Miller Paints was reasonable for a single-product firm. Each individual unit of product can be considered identical to every other one, so trying to trace costs to the individual unit level has no purpose. In a firm with multiple products, however, the benefits of more detailed costing often outweigh the costs. For example, a manager making a pricing decision (accepting a special offer, say) needs cost information at the product level.

Consider the costing system for Sandia Custom Furniture, which makes a variety of products. For our purposes, we will consider only two—a 66-inch mahogany desk, the S-66, and a 72-inch mahogany desk, the S-72. Unlike Miller Paints, Sandia's manufacturing process takes place in a series of discrete steps that differ in detail depending on the product. Basically, each desk (and other types of furniture) goes through three steps. First, wood and other material is delivered to the work area. Second, skilled furniture makers cut, shape, and fit the materials into a finished desk. Finally, the finished piece is moved to the finished goods warehouse.

Three basic resources are used in building the desks: wood, metal sliders, and other parts (direct materials); skilled furniture makers (direct labor); and the necessary support resources (work space, tools, electricity, etc.) that constitute manufacturing overhead. Just as these three types of physical resources are combined to produce an S-66, the cost accounting system has to be designed to take the cost of the three resources, combine them in some way, and produce the cost of an S-66.

The cost diagram in Exhibit 6.3 describes the problem. The cost system we develop must take costs from the three basic cost pools (direct materials, direct labor, and manufacturing overhead) and allocate them to the two cost objects (S-72 and S-66).

Direct materials at Sandia consist primarily of the wood and other major components (hardware, for example) that go into each desk. Because the wood for a specific S-66 or S-72 is brought to the work area for that particular desk, it is relatively easy (i.e., relatively low in cost) to *directly* trace or assign the direct materials cost to each S-66 or S-72. Recall the definition of direct materials in Chapter 2. These are materials that can be identified directly with the product at reasonable cost. In other words, there really is no allocation problem because the work orders and inventory requisitions for the materials are specific to the individual product. In the same way, the skilled furniture makers can easily track their time spent on the individual desk. Therefore, it is also relatively low cost to allocate the direct labor cost directly to the individual desks.

A problem arises, however, with manufacturing overhead. By definition, these costs cannot be identified directly (for a reasonable cost) with individual units of product. If they could be, they would be included in either direct materials (lubricating oil, for example) or direct labor (production supervisors, for example). Therefore, we need to identify one or more allocation bases to use to allocate the manufacturing overhead to the two desk models.

Exhibit 6.3   Cost Flow Diagram: Cost Allocation Bases—Sandia Custom Furniture

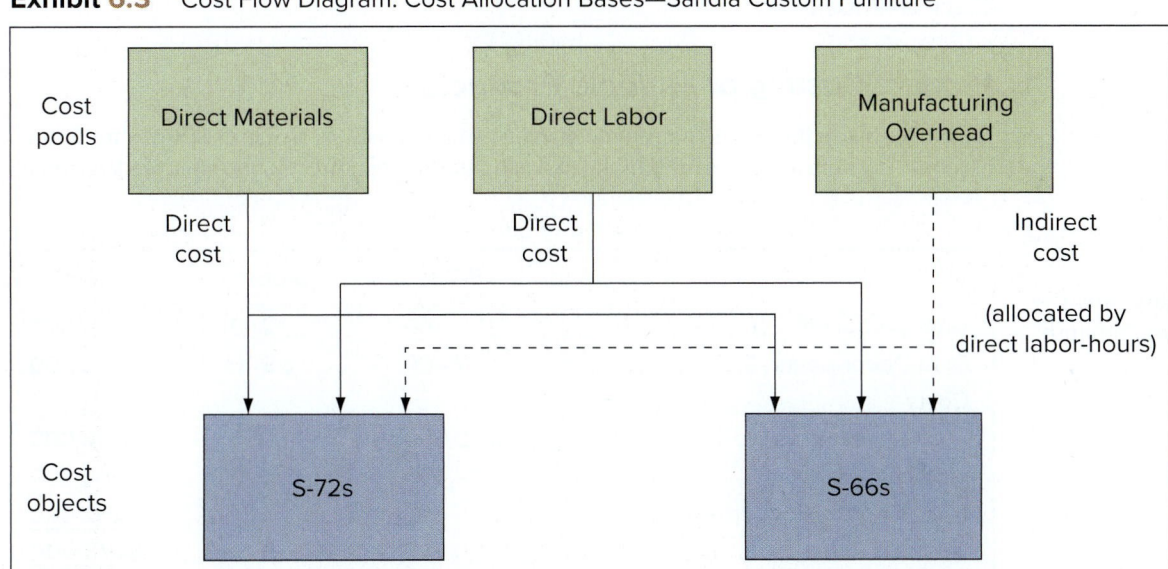

Ideally, an allocation base has a direct, cause-and-effect relationship with the costs incurred. That ideal is unlikely to be met. At a minimum, however, an allocation base needs to be measured for each cost object before it can be used to allocate the manufacturing overhead. One obvious allocation base that is quite common is direct labor. Sandia Custom Furniture keeps track of direct labor-hours (and costs) for each of its products because the furniture makers complete time cards (electronically) that show which product they were working on as well as the starting and ending times. In what follows, we assume that Sandia uses direct labor-hours to allocate manufacturing overhead to products. The cost diagram in Exhibit 6.3 notes how the costs in the cost pools are assigned or allocated to the two products.

Data on manufacturing plans for Sandia Custom Furniture for January, year 2, are shown in Exhibit 6.4. These are budgeted costs, not actual. We use them to estimate the costs for the two desk models. We can use the cost diagram in Exhibit 6.3 to guide us through the development of the product cost. Assigning costs for direct materials and direct labor is straightforward. Based on the cost diagram and the data in Exhibit 6.4, these costs are assigned directly to the individual products.

Predetermined Overhead Rates

LO 6-2

Allocate overhead to products and services in a manner that provides useful information for decision making.

predetermined overhead rate
Cost per unit of the allocation base used to charge overhead to products.

Assigning the cost of manufacturing overhead is not done directly. First, determine how to allocate the budgeted manufacturing overhead costs between the two products. The allocation base we have selected is direct labor-hours. We must allocate $252,000 of budgeted manufacturing overhead costs to products that are expected to use a total of 6,300 direct labor-hours. To do the allocation, we determine the cost per direct labor-hour, or the **predetermined overhead rate,** for manufacturing overhead:

$$\text{Predetermined overhead rate} = \frac{\text{Estimated overhead}}{\text{Estimated allocation base}}$$

In the case of Sandia Custom Furniture, the estimated overhead is $252,000. The allocation base is direct labor, estimated to be 6,300 direct labor-hours. Therefore, the predetermined overhead rate at Sandia Custom Furniture is

$$\text{Predetermined overhead rate} = \frac{\$252,000}{6,300 \text{ direct labor-hours}} = \$40 \text{ per direct labor-hour}$$

This $40 rate is the predetermined overhead rate for Sandia Custom Furniture for January, year 2. When we estimate that a desk uses 1 hour of direct labor, we also estimate that the desk "uses" $40 of manufacturing overhead. This is in addition, of course, to the cost of direct labor itself.

Product Costing of Multiple Products

We can now use the cost system to determine product costs for S-72s and S-66s for Sandia Custom Furniture as shown in Exhibit 6.5. Using the $40 per direct labor-hour predetermined

Exhibit 6.4

Data for January, Year 2— Sandia Custom Furniture

	S-72s	S-66s	Total
Units produced	80	240	320
Direct labor-hours	2,400	3,900	6,300
Costs			
Direct materials	$40,000	$36,000	$ 76,000
Direct labor	72,000	78,000	150,000
Manufacturing overhead			252,000
Total			$478,000

	S-72s	S-66s	Total
Units produced	80	240	320
Direct labor-hours	2,400	3,900	6,300
Costs			
Direct materials	$ 40,000	$ 36,000	$ 76,000
Direct labor.	72,000	78,000	150,000
Manufacturing overhead (@ $40/hour)	96,000	156,000	252,000
Total.	$208,000	$270,000	$478,000
Cost per unit.	$ 2,600	$ 1,125	

Exhibit 6.5

Product Costs for January, Year 2—Sandia Custom Furniture

overhead rate, we can allocate overhead to the two products. Because S-72s are expected to use 2,400 direct labor-hours, we allocate $96,000 (= 2,400 direct labor-hours × $40 per direct labor-hour) to S-72s and $156,000 (= 3,900 direct labor-hours × $40 per direct labor-hour) to S-66s. Alternatively, S-72s are expected to use just over 38.1 percent (= 2,400 hours ÷ 6,300 hours) of the direct labor, so we allocate just over 38.1 percent (= $96,000, or 38.1% of $252,000) to S-72s, and the remaining 61.9 percent ($156,000) to S-66s.

Within the two product categories, we assume that all the S-72s are the same and all the S-66s are the same, so we estimate the individual unit costs as the total cost of the product divided by the number of units produced. In other words, the cost system estimates a cost of $2,600 (= $208,000 ÷ 80 S-72s) to each S-72 and $1,125 (= $270,000 ÷ 240 S-66s) to each S-66. If these were the costs actually calculated for the desks, then when an S-66 or S-72 is moved to finished goods, the accounting system "moves" $2,600 or $1,125 from Work-in-Process Inventory to Finished Goods Inventory.

These product costs are estimates, not actual results. They are useful for decisions about pricing and whether to continue making a particular product.

Choice of the Allocation Base for Predetermined Overhead Rate

In selecting an allocation base, Sandia Custom Furniture chose direct labor-*hours* for two reasons: The cost system already records direct labor-hours by product line and Sandia managers believe that labor-hours reflect the amount of "effort" that goes into each product line. We know from our discussion of cost allocation, however, that the choice of an allocation base is somewhat arbitrary. We can look at alternatives and consider them for the Sandia system.

One obvious alternative is direct labor *cost*. This satisfies the same two criteria used at Sandia. Will the cost allocated to the two product lines be the same? As before, to answer this question, we compute the predetermined overhead rate using direct labor cost. This rate is 168 percent (= $252,000 ÷ $150,000). For every dollar of direct labor cost, we add $1.68 of manufacturing overhead.

Product costing using direct labor dollars is shown in Exhibit 6.6. As we see, S-72s are now allocated $120,960 in overhead (= 168% of $72,000) and S-66s are allocated $131,040 (= 168% of $78,000). Because S-72s use 48 percent (= $72,000 ÷ $150,000) of the direct labor dollars, S-72s are allocated 48 percent of the manufacturing overhead costs. Similarly, S-66s use 52 percent (= $78,000 ÷ $150,000) of the direct labor dollars and so are allocated 52 percent of the manufacturing overhead costs.

Notice that the per-unit cost of the S-72s and S-66s changed when we changed the allocation base for manufacturing overhead: It increased for S-72s and decreased for S-66s. We would expect this because S-72s use more expensive labor than do S-66s. The average direct labor-hour rate for S-72s is $30 (= $72,000 ÷ 2,400 hours) and $20 (= $78,000 ÷ 3,900 hours) for S-66s. As a result, using dollars to allocate the costs leads Sandia Custom Furniture to charge more manufacturing overhead to S-72s and less to S-66s.

Exhibit 6.6

Product Costs for January, Year 2—Sandia Custom Furniture (allocation base is direct labor dollars)

	S-72s	S-66s	Total
Units produced	80	240	320
Direct labor-hours	2,400	3,900	6,300
Costs			
Direct materials	$ 40,000	$ 36,000	$ 76,000
Direct labor.	72,000	78,000	150,000
Manufacturing overhead			
(@ 168%)	120,960	131,040	252,000
Total.	$232,960	$245,040	$478,000
Cost per unit.	$ 2,912	$ 1,021	

Choosing among Possible Allocation Bases

The choice between direct labor-hours and direct labor costs could have important implications for decision making at Sandia Custom Furniture. From the simple example presented, this choice affected the product costs for the two products, S-72s and S-66s. If the choice of allocation bases did not affect the product costs, there would be no benefit to further analysis of the choice because managers' decisions would not be affected.

Before we choose between the two allocation bases, we ask why the relation between direct labor-hours and direct labor cost is not the same for both products. For S-72s, we estimate direct labor costs as $72,000 for 2,400 hours, for an average direct labor rate of $30 per hour. For S-66s, we estimate $78,000 in costs for 3,900 hours, for an average rate of $20 per hour. Why is there a difference? One possibility is that it is just "random." That is, perhaps because of scheduling reasons, more senior employees (whose wage rate could be higher because of seniority) are expected to work on S-72s rather than S-66s this period. In this case, direct labor-hours could be the better allocation base because we do not want to distort the product costs by random scheduling events.

Another possibility is that the wage rate reflects the skill of the employees and that more skilled employees are required for S-72s than for S-66s. In this case, the assignment of employees and the relation between hours and costs is not random but reflects the underlying product process at Sandia Custom Furniture. In this case, the choice between hours and costs should be based on the impact of production activity on overhead costs.

As we said earlier, the allocation base we choose ideally reflects a direct cause-and-effect relationship between overhead costs incurred and the activity represented by the allocation base. In other words, when an additional hour (or dollar) of direct labor is incurred in the production of a good, we want the allocation system to add an "appropriate" amount of overhead cost. In Chapter 5, we discussed several methods for estimating costs. We can apply two of the approaches described there to aid in making the choice.

First, we can analyze the overhead accounts to determine which allocation base seems to be most highly related to overhead. For example, if a large portion of the overhead accounts are employee related and affected by the wage rate (or seniority) of the employees, direct labor cost would be the better allocation base. If the costs are largely determined by the labor activity regardless of the seniority or skills of the employees, direct labor-hours would be the better choice.

Another approach is to estimate the correlation between overhead cost and activity using statistical analysis. Suppose the goal is to use the product costs as estimates of what it costs to produce S-72s and S-66s so that managers can use this information for planning and costing. Then, the more highly overhead costs and activity are correlated, the better our chances that the cost forecast will have given an accurate forecast of activity.

There is no single, obviously "right" choice in this case because, by definition, there is no direct relation between activity and overhead cost that is economically feasible to measure. If such a direct relation existed, we would not classify these costs as overhead. Remember that allocation is inherently imprecise. Our goal is to avoid distorting the product costs "too much."

3. The production manager at Sandia Custom Furniture tells us that she believes that overhead is mostly related to machine-hours. Production of the 80 S-72 desks required 1,400 machine-hours, and the 240 S-66 desks required 4,200 machine-hours. Compute the reported product costs if machine-hours are used as the overhead allocation base.

The solution to this question is at the end of the chapter.

Multiple Allocation Bases and Two-Stage Systems

Exhibit 6.7 provides more detail on the components of manufacturing overhead at Sandia Custom Furniture. The cost accounting system at Sandia uses direct labor costs to allocate all manufacturing overhead, but a closer inspection of the overhead accounts in Exhibit 6.7 suggests that some of the overhead seems to be related more to machine utilization than direct labor. For example, it might be that machine depreciation and utilities are more related to machine-hours than to direct labor-hours or cost. If this is the case, we can use two or more allocation bases to allocate manufacturing overhead to the products.

This process has two steps. First, overhead costs have to be assigned to the two or more intermediate cost pools. Then the costs from each of the intermediate cost pools are allocated to the products using a specified allocation base. This approach is referred to as a **two-stage cost allocation** system. Exhibit 6.8 is a cost flow diagram that shows how this is done.

In Exhibit 6.8, the two intermediate cost pools are "direct labor-related costs" and "machine-related costs." In Sandia's case, this first stage assignment is easy to accomplish because it is based on the accounts in the cost accounting system.

Implementing the two-stage approach at Sandia requires computing two overhead rates, one for labor-related costs and one for machine-related costs. As indicated in Exhibit 6.9, the total machine-related overhead is $100,800 and there are 5,600 machine-hours, so the machine-related rate is $18 per machine-hour (= $100,800 ÷ 5,600 machine-hours). The total labor-related overhead is $151,200, and the direct labor-hours are 6,300, so the labor-related overhead rate is $24 per direct labor-hour (= $151,200 ÷ 6,300 direct labor-hours).

Choice of Allocation Bases

As in the case of a single allocation base, we need to determine which allocation bases to use. The basic approach is the same as before. We want to choose those bases that best reflect the relation between overhead incurrence and activity. A second criterion is the extent to which the choice of allocation base affects reported product costs.

LO 6-3
Allocate costs using a two-stage allocation system.

two-stage cost allocation
Process of first allocating costs to intermediate cost pools and then to the individual cost objects using different allocation bases.

Manufacturing Overhead	
Utilities[a]	$ 3,360
Supplies[b]	3,500
Training[b]	42,000
Supervision[b]	76,860
Machine depreciation[a]	41,370
Plant depreciation[a]	56,070
Miscellaneous[b]	28,840
Total	$252,000

[a] Machine-related overhead.
[b] Direct labor-related overhead.

Exhibit 6.7

Components of Manufacturing Overhead—Sandia Custom Furniture

Exhibit 6.8 Cost Flow Diagram: Two-Stage Cost Allocation System

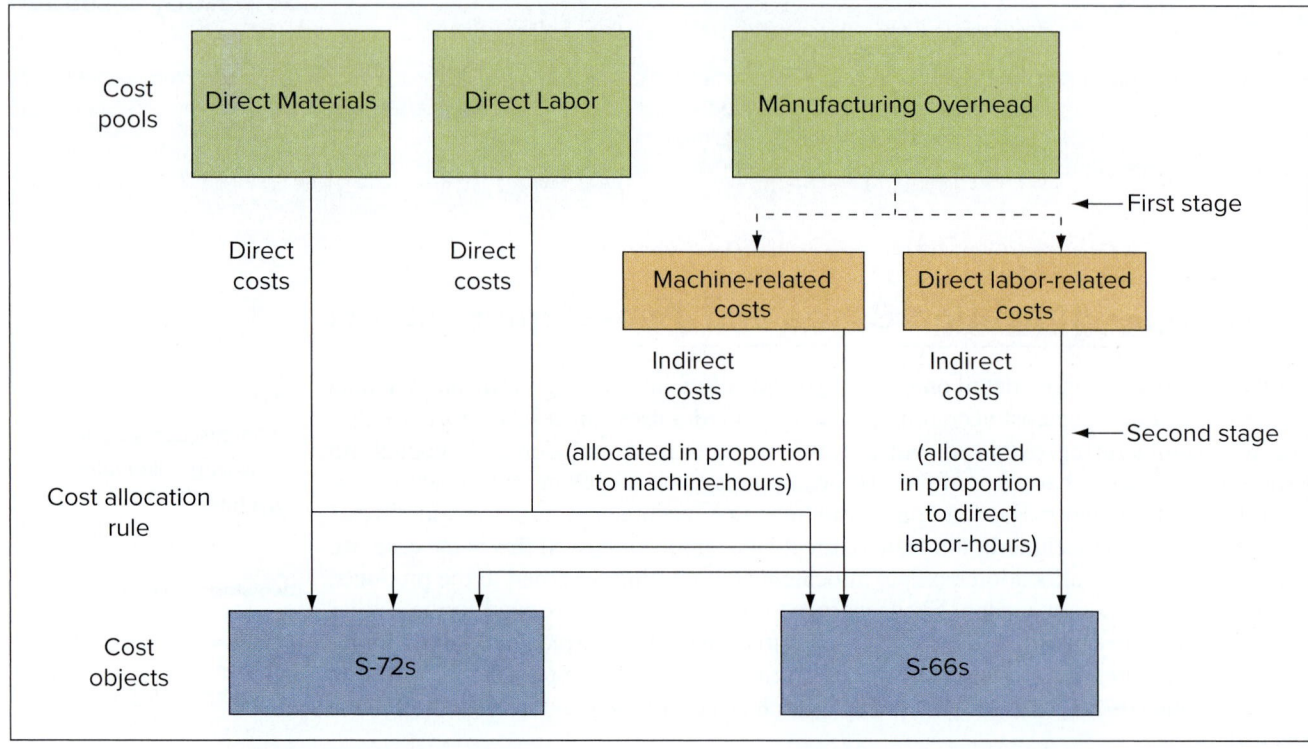

In our *two-stage* allocation system, we used direct labor-hours and machine-hours. In the *single* allocation system, there was a difference between direct labor-hours and direct labor cost because of the employees assigned to S-72 and S-66 production. Similarly, in the two-stage system, there is a difference in the reported product costs when machine-hours are used. This need not be the case.

Consider this example. Suppose that all direct labor at Sandia Custom Furniture is paid the same wage rate per hour. In this case, there would be no difference between using direct labor cost or direct labor-hours in the single allocation base costing system. Now, however, suppose that each direct laborer used one, and only one, machine and that the machine was running whenever the employee was working. In this case, machine-hours would be the same as labor-hours and the two-stage system would result in the same product costs as the single-stage system.

Different Companies, Different Production and Costing Systems

LO 6-4

Describe the three basic types of product costing systems (job, process, and operations), calculate product costs using these systems, and identify the business environments for which each is the best fit.

job

Unit of a product that is easily distinguishable from other units.

Consider our two example companies. Miller Paints manufactures paint, and Sandia Custom Furniture builds custom furniture. The production processes that lead to these two products can be described as *continuous* and *discrete,* respectively. For paint, the (single) product goes through a continuous flow process that all units (gallons of paint) follow. The production process produces a series of identical units. Custom furniture, on the other hand, goes through a discrete set of steps that all units can, but might not, go through. It is relatively easy to distinguish between different units in the custom furniture workshop, but it is impossible to distinguish between units in the paint factory.

The product costing systems in the two factories are different also, reflecting the differences in the production process. In the custom furniture factory, the costing system computes costs for the individual units (or small groups of units) called **jobs.** In the paint factory, because the units are identical, the costing system does not attempt to cost the individual units, but only large "batches."

	S-72s	S-66s	Total
Units produced	80	240	320
Machine-hours	1,400	4,200	5,600
Direct labor-hours	2,400	3,900	6,300
Direct materials	$ 40,000	$ 36,000	$ 76,000
Direct labor	72,000	78,000	150,000
Manufacturing overhead			
Utilities[a]			3,360
Supplies[b]			3,500
Training[b]			42,000
Supervision[b]			76,860
Machine depreciation[a]			41,370
Plant depreciation[a]			56,070
Miscellaneous[b]			28,840
Total manufacturing overhead			$252,000

Predetermined overhead rates	Overhead		Allocation Base		
	$100,800	÷	5,600 machine-hrs	=	$18
	$151,200	÷	6,300 direct labor-hours	=	$24

Product Costing	S-72s	S-66s	Total
Direct materials	$ 40,000	$ 36,000	$ 76,000
Direct labor	72,000	78,000	150,000
Overhead			
Machine-related (@ $18 per machine-hour)	25,200	75,600	100,800
Labor-related (@ $24 per direct labor-hour)	57,600	93,600	151,200
	$ 82,800	$169,200	$252,000
Total cost	$194,800	$283,200	$478,000
Unit cost	$ 2,435	$ 1,180	

[a] Machine-related overhead.
[b] Labor-related costs.

Exhibit 6.9

Two-Stage Cost Allocation—Sandia Custom Furniture

Cost accountants use the terms *job costing* and *process costing* to describe these two extremes. A **job costing** system records costs and revenues for each individual job. By contrast, **process costing** does not separate and record costs for each unit. Process costing is an accounting system used when identical units are produced through uniform production steps. The details of these two systems are discussed in Chapters 7 and 8; in this chapter, we have introduced the basic approach of each system.

Exhibit 6.10 shows a continuum of production methods ranging from those requiring job costing to those needing process costing. Companies using job costing include construction companies such as Morrison-Knudsen, defense contractors such as Boeing, hospitals such as the Memorial Sloan-Kettering Cancer Center (where the jobs would be called *cases*), moviemakers such as Universal Studios, and public accounting firms such as EY (formerly, Ernst & Young) (where the jobs are often called *clients*). These companies produce customized products.

Continuous flow processing is at the opposite end of the spectrum from job shops. A process system generally mass-produces a single, homogeneous product in a continuing process. Process systems are used in manufacturing chemicals, grinding flour, and refining oil. Companies with continuous flow processing use process costing methods.

Many organizations use job systems for some projects and process systems for others. A home builder might use process costing for standardized homes with a similar floor plan. The same builder might use job costing when building a custom-designed

job costing
Accounting system that traces costs to individual units or to specific jobs, contracts, or batches of goods.

process costing
Accounting system used when identical units are produced through a series of uniform production steps.

continuous flow processing
System that generally mass-produces a single, homogeneous output in a continuing process.

Exhibit 6.10

Production Flows and
Product Costing Systems

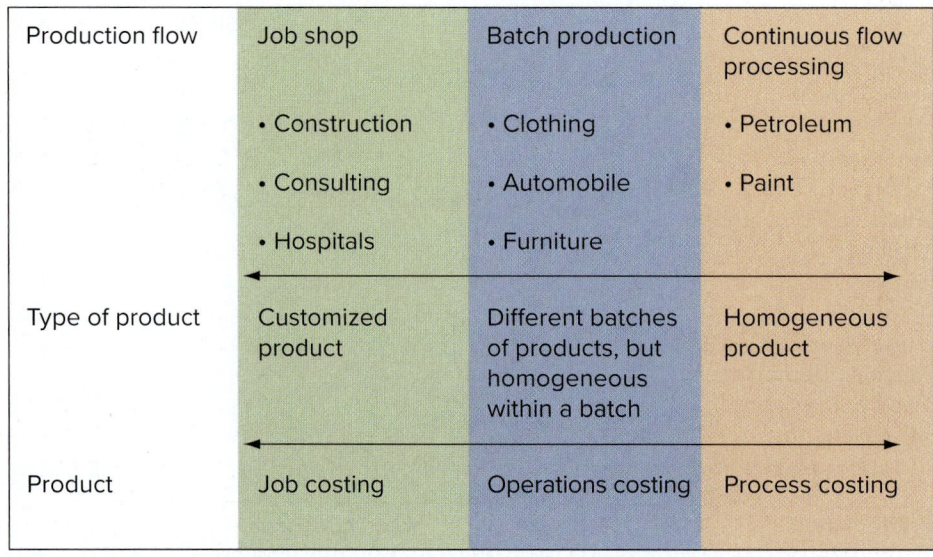

Production flow	Job shop	Batch production	Continuous flow processing
	• Construction	• Clothing	• Petroleum
	• Consulting	• Automobile	• Paint
	• Hospitals	• Furniture	
Type of product	Customized product	Different batches of products, but homogeneous within a batch	Homogeneous product
Product	Job costing	Operations costing	Process costing

operations costing

Hybrid costing system used in manufacturing goods that have some common characteristics and some individual characteristics.

operation

Standardized method or technique that is repeatedly performed in making a product.

home for a single customer. Honeywell International Inc., a high-tech company, uses process costing for most of its furnace thermostats but job costing for specialized defense and space contracting work.

Many companies use a hybrid of job and process costing, called **operations costing.** An **operation** is a standardized method of making a product that is performed repeatedly in production. Like companies using process costing, companies using operations costing produce goods through standardized production methods, but materials can be different for each product.

For example, Nissan manufactures a variety of models of cars and trucks on one assembly line in its manufacturing plant near Nashville, Tennessee. Each car or truck goes through the same work stations such as the painting station. Each vehicle type has a different set of materials, however. For example, trucks and cars have different bodies. This makes operations costing an obvious choice; different products with different materials share a standardized process.

Operations Costing: An Illustration

Miller Paints represents a firm that uses process costing and Sandia Custom Furniture illustrates a firm that uses a job costing system. We finish this chapter with an illustration of an operations costing system.

Bayou Workspaces buys inexpensive, unpainted tables and chairs for use in small offices and cubicles. It then paints the furniture and sells them to office supply stores. The amount of paint and the time to paint each unit is roughly the same regardless of the size of the unit. Bayou never carries any inventories. Exhibit 6.11 shows the basic data for Bayou for the month of November.

Exhibit 6.11

Basic Data, November—
Bayou Workspaces

	Tables	Chairs	Total
Number of units purchased from supplier	500	2,000	2,500
Price per unit	× $80	× $30	
Total costs of unfinished material.	$40,000	$60,000	$100,000
Direct labor in painting operation.			$ 32,000
Paint cost in painting operation			5,000
Overhead in painting operation			43,000
Total cost in painting operation			$ 80,000

Bayou has two types of raw material cost: furniture and paint. It has one manufacturing operation, the painting of tables and chairs. Its cost system is designed to provide information to the managers about the costs of these two products.

Many products are produced in a batch production environment. For example, many processes in snowmobile manufacturing are standard, much like products produced in a continuous process. Different models, however, require different parts, as in a job costing environment.
Purestock/SuperStock

Clearly, the cost of the unfinished tables and chairs can be assigned directly to the two products, so the cost system needs to allocate only the cost of the painting operation to the two products. Because the time and the amount of paint do not depend on whether a table or chair is being painted, Bayou allocates the operations costs (paint, direct labor, and overhead) based on the number of units (tables plus chairs) painted.

For November, the allocation of the painting operations costs and the subsequent product costs are shown in Exhibit 6.12.

The cost system that Bayou uses combines elements of the systems used at Miller Paints and Sandia Custom Furniture. Because it treats the painting process as a continuous process, it mirrors the cost system at Miller Paints. Because it recognizes the differences between the two products, it is similar to that at Sandia Custom Furniture. All three cost systems accomplish one thing. They provide managers with information about the costs of the products and services these companies sell. These three examples also illustrate that the design of the cost system is fundamentally the same in all three firms. All production costs are allocated to the products manufactured. The differences reflect differences in the number of products and the processes used.

	Tables	Chairs	
Total operation cost			$80,000
Total units painted.	500	2,000	÷ 2,500
Cost per unit in paint			$ 32
Allocation of operation cost			
Units	500	2,000	2,500
Operation cost (@ $32 per unit) . . .	$ 16,000	$ 64,000	$80,000
Materials cost (from Exhibit 6.11) . . .	$ 40,000	$ 60,000	
Total cost.	$ 56,000	$124,000	
Number of units.	500	2,000	
Unit cost	$ 112	$ 62	

Exhibit 6.12

Product Costs—Bayou Workspaces

Key Takeaways

1. Cost management systems should be designed so they
   a. Have a decision focus;
   b. Reflect different (relevant) information for different purposes;
   c. Meet the cost-benefit test.
2. The basic cost flow diagram provides a visualization of the product cost allocation process:
   a. Cost pools (direct materials, direct labor, and manufacturing overhead, for example);
   b. Cost objects (products and services, for example);
   c. Cost allocation rule (allocate overhead based on direct-labor hours, for example).
3. Different production systems lead to different cost accumulation systems:
   a. Job shops (customized products or services using a mix of similar and idiosyncratic processes) → Job costing
   b. Continuous flow processing (homogeneous products using a shared, common, process) → Process costing
   c. Batch production (a set of similar products, each produced in a large batch, in which different products share some, but not necessarily all, production processes) → Operations costing

Self-Study Question

4. Pear Computers assembles computer parts into finished systems for sale through mass-market retailers. It sells two models differentiated by the speed of the processor and other peripherals, the X3G and the X2G. Data on the two models for April follow. The time required for either unit is the same. Pear Computers uses operations costing and assigns direct labor and overhead based on the number of units assembled. Compute the cost of the X3G and X2G models for April.

The solution to this question is at the end of the chapter.

	X3G	X2G	Total
Number of units..	6,000	14,000	20,000
Parts cost per unit........	× $ 250	× $ 175	
Parts cost........	$1,500,000	$2,450,000	$3,950,000
Other costs:			
Direct labor....			$ 414,000
Overhead			806,000
Total............			$1,220,000

SUMMARY

This chapter introduced the basic principles of product and service costing systems. It illustrated simple systems for both continuous processing and discrete manufacturing industries. For continuous process products, the costing system focuses on the costs of relatively large production quantities, such as monthly production, with each unit in the month being assigned the same unit costs.

For products in discrete manufacturing industries, costing at the individual unit level (or for small numbers of identical units) is used. Manufacturing overhead is allocated to products using one or more allocation bases to compute predetermined overhead rates.

The following summarizes the key ideas tied to the chapter's learning objectives.

LO 6-1 Describe how a product costing system works and apply these principles to a variety of business environments. Product costing systems provide information to managers for decision making. The basic approach to product costing is first to assign costs that are directly associated with a product to that product. The next step allocates all other product costs to the units produced based on the number of units or some equivalent measure.

LO 6-2 Allocate overhead to products and services in a manner that provides useful information for decision making. Overhead is allocated to products using a cost allocation base that ideally reflects a cause-and-effect relation between the production of the unit and the incurrence of overhead costs. Common allocation bases are direct labor-hours, direct labor cost, and machine-hours.

LO 6-3 Allocate costs using a two-stage allocation system. A two-stage allocation system first allocates overhead costs to two or more cost pools. Ideally, the individual cost pools are relatively homogeneous in their use by products. Each pool is then allocated to products based on separate allocation bases.

LO 6-4 Describe three basic types of product costing systems (job, process, and operations), calculate product costs using these systems, and identify the business environments for which each system is the best fit. *Job costing systems* are used when individual units (or small groups of units) are easily distinguishable and production of each unit can require different resources and process flows. *Process costing* is used when individual units are homogeneous and the production flow is the same for all units. *Operations costing* is a combination of job costing methods with process costing methods. It is often used in environments with standardized processes applied to products that use different materials and parts.

KEY TERMS

continuous flow processing, 257
cost management system, 245
job, 256
job costing, 257
operation, 258

operations costing, 258
predetermined overhead rate, 252
process costing, 257
two-stage cost allocation, 255

REVIEW QUESTIONS

6-1. How are product costing and cost allocation related?

6-2. What are the three criteria for the design of cost management systems?

6-3. Why are cost flow diagrams useful in describing product costing systems?

6-4. What are the characteristics of the following three costing systems: (*a*) job costing, (*b*) process costing, and (*c*) operations costing?

6-5. How are job order, process, and operations costing the same? How are they different?

6-6. Describe the predetermined overhead rate. What is the role of the predetermined overhead rate in product costing?

6-7. Ideally, what does an allocation base reflect between the overhead cost and the activity (production of a product, for example)?

6-8. What is two-stage cost allocation?

6-9. What is continuous flow processing? Give at least three examples of products that might use continuous flow processing.

6-10. What is each component of the basic cost flow model? Describe each component.

CRITICAL ANALYSIS AND DISCUSSION QUESTIONS

6-11. "Cost allocation is arbitrary, so there is nothing gained by it. We should report only the costs that we know are direct." Do you agree? Why?

6-12. When is the basic cost flow model used? Give an example.

6-13. It is your first day at a new job and you talk about the themes of cost system design. One of your new colleagues asks, "If different cost information is used for different purposes, does that mean we do not know what something costs? I thought that was what a cost system reported." How would you respond?

6-14. The business school dean has asked the accounting club to help with a product costing analysis for the school. How would we define the products? What questions would we ask the dean before we accept the task?

6-15. Identify a particular support function in a business school (the library, for example). Discuss possible allocation bases that might be used to allocate costs in the function to programs (degrees) or students.

6-16. What criteria are important in determining the choice of an allocation base?

6-17. Cost allocation bases are ideally based on a cause-and-effect basis, but they are used to allocate fixed overhead. Is this inconsistent?

6-18. Why does it matter what allocation base is used to determine the predetermined rate?

6-19. Why might two companies in the same industry have different cost systems?

6-20. Is it possible for a company to have a two-stage allocation system but use, for example, direct labor-hours to allocate costs from all pools in the second stage? Will the resulting product costs be the same as if it used a single-stage system?

6-21. Your colleague says, "If a company only has one product, it doesn't matter how we allocate cost because the result will always be the same." Do you agree? Explain.

All applicable Exercises are included in Connect.  **EXERCISES**

6-22. Basic Cost Flow Model

The following events occurred at Moore's Hobbies and Crafts store during the most recent fiscal year: **(LO 6-1)**

1. Purchased merchandise costing $99,000.
2. Had sales revenue for the year totaling $145,000; the merchandise sold was purchased for $85,000.
3. Paid $7,500 transportation-in costs.
4. Incurred selling and administrative costs equal to 10 percent of sales revenue.
5. All transactions, sales and purchases, were for cash.
6. An inventory account at the end of the year indicated merchandise costing $94,500 was on hand.

Required

Give the amounts for the following items in the Merchandise Inventory account:

a.   Ending balance (EB).

b.   Transfers-out (TO).

c.   Transfers-in (TI).

d.   Beginning balance (BB).

(LO 6-1)   **6-23. Basic Cost Flow Model**

Cranbrook Used Books experienced the following events during the current year:

1.   Incurred $12,000 in selling costs.

2.   Took an inventory at year-end and learned that goods costing $55,000 were on hand. This compared with a beginning inventory of $72,000 on January 1.

3.   Purchased $124,000 of merchandise.

4.   Incurred $56,000 of administrative costs.

5.   Determined that sales revenue during the year was $187,000.

6.   Paid $4,500 for transportation-in costs.

7.   Debited all costs incurred to the appropriate account and credited to Accounts Payable. All sales were for cash.

Required

Give the amounts for the following items in the Merchandise Inventory account:

a.   Ending balance (EB)

b.   Transfers-in (TI)

c.   Beginning balance (BB)

d.   Transfers-out (TO)

(LO 6-1)   **6-24. Basic Cost Flow Model**

Assume that the following events occurred at Lakewood, Inc. last month.

1.   Incurred direct labor costs of $300,000.

2.   Completed work on 70 percent of the work in process. Costs are assigned equally across all work in process.

3.   Transferred 80 percent of the materials purchased to work in process.

4.   Purchased $550,000 in direct materials.

5.   Determined that manufacturing overhead was $485,000.

6.   The inventory accounts have no beginning balances. All costs incurred were debited to the appropriate account and credited to Accounts Payable.

Required

Give the amounts for the following items in the Work-in-Process account:

a.   Transfers-in (TI)

b.   Transfers-out (TO)

c.   Ending balance (EB)

(LO 6-1)   **6-25. Basic Cost Flow Model**

Fill in the missing items for the following inventories:

	A	B	C
Beginning balance............	$9,750	_____	$14,200
Ending balance..............	8,000	$4,000	12,400
Transferred in	_____	36,000	44,000
Transferred out..............	17,500	42,000	_____

(LO 6-1)   **6-26. Basic Cost Flow Model**

Fill in the missing items for the following inventories:

	A	B	C
Beginning balance...........	$6,700	_____	$ 42,600
Ending balance.............	5,600	$ 5,700	37,200
Transferred in	_____	41,350	132,000
Transferred out.............	17,000	40,750	_____

6-27. Basic Cost Flow Model

(LO 6-1)

Fill in the missing items for the following inventories:

	A	B	C
Beginning balance...........	$6,800	_____	$ 7,500
Ending balance.............	6,400	$10,000	5,500
Transferred in	_____	10,400	52,500
Transferred out.............	7,600	10,800	_____

6-28. Basic Product Costing

(LO 6-1)

Lenox Solvents manufactures a special fluid at its Hazelridge plant. Operating data for June follow.

Materials	$2,499,000
Labor	214,200
Manufacturing overhead........	856,800

The Hazelridge plant produced 1,050,000 liters in June. The plant never has any beginning or ending inventories.

Required

Compute the cost per liter of liquid produced in June.

6-29. Basic Product Costing

(LO 6-1)

Seville Chemicals produces a fuel additive. Operating data for January follow.

Materials	$ 78,000
Labor	14,000
Manufacturing overhead........	310,000

Seville Chemicals produced 25,125 barrels of the additive in January.

Required

Compute the cost per barrel of the additive produced in January.

6-30. Basic Product Costing

(LO 6-1)

In May, Seville Chemicals produced 26,000 barrels of the additive. Labor costs were $16,800 and manufacturing overhead was $313,000. The cost per barrel was $15.80.

Required

What was the materials cost in May?

6-31. Basic Product Costing

(LO 6-1)

In October, Seville Chemicals produced 22,500 barrels of the additive. Manufacturing overhead was $285,000 and the cost per barrel was $16.30. Materials costs were four times greater than labor costs.

Required

a.   What were the labor costs for October?

b.   What were the materials costs for October?

(LO 6-1)   **6-32. Basic Product Costing**

Barrett eSellers is an online retail store offering a variety of products. As a part of its business model, it offers free returns. The returns are processed at the Returns Processing Facility (RPF) near one of the air freight hubs. The RPF checks the returns for documentation (receipt and so on) and condition of the returned item and determines the disposition of the item (return to stock, resale as a "used" item, or trash). The system at RPF is designed so that all returns that start the process on any given day are processed that day.

    During May, the RPF processed 37,500 returns with a dollar sales value of $3,675,000. The costs incurred at the RPF during May were as follows.

Facility labor...............	$58,800
Facility overhead	88,200

Required

a.   Compute the cost per return for May at the RPF.

b.   Compute the cost per dollar sales value for items returned for May at the RPF.

(LO 6-1)   **6-33. Basic Product Costing**

Bostwick Chemicals started business on April 1. The following operations data are available for April for the one solvent it produces.

	Gallons
Beginning inventory...............................	–0–
Started in January	350,000
Ending work-in-process inventory (75% complete)	40,000

Costs incurred in April follow.

Materials	$424,500
Labor	127,600
Manufacturing overhead..............	365,900

There are never any finished goods at Bostwick Chemicals because all production is to order.

Required

a.   Compute cost of goods sold for April.

b.   What is the value of work-in-process inventory on April 30?

(LO 6-1)   **6-34. Basic Product Costing: Ethical Issues**

Cedargrove Cider processes and bottles apple cider for sale through retail and big box grocery outlets. It had no work in process on May 31 in its only inventory account. The company started 19,100 cases during June. On June 30, work in process is 4,000 cases. The production supervisor estimates that the ending work-in-process inventory is 60 percent complete. Cost records at Cedargrove recorded June production costs of $93,750 in materials cost and $107,500 in conversion costs. All production is sold as it is produced.

Required

a.   Compute cost of goods sold for June.

b.   What is the value of work-in-process inventory on June 30?

c.   The president tells the controller that the company has already met its income target for the quarter, which ends on June 30, but whether the target can be met next quarter is in doubt. The president asks the controller to change the production manager's estimate about the ending work-in-process inventory to increase the probability the company can meet the next quarter's income target.

1. To comply with the president's request, would the controller raise or lower the estimated percentage complete from the 60 percent estimate of the production supervisor? Explain.
2. What should the controller do?

6-35. Process Costing

(LO 6-1)

Duffield Lubricants produces oil-based machine lubricants. On December 1, it had no work-in-process inventory. It starts production of 86,000 gallons of lubricant in December and completes 72,000 gallons. The costs of the resources used by Duffield in December consist of the following.

Materials	$187,568
Conversion costs (labor and overhead) . . .	245,424

Required

The production supervisor estimates that the ending work in process is 38 percent complete. Compute the cost of lubricant transferred to finished goods and the amount in work-in-process ending inventory as of December 31.

6-36. Process Costing

(LO 6-1)

Bremen Fitness Products produces a sports drink. On October 1, it had no work-in-process inventory. It started production of 9,000 cases of the drink in October and shipped 7,800 cases to retailers. (Bremen holds no finished goods inventory.) The costs of the resources used by Bremen in October consist of the following.

Materials	$ 87,523
Conversion costs (labor and overhead) . . .	134,975

Required

The production supervisor estimates that the ending work in process is 55 percent complete on October 31. Compute the cost of cases shipped and the amount in work-in-process ending inventory as of October 31.

6-37. Process Costing

(LO 6-1)

Gullen Partners produces cleaning solvents. On September 1, it had no work-in-process inventory. It started production of 56,000 gallons of solvent in September and completed production of 47,000 gallons. Cost records at Gullen show the following for September.

Materials	$47,660
Conversion costs (labor and overhead) . . .	54,871

Required

The production supervisor estimates that the ending work in process is 62 percent complete on September 30. Compute the cost of solvent completed and the cost of the solvent in work-in-process ending inventory as of September 30.

6-38. Predetermined Overhead Rates

(LO 6-2)

Redfern Audio produces audio equipment including headphones. At the Campus Facility, it produces two wireless models, Standard and Enhanced, which differ both in the materials and components used and in the labor skill required. Data for the Campus Plant for the third quarter follow.

	A	B	C	D
1		Standard	Enhanced	Total
2	Units produced	24,000	8,000	32,000
3	Machine hours	14,400	9,600	24,000
4	Direct labor-hours	18,000	18,000	36,000
5				
6	Direct materials cost	$ 480,000	$ 720,000	$ 1,200,000
7	Direct labor costs	288,000	612,000	900,000
8	Manufacturing overhead			864,000
9	Total costs			$ 2,964,000
10				

Required

Compute the predetermined overhead rate assuming that Redfern Audio uses *direct labor-hours* to allocate overhead costs.

(LO 6-2)   **6-39. Predetermined Overhead Rates**

Refer to the data in Exercise 6-38.

Required

Compute the predetermined overhead rate assuming that Redfern Audio uses *direct labor costs* to allocate overhead costs.

(LO 6-2)   **6-40. Predetermined Overhead Rates**

Refer to the data in Exercise 6-38.

Required

Compute the predetermined overhead rate assuming that Redfern Audio uses the *number of units* to allocate overhead costs.

(LO 6-2)   **6-41. Predetermined Overhead Rates**

Refer to the data in Exercise 6-38.

Required

Compute the predetermined overhead rate assuming that Redfern Audio uses *direct material cost*s to allocate overhead costs.

(LO 6-2)   **6-42. Predetermined Overhead Rates**

Refer to the data in Exercise 6-38.

Required

Compute the predetermined overhead rate assuming that Redfern Audio uses *machine-hours* to allocate overhead costs.

(LO 6-1)   **6-43. Overhead Cost Allocation—Cost Diagram**

Refer to the data in Exercise 6-38.

Required

Draw the cost flow diagram assuming that Redfern Audio uses *machine-hours* to allocate overhead costs.

(LO 6-2)   **6-44. Predetermined Overhead Rates**

Kilbourne Appliances produces two models of beverage coolers for homes and offices, the KA-15 and the KA-24. Data on operations and costs for March follow.

	KA-15	KA-24	Total
Units produced	600	400	1,000
Machine-hours.................	360	540	900
Direct labor-hours..............	750	1,750	2,500
Direct materials costs...........	$72,000	$120,000	$192,000
Direct labor costs	15,000	35,000	50,000
Manufacturing overhead costs....			187,200
Total costs			$429,200

Required

a. Compute the predetermined overhead rate assuming that Kilbourne Appliances uses *direct labor-hours* to allocate overhead costs.

b. Compute the predetermined overhead rate assuming that Kilbourne Appliances uses *machine-hours* to allocate overhead costs.

6-45. Predetermined Overhead Rates—Cost Diagram   (LO 6-2)
Refer to the data in Exercise 6-44.

Required

a. Compute the predetermined overhead rate assuming that Kilbourne Appliances uses *direct labor costs* to allocate overhead costs.

b. Draw the cost flow diagram assuming that Kilbourne Appliances uses *direct labor costs* to allocate overhead costs.

6-46. Predetermined Overhead Rates and Product Profitability   (LO 6-1, 2)
Harmon Recycling Services (HRS), a not-for-profit organization, has two drop-off centers, Westside and Eastside. Data for the expected operation in the next quarter follow.

	A	B	C	D	E
1		Eastside	Westside	Total	
2	Clients	25,000	6,250	31,250	
3	Revenues	$270,000	$180,000	$450,000	
4	Staff hours	8,100	2,700	10,800	
5	Staff costs	$99,000	$81,000	$180,000	
6	General operating costs			$270,000	
7					

Required

a. Compute the predetermined overhead rate used to apply general operating costs to the two centers assuming HRS uses the *number of clients* to allocate general operating costs.

b. Based on the rates computed in requirement (*a*), what is the expected surplus (revenues less costs) for each center?

6-47. Predetermined Overhead Rates and Product Profitability   (LO 6-1, 2)
Refer to the data in Exercise 6-46.

Required

a. Compute the predetermined overhead rate used to apply general operating costs to the two centers assuming HRS uses *revenue* to allocate general operating costs.

b. Based on the rates computed in requirement (*a*), what is the expected surplus (revenues less costs) for each center?

6-48. Predetermined Overhead Rates and Product Profitability   (LO 6-1, 2)
Refer to the data in Exercise 6-46.

Required

a. Compute the predetermined overhead rate used to apply general operating costs to the two centers assuming HRS uses the *staff hours* to allocate general operating costs.

b. Based on the rates computed in requirement (*a*), what is the expected surplus (revenues less costs) for each center?

6-49. Predetermined Overhead Rates and Product Profitability   (LO 6-1, 2)
Refer to the data in Exercise 6-46.

Required

a. Compute the predetermined overhead rate used to apply general operating costs to the two centers assuming HRS uses the *staff cost* to allocate general operating costs.

b. Based on the rates computed in requirement (*a*), what is the expected surplus (revenues less costs) for each center?

(LO 6-1, 2, 3)   **6-50. Two-Stage Cost Allocation and Predetermined Rates**

Tacoma Accessories makes two laptop cases, Plastic and Leather, that require direct materials, direct labor, and overhead. The following data refer to operations expected for next quarter:

	Plastic	Leather	Total
Revenue.....................	$480,000	$500,000	$980,000
Direct material	180,000	260,000	440,000
Direct labor	60,000	40,000	100,000
Overhead:			
Material handling overhead..			198,000
Fabrication overhead			140,000

Tacoma uses a two-stage cost allocation system: It uses direct-material costs to allocate material handling overhead and direct-labor costs to allocate fabrication overhead costs.

Required

a.   Compute the material handling overhead rate for next quarter.

b.   Compute the fabrication overhead rate for next quarter.

c.   What is the total overhead allocated to the Plastic case next quarter?

d.   What is the total overhead allocated to the Leather case next quarter?

(LO 6-1, 2, 3)   **6-51. Two-Stage Cost Allocation and Predetermined Rates—Visualization**

Refer to the data in Exercise 6-50

Required

Draw the cost flow diagram that represents the cost system used by Tacoma Accessories.

(LO 6-1, 2, 3)   **6-52. Two-Stage Cost Allocation and Predetermined Rates**

Westover Travel offers travel packages using both air and ocean travel. Westover offers two packages, Tourist and Premier, that differ in the accommodations, class of travel, and so on. Westover has a call center, which handles customer queries and complaints. The call center tracks the number of calls and the number of call-minutes for customers by the package they have purchased. Expected call center data for next month follow.

	Tourist	Premier	
Call center volume:			
Number of calls	20,000	12,000	
Number of call minutes.........	108,000	162,000	
Call center costs:			Total
Call-related			$200,000
Call minute–related............			121,500
Total call center costs			$321,500

The call center at Westover uses a two-stage cost allocation system: It uses the number of calls to allocate call-related costs and the number of call minutes to allocate call minute–related costs.

Required

a.   Compute the call-related overhead rate for next month.

b.   Compute the call minute–related overhead rate for next month.

c.   Compute the total call center costs allocated to the Tourist package.

d.   Compute the total call center costs allocated to the Premier package.

(LO 6-1, 2, 3).   **6-53. Two-Stage Cost Allocation and Predetermined Rates—Visualization**

Refer to the data in Exercise 6-52.

Required

Draw the cost flow diagram that represents the cost system used by Westover Travel.

6-54. Two-Stage Cost Allocation—Multiple Choice   (LO 6-3)

Consider the cost allocation system used at Tacoma Accessories and Westover Travel in Exercises 6-50 through 6-54.

Required

The system is referred to as a two-stage cost allocation system because

a.   Cost is allocated first to intermediate cost pools and from these pools to cost objects.

b.   There are two or more cost pools.

c.   There are two or more cost objects.

d.   There are exactly two cost objects.

e.   None of the above.

6-55. Operations Costing   (LO 6-4)

Witt Recreation Company (WRC) makes e-bikes. The company currently manufactures two models, the Coaster and the Traveler, in one of the WRC factories. Both models require the same assembling operations. The difference between the models is the cost of materials. The following data are available for the second quarter.

	Coaster	Traveler	Total
Number of bikes assembled …	750	450	1,200
Materials cost per bike ……	$624	$1,200	
Other costs:			
Direct labor……………			$297,000
Depreciation and lease……			380,000
Supervision and control ……			245,000
Factory administration……			338,000

Required

Witt Recreation Company uses operations costing and assigns conversion costs based on the number of units assembled. Compute the cost of each model assembled in the second quarter.

6-56. Operations Costing   (LO 6-4)

Refer to the data in Exercise 6-55.

Required

Witt Recreation Company uses operations costing and assigns conversion costs based on the the direct materials costs. Compute the cost of each model assembled in the second quarter.

6-57. Operations Costing   (LO 6-4)

Piper Recreational Vehicles (PRV) modifies vans into recreational vehicles. PRV offers two models, the XC-2 and XC-6, which differ in the quality of the basic van and the workmanship and machining detail that are used. The following data reflect expected operations for the next year.

	XC-2	XC-6	Total
Number assembled…………	54	39	93
Materials cost per RV ………	$40,000	$70,000	
Other costs:			
Direct labor……………			$905,550
Depreciation……………			735,120
Miscellaneous costs ………			633,180

Required

Piper Recreational Vehicles uses operations costing and assigns conversion costs based on the number of units assembled. Compute the expected cost of each model assembled next year.

(LO 6-4)   **6-58. Operations Costing**

Refer to the data in Exercise 6-57.

Required

Piper Recreational Vehicles uses operations costing and assigns conversion costs based on materials cost. Compute the expected cost of each model assembled next year.

(LO 6-4)   **6-59. Operations Costing**

Spring Garden Vegetables (SGV) processes two brands of frozen vegetables, Valu-PAK and Gourmet. The two brands are processed in one factory using the same production process. The only difference between the two brands is the quality (cost) of the raw vegetables. The following data are expected for November.

	Valu-PAK	Gourmet	Total
Number of cases processed ...	14,000	6,000	20,000
Cost of raw vegetables and packaging per case...........	$6	$14	
Other costs:			
Direct labor			$62,300
Depreciation			17,050
Miscellaneous costs			13,050

Required

Spring Garden Vegetables uses operations costing and assigns conversion costs based on the number of cases of vegetables processed. Compute the cost per unit of each brand of frozen vegetables in November.

(LO 6-4)   **6-60. Operations Costing**

Refer to the data in Exercise 6-59.

Required

Spring Garden Vegetables uses operations costing and assigns conversion costs based on materials cost. Compute the cost per unit of each brand of frozen vegetables in November.

PROBLEMS    connect·   All applicable Problems are included in Connect.

(LO 6-2)   **6-61. Product Costing**

Refer to the data in Exercise 6-38.

Required

a. Compute the individual product costs per unit assuming that Redfern Audio uses the *number of units* to allocate overhead to the products.

b. Compute the individual product costs per unit assuming that Redfern Audio uses *direct labor-hours* to allocate overhead to the products.

c. Compute the individual product costs per unit assuming that Redfern Audio uses *machine-hours* to allocate overhead to the products.

(LO 6-2)   **6-62. Product Costing**

Refer to the data in Exercise 6-38.

Required

a. Compute the individual product costs per unit assuming that Redfern Audio uses *direct labor costs* to allocate overhead to the products.

b. Compute the individual product costs per unit assuming that Redfern Audio uses *material costs* to allocate overhead to the products.

6-63. Product Costing—Data Analysis and Visualization

(LO 6-2)

Refer to the data in Exercise 6-38 and the results in Problems 6-61 and 6-62.

Required

The CEO of Redfern Audio is confused by the number of different possible unit costs and how it is possible that "reasonable" accounting calculations can lead to such differences. Write a brief report that helps the CEO understand the results. Be sure to include an analysis of the data and visual material that illustrate the analysis.

6-64. Product Costing

(LO 6-2)

Refer to the data in Exercise 6-44.

Required

a. Compute the individual product costs per unit assuming that Kilbourne Appliances uses the *number of units* to allocate overhead to the products.
b. Compute the individual product costs per unit assuming that Kilbourne Appliances uses *direct labor cost* to allocate overhead to the products.
c. Compute the individual product costs per unit assuming that Kilbourne Appliances uses *direct material costs* to allocate overhead to the products.

6-65. Product Costing

(LO 6-2)

Refer to the data in Exercise 6-44.

Required

a. Compute the individual product costs per unit assuming that Kilbourne Appliances uses *direct labor-hours* to allocate overhead to the products.
b. Compute the individual product costs per unit assuming that Kilbourne Appliances uses *machine-hours* to allocate overhead to the products.

6-66. Product Costing—Data Analysis and Visualization

(LO 6-2)

Refer to the data in Exercise 6-44 and Problems 6-64 and 6-65.

Required

The chief marketing officer (CMO) of Kilbourne Appliances, who uses product cost analyses to make decisions about pricing and promotion, would like an explanation about how it is possible to have different unit costs when accountants are supposed to come up with "the" number. Prepare a report that helps the CMO understand the results. Be sure to include an analysis of the data and visual material that illustrate the analysis.

6-67. Two-Stage Allocation and Product Costing

(LO 6-2, 3)

Hall, Inc. manufactures two components, Standard and Ultra, that are designed for the same function, but are made of different metals for operational performance reasons. The metal used in Standard is easy to work with and there are few quality issues or reworking required on the machines. The metal used in Ultra is more difficult to work with and often needs additional machine time and rework.

Data on expected operations and direct costs for the next fiscal year follow.

	Standard	Ultra	Total
Units produced..................	30,000	7,500	37,500
Direct labor-hours used	90,000	22,500	112,500
Machine-hours used	15,000	22,500	37,500
Direct materials costs	$2,250,000	$1,500,000	$3,750,000
Direct labor costs...............	2,520,000	855,000	3,375,000

The planning process team at Hall, Inc. has estimated the following manufacturing overhead costs for the next fiscal year:

Account	Amount
Administration.	$ 825,400
Engineering.	902,500
Machine operation and maintenance	785,000
Miscellaneous.	540,100
Supervision	884,500
Total	$3,937,500

The cost accounting system at Hall, Inc. calculates product costs by adding allocated overhead to the direct costs of the product. Overhead costs are allocated based on *direct labor-hours.*

Required

a.   Compute the estimated per-unit product costs for the next fiscal year, based on the current cost accounting system.

b.   An analyst on the planning process team suggests that a two-stage system would improve the estimated product costs. The analyst suggests that overhead be first assigned to one of two cost pools: machine related or labor related. Machine-related overhead consists of the accounts "Engineering" and "Machine operation and maintenance." Labor-related overhead consists of the remaining manufacturing overhead. Machine-related costs would be allocated based on *machine-hours.* Labor-related overhead would be allocated based on *direct labor cost.* Compute the estimated per-unit product costs for the next fiscal year, based on the system proposed by the analyst.

(LO 6-2, 3)   **6-68. Two-Stage Allocation and Product Costing—Analysis and Visualization**
Refer to the information in Problem 6-67.

Required
Prepare a report for the managers at Hall, Inc. explaining the differences in the estimated product costs under the current cost system and the system proposed by the analyst. Include cost flow diagrams to illustrate your analysis. Recommend (with reasons) the system the company should adopt.

(LO 6-1, 2, 3)   **6-69. Predetermined Rates and Product Profitability: Two-Stage Cost Allocation**
Refer to the information in Exercise 6-46 for Harmon Recycling Services (HRS). The company is considering using a two-stage cost allocation system and wants to assess the effects on reported product profits.
More detailed financial information for HRS follows:

13		Eastside	Westside	Total
14	Clients	25,000	6,250	31,250
15	Revenues	$270,000	$180,000	$450,000
16	Staff hours	8,100	2,700	10,800
17	Staff costs	$99,000	$81,000	$180,000
18	General operating costs:			
19	User-related			$135,000
20	Staff-related			135,000
21	Total general operating costs			$270,000
22				

The company plans to use Clients to allocate user-related costs and Staff Costs to allocate staff-related costs.

Required

a.   Compute the predetermined overhead rate used to apply the two general operating cost pools to the two centers (Eastside and Westside) assuming HRS uses the proposed two-stage cost system to allocate general operating costs.

b.   Based on the rates computed in requirement (*a*), what is the surplus (revenues minus costs) for each service?

6-70. Predetermined Rates and Product Profitability: Two-Stage Cost Allocation   (LO 6-1, 2, 3)

Refer to the information in Exercise 6-46 and Problem 6-69. An accounting student from the local college, working on a related project at HRS as a part of a course, suggested a further revision after an analysis of the general operating accounts. Specifically, the student suggested that the staff-related costs should be separated into two cost pools instead of one. One pool would be allocated based on *staff hours* and the other pool allocated based on *staff costs*. The user-related pool would remain as described in Problem 6-69. The general operating costs could be summarized as follows (the information on revenues, users, and staff costs remains as in Problem 6-69).

User-related operating costs	$135,000
Staff hour-related operating costs	108,000
Staff cost-related operating costs	27,000
Total general operating costs	$270,000

Required

a.   Compute the predetermined overhead rate used to apply the three general operating cost pools to the two centers (Eastside and Westside) assuming HRS uses the the student's proposed two-stage cost system to allocate general operating costs.

b.   Based on the rates computed in requirement (*a*), what is the surplus (revenues minus costs) for each service?

6-71. Operations Costing and Two-Stage Systems   (LO 6-3, 4)

Larned Recreational builds two models of dune buggies: Sport and Custom. Both models require the same assembly and finishing process and are assembled in the same factory. They differ in the quality and detail of the materials. The following data reflect expected operations for the upcoming year.

	Sport	Custom	Total
Number of units	3,200	1,800	5,000
Direct materials cost per unit	$400	$1,100	
Conversion costs:			
Direct labor			$1,832,000
Overhead			2,608,000
Total			$4,440,000

Required

a.   Larned Recreation uses operations costing and assigns conversion costs based on the number of units assembled. Compute the cost per unit of the Sport and Custom models for the upcoming year.

b.   The financial team at Larned suggests that a two-stage system be used to compute the product cost of the two models. Their recommendation is to assign direct labor cost based on the number of units and overhead cost based on direct materials cost. Compute the cost per unit of the Sport and Custom models for the upcoming year using the team's recommendation.

6-72. Operations Costing and Two-Stage Systems   (LO 6-3, 4)

Lindsay Mobility manufactures two versions of e-scooters: L-4 and L-36. Both models go through the same assembly process and are produced in the same plant. The difference between the models is in quality and cost of the parts (direct materials). The following data represent expected operations for the next month.

	L-4	L-36	Total
Number of units	400	150	550
Parts cost per unit	$120	$280	
Conversion costs:			
Direct labor			$ 60,500
Overhead			49,500
Total			$110,000

Required

a. Lindsay Mobility uses operations costing and assigns conversion costs based on the number of units assembled. Compute the cost per unit of the L-4 and L-36 models for the upcoming month.

b. After attending a seminar on finance and accounting, the marketing director at Lindsay has asked the controller whether the company should use a two-stage system to calculate the product cost of the two models. The controller agrees to do this and to assign direct labor cost based on the number of units produced and overhead cost based on direct materials cost. Compute the cost per unit of the L-4 and L-36 models for the upcoming month using the controller's design.

INTEGRATIVE CASES

(LO 6-1, 2)   **6-73. Product Costing, Cost Estimation, and Decision Making**

I don't understand this. Last year [year 1], we decided to drop our highest-end Red model and only produce the Yellow and Green models because the cost system indicated we were losing money on Red. Now, looking at the preliminary numbers, our profit is actually lower than last year and it looks like Yellow has become a money loser, even though our prices, volumes, and direct costs are the same. Can someone please explain this to me and maybe help me decide what to do next year?

Robert Dolan
President & CEO
Dolan Products

Dolan Products is a small, family-owned audio component manufacturer. Several years ago, the company decided to concentrate on only three models, which were sold under many brand names to electronic retailers and mass-market discount stores. For internal purposes, the company uses the product names Red, Yellow, and Green to refer to the three components.

Data on the three models and selected costs follow.

Year 1	Red	Yellow	Green	Total
Units produced and sold	5,000	10,000	20,000	35,000
Sales price per unit.	$150	$100	$75	
Direct materials cost per unit	$70	$50	$30	
Direct labor-hours per unit.	2	1	0.5	
Wage rate per hour.	$20	$20	$20	
Total manufacturing overhead				$750,000

This year (year 2), the company only produced the Yellow and Green models. Total overhead was $650,000. All other volumes, unit prices, costs, and direct labor usage were the same as in year 1. The product cost system at Dolan Products allocates manufacturing overhead based on direct labor-hours.

Required

a. Compute the product costs and gross margins (revenue less cost of goods sold) for the three products and total gross profit for year 1.

b. Compute the product costs and gross margins (revenue less cost of goods sold) for the two remaining products and total gross profit for year 2.

(LO 6-1, 2)   c. Should Dolan Products drop Yellow for year 3? Explain.

6-74. Product Costing and Decision Making

Brunswick Parts is a small manufacturing firm located in eastern Canada. The company, founded in 1947, produces metal parts for many of the larger manufacturing firms located in both Canada and the United States. It prides itself on high quality and customer service, and many of its customers have been buying at least some of their parts from Brunswick since the 1950s.

Production of the parts takes place in one of two plants. The older plant, located in Fredericton, was purchased when the company was founded, and the last major improvements to the plant took place in the 1970s. A newer plant, located in Moncton, was built in 1995 to take advantage of the expanding markets. The same part can be produced in either plant, and the final scheduling decision is based on capacity, transportation costs, and production costs.

At a weekly production meeting, Sara Hunter, the manufacturing manager, expresses her frustration at trying to schedule production.

> Something isn't right. We build a new plant to take advantage of new manufacturing technology and we struggle to keep it filled. We didn't have this problem a few years ago when we couldn't keep up with demand, but with the current economy, marketing keeps sending orders to the old plant in Fredericton. I know manufacturing, but I guess I must not understand accounting.

The latest order that generated discussion among plant management was placed by Lawrence Machine Tool Company, a long-time customer. The order called for 1,000 units of a special rod (P28) used in one of its many products. The order was received by the marketing department. Following the established procedure at Brunswick, the marketing manager checked the product costs for both plants. Because quality and transportation costs would be the same from either plant, a decision was made to produce and ship from the Fredericton plant.

The cost system at Brunswick is a traditional manufacturing cost system. Plant overhead (including plant depreciation) is allocated to products based on estimated production for the period. Separate overhead rates are computed for each plant. Corporate administration costs are allocated to the plants based on the estimated production in the plant for purposes of executive performance measurement. Production is measured by direct labor-hours. Cost and production information for P28 follows.

Per unit of P28	Moncton	Fredericton
Direct material (1 kilogram @ $25).....	$25	$25
Direct labor-hours..................	3 hours	4 hours
Direct labor wage rate	$9	$10

Corporate and plant overhead budgets are as follows.

	Corporate Administration	Moncton	Fredericton
Corporate			
Marketing	$150,000		
R&D	100,000		
Depreciation	100,000		
General administration....	150,000		
Plant overhead (before corporate allocations):			
Supervision		$ 100,000	$ 150,000
Indirect labor		200,000	250,000
Depreciation		600,000	50,000
Miscellaneous		100,000	150,000
Total...................	$500,000	$1,000,000	$600,000
Estimated production (direct labor-hours):........		100,000	150,000

Required

a. What would be the reported product cost of P28 *per unit* for the two plants?

b. Where should the P28 units for the Lawrence order be produced? Why?

(LO 6-1, 2, 3) **6-75. Multiproduct CVP, Product Costing, Two-Stage Cost Systems, Data Analysis, and Cost Flow Diagrams**

Ferry Electronics produces a wide variety of video and audio systems for home entertainment. One of the Ferry plants (Lakeview) produces home theatre systems. The plant produces three models, Silver, Gold, and Platinum, which differ in the quality of the components and capability to "fill" the room with sound.

The financial team at Ferry is completing the planning for the coming quarter. Information on volumes and costs expected for the quarter follow:

	Silver	Gold	Platinum	Total
2 Units produced	2,000	1,500	500	4,000
3 Machine-hours	590	2,100	1,050	3,740
4 Direct labor-hours	600	1,200	750	2,550
5				
6 Revenues	$ 583,600	$ 793,050	$ 493,350	$ 1,870,000
7 Direct materials cost	310,000	533,250	303,000	1,146,250
8 Direct labor costs	9,600	28,800	25,350	63,750
9 Manufacturing overhead				561,000
10 Operating profit				$ 99,000

The team has been discussing two issues. First, there is disagreement about how best to allocate the manufacturing overhead among the products. The current cost accounting system allocates manufacturing overhead to products based on expected unit sales. (Because Ferry carries no inventory, unit sales are equal to units produced.) Second, there is a concern about a "softening" in the demand for these systems, and the managers at Ferry want to get a better understanding of possible financial implications if demand should be weaker than expected.

Required

a. Compute the unit profit for the three products using the cost accounting system currently used at Ferry.

b. Assume that the expected sales mix will remain the same regardless of the total volume of sales. Assume for this requirement only that the the entire manufacturing overhead can be considered a fixed cost. At the breakeven volume in units, what are the unit sales for each of the three products?

c. Using the per-unit product line unit profits calculated in requirement (*a*), compute the total profits for each of the products at the breakeven volume. Comment on the results.

d. The finance team decides that a two-stage system might improve the information available for management. They do an account analysis and determine that there appear to be two main drivers of overhead: revenue and direct costs. Based on the account analysis, the team splits the manufacturing overhead into two pools as follows:

> Revenue-related overhead $176,341
> Direct cost-related overhead 384,659
> Total overhead. $561,000

Compute total and per-unit profits by product line based on the expected (not breakeven) sales by product line using the two-stage cost allocation system developed by the finance team.

e. Prepare a cost flow diagram illustrating the two-stage cost system developed by the finance team.

f. One of the team members points out that contribution margin is just revenues less variable costs and suggests the team use a single allocation base, contribution margin. Compute total profits by product line based on the expected (not breakeven) sales by product line allocating overhead costs by relative total contribution margins given expected sales.

g. Prepare a memo commenting on the results of using the two-stage system of the finance team versus the single allocation base method using contribution margin as the allocation base. Be sure to discuss when one system would be preferable (or at least as good as) the other.

SOLUTIONS TO SELF-STUDY QUESTIONS

1. The following table summarizes the costs for November.

	Total	Finished Goods	Work in Process, November 30
Production			
Barrels....................	13,000	8,000	5,000
Percentage complete........		100%	60%
Equivalent barrels...........	11,000	8,000	3,000
Costs			
Materials...................	$223,000		
Conversion costs	272,000		
Total cost incurred...........	$495,000		
Cost per equivalent barrel.....	$ 45[a]		
Cost assigned to product......	$495,000	$360,000[b]	$135,000[c]

[a] $45 = $495,000 ÷ 11,000 equivalent units
[b] $360,000 = 8,000 equivalent units × $45
[c] $135,000 = 3,000 equivalent units × $45

2. The following is the cost flow diagram for Lawrence Chemicals:

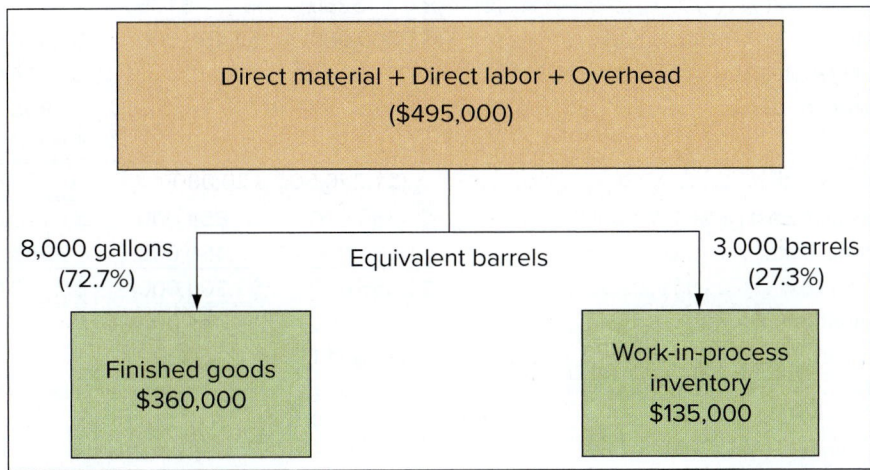

3. The following table reports the cost when machine-hours are used to allocate overhead:

	S-72	S-66	Total
Units produced	80	240	320
Machine-hours......................	1,400	4,200	5,600
Direct labor-hours...................	2,400	3,900	6,300
Direct materials	$40,000	$36,000	$ 76,000
Direct labor........................	72,000	78,000	150,000
Manufacturing overhead			252,000
Total costs.........................			$478,000

Predetermined
overhead rate.... ($252,000 ÷ 5,600 machine-hours) = $45.00

Product Costing	S-72	S-66	Total
Direct material.	$ 40,000	$ 36,000	$ 76,000
Direct labor.	72,000	78,000	150,000
Overhead ($45 per MH × number of machine-hours)	63,000	189,000	252,000
	$175,000	$303,000	$478,000
Number of units.	80	240	
Unit cost	$2,187.50	$1,262.50	

4.

		X3G		X2G	Total
Number of units.		6,000		14,000	20,000
Price per unit	×	$250	×	$175	
Costs.		$1,500,000		$2,450,000	$3,950,000
Direct labor.					$ 414,000
Overhead					806,000
					$1,220,000
Cost per unit		($1,220,000 ÷ 20,000)			$ 61.00
Operation cost (@ $61 per unit)		$ 366,000		$ 854,000	$1,220,000
Material cost.		1,500,000		2,450,000	3,950,000
Total cost		$1,866,000		$3,304,000	$5,170,000
Number of units.		6,000		14,000	
Unit cost		$311		$236	

7

Chapter Seven

Job Costing

LEARNING OBJECTIVES

After reading this chapter, you should be able to:

LO 7-1   Describe what *job* and *job shop* mean and compute product costs in a job cost system.

LO 7-2   Account for overhead using predetermined rates.

LO 7-3   Reconcile and account for the difference between overhead applied to jobs and actual overhead incurred.

LO 7-4   Apply job costing in service organizations.

LO 7-5   Identify ethical issues in job costing and know how to respond to them.

LO 7-6   Describe the difference between *projects* and *jobs* and understand the implications for cost management systems.

Ariel Skelley/Blend Images LLC

> " *I went into this business because I have always liked building things. I don't get much of a chance to do that now because I spend most of my time looking at bids for potential customers. For any bid, we start with calculating the costs using the cost system. We then adjust the cost for various factors including how busy we are, whether we think there is an opportunity for repeat business with the customer, and, finally, how aggressive we think the competition is going to be. I learned a long time ago that understanding the cost* system and how it works is crucial in separating a competitive bid from one that could break a company. "

Ravi Gupta is the founder and president at Gupta Designs. Gupta Designs makes a wide variety of furniture for both offices and homes. Most of the company's business comes from customers who request bids from a variety of vendors. The jobs tend to be reasonably large and often arise when companies decide to relocate or remodel their existing office building.

In Chapter 6, we developed the basics of a cost management system designed to report the costs of products and services. The purpose was to describe the concepts behind product costs, identify some assumptions accountants must make in developing the product costs, and recognize some problems that can arise when these product costs are used for decision making. In this chapter and the next, we discuss the details of a product costing system, including the accounting for the flows of costs through the inventory accounts. We describe a job costing system (also called a *job order costing system*) used in many service and discrete manufacturing settings in this chapter. In Chapter 8, we will continue our discussion by describing process costing and operations costing systems. As we discussed in Chapter 6, the difference in the systems is not conceptual. Rather, it is the level at which costs are aggregated before they are assigned to the individual units of product.

Defining a Job

What do the following have in common? A new, custom-designed home is being built in your city. An antique desk is being refurbished for use in the lobby of the local art museum. You have hired a lawyer to represent you in a civil matter. Each of these products (houses) or services (refurbishing, legal advice) is an example of a job. A **job** is simply a product or service that can be easily (in other words, at reasonable cost) distinguished from other products or services and for which the firm desires that a specific cost be recorded for the product or service. Firms that produce jobs are often called **job shops.**

It is generally possible to distinguish among individual jobs at a firm because, first, the jobs are unique in some way and, second, the firm keeps separate documents that record the costs of the jobs. These records are important for two reasons. First, the firm wants to be able to estimate the costs on similar work in the future. Many job shops obtain business by submitting bids for new work. For example, home remodeling firms generally submit bids that the homeowner compares before making a final selection. Second, the price in job shops for the product or service is commonly related to the cost recorded for the job. For example, the price of legal services is often based on the sum of the costs recorded for a particular client by the law firm.

LO 7-1
Describe what *job* and *job shop* mean and compute product costs in a job cost system.

job
Unit of a product that is easily distinguishable from other units.

job shop
Firm that produces jobs.

Using Accounting Records in a Job Shop

job cost sheet
Record of the cost of the job kept in the accounting system.

subsidiary ledger account
Account that records financial transactions for a specific customer, vendor, or job.

control account
Account in the general ledger that summarizes a set of subsidiary ledger accounts.

The "job" is the cost object of interest in a job shop. If costs are going to be reported for the job, the cost accounting system must be able to record and track the costs incurred by the firm for it. This record is referred to as the **job cost sheet** or record. This job cost sheet is a **subsidiary ledger account** that provides the detail for the Work-in-Process account, which is a **control account.** You are already familiar with control accounts and subsidiary ledger accounts from financial accounting. The Accounts Receivable account on the balance sheet is a control account, which is supported by a subsidiary ledger account for each customer.

Computing the Cost of a Job

We illustrate a job costing system by examining its use at Gupta Designs, a manufacturer of furniture for offices and homes. Although the cost accounting system differs among companies, the following example illustrates the general process that leads to the cost of a job at any job shop, such as Gupta Designs. It also illustrates how the subsidiary ledgers for the individual jobs combine to produce the firm's financial statement.

Production Process at Gupta Designs

Gupta Designs has just been notified that its bid to furnish the executive offices for the new headquarters of Banc25 has been accepted. Gupta Designs's bid was for a fixed price and was based on the designs it submitted for the furniture. You know from Chapter 6 that the basic idea in product costing is for the cost flows to follow the physical flows of the resources that are combined to produce the final product or service, so we describe what happens at Gupta Designs when it wins a bid.

The first step at Gupta Designs is to assign a job number to the Banc25 job. Because it is the first job started in January, it is assigned the number 01-01. (At Gupta Designs, the first two digits represent the month and the last two the order in which the job is entered). Then staff members review the designs and identify the wood, steel, plastic, components, and so on (direct materials) that will be required to produce the furniture. These will be purchased from various vendors or, for standard items such as hardware, pulls, knobs, and some structural pieces, will be taken from items already in the firm's materials inventory. The materials inventory contains both direct material (wood, plastic, and so on) and indirect materials (maintenance materials, oils, and so on).

When the material is available, it is moved to the fabrication and assembly area in the plant. Gupta Designs both manufactures the individual pieces and assembles them into finished items (desks, chairs, and so on). In the fabrication and assembly area, employees (direct labor) build and assemble the various components using a variety of machines and tools (manufacturing overhead).

Once completed, the individual items for the order are moved to the finished goods inventory, where they are kept until the order is complete. When all items have been completed, the order is inspected to ensure that all components are included, and then it is shipped to the customer site. In this case, the furniture will be shipped to the new headquarters building where Banc25 will accept the shipment. At about the same time, Gupta Designs will send an invoice to Banc25. The job is considered sold.

Records of Costs at Gupta Designs

Just as we can describe the flow of the physical resources, the cost accounting system at Gupta Designs records the cost flows as the resources move through the firm. We consider each of the three types of resources used (direct materials, direct labor, and manufacturing overhead) in turn. The Banc25 job is one of three that Gupta Designs is working on in January. Work will continue on Job 12-03 for Jameson Consulting Partners, an order started in December, and a new job (01-02), which started later in January.

Inventory Accounts

On January 1, Gupta Designs has balances in its three inventory accounts: Materials, Work-in-Process, and Finished Goods (for Job 12-02, which is complete, but has not shipped). The beginning balances for the three inventories follow:

Materials Inventory.....................		$30,000
Work-in-Process Inventory..............	(Job 12-03)	$41,000
Finished Goods Inventory..............	(Job 12-02)	$27,000

The cost in the Work-in-Process Inventory account consists of three components of Job 12-03:

Direct materials..................................	$35,000
Direct labor	4,000
Manufacturing overhead...........................	2,000
Total...	$41,000

Direct Materials

All direct materials used in making and assembling jobs at Gupta Designs are received at the materials inventory storage area (the "store") and recorded in the Materials Inventory account. This account also records supplies and other materials that typically are not charged (debited) directly to jobs. We discuss the accounting for these "indirect" materials later, with other items of manufacturing overhead.

In January, Gupta Designs purchases a total of $135,000 in wood, components, and miscellaneous supplies that are placed into the materials inventory. The accounting system at Gupta Designs records these purchases with the following journal entry:

(1)	Materials Inventory...........................	135,000
	Accounts Payable		135,000

During the month, requisitions are sent to the store for $12,000 of material for Job 12-03, $102,000 for the Banc25 Job 01-01, and $15,000 for a new bid won in January, Job 01-02. The following journal entries record these material transfers:

(2)	Work-in-Process Inventory (12-03)..............	12,000	
	Work-in-Process Inventory (01-01)..............	102,000	
	Work-in-Process Inventory (01-02)	15,000	
	Materials Inventory........................		129,000

Exhibit 7.1 shows these cost flows through the T-accounts at Gupta Designs.

Exhibit 7.1

Cost Flows through T-Accounts—Direct Materials

GUPTA DESIGNS
January

Accounts Payable		Materials Inventory		Work-in-Process Inventory	
	17,000 *BB*	*BB* 30,000		*BB* 41,000	
	135,000 (1)	(1) 135,000	129,000 (2)	(2) 129,000	

Direct Labor Recording direct labor cost differs from recording direct materials in one important respect. There is no "store" for direct labor, so the cost is recorded in the Work-in-Process account as it is incurred. The accounting document that records this cost is the *time card*, which includes fields for the job number and the start and end times. The time card can be a physical piece of paper the employee or supervisor fills in or a virtual record updated as the employee checks in and out and enters the job number in a computerized information system. The accounting department collects these cards or downloads the information from the timekeeping system.

The employee's wage (including benefits) is multiplied by the number of hours worked, and this total is used for payroll purposes. At the same time, the cost of each job is posted to the individual job sheets and summarized in the Work-in-Process account. During January, direct labor cost of $98,000 was incurred and assigned to each job as follows:

(3)	Work-in-Process Inventory (12-03).............	16,000
	Work-in-Process Inventory (01-01).............	71,000
	Work-in-Process Inventory (01-02).............	11,000
	Wages Payable	98,000

Exhibit 7.2 shows the direct labor cost flows for January at Gupta Designs.

Exhibit 7.2

Cost Flows through T-Accounts—Direct Labor

GUPTA DESIGNS
January

Accounts Payable	Materials Inventory	Work-in-Process Inventory
17,000 *BB*	*BB* 30,000	*BB* 41,000
135,000 (1)	(1) 135,000 | 129,000 (2)	(2) 129,000
		(3) 98,000

Wages Payable
98,000 (3)

Manufacturing Overhead Accounting for manufacturing overhead tends to be more complicated than accounting for direct labor and direct materials. Manufacturing overhead costs are typically pooled together into one account and then allocated to individual jobs based on a relatively arbitrary allocation base (for example, number of machine-hours or direct labor-hours) as described in Chapter 6. Management must make subjective decisions in establishing the process of allocating manufacturing overhead to each job. We discuss the process of creating predetermined overhead rates later in the chapter.

Manufacturing overhead costs, including indirect materials and indirect labor, are usually accumulated in the Manufacturing Overhead Control account. Each department typically has its own Manufacturing Overhead Control account so each department manager can be held accountable for departmental overhead costs. This helps top management evaluate how well department managers control costs. In this stage, costs are allocated to departments from the accounts in which they were initially entered.

For example, in January, Gupta Designs transfers indirect materials costs of $12,000 from Materials Inventory to Manufacturing Overhead Control for miscellaneous materials that were not charged directly to jobs but were used in the fabrication and assembly processes. Such indirect materials are too difficult or too costly to trace to particular jobs, so their costs are transferred from Materials Inventory to the overhead account. Examples of such items are lubricants for machinery, fasteners (for example, nuts, bolts, and washers), and plastic caps to protect users from hurting themselves on Gupta Designs' products.

Exhibit 7.3

Cost Flows through
T-Accounts—
Manufacturing Overhead

GUPTA DESIGNS
January

Accounts Payable		Materials Inventory		Work-in-Process Inventory	
	17,000 *BB*	*BB* 30,000		*BB* 41,000	
	135,000 (1)	(1) 135,000	129,000 (2)	(2) 129,000	
	13,750 (6)		12,000 (4)	(3) 98,000	

Wages Payable		Manufacturing Overhead Control	
	98,000 (3)	(4) 12,000	
	9,500 (5)	(5) 9,500	
		(6) 29,950	

Prepaid Expense	
	5,000 (6)

Accumulated Depreciation	
	11,200 (6)

Gupta Designs considers $9,500 of the Wages Payable to be for indirect labor costs, which it debits to Manufacturing Overhead Control. Indirect labor is that which is incurred in the production process but is not charged directly to a particular job. Examples include supervisors who oversee the workers on all jobs and maintenance people who repair the equipment used in assembling Gupta Designs' products. Indirect materials and indirect labor costs are recorded as shown in entries (4) and (5) of Exhibit 7.3.

Utilities and other overhead costs credited to Accounts Payable were $13,750. The portion of prepaid taxes and insurance applicable to the period, $5,000, is included in the actual overhead, as is depreciation of $11,200. The total for these latter three items is $29,950 (= $13,750 + $5,000 + $11,200). The amount $29,950 is charged to the Manufacturing Overhead account as described in entry (6) of Exhibit 7.3. Together, manufacturing overhead incurred totals $51,450 and represents the actual overhead incurred during the period.

The journal entries to record manufacturing overhead follow:

(4)	Manufacturing Overhead Control	12,000	
	Materials Inventory		12,000
	To record actual manufacturing overhead for indirect materials.		
(5)	Manufacturing Overhead Control	9,500	
	Wages Payable.		9,500
	To record actual manufacturing overhead for indirect labor.		
(6)	Manufacturing Overhead Control	29,950	
	Accounts Payable		13,750
	Prepaid Expense		5,000
	Accumulated Depreciation.		11,200
	To record actual manufacturing overhead for utilities, prepaid taxes, depreciation, and other overhead costs.		

How Manufacturing Overhead Costs Are Recorded at Gupta Designs

LO 7-2

Account for overhead using predetermined rates.

Manufacturing overhead is the third component of product cost, but because it is not directly incurred in the assembly of the jobs at Gupta Designs, no "transaction" triggers a journal entry. Instead, manufacturing overhead is recorded periodically on the job cost sheet. Two common events that lead to manufacturing overhead being recorded are (1) preparing financial statements for which Work-in-Process Inventory needs to be assessed and (2) completing a job whose costs need to be recorded.

Predetermined Rate

Job shops use predetermined rates to assign manufacturing overhead to jobs. We introduced the concept of predetermined overhead rates in Chapter 6, and we demonstrate its application to job costing in this chapter. The rate is "predetermined" because it is calculated at the beginning of the accounting period, which at Gupta Designs is the year. A year is common, but some firms use other periods such as a month, quarter, or business cycle. We discuss the choice of an appropriate accounting period later in this chapter. The predetermined rate is the estimated manufacturing overhead for the coming year divided by the estimated activity of the allocation base for the year. At Gupta Designs, the allocation base for manufacturing overhead is direct labor cost, so the predetermined rate is

$$\text{Predetermined overhead rate} = \frac{\text{Estimated manufacturing overhead}}{\text{Estimated direct labor cost}}$$

In late December, Gupta Designs' accounting department estimated that manufacturing overhead for the coming year would be $600,000 and that direct labor would be $1,200,000. Therefore, the predetermined overhead rate for January is 50 percent (= $600,000 ÷ $1,200,000).

Application of Manufacturing Costs to Jobs

During January, Gupta Designs completes Jobs 12-03 and 01-01 (the Banc25 job). When they are complete, the accounting department assigns manufacturing overhead to each job by multiplying the direct labor cost for the job by the predetermined overhead rate. This process is referred to as *overhead application* because the manufacturing overhead is "applied" to the jobs based on the direct labor incurred and the predetermined rate. The overhead applied to the two jobs is shown in Exhibit 7.4.

It is important to note that the overhead applied to Job 12-03 in January is based on the direct labor charged to it in January. From the beginning inventory balances, we know that $2,000 of overhead was applied to Job 12-03 in December. This is not affected by the application in January. (Although the overhead rate is the same in both years in this example, it is not always the same.)

The cost of each of the two completed jobs is summarized in Exhibit 7.5.

Exhibit 7.4

Manufacturing Overhead Applied to Completed Jobs—Gupta Designs

Job	Direct Labor Cost	Predetermined Rate	Applied Overhead
12-03......	$16,000	50%	$ 8,000
01-01......	71,000	50	35,500

	Job 12-03		Job 01-01	
Beginning inventory, January 1		$41,000		–0–
Direct materials added in January	$12,000		$102,000	
Direct labor added in January.......	16,000		71,000	
Overhead applied in January	8,000		35,500	
Total costs added in January.........		36,000		208,500
Cost of job		$77,000		$208,500

The applied overhead for Jobs 12-03 and 01-01 is charged to Work-in-Process. The credit could be to the Manufacturing Overhead Account, but in this example, we create a new account, Applied Manufacturing Overhead. The journal entry to record the application to the two completed jobs is

(7)	Work-in-Process Inventory (12-03)............	8,000	
	Work-in-Process Inventory (01-01).............	35,500	
	Applied Manufacturing Overhead...........		43,500

Jobs 12-03 and 01-01 are transferred to finished goods because they are now complete. The journal entry that records this follows:

(8)	Finished Goods Inventory (12-03)	77,000	
	Finished Goods Inventory (01-01)	208,500	
	Work-in-Process Inventory (12-03)...........		77,000
	Work-in-Process Inventory (01-01)...........		208,500

Job 12-02 shipped early in the month and Job 12-03 is shipped shortly after completion. The selling prices of the jobs were $35,000 for Job 12-02 and $95,000 for Job 12-03. The following journal entries were made:

(9)	Cost of Goods Sold (12-02).................	27,000	
	Cost of Goods Sold (12-03).................	77,000	
	Finished Goods Inventory (12-02)...........		27,000
	Finished Goods Inventory (12-03)...........		77,000

(10)	Accounts Receivable (12-02)	35,000	
	Accounts Receivable (12-03)	95,000	
	Revenue (12-02)..........................		35,000
	Revenue (12-03)..........................		95,000

These are entries (8), (9), and (10) in Exhibit 7.6. At the end of January, Gupta Designs prepares the financial statements. Only one job (01-02) is still in process, and one job (01-01) is in finished goods. Accountants at Gupta Designs apply overhead of $5,500 (= 50% of $11,000 of direct labor) to Job 01-02.
The journal entry is

(11)	Work-Process Inventory (01-02)...............	5,500	
	Applied Manufacturing Overhead...........		5,500

This is entry (11) in Exhibit 7.6.
See Exhibit 7.6 for a summary of the cost flows for the month of January and the beginning and ending inventory balances at Gupta Designs on January 31.

Exhibit 7.6

Cost Flows through T-Accounts

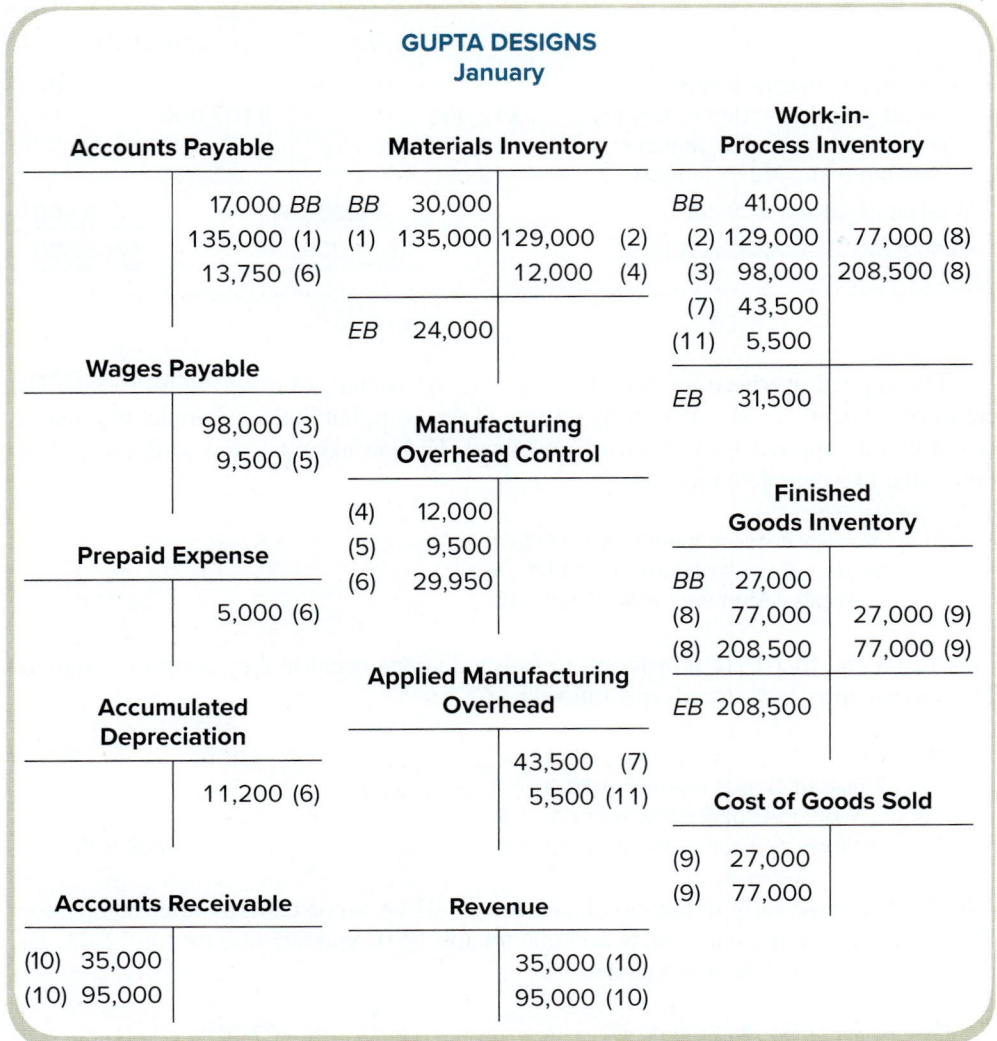

GUPTA DESIGNS
January

Accounts Payable

	17,000 *BB*
	135,000 (1)
	13,750 (6)

Wages Payable

	98,000 (3)
	9,500 (5)

Prepaid Expense

	5,000 (6)

Accumulated Depreciation

	11,200 (6)

Accounts Receivable

(10) 35,000	
(10) 95,000	

Materials Inventory

BB	30,000		
(1)	135,000	129,000	(2)
		12,000	(4)
EB	24,000		

Manufacturing Overhead Control

(4)	12,000	
(5)	9,500	
(6)	29,950	

Applied Manufacturing Overhead

	43,500	(7)
	5,500	(11)

Revenue

	35,000 (10)
	95,000 (10)

Work-in-Process Inventory

BB	41,000		
(2)	129,000	77,000	(8)
(3)	98,000	208,500	(8)
(7)	43,500		
(11)	5,500		
EB	31,500		

Finished Goods Inventory

BB	27,000		
(8)	77,000	27,000	(9)
(8)	208,500	77,000	(9)
EB	208,500		

Cost of Goods Sold

(9)	27,000	
(9)	77,000	

The Job Cost Sheet

For each job at Gupta Designs, the accountant creates a job cost sheet that records the costs for the individual jobs along with some additional information. Exhibit 7.7 shows the job cost sheet for Job 01-01 (the Banc25 job) after it is completed.

There are three basic sections to a job cost sheet at Gupta Designs, as shown in Exhibit 7.7. The top section provides basic information about the job. Each job at Gupta Designs is issued a job number that consists of two parts. As noted earlier in the discussion, the first number is the month the job begins (in this case, January or "01"). The second number notes the order in which the job was entered into the system (this job was the first job entered in January, so it is "01"). The customer name is shown (Banc25) along with the date started and, when the job is finished, the job completion date. A brief description of the job is also given.

The second section shows the costs as they are recorded for the job. This section will be blank for a new job. The third section summarizes the total costs for the job. It also has a field for any notes concerning the job. In addition to recording the costs for the current job, the job cost sheet provides valuable information when bidding on similar jobs in the future.

Exhibit **7.7**

Job Cost Sheet for
Job 01-01

GUPTA DESIGNS

Job number: 01-01

Date started: 1/11

Customer: Banc25

Date completed: 1/26

Description: Manufacture and assemble furniture for delivery to Banc25.

Assembly Area

	Direct Materials			Direct Labor			Factory Overhead	
Date	Requisition Number	Cost	Date	Badge Number	Cost	Date	Cost	
1/13	01-01-001	$62,000	1/13–1/17	507	$627	1/26	$35,500	
1/13	01-01-002	40,000	1/13–1/19	234	966			
			(and many more. Total direct labor cost charged to Job 01-01 was $71,000.)					

Total Costs

Direct materials	$102,000	
Direct labor.	71,000	
Manufacturing overhead	35,500	$208,500
Transferred to finished goods inventory		
Direct materials	$102,000	
Direct labor.	71,000	
Manufacturing overhead	35,500	
Total.	$208,500	

Notes: None.

Over- and Underapplied Overhead

The product costing exercise at Gupta Designs is not quite complete. What about the overhead incurred? In other words, Gupta Designs applied overhead using the predetermined rate based on direct labor costs, but during the month of January, it purchased supplies for the plant, paid for indirect labor, and recorded depreciation on plant and machinery. Recall that Gupta Designs recorded $51,450 in the Manufacturing Overhead account for overhead costs during the month—transactions (4)–(6) in Exhibit 7.6.

As noted earlier, Manufacturing Overhead Control is a control account that summarizes various overhead costs including indirect materials, indirect labor, and depreciation. Debits to the overhead control account reflect purchases of overhead items. When overhead is applied to products, Gupta Designs's accountants credit Applied Manufacturing Overhead. For example, at the end of January, when Gupta Designs applied overhead to the one job remaining in Work-in-Process Inventory, the journal entry was

Work-in-Process Inventory (01-02).	5,500	
Applied Manufacturing Overhead.		5,500

During January, Gupta Designs records a total of $51,450 in the Manufacturing Overhead Control account for its various overhead resources. Also during January, Gupta Designs records $49,000 in Applied Manufacturing Overhead for the overhead charged to work done during the month.

LO 7-3

Reconcile and account for the difference between overhead applied to jobs and actual overhead incurred.

Self-Study Question

1. Jennifer's Home Remodeling worked on three jobs during March. Job 13 was in process on March 1 with total
   charges of $5,500. During the month, the following addi-
   tional transactions occurred:

   a. Purchased $10,000 worth of new materials on account.
   b. Charged materials to jobs as follows: $1,000 to Job
        13, $4,000 to Job 14, $3,000 to Job 15, and $2,000
        as indirect materials.
   c. Charged labor to jobs as follows: $1,000 to Job 13,
        $3,000 to Job 14, $2,000 to Job 15, and $1,000 as
        indirect labor.

   d. Incurred indirect expenses totaling $13,000 including
        depreciation of $4,000. This also included credits of
        $9,000 to Accounts Payable.
   e. Applied manufacturing overhead for March to Work-
        in-Process based on materials used in each job. The
        predetermined rate was based on expected materi-
        als of $80,000 and expected overhead of $120,000
        for this year.

   Show the journal entries to record these transactions.

   The solution to this question is at the end of the chapter.

An Alternative Method of Recording and Applying Manufacturing Overhead

Gupta Designs uses a Manufacturing Overhead Control account to record manufacturing overhead costs and an Applied Manufacturing Overhead account to apply manufacturing overhead to work in process. Some companies combine these two accounts into one account. Accountants in these companies record manufacturing overhead costs as debits and manufacturing overhead costs applied as credits to this account.

If Gupta Designs used only one Manufacturing Overhead account, it would debit Manufacturing Overhead $51,450 for the various overhead resources incurred and credit the same account $49,000 for the overhead charged (applied) to various jobs during the month.

Manufacturing Overhead

51,450	8,000 (12-03)
	35,500 (01-01)
	5,500 (01-02)
51,450	49,000

Whether Gupta Designs uses both an Applied Manufacturing Overhead account and a Manufacturing Overhead Control account or not, at the end of January, there is a net debit balance of $2,450 (= $51,450 − $49,000).

For the remaining discussion, we will assume that Gupta Designs uses both Applied Manufacturing Overhead and Manufacturing Overhead Control accounts. At the end of January, the two accounts appear as follows:

Manufacturing Overhead Control		**Applied Manufacturing Overhead**	
51,450			8,000 (12-03)
			35,500 (01-01)
			5,500 (01-02)
51,450			49,000

underapplied overhead
Excess of actual overhead costs incurred over applied overhead costs.

overapplied overhead
Excess of applied overhead costs over actual overhead incurred during a period.

The $2,450 ($51,450 − $49,000) is **underapplied overhead.** It is underapplied because a total of $49,000 was applied to jobs in January, but a total of $51,450 was incurred. If Gupta Designs had applied more overhead than it had incurred in January, the difference would be **overapplied overhead** because the amount of overhead applied would have been more than the overhead incurred.

Writing Off Over- or Underapplied Overhead   Ultimately, the accounting system needs to account for the amount actually incurred. The Manufacturing Overhead Control and Applied Manufacturing Overhead accounts are accounts that summarize overhead incurred and applied each month. No balance is kept in the account from month to month (they are not balance sheet accounts), so $51,450 must be credited to the Manufacturing Overhead Control account, and $49,000 must be debited to the Applied Manufacturing Overhead account. Where should the underapplied overhead of $2,450 be debited?

Firms vary in their treatment of over- or underapplied overhead. Similar to many firms, Gupta Designs charges cost of goods sold with the underapplied overhead. Any under- or overapplied overhead is simply written off to Cost of Goods Sold for the month. (Alternatively, it could do this at the end of the year.) The intuition is simple. If Gupta Designs has underapplied overhead, this means that "too little" overhead was charged to jobs in January, so the Cost of Goods Sold account needs to be increased. Gupta Designs, therefore, makes the following journal entry at the end of January:

Applied Manufacturing Overhead.	49,000	
Cost of Goods Sold	2,450	
Manufacturing Overhead Control		51,450

As a result, the Manufacturing Overhead Control and Applied Manufacturing Overhead accounts have no remaining balance. Similarly, if Gupta Designs has overapplied overhead, then "too much" overhead was applied in January, so Cost of Goods Sold has to be reduced (credited) to reflect this overapplication of overhead.

Allocating Over- or Underapplied Overhead   A second option for dealing with over- and underapplied overhead is to "allocate" or "prorate" it in some way to the various accounts that contain the cost of the products manufactured during the period. Some units worked on during the period are in work in process, some are in finished goods, and some have been sold. Similarly, the costs of these units are in Work-in-Process Inventory, Finished Goods Inventory, and Cost of Goods Sold.

Suppose Gupta Designs chooses to allocate the underapplied overhead of $2,450 based on the value of overhead in the individual inventory accounts. The total overhead applied in January was $49,000, and the underapplied overhead was $2,450. The underapplied overhead represents 5 percent (= $2,450 ÷ $49,000). An additional 5 percent of overhead will be charged to the jobs worked in January.

Therefore, if Gupta Designs chooses to allocate the underapplied overhead, it will charge the following amounts to the individual jobs:

Job	Stage	Overhead Applied	Charge (5%)
12-03.	Sold	$ 8,000	$ 400
01-01.	Finished goods	35,500	1,775
01-02.	Work in process	5,500	275
Total.		$ 49,000	$2,450

Gupta Designs records the following journal entry:

Applied Manufacturing Overhead.	49,000	
Work-in-Process Inventory (Job 01-02)	275	
Finished Goods Inventory (Job 01-01).	1,775	
Cost of Goods Sold (Job 12-03)	400	
Manufacturing Overhead Control		51,450

Another common approach to allocating over- and underapplied overhead is to use the balances in the job costs, including not only the applied overhead, but also the direct materials and direct labor included in the accounts. These costs are $77,000 for Job 12-03 and $208,500 for Job 01-01 as shown in Exhibit 7.6. Job 01-02 has a total cost before allocating the underapplied overhead of $31,500. This consists of $15,000 in direct materials (journal entry [2]), $11,000 in direct labor (journal entry [3]), and $5,500 in applied manufacturing overhead (journal entry [11]). At the end of January, then, the job cost balances are

Job	Balance before Allocation	Percentage of Total Cost (rounded)
12-03.	$ 77,000	24%
01-01.	208,500	66
01-02.	31,500	10
Total cost	$317,000	100%

If Gupta Designs allocates the underapplied overhead based on job cost balances, it will charge the following amounts to the individual jobs:

Job	Charge	
12-03.	$ 588	(= 24% × $2,450)
01-01.	1,617	(= 66% × $2,450)
01-02.	245	(= 10% × $2,450)
Total cost	$2,450	

Choosing the Time Period for Computing the Predetermined Overhead Rate

Gupta Designs computes the predetermined overhead rate based on the expected overhead and expected production for the upcoming year. The overhead rate is computed in advance so that the cost of jobs can be calculated as they are completed. This means that the firm does not have to wait until the end of the year to determine how much a particular job costs. Gupta Designs uses estimates based on annual activity because it does not want erratic daily or monthly costs or production volumes to affect the calculation of long-run product costs.

For example, if Gupta Designs assigned actual monthly overhead costs to products made during the month, then irregular or unexpected events such as machine breakdowns or a closure for a national holiday might lead to unusually high or low overhead costs or production volume. Even anticipated irregularities, such as the peak production surrounding holidays or the lull in demand that is common in the summer months, would lead to different costs for products made in different seasons if the predetermined overhead rate was not based on annual production figures and costs. This would distort the costs of the jobs.

Following our general principles for cost system design, the choice of the period (annual, monthly, or something else) over which to compute the overhead rate depends on two, related, issues. First, what decisions are managers making that are affected by reported product costs? If the answer is, "no decisions," then the choice for the overhead rate does not matter. Second, does the benefit of using one overhead rate versus another outweigh the costs?

The following example illustrates these points. Consider another company, Lisbon Furniture, which makes a single product, a small table, to order in one of its workshops. The product has the following cost characteristics:

Materials cost per unit.	$10.00
Direct labor cost per unit (.3 hour @ $30)	9.00
Variable overhead cost per unit.	12.00
Total variable cost per unit	$31.00
Fixed cost per month.	$450,000

Month	Estimated Production (Units) (1)	Estimated Direct Labor-Hours (2)	Estimated Overhead (3)	Predetermined Overhead Rate (Monthly) (4)	Reported Unit Cost (5)	Applied Overhead (6)	Actual Overhead (7)	Under (Positive)/Over (Negative) Applied Overhead (8)
January	10,000	3,000	$ 570,000	$ 190	$ 76.00	$ 570,000	$ 570,000	$ -
February	15,000	4,500	630,000	140	61.00	630,000	630,000	-
March	20,000	6,000	690,000	115	53.50	690,000	690,000	-
April	15,000	4,500	630,000	140	61.00	630,000	630,000	-
May	20,000	6,000	690,000	115	53.50	690,000	690,000	-
June	15,000	4,500	630,000	140	61.00	630,000	630,000	-
July	10,000	3,000	570,000	190	76.00	570,000	570,000	-
August	15,000	4,500	630,000	140	61.00	630,000	630,000	-
September	25,000	7,500	750,000	100	49.00	750,000	750,000	-
October	10,000	3,000	570,000	190	76.00	570,000	570,000	-
November	15,000	4,500	630,000	140	61.00	630,000	630,000	-
December	10,000	3,000	570,000	190	76.00	570,000	570,000	-
For the year	180,000	54,000	$ 7,560,000	$ 140		$ 7,560,000	$ 7,560,000	$ -

Notes:
(1) Given.
(2) = Column (1) × .3 direct labor-hour per unit.
(3) = $450,000 + ($12 variable overhead per unit x column (1)).
(4) = Column (3) ÷ Column (2).
(5) = $10 direct materials cost + $9 direct labor cost + (column (4) × .3 direct labor-hour per unit).
(6) = Column (2) × column (4).
(7) = Column (3) by assumption.
(8) = Column (7) — column (6).

Exhibit 7.8

Projections of Reported Unit Costs and Under/Overapplied Overhead: Lisbon Furniture.

The cost accounting system at Lisbon Furniture calculates a predetermined overhead rate monthly. In preparing for the next year, the financial analysts at Lisbon Furniture have put together the projections shown in Exhibit 7.8. Because these are projections, the actual overhead is assumed to be equal to the estimated overhead.

Using the data from Exhibit 7.8, we can analyze the effect visually on reported unit product costs as shown in Exhibit 7.9. We can see in Exhibit 7.9 that the reported unit product costs fluctuate month to month, all caused by the application of fixed overhead to varying levels of products. The reported unit product cost using the annual predetermined rate, however, is constant across the year. Recall that the goal of the product cost system is to reflect the physical flow of resources. In this case, the resources

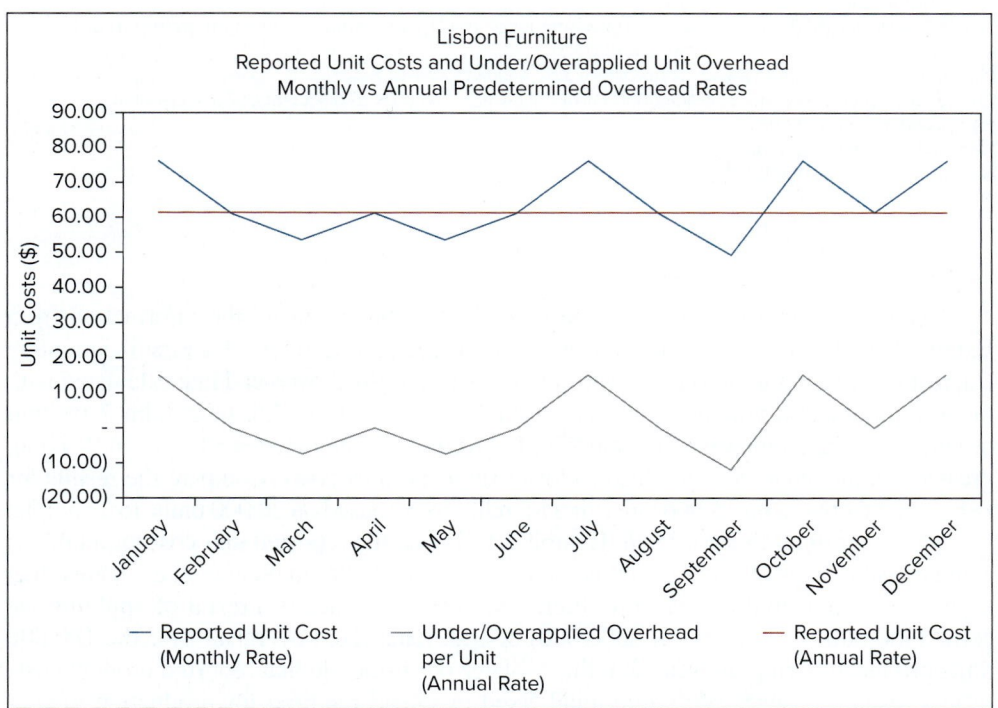

Exhibit 7.9

Graph of Reported Unit Product Costs Using Annual and Monthly Predetermined Rates.

Source: Exhibit 7.8.

used to produce a table do not vary. Production levels vary. Using the annual volume to determine the overhead rate reflects this in the unit costs. The variation has to appear somewhere, and, in the case of the annual predetermined rate, this is in the under- and overapplied overhead. This is shown in the bottom line of the graph in Exhibit 7.9. Recording the variation in the under- or overapplied overhead is less likely to mislead managers into thinking the cost of making a table is changing, while still providing information on the fluctuating volumes.

Using a year is not the answer in every case. If it was, we could just say, "use a year." Consider this modification to the example of Lisbon Furniture. A monthly expenditure of $450,000 in fixed costs supports monthly production levels up to and including 15,000 tables. For production in excess of 15,000 per month, the company can lease, on a month-to-month basis, additional equipment that will the allow for the production of more than 15,000 tables (up to any foreseeable monthly demand). This additional equipment leases for $300,000 per month. Exhibit 7.10 recreates the information in Exhibit 7.8 with the revised overhead estimates and unit costs.

Exhibit 7.10

Projections of Reported Unit Costs and Under/Overapplied Overhead with Additional Monthly Fixed Overhead as Required: Lisbon Furniture.

	A	B	C	D	E	F	G	H	I
1		(1)	(2)	(3)	(4)	(5)	(6)	(7)	(8)
2	Month	Estimated Production (Units)	Estimated Direct Labor-Hours	Estimated Overhead	Predetermined Overhead Rate (Monthly)	Reported Unit Cost	Applied Overhead	Actual Overhead	Under (Positive)/Over (Negative) Applied Overhead
3	January	10,000	3,000	$ 570,000	$ 190	$ 76.00	$ 570,000	$ 570,000	$ -
4	February	15,000	4,500	630,000	140	61.00	630,000	630,000	-
5	March	20,000	6,000	990,000	165	68.50	990,000	990,000	-
6	April	15,000	4,500	630,000	140	61.00	630,000	630,000	-
7	May	20,000	6,000	990,000	165	68.50	990,000	990,000	-
8	June	15,000	4,500	630,000	140	61.00	630,000	630,000	-
9	July	10,000	3,000	570,000	190	76.00	570,000	570,000	-
10	August	15,000	4,500	630,000	140	61.00	630,000	630,000	-
11	September	25,000	7,500	1,050,000	140	61.00	1,050,000	1,050,000	-
12	October	10,000	3,000	570,000	190	76.00	570,000	570,000	-
13	November	15,000	4,500	630,000	140	61.00	630,000	630,000	-
14	December	10,000	3,000	570,000	190	76.00	570,000	570,000	-
15									
16	For the year	180,000	54,000	$ 8,460,000	$ 156.6667		$ 8,460,000	$ 8,460,000	$ -
17									

Notes:
(1) Given.
(2) = Column (1) × .3 direct labor-hour per unit.
(3) = $450,000 + ($12 variable overhead per unit × column (1)) for monthly production less than or equal to 15,000 units.
 = $750,000 + ($12 variable overhead per unit × column (1)) for monthly production greater than 15,000 units.
(4) = Column (3) ÷ Column (2).
(5) = $10 direct materials cost + $9 direct labor cost + (column (4) × .3 direct labor-hour per unit).
(6) = Column (2) × column (4).
(7) = Column (3) by assumption.
(8) = Column (7) — column (6).

Exhibit 7.11 is a recreation of the graph in Exhibit 7.9 using the information from Exhibit 7.10. There are two notable features of the graph in Exhibit 7.11. First the monthly fluctuations in the unit product costs using the predetermined overhead rate calculated with monthly production volumes are smaller than those in Exhibit 7.8. In Exhibit 7.10, unit product costs range between $61 and $76. In Exhibit 7.8, the range is $49 to $76. Second, greater volume alone does not lead to lower (unit) product costs. Compare the results for February, $61 based on 15,000 units, and March, $68.50 based on 20,000 units, for example.

The other thing that we see in Exhibit 7.11 is that the reported unit cost for a table is again constant over the year using the predetermined rate based on annual estimates. It is higher ($66 compared to $61, in Exhibit 7.8). The difference is a result of applying the extra $900,000 (= 3 months × $300,000) of additional fixed overhead over the 180,000 units produced during the year. But this violates our principle that reported product costs reflect resource usage. With additional fixed overhead required for production greater than 15,000 units, units produced in the months of high output "cause" Lisbon Furniture to use more resources, and this should be reflected in the product costs.

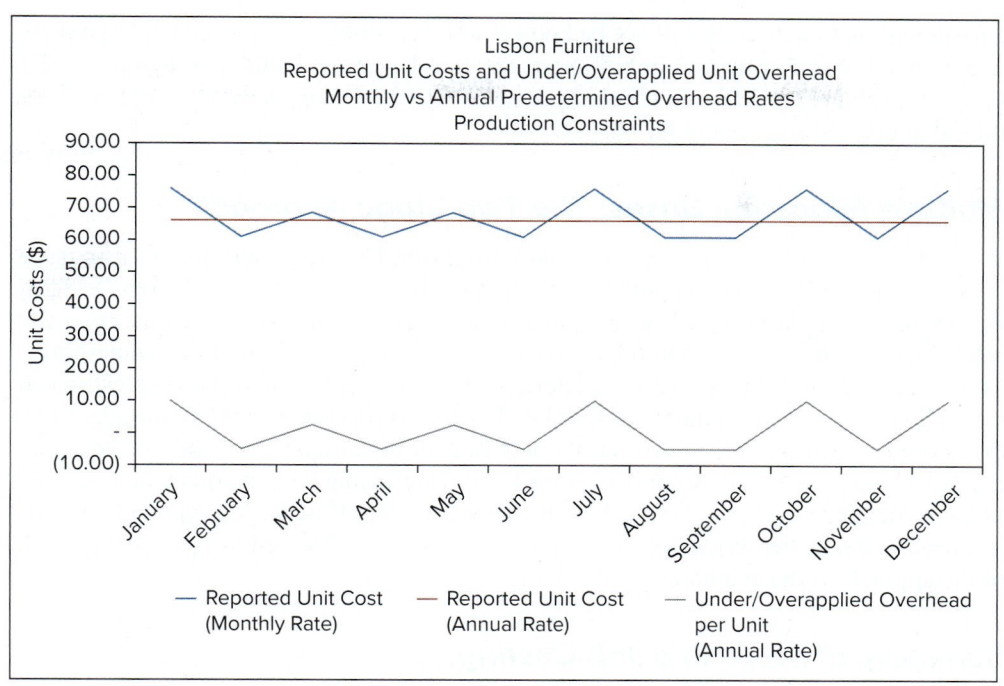

Exhibit 7.11

Graph of Reported Unit Product Costs Using Annual and Monthly Predetermined Rates with Additional Monthly Fixed Overhead as Required.

Source: Exhibit 7.10.

This is not the end of the issue because we still see differences, although smaller, in reported costs in months where volumes were different, but no additional fixed overhead was required. We return to this issue in Chapter 10, which discusses cost management in general and the treatment of the costs of capacity specifically, but these two examples illustrate an approach to deciding on the appropriate period over which to calculate the predetermined overhead that is consistent with proper management cost system design.

Using Normal, Actual, and Standard Costing

When the accountants at Gupta Designs initially recorded manufacturing overhead for the jobs, they multiplied the predetermined overhead rate by the *actual* direct labor cost. This is termed **normal costing,** which is composed of actual direct costs plus overhead applied using a predetermined rate to the actual volume of the allocation base (direct labor cost in this case). With normal costing, the overhead rate is computed using budgeted (estimated) overhead and the estimated level for the allocation base. Recall that the reason for using a predetermined rate is to be able to cost the jobs throughout the period without waiting until the end of the month (or quarter or year) for actual overhead to be known.

An alternative costing method is actual costing. **Actual cost** is composed of actual direct cost plus overhead applied using a rate based on actual overhead and an actual allocation base. When over- or underapplied overhead is allocated using the overhead (or the allocation base) in the individual accounts, the result approximates actual costing. It is not quite the same as actual costing because the amounts in beginning work-in-process inventories might be based on different rates.

A third method—one that is quite common in practice—is standard costing. A **standard cost** is based on budgets (standards) for direct materials and labor. The predetermined overhead rate is estimated using budgeted overhead and budgeted volumes for the allocation base. We discuss standard costing in more detail in Chapter 16, where we use the standard costs as bases for performance measurement.

Choosing between Actual and Normal Costing

The trade-offs between actual and normal costing essentially involve the speed, convenience, and accuracy of the information. *Actual costing* requires management to wait until actual costs are known but, once the costs are known, provides more current information. The information delay to get actual costs is usually short for direct materials and direct labor but is considerably longer for manufacturing overhead. For example, the costs of energy estimated for

normal cost
Cost of job determined by actual direct material and labor cost plus overhead applied using a predetermined rate and an actual allocation base.

actual cost
Cost of job determined by actual direct material and labor cost plus overhead applied using an actual overhead rate and an actual allocation base.

standard cost
Cost of job determined by standard (budgeted) direct material and labor cost plus overhead applied using a predetermined overhead rate and a standard (budgeted) allocation base.

a particular day's activities will not be known until the utility bill is received. Even then, assigning a portion of the utility bill to a particular day of the month and to a particular piece of machinery is difficult, if not impossible. *Normal costing* is a reasonable compromise that uses estimates only for *indirect* costs.

Multiple Allocation Bases: The Two-Stage Approach

We introduced the two-stage cost allocation process in Chapter 6 and discuss it in more detail in Chapter 9. It can be applied easily to the job costing problem at Gupta Designs. For example, Gupta Designs' accountants might believe that some overhead costs are related more to direct labor and other overhead costs are related more to machine-hours. They then need to compute two predetermined overhead rates by assigning estimated overhead to labor-related and machine-related overhead cost pools in the first stage. Next, they compute two predetermined rates, one based on direct labor cost and one based on machine-hours. Finally, they apply overhead to the jobs using both overhead rates as well as the direct labor cost and the machine-hours in each job. If under- or overapplied overhead exists, it is either written off to Cost of Goods Sold or allocated using, possibly, both of the applied overhead amounts in each job.

Summary of Steps in a Job Costing System

The cost of a job using job costing is computed as follows:

1. Select an allocation base for computing the predetermined rate(s).
2. Estimate overhead for each overhead cost pool.
3. Calculate the predetermined rate(s) by dividing the estimated overhead by the estimated allocation base.
4. Record direct costs for each job as they are incurred.
5. Apply overhead using the predetermined rates as jobs are completed or when the financial statements are prepared.
6. If there is over- or underapplied overhead, either write it off directly to Cost of Goods Sold or allocate it to Cost of Goods Sold *and* ending inventories.

Self-Study Question

2. Refer to the data for Jennifer's Home Remodeling in Self-Study Question 1. Suppose that the following additional transactions occurred:

    a. Completed and charged the following jobs to Finished Goods: Job 13 for $9,000 and Job 14 for $13,000.

    b. Sold Job 13 for $12,000 and Job 14 for $15,000, both for cash.

    c. Closed Manufacturing Overhead Control and Applied Manufacturing Overhead. Actual manufac-

turing overhead incurred for the month was $16,000. Any over- or underapplied overhead is written off to Cost of Goods Sold.

Show journal entries for these transactions. Include the entry to close the manufacturing overhead accounts to Cost of Goods Sold for the month of March.

The solution to this question is at the end of the chapter.

Using Job Costing in Service Organizations

LO 7-4

Apply job costing in service organizations.

You will frequently find job operations in service organizations, such as architectural firms, consulting firms, repair shops, and accounting firms. The job costing procedure is basically the same for both service and manufacturing organizations except that service firms generally use fewer direct materials than manufacturing firms do.

    A consulting firm, for example, is very interested in the profitability of each job (referred to as a *client*). Bids to obtain or retain a client are typically based on projected costs, estimated based on actual results for comparable jobs. Therefore, job costing provides management the information necessary to assess job profitability as well as the historical cost data necessary to estimate costs for bidding purposes.

Job costing allows a service firm to assess customer profitability because the cost object (the job) is often the customer. For example, accounting firms regularly review the profitability of each customer by using a job costing system.

Consider the case of a consulting firm, Anything Is Possible (AIP), Inc. AIP has work in process of $75,200 at the beginning of the year, which represents one job in process, Contract 782. AIP's records show $35,200 in direct labor and $40,000 service overhead for Contract 782.

Assume that AIP has the following information for January (the first month of its fiscal year):

1. The personnel department recorded $252,000 in payroll costs for the month: $204,000 is attributed to direct labor costs and charged to Work in Process (Contract 782, $26,000; Contract 783, $102,000; and Contract 784, $76,000). The remaining $48,000 was indirect labor and was charged to Service Overhead.
2. Indirect supplies costs of $3,200 were charged to Service Overhead.
3. Utilities and other costs credited to Accounts Payable were $73,600. The portion of prepaid taxes and insurance applicable to the period, $11,200, is included in the actual overhead, as is depreciation of $30,400. These items total $115,200 and represent the actual overhead incurred during the period (debited to Service Overhead).
4. AIP established a predetermined overhead rate based on estimated annual overhead costs of $2,000,000 and 20,000 associate (employee) hours. This resulted in a rate of $100 per associate hour. The company incurred actual associate hours for each job in January as follows.

> Contract 782 . . . . 200 hours
> Contract 783 . . . . 800 hours
> Contract 784 . . . . 700 hours

Thus, a total of $170,000 [= (200 + 800 + 700) × $100] in Service Overhead was applied to Work in Process in January.

5. Because AIP sells each contract (job) before it begins work, AIP has no finished goods inventory. Instead, costs associated with all completed jobs are transferred out of the Work in Process account into the Cost of Services Billed account. Contracts 782 and 783 were completed by January 31 and were transferred out of Work in Process. Total costs for Contracts 782 and 783 were $121,200 and $182,000, respectively, for a total of $303,200, which appears as a credit to Work in Process and a debit to Cost of Services Billed.
6. Service overhead was overapplied by $3,600 (= $166,400 actual overhead − $170,000 applied overhead). The closing entry for Service Overhead and Service Overhead Applied resulted in $3,600 overapplied service overhead, which was credited to Cost of Services Billed.
7. Clients for Contracts 782 and 783 were billed for $151,500 and $218,500, respectively. Marketing and administrative costs of $36,800 were incurred and recorded in Accounts Payable.

The cost flows through T-accounts for our example are shown in Exhibit 7.12. Exhibit 7.13 shows an income statement for AIP. As you can see from comparing these data and those in Exhibit 7.6 for the Gupta Designs furniture manufacturing company example, job costing is similar for both manufacturing and service organizations. The three primary differences are

1. Service organizations generally use fewer direct materials than manufacturing companies.
2. Service companies' overhead accounts have slightly different names (Service Overhead Control, Applied Service Overhead, and so on).
3. Service companies' finished goods (or services) are charged to Cost of Services Billed rather than to Cost of Goods Sold.

Exhibit 7.12

Cost Flows through
T-Accounts

AIP, INC.
January

Wages Payable		Work-in-Process Inventory		Cost of Services Billed

Wages Payable

	252,000 (1)

Work-in-Process Inventory

BB	75,200	303,200 (5)
(1)	204,000	
(4)	170,000	

Cost of Services Billed

(5)	303,200	
	3,600	(6)

Service Overhead Control

(1)	48,000	
(2)	3,200	
(3)	115,200	
	166,400	(6)

Applied Service Overhead

	170,000 (4)
(6) 170,000	

Accounts Payable

	73,600 (3)
	36,800 (7)

Revenue

	151,500 (7)
	218,500 (7)

Supplies

BB	7,200	3,200 (2)
EB	4,000	

Accumulated Depreciation

	30,400 (3)

Accounts Receivable

(7)	151,500	
(7)	218,500	

Marketing and Administrative Expenses

(7)	36,800	

Prepaid Expenses

	11,200 (3)

Exhibit 7.13

Income Statement—
Service Company

AIP, INC.
Income Statement
For the Month Ended January 31

Sales revenue.		$370,000
Cost of services billed	$303,200	
Subtract overapplied service overhead.	3,600	299,600
Gross margin.		$ 70,400
Marketing and administrative costs		36,800
Operating profit		$ 33,600

Ethical Issues and Job Costing

LO 7-5

Identify ethical issues
in job costing and know
how to respond to
them.

Many organizations have been criticized for improprieties in assigning costs to jobs. For example, major defense contractors have been accused of overstating the cost of jobs for which they were being reimbursed. Several universities have been accused of overstating the cost of research projects (which are jobs for costing purposes). Improprieties in job costing generally are caused by one or more of the following actions: misstating the stage of completion, charging costs to the wrong jobs or categories, or simply misrepresenting the cost.

Misstating the Stage of Completion

Management needs to know the stage of completion of projects to evaluate performance and control costs. If the expenditures on a job are 90 percent of the amount estimated to be spent on the project, but the job is only 70 percent complete, management needs to know as soon as possible that the job will require higher costs than estimated. Job supervisors who report the stage of completion of their jobs can be tempted to overstate it.

Charging Costs to the Wrong Jobs

To avoid the appearance of cost overruns on jobs, job supervisors sometimes instruct employees to charge costs to the wrong jobs. If you work in consulting or auditing, you could encounter superiors who tell you to allocate your time spent on jobs that are in danger of exceeding cost estimates to other jobs that are not in such danger. At a minimum, this practice misleads managers who rely on accurate cost information for pricing, cost control, and other decisions. At worst, it cheats people who are paying for a job on a cost-plus-fee basis that does not really cost as much as claimed. This is unethical and could also be illegal if it constitutes fraud.

Cost Allocation and Government Contracts — *Business Application*

Government organizations (federal, state, and local) purchase a wide variety of goods and services from many different vendors. The prices paid for many of these goods and services are specified in contracts. In some cases, the contracted price is equal to the cost of the product or service plus a fixed fee representing the profit to the vendor. Such contracts are called "cost-plus fixed fee" contracts and are used for a range of products and services from consulting to fighter aircraft and ships for the U.S. Navy. Vendors are allowed to include some portion of their indirect costs in determining the cost and price. As a result, the method used to allocate costs can affect the price paid by the government.

The Cost Accounting Standards Board currently is a function of the Office of Federal Procurement Policy of the Office of Management and Budget. The Board, which is independent, consists of five members. It has

> the exclusive authority to make, promulgate, and amend cost accounting standards and interpretations designed to achieve uniformity and consistency in the cost accounting practices governing the measurement, assignment, and allocation of costs to contracts with the United States.[1]

Several standards deal with cost allocations, but all require judgment. Because of the potentially large amounts of money involved, there is considerable temptation to choose the allocation method that leads to the highest price from the contract.

Source:
1. Office of Management and Budget, https://obamawhitehouse.archives.gov/omb/procurement_casb/

Misrepresenting the Cost of Jobs

Job costs also can be misrepresented in other ways. Managers might know the correct cost of a job but intentionally deceive a customer to obtain a larger payment. They might deceive a banker to obtain a larger loan for the job or for other reasons. Many people insist on audits of financial records to avoid such deception. Government auditors generally work on-site at defense contractors, universities, and other organizations that have contracts for large government jobs.

Another way in which costs can be misrepresented is by choosing to allocate overhead costs using the method that provides the most favorable result, rather than attempting to find an allocation base that truly represents how overhead resources are used. There is always an arbitrary element to the allocation of overhead, but choosing a method because of its result could be unethical, depending on how the costs are used.

For example, in August, Gupta Designs worked on only two jobs, both of which were started and completed in August. Job 08-01 was an unusual job, and the customer and Gupta Designs agreed that the final price would be the cost of the job plus a fixed fee of $10,000. Job 08-02 was a typical order at Gupta Designs and carried a fixed price of $140,000. The costs of the jobs, before the allocation of overhead, were as follows:

	Job 08-01	Job 08-02	Total
Direct materials	$40,000	$20,000	$60,000
Direct labor.	24,000	72,000	96,000

Total overhead for the month was $48,000. Using Gupta Designs's job costing system, which allocates overhead based on direct labor, the overhead rate was 50 percent (= $48,000 ÷ $96,000). The overhead allocated to the jobs and the total job costs using this allocation base were therefore as follows:

	Job 08-01	Job 08-02	Total
Direct materials	$40,000	$ 20,000	$ 60,000
Direct labor.	24,000	72,000	96,000
Applied overhead (50% of direct labor).	12,000	36,000	48,000
Total.	$76,000	$128,000	$204,000

In order to practice the lessons of this chapter, Jason Sills, the marketing manager of Gupta Designs, has decided to see how these allocations and costs would change if the company allocated overhead in proportion to direct materials. In this case, the overhead rate would be 80 percent (= $48,000 ÷ $60,000). Using that overhead rate, the overhead allocated to the two jobs and the total costs reported for the two jobs would be

	Job 08-01	Job 08-02	Total
Direct materials.	$40,000	$ 20,000	$ 60,000
Direct labor	24,000	72,000	96,000
Applied overhead (80% of direct materials). . . .	32,000	16,000	48,000
Total	$96,000	$108,000	$204,000

Although the total costs do not change, the two allocation methods result in different revenues, as follows:

	Allocation Based on	
	Direct Labor	Direct Materials
Revenue from Job 08-01 (unique cost, plus $10,000).	$ 86,000	$106,000
Revenue from Job 08-02 (typical job, fixed price)	140,000	140,000
Total revenue	$226,000	$246,000

Because the total costs are the same under either method, profits would be $20,000 (= $246,000 − $226,000) greater if Gupta Designs used direct materials cost as the allocation base instead of direct labor. Jason Sills complied with the terms of the contract for job 08-01, which specified that the accounting for overhead would be based on direct labor. While he did not face an ethical dilemma, he did begin to understand how ethical issues can arise in job costing.

Managing Projects

Complex jobs (for example, bridges, shopping centers, complex lawsuits) that often take months or years to complete and require the work of many different departments, divisions, or subcontractors are called **projects.**

Jobs can be evaluated relatively quickly, typically within a reporting period, but projects are more difficult to evaluate. Consider the job of painting a small house. The painter might establish an estimate of his costs and bid on the job accordingly. A week later, when the job is complete, the same painter can compare estimated costs to actual costs and evaluate the job's profitability. In contrast, consider a construction firm building a hospital, which will take more than two years to complete. The firm (contractor) must find a way not only to bid on the project but also to evaluate it at specified intervals.

The contractor must first establish a budget of costs to be incurred throughout the project at various stages of completion (described in percentages). Then, as the project progresses, the contractor evaluates two critical areas, budgeted cost of work performed to date versus actual cost of work performed to date and budgeted percentage of completion versus actual percentage of completion. The two graphs in Exhibit 7.14 are simple examples of how the evaluation of costs and scheduling can be performed.

Assuming that the contract is 60 percent complete in the 14th month of construction, the budget indicates that costs should be $4.8 million, as shown in Panel A of Exhibit 7.14. The actual costs line indicates, however, that actual costs were $6.25 million. Thus, at this stage of completion, cost overruns of $1.45 million have been incurred.

Although we know that cost overruns have occurred, we do not know whether the project is on schedule. Panel B shows that the project should be 50 percent complete by month 14. Because the contractor is 60 percent complete by month 14, the project is ahead of schedule.

Given the complex nature of projects, it could be necessary to revise budgeted costs and budgeted stages of completion at certain intervals throughout the project to reflect changes. (Most major projects require changes due to their inherent uncertainty.) Thus, the graphs in Exhibit 7.14 may be updated to reflect revised budgets. This allows managers to be evaluated by comparing actual results against the revised budget.

Depending on the nature of the contract for the project, the estimates of project completion and cost overruns can also lead to ethical or legal issues, as discussed in the Business Application "Fraudulent Reporting of Project Completion to Improve Financial Performance."

LO 7-6
Describe the difference between *projects* and *jobs* and understand the implications for cost management systems.

project
Complex job that often takes months or years to complete and requires the work of many different departments, divisions, or subcontractors.

Buildings, bridges, and other complex jobs are projects. Projects can take many months or even years to complete, complicating the costing process.
Dwight Smith/Shutterstock

Fraudulent Reporting of Project Completion to Improve Financial Performance

Business Application

Estimating how far along a project is or whether actual costs are in line with estimated costs raises ethical (and legal) questions in the case of projects just as with the ethical dilemma discussed earlier in the chapter:

> Two South Carolina companies and two former top executives face civil fraud charges in relation to a failed nuclear power plant expansion project, . . .[1]

> Scana Corporation, a South Carolina company, had been awarded the contract to build two new nuclear reactors for power plants. The company had stopped work on the reactors in 2017 because of costs and delays. However, while the project was active,

> The defendants claimed the project was on track even though they knew it was significantly delayed and wouldn't be completed on time by Jan. 1, 2021, to qualify for $1.4 billion of federal tax credits. . . .[2]

> The Securities and Exchange Commission (SEC) alleged that by claiming to be on time and budget, the company stock value increased, they were able to issue debt at "favorable rates," and, because this project was a public utility project subject to rate regulation, increase rates.

Sources:
1. Mengqi Sun, "SEC Charges South Carolina Companies, Executives in Failed Nuclear Project Case," *The Wall Street Journal,* February 28, 2020.
2. Ibid.

Exhibit 7.14

Project Evaluation Graphs

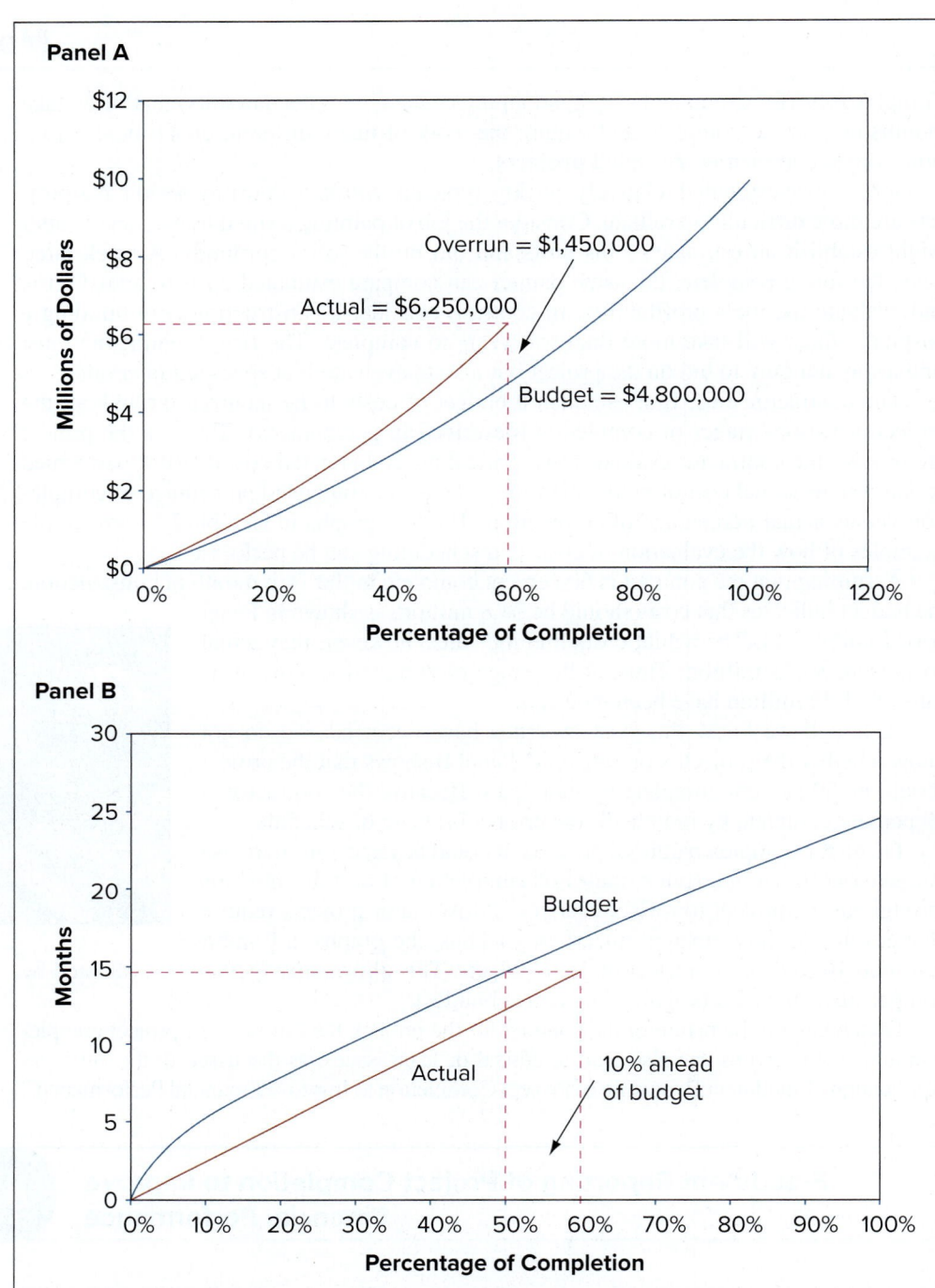

Panel A

Overrun = $1,450,000

Actual = $6,250,000

Budget = $4,800,000

Millions of Dollars (y-axis): $0, $2, $4, $6, $8, $10, $12

Percentage of Completion (x-axis): 0%, 20%, 40%, 60%, 80%, 100%, 120%

Panel B

Budget

Actual

10% ahead
of budget

Months (y-axis): 0, 5, 10, 15, 20, 25, 30

Percentage of Completion (x-axis): 0%, 10%, 20%, 30%, 40%, 50%, 60%, 70%, 80%, 90%, 100%

Key Takeaways

1. Job cost systems are used by companies producing custom or unique products where costs can be traced to individual products or jobs. The product costs include:

    a. Direct materials cost, which are directly traced to the job; and

    b. Direct labor cost, which are directly traced to the job;

    c. Manufacturing overhead, which is applied to the job using a predetermined overhead rate based on units produced, direct labor-hours, or some other allocation base:

    • The predetermined overhead rate is calculated as

    Estimated overhead ÷ Estimated allocation base

(Continued)

(Continued)

2. The overhead applied is generally not equal to the overhead incurred in the period and the difference, under- or overapplied overhead, must be applied to products completed or still in process at the end of the period.

   a. Many companies close the under- or overapplied overhead amount directly to Cost of Good Sold:

      • For underapplied overhead:

      > Dr. Cost of Goods Sold
      > Dr. Applied Overhead
      >   Cr. Overhead Control

      • For overapplied overhead:

      > Dr. Applied Overhead
      >   Cr. Overhead Control
      >   Cr. Cost of Goods Sold

   b. A second approach allocates the under- or overapplied overhead to the inventory accounts, Materials Inventory, Work-in-Process Inventory, and Finished Goods Inventory, based on the balances in the individual accounts;

3. Projects require much longer to complete (often years) and tend to be much more expensive than individual jobs. To manage project costs, companies use two basic measures:

   a. The difference between the cost estimate and the actual costs to date, based on how complete the project is.

   b. The difference between how complete the job is and how complete it should be, given the actual cost incurred.

SUMMARY

This chapter describes the method to account for inventory in a job costing system. Job costing concepts are used when products are easily identifiable as individual units or batches of identical units. Job costing data can be used to bid on jobs and price products, control costs, and evaluate the performance of products, customers, departments, and managers. The flow of costs in Exhibits 7.6 and 7.12 summarizes the discussion of cost flows in the chapter.

The following summarizes key ideas tied to the chapter's learning objectives:

LO 7-1 Describe what *job* and *job shop* mean and compute product costs in a job cost system. A *job* is an easily identified order or service for which a cost is desired. A *job shop* is a firm that produces jobs. Direct materials, direct labor, and manufacturing overhead costs (including indirect materials and indirect labor) are assigned to each job. Direct materials and direct labor are associated directly with the job through purchase requisitions and time cards.

LO 7-2 Account for overhead using predetermined rates. Manufacturing overhead includes all manufacturing costs other than direct materials and direct labor. A predetermined rate based on estimated overhead and the estimated usage of the allocation base is established to assign manufacturing overhead costs to jobs.

LO 7-3 Reconcile and account for the difference between overhead applied to jobs and actual overhead incurred. The difference between overhead incurred and overhead applied is under- or overapplied overhead. Companies treat this in one of two ways. First, they may choose to debit Cost of Goods Sold (in the case of underapplied overhead) or to credit Cost of Goods Sold (in the case of overapplied overhead). Second, they may choose to allocate the under- or overapplied overhead to the inventory accounts according to either the amounts in those accounts or the amount of overhead applied to those accounts.

LO 7-4 Apply job costing in service organizations. Service organizations also use job costing and apply costs to jobs much like manufacturing companies do. The main difference is that service organizations often have no direct materials associated with the job.

LO 7-5 Identify ethical issues in job costing and know how to respond to them. The price of jobs often depends on the costs recorded for the job. This has led to improprieties in assigning costs to jobs. Common causes of these improprieties include misstating the stage of completion of the job, charging costs to the wrong job, and misrepresenting the cost of the job.

LO 7-6 Describe the difference between *projects* and *jobs* and understand the implications for cost management systems. A *project* is a large and complex job whose evaluation is typically based on a percentage of completion at a given point in time.

KEY TERMS

actual cost, *295*

control account, *282*

job, *281*

job cost sheet, *282*

job shop, *281*

normal cost, *295*

overapplied overhead, *290*

project, *301*

standard cost, *295*

subsidiary ledger account, *282*

underapplied overhead, *290*

REVIEW QUESTIONS

7-1. What are characteristics of companies that are likely to use a job cost system?

7-2. Direct labor-hours and direct labor dollars are the most common allocation bases used in the United States (indeed, throughout the world). Why do you suppose they are used more than others?

7-3. What is the purpose of having two manufacturing overhead accounts, the Manufacturing Overhead Control and Applied Manufacturing Overhead?

7-4. How does the accountant know what to record for direct materials for a job or a client? For direct labor cost?

7-5. What are two different ways of treating the difference between applied overhead and actual overhead at the end of the accounting period?

7-6. How is job costing in service organizations (for example, consulting firms) different from job costing in manufacturing organizations?

7-7. What are the costs of a product using normal costing?

7-8. Mega Contractors sells to government agencies using a cost-plus contract and to private firms using fixed price contracts. What choices does Mega have in the design of its job costing system that affect the cost of the government jobs?

7-9. What are three common sources of improprieties in job costing?

7-10. In the context of job costing, what are projects? What additional costing issues are there with projects?

CRITICAL ANALYSIS AND DISCUSSION QUESTIONS

7-11. Why do most companies use normal or standard costing? After all, actual costing gives the actual cost, so the firm could just wait until it knows what the cost will be.

7-12. Why is control of materials important from a managerial planning perspective?

7-13. "Worrying about the choice of an overhead allocation base is a waste of time. In the end, all the overhead is charged to production." Do you agree? Why?

7-14. In computing the predetermined overhead rate, the cost accountant must determine the period over which to estimate the overhead and the allocation base (direct labor-hours, for example). Why are these choices important?

7-15. Interview the manager of a construction company (for example, a company that does house construction, remodeling, landscaping, or street or highway construction) about how the company bids on prospective jobs. Does it use cost information from former jobs that are similar to prospective ones, for example? Does it have a specialist in cost estimation who estimates the costs of prospective jobs? Write a report summarizing the results of your interview.

7-16. Interview the manager of a campus print shop or a print shop in the local area about how the company bids on prospective jobs. Does it use cost information from former jobs that are similar to prospective ones, for example? Does it have a specialist in cost estimation who estimates the costs of prospective jobs? Write a report summarizing the results of your interview.

7-17.   Would a dentist, an architect, a landscaper, and a lawyer use job costing or process costing? Explain.

7-18.   Consider two firms in the same industry. Is it possible that one uses job costing and the other uses process costing? Explain.

7-19.   Is a criminal trial a "job" for costing purposes? Explain.

7-20.   Assume that you have been asked to paint the inside walls of an apartment. State specifically how you would estimate the cost of that job. Include payment for your own labor.

7-21.   Consider Question 7-20. What are some of the allocation bases you considered? Why did you choose the one you used?

7-22.   ABC Consultants works for only two clients: a large for-profit corporation and a small environmental not-for-profit agency. The fee charged for work is based on cost. In deciding how to allocate overhead, the CFO of ABC decides to use the base that allocates the most cost to the large corporation. Is this ethical?

7-23.   Consider the Business Application "Fraudulent Reporting of Project Completion to Improve Financial Performance." Would a solution to the problem of misreporting in the case of projects be solved by writing the contract to make payment when the project is completed? What other issues might this solution create?

All applicable Exercises are included in Connect.      **EXERCISES**

7-24. Assigning Costs to Jobs   (LO 7-1)

Barker Products is a job shop. The following events occurred in September:

1.   Purchased $13,000 of materials.
2.   Issued $14,500 in direct materials to the production department.
3.   Purchased $11,000 of materials.
4.   Issued $900 of supplies from the materials inventory.
5.   Paid for the materials purchased in transaction (1).
6.   Paid $19,200 cash for utilities, power, equipment maintenance, and other miscellaneous items for the manufacturing plant.
7.   Incurred direct labor costs of $22,000, which were credited to Wages Payable.
8.   Issued $1,300 of supplies from the materials inventory.
9.   Applied overhead on the basis of 85 percent of $22,000 direct labor costs.
10.   Recognized depreciation on manufacturing property, plant, and equipment of $11,600.

The following balances appeared in the accounts of Barker Products for September:

	Beginning	Ending
Materials Inventory	$31,700	?
Work-in-Process Inventory	6,100	?
Finished Goods Inventory............	32,000	$29,500
Cost of Goods Sold		52,100

Required

a.   Prepare journal entries to record the transactions.

b.   Prepare T-accounts to show the flow of costs during the period from Materials Inventory through Cost of Goods Sold.

7-25. Assigning Costs to Jobs   (LO 7-1)

Ervin Equipment, a manufacturer of exercise and workout equipment for sale to institutions, uses job costing. The following transactions occurred in January:

1.   Purchased $76,000 of materials.
2.   Paid $81,000 cash for utilities, power, equipment maintenance, and other miscellaneous items for the manufacturing shop.

3. Issued $5,300 of supplies from the materials inventory.
4. Issued $84,000 in direct materials to the production department.
5. Incurred direct labor costs of $74,000, which were credited to Wages Payable.
6. Paid for the materials purchased in transaction (1).
7. Incurred $13,400 in indirect labor costs, which were credited to Wages Payable.
8. Applied overhead on the basis of 155 percent of direct labor costs.
9. Recognized depreciation on manufacturing property, plant, and equipment of $17,500.
10. Returned $1,100 of the materials in transaction (3) to inventory.
11. Paid the for the wages incurred in transaction (5)

The following balances appeared in the accounts of Ervin Equipment for January:

	Beginning	Ending
Materials Inventory	$ 28,300	?
Work-in-Process Inventory	50,400	?
Finished Goods Inventory	179,200	$113,000
Cost of Goods Sold		245,600

Required

a.   Prepare journal entries to record the transactions.

b.   Prepare T-accounts to show the flow of costs during the period from Materials Inventory through Cost of Goods Sold.

(LO 7-1)   **7-26. Assigning Costs to Jobs**

Elmira Tool and Die makes machine tools to order. The following transactions occurred in October:

1. Issued $2,800 of supplies from the materials inventory.
2. Purchased $42,000 of materials.
3. Issued $37,600 in direct materials to the production department.
4. Paid $43,800 for miscellaneous items for the manufacturing plant. Accounts Payable was credited.
5. Returned $5,400 of the materials issued to production in (3) to the materials inventory.
6. Direct labor employees earned $72,000, 50% of which was paid in cash and the remainder credited to Wages Payable.
7. Purchased $12,000 of materials.
8. Recognized depreciation on manufacturing plant of $86,000.
9. Paid for the materials purchased in transaction (2).
10. Applied manufacturing overhead for the month.

Elmira uses normal costing. It applies overhead on the basis of material costs using an annual, predetermined rate. At the beginning of the year, management estimated that materials costs for the year would be $500,000. Estimated overhead for the year was $2,050,000.

The following balances appeared in the inventory accounts of Elmira Tool and Die for October:

	Beginning	Ending
Materials Inventory	?	$ 27,000
Work-in-Process Inventory	?	23,600
Finished Goods Inventory	$7,200	96,300
Cost of Goods Sold	?	175,300

Required

a.   Prepare journal entries to record these transactions.

b.   Prepare T-accounts to show the flow of costs during the period from Materials Inventory through Cost of Goods Sold.

7-27. Assigning Costs to Jobs (LO 7-1, 2)

The following partially complete T-accounts for the month of June along with additional information are from Renfrew & Co.:

Materials Inventory				Work-in-Process Inventory		
BB (6/1)	39,000			BB (6/1)	60,000	
	168,000	144,000				

Finished Goods Inventory				Cost of Goods Sold		
BB (6/1)	115,000					
	262,000	157,000				

Manufacturing Overhead Control				Applied Manufacturing Overhead		
	112,000					

Additional information for June follows:

- Manufacturing overhead is applied at 90 percent of direct labor cost.
- Direct labor-hours recorded on jobs in June totaled 3,900.
- During the month, sales revenue was $351,000, and selling and administrative costs were $67,000.
- The labor wage rate was $25 per hour.
- This company uses no indirect materials or supplies.
- Any products returned by customers are discarded and not resold.

Required

a. What cost amount of direct materials was issued to production during June?
b. How much manufacturing overhead was applied to products during June?
c. What was the cost of products completed during June?
d. What was the balance of the Work-in-Process Inventory account at the end of June?
e. What was the over- or underapplied manufacturing overhead for June?
f. What was the operating profit for June? Any over- or underapplied overhead is written off to Cost of Goods Sold.

7-28. Assigning Costs to Jobs (LO 7-1, 2)

Selected information from the Iowa Instruments accounting records for April follows:

Materials Inventory				Work-in-Process Inventory		
BB (4/1)	25,000			Labor	90,000	
	209,000	174,000		EB (4/30)	91,000	

Finished Goods Inventory				Cost of Goods Sold		
BB (4/1)	87,000				3,500	
	281,000	272,000				

Manufacturing Overhead Control				Applied Manufacturing Overhead		
	77,500					81,000
		77,500			77,500	
					3,500	

Additional information for April follows:

- The labor wage rate was $30 per hour.
- During the month, sales revenue was $320,000, and selling and administrative costs were $73,000.
- This company has no indirect materials or supplies.
- The company applies manufacturing overhead on the basis of direct labor-hours.
- Customer returns are discarded and not resold.

Required

a. What was the cost of direct materials purchased in April?
b. What was the over- or underapplied manufacturing overhead for April?
c. What was the manufacturing overhead application rate in April?
d. What was the cost of products completed during April?
e. What was the balance of the Work-in-Process Inventory account at the beginning of April?
f. What was the operating profit for April? Any over- or underapplied overhead is written off to Cost of Goods Sold.

(LO 7-1, 2)   **7-29. Assigning Costs to Jobs**

Partially completed T-accounts and additional information for Dumfries Designs for the month of August follow:

Materials Inventory				**Work-in-Process Inventory**		
BB (8/1)	165,000			BB (8/1)	307,000	
	682,000	610,000		Labor	576,800	

Finished Goods Inventory				**Cost of Goods Sold**		
BB (8/1)	589,000					
	960,000	777,500				

Manufacturing Overhead Control				**Applied Manufacturing Overhead**		
	462,300					453,200

Additional information for August follows:

- The labor wage rate was $28 per hour.
- During the month, sales revenue was $1,730,000, and selling and administrative costs were $324,600.
- This company has no indirect materials or supplies.
- The company applies manufacturing overhead on the basis of direct labor-hours.

Required

a. What was the cost of direct materials issued to production during August?
b. What was the over- or underapplied manufacturing overhead for August?
c. What was the manufacturing overhead application rate in August?
d. What was the cost of products completed during August?
e. What was the balance of the Work-in-Process Inventory account at the end of August?
f. What was the operating profit for August? Any over- or underapplied overhead is written off to Cost of Goods Sold.

7-30. Assigning Costs to Jobs   (LO 7-1, 2)

The partially completed T-accounts and selected additional information for Hancock Parts for the month of February follow:

Materials Inventory		
BB (2/1)		
		15,000
EB (2/28)		

Work-in-Process Inventory		
BB (2/1)	24,000	
EB (2/28)	41,500	

Finished Goods Inventory		
BB (2/1)	40,000	
EB (2/28)	25,000	

Cost of Goods Sold	

Manufacturing Overhead Control	

Applied Manufacturing Overhead	
	52,500

Additional information for February follows:

- Sales revenue in February was $179,200.
- The operating loss for February was $11,000.
- Hancock applies manufacturing overhead at the rate of 75 percent of direct materials costs.
- Indirect materials in the amount of $15,000 was debited to Manufacturing Overhead Control in February. These materials had been stored in the materials inventory. No other indirect materials were issued in February.
- The Materials Inventory ending balance on February 28 was $30,000 greater than the ending balance on January 31.
- The Cost of Goods Sold in February, including overapplied overhead of $5,600, was $176,400.

Required

a. What was the cost of direct materials issued to production during February?
b. What was the amount of materials purchased in February?
c. What was the cost of goods transferred out of Finished Goods Inventory in February?
d. What was the cost of goods transferred out of Work-in-Process Inventory in February?
e. What were the direct labor costs incurred in February?
f. What was the total amount of actual overhead charged to the Manufacturing Overhead Control account in February?
g. What were the selling and administrative costs incurred in February?

7-31. Predetermined Overhead Rates   (LO 7-2)

Sturgis Manufacturing produces one model of precision tool and accounts for costs using a job cost system. Information from the most recent fiscal year indicates the following.

- Total manufacturing cost during the year was $2,578,125 based on actual direct materials, actual direct labor, and applied manufacturing overhead. Of this amount, 40 percent was comprised of direct costs.
- Manufacturing overhead was applied to work in process at 250 percent of direct materials dollars.

Required

Compute actual direct materials used, actual direct labor, and applied manufacturing overhead.

(LO 7-3)   **7-32. Predetermined Overhead Rates**

Antoine Machining estimated its manufacturing overhead to be $279,000 and its direct materials costs to be $450,000 in Year 1. Three of the jobs that Antoine Machining worked on in Year 1 had actual direct materials costs of $15,000 for Job AM002, $55,000 for Job AM005, and $70,000 for Job AM008. For Year 1, actual manufacturing overhead was $313,000 and total direct materials cost was $540,000. Manufacturing overhead is applied to jobs on the basis of direct materials costs using predetermined rates.

Required

a.   How much overhead was assigned to each of the three jobs, AM002, AM005, and AM008?

b.   What was the over- or underapplied manufacturing overhead for Year 1?

(LO 7-3)   **7-33. Prorate Under- or Overapplied Overhead**

Refer to the information in Exercise 7-32. Overhead applied in each of the inventory accounts is as follows.

Work-in-process inventory	$ 20,088
Finished goods inventory	63,612
Cost of goods sold	251,100

Required

Prepare an entry to allocate the under- or overapplied overhead.

(LO 7-3)   **7-34. Predetermined Overhead Rates**

Linzee Liners estimates that its manufacturing overhead will be $1,725,000 in Year 1. It further estimates that direct labor costs will amount to $750,000. During March, Linzee worked on four jobs with actual direct labor costs of $35,000 for Job 0301, $22,500 for Job 0302, $32,000 for Job 0303, and $16,000 for Job 0304. Actual manufacturing overhead costs for the year were $1,710,000. Actual direct labor costs for the year were $735,000. Manufacturing overhead is applied to jobs based on direct labor costs using predetermined rates.

Required

a.   How much overhead was applied to each of the four jobs, 0301, 0302, 0303, and 0304?

b.   What was the over- or underapplied manufacturing overhead for Year 1?

(LO 7-3)   **7-35. Prorate Over- or Underapplied Overhead**

Refer to the information in Exercise 7-34. The amount of overhead applied in each of the inventory accounts at the end of Year 1 is as follows.

Work-in-process inventory	$ 33,810
Finished goods inventory	270,480
Cost of goods sold	1,386,210

Required

Prepare an entry to allocate the over- or underapplied overhead.

(LO 7-3)   **7-36. Predetermined Overhead Rates**

Marian Manufacturing (2M) applies manufacturing overhead to jobs based on direct labor costs. For Year 2, 2M estimates its manufacturing overhead to be $421,200 and its direct labor costs to be $810,000. 2M worked on three jobs for the year. Job 2M-1, which was sold during year 2, had actual direct labor costs of $420,750. Job 2M-2, which was completed but not sold at the end of the year, had actual direct labor costs of $283,050. Job 2M-3, which is still in work-in-process inventory, had actual direct labor costs of $61,200. Actual manufacturing overhead for Year 2 was $430,000.

Required

a.   How much overhead was applied to each job in Year 2?

b.   What was the over- or underapplied manufacturing overhead for Year 2?

7-37. Prorate Over- or Underapplied Overhead (LO 7-3)
Refer to the information in Exercise 7-36.

Required
Prepare an entry to allocate over- or underapplied overhead to

a. Work in Process.

b. Finished Goods.

c. Cost of Goods Sold.

7-38. Applying Overhead Using a Predetermined Rate (LO 7-3)
Brunswick Home Remodelers (BHM) uses a job order cost system. The following debits (credits) appeared in Work-in-Process Inventory for April:

	Description	Amount
April 1......................	Balance	$ 23,500
For the month	Direct materials	147,000
For the month	Direct labor	96,000
For the month	Factory overhead	95,550
For the month	To finished goods	(290,000)

BHM applies overhead to production at a predetermined rate of 65 percent based on direct materials cost. Job BH-7, which was started during April and is the only job still in process at the end of April, has been charged direct materials of $19,880.

Required
How much direct labor cost was charged to Job BH-7 in April?

7-39. Applying Overhead Using a Predetermined Rate (LO 7-3)
Jason's Custom Tooling (JCT) uses a job order cost system and applies overhead using a predetermined overhead rate based on direct labor costs. The following debits (credits) appeared in Work-in-Process Inventory for November:

	Description	Amount
November 1..................	Balance	$ 37,000
For the month	Direct materials	215,000
For the month	Direct labor	124,000
For the month	Factory overhead	117,800
For the month	To finished goods	(409,000)

Job 13-11, the only job still in process at the end of November, has been charged direct labor of $28,000.

Required
What cost amount of direct materials was charged to Job 13-11?

7-40. Calculating Expected Activity Using the Predetermined Overhead Rate (LO 7-3)
Audubon, Inc. uses a predetermined factory overhead rate based on machine-hours. For October, Audubon recorded $4,500 in overapplied overhead, based on 34,100 actual machine-hours worked and actual manufacturing overhead incurred of $583,725. Audubon estimated manufacturing overhead for October to be $552,000.

Required
What was the estimated number of machine-hours Audubon expected in October?

(LO 7-3, 5) **7-41. Predetermined Overhead Rates: Ethical Issues**

Wanda Instrumentation produces navigational equipment for ships, aircraft (both staffed and drones), and land vehicles. The parts are produced to specification by their customers. Depending on the customer and the type of job, the customer pays according to the terms of either a "fixed-price" contract (the price does not depend directly on the cost of the job) or a "cost-plus" contract (the price is equal to recorded cost plus a fixed fee). Wanda expects only two clients (Ivanhoe Aviation and Rolf's Shipyard) in Year 2. The work done for Ivanhoe will all be done under cost-plus contracts, while the work done for Rolf's will all be done under fixed-price contracts.

Selected budget data for Year 2 include the following:

	Ivanhoe Aviation	Rolf's Shipyard	Unassigned
Direct labor cost ($000)	$ 660	$2,340	
Direct materials cost ($000)	1,980	1,620	
Manufacturing overhead ($000)			$6,480

Required

a. Compute the predetermined rate assuming that Wanda Instrumentation uses direct labor costs to apply overhead.
b. Compute the predetermined rate assuming that Wanda Instrumentation uses direct materials cost to apply overhead.
c. Which allocation base will provide higher income for Wanda Instrumentation?
d. Is it ethical to choose an allocation method based on which one leads to higher income for the firm?

(LO 7-3, 5) **7-42. Predetermined Overhead Rates: Ethical Issues**

Refer to the information in Exercise 7-41. The controller at Wanda Instrumentation chose direct materials cost as the allocation base in Year 2, based on what the financial staff thought reflected the relation between overhead and direct labor cost. Year 3 is approaching and again the company only expects two clients: Rolf's Shipyard and Emily's Trucking Lines (ETL). Work for Rolf's Shipyard will continue to be billed using fixed-price contracts, and ETL will be billed based on cost-plus contracts.

Selected budget data for Year 3 include the following

	Rolf's Shipyard	ETL	Unassigned
Direct labor cost ($000)	$1,500	$2,500	
Direct materials cost ($000)	1,750	1,750	
Manufacturing overhead ($000)			$7,000

Required

a. Compute the predetermined rate assuming that Wanda Instrumentation uses direct labor cost to apply overhead.
b. Compute the predetermined rate assuming that Wanda Instrumentation uses direct materials cost to apply overhead.
c. Which allocation base will provide higher income for Wanda Instrumentation?
d. The controller decides that, for Year 3, the firm will use direct labor cost to apply overhead to jobs. Is this ethical?

(LO 7-4) **7-43. Job Costing in a Service Organization**

At the beginning of the month, Daniel's Business Services had two incomplete consulting engagements (jobs) that had the following costs assigned from previous months.

Job Number	Associate Labor	Applied Overhead
DBS-32	$37,520	?
DBS-35	27,480	?

During the month, Jobs DBS-32 and DBS-35 were completed but not billed to customers. Completion of DBS-32 required an additional $32,100 in associate labor. For DBS-35, an additional $96,000 in associate labor was incurred.

During the month, the only new job, DBS-36, was started but not finished. Total associate labor costs for all jobs amounted to $186,400 for the month. *Overhead* in this company refers to the cost of work that is not directly traced to particular jobs, including supplies, copying, printing, and travel costs to meet with clients. Overhead is applied at a rate of 75 percent of associate labor costs. This rate has not changed for many months. Actual overhead for the month was $137,520.

Required

a.   What are the costs of Jobs DBS-32 and DBS-35 at (1) the beginning of the month and (2) when completed?

b.   What is the cost of Job DBS-36 at the end of the month?

c.   How much was under- or overapplied service overhead for the month?

7-44. Job Costing in a Service Organization   (LO 7-4)

In October, Temptations Event Planners (TEP) planned events for two clients. TEP worked 140 hours for Ward Corporation and 240 hours for Girardin Industries. TEP bills clients at the rate of $350 per hour; labor cost for its planning staff is $140 per hour. The total number of hours worked in October was 380, and overhead costs were $15,600. Overhead is applied to clients at $32 per planner-hour. In addition, TEP had $27,000 in marketing and administrative costs. All transactions are on account. All services were billed.

Required

a.   Show labor and overhead cost flows through T-accounts.

b.   Prepare an income statement for the company for October.

7-45. Job Costing in a Service Organization   (LO 7-4)

Farnsworth Executive Coaching (FEC) offers services to firms in advising executives on improving productivity and leadership. For August, FEC worked 660 hours for Grace Corporation and 390 hours for Temple Construction. In addition, FEC had small engagements with various clients totaling 125 hours. FEC bills clients at the rate of $600 per hour; labor cost for its professional staff is $275 per hour. Overhead costs in August totaled $73,200. Overhead is applied to clients at $65 per labor-hour. In addition, FEC had $179,250 in marketing and administrative costs. All transactions are on account. All services were billed.

Required

a.   Show labor and overhead cost flows through T-accounts.

b.   Prepare an income statement for the company for August.

7-46. Job Costing in a Service Organization   (LO 7-4)

Queenston Professional Support (QPS) provides professional services (IT, payroll and billing, and so on) to firms requiring temporary help in those areas. QPS bills clients for its various services based on the hours its professionals spend. In January, QPS professionals billed 1,875 hours to clients and worked a total of 1,920 hours. (The difference includes time for training, preparing bids, and so on, which are considered administrative costs.) QPS bills clients at the rate of $315 per hour; labor cost for its professionals averaged $145 per hour in January. Overhead costs in January totaled $115,650. Overhead is applied to clients at $60 per labor-hour. In addition, QPS had $155,000 in marketing and administrative costs (not including the professional labor time as described). All transactions are on account. All services were billed.

Required

a.   Show labor and overhead cost flows through T-accounts.

b.   Prepare an income statement for the company for January.

7-47. Evaluating Projects   (LO 7-6)

Clarita Contracting builds roads, tunnels, bridges, and other transportation infrastructure. The following are the budgeted costs and time (months) to a given stage of completion for a project to upgrade a bridge to current standards. The project was originally estimated to take 25 months to complete. Also presented are the actual results through the first 11 months of the project.

	A	B	C	D	E	
1		Cost ($000)		Months to Reach		
2	% Complete	Budget	Actual	Budget	Actual	
3	0%	-	-	0	0	
4	4%	213	112	5	1	
5	8%	471	266	7	1	
6	12%	775	464	8	2	
7	16%	1,125	706	9	3	
8	20%	1,520	990	10	4	
9	24%	1,961	1,317	11	4	
10	28%	2,447	1,688	12	5	
11	32%	2,979	2,102	13	6	
12	36%	3,557	2,559	14	7	
13	40%	4,180	3,059	14	8	
14	44%	4,849	3,603	15	9	
15	48%	5,563	4,189	16	10	
16	52%	6,323	4,819	17	11	
17	56%	7,129		18		
18	60%	7,980		18		
19	64%	8,877		19		
20	68%	9,819		20		
21	72%	10,807		20		
22	76%	11,841		21		
23	80%	12,920		22		
24	84%	14,045		22		
25	88%	15,215		23		
26	92%	16,431		24		
27	96%	17,693		24		
28	100%	19,000		25		
29						
30						

Required

a.   At this time, what is the current cost over- (under-) run on the project?

b.   At this time, by how far ahead or behind schedule is the project in terms of percentage of completion?

(LO 7-6)   **7-48. Evaluating Projects**

Fulton Construction is a general contractor for large construction projects. The budget costs and the time to reach a particular percentage of completion (in months) follow. Also shown are the actual results (cost and months) up to the latest report, which was at the end of month 19.

	A	B	C	D	E	
1		Cost ($000)		Months to Reach		
2	% Complete	Budget	Actual	Budget	Actual	
3	0%	$ -	-	0	0	
4	5%	$ 2,236	774	0	4	
5	10%	$ 3,162	1,545	1	6	
6	15%	$ 3,873	2,308	1	8	
7	20%	$ 4,472	3,061	2	9	
8	25%	$ 5,000	3,799	3	10	
9	30%	$ 5,477	4,520	3	11	
10	35%	$ 5,916	5,221	4	12	
11	40%	$ 6,325	5,899	5	13	
12	45%	$ 6,708	6,553	6	13	
13	50%	$ 7,071	7,182	7	14	
14	55%	$ 7,416	7,783	8	15	
15	60%	$ 7,746	8,356	9	15	
16	65%	$ 8,062	8,900	10	16	
17	70%	$ 8,367	9,416	12	17	
18	75%	$ 8,660	9,902	13	17	
19	80%	$ 8,944	10,361	14	18	
20	85%	$ 9,220	10,791	16	18	
21	90%	$ 9,487	11,194	17	19	
22	95%	$ 9,747		19		
23	100%	$ 10,000		20		
24						
25						

Required

a.   At this time, what is the current cost over- (under-) run on the project?

b.   At this time, by how far ahead or behind schedule is the project in terms of percentage of completion?

All applicable Problems are included in Connect.  **PROBLEMS**

7-49. Applying Overhead Using a Predetermined Rate

(LO 7-2)

Louisiana Metals uses a job costing system. The company applies manufacturing overhead using a predetermined rate based on direct labor cost. The following debits (credits) appeared in the Work-in-Process Inventory for June.

June 1	Balance	???
For the month...................	Direct labor	$ 33,000
For the month...................	Direct materials	43,200
For the month...................	Manufacturing overhead	19,800
For the month...................	To finished goods	(78,700)

Job LM-12, the only job still in production at the end of June, has been charged $13,200 in direct materials cost and $12,400 in direct labor cost.

Required

What was the beginning balance in Work-in-Process Inventory?

7-50. Estimate Direct Labor Costs from Overhead Data

(LO 7-2)

Kenmore Fabrication estimated that direct labor cost for the year would be $640,000. The company also estimated that fixed overhead would be $480,000 and variable overhead would be 35 percent of direct labor cost. Kenmore applies its overhead on the basis of direct labor cost. During the year, all fixed overhead costs were exactly as planned ($480,000) and variable overhead was also incurred as expected. There was $30,000 in underapplied overhead.

Required

How much did Kenmore spend on direct labor cost during the period? Show computations.

7-51. Estimate Hours Worked from Overhead Data

(LO 7-2)

Kingsley Products estimated that direct labor for the year would be 64,000 hours. The company also estimated that the fixed overhead cost for the year would be $160,000. They further estimated the variable overhead cost to be $4.00 per direct labor-hour. All overhead at Kingsley Products is applied on the basis of direct labor-hours. During the year, fixed overhead costs were exactly as planned ($160,000). Variable overhead was incurred at $4.50 per direct labor-hour. Underapplied overhead for the year was calculated as $18,000.

Required

How many direct labor-hours were worked during the period? Show computations.

7-52. Predetermined Rates, Prorate Over- or Underapplied Overhead

(LO 7-3)

Bromley Custom Cabinetry (BCC) uses a job costing system and applies overhead based on direct materials cost. Last year, manufacturing overhead was expected to be $693,000 and direct materials cost was estimated to be $630,000. Actual manufacturing overhead amounted to $693,000, as estimated, and actual direct materials cost was $612,000.

BCC allocates any over- or underapplied overhead to three accounts—Work-in-Process Inventory, Finished Goods Inventory, and Cost of Goods Sold—based on the balances in those accounts. At the end of the year, the total amount in the three accounts (Work-in-Process Inventory, Finished Goods Inventory, and Cost of Goods Sold) was $2 million before any allocation. As a part of the process, you learn that BCC allocated $16,137 to Cost of Goods Sold.

Required

What will Bromley report as Cost of Goods Sold for the year?

(LO 7-1, 2)   **7-53. Assigning Costs: Missing Data**

The following T-accounts for the Fitzpatrick Company represent April activity:

Materials Inventory

BB (4/1)	13,300		
	(a)	2,100	
		(b)	
EB (4/30)	14,700		

Work-in-Process Inventory

BB (4/1)	17,400		
	158,300		
	106,000		
	83,500		
EB (4/30)	17,700		

Finished Goods Inventory

BB (4/1)	12,100		
	(e)	(f)	
EB (4/30)	(g)		

Cost of Goods Sold

343,400	

Applied Overhead Control

	(d)

Wages Payable

	104,100	BB (4/1)
143,700	(c)	
	28,900	
	95,300	EB (4/30)

Manufacturing Overhead Control

112,400	
2,100	
28,900	
15,700	
2,300	

Accounts Payable—Material Suppliers

	87,000

**Accumulated Depreciation—
Plant & Equipment**

	179,600	BB (4/1)
	(h)	
	195,300	EB (4/30)

Prepaid Expenses

BB (4/1)	17,100		
		(i)	
EB (4/30)	14,800		

Required

Compute the missing amounts indicated by the letters (*a*) through (*i*).

(LO 7-2, 3)   **7-54. Assigning Costs: Missing Data**

The following T-accounts represent September activity for Kelly Tools:

Materials Inventory

EB (9/30)	37,600	

Work-in-Process Inventory

BB (9/1)	21,700	
Direct Labor	117,600	

Finished Goods Inventory

EB (9/30)	67,300	

Cost of Goods Sold

Manufacturing Overhead Control

129,150	

Manufacturing Overhead Control

Wages Payable

Sales Revenue

	472,500

Additional Data

- Sales are billed at 175 percent of Cost of Goods Sold before the over- or underapplied overhead is prorated.
- Materials of $75,700 were purchased during the month, and the balance in the Materials Inventory account increased by $5,300.
- Overhead is applied at the rate of 210 percent of direct materials cost.
- The balance in the Finished Goods Inventory account decreased by $19,100 during the month before any proration of under- or overapplied overhead.
- Total credits to the Wages Payable account amounted to $134,700 for direct and indirect labor.
- Factory depreciation totaled $32,100.
- Overhead was overapplied by $16,800. Overhead other than indirect labor, indirect materials, and depreciation incurred was $54,250, which required payment in cash. Overapplied overhead is to be allocated.
- The company has decided to allocate 12 percent of overapplied overhead to Work-in-Process Inventory, 23 percent to Finished Goods Inventory, and the balance to Cost of Goods Sold. Balances shown in T-accounts are before any allocation.

Required

Complete the T-accounts.

7-55. Analysis of Overhead Using a Predetermined Rate   (LO 7-2, 3)

Whitlock Manufacturing uses a job costing accounting system for its production costs. The company uses a predetermined overhead rate based on direct materials costs to apply overhead to individual jobs. The company prepared an estimate of overhead costs at different volumes for the current year as follows:

Direct materials costs	$300,000	$400,000	$ 500,000
Variable overhead costs	$432,000	$576,000	$ 720,000
Fixed overhead costs	384,000	384,000	384,000
Total overhead	$816,000	$960,000	$1,104,000

Whitlock expects to spend $400,000 in direct materials costs over the entire year. The following information is for May, when Jobs WM-52 and WM-53 were completed:

Inventories, May 1	
Materials and supplies	$ 2,600
Work in process (Job WM-52)	13,500
Finished goods	28,100
Purchases of materials and supplies	
Materials.	$ 33,800
Supplies	3,800
Materials and supplies requisitioned for production	
Job WM-52.	$ 11,300
Job WM-53.	9,400
Job WM-54.	6,400
Supplies	1,500
	$ 28,600
Factory direct labor-hours (DLH)	
Job WM-52.	900 DLH
Job WM-53.	750 DLH
Job WM-54.	500 DLH
Labor costs	
Direct labor wages (all hours @ $22).	$ 47,300
Indirect labor wages (500 hours)	8,000
Supervisory salaries	9,000
	(continued)

Building occupancy costs (heat, light, depreciation, etc.)

Factory facilities	$22,500
Sales and administrative offices.	10,500

Factory equipment costs

Power	$12,000
Repairs and maintenance	8,500
Other.	11,500
	$32,000

Required

Answer the following questions:

a. Compute the predetermined overhead rate (combined fixed and variable) to be used to apply overhead to individual jobs during the year.

(*Note:* Regardless of your answer to requirement [a], assume that the predetermined overhead rate is 225% of direct materials cost. Use this rate in answering requirements [b] through [f], as needed.)

b. Compute the total cost of Job WM-52 when it is finished.

c. How much of factory overhead cost was applied to Job WM-54 during May?

d. What total amount of overhead was applied to jobs during May?

e. Compute actual factory overhead incurred during May.

f. At the end of the year, Whitlock Manufacturing had the following account balances:

Underapplied Overhead	$ 48,000
Work-in-Process Inventory	19,800
Finished Goods Inventory.	176,300
Cost of Goods Sold	1,803,900

How would you recommend treating the overapplied overhead, assuming that it is not material? Show the new account balances in the following table.

Underapplied Overhead	_____
Work-in-Process Inventory	_____
Finished Goods Inventory.	_____
Cost of Goods Sold	_____

(LO 7-2, 3)   **7-56. Analysis of Overhead Using a Predetermined Rate**

Sorrento Products uses a job costing accounting system for its manufacturing costs. A predetermined overhead rate based on machine-hours is used to apply overhead to individual jobs. An estimate of overhead costs at different volumes was prepared for the current year as follows.

Machine-hours	180,000	200,000	240,000
Variable overhead costs.	$ 684,000	$ 760,000	$ 912,000
Fixed overhead costs	1,440,000	1,440,000	1,440,000
Total overhead	$2,124,000	$2,200,000	$2,352,000

The expected volume is 200,000 machine-hours for the entire year. The following information is for March, when jobs 302 and 304 were completed:

Inventories, March 1
Raw materials and supplies..................................	$ 90,500
Work in process (Job 302).............................	197,300
Finished goods	497,800

Purchases of raw materials and supplies
Raw materials......................................	$1,362,200
Supplies	174,800

Materials and supplies requisitioned for production
Job 302	$ 603,500
Job 304	508,300
Job 305	101,700
Supplies	33,600
	$1,247,100

Machine-hours (MH)
Job 302	6,700 MH
Job 304	6,600 MH
Job 305	4,000 MH

Direct labor-hours (DLH)
Job 302	9,200 DLH
Job 304	4,000 DLH
Job 305	2,400 DLH

Labor costs
Direct labor wages (all hours @ $32)...................	$ 499,200
Indirect labor wages (1,100 hours)	19,800
Supervisory salaries	28,200

Building occupancy costs (heat, light, depreciation, etc.)
Factory facilities.....................................	$ 28,500
Sales and administrative offices.......................	30,700

Factory equipment costs
Power	$ 46,800
Repairs and maintenance	17,600
Other..	22,200
	$ 86,600

Required

Answer the following questions:

a. Compute the predetermined overhead rate (combined fixed and variable) to be used to apply overhead to individual jobs during the year.

(*Note:* Regardless of your answer to requirement [a], assume that the predetermined overhead rate is $12 per machine-hour. Use this amount in answering requirements [b] through [f], as needed.)

b. Compute the total cost of Job 302 when it is finished.

c. How much of factory overhead cost was applied to Job 305 during March?

d. What total amount of overhead was applied to jobs during March?

e. Compute actual factory overhead incurred during March.

f. At the end of the year, Sorrento Products had the following account balances:

	Balance
Overapplied Overhead............	$ 1,680,000
Work-in-Process Inventory	2,640,000
Finished Goods Inventory..........	960,000
Cost of Goods Sold	20,400,000

How would you recommend treating the underapplied overhead? Show the effect on the account balances in the following table:

Overapplied Overhead............	_____
Work-in-Process Inventory.........	_____
Finished Goods Inventory..........	_____
Cost of Goods Sold	_____

(LO 7-2, 3)   **7-57. Finding Missing Data**

A series of computer and backup system failures caused the loss of most of the company records at Stotter, Inc. Information technology consultants for the company could recover only a few fragments of the company's factory ledger for July as follows:

Materials Inventory			Work-in-Process Inventory		
BB (7/1)	110,000		BB (7/1)	21,700	
	202,000				

Finished Goods Inventory			Cost of Goods Sold		
EB (7/31)	90,000				
	1,800				

Manufacturing Overhead Control			Accounts Payable (Materials)		
	168,000			182,300	
				37,900	EB (7/31)

Further investigation and reconstruction from other sources yielded the following additional information:

- Based on records for January through June, overhead is applied at the rate of $24 per direct labor-hour.
- The production superintendent's cost sheets showed only one job in Work-in-Process Inventory on July 31. Materials of $15,420 had been added to the job, and 270 direct labor-hours had been expended at $30 per hour.
- The employment department has verified that there are no variations in pay rates among direct-labor employees.
- No indirect materials were issued from inventory during the period.
- The controller had just allocated the underapplied overhead to Cost of Goods Sold, Finished Goods Inventory, and Work-in-Process Inventory. (This allocation is done monthly at Stotter, Inc. and is based on account balances.) The controller remembers making the $1,800 entry in Finished Goods Inventory as a part of the allocation and that the total underapplied overhead was $12,000.
- Data used in a study on inventory levels at Stotter, Inc. indicate that the finished goods inventory increased by $17,000 in July.

Required

Determine the following amounts:

a. Work-in-process inventory, July 31, before allocation of underapplied overhead.
b. Cost of goods sold for July, before allocation of underapplied overhead.
c. Direct materials issued from inventory during July.
d. Materials Inventory ending balance on July 31, after the underapplied overhead has been allocated.

(LO 7-2, 3)   **7-58. Data Analysis of Product Costs Using Monthly or Annual Predetermined Rates**

Highway 1 Manufacturing (H1M) produces several, related products in multiple factories. At one facility, which produces only a single product, managers are debating whether to use a predetermined rate calculated on a monthly or annual basis. Overhead is applied on the basis of direct labor-hours at H1M.

Manufacturing data on the product follow:

Direct costs:

Material cost per unit	$51
Direct labor cost per unit (1.5 hours @ $26 per hour)	39

Overhead costs:

Fixed overhead per month	$320,000
Variable overhead per unit (1.5 hours @ $32 per hour).	48

Managers at H1M have estimated monthly production for the coming year according to the following schedule:

	A	B
		Estimated Production
2	Month	(Units)
3	January	3,000
4	February	3,900
5	March	4,800
6	April	6,000
7	May	6,500
8	June	7,800
9	July	8,600
10	August	9,700
11	September	10,800
12	October	11,600
13	November	12,900
14	December	14,400
15		
16	For the year	100,000
17		

Required

Help the managers at H1M in their analysis by recreating the information in Exhibit 7.8 of the text. Assume that estimated values are realized.

7-59. Data Visualization: Product Costs Using Monthly or Annual Predetermined Rates   (LO 7-2, 3)
Refer to the information and data in Problem 7-58.

Required

Help the managers at Highway 1 Manufacturing by illustrating graphically the effect of using monthly rates versus an annual rate for applying overhead.

7-60. Data Analysis of Product Costs Using Monthly or Annual Predetermined Rates   (LO 7-2, 3)
Garvin, Inc. produces a specialized machine tool to order. Garvin uses a job costing system and applies overhead on the basis of direct labor-hours. Each unit varies according to customer specification, but for planning purposes, Garvin uses the following unit cost and quantity information:

Variable costs:

Direct materials cost per unit	$18
Direct labor cost per unit (.75 hour @ $32)	24
Variable overhead (.75 hour @ $20)	15

Demand for Garvin's product fluctuates over the year, so the company leases some of the specialized equipment needed for manufacturing. The leases are structured as month to month to increase flexibility. The following monthly fixed costs, including both equipment owned and leased by Garvin, are given in the following schedule:

Quantity of Output		
For quantity greater than (units)	But less than or equal to (units)	Monthly Fixed Costs
0	7,500	$ 300,000
7,501	10,000	360,000
10,001	15,000	420,000
15,001	--	500,000

Based on current information, the financial planning staff have put together the following monthly forecast of production quantities:

	A	B
2	Month	Estimated Production (Units)
3	January	11,900
4	February	9,400
5	March	19,000
6	April	4,000
7	May	13,100
8	June	9,800
9	July	19,000
10	August	14,400
11	September	5,300
12	October	15,200
13	November	7,000
14	December	21,900
15		
16	For the year	150,000
17		

Required
Recreate the information in Exhibit 7.8 in the text for Garvin, Inc.

(LO 7-2, 3)   **7-61. Data Visualization: Product Costs Using Monthly or Annual Predetermined Rates**
Refer to the information and data in Problem 7-60.

Required
Graphically illustrate the effect of using monthly rates versus an annual rate for applying overhead.

(LO 7-4)   **7-62. Cost Accumulation: Service Company**
Rogell Academic Services (RAS) provides tutoring and test preparation services for children and young adults. Employees include a director and six facilitators. The director manages all marketing and administrative activities, sometimes with the help of one of the other employees. RAS offers four basic services and accounts for each one separately. The services are Group Tutoring (Group), Personalized Tutoring (Pers), Test Prep (Test), and Coding (Code). The facilitators record the time

spent on each service in the RAS computer system. Time spent in training, planning, or when demand is temporarily low is recorded as Not Billed (NB).

Selected operating data for October follow:

	NB	Group	Pers	Test	Code
Sales revenue		$9,100	$8,300	$7,200	$8,100
Direct labor (in hours)	50	450	120	160	170
Direct overhead traceable to departments					
Equipment		$1,600	$ 650	$ 840	$2,000
Supplies		360	280	470	690
Miscellaneous		220	160	490	760

Other Data

- The six facilitators all make $18 per hour. A bonus of $5 per hour is paid for facilitating the coding service.
- The director earns $4,500 per month.
- Overhead that cannot be directly traced to a service, which amounted to $3,420 in October, is allocated among the four services plus the Not Billed "service" based on the number of direct labor-hours used.
- Marketing costs (in addition to the director's salary) in October amounted to $870.
- Other administrative costs (in addition to the director's salary) in October were $560.
- Revenue transactions are cash; all other transactions are on account.

Required

Management wants to know whether each service is contributing to the company's profit. Prepare an income statement for October that shows the revenue and cost for each service. Write a short report to management about service profitability.

7-63. Job Costs: Service Company

(LO 7-4)

Rutland Business Services (RBS) provides miscellaneous consulting and services to local businesses. In August, RBS worked for three clients. It worked 270 hours for Selden Contracting, 170 hours for Moenhart Insurance, and 230 hours for Englewood Medical Center. RBS bills clients at $500 an hour; its labor costs are $125 an hour. A total of 750 hours were worked in August with 80 hours not billable to clients. Overhead costs of $60,000 were incurred and were assigned to clients on the basis of direct labor-hours. Because 80 hours were not billable, some overhead was not assigned to jobs. RBS had $57,000 in marketing and administrative costs. All transactions were on account.

Required

a. What are the revenue and cost per client?
b. Prepare an income statement for August.

7-64. Job Costs in a Service Company

(LO 7-4)

On April 1, two jobs were in process at Hartwell Contracting. Details of the jobs follow:

Job Number	Direct Materials	Direct Labor
HC-34	$4,200	$1,600
HC-37	3,100	5,800

The Materials Inventory account on April 1 totaled $7,900. Materials purchased during the month totaled $17,100. Indirect materials of $1,540 were issued from materials inventory. On April 1, finished goods inventory consisted of two jobs: HC-32, costing $6,780, and HC-35, with a cost of $3,600. Costs for both jobs were transferred to Cost of Services Billed during the month.

Also during April, Jobs HC-34 and HC-37 were completed. Completing Job HC-34 required an additional $4,900 in direct labor. The completion costs for Job HC-37 included $3,200 in direct materials and $10,500 in direct labor.

Hartwell Contracting used a total of $8,900 of direct materials (excluding the $1,540 indirect materials) during the month and $25,600 in total direct labor costs. Overhead has been estimated at 75 percent of direct labor costs, and this relation has been the same for the past few years.

Required
Compute the costs of Jobs HC-34 and HC-37 and the balances in the April 30 inventory accounts.

(LO 7-2, 3)   **7-65. Tracing Costs in a Job Company**

Edwin Parts, a job shop, recorded the following transactions in May:

1. Purchased $87,200 in materials on account.
2. Issued $3,650 in supplies from the materials inventory to the production department.
3. Issued $43,600 in direct materials to the production department.
4. Paid for the materials purchased in transaction (1).
5. Incurred wage costs of $67,200, which were debited to Payroll, a temporary account. Of this amount, $22,300 was withheld for payroll taxes and credited to Payroll Taxes Payable. The remaining $44,900 was paid in cash to the employees. See transactions (6) and (7) for additional information about Payroll.
6. Recognized $34,700 in fringe benefit costs, incurred as a result of the wages paid in (5). This $34,700 was debited to Payroll and credited to Fringe Benefits Payable.
7. Analyzed the Payroll account and determined that 65 percent represented direct labor; 15 percent, indirect manufacturing labor; and 20 percent, administrative and marketing costs.
8. Applied overhead on the basis of 140 percent of direct labor costs.
9. Paid for utilities, power, equipment maintenance, and other miscellaneous items for the manufacturing plant totaling $41,300
10. Recognized depreciation of $26,300 on manufacturing property, plant, and equipment.

Required
a. Prepare journal entries to record these transactions.
b. The balances that appeared in the accounts of Edwin Parts are shown as follows:

	Beginning	Ending
Materials Inventory	$ 89,900	?
Work-in-Process Inventory	25,400	?
Finished Goods Inventory	102,600	$ 93,200
Cost of Goods Sold	—	154,800

Prepare T-accounts to show the flow of costs during the period.

(LO 7-2, 3, 4)   **7-66. Cost Flows through Accounts**

Hyde Restorations rebuilds factory facilities. It employs 130 full-time workers at $25 per hour. Despite operating at capacity, last year's performance was a great disappointment to the managers. In total, nine jobs were accepted and completed, incurring the following total costs:

Direct materials	$1,210,200
Direct labor	4,500,000
Manufacturing overhead	1,152,000

Of the $1,152,000 manufacturing overhead, 25 percent was variable overhead and 75 percent was fixed.

This year, Hyde expects to operate at the same activity level as last year, and overhead costs and the wage rate are not expected to change. For the first quarter of this year, Hyde Restorations completed two jobs and was beginning the third (Job 13). The costs incurred follow:

Job	Direct Materials	Direct Labor
11	$178,360	$612,500
12	120,900	390,500
13	122,200	247,000
Total manufacturing overhead		325,440
Total marketing and administrative costs		156,800

You are a consultant associated with Conway & Company, which has been hired by Hyde to analyze the profitability issue. The managing partner on the engagement has reviewed the accounts at Hyde and suggests you start by classifying the overhead into fixed and variable components for each of the jobs. With the help of the Hyde supervisors on each of the jobs, you arrive at the following split.

	Actual Manufacturing Overhead	
	Variable	Fixed
11....................	$35,880	$ 124,800
12....................	33,000	105,840
13....................	5,520	20,400
	$74,400	$251,040

In the first quarter of this year, 30 percent of marketing and administrative cost was variable and 70 percent was fixed. You are told that Jobs 11 and 12 were sold for $1,090,000 and $690,000, respectively. All over- or underapplied overhead for the quarter is written off to Cost of Goods Sold.

Required

a.   Present in T-accounts the *actual* manufacturing cost flows for the three jobs in the first quarter of this year.

b.   Using last year's overhead costs and direct labor-hours as this year's estimate, calculate predetermined overhead rates per direct labor-hour for variable and fixed overhead.

c.   Present in T-accounts the *normal* manufacturing cost flows for the three jobs in the first quarter of this year. Use the overhead rates derived in requirement (b).

d.   Prepare income statements for the first quarter of this year under the following costing systems:

   1. Actual
   2. Normal

7-67. Show Flow of Costs to Jobs   (LO 7-2, 3)
Manor Painting is a commercial interior and exterior painting contractor specializing in commercial buildings. An inventory of materials and equipment is on hand at all times, so work can start as quickly as possible. Special equipment is ordered as required. On August 1, the Materials Inventory account had a balance of $54,000. The Work-in-Process Inventory account is maintained to record costs of work not yet complete. There were two such jobs on August 1 with the following costs:

	Job 84	Job 87
Materials and equipment....	$23,100	$78,800
Direct labor................	20,300	39,400
Overhead (applied).........	8,120	15,760

Overhead has been applied at 40 percent of the costs of direct labor using an annual rate.

During August, Manor Painting started two new jobs. Additional work was carried out on Jobs 84 and 87. Job 87 was completed and billed to the customer. Details on the costs incurred on jobs during August follow:

Job	84	87	88	90
Materials and equipment........	$4,500	$ 7,200	$6,900	$4,400
Direct labor (wages payable)	7,800	10,100	8,900	2,400

Other August Events

1. Purchased materials and equipment for $14,100.
2. Billed $195,000 to the customer for Job 87 and received payment for $115,000 of that amount.
3. Received $18,600 payment on Job 82 delivered to customer in July.
4. Determined that payroll for indirect labor personnel totaled $2,100.
5. Issued supplies and incidental materials for current jobs costing $750.
6. Recorded overhead and advertising costs for the operation as follows (all cash except equipment depreciation):

Property taxes	$ 900
Storage area rental...........................	1,050
Truck and delivery cost	1,630
Advertising and promotion campaign............	1,200
Inspections....................................	900
Telephone and other miscellaneous	680
Equipment depreciation........................	2,720

Required

a. Prepare journal entries to record the flow of costs for operations during August.
b. Calculate the amount of over- or underapplied overhead for the month. This amount is debited or credited to Cost of Goods Sold.
c. Determine inventory balances for Materials Inventory and Work-in-Process Inventory.

(LO 7-2, 3)   **7-68. Reconstruct Missing Data**

The following financial information about the manufacturing plant of Continental Company for the year-to-date and the month of July appears on the company's records:

Materials inventory, June 30.........................	$ 54,000
Work-in-process inventory, June 30	85,700
Finished goods inventory, June 30	36,200
Cost of goods sold through June 30.................	353,900
Accounts payable (materials suppliers), June 30	22,100
Manufacturing overhead through June 30............	187,800
Payroll payable, June 30...........................	–0–
Withholding and other payroll liabilities, June 30......	11,600
Overhead applied through June 30	176,900

A count of the inventories on hand July 31 shows the following:

Materials inventory........................	$41,700
Work-in-process inventory..................	?
Finished goods inventory	39,200

Interviews with various plant administrative employees August 1 reveal some additional information:

- The company currently owes materials suppliers $51,800.
- The company paid suppliers $38,000 cash during July.

- Plant payroll during July totaled $81,700, of which $15,500 was for indirect labor.
- Manufacturing overhead incurred through July was $219,900.
- Cost of goods sold through July 31 was $401,000.
- Indirect materials cost during July was $2,100.
- Overhead during July was underapplied by $1,300.

Required

Determine the balance of the Work-in-Process Inventory on July 31.

7-69. Find Missing Data

(LO 7-2, 3)

Mechanic Implements manufactures miscellaneous parts for building construction and mainte-nance. The company uses a normal job costing system and overhead is applied on the basis of direct labor cost. Any over- or underapplied overhead is written off to Cost of Goods Sold monthly.

The following journal entries have been recorded in September. (Assume that only one entry is made each month.)

Work-in-Process Inventory (Direct Labor)................	17,500	
Wages Payable.....................................		17,500
Direct Materials Inventory............................	26,250	
Accounts Payable..................................		26,250
Finished Goods Inventory............................	64,750	
Work-in-Process Inventory		64,750
Cost of Goods Sold^a.................................	78,750	
Finished Goods Inventory............................		78,750

^aThis entry does not include any over- or underapplied overhead. Over- or underapplied overhead is written off to Cost of Goods Sold once for the month. For September, the amount written off was 10 percent of overhead applied for September.

The Work-in-Process Inventory ending account balance on September 30 was twice the begin-ning balance. The Direct Materials Inventory ending balance on September 30 was $20,600 less than the beginning balance. The Finished Goods Inventory ending balance on September 30 was $5,250. The September income statement shows Cost of Goods Sold of $79,450.

Required

a. What was the Finished Goods Inventory beginning inventory on September 1?
b. How much manufacturing overhead was applied for September?
c. What was the manufacturing overhead rate for September?
d. How much manufacturing overhead was incurred in September?
e. What was the Work-in-Process Inventory balance on September 1?
f. What was the Work-in-Process Inventory balance on September 30?

7-70. Find Missing Data

(LO 7-2, 3)

Accounting records for Antoinette Designs (AD) for November show the following (each entry is the total of the actual entries for the account for the month):

Work-in-Process Inventory (Direct Labor)................	7,200	
Wages Payable.....................................		7,200
Direct Materials Inventory............................	122,130	
Accounts Payable..................................		122,130
Finished Goods Inventory............................	136,800	
Work-in-Process Inventory		136,800
Cost of Goods Sold^a	131,400	
Finished Goods Inventory............................		131,400

^aThis entry does not include any over- or underapplied overhead. Over- or underapplied overhead is written off to Cost of Goods Sold once for the month. For November, the amount written off was 5 percent of overhead applied for November. Overhead is applied on the basis of direct labor costs.

The Work-in-Process Inventory ending account balance on November 30 was 125 percent of the beginning balance. The Direct Materials Inventory ending balance on November 30 was $2,250 less than the beginning balance. The Finished Goods Inventory beginning balance on November 1 was $13,320.

The September income statement shows revenues of $207,000 and a gross profit of $76,500.

Required

a.   What was the Finished Goods Inventory balance on November 30?

b.   How much manufacturing overhead was applied for November?

c.   What was the manufacturing overhead rate for November?

d.   How much manufacturing overhead was incurred for November?

e.   What was the Work-in-Process Inventory on November 1?

f.   What was the Work-in-Process Inventory on November 30?

(LO 7-2, 3, 4)   **7-71. Incomplete Data: Job Costing**

Plainview Paving Contractors (PPC) is a rapidly growing, recently established company that has not been profitable despite increases in sales. It has hired you as a consultant to find ways to improve profitability. You believe that the problem results from poor cost control and inaccurate cost estimation on jobs. The company has essentially no accounting system from which to collect data. You are able, however, to piece together the following information for April:

- Production
  1. Completed Job 33.
  2. Started and completed Job 41.
  3. Started Job 42.
- Inventory values
- Work-in-process inventory values (excluding applied overhead):

> March 31: Job 33
>   Direct materials .... $ 7,200
>   Labor (850 hours × $36) 30,600

> April 30: Job 42
>   Direct materials .... $ 5,800
>   Labor (920 hours × $36) 33,120

- Job 33 was exactly 60 percent complete as to labor on March 31.
- Job 42 was exactly 40 percent complete as to labor on April 30.
- All direct materials necessary to do the entire job were charged to each job as soon as it was started.
- There were no direct materials inventories or finished goods inventories at either March 31 or April 30.
- Actual overhead was $112,000.
- Cost of goods sold (before adjustment for over- or underapplied overhead):

> Job 33
>   Materials .... $ 7,200
>   Labor ....   ?
>   Overhead ....   ?
>   Total $104,100

```
Job 41

     Materials . . . . . . . . . . . . . . . . . . . . . . .      ?
     Labor . . . . . . . . . . . . . . . . . . . . . . . .        ?
     Overhead . . . . . . . . . . . . . . . . . . . . .          ?
  Total . . . . . . . . . . . . . . . . . . . . . . . . .        ?
```

- Overhead was applied to jobs using a predetermined rate per labor dollar that has been used since the company began operations.
- All direct materials were purchased for cash and charged directly to Work-in-Process Inventory when purchased. Direct materials purchased in April amounted to $16,560.
- Direct labor costs charged to jobs in April were $115,200. All labor costs were the same per hour for all laborers for April.

Required

Write a report to management to show:

a. The cost elements (material, labor, and overhead) of cost of goods sold before adjustment for over- or underapplied overhead for each job sold.

b. The value of each cost element (material, labor, and overhead) for each job in work-in-process inventory at April 30.

c. Over- or underapplied overhead for April.

7-72. Job Costing and Ethics

(LO 7-2, 3, 5)

Jerome Shipyards does work for both the U.S. Navy and private shipping companies. Jerome's major business is renovating ships, which it does at one of two company dry docks referred to by the names of the local towns: Casgrain and Lyndon.

Data on operations and costs for the two dry docks follow:

	Casgrain	Lyndon
Overhead cost ($000).	$16,800	$67,200
Direct labor-hours (000)	140,000	140,000

Virtually all dry dock costs consist of depreciation. The Lyndon dry dock is much newer, so the depreciation on it is much higher. Dry dock overhead is charged to jobs based on direct labor-hours for the specific dock.

Jerome is about to start two jobs, one for the Navy under a cost-plus contract and one for a private shipping company for a fixed fee. Both jobs will require the same number of hours. You have been asked to prepare some costing information. Your supervisor is sure the Navy job will be done at Lyndon and the private job will be done at Casgrain.

Required

a. Compute the overhead rate at the two shipyards.

b. Why do you think your supervisor says that the Navy job will be done at Lyndon?

c. Is the choice of the production location ethical? Why?

7-73. Job Costing and Ethics

(LO 7-5)

Buelow, LLP, is a consulting firm that helps organizations become more efficient. A supervisor on two consulting jobs discusses an issue that arose recently. One of the consulting jobs is for a large technology firm, and the other is for a major automobile company. When the monthly cost reports about the two projects were received three weeks after month-end, the automobile company job report contained bad news. The supervisor explained:

> The automobile job is only half done, but we have already spent all of the $400,000 that we expected to spend on that job. However, we have spent only $200,000 of the $420,000 that we expected to spend on the technology firm job, even though we are 80 percent done with the work. It's too bad because we are reimbursed for costs on the technology job, but the automobile company job is for a fixed price.

Required

a. What should the supervisor do?
b. Does it matter that Buelow is reimbursed for costs on the technology job? Explain.

(LO 7-2, 3, 5) **7-74. Job Costing and Ethics**

Spokane, Inc. is a manufacturing company that produces parts both for inventory and to custom specifications. Parts produced for inventory are sold at prices determined in the market. Custom parts are sold at a price equal to production cost plus a profit based on the cost of production. Although custom parts are different from the standard parts produced for inventory, the same production processes, equipment, labor, and materials are used for both.

The CFO is designing a new cost system and is debating between direct labor-hours and direct labor cost as a basis for applying overhead to products.

Required

a. Why (under what circumstances) would this choice lead to different costs being assigned to standard and custom products?
b. Would it be ethical to decide on the allocation basis by considering the effect of the choice on the relative costs? Explain.

(LO 7-6) **7-75. Evaluating Projects—Data Visualization**

Refer to the information and data in Exercise 7-47 for Clarita Contracting.

Required

Prepare a graphical analysis of the current status of the cost and timing of the project at the current time. **Note:** The graphs in Exhibit 7.14 suggest one approach, but other approaches might also be appropriate.

(LO 7-6) **7-76. Evaluating Projects—Data Visualization**

Refer to the information and data in Exercise 7-48 for Fulton Construction.

Required

Prepare a graphical analysis of the current status of the cost and timing of the project at the current time. **Note:** The graphs in Exhibit 7.14 suggest one approach, but other approaches might also be appropriate.

INTEGRATIVE CASES

(LO 7-2, 3) **7-77. Cost Estimation, Estimating Overhead Rates, Job Costing, and Decision Making**

O'Leary Corporation manufactures special-purpose portable structures (huts, mobile offices, and so on) for use at construction sites. It only builds to order (each unit is built to customer specifications). O'Leary uses a normal job costing system. Direct labor at O'Leary is paid $17 per hour, but the employees are not paid if they are not working on jobs. Manufacturing overhead is assigned to jobs by a predetermined rate on the basis of direct labor-hours. The company incurred manufacturing overhead costs during two recent years (adjusted for price-level changes using current prices and wage rates) as follows:

	Year 1	Year 2
Direct labor-hours worked	67,000	54,000
Manufacturing overhead costs incurred:		
Indirect labor........................	$2,760,000	$2,160,000
Employee benefits	1,005,000	810,000
Supplies..............................	670,000	540,000
Power................................	627,000	522,000
Heat and light........................	138,000	138,000
Supervision	776,250	656,250
Depreciation	1,982,500	1,982,500
Property taxes and insurance	751,250	751,250
Total manufacturing overhead costs.......	$8,710,000	$7,560,000

At the beginning of Year 3, O'Leary has two jobs, which have not yet been delivered to customers. Job MC-270 was completed on December 27, Year 2. It is scheduled to ship on January 7, Year 3. Job MC-275 is still in progress. For the purpose of computing the predetermined overhead rate, O'Leary uses the previous year's actual overhead rate. Data on direct materials costs and direct labor-hours for these jobs in Year 2 follow:

	Job MC-270	Job MC-275
Direct materials costs	$270,000	$495,000
Direct labor-hours	2,500 hours	3,200 hours

During Year 3, O'Leary incurred the following direct materials costs and direct labor-hours for all jobs worked in Year 3, including the completion of Job MC-275:

Direct materials costs	$11,840,000
Direct labor-hours	74,000
Actual manufacturing overhead	$9,120,000

At the end of Year 3, there were four jobs that had not yet shipped. Data on these jobs follow:

	MC-389	MC-390	MC-397	MC-399
Direct materials	$43,200	$67,000	$103,500	$28,900
Direct labor-hours...........	1,740 hours	2,700 hours	6,100 hours	1,300 hours
Job status.................	Finished	Finished	In progress	In progress

Required

a.   What were the amounts in the beginning Finished Goods and beginning Work-in-Process accounts for year 3?

b.   O'Leary incurred direct materials costs of $57,000 and used an additional 300 hours in Year 3 to complete job MC-275. What was the final (total) cost charged to job MC-275?

    c.   What was over- or underapplied overhead for Year 3?

    d.   O'Leary prorates any over- or underapplied overhead to Cost of Goods Sold, Finished Goods Inventory, and Work-in-Process Inventory. Prepare the journal entry to prorate the over- or underapplied overhead computed in requirement (*c*).

    e.   A customer has asked O'Leary to bid on a job to be completed in Year 4. O'Leary estimates that the job will require about $92,500 in direct materials and 5,000 direct labor-hours. Because of the economy, O'Leary expects demand for its services to be low in Year 4, and the CEO wants to bid aggressively but does not want to lose any money on the project. O'Leary estimates that there would be virtually no sales or administrative costs associated with this job. What is the minimum amount O'Leary can bid on the job and still not incur a loss?

(CMA adapted)

(LO 7-3)

7-78. Predetermined Rates, Job Costing, Service Firms, Product-Line Profitability

A&R Quality Advisors is a small consulting firm offering quality audits and advising services to small and mid-sized manufacturing firms. Quality audits entail reviewing, checking, and documenting quality practices within a firm. Quality advising entails making recommendations for new or revised quality practices. Other firms in the area offer one or both of these services, although the competition for quality audit jobs is stronger than for quality advising.

    In addition to senior executives, A&R employees are either staff or managers. Staff employees are usually younger with less experience. Managers, who oversee the staff on jobs, are more experienced. The average hourly wage is $60 for staff and $150 for managers. (Both staff and managers are paid an annual salary; these hourly costs are based on 2,000 average annual hours worked.) Staff are expected to spend at least 90 percent of their time on billable work. Because of administrative work associated with supervising the staff and the expectation that managers will spend a portion of their time seeking new business, managers are expected to spend about 50 percent of their time on billable work. A&R employs 10 staff and two managers.

    In addition to staff and manager costs, A&R has overhead and administrative costs of $4,500,000, of which about $1,500,000 is variable with respect to billable hours. Overhead and administrative costs *include* the nonbillable cost of the staff and managers.

    Selected information on billable hours expected for the next year follows:

	A	B	C	D	E	F	G	H
		Billable Audit Hours		Billable Advising Hours		Total Billable Hours		
1		Staff	Manager	Staff	Manager	Staff	Manager	
2								
3	Client 01	150	12	200	10	350	22	
4	Client 02	70	10	0	0	70	10	
5	Client 03	220	30	80	15	300	45	
6	⋮	⋮	⋮	⋮	⋮	⋮	⋮	
7	Client 49	40	2	0	0	40	2	
8	Client 50	300	20	200	15	500	35	
9	Total	8,500	1,200	9,500	800	18,000	2,000	
10								

    Although not all clients use A&R for both services, about 70 percent do.

    A&R bills audit services based on billable hours and advising services at a fixed fee. The cost for audit services is determined by multiplying the billable hours by the quoted employee rates. Staff rates for the following year are $200 per hour, and manager rates are $500 per hour. The rates are set to meet the competition in the area.

    To determine the cost (not the price) of the job, A&R uses a job costing system. To the employee costs (not the billing rates) is added an amount for overhead based on the predetermined rate and the billable hours in the job. The predetermined rate is based on expected billable hours.

    Total revenue at A&R next year is expected to be $8 million.

    The two founding partners of A&R are looking at these forecasts for next year and trying to decide whether to drop one of these services. "We should probably become more focused, as we sometimes remind our clients."

Required

a. What is the predetermined overhead rate for costing jobs in the following year?

b. How much will Client 02 be billed for audit services next year?

c. How much will the job costing system report as the cost of Client 02 audit services next year?

d. What will be the total revenues from audit services next year based on the expected hours and the billing rates?

e. Based on the job costing system, what will the reported cost of audit services be next year?

f. Based on the job costing system, what will be the cost of advisory services?

g. What is the expected profit of audit services next year?

h. What is the expected profit of advisory services next year?

i. Write a memo for A&R senior executives outlining some issues they should consider when making a decision about the two product lines.

SOLUTIONS TO SELF-STUDY QUESTIONS

1. The journal entries for the transactions follow.

a.	Direct Materials Inventory	10,000	
	Accounts Payable		10,000
b.	Work-in-Process Inventory	8,000	
	Manufacturing Overhead Control	2,000	
	Direct Materials Inventory		10,000
c.	Work-in-Process Inventory	6,000	
	Manufacturing Overhead Control	1,000	
	Wages Payable		7,000
d.	Manufacturing Overhead Control	13,000	
	Accounts Payable		9,000
	Accumulated Depreciation		4,000
e.	Work-in-Process Inventory	12,000	
	Applied Manufacturing Overhead		12,000

Based on a predetermined rate of 150%
(= $120,000 ÷ $80,000) of direct materials cost
(= $8,000 from entry [*b*])

2. The journal entries for the transactions follow:

a.	Finished Goods Inventory	22,000	
	Work-in-Process Inventory		22,000
b.	Cost of Goods Sold	22,000	
	Finished Goods Inventory		22,000
	Cash	27,000	
	Revenue		27,000
c.	Applied Manufacturing Overhead	12,000	
	Cost of Goods Sold	4,000	
	Manufacturing Overhead Control		16,000

8

Chapter Eight

Process Costing

LEARNING OBJECTIVES

After reading this chapter, you should be able to:

LO 8-1   Explain the concept and purpose of equivalent units.

LO 8-2   Assign costs to products using a five-step process.

LO 8-3   Assign costs to products using weighted-average costing.

LO 8-4   Prepare and analyze a production cost report.

LO 8-5   Assign costs to products using first-in, first-out (FIFO) costing.

LO 8-6   Analyze the accounting choice between FIFO and weighted-average costing.

LO 8-7   Know when to use process or job costing.

LO 8-8   Compare and contrast operations costing with job costing and process costing.

Zu Sanchez Photography/Getty Images

" We have developed a pretty good network of stores willing to stock our juices. Most of them are located in the region and I make it a point to visit every one of them at least once a quarter. What I thought might be a pleasant visit has often turned to a pointed exchange on having to reduce our prices. The stores have a lot of choices for juice suppliers. Although I think our juices are better, if the customer is not willing to pay a bit more, we face two choices: reduce our price or go out of business. I am willing to reduce our prices if we can still make some profit. So I have been reviewing our costs carefully. We operate three plants. Two of the plants focus on a single product and are located near our fruit suppliers. The third plant produces multiple specialty juices. We don't seem to face too much pressure on our specialty juices, but the juices from the two focused plants concern me.

I just found out from the plant cost accountant that we have some choices in calculating our costs. I am going to investigate this a bit to see if we have been operating at a disadvantage because of our cost system. I know that the method used to report costs will not change the costs that the plant incurs, but I still want the best information I can get. I need to decide which costing method will give me the best information for decision making and best reflect the results here at the plant."

Jamie Douglas is the owner and founder of Apple State Juices (ASJ). ASJ makes various fruit juices and focuses on organic and specialty juices. The Exeter Plant makes only one product—apple juice. A botanist by training, Jamie has been spending more time with the plant cost accountant to understand better how the cost system works. She wants to make sure that she is making decisions based on good cost information.

We continue our discussion of the details of a product costing system in this chapter by developing a process costing system. As we discussed in Chapter 6, the difference between job order and process costing is not conceptual but is the level at which costs are aggregated before they are assigned to the individual units of product.

Exhibit 8.1 provides a graphical comparison of typical cost flows in a job costing and a process costing system. In job costing, each job

- Is considered unique.
- May or may not follow the same path through production as other jobs.

Process costing assumes that all units

- Are homogeneous.
- Follow the same path through the production processes.

As you will see at the end of this chapter, you can easily adapt either a job costing or process costing system to reflect production flows that are neither as unique as assumed with a job costing system nor as homogeneous as assumed with a process costing system.

Determining Equivalent Units

In Chapter 6, we introduced the concept of product costing in a continuous process industry. The key difference between manufacturing products using a continuous process and manufacturing products in a discrete production environment in terms of product costing is that in a continuous process, individual units are difficult to distinguish because they are homogeneous. A reasonable assumption is that all units in a large group cost the same. As a result, we compute the costs of these large groups, or *batches,* and then assume that all units in each batch have the same cost.

In a continuous production process

- Some product is always just finishing the process.
- Some product is just beginning it.
- Some product is about one-half complete.

LO 8-1
Explain the concept and purpose of equivalent units.

Exhibit 8.1

Comparison of Cost
Flows in Job Costing and
Process Costing

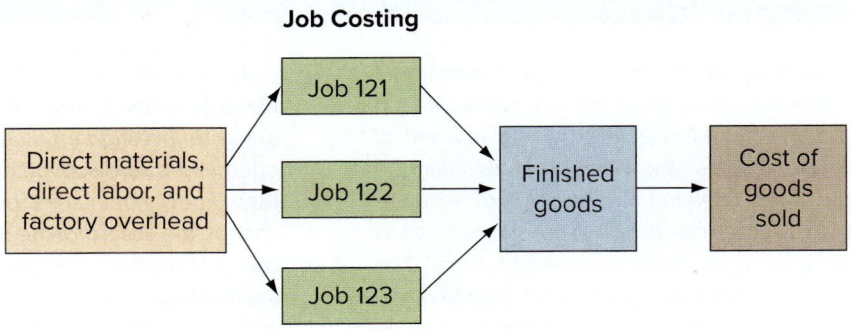

Job Costing

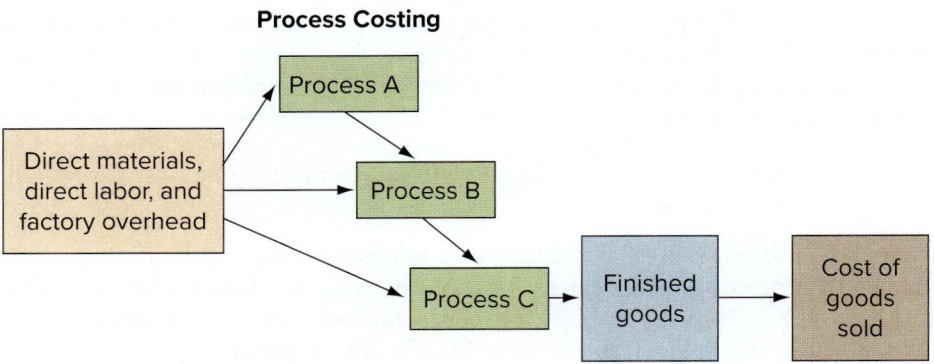

Process Costing

This variation in completion is what defines a continuous production process. In the case of Miller Paints in Chapter 6, we introduced the notion of equivalent units as a measure of output. It allowed us to compare units that were completed with units that were still in process. That is, we cannot consider the physical unit (gallon of paint) that has been finished to be the same as (equivalent to) a gallon of partially complete paint that is in work in process.

If we want to compare the physical units in the work-in-process inventory to completed units, we could ask a knowledgeable manager to estimate "how complete" the units in work in process are relative to a fully complete unit. In other words, we could ask,

"What percentage of the work has been done on the units in work in process, on average?"

equivalent units

Number of complete physical
units to which units in
inventories are equal in terms
of work done to date.

An **equivalent unit** is the number of physical units multiplied by the estimated percentage that an "average" unit in inventory is "complete" with respect to the individual resource.

We can illustrate the concept graphically by continuing the paint example. Suppose that paint production simply consisted of (slowly) filling one-gallon cans of paint along an assembly line. Exhibit 8.2 illustrates that at the end of the month, three cans of paint are filled as indicated. (A can is complete when it is 100 percent full.) Based on the information in Exhibit 8.2, we would say that the ending work-in-process inventory is 65 percent complete, on average. That is, there are three cans, so

$$65\% = \frac{(30\% + 75\% + 90\%)}{3}$$

Exhibit 8.2   Equivalent
Unit Concept

30%

75%

90%

Using Product Costing in a Process Industry

The batches we costed in Chapter 6 were the units that had been transferred out of the department and the units that remained in the department as part of work-in-process ending inventory. We will continue that approach in this chapter. The approach we follow is summarized in the following five steps:

LO 8-2

Assign costs to products using a five-step process.

1. Measure the physical flow of resources.
2. Compute the equivalent units of production.
3. Identify the costs to assign to products.
4. Compute the costs per equivalent unit.
5. Assign product cost to batches of work.

Apple State Juices (ASJ) produces and bottles various fruit juices with an emphasis on being organic and natural. The Exeter Plant at ASJ is a focused plant producing apple juice. Production at ASJ's Exeter Plant takes place in three steps, one in each of three different departments, as shown in Exhibit 8.3. Apples (the primary material) are added at the beginning of the process in the Shredding Department. The apples are shredded using large, high-speed blades. The resulting pulp is then transferred out to the Pressing Department. Finally, the juice from the Pressing Department is finished in the Pasteurization and Packaging Department.

The cost of pulp from the Shredding Department is computed using process costing.

Step 1: Measure the Physical Flow of Resources

We first collect information on the production of juice during March in the Shredding Department.

- On March 1, 20,000 gallons of pulp were in work-in-process inventory.
- During March, Shredding started work on 92,000 gallons of pulp (*not* including the pulp already in process).
- During March, 96,000 gallons of pulp were transferred out to the Pressing Department.
- On March 31, 16,000 gallons remained in work-in-process inventory.

Exhibit 8.4 summarizes these data on the physical flow of resources for the Shredding Department for March. Notice that the information in Exhibit 8.4 uses the inventory equation to ensure that we have accounted for the work done. That is,

$$\begin{array}{ccccccc} \text{Beginning work-in} \\ \text{process inventory} \end{array} + \text{Units started} = \text{Unit transferred out} + \begin{array}{c} \text{Ending work-in-} \\ \text{process inventory} \end{array}$$

$$20,000 \quad + \quad 92,000 \quad = \quad 96,000 \quad + \quad 16,000$$

Step 2: Compute the Equivalent Units of Production

There is one important difference between ASJ and Miller Paints, the company we analyzed in Chapter 6. At Miller, all the resources were added continuously throughout the production process, so we did not consider materials and conversion costs (labor and overhead) separately. At ASJ's Shredding Department, all materials are added at the beginning of the process. Labor and overhead (conversion resources) are added continuously

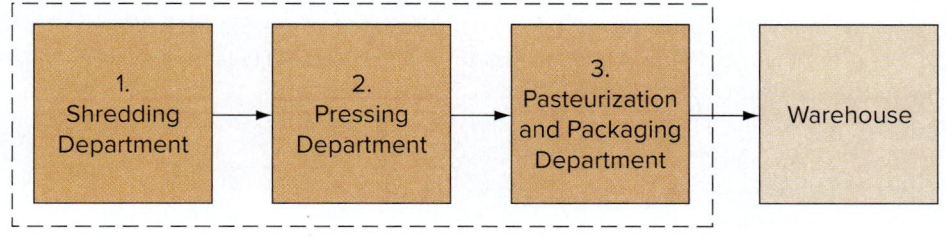

Exhibit 8.3
Production Process—
Apple State Juices (ASJ)

Exhibit 8.4

Shredding Department, March: Physical Flow of Resources

	A	B	C	D
1		Gallons of Pulp		
2				
3	Work in process, March 1	20,000[a]		
4	+ Gallons of pulp started	92,000		
5	Total gallons to account for			112,000
6				
7	= Transferred out to Pressing Department	96,000		
8	+ Work in process, March 31	16,000[b]		
9	Total units accounted for			112,000
10				

[a] 25% complete with respect to conversion costs.
[b] 30% complete with respect to conversion costs.

Exhibit 8.5   Shredding Department, March: Equivalent Units

	A	B	C	D	E
1				Equivalent Units	
2		Physical		Materials	Conversion
3		Units			
4	Transferred out	96,000		96,000	96,000
5	Work in process, March 31	16,000[a]		16,000	4,800
6	Total work			112,000	100,800
7					

[a] 30% complete with respect to conversion.

throughout the process. The calculation of equivalent units, therefore, has to be done separately for each resource (materials and conversion) introduced during the process.

Once started, any gallon of pulp must be fully complete, that is, 100 percent complete, with respect to materials. How complete a gallon of pulp is with respect to conversion costs depends on how far along in the production process it is.

Exhibit 8.5 provides additional detail on operations in the Shredding Department for March including the calculation of equivalent units.

Business Application   **Overstating Equivalent Units to Commit Fraud**

Most managers have incentives to perform well. Their bosses (e.g., top management, the board of directors, the firm's stockholders) use measures of income to measure performance. Consequently, managers have incentives to manipulate income numbers to make them look good. This is not to say that all or even most managers do manipulate the income numbers, just that they have incentives to do so.

One way to manipulate income numbers is to overstate the stage of completion of ending inventory in process costing. Overstating the stage of completion in ending inventory assigns more costs to ending inventory and less costs to goods transferred out of work-in-process inventory. Understating the cost of goods transferred out of work-in-process inventory also understates the cost of goods sold when those goods

are sold. In turn, understating cost of goods sold overstates gross margin and net income, thereby making the business unit appear to be performing better than it actually is.

The Securities and Exchange Commission (SEC) investigated Rynco Scientific Corporation, a manufacturer of contact lenses, for just such a problem. The SEC alleged that Rynco made errors in calculating the equivalent units of ending inventory, which materially overstated ending inventory and understated losses. Because of the SEC's allegations, Rynco agreed to restate its financial statements to conform to generally accepted accounting principles.

Source: Author's research of U.S. Securities and Exchange Commission files.

	A	B	C	D
1		Total	Materials	Conversion
2		Costs	Costs	Costs
3	Work in process, March 1	$ 24,286	$ 16,160	$ 8,126
4	Current costs (March)	298,274	84,640	213,634
5	Total	$ 322,560	$ 100,800	$ 221,760
6				

Exhibit 8.6

Shredding Department,
March: Cost Information

We see from Exhibit 8.5 that 96,000 gallons of pulp have been transferred to the Pressing Department. We also know that each gallon of pulp transferred out is, by definition, 100 percent complete with respect to both materials and conversion. Therefore, 96,000 equivalent units of material resources (= 96,000 gallons × 100%) and 96,000 equivalent units of conversion resources (= 96,000 gallons × 100%) have also been transferred out. The 16,000 gallons of pulp in ending work in process are 100 percent complete as to material resources and 30 percent complete with respect to conversion. Therefore, the work done in March includes 16,000 equivalent units of material resources (= 16,000 × 100%) and 4,800 equivalent units of conversion resources (= 16,000 gallons × 30%). The total work done in March in the Shredding Department is 112,000 equivalent units of material resources and 100,800 equivalent units of conversion resources.

Step 3: Identify the Product Costs for Which to Account

Once we have accounted for the work done, we next collect data on the costs incurred during the period. See Exhibit 8.6 for the costs for the Shredding Department in March. Notice that these costs are collected separately for the two different resources, materials and conversion. Also, the costs in Shredding include not only those incurred for production during March but also those in the beginning work-in-process inventory.

Required: An Assumption about Costs and the Work-in-Process Inventory

If you recall the case of Miller Paints in Chapter 6, the calculation of product cost was simplified by two factors:

1.   All resources at Miller were added continuously, so we did not have to compute different equivalent units for materials and conversion resources.
2.   Miller did not have any beginning work-in-process inventory.

ASJ has both beginning work-in-process inventory and different equivalent units for materials and conversion costs.

The work that has been done in ASJ's Shredding Department in March comes from two sources:

1.   Work done in March (current work).
2.   Beginning work-in-process inventory (work done in February).

In computing product costs, we have two choices:

1.   We can ignore the month in which the work was done and calculate product costs by combining the work (and costs) for February and March.
2.   We can consider the work done in the two months separately and calculate unique costs for the work done in the current month and in the beginning inventory.

The first approach, combining the work and costs, uses the average cost of the current work and the work in inventory. The average is weighted by the number of (equivalent) units in each batch. This approach is called **weighted-average process costing.**

The second approach, separating the costs of the current work and work in beginning inventory, assumes that all beginning work-in-process units are transferred out first. This

weighted-average process costing
Inventory method that for product costing purposes combines costs and equivalent units of a period with the costs and the equivalent units in beginning inventory.

Exhibit 8.7
Comparison of Weighted-Average and FIFO Process Costing: Unit Cost Computations

Costs:	Work-in-process costs	Current period costs
Work (EU)ᵃ:	Work-in-process EU	Current period EU

Weighted average: **Weighted-Average Unit Costs**

$$\frac{\text{Work-in-process costs} + \text{Current period costs}}{\text{Work-in-process EU} + \text{Current period EU}}$$

FIFO: **Work-in-Process Unit Costs**   **Current Period Unit Costs**

$$\frac{\text{Work-in-process costs}}{\text{Work-in-process EU}} \qquad \frac{\text{Current period costs}}{\text{Current period EU}}$$

ᵃ Equivalent unit.

first-in, first-out (FIFO) process costing
Inventory method whereby the first goods received are the first ones charged out when sold or transferred.

means that the ending work in process comes from the work started during the current month. This approach is called **first-in, first-out (FIFO) process costing.**

We continue our example assuming that the Shredding Department uses weighted-average process costing. We then recompute the calculations assuming that the department uses FIFO process costing to illustrate the differences. Keep in mind that, conceptually, the two approaches do the same thing: average the cost of production over all units produced. The difference is the *way* that the costs and work are aggregated. Weighted-average process costing combines the work and the costs for the two periods (the last and current period) and computes a single cost. FIFO process costing keeps the two periods separate. Exhibit 8.7 shows the difference between weighted-average and FIFO process costing by demonstrating the difference in aggregation. We have costs from two periods. In addition to the current period costs, costs from the last period are in the beginning work in process. We also have work (equivalent units) from the last period and the current period.

Weighted-average costing adds the costs together first and then divides this total cost by the total work for the two periods. FIFO keeps the costs and the work separate and, in effect, computes separate unit costs for the two periods.

Which approach is "better"? We compare and contrast the two approaches after we describe how they work. For now, remember that our focus is on *information for decision making*. If the choice does not affect the decisions that managers make, this is not an issue on which the firm should spend much time.

Step 4: Compute the Costs per Equivalent Unit: Weighted Average

LO 8-3
Assign costs to products using weighted-average costing.

Now that we have decided to compute cost using weighted-average process costing, we can continue the computation of product costs for March. Exhibit 8.8 illustrates the calculation of the equivalent unit cost for each of the resources. In the exhibit, the costs for

Exhibit 8.8 Shredding Department, March: Computing Equivalent Unit Costs

	A	B	C	D
1		Total	Materials	Conversion
2		Costs	Costs	Costs
3	Work in process, March 1	$ 24,286	$ 16,160	$ 8,126
4	Current costs (March)	298,274	84,640	213,634
5	Total	$ 322,560	$ 100,800	$ 221,760
6				
7	Total equivalent units (from Exhibit 8.5)		112,000	100,800
8	Cost per equivalent unit		$ 0.90	$ 2.20
9				

Exhibit 8.9   Shredding Department, March: Product Costs

	A	B	C	D	E	F	G	H
1		Total		Materials			Conversion	
2	Transferred out:							
3	Equivalent units			96,000			96,000	
4	Cost per equivalent unit		X	$ 0.90		X	$ 2.20	
5	Cost assigned	$ 297,600			$ 86,400			$ 211,200
6	Work in process, March 31							
7	Equivalent units			16,000			4,800	
8	Cost per equivalent unit		X	$ 0.90		X	$ 2.20	
9	Cost assigned	24,960			14,400			10,560
10	Total cost assigned	$ 322,560			$ 100,800			$ 221,760
11								

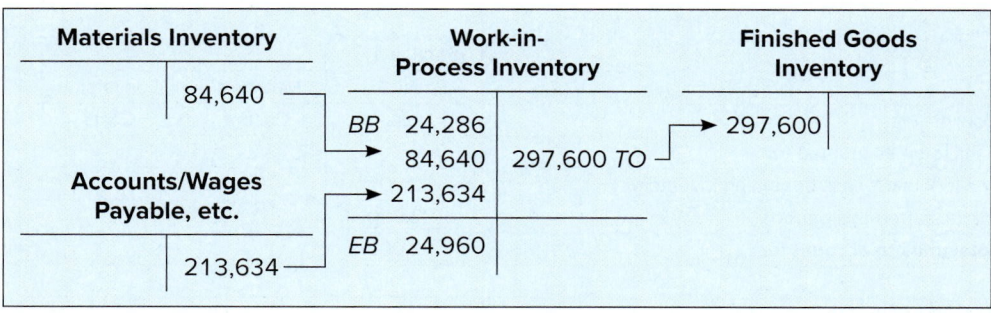

Exhibit 8.10
T-Accounts and Cost Flows: Weighted-Average Process Costing, March

BB: Beginning balance.
EB: Ending balance.
TO: Transferred-out.

current work and work in beginning work in process are combined. This total cost is then divided by the total equivalent units of work for March.

Step 5: Assign Product Cost to Batches of Work: Weighted-Average Process Costing

The final step is to assign the total costs to the two batches of work: pulp transferred out to the Pressing Department and pulp that is not yet complete, that is, the ending work-in-process inventory. We have all the information that we need. We know the number of equivalent units in the two batches (from step 2) and the cost per equivalent unit (from step 4). Exhibit 8.9 shows the calculation. Don't forget to check that the total cost assigned in step 5 ($322,560) is the same as the total cost to account for from step 3 ($322,560).

Recording the Cost Flows in T-Accounts   You may find it helpful for understanding process costing to see how costs flow through T-accounts. Exhibit 8.10 shows the flow of costs through the T-accounts for the Shredding Department for March. Compare these flows with the results in Exhibit 8.9.

production cost report
Report that summarizes production and cost results for a period; generally used by managers to monitor production and cost flows.

Reporting This Information to Managers: The Production Cost Report

The **production cost report** summarizes the production and cost results for a period. It is an important document for managers who monitor the flow of production and costs. Using this report, managers can determine whether inventory levels are getting too high, costs are not low enough, or the number of units produced is too low.

Exhibit 8.11 presents a production cost report for ASJ's Shredding Department at the Exeter Plant for March. Although it may look complex, you will soon see that this report includes the five steps for assigning costs to goods transferred out and to ending

LO 8-4
Prepare and analyze a production cost report.

work-in-process inventory that we described earlier. In fact, this report summarizes the information in Exhibits 8.4, 8.5, 8.6, 8.8, and 8.9. We present the report in five sections, each of which corresponds to a step, to help relate the production cost report to those five steps.

Exhibit 8.11   Production Cost Report: Weighted-Average Process Costing

	A	B	C	D	E	F	G
1	APPLE STATE JUICES						
2	Shredding Department						
3	For the Month Ending March 31						
4							
5				(Section 2)			
6				Equivalent Units			
7							
8		(Section 1)					
9		Physical		Materials		Conversion	
10	*Flow of Units*	Units		Costs		Costs	
11	Units to be accounted for:						
12	In work-in-process beginning inventory	20,000[a]					
13	Units started this period	92,000					
14	**Total units to account for**	112,000					
15							
16	Units accounted for:						
17	Completed and transferred out	96,000		96,000		96,000	
18	In work-in-process ending inventory	16,000		16,000[a]		4,800[b]	
19	**Total units accounted for**	112,000		112,000		100,800	
20							
21				Costs			
22				(Sections 3 through 5)			
23							
24				Materials		Conversion	
25		Total		Costs		Costs	
26	*Flow of Costs*						
27	Costs to be accounted for (Section 3):						
28	Costs in work-in-process beginning inventory	$ 24,286		$ 16,160		$ 8,126	
29	Current period costs	298,274		84,640		213,634	
30	**Total costs to be accounted for**	$ 322,560		$ 100,800		$ 221,760	
31							
32	Costs per equivalent unit (Section 4)			$ 0.90[c]		$ 2.20[d]	
33							
34	Costs accounted for (Section 5):						
35	Costs assigned to transferred-out units	$ 297,600		$ 86,400[e]		$ 211,200[f]	
36	Costs assigned to work-in-process ending inventory	24,960		14,400[g]		10,560[h]	
37	**Total costs accounted for**	$ 322,560		$ 100,800		$ 221,760	
38							

[a] 100% complete with respect to materials.
[b] 30% complete with respect to conversion.
[c] $0.90 = $100,800 ÷ 112,000 equivalent units (EU)
[d] $2.20 = $221,760 ÷ 100,800 EU
[e] $86,400 = 96,000 EU × $0.90 per EU
[f] $211,200 = 96,000 EU × $2.20 per EU
[g] $14,400 = 16,000 EU × $0.90 per EU
[h] $10,560 = 4,800 EU × $2.20 per EU

Sections 1 and 2: Managing the Physical Flow of Units

Sections 1 and 2 of the production cost report correspond to steps 1 and 2 of the cost flow model. Section 1 summarizes the flow of physical units and shows 112,000 units to be accounted for, 96,000 as transfers out and 16,000 in ending inventory. Section 2 shows the equivalent units for direct materials and conversion costs separated into equivalent units transferred out and equivalent units remaining in work-in-process inventory.

Sections 3, 4, and 5: Managing Costs

Sections 3, 4, and 5 provide information about costs. Corresponding to step 3, section 3 shows the costs to be accounted for, $24,286 in beginning inventory and $298,274 incurred during March. Section 4 shows how to compute the cost per equivalent unit for materials ($0.90) and conversion costs ($2.20). Finally, section 5 shows the cost assignment performed in step 5 for direct materials and conversion costs.

We now have assigned costs to units, shown cost flows through T-accounts, and reported the steps performed on the production cost report. Having followed the five-step procedure in the text, you now have an opportunity to practice assigning costs in Self-Study Question 1.

Self-Study Question

1. J&S Lubricants is a small, local operation that makes only one product, a specialty lubricant for manufacturing operations. The following data are available for operations in its Blending Department during October:

	Barrels	Percent Complete	Costs
Beginning work-in-process inventory, October 1	1,000		
Materials costs		25%	$ 1,113
Conversion costs		10	194
Units started in October	5,000		
Costs incurred in October			
Materials costs			22,487
Conversion costs			14,056
Ending work-in-process inventory, October 31	500		
Materials costs		80	?
Conversion costs		40	?

Using weighted-average process costing, prepare a cost of production report for October.

The solution to this question is at the end of the chapter.

Assigning Costs Using First-In, First-Out (FIFO) Process Costing

A disadvantage of weighted-average costing is that it mixes current period costs with the costs of products in beginning inventory, making it impossible for managers to know how much it cost to make a product *this period*. First-in, first-out (FIFO) costing assumes that the first units worked on are the first units transferred out of a production department. Whereas weighted-average costing mixes current period costs and costs from prior periods that are in beginning inventory, FIFO separates current period costs from those in beginning inventory. FIFO costing transfers out the costs in beginning inventory in a lump sum (assuming that the units in beginning inventory were completed during the current period) but does not mingle them with current period costs.

FIFO gives managers better information about the work done in the current period. Managers benefit from this separation of current period costs from costs in beginning inventory because they can identify and manage current period costs.

LO 8-5

Assign costs to products using first-in, first-out (FIFO) costing.

If the production process is a FIFO process, the inventory numbers are more likely to reflect reality under FIFO costing than under weighted-average costing because the units in ending inventory are likely to have been produced in the current period. FIFO costing assigns current period costs to those units, but weighted-average costing mixes current and prior period costs in assigning a value to ending inventory.

To illustrate accounting for process costing using FIFO, we use the data from the ASJ example introduced earlier. This enables us to compare FIFO and weighted-average costing and see how the results differ. Recall the following facts:

	A	B	C	D	E
1				Materials	Conversion
2		Units		Costs	Costs
3	Work in process, March 1	20,000[a]		$ 16,160	$ 8,126
4	Current costs (March)	92,000		84,640	213,634
5	Total			$ 100,800	$ 221,760
6					
7	Transferred out	96,000			
8	Work in process, March 31	16,000[b]			
9					

[a] 25% complete with respect to conversion costs.
[b] 30% complete with respect to conversion costs.

Computing product costs using a FIFO process costing system requires the same five-step procedure as the weighted-average approach. The difference is in the application. For convenience, we repeat the five steps here:

1. Measure the physical flow of resources.
2. Compute the equivalent units of production.
3. Identify the costs to assign to products.
4. Compute the costs per equivalent unit.
5. Assign product cost to batches of work.

Exhibit 8.12 is a production cost report for March using FIFO process costing. We present it now and will refer to it as we go through the five steps, which will reduce the need to repeat the material that is unchanged from the weighted-average method.

Step 1: Measure the Physical Flow of Resources

As with the weighted-average method, we begin the costing process with information on the production of pulp during March in the Shredding Department. As we would expect, the choice of accounting for production costs does not change the physical flow of production, so this part of the report is identical to that for the weighted-average method.

Step 2: Compute the Equivalent Units of Production

Computing equivalent units is different in FIFO costing than in weighted-average costing. Recall that FIFO costing separates what was in beginning inventory from what occurs this period. The FIFO equivalent unit computation is confined only to what was produced this period. Under FIFO, we compute equivalent units in three parts for both direct materials and conversion costs:

1. Equivalent units to complete beginning work-in-process inventory.
2. Equivalent units of goods started and completed during the current period.
3. Equivalent units of goods still in ending work-in-process inventory.

For the Shredding Department, 20,000 units in beginning inventory were 100 percent complete for materials and 25 percent complete for conversion costs at the beginning of the period. Completing the beginning inventory required no additional equivalent units

Exhibit 8.12   Production Cost Report—FIFO Process Costing

	A	B	C	D	E	F	G
1		**APPLE STATE JUICES**					
2		**Shredding Department**					
3		**For the Month Ending March 31**					
4							
5				(Section 2)			
6				Equivalent Units			
7							
8		(Section 1)					
9		Physical		Materials		Conversion	
10	Flow of Units	Units		Costs		Costs	
11	Units to be accounted for						
12	In work-in-process beginning inventory	20,000					
13	Units started this period	92,000					
14	**Total units to account for**	112,000					
15							
16	Units accounted for						
17	Completed and transferred out						
18	From beginning work in process	20,000		20,000		20,000	
19	Started and completed	76,000		76,000		76,000	
20	Total completed and transferred out	96,000		96,000		96,000	
21	In work-in-process ending inventory	16,000		16,000[a]		4,800[b]	
22	**Total units accounted for**	112,000		112,000		100,800	
23	**Less work from beginning work in process**	20,000		20,000		5,000[c]	
24	**New work done in March**	92,000		92,000		95,800	
25							
26			Costs (Sections 3 through 5)				
27							
28	Costs:			Materials		Conversion	
29		Total		Costs		Costs	
30	Flow of Costs						
31	Costs to be accounted for (Section 3)						
32	Costs in work-in-process beginning inventory	$ 24,286		$ 16,160		$ 8,126	
33	Current period costs	298,274		84,640		213,634	
34	**Total costs to be accounted for**	$ 322,560		$ 100,800		$ 221,760	
35							
36	Costs per equivalent unit (Section 4)						
37	(Current period costs ÷ New work done)			$ 0.92[d]		$ 2.23[e]	
38							
39	Costs accounted for (Section 5)						
40	Costs assigned to units transferred out						
41	Costs from beginning work-in-process inventory	$ 24,286		$ 16,160		$ 8,126	
42	Current costs to complete beginning						
43	work-in-process inventory	33,450		–		33,450[f]	
44	Total costs from beginning work-in-process						
45	inventory	$ 57,736		$ 16,160		$ 41,576	
46	Current costs of units started and completed	239,400		69,920[g]		169,480[h]	
47	Total costs transferred out	$ 297,136		$ 86,080		$ 211,056	
48	Costs assigned to work-in-process ending inventory	25,424		14,720[i]		10,704[j]	
49	**Total costs accounted for**	$ 322,560		$ 100,800		$ 221,760	
50							

[a] 100% complete with respect to materials.
[b] 30% complete with respect to conversion.
[c] 5,000 = 20,000 units × 25% complete
[d] $0.92 = $84,640 ÷ 92,000 equivalent units (EU)
[e] $2.23 = $213,634 ÷ 95,800 EU

[f] $33,450 = 15,000 EU × $2.23 per EU
[g] $69,920 = 76,000 EU × $0.92 per EU
[h] $169,480 = 76,000 EU × $2.23 per EU
[i] $14,720 = 16,000 EU × $0.92 per EU
[j] $10,704 = 4,800 EU × $2.23 per EU

for materials [= (100% − 100%) × 20,000 units], and 15,000 equivalent units for conversion costs [= (100% − 25%) × 20,000 units].

The units started and completed can be derived by examining the physical flow of units. Because 92,000 units were started and 16,000 of them remain in ending inventory, according to the FIFO method, the remaining 76,000 were completed. Thus, 76,000 units were started and completed. Another way to get the same result is to observe that of the 96,000 units completed during March, 20,000 came from beginning inventory (according to the FIFO method), so the remaining 76,000 units completed must have been started during March.

Either way you view the physical flow, 76,000 units were started and completed. Because these 76,000 units are 100 percent complete when transferred out of the department, the units started and completed represent 76,000 equivalent units produced during the current period for both direct materials and conversion costs.

Finally, we have the equivalent units of production in ending inventory.[1] Ending inventory of 16,000 units is 100 percent complete with respect to materials and 30 percent complete for conversion costs. Thus, there are 16,000 equivalent units (= 100% × 16,000) for materials in ending work-in-process inventory and 4,800 equivalent units (= 30% × 16,000) for conversion costs in ending work-in-process inventory. These equivalent unit results appear in section 2 of the production cost report in Exhibit 8.12.

You will note that the equivalent units under FIFO are less than or equal to those under weighted average because the FIFO computations refer to the current period's production only. Weighted-average equivalent units consider all units in the department, whether produced this period or in a previous period. (If the department has no beginning inventory, the weighted-average and FIFO equivalent units are equal.)

Step 3: Identify the Product Costs for Which to Account

The total costs to be accounted for under FIFO costing are the same as in weighted-average costing. Whatever our assumption about cost flows, we must account for all costs in the department, composed of those in beginning inventory plus those incurred during the period. For the Shredding Department, these costs are as follows:

	A	B	C	D
1		Total	Materials	Conversion
2		Costs	Costs	Costs
3	Work in process, March 1	$ 24,286	$ 16,160	$ 8,126
4	Current costs (March)	298,274	84,640	213,634
5	Total	$ 322,560	$ 100,800	$ 221,760
6				

Step 4: Compute the Costs per Equivalent Unit: FIFO

Under FIFO, the costs per equivalent unit are confined to the costs incurred this period, $298,274, and the equivalent units produced this period, which were computed in step 2 (92,000 for materials and 95,800 for conversion costs). In formula form,

$$\text{Cost per equivalent unit} = \frac{\text{Current period costs}}{\text{Equivalent units of production this period}}$$

---

[1] For our examples, units in ending inventory come from the current period production. Although it is unlikely, you could encounter cases in practice when the inventory levels are so high relative to current period production that some of the beginning inventory is still in ending inventory. In that case, you should keep the costs and units in ending inventory that come from beginning inventory separate. Having separated those costs and units, you can perform the computations described in the text for the current period costs.

Note that only current period costs are included in the numerator. The FIFO method excludes the beginning work-in-process costs from the cost per equivalent unit calculation. Only the costs of finishing the beginning work-in-process units are included.

For the Shredding Department in March, the cost per equivalent unit under FIFO is calculated here:

Materials Costs:

$$\text{Cost per equivalent unit} = \frac{\$84,640}{92,000 \text{ equivalent units}}$$
$$= \$0.92 \text{ per equivalent unit}$$

Conversion Costs:

$$\text{Cost per equivalent unit} = \frac{\$213,634}{95,800 \text{ equivalent units}}$$
$$= \$2.23 \text{ per equivalent unit}$$

The cost per equivalent unit appears in section 4 of the production cost report.

Step 5: Assign Product Cost to Batches of Work: FIFO

The cost of goods transferred out comprises the first three of the following components, or $297,136.

Costs in beginning work-in-process inventory (March 1)	$ 24,286
Costs to complete beginning inventory	33,450
Cost of the 76,000 units started and completed this period.	239,400
Cost of ending work-in-process inventory	25,424
Total costs accounted for.	$322,560

These results appear in section 5 of the production cost report, Exhibit 8.12. Note that the costs to be accounted for in section 3, $322,560, equal the costs accounted for in section 5, $322,560.

How This Looks in T-Accounts

See Exhibit 8.13 for the flow of costs through the Work-in-Process Inventory T-accounts for the Shredding Department using FIFO. Again, the purpose of presenting the T-accounts is to give you an overview of the cost flows associated with the process costing computations.

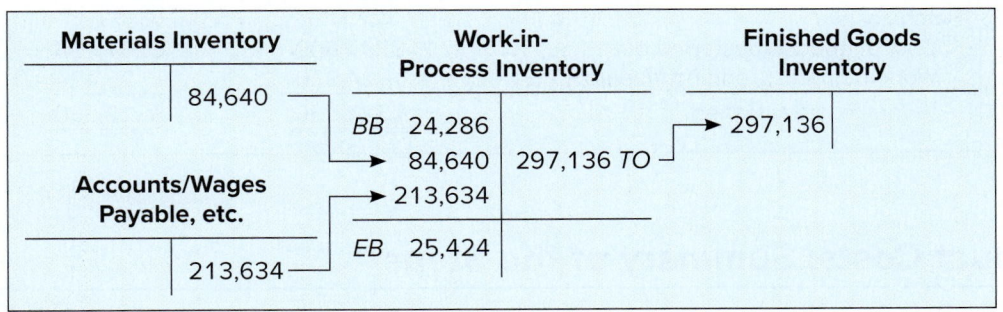

BB: Beginning balance.
EB: Ending balance.
TO: Transferred out.

Exhibit 8.13

T-Accounts and Cost Flows: FIFO Process Costing, March

Self-Study Question

2. Consider the data for October for J&S Lubricants in Self-Study Question 1. Using FIFO process costing, prepare a cost of production report for October.

The solution to this question is at the end of the chapter.

Determining Which Is Better: FIFO or Weighted Average?

LO 8-6

Analyze the accounting choice between FIFO and weighted-average costing.

Weighted-average costing does not separate beginning inventory from current period activity. Unit costs are a weighted average of the two, whereas FIFO costing bases unit costs on current period activity only. The difference in the costs from the two methods is larger when either (or both)

- The number of units in beginning work-in-process inventory is large relative to the number of units started during the period or
- Price changes from period to period are large.

In either or both of these cases, the FIFO method results in unit costs that better reflect current costs. Otherwise, beginning work-in-process inventory has little influence on the average unit cost using the weighted-average approach.

Exhibit 8.14 compares the unit costs, costs transferred out, and ending work-in-process inventory values under the two methods for ASJ's Shredding Department at the Exeter Plant. Although either weighted-average or FIFO costing is acceptable for assigning costs to inventories and cost of goods sold for external reporting, the weighted-average method has been criticized for masking current period costs. Thus, using weighted-average costing, the unit costs reported for March are based not only on the costs incurred in March but also on the costs of previous periods that were in beginning inventory on March 1. For example, synthetic rubber producers such as Goodyear or plastic producers such as DuPont use oil as a raw material in their products. They purchase oil on an international commodities market with frequent price changes. Managers at these companies require knowledge of current period costs. If computational and recordkeeping costs are about the same under both FIFO and weighted average, FIFO costing generally offers greater decision-making benefits.

Exhibit 8.14

Comparison of Weighted-Average and FIFO Process Costing

	Weighted-Average (from Exhibit 8.11)	FIFO (from Exhibit 8.12)
Equivalent unit costs		
Materials..........................	$ 0.90	$ 0.92
Conversion costs	2.20	2.23
Batch costs		
Cost of goods transferred out	$297,600	$297,136
Work in process, ending inventory	24,960	25,424
Total costs assigned.................	$322,560	$322,560

Computing Product Costs: Summary of the Steps

See Exhibit 8.15 for a summary of the steps for assigning costs to units of product using process costing and assuming either a weighted-average or FIFO cost flow. The steps in Exhibit 8.15 correspond to the production cost report used by managers to monitor production and cost flows.

Step 1: Record the physical flow of resources.

Step 2: Compute the equivalent units of production.

Weighted average: EU produced = Units transferred out + EU in ending work-in-process (WIP) inventory

FIFO: EU produced = EU to complete beginning WIP inventory + Units started and finished during the period + EU in ending WIP inventory

Step 3: Identify the total costs to be accounted for.

Total costs to be accounted for = Costs in beginning WIP inventory + Costs incurred this period

Step 4: Compute costs per equivalent unit.

Weighted average:

$$\text{Unit cost} = \frac{\text{Costs in beginning WIP inventory} + \text{Current period costs}}{\text{Units transferred out} + \text{EU in ending WIP inventory}}$$

FIFO:

$$\text{Unit cost} = \frac{\text{Current period costs}}{\text{EU in current work done}}$$

Step 5: Assign costs to batches of work (transferred out and work-in-process ending inventory).

Weighted average: Using weighted average, the cost of goods transferred out equals the total units transferred out times the weighted-average unit cost computed in step 4.

Using weighted average, the cost of goods in ending work-in-process inventory equals the equivalent units in ending work-in-process inventory times the weighted-average unit cost computed in step 4.

FIFO: Using FIFO, the cost of goods transferred out equals the sum of the following three items:

1. The costs already in beginning work-in-process inventory at the beginning of the period.
2. The current period cost to complete beginning work-in-process inventory, which equals the equivalent units to complete beginning work-in-process inventory from step 2 times the current period unit cost computed for FIFO in step 4.
3. The costs to start and complete units, calculated by multiplying the number of units started and finished from step 2 times the cost per equivalent unit computed for FIFO in step 4.

Using FIFO, the cost of goods in ending work-in-process inventory equals the equivalent units in ending work-in-process inventory from step 2 times the cost per equivalent unit computed for FIFO in step 4.

Exhibit 8.15

Summary of Steps for Assigning Costs to Products Using Process Costing

Using Costs Transferred in from Prior Departments

Our discussion so far has treated the Shredding Department as if it existed by itself at ASJ. We know from the description of the production process at ASJ, however, that the Shredding Department transfers finished pulp to the Pressing Department, where additional work is done. As the product passes from one department to another, its costs must follow.

The costs of units transferred out of one department and into another are called **prior department costs** or *transferred-in costs*. The cost of processing cereal at Kellogg's is a prior department cost to the Packaging Department. Equivalent whole units are 100 percent complete in terms of prior department costs, so cost computations for prior department costs are relatively easy.

It is important to distinguish between prior *department* costs and prior *period* costs. Prior department costs are conceptually equivalent to raw materials costs. They differ only by who produced them. Raw materials are purchased from vendors outside the

prior department costs
Manufacturing costs incurred in some other department and transferred to a subsequent department in the manufacturing process.

firm; prior department costs arise from partially completed product produced by another department within the firm.

Prior period costs are costs that were incurred in a previous accounting period and are recorded as Work-in-Process Inventory. Prior period costs might include prior department costs, but prior department costs will never include prior period costs of the current department.

The Pressing Department at ASJ takes the pulp from the Shredding Department and presses the pulp to obtain juice. It adds various stabilizing agents and preservatives when the pulp is 25 percent complete with respect to conversion resources in the Pressing Department. That is, the finished pulp comes into the Pressing Department and some processing begins. When the additional processing is 25 percent complete, the materials (stabilizing agents and preservatives) are added.

See Exhibit 8.16, which is the production cost report for the Pressing Department for March. As you can see in Exhibit 8.16, the Pressing Department uses weighted-average process costing, as does the Shredding Department. We know that the Shredding Department uses weighted-average process costing because the transferred-in costs from the Pressing Department in Exhibit 8.16 are the weighted-average costs computed in Exhibit 8.11. It is important to understand that the two departments could use different costing methods. As far as the Pressing Department is concerned, the pulp it receives from the Shredding Department is just like any other material it uses. The *way* the costs were computed is not a concern, although the *amount* of the cost is.

Who Is Responsible for Costs Transferred in from Prior Departments?

An important question for performance evaluation is whether a department manager should be held accountable for all costs charged to the department. The answer is usually no. A department and its people are usually evaluated on the basis of costs the department added relative to its goods output. A prior department's costs are often excluded when comparing actual department costs with a standard or budget. We discuss this point more

Self-Study Question

3. The Canning Department at J&S Lubricants receives the blended lubricant in barrels and packages it in cans for sale. The following data are available for operations in the Canning Department during August. (Note that the units here are *cans*, not barrels.

	Cans	Percent Complete	Costs
Beginning work-in-process (WIP) inventory, August 1	50,000		
Transferred-in costs		100%	$ 6,998
Materials costs		–0–	–0–
Conversion costs		5	69
Units started in August	240,000		
Costs incurred in August			
Transferred-in costs			$33,602
Materials costs			58,000
Conversion costs			7,611
Ending WIP inventory, August 31	40,000		
Transferred-in costs		100	?
Materials costs		100	?
Conversion costs		15	?

Using weighted-average process costing, prepare a cost of production report for August for the Canning Department.

The solution to this question is at the end of the chapter.

Exhibit 8.16   Production Cost Report—Weighted-Average Process Costing

	A	B	C	D	E	F	G	H	I
1		APPLE STATE JUICES							
2		Pressing Department							
3		For the Month Ending March 31							
4									
5						(Section 2)			
6						Equivalent Units			
7									
8		(Section 1)							
9		Physical		Transferred-		Materials		Conversion	
10	Flow of Units	Units		in Costs		Costs		Costs	
11	Units to be accounted for								
12	In work-in-process beginning inventory	20,000[a]							
13	Units started this period	96,000							
14	**Total units to account for**	116,000							
15									
16	Units accounted for								
17	Completed and transferred out	91,000		91,000		91,000		91,000	
18	In work-in-process ending inventory	25,000		25,000		25,000[b]		15,000[c]	
19	**Total units accounted for**	116,000		116,000		116,000		106,000	
20									
21						Costs			
22						(Sections 3 through 5)			
23									
24				Transferred-		Materials		Conversion	
25		Total		in Costs		Costs		Costs	
26	Flow of Costs								
27	Costs to be accounted for (Section 3)								
28	Costs in work-in-process beginning inventory	$ 56,584		$ 48,664		$ –		$ 7,920	
29	Current period costs	715,780		297,600[d]		208,800		209,380	
30	**Total costs to be accounted for**	$ 772,364		$ 346,264		$ 208,800		$ 217,300	
31									
32	Costs per equivalent unit (Section 4)			$ 2.99[e]		$ 1.80[f]		$ 2.05[g]	
33									
34	Costs accounted for (Section 5)								
35	Costs assigned to transferred-out units	$ 621,988		$ 271,638[h]		$ 163,800[i]		$ 186,550[j]	
36	Costs assigned to work-in-process ending inventory	150,376		74,626[k]		45,000[l]		30,750[m]	
37	**Total costs accounted for**	$ 772,364		$ 346,264		$ 208,800		$ 217,300	
38									

[a] 20% complete with respect to conversion.

[b] 100% complete with respect to materials.

[c] 60% complete with respect to conversion.

[d] See Exhibit 8.11.

[e] $2.99 = $346,264 ÷ 116,000 equivalent units (EU). (This result is rounded.)

[f] $1.80 = $208,800 ÷ 116,000 EU

[g] $2.05 = $217,300 ÷ 106,000 EU

[h] $271,638 = 91,000 EU × $2.99 per EU (based on unit cost before rounding)

[i] $163,800 = 91,000 EU × $1.80 per EU

[j] $186,550 = 91,000 EU × $2.05 per EU

[k] $74,626 = 25,000 EU × $2.99 per EU

[l] $45,000 = 25,000 EU × $1.80 per EU

[m] $30,750 = 15,000 EU × $2.05 per EU

extensively in later chapters on performance evaluation, but we mention it here to empha-size that different information is needed for different purposes. Assigning costs to units for inventory valuation requires that a prior department's costs be included in department product cost calculations. However, assigning costs to departments for performance evalu-ation usually requires that a prior department's costs be excluded from departmental costs.

Choosing between Job and Process Costing

LO 8-7
Know when to use process or job costing.

In job costing, costs are collected for each unit produced, as discussed at the beginning of this chapter. For example, a print shop collects costs for each order, a defense contractor collects costs for each contract, and a custom home builder collects costs for each house. Process costing accumulates costs in a department for an accounting period (for example, a month) and then spreads them evenly, or on an average basis, over all units produced that month. Process costing assumes that each unit produced is relatively uniform. The following example compares cost flows under each method.

Barry's Builders constructs custom homes. In the last year, it started and completed three homes (there were no unfinished homes—no inventory). The cost to build each home follows.

Home 1	$ 100,000
Home 2	200,000
Home 3	450,000
Total	$750,000

Suppose (unrealistically) that Barry's Builders had used process costing and defined each home as a single unit of product. Total costs were $750,000, so each home is assigned a cost of $250,000.

Note that with process costing, Barry's Builders does not maintain a record of the cost of each unit produced. Process costing has less detailed recordkeeping; hence, if a company were choosing between job and process costing, it would generally find lower recordkeeping costs under process costing. Of course, process costing does not provide as much information as job costing because it does not record the cost of each unit pro-duced. The choice of process versus job costing systems involves a comparison of the costs and benefits of each system. The production process being utilized is also a major factor in choosing a cost system.

operations costing
Hybrid costing system used in manufacturing goods that have some common characteristics and some individual characteristics.

The difference between job costing and process costing is in the level of aggregation and detail, not in the basic concepts. To see this, suppose that Barry's Builders built large devel-opments, with each house identical except, perhaps, for some minor design changes. In this case, Barry's Builders might reasonably choose a cost system that resembles a process cost-ing system, or operations costing system, because each house (unit) is essentially identical.

Operations Costing

LO 8-8
Compare and contrast operations costing with job costing and process costing.

Operations costing is a hybrid of job and process costing (see Exhibit 8.17). The costs of resources that are applied to products in a roughly uniform way are assigned to products using process costing methods. The costs of resources that are applied in a unique way to products (special materials, for example) are assigned to the individual products as in job order costing.

Exhibit 8.17   A Comparison of Three Product Costing Methods

Job Costing	Operations Costing	Process Costing
Job shops make customized products.	Operations separate materials for each batch; common processes are used to produce products.	Mass production is used in continuous processes.

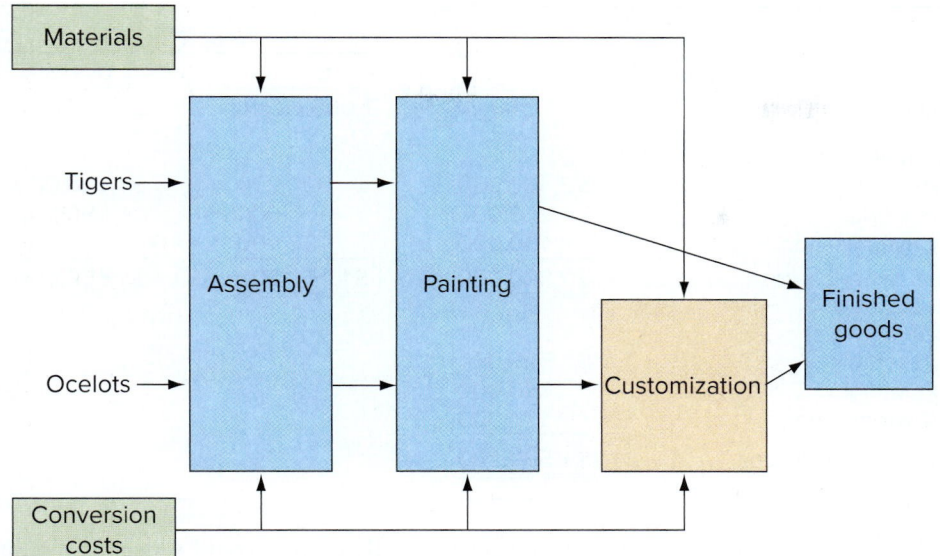

Exhibit 8.18
Operations—St. Ignace Sports Company

Operations costing is used in manufacturing goods that have some common characteristics plus some individual characteristics. An **operation** is a standardized method of making a product that is repeatedly performed. For example, the European company Faurecia makes automobile seats. Different seats use different materials, but attaching the material to the seat assembly is an operation.

operation
Standardized method or technique that is repeatedly performed in making a product.

Product Costing in Operations

The key difference between operations costing and the two methods discussed in this chapter and the previous chapter, job and process costing, is that for each work order or batch passing through a particular operation:

- Direct materials are different.
- Conversion costs (direct labor and manufacturing overhead) are the same.

For example, assume that St. Ignace Sports Company makes two models of snowmobiles, Ocelots and Tigers. The Ocelot has a larger engine and generally more costly materials than the Tiger. See Exhibit 8.18 for the flow of products through St. Ignace's three departments, Assembly, Painting, and Customization. (For our purposes, each department has one operation.) Notice that Tigers pass through only the first two departments, where operations are identical for both types of snowmobiles, but Ocelots pass through all three departments. Materials costs are added to both models in Assembly and Painting and to Ocelots in Customization. Materials are considered separately in the Painting Department for the two models because more costly paint, with better rust protection, is used for the Ocelots. Conversion costs are added to Tigers in the first two departments and to Ocelots in all three departments.

Operations Costing Illustration

Getting ready for the next winter season, the managers at St. Ignace Sports Company issue the following two production work orders for the month of July. Each work order is also called a *batch*. See Exhibit 8.19 for the data on production and costs associated with this work order.

The materials costs are identified easily for the two models because they depend on the engine type, body trim, and so on. For example, assembly materials costs are $450 per snowmobile for Ocelots (= $900,000 ÷ 2,000 units) and $300 per snowmobile for Tigers (= $1,500,000 ÷ 5,000 units). However, the conversion costs are assumed to be the same for each model.

Exhibit 8.19

July Production and
Costs—St. Ignace Sports
Company

| | | Work Order: | |
| | | 07-14 | 07-15 |
Units	Total	2,000 Ocelots	5,000 Tigers
Materials			
Assembly................	$2,400,000	$ 900,000	$1,500,000
Painting.................	250,000	100,000	150,000
Customization............	150,000	150,000	–0–
Total materials cost..........	$2,800,000	$1,150,000	$1,650,000
Conversion			
Assembly................	$ 525,000		
Painting.................	840,000		
Customization............	174,000		
Total conversion cost........	$1,539,000		

The costing of these two products proceeds exactly as you would expect, given our discussion of product costing systems. The system that is used is formally called an *operations costing system.* It assigns materials cost to the specific products for which the underlying materials are used. For example, the engines are taken from the direct materials inventory and the model for which they will be used is recorded. (In this case, of course, such detailed records are not needed because there are only two engines and two models of snowmobiles. Each engine is unique to each model.) Thus, for materials costs, the costing system operates like a job order system.

Within a department at St. Ignace, the products are processed in the same way. That is, Ocelots and Tigers are indistinguishable as far as the use of the conversion resources within a department. Therefore, the cost system treats each snowmobile as one of many homogeneous units. A process costing system is appropriate for the conversion resources.

St. Ignace never has any work-in-process inventories, so the process costing system is extremely simple. It allocates conversion costs to the snowmobiles by simply dividing the total conversion costs by the number of snowmobiles.

See Exhibit 8.20 for the July costing summary for St. Ignace Sports Company. The conversion cost for Painting, for example, is assigned to the two models based on total units. Thus, each snowmobile is assigned $120 of conversion cost in the Painting Department (= $840,000 ÷ 7,000 units). The total Painting Department conversion cost assigned to Ocelots, then, is $240,000 (= $120 per unit × 2,000 units).

Although we combined all labor and overhead costs into conversion costs, we could have assigned the direct labor and manufacturing overhead separately to production as

Exhibit 8.20

July Product Costing
Report—St. Ignace Sports
Company

	Total	2,000 Ocelots	5,000 Tigers
Materials			
Assembly................	$2,400,000	$ 900,000	$1,500,000
Painting	250,000	100,000	150,000
Customization	150,000	150,000	–0–
Total materials cost..........	$2,800,000	$1,150,000	$1,650,000
Conversion			
Assembly................	$ 525,000	$ 150,000	$ 375,000
Painting	840,000	240,000	600,000
Customization	174,000	174,000	–0–
Total conversion cost	$1,539,000	$ 564,000	$ 975,000
Total product cost	$4,339,000	$1,714,000	$2,625,000
Number of units		2,000	5,000
Cost per unit		$ 857	$ 525

Exhibit 8.21   T-Accounts and Cost Flows: FIFO Process Costing for July—St. Ignace Sports Company

Materials Inventory					Wages Payable and Factory Overhead (Conversion Costs)		
BB	3,000,000	900,000	(1-Ocelots)			525,000	(2)
		1,500,000	(1-Tigers)			840,000	(5)
		100,000	(4-Ocelots)			174,000	(8)
		150,000	(4-Tigers)				
		150,000	(7-Ocelots)				

Work-in-Process Inventory Assembly Department				Work-in-Process Inventory Painting Department			
(1-Ocelots)	900,000	1,050,000	(3-Ocelots)	(3-Ocelots)	1,050,000	1,390,000	(6-Ocelots)
(1-Tigers)	1,500,000			(3-Tigers)	1,875,000	2,625,000	(6-Tigers)
(2)	525,000	1,875,000	(3-Tigers)	(4-Ocelots)	100,000		
				(4-Tigers)	150,000		
				(5)	840,000		

Work-in-Process Inventory Customization Department				Finished Goods Inventory			
(6-Ocelots)	1,390,000	1,714,000	(9-Ocelots)	(9-Ocelots)	1,714,000		
(7-Ocelots)	150,000			(6-Tigers)	2,625,000		
(8)	174,000						

(1-Ocelots): Transfer of materials costs to Assembly Department for Ocelots.

(1-Tigers): Transfer of materials costs to Assembly Department for Tigers.

(2): Charge to Assembly Department for conversion costs.

(3-Ocelots): Transfer of Ocelot costs from Assembly Department to Painting Department.

(3-Tigers): Transfer of Tiger costs from Assembly Department to Painting Department.

(4-Ocelots): Transfer of materials costs to Painting Department for Ocelots.

(4-Tigers): Transfer of materials costs to Painting Department for Tigers.

(5): Charge to Painting Department for conversion costs.

(6-Ocelots): Transfer of Ocelot costs from Painting Department to Customization Department.

(6-Tigers): Transfer of Tiger costs from Painting Department to Finished Goods Inventory.

(7-Ocelots): Transfer of materials costs to Customization Department for Ocelots.

(8): Charge to Customization Department for conversion costs.

(9-Ocelots): Transfer of Ocelot costs from Customization Department to Finished Goods Inventory.

well. In many companies, direct labor is such a small portion of the total product cost that the accountants classify direct labor as part of manufacturing overhead. See Exhibit 8.21 for the flow of these costs through T-accounts to Finished Goods Inventory.

Companies generally apply manufacturing overhead using predetermined overhead rates. As noted in Chapter 7, when using predetermined rates, overhead can be over-applied or underapplied compared to actual manufacturing overhead. The treatment of overapplied or underapplied overhead is the same with either process costing or operations costing. It is treated as an expense or allocated to inventories if the goods are still in inventory, as explained in Chapter 7.

Comparing Job, Process, and Operations Costing

We have discussed how to account for product costs in three types of organizations: job shops, such as custom furniture makers, that use job costing; organizations with continuous flow processing, such as beverage manufacturers, that use process costing; and companies with operations, such as automobile manufacturers, that use operations costing.

Operations costing combines the aspect of job costing that assigns materials separately to jobs (also called *work orders* or *batches* in operations costing) with the aspect of process costing that assigns conversion costs equally to each operation. Thus, in our snowmobile example, Ocelots had different per-unit materials costs but the same operations costs per unit for the two operations that both models passed through.

In practice, you are likely to find elements of all three production methods and thus find elements of all three costing methods. When thinking about the appropriate product costing system, do not try to fit all systems into one of these three categories. You will find that every company has its own unique costing methods that do not precisely fit any textbook description. Studying these three basic costing methods will enable you to figure out the variations on the methods presented here and choose the system that provides managers the best information for the decisions they make routinely.

Self-Study Question

4. Rigney Corporation manufactures two models of travel alarms, the M-24 and the D-12, which differ only in the quality of plastic used for the cases. Production takes place in two departments—Manufacturing and Finishing.

Data for the only two work orders for February are shown in the following table. Conversion costs are allocated based on the number of units produced. There are no work-in-process inventories.

	Total	M-24 (5,000 units)	D-12 (9,000 units)
Materials			
Manufacturing	$42,500	$20,000	$22,500
Conversion costs			
Manufacturing	42,000		
Finishing	21,000		
Total conversion costs	$63,000		

What is the cost per unit transferred to finished goods inventory for the two models, M-24 and D-12, in February?

The solution to this question is at the end of the chapter.

Key Takeaways

1. Process costing spreads or averages manufacturing costs (both direct and indirect) across all units of production. Units of production are assumed to be the same (homogeneous) and therefore unit costs are the same.
2. There are two approaches:
   a. Weighted-average process costing assumes all production costs are spread over all production, regardless of whether the work was done in the current or prior period.
   b. First-in, first-out (FIFO) process costing assigns costs incurred in the period to production in the period.

Production costs in work-in-process inventory are assumed to be transferred out first, leaving only current costs in ending work-in-process inventory.
3. Operations costing is a hybrid system with some costs assigned as in job costing (materials, for example) and other costs assigned as in process costing. All three costing methods (job, process, and operations) assign production costs to units of production. The difference among the three is how differentiated the costs are among the different units of production.

SUMMARY

Process costing is used when it is not possible or practical to identify costs with specific units of product. The two most common methods of process costing are *first-in, first-out (FIFO) costing* and *weighted-average costing*. FIFO costing separates current period costs from beginning inventory costs. The weighted-average method makes no distinction between beginning inventory and current period costs. As a result, weighted-average computations are simpler. The FIFO method is potentially more informative, however, because it tracks current and previous period costs separately.

Exhibit 8.15 is a summary of the steps required to assign costs to units. In comparing the weighted-average and FIFO methods, note the importance of matching costs with units. Weighted-average costing includes beginning inventory (that is, work done in a previous period) in computing both equivalent units and unit costs; FIFO costing excludes beginning inventory in computing equivalent units and unit costs.

Process costing systems accumulate costs for each production department but do not maintain separate records of costs for each unit produced. When comparing job and process costing, companies generally find that job costing provides more data but has higher recordkeeping costs. Managers and accountants must decide whether the additional data available under job costing justify these higher costs. For companies that produce relatively homogeneous units in a continuous process, cost-benefit analysis generally favors process costing.

The following summarizes key ideas tied to the chapter's learning objectives:

LO 8-1 Explain the concept and purpose of equivalent units. Equivalent units are used to measure production in continuous production processes and are necessary because when the accounting reports are prepared, some units are not complete but have used resources.

LO 8-2 Assign costs to products using a five-step process. The five-step procedure we develop can be used to summarize the flow of products and costs and then combine them to develop unit costs for determining the costs of inventory.

LO 8-3 Assign costs to products using weighted-average costing. When beginning work-in-process (WIP) inventory exists, we must choose between the weighted-average and FIFO costing methods. The five-step process is crucial in helping allocate production costs to finished goods inventory and ending WIP inventory using unit costs that are a weighted average of the costs in beginning inventory and those from the current period.

LO 8-4 Prepare and analyze a production cost report. The production cost report summarizes the costs allocated to finished goods inventory and ending WIP inventory. Managers use this report to monitor production and cost flows.

LO 8-5 Assign costs to products using first-in, first-out (FIFO) costing. The FIFO costing method assumes that all beginning WIP inventory is completed and transferred out during the period. Costs are tracked accordingly. The five-step process is also used for the FIFO method.

LO 8-6 Analyze the accounting choice between FIFO and weighted-average costing. Weighted-average costing does not separate beginning inventory from current period activity. Unit costs are a weighted average of the two, whereas under FIFO costing, unit costs are based on current period activity only. If computational and recordkeeping costs are about the same under both methods, FIFO costing is generally preferred.

LO 8-7 Know when to use process or job costing. In general, job costing systems are more costly (and reflect unit costs better) than process costing systems. In deciding which system to use, accountants and managers must decide whether the benefits of implementing a job costing system outweigh the costs associated with such a system.

LO 8-8 Compare and contrast operations costing with job costing and process costing. Operations costing is a hybrid of job costing and process costing. Operations costing is often used when different products use common processes but differ in their materials.

KEY TERMS

equivalent units, *336*
first-in, first-out (FIFO) process costing, *340*
operation, *353*
operations costing, *352*

prior department costs, *349*
production cost report, *341*
weighted-average process costing, *339*

REVIEW QUESTIONS

8-1. What are the characteristics of industries most likely to use process costing?
8-2. A manufacturing company has records of its activity during the month in work-in-process inventory and of its ending work-in-process inventory; however, the record of its beginning inventory has been lost. What data are needed to compute the beginning inventory? Express them in equation form.
8-3. If costs increase from one period to another, will costs that are transferred out of one department under FIFO costing be higher or lower than costs transferred out using weighted-average costing? Why?

8-4.   What are the five steps to follow when computing costs using a process costing system?

8-5.   What is the distinction between equivalent units under the FIFO method and equivalent units under the weighted-average method?

8-6.   Which method, weighted-average or FIFO, better reflects the current cost of production when using process costing?

8-7.   It has been said that a prior department's costs behave similarly to direct materials costs. Under what conditions are the costs similar? Why account for them separately?

8-8.   The more important individual unit costs are for making decisions, the more likely it is that process costing will be preferred to job costing. Do you agree?

8-9.   Assume that the number of units transferred out of a department is unknown. What is the formula to solve for units transferred out using the basic cost flow model?

8-10.   In what way are job costing, process costing, and operations costing similar? In what way do they differ?

CRITICAL ANALYSIS AND DISCUSSION QUESTIONS

8-11.   The management of a liquid cleaning product company is trying to decide whether to install a job or process costing system. The manufacturing vice president has stated that job costing gives the best control because it is possible to assign costs to specific lots of goods. The controller, however, has stated that job costing requires too much recordkeeping. Would a process costing system meet the manufacturing vice president's control objectives? Explain.

8-12.   We have discussed two methods for process costing, weighted average and FIFO. Your colleague recommends last-in, first-out (LIFO) process costing to the controller as a new system. The controller is concerned about the recommendation because the cost records are maintained on a FIFO basis. Indeed, the controller has not even heard of using LIFO for process cost accounting. Can you suggest how the controller might resolve the problem?

8-13.   A friend owns and operates a consulting firm that works for a single client under one consulting agreement. The consulting firm bills the client monthly for charges incurred. She asks you whether you would recommend a job costing or process costing system for her business. What would you recommend? Why?

8-14.   The controller of a local firm that uses a continuous production process asks you to recommend whether the company should use weighted-average or FIFO process costing. What factors would you consider in making a recommendation?

8-15.   Throughout the chapter, we treated conversion costs (direct labor and manufacturing overhead) as a single resource. Why could we do this without distorting the resulting costs? When would we need to treat them separately?

8-16.   Consider a manufacturing firm with multiple departments all using continuous production processes and process costing. Suppose Department A transfers product to Department B for completion to the final product. Is it necessary that both departments use the same cost-flow assumption (weighted-average vs. FIFO)? Why?

8-17.   In the chapter, we said that the costs from a prior department are often excluded when comparing a department's cost with its standards or budgets. However, when a department buys materials from an outside firm, those costs would almost always be part of the evaluation process. Why might a firm treat prior period costs differently for evaluation purposes from direct materials costs for items purchased from another firm?

8-18.   Would process costing work well for a service firm? Why or why not?

8-19.   A firm produces a product by sending it through three production departments (A, B, and C). A uses job costing, B uses operations costing, and C uses process costing. Is this possible? Why? Is this likely? Why?

EXERCISES      All applicable Exercises are included in Connect.

(LO 8-1, 3)   **8-20. Compute Equivalent Units: Weighted-Average Method**

Trevor Mills produces agricultural feed at its only plant. Materials are added at the beginning of the process. Information on work-in-process in December follows:

* Beginning inventory, 16,000 partially complete units, 10 percent complete with respect to conversion costs.

- Units started in December, 77,000 units.
- Units transferred out in December, 73,000 units.
- Ending inventory, 20,000 units, 62 percent complete with respect to conversion costs.

Required

Compute the equivalent units for materials and conversion costs for December using the weighted-average method.

8-21. Compute Equivalent Units: FIFO Method
Refer to the data in Exercise 8-20.

(LO 8-1, 5)

Required

Compute the equivalent units for materials and conversion costs for December using the FIFO method.

8-22. Compute Equivalent Units: Weighted-Average Method
Patton Dyes manufactures colorings, primarily for textiles. Information on the work in process follows:

(LO 8-1, 3)

- Beginning inventory, 115,000 partially complete liters.
- Ending inventory, 85,000 liters; units are 25 percent complete with respect to materials and 60 percent complete with respect to conversion costs.
- Started this month, 690,000 liters.

Required
a.   Compute the equivalent units for materials using the weighted-average method.
b.   Compute the equivalent units for conversion costs using the weighted-average method.

8-23. Compute Equivalent Units: FIFO Method
Refer to the data in Exercise 8-22. Assume that beginning inventory is 20 percent complete with respect to materials and 40 percent complete with respect to conversion costs.

(LO 8-1, 5)

Required
a.   Compute the equivalent units for materials using FIFO.
b.   Compute the equivalent units for conversion costs using FIFO.

8-24. Compute Equivalent Units: Weighted-Average Method
Kronk, Inc. provides the following information concerning the work in process at its plant:

(LO 8-1, 3)

- Beginning inventory was partially complete (materials are 100 percent complete; conversion costs are 10 percent complete).
- Started this month, 65,000 units.
- Transferred out, 62,000 units.
- Ending inventory, 36,000 units (materials are 100 percent complete; conversion costs are 65 percent complete).

Required
a.   Compute the equivalent units for materials using the weighted-average method.
b.   Compute the equivalent units for conversion costs using the weighted-average method.

8-25. Compute Equivalent Units: FIFO Method
Refer to the data in Exercise 8-24.

(LO 8-1, 5)

Required
a.   Compute the equivalent units for materials using FIFO.
b.   Compute the equivalent units for conversion costs using FIFO.

8-26. Compute Equivalent Units

Radford Products adds materials at the beginning of the process in Department A. The following information on physical units for Department A for the month of January is available.

Units started in January..	890,000
Units completed in January..	914,000
Work in process, January 1 (25% complete with respect to conversion)	96,000
Work in process, January 31 (40% complete with respect to conversion)	72,000

Required

a. Compute the equivalent units for materials costs and for conversion costs using the weighted-average method.

b. Compute the equivalent units for materials costs and for conversion costs using the FIFO method.

(LO 8-5) **8-27. Equivalent Units: FIFO Process Costing**

When using the FIFO method of process costing, total equivalent units produced for a given period equal

a. The number of units started and completed during the period plus the number of units in beginning work in process plus the number of units in ending work in process.

b. The number of units in beginning work in process plus the number of units started during the period plus the number of units remaining in ending work in process times the percentage of work necessary to complete the items.

c. The number of units in beginning work in process times the percentage of work necessary to complete the items plus the number of units started and completed during the period plus the number of units started this period and remaining in ending work in process times the percentage of work done on the units during the period.

d. The number of units transferred out during the period plus the number of units remaining in ending work in process times the percentage of work necessary to complete the items.

e. None of the above.

(CPA adapted)

(LO 8-3) **8-28. Compute Equivalent Units: Weighted-Average Method**

The following data are taken from the production records at the Bay Plant of Charlevoix Chemicals for May. Work-in-process beginning inventory consisted of 43,000 units fully complete with respect to materials and 22 percent complete with respect to conversion costs. In May, the plant started 240,000 units and transferred out 228,000 units. The work-in-process ending inventory was fully complete with respect to materials and 80 percent complete with respect to conversion costs.

Required

Charlevoix Chemicals uses weighted-average process costing at the Bay Plant for product costing. The following equivalent units (materials; conversion) used to compute production costs for May would be

a. (283,000; 272,000).

b. (240,000; 240,000).

c. (283,000; 262,540).

d. (240,000; 262,540).

e. None of the above.

(LO 8-5) **8-29. Compute Equivalent Units: FIFO Method**

Refer to the data in Exercise 8-28 for Charlevoix Chemicals.

Required

Charlevoix Chemicals uses FIFO process costing at the Bay Plant for product costing. The following equivalent units (materials; conversion) used to compute production costs for May would be

a. (283,000; 272,000).

b. (240,000; 240,000).

c.   (283,000; 262,540).

d.   (240,000; 262,540).

e.   None of the above.

8-30. Compute Equivalent Units: Ethical Issues

(LO 8-1, 3, 5)

Hoyt, Inc. has a process costing system at its Forest Street Plant. All materials are introduced when conversion costs reach 40 percent. The following information is available for physical units during August:

Units started in August.	163,000
Units transferred out to Finishing Department in August.	178,000
Work in process, August 1 (85% complete as to conversion costs).	41,000
Work in process, August 31 (25% complete as to conversion costs)	26,000

Required

a.   Compute the equivalent units for materials costs and for conversion costs using the weighted-average method.

b.   Compute the equivalent units for materials costs and for conversion costs using the FIFO method.

c.   The company president has been under considerable pressure to increase income. He tells the controller to change the estimated completion for ending work in process to 45 percent (from 25 percent).

1.   What effect will this change have on the unit costs of units transferred to finished goods in August?
2.   Would this be ethical?
3.   Is this likely to be a successful strategy for affecting income over a long period of time?

8-31. Equivalent Units and Cost of Production

(LO 8-3)

By mistake, the production supervisor at East Manufacturing transposed the digits on the production report and reported a higher percentage of completion for each inventory component. Assume that there was no beginning inventory.

Required

What is the effect of this error on the following?

a.   The computation of total equivalent units.

b.   The computation of costs per equivalent unit.

c.   Costs assigned to work-in-process ending inventory.

(CPA adapted)

8-32. Compute Costs per Equivalent Unit: Weighted-Average Method

(LO 8-3)

The following information about the work-in-process inventory pertains to the Remington Plant for the month of July (all materials are added at the beginning of the process):

	Materials	Conversion
Beginning work in process (26,000 units):		
Percentage complete with respect to.	100%	20%
Costs.	$83,600	$18,636
Ending work in process (42,000 units)		
Percentage complete with respect to.	100%	60%
Costs.	??	??

The Remington Plant started 216,000 units and transferred out 200,000 in July. Materials costs incurred in July were $594,000 and conversion costs were $979,000.

Required

Compute the cost per equivalent unit for materials and conversion costs using the weighted-average method.

(LO 8-5)   **8-33. Compute Costs per Equivalent Unit: FIFO Method**
Refer to the data in Exercise 8-32.

Required
Compute the cost per equivalent unit for materials and conversion costs using the FIFO method.

(LO 8-1, 5)   **8-34. Compute Equivalent Units and Cost per Equivalent Unit: FIFO Method**
Shirley Processing, Inc. (SPI) makes adhesive tape and uses a FIFO process costing system. The following information shows the physical flow of units and costs for the month of March:

	A	B	C	D
1			Percentage Complete	
2	Quantities	Physical units	Materials	Conversion
3	Beginning work-in-process	105,000	100%	40%
4	Started	956,000		
5	To account for	1,061,000		
6				
7	Transferred out	973,500	100%	100%
8	Ending work-in-process	87,500	100%	20%
9	Accounted for	1,061,000		
10				
11	Costs:	Total	Direct Mat.	Conversion
12	Beginning work-in-process	$ 182,570	$ 165,180	$ 17,390
13	Current Period	1,830,970	1,214,120	616,850
14	Total	$ 2,013,540	$ 1,379,300	$ 634,240
15				
16				

Required
a.   Compute the equivalent units for the materials and conversion cost calculation for March.
b.   Compute the cost per equivalent unit for materials and conversion costs for March.

(LO 8-1, 3)   **8-35. Compute Equivalent Units and Cost per Equivalent Unit: Weighted-Average Method**
Refer to the data in Exercise 8-34.

Required
a.   Compute the equivalent units for the conversion cost calculation for March assuming Shirley Processing, Inc. uses the weighted-average method.
b.   Compute the cost per equivalent unit for materials and conversion costs for March assuming Shirley Processing, Inc. uses the weighted-average method.

(LO 8-3)   **8-36. Cost per Equivalent Unit: Weighted-Average Method**
In computing the cost per equivalent unit, the weighted-average method considers
a.   Current costs less costs in beginning WIP inventory.
b.   Current costs plus the cost of ending WIP inventory.
c.   Current costs plus costs in beginning WIP inventory.
d.   Current costs only.

(CPA adapted)

(LO 8-2, 3)   **8-37. Compute Costs per Equivalent Unit: Weighted-Average Method**
The following cost information is available for July for the Crest Plant at Calvert Company:

Beginning work-in-process inventory
  Materials cost. . . . . $ 56,000
  Conversion cost   35,400
      Total. . . . . $ 91,400
Current costs
  Materials cost $124,000
  Conversion cost   372,600
      Total $496,600

Materials are added at the beginning of the process. The following quantities have been recorded:

- Beginning inventory, 40,000 partially complete gallons, 25 percent complete with respect to conversion costs.
- Units started in July, 80,000 gallons.
- Units transferred out in July, 90,000 gallons.
- Ending inventory, 30,000 gallons, 40 percent complete with respect to conversion costs.

Required
Compute the cost per equivalent unit for direct materials and conversion costs for July using the weighted-average method.

8-38. Assign Costs to Goods Transferred Out and Ending Inventory: (LO 8-2, 3)
Weighted-Average Method
Refer to the data in Exercise 8-37. Compute the cost of goods transferred out and the ending inventory for July using the weighted-average method.

8-39. Compute Costs per Equivalent Unit: FIFO Method (LO 8-2, 5)
Refer to Exercise 8-37. Compute the cost per equivalent unit for direct materials and for conversion costs for July using the FIFO method.

8-40. Assign Costs to Goods Transferred Out and Ending Inventory: FIFO Method (LO 8-2, 5)
Refer to the data in Exercise 8-37. Compute the cost of goods transferred out and the ending inventory for July using the FIFO method.

8-41. Compute Costs per Equivalent Unit: Weighted-Average Method (LO 8-3)
Annin Laboratories uses the weighted-average method to account for its work-in-process inventories. The accounting records show the following information for February:

Beginning WIP inventory	
Direct materials	$ 20,553
Conversion costs	6,805
Current period costs	
Direct materials	225,147
Conversion costs	117,460

Quantity information is obtained from the manufacturing records and includes the following:

Beginning inventory	6,000 units	(40% complete as to materials, 15% complete as to conversion)
Current period units started	44,000 units	
Ending inventory.	11,000 units	(75% complete as to materials, 35% complete as to conversion)

Required
Compute the cost per equivalent unit for direct materials and conversion costs for February.

8-42. Assign Costs to Goods Transferred Out and Ending Inventory: Weighted-Average (LO 8-2, 3)
Method
Refer to the data in Exercise 8-41. Compute the cost of goods transferred out and the ending inventory for February using the weighted-average method.

8-43. Compute Costs per Equivalent Unit: FIFO Method (LO 8-5)
Using the data in Exercise 8-41, compute the cost per equivalent unit for direct materials and for conversion costs for February using the FIFO method.

(LO 8-5)   **8-44. Assign Costs to Goods Transferred Out and Ending Inventory: FIFO Method**
Refer to the data in Exercises 8-41 and 8-43. Compute the cost of goods transferred out and the ending inventory for February using the FIFO method.

(LO 8-3)   **8-45. Compute Costs per Equivalent Unit: Weighted-Average Method**
Bellevue Chemicals had beginning work-in-process inventory of $239,910 on March 1. Of this amount, $101,280 was the cost of direct materials and $138,630 was the cost of conversion. The 24,000 units in the beginning inventory were 45 percent complete with respect to direct materials and 65 percent complete with respect to conversion costs.

During March, 58,000 units were transferred out and 14,000 remained in ending inventory. The units in ending inventory were 70 percent complete with respect to direct materials and 15 percent complete with respect to conversion costs. Costs incurred during March amounted to $820,800 for direct materials and $961,200 for conversion.

Required
Compute the cost per equivalent unit for direct materials and for conversion costs for March using the weighted-average method.

(LO 8-2, 3)   **8-46. Assign Costs to Goods Transferred Out and Ending Inventory: Weighted-Average Method**
Refer to the data in Exercise 8-45. Compute the costs of goods transferred out and the ending inventory for March using the weighted-average method.

(LO 8-5)   **8-47. Compute Costs per Equivalent Unit: FIFO Method**
Refer to the data in Exercise 8-45. Compute the cost per equivalent unit for direct materials and for conversion costs for March using the FIFO method.

(LO 8-2, 5)   **8-48. Assign Costs to Goods Transferred Out and Ending Inventory: FIFO Method**
Refer to the data in Exercise 8-45.

Required
a.   Compute the cost of goods transferred out and the cost of ending inventory for March using the FIFO method.
b.   Is the ending inventory higher or lower under the weighted-average method compared to FIFO? Why?

(LO 8-2, 4, 5)   **8-49. Prepare a Production Cost Report: FIFO Method**
Terminal Industries (TI) produces a product using three departments: Mixing, Processing, and Filtering. New material is added only in the Mixing Department. The following information is given for the Processing Department for August. TI uses process costing.

WIP Inventory—Processing Department: August 1	
Quantity (60% complete)	28,000 units
Transferred-in costs (from Mixing Department)	$33,890
Conversion costs (Processing Department)	13,612
Total WIP cost: August 1	$47,502
Current production and costs (August)	
Units started	75,000 units
Current costs	
Transferred-in costs (from Mixing Department)	$82,500
Conversion costs (Processing Department)	53,060
Total current cost: August	$135,560
WIP Inventory—Processing Department: August 31	
Quantity (20% complete)	13,000 units
Transferred-in costs (from Mixing Department)	??
Conversion costs (Processing Department)	??
Total WIP cost: August 31	??

Required
Prepare a production cost report for August using FIFO.

8-50. Prepare a Production Cost Report: Weighted-Average Method   (LO 8-2, 3, 4, 6)
Refer to the information in Exercise 8-49.

Required

a. Prepare a production cost report for August using the weighted-average method.

b. Is the ending inventory higher using FIFO or the weighted-average method? Why?

c. Would you recommend that Terminal Industries use the FIFO method or the weighted-average method? Explain.

8-51. Prepare a Production Cost Report: Weighted-Average Method   (LO 8-2, 4)
Beverly Plastics produces a part used in precision machining. The part is produced in two depart-ments: Mixing and Refining. The raw material is introduced into the process in the Mixing Department. The cost of the material fluctuates significantly month to month based on market conditions. Information on costs and operations in the Refining Department for September follow:

> WIP inventory—Refining
>   Beginning inventory (17,500 units, 10% complete with respect
>   to Refining costs)
>   Transferred-in costs (from Mixing) $237,055
>   Refining conversion costs 9,676
>   Current work (55,300 units started)
>   Mixing costs $898,625
>   Refining costs 103,140
>   The ending inventory has 22,900 units, which are 90 percent
>   complete with respect to Refining Department costs.

Required
Prepare a production cost report using the weighted-average method.

8-52. Prepare a Production Cost Report: FIFO Method   (LO 8-2, 4, 5, 6)
Refer to the information in Exercise 8-51.

Required

a. Prepare a production cost report using the FIFO method.

b. Is the ending inventory higher using FIFO or the weighted-average method? Why?

c. Would you recommend that Beverly Plastics use the FIFO method or the weighted-average method? Explain.

8-53. Operations Costing   (LO 8-8)
Boulder Toys manufactures powered, ride-on tractors and other equipment for children. There are three models, increasing in features and detail: XL, XLS, and XLT. All three models start in the Assembly Department, where the raw materials are shaped and components, such as tires and motor, are assembled. The XL and XLS models are then sent to the Packaging Department, where they are made ready for delivery to dealers. The XLT models are sent from the Assembly Department to the Customization Department, where they are detailed with various special-order paints and logos.

Boulder Toys uses operations costing and conversion costs are allocated to products based on the number of units produced. No work-in-process inventories exist in any of the three depart-ments. Data for October follow:

	Total	XL	XLS	XLT
Units produced	3,800	1,800	1,350	650
Costs:				
Materials.................	$559,150	$156,600	$180,900	$221,650
Conversion costs				
Assembly	$307,800			
Customization	27,950			
Packaging...............	72,200			
Total conversion costs ...	$407,950			

Required

What is the cost per unit transferred to finished goods inventory for each of the three models in October?

(LO 8-8) **8-54. Operations Costing: Ethical Issues**

Wakefield Instruments manufactures three digital piano models, which differ only in the components included: Solo, Recital, and Concert. Production takes place in two departments, Assembly and Finishing. The Solo and Recital models are complete after the Assembly Department. The Concert model goes from Assembly to Finishing and is completed there. Data for November are shown in the following table. There are no work-in-process inventories.

	Total	Solo	Recital	Concert
Units	3,000	1,500	1,200	300
Expected unit selling price		$210	$375	$525
Costs:				
Materials.	$480,000	$144,000	$240,000	$96,000
Conversion costs:				
Assembly	$268,800			
Finishing	17,820			
Total conversion costs. .	$286,620			

Required

a. Wakefield allocates conversion costs in the Assembly Department based on materials costs. What is the cost per unit transferred to finished goods inventory for each of the three piano models in November?

b. Wakefield has a policy that products have to earn a gross margin percentage of at least 10 percent, where gross margin percentage is computed as the unit gross margin divided by the unit cost of sales. The product manager is concerned about the cost of the Concert model because the competition is strong in this product line. The product manager suggests allocating the Assembly Department costs based on the number of units rather than materials costs as a way to "help" the Concert model.

　　1. What cost would be reported for the three models if the product manager's suggestion is adopted?

　　2. Would this be ethical?

(LO 8-8) **8-55. Operations Costing**

Devereaux Cycles makes three models of scooter: Commuter, Sport, and X-treme. The scooters are produced in four departments: Assembly, Detailing, Customization, and Packaging. All three models are started in Assembly, where all materials are assembled. The Commuter is then sent to Packaging, where it is packaged and transferred to finished goods inventory. The Sport is then transferred to Detailing. Once the detailing process is completed, the Sport models are transferred to Packaging and then finished goods. The X-Treme model is assembled and then transferred to Customization, and then Packaging. When packaged, it is transferred to finished goods.

　　Data for February are shown in the following table. Conversion costs are allocated based on the number of units processed in each department. No work-in-process inventories are maintained in any department.

	Total	Commuter (1,200 units)	Sport (900 units)	X-Treme (400 units)
Materials	$3,670,000	$1,440,000	$1,350,000	$880,000
Conversion costs:				
Assembly	$2,675,000			
Detailing	427,500			
Customization	544,000			
Packaging	367,500			
Total conversion costs . . .	$4,014,000			

Required

a.   Draw the flow of the different models through the production process.

b.   What is the cost per unit transferred to finished goods inventory for each of the three models in February?

8-56. Operations Costing   (LO 8-8)

Hedwig Optical makes three models of binoculars: Travel, Sport, and Pro. The models differ by the size of the casing and the quality of the optics. The binoculars are produced in two departments. The Assembly Department purchases components from vendors and assembles them into binoculars. The Travel and Sport models are complete and ready for sale after completing the assembly process. The Pro model undergoes further processing in the Calibration Department, which is actually just a small area in the same building as the Assembly Department.

Conversion costs in both the Assembly Department and Calibration Department are based on the number of units produced. There are never any work-in-process inventories. Data for production in January are shown in the following table:

	Total	Travel	Sport	Pro
Units produced.............	20,000	10,000	7,500	2,500
Materials cost..............	$1,600,000	$290,000	$847,500	$462,500
Conversion costs				
Assembly	$ 440,000			
Calibration	44,400			
Total conversion costs ...	$ 484,400			

Required

What is the cost per unit transferred to finished goods inventory for each of the three binocular models in January?

PROBLEMS      All applicable Problems are included in Connect.

8-57. Compute Equivalent Units   (LO 8-1, 3, 5)

Select the best answer for each of the following independent multiple-choice questions.

a.   Hillger Paints's production cycle starts in Department A. The following information is available for April:

	Units
Work in process, April 1 (30% complete)	85,000
Started in April	365,000
Work in process, April 30 (70% complete)	63,000

Materials are added at the beginning of the process in Department A. Using the weighted-average method, what are the equivalent units of production for the month of April?

	Materials	Conversion
(1)...............	343,000	368,500
(2)...............	343,000	387,100
(3)...............	450,000	412,500
(4)...............	450,000	431,100
(5)...............	None of the above	

b.   Department S is the fourth, and final, stage of Service Corporation's production cycle. On March 1, beginning work in process contained 95,000 units, which were 80 percent complete as to conversion costs. During March, 610,000 units were transferred in from the third stage of the production cycle. On March 31, ending work in process contained 72,000 units, which were 35 percent complete as to conversion costs. Materials are added when the units are 50 percent complete with respect to conversion costs. Using the weighted-average method, the equivalent units produced during March were as follows:

	Prior Department Costs	Materials	Conversion
(1).........	705,000	633,000	658,200
(2).........	705,000	633,000	633,000
(3).........	750,000	705,000	705,000
(4).........	610,000	659,250	699,500
(5).........	None of the above		

c.   Department X is the first stage of Sarena Solvents's production cycle. The following information is available for conversion costs for the month of December:

	Physical Units
Beginning work-in-process inventory (60% complete).........	45,000
Started in December	530,000
Completed in December and transferred to Department Y	510,000
Ending work-in-process inventory (40% complete)...........	65,000

Using the FIFO method, the equivalent units for the conversion cost calculation are

(1)	554,000
(2)	518,000
(3)	522,000
(4)	536,000
(5)	None of the above

d.   Novera, Ltd. reported the following physical units in work-in-process inventory for July in Department N:

Work-in-process, July 1 (5% complete)	68,000
Work-in-process, July 31 (90% complete)	55,000

Department N is the second stage of the process at Novera. Materials are added at the end of the process. Department N uses FIFO process costing. At the end of July, the equivalent units for transferred-in resources was 293,000 for calculating product cost. What were the equivalent units used in the production cost computation for the month of July for materials and conversion costs using the FIFO method?

	Materials	Conversion
(1)	361,000	407,100
(2)	306,000	352,100
(3)	293,000	352,100
(4)	306,000	290,900
(5)	None of the above	

(CPA adapted)

8-58. FIFO Method   (LO 8-5)

Breckenridge Corporation manufactures a part in a single production process in Department B. The company reports the following information about conversion costs for June:

	Units	Conversion Costs
WIP at June 1 (65% complete)	60,000	$132,600
Units started and costs incurred during June	320,000	939,675
Units completed and transferred to finished goods during June . . .	270,000	?

Work-in-process ending inventory was 45 percent complete with respect to conversion costs. Breckenridge uses FIFO for product costing.

Required

a.   What was the conversion cost of work-in-process inventory in Department B on June 30?

b.   What were the conversion costs per equivalent unit produced last period and this period, respectively?

(CPA adapted)

8-59. Prepare a Production Cost Report: Weighted-Average Method   (LO 8-3, 4)

Mercier Manufacturing produces a plastic part in three sequential departments: Extruding, Fabricating, and Packaging. Mercier uses the weighted-average process costing method to account for costs of production in all three departments. The following information was obtained for the Fabricating Department for the month of September.

Work in process on September 1 had 15,000 units made up of the following:

	Amount	Degree of Completion
Prior department costs transferred in from the Extruding Department . .	$ 75,750	100%
Costs added by the Fabricating Department		
Direct materials	36,000	90
Direct labor.	9,300	70
Manufacturing overhead	8,520	35
	$ 53,820	
Work in process, September 1	$129,570	

During September, 75,000 units were transferred in from the Extruding Department at a cost of $356,250. The Fabricating Department added the following costs:

Direct materials	$214,200
Direct labor.	64,800
Manufacturing overhead	33,480
Total costs added	$312,480

Fabricating finished 60,000 units and transferred them to the Packaging Department.

At September 30, 30,000 units were still in work-in-process inventory. The degree of completion of work-in-process inventory at September 30 was as follows:

Direct materials	100%
Direct labor	60
Manufacturing overhead	50

Required

a.   Prepare a production cost report for September using the weighted-average method.

b.   Management would like to decrease the costs of manufacturing the parts. In particular, it has set the following per-unit targets for this product in the Fabricating Department: Materials, $2.80; labor, $0.90; and manufacturing overhead, $0.55. Has the product achieved management's cost targets in the Fabricating Department? Write a short report to management stating your answer(s).

(CPA adapted)

(LO 8-4, 5)   **8-60. Prepare a Production Cost Report: FIFO Method**
Refer to the facts in Problem 8-59.

Required

a.   Prepare a production cost report using FIFO.

b.   Answer requirement (*b*) in Problem 8-59.

(LO 8-3, 4)   **8-61. Prepare a Production Cost Report: Weighted-Average Method**
Edwina Industrial Products (EIP) manufactures cleaning products. The Grant Street Plant produces a single product in three departments: Mixing, Refining, and Packaging. Additional materials are added in the Refining Process when units are 40 percent complete with respect to conversion. Information for operations in September in the Refining process appear as follows.

Work in process on September 1 consisted of 25,000 units with the following costs:

	Amount	Degree of Completion
Mixing costs transferred in	$12,000	100%
Costs added in Refining		
Direct materials	$27,800	100%
Conversion costs	29,320	80%
	$57,120	
Work in process September 1	$69,120	

During September, 275,000 units were transferred in from Mixing at a cost of $165,000. The following costs were added in Refining in September.

Direct materials	$310,200
Conversion costs	396,800
Total costs added	$707,000

Refining finished 260,000 units in September and transferred them to Packaging. At the end of September, there were 40,000 units in work-in-process inventory. The units were 20 percent complete with respect to conversion costs.

The Refining Department uses the weighted-average method of process costing. The Mixing Department at the Grant Street Plant uses the FIFO method of process costing. If the Mixing Department at the plant had used the weighted-average method, the amount of costs transferred in from Mixing would have been $166,800 for the amount transferred in this month.

Required
Prepare a production cost report for September for the Refining Department.

(LO 8-4, 5)   **8-62. Prepare a Production Cost Report: FIFO Method**
Refer to the data in Problem 8-61. The Refining Department uses the FIFO method of process costing. The Mixing Department at the Grant Street Plant uses the weighted-average method of process costing. If the Mixing Department at the Plant had used the FIFO method, the amount of costs transferred in from Mixing would have been $164,450 for the amount transferred in this month.

Required
Prepare a production cost report for September for the Refining Department.

8-63. Prepare a Production Cost Report and Adjust Inventory Balances: Weighted-Average   (LO 8-3, 4)
Method
The records of Tillman Corporation's initial and unaudited accounts show the following ending inventory balances, which must be adjusted to actual costs:

	Units	Unaudited Costs
Work-in-process inventory.............	48,000	$242,880
Finished goods inventory	15,000	105,300

   As the auditor, you have learned the following information. Ending work-in-process inventory is 35 percent complete with respect to conversion costs. Materials are added at the beginning of the manufacturing process, and overhead is applied at the rate of 90 percent of the direct labor costs. There was no finished goods inventory at the start of the period. The following additional information is also available:

	Units	Direct Materials	Direct Labor
Beginning inventory		*Costs*	
(25% complete as to labor)	32,000	$116,640	$ 14,240
Units started	118,000		
Current costs		436,860	199,600
Units completed and transferred			
to finished goods inventory	102,000		

Required
a. Prepare a production cost report for Tillman using the weighted-average method.
b. Show the journal entry required to correct the difference between the unaudited records and actual ending balances of Work-in-Process Inventory and Finished Goods Inventory. Debit or credit Cost of Goods Sold for any difference.
c. If the adjustment in requirement (b) is not made, will the company's income and inventories be overstated or understated?

(CPA adapted)

8-64. Prepare a Production Cost Report: Weighted-Average and FIFO   (LO 8-3, 4, 5)
Ambassador Lubricants (AL) produces various oil and synthetic-based products. One of the products is produced at the company's Bridge Plant in a single department. Two materials are used in the production process. Material A is introduced at the beginning of the process. Material B is added when the units are 60 percent complete with respect to conversion costs. Data for production during June follows:

	A	B	C	D	E
1		AMBASSADOR LUBRICANTS			
2		For the Month Ending June 30			
5	Quantities	Physical units			
6	WIP Beginning	22,000			
7	Started	63,000			
8	To account for	85,000			
10	Transferred out	69,000			
11	WIP Ending	16,000			
12	Accounted for	85,000			
14	Costs:	Total	Material A	Material B	Conversion
15	WIP Beginning	$ 355,700	$ 163,800	$ 112,800	$ 79,100
16	Current Period	1,023,650	478,800	211,500	333,350
17	Total	$ 1,379,350	$ 642,600	$ 324,300	$ 412,450

The beginning work-in-process inventory was 75 percent complete with respect to conversion resources. The ending work-in-process inventory was 25 percent complete.

Required

a.   Prepare a production cost report assuming that Ambassador Lubricants uses the weighted-average method of process costing.

b.   Prepare a production cost report assuming that Ambassador Lubricants uses the FIFO method of process costing.

(LO 8-3, 5, 6)   **8-65. Choosing between Weighted-Average and FIFO Process Costing: Data Analysis and Data Visualization**
Refer to the facts in Problem 8-64.

Required

The financial managers at Ambassador Lubricants are trying to decide between whether to continue using the weighted-average method or switch to FIFO. They tell you that the June results are fairly typical. What would you recommend and why? Include, as appropriate, any visual support for your arguments.

(LO 8-4, 5)   **8-66. Prepare a Production Cost Report: Weighted-Average and FIFO**
The Erskine Inc. Metals Division manufactures an industrial compound used in metal working at the division's only plant. The production process uses two materials. The first is a lubricant produced by the Chemicals Division of Erskine. The Chemicals Division sells the lubricant to other customers as well as the Metals Division. In January of this year, the Metals Division and the Chemicals Division signed a one-year contract, which went into effect on February 1, whereby the Chemicals Division agreed to sell up to 100,000 units of the lubricant each month to the Metals Division for a fixed price per unit. The second material is a solvent that the Metals Division purchases on the outside market. The solvent is introduced at the beginning of the process in the Metals Division along with the lubricant from the Chemicals Division.

The beginning work-in-process inventory on May 1 consists of 20,000 physical units, 50 percent complete with respect to conversion costs. The beginning work-in-process inventory has a total cost (transferred-in, materials, and conversion) of $276,300, of which $100,000 is for materials.

The ending work-in-process inventory on May 31 consists of 25,000 physical units, 40 percent complete with respect to conversion costs.

During May, 80,000 units were transferred in from the Chemicals Division and started in the Metals Division. The Metals Division incurred total costs (transferred-in, materials, and conversion) of $1,520,700 in May, of which $320,000 was for materials and $697,500 was for conversion costs.

Required

a.   Compute the cost of goods transferred out in May and the cost of work-in-process ending inventory assuming that the Metals Division uses weighted-average process costing.

b.   Compute the cost of goods transferred out in May and the cost of work-in-process ending inventory assuming that the Metals Division uses FIFO process costing.

(LO 8-2, 4)   **8-67. Prepare a Production Cost Report: Weighted-Average Method, Missing Data**
Howell Food Products (HFP) produces the most popular of its canned soup varieties at the Stadium Plant. The Stadium Plant has two departments: Mixing and Canning. Raw materials are added at two points in the production of the soup. First, vegetables are added at the beginning of production in the Mixing Department. After the process is 30 percent complete with respect to conversion, a unique broth is added to the vegetable-water mix. Once the soup is mixed, it is transferred to the Canning Department for cooking and packaging. The following information is available from the Stadium Plant for October. (No new material is added in the Canning Department.)

> Canning Department Production and Costs: October
> Beginning inventory (125,000 units, 60% complete with respect to Canning Department costs)
> Total (Mixing and Canning Departments) cost:
>   Beginning inventory. . . . . $ 241,212
>   Current work (1,225,000 units started)
>   Mixing Department costs . . . . $ 1,724,800
>   Canning Department costs.   766,988
> The ending inventory has 175,000 units, which are 100 percent complete for Mixing Department costs.

Required

a.   Assume that the Canning Department uses weighted-average process costing. The cost per equivalent unit for October for materials (transferred in from the Mixing Plant) in the Canning Department is $1.44 and for conversion costs it is $.60. How complete is ending inventory with respect to conversion costs?

b.   What is the cost of product transferred out of the Canning Department for October?

c.   What is the cost of ending inventory in the Canning Department for October?

8-68. Determine Degree of Completion: FIFO Method, Missing Data   (LO 8-1, 5)

Refer to the information in Problem 8-67. The Mixing Department at the Stadium Plant uses FIFO process costing to account for production. In May, beginning work-in-process inventory consisted of 150,000 units, 40 percent complete with respect to conversion. The cost of vegetables put in production in May was $600,000. The cost of broth introduced into production in May was $225,000. Reported costs per equivalent unit for May were $1 per equivalent unit of vegetables and $.45 per equivalent unit for broth.

Required

Based on the information available, the ending work-in-process inventory in May was:

a.   At least 30 percent complete with respect to conversion cost.

b.   Less than 30 percent complete with respect to conversion cost.

c.   More than 40 percent complete (the value for the beginning inventory) with respect to conversion cost.

d.   There is not enough information to determine the degree of completion.

8-69. Solving for Unknowns: FIFO Method   (LO 8-4, 5)

For each of the following independent cases, use FIFO costing to determine the information requested.

a.   At the start of the period, 7,000 units were in the work-in-process inventory; 5,250 units were in the ending inventory. During the period, 16,625 units were transferred out to the next department. Materials and conversion costs are added evenly throughout the production process. FIFO costing is used. How many units were started during this period?

b.   During May, 227,200 units were completed and transferred out to finished goods inventory. The current cost per equivalent unit for work done in May for conversion costs was $1.15. The conversion costs assigned to units started and completed in May was $226,780. How many physical units were in work-in-process inventory on May 1?

c.   Materials and conversion costs are added evenly throughout the production process. Beginning inventory amounted to 13,000 units. This period, 58,500 units were started and completed. At the end of the period, the 39,000 units in inventory were 50 percent complete. Using FIFO costing, the equivalent production for the period was 83,200 units. What was the percentage of completion of the beginning inventory?

d.   The ending inventory included $29,000 for conversion costs. During the period, 21,000 equivalent units were required to complete the beginning inventory, and 30,000 units were started and completed. The ending inventory represented 5,000 equivalent units of work this period. FIFO costing is used. What were the total conversion costs incurred this period?

8-70. Solving for Unknowns: Weighted-Average Method   (LO 8-3, 4)

For each of the following independent cases, determine the units or equivalent units requested (assuming weighted-average costing).

a.   Beginning inventory consisted of 64,000 units with a direct materials cost of $113,600. The equivalent work represented by all direct materials costs in the WIP Inventory account amounted to 288,000 units. Ending inventory had 32,000 units that were 60 percent complete with respect to materials. The ending inventory had a $30,720 direct materials cost assigned. What was the total materials cost incurred this period?

b.   Beginning inventory had 36,900 units, 90 percent complete with respect to conversion costs. During the period, 31,500 units were started. Ending inventory was 45 percent complete with respect to conversion costs and was assigned $13,230 in conversion costs. The conversion cost per equivalent unit was $1.47. How many units were transferred out?

c. During the period, 105,000 units were transferred into the department. The 160,000 units transferred out were charged to the next department at an amount that included $216,000 for direct materials costs. The ending inventory was 80 percent complete with respect to direct materials and had a direct materials cost of $40,500 assigned to it. How many physical units are in the ending inventory?

d. The WIP Inventory account had a beginning balance of $28,500 for conversion costs on items in process and, during the period, $271,500 in conversion costs were charged to it. Also during the period, $288,000 in conversion costs were transferred out. There were 12,000 units in the beginning inventory, and 144,000 units were transferred out during the period. The units in ending work-in-process inventory are 40 percent complete with respect to conversion costs. How many units were started this period?

(LO 8-7) **8-71. Choosing between Job Costing and Process Costing**

Saratoga Systems produces a single product. The production process requires all material to be brought to the shop floor before any work begins. The material is then processed and assembled and then transferred to finished goods inventory. Every unit is completely identical in specification and use, and no customization is possible. Because of the cost of the product, only a few units are produced in any one month.

During June, only three units were started, and these were labeled ID061, ID062, and ID063. There was no beginning inventory of any kind on June 1. Records from the raw materials store and employee time records show the following requisitions and direct labor costs:

	Direct Materials	Direct Labor
ID061	$17,000	$17,600
ID062	15,300	14,600
ID063	18,700	3,800

The difference in the materials cost represents the historical cost of materials purchased at different times. The difference in labor cost represents the difference in seniority (not skill) of the individual employees.

Overhead for the month of June totaled $63,000.

During March, ID061 and ID062 were completed and transferred to finished goods. ID063 was still in process on June 30.

Required

a. Suppose Saratoga Systems uses a job cost system and applies overhead to products based on direct labor cost. What will be the cost of the units transferred to finished goods? What will be the amount in Work-in-Process Ending Inventory?

b. Suppose Saratoga Systems uses process costing and ID063 was 25 percent complete with respect to conversion costs (direct labor and overhead cost). Assume that direct materials cost is not traced to individual units. What will be the cost of the units transferred to finished goods? What will be the amount in Work-in-Process Ending Inventory?

c. What system (job costing or process costing) would you recommend for Franklin? Why?

(LO 8-8) **8-72. Operations Costing: Work-in-Process Inventory**

Chateaufort Craft (CC) makes three models of sea kayaks: CC-100, CC-200, and CC-500. CC manufactures the boats in two departments: Department A (Assembly) and Department B (Finishing). All three models are processed initially in Department A, where all material is assembled. The CC-100 model is then transferred to finished goods. After processing in Department A, the CC-200 and CC-500 models are transferred to Department B for final detailing, and then transferred to finished goods.

There were no beginning work-in-process inventories on September 1. Data for September are shown in the following table. Ending work in process is 40 percent complete in Department A and 25 percent complete in Department B. Conversion costs are allocated based on the number of equivalent units processed in each department.

	Total	CC-100	CC-200	CC-500
Units started.........................		825	495	330
Units completed in Department A		660	428	297
Units completed in Department B			370	275
Materials...........................	$653,400	$132,000	$207,900	$313,500
Conversion costs:				
Assembly Department (A)	$365,295			
Finishing Department (B)............	89,775			
Total conversion costs	$455,070			

Required

a. What is the unit cost of each model transferred to finished goods in September?

b. What is the balance of work-in-process inventory on September 30 for Department A? Department B?

8-73. Operations Costing: Work-in-Process Inventory   (LO 8-8)

Drew Implements makes four models of utility and light construction tractors. The model names are DI-1400, DI-3800, DI-5000, and DI-8000. Drew manufactures the tractors in two departments—Fabrication and Detailing. All four models are processed initially in Fabrication, where all materials are assembled into the basic tractor. The DI-1400 model is then transferred to finished goods. After processing in Fabrication, the other three models are transferred to Detailing for additional work (though no new materials are added) and then transferred to finished goods.

There were no beginning work-in-process inventories on February 1. Data for February are shown in the following table. Ending work in process is 90 percent complete in Fabrication and 40 percent complete in Detailing. Conversion costs are allocated based on the number of equivalent units processed in each department.

	Total	DI-1400	DI-3800	DI-5000	DI-8000
Units started		700	575	350	175
Units completed in Fabrication..		650	550	325	125
Units completed in Detailing.....			525	300	100
Materials.................	$3,514,500	$392,000	$1,092,500	$1,050,000	$980,000
Conversion costs:					
Fabrication..............	$1,463,700				
Detailing...............	931,125				
Total conversion costs ..	$2,394,825				

Required

a. What is the unit cost of each model transferred to finished goods in February?

b. What is the balance of the Work-in-Process Inventory on February 28 for Fabrication? For Detailing?

8-74. Operations Costing and Process Costing   (LO 8-3, 8)

Refer to the data in Exercise 8-56 (Hedwig Optical). Information for January is copied here. There are never any work-in-process inventories.

	Total	Travel	Sport	Pro
Units produced	20,000	10,000	7,500	2,500
Materials cost	$1,600,000	$290,000	$847,500	$462,500
Conversion costs				
Assembly....................	$ 440,000			
Calibration....................	44,400			
Total conversion costs.....	$ 484,400			

The plant controller believes that keeping track of the three models and separating costs in the Assembly and Calibration Departments is not worth the time and effort. The controller suggests not distinguishing between the three binocular models, treating Assembly and Calibration as a single department, and using process costing to develop product costs for the three binocular models.

Required

a.   Suppose the controller's suggestion is followed. What will be the unit cost of a pair of binoculars produced in January?

b.   Would you recommend adopting the controller's suggestion? Explain.

(LO 8-7, 8)   8-75. Operations Costing and Job Costing

Refer to the data in Exercise 8-56 and Problem 8-74 (Hedwig Optical). The marketing manager cannot believe that the controller wants to treat all binocular models the same. The marketing manager says that in order to understand where to target marketing resources, it is important to understand the profitability (and therefore the costs) of the individual models. The marketing manager suggests treating the individual models as "jobs" and using job costing to calculate the costs of the individual models. The marketing manager also suggested that the conversion costs in both departments should be applied to the jobs based on direct materials costs.

Required

a.   Suppose the marketing manager's suggestion is followed. What will be the unit cost of a pair of binoculars produced in January?

b.   Would you recommend adopting the marketing manager's suggestion? Explain.

(LO 8-3)   8-76. Process Costing and Ethics: Increasing Production to Boost Profits

Pacific Siding Incorporated produces synthetic wood siding used in the construction of residential and commercial buildings. Pacific Siding's fiscal year ends on March 31, and the weighted-average method is used for the company's process costing system.

Financial results for the first 11 months of the current fiscal year (through February 28) are well below the expectations of management, owners, and creditors. Halfway through the month of March, the chief executive officer (CEO) and the chief financial officer (CFO) ask the controller to estimate the production results for the month of March in the form of a production cost report (the company has only one production department). This report is shown in the accompanying exhibit.

Armed with the preliminary production cost report for March, and knowing that the company's production is well below capacity, the CEO and CFO decide to produce as many units as possible for the last half of March, even though sales are *not* expected to increase any time soon. The production manager is told to push his employees to get as far as possible with production, thereby increasing the percentage of completion for ending WIP inventory. However, because the production process takes three weeks to complete, all of the units produced in the last half of March will be in WIP inventory at the end of March.

Required

a.   Explain how the CEO and CFO expect to increase profit (net income) for the year by boosting production at the end of March. Assume that most overhead costs are fixed.

b.   Using the following assumptions, prepare a revised estimate of production results in the form of a production cost report for the month of March. *Assumptions based on the CEO and CFO's request to boost production:*

   1.   Units started and partially completed during the period will increase to 225,000 (from the initial estimate of 70,000). This is the projected ending WIP inventory at March 31.
   2.   Percentage of completion estimates for units in ending WIP inventory will increase to 80 percent for direct materials, 85 percent for direct labor, and 90 percent for overhead.
   3.   Costs incurred during the period will increase to $95,000 for direct materials, $102,000 for direct labor, and $150,000 for overhead (recall that most overhead costs are fixed).
   4.   All units completed and transferred out during March are sold by March 31.

c.   Compare your new production cost report with the one prepared by the controller. How much do you expect profit to increase as a result of increasing production during the last half of March?

d.   Is the request made by the CEO and CFO ethical? Explain your answer.

(Copyright © K. Heisinger, 2006)

Data Entry Section

Unit Information

	Units (board feet)	Percent Complete Direct Materials	Direct Labor	Overhead
Units in beginning WIP inventory (all completed this period)	250,000	n/a	n/a	n/a
Units started and completed during the period	140,000	100%	100%	100%
Units started and *partially* completed during the period	70,000	40	60	30

Cost Information

	Direct Materials	Direct Labor	Overhead
Costs in beginning WIP inventory	$ 76,000	$ 90,000	$ 150,000
Costs incurred during the period	55,000	75,000	135,000

PACIFIC SIDING INCORPORATED
Preliminary Production Cost Report
Month Ending March 31

Step 1: Summary of Physical Units and Equivalent Unit Calculations

Units to be accounted for:	Physical Units
Units in beginning WIP inventory	250,000
Units started during the period	210,000
Total units to be accounted for	460,000

		Equivalent Units		
Units accounted for:	Physical Units	Direct Materials	Direct Labor	Overhead
Units completed and transferred out	390,000	390,000	390,000	390,000
Units in ending WIP inventory	70,000	28,000	42,000	21,000
Total units accounted for	460,000	418,000	432,000	411,000
				0

Step 2: Summary of Costs to Be Accounted For

Costs to be accounted for:	Direct Materials	Direct Labor	Overhead	Total
Costs in beginning WIP inventory	$ 76,000	$ 90,000	$ 150,000	$ 316,000
Costs incurred during the period	55,000	75,000	135,000	265,000
Total costs to be accounted for	$ 131,000	$ 165,000	$ 285,000	$ 581,000
				$ 0

Step 3: Calculation of Cost per Equivalent Unit

	Direct Materials	Direct Labor	Overhead	Total
Total costs to be accounted for (a)	$ 131,000	$ 165,000	$ 285,000	
Total equivalent units accounted for (b)	418,000	432,000	411,000	
Cost per equivalent unit (a) ÷ (b)	$ 0.3134	$ 0.3819	$ 0.6934	$ 1.3888

Step 4: Assign Costs to Units Transferred Out and Units in Ending WIP Inventory

	Direct Materials	Direct Labor	Overhead	Total
Costs assigned to units transferred out	$ 122,225	$ 148,958	$ 270,438	$ 541,621
Costs assigned to ending WIP inventory	8,775	16,042	14,562	39,379
Total costs accounted for				$ 581,000

INTEGRATIVE CASES

(LO 8-5)   **8-77. Show Cost Flows: FIFO Method, Over- or Underapplied Overhead**

Vermont Company uses continuous processing to produce stuffed bears and FIFO process costing to account for its production costs. It uses FIFO because costs are quite unstable due to the volatile price of fine materials it uses in production. The bears are processed through one department. Overhead is applied on the basis of direct labor costs, and the application rate has not changed over the period covered by the problem. The Work-in-Process Inventory account showed the following balances at the start of the current period:

Direct materials	$131,000
Direct labor.	260,000
Overhead applied	325,000

These costs were related to 52,000 units that were in process at the start of the period.

During the period, 60,000 units were transferred to finished goods inventory. Of the units finished during this period, 80 percent were sold. After units have been transferred to finished goods inventory, no distinction is made between the costs to complete beginning work-in-process inventory and the costs of goods started and completed in work in process this period.

The equivalent units for materials this period were 50,000 (using FIFO). Of these, 10,000 were equivalent units with respect to materials in the ending work-in-process inventory. Materials costs incurred during the period totaled $300,400.

Conversion costs of $1,287,000 were charged this period for 62,500 equivalent units (using FIFO). The ending inventory consisted of 22,000 equivalent units of conversion costs. The actual manufacturing overhead for the period was $660,000.

Required

Prepare T-accounts to show the flow of costs in the system. Any difference between actual and applied overhead for the period should be debited or credited to Cost of Goods Sold.

(LO 8-1, 5, 7)   **8-78. Job Costing, Process Costing, Choosing a Costing Method**

Bouwens Corporation manufactures a solvent used in airplane maintenance shops. Bouwens sells the solvent to both U.S. military services and commercial airlines. The solvent is produced in a single plant in one of two buildings. Although the solvent sold to the military is chemically identical to that sold to the airlines, the company produces solvent for the two customer types in different buildings at the plant. The solvent sold to the military is manufactured in building 155 (B-155) and is labeled M-Solv. The solvent sold to the commercial airlines is manufactured in building 159 (B-159) and is labeled C-Solv.

B-155 is much newer and is considered a model work environment with climate control and other amenities. Workers at Bouwens, who all have roughly equal skills, bid on their job locations (the buildings they will work in) and are assigned based on bids and seniority. As workers gain seniority, they also receive higher pay.

The solvent sold to the two customers is essentially identical, but the military requires Bouwens to use a base chemical with a brand name, MX. The solvent for the commercial airlines is called CX. MX is required for military applications because it is sold by vendors on a preferred vendor list.

The company sells solvent for the market price to the airlines. Solvent sold to the military is sold based on cost plus a fixed fee. That is, the government pays Bouwens for the recorded cost of the solvent plus a fixed amount of profit. The cost can be computed according to "commonly used product cost methods, including job costing or process costing methods using either FIFO or weighted-average methods." Competition for the government business is very strong, and Bouwens is always looking for ways to reduce the cost and the price it quotes the government.

Currently, Bouwens uses a job costing system in which each month's production for each customer type is considered a "job." Thus, every month, Bouwens starts and completes one job in B-155 and one job in B-159. (There is never any beginning or ending work in process at Bouwens.) Recently, a dispute arose between Jack, the product manager for the military solvent, and Jill, the product manager for the commercial solvent, over the proper costing system.

> Jack: It is ridiculous to use job costing for this. We are producing solvent. Everyone knows that the chemicals are the same. The fact the B-155 has high-cost labor is because all the senior employees want to work there. We could produce the same product with the employees in B-159. We should be using process costing and consider all the production in both buildings for each month as the batch.

Jill: Jack, the fact is that the military requires us to use a special chemical, and their contracts require we keep track of the costs for their business. If we don't separate the costing, we won't know how profitable either business is.

The following is production and cost information for a typical month, July:

	M-Solv (B-155)	C-Solv (B-159)	Total
Units started..............	2,000	10,000	12,000
Materials costs.............	$14,000	$ 40,000	$ 54,000
Conversion costs...........	30,000	120,000	150,000
Total...................	$44,000	$160,000	$204,000

Required

a. Compute the unit costs of M-Solv and C-Solv for July using the current system (job costing) at Bouwens.

b. Compute the costs of M-Solv and C-Solv for July if Bouwens were to treat all production as the same (combining B-155 and B-159 production).

c. Recommend a costing method that best reflects the cost of producing M-Solv and C-Solv.

d. For your recommended costing system, compute the cost of both M-Solv and C-Solv for July.

SOLUTIONS TO SELF-STUDY QUESTIONS

1. The following is the cost of production report, using the weighted-average method:

J&S LUBRICANTS
Blending Department
for the Month Ending October 31

	(Section 1) Physical Units	(Section 2) Equivalent Units Materials	Conversion
Flow of Units			
Units to be accounted for:			
In work-in-process (WIP) beginning inventory.....	1,000		
Units started in this period	5,000		
Total units to account for.......................	6,000		
Units accounted for:			
Completed and transferred out.................	5,500	5,500	5,500
In WIP ending inventory	500	400[a]	200[b]
Total units accounted for......................	6,000	5,900	5,700

	Costs (Sections 3 through 5) Total	Materials	Conversion
Flow of Costs			
Costs to be accounted for (Section 3):			
Costs in WIP beginning inventory...............	$ 1,307	$ 1,113	$ 194
Current period costs	36,543	22,487	14,056
Total costs to be accounted for	$37,850	$23,600	$14,250
Costs per equivalent unit (Section 4)		$ 4.00[c]	$ 2.50[d]

(Continued)

Costs accounted for (Section 5):

Costs assigned to units transferred out..........	$35,750	$22,000[e]	$13,750[f]
Costs assigned to WIP ending inventory.........	2,100	1,600[g]	500[h]
Total costs accounted for	$37,850	$23,600	$14,250

[a] 80% complete with respect to materials.
[b] 40% complete with respect to conversion.
[c] $4.00 = $23,600 ÷ 5,900 equivalent units (EU)
[d] $2.50 = $14,250 ÷ 5,700 EU
[e] $22,000 = 5,500 EU × $4.00 per EU
[f] $13,750 = 5,500 EU × $2.50 per EU
[g] $1,600 = 400 EU × $4.00 per EU
[h] $500 = 200 EU × $2.50 per EU

2. The following is the cost of production report, using the FIFO method.

J&S LUBRICANTS
Blending Department
for the Month Ending October 31

	(Section 1) Physical Units	(Section 2) Equivalent Units Materials	Conversion
Flow of Units			
Units to be accounted for:			
In work-in-process (WIP) beginning inventory	1,000		
Units started in this period	5,000		
Total units to account for.......................	6,000		
Units accounted for:			
Completed and transferred out			
From beginning WIP	1,000	1,000	1,000
Started and completed	4,500	4,500	4,500
Total completed and transferred out	5,500	5,500	5,500
In WIP ending inventory	500	400[a]	200[b]
Total units accounted for.......................	6,000	5,900	5,700
Less work from beginning WIP	1,000	250[c]	100[d]
New work done in October.......................	5,000	5,650	5,600

	Total	Costs (Sections 3 through 5) Materials Costs	Conversion Costs
Flow of Costs			
Costs to be accounted for (Section 3):			
Costs in WIP beginning inventory...............	$ 1,307	$ 1,113	$ 194
Current period costs	36,543	22,487	14,056
Total costs to be accounted for	$37,850	$23,600	$14,250
Costs per equivalent unit (Section 4)		$ 3.98[e]	$ 2.51[f]
Costs accounted for (Section 5):			
Costs assigned to units transferred out			
Costs from beginning WIP	$ 1,307	$ 1,113	$ 194
Current cost to complete beginning WIP inventory..............................	5,244	2,985[g]	2,259[h]
Total costs from beginning WIP inventory	$ 6,551	$ 4,098	$ 2,453

Current cost of units started and completed.....	29,205	17,910[i]	11,295[j]
Total cost transferred out....................	$35,756	$22,008	$13,748
Costs assigned to WIP ending inventory.......	2,094	1,592[k]	502[l]
Total costs accounted for	$37,850	$23,600	$14,250

[a] 80% complete with respect to materials.
[b] 40% complete with respect to conversion.
[c] 25% complete with respect to materials.
[d] 10% complete with respect to conversion.
[e] $3.98 = $22,487 ÷ 5,650 equivalent units (EU)
[f] $2.51 = $14,056 ÷ 5,600 EU
[g] $2,985 = (100% − 25%) × 1,000 units × $3.98 per EU
[h] $2,259 = (100% − 10%) × 1,000 units × $2.51 per EU
[i] $17,910 = 4,500 EU × $3.98 per EU
[j] $11,295 = 4,500 EU × $2.51 per EU
[k] $1,592 = 400 EU × $3.98 per EU
[l] $502 = 200 EU × $2.51 per EU

3.   The following is the cost of production report, using the weighted-average method.

J&S LUBRICANTS
Canning Department
for the Month Ending August 31

	(Section 1) Physical Units	Transferred-in Costs	Materials Costs	Conversion Costs
			(Section 2) Equivalent Units	
Flow of Units				
Units to be accounted for:				
In work-in-process (WIP) beginning inventory......	50,000			
Units started in this period	240,000			
Total units to be accounted for	290,000			
Units accounted for				
Completed and transferred out..................	250,000	250,000	250,000	250,000
In WIP ending inventory	40,000	40,000	40,000[a]	6,000[b]
Total units accounted for........................	290,000	290,000	290,000	256,000

	Total	Transferred-in Costs	Materials Costs	Conversion Costs
		Costs (Sections 3 through 5)		
Flow of Costs				
Costs to be accounted for (Section 3):				
Costs in WIP beginning inventory................	$ 7,067	$ 6,998	$ −0−	$ 69
Current period costs	99,213	33,602	58,000	7,611
Total costs to account for	$106,280	$40,600	$58,000	$7,680
Costs per equivalent unit (Section 4)		$ 0.14[c]	$ 0.20[d]	$ 0.03[e]
Costs accounted for (Section 5):				
Costs assigned to units transferred out...........	$ 92,500	$35,000[f]	$50,000[g]	$7,500[h]
Costs assigned to WIP ending inventory..........	13,780	5,600[i]	8,000[j]	180[k]
Total costs accounted for	$106,280	$40,600	$58,000	$7,680

[a] 100% complete with respect to materials.
[b] 15% complete with respect to conversion.
[c] $0.14 = $40,600 ÷ 290,000 equivalent units (EU)
[d] $0.20 = $58,000 ÷ 290,000 EU
[e] $0.03 = $7,680 ÷ 256,000 EU
[f] $35,000 = 250,000 EU × $0.14 per EU
[g] $50,000 = 250,000 EU × $0.20 per EU
[h] $7,500 = 250,000 EU × $0.03 per EU
[i] $5,600 = 40,000 EU × $0.14 per EU
[j] $8,000 = 40,000 EU × $0.20 per EU
[k] $180 = 6,000 EU × $0.03 per EU

4. The following is the cost of production report:

	Total	5,000 M-24	9,000 D-12
Materials...................	$ 42,500	$20,000	$22,500
Conversion			
Manufacturing	$ 42,000	$15,000[a]	$27,000[b]
Finishing.................	21,000	7,500[c]	13,500[d]
Total conversion costs	$ 63,000	$22,500	$40,500
Total product cost	$105,500	$42,500	$63,000
Number of units.............		5,000	9,000
Cost per unit...............		$ 8.50	$ 7.00

[a] $15,000 = 5,000 units × [$42,000 ÷ (5,000 + 9,000)]
[b] $27,000 = 9,000 units × [$42,000 ÷ (5,000 + 9,000)]
[c] $7,500 = 5,000 units × [$21,000 ÷ (5,000 + 9,000)]
[d] $13,500 = 9,000 units × [$21,000 ÷ (5,000 + 9,000)]

9

Chapter Nine

Activity-Based Costing

LEARNING OBJECTIVES

After reading this chapter, you should be able to:

LO 9-1 Understand the potential effects of using reported product costs for decision making.

LO 9-2 Explain how a two-stage product costing system works.

LO 9-3 Compare and contrast plantwide and department allocation methods.

LO 9-4 Explain how activity-based costing and a two-stage product costing system are related.

LO 9-5 Compute product costs using activity-based costing.

LO 9-6 Compare activity-based product costing to traditional department product costing methods.

LO 9-7 Demonstrate the flow of costs through accounts using activity-based costing.

LO 9-8 Apply activity-based costing to marketing and administrative services.

LO 9-9 Explain how time-driven activity-based costing works.

Doxieone Photography/Moment Open/ Getty Images

❝ *This morning's conference call really got things moving around here. The marketing managers in Los Angeles are disputing our costs on the two drone models we produce. They claim that company guidelines linking the prices we charge to the reported costs are killing the sales for one of our models. Now I am supposed to investigate whether there is a better way to develop the product costs. I've read about activity-based costing and its benefits, but I'm not sure if it is right for us.*❞

Nancy Chen is the cost accounting manager at the CenterPoint plant of IVC, Inc., a manufacturer of electronic devices and wireless equipment for automotive, marine, and hobby markets. The plant manufactures two of the four models of drones the company makes. The plant manager has asked her to determine if the current cost accounting system is suitable as a basis for pricing. If not, Nancy needs to recommend changes and justify those changes to the senior financial executives at IVC.

Chapters 7 and 8 described product costing systems that most firms around the world use, perhaps with some minor variations. Individual systems can be more complex, but the basic approach is the same: Assign direct costs to products and allocate manufacturing overhead costs to products using a handful of allocation bases, typically based on direct labor, direct material, or machine utilization. These systems are certainly satisfactory for developing product costs for financial reporting. Our focus, however, is on decision making.

In the last 40 years or so, many companies have experimented with and implemented new systems based on a different approach to cost management. These systems are grounded in production processes rather than accounting systems that support financial reporting to shareholders. In certain business environments and for certain decisions, traditional accounting systems have not given managers the information they needed.

In this chapter, we describe one of these approaches, activity-based costing, or ABC, which has been implemented or considered by a number of major firms, including manufacturing firms such as General Motors and Caterpillar, service firms such as Citibank, and even agencies of the U.S. government.

Reported Product Costs and Decision Making

The product costs we computed in Chapters 7 and 8 were used primarily for developing inventory balances and cost of goods sold amounts for financial reporting. Let's see what happens when we use the data to make what seems to be a reasonable decision—whether to keep or drop a product.

LO 9-1
Understand the potential effects of using reported product costs for decision making.

Dropping a Product

Managers at Sandia Custom Furniture (introduced in Chapter 6) are considering dropping the S-72 line of desks. The reported costs of producing it have risen more rapidly than the price Sandia charges for it, and the product line margins have fallen to unacceptable levels. The decision will be based on the impact it has on reported product costs.

Suppose that overhead costs are allocated using direct labor-hours, so we can use the results in Exhibit 6.5, which is reproduced here as Exhibit 9.1, for our product line costs. From the information in Exhibit 9.1, we see that the cost accounting system assigns S-72s a unit cost of $2,600. Sandia currently produces 80 S-72 desks. If that line is eliminated, it might appear that total costs will fall by $208,000 (= $2,600 × 80 desks). Thus, we estimate the total cost to be $270,000 (= $478,000 − $208,000) without S-72s.

We ask Sandia's cost accountant to estimate the company's manufacturing costs at the company if it produces 240 S-66s but no S-72s. See the cost accountant's analysis in Exhibit 9.2.

Exhibit 9.1

Product Costs for January, Year 2—Sandia Custom Furniture (allocation base is direct labor hours)

	S-72s	S-66s	Total
Units produced	80	240	320
Direct labor-hours	2,400	3,900	6,300
Costs:			
Direct materials	$ 40,000	$ 36,000	$ 76,000
Direct labor	72,000	78,000	150,000
Manufacturing overhead (@ $40 per hour)	96,000	156,000	252,000
Total	$208,000	$270,000	$478,000
Cost per unit	$ 2,600	$ 1,125	

Exhibit 9.2

Manufacturing Costs for S-66s—Sandia Custom Furniture

	S-66s
Units produced	240
Machine-hours	6,000
Direct labor-hours	3,900
Direct materials	$ 36,000
Direct labor	78,000
Manufacturing overhead	234,000
Total costs	$348,000
Overhead rate	$ 60
Unit cost	$ 1,450

Clearly, this cost estimate is much higher than that estimated using the product costs produced by the cost accounting system. You can see by comparing the data in Exhibit 9.2 with those in Exhibit 9.1 that the difference is due to the overhead estimate. The overhead rate from Exhibit 9.1 is $40 per direct labor hour. Producing only S-66s using 3,900 direct labor-hours, we would expect that manufacturing overhead costs should be $156,000 (= $40 × 3,900). Instead, the accountant has estimated overhead costs to be $234,000.

Let's consider the manufacturing overhead costs more closely. The cost accountant has provided the overhead estimates with and without the S-72s (Exhibit 9.3). We can readily see where the problem is. Although some overhead estimates decrease if S-72s are

Exhibit 9.3

Cost Estimates

	Original	S-66 Only
Direct materials	$ 76,000	$ 36,000
Direct labor	150,000	78,000
Manufacturing overhead		
Utilities	$ 3,360	$ 2,100
Supplies	3,500	2,240
Training	42,000	26,520
Supervision	76,860	76,860
Machine depreciation	41,370	41,370
Plant depreciation	56,070	56,070
Miscellaneous	28,840	28,840
Total overhead	$252,000	$234,000
Total costs	$478,000	$348,000

not produced, others do not change. Looking closely at the accounts that have remained the same, you can see that these include supervision, depreciation, and miscellaneous overhead items. By computing a predetermined overhead rate, the cost accounting system treats all overhead as if it were variable with respect to the allocation base, which is not true in the case of Sandia Custom Furniture.

If managers at Sandia Custom Furniture rely on the cost accounting system to make the decision to keep or drop the S-72 desk line as a product, the cost system provides potentially inaccurate unit costs. Suppose, as a result of using costs from the cost accounting system, managers decide to drop S-72s. The reported unit costs of desks will increase from $1,125 to $1,450, an increase of about 29 percent. If the managers attempt to increase the price of the S-66s by an equivalent amount, the market is unlikely to accommodate it. As a result, they face two equally unappealing choices: remain in business and lose money, or shut down.

The problem, of course, is that the reported product costs treat *all* overhead costs as if they vary with direct labor, but this might not be true for two reasons. First, some of the overhead could be fixed, and reducing the number of desks made does not result in lower fixed costs. Second, some of the overhead could vary but with cost drivers other than direct labor. In this chapter, we consider some approaches to developing product costing systems that consider this second reason.

The Death Spiral

If managers attempt to recover the costs with a smaller number of units, they are likely to meet resistance in the market, resulting in demand for even fewer units. With the lower production, the reported product costs increase even more. This can set off a vicious cycle of attempting to cover a fixed amount of costs with fewer and fewer units until, at the extreme, the firm is producing no units. This phenomenon is referred to as the **death spiral.**

The death spiral can begin in many ways. For example, if the demand for S-72s falls for some reason—lower economic activity, recession, or a change in tastes for desks—Sandia's cost accounting system will report higher unit costs for both desk models. If a major customer leaves—for example, if a retailer goes bankrupt—the decline in demand will lead to higher reported costs. If the firm attempts to recover the production costs from the remaining customers, they too will reduce or eliminate their demand.

Although the death spiral is easy to see in the case of Sandia Custom Furniture, and therefore is easy to avoid, imagine a company with thousands of products and constantly changing overhead costs. The impact of a reduction in demand would be much more subtle and detection could come too late to avoid serious problems for the firm.

The death spiral can occur even in firms with increasing demand. For example, a firm is likely to add capacity with increasing demand. This can be in the form of new plant and equipment. An increase in capacity is accompanied by an increase in fixed (overhead) costs without a similar increase in output, at least not immediately.

The reason for the capacity increase is an expected increase in *future* demand. However, if the accounting system computes product costs based on relatively short-term demand estimates (for example, for the next year), it will include in the product costs the costs of the excess capacity that exists for growth. Using the reported product costs, managers will attempt to recover the excess capacity costs from current customers, who are unlikely to be willing to pay, assuming there are competitors without the excess capacity. In this case, the death spiral can lead companies to build new plants only to see them idle because of reduced demand. We return to the issue of capacity costs and cost system design in Chapter 10.

death spiral
Process that begins by attempting to increase price to meet reported product costs, losing market, reporting still higher costs, and so on, until the firm is out of business.

Business Application   The Death Spiral

As we noted, the death spiral can arise for many reasons. It may also affect more than one firm and even an entire industry. A recent example is the digital camera industry of Japan. Once the global standard, the Japanese camera industry, composed of well-known brands such as Olympus, Nikon, and Canon, had seen demand fall in the decade of the 2010s, primarily because of competition from smartphones and their ever-increasing camera quality. The onset of the COVID-19 pandemic in early 2020 accelerated this decline.

Industry observers, however, also blame the camera firms themselves for engaging in "excess competition."

> "Digital camera companies intend to strangle their rivals through excessive competition, but in the end they'll strangle themselves," Hiroshi Hamada lamented about 11 years ago. . . . "It looks just like the personal computer industry, . . . A lot of manufacturers competing excessively."[1]

In this context, excess competition refers to something that would drive profits to be less than with perfect competition. The concern of the observer in this case is that competitors are overinvesting in research and development, while updating faster than they can afford to relative to recovering their investment.

After establishing dominance in the market, Japanese camera manufacturers competed against each other by shortening the product cycle (offering more frequent product updates) and dropping prices significantly each year. As the market size declines and less revenue is earned on each model, companies are unable to recover the investments in new technology:

> With the market shrinking at such speed, companies are at great risk of falling into a fixed-costs crisis.[2]

The death spiral here (referred to as the "fixed-costs crisis"), occurs when revenues are falling faster than costs can be reduced. Although consumers benefited from more features and lower prices, some manufacturers such as Casio and Olympus have recently dropped out of the market, and the future of the industry is unclear.

Sources:
1. Hoshi, Masamichi, "Olympus Exit Foreshadows a Japan Camera Sector Shake-up," *Nikkei Asian Review,* July 1, 2020.
2. Ibid.

Self-Study Question

1. Suppose that Sandia Custom Furniture continues to build the two desks and plans the same monthly activity for next year. However, anticipating expansion in the future, its managers plan to lease a new building in which to manufacture the desks. Because this is such a good opportunity, managers decide to move in today even though there will be excess capacity. The net increase in manufacturing overhead (over current costs) from the new lease is $100,800. All other data are the same as shown in Exhibit 9.1. What will be the new reported product costs for the two desk models, assuming that overhead is allocated on the basis of direct labor-hours?

The solution to this question is at the end of the chapter.

Two-Stage Cost Allocation

LO 9-2

Explain how a two-stage product costing system works.

The basic approach in product costing is to allocate costs in the cost pools to the individual cost objects, which are the products or services of interest. We assign, or allocate, these costs to the individual cost objects by using appropriate cost allocation bases, or cost drivers. We continue that approach here by considering alternative cost pools and cost drivers. The basic steps to cost allocation introduced in Chapter 6 continue here, but we consider alternative implementations using two criteria—decision usefulness and cost benefit—to evaluate the new approach.

We start by recalling the two-stage approach to product costing discussed in Chapter 6. See the cost diagram for the two-stage approach in Exhibit 9.4. The first-stage cost objects are the overhead accounts, such as supplies, depreciation, and so on. The two-stage approach allowed us to separate plant, or manufacturing, overhead into two or more cost pools based on the account in which the costs were recorded. The allocation in the first stage, although simple, allowed us then to select multiple cost drivers—direct labor costs and machine-hours, for example—that were used to allocate costs to products.

Exhibit 9.4   Cost Flow Diagram: Two-Stage Cost Allocation System

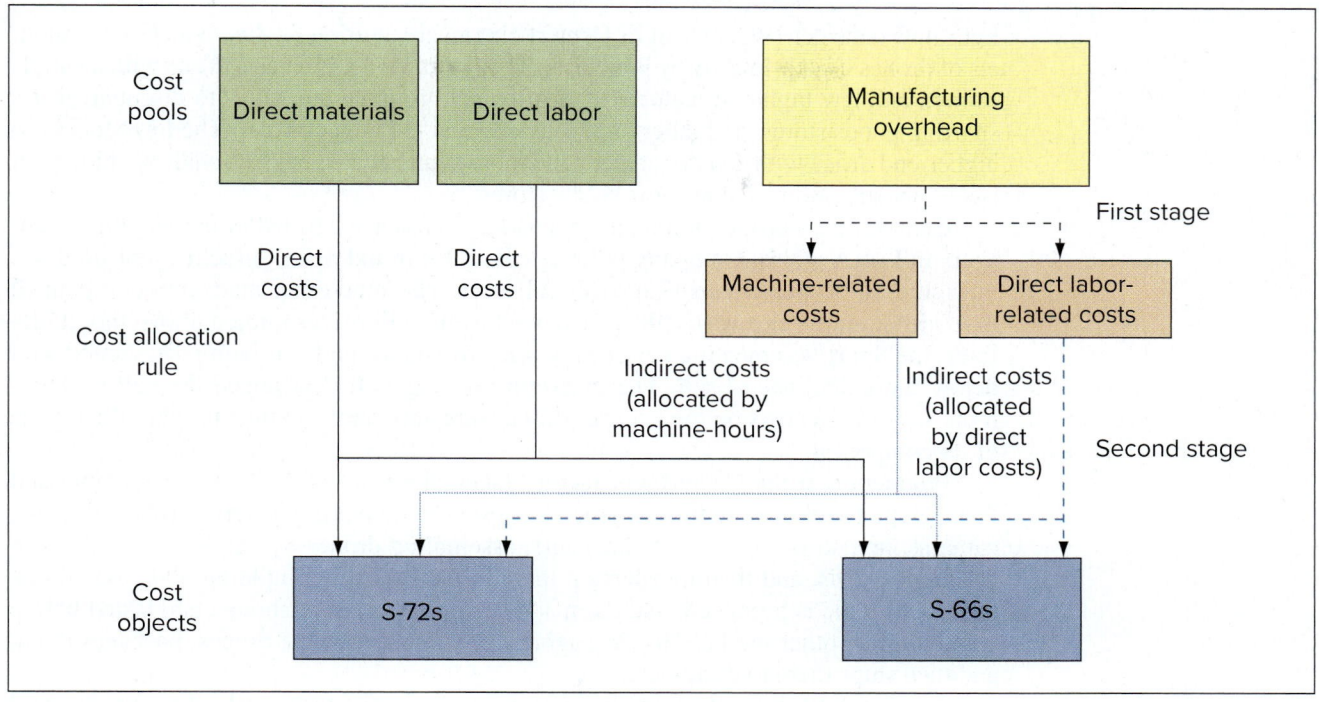

In Chapter 6, we grouped overhead accounts with similar patterns of variability into first-stage cost pools that could be allocated to products using a common cost driver; however, we are not limited to this choice. Another common choice is to use departments within the plant. See Exhibit 9.5 for such a costing system.

We use predetermined overhead rates throughout this chapter. Recall from Chapter 7 that using predetermined rates normally results in over- or underapplied overhead. To keep the examples from becoming too complex, we do not use examples that involve over- or underapplied overhead in this chapter.

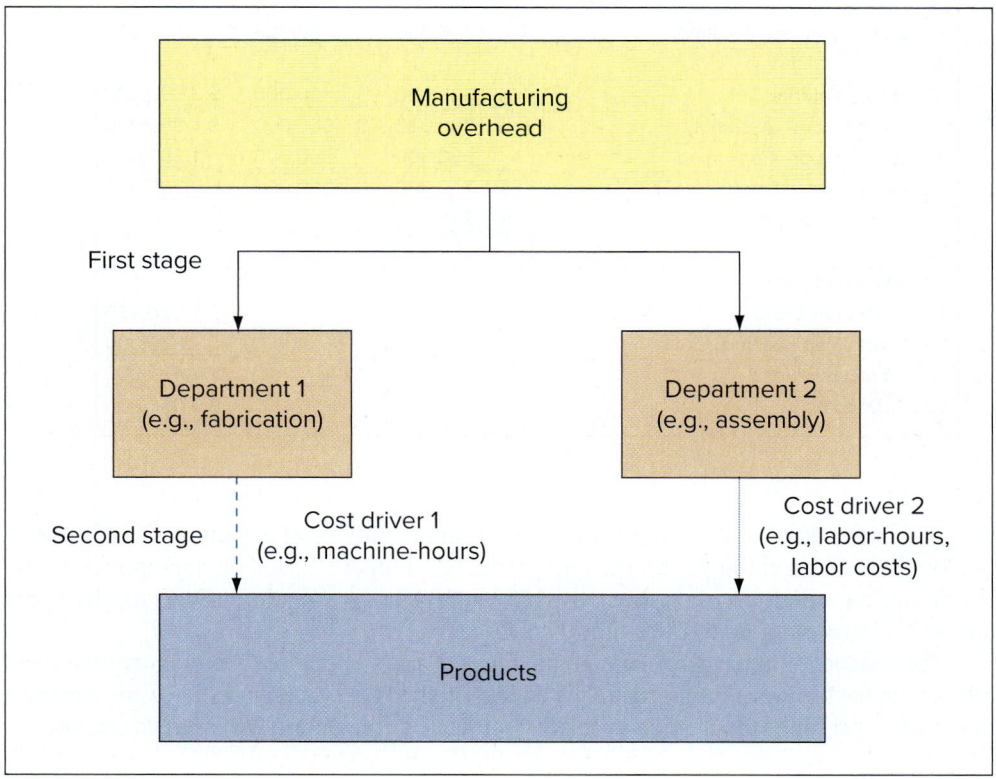

Exhibit 9.5

Two-Stage Cost Allocation: First-Stage Allocation to Departments

Two-Stage Cost Allocation and the Choice of Cost Drivers

Let's now consider IVC, Inc. At its CenterPoint manufacturing facility, it makes two models of drones used primarily by hobbyists. The Sport Model is a basic drone with a simple camera and few high-end features. It is often sold in large quantities to discount stores, sporting goods stores, and other outlets that appeal to budget buyers. The Pro Model is a higher-end drone with a better camera and more sophisticated navigational capabilities. It is sold mostly online and at some hobby stores.

CenterPoint's production managers had a conference call with the marketing managers in Los Angeles. Company policies called for initial price guidelines for products to include a 30 percent markup over full cost. The marketing managers complained that, although the Pro was selling very well even with prices quoted above the guidelines, the Sport was meeting very heavy price resistance and was being discounted well below the guidelines to sell. The marketing managers had arranged the call to determine why IVC's costs on the cheaper drone were apparently so much higher than those of its competitors.

Production at the CenterPoint facility takes place in two buildings, Assembly and Packaging. The drone production process consists of delivering materials (plastic, rotors, cameras, and so on) to the assembly line, assembling drones by employees working in production cells, and then transferring them to the Packaging building. Only one drone model at a time is produced, and the machines have to be recalibrated and tested before beginning the other model. The Packaging Department tests the drones, packages them, and then ships them to customers.

See Exhibit 9.6 for data on the operations of the CenterPoint facility for the third quarter. The facility's cost system is a traditional product costing system that allocates manufacturing overhead to products based on direct labor costs.

Exhibit 9.6

Third Quarter
Production and Cost
Data—CenterPoint
Manufacturing Facility

	A	B	C	D
1		Sport	Pro	Total
2				
3	Number of units	100,000	40,000	140,000
4				
5	Machine-hours—Assembly	6,000	30,000	36,000
6				
7	Direct materials	$ 1,500,000	$ 2,400,000	$ 3,900,000
8	Direct labor—Assembly	$ 750,000	$ 600,000	$ 1,350,000
9	Direct labor—Packaging	990,000	360,000	1,350,000
10	Direct labor—Total	$ 1,740,000	$ 960,000	$ 2,700,000
11	Total direct cost	$ 3,240,000	$ 3,360,000	$ 6,600,000
12				
13	Overhead costs			
14	Assembly building			$ 1,620,000
15	Packaging building			810,000
16	Total overhead			$ 2,430,000
17	Total costs			$ 9,030,000

The overhead allocation rate at the CenterPoint facility is 90 percent (= $2,430,000 ÷ $2,700,000). See Exhibit 9.7 for the unit product cost report. Based on the reported costs, marketing set initial prices on the two drones at $62.48 (= $48.06 × 130%) for the Sport and $137.28 (= $105.60 × 130%) for the Pro.

The production managers claimed that CenterPoint's operations were among the most efficient in the business. Furthermore, when they studied the cost report, they were surprised that the Pro was only about twice as costly to produce as the Sport. That seemed too low.

	A	B	C
		Sport	Pro
1			
2	Units produced	100,000	40,000
3			
4	Direct material	$ 15.00	$ 60.00
5	Direct labor		
6	Assembly	$ 7.50	$ 15.00
7	Packaging	9.90	9.00
8	Total direct labor	$ 17.40	$ 24.00
9	Direct costs	$ 32.40	$ 84.00
10	Applied overhead (@ 90% of direct labor costs)	15.66	21.60
11	Unit costs	$ 48.06	$ 105.60

Exhibit 9.7

Third Quarter Unit Cost Report—CenterPoint Manufacturing Facility

The production managers explained that the Pro requires much more complex equipment and special handling in Assembly. In addition, it requires much shorter production runs, requiring more setups. "Something," they said, "doesn't seem right in the way the costs came out."

As a result of the controversy, Nancy, the cost accounting manager, is now evaluating the product cost accounting system to determine whether it was accurately reporting the costs of making the two models.

Nancy decided to experiment with a two-stage cost allocation system. In the first stage, the overhead costs would be allocated to the two buildings (departments). In the second stage, the overhead costs in each building would be allocated to products using different cost drivers. Because of the use of production cells and the importance of equipment cost in the Assembly building, Nancy decided to use machine-hours to allocate overhead costs in Assembly. She decided that Packaging's direct labor costs were still appropriate as an allocation base in the Packaging building. See Exhibit 9.8 for the cost flow diagram that Nancy developed for the cost system.

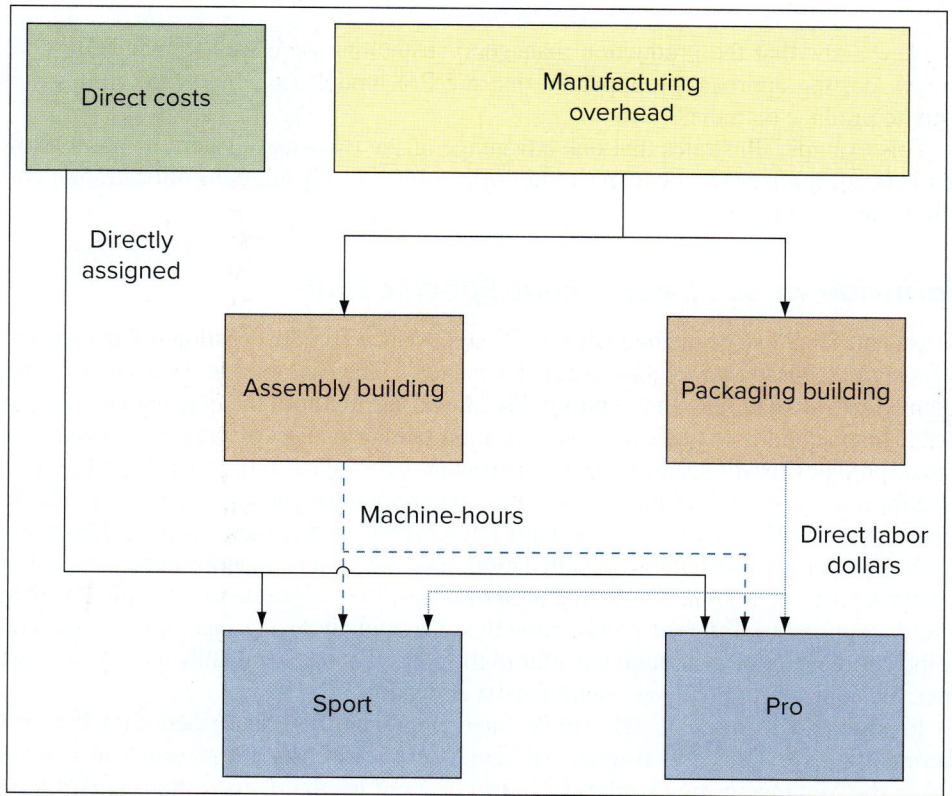

Exhibit 9.8

Cost Flow Diagram, Two-Stage System—CenterPoint Manufacturing Facility

Nancy calculates the overhead rates for the two buildings:

$$\text{Assembly:} \frac{\text{Budgeted overhead}}{\text{Budgeted machine-hours (MH)}} = \frac{\$1,620,000}{36,000 \text{ MH}} = \$45 \text{ per machine-hour}$$

$$\text{Packaging:} \frac{\text{Budgeted overhead}}{\text{Budgeted direct labor cost}} = \frac{\$810,000}{\$1,350,000} = 60\% \text{ of direct labor cost}$$

Based on these overhead rates, Nancy calculated the revised product costs (see Exhibit 9.9). For the Sport, the Assembly overhead costs per unit were $2.70 [($45 × 6,000 MH)/100,000 units]. Note that the 6,000 machine-hours (MH) were shown in Exhibit 9.6, row 5. Also for the Sport, the Packaging overhead costs per unit were $5.94 (= 60% × $9.90), where the $9.90 is the Packaging direct labor cost shown in Exhibit 9.9, row 7. We can use the same methods to find the unit overhead costs for the Pro.

Exhibit 9.9

Third Quarter Unit Cost Report—CenterPoint Manufacturing Facility

	A	B	C
		Sport	Pro
1			
2	Units produced	100,000	40,000
3			
4	Direct material	$ 15.00	$ 60.00
5	Direct labor		
6	Assembly	$ 7.50	$ 15.00
7	Packaging	9.90	9.00
8	Total direct labor	$ 17.40	$ 24.00
9	Direct costs	$ 32.40	$ 84.00
10	Applied overhead		
11	Assembly (@ $45 per machine-hour)	$ 2.70	$ 33.75
12	Packaging (@ 60% of packaging direct labor cost)	5.94	5.40
13	Total overhead	$ 8.64	$ 39.15
14	Unit costs	$ 41.04	$ 123.15
15			

Nancy saw that the production managers' suspicions were well founded. Based on the new costing approach, it appeared that the Pro model was about three times more costly to produce than the Sport.

This example illustrates that one advantage of the two-stage system is that it allows the firm to develop product costing systems that more closely align the allocation of costs with the use of resources.

Plantwide versus Department-Specific Rates

LO 9-3

Compare and contrast plantwide and department allocation methods.

plantwide allocation method
Allocation method using one cost pool for the entire plant. It uses one overhead allocation rate, or one set of rates, for all of a plant's departments.

We used the single-stage method when we first introduced product costing in Chapter 6 and for most of the discussion of job costing in Chapter 7. The examples in those chapters used a plantwide overhead rate. In the **plantwide allocation method,** the cost pool is the entire plant. This method uses one overhead allocation rate, or one set of rates, to allocate overhead to products for *all* departments in a particular plant. We use the term *plant* to refer to an entire factory, store, hospital, or other multidepartment segment of a company. The key word in the definition is *all;* that is, a single rate or set of rates is used for every department.

Although it is called *plantwide* allocation, this allocation concept can be used in both manufacturing and nonmanufacturing organizations. In a hospital, for example, overhead could be applied to different wards, patients, or treatments using just one overhead rate for the entire hospital. Although we refer to the costs that are being allocated as *overhead* costs, the concepts apply to *any* indirect cost allocation.

Plantwide allocation is the single-stage approach first described in Chapter 6. Accounting for overhead is simple. All actual overhead costs are recorded in one cost pool in the Manufacturing Overhead Control account for the plant without regard to the department or activity that caused them. A single overhead rate is used to apply overhead to products, crediting Applied Manufacturing Overhead. For example, if overhead is applied using a predetermined rate per machine-hour, the amount of the credit to the Applied Manufacturing Overhead account and the amount of the debit to Work in Process for overhead costs equal the rate per machine-hour times the total number of machine-hours worked.

Companies using a single plantwide rate generally use an allocation base related to the *volume* of output, such as direct labor-hours, machine-hours, units of output, or materials costs. Later in this chapter, we discuss allocation bases that are not directly related to volume.

Using the **department allocation method,** a company has a separate cost pool for each department. The company establishes a separate overhead allocation rate for each department. (In this chapter, we assume that only one rate is used for each department. The use of multiple rates, specifically dual rates, is discussed in Chapter 12.) Each production department is a separate cost pool. In contrast, the plantwide allocation method considers the entire plant as one cost pool.

department allocation method
Allocation method that has a separate cost pool for each department, which has its own overhead allocation rate or set of rates.

Choice of Cost Allocation Methods: A Cost-Benefit Decision

The choice of whether to use a plantwide rate or departmental rates depends on the products and the production process. If the company manufactures products that are quite similar and that use the same set of resources, the plantwide rate is probably sufficient. If multiple products use the manufacturing facilities in many different ways, departmental rates provide a better picture of the use of manufacturing resources by the different products. Managers need to make a decision about plantwide versus departmental rates based on the costs and benefits of the information inherent in each system. Selecting more complex allocation methods requires more time and skill to collect and process accounting information. Such incremental costs of additional information must be justified by an increase in benefits from improved decisions.

Self-Study Question 2 demonstrates the differences between plantwide (or company-wide) and department rates when computing service costs.

Self-Study Question

2. Mesa Consultants has projects with both private and government clients. Its overhead consists of both negotiations costs (including proposal preparation) and general administrative costs. Mesa has two groups, private and government, each working solely with one type of client. The following estimated operating data are available for next year:

	Government	Private
Direct costs...........	$4,000,000	$1,000,000
Number of contracts.....	20	30

Costs in the two administrative departments are expected to be as follows:

Negotiations.......................	$ 750,000
General administrative..............	850,000
Total	$1,600,000

Mesa management is considering two approaches to assigning overhead costs to projects. One is to use a plantwide rate based on direct costs. The second is to use separate rates for the negotiations and general administrative costs. Under this method, negotiations costs will be allocated based on the number of contracts, and general administrative costs will be allocated based on the direct costs.

Compute the overhead costs allocated to the two groups using (1) the plantwide rate and (2) the individual department rates. What are the advantages and disadvantages of the separate rates compared to the plantwide rate?

The solution to this question is at the end of this chapter.

Activity-Based Costing

LO 9-4

Explain how activity-based costing and a two-stage product costing system are related.

Assume that you are thinking about starting a new business, a restaurant, perhaps. One of the first steps, as you know from your business courses, is to develop a business plan that includes a financial analysis. One aspect of the financial analysis is estimating the cost of operations (food, labor, building, maintenance, and so on) to help you assess the profitability of your venture. How would you proceed in your analysis?

Because you are not now in the business, you have no accounting records to use to help you. Instead, you would probably proceed by identifying the activities that you would need to perform once your restaurant is open for business. You would need to *lease* and *maintain* suitable facilities to serve the meals. Ensuring you have the ingredients for the meals would require *ordering* and *paying* for food and beverages from suppliers (local farmers, for example). You would need to *pay* your staff (and *train* new staff as turnover occurs). You would need to *advertise* your restaurant and new specials, *keep* records for tax authorities, *withhold* and *pay* payroll taxes, and so on in order to operate.

Once you had identified each activity that you would have to accomplish, you would estimate the cost of completing each one. You would then compare the total cost to the expected revenues of the meals to determine whether your venture will be financially viable based on marketing data about the demand for your venture. This approach is the engineering approach to cost estimation we discussed in Chapter 5. It is a natural approach when you do not have data to use to estimate costs.

In this description of the process you would follow, the italicized words are actions that represent tasks that you would complete to make the product (service) available for sale. You do not attempt to determine what department or what overhead account would be used. You use activities. Applying this approach to the two-stage cost allocation system, you assign costs to activities, not departments or buildings, in the first stage. In the second stage, you "allocate" costs to your products (meals, for example) using the appropriate cost drivers for each *activity*.

activity-based costing (ABC)
Costing method that first assigns costs to activities and then assigns them to products based on the products' consumption of activities.

Activity-based costing (ABC) is a two-stage product costing method that assigns costs first to activities and then to the products based on each product's use of activities. An *activity* is any discrete task that an organization undertakes to make or deliver a product or service. Activity-based costing is based on the concept that products consume activities and activities consume resources.

Developing Activity-Based Costs

Activity-based costing involves the following four steps:

1. Identify the activities—such as purchasing food and beverages—that consume resources, and assign costs to them.

cost drivers
Factors that cause, or "drive," costs.

2. Identify the cost driver(s) associated with each activity. A **cost driver** causes, or "drives," an activity's costs. For the food-purchasing activity, the cost driver could be the number of purchase orders.
3. Compute a cost rate per cost driver unit or transaction. The cost driver rate could be the cost per purchase order, for example.
4. Assign costs to products by multiplying the cost driver rate by the volume of cost driver units consumed by the product. For example, the cost per purchase order multiplied by the number of orders processed for a particular food item during the month of March measures the cost of the order processing activity for that menu item during March.

Identifying Activities That Use Resources   Often the most interesting and challenging part of the exercise is identifying activities that use resources because doing so requires understanding all the activities required to make a product. In fact, much of

Machine-hours used	Computer time used
Labor-hours or labor cost incurred	Number of items produced or sold
Pounds of materials handled	Customers served
Pages typed	Flight hours completed
Machine setups	Surgeries performed
Purchase orders completed	Scrap/rework orders completed
Quality inspections performed	Hours of testing time spent
Number of parts installed in a product	Number of different customers served
Miles driven	

Exhibit 9.10

Examples of Cost Drivers

the value of activity-based costing comes from this exercise even without changing the way product costs are computed. When managers step back and analyze the processes (activities) they follow to produce a good or service, they often uncover many nonvalue-added steps that they can eliminate. We discuss this aspect of ABC, often called *activity-based management,* in Chapter 10.

Imagine the activities involved in making a simple product such as a bottle of water: ordering, receiving, and inspecting materials; bottling the water; packing the cases; shipping the cases. Now imagine the number of activities involved in making or providing a complex product or service such as an airplane or an overnight package delivery service. Of course, using common sense and the principle that the benefits of more detailed costs should exceed the costs of getting the information, companies identify only the most important activities.

Choosing Cost Drivers

See Exhibit 9.10 for several examples of the types of cost drivers that companies use. Most are related either to the volume of production or to the complexity of the production or marketing process.

We have already discussed several criteria for selecting allocation bases. The best cost driver is one that is causally related to the cost being allocated. Finding an allocation base that is causally related to the cost is often not possible. In previous chapters, we have used reasonable allocation bases such as direct labor-hours or machine-hours. With an ABC system, the selection of an allocation base, or cost driver, is often easier because we can use a measure of the activity volume. For example, a reasonable allocation base for machine setup costs is machine setup hours. Notice that many of the cost drivers in Exhibit 9.10 refer to an *activity.*

Computing a Cost Rate per Cost Driver

In general, predetermined rates for allocating indirect costs to products are computed as follows:

$$\text{Predetermined rate} = \frac{\text{Estimated indirect cost}}{\text{Estimated volume of allocation base}}$$

This formula applies to any indirect cost, whether manufacturing overhead or administrative, distribution, selling, or any other indirect costs. Workers and machines perform activities on each product as it is produced. Costs are allocated to a product by multiplying each activity's predetermined rate by the volume of activity used in making it.

In the ABC two-stage cost system, the first stage consists of activities, not departments. Instead of a department rate, activity-based costing computes a cost driver rate for each activity center. This means that each activity has an associated cost pool (see Exhibit 9.11). If the cost driver for materials handling is the number of production runs, for example, the company must be able to estimate the costs of materials handling before the period and, ideally, track the actual cost of materials handling as it is incurred during the period.

Exhibit 9.11

Cost Flow Diagram:
Activity-Based Costing
System

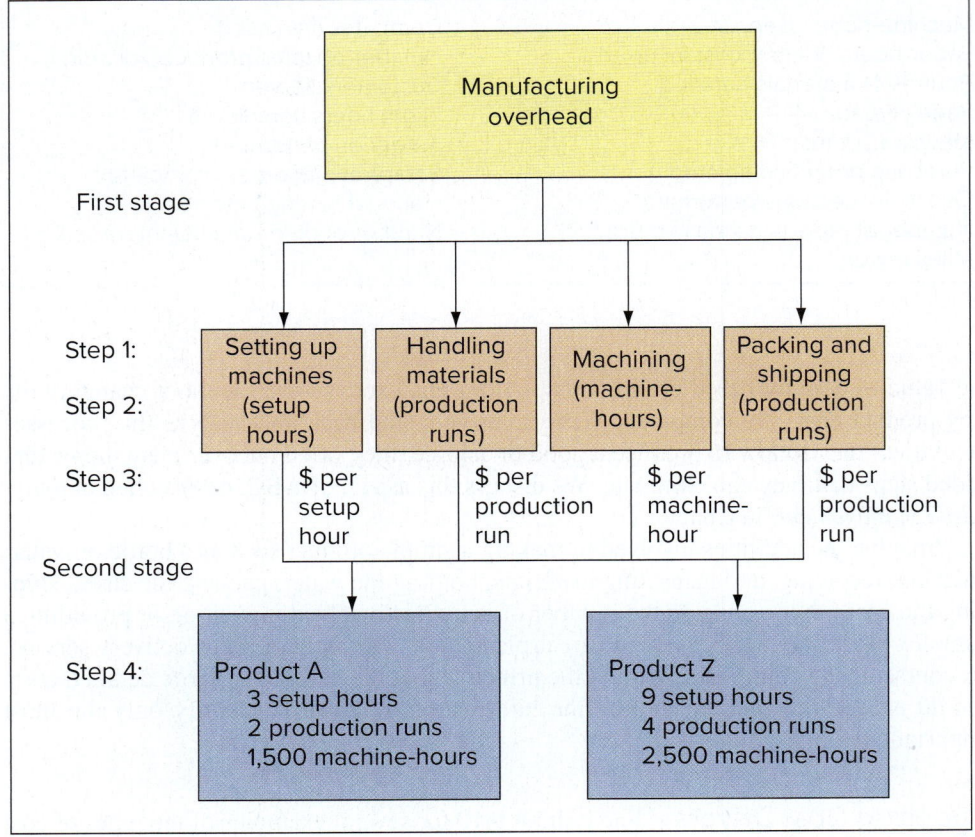

Assigning Costs to Products   The final step in the activity-based costing system is to assign the activity costs to products. We do this just as we have done for the other product costing systems we have considered. We multiply the cost driver rates by the number of units of the cost driver in each product.

The cost flow diagram in Exhibit 9.11 illustrates the four steps of developing activity-based costs graphically:

1. Identify the activities.
2. Identify the cost driver(s) associated with each activity.
3. Compute a cost rate per cost driver unit or transaction.
4. Assign costs to products by multiplying the cost driver rate by the volume of cost driver units consumed by the product.

Exhibit 9.11 depicts a cost flow diagram in a general manufacturing firm. We can think of the general activities that might be required, for example, setting up the machines, bringing material to the assembly line (handling materials), machining the raw material into the final product, and packing and shipping the final product.

Cost Hierarchies

When we look at the cost flow diagram for the activity-based costing system in Exhibit 9.11 and compare it to the two-stage cost flow diagram in Exhibit 9.5, a natural issue is how these two systems differ. The first obvious difference is that in the activity-based costing system, the first-stage allocates costs to *activities,* not *departments.* Although this seems to be a small difference, you will see in Chapter 10 that it has important implications for cost management.

The second, more important difference is the nature of the cost drivers. Notice that in the case of Exhibit 9.5, the cost drivers were direct labor- and machine-hours, both of which are production-volume or simply *volume related*. That is, both cost drivers are proportional to production volume.

In Exhibit 9.11, one cost driver, machine-hours, is volume related, but the other two, production runs and setup hours, are not directly related to volume. In other words, given a setup and production run, it really does not matter how many units are produced. The costs of materials handling, for example, are not volume related; they are production-run or *batch related*. The distinctive feature of activity-based costing is that it recognizes that overhead costs are caused by activities and that some activities are driven by something other than production volume.

A **cost hierarchy** classifies cost drivers by general dimensions or levels of activity. For example, some cost drivers are related to volume and some to production runs (batches), as in Exhibit 9.11. The cost hierarchy can have other levels as well. For example, some costs are caused simply by having a product available for sale. They include the costs of maintaining specifications or designs and could be called *product related*. The costs also include regulatory compliance costs, for example, testing for environmental compliance. Other general costs could be incurred simply to have the manufacturing capability (plant depreciation, for example). These costs might be thought of as *facility related*. See Exhibit 9.12 for a summary of the cost hierarchy and four possible levels.

In a college, the cost hierarchy consists of costs related to students (paper for class handouts), classes (instructors), products (accreditation), and facilities (buildings). Aaron Roeth Photography

cost hierarchy
Classification of cost drivers into general levels of activity, volume, batch, product, and so on.

Hierarchy Level	Example Costs	Cost Driver Examples
Volume related	Supplies	Direct labor cost
	Lubricating oil	Machine-hours
	Machine repair	Number of units
Batch related..........	Setup costs	Setup hours
	Materials handling	Production runs
	Shipping costs	
Product related........	Compliance costs	Number of products
	Design and specification costs	
Facility related	General plant costs	Direct cost
	Plant administration costs	Value added

Exhibit 9.12

Cost Hierarchy

An activity-based costing system can have fewer than four levels in the hierarchy, or it can have more than four. The important factor in distinguishing an activity-based costing system is whether the cost drivers for the activities reflect the cost incurred by the activity, even if cost is not caused by volume.

Activity-Based Costing Illustrated

Let's see how the reported product costs for the two drone models produced by IVC's CenterPoint manufacturing facility are affected by using activity-based costing. Once we have computed the costs, we will contrast the results using activity-based costing with those computed using a single rate and using a two-stage system, using the volume-related cost drivers of direct labor cost and machine-hours.

LO 9-5
Compute product costs using activity-based costing.

Step 1: Identify the Activities

In developing an ABC system at the plant, Nancy Chen, the cost accounting manager, begins by interviewing the production managers to determine the major activities used to manufacture products in the CenterPoint facility. She learns that the Assembly building

Exhibit 9.13

Cost Drivers and Cost
Driver Volumes—
CenterPoint
Manufacturing Facility

	A	B	C	D	E
1				Cost Driver Volume	
2	Activity	Cost Driver	Sport	Pro	Total
3	Assembly building				
4	Assembling	Machine-hours	6,000	30,000	36,000
5	Setting up machines	Setup hours	40	400	440
6	Handling material	Production runs	8	40	48
7	Packaging building				
8	Inspecting and packing	Direct labor-hours	60,000	22,800	82,800
9	Shipping	Number of shipments	100	200	300
10					

has three major activities—assembling, setting up, and handling material—and that the Packaging building has two major activities—inspecting and packing, and shipping. This identification completes step 1 of the activity-based costing process.

Step 2: Identify the Cost Drivers

Next, Nancy interviews the production supervisors in the two buildings to determine the appropriate cost drivers. After some discussion with the line employees, the production supervisors agree on the cost drivers and the expected volume of each driver (Exhibit 9.13). Nancy completes the second step of the ABC process.

Step 3: Compute the Cost Driver Rates

Nancy returns to the production supervisors to complete the third step, computing the cost driver rates. She interviews the production supervisors in the two buildings to determine how much overhead cost is incurred for each of the five activities. She summarizes what she has learned in Exhibit 9.14, which provides more detail about the overhead costs in Exhibit 9.6.

Step 4: Assign Costs Using Activity-Based Costing

Based on these interviews, Nancy develops a cost flow diagram (Exhibit 9.15), which includes the first-stage assignment of costs to activity pools and the second-stage allocation of activity costs to products noting the cost drivers for each activity.

Exhibit 9.14   Third Quarter Overhead Cost Data—CenterPoint Manufacturing Facility

	A	B	C	D	E	F	G	H
1		Overhead	÷		Cost Driver	=		Cost Driver
2	Building and Activity	Cost			Volume			Rate
3	Assembly building							
4	Assembling	$ 1,080,000	÷	36,000	machine-hours	=	$ 30	per machine-hour
5	Setting up machines	396,000	÷	440	setup hours	=	$ 900	per setup hour
6	Handling material	144,000	÷	48	production runs	=	$ 3,000	per production run
7	Total Assembly building overhead	$ 1,620,000						
8								
9	Packaging building							
10	Inspecting and packing	$ 414,000	÷	82,800	direct labor-hours	=	$ 5	per direct labor-hour
11	Shipping	396,000	÷	300	shipments	=	$ 1,320	per shipment
12	Total Packaging building overhead	$ 810,000						
13	Total overhead	$ 2,430,000						
14								

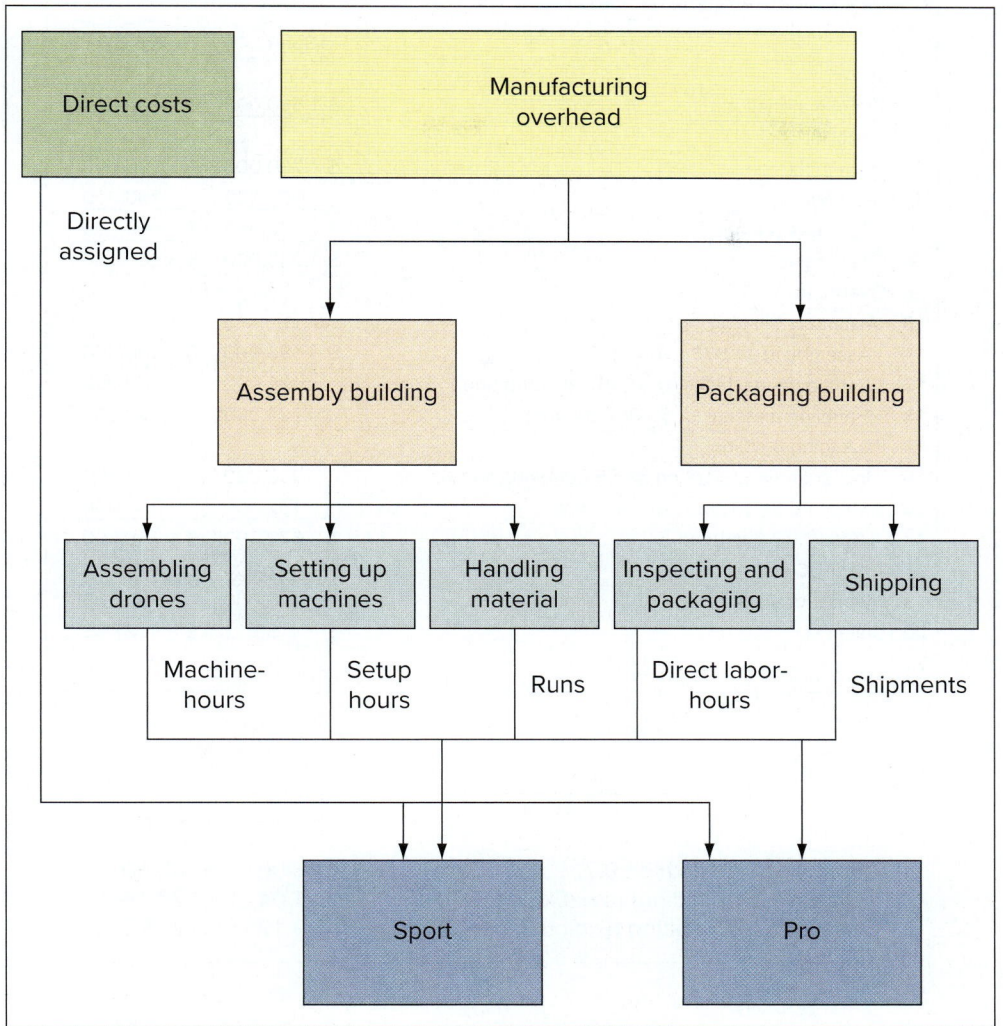

Exhibit 9.15

Cost Flow Diagram, Activity-Based Costing System—CenterPoint Manufacturing Facility

Using the information in the cost flow diagram, Nancy assigns costs to the two products. The direct costs, material and labor, are, of course, the same as in the original system and the two-stage system described earlier in the chapter. There is a difference, however, in the assignment of overhead costs. No longer can Nancy multiply the number of units of the cost driver in a unit of product by the cost driver rate because not all cost drivers are identified at the unit level (i.e., they are not all volume related). In the production cost report that Nancy prepares (Exhibit 9.16), she first calculates the total cost of production for each product and then divides the total cost by the number of units produced to arrive at the unit cost. She could also have calculated the cost-driver rate per unit of product for each of the cost drivers and then calculated the unit cost of the product directly.

Unit Costs Compared

How do the reported product costs compare for the three methods we considered in this chapter? See the summary of the unit product costs under the three systems in Exhibit 9.17. Panel A of Exhibit 9.17 provides the data, but the impact of the three methods is more easily seen in the graph in Panel B, where we see that rather than being about twice the cost of the Sport model, the Pro model, using ABC as the costing system,

LO 9-6

Compare activity-based product costing to traditional department product costing methods.

Exhibit 9.16

Third Quarter Unit Cost
Report, Activity-Based
Costing—CenterPoint
Manufacturing Facility

	A	B	C
1		Sport	Pro
2			
3	Direct material	$ 1,500,000	$ 2,400,000
4	Direct labor		
5	Assembly	$ 750,000	$ 600,000
6	Packaging	990,000	360,000
7	Total direct labor	$ 1,740,000	$ 960,000
8	Direct costs	$ 3,240,000	$ 3,360,000
9	Overhead		
10	Assembly building		
11	Assembling (@ $30 per MH)	$ 180,000	$ 900,000
12	Setting up machines (@ $900 per setup hour)	36,000	360,000
13	Handling material (@ $3,000 per run)	24,000	120,000
14	Packaging building		
15	Inspecting and packing (@ $5 per direct labor-hour)	300,000	114,000
16	Shipping (@ $1,320 per shipment)	132,000	264,000
17	Total ABC overhead	$ 672,000	$ 1,758,000
18	Total ABC cost	$ 3,912,000	$ 5,118,000
19	Number of units	100,000	40,000
20	Unit cost	$ 39.12	$ 127.95
21			

Exhibit 9.17

Panel A: Comparison of
Reported Unit Product
Costs

	Sport	Pro
Plantwide rate (Exhibit 9.7)	$48.06	$105.60
Department (building) rate (Exhibit 9.9).	41.04	123.15
Activity-based costing (Exhibit 9.16)	39.12	127.95

Panel B: Graphical
Comparison of Reported
Unit Product Costs

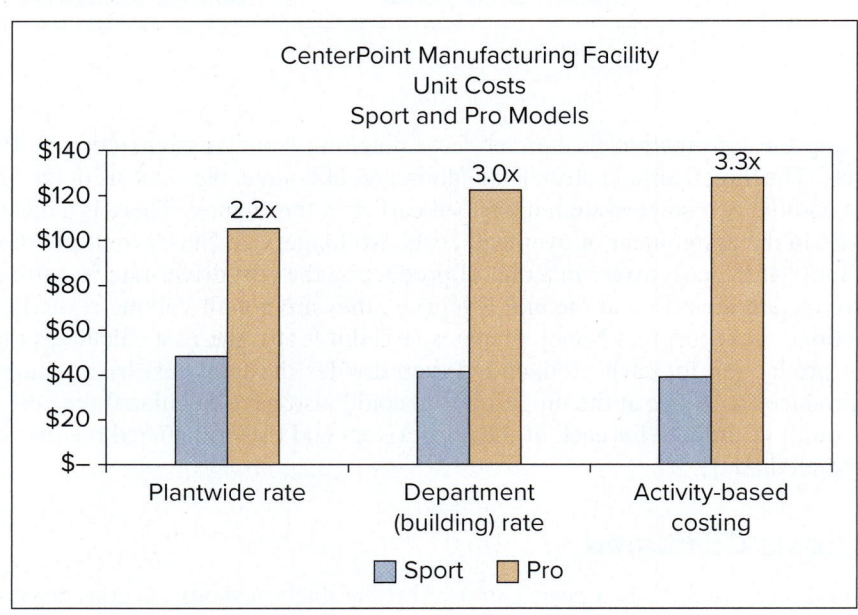

is over three times as costly to produce. This confirms the intuition of production
personnel and is consistent with the description of the manufacturing process. As we
moved from the plantwide rate to the building rate, the cost shifted from the simpler
drone (the Sport) to the more complex drone (the Pro) because using the plantwide

rate allocated all overhead on the basis of direct labor. Notice that the simpler drone uses many fewer machine-hours and more direct labor in Assembly. Because the simpler drone is more labor intensive in Assembly, the plantwide rate cost system charged the simple drone with a large proportion of overhead. When separate departmental (building) rates were used in the two-stage system, some of this overhead shifted to the more complex drone. This was also consistent with the intuition of the production managers.

When the company considered the activities, it recognized that the lower-volume drone used more of some activities (Exhibit 9.13). Moving to an activity-based costing system reflected the use of the activities by the products. Both the plantwide rate system and the department (building) rate system assumed that overhead was incurred proportionally with the volume of output. The activity-based costing system recognized that overhead was related to activity use, not necessarily to the volume of output.

The preceding discussion made the following important points about activity-based costing:

- Different cost allocation methods result in different estimates of how much it costs to make a product.

- Activity-based costing provides more detailed measures of costs than do plantwide or department allocation methods.

- Production also benefits because activity-based costing provides better information about how much each activity costs. In fact, it helps identify cost drivers (that is, the activities that cause costs) that previously were unknown. To manage costs, production managers learn to manage the cost drivers.

- Activity-based costing provides more information about product costs but requires more recordkeeping. Managers must decide whether the benefits of improved decisions justify the additional cost of activity-based costing compared to department or plantwide allocation.

- Installing activity-based costing requires teamwork between accounting, production, marketing, management, and other nonaccounting employees.

Cost Flows through Accounts

See Exhibit 9.18 for the flow of costs through accounts using activity-based costing. The amounts shown in the accounts are from Exhibit 9.16.

LO 9-7
Demonstrate the flow of costs through accounts using activity-based costing.

Self-Study Question

3. The production supervisor at the CenterPoint Manufacturing facility has given more thought to the appropriate cost driver for setups and believes it should be production runs, not setup hours. Compute the activity-based costs for the two drone models at the CenterPoint facility assuming an activity-based costing system where setup cost is allocated based on the number of production runs. Use data from Exhibits 9.13 and 9.14.

The solution to this question is at the end of the chapter.

Exhibit 9.18 Cost Flows in the CenterPoint Manufacturing Facility

Materials Inventory		Work-in-Process—Assembly			
1,500,000		Sport—Material	1,500,000	2,490,000	Sport to Packaging
2,400,000		Sport—Labor	750,000		
		Sport—Overhead	240,000		
		Pro—Material	2,400,000	4,380,000	Pro to Packaging
		Pro—Labor	600,000		
Wages Payable		Pro—Overhead	1,380,000		
750,000					
600,000		**Work-in-Process—Packaging**			
990,000					
360,000		Sport from Assembly	2,490,000	3,912,000	Sport to Finished Goods
		Sport—Labor	990,000		
		Sport—Overhead	432,000		
		Pro from Assembly	4,380,000	5,118,000	Pro to Finished Goods
		Pro—Labor	360,000		
		Pro—Overhead	378,000		

Assembling Activity

Overhead Incurred		Overhead Applied
Actual costs		180,000 (Sport)
		900,000 (Pro)

Setting Up Machines Activity

Overhead Incurred		Overhead Applied
Actual costs		36,000 (Sport)
		360,000 (Pro)

Handling Material Activity

Overhead Incurred		Overhead Applied
Actual costs		24,000 (Sport)
		120,000 (Pro)

Inspecting and Packing Activity

Overhead Incurred		Overhead Applied
Actual costs		300,000 (Sport)
		114,000 (Pro)

Shipping Activity

Overhead Incurred		Overhead Applied
Actual costs		132,000 (Sport)
		264,000 (Pro)

Choice of Activity Bases in Modern Production Settings

When cost systems were first being developed in industry, companies were far more labor intensive than they are today. Much of the overhead cost was incurred to support labor, so it made sense to allocate overhead to products based on the amount of labor in the products. Labor is still a major product cost in many companies, especially service organizations such as consulting, law, and public accounting firms. In those cases, overhead is often allocated to products (called *jobs*) on the basis of the amount of labor in the product.

As companies have become more automated, including those in the service sector such as banks, direct labor has become less appropriate as a basis for allocating overhead. Because direct labor has dropped to less than 5 percent of product costs in many companies and overhead has increased, companies that stubbornly continue to allocate overhead to products based on direct labor are experiencing rates as high as 500 percent or more. (We have seen cases in which overhead rates are more than 1,000 percent of direct labor costs.)

When labor is such a small part of product costs, there is little, if any, relation between labor and overhead. In addition, small errors in assigning labor to products are magnified many times when overhead rates are several hundred percent or more of labor costs. Finally, allocating overhead on the basis of direct labor sends signals that direct labor is more expensive than it really is. This also creates tremendous incentives to reduce the labor content of products. This can be desirable in particular circumstances, but such decisions should be based on accurate cost numbers, not on those that are heavily biased because of an arbitrary cost allocation method.

The magnitude of the overhead rate based on direct labor is of less concern when all resources are used proportionally. For example, if one employee uses only one machine, the number of labor-hours and machine-hours worked on a product will be proportional. Using machine-hours instead of labor-hours will not change the allocation of overhead to products in this case. However, in modern manufacturing settings, proportionality between machine-hours and direct labor-hours is much less common. Workers tend to work with two or more machines at the same time. In this case, a proportional relation between labor-hours and machine-hours for a particular product is no longer likely.

Complexity as a Resource-Consuming Activity

One lesson of activity-based costing has been that costs are a function of both volume and complexity. It might be obvious that a higher volume of production consumes resources, but why does *complexity* consume resources?

To understand the answer to that question, imagine that you produce office desks and chairs. If you made only one model of desk and one model of chair, your production process would be reasonably simple. You might produce desks in one building and chairs in another. As they are finished, they are combined and sold as a set.

One activity that you will perform is order processing. Just as the production process is relatively simple, so is the administrative process for accepting orders. Now consider what happens as you offer variations on your two products. For example, you offer different colors, different materials, chairs with and without arms, and so on. Although you still make only two products, the *complexity* of the product offering has increased costs considerably in the order-processing function. For example, your order taker now must ensure that the color of the chair and desk are compatible; that the fabric for chair arms is specified, but only if the customer orders chairs with arms; and so on. Your simple company has suddenly become more complex and more costly, even if it sells exactly the same number of chairs and desks.

When accountants use allocation rates based on volume, such as direct labor-hours or machine-hours, they naturally allocate costs to products in proportion to volume. High-volume products are allocated a high proportion of overhead costs, and low-volume products are allocated a low proportion. After installing activity-based costing, managers have frequently found that the low-volume products should be allocated more overhead.

Low-volume products could be more specialized, requiring, for example, more drawings, specifications, and inspections.

Low-volume products often require more machine setups for a given level of production output because they are produced in smaller batches. In the furniture example, one production run (batch) of 50 units of a low-volume (but "high-fashion") desk might require as much overhead cost for machine setups, quality inspection, and purchase orders as one run of 10,000 desks of the most popular design. In addition, the low-volume product adds complexity to the operation by disrupting the production flow of the high-volume items. You appreciate this fact every time you stand in a line when someone ahead of you has a special and complex transaction.

As stated, when overhead is applied based on the volume of output, high-volume products are allocated relatively more overhead than are low-volume products. High-volume products "subsidize" low-volume products in this case. Volume-based allocation methods hide the cost effects of keeping a large number of low-volume products. This has led many companies to continue producing or selling products without realizing how costly they are.

Business Application   ABC in Health Care

UPMC, a $21 billion medical system affiliated with the University of Pittsburgh, employs over 90,000 staff and 400 doctors. As a major medical provider, UPMC closely monitors the health system's costs in a variety of areas. The information from the costing system at UPMC allows decision makers to manage costs and improve productivity while maintaining effective care.

> "That's why you're seeing that improved productivity, because we actually reduced our fixed-cost infrastructure," said Robert DeMichiei [UPMC, CFO]. . . . "We had not only the data and the measurements and the insight into our operations, but we also had the management willpower and initiative."[1]

What is the cost system and how is it used?

> That data comes from the activity-based cost accounting system UPMC has spent years building to its current form. Division leaders use it to decide where spending needs to be adjusted based on whether volumes are up or down.[2]

Tracking costs has always been important, of course, but many executives believe that current technology has made better information available. In the past, many healthcare systems relied on rate increases and higher volumes to maintain revenue. That is probably not a sustainable strategy, so many healthcare providers are looking at cost efficiency and productivity improvements. Where will the cost information be that healthcare executives need to help?

> Several leaders cited activity-based costing, or ABC, as an important method of cost accounting that's superior to older strategies, namely those using cost-to-charge ratios.[3]

ABC provides these leaders with a better understanding of their costs with which to make decisions.

Sources:
1. Bannow, Tara, "More Hospitals Calculating Actual Cost of Care," *Modern Healthcare*, May 18, 2019.
2. Ibid.
3. Ibid.

Activity-Based Costing in Administration

LO 9-8

Apply activity-based costing to marketing and administrative services.

Activity-based costing also can be applied to administrative activities. The principles and methods are the same as those previously discussed. Specifically, ABC in administration involves these steps:

1. Identify the activities that consume resources.
2. Identify the cost driver associated with each activity.
3. Compute a cost rate per cost driver for each unit or transaction.
4. Assign costs to the marketing or administration activity by multiplying the cost driver rate by the volume of cost driver units consumed for that activity.

Note that instead of computing the cost of a product, accountants compute a cost of performing an administrative service. For example, the Purchasing Department at the

Activity	Possible Cost Drivers
Reviewing purchase requests.........	Number of requests
	Dollar amount of request
Soliciting bids.......................	Number of bids
	Number of vendors
	Amount of bid
Evaluating bids	Number of bids
	Amount of bid
Placing orders	Number of orders
Preparing invoices	Number of invoices
	Amount of invoices

Exhibit 9.19
Possible Cost Drivers in a Purchasing Department

CenterPoint manufacturing facility of IVC, Inc., is responsible for purchasing materials. Providing this service requires Purchasing Department staff to engage in several activities: reviewing the request, soliciting bids, evaluating bids, placing the orders, preparing the invoice, and so on, all of which require resources, just as making a drone requires resources.

The Purchasing Department can apply activity-based costing by following the same four-step procedure described for manufacturing. Many of the cost drivers in an administrative function (or a service firm) will be time related, but not all will be. See Exhibit 9.19 for some common cost drivers in a Purchasing Department.

Who Uses ABC?

We have described some benefits (and costs) of using ABC in organizations. Is ABC actually used? Exhibit 9.20 lists some of the organizations that have been cited as using ABC for at least some of their operations. The list is not exhaustive by any means. It is only a sample of organizations. Note that there are three problems with identifying users of ABC. First, ABC means different things to different observers; there is no one ABC method. The organizations listed in Exhibit 9.20 have been identified as using ABC either by themselves or by others writing about them; the individual systems could vary substantially. Second, ABC may be applied in parts of an organization but not everywhere. The organizations listed in Exhibit 9.20 may not use ABC throughout. Finally, while firms may publicly announce the adoption of ABC, they are less likely to announce its discontinuance.

Manufacturing:	**Services:**
Boeing	American Airlines
British Telecom	American Express
General Motors	Charles Schwab
Hewlett-Packard	Fireman's Fund
Texas Instruments	Owens & Minor
Weyerhauser	Truliant Federal Credit Union
Health Care:	**Government Agencies:**
Alexandria Hospital	Amtrak
Cambridge Hospital	City of Indianapolis
Froedtert Memorial Lutheran—	City of Phoenix
throughout Hospital	U.S. Marine Corps
Providence Portland Medical Center	U.S. Postal Service

Exhibit 9.20
Organizations Using ABC

Sources: Anonymous, "How ABC Will Save PPMC over $1 Million a Year," *IOMA's Report on Financial Analysis, Planning, and Reporting,* vol. 3, no. 11, 6; Byerly, D., Revell, E., and Davis, S., "Benefits of Activity-Based Costing in the Financial Services Industry," *Cost Management,* vol. 17, no. 6, 25; Grandlich, C., "Using Activity-Based Costing in Surgery," *AORN Journal,* vol. 79, no. 1, 189; Kline, J., "Activity-Based Costing and Benchmarking," *Journal of Government Financial Management,* vol. 52, no. 3, 50; Narayanan, V., "Cambridge Hospital Community Health Network—The Primary Care Unit," *Harvard Business School Case 9-100-054;* Narayanan, V., "Owens & Minor, Inc. (A)," *Harvard Business School Case 9-100-055.*

Regardless of these limitations, the list in Exhibit 9.20 is impressive in two respects. First, it includes a wide range of organizations from manufacturing firms to government agencies. Second, the size of the organizations ranges from a small, regional financial services firm to a multinational manufacturing firm. The list is an indication that *all* organizations are interested in getting better cost information for decision making.

We have considered activity-based costing for computing product and service costs in this chapter. In Chapter 10, we demonstrate how activity-based costing concepts can be used to manage costs.

Time-Driven Activity-Based Costing

LO 9-9

Explain how time-driven activity-based costing works.

As we have seen, product and service costs computed using activity-based costing offer many advantages over costs developed using traditional costing systems. Traditional systems allocate costs primarily on volume-related bases, such as direct labor-hours. An ABC system better reflects the cost drivers for the activities required. The ABC cost drivers might be volume related, but there will be some that are related to batches and so on.

Why, then, might a company choose not to use ABC? In order to provide useful information, an ABC system must be maintained and updated to reflect current activities. For example, managers must be routinely interviewed or surveyed about the allocation of their employees' time and resources across various activities. If the system is not kept up to date, there is a danger that the product costs it produces might be worse than those provided by a simpler traditional system. The process of continually updating the system is costly. We said in Chapter 1 that if the benefits of a cost system do not exceed the costs of the system, managers will not adopt the new system. This is one reason many companies do not use activity-based costing.

A modified version of ABC that addresses the costs of maintaining an ABC system has been developed.[1] This modified approach to ABC is called *time-driven activity-based costing,* or TDABC. We will illustrate the development of a TDABC system by showing how it has been implemented in the Receiving Department at the CenterPoint Facility of IVC, Inc.

Developing Time-Driven Activity-Based Costs

With TDABC, the manager only needs to determine (1) the cost of the resources supplied to a department and (2) the time it takes to complete the various activities of the department. This approach avoids the need to conduct surveys or interviews of multiple managers and employees. This means that it is not as costly to maintain as the unmodified ABC system.

The Costs of Resources Supplied
The Receiving Department at CenterPoint employs five people who conduct three activities: receiving materials, inspecting materials, and transporting materials to a small building used as a warehouse. Receiving has identified these three activities, but any one order of materials might not need to go through each activity. For example, some materials do not need to be inspected. Others might go directly to the factory floor rather than to the warehouse.

The costs of the resources supplied to Receiving include the cost of these five line employees. We add to this cost the cost of the manager of Receiving, the costs of the technology and facilities for Receiving, and so on. Together, these costs total $627,000.

---

[1] See, for example, Robert S. Kaplan and Steven R. Anderson, "Time-Driven Activity-Based Costing," *Harvard Business Review,* November 2004; or Robert S. Kaplan and Steven R. Anderson, *Time-Driven Activity-Based Costing: A Simpler and More Powerful Path to Higher Profits,* (Harvard Business School Publishing, 2007).

The Time Required for Each Activity With TDABC, we do not ask the manager to estimate what proportion of the time the employees spend on each activity. Instead, we ask the manager to estimate how much time each activity takes for a single transaction. In other words, we ask the manager, "How long does it take to inspect an incoming shipment of materials?" Typically, this is a much easier question for an experienced manager to answer.

When Nancy Chen, the cost accounting manager, asked about the time for each of these activities, the manager of Receiving provided the following estimates:

- Receiving materials: 20 minutes.
- Inspecting materials: 45 minutes.
- Transporting materials: 15 minutes.

Calculating the Costs of the Activities Now that we have the cost of the resources supplied and we know the time required for each activity, we can compute the cost of each activity. We start by calculating a cost-driver rate.

Each of the five employees works 50 weeks per year and 40 hours per week. We assume that two hours per week are used for training and other administrative tasks. Therefore, each of the five employees is available to work on these three activities for a total of 1,900 hours ($= 50$ weeks $\times$ 38 hours per week) or 114,000 minutes ($= 1,900$ hours $\times$ 60 minutes per hour) each year. This means that Receiving has 570,000 minutes of capacity available.

The cost-driver rate, then, for the various activities is computed as

$$\text{Cost-Driver Rate} = \text{Cost of Receiving} \div \text{Minutes Available}$$
$$= \$627,000 \div 570,000 \text{ minutes}$$
$$= \$1.10 \text{ per minute}$$

Combining this cost-driver rate with the time required for each activity allows us to compute the activity costs:

- Receiving materials: $22.00 ($= 20$ minutes $\times$ \$1.10 per minute).
- Inspecting materials: $49.50 ($= 45$ minutes $\times$ \$1.10 per minute).
- Transporting materials: $16.50 ($= 15$ minutes $\times$ \$1.10 per minute).

During the year, Receiving gets 7,500 orders. Of these, 4,000 are inspected and 6,500 are stored. Therefore, the costs of Receiving for the year were composed of the following:

	A	B	C	D
1	Activity	Number of Transactions for the Activity	Cost per Unit of Activity	Total Activity Cost
2	Receiving materials	7,500	$ 22.00	$ 165,000
3	Inspecting materials	4,000	49.50	198,000
4	Transporting materials	6,500	16.50	107,250
5	Total			$ 470,250
6				

The total cost of activity for Receiving is $470,250. However, recall that the total cost of Receiving is $627,000. What is the difference? It is idle time. In other words, the total time available to Receiving is 570,000 minutes. The total time used for activities is 427,500 ($= [7,500$ transactions $\times$ 20 minutes$] + [4,000 \times 45] + [6,500 \times 15]$). During the year, employees of Receiving spent 75 percent ($= 427,500 \div 570,000$) of their time working on completing activities. The rest was idle time and represents the excess capacity in Receiving.

How can these calculations help Nancy and the other managers at CenterPoint? The reported costs can be used when considering the demands placed on Receiving by the characteristics of different products. For example, if some products are produced in small quantities, they might still require the same number of shipments as those products with larger volumes. These costs can help managers make better decisions about whether they should keep or drop these products by giving better information about support costs, such as the costs for Receiving.

Business Application   What Are a Hospital's Costs?

Healthcare costs in the United States and elsewhere have been the subject of policy discussion for many years. Hospitals and insurers (including governments) are particularly interested in controlling costs while maintaining effective care. However, to manage costs it is important to understand what the costs are. Because of the methods used to reimburse hospitals in the past, little effort was devoted to the costs of individual services. As one vendor of cost accounting software with over 200 healthcare clients notes:

> A complete strategy should incorporate time-driven costing, which refers to timing procedures in operating rooms to get more precise data. . . .[1]

A project at the University of Utah Hospital is addressing this. The project tracks outcomes and costs at detailed levels.

(There are over two million rows in the database for costs and staff time, for example.) The project team tracks costs for supplies, staff, and so on, at the patient level. As a result, the hospital has detailed cost per minute information that helps them manage patient care and cost. For example,

> The hospital has been able to calculate, for instance, the cost per minute in the emergency room (82 cents), in the surgical intensive care unit ($1.43), and in the operating room for an orthopedic surgery case ($12).[2]

Sources:
1. Bannow, Tara, "More Hospitals Calculating Actual Cost of Care," *Modern Healthcare,* May 18, 2019.
2. Kolata, Gina, "What Are a Hospital's Costs? Utah System Is Trying to Learn," *The New York Times,* September 7, 2015.

Extensions of TDABC

As we have described it, TDABC is all based on a single measure for each activity: time. We can modify this somewhat without adding all of the complications of a regular ABC system.

Cost Drivers Other Than Time   Although TDABC is based primarily on time estimates for different activities, we can easily extend this to accommodate a particular case. For example, Receiving stores the material in the warehouse, which is a part of the resources included in Receiving. We can think of an additional activity (storage, for example). The cost of storage might be more related to the space required instead of time. It is a simple extension of the model to compute the cost per square foot and apply it to materials that are stored in the warehouse.

In the case of Receiving, the cost of the warehouse is $114,000 annually. The warehouse has 10,000 square feet of storage space. Therefore, the cost-driver rate for storage is $11.40 (= $114,000 ÷ 10,000 square feet) per square foot per year.

We would also recompute the time-based cost-driver rate to account for the lower remaining costs in Receiving after splitting out the warehouse cost. The remaining costs are $513,000 (= $627,000 − $114,000). Therefore, the new rate for the other activities is now $0.90 per minute (= $513,000 ÷ 570,000 minutes).

Time Equations   The TDABC system that we have developed so far assumes all orders that go through any one of the activities take the same amount of time. For example, any order that is inspected is assumed to take 45 minutes. We can extend the TDABC system to allow for differences among orders by using what are called **time equations.**

For example, Receiving has a policy of adding a verification step to the receiving materials activity if this is the first order from this vendor. The manager estimates that the

time equations

Time equations allow managers to adjust the times for orders with different characteristics.

extra verification step takes 7 minutes. In addition, if any order that is inspected contains hazardous material, extra handling precautions must be taken by the employee. These precautions are estimated to take an extra 12 minutes.

These extra steps can be expressed in the following time equations:

- Time for receiving order = 20 minutes + 7 minutes (if the vendor is new);
- Time for inspecting order = 45 minutes + 12 minutes (if the order contains hazardous material).

Time equations can also be written if there is a maximum size of an order that can be inspected or transported to the warehouse.

TDABC provides an alternative to an unmodified ABC system that might be too costly to maintain given the benefits the ABC system provides. Most likely, a combination of the two systems might be used depending on the size of the department and the need for improved cost information.

Key Takeaways

1. A two-stage cost system first allocates costs to intermediate cost pools, whether overhead accounts, departments, or some other collection of costs. It then allocates the first-stage costs to products or services using one or more cost drivers, such as direct labor-hours, machine-hours, or so on.

2. Activity-based costing (ABC) is a two-stage cost system where the first stage cost pools are *activities,* rather than departments or overhead accountings. ABC costs are computed using the following four steps:

   Step 1. Identify the activities that consume resources and assign costs to them.

   Step 2. Identify the cost driver(s) associated with each activity.

   Step 3. Compute a cost rate per cost driver unit or transaction.

   Step 4. Assign costs to products by multiplying the cost driver rate by the volume of cost driver units consumed by the product.

3. A key distinguishing feature of an ABC system is the cost hierarchy. With the cost hierarchy, not all overhead costs are assumed to be volume related. Some may be related to batches (production runs, shipments, and so on), product types, or general facility-related costs. An ABC system recognizes a "continuum of cost variability" from unit variable costs to costs that are fixed for the company. In the middle are costs that vary with batch, product, customer, facility, and so on.

4. Because ABC is based on activities, it can be used to understand better costs in service firms, not-for-profit organizations, government agencies, and administrative functions as well as manufacturing companies.

SUMMARY

This chapter deals with the allocation of indirect costs to products. Product cost information helps managers make numerous decisions, such as pricing, keeping or dropping a product, estimating the cost to make a similar product, and determining how to reduce the costs of making products.

Activity-based costing assigns costs first to activities and then to the products based on each product's use of activities. Activity-based costing is based on the premise that products consume activities and activities consume resources. Activity-based costing involves these four steps:

1. Identify the activities that consume resources and assign costs to those activities.
2. Identify the cost driver(s) associated with each activity.
3. Compute a cost rate per cost driver unit or transaction.
4. Assign costs to products by multiplying the cost-driver rate by the volume of cost-driver units consumed by the product.

The following summarizes key ideas tied to the chapter's learning objectives:

LO 9-1 Understand the potential effects of using reported product costs for decision making. When product costs are used for making decisions, the assumption about proportionality of the cost and output can distort decisions.

LO 9-2 Explain how a two-stage product costing system works. A two-stage system first allocates costs to departments or activities and then allocates costs from the departments or activities to the products or services.

LO 9-3 Compare and contrast plantwide and department allocation methods. A single-stage cost allocation system uses a single, plantwide rate to allocate costs. A two-stage cost allocation system, which allocates costs to departments in the first stage, allows managers to choose cost drivers that are appropriate for each department, rather than having to select a single driver.

LO 9-4 Explain how activity-based costing and a two-stage product costing system are related. An activity-based costing system is a two-stage system in which the first stage assigns costs to activities.

LO 9-5 Compute product costs using activity-based costing. Product costs are computed by multiplying the cost-driver rate by the number of units of the cost driver in each product.

LO 9-6 Compare activity-based product costing to traditional department product costing methods. Costs for low-volume products under activity-based costing are typically higher than under traditional department costing systems.

LO 9-7 Demonstrate the flow of costs through accounts using activity-based costing. The flow of activity-based costs through the ledger is the same as their flow using traditional methods except that the accounts are based on activities, not departments.

LO 9-8 Apply activity-based costing to marketing and administrative services. ABC methods can be used in service or administrative units of companies. Activities drive costs, regardless of industry or functional area. ABC information can help decision makers manage these costs.

LO 9-9 Explain how time-driven activity-based costing works. An alternative approach to ABC is based on time estimates to complete activities. These time estimates are multiplied by a cost-driver rate. The rate is computed as the cost of the resources supplied divided by the total time available. Time equations can be used for activities where the work required depends on features of the product or service.

KEY TERMS

activity-based costing (ABC), *394*

cost driver, *394*

cost hierarchy, *397*

death spiral, *387*

department allocation method, *393*

plantwide allocation method, *392*

time equations, *408*

REVIEW QUESTIONS

9-1. Give examples of cost drivers commonly used to allocate overhead costs to products and services.

9-2. What is the *death spiral?* How is it related to the cost accounting system?

9-3. The product costs reported using either plantwide or department allocation are the same. The only difference is in the number of cost drivers used. True or false? Explain.

9-4. Why do companies commonly use direct labor-hours or direct labor cost but not the number of units to allocate overhead?

9-5. What are the costs of moving to an activity-based cost system? What are the benefits?

9-6. What are the basic steps in computing costs using activity-based costing?

9-7. What is the *cost hierarchy?*

9-8. Cost allocation allocates only a given amount of costs to products. The total allocated is the same; therefore, the choice of the system does not matter. True or false? Explain.

9-9. What type of organization is most likely to benefit from using activity-based costing for product costing? Why?

9-10. In what ways is implementing an activity-based costing system in a manufacturing firm's personnel department the same as implementing it in the plant? In what ways is it different?

9-11. How does complexity lead to higher costs? Why is it important for the cost system design to consider complexity?

9-12. What two questions must a manager answer if a company is implementing time-driven activity-based costing?

9-13. In the context of time-driven ABC, what are *time equations?*

CRITICAL ANALYSIS AND DISCUSSION QUESTIONS

9-14. "Activity-based costing does a better job of allocating both direct and indirect costs than traditional methods do." Is this statement true, false, or uncertain? Explain.

9-15. "Activity-based costing is the same as department costing." Is this true, false, or uncertain? Explain.

9-16. Jim, the vice president of marketing, says the company should not adopt activity-based costing because it will result in the costs of some of the products going up, but the market will not allow for raising prices. How would you respond?

9-17. "It is clear after reading this chapter that activity-based costing is the best system. Whenever someone asks, I'll recommend its adoption." Do you agree? Explain.

9-18. "One of the lessons learned from activity-based costing is that all costs are really a function of volume of output." Is this true, false, or uncertain? Explain.

9-19. You have been asked to determine whether a company uses an activity-based costing system. What information would you look for to answer the question?

9-20. "Activity-based costing is just another inventory valuation method. It isn't relevant for making operating decisions." Do you agree with this statement? Explain.

9-21. As the representative of the local accounting club, you have been asked by the dean to help them understand the costs of the different degrees offered at the school. You decide to use an activity-based costing system. Write a report outlining the first two steps of developing an ABC system for this purpose: (1) identify the activities and (2) identify the activities associated with each activity.

9-22. Select an administrative function commonly found in a firm. Examples include personnel, accounts payable, purchasing, and so on. Outline an activity-based costing system for the function, including major activities, potential cost drivers, and relevant cost objects.

9-23. A manager tells you that her company's cost accounting system divides overhead into two pools: (1) inspect material and (2) assemble product. The inspect material pool is allocated on the basis of direct material dollars, and the assemble product pool is allocated on the basis of direct labor costs. She says that her controller claims this is an activity-based cost system, but she is not convinced and has asked your opinion. How would you respond?

9-24. One of the issues we identified with traditional costing systems is that all costs are allocated using volume-related drivers, such as direct labor-hours. How is time-driven ABC, which relies on minutes, different?

9-25. The cost accounting manager at your business says that he is trying to choose between a job costing system and an ABC system. How would you respond?

All applicable Exercises are included in Connect.      **EXERCISES**

9-26. Reported Costs and Decisons

(LO 9-1)

Regular Company produces audio equipment, specifically headphones and speakers. A new CEO has just been hired and announces a new policy that if a product cannot earn a markup of at least 25 percent, it will be dropped. The markup is computed as product gross profit divided by reported product cost.

Manufacturing overhead for year 1 totaled $960,000. Overhead is allocated to products based on direct materials cost. Data for year 1 show the following:

	Headphones	Speakers
Sales revenue.........	$2,156,800	$2,058,000
Direct materials	700,000	900,000
Direct labor	480,000	240,000

Required

a. Which product(s), if any, would be dropped based on the CFO's new policy? Show computations.

b. Regardless of your answer in requirement (a), the CFO decides at the beginning of year 2 to drop the speakers from the product line. The company cost analyst estimates that overhead without the speaker line will be $600,000. The revenue and costs for headphones are expected to be the same as last year. What is the estimated markup for headphones in year 2?

(LO 9-1)   **9-27. Reported Costs and Decisions**

McClellan Recreation manufactures and sells two models of paddle boards: Starter and Pro. The Starter model is a basic board used for instruction and purchased by novices. The Pro model is made with premium materials and comes with several accessories. The boards are produced to order, and there are no inventories at the end of the year.

The cost accounting system at McClellan allocates overhead to products based on direct labor cost. Overhead in year 1, which just ended, was $2,380,000. Data on units sold for year 1 along with the unit sales price and unit direct costs for the two models follow:

	Starter Model (12,000 units)	Pro Model (4,000 units)
Sales price per unit	$310	$600
Direct materials per unit	80	150
Direct labor per unit.	100	125

Required

a.   Compute product line profits for the Starter model and the Pro model for year 1.

b.   A study of overhead shows that without the Starter model, overhead would fall to $1,400,000. Assume all other revenues and costs would remain the same for the Pro model in year 2. Compute product line profits for the Pro model in year 2 assuming the Starter model was not produced or sold.

(LO 9-2, 3)   **9-28. Plantwide versus Department Allocation**

Edlie Accessories (EA) makes travel bags, both for sale under their own label ("Branded") and for other resellers to put their label on the bags ("Private-Label"). The bags sold through the two channels are similar, but they differ slightly in the quality of materials and detail in the manufacturing process.

The manufacturing plant at EA has two departments. Department A-101 was the original manufacturing facility, and many of the machines are original. Department A-102 is new, with state-of-the-art equipment. The new equipment facilitates the additional care taken with the Branded product.

The following information presents financial results for the two models from last year:

	Private Label	Branded	Total
Sales revenue	$768,000	$480,000	$1,248,000
Direct material	216,000	156,000	372,000
Direct labor.	144,000	96,000	240,000
Manufacturing overhead			
Department A-101			$201,600
Department A-102			230,400
Total overhead			$432,000

The product costing system at EA allocates manufacturing overhead on the basis of direct labor costs.

Required

a.   Compute the profit for each product using plantwide allocation.

b.   Compute the profit for each product using department allocation.

c.   Based on the information in the exercise, would you recommend that EA continue using plantwide allocation or switch to department allocation? Explain.

(LO 9-2, 3)   **9-29. Plantwide versus Department Allocation**

West State Furniture (WSF) manufactures desks and desk chairs using two departments within a single facility. The West Department produces the desks, and the State Department produces the chairs. WSF uses plantwide allocation to allocate its overhead to all products. Direct materials cost is the allocation base. The rate used is 60 percent of direct materials cost. Last year, revenue, direct materials, and direct labor were as follows.

	Desks	Chairs
Sales revenue..........	$945,000	$810,000
Direct materials	385,000	247,500
Direct labor	175,000	112,500

Required

a.   Compute the profit for each product using plantwide allocation.

b.   The new CFO at WSF was surprised that the company used a plantwide rate because the two products were produced in separate departments. The cost analyst estimated the overhead rates for each department separately. Using department rates, the West Department rate would be 33 percent of direct materials cost. The State Department rate would be 102 percent of direct materials cost. Recompute the profits for each product using each department's allocation rate (based on direct materials cost in each department).

c.   Which overhead allocation method, plantwide or department, allocates more total overhead to the two products? Explain.

9-30. Plantwide versus Department Allocation   (LO 9-2, 3)

Trombly Travel Products (TTP) manufactures and sells travel bags and accessories. TTP produces backpacks at its West Street plant. The different backpack models are identified by the primary material used: canvas, nylon, or leather. The company uses a plantwide rate based on direct labor-hours. The plantwide rate is $5.00 per labor-hour. All direct labor at TTP is paid $25 per hour. Canvas and nylon backpacks are produced in Department 1. Leather backpacks are produced in Department 2. The product costs (per backpack) follow.

	Canvas	Nylon	Leather
Direct materials	$20.00	$25.00	$35.00
Direct labor......................	37.50	50.00	55.00

Required

a.   Compute the total unit cost of each backpack model using the plantwide allocation method.

b.   The machines in Department 1 are older and almost fully depreciated. The equipment in Department 2 was recently updated, and the process in Department 2 is more highly automated. At the request of the manager of Department 1, a cost analyst at TTP provided the following information on overhead costs, machine-hours, and direct labor-hours for the two departments.

	Department 1	Department 2
Overhead..............	$54,000	$86,000
Machine-hours	15,000	20,000
Labor-hours............	18,000	10,000

Using labor-hours as the department allocation base for Department 1 and machine-hours as the department allocation base for Department 2, compute the allocation rate for each.

c.   Compute the unit cost of each model of backpack using the department allocation rates computed in requirement (b) (labor-hours in Department 1 and machine-hours in Department 2).

d.   Which costing method would you recommend for TTP: plantwide rates or department rates? Explain.

(LO 9-2, 3) **9-31. Unitwide versus Department Allocation—Administrative (Service) Function**

Cranshaw Business Services (CBS) operates an information technology (IT) consulting firm out of two offices: Detroit and Los Angeles. Corporate services, such as legal, finance, and personnel, are centralized at the main office, and the costs of these services are allocated to the two offices for the purposes of profitability assessment. The Detroit office is the original unit of the company and is well established, having long-time clients from the automotive and other manufacturing industries. The Los Angeles office is new with a smaller, much more varied, clientele. The costs of personnel services at CBS are currently allocated on the basis of the number of employees in each office. The annual costs of the personnel department total $350,000. Data for the fiscal year just ended show the following:

	Detroit	Los Angeles
Number of employees	380	120
Number of new hires	7	20
Number of employees departing	3	10

Required

a. Compute the cost allocated to each unit using the current allocation system.

b. The manager of the Detroit office believes that Detroit gets little benefit from the personnel office other than the occasional hire and termination help. The manager asks the controller's office to estimate the amount of Personnel Department cost associated with routine personnel matters (benefits and so on) and those associated with hiring employees and assisting with departing employees (transitions). The controller responds that if they separated the overhead costs on this basis, the cost of the Personnel Department for routine matters is $200,000 and the cost of the Personnel Department for transitions (each hire and each departure counts as one transition) is $150,000.

Recompute the costs allocated to each unit using the separate rates for routine and transitional matters.

(LO 9-1, 2, 3) **9-32. Unitwide versus Department Allocation—Decision Making**

Refer to the information in Exercise 9-31. The manager of the Los Angeles office is now unhappy with the results of the controller's study. The manager asks the controller to develop separate rates for fixed and variable costs in the Personnel Department. The controller reports back to the Los Angeles manager that the costs would be as follows:

Allocation based on	Variable Cost	Fixed Cost	Total Cost
Employees	$80,000	$120,000	$200,000
Transitions	60,000	90,000	150,000

Required

a. The manager claims that the Los Angeles office should only be allocated the variable costs from this system because the company would have to pay the fixed costs even if the Los Angeles office did not exist. Compute the cost allocated to each unit using the approach the Los Angeles manager prefers.

b. Do you agree with the Los Angeles manager? Explain.

(LO 9-4, 5) **9-33. Activity-Based Costing**

After reviewing the new activity-based costing system that Nancy Chen has implemented at IVC's CenterPoint manufacturing facility, Tom Spencer, the production supervisor, believes that he can reduce production costs by reducing the time spent on machine setups. He has spent the last month working with employees in the plant to change over the machines more quickly with the same reliability. He plans to produce 100,000 units of the Sport model and 40,000 units of the Pro model in the first quarter. He believes that with his more efficient setup routine, he can reduce the number of setup hours for both the Sport and the Pro products by one-third.

Required

a. Refer to Exhibits 9.13 through 9.16. Compute the amount of overhead allocated to the Sport and the Pro drones for the first quarter using activity-based costing. Assume that all events are the same in the first quarter as in the third quarter (the text example) except for the number of setup hours. Assume the cost of a setup hour remains at $900.

b. Assume that CenterPoint had used machine-hours and a department allocation method to allocate its overhead and that the setup-hour rate for the first quarter is $900. Could Tom have made the cost reductions that he planned? What are the advantages and disadvantages of activity-based costing compared to the traditional volume-based allocation methods?

9-34. Activity-Based Costing and Cost Driver Rates

(LO 9-4)

Benton Corporation manufactures computer microphones, which come in two models: Standard and Premium. Data for a representative quarter for the two models follow:

	Standard	Premium
Units produced.....................	10,000	2,500
Production runs per quarter.............	50	25
Direct materials cost per unit............	$30	$64
Direct labor cost per unit	50	75

Manufacturing overhead in the plant has three main functions: supervision, setup labor, and incoming material inspection. Data on manufacturing overhead for a representative quarter follow:

Supervision	$206,250
Setup labor......................	240,000
Incoming inspection...............	172,500
Total overhead..................	$618,750

Required

a. Benton currently applies overhead on the basis of direct labor cost. What is the predetermined overhead rate for the quarter?

b. The CFO and the plant controller at Benton are thinking of adopting an ABC system. They have tentatively chosen the following cost drivers: direct labor cost for supervision, production runs for setup labor, and direct material dollars for incoming inspection. Compute the cost driver rates for the proposed system at Benton.

9-35. Activity-Based Costing

(LO 9-4)

Refer to the information in Exercise 9-34.

Required

a. Compute the unit costs for the two products, Standard and Premium, using the current costing system at Benton (using direct labor costs as the allocation basis for overhead).

b. Compute the unit costs for the two products, Standard and Premium, using the proposed ABC system at Benton.

9-36. Activity-Based Costing and Cost Driver Rates

(LO 9-4)

Heidelberg Fabrication manufactures two products, G-09 and G-35:

	G-09	G-35
Units produced	18,000	3,600
Direct materials cost per unit..........	$7	$19
Machine-hours per unit..............	4	7
Production runs per quarter..........	144	72

Production at the plant is automated and any labor cost is included in overhead. Data on manufacturing overhead at the plant follow:

Machine depreciation...............	$ 97,200
Setup labor........................	48,600
Materials handling.................	38,880
Total.........................	$184,680

Required

a. Heidelberg currently applies overhead on the basis of machine-hours. What is the predetermined overhead rate for the quarter?

b. Heidelberg is thinking of adopting an ABC system. It has tentatively chosen the following cost drivers: machine-hours for machine depreciation, production runs for setup labor, and direct material dollars for materials handling. Compute the cost driver rates for the proposed system at Heidelberg.

(LO 9-4)   **9-37. Activity-Based Costing**
Refer to the information in Exercise 9-36.

Required

a. Compute the unit costs for the two products, G-09 and G-35, using the current costing system at Heidelberg (using machine-hours as the allocation basis).

b. Compute the unit costs for the two products, G-09 and G-35, using the proposed ABC system at Heidelberg.

(LO 9-4)   **9-38. Activity-Based Costing, Cost Driver Rates, and the Cost Hierarchy: Not-for-Profit**
The Philip County Historical Society (PCHS) collects and displays historical artifacts from the local area. One of its services is dedicated tours. PCHS offers dedicated tours to two groups: the general public (generally tourists and local residents) and donors. PCHS has two part-time coordinators for these tours—one for the public tours and one for the donor tours.
Data for the quarter on the two groups follow:

	Public Tours	Donor Tours	Total
Number of visitors	500	250	750
Number of tours..................	25	30	55

The operational costs associated with the tours have been collected and are presented in the following table:

Refreshments, audio guides, and other	$18,000
Tour guide salaries and benefits	10,450
Coordinator salaries and benefits (@ $10,450 per coordinator)	20,900
Total..	$49,350

Required

a. PCHS currently applies operational costs of the tours to the two types (public and donor) based on the number of visitors. What is the operational cost per visitor based on the costing system currently used?

b. The financial advisor to PCHS suggests adopting an ABC system to evaluate the costs of the two types of tours. If PCHS did so, it would use the following cost drivers: number of visitors for refreshments, audio guides, and other costs; number of tours for tour guide salaries and benefits; and number of coordinators for coordinator salaries and benefits. Compute the cost-driver rates for the refreshments, information, and audio guides and tour leaders.

c. Match each of the three activity drivers to one of the levels of the cost hierarchy:

> 1. Visitors   A. Facility related
> 2. Tours   B. Batch related
> 3. Coordinators   C. Volume related
>   D. Product related

9-39. Activity-Based Costing: Not-for-Profit   (LO 9-3, 5)
Refer to the data in Exercise 9-38.

Required

a. Compute the unit (per visitor) costs for the two tour types (public and donor) assuming PCHS uses the current cost system.

b. Compute the unit (per visitor) costs for the two tour types (public and donor) assuming PCHS adopts the ABC system the advisor proposes.

9-40. Activity-Based Costing in a Nonmanufacturing Environment   (LO 9-4, 5)
Richard's Events provides catering services, among other services. The company has adopted activity-based costing (ABC) for the catering services. The ABC system classifies activities into two groups based on the cost driver used: diners and events. Each event is limited to 25 guests and requires four people to serve and clean up. Richard's Events offers two types of catered events—an informal, outside party and a formal, seated meal.

The cost accountant at Richard's Events has developed the following cost-driver rates for the individual activities:

Activities (and cost drivers)	Informal Party	Formal Dinner
Advertising (events).	$120 per event	$120 per event
Planning (events)	90 per event	150 per event
Renting equipment (events, diners)	60 per event, plus 12 per diner	90 per event, plus 24 per diner
Obtaining insurance (events)	240 per event	480 per event
Serving (events)	240 per event	360 per event
Preparing food (diners)	24 per diner	36 per diner

Per-event costs do not vary with the number of diners.

Required

a. Compute the cost of a 25-guest informal party.

b. Compute the cost of a 25-guest formal meal.

c. How much should Richard's Events charge for each diner for each type of event if the company is to cover its costs?

9-41. Activity-Based versus Traditional Costing   (LO 9-4, 5, 6)
Asbury Coffee Enterprises (ACE) manufactures two models of coffee grinders: Personal and Commercial. The Personal grinders have a smaller capacity and are less durable than the Commercial grinders. ACE only recently began producing the Commercial model. Since the introduction of the new product, profits have been steadily declining, although sales have been increasing. The management at ACE believes that the problem might be in how the accounting system allocates costs to products.

The current system at ACE allocates manufacturing overhead to products based on direct labor costs. For the most recent year, which is representative, manufacturing overhead totaled $1,902,000 based on production of 30,000 Personal grinders and 10,000 Commercial grinders. Direct costs were as follows:

	Personal	Commercial	Total
Direct materials	$1,437,000	$517,500	$1,954,500
Direct labor	1,020,000	565,000	1,585,000

Management has determined that overhead costs are caused by three cost drivers. These drivers and their costs for last year are as follows:

Cost Driver	Costs Assigned	Activity Level		
		Personal	Commercial	Total
Number of production runs	$ 900,000	50	25	75
Quality tests performed	780,000	15	25	40
Shipping orders processed	222,000	150	50	200
Total overhead	$1,902,000			

Required

a.   How much overhead will be assigned to each product if these three cost drivers are used to allocate overhead? What is the total cost per unit produced for each product?

b.   How much overhead will be assigned to each product if direct labor cost is used to allocate overhead? What is the total cost per unit produced for each product?

c.   How might the results from using activity-based costing in requirement (*a*) help management understand ACE's declining profits?

(LO 9-4, 5, 6)   **9-42. Activity-Based Costing versus Traditional Costing**

Shady Fabrication Group (SFG) manufactures components for manufacturing equipment at several facilities. The company produces two, related, parts at its Park River Plant, the models SF-08 and SF-48. The differences in the models are the quality of the materials and the precision to which they are produced. The SF-48 model is used in applications where the precision is critical and thus requires greater oversight in the production process.

Although sales remain reasonably strong, managers at SFG have noticed that the company is meeting more resistance to the pricing for SF-08, although there seems to be little need for negotiation on the price of the SF-48 model. As a result, the marketing manager at SFG has asked the financial staff to review the costs of the two products to understand better what might be happening in the market.

Manufacturing overhead is currently assigned to products based on their direct labor costs. For the most recent month, manufacturing overhead was $180,000. During that time, the company produced 8,000 units of Model SF-08 and 2,000 units of Model SF-48. The direct costs of production were as follows:

	SF-08	SF-48	Total
Direct materials	$160,000	$90,000	$250,000
Direct labor	120,000	80,000	200,000

Management determined that overhead costs are caused by three cost drivers. These drivers and their costs for last month were as follows:

Cost Driver	Overhead Costs	Activity Level		
		SF-08	SF-48	Total
Direct materials costs	$ 50,000	$160,000	$90,000	$250,000
Number of production runs	54,000	20	40	60
Number of inspections	76,000	8	11	19
Total overhead	$180,000			

Required

a.   How much overhead will be assigned to each product if these three cost drivers are used to allocate overhead? What is the total cost per unit produced for each product?

b.   How much of the overhead will be assigned to each product if direct labor cost is used to allocate overhead? What is the total cost per unit produced for each product?

c.   Draft a memo for the marketing manager explaining why the SF-08 might be experiencing resistance in the market along with your recommendation for which costing system to use.

9-43. Activity-Based Costing in a Service Environment

(LO 9-3, 4, 5)

Heidt Cleaning Services (HCS) is a local custodial service company serving both the residential and commercial markets. The owner is considering dropping the commercial clients because that business seems only marginally profitable.

Twenty-five employees worked a total of 37,500 hours last year, 25,000 on commercial jobs and 12,500 on residential jobs. Wages were $20 per hour for all work done. Any materials used are included in overhead as supplies. All overhead is allocated on the basis of labor-hours worked, which is also the basis for customer charges. Given current economic conditions and competition, HCS bills residential clients $40 per hour and commercial clients $30 per hour.

Required

a.   If overhead for the year was $337,500, what were the profits of the residential and commercial services using labor-hours as the allocation base?

b.   Overhead consists of costs of supervision, equipment used (including vehicle rental), and supplies used, which can be traced as follows:

Activity	Cost Driver	Cost	Cost Driver Volume Commercial	Residential
Supervision	Number of clients served	$ 42,000	20	64
Equipment depreciation and lease	Equipment hours	155,500	3,000	2,000
Miscellaneous supplies . . .	Area serviced in square yards	140,000	76,000	36,000
Total overhead.		$337,500		

Recalculate profits for commercial and residential services based on these activity bases.

c.   What recommendations do you have for management regarding dropping the commercial clients?

9-44. Activity-Based versus Traditional Costing

(LO 9-3, 4, 5)

Spencer's Sports manufactures outdoor equipment at three regional plants. The Freeway Plant produces two models of fishing reels, the Stream and the Surf. The Surf model is heavier and more durable. Overhead costs are currently allocated using direct labor cost. The plant manager has just returned from a week-long executive course where the instructor discussed product costing and, specifically, activity-based costing (ABC). The plant manager has asked the plant controller about implementing ABC at the plant. The controller has collected the following information on plant overhead for the most recent period:

Activity	Cost Driver	Cost	Cost Driver Volume Stream	Surf
Setting up.	Number of setups	$162,000	15	135
Inspecting.	Number of inspections	121,500	36	45
Packing and shipping . . .	Number of packages shipped	76,500	50	200
Total overhead.		$360,000		

The controller also collected the following information on production volume and direct costs for each product:

	Stream	Surf	Total
Units produced.	18,000	4,500	22,500
Direct materials cost	$450,000	$337,500	$ 787,500
Direct labor cost.	180,000	270,000	450,000
Total direct cost	$630,000	$607,500	$1,237,500

Required

a. Compute the unit cost of each model under the current system.

b. Compute the unit cost of each model under the ABC system suggested by the controller's classification of overhead costs.

c. Should the company adopt ABC for product costing?

(LO 9-3, 4, 5)

9-45. Activity-Based versus Traditional Costing—Ethical Issues

Cathedral City Services (CCS) is a not-for-profit organization offering two services in a mid-sized city. The services are "Elder Meals" and "Jobs4U." Elder Meals is a meals-on-wheels type program that delivers meals on a scheduled basis to seniors who are house-bound. Jobs4U is a jobs-training program focused on youth or adults who are looking to change careers. Participants in the program are sponsored by a local government agency, a charitable organization, or a local business. CCS charges a $240 fee per hour for each service. The revenues and costs for the year are shown in the following income statement:

CATHEDRAL CITY SERVICES
Income Statement

	Elder Meals	Jobs4U	Total
Revenue	$96,000	$240,000	$336,000
Expenses:.			
General office costs			56,000
Travel and transportation.			50,400
Equipment lease and maintenance			28,000
Operating profit.			$201,600

The following data have been collected concerning activities at CCS:

		Activity Level	
Activity	Cost Driver	Elder Meals	Jobs4U
General office costs.	Number of clients	100	60
Travel and transportation	Number of visits	550	80
Equipment lease and maintenance	Computer hours	220	900

Required

a. Complete the income statement using activity-based costing and CCS's three cost drivers.

b. Recompute the income statement using direct labor-hours as the only allocation base (400 hours for Elder Meals; 1,000 hours for Jobs4U).

c. How might CCS's decisions regarding pricing or dropping a service be altered if the organization were to allocate all overhead costs using direct labor-hours?

d. Under what circumstances would the labor-based allocation and activity-based costing (using CCS's three cost drivers) result in similar profit results?

e. A regional government agency is looking for worthy causes to support through financial grants. A primary criterion for support is financial need. CCS is thinking of applying for support for the Elder Meals program. Which allocation method would give CCS the best chance of winning a grant? Would it be ethical for CCS to report the income using this method in their application?

9-46. Activity-Based Costing: Cost Flows through T-Accounts   (LO 9-5, 7)

Heintz Products uses activity-based costing to account for product costs. The plant manager has estimated the following cost drivers and rates.

Activity Centers	Cost Drivers	Rate per Cost Driver Unit
Materials inspection	Direct materials cost	15% of materials cost
Equipment maintenance	Machine-hours	$12 per machine-hour
Machine setups	Number of production runs	$6,300 per setup
Packing and shipping	Pounds of finished output	$3.50 per pound

Direct materials costs were $480,000 and direct labor costs were $320,000 during November, when the plant finished 7,000 pounds of product, had 20 setups, and ran the machines for 15,000 hours. There were no work-in-process inventories.

Required
Use T-accounts to show the flow of materials, labor, and overhead costs from the four overhead activity centers through Work-in-Process Inventory and out to Finished Goods Inventory. Use the accounts Materials Inventory, Wages Payable, Work-in-Process Inventory, Finished Goods Inventory, and four overhead applied accounts.

9-47. Activity-Based Costing: Cost Flows through T-Accounts   (LO 9-5, 7)

LaFontaine Accessories makes a variety of computer bags, carrier bags, and so on. LaFontaine uses activity-based costing for its products. The production manager has identified the following cost drivers and rates for overhead. The manufacturing facility at LaFontaine never has any work-in-process at the end of the month.

Activity Centers	Cost Drivers	Rate per Cost Driver Unit
General support	Number of machine-hours	$8 per machine-hour
Materials handling	Direct materials cost	8% of materials cost
Machine setups	Number of machine setups	$4,600 per setup
Quality inspections	Number of inspections	$86 per inspection

Direct materials costs were $850,000 and direct labor costs were $835,000 during January, when the manufacturing facility made 750 inspections, had 36 setups, and ran the machines for 18,000 hours.

Required
Use T-accounts to show the flow of materials, labor, and overhead costs from the four overhead activity centers through Work-in-Process Inventory and out to Finished Goods Inventory. Use the accounts Materials Inventory, Wages Payable, Work-in-Process Inventory, Finished Goods Inventory, and four overhead applied accounts.

9-48. Activity-Based Costing for an Administrative Service   (LO 9-5, 8)

Exeter Group is a large retail company that has brick-and-mortar outlets throughout the Southeast. It has been in business for many years, but two years ago started an online sales channel to offset slowing in-store sales. The human resources (HR) department at Exeter handles tasks for the two divisions that make up Exeter: Retail and Online. Retail Division manages the company's traditional business line. This business, although still profitable, is currently not growing and may be shrinking slightly. Online Division, on the other hand, has experienced double-digit growth from the beginning.

The cost allocation system at Exeter allocates all corporate costs to the divisions based on a variety of cost allocation bases. HR costs are allocated based on the average number of employees in the two divisions.

There are two basic activities in the HR Department. The first is employee maintenance (payroll administration, benefits, and so on), which is an ongoing activity and requires the same amount of work for each employee regardless of the employee's salary. The second, called turnover, handles new and departing employees, including all records and orientations (for new employees) and assurance of procedural integrity (for all departures). Virtually all of this activity occurs when employees are hired or leave the company.

Assorted data for Exeter for the most recent year follow:

	Retail	Online	Total
Number of employees (average)...............	18,000	2,000	20,000
Employees hired/leaving	720	1,480	2,200

The HR Department incurred the following costs during the same year.

Employee maintenance.............	$3,940,000
Turnover	5,060,000
Total...........................	$9,000,000

Required

a. Under the current allocation system, what are the costs that will be allocated from HR to Retail Division? To Online Division?

b. Suppose the company implements an activity-based cost system for HR with the two activities employee maintenance and turnover. Use the average number of employees as the cost driver for employee maintenance costs and the average number of employees hired/leaving for turnover costs. What are the costs that will be allocated from HR to Retail? To Online?

(LO 9-5, 8)   **9-49. Activity-Based Costing for an Administrative Service**

Armada Shipping is a global logistics company. The company is organized into two divisions: Contracts and Retail. The Contracts Division, which is by far the larger division, handles customers who have regular shipping requirements and have signed contracts specifying costs and schedule for up to one year. The Retail Division handles shipments for customers who have only occasional shipping requirements and pay on an as-used basis. Billing for all customers is handled by the corporate Accounts Receivable Department. Accounts Receivable performs two major activities: billing and accounts. Billing refers to preparing and sending the bills as well as processing the payments. Accounts refers to establishing accounts, ensuring credit status, following up on collection, and so on.

The costs of the Accounts Receivable Department are allocated to the two divisions based on the number of bills prepared. The manager of the Contracts Division has complained that the allocated costs from Accounts Receivable are beginning to make the Contracts Division look unprofitable and has asked the Finance Department to recommend some changes to the allocation system.

Data on costs and activities in the Accounts Receivable Department follow:

	Contract	Retail	Total
Number of bills prepared....................	900	300	1,200
Number of new accounts/collections	20	180	200

The Accounts Receivable Department incurred the following costs during the year.

Billing..........................	$ 84,000
Accounts........................	78,000
Total........................	$162,000

Required

a. Under the current allocation system, what is the cost that will be allocated from Accounts Receivable to the Contracts Division? To the Retail Division?

b. Suppose the company implements an activity-based cost system for Accounts Receivable with two activities, billing and accounts. What is the cost that will be allocated from Accounts Receivable to the Contracts Division? To the Retail Division? Use the number of bills prepared as the cost driver for billing costs and the number of new accounts/collections for accounts costs.

9-50. Time-Driven Activity-Based Costing

(LO 9-9)

Meadow Logistics, Inc. (MLI) distributes food purchased in bulk to small retailers. The firm is divided into two divisions: Purchasing and Distribution. Purchasing is responsible for ordering goods from the manufacturer, receiving them, and then moving them to the appropriate location in the warehouse. Distribution is responsible for taking orders from retailers, picking the products from the warehouse for the orders, and packaging the orders for shipment. MLI has a policy of filling every order on the day of the order. If the firm is out of a particular item, it will ship a partial order and complete the order when the item is back in stock. Occasionally, an order will not have to be packaged if the retailer chooses to take delivery at the MLI loading dock.

Distribution has 20 employees who are responsible for the activities, and all 20 are trained to handle any of the three tasks. Each of these employees works 40 hours per week for 50 weeks. There is an allowance of 18 percent of the employees' time for training and other administrative tasks. The total costs of distribution for the coming year are estimated to be $885,600. When asked, the manager of Distribution estimated the following times for each of the three activities:

- Taking orders: 8 minutes.
- Picking orders: 12 minutes.
- Packaging orders: 15 minutes.

During the year, Distribution received 42,000 orders. Because of out-of-stock events, pickers had to pick 49,000 orders; 39,500 orders were packaged.

Required:

a. What is the cost per minute for activities in Distribution?

b. What is the cost of an order that requires all three activities?

c. How many minutes of unused capacity did Distribution have for the year?

d. What was the cost of the unused capacity in Distribution?

9-51. Time-Driven Activity-Based Costing

(LO 9-9)

Lincolnshire Lumber sells boards for many uses including wood floors. For floors, the boards are sold to local installers or do-it-yourself homeowners. The boards go through up to four processes, although only the first two are completed for all sales.

Lincolnshire employs 10 workers in the Flooring Department who are each trained and experienced in all four processes. Each employee works 35 hours per week for 50 weeks per year. Lincolnshire allocates 10 percent of the workers' time to training and staff meetings, The total annual cost for Flooring, excluding the cost of the wood itself but including the tools, machinery, labor, and so on, is $737,100.

The supervisor of the Flooring Department estimates the following time for each of the four processes for a unit of wood as sold:

1. Cutting: 11 minutes
2. Planing: 18 minutes
3. Distressing (optional): 24 minutes
4. Staining (optional): 27 minutes

During the year, Flooring received orders for 12,000 units. Of these, 7,000 units were distressed and 9,500 units were stained.

Required:

a.   What is the cost per minute for activities in Flooring?

b.   What is the cost of a unit that is cut, planed, and stained?

c.   How many minutes of unused capacity did Flooring have for the year?

d.   What was the cost of the unused capacity in Flooring?

(LO 9-8, 9)   **9-52. Time-Driven ABC for an Administrative Service**

The manager of the Personnel Department at Binder City has been reading about time-driven ABC and wants to apply it to that department. The manager has identified four basic activities Personnel Department employees spend most of their time on: Interviewing, Hiring, Evaluation, and Exit. The department employs seven staff members who perform these activities. The manager provides the following estimates for the amount of time it takes to complete each of these activities:

- Interviewing: 40 minutes.
- Hiring: 45 minutes.
- Evaluation: 85 minutes.
- Exit: 105 minutes.

Employees in Personnel work 37.5-hour weeks with four weeks for vacation. Of the 37.5 hours, 5 are reserved for administrative tasks, training, and so on. The costs of the Personnel Department, including any allocated costs from other staff functions, are $1,244,880. During the year, Personnel conducted 1,100 interviews, made 640 hires, made 5,400 evaluations, and had 400 separations.

Required

a.   What is the cost per minute for activities in Personnel?

b.   What is the cost of interviewing and hiring one employee?

c.   How many minutes of unused capacity did Personnel have for the year?

d.   What was the cost of the unused capacity in Personnel?

PROBLEMS    All applicable Exercises are included in Connect.

(LO 9-1, 5, 6)   **9-53. Comparative Income Statements and Management Analysis**

Normandy Office Products (NOP) makes two types of office desks, Manager and Executive. The Executive model is adjustable using electric motors and is made with upgraded materials. The manufacturing process for the Executive model is more complex than that for the Manager model, requiring more frequent inspections and shorter production runs. The Manager model is a basic desk, using good, but easy to work with, materials, and is simpler to manufacture. NOP's results for the last fiscal year are shown in the following statement.

NORMANDY OFFICE PRODUCTS Income Statement			
	Manager	Executive	Total
Sales revenue	$960,000	$1,065,000	$2,025,000
Direct materials	170,000	180,000	350,000
Direct labor	120,000	150,000	270,000
Overhead costs			
Administration			216,000
Machine setup			360,000
Inspection			240,000
Packing and shipping			480,000
Operating profit			$ 109,000

NOP currently uses labor costs to allocate all overhead, but management is considering implementing an activity-based costing system. After interviewing the sales and production staff, management decides to allocate administrative costs on the basis of direct labor costs but to use the following bases to allocate the remaining costs:

| | | Activity Level | |
Activity	Cost Driver	Manager	Executive
Machine setup	Number of production runs	200	100
Inspection	Number of inspections	200	400
Packing and shipping	Number of units shipped	12,000	3,000

Required

a.   Prepare the product line income statement using the proposed activity bases.

b.   Write a brief report indicating how management could use activity-based costing to reduce costs.

c.   Restate the product line income statement for Normandy Office Products using direct labor costs as the only overhead allocation base.

d.   Write a report to management stating why product line profits differ using activity-based costing compared to the traditional approach. Indicate whether activity-based costing provides more accurate information and why (if you believe it does provide more accurate information). Indicate in your report how the use of labor-based overhead allocation could cause NOP management to make suboptimal decisions.

9-54. Comparative Income Statements and Management Analysis

(LO 9-1, 5, 6)

Thatcher Supply manufactures and sells two types of pet doors—Standard and Hi-Tech. The Standard model is a basic opening installed in a door. The Hi-Tech model is automated and includes several safety features using electronics. The Hi-Tech model requires shorter production runs and more frequent inspection to ensure quality standards are met. In August, Thatcher Supply had the following financial results:

| THATCHER SUPPLY | | | |
Income Statement For the Month of August			
	Standard	Hi-Tech	Total
Sales revenue	$262,500	$168,500	$431,000
Direct materials	51,720	34,500	86,220
Direct labor.	95,000	38,000	133,000
Overhead costs			
Administration			51,720
Machine setup...............			54,600
Quality assurance............			20,680
Machine maintenance			48,000
Operating profit...............			$36,780

Other selected information for units produced in August follow:

	Standard	Hi-Tech
Units produced	2,500	500
Direct labor-hours per unit.	2	4
Machine-hours per unit	.8	2

Thatcher Supply currently uses direct labor-hours to allocate all overhead to the two models but is considering implementing an activity-based costing system. After interviewing the sales and production staff, the financial staff suggests they allocate administrative costs on the basis of revenue. They would use the following cost drivers to allocate the remaining three pools of overhead costs:

		Activity Level	
Activity	Cost Driver	Standard	Hi-Tech
Machine setup	Number of production runs	10	25
Quality assurance	Number of inspections	10	10
Machine maintenance...........	Number of machine-hours	2,000	1,000

Required

a. Complete the product-line income statement using the current system using direct labor-hours to allocate overhead costs.

b. Complete the product-line income statement using the proposed ABC system to allocate overhead costs.

c. Write a report to management stating why product-line profits differ using activity-based costing compared to the traditional approach. Indicate whether you believe activity-based costing provides more accurate information and, if so, why. Indicate in your report how the use of labor-based overhead allocation could cause management at Thatcher Supply to make suboptimal decisions.

d. How might using ABC help managers at Thatcher Supply manage costs? Be specific.

(LO 9-1, 5, 6)   **9-55. Ethics and Choice of Accounting Methods**

Refer to Problem 9-54. Assume that you have prepared financial statements that show the operating profit for each of the two models manufactured by Thatcher Supply. Further assume that under the activity-based costing approach (requirement [b] in Problem 9-54), the Hi-Tech model is less profitable than when only direct labor-hours are used to allocate overhead costs (requirement [a] in Problem 9-54). If management sees the activity-based costing results, the company will probably quit producing the Hi-Tech model. You were responsible for the original financial analysis that indicated that the Hi-Tech model would be more profitable than the Standard model.

Required

Should you show the activity-based costing results to management?

(LO 9-3, 5, 6)   **9-56. Activity-Based Costing and Predetermined Overhead Allocation Rates**

Fisher Fixtures manufactures three types of lighting fixtures, with model names of Silver, Gold, and Platinum. It applies all indirect costs according to an annual predetermined rate based on direct labor-hours. The plant controller has recommended that the company switch to an activity-based costing system. The controller's staff prepared the following cost estimates for next year (year 2) for the recommended cost drivers.

Activity	Recommended Cost Driver	Estimated Cost	Estimated Cost Driver Activity
Purchasing material	Number of purchase orders	$ 114,000	240 purchase orders
Receiving material...........	Direct materials cost	216,000	$2,700,000
Setting up equipment.......	Number of production runs	210,000	120 runs
Machine depreciation and maintenance	Machine-hours	72,000	14,400 hours
Ensuring regulatory compliance..............	Number of inspections	421,200	54 inspections
Shipping	Number of units shipped	1,036,800	576,000 units
Total estimated cost		$2,070,000	

In addition, management estimated 45,000 direct labor-hours for year 2.

Assume that the following cost-driver volumes occurred in January, year 2:

	Silver	Gold	Platinum
Number of units produced	32,000	10,000	3,000
Direct labor-hours	2,000	1,200	400
Number of purchase orders	7	6	3
Direct materials costs	$97,500	$60,000	$37,500
Number of production runs	2	3	5
Machine-hours	700	175	100
Number of inspections	0	2	3
Units shipped	32,000	10,000	3,000

Labor costs are based on the contractual rate of $25 per hour.

Required

a. Compute the predetermined rate for year 2 for use in the current product-costing system using direct labor-hours as the allocation base.

b. Compute the per-unit production costs for each model for January using direct labor-hours as the allocation base and the predetermined rate computed in requirement (*a*).

c. Compute the predetermined overhead rate for year 2 for each cost driver using the estimated costs and estimated cost driver units prepared by the controller's staff to be used in an ABC system.

d. Compute the per-unit production costs for each product for January using the cost drivers recommended by the consultant and the predetermined rates computed in requirement (*c*). (*Note:* Do not assume that total overhead applied to products in January will be the same for activity-based costing as it was for the labor-hour-based allocation.)

e. Management has seen your numbers and wants an explanation for the discrepancy between the product costs using direct labor-hours as the allocation base and the product costs using activity-based costing. Write a brief response to management.

9-57. Activity-Based Costing: Analysis and Visualization   (LO 9-5, 6)

Clairepoint Medical Devices, Inc. (CMDI) makes three types of a diagnostic device. For internal purposes, these models are referred to as Alpha, Beta, and Gamma, respectively. Although they are designed to provide the same information, the models differ by the quality of the materials and their electronic capabilities. The Alpha model is a relatively simple device that requires more manual data entry and retrieval. The Gamma model automates much of the interface with the user. As a purveyor of certain medical devices, including these models, CMDI requires certification for each model, regardless of the number of units sold.

CMDI computes product costs by allocating all manufacturing overhead to products based on direct labor costs. After attending a seminar on financial analysis, the chief marketing officer (CMO) of CMDI asked the plant controller about ABC and whether it could be used for the costing of these three models. To respond to the request, the controller collected the following information for the upcoming period:

Activity	Recommended Cost Driver	Estimated Cost
Obtaining certificates	Number of certificates	$ 105,000
Handling materials	Direct materials cost	204,750
Setting up	Production runs	155,500
Engineering	Number of units	320,000
Assuring quality	Number of inspections	104,000
Shipping	Production runs	220,000
		$1,109,250

Product-line information for the upcoming period follows:

	Alpha	Beta	Gamma
Number of units produced	2,500	1,000	500
Direct materials costs (total)	$212,500	$145,000	$130,000
Direct labor cost (total).	$262,500	$105,000	$67,500
Number of certificates	1	1	1
Number of production runs.	5	5	10
Number of inspections.	2	4	10

Required

a. Compute the unit product costs for the upcoming period using the current system, which allocates overhead based on direct labor costs.

b. Compute the unit product costs for the upcoming period based on an ABC system using the activities and cost drivers identified by the controller.

c. Prepare a report for the CMO on the reasons for the differences in the costs, the implications for decisions, and how the results might be used to manage costs. Be sure to include any visual support appropriate to illustrate your analysis.

(LO 9-5, 6) **9-58. Activity-Based Costing: Analysis and Visualization**

Delaware Electronics makes three models of a controller for measurement and testing equipment: Models X-100, X-200, and X-500. The three models differ in their capabilities and also in the materials they use. The X-100 model is a low-technology, standard controller that does not use any unusual materials. The X-200 and X-500 have more capabilities and include some materials that require special treatment both in the production process and in the treatment of wastewater once a production run is complete. Companies that use the materials are required to obtain a permit to purchase and use the materials and must treat the wastewater using a method that meets current environmental regulations. The permits are required regardless of the number of units produced and are valid for a single reporting period.

Delaware currently uses a traditional product-costing system and allocates overhead to products based on direct labor costs. The chief financial officer (CFO) is considering adopting an ABC system for product-costing purposes and has asked the plant cost analyst to study the feasibility and the benefits of doing so. The cost analyst formed a study team with production and other financial staff to respond to the CFO's request. The team first identified activities and cost drivers. The team then estimated production levels, costs, and so on for the next reporting period. The following table summarizes the information gathered about activities, drivers, and costs:

Activity	Proposed Cost Driver	Estimated Cost
Obtaining permits.	Number of permits	$ 84,460
Setting up machines	Number of production runs	176,700
Maintaining equipment	Number of machine-hours	234,600
Checking quality.	Number of inspections	26,240
Treating wastewater	Number of units generating wastewater	389,000
Packaging	Number of units	160,000
Total overhead cost.		$1,071,000

Information from the ABC team about individual products for the next reporting period follow:

	X-100	X-200	X-500
Units produced.	20,000	12,000	8,000
Direct materials cost (total).	$240,000	$216,000	$256,000
Direct labor cost (total)	$600,000	$180,000	$240,000
Machine hours (total).	40,000	30,000	32,000
Number of permits required.	0	1	1
Number of production runs	10	15	32
Number of inspections	2	4	10
Number of units generating wastewater	0	12,000	8,000

Required

a.   Compute the unit product costs for the upcoming period using the current system, which allocates overhead based on direct labor costs.

b.   Compute the unit product costs for the upcoming period based on an ABC system using the activities and cost drivers identified by the ABC study team.

c.   Prepare a report for the CFO on the reasons for the differences in the costs, the implications for decisions, and how the results might be used to manage costs. Be sure to include any visual support appropriate to illustrate your analysis.

9-59. Adopting an Activity-Based Costing System   (LO 9-3, 5, 6)

Ellis Equipment (EE) manufactures three models of lawn tractor: EE-1000, EE-1800, and EE-2800. Because of the different materials used, production processes for each model differ significantly in terms of machine types and time requirements. Once parts are produced, however, assembly time per unit required for each type of tractor is similar. For this reason, EE allocates overhead on the basis of machine-hours. Last quarter, the company shipped 8,000 EE-1000s, 3,200 EE-1800s, and 800 EE-2800s. The revenues and expenses for the last quarter were as follows:

ELLIS EQUIPMENT
Income Statement
For the Quarter ended June 30

	EE-1000	EE-1800	EE-2800	Total
Sales revenue.................	$12,800,000	$8,000,000	$3,520,000	$24,320,000
Direct costs				
Direct materials	4,800,000	3,200,000	1,120,000	9,120,000
Direct labor..................	1,680,000	768,000	230,400	2,678,400
Variable overhead				
Setting up machines				1,400,000
Quality testing..............				1,800,000
Painting				780,000
Operating equipment				155,000
Shipping....................				756,000
Contribution margin...........				$ 7,630,600
Fixed overhead				
Facility administration				1,430,000
Miscellaneous fixed overhead...				3,300,000
Gross profit..................				$ 2,900,600

The plant manager asked the plant controller about the possibility of adopting ABC. After consulting with the production supervisors in the plant, the controller recommended the following:

			Activity Level	
Activity	Cost Driver	EE-1000	EE-1800	EE-2800
Setting up machines	Number of production runs	154	238	308
Quality testing...........	Number of tests	320	200	80
Painting	Units shipped	8,000	3,200	800
Operating equipment	Machine-hours	5,000	8,000	12,000
Shipping...............	Number of units shipped	8,000	3,200	800

The controller also recommended that facility administration and miscellaneous fixed overhead costs not be applied to products, especially in the initial experiment with ABC.

Required

a.   Using machine-hours to allocate production overhead, complete the income statement for Ellis Equipment. Follow the controller's recommendation and do not attempt to allocate facility administration or miscellaneous fixed overhead.

b.   Complete the income statement using the bases recommended by the controller.

c.   How might activity-based costing result in better decisions by Ellis Equipment's management?

d.   After hearing the controller's recommendations, the plant manager has decided to adopt activity-based costing, at least for internal purposes. However, the plant manager is concerned about not allocating all the costs to products. How would you respond to this concern?

(LO 9-3, 5, 6)   **9-60. Adopting an Activity-Based Costing System**

Nall Products manufactures a wide variety of products in several facilities. It produces three models of mobility scooters in its St. Claire plant: models NP-10, NP-20, and NPX-70. The machine and labor times for the three models are similar. The difference in the production process is in the amount of testing, size of the production runs, and so on. The St. Clair plant allocates manufacturing overhead based on machine-hours. Last month, the company shipped 750 NP-10s, 500 NP-20s, and 250 NPX-70s. The revenues and expenses for the last month were as follows:

NALL PRODUCTS
Income Statement
For the Month ended October 31

	NP-10	NP-20	NPX-70	Total
Sales revenue	$412,500	$350,000	$262,500	$1,025,000
Direct costs				
Direct materials	112,500	100,000	70,000	282,500
Direct labor	37,500	37,500	31,250	106,250
Variable overhead				
Machine setups				75,000
Quality assurance				67,500
Assembly				37,500
Machine usage				18,000
Shipping				27,000
Contribution margin				$411,250
Fixed costs				
General plant support				73,000
Other fixed costs				148,000
Gross profit				$190,250

After a review of operational and financial practices at the plant, a consultant recommended that the St. Clair plant adopt an ABC system for computing product costs to provide better information for routine decisions. The consultant also recommended the following activities and drivers be used in the system:

Activity	Cost Driver	Activity Level NP-10	NP-20	NPX-70
Machine setups	Number of production runs	15	20	25
Quality assurance	Number of tests	25	50	50
Assembly	Number of units	750	500	250
Machine usage	Machine-hours	8,625	6,000	4,125
Shipping	Number of units shipped	750	500	250

The consultant also suggested not allocating the fixed costs to products because "there does not seem to be much of a link between the costs and production activity."

Required

a.   Using machine-hours to allocate production overhead, complete the income statement for Nall Products for the month. Follow the consultant's recommendation and do not attempt to allocate general plant support or other fixed costs.

b. Complete the income statement using the bases recommended by the consultant.

c. How might activity-based costing result in better decisions by Nall Product's management?

d. After hearing the consultant's recommendations, the plant manager, with the approval of the company CFO, has decided to adopt activity-based costing, at least for internal purposes. However, the plant manager is concerned about not allocating all the costs to products. How would you respond to this concern?

9-61. Activity-Based Costing, Cost Flow Diagram, Cost Hierarchy, and Predetermined Overhead Rates   (LO 9-3, 5, 6)

Warren Furniture produces three models of desk chairs: Basic, Ergo, and Exec. The cost system at the Warren production facility allocates overhead cost on the basis of direct labor hours. The company is considering updating its cost system to an activity-based costing system and is interested in understanding the effects. A study team composed of the production facility's finance and operations groups has identified three overhead cost pools along with appropriate cost drivers for each pool.

Cost Pools	Costs	Activity Drivers
Assembly..............	$1,215,000	Direct labor-hours
Setup.................	1,080,000	Number of setups
Quality assurance	585,000	Number of tests

The plans for production for the next year and the budgeted direct costs and activity by product line are as follows:

	Products		
	Basic	Ergo	Exec
Direct costs (material and labor).........	$1,440,000	$1,200,000	$960,000
Direct labor-hours.....................	25,200	12,000	7,800
Machine-hours........................	21,600	9,600	7,200
Number of setups.....................	48	72	120
Number of tests......................	140	100	60
Number of units produced	7,200	3,000	1,200

Required

a. The current cost accounting system charges overhead to products based on machine-hours. What unit product costs will be reported for the three products if the current cost system continues to be used?

b. What are the cost driver rates for the three cost pools identified by the study team?

c. Prepare a cost flow diagram of the ABC system proposed by the study team.

d. What unit product costs will be reported for the three products if the ABC system proposed by the study team is adopted?

e. How would the activities identified by the study team be classified in terms of the levels of the cost hierarchy? Use the levels identified in Exhibit 9.12 (volume related, batch related, product related, and facility related).
   1. Assembly
   2. Setup
   3. Quality assurance

9-62. Activity-Based Costing, Cost Flow Diagram, Cost Hierarchy, and Predetermined Overhead Rates   (LO 9-3, 5, 6)

Kensington Electronics (KE) is a wholly owned subsidiary of CWD Enterprises, a global manufacturing company. Unlike most CWD companies, KE uses a traditional costing system to compute product costs. After the last review by CWD staff, the financial management at KE decided to consider switching to activity-based costing. The controller's staff at KE has classified manufacturing overhead costs for the next quarter into four overhead cost pools. They also identified an appropriate cost driver for each pool.

Cost Pools	Costs	Activity Drivers
Production setup..........	$300,000	Production runs
Fabrication...............	551,000	Machine-hours
Certification	66,500	Certificates
Quality assurance.........	315,000	Test-hours

The company manufactures two basic products, which are components of navigation systems. The products are the NAV1 and NAV1-AV. Although similar, the NAV1-AV uses upgraded materials. In addition, the NAV1-AV needs to be certified for use in aircraft navigational equipment. All units produced are tested, but the tests are more extensive for the NAV1-AV model.

The following are data for production for the next quarter:

	Products	
	NAV1	NAV1-AV
Total direct materials costs....................	$480,000	$200,000
Total direct labor costs	$320,000	$100,000
Total machine-hours	10,000	4,500
Total test hours.............................	4,000	3,000
Total number of production runs...............	20	20
Number of certificates.......................	0	1
Number of units produced and shipped	4,000	1,000

Required

a. The current cost accounting system charges overhead to products based on machine-hours. What unit product costs will be reported for the two products if the current cost system continues to be used?

b. What are the cost-driver rates for the four cost pools identified by the controller's staff?

c. Prepare a cost flow diagram of the ABC system proposed by the controller's staff.

d. What unit product costs will be reported for the three products if the ABC system proposed by the controller's staff is adopted?

e. How would the activities identified by the controller's staff be classified in terms of the levels of the cost hierarchy? Use the levels identified in Exhibit 9.12 (volume related, batch related, product related, and facility related).
   1. Production setup
   2. Fabrication
   3. Certification
   4. Quality assurance

(LO 9-3, 5, 6) **9-63. Activity-Based Costing and Predetermined Overhead Rates**

Lauder Company manufactures and distributes various fixtures used primarily in new building construction. At the company's Bayside plant, Lauder produces two models of one widely used fixture designated by model names LC-20 and LC-50. Currently, the Bayside plant uses direct labor-hours to allocate manufacturing overhead costs to products.

The vice president–manufacturing (VP-M) at Lauder has recently been considering updates to the company's costing systems as a way to ensure that managers had the best information available for decision making. However, rather than update throughout the entire firm, the VP–M and CFO agreed to test an ABC system. Because of its size and focus, the Bayside plant was selected for the experiment. An ABC study team, consisting of both plant and corporate employees, was formed to propose an ABC system and compare the product costs with those reported by the current system. Based on the experiment, the executives at Lauder will decide whether to roll out the new cost system to the entire company.

The study team identified four cost pools into which the manufacturing overhead costs could be grouped. There was a great deal of discussion about both the pools and the cost drivers. The final system selected consisted of the following pools and drivers. The costs were based on the forecasts for the coming year.

Cost Pools	Costs	Activity Drivers
Material inspection	$ 396,000	Direct materials cost
Assembly	2,210,000	Machine-hours
Equipment setup	790,000	Production runs
Packaging and shipping. . . .	420,000	Units shipped

Data for production of the two products at the Bayside plant for the coming year of operations follow:

	Products	
	LC-20	LC-50
Total direct materials costs	$540,000	$180,000
Total direct labor costs	$420,000	$210,000
Total machine-hours	92,125	46,000
Total number of production runs	75	50
Number of units produced and shipped	240,000	60,000

All direct labor at the Bayside plant is paid $35 per hour.

Required

a. What unit product costs will be reported for the two products in the coming year if the current cost system continues to be used?

b. What unit product costs will be reported for the two products if the ABC system is used?

c. Would you recommend that the Bayside plant adopt the team's proposed ABC system? Explain.

9-64. Activity-Based Costing and Predetermined Overhead Rates   (LO 9-3, 5, 6)
Refer to Problem 9-63. The study team decides to look more closely at the assembly activity and determines that it can be broken down into two activities: production and engineering. Production covers the costs of ongoing manufacturing, while engineering includes those activities dealing with design changes, equipment calibration, and so on.

The costs attributed to production are $1,657,500, and the costs attributed to engineering are $552,500. After discussion with plant engineers, the team decides that although machine-hours are an appropriate cost driver for production, the best cost driver for engineering is setups because most of the work arises from changes in the way the product is run.

Required

a. What unit product costs will be reported for the two products if the revised ABC system is used?

b. Would you recommend that the Bayside plant adopt the team's revised ABC system? Explain.

9-65. Activity-Based Costing, Cost Drivers, and Support Functions   (LO 9-4, 6)
Burgess Business School has two degree programs, BBA and MBA. The school uses an ABC system to cost the three support services it provides to students from both programs: Career Center, Events, and Library. Following are the costs of these three activities and the cost drivers used in the system:

Activity	Activity Cost	Cost Driver
Career Center	$468,000	Interview-hours
Event planning and hosting.	630,000	Event attendance
Library	561,000	Number of visits

For the most recent year, data collected from the central IT systems indicate the following:

	BBA	MBA
Interview-hours	12,000	7,500
Event attendance	8,000	6,000
Library visits	120,000	12,000

Required

a. Compute the cost-driver rates for the three activities at the school.

b. Suppose that in a future period, no students from the MBA program visited the Library. What amount of the Library cost would be assigned to the MBA program?

c. Does the result in requirement (b) appear to reflect the resource usage at the school? Explain.

(LO 9-5, 6) **9-66. Activity-Based Costing of Jobs**

Miller Manufacturing (2M) makes a variety of components for mechanized agricultural equipment. The products are similar but not identical, and all go through many of the same processes. 2M sells products worldwide and has to comply with various regulations regarding environmental and health and safety compliance. For the most part, 2M manufacturing practices comply with or exceed requirements in the countries to which it ships its products, but depending on the specific part ordered, it might have to go through additional certification processes to make the sale.

The company produces to order and never has any work-in-process inventories. The manufacturing facility uses a job costing system for product costing. Manufacturing overhead is applied to jobs based on direct labor cost. The cost analyst at 2M recently put together an estimate of overhead for the coming year, which is shown in the following table:

Category	Amount
Fabricating	$ 480,000
Machining	960,000
Machine setup	768,000
Shipping	432,000
Certification	240,000
Total	$2,880,000

The following are estimates for the three jobs planned for March:

	Job MM03-11	Job MM03-12	Job MM03-13
Direct materials	$ 9,600	$14,400	$12,000
Direct labor	$24,000	$38,400	$31,200
Number of units	300	750	600
Direct labor-hours	360	1,200	540
Machine-hours	750	1,050	900
Setup-hours	15	30	15
Certification required?	Yes	Yes	No

2M is considering adopting an activity-based costing system. The cost analyst has studied the system and has recommended the following cost drivers for each of the overhead categories. The analyst has also estimated the annual volume for each of the cost drivers. This information follows.

Overhead Category	Cost Driver	Annual Cost Driver Volume
Fabricating	Direct labor-hour	24,000 direct labor-hours
Machining	Machine-hours	30,000 machine-hours
Machine setup	Setup-hours	1,200 setup-hours
Shipping	Units	180,000 units
Certification	Certifications required	20 certifications required

The average direct labor rate at 2M is $40 per hour.

Required

a. What is the unit cost for each of the three jobs started and completed assuming 2M uses its current costing system?

b. What is the unit cost for each of the three jobs started and completed assuming 2M adopts the ABC system as designed by the cost analyst?

9-67. Activity-Based Costing of Jobs

(LO 9-5, 6)

Montana Precision Products (MPP) produces parts for small machine tools. The typical product goes through two processes, machining and finishing, before being packaged and shipped to the customer. All jobs at MMP are produced to order, and the company holds no finished goods inventory or work-in-process inventory. The company uses a traditional cost system and applies overhead to jobs based on machine-hours.

The plant manager and the plant controller have been discussing activity-based costing and the benefits of using it. The controller's staff have been collecting data on the plant costs and activities. Following are estimates of representative annual costs:

Overhead Category	Annual Cost
Materials handling.	$1,500,000
Machining.	3,000,000
Finishing.	1,000,000
Shipping.	750,000
Setups.	150,000
Total.	$6,400,000

The plant manager and the plant controller decide to look at the difference in the unit costs using the two cost systems, by computing costs for three representative jobs completed in October. Data on those jobs follow:

	Job 1004	Job 1005	Job 1008
Direct materials.	$15,000	$28,000	$50,000
Machine hours.	1,280	1,600	3,200
Units.	800	1,000	2,000
Setup-hours.	24.8	40.0	23.2
Orders.	2	4	2

The plant controller has a completed a tentative design for an ABC system to replace the current cost system. The system has five activities. Data on the activities and the annual volume for each of cost drivers follow:

Activity	Costs Driver	Annual Cost Driver Volume
Materials handling.	Materials cost	$3,000,000
Machining.	Machine-hours	160,000
Finishing.	Units	100,000
Shipping.	Orders	625
Setups.	Setup-hours	1,200

Required

a. What is the unit cost for each of the three jobs assuming Montana Precision Products continues to use its current costing system?

b. What is the unit cost for each of the three jobs assuming Montana Precision Products adopts the ABC system as designed by the plant controller?

(LO 9-1, 6)   **9-68. Benefits of Activity-Based Costing**

Chadwick Industries has several manufacturing facilities that make a wide variety of industrial and consumer products. Two of the plants, River North and River South, make components for road construction equipment. The River North plant was built when the demand for the products exceeded the River South plant's capacity. Even though slightly different in age at this point, the production process in both plants is roughly the same. Last year, however, the River North plant manager determined that the plant could use lower-cost utility labor in place of the skilled direct labor to bring raw materials to the assembly line and move finished products to the warehouse. While the total time required remained the same, the new materials handling process was included in overhead rather than being considered as direct labor. Staffing at the River North plant was adjusted to reflect the change.

In looking over the production plans for next year, the Chadwick vice president of operations is surprised by the cost estimates for the two plants. Specifically, the manufacturing overhead rate, which had been comparable between the two plants, is now much higher at the River North plant. The vice president suggests moving some of the production to the River South plant, which has the capacity, to reduce production costs.

Required

Prepare a report that states how an activity-based costing system might benefit Chadwick Industries and address the vice president's concern about costs.

(LO 9-3, 5, 6)   **9-69. Choosing an Activity-Based Costing System**

Commonwealth Devices makes three wearable fitness devices at its Lake Plant: CFit-1, CFit-2, and CFit-Xtra. The company has for many years allocated overhead to products using machine-hours. Last year, the Lake Plant produced and shipped 8,000 units of CFit-1, 14,000 units of CFit-2, and 8,000 units of CFit-Xtra. The plant recorded the following revenues and costs:

	COMMONWEALTH DEVICES **Lake Plant** **Income Statement**			
	CFit-1	CFit-2	CFit-Xtra	Total
Sales revenue	$864,000	$1,260,000	$1,296,000	$3,420,000
Direct costs				
Direct materials	192,000	280,000	240,000	712,000
Direct labor.	40,000	52,500	120,000	212,500
Variable overhead				
Machine setup.				192,000
Order processing				144,000
Materials handling.				192,000
Machining.				96,000
Shipping				72,000
Contribution margin				$1,799,500
Plant administration costs . . .				1,400,000
Gross profit.				$ 399,500

The Lake Plant has put together an employee team to recommend a possible activity-based cost system, including cost allocation bases. The employee team recommends the following:

Activity	Cost Driver	CFit-1	CFit-2	CFit-Xtra
Machine setup	Setups	80	160	160
Order processing	Orders received	9	20	11
Materials handling.	Material movements	3,000	4,500	5,000
Machining.	Machine-hours	10,000	16,000	24,000
Shipping	Units shipped	8,000	14,000	8,000

The employee team further recommends that administration costs not be allocated to products.

Required

a.   Using machine-hours to allocate overhead, complete the income statement for the Lake Plant. Do not allocate administrative costs to products.

b.   Complete the income statement using the activity-based costing method suggested by the employee team.

c.   Write a brief report indicating how activity-based costing might result in better decisions by managers at Commonwealth Devices and the Lake Plant.

d.   After hearing the recommendations, the plant manager expresses concern about failing to allocate administrative costs. If plant administrative costs were to be allocated to products, how would you allocate them?

9-70. Time-Based ABC: Time Equations   (LO 9-9)

Refer to Exercise 9-50. Until now, Meadow Logistics, Inc. (MLI) has used a commercial vendor to ship orders. The manager of Distribution believes the system described in Exercise 9-50 is too simple in two ways. First, if a retailer is ordering from MLI for the first time, Distribution has to take time to verify the retailer details (shipping address, credit, and so on). The manager estimates this additional time to total 20 minutes. In addition, some orders are quite complex. This happens when a retailer orders many different items in one order. The manager estimates that a complex order takes an additional 30 minutes to pick, on average.

Required

a.   Write out the time equation for taking an order.

b.   Write out the time equation for picking an order.

c.   Using the data from Exercise 9-50 and the additional data here, compute the cost of filling a complex order from a new retailer. Assume that all of the items in the order are in stock and that the retailer will not pick the order up at the MLI loading dock.

9-71. Time-Based ABC: Time Equations   (LO 9-9)

Refer to the information in Exercise 9-52. The manager of the Personnel Department decides that the estimate of the activities might be too simple in two ways. First, the time to interview depends on the level of the position for which a candidate is sought. The personnel manager estimates that for a candidate at the manager level, the additional interviewing time is 90 minutes. (Personnel Department employees only conduct the initial interview, but they accompany the candidate for interviews by the hiring executive or CEO.) For a candidate at the executive level, the additional time for interviewing is 180 minutes (in addition to the time required for a manager).

   The second issue the personnel manager identified is that the time for exit processing depends on whether the exit is voluntary. The manager estimates that an involuntary exit requires an additional 150 minutes of personnel time.

Required

a.   Write out the time equation for the interviewing activity.

b.   Write out the time equation for the separation processing activity.

c.   Based on the information in Exercise 9-52 and in this problem, what is the cost of interviewing a manager? An executive?

d.   Based on the information in Exercise 9-52 and in this problem, what is the cost of a voluntary exit? An involuntary exit?

INTEGRATIVE CASES

9-72. Cost Allocation and Environmental Processes—Ethical Issues   (LO 9-1, 3, 5, 6)

California Circuits Company (3C) manufactures a variety of components. Its Valley plant specializes in two electronic components used in circuit boards. These components serve the same function and perform equally well. The difference in the two products is the raw material. The XL-D chip is the older of the two components and is made with a metal that requires a wash prior to assembly. Originally, the plant released the wastewater directly into a local river. Several years ago, the company was ordered to treat the wastewater before its release, and it installed relatively expensive equipment. While the equipment is fully depreciated, annual operating expenses of $250,000 are still incurred for wastewater treatment.

Two years ago, company scientists developed an alloy with all of the properties of the raw materials used in XL-D that generates no wastewater. Some prototype components using the new material were produced and tested and found to be indistinguishable from the old components in every way relating to their fitness for use. The only difference is that the new alloy is more expensive than the old raw material. The company has been test-marketing the newer version of the component, referred to as XL-C, and is currently trying to decide its fate.

Manufacturing of both components begins in the Production Department and is completed in the Assembly Department. No other products are produced in the plant. The following information relates to the two components:

	XL-D	XL-C
Units produced	100,000	25,000
Raw materials costs per unit...................	$12	$14
Direct labor-hours per unit—Production	0.1	0.1
Direct labor-hours per unit—Assembly	0.4	0.4
Direct labor rate per hour—all labor.............	$20	$20
Machine-hours per unit—Production.............	1.6	1.6
Machine-hours per unit—Assembly.............	0.4	0.4
Testing hours per unit (all in Production).........	3.0	3.0
Shipping weight per unit (pounds)..............	1.0	1.6
Wastewater generated per unit (gallons)	10.0	0.0

Annual overhead costs for the two departments follow:

	Production Department	Assembly Department
Supervision	$ 100,000	$240,000
Materials handling	93,000	40,000
Testing	150,000	–0–
Wastewater treatment...............	250,000	–0–
Depreciation on equipment	400,000	100,000
Shipping...........................	7,000	120,000
Total	$1,000,000	$500,000

The company president believes that it's foolish to continue producing two essentially equivalent products. At the same time, the corporate image is somewhat tarnished because of a toxic dump found at another site (not the Valley plant). The president would like to be able to point to the Valley plant as an example of company research and development (R&D) working to provide an environmentally friendly product. The controller points out to the president that the company's financial position is shaky, and it cannot afford to make products in any way other than the most cost-efficient one.

Required

a. 3C's current cost accounting system charges overhead to products based on direct labor cost using a single plantwide rate. What product costs will it report for the two products if the current allocation system is used?

b. The controller recently completed an executive education course describing the two-stage allocation procedure. Assume that the first stage allocates costs to departments and the second stage allocates costs to products. The controller believes that the costs will be more accurate if machine-hours are used to allocate Production Department costs and labor-hours are used to allocate Assembly Department costs. What product costs will be reported for the two products if the two-stage allocation process is used?

c. Explain the results found in requirements (a) and (b).

d. The president argues that an activity-based costing system would provide even better costs. The company decides to compute product costs assuming an ABC system is implemented only in the Production Department. Overhead in Assembly will continue to be allocated based on direct labor cost. The cost drivers selected for the activity-based costing system are as follows.

Overhead Item	Driver
Supervision	Direct labor-hours
Materials handling...............	Materials cost
Testing.........................	Testing hours
Wastewater treatment.............	Wastewater generated
Depreciation on equipment	Machine-hours
Shipping	Weight

What product costs would be reported if this ABC system were implemented? Assume that the production mix and costs would remain as originally planned.

e. Because the two products are identical in their use, the controller argues that the decision should be made on cost alone. Do you agree? Explain.

9-73. Distortions Caused by Inappropriate Overhead Allocation Base

(LO 9-1, 3, 5, 6)

Chocolate Bars, Inc. (CBI) manufactures creamy deluxe chocolate candy bars. The firm has developed three distinct products: Almond Dream, Krispy Krackle, and Creamy Crunch.

CBI is profitable, but management is quite concerned about the profitability of each product and the product costing methods currently employed. In particular, management questions whether the overhead allocation base of direct labor-hours accurately reflects the costs incurred during the production process of each product.

In reviewing cost reports with the marketing manager, Steve Hoffman, who is the cost accountant, notices that Creamy Crunch appears exceptionally profitable and that Almond Dream appears to be produced at a loss. This surprises both him and the manager, and after much discussion, they are convinced that the cost accounting system is at fault and that Almond Dream is performing very well at the current market price.

Steve decides to hire Jean Sharpe, a management consultant, to study the firm's cost system over the next month and present her findings and recommendations to senior management. Her objective is to identify and demonstrate how the cost accounting system might be distorting the firm's product costs.

Jean begins her study by gathering information and documenting the existing cost accounting system. It is rather simplistic, using a single overhead allocation base—direct labor-hours—to calculate and apply overhead rates to all products. The rate is calculated by summing variable and fixed overhead costs and then dividing the result by the number of direct labor-hours. The product cost is determined by multiplying the number of direct labor-hours required to manufacture the product by the overhead rate and adding this amount to the direct labor and direct materials costs.

CBI engages in two distinct production processes for each product. Process 1 is labor intensive, using a high proportion of direct materials and labor. Process 2 uses special packing equipment that wraps each individual candy bar and then packs it into a box of 24 bars. The boxes are then packaged into cases, each of which has six boxes. Special packing equipment is used on all three products and has a monthly capacity of 3,000 cases, each containing 144 candy bars (= 6 boxes × 24 bars).

To illustrate the source of the distortions to senior management, Jean collects the cost data for the three products, Almond Dream, Krispy Krackle, and Creamy Crunch (see Exhibit 9.21).

CBI recently adopted a general policy to discontinue all products whose gross profit margin percentages [(Gross margin ÷ Selling price) × 100] were less than 10 percent. By comparing the selling prices to the firm's costs and then calculating the gross margin percentages, Jean could determine which products, under the current cost system, should be dropped. The current selling prices of Almond Dream, Krispy Krackle, and Creamy Crunch are $85, $55, and $35 per case, respectively. Overhead will remain $69,500 per month under all alternatives.

Required

a. Complete Exhibit 9.21 under the current cost system and determine which product(s), if any, should be dropped.

b. What characteristic of the product that should be dropped makes it appear relatively unprofitable?

Exhibit 9.21

Cost Data for Almond Dream, Krispy Krackle, and Creamy Crunch

	Almond Dream	Krispy Krackle	Creamy Crunch
Product costs			
Labor-hours per case..................	7	3	1
Total cases produced	1,000	1,000	1,000
Materials cost per case...............	$ 8	$ 2	$ 9
Direct labor cost per case............	$ 42	$ 18	$ 6
Labor-hours per product.............	7,000	3,000	1,000
Total overhead = $69,500			
Total labor-hours = 11,000			
Direct labor costs per hour = $6			
Allocation rate per labor-hour = _(a)_			
Costs of products			
Materials cost per case...............	$ 8	$ 2	$ 9
Direct labor cost per case............	42	18	6
Allocated overhead per case			
(to be computed)	(b)	(c)	(d)
Product cost	(e)	(f)	(g)

c. Assume that CBI drops the product(s) identified in requirement (*a*). Calculate the gross profit margin percentage for the remaining products. Assume that CBI can sell all products that it manufactures and that it will use the excess capacity from dropping a product to produce more of the most profitable product. If CBI maintains its current rule about dropping products, which additional products, if any, should CBI drop under the existing cost system?

d. Assume that CBI drops the products identified in requirements (*a*) and (*c*). Recalculate the gross profit margin percentage for the remaining product(s) and ascertain whether any additional product(s) should be dropped.

e. Discuss the outcome and any recommendations you might make to management regarding the current cost system and decision policies.

(LO 9-1, 3, 5, 6)   **9-74. Multiple Allocation Bases**

Refer to Case 9-73. Jean Sharpe decides to gather additional data to identify the cause of overhead costs and figure out which products are most profitable. She notices that $30,000 of the overhead originated from the equipment used. She decides to incorporate machine-hours into the overhead allocation base to determine the effect on product profitability. Almond Dream requires two machine-hours per case, Krispy Krackle requires seven hours per case, and Creamy Crunch requires six hours per case. Additionally, Jean notices that the $15,000 per month spent to rent 10,000 square feet of factory space accounts for almost 22 percent of the overhead. The assignment of square feet is 1,000 to Almond Dream, 4,000 to Krispy Krackle, and 5,000 to Creamy Crunch. Jean decides to incorporate this into the allocation base for the rental costs.

Because labor-hours are still an important cost driver for overhead, Jean decides that she should use labor-hours to allocate the remaining $24,500.

CBI still plans to produce 1,000 cases each of Almond Dream, Krispy Krackle, and Creamy Crunch. Assume that CBI can sell all products it manufactures and that if it drops any products, it will use excess capacity to produce additional cases of the most profitable product. Overhead will remain $69,500 per month under all alternatives.

Required

a. Based on the additional data, determine the product cost and gross profit margin percentages of each product using the three allocation bases (labor-hours, machine-hours, and square feet) to determine the allocation assigned to each product.

b. Would management recommend dropping any product based on the criterion of dropping products with less than 10 percent gross profit margin?

c. Based on the recommendation you make in requirement (*b*), recalculate the allocations and profit margins to determine whether any of the remaining products should be dropped from the product line. If so, substantiate the profitability of remaining products.

(Copyright © Michael W. Maher, 2023)

9-75. Activity-Based Costing: The Grape Cola Caper   (LO 9-1, 3, 5, 6)

Howard Rockness was worried. His company, Rockness Bottling, showed declining profits over the past several years despite an increase in revenues. With profits declining and revenues increasing, Rockness knew there must be a problem with costs.

Rockness sent an e-mail to his executive team under the subject heading "How do we get Rockness Bottling back on track?" Meeting in Rockness's spacious office, the team began brainstorming solutions to the declining profits problem. Some members of the team wanted to add products. (These were marketing people.) Some wanted to fire the least efficient workers. (These were finance people.) Some wanted to empower the workers. (These people worked in the human resources department.) And some people wanted to install a new computer system. (It should be obvious who these people were.)

Rockness listened patiently. When all participants had made their cases, Rockness said, "We made money when we were a smaller, simpler company. We have grown, added new product lines, and added new products to old product lines. Now we are going downhill. What's wrong with this picture?"

Rockness continued, "Here, look at this report. This is last month's report on the cola bottling line. What do you see here?" He handed copies of the following report to the people assembled in his office.

A		B	C	D	E	F
1	Monthly Report on Cola Bottling Line					
2		**Diet**	**Regular**	**Cherry**	**Grape**	**Total**
3	Sales	$ 75,000	$ 60,000	$ 13,950	$ 1,650	$150,600
4	**Less:**					
5	Materials	25,000	20,000	4,680	550	50,230
6	Direct labor	10,000	8,000	1,800	200	20,000
7	Fringe benefits on direct labor	4,000	3,200	720	80	8,000
8	Indirect costs (@ 260% of direct labor)	26,000	20,800	4,680	520	52,000
9	Gross margin	$ 10,000	$ 8,000	$ 2,070	$ 300	$ 20,370
10	Return on sales (see note [a])	13.3%	13.3%	14.8%	18.2%	13.5%
11	Volume	50,000	40,000	9,000	1,000	100,000
12	Unit price	$ 1.50	$ 1.50	$ 1.55	$ 1.65	$ 1.506
13	Unit cost	$ 1.30	$ 1.30	$ 1.32	$ 1.35	$ 1.302
14						
15	a. Return on sales before considering selling, general, and administrative expenses.					
16						

Rockness asked, "Do you see any problems here? Should we drop any of these products? Should we reprice any of these products?" The room was silent for a moment, and then everybody started talking at once. Nobody could see any problems based on the data in the report, but they all made suggestions to Rockness ranging from "add another cola product" to "cut costs across the board" to "we need a new computer system so that managers can get this information more quickly." A not-so-patient Rockness stopped the discussion abruptly and adjourned the meeting.

He then turned to the quietest person in the room—his son, Rocky—and said, "I am suspicious of these cost data, Rocky. Here we are assigning indirect costs to these products using a

260 percent rate. I really wonder whether that rate is accurate for all products. I want you to dig into the indirect cost data, figure out what drives those costs, and see whether you can give me more accurate cost numbers for these products."

Rocky first learned from production that the process required four activities: (1) setting up production runs, (2) managing production runs, and (3) managing products. The fourth activity did not require labor; it was simply the operation of machinery. Next, he went to the accounting records to get a breakdown of indirect costs. Here is what he found:

	A	B
1	Indirect labor	$ 20,000
2	Fringe benefits on indirect labor	8,000
3	Information technology	10,000
4	Machinery depreciation	8,000
5	Machinery maintenance	4,000
6	Energy	2,000
7	Total	$ 52,000
8		

Then, he began a series of interviews with department heads to see how to assign these costs to cost pools. He found that 40 percent of indirect labor was for scheduling or for handling production runs, including purchasing, preparing the production run, releasing materials for the production run, and performing a first-time inspection of the run. Another 50 percent of indirect labor was used to set up machinery to produce a particular product. The remaining 10 percent of indirect labor was spent maintaining records for each of the four products, monitoring the supply of raw materials required for each product, and improving the production processes for each product. This 10 percent of indirect labor was assigned to the cost driver "number of products."

Interviews with people in the information technology department indicated that $10,000 was allocated to the cola bottling line. Eighty percent of this $10,000 information technology cost was for scheduling production runs. Twenty percent of the cost was for recordkeeping for each of the four products.

Fringe benefits were 40 percent of labor costs. The rest of the overhead was used to supply machine capacity of 10,000 hours of productive time.

Rocky then found the following cost-driver volumes from interviews with production personnel:

- Setups: 560 labor-hours for setups.
- Production runs: 110 production runs.
- Number of products: 4 products.
- Machine-hour capacity: 10,000 hours.

Diet cola used 200 setup hours, 40 production runs, and 5,000 machine-hours to produce 50,000 units. Regular cola used 60 setup hours, 30 production runs, and 4,000 machine-hours to produce 40,000 units. Cherry cola used 240 setup hours, 30 production runs, and 900 machine-hours to produce 9,000 units. Grape cola used 60 setup hours, 10 production runs, and 100 machine-hours to produce 1,000 units. Rocky learned that the production people had a difficult time getting the taste just right for the Cherry and Grape colas, so these products required more time per setup than either the Diet or Regular colas.

Required

a. Compute cost driver rates for each of the four cost drivers.

b. Compute unit costs for each of the cola products: Diet, Regular, Cherry, and Grape.

c. Prepare a new "Monthly Report on Cola Bottling Line," but with your revised indirect cost numbers for each product.

d. Prepare a memorandum to Howard Rockness recommending what to do.

(Copyright © Michael W. Maher, 2023)

SOLUTIONS TO SELF-STUDY QUESTIONS

1. The new estimated overhead will be $252,000 + $100,800 = $352,800. The new overhead rate will be $56 per direct labor-hour (= $352,800 ÷ 6,300 hours). Therefore, the cost system will report the following as the new product costs:

	S-72s	S-66s	Total
Units produced	80	240	320
Direct labor-hours	2,400	3,900	6,300
Costs:			
Direct materials	$ 40,000	$ 36,000	$ 76,000
Direct labor	72,000	78,000	150,000
Manufacturing overhead (@ $56)	134,400	218,400	352,800
Total	$246,400	$332,400	$578,800
Cost per unit	$ 3,080	$ 1,385	

2. The single, companywide overhead rate will be 32 percent (= $1,600,000 ÷ $5,000,000). The overhead charged to the two groups will be

Group	Direct Costs	Overhead (@ 32%)
Government	$4,000,000	$1,280,000
Private	1,000,000	320,000

The separate overhead rates will be $15,000 per contract (= $750,000 ÷ 50 contracts) for negotiations and 17 percent (= $850,000 ÷ $5,000,000) for general administrative costs. The overhead charged to the two groups will be

Group	Contracts	Direct Costs	Negotiations Overhead (@ $15,000)	G & A Overhead (@ 17%)	Total Overhead
Government	20	$4,000,000	$300,000	$680,000	$980,000
Private	30	1,000,000	450,000	170,000	620,000

Separate rates allow the company to use allocation bases that are most appropriate for each department. The disadvantage is that separate rates require more recordkeeping costs and the decision-making benefits might not justify the additional costs.

3.   The cost driver rate for setups is now $8,250 per production run (= $396,000 ÷ 48 production runs). The production cost report using this information follows:

	Third Quarter Unit Cost Report, Activity-Based Costing, CenterPoint Manufacturing Facility	
	Sport	Pro
Direct materials.	$1,500,000	$2,400,000
Direct labor		
Assembly	$ 750,000	$ 600,000
Packaging	990,000	360,000
Total direct labor.	$1,740,000	$ 960,000
Direct costs	$3,240,000	$3,360,000
Overhead		
Assembly building		
Assembling (@ $30 per MH).	$ 180,000	$ 900,000
Setting up (@ $8,250 per production run)	66,000	330,000
Material handling (@ $3,000 per run)	24,000	120,000
Packaging building		
Inspecting and packing (@ $5 per direct labor-hour)	300,000	114,000
Shipping (@ $1,320 per shipment)	132,000	264,000
Total ABC overhead.	$ 702,000	$1,728,000
Total ABC cost.	$3,942,000	$5,088,000
Number of units	100,000	40,000
Unit cost.	$39.42	$127.20

10

Chapter Ten

Fundamentals of Cost Management

LEARNING OBJECTIVES

After reading this chapter, you should be able to:

LO 10-1 Describe how activity-based cost management can be used to improve operations.

LO 10-2 Use the hierarchy of costs to manage costs.

LO 10-3 Describe how the actions of customers and suppliers affect a firm's costs.

LO 10-4 Use activity-based costing methods to assess customer and supplier costs.

LO 10-5 Distinguish between resources used and resources supplied.

LO 10-6 Design cost management systems to assign capacity costs.

LO 10-7 Describe how activities that influence quality affect costs and profitability.

LO 10-8 Compare the costs of quality control to the costs of failing to control quality.

❝ *When you run a distribution business, you are really selling a service and not the products. The problem is that you are being paid for products. This means that two people can pay the same amount although they receive different levels of service. What I would like to know is what it costs me to serve different types of customers. Perhaps even more important, I'd like to understand* why *the costs of serving different customers differ. Maybe then I can decide how to manage my costs and improve my profitability.*❞

Anjana Malik is the owner of Lygon Food Distributors (LFD). LFD serves a diverse customer base ranging from small cafes and coffee shops to larger, upscale restaurants and hotels. Customers send an order to LFD, which then delivers food and other restaurant products to the restaurant or hotel. LFD is facing increasing competition as large national distributors enter the market. The competition has resulted in lower margins and a need for better cost information.

In Chapters 6 through 9, we emphasized the design of cost accounting systems and the information provided to managers for decision making. In our discussions, we illustrated the use (and sometimes the misuse) of cost accounting data in making pricing and product portfolio decisions, but we did not dwell on the use of the information for managing costs, which we address in this chapter.

Using Activity-Based Cost Management to Add Value

We'll start with **activity-based cost management** (ABCM), which uses activity-based costing data to evaluate the cost of value-chain activities within the firm and identify opportunities for improvement.

Before diving into ABCM, let's briefly review two key concepts: *activity-based costing* and the *value chain*. Recall from Chapter 9 that activity-based costing (ABC) is a system used to assign costs to products based on the products' use of activities, which are the discrete tasks an organization undertakes to make or deliver the product. Chapter 9 describes, in detail, how to implement ABC. Our goal in this chapter is to understand how to take the information derived from an ABC system and use it to improve operations. The value chain is the set of activities that transforms raw resources into products for customers. Value-added activities in the value chain are the things that customers will pay for. To maximize profits, firms must manage activities and the resources used to fund those activities to minimize costs while providing value for the customer.

Let's look at an example to clarify how ABC and ABCM can be used to improve operations. Consider the cost of setting up equipment to make a batch of units. Say the activity-based costing system indicates a cost driver rate (the predetermined overhead rate in ABC) of $50 per setup. Managers can reduce costs in two ways. They can reduce the number of setups that they perform, perhaps by running larger batches or by eliminating very-small-volume products. Or they can work hard to become more efficient at performing setups so that the cost per setup declines.

Japanese automobile manufacturer Toyota Motor Company became famous for the speed with which its employees could change the tooling of machines. Their speed meant that fewer resources were consumed in the setup activity and less productive capacity was lost to idle changeover time. With a lower cost of setup than their U.S. competitors, they could efficiently run smaller batch sizes, a critical feature of Toyota's operating strategy, which has come to be known as *lean manufacturing*. We'll talk more about lean manufacturing later in the chapter.

Senior managers can urge employees to reduce costs (as determined by the activity-based costing system), but achieving cost reductions requires the company to change either the frequency or the efficiency of an activity. Activity-based cost management can help accomplish this.

When an organization has to work with fewer resources, decision makers may decide to drop products or product features or limit customer services. They could also decide to

LO 10-1
Describe how activity-based cost management can be used to improve operations.

activity-based cost management
Approach that uses activity-based costing data to evaluate the cost of value-chain activities and to identify opportunities for improvement.

introduce new materials or technologies that substitute less costly resources. However, taking these actions without an analysis of the customer experience or the change in perceptions about the product may cause a vicious cycle of reduced demand, further resource reductions, and so on. Employing ABCM or other analytic methods can help managers identify the best way to proceed in the new circumstances. Looking at the two choices noted above, the first set of options adjusts the *frequency of activity* to match resources, while the second set uses fewer or lower-cost resources to *improve efficiencies.* Which of these options is better depends on the specifics of business and the cause of the initial reduction of resources available. The actions of the restaurant mentioned in the Business Application "Responding to a Sudden Drop in Resources" are examples of some of the responses companies make.

Companies that implement ABC and ABCM commonly report two benefits:

1. **Better information about product costs.** Better product cost information helps managers make decisions about pricing and whether to keep or drop products. Although managers must respond to the market, they also consider their product costs in setting prices. Managers also use this information to decide whether to continue selling certain products. If a product's profit margin is too low or if it loses money, managers will probably consider discontinuing it.
2. **Better information about the cost of activities and processes.** Better process and activity cost data help managers gain useful information that may have been hidden by the previous accounting system. It's like lowering the water in a river to expose the rocks. Before lowering the water, you probably suspected the rocks were there. Until you lowered the water, however, you didn't know where the big ones were or how big they were.

Business Application   Responding to a Sudden Drop in Resources

Restaurants are notoriously low profit-margin businesses. Some keys to a successful operation include high customer turnover (or high prices or, preferably, both) and high capacity utilization (closely spaced tables). During the COVID pandemic, restaurants, if they were allowed to open, were restricted to a fraction of the diners they used to serve on any given night. ABCM methods suggest two responses to the new environment. First, restaurant owners had to look for ways to provide some of the same meals, but using fewer resources. Second, they had to determine how to reduce some of the activities that they had been doing for a higher-volume business.

The actions of one restaurant in Melbourne, Australia, illustrate how an owner might react. The restaurant, named Lee Ho Fook, opened in 2013 and had a wide range of options for diners. The options included everything from a quick meal of appetizers at the bar to fine dining in the restaurant. The menu was extensive.

After a period in which the restaurant was closed as part of a COVID lockdown, the owner had developed a different model in response to the new situation, including the distancing requirement for tables and the consequent reduction in the number of diners.

> What he landed on was totally different from the casual excellence for which he'd been known. While still offering a robust to-go menu of fan-favorite dishes, Lee Ho Fook became a tasting-menu restaurant where the price of admission is $160 [approximately $115 US dollars at the time of the article] per person.[1]

In other words, the owner responded in two ways. First, the restaurant reduced the "frequency of activity" by offering many fewer menu options using a tasting menu rather than a full menu. Second, the restaurant provided some of the same services (meals) using fewer resources by changing the delivery method to take out rather than dine in.

Source:
1. Rodell, Besha, "The Pandemic Could End the Age of Midpriced Dining," *The New York Times,* July 28, 2020.

Using Activity-Based Cost Information to Improve Processes

The first step in ABCM is *activity analysis,* which has six steps. We begin by analyzing the costs of key activities:

1. Identify what the customer wants or expects from the firm's products or services, including key features, price, and quality.
2. Chart, from start to finish, the company's activities for completing the product.
3. Develop activity-based costing data for each activity, based on the resources used in each activity.

4. Classify all activities as value-added or nonvalue-added.
5. Compare the costs of each activity with the value that customers assign to it. (The value of nonvalue-added activities would be zero.)
6. Continuously improve the efficiency of all value-added activities. Eliminate or reduce nonvalue-added activities. This changing of operational processes to improve performance, often after examining activity-based costing data to determine opportunities for improvement, is called **process reengineering.**

Activity analysis provides a way for organizations to think systematically about the processes that they use to provide products to their customers. Managers working with accountants can use the analysis to identify and eliminate activities that add costs but not value.

Generally, the following types of activities are candidates for elimination because, from the perspective of the customer, they do not add value to the product:

- **Storing items.** Storing raw materials in a warehouse, storing partially completed products (work in process), and storing finished products (finished goods) are all nonvalue-added activities.

- **Moving items.** Moving parts, materials, and other items around the factory floor does not add value to the finished product. A steel mill in Michigan once had hundreds of miles of railroad tracks to move materials and partially finished products from one part of the factory to another—clearly, a nonvalue-added activity.

- **Waiting for work.** Idle time, as the result of things like waiting for raw materials to arrive to begin production, does not add value to products.

These are only a few examples of nonvalue-added activities. If you observe activities at health care organizations, fast-food restaurants, construction sites, government agencies, and (dare we suggest) universities, you will see numerous examples of nonvalue-added activities.

Using Activity-Based Cost Management in a Service Setting

Let's apply these same concepts to a service organization by looking at a mortgage company that processes loans. Have you ever taken out a loan? Do you wonder why approval cannot be done instantaneously? Exhibit 10.1 tracks activities from the lender's receipt of a loan application to letting the customer know about the loan decision.

Suppose that a loan officer at a bank currently processes 30 loan applications per month. Increasing the efficiency of value-added activities and eliminating nonvalue-added activities can shorten the process. For example, verifying credit, bank, employment, and other key information about the customer delays the process. Using technology can expedite the process.

If the loan officer can reduce the processing time to half a month for 30 loan applications, several good things happen. Happy customers see that their applications are processed faster, the cost per application goes down, and the lender processes more applications per month. The additional capacity will save the firm money as it expands because it will not have to hire and train new loan officers. You can see from this example that activity-based cost management applies to many different types of organizations, including manufacturing, retail, service, nonprofit, and governmental agencies.

Lean Manufacturing and Activity-Based Cost Management

In the business world, you'll often find activity-based cost management paired with *lean manufacturing.* **Lean manufacturing** is an approach to production that tries to significantly reduce production costs using solutions such as just-in-time inventory and production, elimination of waste, and tighter quality control. The key features of lean

process reengineering
Changing operational processes to improve performance, often after examining activity-based costing data to determine opportunities for improvement.

lean manufacturing
Approach to production that looks to significantly reduce production costs using solutions such as just-in-time inventory and production, elimination of waste, and tighter quality control.

```
┌─────────────┐   ┌─────────────┐   ┌─────────────┐   ┌─────────────┐
│   Receive   │ → │   Verify    │ → │    Make     │ → │ Communicate │
│ application │   │ information │   │  decision   │   │  decision   │
└─────────────┘   └─────────────┘   └─────────────┘   └─────────────┘
```

Exhibit 10.1

Activity Flow in the Loan Application Process

manufacturing flow naturally from careful activity analysis. Just as activity-based cost management often prompts firms to begin the journey toward becoming a lean enterprise, becoming lean often prompts firms to revisit their cost accounting practices. What often emerges after firms adopt lean manufacturing is a new approach to cost accounting, termed *lean accounting*. **Lean accounting** is a cost accounting system designed around the value chain of major products and services to support lean manufacturing. It can also refer to applying lean production methods to accounting work itself.

Traditional manufacturing firms often group similar operations together. For example, assume a bicycle manufacturer bends tubing in preparation for welding, welds the tubing into frames, and then paints the welded frames. All of the machines used to bend the tubing are in one area of the plant. All of the welding machines are in another area of the plant. All of the painting equipment is in yet another area of the plant. The workers who operate the machinery in each of the three areas often have their own supervisor for that particular area, and the products typically come through the area in batches.

This approach often results in large work-in-process inventories. To be sure there is enough work to keep the welders busy, the company might have a large batch of bent tubes in inventory waiting for welding. Similarly, the company might have a lot of welded frames in inventory waiting to be painted. Why? Because the company wants to keep these activities going full speed.

Lean manufacturers organize differently. To ensure that a welder is ready to make a bicycle immediately after the preceding operation of bending the tubing—and to avoid inventory buildup—the lean manufacturer places the welding machine near the machine that is bending tubes, and the paint work station. In short, the lean manufacturer organizes its factory around the process flow of a single major product, not around groups of similar machines.

Moreover, if lean manufacturers eliminate inventories and the material-handling functions that accompany them, many of the overhead costs disappear. As a result, the firm's accountants can more directly assign costs to the appropriate value chain. Instead of assigning costs to the welding activity and allocating those costs to the various types of bicycles, accountants assign costs directly to each type of bicycle.

lean accounting
Cost accounting system that provides measures at the work cell or process level and minimizes wasteful or unnecessary transaction processes.

Business Application **The Costs of Lean Production**

We have highlighted the benefits to companies that adopt lean production methods. They reduce costs by reducing activities (storing, moving, fixing defects, and so on). As with all management choices, there are costs as well as benefits and one role of the cost analyst is to provide the decision maker with good information about both the benefits and costs.

By design, lean companies operate with a minimum of inventory. In normal times, this results in a smooth operation with a minimum of extra materials and work-in-process. However, a danger arises when an event seriously disrupts the supply chain. Such an event occurred during the COVID pandemic. For example, at one point during the crisis, "an average of 21% of household paper products were out of stock at US stores. . . ."[1] How did this happen?

The scarcity is rooted in a decades-long quest by businesses at all levels, handling many different products, to eke out more profit by operating with almost no slack. Make only what you can sell quickly. Order only enough materials to keep production lines going.[2]

In other words, companies were operating with a lean production philosophy. The benefits of lean were obvious, and the

philosophy spread from Japanese auto producers to American auto producers and finally to other industries, including services.

The potential costs, or risks, of a lean manufacturing practice were known, at least among some. As the practice became more widespread,

. . . the risk of shortages in an emergency bothered experts in disaster preparedness. Cautions voiced by the worriers had little effect as investors rewarded corporations that held costs low through lean operations.[3]

Of course, this does not mean that the decision to adopt lean manufacturing was a mistake. That would depend on the likelihood of a disaster occurring and the cost to the organization if one did occur. It does mean, however, that the analyst providing information about the cost and benefits of adopting lean would be negligent if the potential impact of disaster was not a part of the analysis.

Sources:
1. Terlep, Sharon, and Annie Gasparro, "Why Are There Still Not Enough Paper Towels?" *The Wall Street Journal*, August 21, 2020.
2. Ibid.
3. Ibid.

Using Cost Hierarchies

Some costs can be associated with units of goods or services; others cannot. Consequently, allocating all costs (such as building leases) to units is misleading if some costs do not vary with the volume of units. As a result, management cannot effectively manage these costs by focusing on the volume of units. For example, the costs of machine setups are generally batch related. A machine setup is required for each new batch of product whether the batch contains 1 unit or 1,000 units. The setup cost is not affected by the number of units but by the number of batches.

Management can establish a hierarchy of costs, as we described in Chapter 9. Strictly variable costs, such as energy costs to run machines, are affected by the volume of units produced. Naturally, any variable costs such as those for direct materials are unit-level costs. At the other extreme are capacity-related costs, which are essentially fixed by management's decisions to have a particular size of store, factory, hospital, or other facility. Although these costs are fixed with respect to volume, it would be misleading to give the impression that they cannot be changed. Managers can make decisions that affect capacity costs; such decisions just require a longer time horizon to implement than do decisions to reduce unit-level costs.

Two middle categories of costs are affected by the way the company manages its activities. A company that makes custom products has more product-level costs than a company that provides limited choices. A company that schedules its work to make one product on Monday, a second product on Tuesday, and so on through Friday has lower batch-related costs than if it produced all five products on Monday, all five again on Tuesday, and so on through the week. In practice, many of the greatest opportunities for reducing costs through activity-based management are in these middle categories of product- or customer-level and batch-related costs.

We gave an example of a cost hierarchy in Chapter 9 (see Exhibit 9.12). Using such a hierarchy, managers analyze only the volume-related costs if they make decisions that affect units, but not batches, products, customers, or capacity. If managers make decisions that affect capacity, however, costs in all levels of the hierarchy—volume, batch, product, and facility—will probably be affected, and activities in all four categories should be analyzed.

> **LO 10-2**
> Use the hierarchy of costs to manage costs.

Self-Study Question

1. Classify the following items as to whether they generate capacity-related costs, product- or customer-related costs, batch-related costs, or unit-level costs.

    a. Piecework labor.
    b. Long-term lease on a building.
    c. Energy to run machines.
    d. Engineering drawings for a product.
    e. Purchase order.
    f. Movement of materials for products in production.
    g. Change order to meet new customer specifications.

    The solution to this question is at the end of the chapter.

Managing the Cost of Customers and Suppliers

We described in Chapter 9 how different products affect firm costs by using resources. The advantage of an activity-based costing system is that it reflects the diverse uses of resources in the product costs so managers can make better decisions about the products. For some firms, however, decisions are not about the products or services but about customers. For example, when a company decides to spend its advertising budget on *Sunday Night Football* rather than *60 Minutes,* it does so because it believes the customers it attracts from one audience will be more profitable than those it might attract from the other audience. One reason a group could be more profitable as customers is that it would buy more product. Another reason is that one group could be less costly to serve.

> **LO 10-3**
> Describe how the actions of customers and suppliers affect a firm's costs.

©Ariel Skelley/Getty Images

©David R. Frazier Photolibrary, Inc./Alamy Stock Photo

Customers making the same transaction in a bank can have a significant impact on the bank's costs. It is generally less costly for the bank if the customers use an automated teller machine (ATM) rather than visit a bank teller.

How can customers "cost" money? Think about the last time you stood in line to purchase a ticket, check in for a flight, or make a transaction in a bank. Many people ahead of you are purchasing the same service (a ticket, a flight, or a deposit), but some take longer (sometimes much longer) to complete the transaction. The additional time those customers take adds cost to the company.

Using Activity-Based Costing to Determine the Cost of Customers and Suppliers

LO 10-4

Use activity-based costing methods to assess customer and supplier costs.

Fortunately, we can apply the concepts of activity-based costing to the question of customer costing (and therefore customer profitability) easily. Consider Lygon Food Distributors (LFD), introduced at the beginning of the chapter. LFD charges a fee for the delivery service based on the value of the order. The current fee is 16 percent of the order value and is designed to just cover the delivery cost.

Recently, some of LFD's best customers have reduced their purchases, and Anjana Malik, the owner, is concerned. She thought the customers were satisfied because they had placed large orders and, although they did not order frequently, always returned.

She still has plenty of customers who generate a great deal of revenue over the year, but she realizes that the customers who have reduced their purchases have different buying patterns than those who continue to order the same amount. She decides to investigate a bit to see why some customers are reducing purchases and whether she can make some changes to reverse this trend.

Anjana decides to look first at her costs and pricing policy. She picks two customers (Mario's Diner and Claire's Cafe) as representative of the types of customers who are staying and leaving, respectively.

Anjana prepares some summary operating data based on the planning for next year (Exhibit 10.2). After preparing the data, Anjana realizes that she cannot determine the cost of delivery at the customer level. She can do this only at the firm level. She decides to investigate even further by studying the delivery service in more detail.

Anjana decides to apply the concepts of activity-based costing to the delivery service itself. Although it could also be useful in analyzing the warehouse operations, Anjana decides that this analysis can wait. Following the four-step procedure described in Chapter 9, Anjana first considers the activities involved with the delivery service and identifies three major activities: entering the order, picking the order (employees going through the warehouse and gathering the individual items in the order), and delivering the order. Anjana identifies a fourth activity, which is supervising and administering delivery. See Exhibit 10.3 for a simplified process flow of the delivery service excluding the administrative activity.

The next step is to identify cost drivers for each of the four activities. After discussing this process with the delivery supervisor, Anjana determines that these are the best drivers.

Activity	Cost Driver
Entering order	Number of orders entered
Picking order	Number of items picked
Delivering order.	Number of deliveries made
Performing general delivery administration	Order value

Anjana considered many drivers for the general administrative activity. Because it is a miscellaneous collection of activities, she decides to use the order value. She believes that the other three cost drivers are appropriate for the respective activities.

The third step in Anjana's analysis is to compute the cost driver rates. Through interviews and an analysis of past accounting records, Anjana computes the rates (Exhibit 10.4), which are based on expected activity for the next year.

	A	B	C	D	E	
1		Mario's	Claire's	All Others	Total	
2	Sales revenue	$ 50,000	$ 50,000	$ 4,900,000	$ 5,000,000	
3	Cost of goods (@ 60%)	(30,000)	(30,000)	(2,940,000)	(3,000,000)	
4	Gross margin	$ 20,000	$ 20,000	$ 1,960,000	$ 2,000,000	
5	Order/delivery charges (@ 16%)	8,000	8,000	784,000	800,000	
6	Delivery costs	?	?	?	(800,000)	
7	Other operating costs				(1,435,000)	
8	Operating profit				$ 565,000	
9						

Exhibit 10.2

Operating Data—Lygon Food Distributors

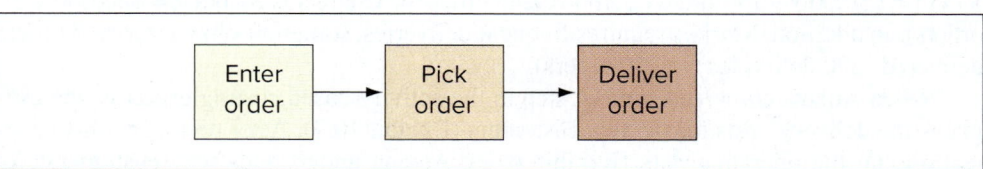

Exhibit 10.3

Process Flow of the Delivery Service—Lygon Food Distributors

Exhibit 10.4

Computation of Cost Driver Rates—Lygon Food Distributors

	A	B	C	D	E	F	G	H
1		Activity		Cost			Cost	
2	Activity	Cost		Driver Volume			Driver Rate	
3	Entering order	$ 100,000	÷	10,000	orders	=	$ 10	per order
4	Picking order	150,000	÷	75,000	items	=	$ 2	per item
5	Delivering order	300,000	÷	12,500	deliveries	=	$ 24	per delivery
6	Performing general							
7	delivery administration	250,000	÷	$ 5,000,000	order value	=	5%	of value
8								

Exhibit 10.5

Cost Driver Information for Two Customers— Lygon Food Distributors

	A	B	C
1	Cost Driver	Mario's	Claire's
2	Number of orders	150	50
3	Number of items	750	750
4	Number of deliveries	200	50
5	Order value (total sales)	$ 50,000	$ 50,000
6			

Exhibit 10.6

Cost Flow Diagram for Cost of Customers— Lygon Food Distributors

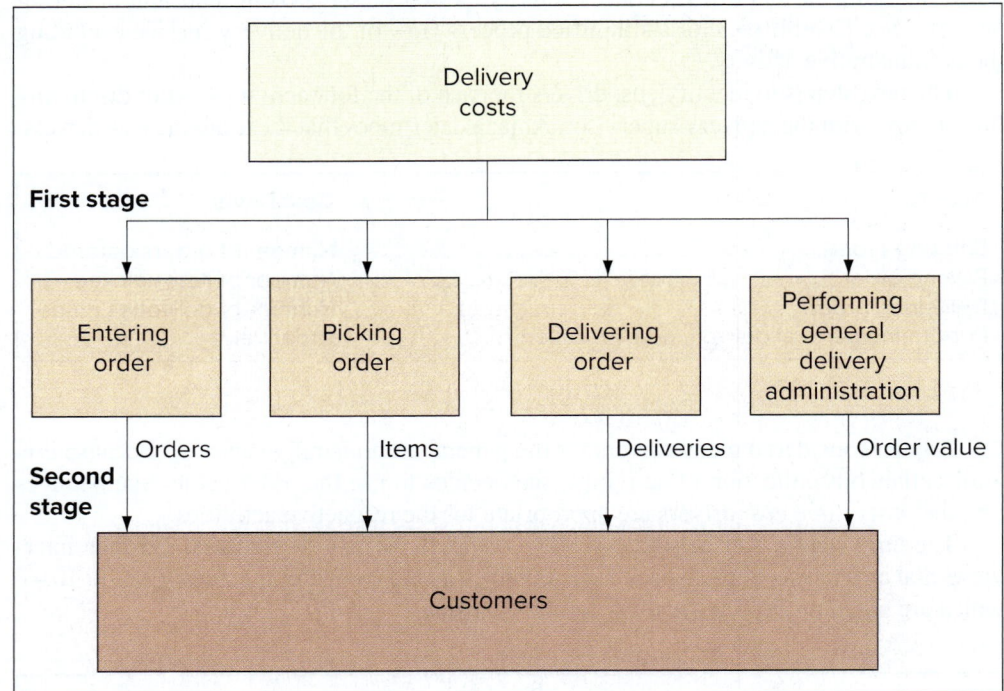

The last step in the costing process is to assign the cost driver rates to the individual customers. To do this, Anjana collects expected cost driver information on the two sample customers, Mario's and Claire's (Exhibit 10.5). See Exhibit 10.6 for the cost flow diagram for the customer cost analysis. After putting together the data in Exhibit 10.5, Anjana notices something interesting. Mario's, a customer who is staying, orders the same number of items as Claire's, a customer who is leaving. However, Mario's makes many relatively small orders; the sales value of an average order for Mario's is about $333 (= $50,000 ÷ 150 orders). An average order for Claire's is $1,000 (= $50,000 ÷ 50 orders). In addition, Mario's requires frequent deliveries, sometimes having partial orders delivered (200 deliveries for 150 orders).

When Anjana completes the last step in the activity-based costing exercise, she estimates the delivery costs for the two customers (Exhibit 10.7). After reviewing this information and the operating data (Exhibit 10.2), Anjana understands why customers like

Exhibit 10.7   Estimated Customer Delivery Costs—Lygon Food Distributors

	A		G	H	I	J	K	L	M
1				Cost		Mario's			Claire's
2	Activity			Driver Rate	Driver Volume	Activity Cost		Driver Volume	Activity Cost
3	Entering order		$ 10	per order	150	$ 1,500		50	$ 500
4	Picking order		$ 2	per item	750	1,500		750	1,500
5	Delivering order		$ 24	per delivery	200	4,800		50	1,200
6	Performing general								
7	delivery administration		5%	of value	$ 50,000	2,500		$ 50,000	2,500
8	Total delivery costs					$ 10,300			$ 5,700
9									

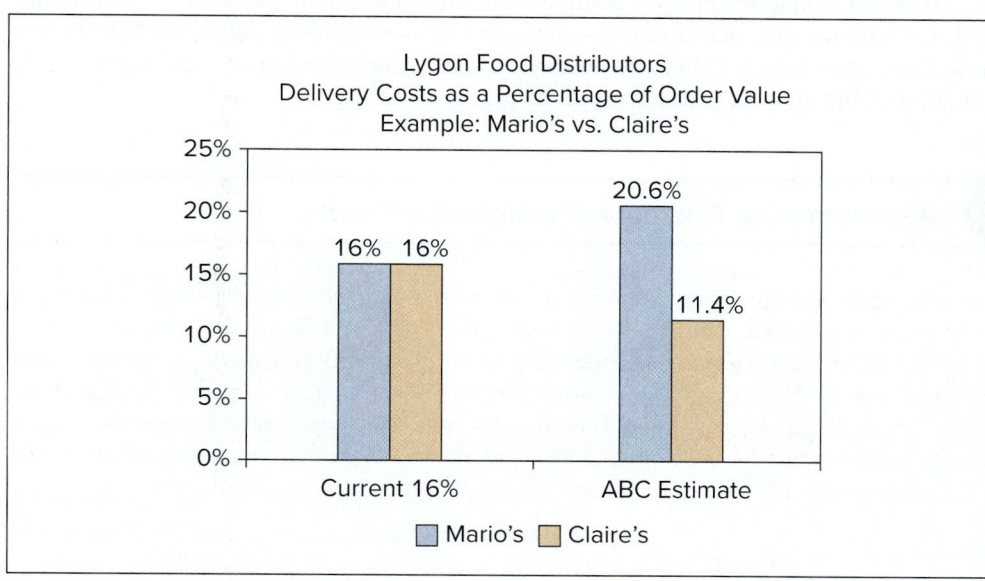

Exhibit 10.8

Estimated Customer Delivery Costs: Current System vs. ABC Estimate—Lygon Food Distributors

Claire's are leaving; they pay the same amount for delivery as Mario's ($8,000), even though it costs much less to provide delivery service to them.

A graphical visualization of the difference in delivery cost as a percentage of order value is shown in Exhibit 10.8. The graph in Exhibit 10.8 shows that the amount spent on delivery costs as a percentage of order value for Mario's is almost double that spent for Claire's. This information will help Anjana decide how to price delivery costs in a way that might keep more profitable customers from leaving.

Determining Why the Cost of Customers Matters

If LFD is the only food distributor in town, the issue of who pays for the delivery cost might not matter much to Anjana. After all, the total delivery cost is $800,000 and collectively customers pay $800,000. However, what happens when a competitor opens a warehouse? The competitor could price delivery services closer to the cost of delivery rather than basing the delivery fee on revenue. In this case, the competitor could attract Claire's away, although Mario's remains LFD's customer. As more and more customers with the same buying patterns as Claire's leave, LFD is left with the higher-cost customers who are similar to Mario's in their purchasing behavior.

Using Cost of Customer Information to Manage Costs

Anjana can use the information from the cost of the customer system to manage delivery costs. Under the current system, customers do not see a link between their buying patterns and the costs of delivery because the delivery fee is a flat percentage of the order value. However, from the cost driver information, we know that the order *patterns,* not the order *values,* drive most of the delivery cost.

Suppose that Anjana changes the way LFD charges for delivery and uses a pricing schedule based on the cost driver rates used to determine customer costs. For example, every time a customer places an order, there would be a $10 charge regardless of the size of the order or the number of units in it. This signals the customer that ordering less frequently but in larger amounts can save delivery costs. In this way, the customer can determine the trade-off between delivery costs and inventory costs. Some customers, such as Mario's, might decide that storing their own inventory is more costly than paying the higher delivery costs of LFD. Other customers, such as Claire's, might decide to save even more in delivery costs by ordering less frequently.

The point is that inventory is being held in the value chain. The issue is who should hold it. Using the cost driver rates to determine delivery pricing causes the firm that is most efficient at storage to hold the inventory. This reduces total cost in the supply chain and allows LFD to manage the cost of delivery.

Business Application   Managing the Customer Portfolio for Profit

The COVID pandemic resulted in unexpected and significant disruptions in many industries. For example, online retail sales increased 32 percent in 2020.[1] Much of that merchandise was delivered by established logistics companies such as United Parcel Service, Inc. (UPS) and FedEx. One possible response to such an increase would be to welcome the increased volume. However, as we have seen, high volume does not always lead to high profit.

Under a new CEO, Carol Tomé, who took over leadership of the company in March 2020, UPS took a different approach.

> UPS has become more selective about which packages it ships. . . . Sales leaders evaluate customers . . . by what they deliver to the bottom line.[2]

This approach has led to several changes at the company. One problem, which UPS identified several years earlier, was the practice of some retailers to forecast large volumes for shipping over the holidays. Based on the forecast, UPS and other carriers would invest in capacity only to have the actual volume be much less. As a result, UPS began

> . . . pushing back against . . . retailers who order up capacity . . . but don't meet their forecasts.[3]

However, UPS is not looking at customer profitability solely on a delivery-by-delivery basis, but as a whole. That is, some customers might not use high-profit services but might provide a reliable volume of business to keep the system capacity busy. Other, smaller businesses might buy a package of services that offer a higher profit margin than simple delivery services. Just as a retail firm might make little money on one product, customers buy a range of products, and it is this package of services that is important. As the CEO of UPS says,

> "As we look at our customer mix, we run it like a portfolio."[4]

Some customers of UPS responded to these changes, including rate hikes of 30 percent or more, by taking their business elsewhere. Ms. Tomé, rather than retreating, responds that UPS requires an appropriate price for what it delivers, adding,

> "If the customer isn't willing to pay and they elect to leave us, then we wish them all the best."[5]

Sources:
1. Ziobro, Paul, "UPS Boss Preaches the Power of No," *The Wall Street Journal,* February 26, 2021.
2. Ibid.
3. Ziobro, Paul, "UPS Asks Retailers to Pitch in—Delivery Company Doesn't Want to Be Left Holding the Bag on Cost for Excess Capacity," *The Wall Street Journal,* May 2, 2017.
4. Ziobro, "UPS Boss Preaches the Power of No."
5. Ibid.

Determining the Cost of Suppliers

The analysis of customer cost also can be applied to suppliers. For example, firms commonly evaluate suppliers based on the price they charge for materials. What such an evaluation policy ignores, however, is that the supplier actually provides other services as well. A good supplier delivers the material that was ordered, on time, and of appropriate quality. If a supplier fails to perform any one of these ancillary activities well, the customer incurs costs to correct the failure.

Consider the case of Lygon Food Distributors (LFD) again. LFD buys food and other products from two suppliers, Pacific Foods and Coastal Supply. Both distributors almost always send the correct order and the products of the right quality, but sometimes deliveries are late. When that happens, LFD has to hire temporary workers or pay its employees overtime to handle the delivery. Because most deliveries from the two distributors consist of similar products, the cost to handle a delivery is roughly proportional to the weight of the products in the delivery. See Exhibit 10.9 for data on deliveries from the two distributors for the year.

The warehouse supervisor at LFD estimates that the cost of late deliveries was $34,000, based on the cost of temporary labor, overtime wages and benefits, and the administrative costs of delaying deliveries to customers.

Anjana can use this information to manage costs by revising her purchasing policy. Based on the data in Exhibit 10.9, 340,000 pounds of product were delivered late (= 600,000 pounds × 50% late deliveries + 400,000 pounds ordered × 10% late deliveries). The cost of the late deliveries was $34,000, or $0.10 per pound delivered late. Anjana has just received two bids for an order of food and other supplies. Pacific Foods bid $2.04 per pound (based on the products in the order) and Coastal Supply bid $2.07. Under its current purchasing policy, LFD would order from Pacific Foods because the price is lower.

Anjana computes the effective cost of buying from Pacific Foods based on its past delivery performance (see Exhibit 10.10). After doing this, Anjana realizes that given the delivery performance, it is actually cheaper to buy from Coastal Supply. In addition, she has a better basis to compare bids in the future. She can simply add $0.05 to the bid from Pacific Foods and $0.01 to the bid from Coastal Supply.

Capturing the Cost Savings

Identifying the costs of customers and pricing the services to reflect the costs is not sufficient to reduce the costs that LFD incurs for delivery. It is important to reduce the resources used by the delivery activities. If, for example, LFD's customers order less frequently because of the new pricing policy, LFD has to take steps to redeploy the assets used in the order-taking activity. Otherwise, the costs will remain the same. LFD will simply have excess capacity in the order-taking group.

	A	B	C	D
1		Pacific Foods	Coastal Supply	Total
2	Weight of product purchases	600,000	400,000	1,000,000
3	Average purchase price per pound	$ 2.01	$ 2.02	$ 2.014
4	Total value of product purchased	$ 1,206,000	$ 808,000	$ 2,014,000
5	Number of deliveries	100	60	160
6	Percentage of late deliveries	50%	10%	35%
7				

Exhibit 10.9

Annual Data on Food and Restaurant Supply Deliveries—Lygon Food Distributors

	A	B	C
1		Pacific Foods	Coastal Supply
2	Initial price per pound	$ 2.04	$ 2.07
3	Additional cost of late delivery per pound	0.10	0.10
4	Probability of late delivery	50%	10%
5	Expected cost of late delivery per pound	0.05	0.01
6	Effective cost per pound		
7	(Initial bid plus expected cost of late delivery) .	$ 2.09	$ 2.08
8			

Exhibit 10.10

Effective Purchase Price of Products When Late Deliveries Are Considered—Lygon Food Distributors

Self-Study Question

2. LFD decides to price delivery service according to the results of the activity-based cost study. That is, LFD charges $10 per order, $2 per item, $24 for delivery, and 5 percent of the order value for the general delivery costs. A year later, LFD collects data from the two customers, Mario's Diner and Claire's Cafe, which follow:

    a. Compute the cost of delivery for the two customers.

    b. Has the cost of delivering to the two customers changed? Why?

Cost Driver	Mario's	Claire's
Number of orders	75	50
Number of items	750	1,500
Number of deliveries	80	50
Order values (total sales)	$50,000	$100,000

The solution to this question is at the end of the chapter.

Managing the Cost of Capacity

In the product costing systems we have designed, the costs of all resources, including the costs of capacity, generally have been divided by an activity measure and included in the resulting product costs. Managers then use these product costs to make pricing decisions, product portfolio decisions, process decisions, and so on. At the beginning of Chapter 9, we indicated that this treatment could lead to the death spiral as managers try to cover increasing reported product costs.

Using and Supplying Resources

LO 10-5

Distinguish between resources used and resources supplied.

In some situations, costs go up and down proportionately with the cost driver. Materials, energy, and piecework labor are excellent examples in a manufacturing firm. Consider the delivery service at Lygon Food Distributors (LFD). Suppose that every time LFD has an order to deliver, it hires temporary workers and pays them $0.80 per item to load them into a delivery truck. The cost driver is obviously the number of items, and the cost driver rate is $0.80 per item.

Now suppose that employees (loaders) are hired for a month for $9 per hour. LFD employs five workers, each of whom works 8-hour days. Each of these workers has the capacity to load 60 items per day. The cost driver might still be the number of items. The cost driver rate is computed by dividing the estimated wages of loaders for the day by their capacity measured in items. This calculation gives a rate of $1.20 per item [= ($9 per hour × 8 hours) ÷ 60 items]. In general, this cost driver rate could be higher, lower, or the same as the piecework rate. We use a rate of $1.20 just to help you recognize that a difference exists between the piecework rate and the cost driver rate when workers are paid by the hour.

Suppose that on Tuesday, the workers loaded 260 items. That means there were 40 items, or $48 (= $1.20 cost driver rate × 40 items), of unused capacity on Tuesday. LFD has costs of $360 computed either of two ways:

$$\$360 = 5 \text{ workers} \times \$9 \text{ per hour} \times 8\text{-hour day}$$
$$\$360 = \$1.20 \text{ per item} \times 300 \text{ item capacity}$$

LFD supplied resources of $360 to the loading activity. Only $312 of loading resources were used ($312 = $1.20 × 260 items actually loaded), however, leaving $48 of unused capacity. LFD knows that the five workers could have loaded more items without increasing the resources supplied to the activity.

In general, activity-based costing estimates the cost of resources used. In activity-based costing, **resources used** for an activity are measured by multiplying the cost driver rate by the cost driver volume. In the case of LFD's delivery service, resources used were $312.

resources used

Cost driver rate multiplied by the cost driver volume.

The **resources supplied** to an activity are the expenditures or the amounts spent on it. In the case of LFD's delivery services, the amount of resources supplied was the $360 paid to the loaders. Resources supplied is the amount that appears on financial statements. The difference between resources used and resources supplied is **unused resource capacity.** Now that we have identified unused resource capacity, we show how to report this information in a way that supports cost management. We do this by combining the concepts of the cost hierarchy and unused resource capacity. Typical reports show costs as line items similar to those shown for LFD in Exhibit 10.11, which itemizes the delivery costs in Exhibit 10.2. It is impossible for managers to distinguish resources used from resources supplied in such reports.

A more informative report for managing capacity costs is shown in Exhibit 10.12. It first categorizes costs into the cost hierarchies. Managers can look at the amount of costs in each level of the hierarchy and find ways to manage those resources effectively. For example, managers see that $400,000 of resources are supplied to batch-related activities such as entering and delivering orders. Managers can investigate to determine how much of that $400,000 can be saved by changing the production process, for example, by using flexible scheduling for the order entry clerks.

Perhaps of more interest, the report shows managers how much of the resources for each type of cost are unused. Here's how it works. The cost driver for picking items is the number of items and the rate is $2 per item. (The cost driver rate includes, in addition to labor costs, a portion of the depreciation and equipment, energy, and other costs.) Based on the information in the income statement, LFD spent $150,000 on picking items. That represents 75,000 items of picking capacity (= $150,000 ÷ $2 per item). However, only 67,500 items were picked (= $135,000 resources used ÷ $2 cost driver rate). The report shows managers that $15,000 (or 7,500 items) of unused picking resources were available.

All other things being equal, perhaps as many as 7,500 additional items could have been picked during the year without increasing expenditures. In reality, managers know that some unused resources are a good thing. Having some unstructured time for ad hoc training, leisure, and thinking about ways to improve the work and work environment can be useful for morale and productivity.

Note that some costs have more unused resources than others. The volume-related costs show 10 percent (= $15,000 ÷ $150,000) unused resources. Many of these costs vary proportionately with output and often have little or no unused resources. Some of the picking labor, for example, is the cost of temporary help that is employed on an as-needed

resources supplied
Expenditures or the amounts spent on a specific activity.

unused resource capacity
Difference between resources used and resources supplied.

LYGON FOOD DISTRIBUTORS
Year 2

Sales revenue		$5,000,000
Costs of goods (@ 60%)		(3,000,000)
Gross margin		$2,000,000
Delivery fees charged to customers		800,000
Delivery costs		
Depreciation and equipment leases	$420,000	
Energy	100,000	
Salaries and wages	250,000	
Other delivery costs	30,000	
Total delivery costs		(800,000)
Other operating costs		(1,435,000)
Operating profit		$ 565,000

Exhibit 10.11

Traditional Income Statement

Exhibit 10.12

Activity-Based Income
Statement—Lygon Food
Distributors

	A	B	C	D	E
1			Unused		
2		Resources	Resource	Resources	
3		Used	Capacity	Supplied	
4	Sales revenue				$ 5,000,000
5	Cost of goods (@ 60%)				(3,000,000)
6	Gross margin				$ 2,000,000
7	Delivery fees				800,000
8	Delivery costs				
9	Volume related				
10	Picking items	$ 135,000	$ 15,000	$ 150,000	
11	Batch related				
12	Entering orders	$ 65,000	$ 35,000	$ 100,000	
13	Delivering orders	200,000	100,000	300,000	
14	Total batch related	$ 265,000	$ 135,000	$ 400,000	
15	Facility related	175,000	75,000	250,000	
16	Total delivery costs	$ 575,000	$ 225,000	$ 800,000	
17	Total delivery costs				(800,000)
18	Other operating costs				(1,435,000)
19	Operating profit				$ 565,000
20					

basis. Summer workers in a food processing plant are another example of short-term labor. However, the report indicates that one-third of the delivering orders activity costs are for unused capacity. Reporting the capacity costs by activity and cost hierarchy helps managers identify areas for further investigation.

Managers at charter airlines need to understand how capacity costs affect profits.
anopdesignstock/Photodisc/ Getty Images

Computing the Cost of Unused Capacity

LO 10-6

Design cost management systems to assign capacity costs.

The importance of managing capacity costs increases with the relative proportion of these costs in an organization's cost structure. Consider Northern Air Charters (NAC), which operates a fleet of small aircraft that flies tourists into remote regions for hunting, fishing, and backpacking trips. NAC purchased planes based on an estimated long-term annual volume of 2,500 passengers. If every seat were filled on every flight, these planes could carry 4,000 passengers. However, under the best practical conditions that can be expected, the planes would be capable of carrying no more than 3,200 passengers annually.

NAC incurs $400,000 of fixed operating costs for depreciation, supervision, and other items annually. It uses a traditional product costing system and computes product cost by allocating the fixed operating costs according to the number of passengers flown. Zack Stryker, NAC's owner, is concerned about the fluctuations in reported product costs over the last few years. He uses the reported costs (along with information on market conditions) to establish trip prices. See Exhibit 10.13 for computations for the last three years. Zack believes that these three years are representative of the business given the fluctuations in weather and economy.

As he considers the data in Exhibit 10.13, Zack notices a weird result. In poor years (such as year 3), when business is down, the cost system reports a relatively high cost. In good years (such as year 2), when business is booming, reported product costs are relatively low. This bothers Zack because he remembers that in year 3, he thought about lowering prices to attract new business, but the information from the cost system suggested that he would have to sell below cost.

What is the cause of the problem? The cost system allocates all costs to expected volume annually. Therefore, in "bad years" (year 3), the costs are allocated among relatively few passengers. In "good years" (year 2), the costs are spread over a larger number of passengers. This process is sending exactly the wrong signal to Zack for his pricing decisions.

Zack knows that he could use variable costing and ignore fixed costs of capacity, but he is afraid he will forget about these costs. Suppose, however, that he defines the allocation base so that it does not vary over time. Then the reported unit fixed cost would remain constant (assuming that the costs remained constant) and there would be no perverse signal on the costs. One possibility is to use a measure of *capacity* as the allocation base.

If Zack chooses to use capacity as the allocation base, he needs to decide how to measure it. There are at least four possibilities for the base. One, the **actual activity,** which is the volume actually produced this period, is used currently. It leads to the problems just described. The highest volume is **theoretical capacity,** which is what could be produced or served under ideal conditions without allowing for normal maintenance and expected downtime. **Practical capacity** is the volume that could be produced allowing for expected breaks and normal (expected) maintenance and downtime. **Normal activity** is the long-run expected volume produced. See Exhibit 10.14 for a comparison of the fixed operating cost per unit under each measure of capacity.

actual activity
Actual volume for the period.

theoretical capacity
Amount of production possible under ideal conditions with no time for maintenance, breakdowns, or absenteeism.

practical capacity
Amount of production possible assuming only the expected downtime for scheduled maintenance and normal breaks and vacations.

normal activity
Long-run expected volume.

	A	B	C	D
1		Fixed		Fixed
2		Operating	Number of	Operating
3		Cost	Passengers	Cost Rate
4	Year 1	$ 400,000	2,000	$ 200
5	Year 2	400,000	2,500	160
6	Year 3	400,000	1,600	250
7				

Exhibit 10.13

Fixed Operating Cost Rate for the Past Three Years—Northern Air Charters

	A	B	C	D	E
1				Fixed	
2		Capacity		Operating Cost	
3	Measure	(passengers)		Rate per Passenger	
4	Theoretical capacity	4,000		$ 100	
5	Practical capacity	3,200		125	
6	Normal activity (year 2)	2,500		160	
7	Actual activity (year 3)	1,600		250	
8					

Exhibit 10.14

Capacity and Cost Driver Rates for Different Measures of Capacity— Northern Air Charters

Suppose Zack chooses to compute fixed operating cost based on normal activity. This means that the costing system charges operations at $160 per passenger (see Exhibit 10.14). How can Zack use this information to help him manage capacity costs? Suppose that, as in year 1, actual activity is 2,000 passengers. Then the cost system charges $320,000 (= 2,000 passengers × $160 per passenger). Actual fixed costs are $400,000. The difference is $80,000, which is a period charge for unused (excess) capacity. When this information is reported to Zack, he can use it to decide whether this year's volume is simply part of the normal business cycle or whether it is part of a long-term trend downward in traffic. If this is part of a long-term trend, Zack can take actions to reduce the capacity.

Notice that if the cost of excess capacity were included in the cost of the service (by using actual volume), the company would still incur the $80,000 of excess capacity cost. The problem is that in this case, the excess capacity cost is hidden from Zack because it is included in each unit of service. Making it explicit enables him to consider the excess capacity and what actions need to be taken to manage it.

The earlier analysis suggests that using actual activity leads to information that can distort pricing decisions. The problem with theoretical capacity is that, by definition, NAC cannot achieve it. This means that if Zack uses it as a basis for pricing, he is in danger of not recovering his costs. To examine more closely the benefits of using practical capacity or normal activity, we need to address another issue.

Assigning the Cost of Unused Capacity

Notice that Northern Air Charters has the capacity to carry 3,200 passengers annually although, when buying the capacity, it expected an annual volume of 2,500 passengers. Why would NAC buy more capacity than it expected to use? There are two general reasons. (We explore other reasons for unused capacity and the appropriate treatment of costs in the problems to this chapter.) First, NAC could be planning to expand its business and may not want to have to buy additional capacity, for whatever reason, when it does. A second possibility is that customers tend to "bunch" their demands. That is, demand in some periods, the summer, for example, is higher than in others, for example, the winter. However, because NAC does not rent the aircraft daily or monthly, it has to have excess capacity during the year to meet the extra demand in the summer. This is called seasonal demand, and it occurs when the demand for the capacity is uneven over some period such as the year.

These two situations are fundamentally different. In the first case (planning for expansion), NAC bought the excess capacity for *its* use, not that of its customers. In this case, the better cost system to report cost would use practical capacity, or some measure of long-term volume. Otherwise, the cost of serving customers is overstated because a smaller fleet of planes (at a lower cost) could have carried the passengers. Using normal or actual activity suggests that current customers should "pay" for NAC's unused capacity. (Of course, the reported product cost is not what a customer pays but is the signal that managers receive about the cost of serving a customer and could influence pricing decisions.)

Seasonal Demand and the Cost of Unused Capacity

In the second case (fluctuating demand), the excess capacity is for the benefit of the customer; it allows NAC to meet the peaks in demand in the summer. Although NAC has the capacity to carry 3,200 passengers, NAC can achieve this volume only if the demand is uniform over the year. We can apply the lesson of the preceding section to the case of seasonal demand. Suppose NAC has one group of customers that wants to fly in the winter and another group that wants to fly in the summer. For convenience, assume that there are only two seasons, each of which is six months long. Also assume that demand is uniform throughout each season.

Demand in the winter totals 800 passengers and in the summer totals 1,600 passengers. We see in this case that the reason that NAC has an annual capacity of 3,200 passengers is to serve the summer market. (An annual capacity of 3,200 passengers is equivalent to a six-month capacity of 1,600 passengers.) How should the product costing system assign capacity cost in order to give Zack useful signals about the cost of the service?

To answer this question, we note that the cost of unused capacity is $100,000. That is, by spreading the 2,400 passengers out uniformly over the year, Zack could reduce the capacity by 25 percent (= 800 excess passenger capacity ÷ 3,200 passenger capacity) or $100,000 (= 25% × $400,000). The question is how to report the unused capacity cost of $100,000. See Exhibit 10.15 for the costs of capacity by season. The shaded areas represent the cost of capacity used; the unshaded square is the cost of the unused capacity.

There are four alternatives for assigning the cost of the unused capacity.

1. Zack can assign it to the idle capacity account, not to any passenger.
2. He can assign it evenly to the costs of serving all (winter and summer) passengers. (Add one-third, or $33,333, of the $100,000 to B, the cost of winter passengers, and two-thirds, or $66,667, to C, the cost of summer passengers. Note that this leads to the same reported costs for passengers as if the distinction between excess and used capacity costs was not considered. That is, he can divide the total annual cost, $400,000, by the total annual number of passengers, 2,400.)
3. He can assign it to the cost of serving the winter passengers. (Add $100,000 in excess capacity costs to B.)
4. He can assign it to the costs of serving the summer passengers. (Add $100,000 in excess capacity costs to C.)

See Exhibit 10.16 for the reported costs per passenger under each alternative.

The first alternative is not appropriate because NAC has the unused capacity for the benefit of the passengers. The second and third alternatives assign some costs to the winter customers in excess of the costs to serve those passengers. If Zack uses this cost to make pricing decisions, he is in danger of losing those customers to competitors that do not have excess capacity. If the costs are assigned only to the winter passengers, for example, information from the cost system tells managers to concentrate on increasing *summer* business because summer passengers are less costly. But in summer, NAC is already at capacity. Therefore, the best solution is to assign the unused capacity costs to the cost of serving passengers in the summer (i.e., alternative 4). These passengers require the excess capacity. It is the summer passengers that should be assigned the cost.

It is important to remember that this analysis does not mean that Zack should raise the price to the summer passengers. Pricing depends not only on costs but also on market conditions. The analysis also assumes that there is no other use for the capacity in the winter (flying passengers to ski resorts, for example). The key factor is what competitors are likely to do. If all competitors must have excess capacity to meet summer demand, it is likely that the market price will reflect the cost of this excess capacity. If a competitor finds an alternative use for the excess capacity, the market price will fall to reflect the lower cost of excess capacity.

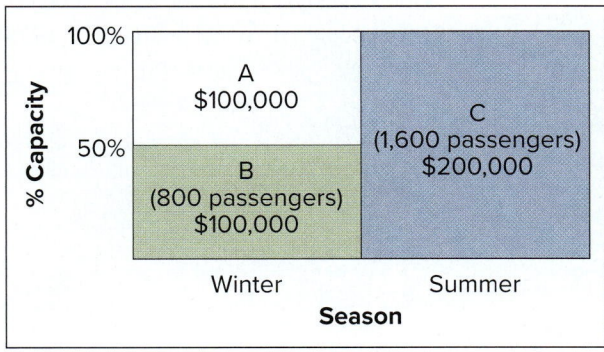

Exhibit 10.15

Seasonality and the Cost of Unused Capacity— Northern Air Charters

Exhibit 10.16

Reported Cost per Passenger: Assigning Cost of Capacity— Northern Air Charters

	A	B	C	D	E	F
1		Reported Costs for Winter Passengers				
2					Reported	
3	Alternative: Assign Unused			Number of	Cost per	
4	Capacity Costs to:	Cost from Exhibit 10.14		Passengers	Passenger	
5	1. Period cost only; none					
6	to passenger costs	$ 100,000	(B)	800	$ 125.00	
7	2. All passengers equally	400,000	(A+B+C)	2,400	166.67	
8	3. Winter passengers only	200,000	(A+B)	800	250.00	
9	4. Summer passengers only	100,000	(B)	800	125.00	
10						
11		Reported Costs for Summer Passengers				
12					Reported	
13	Alternative: Assign Unused			Number of	Cost per	
14	Capacity Costs to:	Cost from Exhibit 10.14		Passengers	Passenger	
15	1. Period cost only; none					
16	to passenger costs	$ 200,000	(C)	1,600	$ 125.00	
17	2. All passengers equally	400,000	(A+B+C)	2,400	166.67	
18	3. Winter passengers only	200,000	(C)	1,600	125.00	
19	4. Summer passengers only	300,000	(A+C)	1,600	187.50	
20						
21	Alternative: Assign Unused	Unassigned (Period Costs)				
22	Capacity Costs to:	Cost from Exhibit 10.14	Cost			
23	1. Period cost only; none					
24	to passenger costs	$ 100,000	(A)	$ 100,000		
25	2. All passengers equally	(None)		–		
26	3. Winter passengers only	(None)		–		
27	4. Summer passengers only	(None)		–		
28						

Business Application   **Managing Excess Capacity Resources—The Case of Employees**

Excess capacity can arise for many reasons. We have discussed some, such as expected growth or seasonal fluctuations in demand. Another reason is a sudden drop in demand. An example is the experience of Hormel, a U.S. processor of meat products during the COVID pandemic. The resources that were suddenly idled? Employees. The immediate issue is not how to assign the excess capacity costs to products or customers, but how to manage the costs of excess capacity. Initially, the company

> . . . chose to furlough roughly 350 workers, but didn't lay them off. These furloughed employees didn't receive pay but got benefits such as health care.[1]

One reason for this is that the company views the employees as assets:

> "Our employees are long-term investments for us and they're a precious resource, so we needed to do what we could. . . ."[2]

The company's cost analysis indicated that paying benefits during a furlough would be less than the costs associated with layoffs, including severance pay, plus the hiring and training costs when demand returns. Of course, if forecasts change and it appears that recovery will be longer than expected, the resulting decrease in cash flows will require layoffs.

This assessment on the benefits of furloughing employees was not limited to Hormel. One survey indicated that approximately 75 percent of the firms listed on the S&P 500 that announced reductions in staff furloughed the affected employees rather than laying them off.[3]

Sources:
1. Shumsky, Tatyana, and Kristin Broughton, "Companies Choose Furloughs over Layoffs to Manage Coronavirus Slowdown," *The Wall Street Journal,* July 6, 2020.
2. Ibid.
3. As referenced in ibid.

3. Anjana, the owner of Lygon Food Distributors, notes with pleasure that her two sample customers have changed their behavior to order more efficiently. In fact, all of her customers have responded this way. However, she is bothered that she does not see a corresponding drop in her costs and that her profits have actually declined. Explain to Anjana how an understanding of resources supplied and resources consumed will help resolve the contradiction.

The solution to this question is at the end of the chapter.

Managing the Cost of Quality

A major theme of this book is that managers need good information to make good decisions. A well-designed cost management system provides the information they need regarding the cost of products, services, and customers as well as the cost of the activities and processes that are used. In the development of our cost systems, we have assumed that one unit of a product or service is like every other unit. However, one important difference is the quality of the product or service produced.

> **LO 10-7**
> Describe how activities that influence quality affect costs and profitability.

How Can We Limit Conflict between Traditional Managerial Accounting Systems and Total Quality Management?

To ensure that they produce high-quality products, many companies have adopted total quality management (TQM) systems that support quality initiatives. However, unless the cost accounting systems are also designed to support these initiatives, companies are likely to find that TQM has little economic benefit. Managers are ultimately evaluated on the cost of their activities, and costs associated with quality must be incorporated in a way that allows managers to make decisions that consider the role of quality and other product characteristics and that increase the value of the firm. Using separate cost and quality systems has the risk that managers will work with and respond to incorrect signals about the value of quality programs. For example, suppose that TQM requires expenditures to train employees to improve quality but increases short-run costs. Suppose also that the company records and reports cost increases but not quality improvements. Given a choice between a recorded cost increase and an unrecorded quality improvement, the manager might choose not to increase cost to improve quality.

Effective implementation of TQM requires five changes to traditional managerial accounting systems:[1]

1. The information should include problem-solving data such as those from quality control charts, not just financial reports. Financial reports would indicate a decline in revenues, for example, but not its causes.
2. The workers themselves should collect the information and use it to obtain feedback and solve problems. Line employees are in the best position to make adjustments to the processes to prevent quality problems.
3. The information should be available quickly (for example, daily) so workers can get feedback quickly. Timely information accelerates identifying and correcting problems.
4. Information should be more detailed than that found in traditional managerial accounting systems. Instead of reporting only the cost of defects, for example, the information system should also report the types and causes of defects.
5. Rewards should be based on quality and customer satisfaction measures of performance to obtain quality. This is the idea that "you get what you reward."

---

[1] See C. Ittner and D. Larcker, "Total Quality Management and the Choice of Information and Reward Systems," *Journal of Accounting Research,* Supplement to Volume 33.

What Is Quality?

Many discussions about the value of quality in the organization are not productive because different managers use quality to mean different things. While we could (and some do) write a book defining quality, we list here two common views of what quality means. Neither of these views is appropriate in all situations, but when designing a cost management system to support quality programs, you need to be sure that you know what view of quality the system is designed to support. We consider two views of the meaning of quality—the external and the internal views.

customer expectations of quality

Customer's anticipated level of product or service (including tangible and intangible features).

External View: Customer Expectations

Customer expectations of quality refer to what customers expect from a product's tangible and intangible features. *Tangible features* include performance, taste, and functionality; *intangible features* include how the product's salespeople treat customers and the time required to deliver the product to the customer after it is ordered. In short, the external view is everything about the product that the customer values. It is about all aspects of a product's purchase and use.

Although customer expectations are clearly important in determining quality, at times they do not provide a useful guide for managers. For example, products and services could be so new or so different that customers have no expectations of them. In these cases, firms have to look inside to evaluate quality.

conformance to specification

Degree to which a good or service meets specifications.

Internal View: Conformance to Specification

Quality also can be defined as **conformance to specification,** the degree to which a product or service performs as designed (or specified). If we establish a specification that a printer will produce one page in 10 seconds, a "quality" printer will do just that (or better).

Conformance to specification, of course, is also not sufficient. We can produce a product that is 100 percent within specifications that no customer wants, at any price. Therefore, there has to be a link between the specifications we develop for our product and the expectations customers have for it.

What Is the Cost of Quality?

LO 10-8

Compare the costs of quality control to the costs of failing to control quality.

Managing costs does not only mean reducing cost. Rather, we manage costs by ensuring that the organization is operating efficiently given the products, customers, and processes that comprise its activities. As with other product characteristics, quality is something the customer values and the firm expends resources to ensure. One cost management system that is designed to help managers make decisions about quality is a so-called cost of quality system.

A **cost of quality system** is based on the idea that a tension exists between incurring costs to ensure that products meet the company's definition of quality and the cost incurred by not meeting that definition. By classifying the firm's quality-related costs into categories, managers can better manage them.

cost of quality system

A system that reflects the tension between incurring costs to ensure quality and the costs incurred with quality failures.

Conformance Costs Ensuring that quality conforms to the firm's requirements involves two costs, prevention costs and appraisal costs. **Prevention costs** are incurred to prevent defects in the products or services being produced. The costs and the associated activities include the following:

prevention costs

Costs incurred to prevent defects in the products or services being produced.

- *Materials inspection.* Inspecting production materials when they are delivered.
- *Process control (process inspection).* Inspecting the production process as it occurs.
- *Process control (equipment inspection).* Acquiring and maintaining the equipment used to track the production process.
- *Quality training.* Training employees to improve quality.
- *Machine inspection.* Ensuring that machines are operating properly within specifications.
- *Product design.* Designing products to reduce manufacturing problems (sometimes referred to as *designing for manufacturability*).

Appraisal costs (also called *detection costs*) are incurred to detect individual units of products that do not conform to specifications. Appraisal costs include these:

- *End-of-process sampling.* Inspecting a sample of finished goods to ensure quality.
- *Field testing.* Testing products in use at customer sites.

One of the services Lygon Food Distributors (LFD) offers is to provide prepackaged assortments of produce to specialty food shops. What quality costs might LFD incur? The kitchen supervisor checks the packaging equipment routinely every morning to ensure that it will not damage the produce. This is an example of a *prevention cost.* After preparing packages for distribution to a particular customer, she randomly checks the packages to ensure they are the right assortment and the produce is fresh and attractively packaged. This is an example of an *appraisal cost.*

Nonconformance Costs   The two costs of failing to control quality are internal failure costs and external failure costs. **Internal failure costs** are incurred when nonconforming products and services are detected before being delivered to customers. They include these:

- *Scrap.* Materials wasted in the production process.
- *Rework.* Correcting product defects before the product is sold.
- *Reinspection/Retesting.* Quality control testing after rework is performed.

External failure costs are incurred when nonconforming products and services are detected after being delivered to customers. They include these costs:

- *Warranty repairs.* Repairing defective products.
- *Product liability.* Accepting company liability resulting from product failure.
- *Marketing costs.* Improving the company's image tarnished from poor product quality.
- *Lost sales.* Experiencing decreased sales resulting from poor-quality products (customers will go to competitors).

LFD might sell at a discount food that has been damaged in handling or purchased food that does not meet strict quality standards. The lost sales value represents an *internal failure cost.* LFD will not sell some food that has been damaged or is past its freshness date because it is concerned about lost customer loyalty (and, thus, lost future sales) as a result of an incorrect mix of produce. Lost future business is an example of an *external failure cost.* See Exhibit 10.17 for a summary of the four main classifications of quality costs.

Trade-Offs, Quality Control, and Failure Costs

The ultimate goal in implementing a quality improvement program is to achieve zero defects while incurring minimal costs of quality. However, managers must make trade-offs between the four cost categories, and total costs of quality must be reduced over time.

Conformance Costs	Nonconformance Costs
Prevention costs: Costs of reducing the possibility of producing low-quality or defective units.	**Internal failure costs:** Costs associated with low-quality or defective units identified before sale or delivery to the customer.
Appraisal costs: Costs of inspecting products before sale or delivery to the customer.	**External failure costs:** Costs associated with delivering low-quality or defective units to the customer.

Exhibit 10.17

Cost of Quality Cost Classifications

How would Anjana at LFD estimate the cost of quality? She would calculate the costs related to ensuring quality. For example, the kitchen supervisor and her staff perform the packaging equipment inspections as part of their daily duties, an activity (prevention cost) that costs $22,000 per year. Anjana must decide how much to spend on packaging equipment inspections versus inspecting the final produce packages (appraisal cost). It could be less costly to inspect the packages rather than the equipment (which takes the equipment out of service). See Exhibit 10.18 for an illustration of the trade-off between conformance and nonconformance costs.

Costs of quality are often expressed as a percentage of sales. An example of a cost of quality report prepared for LFD (Exhibit 10.19) indicates that the firm spent $57,600 on quality training and machine inspections (prevention costs), which represents 1.2 percent of sales. This is the largest amount spent on quality for any of the four categories. LFD spent $30,000 (= 0.6 percent of sales) on appraisal costs and $36,000 (= 0.7 percent of sales) on scrap costs. The cost of dealing with customer complaints totaled $30,000 (= 0.6 percent of sales).

Anjana uses the information to see how she can reduce the overall cost of quality. For example, suppose that "scrap" occurs because produce is cut incorrectly. Adding an

Exhibit 10.18

Cost of Quality: Trade-Off between Conformance and Nonconformance Costs

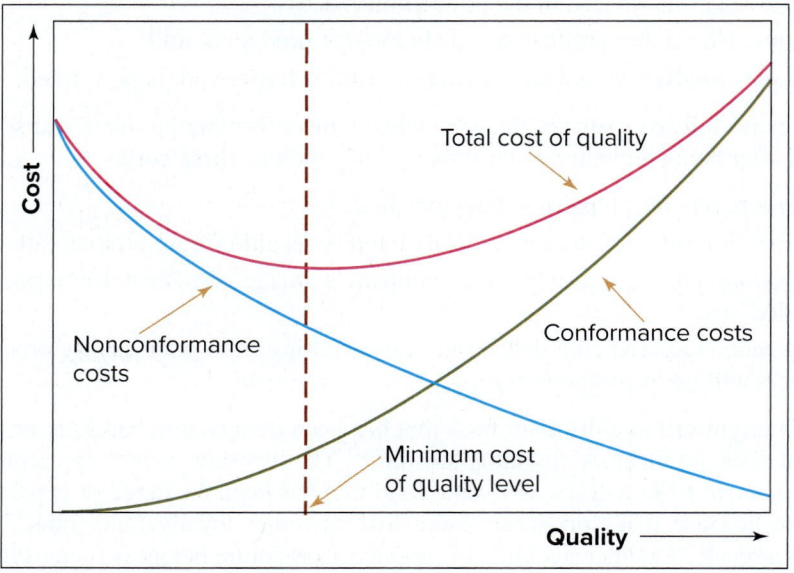

Exhibit 10.19

Cost of Quality Report

	A	B	C	D	E	F
1		LYGON FOOD DISTRIBUTORS				
2		Cost of Quality Report				
3		For the Year				
4						
5				Percent of Sales		
6		Costs of Quality		(Sales = $ 5,000,000)		
7	Prevention costs					
8	Quality training	$ 35,600				
9	Machine inspections	22,000	$ 57,600		1.2%	
10	Appraisal costs					
11	Inspect copies		30,000		0.6%	
12	Internal failure costs					
13	Food scrap		36,000		0.7%	
14	External failure costs					
15	Customer complaints		30,000		0.6%	
16	Total cost of quality		$ 153,600		3.1%	
17						

additional check to ensure that each order is correct could reduce scrap costs. Customer complaints refer to the cost of dealing with customers, including managerial time and reimbursements to irate customers. Perhaps this cost could be reduced by finding the source of customer complaints and dealing with the problem before it becomes a customer complaint.

Anjana's goal is to reduce the total cost of quality ($153,600) as a percentage of sales (3.1 percent) while maximizing the value of each dollar spent on quality. Thus, she could find that spending an additional $30,000 on prevention costs will reduce the cost of scrap by $20,000 and the cost of customer complaints by $25,000, for a total of $45,000 saved for an additional cost of $30,000. This gives a net reduction in the cost of quality of $15,000. As a result, the total cost of quality would be reduced to $138,600, or 2.8 percent of sales.

The cost of quality report can be a valuable decision-making aid for managers, but it is only effective if all quality costs are measured and reported. If a cost of quality system is not comprehensive, there is a danger that decisions will be distorted as managers focus on the costs the system includes but ignore unreported quality costs.

Technology, Data Analysis, Customer Profitability, and Cost of Quality

Business Application

We have discussed both the cost (profitability) of customers and suppliers and the costs of quality in this chapter. Of course, these are not separate issues as, for example, the cost of losing a customer because of poor quality (external failure) depends on the profitability of the customer a firm loses. One of the problems in the past with cost of quality systems was that it was difficult to measure the cost of external failure because there was no "event" that triggered a transaction that would be picked up by the accounting system and, therefore, no way of knowing that an external failure had occurred.

As technological capabilities grow and costs of data acquisition and analysis shrink, companies can track in greater detail the habits of individuals and the choices they might make. In other words,

> Technologies can track how long a customer will wait for a human to answer the phone and how many ads they will tolerate. They can monitor the tone of a customer's voice. Companies know what steps they must take to keep shoppers loyal—and which they can skip.[1]

Consider, for example, a customer of an online retail firm. A delivery of an order to a customer that was late (or lost) would be considered (potentially) an external failure cost, as it could lead the customer to move business to another firm.

Will this cost arise? For online firms, who deal directly with the customer, they have

> . . . data on exactly when, how and why consumers buy—or don't buy—their products. Since they don't use a middleman they can know, for instance, that two delayed shipments won't cost the company business, but three will.[2]

These same data can be analyzed to determine the profitability of customers.

> Just as data can be used to measure customers' threshold for bad service, it also helps pinpoint which shoppers are most profitable and, therefore, worth the effort and expense to please.[3]

Together, this technology makes available to firms the information needed to assess when to make concessions that will keep a profitable customer and when to not yield to requests (perhaps "firing" the customer) when the customer is deemed to be not profitable.

Sources:
1. Terlep, Sharon, "Everyone Hates Customer Service. This is Why," *The Wall Street Journal*, August 3, 2019.
2. Ibid.
3. Ibid.

Because most accounting systems do not collect the cost of lost business and other opportunity costs, a cost of quality system is likely to underestimate external failure costs. In this case, information from the cost of quality system is likely to lead managers to underinvest in prevention and appraisal activities because the cost of external failures is underestimated.

The graphical representation in Exhibit 10.18 is often misinterpreted to imply that some optimal and unchanging level of quality exists, but as competition increases and the costs of technology decrease, both the conformance and nonconformance curves shift to the right. This means that over time, the optimal level of quality increases. However, without a cost management system that routinely reports the cost of quality, managers are unable to monitor these costs at all.

Self-Study Question

4. Walsh Industries manufactures suits for men. Following is its financial information for one year:

    a. Classify these items into prevention (P), appraisal (A), internal failure (IF), or external failure (EF) costs.

    b. Create a cost of quality report for year 2.

    The solution to this question is at the end of the chapter.

	Year 2
Sales revenue.	$4,500,000
Costs	
Materials inspection.	$ 65,000
Scrap	85,000
Employee training	130,000
Returned goods	31,000
Finished goods inspection	150,000
Customer complaints.	80,000

Key Takeaways

1. The methods of activity-based costing (ABC) can be used not only to compute product costs, but also to manage costs. Activity-based cost management (ABCM) gives managers information about the activities that use resources, and this information helps managers make decisions about which activities to

    a. Perform less frequently (running larger batch sizes in each production run, for example).

    b. Do more efficiently (taking less time to set up equipment for a new production run, for example).

2. Customers can impose cost on the organization by using more or fewer services for the same amount of goods purchased. ABC can help the firm assess profitability at a customer level by recording and costing the number of activities a customer requires. Examples of these activities include

    a. Ordering more frequently (in smaller batches).

    b. Returning more items.

    c. Not paying on time.

    d. Requiring more customer service time.

    ABC also makes it possible to compute the costs that suppliers impose on the firm by late deliveries, poor quality, and so on. This information is useful when considering the total cost of supply.

3. The difference between the cost of capacity available (resources supplied) and capacity used (resources consumed) is the cost of excess capacity. The way these costs are assigned to products of customers depends on the reason for the excess capacity.

    a. If it is for the benefit of the firm (because of expected growth, for example), it should be kept separate from the cost of products. This allows managers to determine if the growth is still likely to arise.

    b. If it is for the benefit of a group of customers (because of seasonal demand, for example), it should be assigned to the products or services produced for these benefits.

4. Managing quality in goods and services produced requires two types of costs:

    a. Cost of conformance: the cost of producing quality goods and services.

    • Prevention costs—the costs to ensure high quality (design, equipment, and so on).

    • Appraisal costs—the costs to test products or services during or after production.

    b. Cost of nonconformance: the cost incurred by producing products or services that do not meet quality standards.

    • Internal failure costs—the costs of producing below-standard quality of goods and services (rework, scrap, and so on).

    • External failure costs—the costs of producing and selling below-standard quality of goods and services (warranty costs, liability costs, and so on).

    Managing the cost of quality involves trading off these two types of costs as illustrated in the cost of quality graph (Exhibit 10.18).

SUMMARY

A well-designed cost management system helps firms manage costs. Because activities drive costs, the use of activity-based costing methods represents an important approach for cost management. Activity-based management is the concept of using activity-based costing to be more effective as a manager. In thinking about what affects costs, managers will likely improve decisions by categorizing costs according to major categories of activities.

The effect of customer and supplier actions on a firm's costs and profit can be evaluated using activity-based concepts of costing. Customers affect a firm's activities and costs, and managers can use information about the affected activities to manage their costs.

Capacity cost should be identified with the activities, products, and customers that require the cost. Excess capacity cost that the firm incurs that is not for the benefit of the customer should be reported separately.

Quality programs can be managed by reporting the costs associated with quality. Cost of quality reports break quality costs into four categories: prevention, appraisal, internal failure, and external failure.

The following summarizes key ideas tied to the chapter's learning objectives:

LO 10-1 Describe how activity-based cost management can be used to improve operations. This section explores the benefits of activity-based costing systems from a manager's perspective. The process goes beyond calculating the cost of products using activity-based costing. After a new costing system is in place, management must determine how to use the new, more detailed information to make better decisions.

LO 10-2 Use the hierarchy of costs to manage costs. Establishing a hierarchy of costs can help management understand which production processes must be changed to affect certain costs. For example, reducing unit-level costs would not likely affect capacity-level costs, at least in the short run.

LO 10-3 Describe how the actions of customers and suppliers affect a firm's costs. By their ordering and supply actions, customers and suppliers can impose costs on firms by requiring additional personnel, rework, or support activities. Activity-based costing can help identify these costs.

LO 10-4 Use activity-based costing methods to assess customer and supplier costs. Once the costs of customers and suppliers have been determined, this information can be used to work with customers and suppliers to identify areas in which it is mutually beneficial to change behavior.

LO 10-5 Distinguish between resources used and resources supplied. Companies must pay for activities supplied even if they are not fully utilized. For example, if assembly workers who earn hourly wages are idle for half of an 8-hour shift, the company still must compensate them for 8 hours. Management must try to match activities supplied to activities used to be as efficient as possible.

LO 10-6 Design cost management systems to assign capacity costs. Capacity costs should be assigned to the product or customer that requires them. If capacity costs are for the benefit of the firm (for example, to allow for growth), they should not be assigned to current customers.

LO 10-7 Describe how activities that influence quality affect costs and profitability. Activities that firms implement to improve quality require resources but also return benefits. A cost of quality system makes this trade-off explicit by identifying the costs of maintaining quality (conformance costs) and the costs associated with poor quality (nonconformance costs).

LO 10-8 Compare the costs of quality control to the costs of failing to control quality. The two costs of controlling quality are prevention costs—those incurred to prevent defects in the products or services being produced—and appraisal costs—those incurred to detect individual units of products that do not conform to specifications. The two costs of failing to control quality are internal failure costs—those incurred when nonconforming products and services are detected before being delivered to customers—and external failure costs—those incurred when nonconforming products and services are detected after being delivered to customers.

KEY TERMS

activity-based cost management, *447*

actual activity, *461*

appraisal costs, *467*

conformance to specification, *466*

cost of quality system, *466*

customer expectations of quality, *466*

external failure costs, *467*

internal failure costs, *467*

lean accounting, *450*

lean manufacturing, *449*

normal activity, *461*

practical capacity, *461*

prevention costs, *466*

process reengineering, *449*

resources supplied, *459*

resources used, *458*

theoretical capacity, *461*

unused resource capacity, *459*

REVIEW QUESTIONS

10-1. How are activity-based costing and activity-based management similar? How do they differ?

10-2. Can activity-based management be implemented without an activity-based costing system? Explain.

10-3. Why is it important for managers to assess whether activities are value-added or nonvalue-added? What are some common nonvalue-added activities found in many businesses?

10-4. What are some ways in which customers affect a firm's costs? What are some ways in which suppliers affect a firm's costs?

10-5. How is computing the cost of customers the same as computing the cost of products? How is the computation different?

10-6. What is the difference between resources supplied and resources consumed? Why is the difference important?

10-7. Why does it matter how capacity costs are assigned to products?

10-8. Under what conditions should the cost of excess capacity be assigned to products or customers? When should excess capacity costs not be assigned to products or customers?

10-9. In what ways does quality affect cost?

10-10. What are the four categories in a cost of quality system? Give an example of each.

CRITICAL ANALYSIS AND DISCUSSION QUESTIONS

10-11. What are examples of two nonvalue-added activities that could be found in each of the following service organizations: (*a*) a health clinic and (*b*) a bank?

10-12. What are examples of two nonvalue-added activities that could be found in organizations that manufacture (*a*) lumber and (*b*) furniture?

10-13. Suppose a manager can reduce the processing time for loan applications by reducing the amount of time the application awaits action. How does the reduction add value to the organization?

10-14. "You can get the cost of customers by first computing the cost of the products they buy and then multiplying by the number of units each customer buys." Do you think this approach would assist in cost management? Why?

10-15. Consider the Business Application feature "Technology, Data Analysis, Customer Profitability, and Cost of Quality." Do you think it is easier to estimate the cost savings from adapting a lean manufacturing system or to estimate the costs from a disaster such as the COVID pandemic? Why? Does this make it more or less likely that there will be "too much" lean manufacturing?

10-16. "Customers don't cost money; they bring in revenue." Do you agree? Why?

10-17. Consider the Business Application feature "Technology, Data Analysis, Customer Profitability, and Cost of Quality." What does it mean to "fire a customer"? Why would a firm want to do this? How would a firm do this?

10-18. "I have to pay for capacity whether it is used or not. Therefore, excess or idle capacity really doesn't cost me anything." Do you agree? Why?

10-19. You are working at a hotel in a resort location. The manager says that the hotel must raise the rates in the winter when it has fewer tourists because the cost per room is much higher. How would you respond?

10-20. Many if not most schools in the United States have large excess capacity cost because they are underutilized in the summer months. The dean at the local business school is developing a cost of customer system to assess costs of students in different degree programs. He has asked you for your recommendation on how these excess capacity costs should be assigned. What would you recommend?

10-21. Can you think of any products for which one or several of the elements of service, quality, and cost are *not* important to the customer? If so, explain why.

10-22. How might a manufacturing system differ under a quality-based view versus the traditional view of managing quality?

10-23. Consider the Business Application "Managing Excess Capacity Resources—The Case of Employees." In a related article, the authors write that manufacturers would "probably not try to pass them [excess capacity costs] along to the consumer, at least in the short term." Is this consistent with the appropriate treatment of excess capacity costs as discussed in the chapter? Why?

All applicable Exercises are included in Connect.

EXERCISES

10-24. Activity-Based Cost Management in a Retail Store   (LO 10-1)
Consider the following actions of a retail store trying to manage the costs of its returns service.

Required
Match each of the process improvements listed with how they deliver cost reductions.

Process Improvement	Delivers Cost Reduction
1. The hours at which returns will be processed have been reduced 2. Customers may now generate paperwork for returns online, print the forms at their convenience, and drop off the forms and the returns at a special desk. 3. Consolidating the returns function by establishing one physical location in the store for returns instead of allowing returns at each checkout point.	a. By reducing the frequency of activity. b. By improving the efficiency of the activity. c. By both (a) and (b).

10-25. Activity-Based Management for a College Placement Center   (LO 10-1)
Consider the following actions of a college placement center trying to manage the costs of its placement services.

Required
Match each of the process improvements listed with how it delivers cost reductions.

Process Improvement	Delivers Cost Reduction
1. The center closes on Wednesdays during spring break. 2. Students may now schedule interviews online rather than in person. 3. Résumés of students being interviewed are made available to recruiters online rather than distributed in hard-copy form.	a. By reducing the frequency of activity. b. By improving the efficiency of the activity. c. By both (a) and (b).

10-26. Activity-Based Management in a Manufacturing Firm   (LO 10-1)
Consider the following actions of a manufacturing firm trying to manage the costs of materials handling from the direct materials inventory to the production line.

Required
Match each of the process improvements listed with how it delivers cost reductions.

Process Improvement	Delivers Cost Reduction
1. Production scheduling is changed, resulting in shorter setup times between production runs. 2. Labor moving materials from raw materials inventory to the production area has been reclassified from direct labor to indirect labor (overhead). 3. Finished goods inventory has been moved to be closer to the end of the production.	a. By reducing the frequency of the activity. b. By improving the efficiency of the activity. c. Neither (a) nor (b).

(LO 10-2) **10-27. Cost Hierarchy for a Not-for-Profit**

Brentwood Disaster Relief (BDR) is a local not-for-profit organization working to help victims of disasters.

Required

The following are various resources and activities of the organization. Indicate whether each is likely to apply at the (1) unit level or (2) facility level.

a. Lodging—hotel rooms for victims left homeless.

b. Food and supplies—food, blankets, and so on for victims.

c. Salaries—salaries for administrators.

d. Fund-raising—mailings and wages for phone solicitations.

e. Transportation—travel from disaster site to temporary lodging for victims.

f. Utilities—for main office.

g. Building lease—offices of employees.

h. Communications cost—computers and phone systems at main office.

(LO 10-2) **10-28. Cost Driver Identification**

The following are various activities for Humphrey Insurance Agency.

Required

Suggest a feasible cost driver base for each of the following, and explain why each selected cost driver base is feasible.

a. Consumer contract customer service.

b. Consumer contract review.

c. Sales calls—existing commercial customers.

d. Advertising particular products.

e. Commercial contract customer service.

f. Consumer payment processing.

g. Commercial payment processing.

h. Sales calls—new commercial customers.

i. Commercial contract negotiation.

j. Commercial contract review.

k. Customer file maintenance.

l. Employee relations.

m. Community involvement.

(LO 10-2) **10-29. Cost Driver Identification**

The following are various activities for EMS Law School.

Required

Suggest a feasible cost driver base for each of the following, and explain why each selected cost driver base is feasible.

a. Course registration.

b. Admissions: Attending recruiting fairs.

c. Admissions: Evaluating applications.

d. Course scheduling.

e. Admissions: Interviewing applicants.

f. Career placement: Scheduling interviews.

g. Career placement: Counseling students.

h. Faculty teaching.

(LO 10-3, 4) **10-30. Activity-Based Costing of Customers**

Alter's Home Center (AHC) sells renovation and remodeling products to both contractors and individual home owners. One of the services AHC offers is delivery of the purchased products to the customer's work site. Because not all customers take advantage of the delivery service option, ACH adds 10 percent to the cost of the products purchased to cover the delivery cost. A business intern spent the summer at ACH. The intern's assignment was to analyze the delivery service and recommend a better way to charge customers for using it. The intern, who had studied activity-based costing, identified the following activities and the data related to them:

Activity	Cost Driver	Annual Cost	Annual Driver Volume
Picking order	Number of items	$286,000	357,500 items
Delivering order.	Number of orders	522,500	27,500 orders
Handling complaints.	Number of complaints	32,400	135 complaints
Total delivery cost.		$840,900	

The intern selected two customers, who were frequent customers, to use as an illustration of the system: Wagner Remodeling and Burlington Contractors. The intern collected the following information on these two customers for the most recent six months:

	Wagner Remodeling	Burlington Contractors
Total order value (before delivery charge).	$12,500	$13,000
Number of orders	15	42
Total number of items	310	305
Number of delivery complaints	1	6

Required

a.   What would the delivery charge for each customer be under the current policy of 10 percent of order value?

b.   What would the activity-based costing system estimate as the cost of delivering to each customer?

c.   How could managers at AHC use the information identified by the new costing method to manage costs?

10-31. Activity-Based Costing of Customers   (LO 10-3, 4)

Rupert's Appliance Warehouse (RAW) delivers appliances to retailers throughout the city. The firm adds 6 percent to the cost of the appliances to cover the delivery cost. The delivery fee is meant to cover the cost of delivery. The finance team at RAW has analyzed the delivery service using activity-based costing methods and identified four activities. Data on these activities follow:

Activity	Cost Driver	Activity Cost	Cost Driver Volume
Processing order.	Number of orders	$ 90,000	3,000 orders
Loading truck.	Number of items	180,000	60,000 items
Delivering order.	Number of orders	108,000	3,000 orders
Billing.	Number of invoices	70,000	2,500 invoices
Total overhead.		$448,000	

Two of Rupert's customers are McLean Designs and Neveux Appliances. Data for orders and deliveries to these two customers follow:

	McLean Designs	Neveux Appliances
Order value (total).	$90,000	$96,000
Number of orders	31	66
Total number of items.	360	900
Number of invoices.	7	60

Required

a.   What would the delivery charge for each customer be under the current policy of 6 percent of order value?

b.   What would the activity-based costing system estimate as the cost of delivering to each customer?

c.   How could Rupert's use the information identified by the new costing method to manage costs?

(LO 10-3, 4)   **10-32. Activity-Based Costing of Customers**

Northwestern Bank (NB) offers only checking accounts. Customers can write checks and use a network of automated teller machines. NB earns revenue by investing the money deposited; currently, it averages 4.1 percent annually on its investments of those deposits. To compete with larger banks, NB pays depositors 0.3 percent on all deposits. A recent study classified the bank's annual operating costs into four activities.

Activity	Cost Driver	Cost	Driver Volume
Using ATM	Number of uses	$ 1,800,000	3,000,000 uses
Visiting branch.	Number of visits	1,080,000	225,000 visits
Processing	Number of		
transaction	transactions	7,920,000	120,000,000 transactions
Managing functions	Total deposits	7,200,000	$562,500,000 in deposits
Total overhead.		$18,000,000	

Data on two representative customers follow:

	Emily	Jacob
ATM uses	40	130
Branch visits.	5	45
Number of transactions	200	520
Average deposit	$10,000	$10,000

Required

a.   Compute the operating profit for Northwestern Bank.

b.   Compute the profit from Emily and Jacob, assuming that customer costs are based only on deposits. Interest costs = 0.3 percent of deposits; operating costs are 3.2 percent (= $18,000,000/ $562,500,000) of deposits.

c.   Compute the profit from Emily and Jacob, assuming that customer costs are computed using the information in the activity-based costing analysis.

(LO 10-3, 4)   **10-33. Activity-Based Costing of Customers**

Refer to the data in Exercise 10-32.

Required

a.   How can Northwestern Bank use the information from the activity-based costing analysis to manage its costs?

b.   What does Northwestern Bank need to consider before implementing your suggestions from requirement (a)?

(LO 10-3, 4)   **10-34. Activity-Based Costing of Customers: Ethical Issues**

Lygon Food Distributors (LFD), introduced in the chapter, hired a consultant to update its system for reporting the cost of customers. The consultant showed Anjana Malik, the owner of LFD, an analysis that indicates that customer support costs are significantly higher for customers who order on weekends than for those who order during the week.

Required

a.   What pricing decisions might LFD make based on the consultant's information?

b.   Would these be ethical? Why or why not?

c.   The consultant comes back to Anjana's office and explains that he made a mistake in the analysis. The relation is actually between cost of customer support and the customer's age. Does this affect your answers to requirements (*a*) and (*b*)?

10-35. Activity-Based Costing of Customers: Ethical Issues

(LO 10-3, 4)

Central State College (CSC) is a state-supported college with a large business school. The business school offers an undergraduate degree and training programs for a local manufacturer. The state does not support the training programs, which are paid for by the manufacturer under a fixed-price contract.

The college president has asked the dean of the business school for a breakdown of costs by program. The president will be meeting with state legislators asking for an increase in support for the college's programs. The dean has assigned you to lead the team that will develop the costs by program.

The business school's computer lab is a major cost item. The lab is used during the day for the undergraduate program and in the evening for the training program.

Required

a.   How will you recommend that the cost of the computer lab be allocated to the two programs? Be explicit in your description of the allocation base.

b.   The dean tells you that the training program should not be allocated any costs other than its direct costs. She points out that the college was established for undergraduate education and the training program is an incremental activity. "After all, if we didn't have the training program, we would still have the computer lab," she says. Do you agree with the dean? Is the dean's suggestion ethical?

10-36. Activity-Based Costing of Suppliers

(LO 10-3, 4)

Rex Metal Fabricators (RMF) buys scrap metal and produces components for buildings and other structures. The purchase contracts specify an average quality level of 90 percent. That is, 90 percent of the metal must be ready for use without further processing. Metal that is not ready can be treated at extra cost by RMF, and this is more cost-effective than scrapping the metal and purchasing additional amounts. The cost of treating the metal requiring further processing is $80 per ton.

RMF uses two suppliers: Chopin Yards and Joe Company. During the past year, the purchasing quality data were as follows:

	Chopin Yards	Joe Company	Total
Total purchases (tons).	1,500	1,000	2,500
Average purchase price (per ton).	$124.00	$120.00	$122.40
Percentage requiring further processing	2.0 7.5	4.2	

Required

Assume that the average quality, measured by the percentage of metal purchases requiring further processing, and prices from the two companies will continue as in the past. What is the effective price for metal from the two companies when quality is considered?

10-37. Activity-Based Costing of Suppliers

(LO 10-3, 4)

Refer to the data in Exercise 10-36.

Required

Assume all else remains the same. What percentage of metal from Chopin Yards that requires further processing would make Rex Metal Fabricators indifferent between buying from Chopin Yards and Joe Company?

(LO 10-3, 4)   **10-38. Activity-Based Costing of Suppliers**

Watko Entertainment Systems (WES) buys audio and video components for assembling home entertainment systems from two suppliers, Bacon Electronics and Hessel Audio and Video. The components are delivered in cartons. If the cartons are delivered late, the installation for the customer is delayed. Delayed installations lead to contractual penalties that call for WES to reimburse a portion of the purchase price to the customer.

During the past quarter, the purchasing and delivery data for the two suppliers showed the following:

	Bacon	Hessel	Total
Total purchases (cartons).	5,000	3,000	8,000
Average purchase price (per carton).	$160	$176	$166
Number of deliveries	40	20	60
Percentage of cartons delivered late	30%	15%	25%

The Accounting Department recorded $234,000 as the cost of late deliveries to customers.

Required

Assume that the average quality, measured by the percentage of late deliveries, and prices from the two companies will continue as in the past. Also assume that the number of components is the same for all deliveries from either company. What is the effective price for cartons from the two companies when late deliveries are considered?

(LO 10-3, 4)   **10-39. Activity-Based Costing of Suppliers**

Refer to the data in Exercise 10-38.

Required

Assume all else remains the same. What percentage of late deliveries by Bacon would make WES indifferent between buying from Bacon Electronics and Hessel Audio and Video?

(LO 10-3, 4)   **10-40. Activity-Based Costing of Suppliers**

Ellery Products manufactures various components for the fashion industry. Ellery buys fabric from two vendors: Ewers Textiles and Bramford Materials. Ellery chooses the vendor based on price. Once the fabric is received, it is inspected to ensure that it is suitable for manufacturing purposes. Ellery disposes of fabric that is deemed unsuitable.

The controller at Ellery collected the following information on purchases for the past quarter:

	Ewers	Bramford
Total purchases (yards).	19,800	36,900
Fabric discarded (yards).	990	4,428

The purchasing manager has just received bids on an order for 800 yards of fabric from both Ewers and Bramford. Ewers bid $2,261 and Bramford bid $2,134.

Required

Assume that the average quality, measured by the amounts discarded from the two companies, will continue as in the past. Which supplier would you recommend that the purchasing manager select? Explain.

10-41. Activity-Based Costing of Suppliers (LO 10-3, 4)
Refer to the data in Exercise 10-40.

Required

a. Assume all else remains the same. What bid by Ewers would make Ellery indifferent between buying from Ewer or Bramford?

b. Why, given the information, do you think Ellery continues to buy fabric from Bramford?

10-42. Resources Used versus Resources Supplied (LO 10-5)
Byron Truck Repair uses a specialized hydraulic lift to work on trucks and busses. Data on the lift and its usage follow:

	Cost Driver Rate	Cost Driver Volume
Resources used		
Operation	$6.00 per lift-hour	2,460 lift-hours
Maintenance.	$4.50 per job	480 jobs
Resources supplied		
Operation	$18,000	
Maintenance.	$2,700	

Required
Compute the cost of unused resource capacity in operation and maintenance for Byron Truck Repair.

10-43. Resources Used versus Resources Supplied (LO 10-5, 6)
Refer to Exercise 10-42. Sales revenue from truck repair totaled $32,000.

Required

a. Prepare a traditional income statement like the one in Exhibit 10.11.

b. Prepare an activity-based income statement like the one in Exhibit 10.12.

10-44. Resources Used versus Resources Supplied (LO 10-5)
Wykes Metal Working uses a special lathe to shape components. Data on the lathe and its usage follow:

	Cost Driver Rate	Cost Driver Volume
Resources used		
Energy.	$2.40 per machine-hour	2,130 machine-hours
Repairs	$ 5.40 per job	710 jobs
Resources supplied		
Energy.	$6,250	
Repairs	$5,100	

Required
Compute the cost of unused resource capacity in energy and repairs for Wykes Metal Working.

10-45. Resources Used versus Resources Supplied (LO 10-5, 6)
Refer to Exercise 10-44. Sales revenue from lathe work totaled $17,900.

Required

a. Prepare a traditional income statement like the one in Exhibit 10.11.

b. Prepare an activity-based income statement like the one in Exhibit 10.12.

(LO 10-5)   **10-46. Resources Used versus Resources Supplied**

Boston Home Center (BHC) offers customers the use of a truck at $40 per trip to take purchased merchandise home. BHC reports the following information about the trucks it has for customer usage:

	Cost Driver Rate	Cost Driver Volume
Resources used		
Operation	$.55 per mile	45,000 miles
Administration	$25.00 per trip	1,850 trips
Resources supplied		
Operation	$33,000	
Administration	$60,000	

Required

Compute the cost of unused operation and administration resource capacity for Boston Home Center.

(LO 10-5, 6)   **10-47. Resources Used versus Resources Supplied**

Refer to Exercise 10-46. Sales revenue totaled $74,000.

a.   Prepare a traditional income statement like the one in Exhibit 10.11.

b.   Prepare an activity-based income statement like the one in Exhibit 10.12.

(LO 10-5)   **10-48. Resources Used versus Resources Supplied**

The Shipping Department at Nashville Fabricators reports the following information about resources:

	Cost Driver Rate	Cost Driver Volume
Resources used		
Final inspection	$17 per inspected unit	29,000 units inspected
Certification	$82 per shipment	7,250 shipments
Resources supplied		
Final inspection	$641,000	
Certification	$745,000	

Required

Compute the cost of unused resource capacity in the Shipping Department at Nashville Fabricators.

(LO 10-5)   **10-49. Resources Used versus Resources Supplies**

Abbott Business Services (ABS) generated revenue of $637,800 processing accounts payable and payroll transactions for clients. ABS reports the following information about resources in two functions:

	Cost Driver Rate	Cost Driver Volume
Resources used:		
Process transactions	$.008 per transaction	17,500,000 transactions
Administer accounts.........	$525 per account	430 accounts
Resources supplied		
Process transactions	$210,000	
Administer accounts.........	$280,000	

Required

a.   Compute the cost of unused resource capacity at Abbott Business Services.

b.   Prepare a traditional income statement like the one in Exhibit 10.11.

c.   Prepare an activity-based income statement like the one in Exhibit 10.12.

10-50. Resources Used versus Resources Supplied: Working Backward (LO 10-5)

Hosmer Industries provides the following information about resources and usage:

	Unused Resources Capacity	Cost Driver Volume
Resources used		
Materials....................	$ 4,800	6,400 pounds
Power	3,744	272 hours
Setups.....................	1,800	62 setups
Purchasing.................	4,320	64 purchase orders
Client assistance............	18,240	40 inquiries
Supervision	8,160	256 labor-hours
Facility cost	6,720	3,360 square meters
Resources supplied		
Materials....................	$235,200	
Power	42,912	
Setups.....................	57,600	
Purchasing.................	50,400	
Client assistance............	37,440	
Supervision	69,600	
Facility cost	67,200	

Required

a. Compute the cost driver rate for each resource.

b. Describe what the term *unused resource capacity* means.

10-51. Assigning Cost of Capacity (LO 10-5, 6)

Middle Industries produces a sensor for use in manufacturing. It produces the sensor in a plant with an annual practical capacity of 75,000 units. The variable cost of the sensor is $185.00 per unit, and the fixed costs of the plant are $12,375,000 annually. Current annual demand is 55,000 sensors. Middle Industries bought the plant because it was close to its other manufacturing facilities and was available for sale when they were searching for a location.

Required

a. What cost per sensor should the cost system report to facilitate management decision making?

b. Given your answer to requirement (a), is there any cost of excess capacity? If yes, what is the cost of excess capacity, and how should it be reported? If no, why not?

c. How would your answers to requirements (a) and (b) change if the smallest manufacturing plant that one could build that was suitable for sensor manufacturing (owing to technology) was able to produce 75,000 sensors?

10-52. Assigning Cost of Capacity (LO 10-5, 6)

Basil's Framing manufactures picture frames in one workshop, which has a practical capacity of 40,000 frames. The variable cost of a frame is $24 per unit, and the fixed costs of the workshop are $392,000 annually. Current annual demand is 28,000 frames. Basil's Framing bought the current workshop because of forecasts that demand for the frames would grow.

Required

a. What cost per frame should the cost system report to facilitate management decision making?

b. Given your answer to requirement (a), is there any cost of excess capacity? If yes, what is the cost of excess capacity, and how should it be reported? If no, why not?

c. How would your answers to requirements (a) and (b) change if the smallest manufacturing plant that one could build (owing to technology) was able to produce 35,000 frames?

10-53. Assigning Cost of Capacity (LO 10-5, 6)

Cairney, Inc. manufactures a specialized part used in internal combustion engines. The annual demand for the part is 225,000 units. The facility has a practical capacity of 240,000 units annually. The company leased the current facility because facilities capable of manufacturing the unit require machines that can produce 60,000 units each. The annual cost of the facility is $864,000. The variable cost of a part is $4.

Required

a.   What cost per unit should the cost system report to facilitate management decision making?

b.   Given your answer to requirement (*a*), is there any cost of excess capacity? If yes, what is the cost of excess capacity, and how should it be reported? If no, why not?

(LO 10-7, 8)   **10-54. Costs of Quality**
Fraser Plastics produces plastic parts for use in various products. The following represents accounts in its cost of quality system.

1. Rework	6. Waste
2. Testing equipment	7. Field testing
3. Preventive maintenance	8. Customer complaints
4. Inspection training	9. Warranty repairs
5. Incoming materials inspection	10. Process inspection

Required
Classify each as prevention (P), appraisal (A), internal failure (IF), or external failure (EF).

(LO 10-7, 8)   **10-55. Costs of Quality**
Cass Company has recorded the following information for the last six months of operations from its cost of quality system:

	Quarter 1	Quarter 2
Revenue	$760,000	$920,000
Costs		
Warranty expense	$15,200	$13,800
Machine calibration	3,800	7,360
Customer returns (defects)	22,800	18,400
Material inspection on receiving dock	9,120	5,520
Waste	19,000	14,720
Quality testing equipment	18,700	11,700
Rework	2,280	3,650
Inspection before packaging	7,600	8,900
Training on testing equipment	6,200	9,000

Required

a.   Classify these items into prevention (P), appraisal (A), internal failure (IF), or external failure (EF) costs.

b.   Calculate the ratio of the prevention, appraisal, internal failure, and external failure costs to sales for Quarter 1 and Quarter 2.

(LO 10-7, 8)   **10-56. Trading-Off Costs of Quality**
Refer to the data in Exercise 10-55.

Required
Construct a cost of quality report for Quarter 1 and Quarter 2.

(LO 10-7, 8)   **10-57. Costs of Quality**
The following represents the financial information for Plaza Plastics for May and June:

	May	June
Sales revenue	$735,000	$528,000
Costs		
Scrap.	$ 1,980	$ 1,690
Process inspection	2,860	1,740
Quality training	23,760	11,700
Product testing equipment	5,160	4,320
Field testing	8,400	6,300
Warranty repairs	3,360	3,060
Rework	19,760	16,650
Preventive maintenance	16,200	8,550
Legal expense for warranty claims.	7,800	4,320
Materials inspection	11,280	11,160

Required

a.   Classify these items into prevention (P), appraisal (A), internal failure (IF), or external failure (EF) costs.

b.   Calculate the ratio of the prevention, appraisal, internal failure, and external failure costs to sales for May and June.

10-58. Trading-Off Costs of Quality   (LO 10-7, 8)
Refer to the data in Exercise 10-57.

Required

Construct a cost of quality report for May and June.

10-59. Costs of Quality   (LO 10-7, 8)
One of Camely Chemicals' facilities manufactures a hazardous chemical. The following represents the financial information from the plant for the most recent two years:

	Year 1	Year 2
Sales revenue	$700,000	$1,140,000
Costs		
Redesign manufacturing process.	$ 2,800	$ 5,500
Discard defective batches.	3,700	6,500
Clean up toxic spills	25,000	31,500
Warranty claims.	12,900	26,400
Product liability claims	20,100	23,100
Rework	7,200	14,400
Preventive maintenance	11,400	22,800
Batch testing	30,200	26,400
Training on equipment.	19,000	29,700

Required

a.   Classify these items into prevention (P), appraisal (A), internal failure (IF), or external failure (EF) costs.

b.   Calculate the ratio of the prevention, appraisal, internal failure, and external failure costs to sales for year 1 and year 2.

10-60. Trading-Off Costs of Quality   (LO 10-7, 8)
Refer to the data in Exercise 10-59.

Required

Construct a cost of quality report for year 1 and year 2.

(LO 10-7, 8) **10-61. Cost of Quality: Environmental Issues**

Many companies have adapted the cost of quality framework to environmental issues. They assign costs to one of four categories: prevention (P), appraisal (A), internal failure (IF), and external failure (EF), where the categories refer to environmental activities and consequences of environmental failures.

Required

Classify the following costs incurred for environmental activities into the four categories:

a. Maintenance of machinery that handles hazardous material.

b. Design of processes to minimize leakage and waste.

c. Criminal penalties for illegal dumping.

d. Monitoring costs of chemical processes.

e. Fines for being out of compliance with environmental regulations.

f. Employee training: environmental policies.

g. Cleanup of leaks and spills on the plant floor.

h. Lost sales from bad publicity after toxic spill.

(LO 10-7, 8) **10-62. Cost of Quality: Financial Reporting Issues**

Consider adapting the cost of quality framework to financial reporting issues. Assign costs to one of four categories: prevention (P), appraisal (A), internal failure (IF), and external failure (EF), where the categories refer to financial reporting activities and the consequences of poor, or even illegal, financial reporting.

Required

Classify the following costs incurred for financial reporting activities into the four categories:

a. Design of internal control systems to minimize errors in data entry.

b. Extra work done by external auditors to complete the audit because new employees made a lot of errors.

c. Fines for failing to comply with accounting regulations.

d. Design of information systems to keep out hackers.

e. Internal auditors' review of internal controls in requirement (*a*).

f. Drop in stock price from bad publicity after the chief executive gets sentenced to 10 years in prison.

g. Effects of bad publicity on stock prices because publication of financial statements was delayed in order to correct errors in the statements.

h. Employee training: new accounting regulations.

PROBLEMS

 All applicable Problems are included in Connect.

(LO 10-4, 5) **10-63. Activity-Based Reporting and Capacity**

Refer to Exercise 10-50. Sales revenue for Hosmer Industries is $720,000.

Required

a. Prepare a traditional income statement like the one in Exhibit 10.11.

b. Prepare an activity-based income statement like the one in Exhibit 10.12.

c. Prepare a short report to the managers at Hosmer Industries describing how the activity-based income statement prepared in requirement (*b*) can help them manage costs.

(LO 10-3, 4) **10-64. Activity-Based Reporting: Service Organization**

Lozier Catering and Events (LCE) offers a variety of services from small gatherings to large weddings and corporate retreats. Sales for year 1 totaled $877,500. Information regarding resources for the year includes the following:

	Resources Used	Resources Supplied
Depreciation	$ 56,550	$ 58,175
Training	29,250	35,100
Transportation	52,000	55,575
Publicity	72,800	78,000
Permanent staff	146,250	201,500
Temporary staff	269,750	276,250
Invoicing and records	24,375	27,300
Administrative	45,500	51,350

Required

Management has requested that you do the following:

a. Prepare a traditional income statement.

b. Prepare an activity-based income statement.

c. Write a short report to management explaining why the activity-based income statement provides useful information to managers. Use the information from requirements (*a*) and (*b*) to develop examples for your report.

10-65. Customer Profitability   (LO 10-4)

Kresge Lodging has an elite program for its card members. There are three levels, based on total nights stayed: Diamond (50 nights or more); Platinum (25 nights or more); and Base (fewer than 25 nights). In order to facilitate reservations and answer customer questions, Kresge Lodging provides access to special customer service representatives, who work exclusively with the designated level (Diamond, and so on). Customer representatives receive salaries plus bonuses of 5 percent of customer gross margin. The company provides various perquisites (free nights, upgrades, and so on) to its members, with 75 percent of the cost of the perquisites used for the benefit of Diamond members, 20 percent for Platinum members, and 5 percent for Base members.

Customer Costs	Total	Diamond	Platinum	Base
Number of members	150,000	18,000	50,000	82,000
Average customer representative salary		$75,000	$50,000	$40,000
Number of representatives	28	15	8	5
Perquisite costs	$6,000,000			
Average annual gross margin per customer		$1,200	$400	$200

The gross margin received by Kresge is the amount received from the participating hotels for a customer's stay.

Required

a. What is the excess of gross margin over customer costs for each category of customer?

b. Write a short memo that evaluates customer profitability.

10-66. Customer Profitability   (LO 10-4)

Grand Online Mall (GOM) is an online retailer that sells many different products. GOM offers its customers two options for shipping. First, the "Regular" program charges a flat fee of $9.90 per order within its shipping area. The second ("Elite") program charges customers $100 annually and includes free, regular shipping. The average cost to GOM of shipping an order is $8. In addition to the included shipping, Elite customers also receive a rebate of 5 percent on the sales value of the merchandise purchased for the year. GOM earns an average 30 percent gross margin on its sales, excluding shipping costs and any shipping fees.

Information on the sales to the two customer groups for the most recent year follows:

Customer Costs	Total	Elite	Regular
Number of customers.........................	75,000	15,000	60,000
Average customer sales value per order		$40	$85
Average number of orders annually		12	4

Required

a.   What is the profitability per customer for each category of customer (Elite and Regular)?

b.   Write a short memo that evaluates customer profitability.

c.   The company is revising the rebate policy for the Elite customers and is thinking of raising the rebate percentage. Assuming all other behavior (number of orders, average value of an order, and so on) remains the same, what rebate percentage for the Elite customers would result in profitability for the two categories of customers being the same?

(LO 10-3, 4)   **10-67. Customer Profitability—Data Analysis and Visualization**

Stark Remodeling Center (SRC) is a home renovation showroom that caters primarily to contractors. Customers place orders at SRC, either in person or online, and the merchandise is packaged in standard-sized boxes and delivered to the home or job site. (The delivery service SRC uses charges based on the number of boxes shipped.) SRC sets prices so that they cover the order fulfillment and delivery costs, which SRC estimates to be 15 percent of the total sales value of all orders (order value).

Currently, the financial system at SRC calculates what is called "customer margin" by subtracting two items from the total customer's order value. First, an allowance for cost of goods sold is deducted. This allowance is 75 percent of the order value and approximates the overall experience at SRC. Second, the system deducts an additional 15 percent to reflect the order and fulfillment costs for the customer.

A summer intern working with the cost analysis group at SRC has studied the delivery service using data from the last quarter. The intern identified six major activities, estimated costs, and recommended cost drivers for these activities to use in a customer profitability analysis. The intern's findings follow:

Activity	Cost Driver	Activity Cost	Cost Driver Volume
Verifying order..............	Number of orders	$ 37,500	3,000 orders
Picking order	Number of items	82,500	37,500 items
Delivering order............	Number of boxes	53,460	4,860 boxes
Invoicing order.............	Number of invoices	27,360	3,600 invoices
Leasing warehouse.........	Number of boxes	63,180	4,860 boxes
Administrative costs	Order value	96,000	$2,400,000
Total cost		$360,000	

To illustrate the proposed model, the intern chose two SRC customers who ordered a similar value of products in the last quarter: Eldridge Renovations and Horton Contracting. Data for the last quarter for the two customers follow:

	Eldridge Renovations	Horton Contractors
Total order value	$11,000	$10,800
Number of orders	15	5
Number of items	72	70
Number of boxes.....................	40	14
Number of invoices...................	16	6

Required

a. What would be reported customer margin for each of the two customers under the current customer profitability system?

b. Suppose the intern's ABC system is adopted to measure customer profitability. What would be reported customer margin for each of the two customers under the intern's proposed ABC customer profitability system? Note: The ABC system would continue to subtract 75 percent of the order value to reflect an allowance for cost of goods sold.

c. Prepare a report with recommendations for the management at SRC on how to improve profitability as suggested by the results of the intern's ABC system. Include graphical support as appropriate. Discuss how you would extend the intern's system, if at all. Be sure to identify the additional data that you would need to collect, if any, for the changes you recommend.

10-68. Customer Profitability—Data Analysis and Visualization (LO 10-3, 4)

Huber Supply is a distribution company specializing in providing paper and soap products for institutions such as hospitals, colleges, and so on. Customers place orders online with Huber. Once an order is received, the warehouse verifies the purchaser's basic information (address, drop-off instructions, and so on). The order is then checked for completeness and entered into the warehouse system. Warehouse employees (pickers) then collect the items and package them for delivery. Delivery is completed by an outside firm that charges based on the volume (cubic yards) of the total order. Once the order is received, an invoice is sent to the customer. More than one invoice might be sent for an order. This happens, for example, if deliveries were made to multiple locations or if the customer requests it. In addition to the order value, all customers are charged a flat 4 percent fee (based on order value) to defray part of the delivery cost.

Huber recently hired a new sales and marketing director. The director, in looking through customer histories, noticed what appeared to be a troubling trend. Although Huber continued to be popular with some of the larger institutional customers, it was losing business from some smaller customers, who complained that they could find less expensive products elsewhere. The new director hired a consultant to report on the problem.

The consultant started by looking at the current management reporting system that evaluated customers solely by their order values. Large customers were favored because they placed relatively large orders and seemed satisfied with the service and prices on the goods they purchased. The reporting system did report a profitability number, which was calculated as the order value plus the 4 percent delivery fee less an allowance for the cost of the items. This allowance currently averages 85 percent based on the order value.

The consultant decided to experiment with an ABC system. The consultant identified six activities (including a "Miscellaneous" activity) and associated cost drivers, and estimated annual costs and driver volumes. The consultant's findings follow:

Activity	Cost Driver	Annual Activity Cost	Annual Driver Volume
Verifying order............	Orders	$ 55,000	22,000 orders
Entering order	SKUs*	72,600	1,815,000 SKUs
Packaging order	Items	76,000	190,000 items
Shipping order.............	Cubic yards	216,000	240,000 cubic yards
Invoicing order............	Invoices	54,400	40,000 invoices
Miscellaneous	Order value	150,000	$6,000,000

*Stock keeping units. These are the total SKUs, so 10 orders each for the same product would count as 10 SKUs for the purpose of this ABC system.

Because the sales and marketing director was concerned about the smaller customers, the consultant split the customers into two groups ("Large" and "Small") and eliminated a few that were too difficult to classify. Once the customers were classified, the consultant then collected information on their ordering behavior over the last year. The findings follow:

	Large	Small
Total order value	$2,750,000	$2,800,000
Average cost of items (%).	88%	80%
Number of orders	10,800	10,200
Number of SKUs	600,000	795,000
Number of items	84,000	96,000
Number of cubic yards.	152,000	74,000
Number of invoices.	14,800	11,000

Required

a. What would be reported customer margin for each of the two customer groups under the current customer profitability system?

b. Suppose the consultant's ABC system is adopted to measure customer profitability. What would be reported customer margin for each of the two customer groups under the consultant's proposed ABC customer profitability system? Assume the 4 percent delivery fee would continue to be collected.

c. Prepare a report with recommendations for the sales and marketing director on how to improve profitability as suggested by the results of the consultant's ABC system. Include graphical support as appropriate. Discuss how you would extend the system, if at all. Be sure to identify the additional data that you would need to collect, if any, for the changes you recommend.

(LO 10-3, 4)   **10-69. Activity-Based Costing of Suppliers**

Atwater Chemicals produces an engine additive for machinery. The additive is produced by adding various ingredients to a petroleum-based lubricant. Atwater purchases the lubricant from two suppliers, Woodlawn Petroleum and Spokane Chemicals. The quality of the final product depends directly on the quality of the lubricant. If the lubricant is "off," Atwater has to dispose of the entire batch. Because all lubricant can be "off," Atwater uses a measure it calls the "yield," which is computed as

$$\text{Yield} = \text{Good output} \div \text{Input}$$

where the output and input are both measured in barrels. As a benchmark, Atwater expects to get 12 barrels of good output for every 16 barrels of lubricant purchased, for a yield of 75 percent (= 12 barrels of output ÷ 16 barrels of lubricant).

Data on the two suppliers for the past year follow:

	Woodlawn Petroleum	Spokane Chemicals	Total
Total inputs purchased (barrels)	5,600	3,400	9,000
Good output (barrels)	3,640	2,924	6,564
Average price (per barrel)	$117.00	$150.50	$129.66

Required

Assume that the average quality, measured by the yield, and prices from the two companies will continue as in the past. What is the effective price for lubricant from the two companies when quality is considered?

(LO 10-3, 4)   **10-70. Activity-Based Costing of Suppliers**

Consider the information in Problem 10-69. The sales manager of Woodlawn Petroleum has proposed to the purchasing manager at Atwater that Woodlawn be given an exclusive contract to supply the lubricant. If it receives the contract, Woodlawn will guarantee a 75 percent yield on the lubricant it supplies.

Required

a. Assume that the average quality, measured by the yield, and prices from the two companies will continue as in the past. What is the maximum price for lubricant that Atwater Chemicals should be willing to pay Woodlawn Petroleum under the exclusive contract?

b. Are there other factors that Atwater Chemicals should consider before accepting the offer?

10-71. Activity-Based Costing of Suppliers   (LO 10-3, 4)

Carrie Construction (CC) is a company specializing in building airport runways and major highways. As a part of its business, it receives supplies of aggregate (stone, sand, gravel, and so on) from two suppliers: Austin Aggregate and Granger Materials. The CC purchasing department has a preference for buying from Granger based on price but occasionally has to order from Austin when Granger cannot fill the order.

Carrie Construction has recently had problems with the quality and the timeliness of deliveries. When a supplier delivers a load to CC, it goes through an initial inspection to assure it meets specification. If the load fails the initial inspection, it goes through a secondary inspection to determine the exact issue. Almost always, the issue can be resolved and the load can be used. The initial inspection costs $3,000 per load. A secondary inspection, which is more thorough, costs $15,000 per load. If a delivery is delayed, Carrie has to hire temporary workers or pay overtime to some employees. The average cost of a delayed load is $6,000.

The following are summary statistics from last year's purchases from the two suppliers:

	Granger Materials	Austin Aggregate
Number of loads	600	150
Average tons per load	5,000	10,000
Average price per ton	$7.20	$8.00
Number of initial inspections passed.....	450	141
Number of delayed deliveries..........	120	15

Required

Calculate the effective cost of a ton of aggregate from the two suppliers, assuming that last year's experience is representative.

10-72. Activity-Based Costing of Suppliers   (LO 10-3, 4)

Consider the information in Problem 10-71. The sales manager of Granger Materials has proposed to the purchasing manager at Carrie Construction that Granger be given an exclusive contract to supply the aggregate. Assume that the total annual demand remains the same. If it receives the contract, Granger will deliver the aggregate in the same average-sized load as it does currently.

Required

a.   If Granger receives the exclusive contract, assume the load quality and delivery timeliness will remain the same as current experience. What is the maximum price Carrie Construction should offer Granger Materials for the exclusive contract?

b.   Suppose Granger Materials guarantees that no deliveries will be delayed or it will repay Carrie Construction for the costs associated with the delays. What is the maximum price Carrie Construction should offer Granger Materials for the exclusive contract?

10-73. Activity-Based Reporting: Manufacturing   (LO 10-4, 5)

Barr Plastics makes parts for a variety of manufacturing applications. Sales last year totaled $3,060,000. Information regarding resources for the month follows.

	Resources Used	Resources Supplied
Administrative	$170,000	$252,000
Customer service	34,000	72,000
Depreciation	204,000	360,000
Energy....................	170,000	180,000
Long-term labor............	85,000	126,000
Marketing	238,000	270,000
Materials.................	510,000	540,000
Parts management	102,000	126,000
Quality inspections	153,000	180,000
Setups....................	238,000	360,000
Short-term labor	68,000	86,400

In addition, Barr spent $90,000 on 60 engineering changes with a cost-driver rate of $1,400, and $108,000 on 10 outside contracts with a cost driver rate of $10,800.

Required

The CFO at Barr has requested the following:

a.   A traditional income statement.

b.   An activity-based income statement.

c.   A short report explaining why the activity-based income statement provides useful information to managers. Use the information from requirements (a) and (b) to develop examples for the report.

(LO 10-6)   **10-74. Assigning Capacity Costs**
Located in a small town in upstate New York, Terry's Bakery operates a facility that makes pies for retail sale. The facility has the capacity to make 36,000 pies annually. The plant has only two customers, Panama Food Mart and East Street Coffee. Annual orders for Panama total 18,000 pies, and annual orders for East Street total 9,000 pies. Terry's makes the pies fresh every day and carries no inventory. It also ensures that the customers only sell freshly made pies as well. Variable manufacturing costs are $4.20 per pie, and annual fixed manufacturing costs are $97,200.

Required

What cost per pie should the cost system report? Why? If you need more information to answer the question, describe it.

(LO 10-6)   **10-75. Assigning Capacity Costs: Seasonality**
Refer to the information in Problem 10-74. The pie business in this town has two seasons, summer and winter. Each season lasts exactly six months. Panama Food Mart orders 9,000 pies in the summer and 9,000 pies in the winter. East Street Coffee is closed in the winter and orders all 9,000 pies in the summer.

Required

How would you modify, if at all, the cost system you designed previously for Terry's Bakery in Problem 10-74? Why?

(LO 10-6)   **10-76. Assigning Capacity Costs: Seasonality**
Refer to Problems 10-74 and 10-75. The owner of Terry's Bakery now believes that there are really three seasons instead of two, the third being the fall and spring (as a combined season). Each of the three seasons lasts exactly four months. They also know that East Street Coffee opens in mid-spring and closes in mid-fall.

   The manager at Terry's checks the order patterns and sees the following demand (in pies) in each of the three seasons:

	Winter	Fall and Spring	Summer	Total
Panama Food Mart	6,000	6,000	6,000	18,000
East Street Coffee.	–0–	3,000	6,000	9,000
Total.	6,000	9,000	12,000	27,000

Required

How would you modify, if at all, the cost system you designed previously for Terry's Bakery in Problem 10-75? Why?

(LO 10-6)   **10-77. Assigning Capacity Costs**
Remington Agricultural Products (RAP) produces organic cider with no preservatives. Any production must be sold within a few days, so producing for inventory is not an option. RAP's single plant has the capacity to make 72,000 cases of cider annually. Currently, RAP sells to only two customers: Savery's Organic Produce (SOP) and Griswold Food Stores (a chain of grocery stores). SOP orders 36,000 cases and Griswold orders 12,000 cases annually. Variable manufacturing costs are $15 per case, and annual fixed manufacturing costs are $864,000.

Required

What cost per case should the cost system report? Why? If you need more information to answer the question, describe it.

10-78. Assigning Capacity Costs: Seasonality

(LO 10-6)

Refer to the information in Problem 10-77. The organic cider business has two seasons, holidays and nonholidays. The holiday season lasts exactly four months (although it feels longer), and the nonholiday season lasts eight months. SOP orders the same amount each month, so SOP orders 12,000 packages during the holidays and 24,000 packages in the nonholiday season. Griswold only carries the organic cider during the holidays.

Required

How would you modify, if at all, the cost system you designed previously for Remington Agricultural Products in Problem 10-77? Why?

10-79. Cost of Quality—Data Analysis and Visualization

(LO 10-8)

The production team at Schaefer Manufacturing has been working on improving quality and has been approaching the problem from the technical side (measuring defects, and so on), but also from the financial perspective. They want to develop recommendations they can sell based on the implications of profit and costs. A cost analyst who is a member of the team has been working on developing a cost of quality system. The technical team has developed a way to measure quality at the manufacturing facility, which the cost analyst plans to use.

The quality measure, which the team has assigned to a variable, q, is a numerical scale from 0.1 to 10.0, measured in increments of one-tenth. The low end of the scale, 0.1, represents low quality and 10.0 represents "perfect" quality. Using cost estimates from quality experts and cost data, the cost analyst has estimated, statistically, both the conformance and nonconformance cost relations. Specifically, the analyst estimates that for conformance cost, the relation between conformance cost (C) and quality (q) can be written as

$$C = q^2$$

The relation between nonconformance cost (N) and and quality (q) can be written as

$$N = 100e^{-q}$$

Required

a. Using the two relations, develop a cost of quality diagram depicting (1) conformance cost, (2) nonconformance cost, and (3) the total cost of quality, which is the sum of the conformance cost and the nonconformance cost.

b. Determine the approximate (within 0.1) quality level that minimizes the total cost of quality.

c. Is the minimum you determined in requirement (b) the same level of quality where the conformance cost and nonconformance cost are equal?

10-80. Cost of Quality—Data Analysis and Visualization

(LO 10-8)

Refer to the information and data in Problem 10-79. After working with the quality system for one year, the cost analyst revisits the relations for conformance and nonconformance costs. During the year, the quality team worked on lowering the cost of conformance, specifically reducing the prevention cost. This was accomplished by working with one of the company's vendors to improve the quality of the raw materials used. As a result of the change, the cost analyst now estimates that the relation between conformance cost (C) and quality (q) can be written as

$$C = 0.5q^2$$

The cost of nonconformance relation has not changed.

Required

a. If the conformance cost is lower for every level of quality than it was one year ago and the nonconformance cost is the same, what do you predict will happen to the quality level that results in a minimum cost of quality? Explain.

b. Using the two relations, develop a cost of quality diagram depicting (1) conformance cost, (2) nonconformance cost, and (3) the total cost of quality, which is the sum of the conformance cost and the nonconformance cost.

c. Determine the approximate (within 0.1) quality level that minimizes the total cost of quality.

INTEGRATIVE CASES

(LO 10-1, 2, 3, 4)   **10-81. Cost Hierarchies, Cost of Customers, and Pricing**

WSM Corporation is considering offering an air shuttle service between Sao Paulo and Rio de Janeiro. It plans to offer four flights every day (excluding certain holidays) for a total of 1,400 flights per year (= 350 days × 4 flights per day). WSM has hired a consultant to determine activity-based costs for this operation. The consultant's report shows the following:

Activity	Activity Measure (cost driver)	Unit Cost (cost per unit of activity)
Flying and maintaining aircraft	Number of flights	$1,600 per flight
Serving passengers	Number of passengers	$4 per passenger
Advertising and marketing	Number of promotions	$60,000 per promotion

WSM estimates the following annual information. With 20 advertising promotions, it will be able to generate demand for 40 passengers per flight at a fare of $225. The lease of the 60-seat aircraft will cost $4,000,000. Other equipment costs will be $2,000,000. Administrative and other marketing costs will be $1,250,000.

Required

a.   Based on these estimates, what annual operating income can WSM expect from this new service?

b.   WSM is considering selling tickets over the Internet to save on commissions and other costs. It is estimated that the cost driver rate for *flights* would decrease by $100 as a result of Internet sales. Administrative and other marketing costs would increase by $1 million. WSM estimates that the added convenience would generate a 5 percent increase in demand. All other costs and fares would remain the same. Would you recommend that WSM adopt Internet ticket sales? Explain why or why not.

c.   Assume that WSM management decides *not* to adopt the Internet strategy, regardless of your answer to requirement (b). Instead, it is now considering a plan to sell tickets at two prices. An unrestricted ticket (good for travel at any time on any day) would sell for $250. A discount ticket, good for reservations made in advance, would sell for $150. Management estimates that it can sell 35,000 tickets (25 per flight) at the unrestricted airfare of $250. All other data remain the same.

Ignoring the information in requirement (b), how many discounted tickets would WSM have to sell annually to earn an operating income of $1,700,000? Assume that the annual number of flights remains at 1,400 and that the discounted tickets would be evenly divided across the 1,400 flights.

(LO 10-5, 6)   **10-82. Unused Capacity: The Grape Cola Caper**

Refer to Integrative Case 9-75 in Chapter 9. Assume that all of the facts in Case 9-75 still hold except that the practical capacity of the machinery is 20,000 hours instead of 10,000 hours.

Required

a.   Recompute the unit costs for each of the cola products: Diet, Regular, Cherry, and Grape.

b.   What is the cost of unused capacity? What do you recommend that Rockness Bottling do with this unused capacity?

c.   Now assume that Rockness is considering producing a fifth product: Vanilla cola. Because Vanilla cola is in high demand in Rockness Bottling's market, assume that it would use 10,000 hours of machine time to make 100,000 units. (Recall that the machine capacity in this case is 20,000 hours, while Diet, Regular, Cherry, and Grape consume only 10,000 hours.) Vanilla cola's per-unit costs would be identical to those of Diet cola except for the machine usage costs. What would be the cost of Vanilla cola? Calculate on a per-unit basis, and then in total.

SOLUTIONS TO SELF-STUDY QUESTIONS

1. Cost Category
    a. Unit level
    b. Capacity related
    c. Unit level
    d. Product related
    e. Batch related
    f. Batch related
    g. Customer related
2. a. The cost for the two customers follows:

	Mario's	Claire's
Entering order (@ $10 per order).	$ 750	$ 500
Picking order (@ $2 per item)	1,500	3,000
Delivering order (@ $24 per delivery)	1,920	1,200
Performing general delivery administration (@ 5%).	2,500	5,000
Total delivery costs.	$6,670	$9,700
Delivery costs as a percentage of order value	13.3%	9.7%

   b. Mario's has responded by reducing the frequency of orders. Claire's has responded by increasing volume without increasing the number of orders. Note that both customers have reduced delivery costs as a percentage of the order volume.
3. Although LFD's customers are ordering more efficiently (from LFD's viewpoint), the firm might not be reducing costs. The resources used have fallen, but unless LFD takes steps to reduce the resources supplied, there will not be a reduction in the costs of the delivery service.
4. *a* and *b*.

WALSH INDUSTRIES
Cost of Quality Report
For Year 2

	Costs of Quality		Percent of Sales (Sales = $4,500,000)
Prevention costs			
Employee training	$130,000		
Materials inspections.	65,000	$195,000	4.3%
Appraisal costs			
Finished goods inspection		150,000	3.3
Internal failure costs			
Scrap		85,000	1.9
External failure costs			
Returned goods	31,000		
Customer complaints	80,000	111,000	2.5
Total cost of quality		$541,000	12.0%

11

Chapter Eleven

Service Department and Joint Cost Allocation

LEARNING OBJECTIVES

After reading this chapter, you should be able to:

LO 11-1 Explain why and how service costs are allocated using the direct method, the step method, and the reciprocal method.

LO 11-2 Use the reciprocal method approach for outsourcing decisions.

LO 11-3 Explain why and how joint costs are allocated using the net realizable value method and the physical quantities method.

LO 11-4 Use cost data to make the decision whether to sell or process further.

LO 11-5 Account for by-products.

LO 11-6 (Appendix) Use spreadsheets to solve reciprocal cost allocation problems.

Spaces Images/Blend Images

❝ I don't know how we're supposed to determine the costs of different grades of lumber. First, we have back office operations here at headquarters that support our two forests up north. Second, lumber from the forests comes in two grades, but the costs to harvest are incurred for both.❞

The members of the marketing team at Green Valley Mills (GVM) in the Pacific Northwest were sitting in the company's conference room at corporate headquarters. GVM produces two primary products, #1-Grade and #2-Grade lumber. When GVM harvests lumber at its holdings, this mixture of #1- and #2-Grade lumber is produced in approximately fixed proportions. (Lumber "quality" is determined primarily by the physical appearance of the board.) The company had just received an order for several hundred tons of #1-Grade lumber. The problem, of course, was that GVM would end up with #2-Grade lumber as well and would have to discount it because the company has no room to store it. Somehow, managers had to decide whether the special order was worth accepting and how much cost each product should bear.

Luis Romero, the marketing team member from cost accounting, spoke up:

❝ Cost allocation can be arbitrary, but it is important because of the information it provides. We have two types of allocation problems here. First, what do we do about the support services from the back office operations? Second, how do we treat the joint costs of producing the two grades? Many companies face both of these problems and have developed methods to address them. Give me a day, and I'll have some suggestions.❞

We have seen how cost allocation is used to develop the costs of products, services, and customers. The cost allocation process has other roles, two of which we explore in this chapter. In our discussion of *two-stage cost allocation,* we took the first-stage allocation process as given and concentrated on allocating the cost pools in the second stage. However, part of the first-stage overhead cost is incurred for departments that do not directly produce the service or product. Instead, these departments provide services to the plants and departments that do. For example, personnel, accounting, and purchasing provide services to production departments. In this chapter, we will consider service department cost allocation, which is the process used to allocate the costs of these "service" departments.

Next we consider product costing when multiple products are jointly produced from common inputs in fixed proportions such as the lumber at GVM. In our discussions so far, the companies altered the proportions of the outputs by changing the input mix. For some products, especially in foods, chemicals, and mineral industries, the output proportions are fixed by physical characteristics. When a production process results in outputs in fixed proportion, we use a process called *joint cost allocation* to assign costs to the individual products.

service department
Department that provides services to other subunits in the organization.

user department
Department that uses the functions of service departments.

Service Department Cost Allocation

This section focuses on allocating the costs of a service department to other departments that use the service. **Service departments** provide services to other departments. For example, an information systems department is a service department that provides information systems support to other departments, and a human resources department provides hiring and training services to other departments. **User departments** use the functions of service departments. For example, the production department uses the services provided by the information systems and human resources departments. User departments could be other service departments or production or marketing departments that produce or market the organization's products.

Although our focus in this chapter is on allocating the costs of service departments to production departments, we also discuss how the allocation process can help managers make decisions about keeping or eliminating the service departments. We return to this issue at the end of our discussion on service department cost allocation.

LO 11-1
Explain why and how service costs are allocated using the direct method, the step method, and the reciprocal method.

Many organizations have a food services department that provides meals to employees. Such departments are service departments. Pixtal/AGE Fotostock

Green Valley Mills (GVM) is a midsize forest products and lumber company with many departments, but for simplicity we assume that it has only four. Two, Information Systems (S1) and Administration (S2), are service departments. The other two, Sierra Tract (P1) and Cascades Tract (P2), are user departments. See Exhibit 11.1 for the connections among the departments. Both user departments employ both service departments. That is, Sierra Tract requires support from Information Systems for the automated systems it uses, and it requires support from Administration for most staff functions, such as hiring and training employees. The same is true of Cascades Tract. Notice that Exhibit 11.1 has a dashed line between the two service departments. This indicates that, depending on the situation, each service department also provides service to the other.

Any cost center whose costs are charged to other departments in the organization is called

intermediate cost center
Cost center whose costs are charged to other departments in the organization.

final cost center
Cost center, such as a production or marketing department, whose costs are not allocated to another cost center.

an **intermediate cost center. Final cost centers,** on the other hand, are cost centers whose costs are not allocated to another cost center.

Building companies and home supply retailers use the company's products. GVM's Sierra Tract and Cascades Tract provide these products. To serve their customers, these two user departments require the assistance of Information Systems (to prepare customer statements, for example) and Administration (to provide employees to work in the mills and produce lumber, for example). In Chapter 10, you learned how to compute the cost of a customer. Here, you will consider how to allocate the cost of the service departments (the "back office costs") to the departments that interact with the customers, such as the building supply company.

Service organizations, merchandising organizations, and manufacturing organizations all have production or marketing departments and service departments.

Exhibit 11.1
Service and User Departments—Green Valley Mills

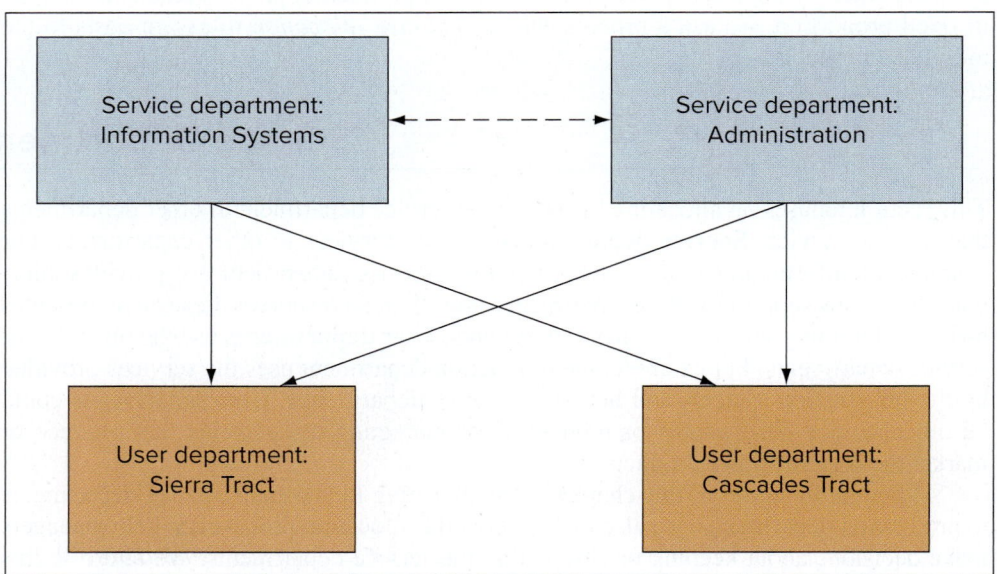

The following are examples of production or marketing and service departments at various organizations:

Organization	Service Department	Production or Marketing Department
Steelcase (office furniture)...........	Order Entry	Computer Furniture Plant
Bank of America	Loan Processing	Palmdale Branch
Los Angeles Unified School District...	Motor Pool	Central High School
City of Grand Rapids...............	Purchasing	Streets and Sanitation

Methods of Allocating Service Department Costs

This section describes three methods used to allocate service department overhead costs: the direct method, the step method, and the reciprocal method. To make each method easier to understand, we use the four departments at GVM as an example.

GVM allocates service department costs to the Sierra and Cascades tracts for two purposes: (1) to determine the cost to produce and market lumber and (2) to encourage operating department managers to monitor service department costs, that is, cross-department monitoring. Because all GVM department managers are evaluated, in part, on the costs of their department, they do not view the allocation of cost as a meaningless exercise. (Performance measurement is discussed in more detail in later chapters of the book.) They make operating decisions, such as pricing, based on the costs of their operations. Therefore, to the managers in these departments, the allocated costs are as "real" as the costs of employees and equipment.

Allocation Bases

Each service department is an intermediate cost center whose costs are recorded as incurred and then distributed to other cost centers. We know from our discussion of cost management systems that an important aspect of cost allocation is deciding which allocation base to use. Because we have already spent a great deal of time on the choice of cost allocation bases, we simply specify that GVM has determined that the best allocation base for Information Systems is computer-hours, and the best allocation base for Administration is number of employees.

See Exhibit 11.2 for the allocation base for each service department and the proportion of costs allocated to user departments. For example, Information Systems' costs are allocated on the basis of the number of computer-hours used by each of the other departments. During the period, Information Systems provided 100,000 hours of service to Administration, which represents 50 percent of the 200,000 total computer-hours provided. Similar methods are used to derive the percentages for allocating Administration costs.

	A	B	C	D	E	
1		Service Department				
2		Information Systems (S1)		Administration (S2)		
3		Usage	Percent	Usage	Percent	
4	Departments	(hours)	of Total	(employees)	of Total	
5	Administration	100,000	50%	–0–	0%	
6	Information Systems	–0–	0	2,000	20	
7	Sierra Tract (P1)	20,000	10	5,000	50	
8	Cascades Tract (P2)	80,000	40	3,000	30	
9	Total	200,000	100%	10,000	100%	
10						

Exhibit 11.2
Basic Data for Service Department Cost Allocation—Green Valley Mills

Direct Method

direct method

Cost allocation method that charges costs of service departments to user departments without making allocations between or among service departments.

The **direct method** allocates costs directly to the final user of a service (Sierra Tract, for example), ignoring intermediate users (Administration, for example). The direct method makes no allocations among service departments. Thus, Information Systems' costs attributable to the Administration Department are not allocated to Administration. Instead, the service department costs are allocated "directly" to the user departments— hence, the name *direct method*.

The use of the direct method of cost allocation at GVM is discussed here (see Exhibit 11.3). Assume that the accounting records show that costs of $800,000 and $5,000,000 are recorded in each service department, Information Systems (S1) and Administration (S2), respectively. Costs are allocated directly to Sierra Tract (P1) and Cascades Tract (P2).

Note that these are direct costs of service departments that become overhead costs of the user departments. Exhibit 11.4 is the cost flow diagram that illustrates the direct method.

Allocate Information Systems Department Costs   Information Systems' costs of $800,000 are allocated to Sierra Tract and Cascades Tract based on the number of computer-hours used by each. According to the facts in Exhibit 11.3, Sierra Tract (P1) used 20 percent and Cascades Tract (P2) used 80 percent of the total Information Systems computer-hours consumed by user departments. Remember that these are *relative* usages that ignore the use of Information Systems services by Administration. Of the total of 200,000 computer-hours used, Administration uses 100,000. This means that the two user departments (Sierra and Cascades Tracts) used 100,000 computer-hours. Sierra Tract uses 20,000 hours (or 20 percent) of the 100,000, and Cascades Tract uses 80,000

Exhibit 11.3   Service Department Cost Allocation Computations: Direct Method—Green Valley Mills

	A	B	C	D	E	F
1		Service Department					
2		Information Systems (S1)		Administration (S2)		
3		Usage of S1	Percent	Usage of S2	Percent	
4	Departments	services (hours)	of Total	services (employees)	of Total	
5	Administration	100,000	50%	–0–	0%	
6	Information Systems	–0–	0	2,000	20	
7	Sierra Tract (P1)	20,000	10	5,000	50	
8	Cascades Tract (P2)	80,000	40	3,000	30	
9	Total usage	200,000	100%	10,000	100%	
10						
11						
12	Direct Method:			Percent Allocable to		
13		Department		Sierra Tract		Cascades Tract
14		Direct Cost		(P1)		(P2)
15	Service Department					
16	Information Systems (S1)	$ 800,000	20.0%	=[B7/(B7+B8)]	80.0%	=[B8/(B7+B8)]
17	Administration (S2)	5,000,000	62.5%	=[D7/(D7+D8)]	37.5%	=[D8/(D7+D8)]
18						
19						
20				Amount Allocable to		
21				Sierra Tract		Cascades Tract
22				(P1)		(P2)
23	Service Department					
24	Information Systems (S1)	$ 800,000	$ 160,000	=(B24*C16)	$ 640,000	=(B24*E16)
25	Administration (S2)	5,000,000	3,125,000	=(B25*C17)	1,875,000	=(B25*E17)
26		$ 5,800,000	$ 3,285,000		$ 2,515,000	
27						

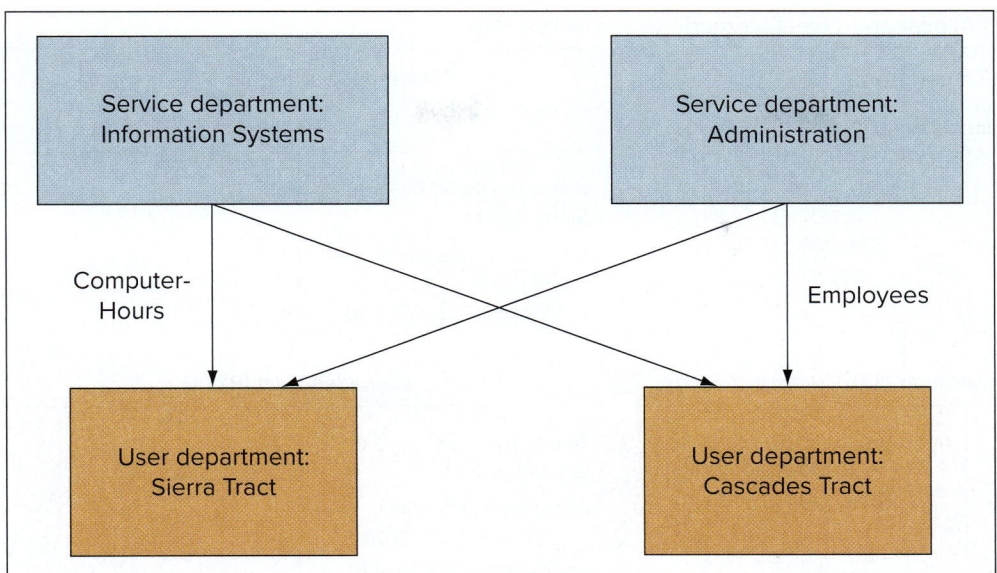

Exhibit 11.4

Cost Flow Diagram: Direct Method—Green Valley Mills

(or 80 percent) of the 100,000. Applying these percentages in exactly the same way in which we have made all of our cost allocation computations, we find that the $800,000 is allocated to the two cost objects (user departments) as follows:

Sierra Tract (P1).........................	20% × $800,000 =	$160,000
Cascades Tract (P2)	80% × $800,000 =	640,000
Total.................................	100% × $800,000 =	$800,000

Allocate Administration Department Costs

Administration costs of $5,000,000 are allocated to Sierra and Cascades Tracts based on the number of employees in the two production departments (tracts). According to the facts in Exhibit 11.3, Sierra Tract (P1) has 62.5 percent and Cascades Tract (P2) has 37.5 percent of the employees in the two user departments. Of the total of 10,000 employees shown in cell D9 of Exhibit 11.2, Information Systems employs 2,000. That means the two user departments (Sierra and Cascades Tracts) employ 8,000. Sierra uses 5,000 (or 62.5 percent) of the 8,000, and Cascades uses 3,000 (or 37.5 percent) of the 8,000. Using the same approach, the $5,000,000 Administration cost is allocated to the two cost objects (user departments) as follows:

Sierra Tract (P1).....................	62.5% × $5,000,000 =	$3,125,000
Cascades (P2)	37.5% × $5,000,000 =	1,875,000
Total...............................	100% × $5,000,000 =	$5,000,000

Adding the allocated costs of the service departments in each of the two user departments assigns the following costs to Sierra Tract and Cascades Tract:

	Sierra Tract	Cascades Tract	Total
Information Systems (S1).......	$ 160,000	$ 640,000	$ 800,000
Administration (S2)	3,125,000	1,875,000	5,000,000
Total......................	$3,285,000	$2,515,000	$5,800,000

Exhibit 11.5   Flow of Cost Allocations: Direct Method—Green Valley Mills

Service Departments		User Departments	
Information Systems (S1)		**Sierra Tract (P1)**	
Direct costs of Information Systems	Allocated to	Direct overhead costs of Sierra Tract	
800,000	160,000 (S1 → P1)	Allocated costs from:	
	640,000 (S1 → P2)	(S1 → P1) 160,000	
		(S2 → P1) 3,125,000	
Administration (S2)		**Cascades Tract (P2)**	
Direct costs of Administration	Allocated to	Direct overhead costs of Cascades Tract	
5,000,000	3,125,000 (S2 → P1)	Allocated costs from:	
	1,875,000 (S2 → P2)	(S1 → P2) 640,000	
		(S2 → P2) 1,875,000	

See Exhibit 11.5 for the flow of costs and the allocations to be recognized by GVM's departments when the direct method is used. The direct costs of service departments are first recorded in those service departments. These costs are shown on the debit side of the service department accounts. Then service department costs are allocated to the user departments.

The user departments also have direct costs such as the department manager's salary. These costs are indicated as the *direct overhead costs of Sierra (or Cascades) Tract* in Exhibit 11.5. These costs do not have to be allocated to the user departments because they are debited to the department accounts when incurred.

Limitations of the Direct Method   Some people have criticized the direct method because it ignores services provided by one service department to another. If one purpose of cost allocation is to encourage cross-departmental monitoring, the direct method falls short because it ignores the costs that service departments themselves incur when they use other service departments. This criticism has led some companies to use other methods of service department cost allocation, which we describe next.

Step Method

step method
Method of service department cost allocation that allocates some service department costs to other service departments.

The **step method** recognizes that one service department can provide services to others and allocates some service department costs to other service departments. Allocations usually are made first from the service department that has provided the largest proportion of its total services to other service departments. Once an allocation is made from a service department, no further allocations are made back to that department. Hence, a service department that provides services to, and receives services from, another service department has only one of these two relationships recognized.

Choosing the allocation order that we just suggested minimizes the percentage of service costs ignored in the allocation process. (Sometimes, the allocation begins from the service department with the largest cost. We explore this possibility in Self-Study Question 2.) When GVM uses the step method, it allocates costs from Information Systems to Administration but not vice versa.

An analysis of service usage among GVM's service departments indicates that Information Systems supplies 50 percent of its services to the other service department, Administration. Administration supplies 20 percent of its services to the other service

1. Modoc Bank is a small retail bank with two branches, Downtown and Mall. It has three service departments: Personnel, Finance, and Building Occupancy. The service departments provide support to both branches as well as to the other service departments. However, the branches are considered the only two profit centers, and the branch managers are evaluated on branch profits after allocation of service department costs.

    During the current period, the following are the direct costs incurred in each of the departments:

Department	Direct Cost
Personnel	$ 202,500
Finance	126,000
Building Occupancy	150,000
Downtown	950,000
Mall	425,000
Total	$1,853,500

Personnel costs are allocated on the basis of number of employees. Finance costs are allocated on the basis of billable transactions. Building Occupancy costs are allo-

cated on the basis of the number of square feet in each user department. For the current period, the following table summarizes the usage of services by other service cost centers and other departments.

	Service Department		
Departments	Personnel (employees)	Finance (transactions)	Building Occupancy (square feet)
Personnel	–0–	13,000	15,000
Finance	30	–0–	10,000
Building Occupancy	15	1,000	–0–
Downtown	60	60,000	30,000
Mall	30	24,000	45,000
Total	135	98,000	100,000

Using the direct method for service cost allocations, what is the total cost for each branch that will be used for determining branch profits?

The solution to this question is at the end of the chapter.

department, Information Systems (see Exhibit 11.2). Based on services provided to other service departments, the rank ordering for step allocation is as follows:

Order	Service Department
1	Information Systems (S1)
2	Administration (S2)

Allocating Service Department Costs
Information Systems' costs are allocated to Administration, but remember that under the step method, once a service department's costs have been allocated to other departments, no costs can be allocated back to it. Therefore, no Administration costs will be allocated to Information Systems. See Exhibit 11.6 for the computation of Information Systems' costs allocated to the other service department at GVM.

Notice that in Exhibit 11.6, the Administration costs that are allocated include both the $5,000,000 costs directly incurred by Administration and the $400,000 costs allocated from Information Systems. The effect of using the step method is that Sierra Tract is allocated more costs than it is with the direct method. The reason is that Sierra uses a larger proportion of Administration resources, and Administration uses half of the Information Systems resources. See Exhibit 11.7 for the cost flow diagram for the step method. The flow of costs through the accounts is shown in Exhibit 11.8.

Limitations of the Step Method
The step method can result in more reasonable allocations than the direct method because it recognizes that some service departments use other service departments. However, it does not recognize reciprocal services, for example, that Information Systems also uses Administration services. The step method

Exhibit 11.6   Service Department Cost Allocation Computations: Step Method—Green Valley Mills

	A	B	C	D	E	F	G
1		Service Department					
2		Information Systems (S1)		Administration (S2)			
3		Usage	Percent	Usage	Percent		
4	Departments	(hours)	of Total	(employees)	of Total		
5	Administration	100,000	50%	–0–	0%		
6	Information Systems	–0–	0	2,000	20		
7	Sierra Tract (P1)	20,000	10	5,000	50		
8	Cascades Tract (P2)	80,000	40	3,000	30		
9	Total usage	200,000	100%	10,000	100%		
10							
11							
12	Step Method:			Percent Allocable to			
13		Department	Information		Sierra	Cascades	
14		Direct Cost	Systems	Administration	Tract	Tract	Total
15	Service Department						
16	Information Systems (S1)	$ 800,000	0.0%	50.0%	10.0%	40.0%	100.0%
17	Administration (S2)	5,000,000	0.0%	0.0%	62.5%	37.5%	100.0%
18		$ 5,800,000					
19							
20			Amount Allocable to				
21			Information		Sierra	Cascades	
22			Systems	Administration	Tract	Tract	
23	From						
24	Direct department costs		$ 800,000	$ 5,000,000	$ –0–	$ –0–	
25	Information Systems (S1)		(800,000)	400,000	80,000	320,000	
26	Administration (S2)		–0–	(5,400,000)	3,375,000	2,025,000	
27	Total		$ –0–	$ –0–	$ 3,455,000	$ 2,345,000	
28							

Exhibit 11.7
Cost Flow Diagram: Step
Method—Green Valley
Mills

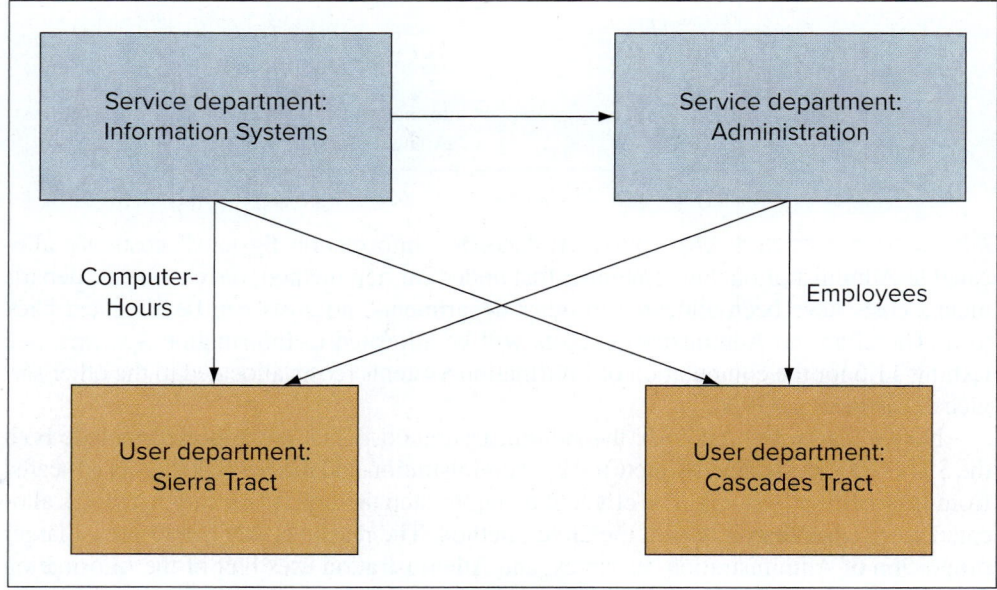

is not necessarily better than the direct method when both the costs and benefits of using cost allocation are considered. A company that already uses the direct method could find it uneconomical to switch methods.

Another limitation of the step method, which is illustrated in Self-Study Question 2, is that the results generally depend on the order in which the allocation is done. Although there are common practices (such as the one followed here) that suggest an order, there is no "right" approach.

Exhibit 11.8   Flow of Cost Allocations: Step Method—Green Valley Mills

Service Departments		User Departments	
Information Systems (S1)		**Sierra Tract (P1)**	
Direct costs of Information Systems	Allocated to:	Direct overhead costs of Sierra Tract	
800,000	Administration	Allocated costs from:	
	400,000 (S1 → S2)	(S1 → P1) 80,000	
	80,000 (S1 → P1)	(S2 → P1) 3,375,000	
	320,000 (S1 → P2)		
Administration (S2)		**Cascades Tract (P2)**	
Direct costs of Administration 5,000,000	Allocated to:	Direct overhead costs of Cascades Tract	
+ Allocated costs from	3,375,000 (S2 → P1)	Allocated costs from:	
(S1 → S2) 400,000	2,025,000 (S2 → P2)	(S1 → P2) 320,000	
		(S2 → P2) 2,025,000	

Self-Study Question

2. Some firms choose the order of allocation based on the costs in the individual service departments. Consider the case of GVM, where Administration is the service department with the higher direct costs. Compute the service cost allocated to each tract (Sierra and Cascades) using the step method. Start by allocating Administration costs.

Recall that Administration's direct cost is $5,000,000 and Information Systems' is $800,000. See Exhibit 11.2 for service department use data.

The solution to this question is at the end of the chapter.

Reciprocal Method

The reciprocal method addresses a limitation of the step method by making a reciprocal, or simultaneous, cost allocation when service departments provide reciprocal services (that is, when they provide services to each other). The **reciprocal method** recognizes all services provided by any department, including those provided to other service departments. This method is identical to the actual process by which services are exchanged among departments within the organization.

reciprocal method
Method to allocate service department costs that recognizes all services provided by any service department, including services provided to other service departments.

With the reciprocal method, the costs of each service department are written in equation form:

$$\text{Total service department costs} = \text{Direct costs of the service department} + \text{Cost allocated to the service department}$$

A single equation for each service department and a single unknown (the total cost of the service department) for each service department in the organization are used. The system of equations is then solved simultaneously using matrix algebra. Solving all equations simultaneously yields all service department allocations, including services provided by service departments to each other. This method is called the *reciprocal method* because it accounts for cost flows in both directions among service departments that provide services to each other. It is also known as the *simultaneous solution method* because it solves a system of equations simultaneously.

Allocating Service Department Costs   We illustrate the use of computer spreadsheets such as Microsoft Excel® for solving reciprocal cost allocation problems in the Appendix to this chapter. However, when there are only two service departments, as in the case of GVM, simple algebra can be used to solve the allocation problem.

From the data in Exhibit 11.2, we can write the equations describing the costs in the two service departments as follows:

$$\begin{array}{c}\text{Total service} \\ \text{department costs}\end{array} = \begin{array}{c}\text{Direct costs of the} \\ \text{service department}\end{array} + \begin{array}{c}\text{Cost allocated to the} \\ \text{service department}\end{array}$$

S1 (Information Systems) =	$ 800,000	+	0.20 S2
S2 (Administration) =	$5,000,000	+	0.50 S1

Substituting the first equation into the second yields:

$$S2 = \$5,000,000 + 0.50\ (\$800,000 + 0.20\ S2)$$
$$S2 = \$5,000,000 + \$400,000 + 0.10\ S2$$
$$0.9\ S2 = \$5,400,000$$
$$S2 = \$6,000,000$$

Substituting the value of S2 back into the first equation gives:

$$S1 = \$800,000 + 0.20\ (\$6,000,000)$$
$$S1 = \$2,000,000$$

Thus, costs are simultaneously allocated between the two service departments. The values for S1 ($2,000,000) and S2 ($6,000,000) are then used as the total costs of the service departments that are to be allocated to the production departments. See Exhibit 11.9 for the allocations.

Exhibit 11.9   Service Department Cost Allocation Computations: Reciprocal Method—Green Valley Mills

	A	B	C	D	E	F	G
1				Service Department			
2		Information Systems (S1)		Administration (S2)			
3		Usage	Percent	Usage	Percent		
4	Departments	(hours)	of Total	(employees)	of Total		
5	Administration	100,000	50%	–0–	0%		
6	Information Systems	–0–	0	2,000	20		
7	Sierra Tract (P1)	20,000	10	5,000	50		
8	Cascades Tract (P2)	80,000	40	3,000	30		
9	Total usage	200,000	100%	10,000	100%		
10							
11							
12	Reciprocal Method:			Percent Allocable to			
13		Department	Information		Sierra	Cascades	
14		Total Cost	Systems	Administration	Tract	Tract	Total
15	Service Department						
16	Information Systems (S1)	$ 2,000,000	0.0%	50.0%	10.0%	40.0%	100.0%
17	Administration (S2)	6,000,000	20.0%	0.0%	50.0%	30.0%	100.0%
18		$ 8,000,000					
19							
20				Amount Allocable to			
21			Information		Sierra	Cascades	
22			Systems	Administration	Tract	Tract	
23	From						
24	Direct department costs		$ 800,000	$ 5,000,000	$ –0–	$ –0–	
25	Information Systems (S1)		(2,000,000)	1,000,000	200,000	800,000	
26	Administration (S2)		1,200,000	(6,000,000)	3,000,000	1,800,000	
27	Total		$ –0–	$ –0–	$ 3,200,000	$ 2,600,000	
28							

The total cost allocated to the production departments (the two tracts) amounts to $5,800,000 (= $3,200,000 + $2,600,000), which equals the costs to be allocated from the service departments ($800,000 + $5,000,000 = $5,800,000). See Exhibit 11.10 for the cost flow diagram for the reciprocal method.

Compare Exhibits 11.8 and 11.11 to identify the key difference between the step and reciprocal methods. Note that the reciprocal method accounts for the reciprocal services between the Information Systems and Administration departments. The step method accounted for only one direction of services, from Information Systems to Administration.

Both the step method and the direct method could understate the cost of running service departments. These methods omit costs of certain services consumed by one service department that were provided by other service departments. For example, only the reciprocal method considers services provided by Administration and Information Systems to each other.

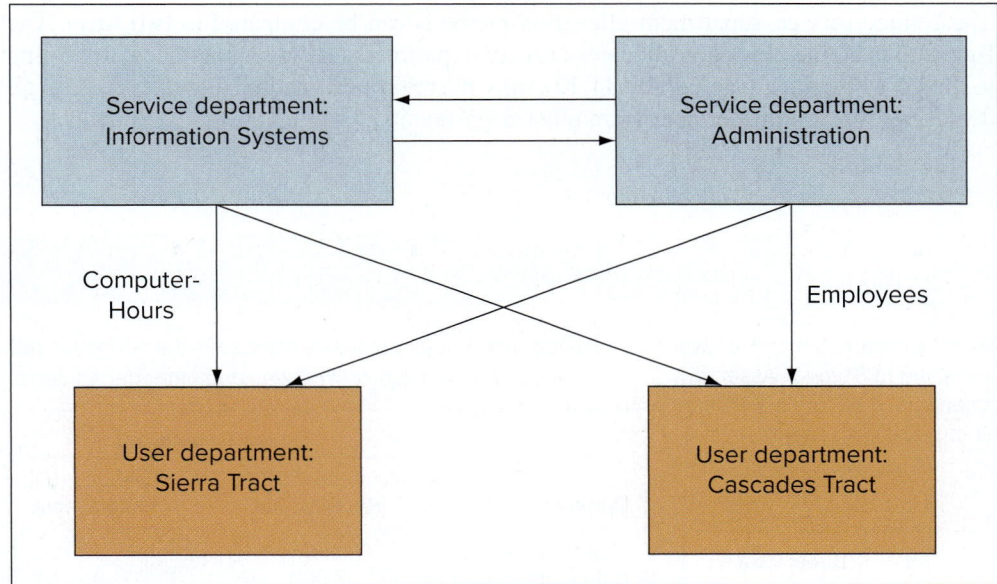

Exhibit 11.10

Cost Flow Diagram: The Reciprocal Method— Green Valley Mills

Exhibit 11.11 Flow of Cost Allocations: Reciprocal Method—Green Valley Mills

Service Departments		Operating Departments	
Information Systems (S1)		**Sierra Tract (P1)**	
Direct costs of Information Systems	Allocated to:	Direct overhead costs of Sierra Tract	
800,000	1,000,000 (S1 → S2)	Allocated costs from:	
(S2 → S1) 1,200,000	200,000 (S1 → P1)	(S1 → P1) 200,000	
	800,000 (S1 → P2)	(S2 → P1) 3,000,000	
Administration (S2)		**Cascades Tract (P2)**	
Direct costs of Administration	Allocated to:	Direct overhead costs of Cascades Tract	
5,000,000	1,200,000 (S2 → S1)	Allocated costs from:	
(S1 → S2) 1,000,000	3,000,000 (S2 → P1)	(S1 → P2) 800,000	
	1,800,000 (S2 → P2)	(S2 → P2) 1,800,000	

Exhibit 11.12   Comparison of Services Provided and Costs Charged Using Each Service Department Cost Allocation Method—Green Valley Mills

Service Department	Services Provided to	Departments Receiving Allocated Costs under the		
		Direct Method	Step Method	Reciprocal Method
Information Systems (S1)	Administration		Administration	Administration
	Sierra Tract	Sierra Tract	Sierra Tract	Sierra Tract
	Cascades Tract	Cascades Tract	Cascades Tract	Cascades Tract
Administration (S2)	Information Systems			Information Systems
	Sierra Tract	Sierra Tract	Sierra Tract	Sierra Tract
	Cascades Tract	Cascades Tract	Cascades Tract	Cascades Tract

Comparison of Direct, Step, and Reciprocal Methods

These three service department allocation methods can be compared in two ways. The first is to examine how each allocates costs to departments receiving services. Returning to the GVM example (see Exhibit 11.12), only the reciprocal method allocates costs to all departments receiving services from other departments.

Self-Study Question

3. Williston Machining is a small manufacturing firm with two production departments, Finishing (P1) and Assembly (P2). Its two service departments, Maintenance (S1) and the Cafeteria (S2), serve both production departments.

The direct costs incurred in each department during the current period follow:

Department	Direct Cost
Maintenance	$ 100,000
Cafeteria	17,600
Finishing	1,200,000
Assembly	640,000
Total	$1,957,600

Maintenance costs are allocated on the basis of repair-hours. Cafeteria costs are allocated on the basis of the number of employees in each department. For the current period, the following table summarizes the usage of services by other service cost centers and other departments.

Departments	Service Department	
	Maintenance (S1) (repair-hours)	Cafeteria (S2) (employees)
Maintenance	–0–	30
Cafeteria.........	3,000	–0–
Finishing (P1)	7,500	20
Assembly (P2)	4,500	50
Total	15,000	100

Using the reciprocal method for service cost allocations, what are the total costs in each of the two production departments, Finishing (P1) and Assembly (P2)?

The solution to this question is at the end of the chapter.

The second way to compare these three methods is to examine the costs that each ultimately allocates to the production departments, Sierra Tract and Cascades Tract, shown in Exhibit 11.13. A graphical visualization of the total service department cost allocated to each production department is shown in Exhibit 11.14. Each method allocates the same total cost for GVM—$5,800,000—but the amounts allocated to either of the two production departments can vary, in this case, by almost 4.5 percent, or $260,000. This might not appear large relative to the total, but to the manager of the Sierra Tract, for example, it can have an important effect on planning and performance measurement.

Method	Sierra Tract	Cascades Tract	Total
	Cost Allocated to		
Direct..............	$3,285,000	$2,515,000	$5,800,000
Step (S1 first)	3,455,000	2,345,000	5,800,000
Reciprocal..........	3,200,000	2,600,000	5,800,000

Exhibit 11.13
Summary of Results: Service Department Cost Allocations—Green Valley Mills

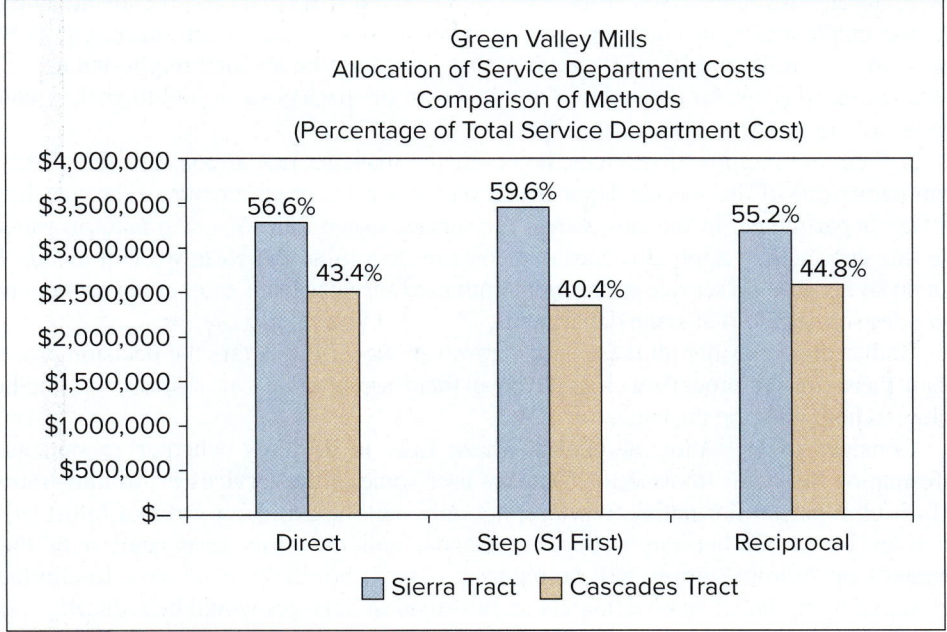

Green Valley Mills
Allocation of Service Department Costs
Comparison of Methods
(Percentage of Total Service Department Cost)

Direct: Sierra Tract 56.6%, Cascades Tract 43.4%
Step (S1 First): Sierra Tract 59.6%, Cascades Tract 40.4%
Reciprocal: Sierra Tract 55.2%, Cascades Tract 44.8%

Exhibit 11.14
Total Service Department Costs Allocated to User Department: Direct, Step, and Reciprocal Methods–Green Valley Mills

The other thing to notice about the different methods summarized in Exhibit 11.13 and Exhibit 11.14 is that, in this example, the direct method results are closer to the reciprocal cost method results than are the results using the step method. This example demonstrates that these methods are not ordered in any sense. That is, the step method sometimes, but not always, results in allocations that are nearer those obtained using the reciprocal method.

In this section, we have considered three approaches to allocating service department costs. We have chosen to present all three, rather than just the reciprocal method, for two reasons. First, the direct and step methods are still in use. Second, the three methods represent an intuitive progression. It is important to remember that all three allocation methods are arbitrary in the following sense. If a production department (Sierra Tract, for example) stops using the services of a service department (Information Systems, for example), the costs saved by the firm are unlikely to be equal to the costs allocated by any one of these methods. This is because, as we learned earlier, there are likely to be some fixed and unavoidable costs at least in the short run.

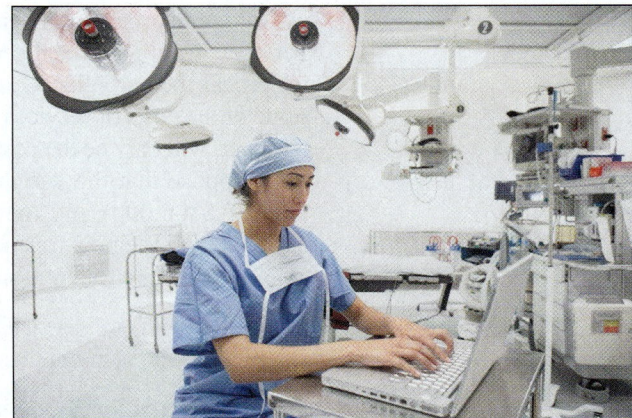

The allocation of service department costs in a hospital can have a major impact on revenues if rates are related to reported costs. ©ERproductions Ltd/Blend Images LLC

The Reciprocal Method and Decision Making

In the previous sections, we allocated service department costs to determine the costs of the production departments. The primary purpose of that exercise was to obtain the manufacturing costs for each of the production departments for product costing purposes. Throughout the text, however, we have stressed the importance of developing cost information to assist managers in making decisions.

LO 11-2
Use the reciprocal method approach for outsourcing decisions.

One decision that Luis Romero is considering is outsourcing some or all of the activities of the Information Services department. Using the methods of Chapter 4, the cost savings will depend on how much an outside vendor will charge and how much cost in Information Services can be eliminated if Luis selects the outsourcing option.

If there are no reciprocal services among the service departments, estimating the cost savings from eliminating a particular department is reasonably straightforward. It is the cost of the service department that is avoidable. This would generally be the variable costs plus any avoidable fixed costs. Examples of fixed costs that could be avoided might include employees who could be used in other activities, leases for space, equipment costs, and so on. Examples of fixed costs that would not be avoided might include allocated overhead costs, for example, corporate costs, or space costs in buildings that would not be sold or used in another capacity.

If there are reciprocal services, however, the manager has to consider the effect of eliminating one of the service departments on the service requirements of the remaining service departments. In the case where the service usage follows a step pattern, we can use the step method applied to variable costs to determine the costs we will avoid. We can do so because no service department both uses services from another department and provides services to that same department.

Rather than consider all these cases, however, we will illustrate the decision process when there are reciprocal services. Even if there are not, we can still use the method below to help with the decision.

Consider the situation at GVM, where Luis is deciding whether to outsource Information Services. Information Services uses some of the services of Administration. If Luis eliminates Information Services, not only will the avoidable costs of Information Services be saved, but the resource demands, and the costs associated with these demands on Administration, will be reduced as well. Similarly, if he were to eliminate Administration, the resource demands on Information Services would be reduced.

How can these additional savings be estimated? Fortunately, the approach we used in the reciprocal method provides a way to do this. Because this method explicitly recognizes the use of one service department by another, it provides an estimate of the costs of Information Services when reciprocal service costs are included. We have to modify the results of the reciprocal method allocation above slightly because if we eliminate Information Services, some of the costs of services of Administration will be lower. The savings in Administration, however, will only be the costs that vary with the output of Administration: the variable costs.

Suppose that the variable cost in Information Services (S1) is $200,000 (out of the total of $800,000) and the variable cost in Administration (S2) is $3,500,000 (out of $5,000,000). We now repeat the reciprocal cost analysis from above substituting the variable costs for the total costs:

$$\text{Total service department costs} = \text{Direct costs of the service department} + \text{Cost allocated to the service department}$$

$$\text{S1 (Information Systems)} = \$\ 200,000 + 0.20\ \text{S2}$$
$$\text{S2 (Administration)} = \$3,500,000 + 0.50\ \text{S1}$$

Substituting the second equation into the first yields

$$\text{S1} = \$200,000 + 0.20\ (\$3,500,000 + 0.50\ \text{S1})$$
$$\text{S1} = \$200,000 + \$700,000 + 0.10\ \text{S1}$$

The first two terms in the equation represent the variable cost savings from eliminating or outsourcing Information Systems. The company would save $200,000 in variable costs from Information Services as well as $700,000 (= 20% × $3,500,000) in variable costs from Administration. We do not need to solve for S1 because we are not allocating costs to departments.

We can repeat the analysis for Administration by setting up the equation for S2.

$$\text{S2} = \$3,500,000 + 0.50\ (\$200,000 + 0.20\ \text{S2})$$
$$\text{S2} = \$3,500,000 + \$100,000 + 0.10\ \text{S2}$$

The variable cost savings from eliminating Administration, considering the effect on Information Systems, is $3,600,000 (= $3,500,000 + $100,000).

This approach works with any number of service departments, but, with only two service departments, it is perhaps simpler to look at the usage of the remaining service department directly. If Information Services is outsourced, for example, the number of employees will be reduced by 2,000. The average variable cost per employee incurred by Administration is $350 (= $3,500,000/10,000 employees). Therefore, the variable cost saved in Administration by outsourcing Information Services is $700,000 (= 2,000 employees × $350 per employee). The total variable cost of Information Services of $200,000 is also saved. Therefore, the total variable costs saved by outsourcing Information Services is $900,000 (= $700,000 + $200,000), as shown.

As noted, this approach works with any number of service departments. However, it is important to understand that it only provides an estimate for eliminating one service department. We cannot combine the results for Information Systems ($900,000) and Administration ($3,600,000) and estimate variable cost savings of $4,500,000 (= $900,000 + $3,600,000). After all, we only spent a total of $3,700,000 (= $200,000 + $3,500,000) in variable costs in the two departments.

The total cost savings that would result from eliminating Information Services are the $900,000 in variable costs calculated plus any of the fixed costs of $600,000 (= $800,000 total cost in Information Services − $200,000 variable costs) that can be avoided.

For example, suppose that Luis determines that $400,000 of the fixed costs in Information Services is avoidable. When he evaluates bids from outside vendors, he can compare the avoidable costs from eliminating Information Services, $1,300,000 (= $900,000 variable costs + $400,000 avoidable fixed costs in Information Services) to the bid by the outside vendor. Of course, Luis will want to consider factors in addition to the cost savings. As the Business Application "The Risks of Outsourcing a Service Center" discusses, outsourcing means giving up a certain amount of control. Although most of the consequences can be foreseen, some may not be.

The Risks of Outsourcing a Service Center | *Business Application*

During the 2000s and 2010s, many firms took advantage of cost savings by outsourcing service centers to offshore entities in countries such as India and the Philippines, where English was widely spoken and wage rates were considerably lower than in the United States and Europe. Such an approach was especially favored for call centers and certain other support activities. A call center is a location or group of locations housing customer service representatives that assist with everything from travel reservations to the use of kitchen appliances. In addition to call centers, other work performed might include claim processing, coding, and hospital billing.

Such work typically relies on access to high-speed internet and other infrastructure that allows employees to communicate seamlessly with customers or with employees located in the home office or other geographical locations. When the COVID-19 pandemic hit in 2020, many of these workers were sent home as a part of mandated lockdowns. For example, Vodofone New Zealand, a wireless and telecommunications provider, had a service center located in the Philippines. When those workers were sent home, even with company-provided equipment, there were unexpected challenges:

Many workers live in cramped spaces crowded with extended family. Few have computers, and many lack basic electricity and broadband internet at home. Client contracts have to be revised or suspended to allow work to be done outside the office. Many companies normally forbid workers from having their mobile phones—and even a pen and paper in certain cases—accessible while they work. Some companies have had to purchase chairs or desks for employees at home.[1]

Other companies that have outsourced work have found it difficult to comply with regulations related to maximum allowed transaction completion times and data and privacy protections when workers work from home.

"This has forced us to go back to a decades-old system of manual processing. We have gone back to the age of ledgers. . . ."[2]

As a result of these challenges, some firms are considering "re-shoring," essentially reversing their original decision.

Sources:
1. Roy, Rajesh, and Jon Emont, "Coronavirus Sends Outsource Workers Home, Causing a Ripple Effect," *The Wall Street Journal*, April 1, 2020.
2. Ibid.

Allocation of Joint Costs

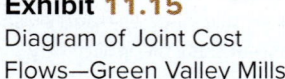

LO 11-3

Explain why and how joint costs are allocated using the net realizable value method and the physical quantities method.

joint cost
Cost of a manufacturing process with two or more outputs.

joint products
Outputs from a common input and common production process.

split-off point
Stage of processing when two or more products are separated.

A **joint cost** is a cost of a manufacturing process with several different outputs. For example, lumber of different quality can come from the same tract. The cost of harvesting the lumber is a joint cost of these **joint products.** The problem in such cases is whether and how to allocate the joint cost of the input (for example, the cost of the tract) to the joint products (for example, #1-Grade and #2-Grade lumber).

Joint Costing Defined

See Exhibit 11.15 for a diagram of the flow of costs incurred to harvest lumber for a month at GVM's Sierra Tract. These costs include materials, labor, and manufacturing overhead (including allocated service department overhead). As the lumber is harvested, two products, #1-Grade and #2-Grade, emerge. (We ignore any other possible products for now.) The stage of processing at which the two products are separated is called the **split-off point.** Processing costs incurred prior to the split-off point are the *joint costs.*

Managers often are interested in another issue. Should a product be sold at the split-off point or processed further? Rather than selling #2-Grade lumber at the split-off point, should GVM process it further to produce a higher-quality product (#2A-Grade)? The higher-quality lumber requires additional processing costs, but the sales price for #2A-Grade lumber is higher than that for #2-Grade Lumber sold at the split-off point.

Reasons for Allocating Joint Costs

Joint costs are allocated for many reasons. Cost allocations are often used to determine departmental or division costs for evaluating executive performance. Many companies compensate executives and other employees, at least partly, on the basis of departmental or division earnings for the year, as we discuss in Chapter 14. When a single raw material is converted into products sold by two or more departments, the cost of the raw material must be allocated to the products involved. For example, if different groups at GVM are responsible for selling #1-Grade lumber and #2-Grade lumber, the cost of harvesting lumber could be allocated to these groups to compute group profit.

Manufacturing companies must allocate joint costs to determine the inventory value of the products that result from the joint process. When companies are subject to rate

Exhibit 11.15

Diagram of Joint Cost Flows—Green Valley Mills

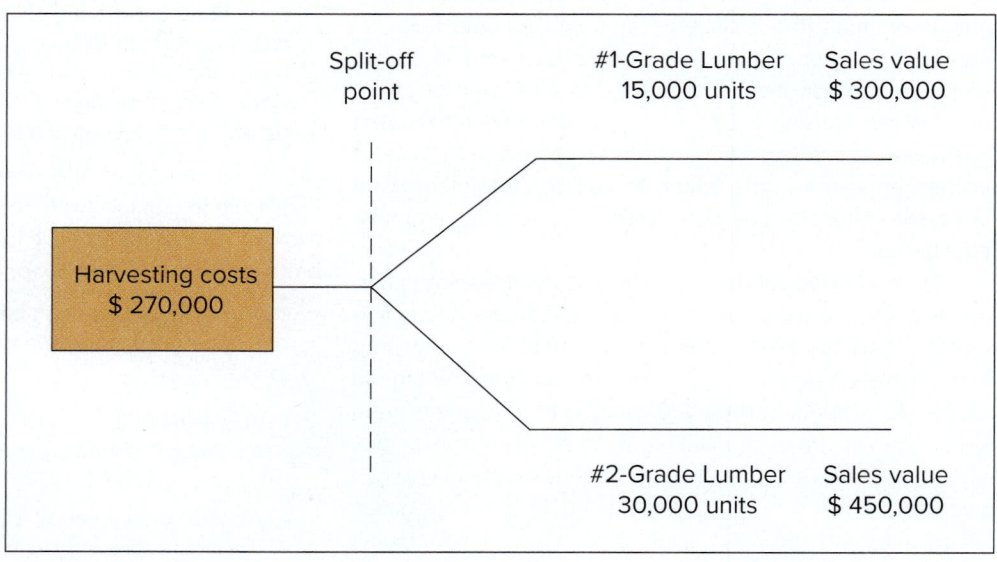

regulation, the allocation of joint costs can be a significant factor in determining the regulated rates. Crude oil and natural gas are usually produced from a common well. In recent years, energy price policies and gas utility rates have been based in part on the allocation of the joint costs of crude oil and natural gas.

When the allocation of costs can impinge on the financial fortunes of opposing parties, both sides critically review the allocation method. For example, neither an insurance company nor an insured party wishes to pay more or receive less than is fair. Executives and employees of one department object to a cost of goods sold figure that they believe is overstated for their department but understated for another department. Both buyers and sellers of regulated products or services are affected by pricing, and neither wishes to give the other an advantage. Each of these cases involves opposing interests.

As always, any cost allocation method contains an element of arbitrariness. No allocation method is beyond dispute. Consequently, allocation methods must be clearly stated before they are implemented.

Joint Cost Allocation Methods

The two major methods of allocating joint costs are (1) the net realizable value method and (2) the physical quantities method.

Net Realizable Value Method

The **net realizable value method** allocates joint costs to products based on their net realizable values at the split-off point. The *net realizable value* is the estimated sales value of each product at the split-off point. If the joint products can be sold at the split-off point, the market value or sales price should be used for this allocation.

net realizable value method
Joint cost allocation based on the proportional values of the joint products at the split-off point.

If the products require further processing before they are marketable, it could be necessary to estimate the net realizable value at the split-off point. This approach is called the **estimated net realizable value,** sometimes referred to as the *netback* or *workback method.* Normally, when a market value is available at the split-off point, it is preferable to use that value rather than the estimated net realizable value method. If the market value is not available, the *net realizable value* at the split-off point is estimated by taking the sales value after further processing and deducting the additional processing costs. Joint costs are then allocated to the products in proportion to their net realizable values at the split-off point.

estimated net realizable value
Sales price of a final product minus additional processing costs necessary to prepare a product for sale.

We use the terms "net realizable value" and "estimated net realizable value" to emphasize that we are attempting to determine the value of the products at the split-off point. The difference is that with net realizable value, we can sell the product at the split-off point, so we do not have to estimate a value. You will see similar terms used in practice and textbooks, such as "sales value at split-off." As always with cost accounting terminology, it is important that you understand the concept referred to by the term and not just memorize the term itself.

We first consider an example of the *net realizable method,* and then we discuss the *estimated net realizable value* method in more detail.

From the information in Exhibit 11.15, we know that GVM produces #1-Grade and #2-Grade lumber. In March, joint harvesting costs (materials, labor, and overhead) totaled $270,000. #1-Grade and #2-Grade lumber have a $750,000 total sales value at the split-off point. #1-Grade has a $300,000 sales value, or 40 percent of the total, and #2-Grade's value is $450,000, or 60 percent of the total. We assume for the purpose of this example that no additional processing is required after the split-off point to process either grade of lumber.

The cost allocation follows the proportional distribution of net realizable values:

	A	B	C	D
1		#1-Grade	#2-Grade	Total
2	Final sales value	$ 300,000	$ 450,000	$ 750,000
3	Less additional processing costs	–0–	–0–	–0–
4	Net realizable value at split-off point	$ 300,000	$ 450,000	$ 750,000
5	Proportionate share			
6	= $ 300,000/$ 750,000 (B4/D4)	40%		
7	= $ 450,000/$ 750,000 (C4/D4)		60%	
8	Allocated joint costs			
9	= $ 270,000 × 40%	$ 108,000		
10	= $ 270,000 × 60%		$ 162,000	
11				

See Exhibit 11.16 for a condensed statement of gross margins at the split-off point. Note that the gross margin as a percentage of sales is 64 percent for both products. This demonstrates an important concept of the net realizable value method, namely that revenue dollars from any joint product are assumed to make the same percentage contribution at the split-off point as the revenue dollars from any other joint product. The net realizable value approach implies a matching of input costs with revenues generated by each output.

Self-Study Question

4. Thumb Beets, Inc., grows sugar beets. After the beets are harvested, they are processed into sugar and livestock feed. One ton (2,000 pounds) of sugar beets yields 0.2 ton of sugar and 0.4 ton of feed. The sugar can be sold for $400 per ton and the feed for $200 per ton at the split-off point. The cost of the sugar beets is $60 per ton. Processing each ton of beets up to the split-off point costs $40 in labor and overhead.

Compute the joint cost allocated to sugar and feed produced from 10 tons of sugar beets using the net realizable value method.

The solution to this question is at the end of the chapter.

Estimation of Net Realizable Value   In the previous example, we assumed that no further processing was required after the split-off point. Not all joint products can be sold at the split-off point, however. Additional processing could be required before a product is marketable. When no sales values exist for the outputs at the split-off point, the *estimated net realizable values* should be determined by taking the sales value of each product at the first point at which it can be marketed and deducting the processing

Exhibit 11.16

Gross Margin Computations: Net Realizable Value Method

	A	B	C	D
1		GREEN VALLEY MILLS		
2		For the Month of March		
3		#1-Grade	#2-Grade	Total
4	Sales value	$ 300,000	$ 450,000	$ 750,000
5	Less allocated joint costs	108,000	162,000	270,000
6	Gross margin	$ 192,000	$ 288,000	$ 480,000
7	Gross margin as a percent of sales	64%	64%	64%
8				

costs that must be incurred after the split-off point. The resulting estimated net realizable value is used for joint cost allocation in the same way as an actual market value at the split-off point.

Suppose that GVM management finds excellent opportunities to sell a refined product, #2A-Grade lumber, but selling it requires that GVM do additional processing to the #2-Grade lumber that comes from the tract. Also assume that no market exists for this #2-Grade lumber. This additional processing costs $50,000 for the #2A-Grade lumber produced in March, after which it could be sold for $550,000. The #1-Grade lumber could still be sold at the split-off point for $300,000. See Exhibit 11.17 for a diagram of the process.

See Exhibit 11.18 for the allocation of the joint cost of $270,000 to #1-Grade lumber and #2A-Grade lumber using the estimated net realizable value method. First, we compute the estimated net realizable values at split-off for #1-Grade and #2A-Grade lumber, which are $300,000 and $500,000, respectively. Next we multiply the ratio of each product's net realizable value to the total estimated net realizable value by the joint cost. To determine the portion of the joint cost allocated to #1-Grade lumber, for example, the computations are ($300,000 ÷ $800,000) times the joint cost of $270,000 (37.5% × $270,000 = $101,250), as shown in Exhibit 11.18.

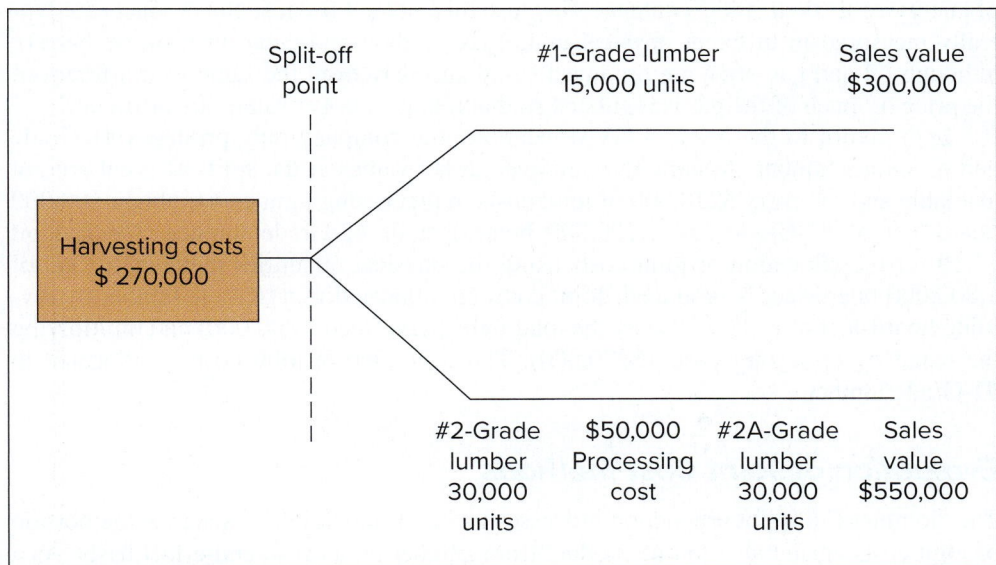

Exhibit 11.17
Further Processing of Lumber Cost Flows—Green Valley Mills

	A	B	C	D
1	GREEN VALLEY MILLS			
2	For the Month of March			
3		#1-Grade	#2A-Grade	Total
4	Sales value	$ 300,000	$ 550,000	$ 850,000
5	Less additional cost to process to #2A-Grade Lumber	–	50,000	50,000
6	Estimated net realizable value at split-off	$ 300,000	$ 500,000	$ 800,000
7	Allocation of joint costs			
8	($ 300,000/$ 800,000) × $ 270,000 = 37.5% × $ 270,000	101,250	–	101,250
9	($ 500,000/$ 800,000) × $ 270,000 = 62.5% × $ 270,000	–	168,750	168,750
10	Gross margin	$ 198,750	$ 331,250	$ 530,000
11	Gross margin as a percent of sales	66%	60%	62%
12				

Exhibit 11.18
Gross Margin Computations Using Net Realizable Value Method: Further Processing

Self-Study Question

Physical Quantities Method

physical quantities method
Joint cost allocation based on measurement of the volume, weight, or other physical measure of the joint products at the split-off point.

The **physical quantities method** of allocation is often used when output product prices are highly volatile. This method is also used when significant processing occurs between the split-off point and the first point of marketability or when product prices are not set by the market. The latter situation could occur when regulators set prices or in cost-based contract situations, for example.

Using the physical quantities method, joint costs are assigned to products based on a physical measure. This could be volume, weight, or any other common measure of physical characteristics.

Many companies allocate joint costs incurred in producing oil and gas on the basis of energy equivalent (BTU content). They use this method because the products are typically measured in different physical units (gas by thousand cubic feet, oil by barrel), although oil and gas often are produced simultaneously from the same well. Moreover, the price of much of the gas is regulated so that relative market values are artificial.

Let's return to the original GVM example; the company only produces #1-Grade and #2-Grade lumber. Assume that relative market values at the split-off point are not available and for every $270,000 of joint costs in processing lumber, we obtain 600,000 board-feet of #1-Grade and 1,200,000 board-feet of #2-Grade lumber. See Exhibit 11.19 for the allocation of joint costs using the physical quantities method. A total of 1,800,000 board-feet is produced. Joint costs are allocated to #1-Grade lumber by dividing board-feet of it (600,000) by the total units harvested (1,800,000) and multiplying the result by total joint costs ($270,000). Thus, $90,000 in joint costs is allocated to #1-Grade lumber.

Evaluation of Joint Cost Methods

The "jointness" of joint production processes makes it impossible to separate the portion of joint costs attributable to one product from another on a cause-and-effect basis. As a result, allocating joint costs is always somewhat arbitrary, although it is often done in

Exhibit 11.19
Gross Margin Computations: Physical Quantities Method

	A	B	C	D
1	GREEN VALLEY MILLS			
2	For the Month of March			
3		#1-Grade	#2-Grade	Total
4	Quantity (Board-feet)	600,000	1,200,000	1,800,000
5				
6	Sales value	$ 300,000	$ 450,000	$ 750,000
7	Allocation of joint costs			
8	(600,000/1,800,000) × $ 270,000 = 33.3% × $ 270,000	90,000	–	90,000
9	(1,200,000/1,800,000) × $ 270,000 = 66.7% × $ 270,000	–	180,000	180,000
10	Gross margin	$ 210,000	$ 270,000	$ 480,000
11	Gross margin as a percent of sales	70%	60%	64%
12				

practice. If allocated joint costs are used for decision-making purposes, they should be used only with full recognition of their limitations. Accountants and managers realize that no one allocation method is appropriate for all situations.

Self-Study Question

6. Refer to Self-Study Question 4. Use the physical quanti-   *The solution to this question is at the end of the chapter.*
    ties method to allocate joint costs.

Deciding Whether to Sell Goods Now or Process Them Further

Many companies have opportunities to sell partly processed products at various production stages. Management must decide whether it is more profitable to sell the output at an intermediate stage or to process it further. In such a sell-or-process-further decision, the relevant data to be considered are (1) the additional revenue after further processing and (2) the additional costs of processing further. This is simply an application of the differential analysis approach discussed in Chapter 4.

LO 11-4

Use cost data to make the decision whether to sell or process further.

Returning to our original example, suppose that GVM can sell #2-Grade lumber for $450,000 at the split-off point or process it further to make a new product, #2A-Grade lumber. The additional processing costs would be $50,000, and the revenue from #2A-Grade lumber produced in March would be $550,000. Should the company sell #2-Grade lumber or process it further?

GVM's profit will be $50,000 higher if #2-Grade lumber is processed further into #2A-Grade lumber (see Exhibit 11.20). It is important to note that the allocation of the $270,000 joint costs between #1-Grade and #2-Grade lumber is irrelevant. The $100,000 additional revenue from processing beyond the split-off point justifies the expenditure of $50,000 for additional processing, regardless of the way joint costs are allocated. *The only costs and revenues relevant to the decision are those that result from it.* Total joint costs incurred prior to the split-off point are not affected by the decision to process further after the split-off point.

Exhibit 11.20   Differential Analysis of the Sell-or-Process-Further Decision—Green Valley Mills

	Sell #2-Grade Lumber	Process Further (#2A-Grade)	Additional Revenue and Costs from Processing Further
Revenues.........................	$450,000	$550,000	$100,000
Less separate processing costs......	–0–	50,000	50,000
Margin.........................	$450,000	$500,000	$ 50,000 Net gain from processing further

We can summarize the sell-or-process-further decision as

Sell at split-off if: Sales value at split-off > Sales value after processing, less additional processing costs

Process further if: Sales value at split-off < Sales value after processing, less additional processing costs

In the case of lumber, when demand increases for one product, the other (joint) product can be stored until demand catches up. However, in the case of fresh meat and produce, long-term storage might not be economically feasible. This creates a problem when the demand for one part increases and the firm has to decide whether it is worthwhile meeting that demand.

For example, an Asian chicken producer is organized according to the part of the chicken being sold. (Because different cultures favor different parts, some parts are delivered fresh while others are frozen.) The company often faces a problem when the marketing managers from one group

(for example, legs) want to increase production because of increased demand. In such cases, the increased production means that the other parts (for example, wings) have to be sold for less. The firm wanted the managers from the group selling legs to consider the depression of prices for wings. By allocating according to net realizable value, the group selling legs now bears a higher percentage of the joint costs because the revenue from selling legs rises relative to that of wings.

While the allocation remains arbitrary, there is now a built-in signal of the impact of increased production of one part on the company's overall profits.

Deciding What to Do with By-Products

LO 11-5

Account for by-products.

by-products

Outputs of joint production processes that are relatively minor in quantity or value.

By-products are outputs from a joint production process that are relatively minor in quantity and/or value when compared to the main products. For example, sawdust is a by-product of lumber harvesting and processing, and kerosene is a by-product of gasoline production. You probably have seen advertisements for carpet and cloth mill ends at bargain prices. These are often by-products of textile production.

Accounting for by-products attempts to reflect the economic relationship between the by-products and the main products with a minimum of recordkeeping for inventory valuation purposes. The two common methods of accounting for by-products are as follows:

- *Method 1:* The net realizable value from sale of the by-product is deducted from the joint costs, effectively allocating to the by-product an amount of joint cost equal to the sales value of the by-product. The remaining joint costs are allocated to the main products.

- *Method 2:* The proceeds from sale of the by-product are treated as other revenue. All joint costs are allocated to the main products.

Assume that in March Green Valley Mills produced 300 tons of sawdust (along with the #1-Grade and #2-Grade lumber). Sales of sawdust total $15,000. All other revenues and costs are as described in Exhibit 11.16.

See Panel A of Exhibit 11.21 for the computation of the gross margin for the two joint products when the net realizable value of the by-product is used to reduce the joint cost (method 1). The $270,000 in joint cost is reduced by the by-product's $15,000 sales value so $255,000 (= $270,000 − $15,000) is allocated to #1-Grade and #2-Grade lumber. Applying method 2 results in no effect on the gross margins of the major products; the by-product shows a gross margin equal to its revenue (see Panel B).

A complication can occur under both methods if the cost of processing by-products occurs in one period but they are not sold until the next period. In such a case, companies could find it necessary to keep an inventory of the by-product processing costs in the Additional By-Product Cost account until the by-products are sold.

In our experience, some companies make by-product accounting as easy as possible by expensing the by-products' costs in the period in which they are incurred and then recording the total revenue from them when they are sold. Using this method, the accountants do not have to keep an inventory of by-product processing costs, nor do they have to compute their net realizable value. Although this simple approach technically violates the principle that revenues and expenses should be matched in the same accounting period, the amounts involved are generally immaterial.

Exhibit 11.21   Gross Margin Computations Using Net Realizable Value Method for Allocating Joint Cost with By-Products

	A	B	C	D	E
1	GREEN VALLEY MILLS				
2	For the Month of March				
3					
4	**Panel A: Method 1**	#1-Grade	#2-Grade	Sawdust	
5	Sales value	$ 300,000	$ 450,000	$ 15,000	$ 765,000
6	Less additional processing costs	–0–	–0–	–0–	–0–
7	Net realizable value at split-off point	$ 300,000	$ 450,000	$ 15,000	$ 765,000
8	Deduct sales value of by-product:			15,000	15,000
9	Proportionate share of remaining joint cost:				
10	$ 300,000/$ 750,000	40%			
11	$ 450,000/$ 750,000		60%		
12	Allocated joint costs				
13	($ 270,000 – $ 15,000) × 40%	$ 102,000			$ 102,000
14	($ 270,000 – $ 15,000) × 60%	–0–	$ 153,000	–0–	153,000
15	Gross margin	$ 198,000	$ 297,000	$ –0–	$ 495,000
16	Gross margin as a percent of sales	66%	66%	–0–%	65%
17					
18					
19	**Panel B: Method 2**				
20	Sales value	$ 300,000	$ 450,000	$ 15,000	$ 765,000
21	Less additional processing costs	–0–	–0–	–0–	–0–
22	Net realizable value at split-off point	$ 300,000	$ 450,000	$ 15,000	$ 765,000
23	Proportionate share of remaining joint cost:				
24	$ 300,000/$ 750,000	40%			
25	$ 450,000/$ 750,000		60%		
26	Allocated joint costs				
27	($ 270,000) × 40%	$ 108,000	–0–	–0–	$ 108,000
28	($ 270,000) × 60%	–0–	$ 162,000	–0–	162,000
29	Gross margin	$ 192,000	$ 288,000	$ 15,000	$ 495,000
30	Gross margin as a percent of sales	64%	64%	100%	65%
31					

Although we have indicated that two methods are used to account for by-products, many variations of these methods are used in practice. By-products are by definition relatively minor products; hence, alternative methods to account for them are not likely to have a material effect on the financial statements for either internal or external reporting.

Key takeaways

1. Production departments contribute directly to the goods and services generated by the organization. Service departments provide support such as administration, purchasing, and so on, to other service departments and to production departments. For purposes of both performance measurement and product costing, service department costs are allocated to production departments.

2. There are three common methods of allocating service department costs. All three allocation methods are based on a measure of usage of the service department's resources, such as employees, hours, IT calls, and so on.

    a. Direct method. The direct method allocates service department costs only to the production departments, regardless of the use of the service department by other service departments.

    b. Step method. The step method starts with a single service department and allocates costs to all departments (both service departments and production departments) that use the services. Once the first service department's costs are allocated, the method moves to the second service department, and so on. At no time is a service department's cost allocated

(Continued)

(Continued)

back to a department whose costs have already been allocated to other departments. The choice of which department to start with is arbitrary, but common bases for the choice include the department with the highest percentage usage going to other service departments or the service department with the largest cost.

c. Reciprocal method. The reciprocal, or simultaneous, method allocates all service department costs to all using departments. It relies on matrix algebra to solve a system of simultaneous equations that reflect the use of resources in any one department.

3. Joint costs arise when one resource is used to produce two or more products in approximately fixed proportion. Producing one product necessarily results in the production of the others. The point at which the resulting

products can be identified is called the "split-off point." Joint costs are allocated to provide product cost information. Two common methods are used to allocate joint costs.

a. Net realizable value method. Under the net realizable value method, the sales value of the resulting products at the split-off point are used to allocate the joint costs. If the product cannot be sold at the split-off point, the estimated sales value (the estimated net realizable value), which is the final sales value less the additional processing costs, is used.

b. Physical quantities method. The physical quantities method uses the quantities (feet, pounds, gallons, and so on) to allocate the joint costs to the individual products.

SUMMARY

Cost allocation is the process of assigning common costs to two or more cost objects. Ideally, cost allocation reflects a cause-and-effect relation between costs and the objects to which they are allocated.

Service department cost allocations are required to ensure that the costs of support services are included in the costs of products. The three major methods of service department cost allocation are the direct method, the step method, and the reciprocal method. The methods differ by the extent to which services provided by one service department to another are considered in the allocation process.

Joint cost allocations arise from the need to assign common costs to two or more products manufactured from a common input. The usual objective of joint cost allocation is to relate the costs of the inputs to the economic benefits received. There is no direct way to do this for joint products, so approximations are necessary. The two methods of joint cost allocation distribute joint costs based on the use of the net realizable value method (or *estimated* net realizable value) or the physical quantities method. These methods are acceptable for financial reporting purposes, but care must be exercised before attempting to use the data for decision-making purposes because of the inherent arbitrariness in joint cost allocations.

The following summarizes key ideas tied to the chapter's learning objectives:

LO 11-1 Explain why and how service costs are allocated using the direct method, the step method, and the reciprocal method. Costs are allocated to provide information on costs of departments and are required for financial reporting and taxes. The three methods used are:

a. Direct method: The direct method allocates service department costs to user departments ignoring the use of one service department by another.

b. Step method: The step method allocates one service department to all other departments based on the resources used. The method then moves to the next service department and allocates its costs, but never allocates costs to a service department whose costs have already been allocated.

c. Reciprocal method: The reciprocal method allocates all service department costs to all using departments. It relies on matrix algebra to solve a system of simultaneous equations that reflect the use of resources in any one department.

LO 11-2 Use the reciprocal method approach for outsourcing decisions. By applying the reciprocal method to the variable costs in the service departments, the resulting costs for these departments provide an estimate of the total variable cost of each service department, accounting for the reciprocal use of other service departments.

LO 11-3 Explain why and how joint costs are allocated using the net realizable value method and the physical quantities method. Companies allocate joint costs to products to establish a cost basis for pricing or performance evaluation. The two methods used are:

a. Net realizable value method: The sales value of the resulting products at the split-off point are used to allocate the joint costs. If the product cannot be sold at the split-off point, the estimated sales value, which is the final sales value less the additional processing costs, is used.

b. Physical quantities method: The physical quantities method uses the physical measures of products to allocate the joint costs.

LO 11-4 Use cost data to make the decision whether to sell or process further. A common decision is whether to sell products at split-off points or process them further. Joint cost allocations are usually irrelevant for these decisions.

LO 11-5 Account for by-products. By-products are relatively minor outputs from a joint production process. The two methods most commonly used to account for by-products are:

a. Reduce the cost of the main product by the net realizable value (sales value minus by-product processing cost) of the by-product.

b. Treat the net realizable value of the by-product as other income.

LO 11-6 (Appendix) Use spreadsheets to solve reciprocal cost allocation problems. Spreadsheets are used to solve complex reciprocal cost allocation problems by inverting the service department usage matrix.

KEY TERMS

by-products, *516*

direct method, *498*

estimated net realizable value, *511*

final cost center, *496*

intermediate cost center, *496*

joint cost, *510*

joint products, *510*

net realizable value method, *511*

physical quantities method, *514*

reciprocal method, *503*

service department, *495*

split-off point, *510*

step method, *500*

user department, *495*

APPENDIX: CALCULATION OF THE RECIPROCAL METHOD USING COMPUTER SPREADSHEETS

The reciprocal method requires that cost relationships be written in equation form. The method then solves the equations for the total costs to be allocated to each department. The direct costs of each department are typically included in the solution. Thus, for any department, we can state the equation

LO 11-6
Use spreadsheets to solve reciprocal cost allocation problems.

$$\text{Total costs} = \text{Direct costs} + \text{Allocated costs}$$

The total costs are the unknowns that we attempt to derive. In what follows, we use S1 for Information Systems, S2 for Administration, P1 for Sierra Tract, and P2 for Cascades Tract to emphasize the generic nature of the approach. The analysis can be expanded to any number of service departments and production departments. Although we ignore the direct costs of the production departments here, they can be easily added to the model.

Following is the series of departmental cost equations. Recall that the direct cost of Information Systems is $800,000 and the direct cost of Administration is $5,000,000. See Exhibit 11.2 for the usage data. The total (unknown) cost of the department is on the left-hand side of the equation and the derivation of the cost is on the right-hand side. The total cost is the sum of the direct cost and the costs allocated from the other departments.

$$\text{Total costs} = \text{Direct costs} + \quad\quad \text{Allocated costs}$$

$$\text{S1} = \$800{,}000 + 0\% \text{ S1} + 20\% \text{ S2} + 0\% \text{ P1} + 0\% \text{ P2}$$

$$\text{S2} = \$5{,}000{,}000 + 50\% \text{ S1} + 0\% \text{ S2} + 0\% \text{ P1} + 0\% \text{ P2}$$

$$\text{P1} = \$0 + 10\% \text{ S1} + 50\% \text{ S2} + 0\% \text{ P1} + 0\% \text{ P2}$$

$$\text{P2} = \$0 + 40\% \text{ S1} + 30\% \text{ S2} + 0\% \text{ P1} + 0\% \text{ P2}$$

We can rewrite the series of equations for the total cost in each department as:

$$100\% \text{ S1} - 20\% \text{ S2} - 0\% \text{ P1} - 0\% \text{ P2} = \$800{,}000$$

$$-50\% \text{ S1} + 0\% \text{ S2} - 0\% \text{ P1} - 0\% \text{ P2} = \$5{,}000{,}000$$

$$-10\% \text{ S1} - 50\% \text{ S2} + 0\% \text{ P1} - 0\% \text{ P2} = \$0$$

$$-40\% \text{ S1} - 30\% \text{ S2} - 0\% \text{ P1} + 0\% \text{ P2} = \$0$$

This set of equations can be expressed in matrix form and solved using the matrix functions of a spreadsheet program such as Microsoft Excel®. Exhibit 11.22 is a screenshot of the spreadsheet set up to solve the reciprocal cost allocation problem at GVM.

Exhibit 11.22   Service Department Cost Allocation Using the Reciprocal Method: Spreadsheet Solution

	A	B	C	D	E	F	G	H	I	J
1	**Panel A: Basic Data**									
2										
3			**Service Department Usage Matrix (S)**							
4			**(Percentage Use)**							
5		**(Positive Numbers: Provide Service – Negative Numbers: Use Service)**								
6			From Department:							
7		Info. Systems	Admin.	Sierra	Cascades					
8	To Department									
9	Information Systems	100.0%	–20.0%	0.0%	0.0%					
10	Administration	–50.0%	100.0%	0.0%	0.0%					
11	Sierra Tract	–10.0%	–50.0%	100.0%	0.0%					
12	Cascades Tract	–40.0%	–30.0%	0.0%	100.0%					
13	Total	0.0%	0.0%	100.0%	100.0%					
14										
15	**Panel B: Department Costs After Reciprocal Service Costs**									
16						Direct				
17			Inverse of Service Matrix (S-Inv)			Department		Allocated		
18						Cost		Cost		
19	Information Systems	111.11%	22.22%	0.00%	0.00%	$ 800,000		$ 2,000,000		
20	Administration	55.56%	111.11%	0.00%	0.00%	$ 5,000,000	=	$ 6,000,000		
21	Sierra Tract	38.89%	57.78%	100.00%	0.00%	$ 0		$ 3,200,000	⇐⋯	Reciprocal
22	Cascades Tract	61.11%	42.22%	0.00%	100.00%	$ 0		$ 2,600,000	⇐⋯	Allocations
23										
24										
25	**Panel C: Alternative Presentation**									
26										
27		Allocation:								
28										
29	**Department**		Info. Systems	Administration	Sierra	Cascades				
30	Information Systems	$ 2,000,000	0.00%	50.00%	10.00%	40.00%	100.00%			
31	Administration	$ 6,000,000	20.00%	0.00%	50.00%	30.00%	100.00%			
32										
33										
34	Direct Costs		$ 800,000	$ 5,000,000	$ 0	$ 0	$ 5,800,000			
35	Information Systems		($ 2,000,000)	$ 1,000,000	$ 200,000	$ 800,000	$ 0			
36	Administration		$ 1,200,000	($ 6,000,000)	$ 3,000,000	$ 1,800,000	$ 0			
37	**Final Allocations**		$ 0	$ 0	$ 3,200,000	$ 2,600,000	$ 5,800,000			
38										

The process has three steps. In the first step, as shown in Panel A, the coefficients of the service matrix are entered. Notice that all coefficients along the diagonal equal 1 (100%). The problem is set up so that the negative coefficients represent the usage of the service department and positive coefficients represent provision of service. Finally, note that the net services used by the service departments are zero. The services ultimately serve the producing department.

In the second step, the inverse of the service matrix is computed. In Microsoft Excel, the following steps accomplish this:

- Highlight the currently empty range (B19:E22) (this is where the inverse will be stored).
- Click the formula bar while leaving the range highlighted.
- Enter the following formula (without the quotation marks) in the formula bar: "=MINVERSE(B9:E12)".
- Simultaneously press CTRL-SHIFT-ENTER (or CTRL-SHIFT-RETURN). (This is the sequence required to perform a function on an array, such as a matrix, in Excel.) See Panel B of Exhibit 11.22 for the result.

The third step is to multiply the inverse matrix by the vector (or array) of direct costs located in the range (F19:F22). Again, this is an array function (matrix multiplication). To do this, perform the following steps:

- Highlight the range (H19:H22) (this is where the cost allocation results will be stored).
- Enter the following formula (inside the quotation marks) in the formula bar: "=MMULT(B19:E22,F19:F22)".
- Simultaneously press CTRL-SHIFT-ENTER (or CTRL-SHIFT-RETURN).

The resulting allocations show the costs of the departments.

Note that the costs allocated to the production departments are exactly the same results shown in Exhibit 11.9. Panel C of Exhibit 11.22 presents the allocation process in a format similar to the analysis shown in Exhibit 11.9 in the text.

REVIEW QUESTIONS

11-1. Why do companies allocate costs? What are some of the advantages and disadvantages to doing so?

11-2. What are the three methods of allocating service department costs?

11-3. What are the similarities and differences among the direct method, the step method, and the reciprocal method of allocating costs?

11-4. What criterion should be used to determine the order of allocation from service departments when the step method is used? Explain why.

11-5. What is a limitation of the direct method of allocating service department costs? The step method?

11-6. What is the objective of joint cost allocation?

11-7. Why would a number of accountants express a preference for the net realizable value method of joint cost allocation over the physical quantities method?

11-8. When would a physical quantities method for allocation be preferred?

11-9. What is the basic difference between the allocation of joint costs to (*a*) joint products and (*b*) by-products?

11-10. What costs are irrelevant for the decision of whether to sell a joint product or process it further?

CRITICAL ANALYSIS AND DISCUSSION QUESTIONS

11-11. If cost allocations are arbitrary and potentially misleading, why do companies, including successful ones, continue to allocate costs?

11-12. One critic of cost allocation noted, "You can avoid the problem of arbitrary cost allocations by not allocating any common costs to other cost objects." What are your thoughts on this comment?

11-13. If the reciprocal method is conceptually superior, why don't all firms use it?

11-14. Service department cost allocation is the first stage in a two-stage system. Suppose a company has a purchasing department that is responsible for buying all materials, including miscellaneous supplies for the company's three production departments. Each production department produces multiple products. Many of the supplies are used in more than one production department. For the service department allocation problem (the first stage), is the cost of the supplies (not the cost of the purchasing activity) a direct or an indirect cost? For the second stage, is the cost of supplies a direct or an indirect cost? Explain.

11-15. What argument(s) could be given in support of the reciprocal method as the preferred method for distributing the costs of service departments?

11-16. Under what conditions are the results from using the direct method of allocation the same as those from using the other two methods? Why?

11-17. Consider a company with two producing departments and one service department. The service department distributes its costs to the producing departments on the basis of the number of employees in each department. If the costs in the service department are fixed, what effect would the addition of employees in one department have on the costs allocated to the other department? Comment on the reasonableness of the situation.

11-18. What are some of the factors that a company needs to consider in addition to cost savings when deciding whether to outsource a service department, such as Information Services?

11-19. Surf Beach State College (SBSC) has a business school with three products: undergraduate degrees, graduate degrees, and executive education. SBSC has three service departments: Computer Support, Career Development, and the Library. The dean would like to measure product line profitability and wants to include an allocation of service department costs in the analysis. How would you recommend the service department costs be allocated?

11-20. Consider a firm with three service departments (S1–S3) with a pattern of usage as follows:

	S1	S2	S3	Production
S1	—	10%	30%	60%
S2	0%	—	0%	100%
S3	20%	30%	—	50%

That is, service department S2 uses 10 percent of the service from S1, service department S3 uses 30 percent, and production departments use 60 percent. If the company uses the step method of service department cost allocation, which service department should be allocated *last?* Explain.

11-21. This chapter indicated that joint costing is used for inventory valuation and regulatory purposes. Under what conditions might the method of joint cost allocation have an impact on other decisions?

11-22. How is joint cost allocation like service department cost allocation?

11-23. In what ways is joint cost allocation similar to the allocation of fixed costs? In what ways is it different?

EXERCISES    connect   All applicable Exercises are included in Connect.

(LO 11-1)

11-24. Why Are Costs Allocated?—Ethical Issues

You are the division president of Wood Division of Underwood Enterprises. The only other division at Underwood Enterprises is Plastics Division. Each division has 12,000 employees. Last year, Wood Division had a turnover of 2,500 employees (2,500 employees left and 2,500 were hired). Plastics Division had a turnover of 6,000 employees. There were no transfers between divisions.

Underwood Enterprise's Human Resources Department only provides services to Wood and Plastics and only when an employee leaves or is hired. The total cost of the Human Resources Department last year was $280,000.

Required

a. As the Wood Division president, how would you recommend the cost of the Human Resources Department be allocated? What arguments would you use to support your claim?

b. How do you think the president of the Plastics Division will recommend allocating the cost of the Human Resources Department? Why?

c. You are going to take over as president of the Plastics Division, but before the transfer, the Underwood CFO asks you to recommend an allocation method. How would you recommend the cost of the Human Resources Department be allocated? What arguments would you use?

d. Is it ethical to recommend different allocation methods depending on which division you will be heading?

11-25. Cost Allocation: Direct Method

(LO 11-1)

Mack Precision Tool and Die has two production departments, Fabricating and Finishing, and two service departments, Repair and Quality Control. Direct costs for each department and the proportion of service costs used by the various departments for the month of March follow:

Department	Direct Costs	Proportion of Services Used by			
		Repair	Quality Control	Fabricating	Finishing
Fabricating	$140,600				
Finishing	98,200				
Repair	42,000	—	0.3	0.4	0.3
Quality Control	78,400	0.3	—	0.2	0.5

Required

Compute the allocation of service department costs to producing departments using the direct method.

11-26. Allocating Service Department Costs First to Production Departments and Then to Jobs

(LO 11-1)

Refer to the facts in Exercise 11-25. Assume that both Fabricating and Finishing work on just two jobs during the month of March: MP-47 and MP-48. Costs are allocated to jobs based on labor-hours in Fabricating and machine-hours in Finishing. The number of labor- and machine-hours worked in each department are as follows:

		Fabricating	Finishing
Job MP-47:	Machine-hours.	20	80
	Labor-hours	70	10
Job MP-48	Machine-hours.	30	45
	Labor-hours	90	15

Required

How much of the service department costs allocated to Fabricating and Finishing using the direct method should be allocated to Job MP-47? How much should be allocated to Job MP-48?

11-27. Cost Allocation: Direct Method

(LO 11-1)

Woodstock Binding has two service departments, IT (Information Technology) and HR (Human Resources), and two operating departments, Publishing and Binding. Management has decided to allocate IT costs on the basis of IT Tickets (issued with each IT request) in each department and HR costs on the basis of employees in each department.

The following data appear in the company records for the current period:

	IT	HR	Publishing	Binding
IT Tickets.	—	1,500	2,400	2,100
Employees	16	—	24	40
Department direct costs. . . .	$150,000	$247,500	$430,000	$390,000

Required
Use the direct method to allocate these service department costs to the operating departments.

(LO 11-1)   **11-28. Cost Allocation: Step Method**
Refer to the data for Mack Precision Tool and Die in Exercise 11-25.

Required
Use the step method to allocate the service costs, using the following:
a.   The order of allocation starts with Repair.
b.   The allocations are made in the reverse order (starting with Quality Control).

(LO 11-1)   **11-29. Cost Allocation: Step Method**
Refer to the data for Woodstock Binding in Exercise 11-27.

Required
Use the step method to allocate the service costs, using the following:
a.   The order of allocation starts with IT.
b.   The order of allocation starts with HR.

(LO 11-1)   **11-30. Cost Allocation: Reciprocal Method**
Refer to the data for Mack Precision Tool and Die in Exercise 11-25.

Required
Use the reciprocal method to allocate the service costs. (Matrix algebra is not required.)

(LO 11-1)   **11-31. Cost Allocation: Reciprocal Method, Two Service Departments**
Activity and selected costs for three production departments (Training, Independent, and Commercial) and two service departments (Accounting and Facilities) at DuBay Films for the past month follow:

	Using Department				
Supplying Department	Accounting	Facilities	Training	Independent	Commercial
Accounting.	—	0.20	0.20	0.40	0.20
Facilities	0.15	—	0.15	0.30	0.40
Direct cost	$80,000	$129,500	$220,000	$190,000	$276,000

Required
Allocate service department costs to Training, Independent, and Commercial using the reciprocal method. What are the total costs of Training, Independent, and Commercial after this allocation?

(LO 11-1)   **11-32. Cost Allocation: Reciprocal Method**
Refer to the data for Woodstock Binding in Exercise 11-27.

Required
Allocate the service department costs using the reciprocal method. (Matrix algebra is not required because there are only two service departments.)

11-33. Cost Allocation: Direct Method

(LO 11-1)

Memorial Services, Inc. (MSI) has three service departments (IT, Accounting, and HR) and two production departments (West and East). The usage data for each of the service departments for the previous period follow:

	IT	Accounting	HR	West	East
IT	—	0%	20%	40%	40%
Accounting	0%	—	0%	40%	60%
HR	10%	10%	—	60%	20%

The direct costs of the service departments in the previous period were $86,750 for IT, $99,000 for Accounting, and $112,500 for HR.

Required

Use the direct method to allocate the service department costs to the production departments.

11-34. Cost Allocation: Step Method

(LO 11-1)

Refer to the data for Memorial Services, Inc. in Exercise 11-33.

Required

Use the step method to allocate the service department costs to the two production departments. Allocate HR costs first, followed by IT, and then Accounting.

11-35. Cost Allocation: Reciprocal Method

(LO 11-1)

Refer to the data for Memorial Services, Inc. in Exercise 11-33.

Required

Use the reciprocal method to allocate the service department costs to the production departments. (Matrix algebra is not required.)

11-36. Evaluate Cost Allocation Methods

(LO 11-1)

Refer to Exercises 11-27, 11-29, and 11-32 (Woodstock Binding).

Required

a.   Which method do you think is best? Why?

b.   How much would it be worth to the company to use the best method compared to the worst of the three methods? (Numbers are not required in this answer.)

11-37. Reciprocal Cost Allocation—Outsourcing a Service Department

(LO 11-1, 2)

Refer to the facts in Exercise 11-25. Mack Precision Tool and Die estimates that the variable costs in the Repair Department total $15,225, and in Quality Control variable costs total $39,200. Avoidable fixed costs in the Repair Department are $12,400.

Required

If Mack Precision Tool and Die outsources the Repair Department, what is the maximum it can pay an outside vendor without increasing total costs?

11-38. Reciprocal Cost Allocation—Outsourcing a Service Department

(LO 11-1, 2)

Refer to the facts in Exercise 11-27. Woodstock Binding estimates that the variable costs in the IT Department total $110,000, and in the HR Department variable costs total $140,000. Avoidable fixed costs in the IT Department are $18,000.

Required

If Woodstock Binding outsources the IT Department functions, what is the maximum it can pay an outside vendor without increasing total costs?

11-39. Net Realizable Value Method: Multiple Choice

(LO 11-3)

Sanford Agricultural Chemicals (SAC) produces two main products, M-4 and M-5, and one by-product, BYP, from a single input, Gen-10. Products M-4 and M-5 can either be sold at split-off or processed further and sold. A given batch begins with 2,500 pounds of Gen-10 with a cost of $160,000. Additional information regarding a batch follows:

| | | | If Processed Further | |
Product	Units Produced	Unit Sales Value at Split-off	Additional Costs (Per Unit)	Sales Value (Per Unit)
M-4.	20,000	$ 8.25	$1.80	$ 15.00
M-5.	12,000	17.50	7.00	25.00
BYP	4,000	0.90	NA	NA

SAC uses the net realizable at split-off approach to allocate joint costs and treats the sales value of the by-product BYP as other income.

Required
The joint cost allocated to product M-5 at Sanford Agricultural Chemicals for a given batch is

a. $60,000.

b. $72,000.

c. $80,000.

d. $89,600.

e. None of the above.

(LO 11-4)   **11-40. Sell or Process Further: Multiple Choice**
Refer to the data in Exercise 11-39. Suppose that Sanford Agricultural Chemicals uses the physical quantities method to allocate joint costs and the revenues from by-products are credited to joint costs.

Required
Under these assumptions, the following product(s) should be processed further and then sold:

a. M-4

b. M-5

c. Both M-4 and M-5

d. Neither M-4 nor M-5

e. Cannot tell from the information given.

(LO 11-3)   **11-41. Net Realizable Value Method**
Monroe Materials processes a purchased material, PM-20, and produces three outputs, Alpha, Beta, and Gamma. In February, the costs to process PM-20 are $524,000 for materials and $196,000 for conversion costs. The results of the processing follow:

	Units Produced	Sales Value per Unit
Alpha.	24,000	$ 9.60
Beta.	19,200	18.00
Gamma	4,800	80.00

Required
Assign costs to Alpha, Beta, and Gamma for February using the net realizable value method.

(LO 11-3)   **11-42. Physical Quantities Method**
Refer to the data for Monroe Materials in Exercise 11-41.

Required
Assign costs to Alpha, Beta, and Gamma for February using the physical quantities method.

(LO 11-3)   **11-43. Estimated Net Realizable Value Method**
St. John Mining operates several facilities. At one, a typical batch of an ore, Pryex, run through the processing plant yields three products: PX-10, PX-20, and PX-30. At the split-off point, the

intermediate products cannot be sold without further processing. A typical batch of PX-10 sells for $110,000 after incurring additional processing costs of $20,000. PX-20 can be sold for $170,000 after additional processing costs of $44,000, and the PX-30 sells for $220,000 but requires additional processing costs of $76,000. The joint costs of processing the Pryex, including the cost of mining, are $240,000 per batch.

Required
Use the estimated net realizable value method to allocate the joint processing costs.

11-44. Estimated Net Realizable Value Method—Solve for Unknowns

(LO 11-3)

Gunston Processing produces two products, ALT-1 and ALT-2, from a batch using a single raw material, ALT-0. Both products require further processing before they be can be sold. A batch of ALT-1 can be sold for $150,000 after processing costs of $30,000. A batch of ALT-2 can be sold for $240,000 after further processing. The cost of ALT-0 is $200,000 for a batch. Using the estimated net realizable value method, a joint cost of $120,000 was allocated to ALT-2 for a batch.

Required
Compute the separable processing cost for a batch of ALT-2.

(CPA adapted)

11-45. Allocation of Joint Costs—Net Realizable Value and Physical Quantities Methods

(LO 11-3)

Milo Manufacturing produces products Kappa and Lambda from a joint process. Total joint costs are $150,000. The sales value at split-off was $162,000 for 1,200 units of Kappa and $63,000 for 1,800 units of Lambda.

Required

a.   What joint costs are allocated to the two products using the net realizable value at split-off approach?

b.   What joint costs are allocated to the two products using the physical quantities method?

11-46. Net Realizable Value Method with By-Products

(LO 11-3, 5)

Denver Fabricators manufactures products DF1 and DF2 from a joint process, which also yields a by-product, BP. The company accounts for the revenues from its by-product sales as other income. Additional information follows:

	DF1	DF2	BP	Total
Units produced	27,000	18,000	15,000	60,000
Allocated joint costs	?	?	?	$560,000
Sales value at split-off.	$561,000	$187,000	$102,000	$850,000

Required
Assuming that joint product costs are allocated using the net realizable value at split-off approach, what joint costs are allocated to each of the joint products DF1 and DF2 and to the by-product, BP?

11-47. Net Realizable Value Method

(LO 11-3)

Barrett Chemicals manufactures four chemicals, Chem-1, Chem-2, Chem-3, and Chem-4, from a joint process. The total joint costs in May were $564,000. Additional information follows:

Product	Units Produced	Sales Value at Split-Off	If Processed Further Additional Costs	If Processed Further Sales Values
Chem-1	288,000	$220,000	$32,700	$ 260,000
Chem-2	176,000	264,000	29,400	290,000
Chem-3	192,000	149,600	24,900	180,000
Chem-4	144,000	246,400	26,300	270,000
	800,000	$880,000	$113,300	$1,000,000

Required

Barrett Chemicals uses the net realizable value method to allocate joint costs. What joint costs would be allocated to each product in May?

(CPA adapted)

(LO 11-3)   **11-48. Physical Quantities Method**

Refer to the facts in Exercise 11-47.

Required

Barrett Chemicals uses the physical quantities method to allocate joint costs. What joint costs would be allocated to each product in May?

(LO 11-4)   **11-49. Sell or Process Further**

Refer to the facts in Exercises 11-47 and 11-48.

Required

Which, if any, of the four products would you recommend Barrett Chemicals sell at split-off (and not process further)? Explain. Does your answer depend on the method used to allocate the joint cost? Why?

(LO 11-3)   **11-50. Physical Quantities Method**

Forest Products, Inc. manufactures three products (FP-10, FP-20, and FP-40) from a single, joint input. None of the products can be sold without further processing. In November, joint product costs were $240,000. Additional information follows:

Product	Units Produced	Sales Values	Processing Costs (After Split-Off)
FP-10..........	66,000	$168,000	$ 28,000
FP-20..........	99,000	308,000	108,000
FP-40..........	55,000	84,000	24,000

Required

Forest Products uses the physical quantities (units produced) method to allocate joint costs. What joint costs would be allocated to each of the three products in November?

(CPA adapted)

(LO 11-3)   **11-51. Estimated Net Realizable Value Method**

Refer to the information in Exercise 11-50 for Forest Products.

Required

Forest Products uses the estimated net realizable value method to allocate joint costs. What joint costs would be allocated to each of the three products in November?

(LO 11-3, 4)   **11-52. Physical Quantities Method; Sell or Process Further**

Refer to the facts in Exercise 11-50. The sale of FP-40 has been banned by a recent law. If FP-40 is produced, disposal in an approved manner costs $120,000 for every 55,000 units produced.

Required

a.   Assume that Forest Products continues to use the physical quantities method of allocation and to manufacture and sell FP-10 and FP-20. What joint costs would be allocated to FP-10 and FP-20, assuming the same production information as in Exercise 11-50?

b.   There is a possibility that a market for FP-10 and FP-20 at split-off will develop. In other words, it will be possible to sell the two products rather than process them further. At what sales value (at split-off) would Forest Products be indifferent between selling them at split-off and processing them further?

c.   How will your answer to requirement (b) change if the disposal cost for FP-40 increases to $150,000 for every 55,000 units of FP-40 produced? Why?

11-53. Physical Quantities Method with By-Product

(LO 11-3, 5)

Lawn Products produces two products (X and Y) and a by-product (Z) from a joint process using a raw material (Alpha). The company chooses to allocate the costs on the basis of the physical quantities method.

Last month, it processed 22,000 pounds of Alpha at a total cost of $98,000. The output of the process consisted of 28,350 units of product X, 34,650 units of product Y, and 7,000 units of by-product Z. By-product Z can be sold for $11,500. This is considered to be its net realizable value, which is deducted from the processing costs of the main products.

Required

What amount of joint costs should be assigned to each of product X and product Y?

All applicable Problems are included in Connect.   **Mc Graw Hill connect**   **PROBLEMS**

11-54. Direct and Step Methods—Data Analysis and Visualization

(LO 11-1)

Tennessee Company manufactures a specialized fitting for industrial machinery at the Stephens Street Facility. The facility has five departments. Two departments (Casting and Finishing) are production departments. The other three departments (Purchasing, Human Resources, and Information Technology) are considered service departments. The accumulated costs in the three service departments in the most recent period were $100,000, $160,000, and $80,000, respectively. The corporate management at Tennessee as been concerned that the costs of the service departments are getting too high. As a result, the plant manager has been told that the bonus payments to plant management (the plant manager and the five department managers) will not be paid if the cost of the allocated service departments is above $9.75 per unit in either production department.

The product costing system at the plant currently uses the step method of service department cost allocation, although that is a decision choice of the plant controller. Information Technology (IT) costs are allocated first, followed by Human Resources (HR), and then Purchasing. IT costs are allocated on the basis of "IT calls" (requests for service). HR costs are allocated on the basis of employees. Purchasing costs are allocated on the basis of purchase orders (POs). The use of each base by all departments during the most recent period follows:

		Used by			
Allocation Base	Purchasing	Human Resources	Information Technology	Casting	Finishing
Purchase orders	500	760	1,140	6,080	1,520
Employees	90	100	180	315	315
IT calls..................	9,600	4,800	30,000	39,600	66,000

Direct costs of the Casting Department (including department overhead, but before allocation of any service department costs) were $450,000 in the most recent period. Direct costs in the Finishing Department (again including department overhead, but before allocation of any service department costs) were $525,000.

Required

a. Using the current system for allocating service department costs, determine the allocated costs and the total costs in each of the two producing departments (Casting and Finishing). (*Hint:* Ignore any of its own services by a service department.)

b. Assume that 20,000 units were processed through these two departments in the most recent period. What is the per-unit allocated service department cost for each of the two production departments?

c. Based on your analysis, will the bonus be paid if the most recent period's costs and activity are repeated? Explain.

d. Repeat the analysis in requirement (*a*) assuming the Stephens Street facility uses the direct method to allocate service department costs.

e. Based on your analysis, will the bonus be paid if the most recent period's costs and activity are repeated and the direct method is used to allocate service department costs? Explain.

f. Prepare a short report to corporate managers on your assessment of the effectiveness of the bonus plan as a means to control service department costs. Use any visualizations that illustrate your points.

(LO 11-1) **11-55. Solve for Unknowns: Direct Method**

Greendale Office Products has a warehouse that supplies office products to its store locations. The warehouse has two service departments, Human Resources (HR) and Information Technology (IT), and two operating departments, Packaging and Delivery. The following are partial cost allocation results for November:

Costs allocated to Packaging	$88,000 from HR
	? from IT
Costs allocated to Delivery	? from HR
	$156,800 from IT

Total costs for the two service departments are $416,000.
   IT's services are provided as follows:

- 17.5 percent to Packaging.
- 70 percent to Delivery.

The direct method of allocating costs is used.

Required

a. What are the total service department costs (HR + IT) allocated to Delivery?

b. Complete the following:

	To	
From	Packaging	Delivery
Human Resources.	$88,000	?
Information Technology	?	$156,800

c. What proportion of HR's costs were allocated to Packaging? To Delivery?

(LO 11-1) **11-56. Solve for Unknowns: Step Method**

Hildale Manufacturing is organized with two service departments (Administration and Maintenance) and two production departments (Assembly and Finishing). The company uses the step method to allocate service department costs, allocating costs from Administration first. In March, $147,000 was allocated from Maintenance to Assembly (including any cost allocated from Administration to Maintenance). In addition, $30,000 was allocated from Administration to Maintenance in March.

Assembly used 49 percent of Maintenance services and Finishing used 21 percent of Maintenance services in March. Finally, Maintenance used 25 percent of Administration services in March.

Required

a. What are the total costs incurred by Administration in March?

b. What are the total costs incurred by Maintenance (before any allocations) in March?

(LO 11-1) **11-57. Comparison of Allocation Methods**

Baldwin Enterprises has two service departments, Personnel and Legal, and two operating divisions, Eastern and Western. Personnel costs are allocated on the basis of employees and Legal costs are allocated on the basis of hours. A summary of Baldwin operations follows:

	Personnel	Legal	Eastern	Western
Employees	—	40	120	40
Hours.	10,800	—	5,400	1,800
Department direct costs.	$300,000	$160,000	$1,200,000	$790,000

Required

a.   Allocate the cost of the service departments to the operating divisions using the direct method.

b.   Allocate the cost of the service departments to the operating divisions using the step method. Start with Legal.

c.   Allocate the cost of the service departments to the operating divisions using the reciprocal method.

d.   Comment on the results.

11-58. Data Analysis and Data Visualization—Direct Method, Step Method, and Allocation Choices   (LO 11-1)

Rohns Manufacturing produces kitchen appliances at its North Roberts plant. The appliances go through two production departments: Fabrication and Assembly. The plant has three service departments: Information Systems Support (ISS), Training, and Administration. A summary of the use of service departments by other service departments as well as by the two producing departments at the plant follows:

			Services Used by		
Service Department	ISS	Training	Administration	Fabrication	Assembly
ISS	NA*	75%	5%	10%	10%
Training	5%	NA*	15%	20%	60%
Administration	20%	20%	NA*	40%	20%
* Not applicable.					

Following are the direct costs in the various departments:

Department	Direct Cost
ISS	$120,000
Training	324,000
Administration	210,000
Fabrication	687,500
Assembly	485,000

The plant controller is evaluating methods for allocating service department costs. Currently three approaches are being considered, and you have been asked to make a recommendation.

Required

a.   Assuming the plant uses the direct method, what is the total service department cost allocated to Fabrication? To Assembly?

b.   Assuming the plant uses the step method, what is the total service department cost allocated to Fabrication? To Assembly? The order of allocation would start with the service department that provides the largest proportion of its services to other service departments. Next would be the service department that provides the next largest proportion to other service departments, and so on.

c.   Assuming the plant uses the step method, what is the total service department cost allocated to Fabrication? To Assembly? The order of allocation would start with the service department that incurs the largest direct cost. Next would be the service department that incurs the next largest direct cost, and so on.

d.   Prepare a brief report recommending one of the three methods considered [those in requirements (*a*) through (*c*)]. Include any visualizations that support your arguments.

(LO 11-1)   **11-59. Data Analysis and Data Visualization—Service Department Cost Allocation**
Bradby Automotive Restoration (BAR) has three service departments (S1, S2, and S3) and two operating departments (P1 and P2). Data on departmental usage of service departments follow:

Supplying Department	Using Department				
	S1	S2	S3	P1	P2
S1......................	NA*	30%	10%	10%	50%
S2......................	0%	NA*	0%	80%	20%
S3......................	0%	60%	NA*	5%	35%
*NA: Not Applicable					

The direct costs for each department in the most recent period were as follows:

S1...............	$240,000
S2...............	150,000
S3...............	210,000
P1...............	444,000
P2...............	565,000

The financial managers at Bradby are evaluating methods for allocating service department costs. All approaches are being considered, although they are "leaning toward the step method."

Required
a.   Assuming the company uses the direct method, what is the total service department cost allocated to P1? To P2?

b.   Assuming the company uses the step method, what is the total service department cost allocated to P1? To P2? The order of allocation would start with the service department that provides the largest proportion of its service to other service departments. Next would be the service department that provides the next largest proportion to other service departments, and so on.

c.   Assuming the company uses the step method, what is the total service department cost allocated to P1? To P2? The order of allocation would start with the service department that incurs the largest direct cost. Next would be the service department that incurs the next largest direct cost, and so on.

d.   Assuming the company uses the reciprocal method, what is the total service department cost allocated to P1? To P2? (You do not need matrix algebra or to read the appendix to complete this requirement.)

e.   Prepare a brief report recommending which method of service department cost allocation you would recommend. You do not have to recommend one of those evaluated in requirements (*a*) through (*d*). However, you should discuss which sequence of departments you would follow should the company decide to use the step method. Include any visualizations that support your arguments.

(LO 11-1)   **11-60. Cost Allocation: Step and Reciprocal Methods**
Dunedin Bank has two operating departments (Retail and Commercial) and three service departments: Operations, Information Technology (IT), and Transactions. For the last period, the following costs and service department usage ratios were recorded:

Supplying	Using Department				
Department	Transactions	IT	Operations	Retail	Commercial
Transactions.........	–0–	–0–	–0–	70%	30%
IT	10%	–0–	20%	30%	40%
Operations	60%	–0–	–0–	10%	30%
Direct cost	$240,000	$660,000	$1,500,000	$3,700,000	$2,250,000

Required

a.   Allocate the service department costs to the two operating departments using the reciprocal method. (You do not need to use a computer or study the appendix in this chapter.)

b.   Allocate the service department costs to the two operating departments using the step method. Allocate IT costs first, followed by Operations, and then Transactions. How does your answer differ from what you obtained in requirement (*a*)? Why?

11-61. Cost Allocation: Reciprocal Method   (LO 11-1)

Hessel Corporation has two operating departments (Domestic and Global) and three service departments: Human Resources (HR), Legal, and Testing. In the most recent period, the following costs and service department usage ratios were recorded:

Supplying	Using Department				
Department	Human Resources	Legal	Testing	Domestic	Global
Human Resources.........	–0–	15%	10%	25%	50%
Legal	10%	–0–	–0–	30%	60%
Testing..................	10%	–0–	–0–	45%	45%
Direct cost	$264,500	$190,000	$90,000	$538,000	$487,000

Required

Allocate the service department costs to the two operating departments using the reciprocal method. (*Hint:* You do not need to use a computer or study the appendix in this chapter.)

11-62. Allocate Service Department Costs: Direct and Step Methods   (LO 11-1)

Western Services has three service departments: Information Systems (IS), Personnel, and Administration. There are two operating departments: Residential and Commercial. A summary of costs and other data for each department prior to allocation of service department costs for the latest period follows:

	IS	Personnel	Administration	Residential	Commercial
Number of IS service tickets	75	105	60	1,410	940
Number of employees	20	25	12	138	162
Square footage occupied ...	3,900	8,000	3,800	16,100	69,500

The costs of the service departments and the allocation basis for each department follow.

Department	Direct Cost	Allocation Base
Information Systems (IS). ...	$14,000	IS service tickets
Personnel	21,000	Employees
Administration	17,700	Square footage occupied

Required

a. Assume that the company allocates service department costs to production departments using the direct method. What amount of Information Systems (IS) Department costs will be allocated to the Commercial Department?

b. Assume the same method of allocation as in requirement (*a*). What amount of Personnel Department costs is allocated to the Residential Department?

c. Assuming that the company allocates service department costs to other departments using the step method (starting with Administration and then IS), what amount of Administration Department costs is allocated to the IS Department?

d. Assume the same method of allocation as in requirement (*c*). What amount of IS Department costs is allocated to Administration?

(CPA adapted)

(LO 11-1)   **11-63. Allocate Service Department Costs: Ethical Issues**

Lothrop Security Group (LSG) provides consulting and security services to various clients, including government agencies and commercial firms. It has two operating departments, Government and Commercial. The Government Department handles contracts with federal and state organizations, and Commercial serves the remaining customers. LSG is organized this way because of the differences in contractual arrangements. Government contracts call for a fee equal to the full cost of the job, including allocated overhead plus a fixed profit amount. Other clients are charged based on the current market environment. LSG has two service departments, Contracts and Information Systems (IS). Contracts Department costs are allocated based on number of contracts, and IS costs are allocated based on employees. Selected percentage use data as well as departmental direct costs follow:

Supplying Department	Using Department			
	Contracts	IS	Government	Commercial
Contracts (contracts)......	0%	10%	36%	54%
IS (employees)..........	20%	–0–	30%	50%
Direct cost	$36,000	$133,600	$320,000	$620,000

Required

a. Suppose LSG allocated service department costs using the direct method. What is the amount of service department costs that will be allocated to each of the operating departments?

b. Suppose that, after reviewing the results, the CFO tells the accountant to change the percentage of classification of contracts so 50 percent is shown as used by the Government Department and 40 percent is shown as used by the Commercial Department. Would this be ethical?

c. Suppose the CFO tells the accountant to use salaries instead of number of employees to allocate IS Department cost. Employees in the Commercial Department earn lower salaries, on average. Would this be ethical?

d. Although LSG's current policy is to allocate service department costs using the direct method, the CFO asks the accountant to allocate the costs using the step method, allocating Information Services Department costs first. What is the amount of service department costs that will be allocated to each of the operating departments?

e. The CFO next asks the accountant to allocate the costs using the reciprocal method. What is the amount of service department costs that will be allocated to each of the operating departments?

f. Suppose the CFO tells the accountant to use the method that allocates the highest cost to the Government Department each period. Would this be ethical?

(LO 11-1, 2)   **11-64. Reciprocal Cost Allocation—Outsourcing a Service Department**

Refer to the facts in Problem 11-57. Baldwin Enterprises estimates that the cost structure in its operations is as follows:

	Personnel	Legal	Eastern	Western
Variable costs.........	$ 125,000	$ 41,000	$ 870,000	$ 560,000
Fixed costs	175,000	119,000	330,000	230,000
Total costs...........	$ 300,000	$160,000	$1,200,000	$ 790,000
Avoidable fixed costs ..	$ 50,000	$ 20,000	$ 150,000	$ 150,000

Required

a.   If Baldwin outsources the Legal Department, what is the maximum it can pay an outside vendor without increasing total costs?

b.   If Baldwin outsources the Personnel Department, what is the maximum it can pay an outside vendor without increasing total costs?

c.   If Baldwin outsources both the Personnel and the Legal Departments, what is the maximum it can pay an outside vendor without increasing total costs? (*Hint:* Stop and think before solving any equations.)

11-65. Reciprocal Cost Allocation—Outsourcing a Service Department   (LO 11-1, 2)

Refer to the facts in Problem 11-60. The cost accountant at Dunedin Bank estimates that the cost structures in its departments are as follows:

	Transactions	IT	Operations	Retail	Commercial
Variable costs...	$180,000	$360,000	$ 480,000	$1,500,000	$1,100,000
Fixed costs	60,000	300,000	1,020,000	2,200,000	1,150,000
Total costs......	$240,000	$660,000	$1,500,000	$3,700,000	$2,250,000
Avoidable fixed costs ...	$ 18,000	$240,000	$ 540,000	$1,300,000	$ 720,000

Required

a.   If Dunedin Bank outsources the Transactions Department, what is the maximum it can pay an outside vendor without increasing total costs?

b.   If Dunedin Bank outsources the IT Department, what is the maximum it can pay an outside vendor without increasing total costs?

c.   If Dunedin Bank outsources the Operations Department, what is the maximum it can pay an outside vendor without increasing total costs?

11-66. Reciprocal Cost Allocation—Outsourcing a Service Department   (LO 11-1, 2)

Refer to the facts in Problem 11-65.

Required

a.   If Dunedin Bank outsources both the Transactions Department and the IT Department, the total savings (before considering the fee paid to the outside vendor) will be
1.   More than the sum of the savings calculated in Problem 11-65(*a*) and (*b*).
2.   Equal to the sum of the savings calculated in Problem 11-65(*a*) and (*b*).
3.   Less than the sum of the savings calculated in Problem 11-65(*a*) and (*b*).
4.   Less than or equal to the savings calculated in Problem 11-65(*a*) and (*b*).
5.   Impossible to determine from the information provided.

b.   In general (not limited to Dunedin Bank), if a firm is considering eliminating more than one service department, the savings will be
1.   Less than or equal to the sum of the savings calculated from eliminating each of the individual service departments.
2.   Less than the sum of the savings calculated from eliminating each of the individual service departments.
3.   Equal to the sum of the savings calculated from eliminating each of the individual service departments.
4.   More than the sum of the savings calculated from eliminating each of the individual service departments.
5.   Impossible to determine from the information provided.

(LO 11-1, 6) **11-67. (Appendix) Cost Allocations—Reciprocal Method (computer required)**
Refer to the information in Problem 11-58 for Rohns Manufacturing.

Required
Assume that Rohns uses the reciprocal method of service department cost allocation. What is the total service department cost allocated to Fabrication? To Assembly? (*Hint:* Use the reciprocal method spreadsheet shown in Exhibit 11.22 as a start to your analysis.)

(LO 11-1, 6) **11-68. (Appendix) Cost Allocations—Reciprocal Method (computer required)**
Filer Fabrication has three service departments (S1, S2, and S3) and two production departments (P1 and P2). Data on service department usage and service direct costs follow.

	Using Department				
	S1	S2	S3	P1	P2
S1............	–	4%	17%	22%	57%
S2............	14%	–	21%	25%	40%
S3............	15%	8%	–	33%	44%
Direct cost	$218,000	$178,000	$155,000	NA*	NA*

*Not applicable for this problem.

Required
Assume that Filer Fabrication uses the reciprocal method of service department cost allocation. What is the total service department cost allocated to P1? To P2? (*Hint:* Use the reciprocal method spreadsheet shown in Exhibit 11.22 as a start to your analysis.)

(LO 11-1, 6) **11-69. (Appendix) Cost Allocations—Reciprocal Method (computer required)**
Morrell Financial Services (MFS) has three service departments: Accounting, Information Technology (IT), and Personnel. MFS also has two operating departments (Advice and Brokerage). Data on service department usage and service direct costs follow:

	Using Department				
	Accounting	IT	Personnel	Advice	Brokerage
Accounting....	–	6%	23%	31%	40%
IT	16%	–	10%	29%	45%
Personnel.....	11%	13%	–	39%	37%
Direct cost	$197,000	$281,000	$264,500	NA*	NA*

*Not applicable for this problem.

Required
Assume that Morrell Financial Services uses the reciprocal method of service department cost allocation. What is the total service department cost allocated to Advice? To Brokerage? (*Hint:* Use the reciprocal method spreadsheet shown in Exhibit 11.22 as a start to your analysis.)

(LO 11-3) **11-70. Net Realizable Value of Joint Products**
Douglass Minerals mines ore and then processes it into other products. At the end of the mining process, the ore splits off into three products: Metal-A, Metal-B, and Metal-C. Douglass sells Metal-C at the split-off point, with no further processing. Metal-A is processed in Plant A, and Metal-B is processed in Plant B. The following is a summary of costs and other related data for the period ended December 31:

Process:	Mining	Plant A	Plant B
Labor....................	$462,000	$390,000	$270,000
Manufacturing overhead ...	$378,000	$327,600	$126,000

Products	Metal-A	Metal-B	Metal-C
Units sold	216,000	144,000	72,000
Units in ending inventory (Dec. 31)	72,000	–0–	48,000
Sales revenue	$853,200	$576,000	$180,000

Douglass Minerals had no beginning inventories on hand at the beginning of the period. The company uses the net realizable value method to allocate joint costs.

Required
Compute the following:
a.   The net realizable value of Metal-C for the period ended December 31.
b.   The joint costs for the period ended December 31 to be allocated.
c.   The cost of Metal-B sold for the period ended December 31.
d.   The value of the ending inventory for Metal-C.

(CPA adapted)

11-71. Estimated Net Realizable Value and Effects of Processing Further   (LO 11-3, 4)
Lipton Liquids produces three products by a joint production process. Raw materials are put into production in Department 1, and at the end of processing in this department, three products appear. Alpha is sold at the split-off point with no further processing. Beta and Gamma require further processing before they are sold. Beta is processed in Department 2, and Gamma is processed in Department 3. Lipton Liquids uses the estimated net realizable value method of allocating joint production costs.

No inventories were on hand at July 1, the beginning of the quarter. No raw material was on hand at September 30. All units on hand at September 30 were fully complete as to processing. Following is a summary of costs and other data for the period ended September 30:

Products	Alpha	Beta	Gamma
Units sold	28,000	82,600	98,000
Units on hand at September 30 ...	70,000	–0–	56,000
Sales revenues	$126,000	$743,400	$1,029,000

Departments	1	2	3
Raw materials cost	$470,400	$ –0–	$ –0–
Direct labor cost	201,600	339,780	805,350
Manufacturing overhead	84,000	88,620	307,650

Required
a.   Determine the following amounts for each product: (1) estimated net realizable value used for allocating joint costs, (2) joint costs allocated to each of the three products, (3) cost of goods sold, and (4) finished goods inventory costs, September 30.
b.   Assume that the entire output of Alpha could be processed further at an additional cost of $12 per unit and then sold for $16.30 per unit. What would have been the effect on operating profits if all of Alpha output for the quarter had been further processed and then sold rather than being sold at the split-off point?
c.   Write a memo to management indicating whether Lipton Liquids should process Alpha further and why.

(LO 11-3)   **11-72. Finding Missing Data: Net Realizable Value**

Troester Manufacturing produces products X, Y, and Z from a joint process. Each product can be processed further and sold as X-Prime, Y-Prime, and Z-Prime. Information on the operations for the most recent period follows:

Product	X	Y	Z	Total
Units produced	76,800	38,400	19,200	134,400
Joint costs	$144,000ᵃ	(b)	(a)	$288,000
Sales value at split-off.	(c)	(d)	$72,000	480,000
Additional costs to convert				
to Prime.	33,600	$ 24,000	14,400	72,000
Sales value as Prime.	336,000	184,000	96,000	576,000

ᵃ This amount is the portion of the total joint cost of $288,000 that had been allocated to X.

Required
Determine the value for each lettered item.

(CPA adapted)

(LO 11-3)   **11-73. Finding Missing Data: Net Realizable Value**

Wadsworth Processes manufactures three produces—ABC, DEF, and GHI—from a joint production process. Data on the operations at Wadsworth for the most recent period are as follow:

	(Dollars in Thousands)			
Product	ABC	DEF	GHI	Total
Allocated joint cost	(b)	$ 67.5	(c)	$ 675.0
Sales value at split-off.	(a)	$ 135.0	(d)	$1,350.0
Additional processing costs	$225.0	$ 90.0	(e)	
Sales value if processed further.	$450.0	$ 247.5	$1,800.0	
Contribution from processing further. . . .	$ 0.0	$ 22.5	$ 540.0	
Units produced	2,500	1,500	6,000	10,000

Required
Determine the value for each lettered item.

(LO 11-3, 5)   **11-74. Joint Costing in a Process Costing Context: Estimated Net Realizable Value Method**

Terry Chemicals processes a single raw material, Clean-Z, in Department 1 of its main production facility. Out of the joint process in Department 1, two products emerge: Azyne and Bethanol. Azyne is further processed in Department 2, which also is a joint production process. After processing in Department 2, two products emerge: AzynePlus and Byzyne. AzynePlus is further processed in Department 3. Bethanol is processed further in Department 4. AzynePlus and Bethanol are considered main products. Byzyne is considered a by-product of AzynePlus. Information on the most recent period's production processes follows:

- In Department 1, 231,000 units of the raw material Clean-Z are processed at a total cost of $1,644,300. After processing in Department 1, 60 percent of the units are transferred to Department 2, and 40 percent of the units (now unprocessed Bethanol) are transferred to Department 4.

- In Department 2, the materials received from Department 1 are processed at an additional cost of $478,800. Seventy percent of the units become AzynePlus and are transferred to Department 3. The remaining 30 percent emerge as Byzyne and are sold at $12.60 per unit. The additional processing costs to make Byzyne salable are $102,060.

• In Department 3, AzynePlus is processed at an additional cost of $207,648. After this processing, AzynePlus can be sold for $30 per unit.

• In Department 4, Bethanol is processed at an additional cost of $2,079,000. A normal loss of 10 percent of the units of good output of Bethanol occurs in this department. The remaining good output is then sold for $72 per unit.

Required
Prepare a schedule showing the allocation of the $1,644,300 joint cost to AzynePlus and Bethanol using the estimated net realizable value approach. Revenue from the sale of by-products should be credited to the manufacturing costs of the related main product (method 1 in the text).

(CPA adapted)

11-75. Find Maximum Input Price: Estimated Net Realizable Value Method (LO 11-3)
Goldsmith Processors produces two joint products from a special type of ore. Product X-1 sells for $8 per unit at the split-off point. After an additional $90,000 of processing costs are incurred, product X-2 sells for $25 per unit. In a typical period, 90,000 units of ore are processed; 72,000 units become product X-1 and 18,000 units become product X-2.

The joint process has only variable costs. In a typical period, the conversion costs of the joint products amount to $243,000. Materials prices for the ore are volatile, and if prices are too high, the company stops production. The company uses the physical quantities method to allocate joint costs to the main products.

Required
The management at Goldsmith is trying to determine the maximum per-unit price that the company should pay for the ore.

a. Calculate the maximum price, per unit, that Goldsmith should pay for the ore.

b. Write a brief memo to management explaining how you arrived at your answer in requirement (a).

c. How would your answer to requirement (a) change if the company switches to the net realizable value method to allocate the joint cost? Explain.

11-76. Effect of By-Product versus Joint Cost Accounting (LO 11-3, 5)
Longwood Corporation processes a liquid into three outputs: K-2, K-4, and K-5. The sales value of each of these products for a single batch follows:

K-2	$579,600
K-4	428,400
K-5	192,000

The joint costs total $850,000. There are no separable production costs. If K-5 is accounted for as a by-product, its sales is credited to the joint manufacturing costs using method 1 described in the text.

Required
a. What are the allocated joint costs for the three outputs
  1. If K-5 is accounted for as a joint product?
  2. If K-5 is accounted for as a by-product?

b. Management does not understand why joint costs are allocated to K-5 differently when it is accounted for as a by-product. Write a brief memo explaining why this occurs.

11-77. Joint Cost Allocation and Product Profitability (LO 11-3, 4)
Elsa Products processes Chem-Z into two products: Chem-A and Chem-B. Chem-Z costs $42,000 per batch. The joint process produces 11,250 units of Chem-A with a market value of $135,000, and 20,000 units of Chem-B with a market value of $33,750. The conversion cost of the joint process is $13,400 per batch. Elsa Products allocates joint costs using the physical quantities method. The company never holds any inventory.

Required

a.   What cost will be the reported (total, not unit) profit for each product using the current method for allocating joint costs?

b.   If the costs of the joint process are allocated on the basis of the net realizable value of the products, what cost will be the reported (total, not unit) profit for each product?

c.   How much will profit at Elsa Products increase or decrease if the company switches to the net realizable value method for allocating joint process costs? Explain.

(LO 11-3, 4)   **11-78. Joint Cost Allocation and Product Profitability**

Hendricks Mining & Manufacturing is a global mineral resource company. At its Taylor site, the company mines and processes three grades of metal—IA, IB, and II—in fixed proportions. The joint costs of mining total $2,550,000. In a typical month, the company will mine 136,000 units of Grade-IA, 204,000 units of Grade-IB, and 68,000 units of Grade-II metal. Market prices have been relatively stable at $15 per unit for Grade-IA, $10 per unit for Grade-IB, and $2.50 per unit for Grade-II. There are no costs to refine the individual grades of metal once it is mined.

Required

a.   What is the reported profitability for each grade assuming the physical quantities method is used to allocate the joint cost of production?

b.   What is the reported profitability for each grade assuming the net realizable value method is used to allocate the joint cost of production?

c.   The marketing manager for Grade-IB comes to you and says that the company is under tremendous price pressure in that market. The marketing manager asks what allocation method would show the lowest cost for Grade-IB. The manager also asks whether treating Grade-II as a by-product would make a difference.

1.   What combination of allocation method and classification of Grade-II product would result in the lowest reported costs for Grade-IB product? (*Hint:* You do not need to do any additional calculations to answer this question.)

2.   Would you recommend the company adopt the method you identify? Explain.

INTEGRATIVE CASE

(LO 11-3, 4)   **11-79. Effect of Cost Allocation on Pricing and Make-versus-Buy Decisions**

Ag-Coop is a large farm cooperative with a number of agriculture-related manufacturing and service divisions. As a cooperative, it pays no federal income taxes. The company owns a fertilizer plant that processes and mixes petrochemical compounds into three brands of agricultural fertilizer: Greenup, Maintane, and Winterizer. The three brands differ with respect to selling price and the proportional content of basic chemicals.

Ag-Coop's Fertilizer Manufacturing Division transfers the completed product to the cooperative's Retail Sales Division at a price based on the cost of each type of fertilizer plus a markup.

The Manufacturing Division is completely automated so that the only costs it incurs are the costs of the petrochemical feedstocks plus overhead that is considered fixed. The primary feedstock costs $1.50 per pound. Each 100 pounds of feedstock can produce either of the following mixtures of fertilizer:

	Output Schedules (in pounds)	
	A	B
Greenup	50	60
Maintane.	30	10
Winterizer	20	30

Production is limited to the 750,000 kilowatt-hours monthly capacity of the dehydrator. Due to different chemical makeup, each brand of fertilizer requires different dehydrator use. Dehydrator usage in kilowatt-hours per pound of product follows:

Product	Kilowatt-Hour Usage per Pound
Greenup	32
Maintane.	20
Winterizer	40

Monthly fixed costs are $81,250. The company currently is producing according to output schedule A. Joint production costs including fixed overhead are allocated to each product on the basis of weight.

The fertilizer is packed into 100-pound bags for sale in the cooperative's retail stores. The sales price for each product charged by the cooperative's Retail Sales Division follows:

	Sales Price per Pound
Greenup	$10.50
Maintane.	9.00
Winterizer	10.40

Selling expenses are 20 percent of the sales price.

The Retail Sales Division manager has complained that the prices charged by the Manufacturing Division are excessive and that he would prefer to purchase from another supplier.

The Manufacturing Division manager argues that the processing mix was determined based on a careful analysis of the costs of each product compared to the prices charged by the Retail Sales Division.

Required

a. Assume that joint production costs including fixed overhead are allocated to each product on the basis of weight. What is the cost per pound of each product, including fixed overhead and the feedstock cost of $1.50 per pound, given the current production schedule?

b. Assume that joint production costs including fixed overhead are allocated to each product on the basis of net realizable value if sold through the cooperative's Retail Sales Division. What is the allocated cost per pound of each product, given the current production schedule?

c. Assume that joint production costs including fixed overhead are allocated to each product on the basis of weight. Which of the two production schedules, A or B, produces the higher operating profit to the firm as a whole?

d. Would your answer to requirement (c) be different if joint production costs including fixed overhead were allocated to each product on the basis of net realizable value? If so, by how much?

SOLUTIONS TO SELF-STUDY QUESTIONS

1. To facilitate solving the problem, first express usage in percentage terms.

	Used by				
Service Center	Personnel	Finance	Building Occupancy	Downtown	Mall
Personnel	—	0.222[a]	0.111	0.444	0.222
Finance	0.133	—	0.010	0.612	0.245
Building Occupancy	0.150	0.100	—	0.300	0.450

[a] 0.222 = 30 ÷ (30 + 15 + 60 + 30). Other computations use the same approach.

Direct method: Use of services by producing departments only.

Service Center	Used by Downtown	Mall
Personnel	0.667[a]	0.333
Finance	0.714[b]	0.286
Building Occupancy	0.400[c]	0.600

[a] 0.667 = 0.444 ÷ (0.444 + 0.222); etc.
[b] 0.714 = 0.612 ÷ (0.612 + 0.245); etc.
[c] 0.400 = 0.300 ÷ (0.300 + 0.450); etc.

Allocation from:	Amount	To Downtown	Mall
Personnel	$202,500	$ 135,000[a]	$ 67,500[a]
Finance	126,000	90,000[b]	36,000[b]
Building Occupancy	150,000	60,000[c]	90,000[c]
Allocated costs		$ 285,000	$193,500
Direct costs		950,000	425,000
Total costs.		$1,235,000	$618,500

[a] $135,000 = $202,500 × 0.667; $67,500 = $202,500 × 0.333
[b] $90,000 = $126,000 × 0.714; $36,000 = $126,000 × 0.286
[c] $60,000 = $150,000 × 0.400; $90,000 = $150,000 × 0.600

2. We can use the analysis in Exhibit 11.6, starting with Administration.

Panel A: Proportions

Service Department	Department's Direct Costs	Information Systems	Administration	Sierra Tract	Cascades Tract	Total
Administration	$5,000,000	20%	–0–%	50%	30%	100%
Information Systems . .	800,000	–0–	–0–	20	80	100
	$5,800,000					

Panel B: Step Method Allocation

From	Cost Allocation to Information Systems	Administration	Sierra Tract	Cascades Tract
Direct costs	$ 800,000	$ 5,000,000	$ –0–	$ –0–
Administration	1,000,000	(5,000,000)	2,500,000	1,500,000
Information Systems	(1,800,000)	–0–	360,000	1,440,000
Total	$ –0–	$ –0–	$2,860,000	$2,940,000

3. We can write the equations for the service department costs as follows:

$$\begin{array}{ccc}
\text{Total service} & = & \text{Direct costs of the} & + & \text{Cost allocated to the} \\
\text{department costs} & & \text{service department} & & \text{service department}
\end{array}$$

$$\begin{aligned}
\text{S1 (Maintenance)} &= \$100{,}000 + 0.30\ \text{S2} \\
\text{S2 (Cafeteria)} &= 17{,}600 + 0.20\ \text{S1}
\end{aligned}$$

Substituting the first equation into the second yields

$$\begin{aligned}
\text{S2} &= \$17{,}600 + 0.20\ (\$100{,}000 + 0.30\ \text{S2}) \\
\text{S2} &= \$17{,}600 + \$20{,}000 + 0.06\ \text{S2} \\
0.94\ \text{S2} &= \$37{,}600 \\
\text{S2} &= \$40{,}000
\end{aligned}$$

Substituting the value of S2 back into the first equation gives

$$\begin{aligned}
\text{S1} &= \$100{,}000 + 0.30\ (\$40{,}000) \\
\text{S1} &= \$112{,}000
\end{aligned}$$

We now use the values for S1 ($112,000) and S2 ($40,000) to allocate costs simultaneously to all the departments, as in Exhibit 11.9.

Panel A: Proportions

Service Department	Department's Total Costs	Maintenance	Cafeteria	Finishing	Assembly	Total
Maintenance	$112,000	–0–%	20%	50%	30%	100%
Cafeteria	40,000	30	–0–	20	50	100
	$152,000					

Panel B: Reciprocal Method Allocation

	Cost Allocation to			
From	Maintenance	Cafeteria	Finishing	Assembly
Direct costs	$100,000	$ 17,600	$ –0–	$ –0–
Maintenance	(112,000)	22,400	56,000	33,600
Cafeteria	12,000	(40,000)	8,000	20,000
Total allocated cost	$ –0–	$ –0–	$ 64,000	$ 53,600
Production department cost . . .			1,200,000	640,000
Total cost.			$1,264,000	$693,600

4. Ten tons of sugar beets yields 2 tons of sugar (10 tons × 0.2) and 4 tons of feed (10 tons × 0.4).

	Sugar	Feed	Total
Final sales value	$800	$800	$1,600
Less additional processing costs	–0–	–0–	–0–
Net realizable value at split-off point.	$800	$800	$1,600
Proportionate share			
$800 ÷ 1,600.	50%		
$800 ÷ 1,600.		50%	
Allocated joint costs			
($60 + $40) × 10 tons × 50%.	$500		
($60 + $40) × 10 tons × 50%.		$500	

5. Subtract the additional processing cost of $200 ($100 per ton × 2 tons) from the net realizable value of the sugar.

	Sugar	Feed	Total
Sales value.	$ 900	$ 800	$1,700
Less additional cost to process sugar beets . . .	200	–0–	200
Estimated net realizable value at split-off	$ 700	$ 800	$1,500
Allocated joint costs			
$\dfrac{\$700}{\$1,500} \times \$1,000 = 46.7\% \times \$1,000$.	467		
$\dfrac{\$800}{\$1,500} \times \$1,000 = 53.3\% \times \$1,000$.		533	1,000
Gross margin	$ 233	$ 267	$ 500
Gross margin as a percent of sales	25.9%	33.3%	29.4%

6. Repeat the analysis for Self-Study Question 4 using physical quantities. Ten tons of sugar beets yield 2 tons of sugar (10 tons × 0.2) and 4 tons of feed (10 tons × 0.4).

	Sugar	Feed	Total
Final quantities.	2 tons	4 tons	6 tons
Proportionate share			
2 tons ÷ 6 tons.	33.3%		
4 tons ÷ 6 tons.		66.7%	
Allocated joint costs			
($60 + $40) × 10 tons × 33.3%.	$ 333		
($60 + $40) × 10 tons × 66.7%.		$ 667	

12

Chapter Twelve

Fundamentals of Management Control Systems

LEARNING OBJECTIVES

After reading this chapter, you should be able to:

LO 12-1 Explain the role of a management control system.

LO 12-2 Identify the advantages and disadvantages of decentralization.

LO 12-3 Describe and explain the basic framework for management control systems, including the relation between organization structure and responsibility centers.

LO 12-4 Understand how managers evaluate performance.

LO 12-5 Analyze the effect of dual- versus single-rate allocation systems.

LO 12-6 Understand the potential link between incentives and illegal or unethical behavior.

LO 12-7 Understand how internal controls can help protect assets.

Morsa Images/Getty Images

The Decision

" *I don't understand these corporate overhead allocations. I'm supposed to meet my budget every quarter, but I never know how much is going to be charged to our operations from headquarters. It's as if I have no control over anything, and it's extremely frustrating. When I question the amounts, I'm told that corporate expenses are incurred to support the divisions. Therefore, the divisions need to be allocated the costs in order to understand the value of the services provided. I know that any "service" I get from corporate, I could get locally for a lot less.* "

Susan Ott, managing director of the European division of Chabot Analytics (CA), was presiding over a meeting of the division's executive committee. CA is a global, U.S.-based consulting firm. The executive committee is made up of the division vice presidents representing the primary staff functions: marketing, operations, finance, and human resources.

The focus of the discussion was the financial summary received earlier that day. Although revenues and most costs were in line with the expected results for the quarter, the division's profit was well below budget. The single largest contributor to the shortfall was the allocation of corporate overhead, which was much higher than expected.

Why a Management Control System?

In the previous chapters, we have considered how information can be developed to help managers make decisions that will increase the organization's performance. For example, better information about the costs of products, customers, and processes can lead to better decisions about pricing, marketing, and operations. Throughout our discussion, the issue has been how the accounting method (for example, activity-based costing) aligns the information that managers receive with the firm's strategy and reflects the underlying economic reality of the business.

> **LO 12-1**
>
> Explain the role of a management control system.

You will notice a change in the nature of the discussion as we describe management control systems. We now explicitly recognize that individuals respond to methods used for performance measurement. Thus, the discussion of the design and use of management control systems considers concepts from human and organizational behavior as well as accounting and economics, although we will be concerned largely with measurement techniques.

As with Chapter 6's coverage of cost management systems, our goal in this chapter is to provide the intuition behind management control systems, not the computational and procedural details. We have three goals in this chapter:

1. To introduce common management control system terms.
2. To introduce a framework for describing and evaluating management control systems.
3. To illustrate some of the ethical issues that arise because of management control systems and to show how internal controls can alleviate some of these issues.

If this is the first time you have studied management control systems, we want you to appreciate why these systems are necessary in all but the smallest organizations. We also want you to understand what the basic issues are and how these systems "fit" the organization. If you have studied management control systems in another course, we want you to step back from the details and consider how these systems help align the goals of the decision makers (the managers) with those of the organization's owners (the shareholders).

Alignment of Managerial and Organizational Interests

An important but generally implicit assumption in our discussion so far is that if given better information, the manager will make better decisions. We have considered the lack of information as the problem to be addressed by the cost management system. In our development of the cost management system, the manager was essentially a machine that processed information and made decisions. If the manager had the "right" information, the manager made the "right" decision.

This focus changes when we discuss management control systems. Managers become "human" and make decisions considering the impact of the decision not only on

the organization but also on their own well-being. In other words, the manager becomes a rational, calculating economic actor who has interests that are not always the same as the organization's. The purpose of the management control system is to align more closely the interests of the manager and the interests of the organization.

Evolution of the Control Problem: An Example

You have decided to start your own business. You have always been interested in accounting (yes, really) and data analytics. While daydreaming in class or at work one day (admit it), you come up with the idea to start your own accounting firm with an emphasis on consulting based on the analysis of data.

Your business has one owner (you), one manager (you), and one worker (you). The decisions that you as the manager make are in the organization's interest, by definition, because you as the manager are also the owner. There is no problem with aligning the interests of the decision maker with those of the owner because they are the same individual and the same interests.

Skip ahead several years. Your small business has been wildly successful. You have developed new services, including software packages that can be purchased. You have formal distribution networks, and you sell your products and services all over the world. Your company's name is Chabot Analytics (CA), and you have people like Susan Ott making decisions for you. You can no longer be sure that the decisions they make are in your interest. The purpose of a management control system is to help you resolve this problem.

Decentralized Organizations

decentralization
Delegation of decision-making authority to a subordinate.

principal–agent relationship
Relationship between a superior, referred to as the *principal,* and a subordinate, called the *agent.*

The manager's task is increasingly difficult as an organization becomes large and complex. Consequently, all but very small organizations delegate managerial duties. The primary managerial responsibility is decision making. **Decentralization** is the delegation of decision-making authority to subordinates in the organization's name.

When authority is decentralized, a superior, whom we call a *principal,* delegates duties to a subordinate, whom we call an *agent.* We find **principal–agent relationships** in many settings, including the following:

Principals	Agents
Southwest Airlines stockholders	Top **Southwest Airlines** management
Corporate **Apple Inc.** managers	Business unit managers (Internet Software and Services)
Citizens	Mayor, governor, and other elected officials
You (as an investor or apartment seeker)	Your stockbroker or real estate agent

centralized
Describes those organizations in which decisions are made by a relatively few individuals in the high ranks of the organization.

decentralized
Describes those organizations in which decisions are spread among relatively many divisional and departmental managers.

A major role of the management control system is to measure the performance of agents (that is, subordinates). For example, accounting information can be used in setting conditions of employment contracts, and employee compensation often is based on accounting performance measures.

Why Decentralize the Organization?

LO 12-2
Identify the advantages and disadvantages of decentralization.

Some organizations are very **centralized;** few decisions are delegated. Many small businesses are good examples of centralized authority with the owner making most or all important decisions. At the other extreme are highly **decentralized** companies in which decisions are delegated to divisional and departmental managers. In many conglomerates, operating decisions are made in the field; corporate headquarters is, in effect, a holding company.

The majority of companies fall between these two extremes. At General Motors, for example, operating units are decentralized, and the research and development (R&D) and finance functions are centralized. Other companies, for example, Johnson & Johnson, decentralize R&D but maintain central control over financing. Many companies begin with a centralized structure but become more and more decentralized as they grow.

As we have emphasized throughout the book, good decisions require good information. In large organizations, especially those that are geographically dispersed, much of the information needed to make the decision is local; that is, it is specific to the local conditions. For example, McDonald's Corporation solicits ideas from franchisees for new menu items that are likely to reflect international and regional taste differences. Although centralization of key decisions about the McDonald's experience is an important part of its standardization strategy, supporting some local variations can capitalize on local knowledge and allow franchisees to earn more than would otherwise be possible. **Local knowledge** is knowledge about these local conditions.

local knowledge
Information about local conditions, markets, regulations, and so on.

Advantages of Decentralization

The larger and more complex an organization is, the more advantages decentralization offers. Some of these advantages follow:

- *Better use of local knowledge.* As companies grow, more and more local knowledge needs to be processed in order to manage the business. It is unlikely that top managers have this local knowledge (for example, the business regulations of a particular country). By delegating decision-making authority to local managers, top managers are delegating decision making to the managers more likely to possess this local knowledge.

- *Faster response.* Local managers can react to a changing environment more quickly than top management can. With centralized decision making, delays occur while information is transmitted to decision makers, and further delays occur while instructions are communicated to local managers.

- *Wiser use of top management's time.* Just as local managers have better information about local conditions, top managers have better knowledge about strategic issues and industry trends. Delegation of many decisions allows top managers to focus on strategic decisions.

- *Reduction of problems to manageable size.* The complexity of problems that humans can solve has limits. Even with the aid of computers, some problems are too complex to be solved by central management. By dividing large problems into smaller, more manageable parts, decentralization reduces the complexity of problems.

- *Training, evaluation, and motivation of local managers.* Decentralization allows managers to receive on-the-job training in decision making. Top management can observe the outcome of local managers' decisions and evaluate their potential for advancement. By practicing with small decisions, managers learn how to make big ones. In addition, ambitious managers are likely to be frustrated if they only implement the decisions of others and never have the satisfaction of making their own decisions and carrying them out. This satisfaction can be an important motivational reward for managers.

Disadvantages of Decentralization

Decentralization has disadvantages as well.

- *Dysfunctional decision making.* The major disadvantage is that local managers can make decisions that are not in the best interests of the organization's top managers and the owners (shareholders). Thus, decentralized companies incur the cost of monitoring and controlling the activities of local managers. They incur the costs that result when local managers make decisions and take actions that are not in the best interests of the organization. **Dysfunctional decision making** is the situation in which local managers make decisions in their interests, which can differ from those of the organization.

dysfunctional decision making
Decisions made in the interests of local managers that are not in the interests of the organization.

- *Administrative duplication.* A second cost of decentralization is administrative duplication. Often in decentralized firms, local managers make the same types of decisions that are being made at headquarters. For example, there could be separate personnel offices, each with its own personnel manager, duplicating many of the same functions.

- *Incomplete information.* A third cost of decentralization is the possibility of poor decisions based on incomplete information. While local information creates a benefit to local decision making, many decisions made at the local level also affect other parts of the firm. For example, division managers unaware of how a decision could affect another business unit might make a decision that is best for their division (and the manager) but damages another unit. Even with the best of intentions and with aligned incentives to pursue what is best for the business unit and the firm, incomplete information can make it difficult to make decisions that have global consequences on the basis of local information alone.

Both the advantages and disadvantages of decentralization listed above must be considered by managers when deciding the level that is economically optimal for the organization. One can assume that the disadvantages of decentralization for highly centralized organizations outweigh the advantages, while the reverse is true for decentralized companies. The optimal level of decentralization is not static. It will change as the organization and the environment change.

The advantages (disadvantages) of centralization mirror the disadvantages (advantages) of decentralization. For example, centralization fails to make use of local knowledge but does not suffer from dysfunctional decision making. We focus on management control systems in decentralized systems because the control problem arises when owners delegate decision making to subordinates.

Business Application   Centralizing as a Cost-Cutting Approach

One of the disadvantages of decentralization discussed in the text is the possibility of increased costs (perhaps because of duplication of effort) that can occur. Some firms have realized this and have centralized certain functions. For example, Pernod Ricard SA (a French beverage company) purchases casks for many of its different products. Initially, casks were purchased separately for each of the brands. However, the company decided to centralize the purchase of casks from a central location in the U.S. The move

> . . . helped the company shave off 2% to 3% of expenses tied to indirect procurement. . . .

Other companies that have centralized certain business activities include PayPal, Inc. and the Royal Bank of Canada.

In addition to the savings from centralizing the service function,

> [m]any companies also opt to place these hubs offshore in lower-cost countries, which can save 20% to 35%. . . .

However, not all companies believe that centralizing functions is the right choice for their organization. For example, Huntington Ingalls Industries, Inc., a military shipbuilding company, has three separate units, each with their own services.

> Our philosophy is to have clear accountability to each of those sector presidents for their profit and loss, and that includes programmatic and financial performance. . . .

Many companies, even those that choose to centralize, recognize that there are lost opportunities when, for example, finance staff are not located with operating managers. As one manager notes,

> [i]t's not all positive. . . . Certainly you get efficiencies, but you also lose connectivity.

Finally, there are other risks associated with centralization, especially to locations away from primary company operations. As described in the Business Application "The Risks of Outsourcing a Service Center," in Chapter 11, when unexpected events (such as the pandemic in 2020) arise, there may be regulatory or logistical issues in maintaining adequate services to the operating units.

Source: Shumsky, Tatyana, and Nina Trentmann, "Finance Chiefs Centralize to Cut Costs, Make Smarter Decisions," *The Wall Street Journal*, October 3, 2017.

Framework for Evaluating Management Control Systems

Once an organization has decided to decentralize, it is important to develop a system to reduce the impact of dysfunctional decision making. This system is called a **management control system,** which is the structure and procedures that the principals (owners) use to influence agents (managers) of the organization to implement the organization's strategies.[1]

As we describe and evaluate components of the management control system in the following chapters, we need a framework that can be used consistently and applied in different settings. Unlike our evaluation of cost management systems, we cannot look solely at the effect of information on decisions. We have to anticipate the decisions that subordinates will make and determine whether their interests are aligned with those of the organization.

> **LO 12-3**
> Describe and explain the basic framework for management control systems, including the relation between organization structure and responsibility centers.

> **management control system**
> System to influence subordinates to act in the organization's interests.

Organizational Environment and Strategy

An appropriate management control system depends on the environment in which the organization operates. This environment is defined by regulations, customs, and industry characteristics, among other factors. In other words, the purpose of the managerial control system is to influence managers operating in a particular environment.

The management control system is also based on the organization's strategy. If the firm's strategy is to be a leader in new product development, for example, the management control system should influence local managers to take actions that promote that strategy. We would expect the management control system in such a firm to be different from the management control system in a firm that is pursuing a strategy of low cost.

Results of the Management Control System

A successful management control system results in higher organization value such as higher share prices. In general, the "right" management control system will lead to the attainment of the organization's goals as articulated in its strategy. The role of the management control system, then, is to provide procedures and practices in an organization that will ensure that organization members work to achieve the best results possible given the strategy and the business environment.

---

[1] This definition is similar to that of Robert N. Anthony, *The Managerial Control Function* (Boston: Harvard Business School Press, 1988), who placed management control between strategic planning on the one hand and task control on the other.

Elements of a Management Control System

Organizational economics is the study of how firms are structured and operated. From the organizational economics literature, management control systems consist of three elements:[2]

1. Delegated decision authority.
2. Performance evaluation and measurement systems.
3. Compensation and reward systems.

delegated decision authority
Specification of the authority to make decisions in the organization's name.

performance evaluation system
System and specification of how the subordinate will be evaluated.

compensation and reward system
System that specifies how the subordinate will be compensated for his or her performance based on a stated measure of performance.

Delegated Decision Authority   The essence of decentralization is **delegated decision authority,** which specifies what decisions the subordinate manager can make in the name of the organization. For example, a division manager could be given the authority to make marketing decisions for the division. These decisions can change over time, but the organization retains the authority for certain other decisions that the local manager is not authorized to make. For example, the same division manager might not have the authority to name the division controller.

Performance Evaluation and Measurement Systems   The **performance evaluation system** specifies how the performance of the subordinate manager is to be measured and how the results of the measurement will be used in evaluating the manager. As you will see in later chapters, performance measures do not have to be financial. They do not even need to be objective. However, our primary focus in this book is on financial and objective (measurable) performance measures. For example, a common example of a performance measure for a division manager is divisional accounting income. Other common measures include costs and various financial ratios, which can be computed in different ways. Common nonfinancial measures include customer satisfaction ratings, defect rates, and delivery times.

Although we focus on financial measures in the next several chapters, we discuss the use of nonfinancial measures in Chapter 18. There, we also discuss subjective performance measures and the implications of using subjective performance measures. We will have less to say about subjective measures because, by their nature, they are more difficult to define in an explicit way.

In public schools, teachers are often evaluated on the performance of their students, and these evaluations can affect teacher compensation through promotion opportunities and tenure. An important public policy question is whether this management control system is effective in attaining educational goals. *Inti St Clair/Digital Vision/Getty Images*

Compensation and Reward Systems   The third element in the management control system is the **compensation and reward system** that defines how the subordinate manager will be paid for their performance. Compensation consists of explicit rewards such as salary and cash bonus, the award of stock or stock options, and perquisites (for example, club memberships). Compensation also includes rewards that are not explicit, such as improved promotion opportunities, the respect of peers and superiors, and general recognition.

Balancing the Elements

An effective, well-functioning management control system balances these three elements and defines them consistently. In the chapters that follow, we present many examples of effective (and ineffective) control systems. Before we describe the elements in more detail, consider the following simple example.

---

[2] See, for example, P. Milgrom and J. Roberts, *Economics, Organization, and Management* (Upper Saddle River, NJ: Prentice-Hall, 1992).

You are the manager of a local retail outlet of a national chain, such as CVS, Lowe's, or Dollar General. You have been delegated the authority to decide how much inventory of each item to order every week (delegated decision authority). Your performance will be measured by the flip of a coin: Heads means good performance and tails means poor performance (performance measurement and evaluation system). Your compensation consists of a straight (fixed) salary, regardless of performance (above a bare minimum), plus a bonus if your performance is "good" (compensation and reward system). Is this management control system effective?

Although the answer seems obvious, we can use the structure just presented to specify exactly what is wrong. Presumably, the goal of the organization is to make money (or at least sell merchandise). As the store manager, you can affect that by making good decisions about the amount and type of inventory to order. The purpose of the management control system is to influence you to make decisions that further the organization's goal. However, because the performance measure (the coin flip) is completely independent of your decisions, it cannot motivate you to make better decisions. The three elements of the management control system are not consistent; that is, they are not balanced.

Delegated Decision Authority: Responsibility Accounting

The cost accounting system in an organization supports the management control system by structuring accounts to reflect the delegation of decision authority. This structure is then used to evaluate the performance of managers in decentralized units. The use of accounting for performance evaluation is often called **responsibility accounting.** It classifies organization units (such as a division, a region, or a store) into centers based on the decision authority delegated to the center's manager.

The four basic kinds of decentralized units are

responsibility accounting
System of reporting tailored to an organizational structure so that costs and revenues are reported at the level within the organization having the related responsibility.

- Cost centers
- Revenue centers
- Profit centers
- Investment centers

The responsibility accounting classification is useful because it suggests the type of performance measure appropriate for a center.

Cost Centers

Managers of **cost centers** are responsible for the cost of an activity for which a well-defined relationship exists between inputs and outputs. Cost centers often are found in manufacturing operations where inputs, such as direct materials and direct labor, can be specified for each output. The production departments of manufacturing plants are examples of cost centers. The concept has been applied in nonmanufacturing settings as well. In banks, for example, standards can be established for check processing, so check-processing departments could be cost centers. In hospitals, food service departments, laundries, and laboratories often are set up as cost centers.

cost center
Organization subunit responsible only for costs.

Managers of cost centers are held responsible for the costs and volumes of inputs used to produce an output. Often these costs and volumes are determined by someone other than the cost center manager, such as the marketplace, top management, or the marketing department. A plant manager often is given a production schedule to meet as efficiently as possible. If the plant is operated as a cost center, manufacturing cost variances typically are used to help measure performance. (See Exhibit 12.1 for how a typical cost center appears on the organization chart.)

Exhibit 12.1
Organizational Structure
and Responsibility
Centers

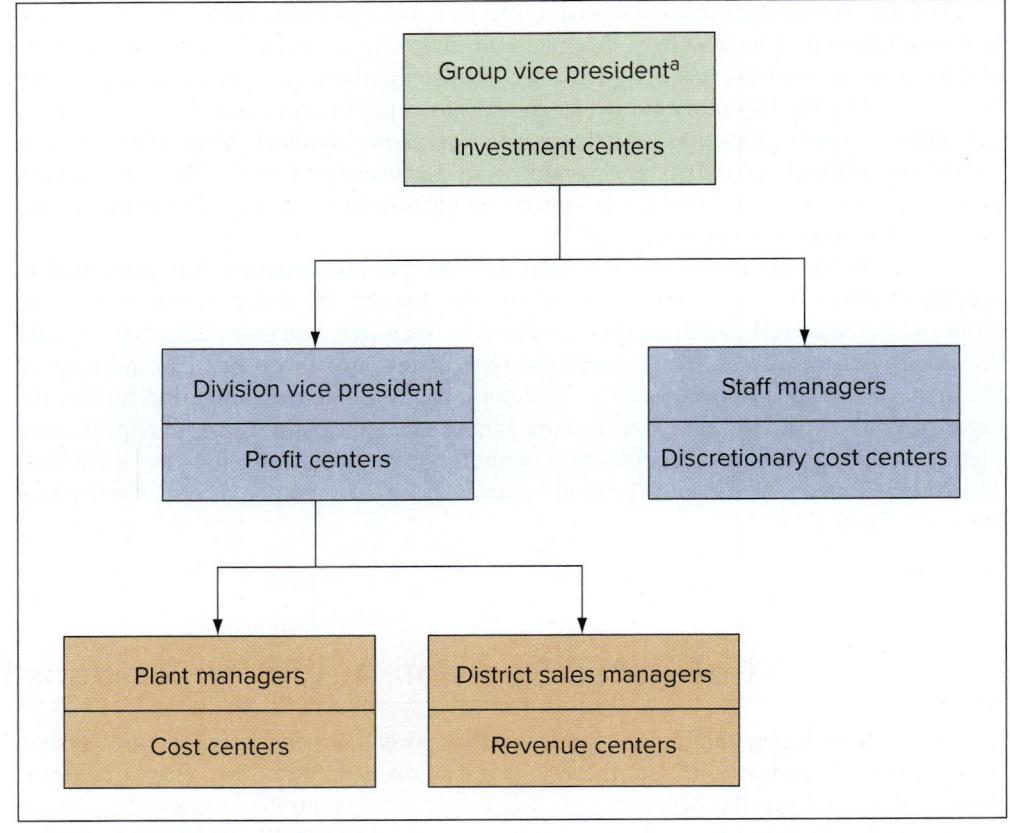

^a *Group* refers to a group of divisions.

standard cost center
Organization subunit whose
managers are held responsible
for costs and in which the
relationship between costs and
output is well defined.

discretionary cost center
Organization subunit whose
managers are held responsible
for costs where the relationship
between costs and outputs is
not well established.

revenue center
Organization subunit
responsible for revenues and,
typically, marketing costs.

profit center
Organization subunit
responsible for profits and thus
revenues, costs, production,
and sales volumes.

investment center
Organization subunit
responsible for profits and
investment in assets.

If the relationship between costs and outputs can be specified, the unit is called a **standard cost center.** When managers are held responsible for costs but the input–output relationship is not well specified, a **discretionary cost center** is established. Legal, accounting, R&D, advertising, and many other administrative and marketing departments are usually discretionary cost centers (for example, see Exhibit 12.1). Discretionary cost centers also are common in government and other nonprofit organizations whose budgets are used as a ceiling on expenditures. Managers are often evaluated on bases other than costs. However, penalties usually exist for exceeding the budget ceiling.

Revenue Centers

Managers of **revenue centers** typically are responsible for selling a product. Consequently, the manager is held responsible for sales price or sales activity variances. An example of a revenue center is the sportswear department of a large department store for which the manager is responsible for merchandise sales.

Profit Centers

Managers of **profit centers** are held accountable for profits. They manage both revenues and costs (see Exhibit 12.1). For example, Home Depot could operate its warehouses as cost centers but its retail stores as profit centers. Managers of profit centers have more autonomy than do managers of cost or revenue centers.

Investment Centers

Managers of **investment centers** have responsibility for profits and investment in assets. These managers have relatively large amounts of money with which to make capital budgeting and other decisions affecting the use of assets. For example, cost center managers are often restricted as to the amount of money they can invest in assets (perhaps $5,000), while investment center managers can make acquisitions costing up to $500,000 without higher approval. Investment centers are evaluated using some measure of profit related to the invested assets in the center.

Responsibility Centers and Organization Structure

The type of responsibility center is closely related to the manager's position in the organization structure (see Exhibit 12.1). For the company shown, plant managers run cost centers, and district sales managers (vice presidents) operate revenue centers. Moving up the organization chart, we find division managers (vice presidents) have responsibility for profits and are in charge of both plant managers and district sales managers.

Of course, every company is organized uniquely (in some highly decentralized companies, manufacturing plants are profit centers, for example). However, it is generally true that profit or investment centers with a broader scope of authority and responsibility are found at higher levels in an organization.

Measuring Performance

Total **goal congruence** exists when all members of an organization have incentives to perform in the common interest. This occurs when the group acts as a team in pursuit of a mutually agreed-upon objective. Individual goal congruence occurs when an individual's personal goals are congruent with organizational goals.

In most business settings, however, personal goals and organizational goals differ. Performance evaluation and incentive systems are designed to encourage employees to behave as if their goals were congruent with organization goals. This results in **behavioral congruence;** that is, an individual behaves in the best interests of the organization regardless of his or her own goals.

You have experienced behavioral congruence in your education. Examinations, homework, and the entire grading process are parts of a performance evaluation and incentive system that encourages students to behave in a certain manner. Sometimes the system appears to encourage the wrong kind of behavior, however. For example, if the goal of education is to encourage students to learn, they might be better off taking very difficult courses. But if students' grades suffer when they take difficult courses, they could have an incentive to take easier courses. As a result, some students take difficult courses and learn more but jeopardize their grade point averages while others take easier courses in an attempt to earn better grades but learn less.

The same problem occurs with managers in units of a firm. The firm can prosper if managers take risks in developing new products. But if the manager's performance is measured by net income, for example, their performance could suffer relative to that of other managers who do not take these same risks.

Just as some managers might have monetary incentives to not take risks that might benefit the firm, other managers have incentives to take "excessive risks" that could threaten the existence of a firm. The 2020 guilty plea by the Malaysia subsidiary of Goldman Sachs in the 1MDB scandal is an example of such excessive risks. As a part of the settlement, Goldman agreed to pay over $5 billion in fees and penalties. It also took back $174 million from executives who received compensation from the firm.[3]

goal congruence
Agreement by all members of a group on a common set of objectives.

behavioral congruence
Alignment of individual behavior with the best interests of the organization regardless of the individual's own goals.

---

[3] Liz Hoffman, "Goldman Sachs Malaysia Subsidiary Pleads Guilty in 1MDB Case," *The Wall Street Journal,* October 22, 2020; Dylan Tokar, "Goldman Promises Greater Scrutiny of Senior Execs Following 1MDB Settlement," *The Wall Street Journal,* October 22, 2020; Liz Hoffman and Dave Michaels, "Goldman Pays Billions—and Takes Millions from Top Execs—to End 1MDB Scandal," *The Wall Street Journal,* October 23, 2020.

Similar problems occur in all organizations. Consider the case of a division manager who believes a promotion and bonus will be given if the plant has high operating profits. If the manager invests in the development of division employees by sending them to executive education classes, short-run profits will be lower, but the company could be better off in the long run. The manager must decide between doing what makes performance look good in the short run and doing what is in the best interest of the company in the long run.

Although such conflicts cannot be totally removed, they can be minimized if they are recognized. To deal with the problem just described, some companies budget training and education separately. Others encourage employees to take a long-run interest in the company through stock option and pension plans tied to long-run performance. Still others retain employees in a position long enough that any short-term counterproductive actions catch up with them.

Two Basic Questions

Managers must answer two basic questions when thinking about their performance evaluation systems:

1. Does the measure reflect the results of those actions that improve the organization's performance?
2. What actions might managers be taking that improve reported performance but are actually detrimental to organizational performance?

As we go about daily life, we see many instances in which performance evaluation systems do not create the appropriate incentives because managers have not satisfactorily answered these two questions. We also see many cases in which people work hard and make the right decisions despite the lack of explicit rewards. Ideally, organization managers should design performance evaluation systems to reward people when they do the right thing. At the most basic level, managers should design systems that do not punish people for doing the right thing.

Cost Centers

The performance of cost centers, such as plants, is typically measured based on the costs incurred. As we will see in Chapters 16 and 17, it is useful to consider the level of output because cost center managers generally do not have the decision-making authority to determine output levels.

It is often more difficult to define performance measures for discretionary cost centers, which include research and development, accounting, and so on, because it is difficult to tie costs to output. For the same reason, it is difficult to evaluate the performance of a discretionary cost center manager. Companies have tried numerous methods to determine appropriate relationships between discretionary costs and activity levels and to compare these costs and activity levels with other firms. Relating costs to activity levels remains primarily a matter of management judgment or discretion. Consequently, managers of discretionary cost centers are typically given a budget and instructed not to exceed it without higher-level authorization. In most governmental units, it is against the law to exceed the budget without obtaining authorization from a legislative body (e.g., Congress, the state legislature, or the city council).

Such situations can invite suboptimal behavior. Managers have incentives to spend all of their budgets even if some savings could be achieved in order to support their request for the same or higher budgets in the following year. Furthermore, often no well-specified relationship exists between the quality of services and their costs. (Would the quality of research and development decrease 10 percent with a 10 percent cut in funds? Would crime increase 10 percent if police department funds were cut 10 percent?)

Ideally, performance should be measured in a well-specified way by comparing actual inputs to standard inputs in a cost center. It is very difficult and costly, however, to measure the performance of the manager and workers in a discretionary cost center. Thus, it also is difficult to provide incentives for employees to perform at the levels that best achieve organization goals.

Revenue Centers

Revenue centers are less common than cost centers or profit centers. The obvious performance measure is the amount of revenue earned. If the manager of the revenue center has decision authority over marketing or sales expenditures, an alternative measure would be the contribution of the center: the difference between the center's revenues and costs.

Profit Centers

Decentralized organizations depend heavily on profit measures to evaluate the performance of decentralized units and their managers. Due to the difficulties of measuring profits, many companies have tried to use multiple performance measures. In the early 1950s, General Electric proposed an extensive and innovative performance measurement system that evaluated market position, productivity, product leadership, personnel development, employee attitudes, public responsibility, and balance between short-range and long-range goals in addition to profitability. Even when a company uses a broad range of performance measures, however, accounting results continue to play an important role in performance evaluation. A commonly heard adage is that "hard" measures of performance tend to drive out "soft" measures. Nevertheless, no accounting measure can fully measure the performance of an organizational unit or its manager.

In profit centers, we encounter the usual problems related to measuring profits for the company as a whole plus an important additional one: How are the company's revenues and costs allocated to each profit center? A profit center that is totally separate from all other parts of the company operates like an autonomous company. The profits of that type of center can be uniquely identified with it.

A completely independent profit center is a highly unusual case, however. Most profit centers have costs (and perhaps revenues) in common with other units. The profit center could share facilities with other units or use headquarters staff services, as does the European division of Chabot Analytics (CA) in the chapter opening example. If so, the company faces a cost allocation problem (see the discussion later in the chapter of how we might improve the management control system at CA).

A related problem involves the transfer of goods or services between a profit center and other parts of the organization. Such transfers must be priced so that the profit center manager has incentives to trade with other units when it is in the organization's best interests. Chapter 15 discusses this transfer pricing problem in more detail.

No easy ways to determine how to measure performance in a profit center exist. Much is left to managerial judgment. No matter what process is chosen, its objectives should be straightforward: Measure employees' performance in ways that motivate them to work in the best interests of their employers and compare that performance to standards or budget plans.

Investment Centers

Investment center managers have decision authority that affects revenues and costs and, hence, profits, but they also have authority as to asset usage. As you will see in Chapter 14, effective performance measures for investment centers, commonly called *business units,* combine both a measure of profit and a measure of asset usage.

Evaluating Performance

LO 12-4
Understand how managers evaluate performance.

Once the organization has measured a manager's performance, how does it determine whether the performance was "good"? For example, suppose that Susan Ott, the managing director of the European division of CA, showed a quarterly loss of $100,000. How would you evaluate her performance?

Relative Performance versus Absolute Performance Standards

A company often is tempted to compare the performance of its centers and even to encourage competition among them. As you will see, the problems inherent in performance measurement complicate such comparisons. In addition, the various centers can be in very different businesses. It is difficult to compare the performance of a manufacturing center with the performance of a center that provides a consulting service and has a relatively small investment base. Investment centers operating in different countries face different risks. When comparing the performance of investment centers, all such differences should be considered.

When diverse centers exist, management frequently establishes target levels of performance for the individual investment centers. We discuss appropriate measures for investment centers in Chapter 14, but suppose for now that performance is measured as division income. The center might be evaluated by comparing the actual division income with the target income. It sometimes makes more sense to compare the income of an investment center with that of a company in the same industry than to compare it with that of other investment centers in the company.

Evaluating Managers' Performance versus Economic Performance of the Responsibility Center

The evaluation of a manager is not necessarily identical to the evaluation of the cost, profit, or investment center. As a general rule, managers are evaluated based on a comparison of actual results to targets. A manager who is asked to take over a marginal operation and turn it around could be given a minimal income target that is consistent with the division's past performance. A manager who meets or exceeds that target would be rewarded. However, it could be that, even with the best management, a division cannot be turned around. Thus, it is entirely possible that the center would be disbanded even though the manager had received a highly positive evaluation. A company should be willing to abandon a bad operation if a better use can be made of company resources. However, top management would like to reward the manager who performs well in an adverse situation. Today, the **controllability concept** is widely used as a basis for managerial performance evaluation.

controllability concept
Idea that managers should be held responsible for costs or profits over which they have decision-making authority.

An interesting problem arises in implementing this concept in a currently operating division. How does one evaluate the performance of a manager who takes over an existing division whose assets, operating structure, and markets are established prior to the manager's arrival at the helm? The new manager cannot control the assets that are on hand or the markets in which the division operates when they take over. However, in time, the new manager can change all of these factors.

As a general rule, evaluating the manager on the basis of performance targets, as suggested earlier in this chapter, overcomes this problem. The new manager establishes a plan for operating the division and works with top management to set targets for the future. Those targets are compared to actual results as the plan is enacted, and the manager is evaluated based on those results. In short, the longer the manager is at the division, the more responsibility the manager takes for its success.

Relative Performance Evaluations in Organizations

A major issue in evaluating divisional performance is the separation of performance results that are controllable by division managers from the effect of environmental factors that are outside their control. As the previous section noted, division managers are generally held accountable for meeting or exceeding targets established for that particular division. However, these targets are often independent of the manager's performance as compared to those of peers (e.g., other divisions operating in similar product markets). **Relative performance evaluation (RPE)** addresses this issue by comparing managers of one division to their peers. A division earning a 10 percent profit margin would be evaluated more favorably if the peers averaged 5 percent instead of 20 percent, for example.

The purpose of RPE is to go beyond setting internal targets (for example, divisional return on investment) and compare managers or divisions to other comparable divisions. It is possible for a division to meet or exceed its internal targets yet to perform much worse than its peer group. The only way to identify such a problem is to compare the division with its peers.

relative performance evaluation (RPE)
Managerial evaluation method that compares divisional performance with that of peer group divisions (i.e., divisions operating in similar product markets).

Compensation Systems

Our focus in this book is on measurement, so we describe the characteristics of compensation systems that are important for our discussion of management control systems. Because managers are free to leave to join other organizations, the firm needs to pay them the equivalent of the best alternative offer. We assume, therefore, that if the manager is willing to work for the organization, the pay is "sufficient."

An effective management control system provides the appropriate incentives for the manager to make decisions in the organization's best interests. The compensation system has to reward the manager for measured performance to provide sufficient incentives to influence the manager's decisions. We can classify the compensation into two categories: fixed compensation and contingent compensation. **Fixed compensation** is paid to the manager independent of measured performance. A good example of fixed compensation is salary. **Contingent compensation** is the amount of compensation that is paid based on measured performance. An example of contingent compensation is the commission paid to the sales staff.

An important design feature of the management control system is the mix of fixed and contingent compensation. If the proportion of contingent compensation is too small, its incentive effect will not be sufficient to motivate the manager to make the decisions intended by the control system. If, instead, the proportion of contingent compensation is too large, the manager will view his compensation as being too risky. In this case, the firm will have to compensate the manager for bearing the risk, but this will be inefficient. Because the shareholders can diversify, they are better able to bear risks than the manager, who cannot diversify as easily.

The compensation system also is used to better align the risk preferences of the manager and the firm. Consider the case of the firm that would benefit from the manager's risky investment in new products as described earlier. By including stock options in the manager's compensation, the firm gives them an incentive to adopt risky projects. With an option, the manager benefits if the product succeeds but does not risk any compensation if the product fails. As the Business Application "Beware of the 'Kink'" shows, designers of compensation plans have to avoid situations where small changes in a performance measure (firm profit, for example) lead to large changes in contingent compensation. The reason is that it is in these situations that managers have the most to gain from difficult-to-detect manipulations of the performance measure.

Perquisites, such as the use of a corporate jet, are important components of executive compensation. *Miles Schuster/ Purestock/Superstock*

fixed compensation
Compensation that is not directly linked to measured performance.

contingent compensation
Compensation that is based on measured performance.

A common approach to linking compensation with perfor-mance at the executive level is to pay a bonus for perfor-mance that exceeds some level. For example, in a typical bonus plan, the company pays into a bonus pool a fixed per-centage of income (for example, 5 percent) if income achieves a particular level (target). Such a plan is shown in the following illustration:

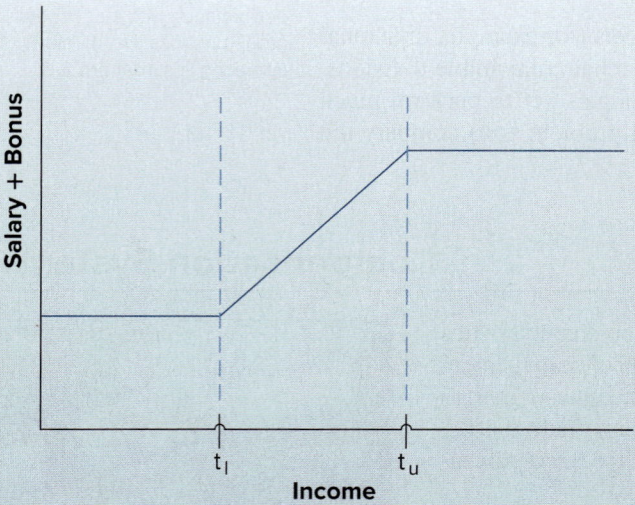

The manager is paid a salary for income below the target, t_l. For income above t_l, the manager is paid the salary plus a bonus. It is common in these plans to pay a maximum bonus so that for income above t_u, no additional bonus, above the maximum, is paid.

The thresholds, t_l and t_u, can lead to dysfunctional behav-ior on the part of managers.

If income is slightly below t_l, the manager has strong incentives to take actions to get income above t_l. On the other hand, if income is far below t_l, the manager has no incentive to increase income and could, in fact, make decisions that defer recognizing income until the next period.

For income above t_u, the manager's incentive is to defer income and recognize it in the next period. The manager could, for example, ask customers to defer orders. Again, these deci-sions are not in the interest of the firm, but they result from the incentives in the management control system.

Using data from 94 large U.S. firms, one researcher found evidence consistent with managers altering accounting accrual decisions in years when the upper or lower threshold was bind-ing. That is, managers tended to adopt income-decreasing accru-als when the thresholds were binding and income-increasing accruals when income was between the two thresholds.

If there are thresholds, one recommendation is to set them so they are unlikely to be close to the actual outcomes. In this way, they are unlikely to distort the manager's decisions.

Sources: Healy, Paul, "The Effect of Bonus Schemes on Accounting Decisions," *Journal of Accounting and Economics* vol. 7, September 1984, pp. 85–107; Jensen, Michael, "Corporate Budgeting Is Broken—Let's Fix it," *Harvard Business Review* vol. 79, no. 10, November 2001, pp. 95–104.

Self-Study Question

2. In some firms, manufacturing plants are cost centers, and in others, they are profit centers. Both approaches can represent effective management control systems. How do you explain this?

The solution to this question is at the end of the chapter.

Illustration: Corporate Cost Allocation

LO 12-5

Analyze the effect of dual- versus single-rate allocation systems.

In the discussion of cost allocation in the previous chapters, the focus was on providing better information to managers making decisions. If the cost allocations are used in part to measure performance, the cost accountant has to consider the role of cost allocation in the management control system. As illustrated in the opening to the chapter, one role of cost allocation is to assign corporate support costs (staff functions, for example) to operating units.

Before we describe and evaluate the allocation process, it is helpful to ask why companies assign some or all of the corporate overhead to individual units. The Business Application "Why Allocate Corporate Costs?" mentions seven reasons identified by executives:

1. Reflect costs to the correct responsibility center.
2. Provide information on the cost of service.
3. Facilitate awareness of cost control.
4. Tax or regulatory reasons.
5. Encourage proper use of corporate services.
6. Reduce costs for corporate results.
7. Other external reporting reasons.

It is important to keep these reasons in mind as we evaluate alternative allocation methods. As with the discussion of allocation in the cost management systems discussion of Chapters 6–11, the effectiveness of a method depends on how the information generated will be used.

Why Allocate Corporate Costs? *Business Application*

Corporate cost allocation is practiced widely, but why do firms use it, and how effective is it? McKinsey & Company, the global consulting firm, conducted a survey of 30 senior managers of firms of various sizes. Of the 30 surveyed, 29 reported allocating some, if not all, of the corporate costs. They then asked the managers how effective their allocation process was in meeting certain objectives. The results are summarized in the following table:

Reason for Allocation	Percentage of Firms Allocating for this Reason	Percentage of Firms for Which the Allocation was "Very Effective" in Meeting the Goal
1. Reflect costs to correct profit-and-loss line based on usage	79%	41%
2. Provide transparency on true cost of service	69	28
3. Facilitate meaning dialogue on cost control	48	21
4. Tax and regulatory reasons	45	58
5. Drive correct behavior in using centralized service	38	15
6. Reduce burden on central P&L	21	33
7. External reporting (other than tax or regulatory)	10	16

Source: Edlich, Alexander, Kyle Hawke, Alison Watson, and Ed Woodcock, "Who Should Pay for Support Functions," McKinsey & Company, January 23, 2017. Available at https://www.mckinsey.com/business-functions/operations/our-insights/who-should-pay-for-support-functions#

Why was the allocation not effective? For many firms, the allocation process was "too simple." In about 50 percent of the cases, the firms were employing a single allocation method, using as a basis "the percentage of enterprise revenues or head count." In other cases, the methods were "too complex" and resulted in measuring and tracking efforts that were not worth the additional detail.

The authors summarized their research with three conclusions:

1. Allocate costs as required for compliance.

2. Allocate in a way that local managers have incentives to manage costs.

3. Allocate costs to encourage decisions that relate to the units' revenues and cost.

Source: Edlich, Alexander, Kyle Hawke, Alison Watson, and Ed Woodcock, "Who Should Pay for Support Functions," McKinsey & Company, January 23, 2017. Available at https://www.mckinsey.com/business-functions/operations/our-insights/who-should-pay-for-support-functions#

Exhibit 12.2

Partial Income
Statement—European
Division, Chabot
Accounting

	A	B	C
1	**CHABOT ANALYTICS**		
2	**European Division**		
3	**Income for the Year**		
4	**($000)**		
5			
6		Actual	Target
7	Sales revenue	$ 70,000	$ 70,000
8	(Percentage of corporate revenue)	16%	14%
9	Direct division cost	$ 51,800	$ 51,800
10	Division margin*	$ 18,200	$ 18,200
11	Allocated corporate overhead	$ 4,800	$ 3,500
12	Operating profit	$ 13,400	$ 14,700
13			
14	*Division margin = Division revenues − Division direct costs.		
15			

Incentive Problems with Allocated Costs

We illustrate the link between cost allocation and management control by returning to the case of Susan Ott, the managing director of the European division of Chabot Accounting (CA). Susan is meeting again with her managers to discuss the issue of corporate cost allocation. See Exhibit 12.2 for an abbreviated income statement and target for the European division. The source of Susan's frustration is clear from looking at the statement. Actual revenues and division direct costs are exactly at the target level, but operating profit, the measure used to assess her performance, shows a $1.3 million shortfall. All of this difference is due to the corporate overhead allocation.

CA allocates corporate overhead to the divisions based on relative revenues. The target revenue for Europe was $70 million, which was 14 percent of corporate revenues, so the target corporate revenue must have been $500 million (= $70,000,000 ÷ 14%). Similarly, the target corporate cost for support functions at the corporate headquarters must have been $25 million (= $3,500,000 ÷ 14%).

The actual corporate revenue was $437.5 million (= $70 million ÷ 16%), and actual corporate overhead was $30 million (= $4.8 million ÷ 16%). The corporate cost allocated to the European division is above target for two reasons:

- The percentage of firm revenues earned by the European division is higher than targeted.
- Corporate costs are higher than targeted.

The management control system is not effective because the manager being measured by the corporate cost allocation (Susan) is not the manager who has the decision-making authority to influence those costs. In other words, Susan does not have control over corporate costs (or revenues from other divisions), so she does not have control over her performance measure.

Effective Corporate Cost Allocation System

An effective cost allocation system ensures that the performance of managers who have decision-making authority over factors that affect the costs will be measured by the costs. At CA, a study determined that expected (or target) corporate costs consisted of a fixed portion ($15 million) and a portion that varied with revenue. The estimated rate for the latter was 2 percent of revenue. Therefore, targeted corporate overhead could be expressed as

dual-rate method
Cost allocation method that separates a common cost into fixed and variable components and then allocates each component using a different allocation base.

$$\text{Corporate overhead} = \$15 \text{ million} + 2\% \times \text{Revenue}$$

Accountants often use the dual-rate method when common costs have both a fixed and a variable component. Under a **dual-rate method,** fixed and variable costs are allocated using different allocation bases. We can examine the dual-rate method by applying it to our CA example. To determine the appropriate bases and rates, consider the four reasons why allocated actual corporate overhead at CA varies from the target:

1. Actual fixed costs are different from targeted fixed costs.
2. The actual variable overhead rate is different from the targeted rate (2 percent).
3. Other divisions earn revenues that differ from their targets.
4. The European division earns revenues that differ from its target.

The only factor that Susan controls is the fourth one. Therefore, an effective cost allocation system that provides incentives for her to monitor and manage the costs she can control should not result in higher cost allocations because of decisions made by others in the organization.

Such an allocation is one that allocates corporate costs to the European division as follows:

Fixed costs	14% of targeted fixed costs	($15 million × 14% =)	$2,100,000
Variable costs.	2% of actual division revenues	($70 million × 2% =)	1,400,000
Actual allocation . .			$3,500,000

This dual-rate allocation method shields Susan from decisions at corporate headquarters that affect corporate costs. There are more points to make about this method.

First, the fixed costs could be allocated in any way as long as it is done the same way for the target and for the actual computation of operating profit. The important thing is that the system allocates only the target, and not the actual, corporate fixed costs. Second, the costs allocated from the corporate department usually are not the same as the actual costs incurred. This means that there can be unallocated costs that remain in the corporate department's account. The difference between the costs allocated and the costs incurred can be used as a performance measure for the corporate-level manager.

These results can be illustrated graphically as shown in Exhibit 12-3. The three sets of bars on the left represent those items that the manager, Susan Ott, can control.

Exhibit 12.3   Graphical Illustration of the Differences in Allocation Methods and Identification of the Elements the Manager Controls—Chabot Analytics

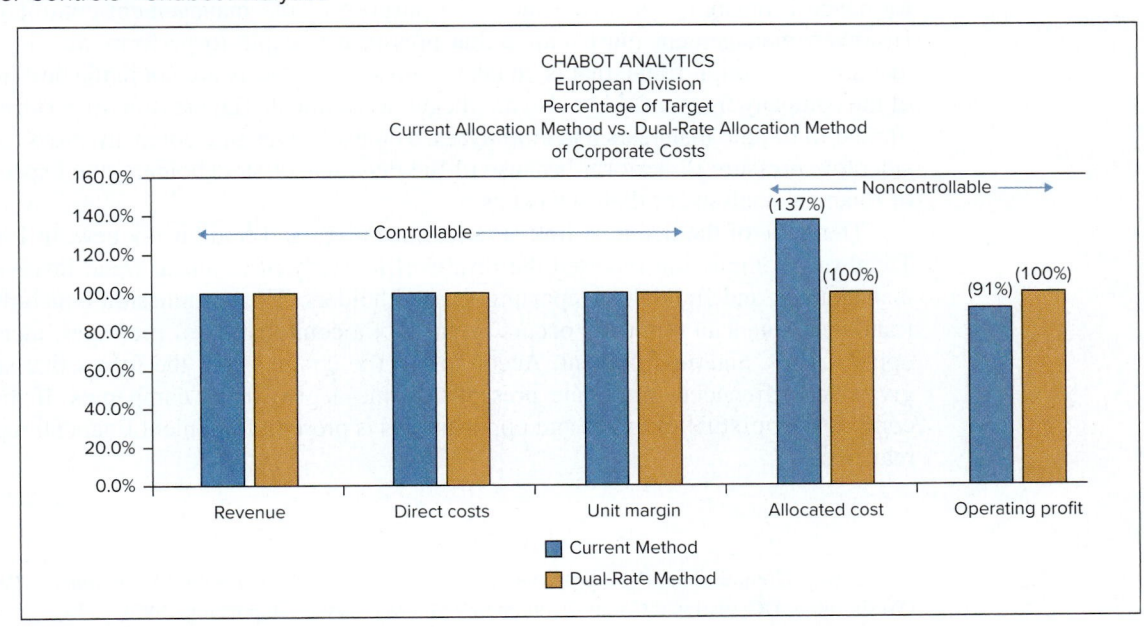

As shown, there is no difference between the actual and target amounts. The two sets of bars on the right, however, show that when the current allocation system is used, the European Division ends up with higher-than-targeted costs and lower-than-targeted operating profit. However, the reasons for this difference are, first, other divisions earning less than targeted revenue and, second, corporate managers spending more than targeted. These two factors are both outside Susan's control.

Self-Study Question

3. Consider the proposed dual-rate method for Chabot Analytics (CA). Suppose that next year's targets are as follows:

Revenue ($000)	
European division	$ 75,000
Total CA revenue	$600,000
Fixed corporate costs ($000)	$ 18,000
Variable cost as a percentage of revenue	2.5%

a. Fixed corporate costs are allocated on the basis of relative revenue. What is the target corporate cost for the European division?

b. Suppose that actual European division revenues next year are $80 million, actual corporate revenues are $800 million, and actual corporate costs are $35 million. Compare the corporate costs that would have been allocated under the old method at CA and under the dual-rate method.

The solution to this question is at the end of the chapter.

Do Performance Evaluation Systems Create Incentives to Commit Fraud?

LO 12-6

Understand the potential link between incentives and illegal or unethical behavior.

We noted earlier that in designing performance measurement systems, management should address two fundamental questions in evaluating how well the company's performance evaluation system works:

1. Does the measure reflect the results of those actions that improve the organization's performance?
2. What actions might managers be taking that improve reported performance but are actually detrimental to organizational performance?

Management could find that employees are highly motivated by high-pressure performance evaluation systems. That is the purpose of the management control system. However, management must realize that pressuring people to perform well is also an incentive to commit fraud, that is, to take actions that not only are *not* in the best interests of the company financially but also are illegal or unethical. The pressure to perform is not limited to middle managers and employees. Top executives in a company often feel considerable pressure to perform because of the demands of stockholders, the expectations of financial analysts, or their own egos.

The issue of the potential link between incentives and fraud is not new. In 1987, the Treadway Commission reported the results of its study of financial fraud involving top management and fraudulent reporting to stockholders. The commission concluded that fraudulent financial reporting occurs because of a combination of pressures, incentives, opportunities, and environment. According to the commission, the forces that seem to give rise to financial fraud "are present to some degree in all companies. If the right combustible mixture of forces and opportunities is present, fraudulent financial reporting may occur."[4]

---

[4] Treadway Commission, *Report of the National Commission on Fraudulent Financial Reporting* (Washington, DC: National Commission on Fraudulent Financial Reporting, 1987), p. 23.

The commission went on to say that a frequent incentive for fraud in financial reporting is the desire to improve a company's financial appearance to obtain a higher stock price or escape a penalty for poor performance. The commission listed examples of pressures that can lead to financial fraud, including the following:

- *Unrealistic budget pressures, particularly for short-term results.* These pressures occur when headquarters arbitrarily determines profit objectives and budgets without considering actual conditions.
- *Financial pressure resulting from bonus plans that depend on short-term economic performance.* This pressure is particularly acute when the bonus is a significant component of the individual's total compensation.[5]

It is particularly important to note the Treadway Commission's reference to companies' emphasis on short-term performance. Management is willing to take a chance on the future to make the current period look good. Why? Because companies emphasize short-term results for top managers and everyone else in the organization.

The Treadway Commission also noted that unrealistic profit objectives in budgets have been a cause of financial fraud. It is difficult for top management in large and widely dispersed companies to know what is realistic to expect in their far-flung divisions. This is one of the tensions in the management control system. With geographically dispersed operations, top managers delegate many decisions to local managers because of their superior local knowledge. This dependence on the local managers could also prevent corporate managers from learning about local activities that are fraudulent.

Performance Incentives and Accounting Manipulation — *Business Application*

The purpose of performance measures is to give managers an incentive to achieve certain organization goals. For example, if firm profitability is a goal, a natural performance measure would be firm profits. At the same time, these incentives can lead managers to take actions that improve the performance measure without improving (and perhaps harming) company performance. If a manager sold products to a customer with the implicit understanding that they could be returned in the next accounting period, the performance measure, firm profits, will increase (at least in the current period), but overall firm profitability will not be improved.

In one recent case,

> [t]he former chief executive of Hertz Global Holdings Inc. agreed to pay nearly $2.2 million to settle claims that he pressured subordinates to "find money" to meet financial targets, causing employees to violate accounting rules, according to regulators.

As a result of the CEO's pressure, employees changed "methodologies they used to estimate how much money the company could recover for vehicle damages caused by car renters." The result raised Hertz's income by "millions of dollars" and, in some cases, violated GAAP.

In a second example, the founder of Under Armour, Inc. and its CFO were warned by the Securities and Exchange Commission (SEC) that they might be subject to an enforcement action due to accounting practices. This resulted from employees of the company "borrowing" revenue from future quarters to offset reduced demand for the company's merchandise in 2016. One purpose of the aggressive accounting was to ensure a continued record of quarterly sales growth exceeding 20 percent.

It is important to understand that not all problems with performance measures and their links to firm goals are as straightforward as in these examples. For example, an operational performance measure may be used because the firm believes it is linked to profit. Many call center personnel are evaluated by the number of calls handled in a certain time period. Managers or employees can manage this measure by being more efficient (that is good for firm profit) or by rushing customers off the call, perhaps reducing future business (that is, presumably, not good for the firm). Determining why a performance measure improved is not always easy.

Sources: Michaels, Dave, "Former Hertz CEO Agrees to Settle Claims Tied to Accounting Misconduct," *The Wall Street Journal*, August 13, 2020; Safdar, Khadeeja, "Under Armour Receives Wells Notices from SEC," *The Wall Street Journal*, July 27, 2020.

---

[5] Ibid., p. 24.

Internal Controls to Protect Assets and Provide Quality Information

LO 12-7

Understand how internal controls can help protect assets.

internal control
A process designed to provide reasonable assurance that an organization will achieve its objectives.

separation of duties
No one person has control over an entire transaction.

Companies set up internal control systems to deal with problems such as financial fraud. At a general level, internal controls provide management with reasonable assurances that their company's assets are protected and the company's accounting is reliable. More specifically, **internal control** is a process designed to provide reasonable assurance that an organization will achieve its objectives in the following categories:

- Effectiveness and efficiency of operations.
- Reliability of financial reporting.
- Compliance with applicable laws and regulations.

The top management of an organization and its board of directors are responsible for providing an adequate system of internal controls. The Sarbanes–Oxley Act of 2002 (SOX) requires that management of publicly traded companies report on the adequacy of their company's internal control over financial reporting. This law also requires that the company's external auditors attest to the effectiveness of the company's internal controls.

In practice, internal controls are detailed methods of protecting assets and assuring reliable information. One of the key internal controls is separation of duties. **Separation of duties** means that no one person has control over the entire transaction. With separation of duties, one person cannot prepare the payroll, authorize the payroll checks, prepare the payroll checks, sign the payroll checks, and distribute the payroll checks to the employees. Similarly, one person cannot make the sale, prepare the invoice, deposit the cash payment, and reconcile the bank statement to the company's books. Of course, employees can collude to beat the internal control system. Two or three employees can work together to handle all parts of a transaction. Many of the biggest financial frauds have been orchestrated by only two or three high-level employees.

Companies use many types of internal controls besides separation of duties. Here are some examples:

- Setting limits on the amount of expenditures (for example, no more than $100 per person for an expense account dinner).
- Requiring management authorization for the use of a company's assets (for example, use of a company car).
- Reconciling various sets of books (for example, reconciling accounts receivable with the collections of cash from customers).
- Prohibiting particular activities or behavior (for example, prohibiting a company's purchasing agents from accepting gifts from present and prospective vendors).
- Rotating personnel and requiring employees to take vacations (for example, requiring the person who reconciles bank statements with the company's cash accounts to rotate duties so someone else can check that the cash on the books is actually in the bank).

Internal controls are not just good business practice but also legally required for publicly traded companies. The Foreign Corrupt Practices Act of 1977 was the first law to require that publicly traded companies have adequate internal controls. This law was intended primarily to reduce the bribery of foreign government officials. Regulators found many instances in which companies' middle managers were paying bribes without the authorization of top management, which was an example of weak internal controls. In addition to outlawing the bribery of foreign government officials, the U.S. Congress required publicly traded companies to have adequate internal controls.

Twenty-five years later, the U.S. Congress passed SOX in response to a large number of business and accounting scandals that came to light in 2001 and 2002. These included the large frauds and subsequent bankruptcies of Enron and WorldCom. SOX will likely cause improvements in the internal controls—and the documentation of internal controls—in many organizations. In addition, SOX might improve investor confidence in companies' internal controls. However, these benefits come at a cost. Consider the separation of duties. Suppose one person handled a transaction before SOX, but two people are required to handle it after SOX. That added separation of duties creates better controls but comes at a cost. An open question is: Do the benefits justify the costs of investing in better internal controls?

When the Internal Control System Fails — *Business Application*

We mentioned the 1MDB scandal involving the investment bank Goldman Sachs earlier in the chapter when discussing executive compensation. However, there is another (related) aspect to that case concerning internal controls. The U.S. Justice Department's case against the bank was based, in part, on the breakdown of the bank's internal control system. Although Goldman initially blamed two of its senior executives as having "circumvented" the system, the Justice Department believed that blame for the fraud included more than the pair of executives separately charged. As is general banking practice,

> [t]he bank's control functions vetted [the principal 1MDB] in 2009 and refused to onboard him as a client.

Although this would seem to end the deal, the Goldman executives continued to pursue it. The control staff suspected that the person they had declined as a client continued to be a participant, but

they repeatedly failed to do anything other than ask members of the deal team whether he was involved. . . .

In their case, the Justice Department specifically "faulted" the control functions and in documents related to the case

portray a business environment where compliance officers and other institutional checks had little power to override high-profile bankers or lucrative investment deals.

As noted earlier, Goldman has reached a settlement with the Justice Department and other parties agreeing to payments of over $5 billion and return of executive compensation to the company by recipients of $174 million.

Source: Tokar, Dylan, "Goldman Promises Greater Scrutiny of Senior Execs Following 1MDB Settlement," *The Wall Street Journal*, October 22, 2020.

Internal Auditing

Internal auditors monitor internal controls. By reviewing internal controls and ensuring that controls are working, internal auditors are often a company's first defense against fraud. One of the best-known fraud detections was that of WorldCom's internal auditor, Cynthia Cooper. Cooper worked as the vice president of Internal Audit at WorldCom. After conducting a thorough investigation in secret, she informed WorldCom's board that the company had covered up $3.8 billion in losses through phony bookkeeping. At the time, this was the largest incident of accounting fraud in U.S. history. For her findings and gutsy reporting to the board of directors, Cooper was named one of three "People of the Year" by *Time* magazine in 2002.

Key Takeaways

1. Management control systems have three elements:
   a. Delegated decision authority, which specifies the decisions a manager may make.
   b. Performance evaluation and measurement systems, which specify how the performance of the subordinate manager is to be measured and how the results of the measurement will be used in evaluating the manager.
   c. Compensation and reward systems, which specify how the subordinate manager will be paid for his or her performance.

2. Responsibility accounting provides an organizational design that facilitates the management control system. There are four types of responsibility centers:
   a. Cost centers:
      - A cost center manager has decision authority that primarily affects costs.
      - Appropriate performance measures tend to be cost-based, such as cost relative to a budget or cost per unit of output.
      - In some cases, such as corporate staff functions, the output might be difficult to measure. The

(Continued)

(Continued)

term *discretionary cost center* is often used to distinguish between a corporate staff function and an operational cost center, such as a manufacturing plant.

b.   Revenue centers:

- Although not common, a revenue center manager has decision authority that primarily affects revenues, but not costs. Examples might include sales functions.
- Appropriate performance measures would be revenue-based, such as total revenue or price received per unit.

c.   Profit centers:

- A profit center manager has decision authority that affects revenues and costs, but not asset acquisition or disposal.
- Appropriate performance measures include accounting profit (revenues minus costs) and financial ratios including revenues and costs (return on sales, for example).

d.   Investment centers:

- An investment center manager has decision authority that affects revenues, costs, and asset acquisition and utilization.

- Appropriate performance measures include indicators that include revenues, costs, and some measure of asset utilizations, such as return on assets.

3.   One approach to providing incentives for unit managers is to allocate the costs of corporate overhead and include those costs in the unit manager's performance evaluation:

a.   Some common (and simple) allocation methods, such as based on relative revenues, have the possibility to encourage behavior that is not in the firm's interest.

b.   A better approach is a dual-rate method, where

- The fixed costs of the corporate function are allocated on the basis of something unchanging between the target and actual results.
- The variable costs are allocated based on the actual use of the driver of the variable costs.
- In both cases, the costs used (whether total or per unit of the cost driver) are based on budgeted amounts.

SUMMARY

A management control system provides procedures for aligning individual goals with organizational goals when managers have been delegated the authority to make decisions. The management control system organizes the firm's activities into responsibility centers whose type reflects the nature of the decisions delegated. The three elements of a managerial control system are (1) delegation of decision authority, (2) performance measurement and evaluation systems, and (3) compensation and reward systems. Each element has to be consistent with the others for the management control system to be effective.

The following summarizes key ideas tied to the chapter's learning objectives:

LO 12-1 Explain the role of a management control system. The management control system aligns interests in decentralized organizations.

LO 12-2 Identify the advantages and disadvantages of decentralization. Decentralization allows managers to take advantage of local knowledge, reduce information costs, and provide learning opportunities for managers. The disadvantages are administrative duplication and, more important, dysfunctional decision making.

LO 12-3 Describe and explain the basic framework for management control systems, including the relation between organization structure and responsibility centers. The three elements of a management control system are the delegation of decision authority, performance measurement and evaluation systems, and compensation and reward systems. Cost centers, revenue centers, and profit centers are usually defined based on the decisions a manager has been delegated and their effect on costs and revenues.

LO 12-4 Understand how managers evaluate performance. Relative performance evaluation compares the performance of similar types of responsibility centers. Managers often distinguish between evaluating the performance of the people from that of the responsibility center.

LO 12-5 Analyze the effect of dual- versus single-rate allocation systems. When a single allocation base is used to allocate costs, we assume that the allocation base reflects the best causal relationship between the cost object and the cost. It might be more appropriate, however, to use two (or dual) allocation bases to allocate costs. This is especially true when there are fixed and variable elements and the manager does not control many of the allocated costs.

LO 12-6 Understand the potential link between incentives and illegal or unethical behavior. Performance measures provide incentives to managers to improve reported performance. This also leads to incentives to engage in fraud.

LO 12-7 Understand how internal controls can help protect assets. Internal controls provide management with reasonable assurances that their company's assets are protected and the company's accounting is reliable. It is a process designed to provide reasonable assurance that an organization will achieve its objectives of effective and efficient operations, reliable financial reporting, and compliance with applicable laws and regulations.

KEY TERMS

behavioral congruence, *555*
centralized, *548*
compensation and reward system, *552*
contingent compensation, *559*
controllability concept, *558*
cost center, *553*
decentralization, *548*
decentralized, *548*
delegated decision authority, *552*
discretionary cost center, *554*
dual-rate method, *562*
dysfunctional decision making, *549*
fixed compensation, *559*

goal congruence, *555*
internal control, *566*
investment center, *554*
local knowledge, *549*
management control system, *551*
performance evaluation system, *552*
principal–agent relationship, *548*
profit center, *554*
relative performance evaluation (RPE), *559*
responsibility accounting, *553*
revenue center, *554*
separation of duties, *566*
standard cost center, *554*

REVIEW QUESTIONS

12-1. What does decentralization mean in the context of a management control system?

12-2. Why is performance measurement an important component of a management control system in a decentralized organization?

12-3. What are the advantages of decentralization? What are some major disadvantages of decentralization?

12-4. What does dysfunctional decision making refer to?

12-5. What are the three elements of a management control system?

12-6. What are the five basic kinds of decentralized units in a responsibility accounting system?

12-7. What is goal congruence? How is it different from behavioral congruence?

12-8. What is the controllability concept?

12-9. What is relative performance evaluation (RPE)?

12-10. What is contingent compensation?

12-11. What is the dual-rate method of corporate cost allocation?

12-12. How does the separation of duties help prevent financial fraud?

CRITICAL ANALYSIS AND DISCUSSION QUESTIONS

12-13. The management control system collects information from local managers for planning purposes. It then uses the plan to evaluate the local managers. What are the advantages of this? What are the disadvantages?

12-14. Salespeople are often paid a commission based on sales revenue. How might that incentive system lead to dysfunctional consequences?

12-15. Is the CEO ever an agent in the principal–agent relationship as discussed in the chapter? Is a division president ever a principal in the principal–agent relationship as discussed in the chapter? Explain.

12-16. On December 30, a manager determines that income is about $9.9 million. The manager has a compensation plan that calls for a bonus of 25 percent (of salary) if income exceeds $10 million and no bonus if it is below $10 million. What problems might arise with this bonus plan?

12-17. Accounting is objective and precise. Therefore, performance measures based on accounting numbers must be objective and precise. Do you agree? Explain.

12-18. Surveying the accounts payable records, a clerk in the controller's office noted that expenses appeared to rise significantly within one month of the close of the budget period. The organization did not have a seasonal product or service to explain this behavior. Can you suggest an explanation?

12-19. The manager of an operating department just received a cost report and has made the following comment with respect to the costs allocated from one of the service departments: "This charge to my division doesn't seem right. The service center installed equipment with more capacity than our division requires. Most of the service department costs are fixed, but we seem to be allocated more costs in periods when other departments use less. We are paying for the excess capacity of other departments when other departments cut their usage levels." How could this manager's problem be solved?

12-20. In the previous chapters, we considered different allocation methods and considered which one might be "better." Why might a manager have a different opinion about the "best" allocation system after moving to another business unit? Is this ethical?

12-21. A company has a bonus plan that states that managers with division income ranked below the average of all managers receive no bonus for the year. What biases might arise in this system?

12-22. Many companies argue that they do not pay their managers a bonus because they believe their employees will work hard for a "fair" wage and do not need to be motivated with a bonus. Why would managers in such a system work hard? Is there a financial incentive even without a bonus?

12-23. Each April, it is common to find news articles contrasting executive pay with firm performance. For example, on April 9, 2009, *The Wall Street Journal* reported that the top three executives at Kilroy Realty (a California property developer and manager) were paid the "highest amount permitted by their compensation agreement in 2008" although occupancy rates declined and share prices fell 39 percent in 2008 and 41 percent (as of the time of the article) in 2009. Why might a firm pay managers high compensation although performance is worsening?

12-24. The Treadway Commission commented that the forces leading to financial fraud were present in all companies to some extent, but fraudulent financial reporting resulted from the right combustible mixture of forces and opportunities to commit fraud. Based on your reading of current news stories, give examples of the combustible mixture that the Treadway Commission mentioned.

12-25. The Treadway Commission commented that a factor giving rise to fraud is the existence of pressures on division managers to achieve unrealistic profit objectives. Why might top management set unrealistic profit targets?

12-26. The Treadway Commission indicated that bonus plans based on achieving short-run financial results have been a factor in financial frauds, particularly when the bonus is a large component of an individual's compensation. Why is this so?

12-27. Evaluating Management Control Systems   (LO 12-1, 3)

Lamont Copy Centers (LCC) operates several stores in the upper midwest. The company is decentralized. At the corporate level, there are two operating managers: chief personnel officer (CPO)
and chief operating officer (COO). The CPO's performance is measured by the total labor cost of
store personnel (excluding store managers) relative to a target. The CPO is responsible for all hiring decisions, but in general follows the recommendation of the store manager for nonmanagerial
employees. The COO's performance is based on store profits relative to targeted profits. The compensation for both the CPO and COO includes a contingent portion, which is equal to 25 percent of
their base salary in each quarter they meet or beat their target.

Information on performance for the last year follows:

	CPO		COO	
Quarter	Target Labor Cost	Actual Labor Cost	Target profit	Actual Profit
1	$520,000	$530,000	$260,000	$252,000
2	535,000	532,000	300,000	304,000
3	495,000	515,000	250,000	235,000
4	525,000	518,000	275,000	280,000

Required

a.   Evaluate the performance of the CPO and the COO based on the performance measures the
     company uses.
b.   Assess the management control system used at Lamont Copy Centers and provide recommen-
     dations for changes, if any are required. Be sure to discuss
     • Decision authority.
     • Performance measures.
     • Compensation.

12-28. Evaluating Management Control Systems—Ethical Considerations   (LO 12-1, 3, 4, 6)

Westphalia Corporation produces audio equipment for home, office, and vehicles. The production
manager (PM) and marketing manager (MM) are both are paid a flat salary and are eligible for
a bonus. The bonus is equal to 2 percent of company profit that is in excess of a specified target
profit. (All profit numbers exclude any bonus.) The maximum bonus is 10 percent of base salary.
The PM's base salary is $200,000, and the MM's is $250,000.

The target profit for this year is $8 million. The production manager has been approached by
an engineering consulting firm that is willing to license to Westphalia a new manufacturing technique that would increase annual profit by 15 percent, after deducting the licensing fee. The PM is
unsure whether to employ the new technique this year, wait, or not employ it at all. Using the new
technique will not affect the target.

Required

a.   Suppose that profit without using the technique this year will be $8 million. By how much
     will the PM's bonus change if the new technique is adopted? By how much will the MM's
     bonus change if the PM decides to adopt the new technique?
b.   Suppose that profit without using the technique this year will be $9 million. By how much
     will the PM's bonus change if the new technique is adopted? By how much will the MM's
     bonus change if the PM decides to adopt the new technique?
c.   Suppose that profit without using the technique this year will be $7 million. By how much
     will the PM's bonus change if the new technique is adopted? By how much will the MM's
     bonus change if the PM decides to adopt the new technique?

d.   Is it ethical for the production manager to consider the impact of the new technique on their bonus when deciding whether or not to use it? Explain.

e.   Assess the management control system used at Westphalia Corporation and provide recommendations for changes, if any are required. Be sure to discuss
  •   Decision authority.
  •   Performance measures.
  •   Compensation.

(LO 12-1, 3, 4, 6)   **12-29. Evaluating Management Control Systems—Ethical Considerations**

Wreford Components produces testing equipment for hospitals and other health care facilities. The vice president for operations (VP-Ops) and vice president for sales (VP-Sales) are paid a flat salary. The base salary is $200,000 for the VP-Ops and $300,000 for the VP-Sales. The company also has a contingent compensation plan that pays eligible managers, including these two vice presidents, a bonus equal to a percentage of their salary depending on actual income (excluding the bonus). The bonus schedule is as described in the following table:

Actual Income Is		Bonus Amount	
At least . . .	But less than . . .	Percentage of Salary	But no greater than . . . .
$20,000,000	$22,000,000	3%	$20,000
$22,000,000	$24,000,000	6%	$20,000
$24,000,000	$27,000,000	9%	$25,000
$27,000,000	$30,000,000	12%	$25,000
$30,000,000	--	15%	$30,000

An employee in sales has suggested to the VP-Sales a modification to the existing distribution process. If implemented, staff analysis indicates it will increase net profits (including costs of the modified process) by $2 million. The VP-Sales is undecided on whether or not to adopt the new process. If the new process is adopted, the compensation schedule will not be modified.

Required

a.   Suppose that income without using the new process this year will be $21 million. By how much will the bonus for the VP-Ops change if the new process is adopted? By how much will the bonus for the VP-Sales change if the new process is adopted?

b.   Suppose that income without using the new process this year will be $24 million. By how much will the bonus for the VP-Ops change if the new process is adopted? By how much will the bonus for the VP-Sales change if the new process is adopted?

c.   Suppose that income without using the new process this year will be $26 million. By how much will the bonus for the VP-Ops change if the new process is adopted? By how much will the bonus for the VP-Sales change if the new process is adopted?

d.   Is it ethical for the VP-Sales to consider the impact of the new process on their bonus when deciding whether or not to use it? Explain.

e.   Assess the management control system used at Wreford Components and provide recommendations for changes, if any are required. Be sure to discuss
  •   Decision authority.
  •   Performance measures.
  •   Compensation.

(LO 12-1, 3, 4)   **12-30. Management Control Systems and Incentives**

Shadownook Industries is a multinational firm operating in many businesses, including manufacturing, mining, and agriculture. Top management focuses on the annual earnings in evaluating the performance of sector managers. (Sector managers include a mix of both industrial and geographic sectors.) Targets in the incentive compensation plan are reset annually.

The incentive plan includes an annual bonus that ranges from 5 to 50 percent of sector managers' salaries. Target earnings for each sector manager are based, in part, on the performance of other firms in the sector. Once the target is set, it is not changed during the year.

Failing to meet a sector's target has serious consequences for the sector manager. First, the manager loses some or all of the potential bonus. Second, managers who miss a target will find their jobs in jeopardy. Missing a target two years in a row generally leads to termination.

Required

a.   What incentives does this plan give to sector managers?

b.   Is this a good plan? Would you want to be a sector manager in this company?

12-31. Management Control Systems and Incentives   (LO 12-1, 3, 4)
Zender Fabrication is a long-established manufacturer of various industrial products located in the United States. This company's products have a well-respected brand name and receive a premium price in the market. The unionized workforce is well paid and does quality work.

Like many companies, Zender faces challenges from foreign companies or other U.S. companies located in countries or areas that pay lower wages or have more modern and more efficient production equipment. A competitive study recently conducted by Zender indicated the importance of reducing costs without compromising the quality of its products.

The company is considering the introduction of a profit-sharing arrangement whereby workers receive a share of profits in profitable years. The workers would forgo a wage increase to obtain this profit-sharing arrangement.

Required

Evaluate the advantages and disadvantages of giving the workers a profit-sharing bonus instead of a wage increase.

12-32. Advantages and Disadvantages of Decentralization   (LO 12-2)
Consider the Business Application, "Centralizing as a Cost-Cutting Approach."

Required

What best describes the benefits that the companies cited that chose not to centralize likely hoped to receive by keeping certain staff functions, such as finance, decentralized?

  A. Faster response
  B. Wiser use of management's time
  C. Training, evaluation, and motivation of local managers
  D. Better use of local knowledge
  E. A, C, and D
  F. Both C and D

12-33. Advantages and Disadvantages of Decentralization   (LO 12-2)
Consider the Business Application, "Centralizing as a Cost-Cutting Approach."

Required

What best describes the cost(s) Pernod Ricard SA likely hoped to reduce by removing some of the authority of local managers to source casks?

  A. Administrative duplication
  B. Dysfunctional decision making
  C. Both A and C
  D. Neither A nor B

12-34. Organization Structure and Responsibility Centers   (LO 12-3)
Evergreen Transportation is a domestic logistics company offering warehousing and transportation services. It is organized along product lines with three sectors: Agricultural, Manufactured Goods, and Petro-Chemicals. Each of the three sectors is further organized into geographic divisions: Eastern, Midwestern, Southern, and Western. Division vice presidents oversee both the marketing and operations for their units. Evergreen is highly decentralized with division presidents given authority to operate the business independently in terms of operations, investments, and marketing.

Required

Match the following executives to the responsibility center that best represents their likely deci-sion-making authority.

Executive	Responsibility Center
1. Warehouse manager, Manufactured Goods	A. Cost center
2. Sector President, Agriculture	B. Discretionary cost center
3. Manager, Evergreen Corporate Human Resources (HR)	C. Investment center
4. Sales Manager, Petro-Chemicals	D. Profit center
5. Vice President, Agriculture–Southern Division	E. Revenue center

(LO 12-5)   **12-35. Alternative Allocation Bases**

Mackenzie Mining has two operating divisions, Northern and Southern, that share the common costs of the company's human resources (HR) department. The annual costs of the HR department total $14,000,000 a year. You have the following selected information about the two divisions:

	Number of Employees	Wage and Salary Expense ($000)
Northern..............	2,310	$173,600
Southern.............	1,890	106,400

Required

a.   What is the HR cost that is charged to each division if the number of employees is used as the allocation basis?

b.   What is the HR cost that is charged to each division if the wage and salary expense total is used as the allocation basis?

c.   The cost of HR is necessary regardless of which division uses it. Why is the method of alloca-tion important?

(LO 12-6)   **12-36. Single versus Dual Rates**

Refer to data for Mackenzie Mining in Exercise 12-35.

Required

Determine the cost allocation if $9.5 million of the HR costs are fixed and allocated on the basis of employees, and the remaining costs, which are variable, are allocated on the basis of the wage and salary expense total.

(LO 12-5)   **12-37. Alternative Allocation Bases**

Giardin Outdoors is a recreational goods retailer with two divisions: Online and Stores. The two divisions both use the services of the corporate Finance and Accounting (F&A) Department. Annual costs of the F&A Department total $5.2 million a year. Managers in the two operating divi-sions are measured based on division operating profits.

The following selected data are available for the two operating divisions:

	Revenues ($000)	Transactions (000)
Online.......................	$74,100	1,066.5
Stores......................	39,900	283.5

Required

a.   What is the F&A cost that is charged to each division if divisional revenues are used as the allocation basis?

b.   What is the F&A cost that is charged to each division if the the number of transactions is used as the allocation basis?

c. Why would the manager of the Online Division be concerned with the choice of the allocation basis for F&A costs?

d. Why would the company allocate F&A costs?

12-38. Single versus Dual Rates

(LO 12-6)

Refer to data for Giardin Outdoors in Exercise 12-37.

Required

Determine the cost allocation if $3.8 million of the F&A costs are fixed and allocated on the basis of revenues, and the remaining costs, which are variable, are allocated on the basis of transactions.

12-39. Alternative Allocation Bases—Ethical Considerations

(LO 12-5)

Kentfield Advisory Services (KAS) is a large management consulting firm organized into two groups: Governmental Services (GS) and Commercial Support (CS). Corporate information technology (IT) services support both groups. The cost of computer support is $33 million. The following information is given:

	Utilization	Revenues ($000)
Governmental Services.............	57%	$221,520
Commercial Support	43	402,480

Required

a. What is the cost charged to each group if the allocation is based on the utilization?

b. What is the cost charged to each group if revenue is the allocation basis?

c. Most of the business in Commercial Support is priced on a fixed fee basis, and most of the work in the Governmental Services Department is priced on a cost-plus fixed fee basis. Will this affect the choice of the allocation base? Should it?

12-40. Single versus Dual Rates

(LO 12-5, 6)

Refer to data for Kentfield Advisory Services in Exercise 12-39.

Required

What is the cost allocation if fixed IT costs of $22.4 million are allocated on the basis of utilization and the remaining costs (all variable) are allocated on the basis of group revenues?

12-41. Alternative Allocation Bases

(LO 12-5)

Dill Shipyards operates a dry dock on the East Coast, where it builds and repairs ships. The company's Payroll Department supports its two divisions, Naval and Private. The Naval division has contracts with the Department of Defense and the Private division works primarily with commercial shippers, specializing in tankers. The annual cost of the Payroll Department is $8.3 million.

Selected data for the two divisions for the most recent year follow:

	Number of Employees	Total Payroll ($000)
Naval.....................	10,080	$526,400
Private..................	13,920	413,600

Required

a. What is the cost charged to each division if Dill allocates Payroll Department costs based on the number of employees?

b. What is the cost charged to each division if Dill allocates Payroll Department costs based on the total payroll?

c. Contracts with the Defense Department are on a cost-plus fixed fee basis, meaning the price is based on the cost of repairing or building the ship, including any overhead assigned to the division. Contracts with commercial shipping companies are almost all fixed price, meaning the price does not depend directly on the cost. Will this affect Dill's choice of an allocation base? Should it?

(LO 12-5, 6)   **12-42. Single versus Dual Rates**
Refer to data for Dill Shipyards in Exercise 12-41.

Required
What is the cost allocation if fixed Payroll costs of $5.6 million are allocated on the basis of number of employees and the remaining costs (all variable) are allocated on the basis of total payroll?

(LO 12-7)   **12-43. Internal Controls**

One of the authors of this book has a favorite sandwich shop where one person makes the sandwich and another person rings up the sale and takes the customer's cash. At first, this author thought that having two people involved had something to do with him. After carefully observing the sandwich shop's operations, he observed that two employees were involved in every sandwich production and sale. The person who made the sandwich did not ring up the sale or take the money from the sale.

Required
a.   What type of internal control is provided in this example? Why is the shop manager/owner providing that internal control?
b.   Is there an even better internal control?
c.   Could the employees get around this internal control?

(LO 12-7)   **12-44. Internal Controls**
Commonly in many organizations, including corporations, universities, and government agencies, when more than one employee from the organization is having a business meal paid by the organization, the most senior person (in terms of authority, not age) pays the bill and submits it for reimbursement.

Required
a.   What type of internal control is provided in this example? Why is some form of internal control needed in this case?
b.   Is there an alternative internal control that might be effective?
c.   Could the employees get around this internal control?

PROBLEMS      All applicable Problems are included in Connect.

(LO 12-3, 4)   **12-45. Evaluating Management Control Systems**
Montgomery Fashions produces and sells clothing through various retailers. Montgomery is highly decentralized and allows its managers discretion in managing with little direct oversight. This latitude in decision making is checked by using a performance measurement and compensation system that rewards results. The vice president of production (VPP) is responsible for the production of the clothing, including the sourcing of fabrics and textiles, hiring labor, and scheduling production. The vice president of marketing (VPM) is responsible for sales and marketing, including developing new customer relations, distribution, and advertising. The VPP is measured on the cost of production relative to a budget. The budgeted cost is adjusted for the product mix and product quantity. The VPM is evaluated on actual "marketing margin" relative to a target marketing margin set at the beginning of the period. The marketing margin is calculated as the gross margin (sales minus cost of goods) less the cost of the marketing department. The advertising costs are included in the costs of the marketing department. If a manager meets or beats the target, the manager receives a bonus equal to 80 percent of salary. Failure to achieve the targeted performance results in no bonus.

Information on performance last year follows:

Cost of Production		Marketing Margin	
Target costs	$21,000,000	Target margin.........	$43,000,000
Actual costs	20,487,500	Actual margin.........	41,220,100

Required

a.   Assess the performance of the vice presidents of marketing and production.

b.   What recommendations would you make concerning the management control system at Montgomery Fashions, with respect to the two vice-president positions.

12-46. Evaluating Management Control Systems   (LO 12-3, 4)

Burt Management Consultants (BMC) is a multinational consulting group organized geographically. In the U.S. Division, the managing partner for sales (MPS) is responsible for client acquisition. The MPS negotiates project scopes and budgets with the clients. This is done in consultation with the managing partner for projects (MPP), but the MPS has ultimate decision authority for signing agreements. The MPP is responsible for overseeing the completion of the projects and has authority over project staffing and all project work.

The MPS is measured based on total bookings, which are the projected revenues for signed contracts less the costs of the sales department. The MPP is measured on the actual costs incurred relative to the budgeted costs. The budget is adjusted for any modifications to the contracts with respect to either timing or scope of work.

Both managing partners are paid a fixed salary plus a bonus for meeting or exceeding their performance target. The annual fixed salaries of both partners are set at $600,000. The bonus is set at 2 percent of the amount by which the actual result exceeds the target.

Information on results in the most recent period follows:

Bookings		Project Costs	
Target bookings.......	$167,000,000	Target project costs	$152,000,000
Actual bookings.......	168,456,000	Actual project costs	154,235,000

Required

a.   Assess the performance of the two managing partners.

b.   What is the bonus earned by the managing partner of sales?

c.   What is the bonus earned by the managing partner of projects?

d.   What recommendations would you make concerning the management control system at the U.S. Division of Burt Management Consultants, with respect to the two managing partner positions.

12-47. Analyze Performance Report for Decentralized Organization   (LO 12-4)

Cherrylawn Appliance Stores is a nationwide chain of kitchen appliance stores. The company operates with a widely based retail and distribution system that has led to a highly decentralized management structure. Each area manager is responsible for purchasing and distributing products (from an approved corporate list) in one of eight geographical areas of the country.

Area managers are evaluated using a performance measure that is calculated as the area's contribution to corporate profits before taxes less a 12 percent investment charge on the area's investment base. The investment base of each area is the sum of its year-end balances of accounts receivable, inventories, and other assets. Corporate policies dictate that areas minimize their investments in receivables and inventories. Investments in other assets are decisions jointly made by the area and corporate managers based on proposals made by area managers, available corporate funds, and general corporate policy.

The Southeast Area Manager (SAM) prepared the year 1 and preliminary year 2 budgets for the area late in year 0. Final approval of the year 2 budget took place in late year 1 after adjustments for trends and other information developed during year 1. Preliminary work on the year 3 budget also took place at that time. In early November of year 2, the area manager asked the area controller to prepare a report that presents performance for the first nine months of year 2. The report follows:

CHERRYLAWN APPLIANCE STORES
Southeast Area
$(000)

	Year 2			Year 1	
	Annual Budget	Three-Quarter Budget[a]	Actual (to Date)	Annual Budget	Actual
Sales.	$25,480	$19,110	$20,020	$22,750	$22,113
Area costs and expenses					
Cost of sales	$14,896	$11,172	$11,930	$12,600	$12,460
Leases	780	585	620	620	755
Maintenance and repairs	560	420	168	490	448
Depreciation on leasehold improvements. . .	924	693	693	847	847
Administration.	1,008	756	756	756	840
Total area costs and expenses	$18,168	$13,626	$14,167	$15,313	$15,350
Area margin.	$ 7,312	$ 5,484	$ 5,853	$ 7,437	$ 6,763
Allocated corporate fixed costs.	3,528	2,646	2,352	3,332	3,136
Area profits	$ 3,784	$ 2,838	$ 3,501	$ 4,105	$ 3,627

	Year 2			Year 1	
	Budgeted Balance 12/31/Year 2	Budgeted Balance 9/30/Year 2	Actual Balance 9/30/Year 2	Budgeted Balance 12/31/Year 1	Actual Balance 12/31/Year 1
Area investment					
Accounts receivable	$ 2,352	$ 2,842	$ 2,450	$ 2,450	$ 2,450
Inventories.	14,000	14,000	18,200	12,600	13,300
Other assets	2,310	2,362	1,925	2,010	1,925
Total	$18,662	$19,204	$22,575	$17,060	$17,675

[a] The area's sales occur uniformly throughout the year.

Required

a. Evaluate the performance of the Southeast Area Manager (SAM) for the nine months ending September 30, year 2. Support your evaluation with pertinent facts from the problem.

b. Identify the features of Cherrylawn's division performance measurement reporting and evaluation system that need to be revised if it is to effectively reflect the responsibilities of the area managers.

(CMA adapted)

(LO 12-3, 5) **12-48. Divisional Performance Measurement: Behavioral Issues**
Racine Chemicals' division managers have been expressing growing dissatisfaction with the methods the company uses to measure division performance. Division operations are evaluated every quarter by comparing them with a budget prepared during the prior year. Division managers claim

that many factors that are completely out of their control are included in this comparison, resulting in an unfair and misleading performance evaluation.

The managers have been particularly critical of the process used to establish budgets. The annual budget, stated by quarters, is prepared six months prior to the beginning of the operating year. Pressure by top management to reflect increased earnings has often caused divisional managers to overstate revenues and/or understate expenses. In addition, after the budget is established, no changes are made. Frequently, the budgets that top management has supplied to the divisions have not recognized external factors such as the state of the economy, changes in consumer preferences, and actions of competitors. The credibility of the performance review is damaged when the budget cannot be adjusted to incorporate these changes.

Recognizing these problems, top management has agreed to establish a committee to review the situation and to make recommendations for a new performance evaluation system. The committee consists of each division manager, the corporate controller, and the executive vice president. At the first meeting, one division manager outlined a proposed "Racine Reach for Excellence" (RRE) performance measurement plan. This performance evaluation system evaluates division managers according to three criteria:

- *Is there improvement?* How do certain selected measures compare to the same measures for the prior year.
- *Are the goals tough but attainable?* Is the current performance being measured relative to a set of realistic, but tough-to-meet, goals?
- *Are current assets used effectively?* Are current assets being underutilized?

One division manager believes that this system would overcome many of the inconsistencies of the current system because divisions could be evaluated from three different viewpoints. In addition, managers would have the opportunity to show how they would react and account for changes in uncontrollable external factors.

Another manager cautions that the success of a new performance evaluation system will be limited unless it has top management's complete support.

Required

a.   Explain whether the proposed RRE plan would be an improvement over the evaluation system of division performance currently used by Racine Chemicals.

b.   Develop specific performance measures for each of the three criteria in the proposed RRE plan that could be used to evaluate division managers.

c.   Discuss the motivational and behavioral aspects of the proposed performance system. Also recommend specific programs that could be instituted to promote morale and give incentives to divisional management.

12-49. Corporate Cost Allocation and Performance Measurement   (LO 12-5)

Lilac Group is organized into two geographic divisions (Americas and Rest of the World, or ROW) and a corporate headquarters. Late last year, the Lilac CFO prepared financial operating plans (budgets) for the two divisions for the current year, shown as follows:

	Americas	ROW
Revenues	$58,500,000	$71,500,000
Direct division costs	46,200,000	51,250,000
Operating profit before allocation	$12,300,000	$20,250,000

Corporate overhead costs are expected to be $10.4 million in the current year. Of the $10.4 million, $6.5 million is fixed, and the remainder is variable, with respect to revenue. Division managers are evaluated and compensated in part on division operating profit relative to the budget.

Required

a.   Suppose corporate overhead is allocated to the two divisions based on relative revenue. What are the budgeted operating profits in each division for the current year after the corporate costs are allocated?

b.   At the end of the current year, actual corporate costs incurred were $11.0 million. Of the $11.0 million, $6.6 was fixed. Actual results in the two divisions are as follows:

	Americas	ROW
Revenues..................................	$58,500,000	$87,750,000
Direct costs	46,200,000	62,550,000
Operating profit before allocation...........	$12,300,000	$25,200,000

What are the operating profits in each division for the current year after the corporate costs are allocated?

c.   Comment on the results from requirements (a) and (b).

(LO 12-5, 6)   **12-50. Dual and Single Allocation Rates—Data Analysis and Visualization**
Refer to the information in Problem 12-49 for Lilac Group.

Required
Recommend a corporate cost allocation system that would improve the performance measurement system used for the two divisions and would address any issues you may have raised in Problem 12-49, requirement (c). Illustrate your recommendation by calculating the actual division operating profits. Use any graphics that illustrate your analysis.

(LO 12-5)   **12-51. Corporate Cost Allocation and Performance Measurement**
Elba Consulting Associates (ECA) is organized into three divisions (Manufacturing, Retail, and Entertainment). Many support services, such as human resources, legal, and information technology, are provided by corporate staff. The corporate staff costs are allocated to the divisions based on divisional revenue. The resulting divisional operating profit (computed as divisional revenues less divisional direct costs less corporate cost allocations) is used to evaluate and compensate all division managers. The compensation plan consists of a fixed salary plus a bonus, which depends on the actual divisional operating profit compared to the target profit. The fixed salary for all three division managers is $500,000. The bonus consists of two parts. First, there is a "target bonus," which is a flat $25,000 for meeting the operating profit target. Second, there is an "incentive bonus," which is equal to 0.2% of salary for every thousand dollars of operating profit in excess of the target. The bonus amounts are not included in divisional operating profits.
   Partial target and actual results for the most recent year were as follows:

Target ($000):	Manufacturing	Retail	Entertainment
Division revenues..................	$20,000	$50,000	$30,000
Division direct costs...............	11,500	28,000	22,000
Division margin....................	$ 8,500	$22,000	$ 8,000

Actual ($000):	Manufacturing	Retail	Entertainment
Division revenues..................	$19,000	$48,000	$29,000
Division direct costs...............	11,000	27,000	21,500
Division margin....................	$ 8,000	$21,000	$ 7,500

The target and actual corporate costs for the most recent year were as follows:

	Target ($000)	Actual ($000)
Variable costs	$10,000	$ 9,600
Fixed costs...............................	15,000	12,000
Total corporate costs	$25,000	$21,600

Required

a.   What are the target operating profits in each division for the most recent year after the corporate costs are allocated?

b.   What are the reported (actual) operating profits in each division for the most recent year after the corporate costs are allocated?

c.   What is the total bonus that will be paid to each of the three managers? How does this compare to the bonus that would be paid if performance was at the target level?

d.   Comment on the results from requirements (*a*) through (*c*).

12-52. Dual and Single Allocation Rates—Data Analysis and Visualization (LO 12-5, 6)
Refer to the information in Problem 12-51 for Elba Consulting Associates.

Required

Recommend a corporate cost allocation system that would improve the performance measurement system used for the three divisions and would address any issues you may have raised in Problem 12-51, requirement (*d*). Illustrate your recommendation by calculating the actual division operating profits and bonus compensation that would be paid. Use any graphics that illustrate your analysis.

12-53. Dual and Single Allocation Rates (LO 12-6)
Burwell Manufacturing is organized into two divisions (Agriculture and Mining) and a corporate headquarters. The financial group of the corporate staff prepared financial operating plans (budgets) for the two divisions for the upcoming year (year 1). Selected information from the plans is as follows:

	Agriculture	Mining
Employees (full-time equivalent, or FTE)	23	52
Revenues ($000)	$8,000	$17,000
Direct division costs ($000)	5,200	13,300
Operating profit before allocation ($000)	$2,800	$ 3,700

Corporate overhead costs are expected to be $3.5 million in year 1. Of the $3.5 million, $1.25 million is fixed and the remainder is variable. Two-thirds of the variable cost is variable with respect to revenue. The other third is variable with respect to the number of FTE employees. Division managers are evaluated and compensated in part on division operating profit (including any allocated corporate costs) relative to the budget. Corporate overhead at Burwell is allocated based on relative revenues to determine both budgeted and actual operating profit.

Required

a.   What are the budgeted operating profits in each division for year 1 after the corporate costs are allocated?

b.   At the end of year 1, actual corporate costs incurred were $3.7 million. Of the $3.7 million, $1.44 million was fixed, $1.3 million was variable with respect to revenues, and $0.96 million was variable with respect to FTEs. Actual division results in year 1, prior to any allocation, are as follows:

	Agriculture	Mining
Employees (FTE)	25	55
Revenues ($000)	$10,400	$15,600
Direct costs ($000)	7,400	13,600
Operating profit before allocation ($000)	$ 3,000	$ 2,000

What are the actual (reported) operating profits in each division for year 1 after the corporate costs are allocated?

c. Comment on the results from requirements (*a*) and (*b*).

d. Recommend a corporate cost allocation system that would address the issues you raised in requirement (*c*). Illustrate your recommendation by calculating the actual division operating profits using your recommended allocation system.

(LO 12-6)   **12-54. Dual and Single Allocation Rates**

Loretto Outfitters is a retail chain of stores organized into two divisions (East and West) and a corporate headquarters. Corporate planners have prepared financial operating plans (budgets) for the two divisions for the upcoming year (year 2). Selected information from the plans is as follows:

	East	West
Number of stores	20	30
Revenues ($000)	$36,000	$60,000
Direct costs ($000)............................	18,000	28,000
Division margin ($000)	$18,000	$32,000

Based on information from various corporate staff, the planning team estimates that corporate overhead costs are expected to be $20 million in year 1. Of the $20 million, $7.2 million is fixed and the remainder is variable. With respect to the variable overhead, $4.8 million is variable with respect to revenue and the remainder is variable with respect to the number of stores. The two division managers are evaluated and compensated in part on division operating profit (including any allocated corporate costs) relative to the budget. Corporate overhead at Loretto is allocated based on relative revenues to determine both budgeted and actual operating profit.

Required

a. What are the budgeted operating profits in each division for year 1 after the corporate costs are allocated?

b. At the end of year 1, actual corporate costs incurred were $19 million. Of the $19 million, $7.3 million was fixed, $4.5 million was variable with respect to revenues, and $7.2 million was variable with respect to the number of stores. Actual division results in year 1, prior to any allocation, are as follows:

	East	West
Number of stores	16	32
Revenues ($000)	$21,000	$79,000
Direct costs ($000)............................	13,000	44,500
Division margin ($000)	$ 8,000	$34,500

What are the actual (reported) operating profits in each division for year 1 after the corporate costs are allocated?

c. Comment on the results from requirements (*a*) and (*b*).

d. Recommend a corporate cost allocation system that would address the issues you raised in requirement (*c*). Illustrate your recommendation by calculating the actual division operating profits using your recommended allocation system.

(LO 12-6)   **12-55. Cost Allocations: Comparison of Dual and Single Rates**

Manning Systems is a commercial software vendor that sells billing and other financial software to companies around the globe. Manning operates a centralized call center for customer support calls. Costs associated with use of the center are charged to the division with primary responsibility for the client. There are four geographical divisions: North America (NA), Central and South America (SA), Europe, and Asia-Pacific (APAC). The allocation is based on the length of time of calls made (Minutes). Idle time of the reservation agents and the fixed cost of the equipment are allocated based on the number of calls received (Calls) from clients in each division. Due to recent increased competition in the commercial software business, Manning has decided that it is necessary to better allocate its costs in order to price its services competitively and profitably. During the most recent period for which data are available, the use of the call center for each division was as follows:

Division	Minutes (Thousands)	Calls (Thousands)
Asia-Pacific	240	180
Central and South America.....................	480	144
Europe	960	432
North America.................................	720	1,044

During this period, the cost of the call center amounted to $2,520,000 for personnel and $1,950,000 for equipment and other costs.

Required

a. Determine the allocation to each of the divisions using the following:
   1. A single rate based on time used (minutes).
   2. Dual rates based on time used (for personnel costs) and number of calls (for equipment and other costs).

b. Write a short report to management explaining whether a single rate or dual rates should be used, and why.

12-56. Cost Allocation for Travel Reimbursement   (LO 12-1, 7)

Burchill Consultants is a global consulting firm. The firm has a travel policy that reimburses employees for the "ordinary and necessary" costs of business travel and reimburses business-class airfare for international and "long" domestic flights. Associates at the firm often mix a business trip with pleasure by either extending the time at the destination or traveling from the business destination to a nearby resort or other personal destination. When this happens, an allocation must be made between the business and personal portions of the trip, so that only the business portion is reimbursed. However, the travel policy is unclear on the allocation method to follow.

Consider this example. An employee obtained a business-class ticket for $8,557 and traveled the following itinerary.

From	To	Miles	One-Way Regular Fare	Purpose
Los Angeles	Singapore	8,770	$3,396	Business
Singapore	Sydney	3,908	2,150	Personal
Sydney	Los Angeles	7,488	3,618	Return

On the date of the flights between Los Angeles and Singapore (and return), a restricted round-trip business-class fare of $4,038 was available.

Required

a. Compute the business portion of the airfare and state the basis for the indicated allocation that is appropriate according to each of the following independent scenarios:
   1. Based on the maximum reimbursement for the employee.
   2. Based on the minimum cost to the company.

b. Write a short report to management explaining the method that you think should be used and why. You do not have to restrict your recommendation to either of the methods in requirement (a).

INTEGRATIVE CASES

(LO 12-1, 2, 3, 4)   **12-57. River Beverages Case: Budget Preparation**

Overview

River Beverages is a food and soft drink company with worldwide operations. The company is organized into five regional divisions with each vice president reporting directly to the CEO, Cindy Wilkins. Each vice president has a strategic research team, controller, and three divisions: Carbonated Drinks, Noncarbonated Drinks, and Food Products (see Exhibit 12.4). Management believes that the structure works well for River because different regions have different tastes and the division's products complement each other.

Industry

The U.S. beverage industry has become mature, its growth matching population growth. Consumers drank about 50 billion gallons of fluids in 1995. Most of the industry growth has come from the non-alcoholic beverage market, which is growing by about 1.1 percent annually. In the nonalcoholic arena, soft drinks are the largest segment, accounting for 53.4 percent of the beverages consumed. Americans consume about 26 billion gallons of soft drinks, ringing up retail sales of $50 billion every year. Water (bottled and tap) is the next largest segment, representing 23.7 percent of the market. Juices represent about 12 percent of the beverages consumed. The smallest segment is ready-to-drink teas, which is growing rapidly in volume but accounts for less than 5 percent of the beverages consumed.

Sales Budgets

Susan Johnson, plant manager at River Beverages's Noncarbonated Drinks plant in St. Louis (see Exhibit 12.5), recently completed the annual budgeting process. According to Johnson, division managers have decision-making authority in their business units except for capital financing activities. Budgets keep the division managers focused on corporate goals.

At the beginning of December, division managers submit a report to the vice president for the region summarizing capital, sales, and income forecasts for the upcoming fiscal year beginning July 1. Although the initial report is not prepared with much detail, it is prepared with care because it is used in the strategic planning process.

Exhibit 12.4

Organization Chart—River Beverages

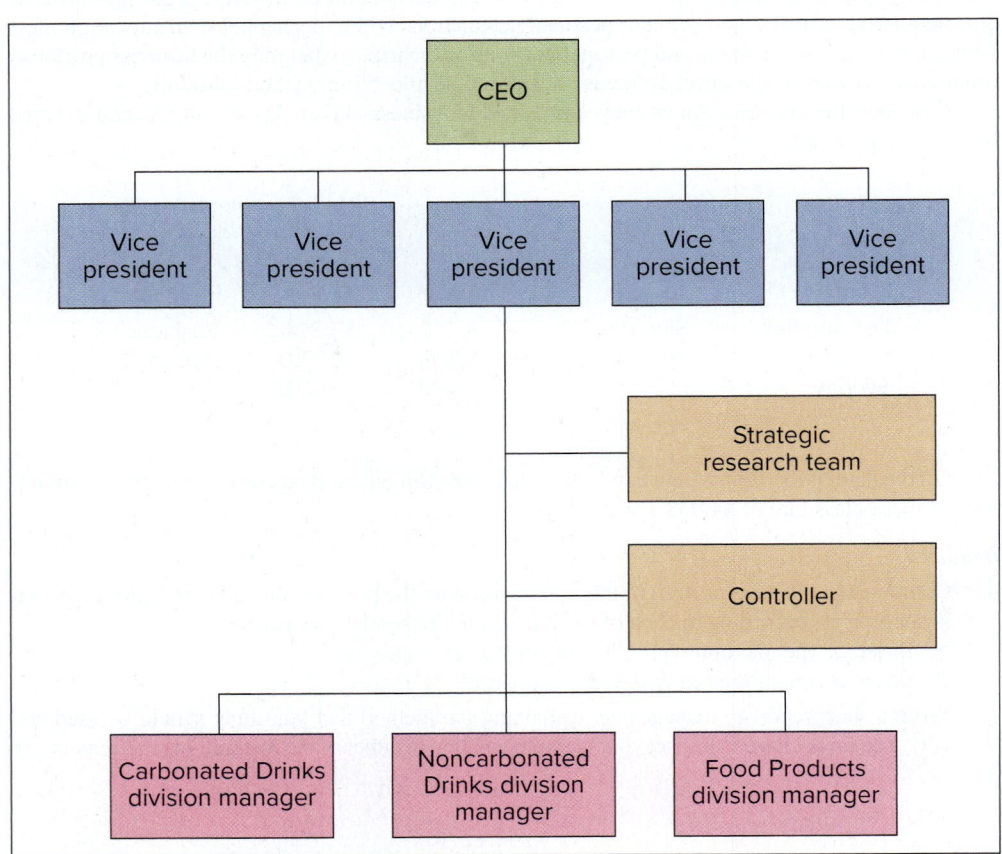

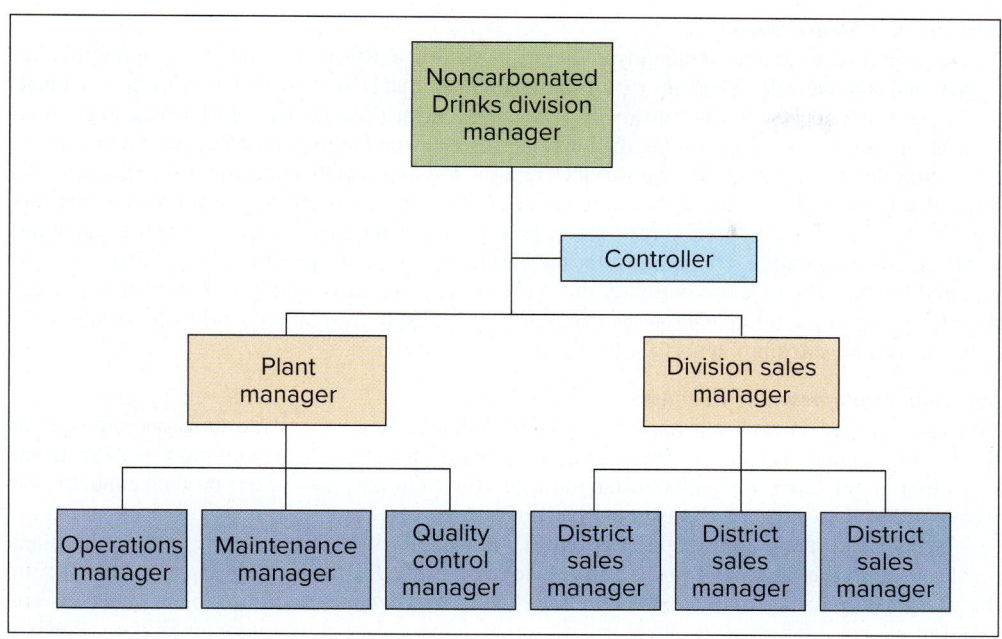

Exhibit 12.4
Division Organization
Chart—River Beverages

Next, the strategic research team begins a formal assessment of each market segment in its region. The team develops sales forecasts for each division and compiles them into a company forecast. The team considers economic conditions and current market share in each region. Management believes the strategic research team is effective because it is able to integrate division products and more accurately forecast demand for complementary products. In addition, the team ensures continuity of assumptions and achievable sales goals.

When the corporate forecast has been completed, the district sales managers estimate sales for the upcoming budget year. The district sales managers are ultimately responsible for the forecasts they prepare. The district sales forecasts are then compiled and returned to the division manager. The division manager reviews the forecast but cannot make any revisions without discussing the changes with the district sales managers. Next, the district sales forecasts are reviewed by the strategic research team and the division controller. Finally, top management reviews each division's competitive position, including plans to increase market share, capital spending, and quality improvement plans.

Plant Budgets

After top management approves the sales budget, it is separated into a sales budget for each plant. Plant location is determined by product type and where the product needs to be distributed. The budget is broken down further by price, volume, and product type. Plant managers budget contribution margins, fixed costs, and pretax income using information from the plant sales budget.

Budgeted profit is determined by subtracting budgeted variable costs and budgeted fixed costs from the sales forecast. If actual sales fall below forecasts, the plant manager is still responsible for achieving the budgeted profit. One of the most important aspects of the plant budgeting process is that plant managers break down the budget into various departments.

Operations and maintenance managers work together to develop cost standards and cost reduction targets for all departments. Budgeted cost reductions from productivity improvements, unfavorable variances, and fixed costs are developed for each department, operation, and cost center in the plant.

Before plant managers submit their budgets, a member of the strategy team and the regional controller visit the plant to keep corporate-level managers in touch with what is happening at the plant level and to help them understand how plant managers determine their budgets. The visits also allow corporate managers to provide budget preparation guidance if necessary. The visits are especially important because they force plant managers to communicate with corporate-level managers.

The final budgets are submitted and consolidated by April 1. The vice presidents review them to ensure that they are in line with corporate objectives. After the vice presidents and the chief executive officer (CEO) have made all changes, the budgets are submitted to the board of directors for approval. The board votes on the final budget in early June.

Performance Measurement

Variance reports are generated monthly at the corporate office. River has a sophisticated information system that automatically generates reports based on input that is downloaded daily from each plant. The reports also can be generated manually by managers in the organization. Most managers generate variance reports several times during the month to solve any problems before they get out of control.

Corporate managers review the variance reports, looking closely at overbudget variance problems. Plant managers are questioned only about overbudget items. Management believes that this ensures that the plant managers stay on top of problem areas and that this keeps the plant operating as efficiently as possible. One week after the variance reports are generated, plant managers are required to submit a response outlining the causes of any variances and how they plan to prevent the problem(s) in the future. Corporate can send a specialist to the plant to work with a plant manager who has repeated problems to solve them.

Sales and Manufacturing Relations

"We are expected to meet our approved budget," remarks Kevin Greely, a division controller at River. Greely continues, "A couple of years ago, one of our major restaurant customers switched to another brand. Even though the restaurant sold over 1 million cases of our product annually, we weren't allowed to make revisions to our budget."

Budgets are rarely adjusted after approval. However, if sales decline early in the year, plant managers may file an appeal to revise the budgeted profit for the year. If sales decline late in the year, management usually does not revise the budgeted amounts. Instead, plant managers are asked to cut costs wherever possible and delay any unnecessary expenditures until the following year. It is important to remember that River sets budgets so it is able to see where to make cuts or where operating inefficiencies exist. Plant managers are not forced to meet their goals, but they are encouraged to cut costs below budget.

The Sales Department is primarily responsible for product price, sales volume, and delivery timing; plant managers are responsible for plant operations. As you might imagine, problems between plant and regional sales managers occur from time to time. For example, rush orders can cause production costs to be higher than normal for some production runs. Another problem can occur when a sales manager runs a promotional campaign that causes margins to shrink. Both problems negatively affect a plant manager's profit budget but positively affect a sales manager's forecasted sales budget. Such situations are often passed up to the division level for resolution; however, it is important to remember that the customer is always the primary concern.

Incentives

River Beverages's management has devised what it thinks is an effective system to motivate plant managers. First, plant managers are promoted only when they have displayed outstanding performance in their current position. River also has monetary incentives in place to reward plant managers for reaching profit goals. Finally, charts that display budgeted items versus actual results are produced each month. Although not required to do so, most plant managers publicize the charts and use them as a motivational tool. The charts allow department supervisors and staff to compare activities in their departments to similar activities in other plants around the world.

CEO's Message

Cindy Wilkins, CEO of River Beverages, looks to the future and comments, "Planning is an important aspect of budget preparation for every level of our organization. I would like to decrease the time spent on preparing the budget, but I believe that the budgeting process keeps people thinking about the future. The negative aspect of budgeting is that sometimes it overcontrols our managers. We need to stay nimble enough to react to customer demands while staying structured enough to achieve corporate objectives. For the most part, our budget process keeps our managers aware of sales goals and alerts them when sales or expenses are offtrack."

Required

a.   Discuss each step in the budgeting process at River Beverages. Begin with the division managers' initial reports and end with the board of directors' approval. Discuss why each step is necessary.

b.   Should plant managers be held responsible for costs or profits?

c.   Write a report to River Beverages management stating the advantages and disadvantages of the company's budgeting process. Start your report by stating your assumption(s) about what River Beverages management wants the budgeting process to accomplish.

(Copyright © Michael W. Maher, 2006)

12-58. Pepsi and Old Bottles   (LO 12-1, 3, 4, 6, 7)

When the fraud at PepsiCo occurred, the company had five somewhat diverse groups of divisions: food products, such as Frito-Lay, Inc.; transportation, such as North American Van Lines, Inc.; sporting goods, such as Wilson Sporting Goods Co.; food service, such as Pizza Hut, Inc., and Taco Bell; and its primary business, beverages. The beverage group included United Beverages International (UBI), a company that bottled soft drinks in 11 foreign countries.

The fraud was committed by employees in the UBI subsidiary in two countries: Mexico and the Philippines. These employees used numerous techniques to falsify income, including keeping inventories of broken or unusable bottles on the books, failing to write off uncollectible accounts receivable, writing up the value of bottle inventory above cost, and falsifying expense accounts. These activities required extensive collusion. In the Philippines, employees kept more than $45 million of obsolete bottles on the books to satisfy the country's debt-to-equity requirements. (Writing off the bottle inventory would have reduced both assets and equity, thus creating a problem with the country's debt-to-equity requirements.)

PepsiCo's net income was overstated by a total of approximately $92 million over a five-year period from these fraudulent activities. At its highest, the overstatement was $36 million, which was 12 percent of PepsiCo's net income from all five of its main groups.

Consistent with its management style of granting considerable autonomy to division managers, PepsiCo's Internal Audit Department acted less like a watchdog and more like a management consultant. For example, at PepsiCo, the Internal Audit Department did not conduct surprise audits but notified division managers in advance of its visits to ensure that key employees were present.

Despite their role as consultants, PepsiCo's internal auditors uncovered the fraudulent activities at PepsiCo's Mexico and Philippines operations. After discovering the fraud, the Internal Audit Department at PepsiCo became less consulting-oriented and started conducting surprise audits. Some people in the company believe that the reorientation of internal audit away from consulting was a major negative repercussion of the fraud.

During the period in which the fraud was committed, PepsiCo portrayed itself as an aggressive, high-performance, results-oriented company. Prior to the fraud, PepsiCo prided itself on the company's morale and sense of community. Its policy of decentralization supported the notion that the company had aggressive, hard-working, and trustworthy employees. After the fraud was discovered, PepsiCo's top management was distressed about the conspiracy among those trusted employees who committed the fraud.

In all, the Securities and Exchange Commission filed formal complaints against 12 employees in the two countries. PepsiCo terminated the people involved, as well as the U.S.-based manager of the bottling unit of UBI.

Required

What factors contributed to the fraud at PepsiCo?

Sources: Interviews conducted by one of the authors and Securities and Exchange Commission documents.

SOLUTIONS TO SELF-STUDY QUESTIONS

1. *a.* The decision is delegated because the real estate agent has superior local knowledge about what is available on the market. If the person is looking for housing in a new city, the real estate agent also has better local knowledge about neighborhoods and other factors. This information is costly for the new person to obtain.

   b. The person looking for housing is the principal. The real estate agent is, appropriately enough, the agent.

   c. The agent might be paid a commission based on the rental rate or sales price, so they have an incentive to show the most expensive housing they think the individual can afford. Of course, this incentive is offset somewhat by the agent's desire for repeat business.

2. The choice of responsibility center type depends on the decision authority delegated to the manager. If one plant manager has responsibility for sales as well as production, a profit center is appropriate. If the plant manager produces only as orders are received, a cost center is appropriate.

3. *a.*

Target fixed corporate costs ($000)	$ 18,000
Target variable cost as a percentage of revenue ($000)	
(2.5% × $600,000)...	15,000
Target total corporate cost...................................	$33,000
Target European division revenues as a percentage of	
total corporate revenues (= $75 million ÷ $600 million)	× 12.5%
Target allocation of corporate cost to European division ($000).....	$ 4,125

b.

		Old Method
Actual revenue as percentage		
of total ($000)..........................	($80 ÷ $800)	10.0%
Corporate cost ($000).......................		$35,000
Allocation to European division ($000)		
(10% × $35,000)		$ 3,500

		Dual Rate
Target revenue as a percentage of total	($75 ÷ $600)	12.5%
Target fixed corporate cost ($000)	$18,000	
Allocated fixed costs ($000).................	12.5% × $18,000	$2,250
Actual division revenue ($000)	$80,000	
Allocated variable cost ($000)...............	2.5% × $80,000	2,000
Total ($000).............................		$4,250

13

Chapter Thirteen

Planning and Budgeting

LEARNING OBJECTIVES

After reading this chapter, you should be able to:

LO 13-1 Understand the role of budgets in overall organization planning and the importance of people in the budgeting process.

LO 13-2 Estimate sales.

LO 13-3 Develop production and cost budgets.

LO 13-4 Estimate cash flows.

LO 13-5 Develop budgeted financial statements.

LO 13-6 Explain budgeting in merchandising and service organizations.

LO 13-7 Identify common ethical dilemmas associated with budgeting.

LO 13-8 Explain how to use sensitivity analysis to budget under uncertainty.

LO 13-9 (Appendix) Describe zero-based budgeting and illustrate its use.

Eric Audras/Onoky/SuperStock

The Decision

" *Last year was a tough one. The economy did not recover as much as we had hoped, and there was increased competition from overseas. It is crucial for our budget to be realistic. We will probably have to ask the bank for some additional financing. I need you to answer one question for me—How much cash will we need to get us through next year so we will be ready when the economy recovers? We have a high level of debt already, so while I want you to be realistic in identifying our needs, there is no room for extras that you would like to have.*

There are two other issues I want you to address. First, although I am concerned about the cash needs for the year, I am particularly concerned about the first three months. Will our cash collections cover the disbursements for the first quarter? Second, I know that sales forecasts are just that—forecasts. Is there some way you can summarize the uncertainty in the forecasts and what it means for our financials next year? "

Roberto Cruz, the chief financial officer of Rainy Days Umbrellas, left the budgeting task force with this assignment. It was late October, and the task force was just starting to develop plans for the coming year. Rainy Days Umbrellas is a manufacturer of umbrellas that are sold under various labels. The company is small, but it has long-term goals that include diversified clothing products and a move to other markets.

Budgeting is a process that is widely used and necessary, at least in some form, for success, yet it is one of the least popular management processes practiced. Budgeting has become the target of criticism in the management press recently as being outdated and "fundamentally flawed."[1]

These are provocative statements for a process that is widely practiced. However, a closer reading of the commentary reveals that the problem is not the budgeting process itself, though it also comes in for its share of criticism. The problems the authors identify are the use of budgets as targets and the dysfunctional effects caused by that use.

In this chapter, we focus on the planning role of the budgeting process. For our purposes here, a **budget** is the plan, stated in financial terms, of how the organization expects to carry out its activities and meet the financial goals established in the planning process. We show how a master budget is developed and how it fits into the overall plan for achieving organization goals. Before we investigate the details of developing a master budget, we discuss the way that strategic planning can increase competitiveness and affect global operations.

> **LO 13-1**
> Understand the role of budgets in overall organization planning and the importance of people in the budgeting process.

> **budget**
> Financial plan of the revenues and resources needed to carry out activities and meet financial goals.

How Strategic Planning Increases Competitiveness

During the strategic planning process, companies often outline their **critical success factors,** which are the strengths that are responsible for making them successful. Critical success factors enable a company to outperform its competitors. By identifying these factors and ensuring that they are incorporated into the strategic plan, companies are able to maintain an edge over competitors. In addition, important critical success factors can be exploited to improve the company's overall competitiveness.

For example, Walmart has relied on several factors to maintain its competitive edge, one of which is to keep its prices consistently low by leveraging its purchasing power. The company knows that this is a critical success factor and has continued to increase its competitiveness by building this factor into its strategic planning process.

> **critical success factors**
> Strengths of a company that enable it to outperform competitors.

---

[1] Michael Jensen, "Corporate Budgeting Is Broken—Let's Fix It," *Harvard Business Review* 79, no. 10 (November 2001): 95; and Jeremy Hope and Robin Fraser, *Beyond Budgeting* (Watertown, MA: Harvard Business School Press, 2003). The Hope and Fraser criticism of budgeting is focused in large part on its use as a performance target and less about its role as part of the planning process.

Overall Plan

master budget
Financial plan of an organization for the coming year or other planning period.

A **master budget** is part of an overall organization plan for the next year made up of three components: (1) the organization goals, (2) the strategic long-range profit plan, and (3) the tactical short-range profit plan.

Organization Goals

organization goals
Company's broad objectives established by management that employees work to achieve.

Top managers establish broad objectives, which serve as **organization goals** that company employees work to achieve. These goals often include financial goals, such as income growth, as well as more general goals focusing on employee learning, innovation, and community involvement. Such broad goals provide a philosophical statement that the company is expected to follow in its operations. Many companies include their goal statements in published codes of conduct, annual reports to stockholders, and websites.

Strategic Long-Range Profit Plan

strategic long-range plan
Statement detailing steps to take to achieve a company's organization goals.

Although a statement of goals is necessary to guide an organization, it is important to detail the specific steps required to achieve them. These steps are expressed in a **strategic long-range plan.** Because the long-range plans look into the intermediate and distant future, they are usually stated in rather broad terms. Strategic plans discuss the major capital investments required to maintain present facilities, increase capacity, diversify products and/or processes, and develop particular markets. An example of the goals and how they might be attained is shown in Exhibit 13.1.

Master Budget (Tactical Short-Range Profit Plan): Tying the Strategic Plan to the Operating Plan

Long-range plans are achieved in year-by-year steps. The guidance they provide is more specific for the coming year than it is for more distant years. The plan for the coming year,

Exhibit 13.1   Goals and Strategies—Microsoft Corporation

"Our Future Opportunity"

The following is taken from the 2020 annual report for Microsoft Corporation:

"In a time of great disruption and uncertainty, customers are looking to us to accelerate their own digital transformations as software and cloud computing play a huge role across every industry and around the world. We continue to develop complete, intelligent solutions for our customers that empower people to stay productive and collaborate, while safeguarding businesses and simplifying IT management. Our goal is to lead the industry in several distinct areas of technology over the long-term, which we expect will translate to sustained growth. We are investing significant resources in:

- Transforming the workplace to deliver new modern, modular business applications to improve how people communicate, collaborate, learn, work, play, and interact with one another.
- Building and running cloud-based services in ways that unleash new experiences and opportunities for businesses and individuals.
- Applying AI to drive insights and act on our customer's behalf by understanding and interpreting their needs using natural methods of communication.
- Using Windows to fuel our cloud business and Microsoft 365 strategy, and to develop new categories of devices—both our own and third-party—on the intelligent edge.
- Inventing new gaming experiences that bring people together around their shared love for games on any devices and pushing the boundaries of innovation with console and PC gaming by creating the next wave of entertainment.

Our future growth depends on our ability to transcend current product category definitions, business models, and sales motions. We have the opportunity to redefine what customers and partners can expect and are working to deliver new solutions that reflect the best of Microsoft."

Source: https://www.microsoft.com/investor/reports/ar20/index.html.

which is more specific than long-range plans, is called the *master budget,* also known as the *static budget,* the *budget plan,* or the *planning budget.* The income statement portion of the master budget is often called the **profit plan.** The master budget indicates the level of sales, production, and cost as well as income and cash flows anticipated for the coming year. In addition, these budget data are used to construct a budgeted statement of financial position (balance sheet).

profit plan
Income statement portion of the master budget.

Budgeting is a dynamic process that ties together goals, plans, decision making, and employee performance evaluation. The master budget and its relationship to other plans, accounting reports, and management decision-making processes is diagrammed in Exhibit 13.2. On the left side are the organizational goals and strategies that set the company's long-term plan. The master budget is derived from the long-range plan in consideration of conditions expected during the coming period. Such plans are subject to change as the events of the year unfold. An economic crisis, a natural disaster, or political instability will often lead firms to defer planned expansion into new markets.

The pandemic of 2020 is an example of how external events can disrupt even the most careful planning. The Business Application "Planning and Budgeting in a Time of Great Uncertainty" reveals what managers need given the changed business environment and some suggestions on what they might do.

Planning and Budgeting in a Time of Great Uncertainty — *Business Application*

During most of 2020, managers were faced with rapidly changing business conditions that depended on both the industry and location of their operations. They also realized that the plans that they had initially made for the period would not be useful in responding. A survey by McKinsey & Company, the international consulting firm, found that 43 percent of CFOs responding believed that the budgeting process had to be refined to respond more rapidly to the changing environment. In addition, 65 percent of the survey respondents thought that rather than relying on static budgets, they would be making greater use of rolling forecasts.

To respond to this need, McKinsey recommended five changes that could be made in the current processes:

1. Stress-test scenarios and assumptions to counter uncertainty.
2. Reimagine the business from a zero base to determine key business drivers.
3. Hold back some spending centrally—as contingent resources—to build flexibility and optionality into budgets.

4. Assign finance talent to the highest-priority areas or topics to prevent burnout.
5. Rethink decision making to speed up and debias processes.

The planning and budgeting process is at least as important in times of uncertainty, but it needs to be capable of adapting to a changing economic environment. Of course, it is in just such times that firms believe they cannot afford to spend resources on activities such as planning and budgeting. However, all five of the steps above are useful in any period, but especially so in times of a global crisis.

Source: Agrawal, Ankur, Matthew Maloney, Ishaan Seth, Michael Bishran, and Christian Grube, "Memo to the CFO: A New Approach to 2021 Budgeting Starts Now," McKinsey & Company, September 10, 2020, https://www.mckinsey.com/business-functions/strategy-and-corporate-finance/our-insights/memo-to-the-cfo-a-new-approach-to-2021-budgeting-starts-now.

The conditions anticipated for the coming year are based in part on managers' near-term projections. Companies can gather this information from production managers, purchasing agents (materials prices), the accounting department, and employee relations (wage agreements), among others. As part of a benchmarking activity, some companies gather information through "competitive intelligence," speaking to their competitors, customers, and suppliers.

Exhibit 13.2
Organizational and
Individual Interaction in
Developing the Master
Budget

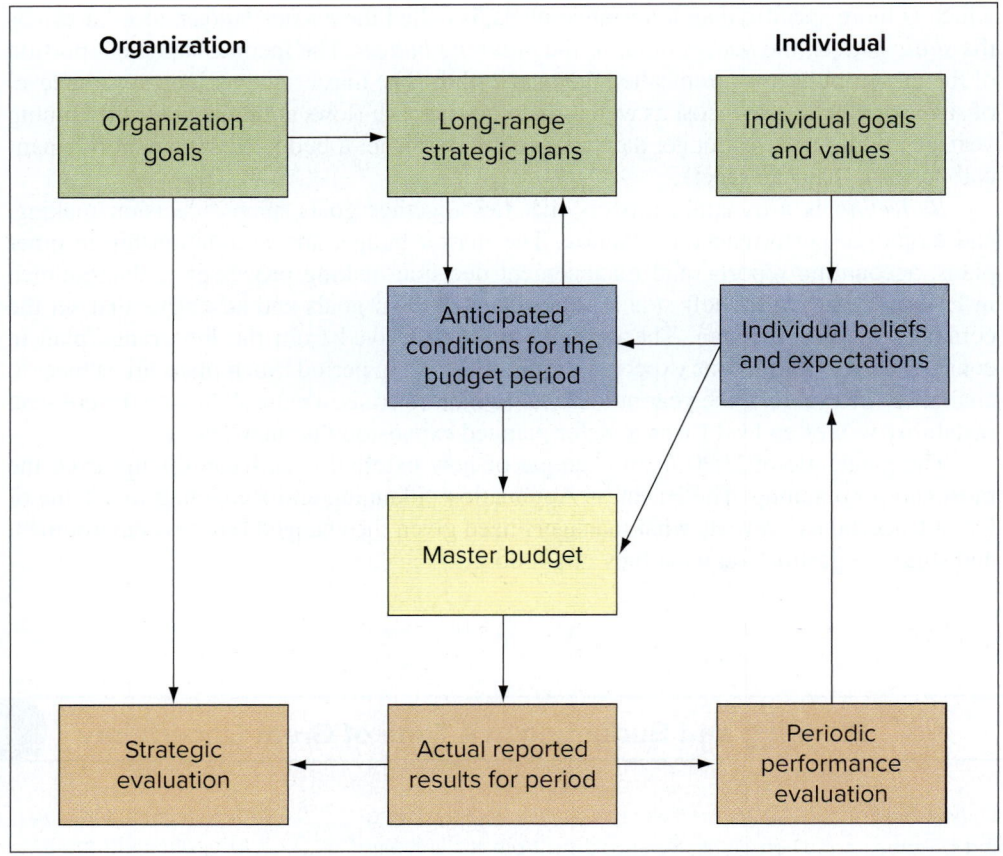

Human Element in Budgeting

A number of factors, including personal goals and values, affect managers' expectations about the coming period. Although budgets are often viewed in purely quantitative, technical terms, the importance of this human factor cannot be overemphasized. The individual's relationship to the budget is diagrammed on the right side of Exhibit 13.2.

Budget preparation rests on human estimates of an unknown future. Forecasts are likely to be greatly influenced by the forecasters' experiences with various segments of the company. For example, district sales managers are in an excellent position to project customer orders over the next several months, but market researchers are usually better able to identify long-run market trends and make macro forecasts of sales. One challenge of budgeting is to identify who in the organization is best able to provide the most accurate information about particular topics.

Value of Employee Participation

participative budgeting
Use of input from lower-
and middle-management
employees; also called *grass
roots budgeting.*

The use of input from lower- and middle-management employees is often called **participative budgeting** or *grass roots budgeting.* The use of lower and middle managers in budgeting has an obvious cost: It is time-consuming. It also has some benefits: It enhances employee motivation and acceptance of goals and provides information that enables employees to associate rewards and penalties with performance. It can serve a training or development role for managers. Participative budgeting can yield information that employees know but managers do not.

A number of studies have shown that managers often provide inaccurate data when asked to give budget estimates. They might request more money than they need because they expect their request to be cut. Managers who believe that the budget will be used as a norm for evaluating their performance could provide an estimate that will not be much of a challenge to achieve.

Thus, managers usually view the technical steps required to construct a comprehensive tactical budget plan in the context of the effect that people have on the budget and the effect that the budget will have on them. Ideally, the budget will motivate people and facilitate their activities so that the organization can achieve its goals.

Developing the Master Budget

Although each organization is unique in the way it puts together its budget, all budgeting processes share some common elements. After organizational goals, strategies, and long-range plans have been developed, work begins on the master budget, a detailed budget for the coming fiscal year with some less-detailed figures for subsequent years. Although budgeting is an ongoing process in most companies, the bulk of the work is usually done in the six months immediately preceding the beginning of the coming fiscal year. Final budget approvals by the chief executive and board of directors are made one month to six weeks before the beginning of the fiscal year.

To envision the master budgeting process, picture the financial statements most commonly prepared by companies: the income statement, the balance sheet, and the cash flow statement. Then imagine preparing these statements before the beginning of the fiscal period.

Where to Start?

Where do you start when preparing a master budget? One way to think about the question is to understand that the organization has more control over some aspects of the business (for example, how much to produce) and less control over other aspects (the demand for its products and services, for example). For most organizations, sales are most uncertain. Therefore, beginning with a sales forecast, the firm can plan the activities over which it has more control. As better information about sales becomes available, it is reasonably easy to adjust the rest of the budget. If, on the other hand, production is more uncertain than sales because the firm relies on a material that is rationed and the supply is uncertain, the firm may want to begin with a raw material and production forecast. Firms that rely on natural resources that are rationed or firms operating in economies in which a government agency controls supply (e.g., centrally planned economies) are examples of companies that start the process by preparing a forecast of production.

Sales Forecasting

In most firms, forecasting sales is the most difficult aspect of budgeting because it involves considerable subjectivity. To reduce subjectivity and gather as much information as possible, management often uses a number of different methods to obtain forecasts from a number of different sources. We begin with a forecast of revenues for the budget period.

LO 13-2
Estimate sales.

Sales Staff   Salespeople are in the unique position of being close to the customers, and they could be the people in the company who possess the best information and the best local knowledge about customers' immediate and near-term needs. As we discussed in Chapter 12, salespeople also realize that they will be evaluated based, at least in part, on their actual performance compared to the budget. As a result, they have an incentive to bias their sales forecasts.

One of the first things the budgeting task force at Rainy Days Umbrellas (RDU) did was to ask Amy Johnston, the company sales manager, to join them for an afternoon to begin developing the sales forecast. For the coming budget year, she expects sales to be about $7.5 million, although they could drop as low as $6 million or run as high as $9 million. Her bonus at the end of next year will be 1 percent of the excess of actual sales over the sales budget. So if the budget is $7 million and actual sales are also $7 million, she will receive no bonus.

The task force is aware that Amy faces conflicting incentives when it comes to providing a sales forecast. On the one hand, if she forecasts sales that are too high, she risks losing her bonus. On the other hand, if she forecasts sales that are too low, the approved budget might not include production necessary to meet sales. In the umbrella business, customers will not wait for RDU to increase production. Instead, they will buy umbrellas from competitors. In addition, Amy might have her sales force reduced, which will also have a negative effect on sales.

Thus, Amy decides on a conservative but reasonable sales forecast of $7 million, which, she believes, will give her a high probability of getting a bonus and a low risk of failing to meet her other objectives.

Incentive compensation plans can be designed to motivate different behaviors, each with their own strengths and weaknesses. If, for instance, her bonus were a fixed percentage of sales, she would have an incentive to maximize sales. Then she might be motivated to make an optimistic sales forecast to justify obtaining a larger sales staff. The high sales forecast also would be used to estimate the amount of production capacity needed, thus ensuring that adequate inventory would be available to satisfy any and all customer needs. Of course, the managers and staff who receive forecasts usually recognize the subjectivity of the situation. As Pablo Suarez, the head of the budgeting task force, put it, "We've received sales forecasts from her for several years, and they are always a bit conservative. We don't ask her to revise her estimates. We simply take her conservatism into account when we put together the overall sales forecast."

Market Researchers   To provide a check on forecasts from local sales personnel, management often turns to market researchers. This group probably does not have the same incentives that sales personnel have to bias the budget. Furthermore, researchers have a different perspective on the market. They may know little about customers' immediate needs, but they can predict long-term trends in attitudes and the effects of social and economic changes on the company's sales, potential markets, and products.

Delphi technique
Forecasting method in which individual forecasts of group members are submitted anonymously and evaluated by the group as a whole.

Delphi Technique   The **Delphi technique** is another method used to enhance forecasting and reduce bias in estimates. With this method, members of the forecasting group prepare individual forecasts and submit them anonymously. Each group member obtains a copy of all forecasts but is unaware of their sources. The group then discusses the results. In this way, differences among individual forecasts can be addressed and reconciled without involving the personality or position of individual forecasters. After the differences are discussed, each group member prepares a new forecast and distributes it anonymously to the others. These forecasts are then discussed in the same manner as before. The process is repeated until the forecasts converge on a single best estimate of the coming year's sales level.

trend analysis
Forecasting method that ranges from a simple visual extrapolation of points on a graph to a highly sophisticated computerized time series analysis.

Trend Analysis   **Trend analysis,** which can range from a simple visual extrapolation of points on a graph to a highly sophisticated computerized time series analysis, also can be helpful in preparing sales forecasts.

Time series techniques use only past observations of the data series to be forecasted. No other data are included. This methodology is justified on the grounds that because all factors that affect the data series are reflected in the actual past observations, the past data are the best reflection of available information. This approach is also relatively economical because only a list of past sales figures is needed. No other data are gathered.

Forecasting techniques based on trend analysis often require long series of past data to derive a suitable solution. Generally, when these models are used in accounting applications, monthly data are required to obtain an adequate number of observations.

Econometric Models

Another forecasting approach is to enter past sales data into a regression model to obtain a statistical estimate of factors affecting sales. For example, the predicted sales for the coming period can be related to such factors as economic indicators, consumer-confidence indexes, back-order volume, and other internal and external factors that the company deems relevant.

Advocates of these **econometric models** contend that they can include many relevant predictors. Manipulating the assumed values of the predictors makes it possible to examine a variety of hypothetical conditions and relate them to the sales forecast. This is particularly useful for performing sensitivity analysis, which we discuss later in this chapter.

econometric models
Statistical methods of forecasting economic data using regression models.

Artificial Intelligence

One characteristic the Delphi technique, trend analyses, and econometric models share is a reliance on historical sales data. Recently, researchers have worked to develop improved methods of sales forecasting based on **artificial intelligence (AI)** approaches, which help identify future patterns in demand. This allows firms to develop better forecasts that reflect both past demand and the firm's ability to meet that demand by considering not just prior period sales but also consumer preferences. As discussed in the Business Application "Using AI to Enhance Sales Predictions," companies are employing AI methods to improve sales forecasts as well as target product and service offerings geographically.

artificial intelligence (AI)
The simulation of human intelligence and behavior by computers.

As this section indicates, sophisticated analytical models using a variety of methods are available for forecasting sales. Most companies have affordable access to these models. Nonetheless, as indicated by the example in the related Business Application, it is important to remember that no model removes the uncertainty surrounding sales forecasts. Management might find in certain situations that the intuition of local sales personnel can refine and improve the sophisticated analyses and models. Finally, as in any management decision, cost-benefit tests should be used to determine which methods are most appropriate.

Using AI to Enhance Sales Predictions   *Business Application*

Traditional sales forecasting techniques typically rely, in large part, on past sales to forecast future sales. Implicit in this approach is that current practices such as product offerings, customer service levels, and other firm-specific practices will be much the same as in the past. Some firms, however, are using artificial intelligence (AI) methods to actively adapt to changes in consumer tastes both over time and across locations.

For example, the Swedish clothing retailer H&M is using data analytic techniques and AI to plan what is offered in different stores, rather than featuring the same portfolio of products everywhere. Historically, H&M, like many retailers, relied on buyers and other staff to predict trends.

Now, it's using algorithms to analyze store receipts, returns and loyalty-card data to better align supply and demand, with the goal of reducing markdowns. As a result, some stores have started carrying more fashion and fewer basics such as T-shirts and leggings.

This approach does include historical data. There are two refinements that data analytics and AI make possible. First, the data incorporate more than summary data from stores or geographic regions. The data analyzed include, for example, detailed purchase and returns information from the more than 5,000 H&M stores worldwide. H&M relies on other data in addition to historical store-level information.

To detect trends three-to-eight months in advance, H&M is analyzing data on a large scale from blog posts, search engines and other sources rather than relying mainly on staff.

Of course, as with any forecasting method, there is always error.

Algorithms late last year suggested that H&M promote reindeer-printed sweaters in January. Executives adjusted the algorithm to account for Christmas.

Data analytics and AI may not be a solution to long-term trends in the competitive environment of retailing firms. However, as this example shows, they can be used to not only forecast sales, but to adapt to changing demands and consumers' tastes.

Source: Chaudhuri, Saabira, "H&M Pivots to Big Data to Spot Next Big Fast-Fashion Trends," *The Wall Street Journal,* May 7, 2018.

Comprehensive Illustration

To make our discussion of the budgeting process more concrete, we'll develop the budget for Rainy Days Umbrellas (RDU). We use a manufacturing example because it includes most aspects of a firm's operations. The methods we discuss also apply to nonmanufacturing and not-for-profit organizations. Later in the chapter, we consider some of the unique budgeting issues in these organizations.

After evaluating the sales forecasts derived from various sources, the budgeting task force at RDU arrived at the following sales budget for the next budget year:

	Units	Price per Unit	Total Sales Revenue
Estimated sales . . .	240,000	$30	$7,200,000

Forecasting Production

LO 13-3
Develop production and cost budgets.

production budget
Production plan of resources needed to meet current sales demand and ensure that inventory levels are sufficient for future sales.

The **production budget** plans the resources needed to meet current sales demand and ensure that inventory levels are sufficient for expected activity levels. It is necessary, therefore, to determine the required inventory level for the beginning and end of the budget period. The production level may be computed from the basic cost flow equation (also known as the *basic inventory formula*):

$$\text{Beginning balance} + \text{Transfers in} - \text{Transfers out} = \text{Ending balance}$$
$$BB + TI - TO = EB$$

Adapting that equation to inventories, production, and sales, we have

$$\text{Units in beginning inventory} + \text{Required production (units)} - \text{Budgeted sales (units)} = \text{Units in ending inventory}$$

Rearranging terms to solve for required production results in

$$\text{Required production (units)} = \text{Budgeted sales (units)} + \text{Units in ending inventory} - \text{Units in beginning inventory}$$

This equation states that production equals the sales demand plus or minus an inventory adjustment. Production and inventory are stated in equivalent finished units.

RDU's sales budget projects sales of 240,000 units. Management estimates that 20,000 units will be in the beginning inventory of finished goods with an estimated cost of $320,000. Based on management's analysis, the required ending inventory is estimated to be 30,000 units. We assume for simplicity that there is no beginning or ending work-in-process inventory. With this information, the budgeted level of production is computed as follows:

$$\text{Required production (units)} = \begin{matrix} 240,000 \text{ units} \\ \text{(sales)} \end{matrix} + \begin{matrix} 30,000 \text{ units} \\ \text{(ending} \\ \text{inventory)} \end{matrix} - \begin{matrix} 20,000 \text{ units} \\ \text{(beginning} \\ \text{inventory)} \end{matrix}$$

$$= \underline{250,000 \text{ units}}$$

See Exhibit 13.3 for the production budget for RDU. The production manager reviews the production budget to ascertain whether the budgeted level of production can be reached with the capacity available. If not, management can revise the sales forecast or consider ways to increase capacity. If it appears that production capacity will exceed requirements, management might want to consider other opportunities for using the capacity.

Chapter 13 Planning and Budgeting

	A	B
1	RAINY DAY UMBRELLAS	
2	Production Budget	
3	For the Budget Year Ended December 31	
4	(in units)	
5		
6	Expected sales	240,000
7	Add desired ending inventory of finished goods	30,000
8	Total needs	270,000
9	Less beginning inventory of finished goods	20,000
10	Units to be produced	250,000
11		

Exhibit 13.3

Production Budget

One benefit of the budgeting process is that it facilitates the coordination of activities. As the sales forecast increases, for example, the budget communicates to the production manager that more umbrellas need to be produced. Conversely, if production capacity falls, the sales manager can avoid accepting orders the company cannot fill, thus reducing the possibility of dissatisfied customers. It is far better to learn about discrepancies between the sales forecast and production capacity in advance so that remedial action can be taken.

Forecasting Production Costs

After the sales and production budgets have been developed and the efforts of the sales and production groups have been coordinated, the budgeted cost of goods sold (production costs) can be prepared. The primary job of this budget is to estimate the costs of direct materials, direct labor, and manufacturing overhead at budgeted levels of production.

Direct Materials   Direct materials purchases needed for the budget period are derived from this equation:

$$\text{Required materials purchases} = \text{Materials to be used in production} + \text{Estimated ending materials inventory} - \text{Estimated beginning materials inventory}$$

The beginning and ending levels of materials inventory for the budget period are estimated, often with the help of an inventory control model. The materials to be used in production are based on production requirements.

Production at RDU for the coming period will require two kinds of materials, fabric (for the canopy) and metal (for the shaft and other structural components). Fabric has an estimated beginning inventory of 10,000 yards and estimated ending inventory of 15,000 yards. Metal has estimated beginning and ending inventories of 1,000 pounds, shown as follows:

	A	B	C	D	E
1		Estimated Production			
2		Material Data			
3		Fabric		Metal	
4	Material per unit of output	3.0	yards	2.0	pounds
5	Beginning materials inventory	10,000	yards	1,000	pounds
6	Ending materials inventory	15,000	yards	1,000	pounds
7	Cost per yard/pound	$ 2		$ 1	
8					

The cost per yard or pound is expected to remain constant during the coming budget period. Required production (from the production budget) is 250,000 units.

Computation of the required materials purchases in units of each material follows:

$$\text{Fabric} = (250,000 \times 3.0) + 15,000 - 10,000$$
$$= 755,000 \text{ yards}$$

$$\text{Metal} = (250,000 \times 2.0) + 1,000 - 1,000$$
$$= 500,000 \text{ pounds}$$

In dollar terms, this amounts to estimated purchases of $1,510,000 for fabric (= 755,000 × $2) and $500,000 for metal (= 500,000 × $1).

The direct materials budget (Exhibit 13.4) shows the materials required for production.

Direct Labor

Estimates of direct labor costs often are obtained from engineering and production management. For RDU, the direct labor costs are estimated at 0.25 hour per unit at $24 per hour (or $6 per output unit produced). Thus, for the budget year, the budgeted direct labor cost of production of 250,000 units is $1,500,000 (see Exhibit 13.5).

Overhead

Unlike direct materials and direct labor, which often can be determined from an engineer's specifications for a product, overhead is composed of many different types of costs with varying cost behaviors. Some overhead costs vary in direct proportion to production (variable overhead); some costs vary with production but in a step fashion (for example, supervisory labor); and other costs are fixed and remain the same unless capacity or long-range policies are changed. Still other costs (for example, plant depreciation) do not necessarily vary with production but can be changed at management's discretion.

Budgeting overhead requires an estimate based on production levels, management discretion, long-range capacity and other corporate policies, and external factors such as increases in property taxes. Due to the complexity and diversity of overhead costs, several cost estimation methods are frequently used. To simplify the budgeting process, costs usually are divided into fixed and variable components, with discretionary and semi-fixed costs treated as fixed costs within the relevant range.

Exhibit 13.4
Direct Materials Budget

	A	B	C	D	E
1	RAINY DAY UMBRELLAS				
2	Direct Materials Budget				
3	For the Budget Year Ended December 31				
4					
5	Units to be produced (from the production budget Exhibit 13.3)	250,000			
6		Fabric		Metal	
7	Direct materials needed per unit	3.0	yards	2.0	pounds
8	Total production needs (amount per unit times 250,000 units)	750,000		500,000	
9	Add desired ending inventory	15,000		1,000	
10	Total direct materials needed	765,000		501,000	
11	Less beginning inventory of materials	10,000		1,000	
12	Direct materials to be purchased	755,000	yards	500,000	pounds
13	Cost of materials, per yard/pound	$ 2		$ 1	
14	Total cost of direct materials to be purchased	$ 1,510,000		$ 500,000	
15					
16	Sum of materials (fabric and metal) to be purchased ($1,510,000 + $500,000)			$ 2,010,000	
17					

Exhibit 13.5
Direct Labor Budget

	A	B
1	RAINY DAY UMBRELLAS	
2	Direct Labor Budget	
3	For the Budget Year Ended December 31	
4		
5	Units to be produced (from the production budget Exhibit 13.3)	250,000
6	Direct labor time per unit (in hours)	0.25
7	Total direct labor-hours needed	62,500
8	Direct labor cost per hour	$ 24
9	Total direct labor cost	$ 1,500,000
10		

Exhibit 13.6

Manufacturing Overhead
Budget

	A	B	C	D
1	**RAINY DAY UMBRELLAS**			
2	**Schedule of Budgeted Manufacturing Overhead**			
3	**For the Budget Year Ended December 31**			
4	Variable overhead	Variable	For Total	
5		Overhead	Production	
6		Per Unit	(Exhibit 13.3)	
7	Units to be produced (from the production budget Exhibit 13.3) .		250,000 units	
8				
9	Indirect materials and supplies	$ 0.15	$ 37,500	
10	Materials handing	0.20	50,000	
11	Other indirect labor	0.05	$ 12,500	$ 100,000
12				
13	Fixed manufacturing overhead			
14	Supervisory labor		83,000	
15	Maintenance and repairs		50,000	
16	Plant administration		85,000	
17	Utilities		55,000	
18	Depreciation		140,000	
19	Insurance		30,000	
20	Property taxes		60,000	
21	Other		22,000	525,000
22	Total manufacturing overhead			$ 625,000
23				

Exhibit 13.7

Budgeted Statement of
Cost of Goods Sold

	A	B	C	D	E	F
1	**RAINY DAY UMBRELLAS**					
2	**Budgeted Statement of Cost of Goods Sold**					
3	**For the Budget Year Ended December 31**					
4						
5	Beginning work in process inventory				$ -	
6	Manufacturing costs					
7	Direct materials					
8	Beginning inventory	$ 21,000				
9	Purchases (from the direct materials budget Exhibit 13.4)	2,010,000				
10	Materials available for manufacturing	2,031,000				
11	Less ending inventory	(31,000)				
12	Total direct materials cost			$ 2,000,000		
13	Direct labor (from the direct labor budget Exhibit 13.5)			1,500,000		
14	Manufacturing overhead (from the schedule of manufacturing overhead Exhibit 13.6)			625,000		
15	Total manufacturing costs				$ 4,125,000	
16	Less ending work-in-process inventory				-	
17	Cost of goods manufactured				$ 4,125,000	
18	Add beginning finished goods inventory (20,000 units)				320,000	a
19	Less ending finished goods inventory (30,000 units)				(495,000)	b
20	Cost of goods sold				$ 3,950,000	
21						

[a] Management estimate.

[b] Finished goods are valued at $16.50 per unit ($4,125,000 ÷ 250,000 units produced) assuming FIFO. Hence, ending finished goods inventory is estimated to be $495,000 (30,000 units × $16.50).

See Exhibit 13.6 for RDU's schedule of budgeted manufacturing overhead. For convenience, after consultation with department management, the budgeting task force at RDU has divided all overhead into fixed and variable costs. The budgeting task force now can determine the budgeted total manufacturing costs by adding the three components: materials, labor, and overhead. This total is $4,125,000 (see Exhibit 13.7).

Completing the Budgeted Cost of Goods Sold

We need only include the estimated beginning and ending work-in-process and finished goods inventories to determine the required number of units produced: 250,000. As previously indicated, no work-in-process inventories exist.[2] Finished goods inventories are as follows, given the management estimate of beginning inventory and the estimated $16.50 cost of producing an umbrella this year.

	Units	Dollars
Beginning finished goods inventory....	20,000	$320,000 (management estimate)
Ending finished goods inventory.......	30,000	495,000 (= 30,000 units × $16.50)

Adding the estimated beginning finished goods inventory to the estimated cost of goods manufactured and then deducting the ending finished goods inventory yields a cost of goods sold of $3,950,000 (Exhibit 13.7).

---

[2] If the company has beginning and ending work-in-process inventories, units are usually expressed as equivalent finished units and treated the way we have treated finished goods inventories. In most companies, estimates of work-in-process inventories are omitted from the budget because they have a minimal impact.

This completes the second major step in the budgeting process: determining budgeted production requirements and the cost of goods sold. Obviously, this part of the budgeting effort can be extremely complex for manufacturing companies. It can be very difficult to coordinate production schedules among numerous plants, some of which use other plants' products as their direct materials. It also is difficult to coordinate production schedules with sales forecasts. New estimates of material availability, labor shortages, strikes, availability of energy, and production capacity often require reworking the entire budget.

Revising the Initial Budget

At this point in the budget cycle, a first-draft budget has been prepared. It usually undergoes a good deal of coordinating and revising before it is considered final. For example, projected production figures could call for revised estimates of direct materials purchases and direct labor costs. Bottlenecks could be discovered in production that will hamper the company's ability to deliver a particular product and thus affect the sales forecast. The revision process can be repeated several times until a coordinated, feasible master budget evolves. No part of the budget is formally adopted until the board of directors finally approves the master budget.

Self-Study Question

1. The self-study questions in this chapter provide a comprehensive budgeting problem based on data from the Rainy Days Umbrellas example in the chapter. Refer to the data for Rainy Days Umbrellas in the chapter example. Assume that the sales forecast was decreased to 220,000 units with no change in price. Managers revised their estimate of property taxes to $52,500 (reduced from $60,000) based on a recent property tax law change. The new target ending inventories follow:

Finished goods.....	25,000 units
Fabric.............	7,000 yards
Metal	400 pounds

Prepare a budgeted manufacturing overhead statement and a budgeted cost of goods sold statement with these new data. (Assume first-in, first-out.)

The solution to this question is at the end of the chapter.

Marketing and Administrative Budget

Creating budgets for marketing and administrative costs is often more difficult than creating the production cost budget because managers have discretion about how much money they spend and the timing of these expenditures.

It is also often difficult to establish the link between the costs and the benefits for the company. For example, the marketing department is responsible for developing sales opportunities for the company's products. This requires spending money on advertising, promotions, staff, and so on. The link between these expenditures and the forthcoming sales is not as direct as, for example, the link between costs and outputs in a production department. As a result, it is more difficult to know whether a reduction in sales is the result of reduced spending by the marketing department or a change in the economic environment. In addition, the budget for marketing and other administrative departments may also be used to fund activities or materials, such as travel and entertainment. These costs might be thought unnecessary, but if managers or other personnel consider these activities as part of the compensation, cutting them might lead to hiring and retention issues.

The budgeting objective here is to estimate the amount of marketing and administrative costs required to operate the company at its projected level of sales and production and to achieve long-term company goals. For example, the budgeted sales figures can be based on a new product promotion campaign. If production and sales

Exhibit 13.8

Marketing and
Administrative Costs
Budget

	A	B	C	D
1	RAINY DAY UMBRELLAS			
2	Schedule of Budgeted Marketing and Administrative Costs			
3	For the Budget Year Ended December 31			
4				
5		Variable	For Total	
6		Marketing	Sales	
7		Per Unit	240,000 units	
8	Variable marketing costs	Sold	(Exhibit 13.3)	
9	Sales commissions	$ 1.50	$ 360,000	
10	Other marketing	0.75	180,000	
11	Total variable marketing costs			$ 540,000
12	Fixed marketing costs			
13	Sales salaries		$ 130,000	
14	Advertising		153,000	
15	Other		67,000	
16	Total fixed marketing costs			350,000
17	Total marketing costs			$ 890,000
18	Administrative costs (all fixed)			
19	Administrative salaries		$ 241,000	
20	Legal and accounting staff		136,000	
21	Data processing services		127,000	
22	Outside professional services		32,000	
23	Depreciation—building, furniture, and equipment		84,000	
24	Other, including interest		36,000	
25	Taxes—other than income taxes		140,000	
26	Total administrative costs			796,000
27	Total budgeted marketing and administrative costs			$ 1,686,000
28				

are projected to increase, an increase in support services—data processing, accounting, personnel, and so forth—likely will be needed to operate the company at the higher projected levels.

An easy way to deal with the problem is to start with a previous period's actual or budgeted amounts and make adjustments for inflation, changes in operations, and similar changes between periods. This method has been criticized and can be viewed as being very simplistic, but it has one advantage: It is relatively easy and inexpensive. As always, the benefits of improving budgeting methods must justify their increased costs.

At Rainy Days Umbrellas, each management level submits a budget request for marketing and administrative costs to the next higher level, which reviews it and approves it, usually after making some adjustments. The budget is passed up through the ranks until it reaches top management. The schedule of marketing and administrative costs is divided into variable and fixed components (see Exhibit 13.8). In this case, variable marketing costs are those that vary with sales (not production). Fixed marketing costs are usually those that can be changed at management's discretion—for example, advertising.

Pulling It Together into the Income Statement

According to Pablo Suarez, head of the budgeting task force at Rainy Days Umbrellas, "At this point, we're able to put together the entire budgeted income statement for the period (Exhibit 13.9) so we can determine our projected operating profits. By making whatever adjustments are required to satisfy generally accepted accounting principles for external reporting, we can project net income after income taxes and earnings per share. If we don't like the results, we go back to the budgeted income statement and, starting at the top, go through each step to see if we can increase sales revenues or cut costs. We usually find some plant overhead, marketing, or administrative costs that can be cut or postponed without doing too much damage to the company's operations."

The board of directors at Rainy Days Umbrellas approved the sales, production, and marketing and administrative budgets and the budgeted income statement as submitted. Note that the budgeted income statement also includes estimated federal and other income taxes, which the tax staff provided. We will not detail the tax estimation process because it is a highly technical area separate from cost accounting.

Exhibit 13.9

Budgeted Income
Statement

	A	B	C	D
1	RAINY DAY UMBRELLAS			
2	Budgeted Income Statement			
3	For the Budget Year Ended December 31			
4				
5	Budgeted revenues			
6	Budgeted price per unit	$30		
7	Budgeted sales volume (Exhibit 13.3)	240,000		$ 7,200,000
8	Costs			
9	Costs of goods sold (Exhibit 13.7)		$ 3,950,000	
10	Marketing and administrative costs (Exhibit 13.8)		1,686,000	
11	Total budgeted costs			5,636,000
12	Budgeted operating profit			$ 1,564,000
13	Federal and other income taxes (@ 25%)			391,000
14	Budgeted profit after taxes			$ 1,173,000
15				

Self-Study Question

2. Refer to Self-Study Question 1. Recall that Rainy Days Umbrellas has a sales forecast of 220,000 units and new target ending inventories as follows:

Finished goods.....	25,000 units
Fabric.............	7,000 yards
Metal.............	400 pounds

In addition, you learn that depreciation expenses on administrative assets are now expected to be $90,000. Variable marketing costs change proportionately with sales volume; that is, the amount now is (220,000 ÷ 240,000) of the amount in the text example.

Prepare a budgeted schedule of marketing and administrative costs and a budgeted income statement.

The solution to this question is at the end of the chapter.

Key Relationships: The Sales Cycle

Assembling the master budget demonstrates some key relations among sales, accounts receivable, and cash flows in the sales cycle. Advantages of understanding these relations include the ability to solve for unknown amounts and to audit the master budget to ensure that the basic accounting equation has been correctly applied.

At Rainy Days Umbrellas, for example, the relations among budgeted sales, accounts receivable, and cash receipts are as follows (sales are assumed to be on account):

Sales (Exhibit 13.8)	Accounts Receivable		Cash (Exhibit 13.9)	
	(BB) 540,000		(BB) 830,000	
7,200,000	7,200,000	6,840,000	6,840,000	7,399,000
	(EB) 900,000		100,000	
			(EB) 371,000	

Note: *BB* and *EB* refer to beginning and ending balances. These balances for accounts receivable appear in later exhibits. We present them here to help you see how cash, sales, and accounts receivable are interrelated.

If an amount in the sales cycle is unknown, the basic accounting equation can be used to find it. For example, suppose that all of the amounts in the preceding diagram are known except ending cash balance and sales. Using the basic cost flow equation

$$BB + TI - TO = EB$$

we find sales from the Accounts Receivable account:

$$\$540,000 + TI \text{ (sales)} - \$6,840,000 = \$900,000$$
$$TI = \$900,000 - \$540,000 + \$6,840,000$$
$$TI = \$7,200,000$$

We can find the ending cash balance from the Cash account:

$$\$830,000 + (\$6,840,000 + \$100,000) - \$7,399,000 = EB$$
$$EB = \$371,000$$

Using Cash Flow Budgets to Estimate Cash Needs

Although the budgeted income statement is an important tool for planning operations, a company also requires cash to operate. Cash budgeting is important to ensure company solvency, maximize interest earned on cash balances, and determine whether the company is generating enough cash for present and future operations.

LO 13-4
Estimate cash flows.

Preparing a **cash budget** requires that all revenues, costs, and other transactions be examined in terms of their effects on cash. The budgeted cash receipts are computed from the collections from accounts receivable, cash sales, sale of assets, borrowing, issuing stock, and other cash-generating activities. Disbursements are computed by counting the cash required to pay for materials purchases, manufacturing and other operations, federal income taxes, and stockholder dividends. In addition, the cash disbursements necessary to repay debt and acquire new assets also must be incorporated into the cash budget.

cash budget
Statement of cash on hand at the start of the budget period, expected cash receipts, expected cash disbursements, and the resulting cash balance at the end of the budget period.

See Exhibit 13.10 for the cash budget for Rainy Days Umbrellas (RDU). The source of each item is indicated.

Multiperiod Cash Flows

Although the cash budget for RDU shows a surplus for the end of the year, we cannot be sure that the company will not run out of cash *during* the year. For that reason, cash flows often are analyzed in more detail than shown in the RDU example so far. Assume that

	A	B	C	D
1	**RAINY DAY UMBRELLAS**			
2	**Cash Budget**			
3	**For the Budget Year Ended December 31**			
4	Cash balance beginning of period		[a]	$ 830,000
5	Receipts			
6	Collections on accounts	$ 6,840,000	[a]	
7	Collection on employee loans	100,000	[a]	
8	Total receipts			6,940,000
9	Less disbursements			
10	Payments for accounts payable	1,880,000	[a]	
11	Direct labor from the direct labor budget (Exhibit 13.5)	1,500,000		
12	Manufacturing overhead requiring cash less noncash depreciation charges			
13	from manufacturing overhead budget (Exhibit 13.6)	485,000		
14	Marketing and administrative costs less noncash charges form marketing			
15	and administrative budget (Exhibit 13.8)	1,602,000		
16	Payments for federal income taxes (per discussion with the tax staff)	350,000		
17	Dividends	30,000	[a]	
18	Reduction in long-term debts	23,000	[a]	
19	Acquisition of new assets	1,529,000	[b]	
20	Total disbursements			7,399,000
21	Budgeted ending cash balance (ties to Exhibit 13.13)			$ 371,000
22				

Exhibit 13.10
Cash Budget

[a] Estimated by the treasurer's office.
[b] Estimated by the treasurer's office per the capital budget.

the following is consistent with the experience of RDU concerning its monthly collection experience for sales on credit:

Cash collected from current month's sales	20%
Cash collected from last month's sales	75
Cash discounts taken (percentage of gross sales).	2
Written off as bad debt	3
Total disposition of credit sales in current month.	100%

This means that if January's credit sales are $500,000, expected collections are $100,000 in January and $375,000 in February; $10,000 is not expected to be collected because the customers paid early enough to get a discount; and $15,000 is not expected to be collected because these accounts will be written off as bad debts. See Exhibit 13.11 for a multiperiod schedule of cash collections for the three months of the quarter ending March 31 for RDU. Assume that the beginning accounts receivable balance on January 1 is expected to be $540,000 (net of discounts and bad debts), all of which is anticipated to be collected during January. The expected sales for the three months follow:

January sales	$500,000
February sales	450,000
March sales.	600,000

The same approach is used for cash disbursements. See the cash disbursements in Exhibit 13.12 for RDU, which pays for 50 percent of its purchases in the month of purchase and 48 percent in the following month, and takes a 2 percent discount

Exhibit 13.11   Multiperiod Schedule of Cash Receipts

	A	B	D	F	G
1	RAINY DAYS UMBRELLAS				
2	Multiperiod Schedule of Cash Collections				
3	For the Quarter Ended March 31				
4					
5			Month		Total for
6		January	February	March	Quarter
7					
8	Beginning accounts receivable, January 1, $ 540,000	$ 540,000			$ 540,000
9	January sales, $ 500,000[a]	100,000	$ 375,000		475,000
10	February sales, $ 450,000[b]		90,000	$ 337,500	427,500
11	March sales, $ 600,000			120,000	120,000
12	Total cash collections	$ 640,000	$ 465,000	$ 457,500	$ 1,562,500
13					
14					

| ⊲ ⊳ ⊳⊳ \ **Collections** ⟋ Disbursements ⟋ Sheet 3 ⟋ | ⊲ |

Note: Assumptions for the budget: 20 percent of a month's sales is collected in cash during the month; 75 percent is collected in the next month; 2 percent is taken as a cash discount for early payments; and 3 percent will not be collected because it is written off as bad debts.

[a] 20 percent collected in January, 75 percent collected in February, and 5 percent not collected, according to the preceding assumption.

[b] 20 percent collected in February, 75 percent collected in March, and 5 percent not collected, according to the preceding assumption.

Exhibit 13.12   Multiperiod Schedule of Cash Disbursements

	A	B	C	D	E	F	G	H	
1		RAINY DAYS UMBRELLAS							
2		Multiperiod Schedule of Cash Disbursements							
3		For the Quarter Ended March 31							
4			Month					Total for	
5			January		February		March	Quarter	
6									
7	Beginning accounts payable, January 1, $ 256,000		$ 256,000					$ 256,000	
8	January purchases, $ 120,000[a]		60,000		$ 57,600			117,600	
9	February purchases, $ 200,000[b]				100,000		$ 96,000	196,000	
10	March purchases, $ 250,000						125,000	125,000	
11	Additional cash payments		250,000		250,000		250,000	750,000	
12	Total cash disbursements		$ 566,000		$ 407,600		$ 471,000	$ 1,444,600	
13									

|◄ ◄ ► ►|\   Collections \   **Disbursements** / Sheet 3 /   ◄

Note: Assumptions for the budget: 50 percent of a month's purchases is paid in cash during the month; 48 percent is paid in the next month; and 2 percent is taken as a cash discount for early payments.

[a] 50 percent paid in January, 48 percent paid in February, and 2 percent discounts taken, according to the preceding assumption.

[b] 50 percent paid in February, 48 percent paid in March, and 2 percent discounts taken, according to the preceding assumption.

for paying on time. Following is a list of purchases for the three months January through March:

January.....................	$120,000
February....................	200,000
March	250,000

In addition, all other cash payments are expected to be $250,000 per month. RDU had accounts payable of $256,000 on January 1, all of which it paid in January.

Self-Study Question

3. This question is based on the previous Self-Study Questions in this chapter and on the Rainy Days Umbrellas example in the text. Prepare a cash budget given the revised figures for Rainy Days Umbrellas provided in Self-Study Questions 1 and 2. Assume, however, that cash collections will decrease by the same amount as the decrease in sales except that the ending accounts receivable level will decrease by another $20,000. Lower payments for purchases of materials equal to the reduction in purchases will be required, but ending accounts payable also will decrease by $2,000. Payments for income taxes will decrease to $300,000.

The solution to this question is at the end of the chapter.

Planning for the Assets and Liabilities on the Budgeted Balance Sheets

Budgeted balance sheets, or statements of financial position, combine an estimate of financial position at the beginning of the budget period with the estimated results of operations for the period (from the income statements) and estimated changes in assets and liabilities. The latter result from management's decisions about optimal levels of capital investment in long-term assets (the capital budget), investment in working capital, and financing decisions. Decision making in these areas is, for the most part, the treasurer's function. We assume that these decisions have been made and incorporate their results in the budgeted balance sheets. See Exhibit 13.13 for the budgeted balance sheets for Rainy Days Umbrellas at the beginning and end of the budget year.

LO 13-5
Develop budgeted financial statements.

budgeted balance sheets
Statements of budgeted financial position.

Exhibit 13.13   Budgeted Balance Sheet

	A	B	C	D	E	F	G	H	I
1	RAINY DAYS UMBRELLAS								
2	Budgeted Balance Sheets								
3	For the Budget Year Ended December 31								
4	($000)								
5									
6		Budget Year							
7		Balance						Balance	
8		(January 1)		Additions		Subtractions		(December 31)	
9	Assets								
10	Current assets								
11	Cash	$ 830	a	$ 6,940	a	$ 7,399	a	$ 371	a
12	Accounts receivable	540	b	7,200	c	6,840	a	900	
13	Inventories	341	d	4,135	e	3,950	f	526	g
14	Other current assets	161	b	–	b	100	h	61	
15	Total current assets	$ 1,872		$ 18,275		$ 18,289		$ 1,858	
16	Long-term assets								
17	Property, plant, and equipment	1,866	b	1,529	a	–	b	3,395	
18	Less accumulated depreciation	(1,246)	b	(224)	i	–	b	(1,470)	
19	Total assets	$ 2,492		$ 19,580		$ 18,289		$ 3,783	
20	Liabilities and shareholder's equity								
21	Current liabilities								
22	Accounts payable	$ 256	b	$ 2,010	j	$ 1,880	a	$ 386	
23	Taxes payable	373	b	391	c	350	a	414	
24	Current portion of long-term debt	23	b	23	b	23	a	23	
25	Total current liabilities	$ 652		$ 2,424		$ 2,253		$ 823	
26	Long-term liabilities	258	b	–	b	23	b	235	
27	Total liabilities	$ 910		$ 2,424		$ 2,276		$ 1,058	
28	Shareholders' equity								
29	Common stock	437	b	–	b	–	b	437	
30	Retained earnings	1,145	b	1,173	k	30	a	2,288	
31	Total shareholders equity	$ 1,582		$ 1,173		$ 30		$ 2,725	
32	Total liabilities and shareholders equity	$ 2,492		$ 3,597		$ 2,306		$ 3,783	

[a] From cash budget (Exhibit 13.10).

[b] Estimated by personnel in the company's accounting department.

[c] From budgeted income statement (Exhibit 13.9). Assumes that all sales are on account.

[d] From budgeted statement of cost of goods sold (Exhibit 13.7), sum of beginning direct materials, work-in-process, and finished goods inventories ($21 + $0 + $320 = $341).

[e] From budgeted statement of costs of goods sold (Exhibit 13.7), sum of materials purchases, direct labor, and manufacturing overhead ($2,010 + $1,500 + $625 = $4,135).

[f] From budgeted statement of cost of goods sold (Exhibit 13.7).

[g] From budgeted statement of cost of goods sold (Exhibit 13.7), sum of ending direct materials, work-in-process, and finished goods inventories ($31 + $0 + $495 = $526).

[h] From employee loans.

[i] Depreciation of $140 from schedule of budgeted manufacturing overhead (Exhibit 13.6), plus depreciation of $84 from the schedule of budgeted marketing and administrative costs (Exhibit 13.8) equals $224 increase in accumulated depreciation.

[j] From budgeted statement of cost of goods sold (Exhibit 13.7). Accounts payable increases are assumed to be for materials purchases only.

[k] From budgeted income statement (Exhibit 13.9), operating profit after taxes.

Big Picture: How It All Fits Together

We have completed the development of a comprehensive budget for Rainy Days Umbrellas. See Exhibit 13.14 for a model of the budgeting process. Although we have simplified the presentation, you can still see that assembling a master budget is a complex process requiring careful coordination of many different organization segments.

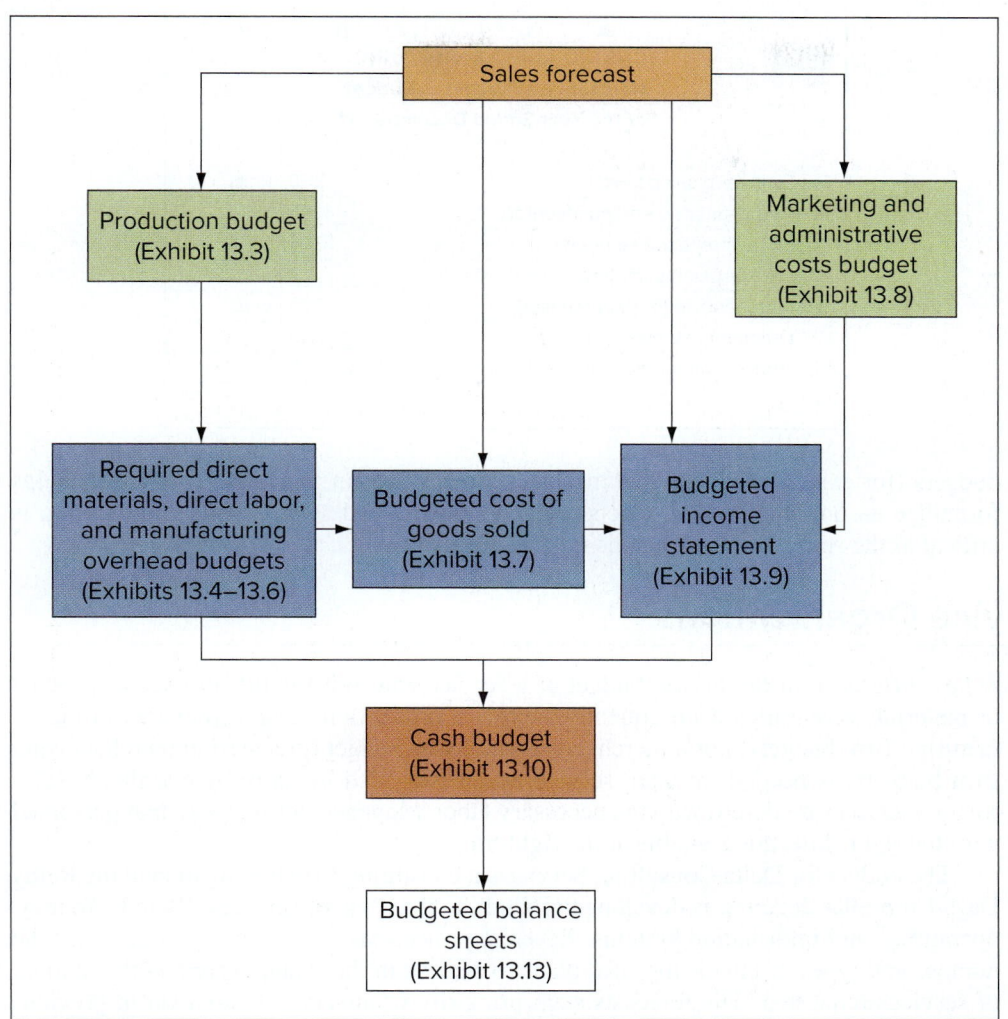

Exhibit 13.14

Assembling the Master Budget for a Manufacturing Firm

Budgeting in Retail and Wholesale Organizations

We used a manufacturing example, Rainy Days Umbrellas, to illustrate the construction of the master budget because it allowed us to include the effects of inventories and inventory balances on the budgeting process. Although a manufacturing operation provides a good comprehensive example, budgeting is used extensively in other environments as well, and we now consider some of the unique features of budgeting in these settings.

As in manufacturing, the sales budget in retail and wholesale (often called *merchandising*) organizations drives the rest of the budgeted income statement. A merchandiser does not have a production budget but instead has a merchandise purchases budget, which is much like the direct materials purchases budget in manufacturing. For example, managers at Castro Audio & Video, Inc., prepared the following purchases budget for a particular home entertainment system:

LO 13-6
Explain budgeting in merchandising and service organizations.

Estimated sales..................	300 units
Estimated ending inventory........	5
Estimated beginning inventory.....	2
Estimated cost per unit...........	$1,725

See Exhibit 13.15 for the merchandise purchases budget for Castro.

As you can see, this budget requires extensive coordination between the managers responsible for sales and those in charge of buying. Because of the critical importance of timing and seasonality in merchandising, special attention is usually given to short-term

Exhibit 13.15

Purchases Budget

	A	B	C
1	**CASTRO AUDIO & VIDEO, INC.**		
2	**Merchandise Purchases Budget**		
3	**For the Year Ended December 31**		
4			
5	Estimated sales (units)	300	units
6	Add estimated ending inventory	5	
7	Total merchandise needs	305	
8	Less beginning inventory	2	
9	Merchandise to be purchased	303	units
10	Estimated cost per unit	× $ 1,725	
11	Total estimated cost of merchandise	$ 522,675	
12			

budgets (for example, spring, summer, and holiday season budgets). The budget helps formalize an ongoing process of coordinating buying and selling. This coordination is critical to the success of merchandising enterprises.

Budgeting in Service Organizations

A key difference in the master budget of a service enterprise is the absence of product or materials inventories. Consequently, neither a production budget (prepared in manufacturing firm budgets) nor a merchandise purchases budget (prepared in merchandising firm budgets) is needed. Instead, service businesses need to carefully coordinate sales (that is, services rendered) with the necessary labor. Managers must ensure that personnel with the right skills are available at the right times.

The budget for Delta Consulting Services, a consulting firm hoping to land the Rainy Days Umbrellas account, is developed around the three major services offered: strategy, operations, and information systems. Revenue projections are based on estimates of the number and types of clients the firm plans to service in the budget year and the amount of services requested. The forecasts stem primarily from services provided in previous years with adjustments for new clients, new services to existing clients, loss of clients, and changes in the rates charged for services.

Once the amount of services (expressed in labor-hours) is forecast, the firm develops its budget for personnel. Staffing to meet client needs is a very important part of the budgeting process. Norm Agnew, a founder of the firm, explains, "Budgeting is critical in a service business like ours. Virtually all of our costs are people. If we hire based on expected business, we cannot easily adjust our staffing if some projects do not materialize. Therefore, we always face a trade-off between not having the staff to do the work and having costly staff who are underemployed."

Ethical Problems in Budgeting

LO 13-7

Identify common ethical dilemmas associated with budgeting.

Budgeting creates serious ethical issues for many people. Managers and employees provide much of the information for the budget; their performance then is compared to the budget they helped develop. For example, as a manager, suppose that you believe that although it is possible to achieve a 10 percent increase in your department's sales, a 2 percent increase is almost certain. If you tell upper management that a 10 percent increase is an appropriate budget but you fall short of it, you will lose opportunities for merit pay increases and a promotion. Management could assume that you fell short of 10 percent not because of market circumstances beyond your control but because you did not perform well in making sales. On the other hand, if you report that only a 2 percent increase is possible, the company will not provide enough production capacity to fill the sales orders if the 10 percent increase comes through. Should you do what is in your best interest or give your best estimate of reality?

Part of the problem, as we will discuss in Chapter 14, is the form of the merit pay schedule that creates strong incentives as actual performance approaches the performance target. As we noted in Chapter 12, the company must recognize the trade-off between encouraging unbiased reporting by local managers and using this information in performance evaluation and reward systems. While the conflicts cannot be avoided in a decentralized firm, managers who are aware of the potential problems that this conflict creates are in a position to take steps to mitigate the consequences.

Budgeting in Government Agencies   *Business Application*

We have emphasized the planning purpose of budgeting in this chapter. However, in governmental organizations, the budget serves as an expression of the legislature's (voters') desires and as such it is a legally binding spending authorization. This can often lead to unintended conflicts between making good decisions and complying with the budget.

A government agency's budget includes details on planned spending for different purposes. It is not enough for the agency to spend only the total amount of the budget. It must use the funds in the ways that are anticipated by the budget. As an example, a department's budget is typically made up of funds for different purposes, such as capital procurement—buying machines, say—and operating and maintenance (O&M) activities—renting or leasing equipment. Suppose a department needs a computer. If the department is short of O&M funds and has excess capital procurement funds, it has an incentive to buy the computer rather than lease it, regardless of what a lease-versus-buy analysis suggests.

A second way in which the budgeting process can distort decisions is caused by the fact that next period's budget is based on this period's budget (and expenditures). This leads to requests for as large a budget as possible. Typically, however, money that is not spent in one fiscal year does not "roll over" and become available the next year. This creates a perverse incentive to spend any unused funds before the fiscal year ends. This is referred to as the "use it or lose it" phenomenon. There are two reasons for this. First, the funds will not be available in the next year so any purchases made are "free." Second, it is relatively common that spending less than the budgeted amount will result in a lower budget for the following year.

Some government agencies have tried to counteract these effects by employing zero-based budgeting, which we discuss in the Appendix to this chapter. Its adoption, however, is not widespread. As a result, virtually every year there are news stories about some of the more blatant (depending on the reporting source's views) misuses of government funds this incentive engenders.

Source: Based on the authors' research.

Budgeting under Uncertainty

LO 13-8

Explain how to use sensitivity analysis to budget under uncertainty.

A major benefit of formal planning models is that they allow you to explore many alternatives and options in the planning process. Although it is beyond the scope of this book to go into the details of formal corporate planning models, we believe that you can see how to integrate the budget plan with formal planning models that set forth mathematical relationships among an organization's operating and financial activities.

For example, a central element of enterprisewide risk management is evaluating the firm's exposure to events that would materially affect the firm's financial prospects. Recognizing this, managers often perform *sensitivity analysis* on their projections. This analysis consists of hypothetical questions such as these: What if labor costs are 10 percent higher (or lower) than projected? What if new health and safety regulations that increase our costs of operations are passed? What if our major supplier of direct materials goes bankrupt? By asking and answering such questions during the planning phase, management can determine the risk of various phases of its operations and develop contingency plans.

As part of the budget plan at Rainy Days Umbrellas (RDU), for example, local managers were asked to provide three forecasts of selling price and selling quantity: their best estimate, an optimistic estimate (defined as "an estimate so high that there is only a 10 percent or less chance that conditions will be better than the optimistic estimate"), and a pessimistic estimate (defined as "an estimate so low that there is only a 10 percent or less chance that conditions will be worse than the pessimistic estimate"). The optimistic and pessimistic forecasts were not as detailed as the best estimates, but they did highlight some potential problems and risks. This exercise led to nine possible scenarios defined by selling price and sales quantity.

Spreadsheets are extremely helpful in preparing budgets, which require considerable sensitivity, or what-if, thinking. Spreadsheets help link the various what-if scenarios to changes in financial variables and to financial consequences.

For example, the simple spreadsheet in Exhibit 13.16 shows the nine scenarios reflecting the estimated sales prices and sales quantities just described. Each scenario is associated with estimated changes in cost of goods sold and in marketing and administrative costs. (Row 9 presents the budget used in the text ignoring inventories; assume that the other scenarios were worked out by management and presented to us.) Note that the amount shown for operating profits varies considerably between the worst scenario in row 4 and the best scenario in row 14. This analysis alerts management that RDU will earn less than half the expected profits under the worst scenario. Given the company's precarious cash position, this analysis will motivate managers at RDU to develop contingency plans for obtaining cash to meet operating expenses in the event that the more pessimistic scenarios are realized.

Although the results of different scenarios are easy to determine in Exhibit 13.16, it would become increasingly difficult as the number of scenarios increased. Data visualizations can be helpful in such cases. The visualizations will depend on the scenarios being modeled, the detail in the assumptions for each scenario, and many other factors. In this relatively simple case, the heat map shown in Exhibit 13.17 can be used to highlight those scenarios that meet certain criteria. For example, suppose that managers have a target operating profit of $1.5 million. The heat map shows that the target cannot be achieved with a sales price of $25 per unit or if the sales price is $30 per unit and the sales quantity is 225,000 units.

A second visualization uses bar charts to identify scenarios that meet the operating profit goal in graphical, rather than tabular, form and that hides some of the intermediate data, such as gross margin. Exhibit 13.18 Panel A presents operating profit as a function of sales volume for three different sales prices. As shown in Panel A, the scenarios

Exhibit 13.16
Spreadsheet Analysis of Alternative Budgeting Scenarios

	A	B	C	D	E	F	G
1	**Sales**	**Sales**		**Cost of**	**Gross**	**Marketing**	**Operating**
2	**Price**	**Quantity**	**Revenue**	**Goods Sold**	**Margin**	**& Admin**	**Profit**
3							
4	$25	225,000	$5,625,000	$3,712,500	$1,912,500	$1,652,250	$260,250
5	$30	225,000	$6,750,000	$3,712,500	$3,037,500	$1,652,250	$1,385,250
6	$35	225,000	$7,875,000	$3,712,500	$4,162,500	$1,652,250	$2,510,250
7							
8	$25	240,000	$6,000,000	$3,960,000	$2,040,000	$1,686,000	$354,000
9	$30	240,000	$7,200,000	$3,960,000	$3,240,000	$1,686,000	$1,554,000
10	$35	240,000	$8,400,000	$3,960,000	$4,440,000	$1,686,000	$2,754,000
11							
12	$25	260,000	$6,500,000	$4,290,000	$2,210,000	$1,731,000	$479,000
13	$30	260,000	$7,800,000	$4,290,000	$3,510,000	$1,731,000	$1,779,000
14	$35	260,000	$9,100,000	$4,290,000	$4,810,000	$1,731,000	$3,079,000
15							

Exhibit 13.17
Heat Map for Scenario Analysis: Desired Operating Profit Greater Than $1.5 Million

	A	B	C	D	E	F	G
1	**Sales**	**Sales**		**Cost of**	**Gross**	**Marketing**	**Operating**
2	**Price**	**Quantity**	**Revenue**	**Goods Sold**	**Margin**	**& Admin**	**Profit**
3							
4	$25	225,000	$5,625,000	$3,712,500	$1,912,500	$1,652,250	$260,250
5	$30	225,000	6,750,000	3,712,500	3,037,500	1,652,250	1,385,250
6	$35	225,000	7,875,000	3,712,500	4,162,500	1,652,250	2,510,250
7							
8	$25	240,000	$6,000,000	$3,960,000	$2,040,000	$1,686,000	$354,000
9	$30	240,000	7,200,000	3,960,000	3,240,000	1,686,000	1,554,000
10	$35	240,000	8,400,000	3,960,000	4,440,000	1,686,000	2,754,000
11							
12	$25	260,000	$6,500,000	$4,290,000	$2,210,000	$1,731,000	$479,000
13	$30	260,000	7,800,000	4,290,000	3,510,000	1,731,000	1,779,000
14	$35	260,000	9,100,000	4,290,000	4,810,000	1,731,000	3,079,000
15							

Exhibit 13.18   Bar Charts for Scenario Analysis: Desired Operating Profit Greater Than $1.5 Million

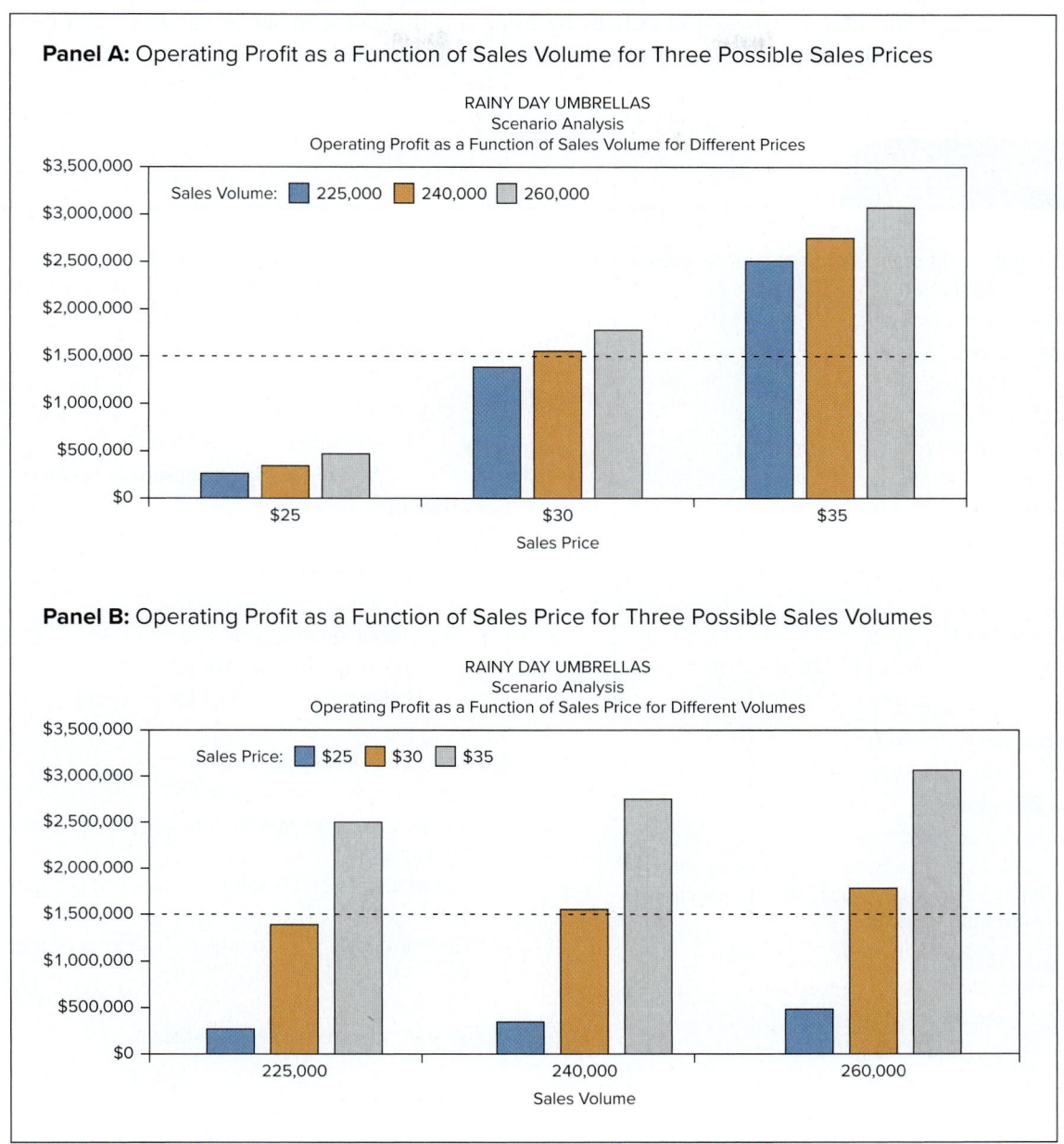

Panel A: Operating Profit as a Function of Sales Volume for Three Possible Sales Prices

RAINY DAY UMBRELLAS
Scenario Analysis
Operating Profit as a Function of Sales Volume for Different Prices

Sales Volume: ▮ 225,000   ▮ 240,000   ▯ 260,000

Panel B: Operating Profit as a Function of Sales Price for Three Possible Sales Volumes

RAINY DAY UMBRELLAS
Scenario Analysis
Operating Profit as a Function of Sales Price for Different Volumes

Sales Price: ▮ $25   ▮ $30   ▯ $35

assuming a unit sales price of $35 for any of the three possible volumes or a sales price of $30 with a sales volume of 240,000 units or 260,000 units meet the criteria.

In Panel B of Exhibit 13.18, the bar chart is repeated, but with operating profit as a function of sales price for three different sales volumes. Again, the scenarios that meet the criteria are easy to identify.

These are only a few of the numerous scenarios that management could develop. Furthermore, managers could develop alternative scenarios for any of the budgets that we have discussed. Large companies usually develop complex financial models to deal with the numerous interactions of the budget, and these models involve considerably more than just the sensitivity analysis illustrated in Exhibits 13.16–13.18.

For example, a decision support system model has been developed to help managers assess the trade-offs of different business approaches. Most budgeting activities involve decisions having more than one strategic objective. A company could have two objectives, to maximize income and minimize labor overtime. As the number of objectives increases and they begin to conflict, the decision-making process becomes more complex. An interactive, multiple-objective, programming model allows managers to deal with often-conflicting objectives by using a straightforward set of equations and constraints. The result is a solution that maximizes each objective.

Key Takeaways

1. The master budget is part of an overall organization plan made up of three components:
   a. Organization goals, including
      - Financial goals.
      - Operational goals.
      - Social involvement goals.
   b. Strategic long-range plan.
      - Capital investments.
      - New markets.
      - New product areas.
   c. Tactical short-range profit plan.
      - Detailed financial planning for the upcoming budget period.
      - Provides pro-forma ("as-if") financial statements.

2. The master budget consists of
   a. Pro-forma income statement
      - Revenue forecast from one or more sources:
         - Sales staff.
         - Market researchers.
         - Forecasting techniques including Delphi analysis, trend analysis, and econometric methods.
      - Cost of goods sold budget:
         - Production forecast based on
            - Expected sales.
            - Desired ending inventories.
            - The inventory equation: Beginning inventory + Production = Sales + Ending Inventory.
         - Direct costs
            - Direct materials.
            - Direct labor.
         - Manufacturing overhead costs
            - Marketing and administrative budget.
   b. Cash budget
      - Cash collections based on
         - Forecasted sales.
         - Accounts receivable history.
      - Cash disbursements based on
         - Cost of goods sold budget.
         - Marketing and administrative budget.
         - Planned capital investments.
   c. Pro-forma balance sheet
      - Cash from the cash budget.
      - Receivables from the sales forecast and collections history.
      - Inventories from the sales forecast and production budget.
      - Capital assets from planned investments and disposals.
      - Liabilities from funding plans.
      - Shareholders' equity as a residual.

SUMMARY

This chapter has discussed and illustrated the budget process. The budget is part of the overall plan for achieving an organization's objectives. The master budget is usually a one-year plan that encompasses budgeted sales and production, the budgeted income statement, the balance sheet, and the cash flow statement, as well as supporting schedules.

The following summarizes key ideas tied to the chapter's learning objectives:

LO 13-1 Understand the role of budgets in overall organization planning and the importance of people in the budgeting process. Budgets, which are used as a blueprint for operations, help companies determine the means for achieving their goals by outlining projected sales, production costs, and marketing and administrative costs. Budgets are based on people's estimates, which are affected by their own goals, values, and abilities. Managers should consider these "soft" factors when collecting information for budgets.

LO 13-2 Estimate sales. The key to the budget is a good sales forecast because many other parts of the budget depend on the sales forecast. The sales forecast usually is derived from multiple sources of data, including data provided by sales personnel, market researchers, and statistical analyses.

LO 13-3 Develop production and cost budgets. After sales forecasts have been developed, the number of units to be produced is estimated. This process derives the cost of goods sold. An estimate of marketing and administrative costs also is made based on the previous period's actual and budgeted amounts adjusted for several factors, including inflation and changes in operations.

LO 13-4 Estimate cash flows. Preparing a cash budget requires that all revenues, costs, and other transactions be examined in terms of their effects on cash.

LO 13-5 Develop budgeted financial statements. Budgeted sales, production costs, and marketing and administrative costs are combined to form the budgeted income statement. To complete the budgeted financial statements, projected cash flows and a balance sheet are prepared.

LO 13-6 Explain budgeting in merchandising and service organizations. Retail and wholesale organization budgets are similar to manufacturing budgets except that they have no production budget. Service organizations are similar except that they have no inventories. The budget is not only a planning tool but also a legal authorization for expenditure in governmental (nonprofit) units.

LO 13-7 Identify common ethical dilemmas associated with budgeting. Conflicts of interest often arise when employees are asked for input to help establish a budget. Incentives exist for employees to provide targets that are relatively easy to achieve. Conversely, companies typically hope to establish challenging goals and reward employees for meeting the challenge. As a result, employees do not always provide accurate information for the budgeting process. In addition, if budget targets are difficult to meet, employees could turn to fraudulent financial reporting.

LO 13-8 Explain how to use sensitivity analysis to budget under uncertainty. Uncertainty is an important part of preparing budgets and plans. In addition to many formal models, managers use sensitivity analyses to better understand the range of outcomes likely to occur. Spreadsheet software has made sensitivity analysis much easier to perform.

LO 13-9 (Appendix) Describe zero-based budgeting and illustrate its use. Zero-based budgeting is a management process that develops a budget without basing it on previous expenditures. It is designed to give managers information about alternative projects or activities, ranking these activities and funding the highest-ranked activities based on funding availability.

KEY TERMS

artificial intelligence (AI), *597*
budget, *591*
budgeted balance sheets, *607*
cash budget, *605*
critical success factors, *591*
Delphi technique, *596*
econometric models, *597*

master budget, *592*
organization goals, *592*
participative budgeting, *594*
production budget, *598*
profit plan, *593*
strategic long-range plan, *592*
trend analysis, *596*

APPENDIX: ZERO-BASED BUDGETING

A criticism of the traditional budgeting approach as described in the chapter concerns how the budget is prepared. In many organizations, the starting point for next period's budget is the actual expenditures for the current period. To this figure are added (or subtracted) amounts for known changes in activities, resource prices, economic conditions, and so on. If there are any inefficiencies in the current activities, this can lead to inefficiencies or unnecessary activities being "baked in" to the current budget. Once we accept that this is a danger of the budgeting process, the solution is obvious. What if we started

LO 13-9

Describe zero-based budgeting and illustrate its use.

each budget period as if we were operating a totally new enterprise? We could then determine what is necessary to operate in the following period.

This is the thinking of proponents of "zero-based budgeting" (ZBB). First formalized at the technology firm Texas Instruments in the early 1970s, ZBB was also popular in some government agencies.[3] Interest in the approach was initially strong, but problems with implementation and resource commitments led to a decline in use. However, as we describe in the Business Application "Current Experiences with Zero-Based Budgeting" below, several large firms are once again using the ideas of ZBB, at least in some areas.

Advocates of ZBB view the concept as a management tool rather than a budgeting approach, at least in the traditional sense. It is designed to focus management attention on the most important issues, rather than on repeated iterations at arriving at an agreed-upon budget. The following is an outline of the general ZBB process, although as with many cost accounting approaches, details differ greatly among adopters.

We provide an outline of the general development of ZBB by applying it to Rainy Days Umbrellas. There are two things to remember as we develop the example. First, ZBB is a *process* to assist management in choosing among alternative levels of effort in different units of the organization. It is not a different method to calculate required production levels, input requirements, or estimates of cash flows. Second, the specific implementation of ZBB and the business activities to which it is applied differ among adopters. However, the following sketch will highlight the main features of a generic ZBB system.

Once the decision is made to apply ZBB in an organization, management needs to choose where to apply it. Although it could be applied to all units, this is generally not done for two reasons. First, it is time-consuming to apply. Second, the biggest benefit is in those areas where the link between effort or inputs and outputs is the most difficult to determine. Corporate staff functions are more promising sites for applying ZBB than production activities. Once the level of production is selected, the budgeting for the manufacturing department is determined primarily by engineering factors and market prices. However, the link between marketing department spending and increased sales is more difficult to determine.

The management at Rainy Days Umbrellas (RDU) has decided to experiment with ZBB by applying it to the Product Development Group (PDG), which works on bringing new ideas to market. There are three areas (departments) in the PDG: PDA-1, PDA-2, and PDA-3. Each of these areas is responsible for a different market. The current-year budget for the three areas is shown in Exhibit 13.19.

The four general steps in the ZBB process that RDU will follow are:

1. Determine at what level the initial analysis will be developed and proposals ranked: individual project, PDA, or all of PDG.
2. Prepare "packages" describing resources required and outcomes achieved at different levels of "effort" determined by the head of the PDG (or higher-ranking executive). This will be done by each manager at the level selected in step 1.
3. Combine all packages from the initial effort into a single ranking for the PDG.
4. Determine packages to be supported based on the PDG resource budget and the macro-level ranking.

Exhibit 13.19

Current-Year Authorized Budget—Rainy Days Umbrellas Product Development Group

Product Development Area	Current-Year Budget
PDA-1	$100,000
PDA-2	140,000
PDA-3	72,000
Total	$312,000

---

[3] Pyhrr, Peter, *Zero-Base Budgeting: A Practical Management Tool for Evaluating Expenses* (New York: Wiley, 1973).

Step 1: *Determine where the initial levels of effort will be developed and ranked.*

The manager of the PDG could do the ZBB analysis for all subordinate units (the PDAs) analyzing each individual project for benefits and costs in order to determine the projects to support. At the other extreme, each project manager (and there might be several in a PDA) could do the analysis. The first approach requires significant management time because of the variation in the nature of the projects and the markets served by the individual PDAs. The second approach is unlikely to provide meaningful information because it is too narrow and the managers too invested in their projects to offer a critical assessment of alternatives. For these reasons, the PDG manager decides that the initial analysis will be completed in the PDAs.

Step 2: *Prepare "packages" describing resources required and outcomes achieved at different levels of "effort."*

The next step is for each PDA manager to develop the alternative projects that the PDA proposes funding. The alternatives are often referred to as *budget alternatives* or *decision packages.* We will use the term *package* to refer to a development project a PDA is working on. There might be any number of packages, but they should be sufficiently well-defined that the decision to support the effort or not can be made at the package level. It might consist of a single project, a group of projects, or a significant step in a particular project.

One of the defining features of ZBB is that managers are asked to develop packages that would not simply be a continuation of current-year activities but could be supported by levels of effort below, at, or above the current-year level by a specified amount. At RDU, the process is going to be applied assuming effort levels equal to 75 percent, 100 percent, and 120 percent of the current-year level. It is important to note that the levels are based on current-year *effort,* measured, perhaps, by staffing, material usage, or some other measure of input. It is not relative to the current-year *expenditures* or budget. As we will see, the packages included for the 100 percent alternative might require a budget above or below the current-year budget because of input price changes, efficiency gains, or other factors. A statement assessing the effect of eliminating support completely is commonly required. This represents the "zero base."

For each package, the PDA manager prepares supporting information outlining expected benefits or outputs, listing resources required, noting the impact of failing to support the package, and so on. The PDA manager ranks each of the packages from 1 (most important) to *n,* where *n* is the number of packages analyzed.

As an example, the manager of PDA-1 has completed the initial analysis with the results shown in Exhibit 13.20. There, we see that two packages, PDA-1_1 and PDA-1_2, can be supported at the 100 percent effort level. Package PDA-1_1 requires $74,000 in resources and Package PDA-1_2 requires $24,000 (= $98,000 − $74,000). The total requirement is $98,000, which is 98 percent of the current-year budget (= $98,000 ÷ $100,000). The Product Area is also required to assess the impact of not supporting each package. For example, for Package PDA-1_2, the manager of the Area stated:

> Failure to proceed with Package PDA-1_2 will result in a delay of market readiness for Apollo [a product code name] of seven months. Because of demand seasonality for the product, this will eliminate our advantage of an early market entry and reduce market share by an estimated 20 percent.

Although the "eliminate" scenario is often dealt with quickly, it is more difficult for managers to address the reduced resources, in this case 75 percent, scenario. ZBB forces managers to decide which activities are most important.

Step 3: *Combine all packages from the PDAs and rank them at the PDG level.*

The PDG manager now considers the packages from each of the PDAs along with the individual rankings. A combined ranking of the individual packages is then made.

Exhibit 13.20

Budget Packages—Rainy Days Umbrellas Product Development Group Area PDA-1 for Alternative Levels of Effort Relative to the Current Year

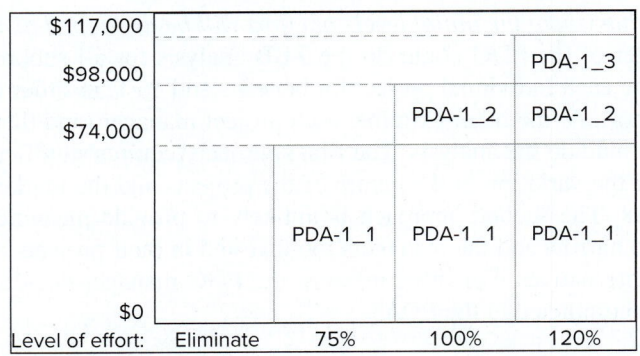

Step 4: *Determine packages to be supported based on the PDG resource budget and the macro-level ranking.*

Once the budget is determined for the PDG, the packages that will be supported are determined based on the overall ranking. The resources required for each package are added one at a time until the overall budget is reached. Any packages not included once the budget is reached are not supported. After Step 4 is complete, the PDA managers will develop the detailed budgets in much the same way as described earlier in the chapter.

Exhibit 13.21 illustrates these last two steps. The three PDAs have put forward a total of 12 packages ranked by PDA along with required resources. The right side of the exhibit shows the final PDG ranking by package. The PDG budget for the coming year has been set at $338,000, which allows funding for the top 10 packages. Note that PDA-2 has all packages funded, while PDA-1 is limited to the 100 percent level of effort.

Zero-based budgeting can help companies manage costs by rethinking what activities are important and the best way to accomplish them. It also provides useful information in uncertain times by forcing managers to prioritize activities so changes can be made quickly if there is a sudden, unexpected change in funding. This is in line with the recommendation noted in the Business Application "Planning and Budgeting in a Time of Great Uncertainty," at the beginning of the chapter.

At the same time, ZBB is also resource intensive, requiring managers to develop every year the analysis for their operations. This is one reason that firms that use ZBB tend to focus on a few areas and not require it throughout the organization. As the Business Application "Current Experiences with Zero-Based Budgeting" indicates, firms have had differing results using ZBB. As with many management approaches, ZBB is conceptually quite useful. Its practical value depends on how and where it is deployed and the current business environment the organization faces.

Exhibit 13.21

Final Budget and Package Selection—Rainy Days Umbrellas Product Development Group

		Final PDG Ranking	
		PDA-3_4	(12)
$338,000		PDA-1_3	(11)
		PDA-2_5	(10)
		PDA-2_4	(9)
	PDA Budget Packages	PDA-3_3	(8)
		PDA-2_3	(7)
		PDA-2_2	(6)
	PDA-2_5	PDA-3_2	(5)
	PDA-2_4 / PDA-3_4	PDA-3_1	(4)
PDA-1_3	PDA-2_3 / PDA-3_3	PDA-1_2	(3)
PDA-1_2	PDA-2_2 / PDA-3_2	PDA-2_1	(2)
PDA-1_1	PDA-2_1 / PDA-3_1	PDA-1_1	(1)

| PDG Area: | PDA-1 | PDA-2 | PDA-3 | PDG Combined | Ranking |

Current Experiences with Zero-Based Budgeting   *Business Application*

The pandemic of 2020 forced many businesses to reconsider their activities and spending because of both reduced revenues and increased uncertainty for both short- and long-term prospects. Many firms began using (or continued to use) zero-based budgeting (ZBB) to help cope with the new environment. The companies adopting ZBB ranged from companies such as Guess (clothing) and Signet Jewelers to General Motors. A survey by Gartner, Inc. (a research firm) found that 26 percent of 300 executives surveyed planned to apply ZBB during the pandemic.

The benefits of ZBB varied among the users. For example,

At Guess, zero-based budgeting allowed the Los Angeles–based clothing retailer to identify ways to quickly cut millions in costs during its fiscal first quarter, which ended May 2[, 2020], in response to a drop-off in sales as governments temporarily closed retail stores to stem the virus's spread.

Although many firms have found that ZBB analyses have resulted in cost savings and increased flexibility, other firms have discontinued the use of the technique or have had mixed results. For example,

Analysts have blamed Kraft Heinz's [a food company] wide ranging use of the budgeting tool [ZBB] that forces managers to start planning from scratch and question every expense for its previous slump.

Although Kraft Heinz does not plan to abandon ZBB, other companies in the food industry have or are reducing its use. These include companies such as Mondelez International (a part of former Kraft Foods and the maker of products such as Oreos and Philadelphia Cream Cheese), Campbell Soup, and Kellogg Co.

Sources: Broughton, Kristin, "Companies Turn to Zero-Based Budgeting to Cut Costs during the Pandemic," *The Wall Street Journal,* June 17, 2020; Trentman, Nina, "Kraft Heinz CFO Wants to Make Sure Cost Cuts Endure," *The Wall Street Journal,* September 16, 2020.

REVIEW QUESTIONS

13-1. Which has more detail, the budget for the coming period or a long-range forecast? Why?

13-2. What is the purpose of the cash budget if the budgeted income statement will indicate whether the firm expects to be profitable?

13-3. Describe four methods used to estimate sales for budgeting purposes.

13-4. What role does the master budget play in the planning and budgeting exercise?

13-5. What problems might arise if a firm relies solely on management estimates in preparing the master budget?

13-6. What is the coordinating role of budgeting?

13-7. What is participative budgeting? What are some advantages of participative budgeting? What are some disadvantages?

13-8. Write out the inventory equation that is used to determine required production in the production budget for a manufacturing firm.

13-9. What makes creating budgets for marketing and administration more difficult than creating, for example, the production cost budget?

13-10. What does the phrase "use it or lose it" mean in the context of budgeting?

13-11. What role do "packages" play in zero-based budgeting? How do these roles address critiques of traditional budgeting?

CRITICAL ANALYSIS AND DISCUSSION QUESTIONS

13-12. "Preparing a budget is a waste of time. The strategic plan is what we work to accomplish." How would you respond to this comment?

13-13. What are the advantages and disadvantages of starting the budgeting process early in the year versus later in the year prior to the budget year?

13-14. Would the budgeting plans for a company that uses a just-in-time (JIT) inventory system be different from those for a company that does not? Why?

13-15. Government agencies are limited in spending by budget categories, not just by an overall spending limit. What purpose does this serve? What problems does it create?

13-16. What is the difference between the planning and the control functions of the budget? What problems do these differences create?

13-17. When might the master budget start with a forecast of something other than sales—production, for example? Why?

13-18. In some organizations (firms, universities, government agencies), spending appears to increase as the end of the budgeting period approaches, even if there are no seasonal differences. What might cause this?

13-19. "Our cash budget shows a surplus for the quarter so we do not have to think about arranging any bank financing." Comment on this statement.

13-20. Your boss asks for your estimate on the costs of a major project for which you have responsibility. Your future with the company depends on your performance relative to this budget. Your best guess is, for example, $1,000,000. What will you say? Why?

13-21. The chapter identified four techniques used for forecasting sales (market researchers, Delphi technique, trend analysis, and econometric models). What are some factors that would lead you in preparing a sales forecast to rely on one or two of these techniques more than the others? Explain.

13-22. Consider the Business Application "Recent Experiences with Zero-Based Budgeting." According to the Application, the company Kraft Heinz intends to keep using zero-based budgeting while other firms in the same industry are dropping it. What might lead one firm to drop zero-based budgeting even though others continue to use it?

EXERCISES      All applicable Exercises are included in Connect.

(LO 13-1) **13-23. Role of Budgets and Plans**

Raynor Testing Services (RTS) is a new company that has not yet developed a formal planning and budgeting process. RTS is unsure how to proceed. It understands that the following five steps need to be completed. It is unsure, however, in what order the steps should be done.

Planning and Budgeting Element
A. Develop the master budget
B. Make changes (corrections) to the operations and the plan
C. Develop the strategic long-range profit plan
D. Develop the organization's goals
E. Evaluate actual results with the budget

Required

List the planning and budgeting elements in the correct order.

(LO 13-1) **13-24. Human Element in Budgeting**

Stockton Distributors is a large, privately held warehousing and freight company with managers assigned to each region of the U.S. The company managers are developing Stockton's sales budget for the following year. The budget department of the CFO's office, using econometric analysis, has set a sales budget for the Southeast Region of $27 million. The region's manager has sent an email to the budget team that addresses the team's forecast:

> *I am not sure where the $27 million forecast comes from, but given that the region is just now recovering from the latest economic slump, it is not achievable. The region is especially dependent on shipments to and from the Gulf ports, and global trade has been especially hard hit. We might be able to hit $25 million or, at a stretch, $26. A $27 million budget is just setting us up for failure.*

Required

a.   What would be an advantage of using the regional manager's forecast?

b.   What would be a disadvantage of using the regional manager's forecast?

c.   Identify two pieces of information that are likely to be available prior to the period you would want in order to choose between the forecasts.

(LO 13-2) **13-25. Estimate Sales Revenues**

Emmons Lawn Maintenance (ELM) provides lawn and garden care for residential properties. In the current year, ELM maintains 75 properties and earns an average of $5,000 annually for each property. The owner of ELM is planning for the coming year. New building in the area is expected to increase volume by 20 percent. In addition, the owner estimates that the number of homeowners that will want ELM's service will increase by 10 percent.

ELM plans to increase the price of service by 12.5 percent to cover expected increased wage and equipment costs.

Required
Estimate revenues for Emmons Lawn Maintenance for the coming year.

13-26. Estimate Sales Revenues   (LO 13-2)
Bramell Park is an amusement park with an entrance fee that allows unlimited rides. Last year, the company sold 88,000 one-day admission tickets with an average price of $125 and 30,000 three-day admission tickets with an average price of $280. The park management expects one-day admission ticket volume to decrease by 12 percent and three-day admission ticket volume to increase by 4 percent.

At the same time, increased competition is expected to result in one-day ticket prices that are 15 percent lower than the current level and three-day ticket prices that are 10 percent lower than the current price.

Required
Estimate admission revenues for Bramell Park for the coming year.

13-27. Estimate Sales Revenues   (LO 13-2)
Gladys Bank & Trust has $360 million in consumer loans with an average interest rate of 7.25 percent. The bank also has $240 million in home equity loans with an average interest rate of 5 percent. Finally, the company owns $60 million in government securities with an average rate of 3 percent.

Managers at Gladys Bank & Trust estimate that next year its consumer loan portfolio will fall to $320 million and the interest rate will increase to 8.75 percent. They also estimate that its home equity loans will increase to $280 million with an average interest rate of 7 percent, and its government securities portfolio will increase to $75 million with an average rate of 6.5 percent.

Required
Estimate the revenues for the coming year for Gladys Bank & Trust.

13-28. Estimate Sales Revenues   (LO 13-2)
Ethel Company manufactures and sells desk lamps for hotel and motel rooms. Last year, it sold 120,000 units of its model Y lamp for $45 per unit. The company estimates that this volume represents a 24 percent share of the current market. The market is expected to increase by 8 percent next year. Marketing specialists have determined that as a result of new competition, the company's market share will fall to 20 percent (of this larger market). Due to changes in production costs and competitive models, the new price for the lamps will be $48 per unit. The revised volume estimates are based on the $48 price.

Required
Estimate Ethel Company's sales revenues from model Y lamps for the coming year.

13-29. Estimate Production Levels   (LO 13-3)
Bortle Manufacturing Group estimates that sales for the coming year will be 576,000 units. Company policy is to maintain a finished goods inventory of one and one-half months' unit sales. Beginning inventory is 75,000 units. Assume sales occur uniformly throughout the year.

Required
Estimate the production level for the coming year for Bortle to meet these objectives.

13-30. Estimate Production Levels   (LO 13-3)
Kirby Soups has just made its sales forecasts, and its marketing department estimates that the company will sell 3,900,000 units of its vegetable soup during the coming year. In the past, management has maintained inventories of finished goods at approximately two weeks' sales. The inventory at the start of the budget period is 95,000 units. Sales occur evenly throughout the year.

Required
Estimate the production level of vegetable soup required for the coming year to meet these objectives.

(LO 13-3)   **13-31. Estimate Sales Levels Using Production Budgets**
Dolson Appliances makes coffee machines for offices and homes. For next year, the production budget is 125,000 units. Beginning inventories will be 10,000 units and the desired ending inventory will be 8,000 units.

Required
What is the sales budget for the coming year for Dolson Appliances?

(LO 13-3)   **13-32. Estimate Inventory Levels Using Production Budgets**
Benham Foundries manufactures metal components. The inventory policy at Benham is to hold inventory equal to 150 percent of the average monthly sales for its main product. Sales for the main product for the following year are expected to be 480,000 units. Based on the inventory policy, the budget calls for the production of 450,000 units.

Required
What is the beginning inventory of the main product?

(LO 13-3)   **13-33. Estimate Production Levels: Capacity Constraints**
Sauer Instruments manufactures a surgical tool used in cardiovascular procedures. The demand for the instrument has been strong after a competitor's instrument was deemed defective and is currently off the market. Sauer management is developing the production budget for next year. The inventory policy at Sauer is to hold two months' worth of sales, which allows them to meet fluctuations in demand. The sales budget for next year is 300,000 units, spread evenly over the year. Because of an unexpected increase in demand resulting from the competitor's withdrawal from the market, inventory at the end of this year is expected to be only 15,000 units. The capacity of the plant is 320,000 units annually.

Required
a.   What production level next year will be required to meet the targets?
b.   What problems might confront the management at Sauer in the coming year?
c.   What would be some alternatives to address any problem they might face?

(LO 13-3)   **13-34. Estimate Production and Materials Requirements**
Cherboneau Novelties produces drink coasters (among many other products). During the current year (year 0), the company sold 520,000 units (packages of 6 coasters). In the coming year (year 1), the company expects to sell 540,000 units, and, in year 2, it expects to sell 624,000 units. The target ending finished goods inventory for each month is equal to the next month's sales. However, because of production issues, the ending inventory in the current year is expected to be only 12,000 units.
   Each unit requires 0.5 pound of cork. At the end of the current year, management expects to have 18,750 pounds of cork in inventory. Management has set a target to have cork on hand equal to one-half of next month's sales requirements. Sales and production take place evenly throughout the year.

Required
a.   Compute the total targeted production of the finished coaster for the coming year.
b.   Compute the required amount of cork to be purchased for the coming year.

(LO 13-3, 4)   **13-35. Estimate Purchases and Cash Disbursements**
Dawes Designs buys T-shirts for clubs, teams, and other organizations. Dawes takes the shirts and adds the organization's logo. Because of the uncertainty in the timing of the sales and to avoid stock outages, Dawes tries to maintain an inventory of shirts equal to two months of sales. The shirts cost $4.50 each and must be paid for in cash. On June 30 of the current year, the company expects to have 15,400 shirts in stock. Sales estimates, based on contracts received and historical data, are as follows for the next six months:

July.	6,820
August.	9,790
September	7,260
October.	7,810
November.	5,280
December.	3,960

Required

a. Estimate purchases (in units) for July, August, and September.

b. Estimate cash required to make purchases in July, August, and September.

13-36. Estimate Purchases and Cash Disbursements   (LO 13-3, 4)

Eliot Sprinkler Systems produces equipment for lawn irrigation. One of the parts used in selected Eliot equipment is a specialty nozzle. The budgeting team is now determining the purchase requirements and monthly cash disbursements for this part.

Eliot wishes to have in stock enough nozzles to use for the coming month. On August 1, the company has 16,800 nozzles in stock, although the latest estimate for August production indicates a requirement for only 15,000 nozzles. Total uses of the nozzle are expected to be 14,700 in September and 15,540 in October.

Nozzles are purchased at a wholesale price of $8. Eliot pays 25 percent of the purchase price in cash in the month when the parts are delivered. The remaining 75 percent is paid in the following month. Eliot purchased 21,000 parts in July.

Required

a. Estimate purchases of the nozzle (in units) for August and September.

b. Estimate the cash disbursements for nozzles in August and September.

13-37. Estimate Purchases and Cash Disbursements   (LO 13-3, 4)

Montrose Instrumentation produces measurement equipment. One component, used in a variety of the company's products, is critical, and the supply chain often breaks. For that reason, Montrose has a policy to hold in inventory enough of the component to produce three months' worth of sales (one component is used in each unit of product in which it is used). On February 1, the company has 30,000 components in stock. Sales of the units in which the component is used in each of the next six months are estimated to be as follows:

February	32,250
March	26,250
April	27,750
May	33,300
June	29,900
July	41,860

Parts are purchased at a wholesale price of $45. The vendor has a financing arrangement by which Montrose pays 40 percent of the purchase price in the month when the components are delivered and 60 percent in the following month. Montrose purchased 37,500 parts in January.

Required

a. Estimate purchases of the component (in units) for February and March.

b. Estimate the cash disbursements for the component in February and March.

13-38. Estimate Cash Disbursements   (LO 13-4)

Evergreen Furniture, a retailing company, is preparing the cash budget for August. The following inventory information is available:

Estimated payments in August for purchases in August	70%
Estimated purchases for August	$2,376,000
Estimated cost of goods sold for August	2,430,000
Estimated payments in August for purchases in July	594,000
Estimated payments in August for purchases prior to July	108,000
Inventories at beginning of August	606,000

Required

What are the estimated cash disbursements in August?

(LO 13-4) **13-39. Estimate Cash Collections**

Hackett Produce Supply is preparing its cash budget for April. The following information is available:

Estimated credit sales for April.	$198,000
Actual credit sales for March	$148,500
Estimated collections in April for credit sales prior to March	$ 15,840
Estimated write-offs in April for uncollectible credit sales.	$ 7,920
Estimated provision for bad debts in April for credit sales in April	$ 6,930
Estimated collections in April for credit sales in April.	30%
Estimated collections in April for credit sales in March	65%

Required

What is the estimated amount of cash receipts from accounts receivable collections in April?

(CPA adapted)

(LO 13-4) **13-40. Estimate Cash Collections**

All sales at Alaska Company are on credit. The company is preparing a cash budget for November. The following information on accounts receivable collections is available from customer payment history:

Percent of current month's sales collected this month	30%
Percent of prior month's sales collected this month.	60
Percent of sales two months prior to current month collected this month.	5
Percent of sales three months prior to current month collected this month	3

The remaining 2 percent is not collected and is written off as bad debts. Sales to date are as follows:

November (estimated)	$370,000
October.	410,000
September	340,000
August.	480,000

Required

What are the estimated cash receipts from accounts receivable collections in November?

(CPA adapted)

(LO 13-4) **13-41. Estimate Cash Receipts**

Curtis Party Rentals offers party equipment such as tents, tables, chairs, and so on for outdoor events. The rental fees average $750 per event. Curtis receives a 15 percent deposit two months before the event, 60 percent the month before, and the remainder on the day the equipment is delivered and set up. Planners at Curtis estimate the following number of events for the last half of the current year:

July.	140
August.	160
September	210
October.	120
November.	80
December.	110

Required

a. What are the expected revenues for Curtis Party Rentals for each month, July through December? Revenues are recorded in the month of the event.

b. What are the expected cash receipts for each month, July through October?

13-42. Estimate Cash Receipts (LO 13-4)

Cornwall Mobile Detailing (CMD) is a service that washes and details a customer's vehicle at their home or office. It operates on a membership basis. Members pay $200 dues per month, which entitle them to a complete wash and detail service monthly. Members may also order additional car washes during the month at a fee of $75. Additional washes are common in both summer and winter months. The number of members also varies with the season. The number of members and the average number of additional washes by members for the months of interest follow:

	Members	Additional Washes (Average per Member)
January..................	360	0.8
February...............	420	1.1
March	980	0.7
April..................	1,120	0.6
May	1,150	0.9
June	1,300	1.4

Cornwall allows members to pay for dues on credit. Cornwall's experience is that 40 percent of its members pay cash for the dues, 50 percent of the members pay the dues for a month in the next month, 5 percent in the second month after. The remainder is uncollectible. Additional washes are payable in cash.

Required

What are Cornwall Mobile Detailing's expected cash receipts for March, April, May, and June?

13-43. Prepare Budgeted Financial Statements (LO 13-5)

Refer to the data in Exercise 13-42. Cornwall estimates that the number of members in July should increase 20 percent above June levels, and the number of additional washes per member should increase by an estimated 12.5 percent. The following information is available for costs incurred in June. All costs except depreciation are paid in cash.

Service costs	
Variable costs...........................	$ 44,000
Equipment maintenance	40,000
Depreciation (fixed)......................	75,000
Total	$159,000
Marketing and administrative costs	
Marketing (variable)......................	$ 32,000
Administrative (fixed).....................	105,000
Total	$137,000
Total costs...............................	$296,000

Variable service and marketing costs change with volume, measured by number of members. Fixed depreciation will remain the same, but fixed administrative costs will increase by 10 percent beginning July 1. Equipment maintenance is outsourced and the contract calls for a 5 percent increase beginning July 1.

Required

Prepare a budgeted income statement for July.

(LO 13-5)   **13-44. Prepare Budgeted Financial Statements**

Cymbal E-Motors is a fast-growing start-up firm that manufactures electric motors for bicycles. The following income statement is available for April:

Sales revenue (720 units @ $400 per unit)	$288,000
Less	
Manufacturing costs	
Variable costs.	57,600
Depreciation (fixed).	46,000
Marketing and administrative costs	
Fixed costs (cash)	120,500
Depreciation (fixed).	54,000
Total costs.	$278,100
Operating profits	$ 9,900

Sales volume is expected to increase by 30 percent in May, but the sales price is expected to fall 5 percent. Variable manufacturing costs are expected to increase by 7.5 percent per unit in May. In addition to these cost changes, variable manufacturing costs also will change with sales volume. Marketing and administrative cash costs are expected to increase by 15 percent.

All revenues and costs at Cymbal are cash transactions, except for depreciation. Cymbal maintains no inventories. Depreciation is fixed and is forecast to remain unchanged in the next six months.

Required

Prepare a budgeted income statement for May.

(LO 13-5)   **13-45. Prepare Budgeted Financial Statements**

Felch Tacos is a drive-thru restaurant in a coastal town with significant seasonal changes in business. The owners are trying to decide whether to remain open during the fourth quarter of the year (October through December) given the reduced business. They estimate that the number of meals sold in the fourth quarter will only be 40 percent of those sold in the third quarter. The number of meals sold in the third quarter was 22,000 at an average price of $7.80. The owners plan to offer a somewhat smaller menu during the fourth quarter and expect the average meal to sell for $7. The variable meal costs and the marketing cost per meal are not expected to change. The fixed meal costs will decline by 10 percent and the administrative costs will decline by 20 percent as the restaurant will be open fewer hours. The following cost information is available for third quarter:

Meal costs	
Food costs (variable).	$ 23,100
Labor (variable)	67,200
Other meal costs (variable)	11,500
Fixed meal costs	19,200
Total meal costs.	$121,000
Marketing and administrative costs	
Marketing (variable with respect to meals)	12,600
Administrative (fixed).	10,000
Total marketing and administrative costs	$ 22,600
Total costs.	$143,600

Required

Prepare a budgeted income statement for the fourth quarter.

13-46. Budgeting in a Service Organization   (LO 13-5, 6)

Mansfield Information Systems (MIS) is an IT support firm. Managers and staff are billed to clients on an hourly basis. The senior administrative staff does not directly provide client support. Because of the clientele of MIS, there is significant fluctuation from month to month.

Managers are billed to clients at a rate of $700 per hour and staff at a rate of $350 per hour. Managers are paid $210 per hour worked (including nonbillable time), and staff are paid $130 per hour. The current plan calls for managers to bill 800 hours in November and 620 hours in December. Staff are expected to bill 6,100 hours in November and 4,800 hours in December. Managers will work a total of 1,120 hours in both months, and staff will work a total of 7,800 hours in November and 6,000 hours in December.

Other monthly costs (all fixed) are $750,000 SG&A, $150,000 in depreciation, and $250,000 in marketing.

Required

Prepare a budgeted income statement for Mansfield Information Systems for November and December (separately).

13-47. Budgeting in a Service Organization   (LO 13-5, 6)

Lambie Custodial Services (LCS) offers residential and commercial janitorial services. Clients are billed monthly but can cancel the service at the end of any month. In addition to the employees who do the actual cleaning, the firm employs two managers who handle the administrative tasks (human resources, accounting, and so on) and one dispatcher, who assigns the cleaning employees to jobs on a daily basis.

On average, residential clients pay $400 per month for weekly cleaning services and the commercial clients pay $1,800 per month for daily service (weekdays only). A typical residential client requires 12 hours a month for cleaning and a typical commercial client requires 65 hours a month. In September, LCS had 75 commercial clients and 80 residential clients. Cleaners are paid $16 per hour and are only paid for the hours actually worked. Supplies and other variable costs are estimated to cost $6 per hour of cleaning.

Other monthly costs (all fixed) are $25,000 SG&A, including managerial and dispatcher salaries, and $4,800 in other expenses.

With the changing economic conditions, the customer mix at LCS is expected to change to one with more residential and fewer commercial clients. Already, for October, company managers forecast a 10 percent increase in residential clients and a 20 percent decrease in commercial clients.

Required

Prepare a budgeted income statement for Lambie Custodial Services for October.

13-48. Budgeting in a Service Organization: Solving for Unknown   (LO 13-6)

Refer to the information in Exercise 13-47. For November, Lambie Custodial Services has budgeted profit of $1,620 based on 50 commercial clients. All information about unit costs for cleaners and supplies, about fixed monthly costs, and about hourly cleaning requirements is the same as in Exercise 13-47.

Required

How many residential clients are budgeted for November?

13-49. Incentives and Sales Forecasts: Ethical Issues   (LO 13-1, 2, 7)

Avery Equipment Rental is a regional firm servicing agricultural and construction clients in the northern plains states. The CFO of Avery is preparing next quarter's budget and has two forecasts for sales in the Western Branch. The market research group in the planning division estimates sales of $12.5 million based on econometric forecasts. The branch manager estimates sales of $11 million.

Required

a.   What are two possible explanations for the difference between the planning division's and the branch manager's estimates?

b.   Suppose that instead of $11 million, the branch manager estimates $13.4 million in sales. What are two possible explanations for the difference between the planning division's and the branch manager's estimates?

c.   Do any of these explanations suggest unethical behavior by the branch manager?

(LO 13-7, 9) **13-50. Zero-Based Budgeting—Ethical Issues**

The director of marketing for Marbud Hardware is responsible for, among other things, identifying new geographic regions for the company to enter. As part of the company's zero-based budgeting process, the director submitted the following funding request as part of the process:

Project	Ranking	Funding Request
Expand online sales and distribution...............	(1)	$1,200,000
Explore Australia and New Zealand market for expansion	(2)	350,000
Develop new advertising strategy.................	(3)	1,600,000
Explore Asia for expansion	(4)	350,000
Total request		$3,500,000

The senior management of Marbud has discussed the entry into Asia with the board of directors and securities analysts extensively. It is considered a logical extension of the current company footprint. The director of marketing is one of the few advocates of an entry into Australia and New Zealand and is sure that such a direction can be shown to be superior. It is not uncommon at Marbud for the company to consider budget requests and then decide to only fund 85–95 percent of the requested amounts.

Required

a.   What do you think the director of marketing is trying to accomplish with the project ranking? Is this ethical?

b.   Is the marketing director likely to be successful in achieving the goal you identified in requirement (*a*)?

(LO 13-8) **13-51. Sensitivity Analysis**

Lamphere Lawn Care provides lawn and gardening services. The price of the service is fixed at a flat rate for each service, and most costs of providing the service are the same, given the similarity in the lawns and lots. The owner budgets income by estimating two factors that fluctuate with the economy: the contribution margin associated with each service call and the number of customers who will request lawn service. Looking at next year, the owner develops the following estimates of contribution margin (price less variable cost of the service, including labor) and the estimated number of service calls. Although the owner understands that it is not strictly true, the owner assumes that the cost of fuel and the number of customers are independent.

Scenario	Contribution Margin per Service Call (Price – Variable cost)	Number of Service Calls
Excellent	$30	10,200
Fair...............	20	7,800
Poor	12	5,500

In addition to the variable costs of service, the owner estimates that other costs are $43,000 plus $8 for each service call in excess of 3,000 calls. Annual administrative and marketing costs are estimated to be $25,000 plus 15 percent of the contribution margin.

Required

Use a spreadsheet to prepare an analysis of the possible operating income for Lamphere Lawn Care similar to that in Exhibit 13.16. What is the range of possible operating incomes?

(LO 13-8) **13-52. Sensitivity Analysis**

Gladstone Mini-Golf operates in a tourist area. The population grows significantly in the summer but is relatively small the rest of the year. For that reason, the business operates only during the roughly four-month (125-day) period from mid-May to mid-September. The owner is currently developing a budget for the coming season and knows that the business is subject to two specific factors: the number of rainy days and the availability of part-time labor to operate the concession.

The tighter the market for the temporary workers, the higher the hourly pay Gladstone has to pay to ensure the course can operate.

The owner's experience is that for every day the course is open, 72 rounds will be played. The course does not open on a rainy day. At a minimum, the owner expects at least 6,500 rounds played over the season. The reason for the minimum is that there are several regulars who will adjust their schedule if rain closes the course on the day they originally planned to visit. To illustrate the owner's forecasting method, if there are 25 rainy days (meaning the course does not open on those days), the expected number of rounds for the season will be 7,200 [= 72 × (125 total days − 25 rainy days)]. However, if there are 45 rainy days, the seasonal demand would be 6,500 rounds because that is greater than the demand of 5,760 rounds [= 72 × (125 total days − 45 rainy days)] that would otherwise be expected.

For the upcoming season, the owner has determined that best estimates of the number of rainy days are 15, 20, and 40. The course has two part-time employees on-site at all times. The best estimates of the hourly wage are $10, $12, and $14. If the course opens, it is open for 12 hours and the labor would be paid for a full day of work. The average price for a round of golf (based on the historical mix of child and adult players) will be $9 per round.

In addition to the variable labor costs noted, the other costs at Gladstone are expected to be fixed seasonal operating costs of $20,000 and variable marketing and space rental costs of 20 percent of sales revenue.

Required

Use a spreadsheet to prepare an analysis of the possible operating income for Gladstone Mini-Golf similar to that in Exhibit 13.16. What is the range of possible operating incomes?

13-53. Sensitivity Analysis   (LO 13-8)

Chatsworth Theatre Group (CTG) is a not-for-profit organization that stages plays and other performances in a medium-sized city. Ticket revenues cover a portion of the operating costs, but CTG also relies on donations from local donors. In preparing the budget for the following year, the director of CTG is concerned about the ability of the company to continue because of uncertainty about the local economy.

The director has analyzed data on program donations and costs and how they vary with two measures of the local economy: median income and the unemployment rate. The analysis suggests that annual donations to the company average about $300,000 plus $6 for every dollar median income is above (or less $6 for every dollar median income is below) $70,000. Donations are also estimated to be $30,000 less (more) for every percentage point the unemployment rate is above (below) 5 percent. Average annual program costs, net of ticket revenue, are $275,000 plus $20,000 for every percentage point the unemployment rate is below 5.0 percent (because of the impact on labor costs).

In looking at the economic forecasts for next year, the director determines that the expected median income will be $70,000 and the expected unemployment rate is 5.0 percent. However, some forecasts have median income at $65,000 and others at $73,000. In addition, some forecasters believe that the unemployment rate could be as low as 4.2 percent and others believe it could be 5.5 percent.

CTG measures financial performance by its operating surplus, which is the difference between program donations and net program costs. The director is quite concerned that this program will end up with a negative surplus and might face having to disband.

Required

Use a spreadsheet to prepare an analysis of the possible operating surplus for Chatsworth Theatre Group, similar to that in Exhibit 13.16. What is the range of possible operating surpluses? Assume, perhaps unrealistically, that the median income and unemployment rates are independent.

13-54. Critiques of Traditional Budgeting—Zero-Based Budgeting   (LO 13-9)

Refer to the information in Exhibits 13.20 and 13.21 that are part of the test of zero-based budgeting at Rainy Days Umbrellas. Information concerning the funding requests for PDG Areas 2 and 3 are as follows:

PDG Area 2 Package	Funding Request	PDG Area 3 Package	Funding Request
2-1	$48,000	3-1	$16,000
2-2	30,000	3-2	35,000
2-3	26,000	3-3	29,000
2-4	35,000	3-4	17,000
2-5	21,000		

Required

As a result of the loss of a major account, funding for the Product Development Group has been reduced even further to $255,000. Complete the table below to indicate whether a package would be funded under the new funding amount.

PDG Area 1		PDG Area 2		PDG Area 3	
Package	Funded?	Package	Funded?	Package	Funded?
1 ($74,000)	Yes	1 ($48,000)		1 ($16,000)	
2 ($24,000)		2 ($30,000)		2 ($35,000)	
3 ($19,000)		3 ($26,000)		3 ($29,000)	
		4 ($35,000)		4 ($17,000)	
		5 ($21,000)			

(LO 13-9)   **13-55. Critiques of Traditional Budgeting—Zero-Based Budgeting**

Refer to the data in Exercise 13-54 and in Exhibits 13.20 and 13.21.

Required

To what level or levels would funding for Product Development Group have to drop such that one, but only one, of the PDG Areas received no funding? Explain.

PROBLEMS

 All applicable Problems are included in Connect.

(LO 13-5)   **13-56. Prepare Budgeted Financial Statements**

Coyle Manufacturing reports the following information for year 1:

Sales revenue (60,000 units)	$5,130,000
Manufacturing costs	
Materials	$ 302,000
Variable cash costs	256,000
Fixed cash costs	590,000
Depreciation (fixed)	1,800,000
Marketing and administrative costs	
Marketing (variable, cash)	760,000
Marketing depreciation	269,000
Administrative (fixed, cash)	916,000
Administrative depreciation	134,000
Total costs	$5,027,000
Operating profits (losses)	$ 103,000

All depreciation charges are fixed. Manufacturing depreciation is expected to increase by 10 percent in year 2. Marketing and administrative depreciation are expected to remain the same for year 2. Sales volume is expected to increase by 5 percent, but prices are expected to fall by 10 percent. Materials costs per unit are expected to decrease by 8 percent. Unit variable cash manufacturing costs are expected to increase by 15 percent. Fixed cash costs are expected to increase by 6 percent.

Variable marketing costs will change with unit volume. Administrative cash costs are expected to decrease by 10 percent. Inventories are kept at zero. Coyle Manufacturing operates on a cash basis.

Required

Prepare a budgeted income statement for year 2 for Coyle Manufacturing.

(LO 13-4)   **13-57. Estimate Cash from Operations**

Refer to the data in Problem 13-56. Estimate the cash from operations expected in year 2 for Coyle Manufacturing.

(LO 13-5)   **13-58. Prepare Budgeted Financial Statements**

The following information is available for Fairmount Industries from year 1 operations:

Sales revenue (45,000 units)	$1,575,000
Manufacturing costs	
Materials.........................	$ 240,000
Variable cash costs...............	545,000
Fixed cash costs	327,000
Depreciation (fixed)...............	160,000
Marketing and administrative costs	
Marketing (variable, cash)	171,000
Marketing depreciation	41,000
Administrative (fixed, cash)	162,000
Administrative depreciation	15,000
Total costs	$1,661,000
Operating profits (losses)............	$ (86,000)

All depreciation charges are fixed. Old manufacturing equipment with an annual depreciation charge of $22,000 will be fully depreciated by the end of year 1 and will not be replaced with new equipment because it is still operating to specification. Sales volume is expected to decrease by 2 percent. Sales price is expected to increase by 8 percent. On a per-unit basis, expectations are that materials costs will decrease by 5 percent and variable manufacturing cash costs will increase by 4 percent. Fixed cash manufacturing costs are expected to increase by 12 percent.

Variable marketing costs will change with volume. Administrative cash costs are expected to decrease by 15 percent. Inventories are kept at zero. Fairmount Industries operates on a cash basis. No change is expected in marketing or administrative depreciation.

Required
Prepare a budgeted income statement for year 2.

13-59. Estimate Cash from Operations   (LO 13-4)
Refer to the data in Problem 13-58. Estimate the cash from operations expected in year 2.

13-60. Prepare a Production Budget   (LO 13-3)
Clairpointe Accessories manufactures products for food preparation at several different manufacturing sites. The following costs and other data apply to unit production from the year just ending:

Direct materials per unit	
4.2 board feet of wood at $6 per board foot	
0.8 pound of plastic at $0.50 per pound	
Direct labor per unit	
0.4 hour at $25 per hour	
Overhead per unit	
Indirect labor	$1.70
Indirect materials.....................	0.75
Power	0.25
Equipment............................	1.80
Facilities	1.90
Total overhead per unit..................	$6.40

The plant controller at the Norfolk Street facility is preparing the budget for the coming year. You learn that equipment and facilities costs are fixed and are based on a normal production of 30,000 units per year. Other overhead costs are variable. Plant capacity is sufficient to produce 37,500 units per year.

Direct labor costs per hour are expected to rise by 5 percent this year. Wood prices are expected to remain unchanged, but plastic prices are expected to decrease by 8 percent. A new production method, which will be put into use at the beginning of the coming year, will result in a reduction of the wood required to produce a unit by 3 percent. No other costs are expected to change.

During the coming budget period, Clairpointe expects to sell 32,000 units. Finished goods inventory is targeted to decrease from the current balance of 4,000 units to 3,500 units as part of a corporatewide initiative to lower inventory levels. Production will occur evenly throughout the year. Inventory levels for wood and plastic are expected to remain unchanged throughout the year. There is no work-in-process inventory.

Required

Prepare a production budget and estimate the materials, labor, and overhead costs for the coming year.

(LO 13-3)   **13-61. Prepare a Production Budget**

West Partners manufactures metal fixtures. Each fitting requires both steel and an alloy that can withstand extreme temperatures. The following data apply to the production of the fittings for year 1:

Direct materials per unit
   2.0 pounds of steel at $0.80 per pound
   1.2 pounds of alloy at $16.00 per pound
Direct labor per unit
   0.04 hour at $30 per hour
Overhead per unit

Indirect materials.	$0.40
Indirect labor	0.80
Utilities.	0.60
Machine depreciation.	1.10
Other overhead	0.60
Total overhead per unit.	$3.50

The machine depreciation and other overhead costs are fixed and are based on production of 100,000 units annually. Plant capacity is 120,000 units annually. All other overhead costs are variable.

The following are forecast for year 2. A wage increase of 6 percent for both direct and indirect labor, which was negotiated recently, will go into effect. Steel prices are expected to decrease by 5 percent while alloy prices are expected to increase by 10 percent. Machine depreciation costs are expected to increase by 4 percent. All other unit overhead costs are expected to remain constant.

West Partners expects to sell 84,000 units in year 2. The current inventory of fittings is 8,000 units. Management is forecasting much higher sales volume in year 3, so it wants to have 11,000 units on hand by the end of year 2. Steel and alloy inventories will not change. Sales are approximately uniform over the year.

Required

Prepare a production budget and estimate the materials, labor, and overhead costs for year 2.

(LO 13-3)   **13-62. Sales Expense Budget**

New Town Foods sells a variety of packaged foods through supermarkets and other outlets using a dedicated sales team. The budget planning group has just received the sales team expense summary for the third quarter, which follows:

Item	Amount
Sales commissions	$510,000
Sales staff salaries	121,000
Building lease payment	75,600
Telephone and mailing.	60,000
Packaging and delivery	103,600
Utilities	15,500
Depreciation	47,300
Marketing consultants	74,500

You have been asked to develop budgeted costs for the coming year. Because the third quarter is typical, the budget team develops the annual budget by starting with the budget for a "typical" quarter, based on the current experience adjusted for expected changes in the coming period. These expected changes include the following:

- Sales volume is expected to increase by 10 percent.
- Sales prices are expected to increase by 5 percent.
- Commissions are based on a percentage of sales revenue.

- Sales staff salaries will increase 3 percent next year regardless of sales volume.
- Building lease cost is based on a five-year lease that expires this year. Based on the local real estate market, the cost of the lease is expected to increase by 6 percent.
- Telephone and mailing expenses are variable with the number of units sold. In addition, the unit costs for these expenses are expected to decrease by 8 percent even with no change in sales volume.
- Packaging and delivery costs are variable with unit sales volume. Unit packaging and delivery costs are expected to increase by 5 percent next year.
- Utilities costs are scheduled to decrease by 6 percent regardless of sales volume.
- Depreciation includes furniture and fixtures used by the sales staff. The company has just acquired an additional $76,800 in furniture that will be received at the start of next year and will be depreciated over an 8-year life using the straight-line method. At the same time, fixtures with a quarterly depreciation of $6,200 will be scrapped.
- Marketing consultant expenses were for a special advertising campaign that runs from time to time. During the coming year, these costs are expected to average $92,000 per quarter.

Required
Prepare a budget for sales expenses for a typical quarter in the coming year.

13-63. Budgeted Purchases and Cash Flows   (LO 13-3, 4, 5)

Oakley Wholesale Hardware and Supplies (OWHS) sells tools, lumber, and other remodeling supplies to commercial contractors. The company controller is compiling cash and other budget information for July, August, and September. On June 30, the company had inventories of $462,500.

OWHS sells a wide variety of products, but for budgeting and inventory planning purposes, the company has developed a standard "unit" of inventory that reflects roughly the mix and purchase costs of the items found in inventory and expected sales volume. The inventory value of $462,500 reported above is based on these inventory units. Each inventory unit is assumed to have a purchase price from vendors (for planning purposes) of $25. This number is not expected to change in the next three months.

The budget is to be based on the following assumptions:

- Each month's sales are billed on the last day of the month.
- Customers are allowed a 3 percent discount if payment is made within 10 days after the billing date. Receivables are recorded in the accounts at their gross amounts (not net of discounts).
- The billings are collected as follows: 75 percent within the discount period, 15 percent by the end of the month, and 8 percent by the end of the following month. Two percent is uncollectible.

Purchase data are as follows:

- For both purchases of inventory merchandise and selling, general, and administrative expenses, 70 percent is paid in the month purchased and the remainder in the following month.
- The number of units in each month's ending inventory equals 90 percent of the next month's units of sales.
- Selling, general, and administrative expenses, of which $8,000 is depreciation, equal 20 percent of the current month's sales.
- Actual and projected sales follow:

	Dollars	Units
May	$675,400	17,700
June	690,800	18,100
July	680,200	17,900
August	649,800	17,100
September	684,000	18,000
October	695,400	18,300

Required
Compute the following:

a. Budgeted inventory purchases in dollars for July.

b. Budgeted inventory purchases in dollars for August.

c. Budgeted cash collections during July.

d. Budgeted cash disbursements during August.

e. The budgeted number of units of inventory to be purchased during September.

(CPA adapted)

(LO 13-5, 6) **13-64. Prepare Budgeted Financial Statements**

Vernon Cabins is a small motel chain located near state and national parks. Each property is made up of separate cabins. The chain has 10 properties with an average of 15 cabins at each property. In year 1, the occupancy rate (the number of rooms filled divided by the number of rooms available) was 80 percent, based on a 180-day season. The properties are closed from late fall until early spring. The average rate was $225 per night per cabin. The basic unit of operation is the "night," which is one cabin occupied for one night.

The operating income for year 1 is as follows.

	A	B
1	Vernon Cabins	
2	Operating Income	
3	Year 1	
4		
5	Sales revenue	
6	Lodging	$ 4,860,000
7	Incidentals	475,200
8	Forfeited deposits	129,600
9	Total revenues	$ 5,464,800
10		
11	Costs	
12	Labor	$ 1,748,000
13	Incidentals	451,200
14	Miscellaneous	86,400
15	Utilities, etc.	95,000
16	Depreciation	550,000
17	Management	120,000
18	Marketing	230,000
19	Property taxes	1,640,000
20	Total costs	$ 4,920,600
21		
22	Operating profit	$ 544,200
23		

Other revenues consist of incidentals (vending machine purchases, supplies, and so on) and forfeited deposits. In year 1, incidentals revenue averaged $22 per night. Reservations require a deposit. Guests who fail to cancel before three nights prior to a stay forfeit the deposit. In year 1, forfeited deposits averaged $6 per night.

In year 1, the average fixed labor cost was $110,000 per property. The remaining labor cost was variable with respect to the number of nights. The costs of incidentals include $30,000 per season per property. The remaining cost of incidentals is variable with respect to the number of nights. Miscellaneous costs are all variable with respect to the number of nights. Utilities and depreciation are fixed for each property. The remaining costs (management, marketing, and property taxes) are fixed for the firm.

At the beginning of year 2, Vernon will close one of its properties with no change in the average number of rooms per property. The occupancy rate is expected to decrease to 70 percent. Management has made the following additional assumptions for year 2:

• The average room rate will increase by 10 percent.

• Incidental revenues per night are expected to increase by 5 percent.

• The forfeited deposit revenue per night is not expected to change.

- The fixed labor cost is expected to increase by 12 percent per property. The variable labor cost per night is not expected to change.
- Incidental cost factors are not expected to change.
- The miscellaneous cost for a night is expected to increase by 25 percent.
- Utilities costs per property are expected to increase by 20 percent.
- Depreciation costs per property are forecast to remain unchanged.
- Management costs will increase by 4 percent and marketing costs will decrease by 6 percent.
- Property taxes will decrease by $180,000 with the closing of the one property.

Required
Prepare a budgeted income statement for year 2.

13-65. Prepare Budgeted Financial Statements: Comparing Alternatives   (LO 13-5, 6)
Refer to the data in Problem 13-64. The managers of Vernon Cabins are considering different pricing strategies for year 2. Under the first strategy (High Price), they will work to maintain an average price of $260 per night. They realize that this will reduce demand and estimate that the occupancy rate will fall to 65 percent with this strategy. Under the alternative strategy (High Occupancy), they will work to maintain the year 1 occupancy rate of 80% by lowering the average price to $215 per night. Under either strategy, Vernon Cabins will close one of the properties.

For either of the two strategies, all the other estimates for year 2 (cost per night, property costs, and so on) will be the same as in Problem 13-64.

Required
a.   Prepare a budgeted income statement for year 2 if the High Price strategy is adopted.
b.   Prepare a budgeted income statement for year 2 if the High Occupancy strategy is adopted.
c.   Make a recommendation to management for a pricing strategy for year 2. Explain your reasons.

13-66. Comprehensive Budget Plan   (LO 13-3, 4, 5)
Lane Products manufactures a popular kitchen utensil. The company recently expanded, and the controller believes that it will need to borrow cash to continue operations. It opened negotiations with the local bank for a one-month loan of $40,000 starting March 1. The bank would charge interest at the rate of 0.5 percent per month and require the company to repay interest and principal on March 31. In considering the loan, the bank requested a projected income statement and cash budget for March.

The following information is available:

- The company budgeted sales at 12,000 units per month in February, April, and May and at 9,000 units in March. The selling price is $60 per unit.
- The company offers a 2 percent discount for cash sales. The company's experience is that bad debts average 1 percent of credit sales.
- The inventory of finished goods on February 1 was 2,400 units. The desired finished goods inventory at the end of each month equals 25 percent of sales anticipated for the following month. There is no work in process.
- The inventory of raw materials on February 1 was 2,280 pounds. At the end of each month, the raw materials inventory equals no less than 20 percent of production requirements for the following month. The company purchases materials in quantities of 250 pounds per shipment.
- Selling expenses are 6 percent of gross sales. Administrative expenses, which include depreciation of $750 per month on office furniture and fixtures, total $68,400 per month.
- The manufacturing budget for the utensil, based on normal production of 10,000 units per month, follows.

Materials (½ pound per utensil, 5,000 pounds, $30 per pound).	$150,000
Labor	120,000
Variable overhead	60,000
Fixed overhead (includes depreciation of $20,000)	120,000
Total	$450,000

Required

a.   Prepare schedules computing inventory budgets by months for
   1. Production in units for February, March, and April.
   2. Raw materials purchases in pounds for February and March.

b.   Prepare a projected income statement for March. Cost of goods sold should equal the variable manufacturing cost per unit times the number of units sold plus the total fixed manufacturing cost budgeted for the period. Assume that 40 percent of sales are cash sales.

(CPA adapted)

(LO 13-3, 4, 5)   **13-67. Comprehensive Budget Plan**

The management at Inverness Manufacturing feels confident about the company's prospect in the current year (year 2). Sales in the first quarter were one-third ahead of last year, and the sales department predicted that this rate would continue throughout the entire year. The controller asked the budget team to prepare a draft forecast for the year and to analyze the differences from last year's results. They decided to base the forecast on actual results obtained in the first quarter plus the expected costs of production to be completed in the remainder of the year. They worked with various department heads (production, sales, and so on) to get the necessary information. The results of these efforts follow:

INVERNESS MANUFACTURING
Expected Account Balances for December 31, Year 2

Cash	$ 6,200	
Accounts receivable.	240,000	
Inventory (January 1, year 2)	144,000	
Plant and equipment	390,000	
Accumulated depreciation		$ 123,000
Accounts payable.		135,000
Notes payable (due within one year). . .		150,000
Accrued payables.		69,750
Common stock		210,000
Retained earnings.		337,200
Sales revenue		1,800,000
Other income.		27,000
Manufacturing costs		
Materials.	639,000	
Direct labor	654,000	
Variable overhead	390,000	
Depreciation	15,000	
Other fixed overhead.	23,250	
Marketing		
Salaries.	48,000	
Commissions.	60,000	
Promotion and advertising	145,000	
Administrative		
Salaries.	48,000	
Travel	7,500	
Office costs	27,000	
Income taxes.	—	
Dividends.	15,000	
	$2,851,950	$2,851,950

Adjustments for the change in inventory and for income taxes have not been made. The scheduled production for this year is 225,000 units, and planned sales volume is 200,000 units. Sales and production volume was 150,000 units last year. The company uses a full-absorption costing and FIFO inventory system and is subject to a 20 percent income tax rate. The actual income statement for last year follows:

INVERNESS MANUFACTURING
Statement of Income and Retained Earnings
For the Budget Year Ended December 31, Year 1

Revenues			
Sales revenue.		$1,350,000	
Other income		45,000	$1,395,000
Expenses			
Cost of goods sold			
Materials.	$ 396,000		
Direct labor	405,000		
Variable overhead	243,000		
Fixed overhead.	36,000		
	$1,080,000		
Beginning inventory.	144,000		
	$1,224,000		
Ending inventory.	144,000	$1,080,000	
Selling			
Salaries.	$ 40,500		
Commissions.	45,000		
Promotion and advertising	94,500	180,000	
General and administrative			
Salaries.	$ 42,000		
Travel	6,000		
Office costs	24,000	72,000	
Income taxes.		12,600	1,344,600
Operating profit			50,400
Beginning retained earnings			301,800
Subtotal			$ 352,200
Less dividends			15,000
Ending retained earnings			$ 337,200

Required

Prepared a budgeted income statement and balance sheet for year 2.

(CMA adapted)

13-68. Budgeted Financial Statements in a Retail Firm   (LO 13-5, 6)

Owen Surf Sports is an idea of two budding entrepreneurs. Their plan is to sell kiteboards from a store in the local town. Between them, they invest $30,000 in capital and are in the process of applying for a bank loan, also for $30,000. The loan would be repaid in four years. The owners will also pay the bank annual interest at a rate of 6 percent.

The owners are working on a business plan that the bank has requested. The store would sell only two models of kites initially, the X-1 and the X-2. Data on the kites is given as follows:

	X-1	X-2
Expected annual sales (units)	400	200
Retail price (per unit).	$800	$1,400
Purchase cost (per unit)	580	1,000

Additional information on the planned operations for the year includes the following:

1. Equipment costing $48,000 will be purchased for cash when the store opens. The equipment will be depreciated over five years using straight-line depreciation.
2. The owners expect sales to occur uniformly over the year. Sales will be both for cash (60 percent) and on account (40 percent). Sales on account are assumed to be collected in two months.
3. The owners will maintain inventory equal to one-half of a month's sales. All kites will be purchased from the manufacturer on credit with payment made one month after purchase.
4. Annual cash selling, general, and administrative expenses are $45,000 fixed plus 15 percent of revenues.
5. The applicable income tax rate is 20 percent.

Required

Prepare the following budgeted statements based on the data and assumptions available:

a.   Income statement for the year.

b.   Year-end (December 31) balance sheet.

(LO 13-4, 5, 6, 8)   **13-69. Cash Budgets and Sensitivity Analysis in a Retail Firm**

Refer to the data in Problem 13-68.

Required

a.   Prepare a cash budget for the year.

b.   The owners want to ensure that they have cash on hand at the end of the year equal to the current accounts payable balance on December 31. Will the store meet that requirement?

c.   Consider only the assumption about the percentage of sales that will be made on account (currently 40 percent). What assumption about this percentage would exactly achieve the goal set by the owners in requirement (b)?

(LO 13-8)   **13-70. Sensitivity Analysis—Data Analysis and Visualization**

Norcross Carpet Cleaning (NCC) is a commercial service specializing in maintaining floor coverings in high-traffic areas such as malls and office buildings. The business is highly seasonal, with high demand in the winter and low demand in the summer. In both seasons, the demand depends on the weather, among other factors. Managers at the company are working on the budget for the following winter season to determine personnel and funding needs. Based on expertise, experience, and regional economic forecasts, they develop the following:

Scenario	Gross Margin per Client (Price – Cost of Cleaning)	Number of Clients
Good	$120	2,000
Fair	90	1,250
Poor	75	750

For simplicity, the managers assume that the gross margin and the estimated number of customers are independent. Thus, there are nine possible scenarios. In addition to the cost of the cleaning (included in the gross margin estimates), the managers estimate staffing costs to be $35,000 plus $120 for every client in excess of 1,000. The marketing and administrative costs are estimated to be $20,000 plus 5 percent of the gross margin.

Required

a.   Use a spreadsheet to prepare an analysis of the possible operating income for Norcross Carpet Cleaning similar to that in Exhibit 13.16. What is the range of operating incomes?

b.   The managers at Norcross would like to be able to visualize these results, to present to the board. Create a graph that illustrates the effect of the number of clients on operating profit for each possible value of gross margin per client.

c.   What conclusions about the most favorable scenarios for Norcross do these visualizations suggest? Prepare a short memo that will help the board members understand these conclusions.

(LO 13-8)   **13-71. Sensitivity Analysis—Data Analysis and Visualization**

Refer to the data in Exercise 13-51. Recent economic events in the local area have led the owner of Lamphere Lawncare to revise some estimates in budgeting the operating income for the following year. First, unexpected competition has depressed prices. The revised estimates for the contribution margin appear as follows. At these new assumed prices, the owner believes there is no reason to revise the estimated number of service calls.

Scenario	Contribution Margin per Service Call (Price – Variable cost)	Number of Service Calls
Excellent	$25	10,200
Fair	18	7,800
Poor	10	5,500

The second revision the owner has to make is to incorporate high prices for the variable factors included in "other costs." At the same time, the fixed other costs are expected to be significantly lower. Specifically, the owner now estimates that other costs are $10,000 plus $20 for each service call in excess of 6,000 calls. All other information remains the same as in Exercise 13-51.

Required

a.   Use a spreadsheet to prepare an analysis of the possible operating income for Lamphere Lawn Care using the new assumptions similar to that in Exhibit 13.16. What is the range of possible operating incomes?

b.   The owner of Lamphere Lawncare would like to be able to visualize these results. Create a graph that illustrates the effect of the number of service calls on operating profit for each possible value of contribution margin per service call.

c.   What conclusions about the most favorable scenarios for Lamphere Lawncare do these visualizations suggest? Prepare a short memo that will help the owner understand these conclusions.

INTEGRATIVE CASES

13-72. Prepare Cash Budget for Service Organization   (LO 13-3, 4, 5, 6)

The board of directors of the Cortez Beach Yacht Club (CBYC) is developing plans to acquire more equipment for lessons and rentals and to expand club facilities. The board plans to purchase about $50,000 of new equipment each year and wants to begin a fund to purchase a $600,000 piece of property for club expansion.

The club manager is concerned about the club's capability to purchase equipment and expand its facilities. One club member has agreed to help prepare the following financial statements and help the manager ascertain whether the plans are realistic. Additional information follows the financial statements.

CORTEZ BEACH YACHT CLUB
Statement of Income (Cash Basis)
For the Year Ended October 31

	Year 9	Year 8
Cash revenues		
Annual membership fees.	$ 710,000	$600,000
Lesson and class fees	468,000	360,000
Miscellaneous	4,000	3,000
Total cash received.	$1,182,000	$963,000
Cash costs		
Manager's salary and benefits	$ 72,000	$ 72,000
Regular employees' wages and benefits	380,000	380,000
Lesson and class employees' wages and benefits. .	390,000	300,000
Supplies	32,000	31,000
Utilities (heat and light).	44,000	30,000
Mortgage interest	46,800	50,400
Miscellaneous	4,000	3,000
Total cash costs.	$ 968,800	$866,400
Cash income	$ 213,200	$ 96,600

Additional Information

1.   Other financial information as of October 31, year 9:
    a.   Cash in checking account, $14,000.
    b.   Petty cash, $600.
    c.   Outstanding mortgage balance, $720,000.
    d.   Accounts payable for supplies and utilities unpaid as of October 31, year 9, and due in November, year 9, $5,000.

2. The club purchased $50,000 worth of sailing equipment during the current fiscal year (ending October 31, year 9). Cash of $20,000 was paid on delivery, with the balance due on October 1, which had not been paid as of October 31, year 9.

3. The club began operations in year 3 in rental quarters. In October, year 5, it purchased its current property (land and building) for $1,200,000, paying $240,000 down and agreeing to pay $60,000 plus 6 percent interest annually on the previously unpaid loan balance each November 1, starting November 1, year 6.

4. Membership rose 3 percent during year 9, approximately the same annual rate of increase the club has experienced since it opened and that is expected to continue in the future.

5. Membership fees were increased by 15 percent in year 9. The board has tentative plans to increase them by 10 percent in year 10.

6. Lesson and class fees have not been increased for three years. The number of classes and lessons has grown significantly each year; the percentage growth experienced in year 9 is expected to be repeated in year 10.

7. Miscellaneous revenues are expected to grow in year 10 (over year 9) at the same percentage as experienced in year 9 (over year 8).

8. Lesson and class employees' wages and benefits will increase to $604,650. The wages and benefits of regular employees and the manager will increase 15 percent. Equipment depreciation and supplies, utilities, and miscellaneous expenses are expected to increase 25 percent.

Required

a. Construct a cash budget for year 10 for Cortez Beach Yacht Club.

b. Identify any operating problem(s) that this budget discloses for CBYC. Explain your answer.

c. Is the manager's concern that the board's goals are unrealistic justified? Explain your answer.

(LO 13-1)   **13-73. The Role of Budgets and People in the Budgeting Process**

Fargo Industries manufactures and sells snowmobiles. The company has eight business units strategically located near the major markets, each with a sales force and two to four manufacturing plants. These business units operate as autonomous profit centers responsible for purchasing, operations, and sales.

The corporate controller describes the business unit performance measurement system as follows: "We allow the business units to control the entire operation from the purchase of materials to the sale of the product. We at corporate headquarters are involved only in strategic decisions such as developing new product lines. Each business unit is responsible for meeting its market needs by providing the right products at low cost on a timely basis. Frankly, the business units need to focus on cost control, delivery, and services to customers. Being as close to the markets as they are, they are best qualified to determine how to do this."

The corporate controller continued, "We give the business units considerable autonomy, but we watch their monthly income statements like a hawk! Each month's actual performance is compared to the budget in considerable detail. If actual sales or contribution margin is more than 4 or 5 percent below budget, we demand an immediate report from the business unit managers. I might add that we don't have much trouble getting their attention. All of the management people at the plant and the business unit level can add appreciably to their annual salaries with bonuses if they exceed their budgets."

The budgeting process begins in April when the business unit sales managers consult their sales personnel to estimate sales for the next fiscal year (the fiscal year runs between July 1 and June 30). These estimates are sent to the plant managers, who use them to prepare the production estimates. At the plants, production statistics including direct materials, labor hours, production schedules, and output quantities are developed by plant personnel. Using the statistics prepared by the plant personnel, the plant accounting staff estimates costs and the plant's budgeted variable cost of goods sold and other plant expenses for each month of the coming fiscal year. In the first week of June, each business unit accounting staff combines the plant budgets with sales estimates.

The corporate controller continued, "It's really hard to predict the demand for snowmobiles. We think both the plant managers and the sales personnel are too conservative. They both prefer to underestimate the sales of snowmobiles. If they are wrong and sales of snowmobiles are better than projected, they could charge a premium. But that doesn't agree with corporate wishes because that means prospective customers will go elsewhere to get their snowmobiles."

Required

a. Identify and explain biases of the corporate management of Fargo Industries that should be expected in the communication of budget estimates by business units staff and plant personnel.

b. What sources of information can Fargo Industries' top management use to monitor the budget estimates prepared by business units and plants?

c. What services could Fargo Industries' top management offer the business units to help them develop their budget without interfering with the business unit's decisions?

d. Assume you are consulting with Fargo Industries. They ask your advice about getting more involved in the business units and plants budgeting activities. Identify and explain what management needs to consider in reaching its decision.

(CMA adapted)

SOLUTIONS TO SELF-STUDY QUESTIONS

1. Budgeted production is

$$\frac{\text{Required}}{\text{production (units)}} = \frac{220{,}000 \text{ units}}{\text{(sales)}} + \frac{25{,}000 \text{ units}}{\text{(ending inventory)}} - \frac{20{,}000 \text{ units}}{\text{(beginning inventory)}}$$

$$= \underline{225{,}000 \text{ units}}$$

RAINY DAYS UMBRELLAS
Schedule of Budgeted Manufacturing Overhead
For the Budget Year Ended December 31
(Compare to Exhibit 13.6)

Variable overhead needed to produce 225,000 units[a]		
Indirect materials and supplies (= 90% of $37,500)....	$ 33,750	
Materials handling (= 90% of $50,000)...............	45,000	
Other indirect labor (= 90% of $12,500)	11,250	$ 90,000
Fixed manufacturing overhead (same as for production of 250,000 units)		
Supervisory labor	83,000	
Maintenance and repairs..........................	50,000	
Plant administration	85,000	
Utilities	55,000	
Depreciation	140,000	
Insurance	30,000	
Property taxes[b]	52,500	
Other..	22,000	517,500
Total manufacturing overhead		$607,500

[a] Variable overhead to produce 225,000 units will be 90 percent (= 225,000 ÷ 250,000) of the variable overhead to produce 250,000 units.

[b] Change in management's estimate.

RAINY DAYS UMBRELLAS
Budgeted Statement of Cost of Goods Sold
For the Budget Year Ended December 31
(Compare to Exhibit 13.7)

Beginning work-in-process inventory...................................		–0–
Manufacturing costs		
Direct materials		
Beginning inventory (10,000 fabric @ $2 + 1,000 metal @ $1)........	$ 21,000	
Purchases[a]..	1,793,400	
Materials available for manufacturing.............................	1,814,400	
Less ending inventory (7,000 fabric @ $2 + 400 metal @ $1).........	(14,400)	

(Continued)

Total direct materials costs	$1,800,000	
Direct labor[b].	1,350,000	
Manufacturing overhead.	607,500	
Total manufacturing costs		$3,757,500
Less ending work-in-process inventory		–0–
Cost of goods manufactured		$3,757,500
Add beginning finished goods inventory (20,000 units)[c]		320,000
Less ending finished goods inventory (25,000 units)[d].		(417,500)
Cost of goods sold		$3,660,000

[a]Additional computations:

Required production:

Beginning Balance (BB) + Production = Sales + Ending Balance (EB)

20,000 + Production = 220,000 + 25,000

Production = 225,000

Materials requirements:

Fabric: BB + Purchases = Production + EB

10,000 + Purchases = (225,000 × 3.0) + 7,000

Purchases = 672,000 units or $1,344,000 (= 672,000 × $2)

Metal: BB + Purchases = Production + EB

1,000 + Purchases = (225,000 × 2.0) + 400

Purchases = 449,400 units or $449,400 (= 449,400 × $1)

Total materials purchases = $1,344,000 + $449,400 = $1,793,400

[b]$1,350,000 = 225,000 units × 0.25 hour per unit × $24 per hour

[c]Management estimate.

[d]Ending finished goods inventory (assuming FIFO): Average unit cost = (Cost of goods manufactured ÷ Units produced) = ($3,757,500 ÷ 225,000) = $16.70

Ending inventory = 25,000 units × $16.70 = $417,500

2.

RAINY DAYS UMBRELLAS
Schedule of Budgeted Marketing and Administrative Costs
For the Budget Year Ended December 31
(Compare to Exhibit 13.8)

Variable marketing costs: (220 ÷ 240) × amounts in Exhibit 13.7		
Sales commissions	$330,000	
Other marketing.	165,000	
Total variable marketing costs.		$ 495,000
Fixed marketing costs.		
Sales salaries	$130,000	
Advertising	153,000	
Other	67,000	
Total fixed marketing costs		350,000
Total marketing costs		$ 845,000
Administrative costs (all fixed)		
Administrative salaries	$241,000	
Legal and accounting staff.	136,000	
Data processing services.	127,000	
Outside professional services.	32,000	
Depreciation—building, furniture, and equipment.	90,000	
Other, including interest.	36,000	
Taxes—other than income	140,000	
Total administrative costs.		802,000
Total budgeted marketing and administrative costs		$1,647,000

RAINY DAYS UMBRELLAS
Budgeted Income Statement
For the Budget Year Ended December 31
(compare to Exhibit 13.9)

Budgeted revenues		
Sales revenue (220,000 units at $30).................		$6,600,000
Costs		
Cost of goods sold[a]	$3,660,000	
Marketing and administrative costs..................	1,647,000	
Total budgeted costs		5,307,000
Budgeted operating profit...........................		$1,293,000
Federal and other income taxes (@ 25%)		323,250
Budgeted profit after tax		$ 969,750

[a] From solution to Self-Study Question 1.

3.

RAINY DAYS UMBRELLAS
Cash Budget
For the Budget Year Ended December 31

Cash balance beginning of period[a]		$ 830,000
Receipts		
Collections on accounts[b]..	$6,260,000	
Collection on employee loans	100,000	
Total receipts		6,360,000
Less disbursements		
Payments for accounts payable[c]	$1,665,400	
Direct labor[d]..	1,350,000	
Manufacturing overhead less noncash depreciation charges[e]........................	467,500	
Marketing and administrative costs less noncash charges[f]........................	1,557,000	
Payments for federal income taxes (per discussion with the tax staff)	300,000	
Dividends	30,000	
Reduction in long-term debts[g]	23,000	
Acquisition of new assets	1,529,000	
Total disbursements		6,921,900
Budgeted ending cash balance		$ 268,100

[a] Estimated by the treasurer's office.

[b] Collections on accounts per Exhibit 13.10	$6,840,000
Reduced sales ($7,200,000 − $6,600,000)	(600,000)
Plus decrease in receivables	20,000
	$6,260,000

[c] Payments on accounts per Exhibit 13.10....................	$1,880,000
Reduced materials purchases ($2,010,000 − $1,793,400)....	(216,600)
Plus decrease in payables................................	2,000
	$1,665,400

[d] See solution to Self-Study Question 1.

[e] From solution to Self-Study Question 1, total manufacturing overhead (which includes $140,000 of depreciation) is $607,500, so the cash portion is $467,500 (= $607,500 − $140,000).

[f] From solution to Self-Study Question 2, total marketing and administrative costs (including depreciation of $90,000) are $1,647,000, so the cash portion is $1,557,000 (= $1,647,000 − $90,000).

[g] Difference in the long-term liabilities shown in the budgeted balance sheets (Exhibit 13.13).

Design Elements: Ethics icon: ©Photodisc/Getty Images.

14

Chapter Fourteen

Business Unit Performance Measurement

LEARNING OBJECTIVES

After reading this chapter, you should be able to:

LO 14-1 Evaluate divisional accounting income as a performance measure.

LO 14-2 Interpret and use return on investment (ROI).

LO 14-3 Interpret and use residual income (RI).

LO 14-4 Interpret and use economic value added (EVA).

LO 14-5 Explain how historical cost and net book value–based accounting measures can be misleading in evaluating performance.

Stella Kalinina/Blend Images/
Getty Images

> *Tomorrow I have to recommend to the board of directors the regional manager who I believe did the best job last year. The board wants to begin thinking about preparing a successor for me as my retirement nears. My problem is that I need to be able to show the board evidence about why one manager gets my vote over the others. There are a lot of qualitative factors, and I can explain those. What the board will want to see is some evidence of performance that members can use to evaluate managers they know less well.*

John O'Neil, CEO of Monarch Enterprises, a national restaurant chain, was discussing his problem with Sonia Jobim from Paulista Partners, a local management consulting firm. Jobim has been working with Monarch Enterprises to develop a performance evaluation and compensation plan for corporate and regional executives. The effect of applying the different evaluation systems and the implications for how individual managers will fare under each have been identified, but the consulting team is not yet ready with its recommendation. Once he has the team's recommendation, O'Neil will use it to decide on a measure (or measures) to present to the board.

We described the organization of the firm in Chapter 12 by referring to responsibility centers: cost centers, profit centers, and investment centers. The advantage of this classification is that it describes the delegation of decision authority and suggests the appropriate performance measures. For example, because cost center managers have authority to make decisions primarily affecting costs, an appropriate performance measure is one that focuses on costs.

Divisional Performance Measurement

In this chapter, we develop and analyze performance measures for investment centers or business units. The distinguishing feature of business unit managers is that they have responsibility for asset deployment, at least to some extent, in addition to revenue and cost responsibility. We will refer in our discussion to business units as *divisions*—a common term for an investment center—but the concepts and methods we discuss here are appropriate for any organizational unit for which the manager has responsibility for revenues, costs, and investment.

As we develop performance measures, our discussion will be guided by three considerations:

1. Is the performance measure consistent with the decision authority of the manager?
2. Does the measure reflect the results of those actions that improve the performance of the organization?
3. What actions might managers be taking that improve reported performance but are actually detrimental to organizational performance?

The last question is particularly important for the designer of performance measurement systems. No performance measurement system perfectly aligns the manager's and organization's interests. Therefore, the systems designer has to be aware of possibly dysfunctional decisions that managers might make.

Business Application   What Performance Measure(s) Do Companies Use?

One of the challenges of cost accounting is learning what other companies are doing. Unlike financial accounting practices such as inventory or depreciation methods, companies are not required to disclose how they compute product costs, allocate corporate overhead, or prepare budgets. However, publicly traded firms (firms that sell securities to the public) are required to disclose the amount and basis of compensation for the CEO, CFO, and the three other most highly paid executives. In addition, the company must disclose,

> . . . the criteria used in reaching executive compensation decisions and the relationship between the company's executive compensation practices and corporate performance.

This information is included in the firm's proxy statement, which is filed with other financial reports such as the 10-K (annual report). In the proxy statement, there will be a section related to compensation discussing both the amount and the basis of the compensation (though not the actual results of the performance measures). Although the proxy statement generally does not include information at lower levels of the firm, it does indicate what factors the managers and company directors believe are important in evaluating their executives.

For example, in the 2020 Proxy Statement for McDonald's Corporation, we find that the compensation of the CEO in 2019 was based on the following measures:

Key Compensation Elements	Share of CEO "Pay Opportunity"	Primary Measures
Base salary	9%	(Not applicable)
Short-term incentive plan	15%	• Operating income growth • Comparable guest count growth
Long-term incentives: Restricted stock	38%	• Earnings per share • Return on incremental invested capital
Long-term incentives: Stock options	38%	• Share price

If "comparable guest count" is important in evaluating and compensating the CEO, it is likely an important component in the evaluations of lower-level managers as well.

Sources: US Securities and Exchange Commission, "Executive Compensation," https://www.investor.gov/introduction-investing /investing-basics/glossary/executive-compensation; McDonald's Corporation, "Notice of Annual Shareholders' Meeting and Proxy Statement," 2020, https://corporate.mcdonalds.com/content/dam /gwscorp/nfl/investor-relations-content/company-overview/2020 _proxy.pdf.

Accounting Income

LO 14-1

Evaluate divisional accounting income as a performance measure.

divisional income
Divisional revenues minus divisional costs.

Because divisions have both revenue and cost responsibility, an obvious performance measure is accounting income (divisional income). Investors use accounting income to assess the performance of the firm, so it is natural for the firm to consider the division's income when assessing divisional performance. Furthermore, divisional income serves as a useful summary measure of performance by equally weighting the division's performance on revenue and cost activities. **Divisional income** is simply divisional revenues minus divisional costs.

Computing Divisional Income

The computation of divisional income follows that of accounting income in general. Remember, however, that because divisional income statements are internal performance measures, they are not subject to compliance with generally accepted accounting principles (GAAP). Firms might choose to use firmwide averages for some accounts or ignore other accounts (taxes, for example).

See Exhibit 14.1 for the divisional income statements for Monarch Enterprises for year 1. We observe in the exhibit that Monarch Enterprises is organized into two divisions based on geography—Western and Eastern. Many firms organize into geographical responsibility units. Another common basis for organization is product line.

	A	B	C	D
1		MONARCH ENTERPRISES		
2		Divisional Income Statements		
3		For the Year 1		
4		($ 000)		
5		Western	Eastern	
6		Division	Division	Total
7	Sales revenue	$ 5,200.0	$ 2,800.0	$ 8,000.0
8	Costs of sales	2,802.0	1,515.0	4,317.0
9	Gross margin	$ 2,398.0	$ 1,285.0	$ 3,683.0
10	Allocated corporate overhead	468.0	252.0	720.0
11	Local advertising	1,200.0	500.0	1,700.0
12	Other general and admin	250.0	227.0	477.0
13	Operating income	$ 480.0	$ 306.0	$ 786.0
14	Tax expense (@ 30%)	144.0	91.8	235.8
15	After-tax income	$ 336.0	$ 214.2	$ 550.2
16				

Exhibit 14.1

Division Income Statements—Monarch Enterprises

The managers of Monarch Enterprises' two divisions have responsibility for sales (revenues), costs (including purchasing and operating costs), and some investment decisions. Specifically, the company's division managers are responsible for choosing store (restaurant) location and lease terms, credit and payables policy, and store equipment. Monarch Enterprises' central staff provides support for legal and financial services. Thus, the company's division managers are investment center (business unit) managers.

In reviewing Exhibit 14.1, we see that the after-tax income (profit) was $336,000 and $214,200 in the Western and Eastern Divisions, respectively. If we used after-tax income as the performance measure, we would conclude that the manager of the Western Division performed better than the manager of the Eastern Division.

Advantages and Disadvantages of Divisional Income

There are several advantages to using after-tax income as a performance measure. First, it is easy to understand because it is financial accounting income computed in the same way that income for the firm is computed. Second, it reflects the results of decisions under the division manager's control. Third, it summarizes the results of decisions affecting revenues and costs. Finally, it makes comparison of divisions easy because they use the same measure, dollars of income.

There are two important disadvantages to using divisional income as a performance measure, however. First, although the results of the Eastern and Western Divisions can be compared, it is not clear that the comparison reflects only the performance of the managers. One obvious problem is that the divisions may be of different sizes. That is, if the Western Division is much larger, it might be easier for its manager to report higher income.

The second disadvantage is that the measure does not fully reflect the manager's decision authority. In the case of Monarch Enterprises, the managers have responsibility for investment (assets), but other than depreciation expense, the effects of asset decisions are not reflected directly in the division's performance measure. This results in an inconsistency between decision authority and performance measurement. From the discussion in Chapter 12, we know that when such an inconsistency exists, the management control system might be ineffective.

Some Simple Financial Ratios

One approach to correcting the first problem—that the divisions are different sizes and, therefore, difficult to compare—is to use financial ratios. Because we have information only on income, we are limited (for the moment) in the ratios we can compute. However, we can use the three profitability ratios in Exhibit 14.2 to see how well the two divisions performed.

Exhibit 14.2

Selected Financial Ratios—Monarch Enterprises

	A	B	C	D
1			Western	Eastern
2	Ratio	Definition	Division	Division
3	Gross margin percentage	(Gross margin ÷ Sales)	46.12%	45.89%
4	Operating margin	(Operating income ÷ Sales)	9.23	10.93
5	Profit margin	(After-tax income ÷ Sales)	6.46	7.65
6				

gross margin ratio
Gross margin divided by sales.

The gross margin ratio reflects the performance of the manager regarding sales and the cost of goods sold. The **gross margin ratio** is the gross margin (sales minus cost of goods sold) divided by sales. Using the gross margin ratio as the performance measure, Exhibit 14.2 indicates that the manager of the Western Division performed better than the manager of the Eastern Division. However, the gross margin ratio ignores costs other than the cost of goods sold.

operating margin ratio
Operating income divided by sales.

A more comprehensive performance measure is the **operating margin ratio,** which is the operating income divided by sales. This measure includes the effect of not only the cost of goods sold but also operating costs. We see in Exhibit 14.2 that, based on operating margin as the performance measure, the manager of the Eastern Division performed better than the manager of the Western Division.

profit margin ratio
After-tax income divided by sales.

A third ratio is the **profit margin ratio,** which is after-tax income divided by sales. This measure includes the effect of divisional activities on taxes. In this case, with the same tax rate, the relative performance of the two divisions remains the same; the Eastern Division shows better performance.

These three ratios are only examples of how we could adjust divisional income for size differences. The important issue is that none of these adjustments addresses the second disadvantage of divisional income, the omission of asset usage in the performance measure.

Self-Study Question

1. Home Furnishings, Inc., is a nationwide retailer of home furnishings. It is organized into two divisions, Kitchen Products and Bath Products. Selected information on performance for year 2 follows:

   a. Compute after-tax divisional income for the two divisions. The tax rate is 35 percent. Comment on the results.

   b. Using the information from part (a), assess the relative performance of the two division managers at Home Furnishings, Inc.

	Kitchen	Bath
	($000)	
Revenue	$10,000	$5,000
Cost of sales.	5,400	3,000
Allocated corporate overhead. . . .	460	200
Local advertising	2,000	500
Other general and admin	500	260

The solution to this question is at the end of the chapter.

Return on Investment

LO 14-2
Interpret and use return on investment (ROI).

If managers have responsibility for asset acquisition, usage, and disposal, an effective performance measure must include the effect of assets. One of the most common performance measures for divisional managers is **return on investment (ROI),** which is computed as follows:

return on investment (ROI)
Ratio of profits to investment in the asset that generates those profits.

$$ROI = \frac{\text{After-tax income}}{\text{Divisional assets}}$$

Later in this chapter, we discuss some of the choices associated with computing income and assets, but for now, we will use very simple calculations for these accounting and investment measures (profits and assets).

	A	B	C	D
1	**MONARCH ENTERPRISES**			
2	**Balance Sheets**			
3	**January 1, Year 1**			
4	**($ 000)**			
5				
6		Western	Eastern	
7		Division	Division	Total
8	Assets			
9	Cash	$ 250	$ 150	$ 400
10	Accounts receivable	225	250	475
11	Inventory	250	150	400
12	Total current assets	$ 725	$ 550	$ 1,275
13	Fixed assets (net)	775	350	1,125
14	Total assets	$ 1,500	$ 900	$ 2,400
15				
16	Liabilities and Equities			
17	Accounts payable	$ 125	$ 95	$ 220
18	Other current liabilities	227	280	507
19	Total current liabilities	$ 352	$ 375	$ 727
20	Long-term debt	–0–	–0–	–0–
21	Total liabilities	$ 352	$ 375	$ 727
22	Total shareholders' equity	1,148	525	1,673
23	Total liabilities and equities	$ 1,500	$ 900	$ 2,400

Exhibit 14.3

Division Balance Sheets—Monarch Enterprises

See Exhibit 14.3 for the divisional balance sheets for Monarch Enterprises. Notice that although Monarch Enterprises wholly owns the two divisions, the company prepares balance sheets as if the divisions were separate entities. This is not important for our development of performance measures, but we include it to show that the measures presented here apply to investment centers that could be separate legal entities, such as subsidiaries.

Based on the information in Exhibit 14.1 and Exhibit 14.3, we can compute the ROI for the two divisions at Monarch Enterprises (see Exhibit 14.4). It is important to remember that there is a large volume of literature on the "correct" way to compute financial ratios. It is not our purpose here to discuss and critique these differences, although we will discuss some of the basic issues involved in computing income and investment later in this chapter. Instead, we focus on the general issue of ratio-based performance measures, such as ROI.

The computation of ROI in Exhibit 14.4 is based on beginning-of-the-year investment (the balance sheet is dated January 1). This is how Monarch Enterprises defines ROI. Later in this chapter, we discuss the use of the beginning-of-the-year, end-of-year, and average investment as the base for the ROI calculation.

Performance Measures for Control: A Short Detour

The focus in this chapter is on performance measurement, but before we evaluate ROI as a performance measure, we illustrate the role it can play in control. That is, we can use information from ROI to highlight the areas of the business that require attention.

	A	B	C
1		Western	Eastern
2		Division	Division
3	After-tax income from income statement, Exhibit 14.1 ($ 000)	$ 336.0	$ 214.2
4	Divisional investment from balance sheet, Exhibit 14.3 ($ 000)	1,500.0	900.0
5			
6	ROI (= After-tax income ÷ Divisional investment)	22%	24%
7			

Exhibit 14.4

ROI for Western and Eastern Divisions—Monarch Enterprises

Suppose that Western Division's ROI has been declining over time. We would like information that indicates where the problem could be. One approach is to decompose ROI into two or more ratios, which, when multiplied, equal ROI.

$$
\begin{aligned}
\text{ROI} &= \frac{\text{After-tax income}}{\text{Divisional assets}} \\
&= \frac{\text{After-tax income}}{\text{Sales}} \times \frac{\text{Sales}}{\text{Divisional assets}} \\
&= \text{Profit margin ratio} \times \text{Asset turnover}
\end{aligned}
$$

The managers at Monarch Enterprises and its divisions can now determine whether the decline in ROI is due to declining profit margins, which might suggest the need to implement cost controls, or to lower asset turnover, which might suggest the need to review asset utilization (evaluating inventory levels, for example). By decomposing the ratio, managers can anticipate where problems will occur in achieving acceptable ROIs and can take action early.

The profit margin ratio is a measure of the investment center's ability to control its costs for a given level of revenues. The lower the costs required to generate a dollar of revenue, the higher the profit margin. The asset turnover ratio is a measure of the investment center's ability to generate sales for each dollar of assets invested in the center.

Relating profits to capital investment is an intuitively appealing concept. Capital is a scarce resource. If one unit of a company shows a low return, the capital could be better employed in another unit where the return is higher, invested elsewhere, or paid to stockholders. Relating profits to investment also provides a scale for measuring performance.

Limitations of ROI

Although ROI is a commonly used performance measure, it has two limitations. First, the many difficulties in measuring profits affect the numerator, and problems in measuring the investment base affect the denominator. Consequently, making precise comparisons among investment centers is difficult. Because accounting results are necessarily based on historical information, these numbers tend to focus on current activities, which makes the measures *myopic*.

More important, however, is that the use of ROI can, at least conceptually, give incentives to managers that lead to lower organizational performance. Thus, using ROI can lead the manager to make suboptimal decisions.

Short-Term Focus (Myopia) from Accounting Information
What do we want managers in the divisions of a firm to do? We want them to take steps that, among other things, will increase the organization's value. Ideally, we would measure performance based on the change in the value of the firm that results from the managers' actions.

The problem we face is that we cannot directly measure this value, especially for business units in the organization. The division is not publicly traded, so we cannot look at how investors assess managers' actions. We must use accounting information, which is an imperfect reflection of the change in value. Accounting measures suffer from three general problems.

First, accounting income—the numerator in ROI—is "backward looking." That is, it reflects what has happened but does not include all changes in value that may happen as a result of the decisions that managers make. For example, a decision today to buy a new plant would not necessarily result in increased sales this period but may lead to increased sales next period. By dividing the activities of the firm into periods of a year, accounting information omits many of the benefits (and some of the costs) of actions in a particular year.

A second, related problem is the accounting treatment of certain expenditures, especially expenditures on intangible assets such as research and development (R&D), advertising, and leases. Although these expenditures are made by managers who believe that these expenditures will have long-term returns, accounting conventions often result in recording the entire expenditure as an expense in the period it is made.

Finally, while accounting treatment for intangibles often results in early recognition of the costs, but not the benefits, it also treats many sunk costs as providing benefits in the future. This is true of expenditures for plant assets, for example, which are depreciated over the life of the asset and might not be written off even after the asset is no longer used.

As we will see in the following discussion, each of these three problems can be addressed by developing a particular performance measure specifically designed for a given situation. However, for most firms, one advantage of using ROI is that the information needed to compute it already exists in the accounting records.

Conflicting Incentives for Managers (Suboptimization)
A more serious problem with ratio-based measures is that a manager can make decisions that lower organizational performance but increase the manager's reported performance. We illustrate this with an example.

Samuel Paige is the manager of Monarch Enterprises' Western Division. Samuel's assistant has presented him an analysis that outlines the benefits of a new type of kitchen exhaust equipment (see Exhibit 14.5).[1] The new equipment requires less maintenance, so the benefits are the cash savings in maintenance. The equipment will last three years and will be depreciated over that period using straight-line depreciation, which is used throughout the company. Samuel's performance is measured on the basis of ROI. He is expected to meet his target of 20 percent return on investment, which is the same as Monarch Enterprises' after-tax cost of capital.

Exhibit 14.5   Present Value Analysis: Exhaust Equipment, Western Division—Monarch Enterprises

	A	B	C	D	E	F	G
1	Investment		$ 480,000				
2	Annual cash flow		270,000	(assumed to be received at the end of each year)			
3	Economic life of the investment		3	years			
4	Annual depreciation		160,000	(= Investment ÷ Economic life of the investment)			
5	Increase in operating income		110,000	(= Annual cash flow – Annual depreciation)			
6	Income tax rate		30%				
7	Increase in income tax		33,000	(= Increase in operating income × Income tax rate)			
8	Cost of capital		20%				
9							
10			Before-Tax		Income Tax		After-Tax
11			Cash Flow		(@ 30%)		Cash Flow
12	Initial outlay		$ (480,000)		–0–		$ (480,000)
13	End of year 1		270,000		$ 33,000		237,000
14	End of year 2		270,000		33,000		237,000
15	End of year 3		270,000		33,000		237,000
16							
17			Present Value Analysis				
18			Present				Present
19			Value		Cash		Value
20			Factor		Flow		(@ 20%)
21	Initial outlay, year	0	1		$ (480,000)		$ (480,000)
22	End of year	1	0.833333		237,000		197,500
23	End of year	2	0.694444		237,000		164,583
24	End of year	3	0.578703		237,000		137,153
25	Net present value						$ 19,236
26							

[1] The analysis in Exhibit 14.5 assumes that you are familiar with present values and the basics of capital budgeting. We present a review of this material in the appendix to the book.

Exhibit 14.6   ROI Calculations, Western Division—Monarch Enterprises

	A	B	C	D	E	F	G	H	I
1								Beginning-of-	ROI
2								Year Net	(After-Tax
3								Investment	Income ÷
4								(Net of	Beginning-of-
5					Before-Tax	Income Tax	After-Tax	Accumulated	Year Net
6		Year	Cash Flow	Depreciation	Income	(@ 30%)	Income	Depreciation)	Investment)
7		1	$ 270,000	$ 160,000	$ 110,000	$ 33,000	$ 77,000	$ 480,000	16%
8		2	270,000	160,000	110,000	33,000	77,000	320,000	24
9		3	270,000	160,000	110,000	33,000	77,000	160,000	48
10									

If Samuel's performance measure is ROI, he will be concerned with the impact of the new investment opportunity on this measure. See Exhibit 14.6 for the calculation of ROI for the proposed investment. Notice that the ROI changes each year, but in the first year, the ROI is less than the level the company expected of Samuel.

As a performance measure, ROI is not consistent with the investment analysis. The net present value of the investment in the exhaust equipment is positive, which means that the firm will benefit from acquiring the equipment. However, the performance measure signals the manager that it is not a good investment because the ROI (at least for the first year) is less than the required rate of return. As a result, ROI does not provide a signal that is consistent with the decision criterion used for the investment.

There is a second, related way in which ROI can lead to suboptimization by the manager. Suppose, for example, that the ROI expected next year in the Western Division is 25 percent, and in the Eastern Division it is 10 percent. When the two division managers evaluate the same decision (whether to buy the exhaust equipment), they could make different decisions. Samuel, the manager of the Western Division, will compare the ROI of the investment to his expected ROI. The ROI of the investment is less than the expected ROI, so he has an incentive *not* to make the investment.

Joan Robinson, the manager of the Eastern Division, has a different incentive. Because the Eastern Division's expected ROI is below the 16 percent ROI for the exhaust equipment, Joan has an incentive to make the investment. Thus, using ROI as the performance measure leads to a situation in which the division performing more poorly, based on ROI, has the incentive to adopt more projects.

If the manager adopts the new project, the ROI of the division will be the weighted average of the ROI of the project and the ROI of the division without the project. The weights are the relative investments in the new project and the division's performance prior to the project. This means that any project with an ROI below that of the division without the project will lower the division's reported performance. A manager compensated on annual ROI performance might choose not to adopt a project that increases firm value.

Both myopia and suboptimization are problems with ROI as a performance measure. We next discuss alternatives to ROI that some companies have adopted. We note, however, that many companies continue to use ROI. It is important to understand that in our identification of these limitations, the manager looked at the effect on ROI of his or her decision and reacted only to the result. The environment of performance measurement is much richer. Corporate managers who were once division managers understand these incentives and watch for certain behavior. Division managers are motivated by a complex mix of compensation, reputation, loyalty

With ROI as a performance measure, managers have incentives to forgo investment in new plant and equipment in order to keep the asset base low, often below the optimal level.
Ingram Publishing/SuperStock

to the firm, and an understanding of what is "right." In identifying these limitations, we simply note that the potential for managers having incentives to take actions that are not in the organization's interest exists and that the designer of the management control system must be aware of these potentially dysfunctional incentives.

Performance Measurement at Walmart   *Business Application*

Although we have identified important limitations of ROI as a measure of managerial performance, it remains a popular metric for companies. Often, it is used with other accounting information to provide an indication of overall performance and is an informative, if flawed, reflection of the trade-off between generating income and using valuable assets. For example, at Walmart

> Our incentive compensation programs reward performance based on a mix of operating income-based metrics, sales-based metrics, and return on investment. We believe that this mix of performance metrics mitigates any incentive to seek to maximize performance under one metric to the detriment of performance under other metrics. For example, our long-term performance share plan is based equally on sales and ROI performance. We believe that this structure mitigates any incentive to

pursue strategies that would increase our sales at the detriment of ROI performance.

We also note at the end of the chapter that different companies compute ROI in alternative ways. As Walmart explicitly notes for its investors

> Although return on investment is a standard financial measure, our calculation of ROI may differ from other companies' calculations of their return on investment.

Therefore, it is always important to determine exactly how ROI (or any measure) is computed and not assume that it is the same across companies.

Source: Walmart, "Notice of Annual Shareholders' Meeting and Proxy Statement," pp. 67, 114, https///corporate.walmart.com/media-library/document/2020-walmart-proxy-statement/_proxy Document?id=00000171-a3e6-de83-a7fd-f7eeef900000.

Self-Study Question

2. Consider the case of Home Furnishings, Inc., which was described in Self-Study Question 1. Divisional assets are $8,200,000 in Kitchen Products and $4,000,000 in Bath Products.
   a. Compute ROI for the two divisions.

   b. Assess the relative performance of the two division managers at Home Furnishings, Inc., using ROI.

   The solution to this question is at the end of the chapter.

Residual Income Measures

One of the problems we identified with divisional income as a business unit performance measure is that it does not explicitly consider the investment usage by the unit. The reason is that accounting income is designed to report the return to the owners of the organization and then let them compare the return to their **cost of capital.** One approach to incorporate investment usage, which we just described, divides income by investment. A second approach is to modify divisional income by subtracting the **cost of invested capital** (the cost of capital multiplied by the division's assets, which measures the investment in the division) from accounting income.

Specifically, we define **residual income (RI)** as

$$\text{Residual income} = \text{After-tax income} - (\text{Cost of capital} \times \text{Divisional assets})$$

In other words, residual income is the divisional income less the cost of the investment required to operate the division. The cost of capital is the payment required to finance projects. The computation of the cost of capital is a subject for finance courses.

LO 14-3
Interpret and use residual income (RI).

cost of capital
Opportunity cost of the resources (equity and debt) invested in the business.

cost of invested capital
Cost of capital multiplied by the assets invested.

residual income (RI)
Excess of actual profit over the cost of capital invested in the unit.

In this book, we take it as given. Residual income is similar to the economist's notion of profit as being the amount left over after *all* costs, including the cost of the capital employed in the business unit, are subtracted.

The residual income for the Western Division of Monarch Enterprises is computed assuming a cost of capital of 20 percent (see Exhibit 14.7). The $36,000 residual income in the Western Division can be interpreted as follows: The operations (the manager) in the Western Division earned $36,000 for Monarch Enterprises after covering the cost of the restaurants, the division operations, *and the cost of the capital that has been invested in the Western Division.*

One advantage of residual income over ROI is that it is not a ratio. Managers evaluated using residual income invest only in projects that increase residual income. Therefore, there is no incentive for managers in divisions with low residual incomes to invest in projects with negative residual incomes. The reason is that the residual income for the division is the sum, not the weighted average, of the residual income for the project and the residual income for the division prior to the investment in the project.

Limitations of Residual Income

Residual income does not eliminate the suboptimization problem. See Exhibit 14.8 for an analysis of the investment in exhaust equipment, assuming that residual income is the performance measure. Again, there is a conflict between the decision criterion, net present value, and the performance measure, residual income. The project has a positive net present value but a negative residual income in year 1. However, residual income reduces the suboptimization problem. As Exhibit 14.8 illustrates, the present value of the residual income is equal to the net present value of the project. Therefore, if the manager considers the impact of the investment on residual income over the life of the project, the incentives of the manager and the incentives of the firm will be aligned. In addition,

Exhibit 14.7   Residual Income for Western and Eastern Divisions—Monarch Enterprises

	A	B	C	D	E
1			Western		Eastern
2			Division		Division
3	After-tax income from income statement, Exhibit 14.1 ($ 000)		$ 336.0		$ 214.2
4	Divisional investment from balance sheet, Exhibit 14.3 ($ 000)	$ 1,500.0		$ 900.0	
5	Cost of capital	20%		20%	
6	Cost of invested capital (= Cost of capital × Divisional investment)		300.0		180.0
7	Residual income ($ 000)		$ 36.0		$ 34.2
8					

Exhibit 14.8   Residual Income for the Acquisition of Exhaust Equipment, Western Division—Monarch Enterprises ($000)

	A	B	C	D	E	F	G	H
1				Beginning-of-		Residual		
2				Year Net		Income		
3				Investment	Cost of	(After-Tax		
4				(Net of	Invested	Income −	Present	
5			After-Tax	Accumulated	Capital	Cost of	Value	Present Value
6		Year	Income	Depreciation)	(@ 20%)	Invested Capital	Factor	(@ 20%)
7		1	$ 77,000	$ 480,000	$ 96,000	$ (19,000)	0.833333	$ (15,833)
8		2	77,000	320,000	64,000	13,000	0.694444	9,028
9		3	77,000	160,000	32,000	45,000	0.578703	26,042
10					Present value of residual income			$ 19,237
11								

if residual income for the year is positive, the manager has an incentive to invest in the project regardless of the division's residual income prior to the investment.

One approach to reducing the problem of managerial myopia, the distortion in incentives that results from problems with accounting measures, is to modify divisional income so that it better reflects economic performance. Such an approach is the idea behind economic value added (EVA).

Economic Value Added (EVA)

Although the concept of residual income has a well-established history in economics, few firms have adopted it as a performance measure.[2] More recently, a concept closely related to residual income, called *economic value added* (EVA), has received attention as a performance measure for business units, and has been adopted by companies such as Coca-Cola, Herman Miller, and Diageo.

Economic value added (EVA) makes adjustments to after-tax income and capital to "eliminate accounting distortions."[3] The "accounting distortions" commonly adjusted are the treatment of inventory costs, the expensing of many intangibles, and so on. For example, pharmaceutical firms, such as Glaxo, invest heavily in research and development (R&D). Generally accepted accounting principles (GAAP) in the United States require firms to expense R&D. Firms invest in R&D, however, because they believe that the expenditure of funds today will result in benefits (returns) in the future. Treating R&D as an expense when managers are evaluated using accounting income–based measures can reduce their willingness to invest in R&D. One solution is to capitalize the expenditure and amortize it over the economic life of the project. Of course, accounting principles change (International Financial Reporting Standards or IFRS, for example) and new standards might reflect better the economics of the transactions.

The capital employed is also adjusted for these same accounting treatments. If, for example, R&D is capitalized, the portion of its expenditures not included in income is recorded on the balance sheet and represents additional investment in the business unit. A second adjustment to capital that is typically made is to deduct current liabilities that do not represent debt from the calculation of capital. Many current liabilities, for example, accounts payable, do not carry explicit costs of capital; any capital cost is included in the acquisition cost and, ultimately, in cost of goods sold.

Thus, advocates of EVA argue that accounting income measures (and the capital employed) need to be adjusted for these distortions in order to compute an appropriate measure of performance. We illustrate the computation and use of EVA with Monarch Enterprises. We caution you that many implementations of EVA differ in the details of the computation. In this book, we take a very simple approach to the calculation in order to illustrate the concept.

We assume that only one accounting treatment—of advertising—requires adjustment. Advertising expenditures at Monarch Enterprises have been expensed in the year incurred, but management believes that the favorable brand image resulting from the advertising campaign will

LO 14-4
Interpret and use economic value added (EVA).

economic value added (EVA)
Annual after-tax (adjusted) divisional income minus the total annual cost of (adjusted) capital.

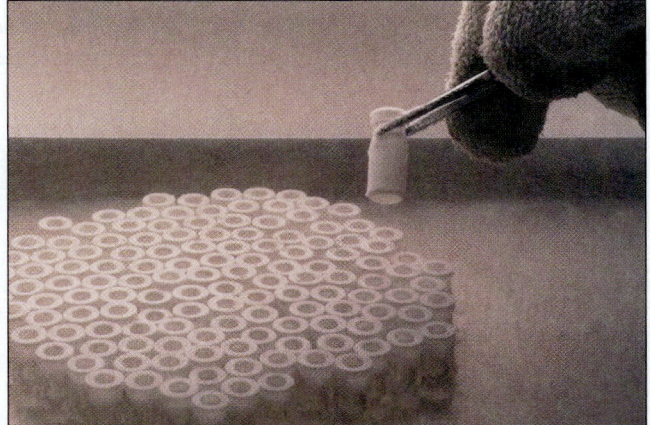

Generally accepted accounting principles (GAAP) require expensing R&D, such as costs for research into new pharmaceuticals. Using EVA, managers can design a performance measure that eliminates this accounting "distortion." Charles Smith/Corbis/VCG/ Getty Images

---

[2] An exception is the use of the residual income concept by General Electric in the 1960s. In fact, according to David Solomons, "The General Electric Company has given the name residual income to this quantity" [the excess of net earnings over the cost of capital]. See Solomons *Divisional Performance: Measurement and Control* (Homewood, IL: Irwin, 1965), p. 63.

[3] G. Bennett Stewart III, *The Quest for Value* (New York: HarperBusiness, 1991), p. 90.

have a two-year life. In other words, expenditures on advertising are the same as any expenditure on an asset that has a two-year life. Last year (year 0), Western Division recorded $800,000 in advertising expenditures and Eastern Division spent $300,000. We also assume—for simplicity—that last year was the first in which Monarch Enterprises made advertising expenditures.

See Exhibit 14.9 for the computation of EVA for Monarch Enterprises. Several comments about these computations are in order.

1. The after-tax income is used, but the tax expense is not adjusted for the adjustment to advertising expenditures. The tax implications of advertising are not affected by their treatment for performance measurement purposes. To provide a useful signal for management decision making, we want to include actual taxes because they will be computed based on the expenditures (the decision choice by managers).
2. Current liabilities are deducted from divisional investment.
3. We have assumed that advertising expenditures are made uniformly throughout the year. Therefore, 50 percent (= 1 year ÷ 2-year life) of the advertising expenditures made last year are expensed this year. Only 25 percent of the expenditures made this year are expensed because we assume that advertising expenditures are made uniformly over the year. A general amortization schedule is shown at the bottom of Exhibit 14.9.

Exhibit 14.9   EVA for Western and Eastern Divisions—Monarch Enterprises Year 1 ($000)

	A	B	C	D	E
			Western		Eastern
1			Division		Division
2					
3	After-tax income from income statement, Exhibit 14.1		$ 336.0		$ 214.2
4	Add back advertising expense, Exhibit 14.1		1,200.0		500.0
5			$ 1,536.0		$ 714.2
6	Less amortization of advertising (see amortization table below)				
7	Advertising expenditure in year 0 (@ 50% of the $ 800,000 expenditure in year 0)	$ 400.0		$ 150.0	
8	Advertising expenditure in year 1 (@ 25% of the $ 1,200,000 expenditure in year 1)	300.0	700.0	125.0	275.0
9	Adjusted income		$ 836.0		$ 439.2
10					
11	Divisional investment, Exhibit 14.3		$ 1,500.0		$ 900.0
12	Less current liabilities, Exhibit 14.3		352.0		375.0
13	Net Investment		$ 1,148.0		$ 525.0
14	Unamortized advertising, beginning of year (see amortization table below)				
15	Advertising expenditure in year 0 [@ (1.0 − 25%) of the $ 800,000 expenditure in year 0]		600.0		225.0
16	Adjusted divisional investment		$ 1,748.0		$ 750.0
17					
18	Calculation of EVA:				
19	Adjusted income (from above)		$ 836.0		$ 439.2
20	Cost of adjusted divisional investment (@ 20%)		349.6		150.0
21	EVA		$ 486.4		$ 289.2
22					
23					
24			Amortization Rate in Year		
25	Amortization of advertising expenditures:	0	1	2	4
26	Expenditures made in year				
27	0	25%	50%	25%	0%
28	1	0	25%	50%	25%
29	2	0	0	25%	50%
30					

These computations appear complicated, but they are exactly the same as those you would make if the accountant mistakenly recorded the entire cost of a machine as an expense instead of properly recording it as an asset and then depreciating it over its useful life. In the case of Monarch Enterprises, the accountant recorded advertising as an expense, as required by GAAP, but the economics of the transaction require a correction to record it as an asset.

EVA as a Performance Measure   *Business Application*

The number of firms that use EVA (or the related measure residual income) for performance evaluation and compensation is unclear, but it is almost certainly many fewer than the number of firms that use ROI or other accounting ratios. One likely reason is the necessity to make unfamiliar adjustments to the numbers from the financial statements. Recently, however, the proxy advisory services company Institutional Shareholder Services (ISS) acquired EVA Dimensions. (A proxy advisory services firm advises clients on voting at shareholder meetings. The services may include recommendations on issues in addition to research and technical support.) EVA Dimensions is an EVA research firm founded by Stern Stewart & Co., early advocates of the EVA concept. One of the services provided by ISS is an assessment of firm performance measured in various ways. Although ISS has not indicated that EVA measures will influence its recommendation, it has advocated for the use of EVA in assessing firm performance.

One company that does use EVA to assess performance at the divisional level is Genesco, Inc., a Nashville-based retailer of shoes and accessories. Genesco operates stores under various names including Journeys, Journeys Kidz, and Johnston & Murphy among others. As described in its proxy statement,

> Presidents of the Company's operating divisions were eligible to earn cash awards equal to the sum of (a) 75% of their bonus targets multiplied by a factor determined by changes in Economic Value Added (EVA) (the "EVA change factor") for their respective business units for the year, and (b) 25% of the targets multiplied by (i) the EVA change factor for their respective business units for the year and (ii) the percentage of achievement of individual strategic goals (discussed in greater detail below) agreed upon by the participant and the chief executive officer during the first quarter of the fiscal year.

Source: Genesco, "Proxy Statement for Annual Meeting of Shareholders June 25, 2020," http://genesco.gcs-web.com/static-files/bf8dcdd9-f43e-49f5-a926-e05ac9ecd9e1, p. 21.

Limitations of EVA

Conceptually, EVA addresses many of the problems associated with ROI and residual income. It is not a ratio, so managers invest in projects as long as EVA is positive. It corrects for many of the accounting distortions that make the other measures myopic. While we have illustrated how to adjust for advertising expenditures, the same approach can be used for any accounting convention that distorts performance.

The difficulty is that EVA replaces one accounting system for another. In the Monarch Enterprises illustration, we determined that it was inappropriate to expense advertising costs as they were incurred. Instead, we amortized those costs over a two-year period because we made the assumption that advertising outlays would benefit the firm for two years.

This illustrates some of the implementation problems with EVA. Who determines the appropriate life for the advertising expenditures? The division managers could be in the best position to do this, but they are being evaluated using the result. Should the same life be used in both regions? These questions can be answered, but it is unlikely that there will be full agreement among the managers.

EVA also does not resolve the suboptimization problem (see Self-Study Question 3). The fundamental problem is that EVA is based on accounting income while the decision to invest is based on the present value of cash flows.

Sensitivity of EVA to the Cost of Capital
One approach to addressing some of these limitations is to evaluate how confident we are in our decisions given these limitations. For example, our discussion of EVA has focused on the calculation of divisional income and divisional investment. We have taken the cost of capital as a given for the reasons discussed earlier in the chapter. However, as cost accountants interested in using

EVA as a performance measure for divisional executives, we should be aware of the sensitivity of our conclusions to the assumed cost of capital rate.

Advocates of EVA often illustrate its use at the firm level for measuring the performance of the CEO. From that, the application to the divisional level seems straightforward. A question arises (or should arise) about whether the cost of capital for the firm is the appropriate cost of capital for the divisions. Many discussions of EVA implicitly assume this. However, the cost of capital is meant to measure the price investors demand for bearing risks (business, economic, political, and so on) with their investments. We expect firms operating in different businesses or different countries to have different costs of capital. Similarly, we should expect that divisions that operate in different businesses or countries should have different costs of capital.

A problem arises, however, with measuring the cost of capital for a division of the firm. Most modern methods of estimating cost of capital assume that the firm's equity securities, at a minimum, trade in a market with observable prices. This allows us to measure the equity cost of capital. Combining that with a debt cost of capital provides a number we can use to assess capital projects in the firm or measure EVA. The problem is that divisions typically do not have equity securities that trade in a market.

Probably the most common way firms that use EVA deal with this is to assume a common cost of capital across divisions. Although this simplifies the calculations, it is not clear that the resulting EVA measures what was intended. A second approach is to use various techniques that look to accounting measures of risk (in place of market measures) and use these to estimate a divisional cost of capital. Both approaches have their advantages and disadvantages, but both introduce error into the performance measurement analysis.

We may not be able to measure the divisional cost of capital precisely, but we can assess how sensitive our assessments of relative divisional performance are to the assumed value we use. We illustrate how we might use sensitivity analysis by asking two questions:

1. At what common cost of capital will the computed EVA for Western and Eastern Divisions of Monarch be equal?
2. If we assume that the correct cost of capital for the Eastern Division is 20 percent (as assumed in Exhibit 14.9), at what cost of capital for the Western Division would the computed EVA for the Western Division equal that of the Eastern Division?[4]

We can answer these questions using the breakeven analysis approach from Chapter 3. We express EVA as a function of the cost of capital and determine the value that equates the two EVAs. Consider the first question above where we assume a common cost of capital for both divisions. We can write EVA as

$$EVA = Divisional\ income - (Divisional\ investment \times r)$$

where r is the assumed cost of capital. For example, using the information from Exhibit 14.9, the EVA for the Western Division is (in thousands of dollars)

$$EVA = Divisional\ income - (Divisional\ investment \times r)$$
$$= \$836.0 - (\$1,748.0 \times 20\%)$$
$$= \$836.0 - \$349.6$$
$$= \$486.4$$

Setting the divisional EVAs equal leads to the following (recall that we assume a common cost of capital, r):

$$Western\ Division = Eastern\ Division$$
$$\$836.0 - (\$1,748.0 \times r) = \$439.2 - (\$750.0 \times r)$$
$$\$998.0\ r = \$396.8$$
$$r = 39.8\%$$

---

[4] In order to illustrate how we might answer this question, we suspend for the moment the assumption that the firm's cost of capital is 20 percent.

We can also provide a visualization of the analysis to illustrate how the computed EVAs change with changes in the assumed (common) cost of capital. Exhibit 14.10 presents one such visualization, which shows that the Western Division's EVA is higher than the Eastern Division's for costs of capital up to about 40 percent. This is consistent with our analysis above. The visualization also shows that the EVA in the Western Division falls more quickly as the cost of capital increases and becomes negative sooner than the Eastern Division EVA.

We see that there is a large difference between the assumed cost of capital and the breakeven cost of capital. We can be reasonably confident that even if we do not have a precise measure of the cost of capital, this will not affect the assessment of relative performance between the two divisions.

We use the same approach to answer the second question: What cost of capital would make the two EVAs equal, assuming that the correct value for the Eastern Division is 20 percent. Setting up the analysis, we have

$$\text{Western Division} = \text{Eastern Division}$$
$$\$836.0 - (\$1,748.0 \times r) = \$289.2$$
$$\$1,748.0 \, r = \$546.8$$
$$r = (\$546.8 \div \$1,748.0)$$
$$= 31.3\%$$

If the cost of capital is 20 percent for the Eastern Division, a cost of capital of about 31.3 percent will result in the Western Division also having an EVA of about $289.2. We provide a visualization of this analysis in Exhibit 14.11.

This difference is not as large, but still substantial. These analyses suggest that measurement error in the cost of capital should not affect our conclusions on relative performance.

These are only two questions we might ask. The EVA numbers calculated here are based on many assumptions including the period of time over which advertising expenditures generate benefits and when those expenditures are incurred (at one time, uniformly over the year, or some other pattern). The fact that we are uncertain about these assumptions should not make us hesitate to use EVA, if we believe it is the best measure of divisional performance. We should, however, evaluate the sensitivity of our decisions to these assumptions to ensure confidence in our conclusions.

Exhibit 14.10   Divisional EVA as a Function of a Common Cost of Capital

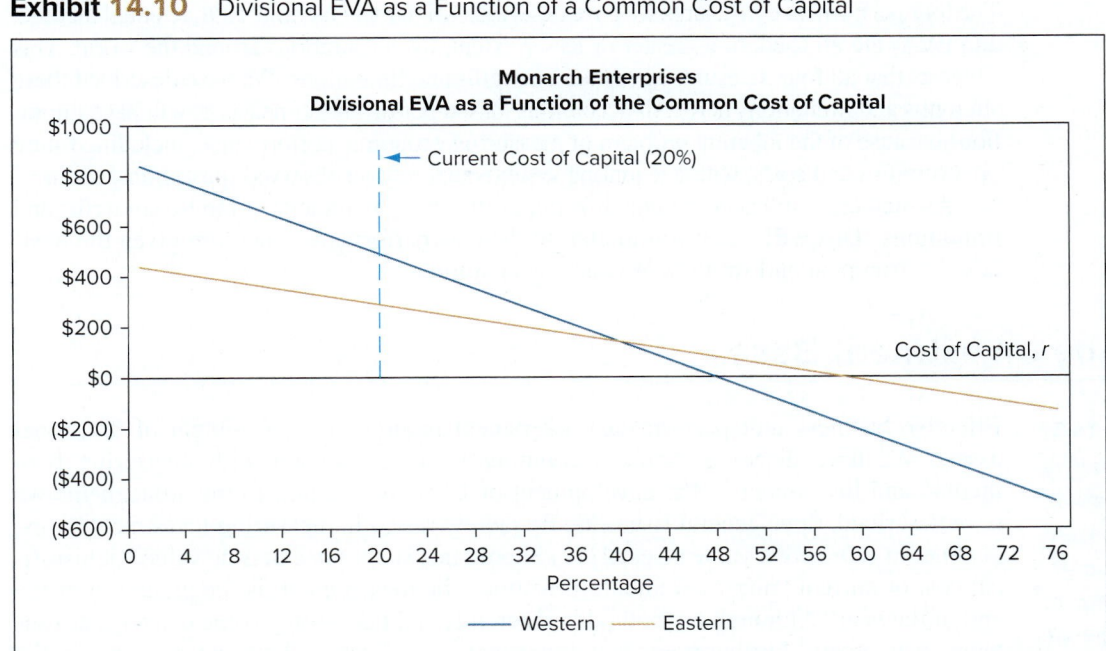

Exhibit 14.11   Divisional EVA as a Function of a Common Cost of Capital

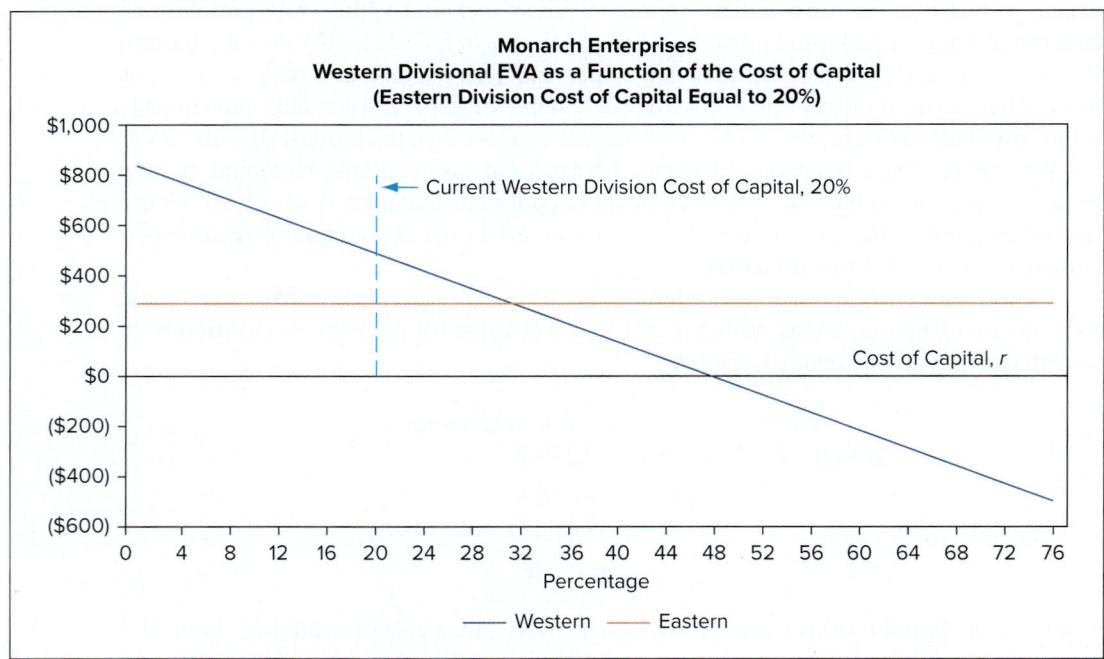

Monarch Enterprises
Western Divisional EVA as a Function of the Cost of Capital
(Eastern Division Cost of Capital Equal to 20%)

Self-Study Question

3. Suppose that Monarch Enterprises uses EVA as the per-   *The solution to this question is at the end of the chapter.*
    formance measure for divisional managers. Will the man-
    ager of either division (Eastern or Western) want to invest
    in the exhaust equipment? Why?

Divisional Performance Measurement: A Summary

The four performance measures we have described (divisional income, ROI, residual income, and EVA) are all used, to a greater or lesser extent, by corporations around the world. This suggests that all four measures have their strengths and limitations. We have described these strengths and limitations here. All accounting-based performance measures will have limitations because of the inherent problem of measuring economic performance, including future opportunities and costs, with accounting systems that rely on observed (past) transactions.

As managers and accountants, it is important that you understand these strengths and limitations. This will allow you to choose the best performance measure given the business environment and strategy of your organization.

Measuring the Investment Base

LO 14-5

Explain how historical
cost and net book
value–based
accounting measures
can be misleading in
evaluating performance.

Effective business unit performance assessment requires a measurement of divisional assets. We have discussed some accounting issues associated with measuring both income and investment in the development of EVA. In addition to the adjustments we have described, three general issues are frequently raised in measuring investment bases: (1) Should *gross* book value be used? (2) Should investment in assets be valued at historical cost or current value? (3) Should investment be measured at the beginning or at the end of the year? Although no method is inherently right or wrong, some can have advantages over others. Furthermore, it is important to understand how the measure of the investment base will affect ROI, residual income, and EVA. We illustrate these methods assuming that ROI is used for performance measurement, although the same comments will apply to the residual income measures, including EVA.

Gross Book Value versus Net Book Value

Suppose that a company uses straight-line depreciation for a physical asset with a 10-year life and no salvage value. The reported cost (expense) of the asset does not change; it is the same in year 3 as in year 1. See Exhibit 14.12 for a comparison of ROI under net book value and gross book value for the first three years. For simplicity, we assume that all operating profits before depreciation are earned at the end of the year, ROI is based on the year-end value of the investment, and there are no taxes.

Note that the ROI increases each year under the net book value method even though no operating changes take place. This occurs because the numerator remains constant while the denominator decreases each year as depreciation accumulates.

Historical Cost versus Current Cost

The previous example assumed no inflation. Working with the same facts, assume that the current replacement cost of the asset increases about 20 percent per year, as do operating cash flows. See Exhibit 14.13 for a comparison of ROI under the original or **historical cost** and the **current cost,** what it would cost to acquire the asset today.

historical cost
Original cost to purchase or build an asset.

current cost
Cost to replace or rebuild an existing asset.

Exhibit 14.12

Impact of Net Book Value versus Gross Book Value Methods on ROI

Facts
Amounts in thousands of dollars.
Profits before depreciation (all in cash flows at end of year): year 1, $100; year 2, $100; and year 3, $100.
Asset cost at *beginning* of year 1, $500. The only asset is depreciable, with a 10-year life and no salvage value. Straight-line depreciation is used at the rate of 10% per year. The denominator in the ROI calculations is based on *end-of-year* asset values.

Year	Net Book Value			Gross Book Value
1	$\text{ROI} = \dfrac{\$100^a - (.1 \times \$500)^b}{\$500^d - (.1 \times \$500)^e}$		ROI =	$\dfrac{\$50^c}{\$500}$
	=	$\$50 \div \$450$	= 11.1%	=	10%
2	$\text{ROI} = \dfrac{\$100 - (.1 \times \$500)}{\$450 - (.1 \times \$500)}$		ROI =	$\dfrac{\$50}{\$500}$
	=	$\$50 \div \$400$	= 12.5%	=	10%
3	$\text{ROI} = \dfrac{\$100 - (.1 \times \$500)}{\$400 - (.1 \times \$500)}$		ROI =	$\dfrac{\$50}{\$500}$
	=	$\$50 \div \$350$	= 14.3%	=	10%

[a] The first term in the numerator is the annual cash profit.
[b] The second term in the numerator is depreciation for the year.
[c] Net income = $50 = $100 − ($500 × .1). Companies sometimes use only cash flows in the numerator.
[d] The first term in the denominator is the beginning-of-year value of the assets used in the investment base.
[e] The second term in the denominator reduces the beginning-of-year value of the asset by the amount of the current year's depreciation.

Exhibit 14.13

Impact of Net Book Value versus Gross Book Value Methods on ROI (Historical & Current Costs)

Facts

Amounts in thousands of dollars.

Operating profits before depreciation (all in cash flows at end of year): year 1, $100; year 2, $120; and year 3, $144.

Annual rate of price changes is 20 percent.

Asset cost at *beginning* of year 1 is $500. At the *end* of year 1, the asset would cost $600; at the end of year 2, it would cost $720; and at the end of year 3, it would cost $864. The only asset is depreciable with a 10-year life and no salvage value.

Straight-line depreciation is used; the straight-line rate is 10 percent per year. The denominator in the ROI computation is based on *end-of-year* asset value for this illustration.

Net Book Value[a]

Year	Historical Cost			Current Cost[b]		
1..	ROI = $\dfrac{\$100 - (.1 \times \$500)}{\$500 - (.1 \times \$500)}$			ROI = $\dfrac{\$100 - (.1 \times \$600)}{\$600 - (.1 \times \$600)}$		
	=	$\$50 \div \$450$	= 11.1%	=	$\$40 \div \$540$	= 7.4%
2..	ROI = $\dfrac{\$120 - (.1 \times \$500)}{\$500 - (.2 \times \$500)}$			ROI = $\dfrac{\$120 - (.1 \times \$720)}{\$720 - (.2 \times \$720)}$		
	=	$\$70 \div \$400$	= 17.5%	=	$\$48 \div \$576$	= 8.3%
3..	ROI = $\dfrac{\$144 - (.1 \times \$500)}{\$500 - (.3 \times \$500)}$			ROI = $\dfrac{\$144 - (.1 \times \$864)}{\$864 - (.3 \times \$864)}$		
	=	$\$94 \div \$350$	= 26.9%	=	$\$57.6 \div \$604.8$	= 9.5%

Gross Book Value

Year	Historical Cost			Current Cost[b]		
1..	ROI = $\dfrac{\$100 - \$50}{\$500}$			ROI = $\dfrac{\$100 - \$60}{\$500}$		
	=	$\$50 \div \$500$	= 10.0%	=	$\$40 \div \$600$	= 6.7%
2..	ROI = $\dfrac{\$120 - \$50}{\$500}$			ROI = $\dfrac{\$120 - \$72}{\$720}$		
	=	$\$70 \div \$500$	= 14.0%	=	$\$48 \div \$720$	= 6.7%
3..	ROI = $\dfrac{\$144 - \$50}{\$500}$			ROI = $\dfrac{\$144 - \$86.4}{\$864}$		
	=	$\$94 \div \$500$	= 18.8%	=	$\$57.6 \div \$864$	= 6.7%

[a] The first term in the numerator is the annual profit before depreciation. The second term in the numerator is depreciation for the year. The first term in the denominator is the beginning-of-the-first-year value of the assets used in the investment base. The second term in the denominator reduces the beginning-of-year value of the asset by the amount of accumulated depreciation: by 10 percent for accumulated depreciation at the end of year 1, by 20 percent at the end of year 2, and by 30 percent at the end of year 3.

[b] Operating income is assumed to exclude any holding gains or losses.

Note that ROI increases each year under the historical cost method even though no operating changes take place. This occurs because the numerator is measured in current dollars to reflect current cash transactions while the denominator and depreciation charges are based on historical cost. The current cost methods reduce the effect by adjusting both the depreciation in the numerator and the investment base in the denominator to reflect price changes. Measuring current costs can be a difficult and expensive task, however, so there is a trade-off in the choice of performance measures.

We derived a level ROI in the current cost, gross book value method because the asset and all other prices increased at the same rate. If inflation affecting cash flows in the numerator increases faster than the current cost of the asset in the denominator, ROI will increase over the years until asset replacement under the current cost method. Of course, ROI will decrease over the years until asset replacement if the denominator increases faster than the numerator does.

Although current cost might seem to be a superior measure of ROI, recall that there is no single right or wrong measure. Surveys of corporate practice show that the vast majority of companies with investment centers use historical cost net book value. In a number of cases, many assets in the denominator are current assets that are not subject to distortions from changes in prices.

In general, how a performance measure is *used* is more important than how it is *calculated*. All of the measures we have presented can offer useful information. As long as the measurement method is understood, it can enhance performance evaluation.

Beginning, Ending, or Average Balance

An additional problem arises in measuring the investment base for performance evaluation. Should the base be the beginning, ending, or average balance? Using the beginning balance could encourage asset acquisitions early in the year to increase income for the entire year. Asset dispositions would be encouraged at the end of the year to reduce the investment base for next year. If end-of-year balances are used, similar incentives to manipulate purchases and dispositions exist. Average investments would tend to minimize this problem, although computing average investments could be more difficult. In choosing an investment base, management must balance the costs of the additional computations required for average investment against the potential negative consequences of using the beginning or ending balances.

Self-Study Question

4. Winter Division of Seasons, Inc., acquired depreciable assets costing $4 million. The cash flows from these assets for three years were as follows:

Year	Cash Flow
1	$1,000,000
2	1,200,000
3	1,420,000

Depreciation of these assets was 10 percent per year; the assets have no salvage value after 10 years. The denominator in the ROI calculation is based on end-of-year asset values. If replaced with identical new assets, these assets would cost $5,000,000 at the end of year 1, $6,250,000 at the end of year 2, and $7,800,000 at the end of year 3.

Compute the ROI for each year under each of the following methods (ignore holding gains and losses):

a. Historical cost, net book value.
b. Current cost, net book value.
c. Historical cost, gross book value.
d. Current cost, gross book value.

The solution to this question is at the end of the chapter.

Other Issues in Divisional Performance Measurement

Divisional income, ROI, residual income, and EVA are financial performance measures that consider the activities of the business unit independently of other units in the firm. Business units are a part of the firm, not separate businesses, because something—products, research activities, markets, and so on—keeps them together. Measuring the manager only on the division's results risks suboptimal decision making because the manager ignores the effect of the decisions on other business units.

In Chapter 15, we discuss how transfer prices can help the performance measurement of business units by signaling the value of the good or service being exchanged between units to each of the business unit managers. Nonfinancial measures of performance, including subjective measures, are described in Chapter 18.

Key Takeaways

1. Investment center managers have decision-making authority affecting revenues, costs, and asset utilization. Effective performance measures for these managers will incorporate information about the manager's decisions on these factors.
2. Four common performance measures used by firms are:
   a. Divisional income
      - Is similar to firm income using divisional information.
      - Reflects how firm performance is assessed.
      - Ignores investment utilization.
   b. Return on investment (ROI)
      - Is measured as Divisional income ÷ Divisional assets.
      - Is simple to compute and understand.
      - Adjusts for the size of the division.
      - If maximized, might not maximize firm profit because it is a ratio.
      - Is based on accounting measures that may lead to managers forgoing profitable investments (suboptimization).
   c. Residual income (RI)
      - Is measured as Divisional income − (Divisional assets × Cost of capital).

   - Can be maximized to maximize profit because it is not a ratio.
   - It is also based on accounting measures, so it may still suffer from suboptimization.
   d. Economic value added (EVA)
      - Is measured in the same way as RI, but income and investment are adjusted to correct accounting mismeasurements.
      - Can involve common adjustments including
        - Subtracting current liabilities from divisional investment.
        - Treating certain expenditures (notably R&D) as long-lived assets rather than being expensed.
      - Is conceptually superior, but because it substitutes one set of accounting measures for another, the result depends on the validity of the new assumptions.
3. Firms use the same names for measures that are computed in different ways. Examples include measuring ROI using gross or book assets, historical or current costs, and so on. Before using measures to assess performance, it is important to ensure you have an understanding of how they are computed in any given situation.

SUMMARY

Business unit performance measures rely on information from the accounting system, especially measurements of unit income and unit investment. Return on investment, residual income, and EVA are measures that explicitly include the investment in the unit. These measures correct for some of the problems of using accounting income as a measure. However, because they are based on accounting income, they do not completely align the interest of the manager with the interest of the organization.

The following summarizes key ideas tied to the chapter's learning objectives.

LO 14-1 Evaluate divisional accounting income as a performance measure. Divisional income provides one measure that is consistent with the firm's profit goal, but it ignores the capital invested in the unit.

LO 14-2 Interpret and use return on investment (ROI). ROI is the ratio of profits to investment in the asset that generates those profits. This measure facilitates comparisons among units of different sizes. Because it is a ratio, managers might not invest in projects that are profitable for the firm.

LO 14-3 Interpret and use residual income (RI). Residual income is the difference between profits and the cost of the assets that generate those profits. Because it is not a ratio, managers will invest as long as the residual income in the project is positive, regardless of what residual income currently is.

LO 14-4 Interpret and use economic value added (EVA). EVA is a variation of residual income that adjusts income to better reflect the economics underlying certain transactions, such as investment in R&D.

LO 14-5 Explain how historical cost and net book value–based accounting measures can be misleading in evaluating performance. Both of these measures can be misleading in evaluating performance. Investment center managers have an incentive to postpone replacing old assets using these measures.

KEY TERMS

cost of capital, *653*
cost of invested capital, *653*
current cost, *661*
divisional income, *646*
economic value added (EVA), *655*
gross margin ratio, *648*

historical cost, *661*
operating margin ratio, *648*
profit margin ratio, *648*
residual income (RI), *653*
return on investment (ROI), *648*

REVIEW QUESTIONS

14-1. What are the advantages of divisional income as a business unit performance measure? What are the disadvantages?

14-2. How is divisional income like income computed for the firm? How is it different?

14-3. How is return on investment (ROI) computed?

14-4. What are the advantages of using an ROI-type measure rather than the absolute value of division profits as a performance evaluation technique for business units?

14-5. How can ratios, such as ROI, be used for control as well as performance evaluation?

14-6. If a division's ROI falls from one period to the next, does that mean that the division's performance is declining? Why?

14-7. How does residual income differ from ROI?

14-8. If a division's residual income falls from one period to the next, does that mean that the division's performance is declining? Why?

14-9. How does EVA differ from residual income?

14-10. What impact does the use of gross book value or net book value in the investment base have on the computation of ROI?

14-11. What are the dangers of using only business unit measures to evaluate the performance of business unit managers?

CRITICAL ANALYSIS AND DISCUSSION QUESTIONS

14-12. A company prepares the master budget by taking each division manager's estimate of revenues and costs for the coming period and entering the data into the budget without adjustment. At the end of the year, division managers are given a bonus if their actual division profit exceeds the budgeted profit. What problems do you see with this system?

14-13. "If every division manager maximizes divisional income, we will maximize firm income. Therefore, divisional income is the best performance measure." Comment.

14-14. What problems might there be if the same methods used to compute firm income are used to compute divisional income? Does your answer depend on the type of business a firm is in?

14-15. Give an example in which the use of ROI measures might lead the manager to make a decision that is not in the firm's interests.

14-16. The chapter identified some problems with ROI-type measures and suggested that residual income reduces some of them. Why do you think that ROI is a more common performance measure in practice than residual income?

14-17. "Failure to invest in projects is not a problem when you use ROI. If there is a good project, corporate headquarters will just tell the division manager to invest." What are the difficulties with this view?

14-18. How would you respond to the following comment? "Residual income and economic value added are identical."

14-19. "I think that EVA is the best performance measure. I am going to recommend that we evaluate all managers, of plants, divisions, subsidiaries, up to the chief executive officer (CEO), using it." Do you think this statement is appropriate? Explain.

14-20. Management of Division A is evaluated based on residual income measures. The division can either rent or buy a certain asset. Might the performance evaluation technique have an impact on the rent-or-buy decision? Why or why not? Will your answer change if EVA is used?

14-21. "Every one of our company's divisions has a return on investment in excess of our cost of capital. Our company must be a blockbuster." Comment on this statement.

14-22. "Residual income solves some of the problems with ROI, but because it is an absolute number, it is difficult to compare divisions. We should use residual income divided by assets and then we would have the best of both measures." Do you agree with this statement? Explain.

14-23. By using economic value added, we avoid managers focusing on short-term gains like they would with accounting income. Do you agree with this statement? Explain.

EXERCISES

 All applicable Exercises are included in Connect.

(LO 14-1) **14-24. Compute Divisional Income**

Lauderdale Corporation is organized in three geographical divisions (regions) with managers responsible for revenues, costs, and assets in their respective regions. The firm is highly decentralized and managers are evaluated solely on divisional performance. Corporate overhead (all fixed) is allocated to the regions based on regional gross margin (regional revenue minus regional cost of sales).

The following information is from Lauderdale's first year of operations:

	Region I	Region II	Region III	Total Corporation
Revenues..................	$1,200,000	$1,650,000	$2,250,000	$5,100,000
Cost of sales..............	450,000	810,000	1,140,000	2,400,000
SG&A (all fixed)............	420,000	630,000	850,000	1,900,000
Corporate overhead				432,000

Required

Compute divisional operating income for the three regions. Ignore taxes. How have these regions performed?

(LO 14-1) **14-25. Compute Divisional Income**

Owen Audio shows the following information for its two divisions for year 1.

	Consumer Division	Commercial Division
Sales revenue.....................	$1,836,000	$5,814,000
Cost of sales	1,101,600	3,779,100
SG&A	275,400	348,840
Allocated corporate overhead........	128,520	406,980

Required

Compute divisional operating income for the two divisions. Ignore taxes. How have these divisions performed?

14-26. Compute Divisional Income

(LO 14-1)

Refer to Exercise 14-25. The results for year 2 have just been posted:

	Consumer Division	Commercial Division
Sales revenue........................	$2,686,000	$5,814,000
Cost of sales.......................	1,477,300	3,779,100
SG&A	287,402	348,840
Allocated corporate overhead........	169,218	366,282

Required

Compute divisional operating income for the two divisions. How have these divisions performed?

14-27. Computing Divisional Income: Incomplete Information and Financial Ratios

(LO 14-1)

The following partial financial information (in thousands of dollars) is available for Thole, Inc.:

	A	B	C	D	E	F
1			(Thousands of Dollars)			
2		**Pacific**		**Southern**		**Total**
3	Sales					
4	Cost of sales					
5	Gross margin					
6	SG&A					
7	Allocated corportate costs	20.0				100.0
8	Operating income					
9	Tax expense (@ 20%)					
10	After-tax income					$ 393.6
11						
12						
13	Gross margin percentage	40.00%		50.00%		48.00%
14	Operating margin	20.00%		36.00%		32.80%
15	Profit margin	16.00%		28.80%		26.24%
16						

Corporate overhead costs at Thole are allocated to divisions based on relative sales.

Required

a.   Complete the income statements for both divisions and the corporation as a whole.

b.   What recommendation(s) would you make about computing divisional income for divisional performance measurement at Thole, Inc.?

14-28. Compute ROI

(LO 14-2)

Refer to the information in Exercise 14-24. Information on the division assets in the three regions of Lauderdale Corporation follows:

Region I.........................	$ 700,000
Region II........................	630,000
Region III.......................	1,287,500

Required

Compute the division ROI for each of the three regions. How have these regions performed?

14-29. Compute RI and ROI

(LO 14-2, 3)

The Custodial Division of Clark's Corporate Services (CCS) has assets of $1.2 million. During the past year, the division had profits of $216,000. CCS has a cost of capital of 7.5 percent. Ignore taxes.

Required

a.   Compute the divisional ROI for the Custodial Division.

b.   Compute the divisional RI for the Custodial Division.

(LO 14-2, 3)   **14-30. ROI versus RI**

Albany Division is considering the acquisition of a new asset that will cost $540,000 and have a cash flow of $180,000 per year for each of the four years of its life. Depreciation is computed on a straight-line basis with no salvage value. Ignore taxes.

Required

a.   What is the ROI for each year of the asset's life if the division uses beginning-of-year asset balances and net book value for the computation?

b.   What is the residual income each year if the cost of capital is 9 percent? Assume the division uses beginning-of-year asset balances and net book value for the computation.

(LO 14-2, 4)   **14-31. Compare Alternative Measures of Division Performance**

The following data are available for two divisions of Ryan Enterprises:

	Alpha Division	Beta Division
Division operating profit	$ 7,200,000	$1,080,000
Division investment	32,000,000	3,000,000

The cost of capital for the company is 7 percent. Ignore taxes.

Required

a.   If Ryan measures performance using ROI, which division had the better performance?

b.   If Ryan measures performance using economic value added, which division had the better performance? (The divisions have no current liabilities.)

c.   Would your evaluation change if the company's cost of capital was 10 percent? Why?

(LO 14-3)   **14-32. Comparing Business Units Using Residual Income**

Refer to the data in Exercises 14-24 and 14-28. Lauderdale Corporation has a cost of capital of 8.6 percent.

Required

Compute residual income for the three regions. Ignore taxes. How have these regions performed?

(LO 14-2)   **14-33. Comparing Business Units Using ROI**

Lasky Manufacturing has two divisions: Carolinas and Northeast. Lasky has a cost of capital of 7.5 percent. Selected financial information (in thousands of dollars) for the first year of business follows:

	Carolinas	Northeast
Sales revenue.	$ 800	$4,000
Income	160	312
Divisional assets (beginning of year)	1,000	1,500
Current liabilities (beginning of year)	160	160
R&D expenditures[a].	400	320

[a] R&D is assumed to benefit two periods. All R&D is spent at the beginning of the year.

Required

Evaluate the performance of the two divisions assuming Lasky uses return on investment (ROI).

(LO 14-3)   **14-34. Comparing Business Units Using Residual Income**

Refer to the data in Exercise 14-33.

Required

Evaluate the performance of the two divisions assuming Lasky Manufacturing uses residual income.

14-35. Comparing Business Units Using Economic Value Added (EVA) (LO 14-4)
Refer to the data in Exercise 14-33.

Required
Evaluate the performance of the two divisions assuming Lasky Manufacturing uses economic value added (EVA).

14-36. Comparing Business Units Using Economic Value Added (EVA) (LO 14-4)
Refer to the data in Exercises 14-24, 14-28, and 14-32. The individual regions are responsible for research and development (R&D) decisions and for current liabilities. Information on R&D expenditures (which are included in SG&A) for the year and current liabilities for the three regions follows:

	Region I	Region II	Region III
R&D expenditures	$150,000	$210,000	$450,000
Current liabilities	90,000	140,000	190,000

R&D expenditures are assumed to be incurred uniformly over the period and are expected to generate benefits for three years.

Required
Compute economic value added for the three regions. Ignore taxes. How have these regions performed?

14-37. Comparing Business Units Using ROI (LO 14-2)
Houghton Chemicals, which started operations one year ago, has two divisions: Alloys and Petro. Both divisions invest heavily in R&D, which is assumed to generate benefits for five years. R&D spending is made uniformly throughout the year. Houghton Chemicals has a cost of capital of 11 percent. Selected financial information for the two divisions (in thousands of dollars) for the year just completed follows:

	Alloys	Petro
Sales revenue.....................	$7,400	$5,500
Divisional income..................	777	945
Divisional investment	5,550	7,000
Current liabilities	160	200
R&D	200	300

Required
Evaluate the performance of the two divisions assuming Houghton uses return on investment (ROI).

14-38. Comparing Business Units Using Residual Income (LO 14-3)
Refer to the data in Exercise 14-37.

Required
Evaluate the performance of the two divisions assuming Houghton Chemicals uses residual income.

14-39. Comparing Business Units Using Economic Value Added (EVA) (LO 14-4)
Refer to the data in Exercise 14-37.

Required
Evaluate the performance of the two divisions assuming Houghton Chemicals uses economic value added (EVA).

14-40. Impact of New Asset on Performance Measures (LO 14-2)
The Plastics Division of Minock Manufacturing currently earns $2.87 million and has divisional assets of $35.0 million. The division manager is considering the acquisition of a new asset that

will add to profit. The investment has a cost of $5,400,000 and will have a yearly cash flow of $1,442,000. The asset will be depreciated using the straight-line method over a five-year life and is expected to have no salvage value. Divisional performance is measured using ROI with beginning-of-year net book values in the denominator. The company's cost of capital is 7 percent. Ignore taxes.

Required

a. What is the divisional ROI before acquisition of the new asset?
b. What is the divisional ROI in the first year after acquisition of the new asset?

(LO 14-2) **14-41. Impact of Leasing on Performance Measures**
Refer to the data in Exercise 14-40. The division manager learns that there is an option to lease the asset on a year-to-year lease for $1,162,000 per year. All depreciation and other tax benefits would accrue to the lessor.

Required
What is the divisional ROI if the asset is leased?

(LO 14-3) **14-42. Residual Income Measures and New Project Consideration**
Refer to the information in Exercises 14-40 and 14-41.

Required

a. What is the division's residual income before considering the project?
b. What is the division's residual income if the asset is purchased?
c. What is the division's residual income if the asset is leased?

(LO 14-2, 3) **14-43. Impact of an Asset Disposal on Performance Measures**
Veach Division has total assets (net of accumulated depreciation) of $462,000 at the beginning of year 1. One of the assets is a machine that has a net book value of $42,000. Expected divisional income in year 1 is $55,440 including $2,940 in income generated by the machine (after depreciation). Veach's cost of capital is 10 percent. Veach is considering disposing of the asset today (the beginning of year 1).

Required

a. Veach computes ROI using beginning-of-year net assets. What will the divisional ROI be for year 1 assuming Veach retains the asset?
b. What would divisional ROI be for year 1 assuming Veach disposes of the asset for its book value and there is no gain or loss on the sale?
c. Veach computes residual income using beginning-of-year net assets. What will the divisional residual income be for year 1 assuming Veach retains the asset?
d. What would divisional residual income be for year 1 assuming Veach disposes of the asset for its book value and there is no gain or loss on the sale?

(LO 14-2, 3) **14-44. Impact of an Asset Disposal on Performance Measures**
Refer to the facts in Exercise 14-43, but assume that Veach has been leasing the machine for $7,200 annually. Assume also that the machine generates income of $2,940 annually after the lease payment. Veach can cancel the lease on the machine without penalty at any time.

Required

a. Veach computes ROI using beginning-of-year net assets. What will the divisional ROI be for year 1 assuming Veach retains the asset?
b. What would divisional ROI be for year 1 assuming Veach disposes of the asset?
c. Veach computes residual income using beginning-of-year net assets. What will the divisional residual income be for year 1 assuming Veach retains the asset?
d. What would divisional residual income be for year 1 assuming Veach cancels the lease on the machine?

14-45. Compare Historical Cost, Net Book Value to Gross Book Value (LO 14-2, 5)

The Street Division of Labrosse Logistics just started operations. It purchased depreciable assets costing $36 million and having a four-year expected life, after which the assets can be salvaged for $7.2 million. In addition, the division has $36 million in assets that are not depreciable. After four years, the division will have $36 million available from these nondepreciable assets. This means that the division has invested $72 million in assets with a salvage value of $43.2 million. Annual operating cash flows are $12 million. In computing ROI, this division uses *end-of-year* asset values in the denominator. Depreciation is computed on a straight-line basis, recognizing the salvage values noted. Ignore taxes.

Required

a. Compute ROI, using net book value for each year.
b. Compute ROI, using gross book value for each year.

14-46. Compare ROI Using Net Book and Gross Book Values (LO 14-2, 5)

Refer to the data in Exercise 14-45. Assume that the division uses *beginning-of-year* asset values in the denominator for computing ROI.

Required

a. Compute ROI, using net book value.
b. Compute ROI, using gross book value.
c. If you worked Exercise 14-39, compare those results with those in this exercise. How different is the ROI computed using end-of-year asset values, as in Exercise 14-39, from the ROI using beginning-of-year values in this exercise?

14-47. Compare Current Cost to Historical Cost (LO 14-2, 5)

Refer to the information in Exercise 14-45. In computing ROI, this division uses end-of-year asset values. Assume that all cash flows increase 10 percent at the end of each year. This has the following effect on the assets' replacement cost and annual cash flows:

End of Year	Replacement Cost	Annual Cash Flow
1	$72,000,000 × 1.1 = $79,200,000	$12,000,000 × 1.1 = $13,200,000
2	$79,200,000 × 1.1 = $87,120,000	$13,200,000 × 1.1 = $14,520,000
3	Etc.	Etc.
4		

Depreciation is as follows.

Year	For the Year	"Accumulated"
1	$ 7,920,000	$ 9,900,000 (= 10% × $79,200,000)
2	8,712,000	21,780,000 (= 20% × $87,120,000)
3	9,583,200	28,749,600
4	10,541,520	42,166,080

Note that "accumulated" depreciation is 10 percent of the gross book value of depreciable assets after one year, 20 percent after two years, and so forth.

Required

a. Compute ROI using historical cost, net book value.
b. Compute ROI using historical cost, gross book value.
c. Compute ROI using current cost, net book value.
d. Compute ROI using current cost, gross book value.

(LO 14-2, 5)   **14-48. Effects of Current Cost on Performance Measurements**

Exeter Division of Wetherby Labs acquired an asset with a cost of $800,000 and a four-year life. The cash flows from the asset, considering the effects of inflation, were scheduled as follows:

Year	Cash Flow
1	$250,000
2	275,000
3	290,000
4	300,000

The cost of the asset is expected to increase at a rate of 5 percent per year, compounded each year. Performance measures are based on beginning-of-year gross book values for the investment base. Ignore taxes.

Required

a.   What is the ROI for each year of the asset's life, using a historical cost approach?

b.   What is the ROI for each year of the asset's life if both the investment base and depreciation are determined by the current cost of the asset at the start of each year?

PROBLEMS

 All applicable Exercises are included in Connect.

(LO 14-1, 2, 3)   **14-49. Comparing Business Units Using Divisional Income, ROI, and Residual Income**

Navarre Energy Research specializes in developing and commercializing new products. It is organized into two divisions, which are based on the products they produce. Canal Division is smaller, and the lives of the products it produces tend to be shorter than those produced by the larger Lake Division. Selected financial data for the past year are shown in the following table. Divisional investment is as of the beginning of the year. Navarre uses an 8 percent cost of capital and beginning-of-year investment when computing ROI and residual income. Ignore income taxes.

	A	B	C
1		Division	
2		Canal	Lake
3		($000)	($000)
4	Allocated corp. overhead	$ 4,100	$ 9,600
5	Cost of goods sold	20,000	30,000
6	Divisional investment	60,100	400,000
7	R&D	12,000	32,000
8	Sales	50,000	100,000
9	SG&A (excl. R&D)	4,500	8,000
10			

Required

a.   Compute divisional income for the two divisions.

b.   Calculate the operating margin, which is equivalent to the return on sales, for the two divisions.

c.   Calculate ROI for the two divisions.

d.   Compute residual income for the two divisions.

e.   Assess the financial performance of the two divisions based on your analysis.

(LO 14-4)   **14-50. Comparing Business Units Using Economic Value Added (EVA)**

Refer to the data in Problem 14-49. R&D is assumed to have a three-year life in Canal Division and an eight-year life in Lake Division. All R&D expenditures are spent at the beginning of the year. Assume there are no current liabilities and (unrealistically) that no R&D investments had taken place before this year.

Required

a.   Compute EVA for the two divisions.

b.   How, if at all, does this change your assessment of the performance of the two divisions?

14-51. Comparing Business Units Using EVA: Sensitivity Analysis   (LO 14-4)
Refer to the data in Problems 14-49 and 14-50. The manager of the Canal Division complains that the calculation of EVA is unfair because a much longer life is assumed for the Lake Division in calculating EVA. The manager of Lake Division responds that EVA is supposed to reflect economic reality and that the reality is that R&D investments in Lake Division do have a longer life.

Required

a.   Assume that the economic life of R&D investments is three years in the Canal Division. What economic life would the R&D investments in the Lake Division have to have to make EVA in the two divisions equal?

b.   Are there other disputes that might arise about the calculation of EVA used for performance evaluation? Explain.

14-52. Equipment Replacement and Performance Measures   (LO 14-2)
Leidich Corporation manufactures hospital equipment. The Measurement Division (MD) manufactures testing and measurement equipment including a special cardiovascular instrument. MD started the year with $6.25 million in other assets. At the beginning of the current year, MD invested $7.5 million in automated equipment for instrument assembly. The division's expected income statement at the beginning of the year was as follows:

Sales revenue....................	$24,000,000
Operating costs	
Variable	2,970,000
Fixed (all cash)	11,600,000
Depreciation	
New automated equipment.....	2,500,000
Other	1,650,000
Division operating profit	$ 5,280,000

A sales representative from South Street Manufacturing (SSM) approached the manager of MD in late November. SSM is willing to sell for $9.4 million a new assembly machine that offers significant improvements over the automated equipment MD acquired at the beginning of the year. The new equipment would expand division output by 12 percent while reducing cash fixed costs by $828,400. It would be depreciated for accounting purposes over a four-year life. Depreciation would be net of the $600,000 salvage value of the new machine. The new equipment meets Leidich's cost of capital criterion. If MD purchases the new machine, it must be installed prior to the end of the year. For practical purposes, though, MD can ignore depreciation on the new machine because it will not go into operation until the start of the next year.

MD will have to dispose of the old machine because the new machine would be installed in the same area. The old machine has no salvage value.

Leidich has a performance evaluation and bonus plan based on ROI. The return includes any losses on disposal of equipment. Investment is computed based on the end-of-year balance of assets, net book value. Ignore taxes.

Required

a.   What is Measurement Division's ROI if it does not acquire the new machine?

b.   What is Measurement Division's ROI this year if it does acquire the new machine?

c.   If MD acquires the new machine and it operates according to specifications, what ROI is expected for next year?

14-53. Evaluate Trade-Offs in Return Measurement   (LO 14-2)
Refer to the information in Problem 14-52. The manager is still assessing the problem of whether to acquire SSM's assembly machine. SSM tells the manager that the new machine could be acquired next year, but it will cost 20 percent more. The salvage value would still be $600,000. Other costs or revenue estimates would be apportioned on a month-by-month basis for the time each machine (either the current machine or the machine the manager is considering) is in use. Fractions of months may be ignored. Ignore taxes.

Required

a. When would the manager of the Measurement Division want to purchase the new machine if he waits until next year?

b. What are the costs that must be considered in making this decision?

(LO 14-3)   **14-54. Residual Income**

Refer to the facts in Problem 14-52. Assume that the performance measurement and bonus plans at Leidich Corporation are based on residual income instead of ROI. The company uses a cost of capital of 10 percent in computing residual income.

Required

a. What is Measurement Division's residual income if it does not acquire the new machine?

b. What is Measurement Division's residual income this year if it does acquires the new machine?

c. If the division acquires the new machine and operates it according to specifications, what residual income is expected for next year?

(LO 14-3)   **14-55. Evaluate Trade-Offs in Performance Measurement and Decisions**

Refer to the facts in Problem 14-52 through 14-54. Assume that the Leidich Corporation performance measurement and bonus plans are based on residual income instead of ROI. The company uses a cost of capital of 10 percent in computing residual income.

Required

a. When would the manager of the Measurement Division want to purchase the new machine if he waits until next year?

b. What are the costs that must be considered in making this decision?

(LO 14-2)   **14-56. ROI and Management Behavior: Ethical Issues**

Division managers at Lesure, Inc. are granted a wide range of decision authority. With the exception of managing cash, which is done at corporate headquarters, divisions are responsible for sales, pricing, production, costs of operations, and management of accounts receivable, inventories, accounts payable, and use of existing facilities.

If divisions require funds for investment, division executives present investment proposals to corporate management, who analyze and document them. The final decision to commit funds for investment purposes rests with corporate management.

The corporation evaluates divisional executive performance by using the ROI measure. The asset base is composed of fixed assets employed plus working capital, exclusive of cash. The ROI performance of a division executive is the most important appraisal factor for salary changes. In addition, each executive's annual performance bonus is based on ROI results, with increases in ROI having a significant impact on the amount of the bonus.

Lesure adopted the ROI performance measure and related compensation procedures about 10 years ago and seems to have benefited from it. The ROI for the corporation as a whole increased during the first years of the program. Although the ROI continued to increase in each division, corporate ROI has declined in recent years. The corporation has accumulated a sizable amount of short-term marketable securities in the past three years.

Corporate management is concerned about the increase in the short-term marketable securities. A recent article in a financial publication suggested that some companies have overemphasized the use of ROI, with results similar to those experienced by Lesure.

Required

a. Describe the specific actions that division managers might have taken to cause the ROI to increase in each division but decrease for the corporation. Illustrate your explanation with appropriate examples.

b. Using the concepts of goal congruence and motivation of division executives, explain how the overemphasis on the use of the ROI measure at Lesure Company might have resulted in the recent decline in the company's ROI and the increase in cash and short-term marketable securities.

c. What changes could be made in Lesure's compensation policy to avoid this problem? Explain your answer.

d. Is it ethical for a manager to take actions that increase the division ROI but decrease the firm's ROI?

(CMA adapted)

14-57. Impact of Decisions to Capitalize or Expense on Performance Measurement: Ethical Issues (LO 14-1, 2)

Technology firms, pharmaceutical firms, oil and gas companies, and other ventures inevitably incur costs on unsuccessful investments in new projects (e.g., new technologies or new drugs). For oil and gas firms, a debate continues over whether those costs should be written off as a period expense or capitalized as part of the full cost of finding profitable oil and gas ventures. However, GAAP in the United States is clear that R&D costs are to be expensed when incurred.

Luther Technologies, an automotive supplier, has been writing R&D costs off to expense as incurred for both financial reporting and internal performance measurement. However, this year a new management team was hired to improve the profit of Luther's Self-Driving Division. The new management team was hired with the provision that it would receive a bonus equal to 12.5 percent of any profits in excess of base-year profits of the division. However, no bonus would be paid if profits were less than 15 percent of end-of-year investment. The following information was included in the performance report for the division:

	This Year	Base Year	Increase over Base Year
Sales revenues	$12,500,000	$12,000,000	
Costs incurred			
R&D expense	–0–	2,400,000	
Depreciation and other amortization	2,300,000	2,200,000	
Other costs	4,800,000	4,700,000	
Division profit	$ 5,400,000	$ 2,700,000	$2,700,000
End-of-year investment	$35,000,000[a]	$30,000,000	

[a] Includes other investments not at issue here.

During the year, the new team spent $3.4 million on R&D activities, of which $3.0 million was for unsuccessful ventures. The new management team has included the $3.0 million in the current end-of-year investment base because "not all great ideas make it to development."

Required

a. What is the ROI for the base year and the current year? Ignore taxes.

b. What is the amount of the bonus that the new management team is likely to claim? Is this ethical?

c. If you were on Luther's board of directors, how would you respond to the new management's claim for the bonus?

14-58. Evaluate Performance Evaluation System: Behavioral Issues (LO 14-1)

Several years ago, Humboldt Products acquired Crescent Fabrication. Prior to the acquisition, Crescent manufactured and sold metal and plastic components to third-party customers. Since becoming a division of Humboldt, Crescent has manufactured components only for products made by Humboldt's Marine Division.

Humboldt's corporate management gives the Crescent Division management considerable latitude in running the division's operations. However, corporate management retains authority for decisions regarding capital investments, product pricing, and production quantities.

Humboldt has a formal performance evaluation program for all division managements. The evaluation program relies substantially on each division's ROI. Crescent Division's income statement provides the basis for the evaluation of Crescent's management. (See the following income statement.)

The corporate accounting staff prepares the divisional financial statements. Corporate general services costs are allocated on the basis of sales dollars, and the computer department's actual costs are apportioned among the divisions on the basis of use. The net divisional investment includes divisional fixed assets at net book value (cost less depreciation), divisional inventory, and corporate working capital apportioned to the divisions on the basis of sales dollars.

HUMBOLDT PRODUCTS
Crescent Division
Income Statement
For the Year Ended December 31
($000)

Sales revenue..........................		$21,000
Costs and expenses		
Product costs		
Direct materials........................	$ 2,500	
Direct labor.........................	5,000	
Factory overhead....................	6,400	
Total product costs....................	$13,900	
Less increase in inventory	1,500	$12,400
Engineering and research		600
Shipping and receiving..................		1,200
Division administration		
Manager's office.....................	$ 900	
Cost accounting.....................	190	
Personnel	360	1,450
Corporate cost		
General services	$ 1,100	
Computer	250	1,350
Total costs and expenses.................		$17,000
Divisional operating profit		$ 4,000
Net plant investment.....................		$25,000
Return on investment....................		16%

Required

a.   Discuss Humboldt Product's financial reporting and performance evaluation program as it relates to the responsibilities of Crescent Division.

b.   Based on your response to requirement (*a*), recommend appropriate revisions of the financial information and reports used to evaluate the performance of Crescent's divisional management. If revisions are not necessary, explain why.

(CMA adapted)

(LO 14-1, 2, 4)   **14-59. ROI, Residual Income, and Different Asset Bases**

Vermont Automotive is a regional chain of auto parts stores. The managers of the individual stores are evaluated using ROI. Vermont requires managers to earn an ROI of at least 10 percent of assets. The manager of the Erie store estimates revenues in the following year will be $3,750,000, cost of goods sold will be $2,180,000, and operating expenses for this level of sales will be $310,000. Investment in the store assets throughout the year is $3,500,000 before considering any changes.

A representative of Hoffman Audio approached the manager about carrying Hoffman's line of car audio systems. This line is expected to generate $1,000,000 in sales in the coming year at the Erie store with a merchandise cost of $780,000. Annual operating expenses for this additional merchandise line total $120,000. To carry the line of goods, an inventory investment of $750,000 throughout the year is required. Hoffman is willing to "floor-plan" the merchandise so that the Erie store will not have to invest in any inventory. The cost of floor planning would be $65,000 per year. Vermont's marginal cost of capital is 7 percent. Ignore taxes.

Required

a. What is the Erie store's expected ROI for the coming year if it does not carry Hoffman's merchandise?

b. What is the store's expected ROI if the manager invests in Hoffman's inventory and carries the audio line?

c. What would the store's expected ROI be if the manager elected to take the floor-plan option?

d. Would the manager prefer requirement (*a*), (*b*), or (*c*)? Why?

e. Would your answers to any of the above change if residual income was used to evaluate performance?

14-60. Economic Value Added (LO 14-4)

Normandy Instruments invests heavily in research and development (R&D), although it must currently treat its R&D expenditures as expenses for financial accounting purposes. To encourage investment in R&D, Normandy evaluates its division managers using EVA. The company adjusts accounting income for R&D expenditures by assuming these expenditures create assets with a two-year life. That is, the R&D expenditures are capitalized and then amortized over two years.

Aerospace Division of Normandy shows after-tax income of $18.0 million for year 2. R&D expenditures in year 1 amounted to $7.2 million and in year 2, R&D expenditures were $12.0 million. For purposes of computing EVA, Normandy assumes all R&D expenditures are made uniformly over the year. Before adjusting for R&D, Aerospace Division shows assets of $72 million at the beginning of year 2 and current liabilities of $1,500,000. Normandy computes EVA using divisional investment at the beginning of the year and a 12 percent cost of capital.

Required

Compute EVA for Aerospace Division for year 2.

14-61. Economic Value Added (LO 14-4)

Gable Corporate Services uses EVA to evaluate the performance of division managers. For the Media Division, after-tax divisional income was $3,100,000 in year 3.

The company adjusts the after-tax income for advertising expenses. First, it adds the annual advertising expenses back to after-tax divisional income. Second, the company managers believe that advertising has a three-year positive effect on the sale of the company's products, so it amortizes advertising over three years. Advertising expenses in year 1 will be expensed 40 percent, 35 percent in year 2, and 25 percent in year 3. Advertising expenses in year 2 will be expensed 40 percent, 35 percent in year 3, and 25 percent in year 4. Advertising expenses in year 3 will be amortized 40 percent, 35 percent in year 4, and 25 percent in year 5. Third, unamortized advertising expenses become part of the divisional investment in the EVA calculations. Media Division incurred advertising expenses of $540,000 in year 1 and $1,050,000 in year 2. It incurred $1,260,000 of advertising in year 3.

Before considering the unamortized advertising, the Media Division had total assets of $28,600,000 and current liabilities of $3,600,000 at the beginning of year 3. Gable calculates EVA using the divisional investment at the beginning of the year. The company uses a 14 percent cost of capital to compute EVA.

Required

Compute the EVA for the Media Division for year 3. Is the division adding value to shareholders?

14-62. Decision Making, ROI, and Residual Income (LO 14-2, 3)

Leland Pharmaceuticals develops both over-the-counter (OTC) and prescription medicines. It is organized into two divisions, which are evaluated as investment centers. The cost of capital used in evaluating the divisions is 9 percent.

A local engineering firm has developed and patented a process that significantly shortens packaging times and costs. The engineering firm has offered to either sell the patent to Leland's

OTC Division or lease the exclusive rights to the process. (The process is not usable in the Prescription Division). The lease (and the estimated economic life of the process) is eight years. If purchased, the technology would cost $4.0 million. An eight-year lease would require annual payments of $900,000.

The division manager of OTC estimates that annual income using the process (before considering any depreciation or lease payments) would be $8 million. The investment for OTC (before considering any impact from the new technology) is $50 million.

Assume that the patent would be amortized on a straight-line basis if purchased. Ignore any income tax effects.

Required

a. Suppose the manager of OTC is evaluated using return on investment (ROI). Will the manager prefer to lease or purchase the technology?

b. Suppose the manager of OTC is evaluated using residual income. Will the manager prefer to lease or purchase the technology?

c. Suppose the manager of OTC is evaluated using return on investment (ROI). What is the lease payment that would make the manager indifferent between leasing and purchasing the technology?

d. Suppose the manager of OTC is evaluated using residual income. What is the lease payment that would make the manager indifferent between leasing and purchasing the technology?

(LO 14-1, 2, 3)   **14-63. Divisional Income, ROI, and Residual Income**

Bentler Industries provides high-technology navigation and communication equipment for the aerospace and shipbuilding industries. It is organized into two divisions, Aeronautics and Marine. The division presidents are given wide decision-making authority that covers operations, marketing, and asset acquisition and disposal. Bentler evaluates the division presidents on, among other things, ROI in their respective divisions. ROI is based on after-tax divisional income and beginning-of-year assets. Divisional income includes allocated corporate overhead.

For the most recent year (year 3), data from the two divisions shows the following:

	A	B	C
1		Aeronautics Division	Marine Division
2	Allocated corporate overhead	$ 15,000	$ 9,000
3	Cost of sales	16,100	13,600
4	Other general and administrative costs	830	1,250
5	R&D costs	15,000	2,400
6	Sales	50,000	30,000
7	Total assets (January 1, Year 3)	30,000	20,000

The tax rate applied at Bentler is 20 percent.

Required

a. Compute divisional income for year 3 for each of the divisions.

b. Evaluate the two divisions based on the information from the divisional income computed in requirement (a). Which division performed better?

c. Compute ROI for year 3 for each of the divisions. Which division performed better?

d. Compute residual income for year 3 for each of the divisions. Which division performed better? Bentler uses a cost of capital of 12 percent.

(LO 14-4)   **14-64. Economic Value Added (EVA)**

Refer to the information in Problem 14-63. Looking at the ROI results for year 3, the president of Aeronautics Division complains that the division is evaluated unfairly because of the accounting rules that R&D expenditures be expensed in the year incurred. The president believes that the type of R&D performed in both Aeronautics and Marine Division generate benefits over a three-year period.

In order to consider the president's complaint, the company considers some additional information. First, divisional balance sheets as of January 1, year 3, follow.

	A	B	C	D
1		**BENTLER RESEARCH, INC.**		
2		**Divisional Income Statements**		
3		**January 1, Year 3**		
4		**($000)**		
5		Aeronautics	Marine	
6		Division	Division	Total
7	Assets			
8	Cash	$ 900	$ 500	$ 1,400
9	Accounts receivable	800	900	1,700
10	Inventory	900	600	1,500
11	Total current assets	$ 2,600	$ 2,000	$ 4,600
12	Fixed assets (net)	27,400	18,000	45,400
13	Total assets	$ 30,000	$ 20,000	$ 50,000
14				
15	Liabilities and Equities			
16	Accounts payable	$ 450	$ 400	$ 850
17	Other current liabilities	1,050	1,300	2,350
18	Total current liabilities	$ 1,500	$ 1,700	$ 3,200
19	Long-term debt	-	-	-
20	Total liabiliities	$ 1,500	$ 1,700	$ 3,200
21	Total shareholders equity	28,500	18,300	46,800
22	Total liabilities and equities	$ 30,000	$ 20,000	$ 50,000
23				

Historical information on R&D expenditures follow here:

	J	K	L
		R&D Expenditures ($000)	
		Years 1-3	
		Aeronautics	Marine
		Division	Division
	Year 1	$ 9,000.0	$ 1,800.0
	Year 2	12,600.0	3,000.0
	Year 3 (Current Year)	15,000.0	2,400.0

Required

a.   Compute the economic value added (EVA) for each division for year 3. Assume that the R&D expenditures are incurred uniformly over the year.

b.   Which division performed better?

14-65. Economic Value Added (EVA)—Data Analysis and Data Visualization   (LO 14-4)

Refer to the information in Problems 14-63 and 14-64. The executives at Bentler's corporate headquarters are intrigued and interested by the EVA findings. They are concerned, however, about the estimated cost of capital that is used (12 percent) and how sensitive the findings of Problem 14-64 are to the cost of capital used in the calculation.

Required

a.   Determine the cost of capital at which the EVA for Aeronautics Division and Marine Division would be equal. Assume that a common cost of capital would be used for both divisions.

b.   Prepare a data visualization that would help the executives better understand this sensitivity.

14-66. Economic Value Added (EVA)—Data Analysis and Data Visualization   (LO 14-4)

Refer to the information in Problems 14-63 and 14-64. Looking at the EVA results for year 3, the president of Marine Division complains that the division is evaluated unfairly because a common cost of capital is used. The president believes that the R&D investments in Aeronautics Division are much riskier than those in the Marine Division.

Required

a. Determine the cost of capital at which the EVA for Aeronautics Division and Marine Division would be equal. Assume that a cost of capital of 12 percent would continue to be used for Marine Division.

b. Prepare a data visualization that would help the executives at Bentler's headquarters and the two Division presidents better understand this sensitivity.

(LO 14-3, 5)   **14-67. Compare Historical, Net Book Value to Gross Book Value, Residual Income**
Refer to the information in Exercise 14-45. Assume that the company uses an 8 percent cost of capital.

Required

a. Compute residual income, using net book value for each year.

b. Compute residual income, using gross book value for each year.

(LO 14-3, 5)   **14-68. Effects of Current Cost on Performance Measurements, Residual Income**
Refer to the information in Exercise 14-48. Assume that the company uses a 12 percent cost of capital. As in Exercise 14-48, performance measures are based on beginning-of-year gross book values for the investment base.

Required

a. What is the residual income for each year of the asset's life, using a historical cost approach?

b. What is the residual income for each year of the asset's life if both the investment base and depreciation are determined by the current cost of the asset at the start of each year?

INTEGRATIVE CASES

(LO 14-1, 2, 3, 4)   **14-69. Barrows Consumer Products (A)**

> I thought evaluating performance would be easier than this. I have three vice presidents, operating the same business in three different countries. I need to be able to compare them in order to prepare compensation recommendations to the board. The problem is that there are so many variables that each of the managers can make some claim to having the best performance. I hope our consultant can help me sort this out.

> *Alice Karlson, Executive Vice President*
> *Southeast Asia Emerging Markets Sector*
> *Barrows Consumer Products*

Organization

Barrows Consumer Products is a large, multinational consumer products firm based in the United States. In the mid-1990s, Barrows made a strategic decision to enter the transitional and emerging markets. Each of the new markets was led by an executive vice president and organized along country lines. Barrows believed this form of organization made it easier to evaluate each country, and also made it easier to exit from a country it identified as unprofitable.

One of the new markets developed by Barrows was Southeast Asia. Although there was significant competition in the region from other Asian and European competitors, the management of Barrows believed its advantage was in its portfolio of products with widely recognized brand names. Barrows chose three countries to enter initially: Indonesia, the Philippines, and Vietnam. At the time of the decision, all three appeared to represent significant growth opportunities.

Barrows's policy in these new markets was to install a Barrows manager originally from the country who was willing to return and manage the business. Barrows believed that this policy resulted in additional goodwill and also allowed the managers to use their knowledge of local business customs. (It also hoped to take advantage of any personal ties the managers might have in business and government, but this was not included in its policy statement.) A simplified organization chart for the Southeast Asia Emerging Markets Sector is provided in Exhibit 14.14.

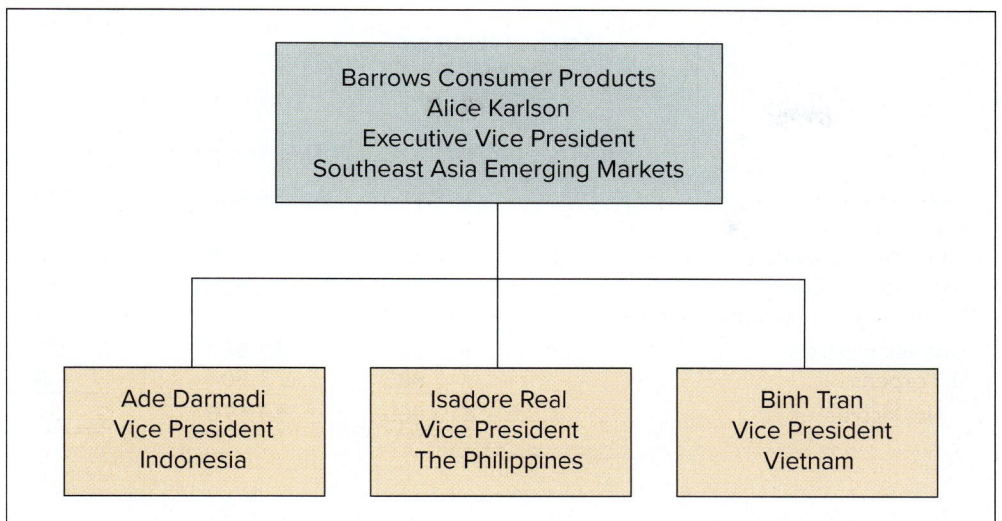

Exhibit 14.14

Organization Chart, Southeast Asia Emerging Markets Sector—Barrows Consumer Products

	Indonesia	The Philippines	Vietnam
Population (millions—approximate)..	225	80	80
GDP per capita (in U.S. dollars)	$2,830	$3,500	$1,700

Exhibit 14.15

Selected Demographic Data, Southeast Asia Emerging Markets Sector—Barrows Consumer Products

Although all three countries could be classified as emerging or transitional economies, there are considerable differences among them. Indonesia has a very large population, while the Philippines and Vietnam are smaller. The Philippines, however, has a higher level of per capita income; Vietnam is the poorest of the three countries. Selected demographic data for the three countries are shown in Exhibit 14.15.

Performance Evaluation

Barrows has a well-developed set of performance measures that are used for managerial evaluation. The two primary measures that are used for groups in the United States, Canada, Western Europe, and Japan are division (or country) profit and return on investment (ROI). Return on investment is computed by dividing division (or country) operating income (essentially, income before taxes) by division (or country) total assets. While profit and ROI are commonly used in much of the company, the executive vice presidents in emerging market sectors are given considerable leeway in evaluating their individual country vice presidents. This performance evaluation is important to these managers. Compensation in the Southeast Asia Sector consists of salary and bonus. The bonus pool for the three managers is dictated by corporate headquarters of Barrows in the United States. The bonus pool formula is not explicitly defined, although there is a clear correlation between the size of the pool and the profitability of the sector, however measured.

The allocation of the pool to the individual country managers is at the discretion of Ms. Karlson, the sector executive vice president. In March of year 9, the financial results from the three countries for year 8 have been tabulated and she is now evaluating them. Because this is her first year in this position, she has not had to perform this task in the past. She has hired a local compensation consultant to advise her on the relative performance of the three managers.

The financial staff at sector headquarters receives the financial statements from the controller's staff in each of the three countries and ensures that the statements are consistently prepared in a common currency. The income statements for year 8 are shown in Exhibit 14.16. The balance sheets as of the beginning of year 8 are shown in Exhibit 14.17. Ms. Karlson discusses the source of her concern.

> When I look at the financial statements, I can see immediately that Ade [Darmadi, VP—Indonesia] has outperformed Isadore [Real, VP—Philippines]. But Indonesia is a much larger market than the Philippines. So I calculate ROI to try and adjust for size and now Isadore is outperforming Ade. When I mention this to Ade, she counters that although

Exhibit 14.16

Country-Level Income Statements, Southeast Asia Emerging Markets Sector—Barrows Consumer Products

Income Statement For Year 8 ($000)	Indonesia	The Philippines	Vietnam
Sales revenue..........................	$18,000	$9,500	$2,500
Cost of sales.........................	8,650	4,200	1,100
Allocated corporate overhead............	432	228	60
Local advertising	5,100	2,955	960
Other general and administration.........	868	437	350
Operating income	$ 2,950	$1,680	$ 30
Tax expense	885	504	9
Net Income..........................	$ 2,065	$1,176	$ 21

Exhibit 14.17   Country-Level Balance Sheets, Southeast Asia Emerging Markets Sector—Barrows Consumer Products

Balance Sheet as of January 1 ($000)	Indonesia		The Philippines		Vietnam	
	Year 8	Year 9	Year 8	Year 9	Year 8	Year 9
Assets						
Cash..........................	$ 750	$ 900	$ 500	$ 510	$ 320	$ 300
Accounts receivable..............	1,600	1,800	450	600	500	640
Inventory	1,350	1,300	500	900	320	490
Total current assets	$3,700	$4,000	$1,450	$2,010	$1,140	$1,430
Plant assets (net)	3,500	3,400	2,550	2,402	740	810
Total assets...................	$7,200	$7,400	$4,000	$4,412	$1,880	$2,240
Liabilities and equities						
Accounts payable	$ 575	$ 620	$ 250	$ 315	$ 190	$ 380
Other current liabilities	680	720	454	450	560	709
Total current liabilities	$1,255	$1,340	$ 704	$ 765	$ 750	$1,089
Long-term debt.................	–0–	–0–	–0–	–0–	–0–	–0–
Total liabilities.................	$1,255	$1,340	$ 704	$ 765	$ 750	$1,089
Common stock..................	$ 745	$ 745	$ 496	$ 496	$ 450	$ 450
Retained earnings	5,200	5,315	2,800	3,151	680	701
Total shareholders' equity	$5,945	$6,060	$3,296	$3,647	$1,130	$1,151
Total liabilities and equities	$7,200	$7,400	$4,000	$4,412	$1,880	$2,240

Indonesia is larger, it is also poorer and geographically dispersed, leading to higher distribution costs. The only thing I can say for sure is that Binh [Tran, VP—Vietnam] has not developed much of a market.

I also wonder whether headquarters is looking at the right performance measure. I recently attended a seminar on new performance evaluation measures, and the seminar speaker spent quite a bit of time on something called economic value added (EVA). The way I understand it, EVA adjusts profit and subtracts a capital charge from it. The capital charge is the cost of capital multiplied by the net assets (total assets less current liabilities) employed. I guess I would use the cost of capital of 20 percent after-tax that corporate policy requires I use for investment decisions. The problem I have is I am not sure how to adjust income, which is an accounting measure, into something more meaningful.

Year	Indonesia	The Philippines	Vietnam	Total
Year 7	$5,100	$2,502	$600	$8,202
Year 6	4,200	2,400	549	7,149
Year 5	4,500	2,700	570	7,770

Exhibit 14.18

Historical Advertising Expenses, Southeast Asia Emerging Markets Sector—Barrows Consumer Products

We don't do any R&D here, so the only item on the statements that was mentioned at the seminar is advertising. (*Note:* Advertising expenses for the previous three years are shown in Exhibit 14.18.) When I was working in the United States, I came across a study stating that advertising expenditures in our industry have an expected life of about three years. If that's true, then clearly the way we account for advertising is wrong and I should adjust these results accordingly.

There are other issues that I think are more ambiguous. For one thing, Binh developed a new approach for delivering products that cut distribution costs in Vietnam. At our annual retreat, he shared his ideas with Ade and Isadore about how they could adapt this to their markets. In addition, many customers want their stores in Vietnam and Indonesia to be entirely served from Indonesia, so Binh receives no credit for that business.

Required

a. What are some of the factors causing the problems in measuring performance in the Southeast Asia Sector?

b. Rank the three countries using each of the following measures of performance:
   1. Country profit.
   2. Return on investment.
   3. Economic value added (EVA).

c. Are there other performance measures you would suggest? How would you measure these?

d. Write a one-page memo to Ms. Karlson explaining which country performed best. Be sure to explain your reasoning.

(© Copyright William N. Lanen, 2023)

14-70. Capital Investment Analysis and Decentralized Performance Measurement   **(LO 14-2, 3, 4)**
The following exchange occurred just after the finance staff at Diversified Electronics rejected a capital investment proposal:

David Parker (Product Development): I just don't understand why you rejected my proposal. We can expect to make $230,000 on it before tax.

Shannon West (Finance): David, get real. This product proposal does not meet our short-term ROI target of 15 percent after tax.

David: I'm not so sure about the ROI target, but it is profitable—$230,000 worth.

Shannon: We believe that a company like Diversified Electronics should have a return on investment of 15 percent after tax. The Professional Services division consistently comes in with a 15 percent or better ROI, while your division, Residential Products, has managed to get only 10 percent. The performance of the Aerospace Products division has been especially dismal, with an ROI of only 6 percent. We expect divisions in the future to carry their share of the load.

Diversified Electronics, a growing company in the electronics industry, had grown to its present size of more than $140 million in sales. (See Exhibits 14.19 and 14.20 for Diversified's year 1 and year 2 income statements and balance sheets, respectively.) Diversified Electronics has three divisions, Residential Products, Aerospace Products, and Professional Services, each of which accounts for about one-third of Diversified Electronics's sales. Residential Products, the oldest division, produces furnace thermostats and similar products. The Aerospace Products division is a large job shop that builds electronic devices to customer specifications. A typical job or batch takes several months to complete. About one-half of Aerospace Products's sales are to the U.S. Defense Department. The newest of the three divisions, Professional Services, provides consulting engineering services. This division has grown tremendously since Diversified Electronics acquired it seven years ago.

Exhibit 14.19

Income Statements—
Diversified Electronics

DIVERSIFIED ELECTRONICS
Income Statements for Year 1 and Year 2
(all dollar amounts in thousands, except earnings-per-share figures)
Year Ended December 31

	Year 1	Year 2
Sales.	$141,462	$148,220
Cost of goods sold.	108,118	113,115
Gross margin.	$ 33,344	$ 35,105
Selling and general	13,014	13,692
Profit before taxes and interest	$ 20,330	$ 21,413
Interest expense.	1,190	1,952
Profit before taxes	$ 19,140	$ 19,461
Income tax expense	7,886	7,454
Net income	$ 11,254	$ 12,007
Earnings per share.	$ 5.63	$ 6.00

Exhibit 14.20

Balance Sheets—
Diversified Electronics

DIVERSIFIED ELECTRONICS
Balance Sheets for Year 1 and Year 2
(all dollar amounts in thousands)
Year Ended December 31

	Year 1	Year 2
Assets		
Cash and temporary investments	$ 1,404	$ 1,469
Accounts receivable.	13,688	15,607
Inventories	42,162	45,467
Total current assets.	$ 57,254	$ 62,543
Plant and equipment:		
Original cost.	$107,326	$115,736
Accumulated depreciation	42,691	45,979
Net.	$ 64,635	$ 69,757
Investments and other assets.	3,143	3,119
Total assets.	$125,032	$135,419
Liabilities and owners' equity		
Accounts payable.	$ 10,720	$ 12,286
Taxes payable	1,210	1,045
Current portion of long-term debt	–0–	1,634
Total current liabilities.	$ 11,930	$ 14,965
Deferred income taxes.	559	985
Long-term debt	12,622	15,448
Total liabilities	$ 25,111	$ 31,398
Common stock	$ 47,368	$ 47,368
Retained earnings.	52,553	56,653
Total owners' equity	$ 99,921	$104,021
Total liabilities and owners' equity	$125,032	$135,419

Each division operates independently of the others, and corporate management treats each as a separate entity. Division managers make many of the operating decisions. Corporate management coordinates the activities of the various divisions, including the review of all investment proposals over $400,000.

Diversified Electronics measures return on investment as the division's net income divided by total assets. Each division's expenses include the allocated portion of corporate administrative expenses. Because each of Diversified Electronics's divisions is located in a separate facility, management can easily attribute most assets, including receivables, to specific divisions. Management allocates the corporate office assets, including the centrally controlled cash account, to the divisions on the basis of divisional revenues.

Exhibit 14.21 shows the details of David Parker's rejected product proposal.

Required

a.   Was the decision to reject the new product proposal the right one? If top management used the discounted cash flow (DCF) method instead, what would the results be? The company uses a 15 percent after-tax cost of capital (i.e., discount rate) in evaluating projects such as these.

b.   Evaluate the manner in which Diversified Electronics has implemented the investment center concept. What pitfalls did it apparently not anticipate? What, if anything, should be done with regard to the investment center approach and the use of ROI as a measure of performance?

c.   What conflicting incentives for managers can occur when yearly ROI is used as a performance measure and DCF is used for capital budgeting?

(© Copyright Michael W. Maher, 2023)

Exhibit 14.21

Data—New Product Proposal

DIVERSIFIED ELECTRONICS
Financial Data for New Product Proposal

1. Projected asset investment:

Land purchase	$ 200,000
Plant and equipment[a]	800,000
	$1,000,000

2. Cost data, before taxes (first year):

Variable cost per unit	$ 3.00
Differential fixed cost[b]	$ 170,000

3. Price/market estimate (first year):

Unit price	$ 7.00
Sales volume	100,000 units

4. Taxes: The company assumes a 40 percent tax rate for income and gains on land sale. Depreciation of plant and equipment according to tax law is as follows: year 1: 20 percent; year 2: 32 percent; year 3: 19 percent; year 4: 14.5 percent; and year 5: 14.5 percent. Taxes are paid for taxable income in year 1 at the end of year 1; taxes are paid for taxable income in year 2 at the end of year 2; and so on.

5. The new product is in a growth market with expected price increases of 10 percent per year. This 10 percent applies to revenues and costs except depreciation and land for years 2 through 8 (i.e., year 2 amounts will reflect a 10 percent increase over the year 1 amounts shown in the data above).

6. The project has an eight-year life. Land will be sold for $400,000 at the end of year 8.

7. Assume the gain on the sale of land is taxable at the 40 percent rate.

[a] Annual capacity of 120,000 units.
[b] Includes straight-line depreciation on new plant and equipment, depreciated for eight years with no net salvage value at the end of eight years.

SOLUTIONS TO SELF-STUDY QUESTIONS

1. *a.* Divisional income:

HOME FURNISHINGS, INC.
Divisional Income
For Year 2
($000)

	Kitchen	Bath	Total
Sales revenue	$10,000	$5,000	$15,000
Cost of sales	5,400	3,000	8,400
Gross margin	$ 4,600	$2,000	$ 6,600
Allocated corporate overhead	460	200	660
Local advertising	2,000	500	2,500
Other general and administrative	500	260	760
Operating income	$ 1,640	$1,040	$ 2,680
Taxes (@ 35%)	574	364	938
After-tax income	$ 1,066	$ 676	$ 1,742

Kitchen has higher accounting income, but the two divisions are of different sizes. The gross margin ratio for Kitchen was 46 percent (= $4,600 ÷ $10,000) and for Bath was 40 percent (= $2,000 ÷ $5,000). These results suggest that the performance of the manager of Kitchen Products was better than that of the manager of Bath Products. The operating margin ratio of Kitchen Products was 16.4 percent (= $1,640 ÷ $10,000), and the operating margin of Bath Products was 20.8 percent (= $1,040 ÷ $5,000). The profit margin ratio for Kitchen Products was 10.7 percent (= $1,066 ÷ $10,000) and for Bath Products was 13.5 percent (= $676 ÷ $5,000). Based on the operating margin ratio and the profit margin, the performance of the Bath Products manager was better.

   b. From these results, we can see that the Kitchen Products manager appears to have earned higher margins on what was sold (higher gross margin ratio) while the Bath Products manager appears to have operated the division more efficiently (higher operating margin ratio). These comparisons are difficult because the managers operate in different markets.

2. *a.* Return on investment (ROI) is after-tax income (computed in the solution to Self-Study Question 1) divided by divisional assets (given in Question 2).

	Kitchen	Bath
	($000)	
After-tax income	$1,066	$ 676
Divisional investment	8,200	4,000
ROI	$\dfrac{\$1,066}{\$8,200} = 13\%$	$\dfrac{\$676}{\$4,000} = 17\%$

   b. Based on the cost of the assets employed in the two divisions, the manager of Bath Products reported better performance, based on ROI.

3. In the case of the exhaust equipment, the analysis of residual income is the same as that of EVA. There are no issues of amortizing the investment because the investment in exhaust equipment is already being depreciated. Therefore, neither manager has an incentive, at least based on the results in the first year of the investment, to invest in the exhaust equipment. (See Exhibit 14.8.)

4.   (The following computations are in thousands.)

Net Book Value[a]

Year	a. Historical Cost	b. Current Cost

Year 1

a. Historical Cost:
$$\text{ROI} = \frac{\$1,000 - (.1 \times \$4,000)}{\$4,000 - (.1 \times \$4,000)}$$
$$= \frac{\$600}{\$3,600} = \underline{16.7\%}$$

b. Current Cost:
$$\text{ROI} = \frac{\$1,000 - (.1 \times \$5,000)}{\$5,000 - (.1 \times \$5,000)}$$
$$= \frac{\$500}{\$4,500} = \underline{11.1\%}$$

Year 2

a. Historical Cost:
$$\text{ROI} = \frac{\$1,200 - (.1 \times \$4,000)}{\$4,000 - (.2 \times \$4,000)}$$
$$= \frac{\$800}{\$3,200} = \underline{25\%}$$

b. Current Cost:
$$\text{ROI} = \frac{\$1,200 - (.1 \times \$6,250)}{\$6,250 - (.2 \times \$6,250)}$$
$$= \frac{\$575}{\$5,000} = \underline{11.5\%}$$

Year 3

a. Historical Cost:
$$\text{ROI} = \frac{\$1,420 - (.1 \times \$4,000)}{\$4,000 - (.3 \times \$4,000)}$$
$$= \frac{\$1,020}{\$2,800} = \underline{36.4\%}$$

b. Current Cost:
$$\text{ROI} = \frac{\$1,420 - (.1 \times \$7,800)}{\$7,800 - (.3 \times \$7,800)}$$
$$= \frac{\$640}{\$5,460} = \underline{11.7\%}$$

Gross Book Value[b]

Year	c. Historical Cost	d. Current Cost

Year 1

c. Historical Cost:
$$\text{ROI} = \frac{\$600}{\$4,000} = \underline{15\%}$$

d. Current Cost:
$$\text{ROI} = \frac{\$500}{\$5,000} = \underline{10\%}$$

Year 2

c. Historical Cost:
$$\text{ROI} = \frac{\$800}{\$4,000} = \underline{20\%}$$

d. Current Cost:
$$\text{ROI} = \frac{\$575}{\$6,250} = \underline{9.2\%}$$

Year 3

c. Historical Cost:
$$\text{ROI} = \frac{\$1,020}{\$4,000} = \underline{25.5\%}$$

d. Current Cost:
$$\text{ROI} = \frac{\$640}{\$7,800} = \underline{8.2\%}$$

[a] The first term in the numerator is the annual cash flow. The second term is the annual depreciation. The first term in the denominator is the gross book value of the assets before accumulated depreciation. The second term is the accumulated depreciation. The denominator is the original (or the replacement) cost of the asset less accumulated depreciation. Accumulated depreciation is 10 percent of the gross book value after one year, 20 percent after two years, and 30 percent after three years.
[b] The numerator is the adjusted (historical or current cost) annual net income. The denominator is the gross book value of the assets.

15

Chapter Fifteen

Transfer Pricing

LEARNING OBJECTIVES

After reading this chapter, you should be able to:

LO 15-1 Explain the basic issues associated with transfer pricing.

LO 15-2 Explain the general transfer pricing rules and understand the underlying basis for them.

LO 15-3 Identify the behavioral issues and incentive effects of negotiated transfer prices, cost-based transfer prices, and market-based transfer prices.

LO 15-4 Explain the economic consequences of multinational transfer prices.

LO 15-5 Describe the role of transfer prices in segment reporting.

Visionsi/Shutterstock

"This new organizational structure has resulted in smoother operations, and we have been more responsive to customer demands. Unfortunately, we are still trying to smooth out a few rough spots. Both Milk Division and Cheese Division managers are being evaluated on division profit. Determining how we price milk for sale to the cheese factories, which are part of Cheese Division, has generated more disagreements than we expected. Still, I think we can come up with a policy that both managers will accept."

Sumi Matsumoto, the controller of Canyon Dairies, was meeting with the consulting team that had recommended a new, more decentralized organizational structure for the company. Canyon Dairies is a national, fully integrated dairy products company with, among other things, dairy farms producing milk and cheese factories producing a variety of cheeses.

The consulting firm recommended an organizational structure based on products, and the company formed two new divisions, Milk and Cheese. Each division is evaluated based on division profit. Milk products are a fundamental input to cheese production, and the new organization has resulted in sales from one division to another. Because both divisions are evaluated as profit centers, the controller has to determine a transfer pricing policy that will determine the price at which these interdivisional sales are recorded.

What Is Transfer Pricing and Why Is It Important?

We said in Chapter 12 that decentralization in the firm—the delegation of decision-making authority to subordinates—is often beneficial. It lowers the information costs associated with attempting to make decisions centrally, and the organization benefits by using managers' local knowledge. For example, regional managers are generally better informed about local market conditions than are headquarters managers. Along with the benefits of decentralization, however, come the costs of dysfunctional decision making that occur when local managers, making decisions based on local interests, make choices that are suboptimal for the organization as a whole.

A common example of decentralized decision making occurs when business units (divisions) within the organization buy and sell goods and services from one another and when each is treated as a profit center (i.e., when each unit manager is evaluated on reported unit profit). When such an exchange occurs, the accounting systems in the two divisions record the transaction as if it were an ordinary sale (purchase) to (from) an external customer (supplier). The price at which the transaction is recorded is the transfer price. The profit on the sale that accrues to the selling division is simply the transfer price less the cost of the goods sold. The profit that will accrue to the buying division when the item is sold to an external customer is the revenue from the external sale less the transfer price less any additional cost incurred by the buying division to complete the product.

The **transfer price** is the value or amount recorded in a firm's accounting records when one business unit sells (transfers) a good or service to another business unit. The accounting records in the two units (responsibility centers) treat this transaction in exactly the same way as a sale to an outside customer. Because the exchange takes place within the organization, however, the firm has considerable discretion in setting this transfer price. Just as with prices determined on an open market, transfer prices are widely used for decision making, product costing, and performance evaluation. Therefore, it is important to consider alternative transfer-pricing methods and their advantages and disadvantages.

LO 15-1
Explain the basic issues associated with transfer pricing.

transfer price
Value assigned to the goods or services sold or rented (transferred) from one unit of an organization to another.

From the corporation's viewpoint, of course, the total profit associated with the item is simply the price paid by the external buyer less the costs incurred by the selling division and less the additional cost incurred by the buying division before the item is sold. The transfer price is not a factor in this calculation and, therefore, does not affect corporate profit *if the transaction occurs.*

What makes the transfer price important is that it affects the division managers' decisions about whether to engage in the transaction. Because the managers of both the selling division and the buying division are evaluated on division rather than company profit, they consider the effect of all internal and external sales on their *division,* not company, profit. This aspect of decentralized decision making means that the definition of the transfer price can affect corporate profitability. If one of the managers decides not to participate in the transaction, even though the transaction is profitable for the corporation, the corporation forgoes any profit from the opportunity. The **optimal transfer price,** then, is the price that leads both division managers, each acting in their own self-interest, to make decisions that are in the firm's best interest. In other words, if a transaction would increase firm profits, it must be profitable for both divisions to make the transaction at the given transfer price. Otherwise, the given transfer price cannot be the optimal price. If a transaction is not profitable for the corporation, the transfer price, to be optimal, must make the sale unprofitable for at least one of the two transacting divisions.

Responsibility centers in decentralized firms frequently exchange products and services. Like Canyon Dairies, units of vertically integrated companies in a variety of industries, such as food, paper, and oil and gas, sell basic products such as grain or milk, wood, or crude oil to other units of their own companies as well as to other companies in the industry. As another example, banks, such as Wells Fargo, have deposit units that "sell" funds to loan units. In all these cases, the transfer price becomes a cost to the buying unit and revenue to the selling unit.

If business unit profitability is used to evaluate performance, perhaps by return on investment (ROI) or economic value added (EVA), the transfer price will affect the evaluation of the unit and the unit manager. For example, the higher the transfer price is, the lower the profit (and ROI or EVA) in the buying unit will be and the higher the profit in the selling unit will be, all other things being equal.

This chapter focuses on transfer pricing as a method to ensure that managers of profit centers that exchange goods make decisions in the company's interest. However, we have seen uses of transfer prices earlier in the text, although we did not use this term. For example, in Chapter 12, we discussed the allocation of corporate costs to profit centers. These allocations, specifically an individual allocation rate, can be thought of as a type of transfer price. They represent prices charged to divisions for the use of corporate services. The "service," whether finance, human resources, or IT, is measured in the units of the allocation base, transactions, employees, or technician support hours. The same principles for optimal corporate cost allocation methods you learned in Chapter 12 will be applied in this chapter. The Business Application "Pricing Intellectual Property in Multinational Tech Companies" describes how Facebook allegedly transferred intellectual property (IP), software, trademarks, and other intangible items to an Irish subsidiary to reduce its tax liability. In this example, the goods and services being transferred are not tangible items and are not direct services (such as corporate support). They are, however, property of value, and the determination of the "value" for appropriate transfer pricing is a contentious issue.

optimal transfer price
The transfer price that leads both division managers to make decisions that are in the firm's best interests.

Allocating the cost of a corporate function, which we discussed in Chapter 12, is conceptually the same as charging divisions a transfer price for corporate services. For computer services, a company could use the market prices for similar services or use the costs incurred by the computer department.
Fuse/Corbis/Getty Images

Pricing Intellectual Property in Multinational Tech Companies *Business Application*

High-tech companies such as Google and Apple have assets that include land, buildings, and other tangible items. They also, however, hold assets of substantial value in the form of intangible assets, such as software they have developed, patents for their inventions, trademarks, and so on. These assets generate value not only for the corporate entity, but also subsidiary units operating in other countries. As we will see in this chapter, setting the right "price" at which to transfer an asset that consists of intellectual property (IP) is difficult to determine because these are unique assets, so prices cannot be observed. Further, these assets were generated internally, so even the cost to develop the asset is frequently unknown or unreliable. Such a determination has to be made, however, to obtain an appropriate measure of income earned by the subsidiary.

When this is done to determine taxable income, the amount of the compensation assigned to a particular jurisdiction, the United States, for example, affects reported income and the related income tax liability. This is one example where the transfer price chosen affects total firm profitability. Of course, the Internal Revenue Service (IRS) evaluates the allocation method (the transfer price). Frequently, disagreements between firms and the IRS end up being resolved in the courts. In a recent case, the IRS accused the social media company Facebook of understating the value of IP that it transferred to its Irish business unit. The transfer price of the IP was meant to reflect costs to develop as well as future earnings from the IP; in other words, what the IP would have been worth in an arm's-length sale. Both the cost to develop and the future earnings are difficult to determine. The potential cost to the company, should the IRS prevail, is estimated to exceed $9 billion.

> The trial at San Francisco's tax court centres on how the Silicon Valley company valued intellectual property such as software and trademarks transferred to an Irish subsidiary. . . .

The issue concerned how companies divided their costs with business units located in foreign countries, which often have lower tax rates than the U.S.

> Ireland's headline corporate tax rate is 12.5 percent compared with the 35 percent federal tax rate in the US at the time.

Facebook has denied the allegations, claiming, in part, the Irish subsidiary created some technology on its own.

Source: Murphy, Hannah, "Facebook Accused of Downplaying IP Value in $9bn US Tax Case," *Financial Times*, February 18, 2020.

Determining the Optimal Transfer Price

Keeping separate accounting records and using transfer prices to record exchanges among divisions allows firms to delegate decisions to local managers (and benefit from better decisions) while holding these same managers responsible for divisional performance.[1] The transfer price is a device to motivate managers to act in the best interests of the company.

LO 15-2
Explain the general transfer pricing rules and understand the underlying basis for them.

The Setting

We use the example of Canyon Dairies described at the beginning of the chapter to illustrate the analysis used to determine the optimal transfer price. Canyon Dairies consists of two divisions, Milk and Cheese. Milk Division "makes" milk (manages dairy farms), which can be sold as milk or used as an input in "manufacturing" (making) cheese. In addition to customers not affiliated with Canyon Dairies, it "sells" the milk to Cheese Division, which uses it to make cheese. Cheese Division then sells its products (cheese) to customers that are external to Canyon Dairies. Both Milk and Cheese Divisions are profit centers under the company's new organization, and the division managers are evaluated and compensated based on divisional profits. See Exhibit 15.1 for some basic data

---

[1] The transfer pricing issue usually occurs at the division level, so we frequently refer to divisions (and division managers) instead of the more generic "responsibility centers" or "business units."

Exhibit 15.1

Cost and Production Data—Canyon Dairies

A		B	C	
1		Milk	Cheese	
2	Average units produced	100,000		
3	Average units sold		100,000	
4	Variable manufacturing cost per unit	$ 20		
5	Variable finishing cost per unit		$ 30	
6	Fixed divisional costs (unavoidable)	$ 2,000,000	$ 4,000,000	
7				

Exhibit 15.2

Resource Flows—Canyon Dairies

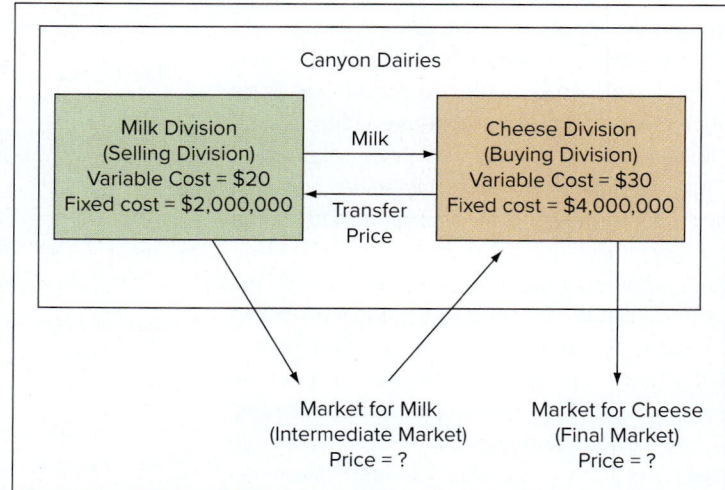

for Canyon Dairies and Exhibit 15.2 for an illustration of the resource flow and certain cost data for the company. Notice in Exhibit 15.2 that Milk Division might sell its products in the milk market, which we refer to as the *intermediate market*. Cheese Division might purchase milk from the intermediate market, but it sells cheese in the final market.

Determining Whether a Transfer Price Is Optimal

Before we describe the analysis to follow in computing the optimal transfer price, we provide a simple test to determine whether the calculated transfer price is optimal. This test is an application of the differential profitability analysis developed in Chapter 4 and is applied three times: once for the firm and once for each of the two divisions.

1. Given the market prices and the costs in the *firm,* does the transfer increase *firm* profit?
2. Given the transfer price, the intermediate market prices, and the *divisional* costs, does the transfer increase the *selling division* profit?
3. Given the transfer price, the final market prices, and the *divisional* costs, does the transfer increase *buying division* profit?

If the answer to the first question is yes, the answers to questions 2 and 3 must also be yes or the transfer price is not optimal. It is not optimal because the transfer increases the firm's profits, but one (or both) of the division managers will not make the transfer because it lowers the division's profits.[2] If the answer to the first question is no, the answer to either question 2 or 3 (or both) must be no or the transfer price is not optimal.

---

[2] Throughout the chapter, we assume that if the transfer has no effect on divisional profit, the divisional manager will be indifferent between making the transfer or not. In this case, we assume that the manager will do whatever is in the best interest of the company because it does not affect divisional performance.

In determining the optimal transfer price, the important issue is the nature of the intermediate market, the market for the good being transferred. Our analysis considers two cases: (1) a perfect intermediate market and (2) no intermediate market. (If there is an intermediate market, but company policy forbids divisions from buying or selling from the outside, the analysis is the same as case 2, no intermediate market.) These are clearly extreme cases, but they are useful in illustrating the nature of the analysis to determine the optimal transfer price. We discuss other cases after we develop a general rule for the optimal transfer price.

Case 1: A Perfect Intermediate Market for Milk

Consider first the case in which there is a "perfect" intermediate market for milk used in cheese making. Economists call a market perfect if buyers can buy and sellers can sell any quantity without affecting the price. This means, of course, that the product being sold is not differentiated by quality, service, or other characteristics. In the case of Canyon Dairies, it means that the milk that Milk Division produces is indistinguishable from all other milk in the market. In this case, the divisions of Canyon Dairies are *price takers.*

The optimal transfer price in this case is clear: It is the intermediate market price, which is the only viable price. At any price lower than the intermediate market price, Milk Division will supply no output to Cheese Division, and at any higher price, Cheese will not purchase any milk from Milk Division. In this case, of course, Canyon Dairies is indifferent to the arrangements because any product not transferred can be replaced at the market price.

Although the optimal transfer price is easy to determine in this case, it is a useful case for illustrating a more general approach to determining the right price. Notice that in Exhibit 15.2 we specified neither the intermediate market price nor the final market price. With an efficient transfer-pricing system, Canyon Dairies does not have to change the transfer-price policy for milk as the external market prices change (although the actual transfer price itself will change). This is an important factor because the point of decentralization is to delegate decision-making authority to subordinates. If the corporate staff had to determine the transfer price with every change in the external market, it might as well make the decision on the quantity to transfer.

To test whether the market price is the best transfer price, consider various prices in the intermediate (milk) and final (cheese) markets. If the market price is the best transfer price, then, regardless of these external market prices, the two division managers, acting independently, will make the transfer that the corporate staff would set if it had all the information that the division managers have. For example, suppose the final market price for cheese is $120 and the intermediate market price for milk is $50, summarized as follows:

	A	B
1	Variable manufacturing cost (Milk Division) per unit	$ 20
2	Variable finishing cost (Cheese Division) per unit	30
3	Other data	
4	Final market (cheese) price	120
5	Intermediate market (milk) price	50
6		

Banks evaluate the profitability of their products using a transfer price for deposits that is used for funding loans. Financial markets are close to "perfect"; the market rate is generally the optimal transfer price. Tom Grill/Photographer's Choice RF/Getty Image

Using the intermediate market price as the transfer price, the transfer price is set at $50. At these market prices, does Canyon Dairies (as a firm) want to sell cheese? The company receives $120 for every unit sold. The total variable cost is $50 (= $20 Milk cost + $30 Cheese cost). The firm wants to make the sale. Milk Division is indifferent between selling milk internally or on the intermediate market. Cheese Division is indifferent between buying milk from Milk Division or the intermediate market. Therefore, the sale will be made and the source of milk to Cheese Division does not affect firm profits.

The case of perfect intermediate markets is not particularly interesting because there is really little opportunity for managerial discretion. Suppose, however, that there are two grades of milk, grade A (better) and grade B. Suppose that either grade can be used to make cheese and that there are perfect markets for the different grades. The intermediate market price for grade A milk is $60 and the intermediate market price for grade B milk is $50 per unit, as summarized in the following table. Milk Division supplies grade A. What is the optimal transfer price?

	A	B
1	Variable manufacturing cost (Milk Division) per unit	$ 20
2	Variable finishing cost (Cheese Division) per unit	30
3	Other data	
4	Final market (cheese) price	120
5	Intermediate market (grade A milk) price	60
6	Intermediate market (grade B milk) price	50
7		

We know from the discussion of case 1 that the optimal transfer price is the intermediate market price, but which market do we use? If we allow the division managers to choose where to buy and sell, we know that Milk Division will sell its output on the intermediate (grade A) market for $60 and Cheese Division will buy milk on the intermediate (grade B) market for $50. These are also the optimal decisions from the firm's perspective.

The optimal transfer price in this case, even though no transfers will take place, is the intermediate market price for grade A milk. This is the value of the milk that Milk Division produces. By using the intermediate market price for grade A milk as the transfer price, the firm ensures that the managers understand the opportunity cost of using the milk from Milk Division in cheese making. The manager loses the opportunity to sell it in the intermediate market, where the current price is $60. Thus, the Cheese Division manager will face the same decision the firm would if it were making the decision: Use grade A milk at a cost of $60 or grade B milk at a cost of $50. The optimal transfer price is sending the correct "signal" to the subordinate managers.

Case 2: No Intermediate Market

Suppose that no intermediate market for milk exists or that, for whatever reason, the company has decided that it will not allow the divisions to buy or sell milk on the outside market. In this case, the only outlet for Milk Division is Cheese Division, and the only source of supply for Cheese Division is Milk Division. Some potential transfer prices can be disregarded immediately as being suboptimal. At any transfer price below $20—the variable cost in Milk Division—no transfers will take place because Milk will lose money on each unit sold. Any transfer price above the final (cheese) market price less the $30 variable processing cost of Cheese Division will also not be optimal because Cheese will not buy any milk. Where, between these two extremes, is the optimal transfer price?

To understand the analysis, pick any price higher than the variable cost in Milk Division and ask whether it can be the optimal transfer price. If it is, it must lead both division managers to make the correct decision. Because no intermediate market for milk exists, we need to consider only the final (cheese) market price. Suppose this price is $120 as it was earlier. If the transfer price is $50, will both managers choose to transfer the product? We know from the analysis of case 1 that this is the decision the firm prefers. For Cheese Division's manager, the transfer will lead to an additional $40 in contribution margin (and divisional profit). This is the $120 in revenue from the sale to the cheese market less the $50 transfer price paid to Milk Division less the additional $30 variable processing cost.

What about Milk Division? For each unit transferred, its manager receives another $30 in contribution margin (divisional profit). This is the $50 received as revenue from the Cheese Division less the $20 variable production cost. Therefore, both managers have an incentive to transfer the product. A transfer price of $50 will work *as long as* the external price is $120.

To be optimal in general, however, the transfer price cannot depend on the current external price. Suppose the external market price for cheese drops to $70. In this case, the firm will still benefit from the transfer because total contribution margin will be $20 (remember that the fixed costs are unavoidable). This is the $70 revenue less the $20 variable cost in Milk Division and the $30 variable cost in Cheese Division. Milk Division will be willing to transfer the product because its contribution margin will increase by $30 (the $50 transfer price less the $20 variable production cost). However, Cheese Division will not be willing to buy any milk because it will lose $10 on every unit (the $70 revenue less the $50 transfer price less the $30 variable processing cost). From this analysis, we know that $50 cannot be the optimal transfer price because the actions of the two division managers do not lead to the outcome desired by the firm.

Following this reasoning, it is easy to see that the only price that will work, for all possible external market prices, is $20, the variable cost in Milk Division. Any transfer price higher than the variable cost in Milk Division will potentially cause Cheese Division not to buy the milk when it is in the best interests of the firm to do so.

We can illustrate this reasoning numerically to support our analysis that leads to the conclusion that $20 per unit is the optimal transfer price. Recall that there are three questions we ask of any potential transfer price:

1. Does Canyon Dairies want this transfer to be made given the outside price? (Remember that the company is indifferent about the transfer price given that the transfer is made or not made.)
2. Does Milk Division want this transfer (sale) to be made given the outside price and the transfer price?
3. Does Cheese Division want this transfer (purchase) to be made given the outside price and the transfer price?

We continue with the assumptions made above. Specifically,

- Canyon Dairies will sell 100,000 units if it wants to sell any quantity and that there is no intermediate market for the output of Milk Division.
- The variable costs remain $20 per unit in Milk Division and $30 in Cheese Division.
- Division managers alone make the decision to transfer (or not transfer) units from Milk Division to Cheese Division.

For any given final market price, *FP,* and any transfer price, *TP,* we can summarize firm and division contribution margins, *assuming the transfer occurs,* as

$$\text{Contribution margin (Canyon Dairies)} = 100{,}000 \text{ units} \times (FP - \$20 - \$30). \text{ (1)}$$
$$\text{Contribution margin (Milk Division)} = 100{,}000 \text{ units} \times (TP - \$20). \text{ (2)}$$
$$\text{Contribution margin (Cheese Division)} = 100{,}000 \text{ units} \times (FP - TP - \$30). \text{ (3)}$$

If the result in equation (1) is negative, the company does not want the transfer and sale to the final market to occur. Similarly, if the results in equations (2) or (3) are negative, the division manager in at least one of the divisions will not want the transfer to occur. A conflict occurs when the company (Canyon Dairies) wants to make the sale in the final market, but one or both of the division managers do not.[3]

---

[3] Technically, a conflict also occurs if Canyon Dairies does not want to make the sale, but both of the division managers do. However, this cannot happen in this example because the company contribution margin is the sum of the contribution margins in the two divisions. If the company contribution margin is negative, the contribution margin in at least one of the divisions must be as well. Therefore, we do not consider this case.

We can summarize the overall company contribution margin by rewriting equation (1) as

$$\text{Contribution margin (Canyon Dairies)} = Transfer \times \max\{0,\ 100{,}000 \text{ units} \times (FP - \$20 - \$30)\} \quad (1a)$$

where the variable *Transfer* takes on the value 1 if both divisions want to make the transfer and −1 if at least one division does not.

Exhibit 15.3 provides a visual depiction of this analysis for selected final market and transfer prices. Along the top row (Row 2) of the spreadsheet are possible transfer price alternatives. The left-hand column contains alternative prices in the final market. An individual cell contains the result of equation (1a), the contribution margin (in thousands of dollars) Canyon Dairies receives (or forgoes).

Panel A of Exhibit 15.3 highlights the spreadsheet for the analysis made above. The highlighted cells indicated by the arrow represent the results when the transfer price is $50 per unit and the final market price is either $120 per unit or $70 per unit. When the final market price is $120 per unit, both divisions are willing to make the transfer and the contribution margin for Canyon Dairies is $7 million. If the final market price is $70 per unit (and the transfer price is $50 per unit), one of the divisions (Cheese Division in this case) is not willing to make the transfer. The lost contribution margin for Canyon Dairies is $2 million.

There are many ways to develop the individual cells in Excel. One is as follows. This is shown in two parts for clarity. First, calculate the value of the variable *Transfer* with the

Exhibit 15.3

Analysis of Alternative Transfer Prices When There Is No Intermediate Market for Milk—Canyon Dairies

Panel A: Canyon Dairies' Contribution Margin for Selected Transfer Prices ($000)

	A	J	K	L	M	N
1				**Transfer Price**		
2		$40	$45	$50	$55	$60
3	**Final Market Price**					
8	$48	$0	$0	$0	$0	$0
9	$50	$0	$0	$0	$0	$0
16	$64	($1,400)	($1,400)	($1,400)	($1,400)	($1,400)
17	$66	($1,600)	($1,600)	($1,600)	($1,600)	($1,600)
18	$68	($1,800)	($1,800)	($1,800)	($1,800)	($1,800)
19	$70	$2,000	($2,000)	($2,000)	($2,000)	($2,000)
20	$72	$2,200	($2,200)	($2,200)	($2,200)	($2,200)
21	$74	$2,400	($2,400)	($2,400)	($2,400)	($2,400)
22	$76	$2,600	$2,600	($2,600)	($2,600)	($2,600)
36	$104	$5,400	$5,400	$5,400	$5,400	$5,400
37	$106	$5,600	$5,600	$5,600	$5,600	$5,600
38	$108	$5,800	$5,800	$5,800	$5,800	$5,800
39	$110	$6,000	$6,000	$6,000	$6,000	$6,000
40	$112	$6,200	$6,200	$6,200	$6,200	$6,200
41	$114	$6,400	$6,400	$6,400	$6,400	$6,400
42	$116	$6,600	$6,600	$6,600	$6,600	$6,600
43	$118	$6,800	$6,800	$6,800	$6,800	$6,800
44	$120	$7,000	$7,000	$7,000	$7,000	$7,000
45	$122	$7,200	$7,200	$7,200	$7,200	$7,200
46	$124	$7,400	$7,400	$7,400	$7,400	$7,400
47	$126	$7,600	$7,600	$7,600	$7,600	$7,600
56	$144	$9,400	$9,400	$9,400	$9,400	$9,400
57	$146	$9,600	$9,600	$9,600	$9,600	$9,600
58	$148	$9,800	$9,800	$9,800	$9,800	$9,800
59						

Exhibit 15.3 *(Continued)*

Panel B: Heat Map Showing Contribution Margin Earned (Forgone) at Different Transfer Prices ($000)

	Transfer Price																				
Final Market Price	$10	$15	$20	$25	$30	$35	$40	$45	$50	$55	$60	$65	$70	$75	$80	$85	$90	$95	$100	$105	$110
$48	$0	$0	$0	$0	$0	$0	$0	$0	$0	$0	$0	$0	$0	$0	$0	$0	$0	$0	$0	$0	$0
$50	$0	$0	$0	$0	$0	$0	$0	$0	$0	$0	$0	$0	$0	$0	$0	$0	$0	$0	$0	$0	$0
$52	($200)	($200)	$200	($200)	($200)	($200)	($200)	($200)	($200)	($200)	($200)	($200)	($200)	($200)	($200)	($200)	($200)	($200)	($200)	($200)	($200)
$54	($400)	($400)	$400	($400)	($400)	($400)	($400)	($400)	($400)	($400)	($400)	($400)	($400)	($400)	($400)	($400)	($400)	($400)	($400)	($400)	($400)
$56	($600)	($600)	$600	$600	($600)	($600)	($600)	($600)	($600)	($600)	($600)	($600)	($600)	($600)	($600)	($600)	($600)	($600)	($600)	($600)	($600)
$58	($800)	($800)	$800	$800	($800)	($800)	($800)	($800)	($800)	($800)	($800)	($800)	($800)	($800)	($800)	($800)	($800)	($800)	($800)	($800)	($800)
$60	($1,000)	($1,000)	$1,000	$1,000	$1,000	($1,000)	($1,000)	($1,000)	($1,000)	($1,000)	($1,000)	($1,000)	($1,000)	($1,000)	($1,000)	($1,000)	($1,000)	($1,000)	($1,000)	($1,000)	($1,000)
$62	($1,200)	($1,200)	$1,200	$1,200	$1,200	($1,200)	($1,200)	($1,200)	($1,200)	($1,200)	($1,200)	($1,200)	($1,200)	($1,200)	($1,200)	($1,200)	($1,200)	($1,200)	($1,200)	($1,200)	($1,200)
$64	($1,400)	($1,400)	$1,400	$1,400	$1,400	($1,400)	($1,400)	($1,400)	($1,400)	($1,400)	($1,400)	($1,400)	($1,400)	($1,400)	($1,400)	($1,400)	($1,400)	($1,400)	($1,400)	($1,400)	($1,400)
$66	($1,600)	($1,600)	$1,600	$1,600	$1,600	$1,600	($1,600)	($1,600)	($1,600)	($1,600)	($1,600)	($1,600)	($1,600)	($1,600)	($1,600)	($1,600)	($1,600)	($1,600)	($1,600)	($1,600)	($1,600)
$68	($1,800)	($1,800)	$1,800	$1,800	$1,800	$1,800	($1,800)	($1,800)	($1,800)	($1,800)	($1,800)	($1,800)	($1,800)	($1,800)	($1,800)	($1,800)	($1,800)	($1,800)	($1,800)	($1,800)	($1,800)
$70	($2,000)	($2,000)	$2,000	$2,000	$2,000	$2,000	$2,000	($2,000)	($2,000)	($2,000)	($2,000)	($2,000)	($2,000)	($2,000)	($2,000)	($2,000)	($2,000)	($2,000)	($2,000)	($2,000)	($2,000)
$72	($2,200)	($2,200)	$2,200	$2,200	$2,200	$2,200	$2,200	($2,200)	($2,200)	($2,200)	($2,200)	($2,200)	($2,200)	($2,200)	($2,200)	($2,200)	($2,200)	($2,200)	($2,200)	($2,200)	($2,200)
$74	($2,400)	($2,400)	$2,400	$2,400	$2,400	$2,400	$2,400	($2,400)	($2,400)	($2,400)	($2,400)	($2,400)	($2,400)	($2,400)	($2,400)	($2,400)	($2,400)	($2,400)	($2,400)	($2,400)	($2,400)
$76	($2,600)	($2,600)	$2,600	$2,600	$2,600	$2,600	$2,600	$2,600	($2,600)	($2,600)	($2,600)	($2,600)	($2,600)	($2,600)	($2,600)	($2,600)	($2,600)	($2,600)	($2,600)	($2,600)	($2,600)
$78	($2,800)	($2,800)	$2,800	$2,800	$2,800	$2,800	$2,800	$2,800	($2,800)	($2,800)	($2,800)	($2,800)	($2,800)	($2,800)	($2,800)	($2,800)	($2,800)	($2,800)	($2,800)	($2,800)	($2,800)
$80	($3,000)	($3,000)	$3,000	$3,000	$3,000	$3,000	$3,000	$3,000	$3,000	($3,000)	($3,000)	($3,000)	($3,000)	($3,000)	($3,000)	($3,000)	($3,000)	($3,000)	($3,000)	($3,000)	($3,000)
$82	($3,200)	($3,200)	$3,200	$3,200	$3,200	$3,200	$3,200	$3,200	$3,200	($3,200)	($3,200)	($3,200)	($3,200)	($3,200)	($3,200)	($3,200)	($3,200)	($3,200)	($3,200)	($3,200)	($3,200)
$84	($3,400)	($3,400)	$3,400	$3,400	$3,400	$3,400	$3,400	$3,400	$3,400	($3,400)	($3,400)	($3,400)	($3,400)	($3,400)	($3,400)	($3,400)	($3,400)	($3,400)	($3,400)	($3,400)	($3,400)
$86	($3,600)	($3,600)	$3,600	$3,600	$3,600	$3,600	$3,600	$3,600	$3,600	$3,600	($3,600)	($3,600)	($3,600)	($3,600)	($3,600)	($3,600)	($3,600)	($3,600)	($3,600)	($3,600)	($3,600)
$88	($3,800)	($3,800)	$3,800	$3,800	$3,800	$3,800	$3,800	$3,800	$3,800	$3,800	($3,800)	($3,800)	($3,800)	($3,800)	($3,800)	($3,800)	($3,800)	($3,800)	($3,800)	($3,800)	($3,800)
$90	($4,000)	($4,000)	$4,000	$4,000	$4,000	$4,000	$4,000	$4,000	$4,000	$4,000	$4,000	($4,000)	($4,000)	($4,000)	($4,000)	($4,000)	($4,000)	($4,000)	($4,000)	($4,000)	($4,000)
$92	($4,200)	($4,200)	$4,200	$4,200	$4,200	$4,200	$4,200	$4,200	$4,200	$4,200	$4,200	($4,200)	($4,200)	($4,200)	($4,200)	($4,200)	($4,200)	($4,200)	($4,200)	($4,200)	($4,200)
$94	($4,400)	($4,400)	$4,400	$4,400	$4,400	$4,400	$4,400	$4,400	$4,400	$4,400	$4,400	($4,400)	($4,400)	($4,400)	($4,400)	($4,400)	($4,400)	($4,400)	($4,400)	($4,400)	($4,400)
$96	($4,600)	($4,600)	$4,600	$4,600	$4,600	$4,600	$4,600	$4,600	$4,600	$4,600	$4,600	$4,600	($4,600)	($4,600)	($4,600)	($4,600)	($4,600)	($4,600)	($4,600)	($4,600)	($4,600)
$98	($4,800)	($4,800)	$4,800	$4,800	$4,800	$4,800	$4,800	$4,800	$4,800	$4,800	$4,800	$4,800	($4,800)	($4,800)	($4,800)	($4,800)	($4,800)	($4,800)	($4,800)	($4,800)	($4,800)
$100	($5,000)	($5,000)	$5,000	$5,000	$5,000	$5,000	$5,000	$5,000	$5,000	$5,000	$5,000	$5,000	$5,000	($5,000)	($5,000)	($5,000)	($5,000)	($5,000)	($5,000)	($5,000)	($5,000)
$102	($5,200)	($5,200)	$5,200	$5,200	$5,200	$5,200	$5,200	$5,200	$5,200	$5,200	$5,200	$5,200	$5,200	($5,200)	($5,200)	($5,200)	($5,200)	($5,200)	($5,200)	($5,200)	($5,200)
$104	($5,400)	($5,400)	$5,400	$5,400	$5,400	$5,400	$5,400	$5,400	$5,400	$5,400	$5,400	$5,400	$5,400	($5,400)	($5,400)	($5,400)	($5,400)	($5,400)	($5,400)	($5,400)	($5,400)
$106	($5,600)	($5,600)	$5,600	$5,600	$5,600	$5,600	$5,600	$5,600	$5,600	$5,600	$5,600	$5,600	$5,600	$5,600	($5,600)	($5,600)	($5,600)	($5,600)	($5,600)	($5,600)	($5,600)
$108	($5,800)	($5,800)	$5,800	$5,800	$5,800	$5,800	$5,800	$5,800	$5,800	$5,800	$5,800	$5,800	$5,800	$5,800	($5,800)	($5,800)	($5,800)	($5,800)	($5,800)	($5,800)	($5,800)
$110	($6,000)	($6,000)	$6,000	$6,000	$6,000	$6,000	$6,000	$6,000	$6,000	$6,000	$6,000	$6,000	$6,000	$6,000	$6,000	($6,000)	($6,000)	($6,000)	($6,000)	($6,000)	($6,000)
$112	($6,200)	($6,200)	$6,200	$6,200	$6,200	$6,200	$6,200	$6,200	$6,200	$6,200	$6,200	$6,200	$6,200	$6,200	$6,200	($6,200)	($6,200)	($6,200)	($6,200)	($6,200)	($6,200)
$114	($6,400)	($6,400)	$6,400	$6,400	$6,400	$6,400	$6,400	$6,400	$6,400	$6,400	$6,400	$6,400	$6,400	$6,400	$6,400	($6,400)	($6,400)	($6,400)	($6,400)	($6,400)	($6,400)
$116	($6,600)	($6,600)	$6,600	$6,600	$6,600	$6,600	$6,600	$6,600	$6,600	$6,600	$6,600	$6,600	$6,600	$6,600	$6,600	$6,600	($6,600)	($6,600)	($6,600)	($6,600)	($6,600)
$118	($6,800)	($6,800)	$6,800	$6,800	$6,800	$6,800	$6,800	$6,800	$6,800	$6,800	$6,800	$6,800	$6,800	$6,800	$6,800	$6,800	($6,800)	($6,800)	($6,800)	($6,800)	($6,800)
$120	($7,000)	($7,000)	$7,000	$7,000	$7,000	$7,000	$7,000	$7,000	**$7,000**	$7,000	$7,000	$7,000	$7,000	$7,000	$7,000	$7,000	$7,000	($7,000)	($7,000)	($7,000)	($7,000)
$122	($7,200)	($7,200)	$7,200	$7,200	$7,200	$7,200	$7,200	$7,200	$7,200	$7,200	$7,200	$7,200	$7,200	$7,200	$7,200	$7,200	$7,200	($7,200)	($7,200)	($7,200)	($7,200)
$124	($7,400)	($7,400)	$7,400	$7,400	$7,400	$7,400	$7,400	$7,400	$7,400	$7,400	$7,400	$7,400	$7,400	$7,400	$7,400	$7,400	$7,400	($7,400)	($7,400)	($7,400)	($7,400)
$126	($7,600)	($7,600)	$7,600	$7,600	$7,600	$7,600	$7,600	$7,600	$7,600	$7,600	$7,600	$7,600	$7,600	$7,600	$7,600	$7,600	$7,600	$7,600	($7,600)	($7,600)	($7,600)
$128	($7,800)	($7,800)	$7,800	$7,800	$7,800	$7,800	$7,800	$7,800	$7,800	$7,800	$7,800	$7,800	$7,800	$7,800	$7,800	$7,800	$7,800	$7,800	($7,800)	($7,800)	($7,800)
$130	($8,000)	($8,000)	$8,000	$8,000	$8,000	$8,000	$8,000	$8,000	$8,000	$8,000	$8,000	$8,000	$8,000	$8,000	$8,000	$8,000	$8,000	$8,000	$8,000	($8,000)	($8,000)
$132	($8,200)	($8,200)	$8,200	$8,200	$8,200	$8,200	$8,200	$8,200	$8,200	$8,200	$8,200	$8,200	$8,200	$8,200	$8,200	$8,200	$8,200	$8,200	$8,200	($8,200)	($8,200)
$134	($8,400)	($8,400)	$8,400	$8,400	$8,400	$8,400	$8,400	$8,400	$8,400	$8,400	$8,400	$8,400	$8,400	$8,400	$8,400	$8,400	$8,400	$8,400	$8,400	($8,400)	($8,400)
$136	($8,600)	($8,600)	$8,600	$8,600	$8,600	$8,600	$8,600	$8,600	$8,600	$8,600	$8,600	$8,600	$8,600	$8,600	$8,600	$8,600	$8,600	$8,600	$8,600	$8,600	($8,600)
$138	($8,800)	($8,800)	$8,800	$8,800	$8,800	$8,800	$8,800	$8,800	$8,800	$8,800	$8,800	$8,800	$8,800	$8,800	$8,800	$8,800	$8,800	$8,800	$8,800	$8,800	($8,800)
$140	($9,000)	($9,000)	$9,000	$9,000	$9,000	$9,000	$9,000	$9,000	$9,000	$9,000	$9,000	$9,000	$9,000	$9,000	$9,000	$9,000	$9,000	$9,000	$9,000	$9,000	$9,000
$142	($9,200)	($9,200)	$9,200	$9,200	$9,200	$9,200	$9,200	$9,200	$9,200	$9,200	$9,200	$9,200	$9,200	$9,200	$9,200	$9,200	$9,200	$9,200	$9,200	$9,200	$9,200
$144	($9,400)	($9,400)	$9,400	$9,400	$9,400	$9,400	$9,400	$9,400	$9,400	$9,400	$9,400	$9,400	$9,400	$9,400	$9,400	$9,400	$9,400	$9,400	$9,400	$9,400	$9,400
$146	($9,600)	($9,600)	$9,600	$9,600	$9,600	$9,600	$9,600	$9,600	$9,600	$9,600	$9,600	$9,600	$9,600	$9,600	$9,600	$9,600	$9,600	$9,600	$9,600	$9,600	$9,600
$148	($9,800)	($9,800)	$9,800	$9,800	$9,800	$9,800	$9,800	$9,800	$9,800	$9,800	$9,800	$9,800	$9,800	$9,800	$9,800	$9,800	$9,800	$9,800	$9,800	$9,800	$9,800

following entry into a cell, for example, cell L44 (corresponding to a final market price of $120 per unit and a transfer price of $50 per unit):

$$Transfer = \text{IF((100000*(L\$3-20))<0,-1, IF((100000*(\$A44-L\$3-30))<0,-1,1))}$$

The first IF statement checks to see if the Milk Division manager is willing to make the transfer of 100,000 units. (The values "20" and "30" are the given variable costs in the Milk and Cheese Divisions, respectively.) If the contribution margin is negative, the transfer will not be made and *Transfer* is assigned the value −1 (because the statement that the contribution margin is negative is true). If the contribution margin is positive, the next IF statement proceeds to the next logical test. This is a test of whether the contribution margin of Cheese Division will be at least zero if 100,000 units are transferred. If this contribution margin in negative, a value of −1 for *Transfer* is returned. If neither divisional contribution margin is negative, the value +1 for *Transfer* will be returned, meaning that the transfer will occur.

The second part of the cell entry is the contribution to the firm from making the sale in the final market. This can be entered as

$$= \text{MAX(0,100000*(\$A44-20-30))}$$

Notice that there is no transfer price in this formula because for the firm, the transfer price is irrelevant, given the transfer. Finally, the cell value is calculated by multiplying the two individual formulas and then multiplying by 0.001 (to express the value in thousands of dollars):

$$= \text{0.001*MAX(0,100000*(\$A44-20-30))*}Transfer$$

Cells that contain a negative contribution margin show combinations of transfer price and final market price where Canyon Dairies would want the transfer to occur, but at least one of the division managers did not. The value in the cells with the negative numbers indicates the contribution margin that Canyon Dairies forgoes because of a transfer not made.

Panel B of Exhibit 15.3 uses a heat map to identify combinations of final market price and transfer price that result in conflicting decisions between Canyon Dairies and one or both of the divisions. These combinations are highlighted in red. As we can see from the heat map, there is only one transfer price that never results in a conflict, regardless of the final market price. That transfer price is $20 per unit, confirming our analysis above.

What about the fixed cost in Milk Division? At a $20 transfer price, Milk Division will operate at a loss (equal to its fixed costs). Why will the manager be willing to transfer milk? The fixed costs are assumed to be unavoidable (this assumption will be relaxed later). As a result, Milk Division will incur these fixed costs regardless of whether the transfer is made. Therefore, the manager is indifferent about transferring product. (Perhaps a better question is why Milk Division is organized as a profit center. It seems that a cost center structure would be more appropriate. In that case, Cheese Division would order milk from Milk Division and Milk Division's manager would be evaluated on the costs incurred to fulfill the order.)

Optimal Transfer Price: A General Principle

The optimal transfer price has been determined in two relatively extreme cases, neither of which might occur. However, we can infer the optimal transfer price in general from these extreme cases. In both cases, the transfer price that is optimal (i.e., that leads to correct decisions) represents the value of the milk to Canyon Dairies at the transfer point. That is, by providing both managers the information about the value of milk at the point of transfer and using this value as the transfer price, the division managers will use the same information for their local decisions that the corporate staff would use in making a decision that is optimal for the company.

The value of the milk at the point of transfer consists of two parts:

1. The incremental cost to produce milk and bring it to the point of transfer (outlay cost).
2. The opportunity cost of choosing to transfer the milk to Cheese Division and not sell it on the outside (intermediate) market (opportunity cost).[4]

Thus, a general principle on setting the transfer price that leads managers to make decisions in the firm's best interests is

$$\frac{\text{Transfer}}{\text{price}} = \frac{\text{Outlay}}{\text{cost}} + \frac{\text{Opportunity cost of the resource}}{\text{at the point of transfer}}$$

In the case of a perfect intermediate market for milk, its value to Canyon Dairies is equal to what it can be sold for in the intermediate market. In other words, from the firm's perspective, if Milk Division forgoes the opportunity to sell the milk in the intermediate market, the firm forgoes the value represented by the (intermediate) market price less the outlay cost to produce the milk. Therefore, by using a transfer price equal to the (intermediate) market price, Milk Division faces the same decision, with the same prices and costs as the firm. Similarly, from Cheese Division's perspective, the transfer price represents the value of the milk to the firm. Unless Cheese Division can find a use for the milk that makes it worth paying that price to Milk Division, it will not order any milk from Milk Division.

At the other extreme, if there is no intermediate market, there is no opportunity cost of the milk (because there is no alternative use) and the only cost is the variable, or outlay, cost incurred to produce it, assuming that Milk Division is not operating at capacity. Again, setting the transfer price equal to the outlay cost (in this case, the variable cost in Milk Division) plus the opportunity cost (zero), the two division managers face the same prices and costs when making decisions about the production and the use of the intermediate product—the milk—as the firm does.

Other Market Conditions

Case in Which Milk Division Is at Capacity   If Milk Division is operating at capacity, the opportunity cost is more difficult to assess because this situation requires

---

[4] Recall from Chapter 2 that we define opportunity cost to exclude any outlay cost. In this case, the opportunity cost only includes the forgone contribution margin from the sale of milk in the intermediate market.

identifying the next best alternative use of the milk. If a market for milk exists, its market price should be used. This provides the correct information to Milk Division and the firm about the value of adding capacity. If there is no intermediate market, the opportunity cost of additional milk depends on the cost of adding capacity.

Imperfect Intermediate Markets   The transfer price has been derived in the two extreme cases of a perfect intermediate market and no intermediate market. If the intermediate market exists but is imperfect (i.e., if the intermediate market price is affected by the quantity of milk sold), the optimal transfer price is still the outlay cost plus the opportunity cost. However, in this case, the opportunity cost is less than the current intermediate market price less the outlay cost. If Milk Division sells milk in the intermediate market, the price will fall. Therefore, the opportunity cost to the firm of using milk from Milk Division in Cheese Division is less than the excess of current market price over outlay cost.

Applying the General Principle

The general principle stated previously can be easily applied with the following two general rules when establishing a transfer price:

1. If an intermediate market exists, the optimal transfer price is the market price.
2. If no intermediate market exists, the optimal transfer price is the outlay cost for producing the goods (generally, the variable costs).

These general rules should ensure that in their decisions, both managers use the value of the transferred product to the firm and incorporate this value in their individual decisions. In other words, this transfer price ensures that if the managers make the correct decision for their division, the result (transfer or no transfer) will also be the correct decision for the firm.

Self-Study Questions

1. Elmhurst Enterprises consists of two divisions: Flavorings and Foods. Flavorings Division manufactures a food flavoring that can be used in the packaged dinners that Foods Division produces and sells. Both divisions are considered profit centers, and the division managers are evaluated and compensated based on divisional profits. The following data are available concerning the flavoring and the two divisions:

	Flavorings Division	Food Division
Average units produced	200,000	
Average units sold		200,000
Variable manufacturing cost per unit..............	$1	
Variable processing cost per unit..............		$4
Fixed divisional costs (unavoidable).............	$50,000	$200,000

Flavorings Division can sell all of its output to other food manufacturers for $2 per unit. Foods Division can buy flavorings from other firms (of the same quality, etc.) for $2. Foods Division sells its dinners for $10 per unit.

a. What is the optimal transfer price in this case?

b. If both division managers are given the decision authority to decide where to buy and sell flavoring, are there likely to be many disputes about the transfer price?

2. Consider the same facts as in Self-Study Question 1, but assume there is no intermediate market for flavorings.

a. If the transfer price for flavoring is set at $2 per unit, what is the minimum price that Foods Division can charge for its product and still cover its differential costs?

b. What is the optimal transfer price?

c. What profit will the two divisions report at the optimal transfer price from part (b)?

The solutions to these questions are at the end of the chapter.

How to Help Managers Achieve Their Goals While Achieving the Organization's Goals

The general transfer pricing rules are easy to state, but they are often difficult to apply in practice. A conflict can occur between the company's interests and the individual manager's interests when transfer price–based performance measures are used. The following describes such a conflict that has occurred at Canyon Dairies.

Milk Division is operating below capacity. Cheese Division has received a contract to produce 20,000 units of cheese that requires 20,000 units of milk. Emma Larson, the vice president of Cheese Division, has called Rajiv Dutta, the vice president of Milk Division, and made a proposal.

Emma: Rajiv, I'm bidding on a job with Mid-Atlantic Foods. I can make a competitive bid if I can buy 20,000 units of milk at $30. This will give us a $10 profit per unit, barely enough to make it worthwhile. I know you're running below capacity out there in Milk Division. This price will help us get the job and enable you to keep your dairy farming operations busy.

Rajiv: Emma, you and I both know that it would cost you a lot more to buy milk from an outside supplier. We aren't going to accept less than $50 per unit, which gives us our usual markup and covers our costs.

Emma: But, Rajiv, your variable costs are only $20. I know I'd be getting a good deal at $30, but so would you. You should treat this as a special order. Anything over your variable costs on the order is pure profit. If you can't do better than $50, I'll have to solicit prices from other companies.

Rajiv: The $50 is firm. Take it or leave it.

Cheese Division subsequently sought bids on the milk and was able to obtain a quote from an outside supplier for $30 per unit and won the job with Mid-Atlantic Foods because the bid price was $5 lower than the next best bid. Milk Division continued to operate below capacity. The actions of the two divisions cost the company $200,000. This is the amount paid to the outside supplier ($30) less the variable cost to Milk ($20) multiplied by the 20,000 units of milk in the order. The transfer price would not have affected company profit *if* Cheese Division had won the Mid-Atlantic order and used milk from the Milk Division, but it did affect the decisions made in the two divisions.

How can a decentralized organization avoid this type of cost? Although there is no easy solution, there are three general approaches to this type of problem:

1. Direct intervention by top management.
2. Centrally established transfer price policies.
3. Negotiated transfer prices.

Top-Management Intervention in Transfer Pricing

Sumi Matsumoto, Canyon Dairies's controller, could have directly intervened in this pricing dispute and ordered Milk Division to produce the milk and transfer it to Cheese Division at a management-specified transfer price. If this were an extraordinarily large order or if internal transfers were rare, direct intervention could be the best solution to the problem.

The disadvantage of direct intervention is that top management could become swamped with pricing disputes, and individual division managers lose the flexibility and other advantages of autonomous decision making. Thus, direct intervention promotes short-run profits by minimizing the type of uneconomic behavior demonstrated in the Canyon Dairies case, but it reduces the benefits from decentralization.

As long as transfer pricing problems are infrequent, the benefits of direct intervention could outweigh the costs. However, if transfer transactions are common, direct intervention can be costly by requiring substantial top-management involvement in decisions that should be made at the divisional level.

Centrally Established Transfer Price Policies

A transfer pricing policy should allow divisional autonomy yet encourage managers to pursue corporate goals consistent with their division goals. The transfer pricing policy should also be established keeping in mind the performance evaluation system used and the impact that alternative transfer prices will have on managerial performance evaluation. We know from the two general rules we established earlier that corporate managers have two economic bases on which to establish transfer price policies: market prices and cost.

Establishing a Market Price Policy

Externally based market prices are generally considered the best basis for transfer pricing when a competitive market exists for the product and market prices are readily available. An advantage of market prices is that both the buying and selling divisions are indifferent between trading with each other or with outsiders. From the company's perspective, this is fine as long as the supplying unit is operating at capacity.

Situations in which such a market exists are rare, however. Usually, there are differences between products produced internally and those that can be purchased from outsiders, such as distribution costs, quality (as discussed above in Case 1 with a perfect intermediate market), or product characteristics. The very existence of two divisions that trade with each other in a company tends to indicate that there may be advantages to dealing internally instead of with outside markets.

When such advantages exist, it is in the company's best interest to create incentives for internal transfer. Top management could establish policies that direct two responsibility centers to trade internally unless they can show good reason why external trades are more advantageous. A common variation on this approach is to establish a policy that provides the buying division a discount for items produced internally. The discount can reflect many factors. For example, transportation or purchasing costs could be lower when buying material from another division. Perhaps testing costs to ensure quality or costs associated with erratic delivery can be avoided when the transactions occur between units of the same company.

To encourage transfers that are in the best interest of the company, management can set a transfer pricing policy based on market prices for the intermediate product, such as milk. As a general rule, a **market price–based transfer pricing** policy contains the following guidelines:

- The transfer price is usually set at a discount from the cost to acquire the item on the open market.
- The selling division may elect to transfer or to continue to sell to the outside.

market price–based transfer pricing
Transfer pricing policy that sets the transfer price at the market price or at a small discount from the market price.

Establishing a Cost-Based Policy

A cost-based transfer pricing policy should adhere to the following rule, which restates the general principle: Transfer at the differential outlay cost to the selling division (typically variable costs) plus the forgone contribution to the company of making the internal transfers ($0 if the seller has idle capacity; selling price minus the variable costs if the seller is operating at capacity).

Using the Canyon Dairies example to demonstrate this policy, recall that the seller (Milk Division) could sell in outside markets for $50 and had a variable cost of $20, which we assume is its differential cost.

Now consider two cases. In case A, the seller (Milk Division) operates below capacity, in which case there is no lost contribution on the internal transfer because no outside sale is forgone. In case B, the seller operates at capacity and would have to give up one unit of outside sales for every unit transferred internally.

In case B, the opportunity cost of transferring the product to a division inside the company is the cost of producing the product plus the forgone contribution of selling the unit in an outside market. Consequently, the optimal transfer price for Canyon Dairies is $20 for the below-capacity case (case A) or $50 for case B, the at-capacity case (see Exhibit 15.4).

A seller operating at capacity is indifferent between selling in the outside market for $50 or transferring internally at $50. Note that this is the same solution as the market price rule for competitive markets because sellers can sell everything they can produce at the market price. Consequently, as a rule of thumb, the economic transfer pricing rule can be implemented as follows:

- A seller operating below capacity should transfer at the differential cost of production (variable cost).
- A seller operating at capacity should transfer at the market price.

A seller operating below capacity is indifferent between providing the product and receiving a transfer price equal to the seller's differential outlay cost (generally, variable production cost) or not providing the product at all. For example, if Milk Division received $20 for the product, it would be indifferent between selling it or not. In both the below-capacity and at-capacity cases, the selling division is no worse off if it makes the internal transfer.

The selling division does not earn a contribution on the transaction in the below-capacity case, however. It earns only the same contribution for the internal transfer as it would for a sale to the outside market in the at-capacity case. The general rule as stated is optimal for the company but does not benefit the selling division for an internal transfer.

Alternative Cost Measures

Full Absorption Cost–Based Transfers

Although the transfer pricing rule—differential outlay cost to the selling division plus the opportunity cost of making the internal transfer to the company—assumes that the company has a reliable estimate of differential or variable cost, this is not always the case. Consequently, manufacturing firms sometimes use full absorption cost as the transfer price.

Similarly, if measures of market prices are not available, it is impossible to compute the opportunity cost required by the general rule. Consequently, companies frequently use full absorption costs, which are higher than variable costs but probably less than the market price.

Exhibit 15.4

Application of General Transfer Pricing Principle—Canyon Dairies

	Outlay cost	+	Opportunity cost (forgone contribution of trans- ferring internally)	=	Transfer price (outlay cost plus opportunity cost at the point of transfer)
If the seller (Milk Division) has idle capacity	$20	+	$–0–	=	$20
If the seller has no idle capacity	$20	+	$30[a]	=	$50

[a] $50 selling price – $20 variable cost.

The use of full absorption costs does not necessarily lead to the profit-maximizing solution for the company; however, it has some advantages. First, these costs are available in the company's records. Second, they provide the selling division a contribution equal to the excess of full absorption costs over the variable costs, which gives the selling division an incentive to transfer internally. Third, the full absorption cost can sometimes be a better measure of the differential costs of transferring internally than the variable costs. For example, the transferred product could require engineering and design work that is buried in fixed overhead. In these cases, the full absorption cost could be a reasonable measure of the differential costs, including the unknown engineering and design costs.

Cost-Plus Transfers
We also find companies using **cost-plus transfer pricing** based on either variable costs or full absorption costs. These methods generally apply a normal markup to costs as a surrogate for market prices when intermediate market prices are not available.

cost-plus transfer pricing Transfer pricing policy based on a measure of cost (full or variable costing, actual or standard cost) plus an allowance for profit.

Standard Costs or Actual Costs
If actual costs are used as the basis for the transfer, any variances or inefficiencies in the selling division are passed to the buying division. The problem of isolating the variances that have been transferred to the subsequent buying divisions becomes extremely complex. To promote responsibility in the selling division and to isolate variances within divisions, standard costs are generally used as a basis for transfer pricing in cost-based systems.

For example, suppose that Canyon Dairies makes transfers based on variable costs for milk. The standard variable cost of producing the milk is $20, but the actual cost is $22 because of inefficiencies in Milk Division. Should this inefficiency be passed on to Cheese Division? The answer is usually no in order to give Milk Division incentives to be efficient. In these cases, companies use standard costs for the transfer price. If standards are out of date or otherwise do not reflect reasonable estimates of costs, the actual cost could be a better measure to use in the transfer price.

Remedying Motivational Problems of Transfer Pricing Policies

When the transfer pricing policy does not give the supplier a profit on the transfer, motivational problems can occur. For example, if transfers are made at differential cost, the supplier earns no contribution toward profits on the transferred goods. Then the transfer price policy does not motivate the supplier to transfer internally because there is no likely profit from internal transfers. This situation can be remedied in many ways.

A supplier whose transfers are almost all internal is usually organized as a cost center. The center manager is normally held responsible for costs, not revenues. Hence, the transfer price does not affect the manager's performance measures. In companies in which such a supplier is a profit center, the artificial nature of the transfer price should be considered when evaluating the results of that center's operations.

A supplying center that does business with both internal and external customers could be set up as a profit center for external business when the manager has price-setting power and as a cost center for internal transfers when the manager does not have such power. Performance on external business could be measured as if the center were a profit center; performance on internal business could be measured as if the center were a cost center.

Dual Transfer Prices
A **dual transfer pricing** system could be installed to provide the selling division with a profit but to charge the buying division only for costs. That is, the buyer could be charged the cost of the unit, however cost is determined, and the selling division could be credited for cost plus some profit allowance. The difference could be accounted for in a specialized centralized account. This system would preserve the

dual transfer pricing Transfer pricing system that charges the buying division with costs only and credits the selling division with cost plus some profit allowance.

cost data for subsequent buyer divisions and would encourage internal transfers by providing a profit on such transfers for the selling divisions.

Some companies use dual transfer pricing systems to encourage internal transfers. The disadvantage of dual price systems is that they reduce the value of the transfer price as a signal to division managers of the value of the intermediate good to the firm. These systems can also tend to remove some of the performance evaluation value because both managers benefit and the difference in the central account is often ignored.

There are other ways to encourage internal transfers. For example, many companies recognize internal transfers and incorporate them explicitly into their reward systems. Other companies base part of a supplying manager's bonus on the purchasing center's profits.

Negotiating the Transfer Price

negotiated transfer pricing
System that arrives at transfer prices through negotiation between managers of buying and selling divisions.

An alternative to a centrally administered transfer pricing policy is to permit managers to negotiate the price for internally transferred goods and services. Under a **negotiated transfer pricing** system, the managers involved act in much the same way as the managers of independent companies. The major advantage of negotiated transfer pricing is that it preserves the autonomy of the division managers. However, the two primary disadvantages are that a great deal of management effort can be consumed in the negotiating process and that the final price and its implications for performance measurement could depend more on the manager's ability to negotiate than on what is best for the company.

In the Canyon Dairies case, the two managers have room to negotiate the price between $20 and $50. They could choose to "split the difference" or develop some other negotiating strategy.

Imperfect Markets

Transfer pricing can be quite complex when selling and buying divisions cannot sell and buy all they want in perfectly competitive markets. In some cases, there may be no outside market at all. In others, the market price could depend on how many units the divisions want to buy or sell on the market. As a result, companies often find that not all transactions between divisions occur as top management prefers. In extreme cases, the transfer pricing problem is so complex that top management reorganizes the company so that buying and selling divisions report to one manager who oversees the transfers.

Self-Study Question

3.   Suppose that Sumi Matsumoto, as the controller of Canyon Dairies, decides to use a dual transfer pricing policy. Milk Division will sell milk to Cheese Division for $50, and Cheese Division will buy milk from Milk Division for $20. Cheese can sell its product for $120 per unit, and all other data are unchanged from Exhibit 15.1.

What is income for each of the divisions and for Canyon Dairies under this transfer pricing policy?

The solution to this question is at the end of the chapter.

Method Used	United States[a]	Canada[b]	Japan[c]
Cost-based......................	45%	47%	47%
Market-based....................	33	35	34
Negotiated transfer prices.	22	18	19
Total........................	100%	100%	100%

Exhibit 15.5
Transfer Pricing Practices

Note: Companies using other methods were omitted from this illustration. These companies were 2 percent or less of the total.

[a] S. Borkowski, "Environmental and Organizational Factors Affecting Transfer Pricing: A Survey," *Journal of Management Accounting Research* 2 (Fall 1990): 78–99.

[b] R. Tang, "Canadian Transfer Pricing Practices," *CA Magazine* 113 , no. 3 (1980): 32–38.

[c] R. Tang, C. Walter, and R. Raymond, "Transfer Pricing—Japanese vs. American Style," *Management Accounting* 60, no. 7 (1979): 12–16.

Global Practices

The authors of surveys of corporate practices (summarized in Exhibit 15.5) report that nearly 45 percent of the U.S. companies surveyed use a cost-based transfer pricing system, 33 percent use a market price–based system, and 22 percent use a negotiated system. Similar results have been found for companies in Canada and Japan.

Generally, we find that when negotiated prices are used, they are between the market price at the upper limit and some measure of cost at the lower limit.

No transfer pricing policy applied in practice is likely to dominate all others. An established policy most likely will be imperfect in the sense that it will not always work to induce the economically optimal outcome. As with other management decisions, however, the cost of any system must be weighed against its benefits. Improving a transfer pricing policy beyond some point (for example, by obtaining better measures of variable costs and market prices) will result in the system's costs exceeding its benefits. As a result, management tends to settle for a system that seems to work reasonably well rather than devise a "textbook" perfect system.

Multinational Transfer Pricing

In international (or interstate) transactions, transfer prices can affect tax liabilities, royalties, and other payments because of different laws in different countries (or states or provinces). Because tax rates vary among countries, companies have incentives to set transfer prices that will increase revenues (and profits) in low-tax countries and increase costs (thereby reducing profits) in high-tax countries.

LO 15-4
Explain the economic consequences of multinational transfer prices.

Tax avoidance by foreign companies using inflated transfer prices has been a major issue in U.S. presidential campaigns. Foreign companies that sell goods to their U.S. subsidiaries at inflated transfer prices artificially reduce the profit of the U.S. subsidiaries.

To understand the effects of transfer pricing on taxes, consider the case of Diego Pharmaceuticals. Its Puerto Rico unit imports bulk drugs from the company's U.S. manufacturing division. The Puerto Rico unit then packages them for sale directly to consumers in the United States. Suppose the U.S. tax rate is 21 percent, but in Puerto Rico it is 10 percent (with incentives).

During the current year, Diego incurred production costs of $20 million in its U.S. manufacturing operation. Costs incurred in Puerto Rico, in addition to the cost of the bulk pharmaceuticals, amounted to $5 million. (We call these *third-party* costs.) The sales revenues from the U.S. sales of the packaged drugs totaled $50 million.

A useful market price for pharmaceuticals is difficult to obtain because good substitutes are rare, so the market value at the point of transfer must be estimated. One estimate is $45 million. This is the $50 million ultimate sales value less the packaging costs of $5 million. A second estimate is $20 million, the cost of producing the bulk product. What would Diego's total tax liability be if it used the $20 million transfer price? What would the liability be if it used the $45 million transfer price?

Assuming the $20 million transfer price, the tax liabilities are computed as follows:

	A	B	C	D
1		United States		Puerto Rico
2	Revenues	$ 20,000,000		$ 50,000,000
3	Third-party costs	20,000,000		5,000,000
4	Transferred goods costs	–		20,000,000
5	Taxable income	$ –		$ 25,000,000
6	Tax rate	21%		10%
7	Tax liability	$ –		$ 2,500,000
8	Total tax liability		$ 2,500,000	
9				

Assuming the $45 million transfer price, the tax liabilities are computed as follows.

	A	B	C	D
1		United States		Puerto Rico
2	Revenues	$ 45,000,000		$ 50,000,000
3	Third-party costs	20,000,000		5,000,000
4	Transferred goods costs	–		45,000,000
5	Taxable income	$ 25,000,000		$ –
6	Tax rate	21%		10%
7	Tax liability	$ 5,250,000		$ –
8	Total tax liability		$ 5,250,000	
9				

Diego Pharmaceuticals can save $2.75 million in taxes simply by changing its transfer price!

To say the least, international taxing authorities look closely at transfer prices when examining the returns of companies engaged in related-party transactions that cross national boundaries. Companies must have adequate support for the use of the transfer price that they have chosen for such a situation. Transfer pricing disputes frequently end in costly litigation between the company and the taxing authority.

Self-Study Question

4. Refer to the information for Diego Pharmaceuticals in the text. Assume that the tax rate for both countries is 25 percent. What would be Diego's tax liability if the transfer price were set at $20 million? At $45 million?

The solution to this question is at the end of the chapter.

Tax Considerations in Transfer Pricing   *Business Application*

Multinational firms often face conflicting pressures when developing transfer pricing policies. Management control considerations suggest that the transfer price should reflect the value of the good or service being transferred. However, if there are differences in tax rates at which the parties to the transfer are taxed, the transfer pricing policy affects the company's tax liability. For many firms, the tax issues are more important and the focus of the transfer pricing policy is to reduce total taxes paid.

For example, a U.S. Tax Court recently ruled that Coca-Cola Company allocated too much profit (too little cost) to selected foreign subsidiaries. In the dispute, the IRS sought more than $3 billion covering the tax years being contested. One primary issue is how Coca-Cola accounts for profits from its sales of the material (concentrate) that is used to make the final drink.

Although companies are generally required to allocate profits in a way that reflects how profits would be earned if the entities were unrelated, this can be difficult to determine,

especially when companies profit from mobile, intangible assets like trademarks and patents.

However, as the Tax Court Judge commented,

. . . Coca-Cola's foreign subsidiaries had few trademarks or intellectual property and had little discretion over marketing, strategy and other decisions controlled by U.S. executives.

He further noted that the subsidiaries perform "routine contract manufacturing" and asked,

"And why does their profitability dwarf that of [Coca-Cola], which owns the intangibles upon which the Company's profitability depends?"

Source: Rubin, Richard, "Coca-Cola Improperly Shifted Profits Abroad, Tax Court Rules," *The Wall Street Journal,* November 19, 2020.

Segment Reporting

The Financial Accounting Standards Board (FASB) requires companies engaged in different lines of business to report certain information about segments that meet the FASB's technical requirements.[5] This reporting requirement is intended to provide a measure of performance for those segments that are significant to the company as a whole. The definition of a segment for financial reporting purposes has evolved over time. Currently, one of the criteria is that a unit of the enterprise is one whose "operating results are reviewed regularly by the public entity's chief operating decision maker to make decisions about resources to be allocated to the segment and assess its performance."[6]

LO 15-5
Describe the role of transfer prices in segment reporting.

The following are the principal items that must be disclosed about each segment:

- Segment revenue, from both internal and external customers.
- Interest revenue and expense.
- Segment operating profit or loss.
- Identifiable segment assets.
- Depreciation and amortization.
- Capital expenditures.
- Certain specialized items.

In addition, if a company has significant foreign operations, it must disclose revenues, operating profits or losses, and identifiable assets by geographical region.

The financial reporting of internal transactions requires that firms report segment profit as computed for use by the chief operating decision maker in assessing segment performance. This means that the transfer pricing method used for performance evaluation will be reflected in reported segment income and can be either cost- or market-based.

---

[5] The requirements, which are too detailed to cover here, are summarized in Joanne M. Flood, *Wiley Practitioner's Guide to GAAP 2021* (Hoboken, NJ: Wiley, 2021), chapter 15, ASC-280.

[6] Ibid., p. 189.

Transfer pricing is important for evaluation of segment profit in many industries where there is a significant transfer of goods and services between divisions. One example is financial services where one business unit (or business activity) attracts deposits and a second lends money. Another example is the paper industry where the firm raises its own raw materials (pulp and lumber) for use in making paper. One large paper company in the United States is Weyerhaeuser. In its 2019 Annual Report, it explains the basis of its transfer pricing policy for determining segment income.

We also transfer raw materials, semi-finished materials and end products among our business segments. Because of this intracompany activity, accounting for our business segments involves pricing products transferred between our business segments at *current market values* (emphasis added).

Unallocated Items are gains or charges related to company level initiatives or previous businesses that are not allocated to our current business segments. They include all or a portion of items such as *share-based compensation* (emphasis added). . . .

Source: Weyerhauser 2019 Annual Report and Form 10K, p. 65, 2020.

Other financial reporting requirements can also dictate the method used. For example, oil and gas firms must use market prices for transfers when reporting segment results.[7]
Example disclosures of transfer pricing methods include the following:

> Transactions among Automotive segments generally are presented on a "where-sold," absolute-cost basis, which reflects the profit/(loss) on the sale within the segment making the ultimate sale to an external entity. This presentation generally eliminates the effect of legal entity transfer prices within the Automotive sector for vehicles, components, and product engineering. [Ford Motor Company, 2008]

and

> The net interest income of the businesses includes the results of a funds transfer pricing process that matches assets and liabilities with similar interest rate sensitivity and maturity characteristics. [Bank of America, 2008]

These examples indicate that, as shown in Exhibit 15.5, firms use different methods for transfer pricing when computing divisional profit for performance evaluation. This change in financial reporting requirements represents one of the few examples in which accounting for external reporting recognizes differences in the way firms use financial information for internal decision making.

---

[7] See, for example, FASB, *ASC 932-235-50-24*, which specifies the use of market-based transfer prices when calculating the results of operations for an oil and gas exploration and production operation.

Key Takeaways

1. Transfer prices are the prices one division of a company charges (pays to) another division of the same company for goods or services. Division managers use these prices to make decisions that maximize division profits. Transfer prices do not affect total firm profits *as long as the transaction takes place*.

2. The general rule for an optimum transfer price is Transfer price = Outlay cost + Opportunity cost at the point of transfer.

    a. If there is a perfect intermediate (outside) market, meaning buyers and sellers cannot affect the price, the optimum transfer price is the market price. The opportunity cost is the contribution the firm forgoes by not selling the good or service in the market.

    b. If there is no intermediate (outside) market for the good or service being transferred, the optimum transfer price is the outlay cost (generally the variable cost) of the product or service transferred. Without an outside market, the opportunity cost of transfer is zero.

    c. Other transfer prices include cost-based and negotiated transfer prices.

3. Transfer pricing in multinational firms is often more concerned with minimizing tax impacts rather than management control. Firms use transfer prices that increase (lower) costs and lower (increase) profits for divisions located where tax rates are higher (lower).

SUMMARY

This chapter discussed scenarios in which transactions between units of a firm can result in decisions that are not in the firm's best interests. The problems associated with such situations can be mitigated by setting an appropriate transfer price that reflects the value of the good or service being transferred.

The following summarizes key ideas tied to the chapter's learning objectives:

LO 15-1 Explain the basic issues associated with transfer pricing. When companies transfer goods or services between divisions, they assign a price to that transaction. This transfer price becomes part of the recorded revenues and costs in the divisions involved in the transfer. As a result, the dollar value assigned to the transfer can have significant implications in evaluating divisional performance. Establishing transfer prices can be a difficult task and depends on individual circumstances. The chapter outlined four common scenarios.

LO 15-2 Explain the general transfer pricing rules and understand the underlying basis for them. Two general rules exist when establishing a transfer price: (1) If there is a market for the intermediate product, the transfer price should be the market price, and (2) if there is no intermediate market, the transfer price should equal the variable cost to produce the goods.

LO 15-3 Identify the behavioral issues and incentive effects of negotiated transfer prices, cost-based transfer prices, and market-based transfer prices. Transfer pricing systems can be based on direct intervention, market prices, costs, or negotiation among the division managers. The appropriate method depends on the markets in which the company operates and management's goals. Top management usually tries to choose the appropriate method to promote corporate goals without destroying the autonomy of the division managers. Different approaches to transfer pricing create different motivations for behavior. In creating a basis for establishing transfer prices (e.g., negotiated, cost-based, or market-based), management must consider the behavior that such a plan motivates.

LO 15-4 Explain the economic consequences of multinational transfer prices. Because tax rates vary in different countries, companies have incentives to set transfer prices to increase revenues (and profits) in low-tax countries and increase costs (thereby reducing profits) in high-tax countries.

LO 15-5 Describe the role of transfer prices in segment reporting. Companies with significant segments are required to report on those segments separately in their financial statements. The accounting profession has indicated a preference for market-based transfer prices when reporting on a segment of a business.

KEY TERMS

cost-plus transfer pricing, *703*
dual transfer pricing, *703*
market price–based transfer pricing, *701*

negotiated transfer pricing, *704*
optimal transfer price, *690*
transfer price, *689*

REVIEW QUESTIONS

15-1. What is the purpose of a transfer price?

15-2. In Chapter 12, we discussed corporate cost allocation and the incentive problems associated with these allocations. How is the problem of corporate cost allocations similar to the transfer pricing problems studied in this chapter? Is the approach suggested in Chapter 12 as a solution to the corporate cost allocation problem consistent with the optimal transfer pricing approach discussed in this chapter?

15-3. Do transfer prices exist in centralized firms? Why?

15-4. Many firms prefer to use market prices for transfer prices. Why would they have this preference?

15-5. What are the limitations of market-based transfer prices? What are the limitations of cost-based transfer prices?

15-6. When would you advise a firm to use direct intervention to set transfer prices? What are the disadvantages of such a practice?

15-7. When would you advise a firm to use prices other than market prices for interdivisional transfers?

15-8. What is the basis for choosing between actual and standard costs for cost-based transfer pricing?

15-9. What are the advantages and disadvantages of a negotiated transfer price system?

15-10. What is the general transfer pricing rule? What is the transfer price that results from this rule when

    a.   There is a perfect market for the product?

    b.   The selling division is operating below capacity?

15-11. Why is transfer pricing important in tax accounting?

15-12. Why is transfer pricing important in segment reporting for financial accounting?

CRITICAL ANALYSIS AND DISCUSSION QUESTIONS

15-13. What should an effective transfer pricing system accomplish in a decentralized organization?

15-14. Alpha Division and Beta Division are both profit centers. Alpha has no external markets for its one product, an electrical component. Beta uses the component but cannot purchase it from any other source. What transfer pricing system would you recommend for the interdivisional sale of the component? Why?

15-15. Refer to Question 15-14. What type of responsibility center would you recommend the company make Alpha Division? Beta Division? Explain your reasons.

15-16. Refer to the Business Application item "Transfer Pricing at Weyerhaeuser." Why might the company use market prices instead of costs for product transfers?

15-17. How does the choice of a transfer price affect the operating profits of both segments involved in an intracompany transfer? Why is the choice of a transfer price important if the total profits of the firm are unaffected by this choice?

15-18. When setting a transfer price for goods that are sold across international boundaries, what factors should management consider?

15-19. In what ways is transfer pricing like cost allocation? In what ways is it different?

15-20. Consider a company that leases a fleet of aircraft for passenger service. Because the planes often fly with room in the cargo area, the company adds a new business shipping time-sensitive freight. The company organizes into two profit centers—Passenger Service and Freight Service—and evaluates the division managers based on divisional return on investment. What transfer pricing issues might arise?

15-21. Consider a university setting with many colleges, such as the Engineering College, the Business College, Arts & Sciences College, and so on. The central administration is responsible for finance, personnel, legal, and other costs. Because the university is organized as a not-for-profit entity, it has no transfer pricing issues. Do you agree? Why or why not?

EXERCISES      All applicable Problems are included in Connect.

(LO 15-1)   **15-22. Basic Transfer Pricing Issues**

Philadelphia Supply Corporation (PSC) produces and distributes various products for the hospitality industry. It is organized in two divisions: Assembly and Packaging. The managers of both divisions are evaluated and compensated based on divisional income. Assembly only "sells" to Packaging. Packaging prepares the items for a particular customer (adding labels, logos, and so on), prepares them for delivery, and ships them to the customer.

Information on revenues and costs for the latest quarter for each division follows. Production and sales quantities, measured in "standard units," were 3,000 units for the quarter.

	Assembly	Packaging
Sales revenue	$195,000	$900,000
Direct materials	105,000	385,000
Direct labor	55,000	170,000
Variable overhead	20,000	45,000
Fixed costs	40,000	180,000

A local hotel is hosting a special convention next month and has asked for a special price for 500 units at a total price of $102,500. After hearing about the order, the Assembly Division manager insists that the transfer cost (the transfer price multiplied by 500 units) be set at $40,000. There is sufficient excess capacity in Assembly to handle the special order.

Required

a. What is the current transfer price for a unit?

b. Does PSC (the corporation) want to accept this order?

c. Will the Assembly Division manager be willing to accept this order if the transfer cost is $40,000?

d. Will the Packaging Division manager be willing to accept this order if the transfer cost is $40,000?

15-23. Basic Transfer Pricing Issues
(LO 15-1)

Refer to the data in Exercise 15-22. PSC management has disallowed any change in transfer prices for special orders.

Required

a. Does PSC want to accept this order?

b. Will the Assembly Division manager be willing to accept this order?

c. Will the Packaging Division manager be willing to accept this order?

15-24. Basic Transfer Pricing Issues
(LO 15-1)

Hamlet Industries is organized into two divisions, Fabrication and Finishing. Both divisions are considered to be profit centers, and the two division managers are evaluated in large part on divisional income. The company makes a single product. It is manufactured in Fabrication and then packaged and sold in Distribution. There is no intermediate market for the product.

The monthly income statements, in thousands of dollars, for the two divisions follow. Production and sales amounted to 32,000 units.

	Fabrication ($000)	Distribution ($000)
Revenues	$4,800	$8,000
Variable costs	3,840	5,920
Contribution margin	$ 960	$2,080
Fixed costs	800	1,280
Divisional profit	$ 160	$ 800

The company has just received an offer to buy 3,200 units of the product this month at a price of $200 per unit. The Distribution Division manager suggests that for the special order only, the transfer price be set at 50 percent of the sales price, or $100 per unit.

Required

a. What is the current transfer price for a unit?

b. Does Hamlet Industries want to accept this order?

c. Will the Distribution Division manager be willing to accept this order if the transfer price is $100 per unit?

d. Will the Fabrication Division manager be willing to accept this order if the transfer price is $100 per unit?

(LO 15-1) **15-25. Basic Transfer Pricing Issues**

Refer to the data in Exercise 15-24. Assume the transfer price is unchanged from the current transfer price.

Required

a. Does Hamlet Industries want to accept this order?

b. Will the Distribution Division manager be willing to accept this order?

c. Will the Fabrication Division manager be willing to accept this order?

(LO 15-2) **15-26. Apply Transfer Pricing Rules**

Lamothe Solutions is a management consulting firm. Its Business Division advises firms on the adoption and use of financial systems. Civic Division consults with state and local governments. Civic Division has a client that is interested in implementing a new costing system in its public works department. The division's head approached the head of Business Division about using one of its associates. Corporate Division charges clients $750 per hour for associate services, the same rate other consulting companies charge. The Civic Division head complained that it could hire its own associate at an estimated variable cost of $350 per hour, which is what Business pays its associates.

Required

a. What is the maximum price that Civic Division should pay?

b. What is the maximum transfer price that Business Division should obtain for its services, assuming that it is operating at capacity?

c. Would your answers in requirement (*a*) or (*b*) change if Business Division had idle capacity? If so, which answer would change, and what would the new amount be?

(LO 15-2) **15-27. Evaluate Transfer Pricing System**

Lola Metals has two decentralized divisions, Stamping and Finishing. Finishing always has purchased certain units from Stamping at $36 per unit. Stamping plans to raise the price to $48 per unit, the price it receives from outside customers. As a result, Finishing is considering buying these units from outside suppliers for $36 per unit. Corporate policy allows division managers to choose both customers and suppliers regardless of the transfer price. Stamping's costs follow:

Variable costs per unit	$ 34
Annual fixed costs	$60,000
Annual production of these units sold to Alpha	27,000 units

Required

a. If Finishing buys from an outside supplier, the facilities that Stamping uses to produce these units will remain idle. What will be the impact on corporate profits if Lola Metals enforces a transfer price of $48 per unit between Stamping and Finishing?

b. Suppose Lola Metals enforces a transfer price of $36 and insists that Stamping sell to Finishing before selling to outside customers. Stamping currently operates at capacity and can easily sell on the outside market the units it sells to Finishing. What cost will Lola Metals incur as a result of this policy?

(CPA adapted)

(LO 15-2) **15-28. Evaluate Transfer Pricing System**

Pilgrim Logistics operates a network of delivery vans. Pilgrim allows its decentralized units (divisions) to "rent" vans to another Pilgrim division. Commercial Division has leased some of its idle vans to Retail Division for $450 per month. Recently, Commercial obtained a new contract with a local distribution center, which will increase its load sufficiently so that the idle vans are more valuable to it. Commercial has told Retail that the rental price will increase to $620 per month. Retail can lease vans for $510 per month from an outside company but would rather use the vans from Commercial. If Retail Division continues to use the vans from Commercial, Commercial will have to rent other vans for $600 per month. (The difference in rental prices occurs because Commercial Division requires larger vans than does Retail Division.)

Required

Recommend a transfer price and explain your reasons for choosing that price.

15-29. Evaluate Transfer Pricing System

(LO 15-2)

Southfield Division offers its product to outside markets for $115. It incurs variable costs of $40 per unit and fixed costs of $139,000 per month based on monthly production of 22,000 units. Northfield Division can acquire the product from an alternate supplier for $120 per unit or from Southwest Division for a transfer price of $115 plus $7 per unit in transportation costs.

Required

a. What are the costs and benefits of the alternatives available to Southfield Division and Northfield Division with respect to the transfer of Southfield Division's product? Assume that Southfield Division can market all that it can produce.

b. How would your answer change if Southfield Division had idle capacity sufficient to cover all of Northfield Division's needs?

15-30. Evaluate Transfer Pricing System

(LO 15-2, 3)

Hardyke Group operates a local after-school recreation and activities program. The Education Department is a state governmental agency. Hardyke has an agreement with the Department to provide services to students in need for a nominal $1 per day, to be paid by the student. The government will reimburse Hardyke for the "cost" of providing daily services used by a student.

The regular price to participate in the program is $5.00 per day. After analyzing its costs, Hardyke calculates that, with its operating deficit, the full cost of each student for a day is $7.50. All programs that Hardyke offers are unaffected by the number of students paying the nominal fee.

Required

a. What alternative prices could be used to determine the governmental reimbursement to Hardyke Group?

b. Which price would Hardyke Group prefer? Why?

c. Which price would the Education Department prefer? Why?

d. If Hardyke provides an average of 3,000 student-days for in-need children in a given month, what is the monthly value of the difference between the prices in requirements (b) and (c)?

15-31. International Transfer Prices: Ethical Issues

(LO 15-4)

Whitehill Chemicals has two operating divisions. Its Formulation Division in the United States mixes, processes, and tests basic chemicals, and then ships them to Ireland, where the company's Commercial Division uses the chemicals to produce and sell various products. Operating expenses amount to $26 million in the U.S. and $78 million in Ireland exclusive of the costs of any goods transferred from the U.S. Revenues in Ireland are $195 million.

If the chemicals were purchased from one of the company's Irish mixing divisions, the costs would be $39 million. However, if it had been purchased from an independent U.S. supplier, the cost would be $52 million. The marginal income tax rate is 20 percent in the U.S. and 12 percent in Ireland.

Required

a. What is the company's total tax liability to both jurisdictions for each of the two alternative transfer pricing scenarios ($39 million and $52 million)?

b. Is it ethical to choose the transfer price based on the impact on taxes? Explain.

15-32. Transfer Pricing Policies: Ethical Issues

(LO 15-4)

Refer to the data in Exercise 15–26. Suppose that Civic Division will charge the client interested in implementing a costing system by the hour based on cost plus a fixed fee, where the cost is primarily the consultant's hourly pay. Assume also that Civic Division cannot hire additional consultants. That is, if it is to do this job, it will need to use a consultant from Business Division.

Required

a. What is the minimum transfer price that Business Division should obtain for its services, assuming that it is operating at capacity? Would this be an ethical price to charge the government client? Explain.

b. What is the transfer price you would recommend if Corporate Division was not operating at capacity? Would this be an ethical price to charge the government client? Explain.

(LO 15-2, 4)   **15-33. International Transfer Pricing and Taxes**

Cascade Containers is organized into two divisions—Manufacturing and Distribution. Manufacturing produces a product that can be sold immediately or transferred to Distribution for further processing and then sold. Distribution only buys from Manufacturing for quality control reasons.

Manufacturing currently sells 2,400 units annually at a price of $600 per unit to outside customers. It sells an additional 1,200 units to Distribution. The unit variable cost in Manufacturing is $300 and annual fixed costs are $300,000. Manufacturing is located in a country with a 20 percent tax rate.

Distribution can sell units that have had further processing for $1,200 each. In addition to what it pays Manufacturing, the variable costs in Distribution are $150 per unit. Annual fixed costs in Distribution are $360,000. Distribution is located in a country with a 10 percent tax rate.

Required

a.   Suppose Manufacturing would have excess capacity even with the demand from Distribution. Ignoring tax implications, what transfer price would you recommend Cascade Containers adopt?

b.   What would be the total taxes Cascade Containers paid under the policy you recommend in requirement (*a*)?

c.   Suppose Manufacturing has no excess capacity. Ignoring tax implications, what transfer price would you recommend Cascade Containers adopt?

d.   What would be the total taxes Cascade Containers paid under the policy you recommend in requirement (*c*)?

(LO 15-2)   **15-34. Evaluate Transfer Pricing System**

Carol Components operates a Production Division and a Packaging Division. Both divisions are evaluated as profit centers. Packaging buys components from Production and assembles them for sale. Production sells many components to third parties in addition to Packaging. Selected data from the two operations follow:

	Production	Packaging
Capacity (units)	50,000	25,000
Sales price[a]	$ 240	$ 780
Variable costs[b]	$ 96	$ 288
Fixed costs.	$3,000,000	$1,800,000

[a] For Production, this is the price to third parties.
[b] For Packaging this does not include the transfer price paid to Production.

Required

a.   Current output in Production is 25,000 units. Packaging requests an additional 5,000 units to produce a special order. What transfer price would you recommend? Why?

b.   Suppose Production is operating at full capacity. What transfer price would you recommend? Why?

c.   Suppose Production is operating at 47,500 units. What transfer price would you recommend? Why?

(LO 15-4)   **15-35. International Transfer Prices**

Refer to the information in Exercise 15-34. Suppose Production is located in Country A with a tax rate of 30 percent and Distribution in Country B with a tax rate of 10 percent. All other facts remain the same.

Required

a.   Current output in Production is 25,000 units. Packaging requests an additional 5,000 units to produce a special order. What transfer price would you recommend? Why?

b.   Suppose Production is operating at full capacity. What transfer price would you recommend? Why?

c.   Suppose Production is operating at 47,500 units. What transfer price would you recommend? Why?

15-36. Evaluate Transfer Pricing System: Dual Rates

(LO 15-2, 3)

Anstell Corporation operates a Manufacturing Division and a Marketing Division. Both divisions are evaluated as profit centers. Marketing buys products from Manufacturing and packages them for sale. Manufacturing sells many components to third parties in addition to Marketing. Selected data from the two operations follow:

	Manufacturing	Marketing
Capacity (units)	250,000	125,000
Sales price*	$ 280	$ 910
Variable costs†	$ 112	$ 336
Fixed costs	$100,000	$720,000

* For Manufacturing, this is the price to third parties.

† For Marketing this does not include the transfer price paid to Manufacturing.

Required

a. Current output in Manufacturing is 150,000 units. Marketing requests an additional 25,000 units to produce a special order. What transfer price would you recommend? Why?

b. Suppose Manufacturing is operating at full capacity. What transfer price would you recommend? Why?

c. Suppose Anstell management decides that a dual-rate system will lead the two divisions to cooperate. Manufacturing continues to operate at full capacity. Management sets a transfer price for Manufacturing to receive (as revenue) at $280 and a transfer price for Marketing to pay (as a cost) at $112. From a management control viewpoint, assess the value of the dual-rate system to your recommended system obtained in requirement (b).

15-37. Evaluate Transfer Pricing System: Negotiated Rates

(LO 15-2, 3)

Refer to the information in Exercise 15-24. Assume there is no special order pending.

Required

a. What transfer price would you recommend for Hamlet Industries?

b. Using your recommended transfer price, what will be the income of the two divisions, assuming monthly production and sales of 32,000 units?

c. The manager of the Fabrication Division complains about the transfer price, saying that division profits are unfairly low. The two division managers meet and negotiate a transfer price of $148. What will be the income of the two divisions, assuming monthly production and sales of 32,000 units?

d. From a management control viewpoint, assess the value of the negotiated transfer price relative to your recommended price in requirement (a).

15-38. International Transfer Prices

(LO 15-4)

Refer to the information in Exercise 15-36. Suppose Manufacturing is located in Country X with a tax rate of 35 percent and Marketing in Country Y with a tax rate of 15 percent. All other facts remain the same.

Required

a. Current output in Manufacturing is 125,000 units. Marketing requests an additional 25,000 units to produce a special order. What transfer price would you recommend? Why?

b. Suppose Manufacturing is operating at full capacity. What transfer price would you recommend? Why?

c. Suppose Manufacturing is operating at 230,000 units. What transfer price would you recommend? Why?

15-39. Segment Reporting

(LO 15-5)

Burdeno Appliances has two divisions, Sales and Financing. Sales is responsible for selling Burdeno's inventory and maintaining inventory for future sale. Financing Division takes loan applications, packages loans into pools, and sells them in the financial markets. It also services the loans. Both divisions meet the requirements for segment disclosures under accounting rules.

Sales Division had $8 million in sales last year. Costs, other than those charged by Financing Division, totaled $6 million. Financing Division earned revenues of $2.5 million from servicing loans and incurred outside costs of $3 million. In addition, Financing charged Operations $900,000 for loan-related fees. Sales' manager complained to corporate that Financing was charging 150 percent of the commercial rate for loan-related fees and that Sales would be better off sending its buyers to an outside lender.

Financing's manager replied that although commercial rates could be lower, servicing these loans is more difficult, thereby justifying the higher fees.

Required

a.   What are the reported segment operating profits for each division, ignoring income taxes and using the $900,000 transfer price for the loan-related fees?

b.   What are the reported segment operating profits for each division, ignoring income taxes and using a $600,000 (= $900,000 ÷ 150%) commercial rate as the transfer price for the loan-related fees?

c.   Write a memo to the management at Burdeno suggesting an appropriate transfer pricing policy along with your reasons.

(LO 15-5)   **15-40. Segment Reporting**
Eastlawn Travel has two operating divisions, Tours and Resorts. The two divisions meet the requirements for segment disclosures. Before transactions between the two divisions are considered, revenues and costs are as follows:

	Tours	Resorts
Revenues	$35,200,000	$24,200,000
Costs	19,800,000	17,600,000

The two divisions have an arrangement by which Resorts gives coupons redeemable for tours and Tours gives discount coupons good for stays at a resort. The value of the coupons for the tours redeemed during the past year totaled $5.3 million. The discount coupons redeemed at the resorts totaled $2.2 million. As of the end of the year, all coupons for the current year expired.

Required
What are the operating profits for each division considering the effects of the costs arising from the joint agreement?

PROBLEMS      All applicable Problems are included in Connect.

(LO 15-2)   **15-41. Transfer Pricing with Imperfect Markets: ROI Evaluation, Normal Costing**
Washburn Associates has two divisions. Western Division, which has an investment base of $50,000,000, produces and sells 1,400,000 units of a product at a market price of $60 per unit. Its variable costs total $25 per unit. The division also charges each unit $20 of fixed costs based on a capacity of 1,500,000 units.

Eastern Division wants to purchase 200,000 units from Western. However, it is willing to pay only $40 per unit because it has an opportunity to accept a special order at a reduced price. The order is economically justifiable only if Eastern can acquire Western's output at a reduced price.

Required

a.   What is the ROI for Western without the transfer to Eastern?

b.   What is Western's ROI if it transfers 200,000 units to Eastern at $40 each?

c.   What is the minimum transfer price for the 200,000-unit order that Western would accept if it were willing to maintain the same ROI with the transfer as it would earn by only selling its 1,400,000 units to the outside market?

15-42. Transfer Pricing with Imperfect Markets: RI Evaluation, Normal Costing

(LO 15-2)

Refer to the data in Problem 15-41. Division managers are evaluated using residual income using a 9 percent cost of capital.

Required

a.   What is the residual income for Western without the transfer to Eastern?

b.   What is Western's residual income if it transfers 200,000 units to Eastern at $40 each?

c.   What is the minimum transfer price for the 200,000-unit order that Western would accept if it were willing to maintain the same residual income with the transfer as it would earn by only selling its 1,400,000 units to the outside market?

15-43. Evaluate Profit Impact of Alternative Transfer Decisions

(LO 15-2, 3)

Mack's Juices produces and bottles a line of fruit juices. The manufacturing process entails mixing and adding juices and other ingredients at the bottling plant, which is a part of Blending Division. The finished product is packaged in a company-produced glass bottle and packed in cases of 24 bottles each.

Because the appearance of the bottle heavily influences sales volume, Mack's developed a unique bottle production process at the company's container plant, which is a part of Packaging Division. Blending Division uses all of the container plant's production. Each division (Blending and Packaging) is considered a separate profit center and evaluated as such. As the new corporate controller, you are responsible for determining the proper transfer price to use for the bottles produced for Blending Division.

At your request, Packaging Division's general manager asked other bottle manufacturers to quote a price for the number and sizes demanded by Blending Division. These competitive prices follow:

Volume	Total Price	Price per Case
100,000 equivalent cases[a]	$2,160,000	$21.60
200,000	3,750,000	18.75
300,000	4,860,000	16.20

[a]An equivalent case represents 24 bottles.

Packaging Division's cost analysis indicates that it can produce bottles at these costs.

Volume	Total Price	Price per Case
100,000 equivalent cases	$1,800,000	$18.00
200,000	3,000,000	15.00
300,000	4,200,000	14.00

These costs include fixed costs of $600,000 and variable costs of $12 per equivalent case. These data have caused considerable corporate discussion as to the proper price to use in the transfer of bottles from Packaging Division to Blending Division. This interest is heightened because a significant portion of a division manager's income is an incentive bonus based on profit center results.

Blending Division has the following costs in addition to the bottle costs:

Volume	Total Price	Price per Case
100,000 equivalent cases	$1,350,000	$13.50
200,000	1,950,000	9.75
300,000	2,550,000	8.50

The corporate marketing group has furnished the following price–demand relationship for the finished product:

Sales Volume	Total Sales Revenue	Sales Price per Case
100,000 equivalent cases........	$ 6,000,000	$60
200,000	10,800,000	54
300,000	13,500,000	45

Required

a. Mack's Juices has used market price–based transfer prices in the past. Using the current market prices and costs and assuming a volume of 300,000 cases, calculate operating profits for
1. Packaging Division.
2. Blending Division.
3. Mack's Juices.

b. Is this production and sales level the most profitable volume for
1. Packaging Division?
2. Blending Division?
3. Mack's Juices?

Explain.

(CMA adapted)

(LO 15-4)   **15-44. International Transfer Prices**

Santos Shipping Lines (SSL) operates a fleet of container ships in international trade between Brazil and Ireland. All of the shipping income (that is, that related to SSL's ships) is deemed to be earned in Brazil. SSL also owns a dock facility in Ireland that services SSL's fleet. Income from the dock facility is deemed to be earned in Ireland. SSL's income deemed attributable to Brazil is taxed at a 34 percent rate. Its income attributable to Ireland is taxed at a 12.5 percent rate. Last year, the dock facility had operating revenues of $15 million, excluding services performed for SSL's ships. SSL's shipping revenues for last year were $70 million.

Operating costs of the dock facility totaled $19 million last year and operating costs for the shipping operation, before deduction of dock facility costs, totaled $45 million. No similar dock facilities in Ireland are available to SSL.

However, a facility in the United Kingdom (UK) would have charged SSL an estimated $14 million for the services that SSL's Ireland dock provided to its ships. SSL management noted that had the services been provided in Brazil, the costs for the year would have totaled $20 million. SSL argued to the Brazilian tax officials that the appropriate transfer price is the price that would have been charged in Brazil. Brazilian tax officials determined that the UK price is the appropriate one.

Required

What is the difference in tax costs to SSL between the alternate transfer prices for dock services, that is, its price in Brazil versus that in the UK?

(LO 15-4)   **15-45. International Transfer Prices**

Maple Cargo is an all-cargo airline that operates on four continents. Its headquarters are in New Zealand. It has two divisions, Cargo and Maintenance. Cargo Division flies cargo to and from international locations. Maple Cargo also has a maintenance facility located in Hong Kong and schedules its planes in such a way that most maintenance can be done there. In addition to Maple aircraft, Maintenance Division also provides services to several other passenger and cargo air companies.

All of the Cargo Division income is deemed to be earned in New Zealand. Income from the Maintenance Division is deemed to be earned in Hong Kong. Maple's income deemed attributable to New Zealand is taxed at a 28 percent rate. Its income attributable to Hong Kong is taxed at a 16.5 percent rate. Last year, Maintenance Division had operating revenues of $39 million, excluding services performed for Cargo Division aircraft. Cargo Division revenues last year were $150 million.

Operating costs of Maintenance Division were $24 million last year and operating costs for the Cargo Division, before considering maintenance costs, totaled $74 million. No similar maintenance facilities in Hong Kong are available to Maple.

Recently, a maintenance facility opened in Malaysia. That facility proposed to Cargo Division that it could conduct the maintenance in Malaysia. The facility proposed a price of $33 million for the services that Maintenance Division in Hong Kong provided to Cargo Division. Maple management estimated that had the services been provided in New Zealand, the costs for the year would have totaled $50 million. In its latest tax filing, Maple assigned the $50 million as the appropriate transfer price Cargo paid for the services from Maintenance. The New Zealand tax authorities denied that expense and instead applied $33 million as the appropriate transfer price.

Required

What is the difference in tax costs to Maple between the alternate transfer prices for maintenance services, that is, the difference between transfer prices of $33 million and $50 million?

15-46. International Transfer Prices

(LO 15-4)

Pallister Medical, Inc. (PMI) produces and sells a single drug. The company is organized into three divisions: Production, Packaging, and Distribution. Production, located in country A, manufactures the drug producing a single-dose capsule. The variable cost of a capsule is $25. The fixed costs of Production are $2.5 million and Production produces 400,000 capsules annually.

Packaging is located in country B. Packaging takes the pills that are sent by Production in bulk and packages them in boxes containing 20 capsules each. The variable costs of packaging are $100 per box excluding any costs from Production. The pills from Production are transferred at average (variable plus fixed) costs. Fixed costs in packaging are $1 million annually.

Distribution, like Production, is located in country A. Distribution takes the boxes prepared by Packaging and sells them to distributors in country A. The variable costs of Distribution are $125 per box excluding any costs from Packaging. Fixed costs in Distribution are $800,000 annually.

The pill produced by PMI is a generic drug with many competitors. The market value before distribution costs is determined to be $1,000 per box. Distribution Division sells boxes to its customers for $1,250 per box. The tax rates are 30 percent in country A and 10 percent in country B.

Required

a.   The company decides that for tax purposes, it will use the market value of the pills (before distribution costs) for the transfer price between Packaging and Distribution. What is the total tax PMI will pay in income tax to the two countries?

b.   The tax authorities in country A object and argue that this drug is not that similar to other generics of this type. Therefore, the transfer price should be the average total cost (variable plus fixed) of Packaging. If that transfer price is used, what is the total tax PMI will pay in income tax to the two countries?

15-47. Analyze Transfer Pricing Data

(LO 15-2)

Dakota Security Systems (DSS) is a decentralized organization that evaluates divisional management based on measures of divisional contribution margin. Residential Division and Commercial Division both sell security and monitoring equipment. Residential sells primarily to home owners and apartment management companies. Commercial focuses on small to medium-sized businesses. Residential sells a particular alarm to the outside market for $216 per unit. The outside market can absorb up to 43,750 units per year. These units require 3 direct labor-hours each.

If Residential modifies the units with an additional 0.75 hour of labor time, it can sell them to Commercial for $243 per unit. Commercial will accept up to 37,500 of these units per year.

If Commercial does not obtain 37,500 units from Residential, it purchases them for $252 each from the outside. Commercial incurs $108 of additional labor and other out-of-pocket costs to convert the alarm (either from Residential or outside) into one that fits in an existing Commercial Division system. The units can be sold to the outside market for $612 each.

Residential estimates that its total costs are $1,485,000 for fixed costs, $20.00 per direct labor-hour, and $21.60 per alarm for materials and other variable costs besides direct labor. Its capacity is limited to 187,500 direct labor-hours per year.

Required

Determine the following:

a. Total contribution margin to Residential if it sells 43,750 units outside.

b. Total contribution margin to Residential if it sells 37,500 units to Commercial.

c. The costs to be considered in determining the optimal company policy for sales by Residential.

d. The annual contributions and costs for Residential and Commercial under the optimal policy.

(LO 15-2, 3)   **15-48. Transfer Pricing: Performance Evaluation Issues**

LGA's Energy Division is operating at capacity. It has been asked by Products Division to supply it a thermal switch, which Energy sells to its regular customers for $72 each. Products, which is operating at 75 percent capacity, is willing to pay $48 each for the switch. Products will put the switch into a sensor that it is manufacturing on a cost-plus basis for a larger manufacturing firm, based in South America. Energy has a $40 variable cost of producing the switch.

The cost of the sensor as built by Products follows:

Purchased parts—outside vendors.	$216
Energy thermal switch	48
Other variable costs	135
Fixed overhead and administration	77
Total cost.	$476

Products Division believes that the price concession is necessary to get the job.

The company uses ROI and dollar profits in evaluating the division's and divisional manager's performance.

Required

a. If you were Energy Division's controller, would you recommend supplying the switch to Products Division? (Ignore any income tax issues.) Why or why not?

b. Would it be to the short-run economic advantage of LGA for Energy to supply Products with the switch at $48 each? (Ignore any income tax issues.) Explain your answer.

c. Discuss the organizational and managerial behavior difficulties, if any, inherent in this situation. As LGA's controller, what would you advise the corporation's president to do in this situation?

(CMA adapted)

(LO 15-2, 3)   **15-49. Evaluate Transfer Pricing System**

Fenton Supplies manufactures and sells food products for restaurants and other institutional food providers. Produce Division does both manufacturing (blending, canning, bottling) and storing of products until shipping. Produce Division workers then load trucks with products for distribution using third-party trucking companies to customers' regional distribution centers.

Fenton recently started a new enterprise, Logistics, which would focus on shipping alone, providing transportation services to both other Fenton divisions and third parties. The manager of Logistics proposes using the warehouse facility of Produce Division, at least to start. Produce Division employees would load the trucks for the Logistics business as well as the Produce Division business.

All divisions at Fenton are treated as profit centers with managers evaluated on division profit. The best estimates of the current warehouse activity and costs of Produce Division follow:

	Produce Division
Capacity (containers).	150,000
Produce Division activity (containers)	90,000
Variable costs (per container)	$8
Fixed costs	$2,400,000

Required

a. The current activity estimated for Logistics Division is 30,000 cases. The company has asked you to recommend a transfer price policy to implement. What transfer price would you recommend? Why?

b. How would the division manager for Produce Division likely respond? How would you answer?

c. The manager of a third division at Fenton Supplies has identified another opportunity and also proposes using the Produce Division facility. Estimated activity for this third division is expected to be 45,000 cases. How would you modify, if at all, your recommendation in requirement (*a*)?

15-50. Evaluate Transfer Price System   (LO 15-2, 3)

Norfolk, Inc. consists of three divisions—Tidal, Hill, and Wood—that operate as if they were independent companies. Each division has its own sales force and production facilities. Each division manager is responsible for sales, cost of operations, acquisition and financing of divisional assets, and working capital management. Norfolk corporate management evaluates the performance of each division and its managers on the basis of residual income using a cost-of-capital of 8 percent.

Wood Division has just been awarded a contract for a product that uses a component manufactured by outside suppliers as well as by Hill Division, which is operating well below capacity. Wood Division used a cost figure of $58 for the component in preparing its bid for the new product. Hill Division supplied this cost figure in response to Wood Division's request for the average variable cost of the component; it represents the standard variable manufacturing cost and variable marketing costs.

The regular selling price for the Hill Division component that Wood Division needs is $95. Hill Division's management indicated that it could supply Wood Division the required quantities of the component at the regular selling price less variable selling and distribution expenses. Wood Division's management responded by offering to pay standard variable manufacturing cost plus 25 percent.

The two divisions have been unable to agree on a transfer price. Corporate management has never established a transfer price policy. The corporate controller suggested a price equal to the standard full manufacturing cost (that is, no selling and distribution expenses) plus a 20 percent markup. The two division managers rejected this price because each considered it grossly unfair.

The unit cost structure for the Hill Division component and the suggested prices follow:

Costs	
Standard variable manufacturing cost.	$48
Standard fixed manufacturing cost.	17
Variable selling and distribution expenses	10
Total cost.	$75
Alternative transfer prices	
Regular selling price	$95
Regular selling price less variable selling and	
distribution expenses ($95 − $10).	85
Variable manufacturing plus 25% ($48 × 1.25)	60
Standard full manufacturing cost plus 20% ($65 × 1.20).	78

Required

a. Discuss the effect that each of the proposed prices could have on the attitude of Hill Division's management toward intracompany business.

b. Is the negotiation of a price between Hill Division and Wood Division a satisfactory method to solve the transfer price problem? Explain your answer.

c. Should Norfolk's corporate management become involved in this transfer price controversy? Explain your answer.

(CMA adapted)

(LO 15-4) **15-51. Transfer Prices and Tax Regulations: Ethical Issues**

Northfield Manufacturing has two operating divisions in a semiautonomous organizational structure. Americas Division, based in the United States, produces a specialized memory chip that is an
input to Asia Division, based in Japan. Americas Division uses idle capacity to produce the component, which has a domestic market price of $72. Its variable costs are $30 per unit. Northfield's
U.S. tax rate is 25 percent of income.

In addition to the transfer price for each component received from Americas, Asia
Division pays an $18-per-unit shipping fee. The chip becomes a part of its assembled product,
which costs an additional $12 to produce and sells for an equivalent of $138. Asia could purchase the component from an Asian supplier for $60 per unit. Northfield's tax rate in Japan
is 30 percent of income. Assume that Japanese tax laws permit transferring at either variable
cost or market price.

Required

a.   What transfer price is economically optimal for Northfield Manufacturing? Show computations.

b.   Is it ethical to choose a transfer price for tax purposes that is different from the transfer price
used to evaluate a business unit's performance?

c.   Suppose Northfield Manufacturing had a third operating division, APAC, in Singapore,
where the tax rate is below that of the United States. Would it be ethical for Northfield to use
different transfer prices for transactions between Americas and Asia and between Americas
and APAC?

(LO 15-5) **15-52. Segment Reporting**

Wager Enterprises has four operating divisions: Tours, Hotels, Concerts, and Ticket Services. Each
division is a separate segment for financial reporting purposes. Revenues and costs related to outside transactions were as follows for the past year (dollars in thousands):

	Tours	Hotels	Concerts	Ticket Services
Revenues	$8,840	$19,600	$ 7,120	$2,560
Costs	5,680	12,560	5,280	2,400

Tours Division participates in a "frequent explorer" program with Hotels Division.
During the past year, Tours reported that it traded lodging award coupons for tours that had
a retail value of $850,000, assuming that the tours were redeemed at full prices. Concerts
Division offered 20 percent discounts to Wager's tour customers and hotel guests. These discounts to tour customers were estimated to have a retail value of $240,000. Wager's hotel
guests redeemed $560,000 in concert discount coupons. The Hotels Division also provided
rooms for employees of the Tours Division (drivers and guides). The value of the rooms for
the year was $2.4 million.

Ticket Services Division sold tickets on behalf of Tours Division valued at $320,000 for the
year. This service for intracompany lodging was valued at $160,000. It also sold concert tickets for
Concerts; tickets for intracompany concert admission were valued at $80,000.

While preparing all of these data for financial statement presentation, Tour Division's controller stated that the value of the hotel rooms used for Tours Division employees should be based on
their differential and opportunity costs, not on the full price. This argument was based on the fact
that the hotel rooms are usually those that would otherwise be empty or sold at a discount. If the
differential and opportunity costs were used for this transfer price, the value would be $460,000
instead of $2.4 million. Hotel Division's controller made a similar argument concerning the con-
cert discount coupons. If the differential cost basis were used for the concert coupons, the transfer
price would be $80,000 instead of $560,000.

Wager Enterprises reports assets in each division as follows (dollars in thousands):

Tours	$30,800
Hotels	76,400
Concerts	25,680
Ticket Services.	5,200

Required

a.   Using the retail values for transfer pricing for segment reporting purposes, what are the operating profits for each Wager Enterprises division?

b.   What are the operating profits for each Wager Enterprises division using the differential cost basis for pricing transfers?

c.   Rank each division by ROI using the transfer pricing methods in requirements (*a*) and (*b*). What difference does the transfer pricing system have on the rankings?

15-53. Segment Reporting

(LO 15-5)

Grand Amusements, Inc. (GAI) has two operating divisions, Parks and Foods. The two divisions have a marketing agreement to provide incentives to customers. Parks Division offers vouchers good for meals at the restaurants of Foods Division, and Foods Division offers coupons for discounted admission at Parks Division amusement parks. Annual profits are $16.8 million. The two divisions meet the requirements for segment disclosures.

Before the transactions are considered, revenues and costs (in thousands of dollars) for the two divisions are as follows:

	Parks	Foods
Revenue	$21,000	$36,000
Costs	?	?
Profit	?	?

After adjusting appropriately for the effect of the marketing agreement, the revenues and costs are as follows:

	Parks	Foods
Revenues	?	?
Costs	$18,900	?
Profit	?	$13,200

The value of the vouchers issued by the Foods Division was 150 percent the value of the coupons issued by the Parks Division.

Required

What was the value of the coupons issued by Parks Division? By Foods Division?

15-54. Two-Part Transfer Prices

(LO 15-1, 2)

Radom Manufacturing produces various products. The company operates a landfill, which it uses to dispose of nonhazardous trash. The trash is hauled from the two nearby manufacturing facilities in trucks that can carry up to five tons of trash in a load. The landfill operation requires certain preparation activities regardless of the amount of trash in a truck (i.e., for each load). The budget for the landfill for next year follows:

Volume of trash	2,250 tons (450 loads)
Preparation costs (varies by loads)	$ 108,000
Other variable costs (varies by tons)	108,000
Fixed costs	270,000
Total budgeted costs	$486,000

Radom plans to make the landfill a profit center and charge the manufacturing plants for disposal of the trash. The landfill has sufficient capacity to operate for at least the next 20 years. Other landfills are available in the area (both private and municipal), and both Radom manufacturing plants would be free to decide which landfill to use.

Required

a. What transfer pricing rule should Radom implement at the landfill so that its plant managers would independently make decisions regarding landfill use that would be in the company's best interests?

b. Illustrate your rule by computing the transfer price that would be applied to a three-ton load of trash from one of the plants.

(LO 15-3)   **15-55. Budget versus Actual Costs**

Refer to the data in Problem 15-54. At the end of the year, the following data are available on actual operations at the landfill:

Volume of trash	1,875 tons (600 loads)
Preparation costs (per load)	$129,600
Other variable costs (per ton)	93,750
Fixed costs	266,400
Total actual costs	$489,750

Required

Based on the actual activities and costs, would you change the recommendation you made in Problem 15-54? Why or why not?

(LO 15-1, 2)   **15-56. Two-Part Transfer Prices**

Milner Technologies is a large, multidivision firm. One division, Testing, is well known inside Milner for its efficient information technology (IT). A smaller division, Energy, has approached Testing with a proposal that Testing provide IT support in the form of machine time for some of Energy's administrative work.

After an analysis of the demands that Energy would place on the system, the IT manager of Testing notes that Testing would have to lease a new server because of the additional load. The lease rates for the current server are a fixed annual lease of $2,600, and it averages machine time of 4,200 hours annually. The new server leases for an annual rate of $4,000. Because the new server is a faster machine, Testing can complete its current requirements in only 3,000 hours. The work for Energy is estimated to be 1,500 hours.

In addition to leasing a new server, there are two other changes Testing would have to make in IT. First, it will have to upgrade its server support position. The IT manager estimates that it will cost an additional $16,000 per year to get an individual with the necessary advanced training. In addition, Testing has a contract for service from the machine vendor. The support contract is a fixed-price contract of $2 per hour of machine usage. The current lease contract can be canceled at no cost if Testing leases a more expensive machine.

Required

a. Assume that no outside market exists for this service and that Testing would have excess capacity on the new server. What is the optimal transfer price rule Testing should use to charge Energy?

b. Suppose Energy uses 1,500 hours on the new machine. What is the average cost per hour Energy would pay using the rule you developed in requirement (a)?

c. Suppose Energy uses 150 hours on the new machine. What is the average cost per hour Energy would pay using the rule you developed in requirement (a)?

(LO 15-1, 2)   **15-57. Two-Part Transfer Prices**

Refer to Problem 15-56. Suppose Testing could sell time on the machine to other companies in the area on a per-hour basis. Further, it can sell all the time available for $22 per hour.

Required

a. What is the optimal transfer price rule Testing should use to charge Energy?

b. Suppose Energy uses 1,500 hours on the new machine. What is the average cost per hour Energy would pay using the rule you developed in requirement (a)?

c. Suppose Energy uses 150 hours on the new machine. What is the average cost per hour Energy would pay using the rule you developed in requirement (a)?

15-58. Transfer Prices—Analysis and Visualization   (LO 15-1, 2, 3)

Whipple Parts is organized in two divisions: Stamping and Assembly. Managers in both divisions are evaluated as profit centers using divisional income. All orders at Whipple come to Assembly Division. The company makes a single product, which is a specialized part. Production of the part begins in Stamping. The partially complete unit is transferred to Assembly, where other materials are added and the part is tested, packaged, and shipped. The transfer price is set quarterly.

Divisional income from the most recent quarter follows. Activity in the most recent quarter was 24,000 units, which is significantly below capacity.

	Stamping	Assembly
Revenues	$2,520,000	$4,176,000
Variable costs		
Materials	1,080,000	2,808,000
Labor	624,000	30,000
Overhead	96,000	13,000
Fixed costs	450,000	677,000
Total costs	$2,250,000	$3,528,000
Divisional income	$ 270,000	$ 648,000

Required

a. What was the transfer price applied in the most recent quarter?

b. Is the transfer price applied in the most recent quarter the optimal transfer price for managerial decision making? If it is, why? If not, what transfer price would you recommend?

c. Write a short memo explaining your recommendation in requirement (*b*), including support for the existing price, if that is your recommendation. Include visual support for your recommendation.

15-59. Transfer Prices—Analysis and Visualization   (LO 15-1, 2, 3)

Rogge Corporation makes a specialized sensor that is used in testing equipment. The company is organized in two divisions: Assembly and Shipping. Managers in both divisions are evaluated as profit centers using divisional income. Orders are received in Shipping. All orders consist of 100 units. If a customer wants 150, for example, an order of 200 units has to be placed. Each order is produced separately. The initial step in production takes place in Assembly, which then transfers the unfinished part to Shipping. Shipping conducts tests and calibration, applies labels identifying the customer and the date of shipment, and sends the part to the customer.

Production costs in Assembly consist of three factors. Setup costs of $10,000 are incurred for each order. Direct materials, direct labor, and variable overhead amount to $175 per unit. The third factor is fixed manufacturing overhead, which consists of depreciation ($1,800,000 annually) and fixed cash overhead ($640,000 annually). Production costs in Shipping are made up of direct labor ($100 per unit), variable overhead ($60 per unit), and fixed overhead of $2,400,000 annually.

Required

a. What is the optimal transfer price per unit for units transferred between Assembly and Shipping?

b. Write a short memo explaining your recommendation in requirement (*a*), including support for the existing price, if that is your recommendation. Include visual support for your recommendation.

INTEGRATIVE CASES

15-60. Custom Freight Systems (A): Transfer Pricing   (LO 15-1, 2, 3)

"We can't drop our prices below $210 per hundred pounds," exclaimed Greg Berman, manager of Forwarders, a division of Custom Freight Systems. "Our margins are already razor thin. Our costs just won't allow us to go any lower. Corporate rewards our division based on our profitability, and I won't lower my prices below $210."

Exhibit 15.6

Custom Freight Systems's Operations

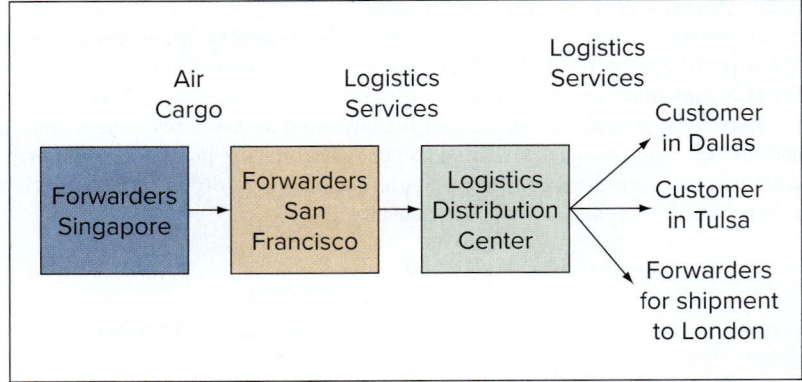

Custom Freight Systems is organized into three divisions: Air Cargo provides air cargo services, Logistics Services operates distribution centers and provides truck cargo services, and Forwarders provides international freight forwarding services (see Exhibit 15.6). Freight forwarders typically buy space on planes from international air cargo companies. This is analogous to a charter company that books seats on passenger planes and resells them to passengers. In many cases, freight forwarders hire trucking companies to transport the cargo from the plane to the domestic destination.

Management believes that the three divisions integrate well and are able to provide customers with one-stop transportation services. For example, a Forwarders branch in Singapore would receive cargo from a shipper, prepare the necessary documentation, and then ship the cargo on Air Cargo to a domestic Forwarders station. The domestic Forwarders station would ensure that the cargo passes through customs and would ship it to the final destination with Logistics Services as in Exhibit 15.6.

Management evaluates each division separately and rewards divisional managers based on profit and return on investment (ROI). Responsibility and decision-making authority are decentralized. Similarly, each division has a sales and marketing organization. Divisional salespeople report to the vice president of operations for Custom Freight Systems. See Exhibit 15.7. Custom Freight Systems believes that it successfully motivates divisional managers by paying bonuses for high divisional profits.

Recently, the Logistics division needed to prepare a bid for a customer. The customer had freight to import from an overseas supplier and wanted Logistics to submit a bid for a distribution package that included supplying air freight, receiving the freight and providing customs clearance services at the airport, warehousing, and then distributing packages to customers.

Because this was a contract for international shipping, Logistics needed to contact different freight forwarders for shipping quotes. Logistics requested quotes from Forwarders and United Systems, a competing freight forwarder. Divisions of Custom Freight Systems are free to use the most appropriate and cost-effective suppliers.

Logistics received bids of $210 per hundred pounds from Forwarders and $185 per hundred pounds from United Systems. Forwarders specified in its bid that it will use Air Cargo, a division of Custom Freight Systems. Forwarders's variable costs were $175 per hundred pounds, which included the cost of subcontracting air transportation. Air Cargo, which was experiencing a period of excess capacity, quoted Forwarders the market rate of $155. Typically, Air Cargo's variable costs are 60 percent of the market rate.

The price difference between the two different bids alarmed Susan Burns, a contract manager at Logistics. She knows this is a competitive business and is concerned because the difference between the high and low bids was at least $1 million (current projections for the contract estimated 4,160,000 pounds during the first year). Susan contacted Greg Berman, the manager of Forwarders, and discussed the quote. "Don't you think full markup is unwarranted due to the fact that you and the airlines have so much excess capacity?" she asked.

Susan soon realized that Greg was not going to drop the price quote. "You know how small the margins in this business are. Why should I cut my margins even smaller just to make you look good?" he asked.

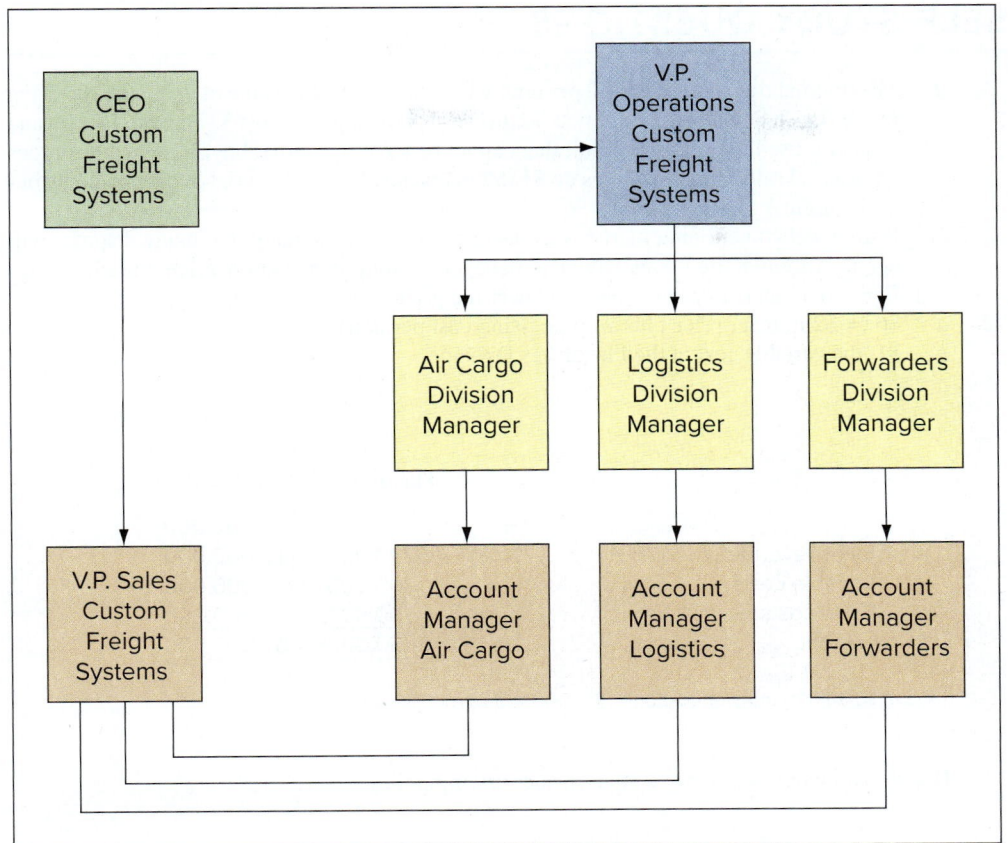

Exhibit 15.7

Organization Chart—
Custom Freight Systems

Susan went to Bennie Espinosa, vice president of operations for Custom Freight Systems and chairperson for the corporate strategy committee. "That does sound strange," he said. "I need to examine the overall cost structure and talk to Greg. I'll get back to you by noon Monday."

Required

a.   Which bid should the Logistics Services division accept—the internal bid from the Forwarders division or the external bid from United Systems?

b.   What should the transfer price be on this transaction?

c.   What should Bennie Espinosa do?

d.   Do the reward systems for divisional managers support the best interests of both the Forwarders division and Custom Freight Systems? Give examples that support your conclusion.

(Prepared by Thomas B. Rumzie under the direction of Michael W. Maher.
© Copyright Michael W. Maher, 2017.)

15-61. Custom Freight Systems (B): Transfer Pricing   (LO 15-1, 2, 3)

Assume that all of the information is the same as in Integrative Case 15-60, but instead of receiving only one outside bid, Logistics Services receives two. The new bid is from World Services for $195 per hundred pounds. World has offered to use Air Cargo for transporting packages. Air Cargo will charge World $155 per hundred pounds. The bids from Forwarders and United Systems remain the same as in Integrative Case 15-60, $210 and $185, respectively.

Required

Which bid should Logistics Services take? Why?

(Prepared by Thomas B. Rumzie under the direction of Michael W. Maher.
© Copyright Michael W. Maher, 2023.)

SOLUTIONS TO SELF-STUDY QUESTIONS

1.   *a.*   The optimal transfer price is $2 per unit, which represents the value of using the flavoring in the Foods Division of Elmhurst because the flavoring will cost $1 to manufacture and each unit used internally is a unit that cannot be sold to external buyers. When it forgoes an external sale, Elmhurst gives up $1 ($2 in revenue less $1 of variable cost) in contribution margin.

    b.   With a well-functioning market such as this one, it is less likely that many disputes will occur. Although the Foods Division manager would prefer a lower price, the Flavorings Division manager has no reason to lower the price.

2.   *a.* $6 (= $2 transfer price plus $4 processing cost per unit).

    b. $1, the variable cost in the Flavorings Division.

    c.

	Flavorings	Foods
Units	200,000	200,000
Sales revenue	$200,000	$2,000,000
Variable costs	200,000	1,000,000[a]
Fixed costs	50,000	200,000
Profit	$ (50,000)	$ 800,000

[a] $200,000 transfer cost plus 200,000 × $4 processing cost.

3.   Divisional income assuming a dual transfer pricing policy.

	Milk Division	Cheese Division	Canyon Dairies
Units	100,000	100,000	
Sales revenue	$5,000,000[a]	$12,000,000[b]	$12,000,000[b]
Variable costs			
Transfer	–0–	2,000,000[c]	–0–
Directly incurred	2,000,000[c]	3,000,000[d]	5,000,000[e]
Fixed costs	2,000,000	4,000,000	6,000,000
Profit	$1,000,000	$ 3,000,000	$ 1,000,000

[a] $50 × 100,000.
[b] $120 × 100,000.
[c] $20 × 100,000.
[d] $30 × 100,000.
[e] $2,000,000 + $3,000,000.

4.   If the tax rates are the same, the transfer price will not affect tax liability. At a $20 million transfer price, the tax liability is as follows:

	United States	Puerto Rico
Sales revenue	$20,000,000	$50,000,000
Third-party costs	20,000,000	5,000,000
Transferred goods costs		20,000,000
Taxable income	$ –0–	$25,000,000
Tax rate	25%	25%
Tax liability	$ –0–	$ 6,250,000
Total tax liability	$6,250,000	

At a $45 million transfer price:

	United States	Puerto Rico
Sales revenue.	$45,000,000	$50,000,000
Third-party costs	20,000,000	5,000,000
Transferred goods costs.		45,000,000
Taxable income	$25,000,000	$ –0–
Tax rate	25%	25%
Tax liability	$ 6,250,000	$ –0–
Total tax liability	$6,250,000	

16

Chapter Sixteen

Fundamentals of Variance Analysis

LEARNING OBJECTIVES

After reading this chapter, you should be able to:

LO 16-1 Use budgets for performance evaluation.

LO 16-2 Develop and use flexible budgets.

LO 16-3 Compute and interpret the sales activity variance.

LO 16-4 Prepare and use a profit variance analysis.

LO 16-5 Compute and use variable cost variances.

LO 16-6 Compute and use fixed cost variances.

LO 16-7 (Appendix) Understand how to record costs in a standard costing system.

For the second month in a row, profits at our Peak Division are down and I don't know why. We budgeted $190,000 in profit for August, but the actual result was only $114,500. We thought we had developed realistic monthly budgets. I know sales were down some, but I'm not sure that is the only problem there is.

What I need to know is whether we should focus on improving the marketing of the division or if we need to take a look at our production activities there. I have asked Claudia [Ramos, the president of Peak] to identify the primary cause of the shortfall—revenues or costs—and report back to me next week. If Peak can't improve, we may have to dispose of it.

Keith Hunter, the CFO of Brunswick, Inc., was discussing his concern about the performance of the company's Peak Division. Brunswick purchased Peak just over one year ago in hopes of building some synergies between Brunswick's specialty supplements and Peak's sole product, an energy drink popular with students and young adults. The Peak Division operates as a profit center. The synergies have been slow to develop. In addition, Peak's profit performance has been disappointing and Peak's management has been under considerable pressure to show improvement.

Using Budgets for Performance Evaluation

In Chapter 13, we described the development of the master budget as a first step in the budgetary planning and control cycle. The budgeting process provides a means to coordinate activities among units of the organization, to communicate the organization's goals to individual units, and to ensure that adequate resources are available to carry out the planned activities. Typically, the budget is set prior to the beginning of the accounting period, although it is common for budgets to be revised during the accounting period as major changes in operations are encountered (e.g., large changes in expected sales).

While this planning aspect of budgets is important, it is not the only role that budgets can play. In the control and evaluation activity, the performance of units and managers is evaluated and actions are taken in an attempt to improve performance. As we discussed in Chapter 14, evaluation requires a benchmark against which to measure performance. When evaluating a firm's performance, it is common to select other firms in the same industry as benchmarks. Financial performance, as reported in publicly available accounting records, is one measure of performance. For units of the firm or for organizations that don't routinely prepare public reports (for example, government organizations and not-for-profit firms), these benchmarks are much more difficult to collect. One obvious alternative is the budget; this is management's plan for financial performance.

The master budget includes **operating budgets** (for example, the budgeted income statement, the production budget, the budgeted cost of goods sold) and **financial budgets** (for example, the cash budget, the budgeted balance sheet). When management uses the master budget for control purposes, it focuses on the key items that must be controlled to ensure the company's success. Most of these items are in the operating budgets, although some also appear in the financial budgets. In this chapter, we focus on the income statement because it is the most important financial statement that managers use to control operations.

When actual results are compared to budgeted, or planned, results, there is almost always a difference, or **variance.** Variance analysis uses the difference between actual performance and budgeted performance to

1. Evaluate the performance of individuals and business units.
2. Identify possible sources of deviations between budgeted and actual performance.

LO 16-1
Use budgets for performance evaluation.

operating budgets
Budgeted income statement, production budget, budgeted cost of goods sold, and supporting budgets.

financial budgets
Budgets of financial resources—for example, the cash budget and the budgeted balance sheet.

variance
Difference between planned result and actual outcome.

As with all management accounting practices, firms and organizations may develop many variances for their own needs. The basic idea, however, is always the same:

1. Calculate the difference between actual performance and a planned (budgeted) number.
2. Attempt to explain the causes of the difference.

Profit Variance

The simplest measure of performance is the variance, or difference, between actual income and budgeted income. Peak's profit variance, for example, is $75,500. That is the actual profit of $114,500 less the budgeted profit of $190,000. Because actual income was less than budgeted income, this is typically referred to as an *unfavorable variance*. For evaluation purposes, we could stop here and say that Peak's performance did not meet expectations because actual income was less than budgeted. However, this does not provide much information about the causes of its actual performance. We want to look more closely at the information available and try to use it to obtain more insight into operations.

See Exhibit 16.1 for Peak Division's actual income statement and the master budget for August. The master budget represents the financial plan for Peak for the month, and the actual results reflect the performance.

Before we analyze the variances in more detail, it is important to understand what the labels "favorable" and "unfavorable" mean. Traditionally, they are used to indicate how actual income differs from budgeted income. That is,

favorable variance
Variance that, taken alone, results in an addition to operating profit.

- A **favorable variance** increases operating profits.
- An **unfavorable variance** decreases operating profits.

unfavorable variance
Variance that, taken alone, reduces operating profit.

Thus, when discussing revenue, income, or contribution margin, a favorable variance means the actual result is greater than the budgeted result. When discussing costs, a favorable variance indicates that actual costs are less than budgeted costs. The labels "favorable" and "unfavorable" should not be considered as indications of good or bad performance without additional investigation:

- A favorable variance is not necessarily good.
- An unfavorable variance is not necessarily bad.

Exhibit 16.1

Budget and Actual Results, August—Peak Division

	A	B	C	D
1		Actual	Master Budget	
2	Sales (units)	80,000	100,000	
3				
4	Sales revenue	$ 840,000	$ 1,000,000[a]	
5	Less			
6	Variable costs			
7	Variable manufacturing costs	329,680	380,000[b]	
8	Variable selling and administrative	68,000	90,000[c]	
9	Total variable costs	$ 397,680	$ 470,000	
10	Contribution margin	$ 442,320	$ 530,000	
11	Fixed costs			
12	Fixed manufacturing overhead	195,500	200,000	
13	Fixed selling and administrative costs	132,320	140,000	
14	Total fixed costs	$ 327,820	$ 340,000	
15	Profit	$ 114,500	$ 190,000	
16				
17	Calculation for master budget:			
18	[a]100,000 units at $ 10.00 per unit.			
19	[b]100,000 units at $ 3.80 per unit.			
20	[c]100,000 units at $ 0.90 per unit.			
21				

When a Favorable Variance Might Not Mean "Good" News   *Business Application*

Although it is common to consider favorable variances as good news, we should recognize that any variance represents a difference from what we expected (the budget or standard). When a unit or a firm reports higher-than-expected profits, it is important to understand why. It might be that the managers found more efficient ways to operate or a marketing campaign was more successful than expected. If so, it would be important to share this with other units. It could also be that managers have found ways to manipulate operations or reported financial results to make performance look better than it really is. It is not uncommon when accounting fraud cases come to light that supervisors were surprised given the "favorable" results that the guilty managers had generated.

Another possibility is that the favorable results this period point to future events that will depress profits. One example is the health insurance industry during the COVID-19 pandemic.

The profits of one insurer, UnitedHealth Group, doubled in one quarter. The reason?

> . . . [E]lective procedures the large health insurer pays for were postponed or delayed amid the spread of the Coronavirus strain Covid-19.

In this case, executives at UnitedHealth Group recognized that this profit windfall did not indicate future good news.

> . . . UnitedHealth Group didn't raise its earnings expectations or change its 2020 financial guidance as the health insurer braced for patients to seek care later this year and into 2021 that might even be more costly than anticipated.

Source: Japsen, Bruce, "UnitedHealth Group Doubles Profits as Patients Defer Care in Pandemic," Forbes.com, July 15, 2020. https://www.forbes.com/sites/brucejapsen/2020/07/15/unitedhealth-group-profits-double-as-patients-defer-treatment-in-pandemic/?sh=53b99087506c.

Although the fact that profit is $75,500 below budget provides some information, it does not indicate where the managers at Peak should look for improvement. At a more detailed level, we can compute the variance of each income statement line item (see Exhibit 16.2). Notice that the data in the Variance column of Exhibit 16.2 provides information useful for understanding the source of the difference between planned and realized profit performance. Although a simple comparison of planned and actual profit suggests that performance was worse than planned, the additional data in Exhibit 16.2 provide information on the impact on profit performance of each of the revenue and cost categories.

This information can be useful for two reasons. First, it allows the manager to investigate more efficiently the causes of off-budget performance. That is, the manager can analyze those areas with a relatively large variance and, if the investigation identifies the

	A	B	C	D	E
1		Actual	Variance		Master Budget
2	Sales (units)	80,000	20,000	U	100,000
3					
4	Sales revenue	$ 840,000	$ 160,000	U	$ 1,000,000
5	Less				
6	Variable costs				
7	Variable manufacturing costs	329,680	50,320	F	380,000
8	Variable selling and administrative	68,000	22,000	F	90,000
9	Total variable costs	$ 397,680	$ 72,320	F	$ 470,000
10	Contribution margin	$ 442,320	$ 87,680	U	$ 530,000
11	Fixed costs				
12	Fixed manufacturing overhead	195,500	4,500	F	200,000
13	Fixed selling and administrative costs	132,320	7,680	F	140,000
14	Total fixed costs	$ 327,820	$ 12,180	F	$ 340,000
15	Profit	$ 114,500	$ 75,500	U	$ 190,000
16					
17	U = Unfavorable variance.				
18	F = Favorable variance.				
19					

Exhibit 16.2

Budget and Actual Results, August—Peak Division

problem and it can be corrected, the organization will be more likely to improve its per-formance in the following period. Second, the information allows the manager to evalu-ate subordinate managers responsible for various aspects of the firm's operations (for example, marketing and production).

Why Are Actual and Budgeted Results Different?

The decomposition of the profit variance into revenue and cost components is more infor-mative than the simple profit variance itself, but it does not give information that would be useful for control purposes. Managers at Peak want to know how they should change its marketing or production operations to improve results. In other words, managers want to know *why* the individual line items in Exhibit 16.2 differ. An important part of variance analysis is understanding, first, what might cause a difference between actual and budgeted results and, second, what portion of the total profit variance is due to each cause.

Flexible Budgeting

LO 16-2

Develop and use flexible budgets.

static budget
Budget for a single activity level; usually the master budget.

flexible budget
Budget that indicates revenues, costs, and profits for different levels of activity.

flexible budget line
Expected monthly costs at different output levels.

One obvious reason that actual results might differ from budgeted results is that the actual activity itself sometimes differs from the budgeted or expected activity. A master budget presents a comprehensive view of anticipated operations. Such a budget is typi-cally a **static budget;** that is, it is developed in detail for one level of anticipated activity. A **flexible budget,** in contrast, indicates budgeted revenues, costs, and profits for virtu-ally all feasible levels of activities. Because variable costs and revenues change with changes in activity levels, these amounts are budgeted to be different at each activity level in the flexible budget.

For example, by reviewing the master budget information in Exhibits 16.1 and 16.2, we see that the total cost of producing and selling 100,000 units (cases) of the energy drink at Peak is $810,000. This consists of $470,000 in variable costs and $340,000 in fixed costs. In developing the budget, Peak used the following budgeting formula to determine costs at the master budget level:

$$\text{Total cost} = \$340,000 + (\$4.70 \times \text{Units produced and sold})$$

Total variable costs are $470,000 for 100,000 units, or $4.70 per unit. See Exhibit 16.3 for a graph of this cost function. This is the same type of cost line used for the cost-volume-profit (CVP) analysis that we described in Chapter 3. The expected activity level for the period is budgeted at 100,000 units. From the **flexible budget line** in Exhibit 16.3, we find the budgeted costs at a planned activity of 100,000 units to be $810,000 [= $340,000 + ($4.70 × 100,000 units)].

At first glance, it might appear that the division had done a good job of cost con-trol because actual costs were $84,500 lower than the budget plan (variable costs were $72,320 lower and fixed costs were $12,180 lower). In fact, Peak actually produced and sold only 80,000 units. According to the flexible budget concept, the master budget must be adjusted for this change in activity. The adjusted budgeted costs for control and per-formance evaluation purposes would be the flexible budget for actual activity, $716,000 [= $340,000 + ($4.70 × 80,000 units)], which is *less* than the actual costs.

The estimated cost-volume line in Exhibit 16.3 is known as the *flexible budget line* because it shows the budgeted costs allowed for each level of activity. For example, if activity increased to 120,000 units, budgeted costs would be $904,000 [= $340,000 + ($4.70 × 120,000 units)]. If activity dropped to 50,000 units, budgeted costs would drop to $575,000 [= $340,000 + ($4.70 × 50,000 units)].

You can compare the master budget with the flexible budget by thinking of the mas-ter budget as an ex-ante (before-the-fact) prediction of the activity (*X*); the flexible bud-get is based on ex-post (after-the-fact) knowledge of the actual activity.

Exhibit 16.3   Flexible Budget Line Costs—Peak Division

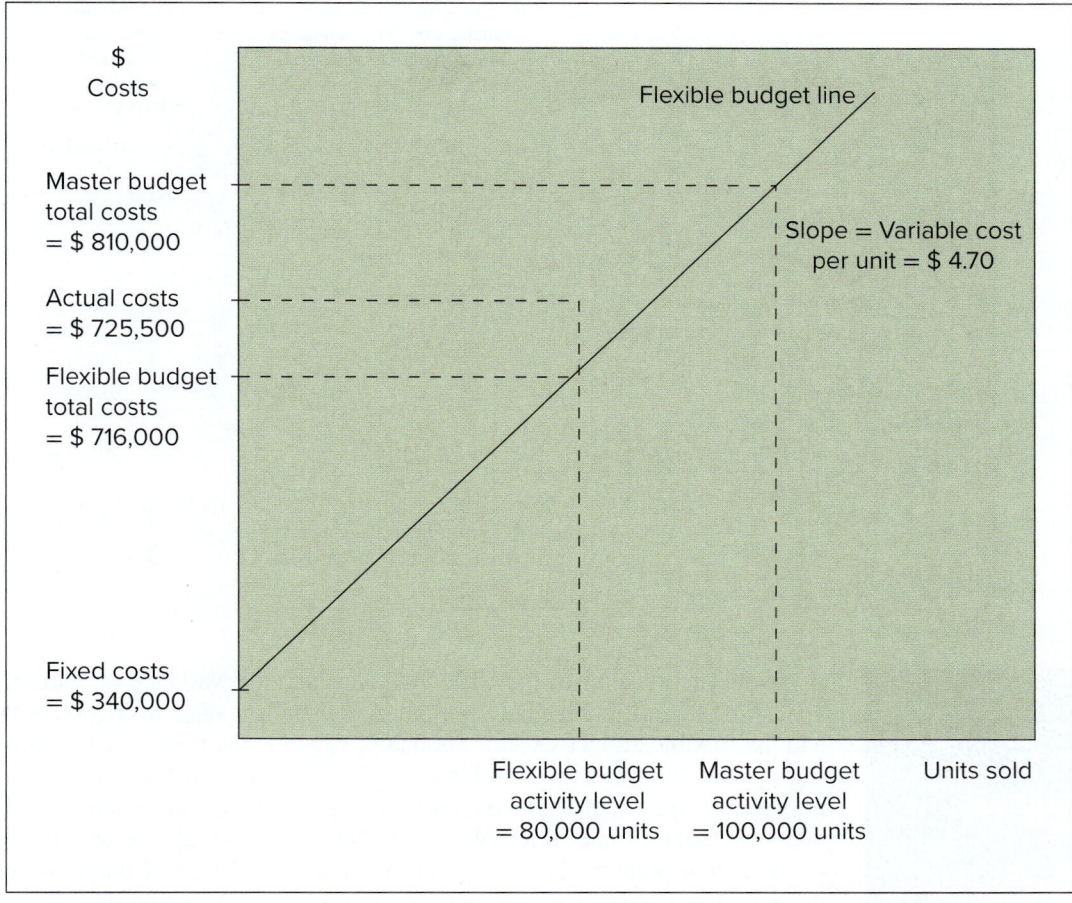

Comparing Budgets and Results

A comparison of the master budget with the flexible budget and with actual results is the basis for analyzing differences between plans and actual performance. The flexible budget (see Exhibit 16.4) is based on *actual* activity. In August, Peak actually produced and sold 80,000 units. We start by understanding the difference in operating profits that results from the sales activity at Peak.

Sales Activity Variance

The difference between operating profits in the master budget and operating profits in the flexible budget is called a **sales activity variance.** The $106,000 unfavorable variance is due to the activity that resulted in a 20,000-unit difference between actual sales and planned sales.

The information in Exhibit 16.4 is useful for management. First, it isolates the decrease in operating profits caused by the decrease in activity from the master budget. Furthermore, the resulting flexible budget shows budgeted sales, costs, and operating profits *after* considering the activity decrease but *before* considering differences in *unit* selling prices, variable costs, and fixed costs from the master budget. As noted, we refer to this change from the master budget plan as the sales activity variance, also known as *sales volume variance.*

sales activity variance
Difference between operating profit in the master budget and operating profit in the flexible budget that arises because the actual number of units sold is different from the budgeted number; also known as sales volume variance.

Exhibit 16.4

Flexible and Master Budget, August—Peak Division

	A	B	C	D	E
1		Flexible Budget (based on actual activity of 80,000 units)	Sales Activity Variance (based on variance in sales volume)		Master Budget (based on planned activity of 100,000 units)
2	Sales units	80,000	20,000		100,000
3					
4	Sales revenue	$ 800,000	$ 200,000	U	$ 1,000,000
5	Less				
6	Variable costs				
7	Variable manufacturing costs	304,000	76,000	F	380,000
8	Variable selling and administrative	72,000	18,000	F	90,000
9	Total variable costs	$ 376,000	$ 94,000	F	$ 470,000
10	Contribution margin	$ 424,000	$ 106,000	U	$ 530,000
11	Fixed costs				
12	Fixed manufacturing overhead	200,000	–0–		200,000
13	Fixed selling and administrative costs	140,000	–0–		140,000
14	Total fixed costs	$ 340,000	–0–		$ 340,000
15	Profit	$ 84,000	$ 106,000	U	$ 190,000
16					

When sales fall and plants reduce production, manufacturing costs decrease. Companies compute a sales activity variance to distinguish between lower sales and increased manufacturing efficiency as explanations for the lower reported costs.
Steve Allen/Brand X Pictures/Getty Images

Note the makeup of the $106,000 sales activity variance in Exhibit 16.4. First, the difference between the master budget sales of $1,000,000 and the flexible budget sales of $800,000, which is the budgeted $10 unit sales price multiplied by the 80,000 units actually sold, is $200,000. This is based on the 20,000-unit decrease in sales volume multiplied by the budgeted $10 unit sales price. We use the *budgeted* unit sales price instead of the *actual* price because we want to isolate the impact of the activity decrease from changes in the sales price. We want to focus on the effects of volume alone. Thus, the sales amount in the flexible budget is *not the actual revenue* (actual price times actual volume) but the *budgeted unit sales price times the actual number of units sold.* Second, variable costs are *expected* to decrease by $94,000, giving an unfavorable contribution margin of $106,000 (= $200,000 − $94,000), which is the unfavorable sales activity variance.

Interpreting Variances   Holding everything else constant, the 20,000-unit decrease in sales creates an unfavorable sales activity variance as shown in Exhibit 16.4. Does this indicate poor performance? Perhaps it does not. Economic conditions could have been worse than planned, decreasing the volume demanded by the market. Hence, perhaps, the 20,000-unit decrease in sales volume could have been even greater, taking everything into account.

Note that both variable cost variances are labeled *favorable,* but this doesn't mean that they are good for the company. Variable costs are expected to decrease when volume is lower than planned.

Self-Study Question

1. Prepare a flexible budget for Peak Division for August with the same master budget as in Exhibit 16.4 but assuming that 110,000 units were actually sold.

The solution to this question is at the end of the chapter.

Profit Variance Analysis as a Key Tool for Managers

The **profit variance analysis** shows additional detail about the differences between budgeted profits and actual profits earned. The actual results can be compared with both the flexible budget and the master budget in a profit variance analysis (Exhibit 16.5). Columns (5), (6), and (7) are carried forward from Exhibit 16.4.

Column (1) is the reported income statement based on the actual sales (see Exhibit 16.1). Column (2) summarizes manufacturing (production) variances, which are discussed in more detail later in this chapter, and Column (3) shows marketing and administrative variances. Costs have been divided into fixed and variable portions here and would be presented in more detail to the managers of centers having responsibility for them.

Cost variances result from deviations in input prices and efficiencies in operating the company. They are important for measuring productivity and helping to control costs.

profit variance analysis
Analysis of the causes of differences between budgeted profits and the actual profits earned.

Sales Price Variance

The **sales price variance,** Column (4) in Exhibit 16.5, is derived from the *difference between the actual revenue and budgeted selling price multiplied by the actual number of units sold* [$40,000 = ($840,000 − {$10 × 80,000 units})]. This is equivalent, of course, to the difference between the average actual selling price ($10.50 = $840,000 ÷ 80,000 units) and the budgeted selling price ($10) multiplied by the actual quantity sold [= $40,000 = ($10.50 − $10) × 80,000 units].

sales price variance
Difference between actual revenue and actual units sold multiplied by budgeted selling price.

Variable Production Cost Variances

Be careful to distinguish the variable cost variances in Columns (2) and (3) of Exhibit 16.5, which are *input* variances, from the variable cost variances in Column (6), which are part of the *sales activity* variance. Management expects the costs in the flexible budget to be lower than the master budget, creating a sales activity variance, because the sales volume is lower than planned.

As indicated in Column (5), variable production costs *should have been* $304,000 for a production and sales volume of 80,000 units, not $380,000 as expressed in the master budget in Column (7). Column (1) indicates that the *actual* variable production costs were $329,680, or $50,320 (= $76,000 F − $25,680 U) lower than the master budget, but $25,680 higher than the flexible budget. Which number should be used to evaluate production cost control, the $50,320 F variance from the master budget or the $25,680 U variance from the flexible budget?

The number to use to evaluate production performance is the $25,680 U variance from the flexible budget. This points out a benefit of flexible budgeting. A superficial comparison of the master budget plan with the actual results would have indicated a favorable variance of $50,320. In fact, production is actually responsible for an unfavorable variance of $25,680, which is caused by deviation from production norms. We discuss the source of this $25,680 in more detail in the following section.

Fixed Production Cost Variance

The fixed production cost variance is simply the difference between actual and budgeted costs. Fixed costs are treated as period costs here; they should not be affected by activity levels within a relevant range. Hence, the flexible budget's fixed costs equal the master budget's fixed costs.

Marketing and Administrative Variances

Marketing and administrative costs are treated like production costs. Variable costs are expected to change as activity changes; hence, variable costs were expected to decrease

Exhibit 16.5 Profit Variance Analysis, August—Peak Division

	A	B	C	D	E	F	G	H	I	J	K	L	M
1		(1)	(2)			(3)		(4)		(5)	(6)		(7)
2		Actual (based on actual activity of 80,000 units)	Manufacturing Variances			Marketing and Administrative Variances		Sales Price Variance		Flexible Budget (based on actual activity of 80,000 units)	Sales Activity Variance		Master Budget (based on planned activity of 100,000 units)
3	Sales revenue	$ 840,000						$ 40,000	F	$ 800,000	$ 200,000	U	$ 1,000,000
4	Less												
5	Variable costs												
6	Variable manufacturing costs	329,680	$ 25,680	U	a					304,000	76,000	F	380,000
7	Variable selling and administrative	68,000				$ 4,000	F			72,000	18,000	F	90,000
8	Contribution margin	$ 442,320	$ 25,680	U		$ 4,000	F	$ 40,000	F	$ 424,000	$ 106,000	U	$ 530,000
9	Fixed costs												
10	Fixed manufacturing overhead	195,500	4,500	F						200,000	–0–		200,000
11	Fixed selling and administrative costs	132,320				7,680	F			140,000	–0–		140,000
12	Profit	$ 114,500	$ 21,180	U		$ 11,680	F	$ 40,000	F	$ 84,000	$ 106,000	U	$ 190,000
13													
14	aThe individual cost variances are shown in Exhibit 16.11.												
15													

by $18,000 between the flexible and master budgets (Exhibit 16.5) because volume decreased by 20,000 units. The $4,000 favorable variance for variable marketing and administrative costs must be caused by factors other than sales activity. Comparing actual costs with the flexible budget reveals a $7,680 favorable variance for fixed marketing and administrative costs. Fixed marketing and administrative costs do not change as volume changes; hence, the flexible and master budget amounts are the same.

Visualizing Profit Variances

Recall that Keith Hunter, the CEO of Brunswick, Inc., wanted to understand the role of revenues versus costs in explaining the disappointing financial results. The variance analysis we just completed will allow Claudia Ramos, the president of Peak Division, to answer this question. Rather than just presenting the results in Exhibit 16.5, however, she decides to prepare the information in visual form to highlight the key findings. Her visualization is shown in Exhibit 16.6, which shows the relative effect of sales versus operating costs on Division profits.

Although the information in Exhibit 16.6 answers the question about sales versus costs in the impact on profit, it is not particularly informative. A fuller picture is possible using the information in Exhibit 16.5. Exhibit 16.7 breaks down the sales and cost information into components to help managers focus attention on areas that might be worthwhile looking at to improve results.

As we see in Exhibit 16.7, the largest variances are sales and variable manufacturing costs. For sales, this includes both the sales activity variance, which is unfavorable, and sales price variance, which is favorable. By comparison, the other variances (fixed manufacturing costs, and marketing and administration costs) are small (and favorable). In Chapter 17, we consider the sales activity variance in more detail to determine whether the unfavorable variance is due to a decline in activity in the industry or to a reduced market share (or both). A general decline in industrial volume is generally more difficult for the firm to overcome. One last possibility is that with a favorable price variance, it might be that the higher price led to sales declines sufficiently large that the overall effect was to reduce profits.

Exhibit 16.6   Visualization of Variances Results for Peak Division

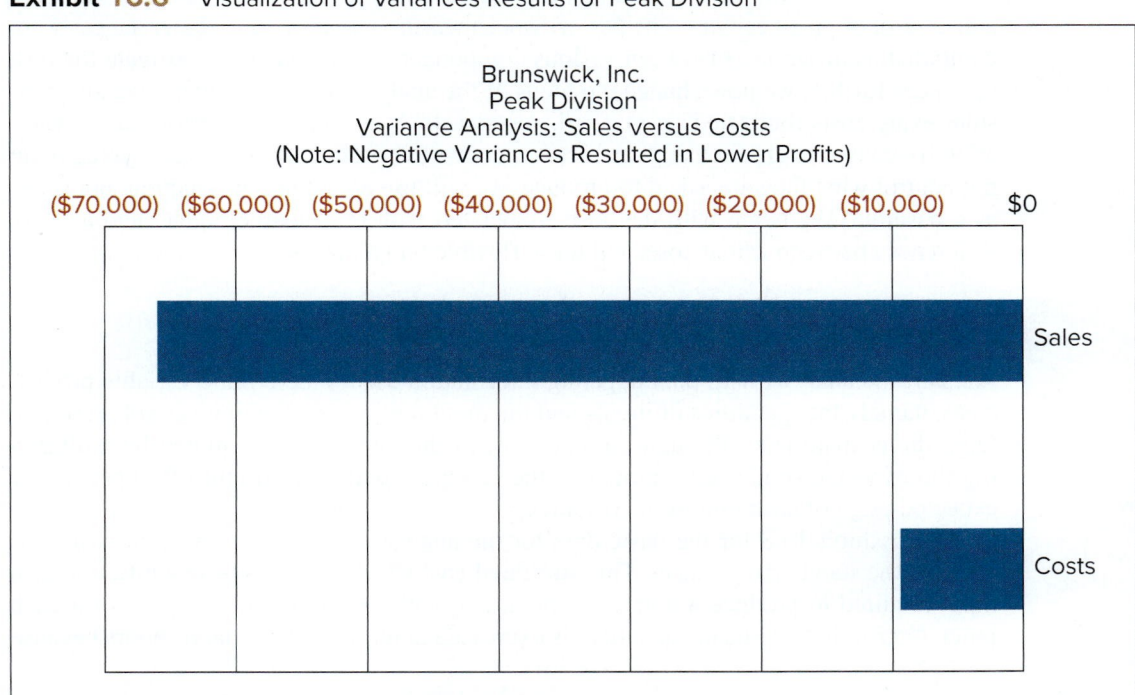

Exhibit 16.7   Visualization of Variances Results for Peak Division: Variances by Profit Category

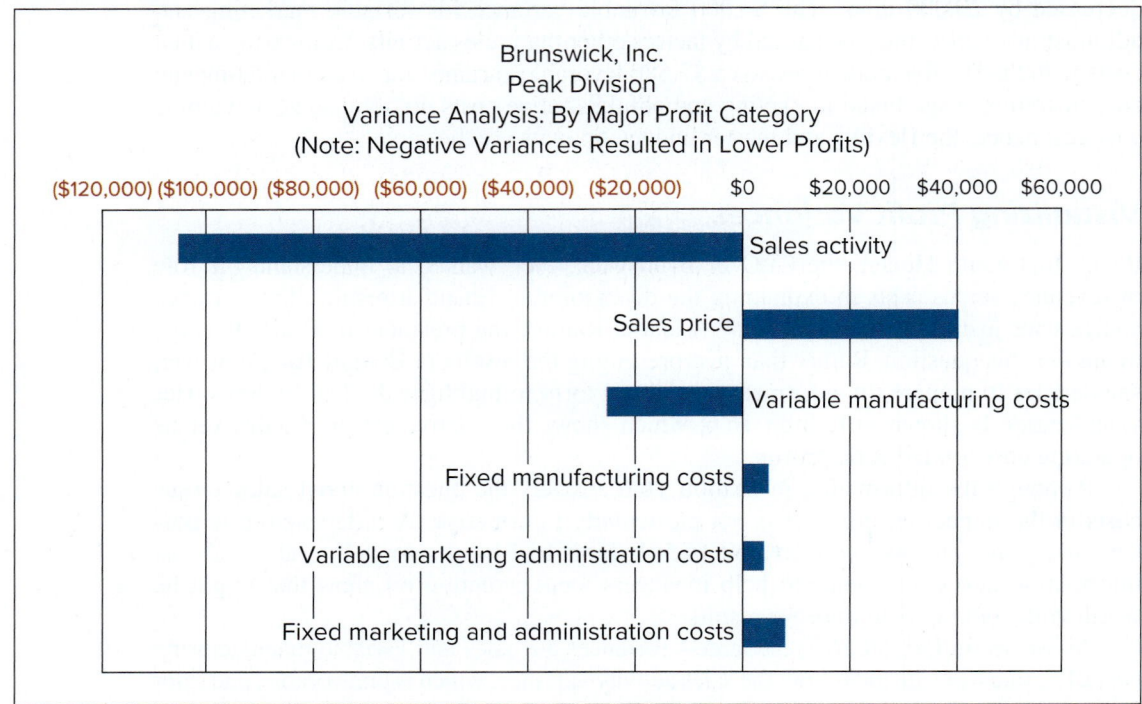

In the next section, we consider the manufacturing cost variances in more detail in a way that provides managers information they can use to identify and possible areas for improvement.

Performance Measurement and Control in a Cost Center

Before this point, we have considered the measurement of variances for the evaluation and control of profit centers. The performance measure was profit and the variances were computed as differences between various components of profits. To investigate the cost variances further, we now change the focus of the analysis to a cost center level and consider using costs (budgeted, or planned, versus actual) as a basis for performance evaluation. Because we are focusing on cost centers whose production managers typically do not control what they are asked to produce, we will use actual unit production, not sales, as a baseline. We begin with the costs associated with the flexible budget and analyze differences between actual costs and these flexible budget costs.

Variable Production Costs

We start the analysis with the budgeting information used to determine variable product costs, namely the quantities of inputs and the input unit prices. For any variable resource (e.g., direct materials), the unit variable cost in the budget is determined by multiplying the expected (budgeted) amount of the resource used in each unit of output by the expected price of each unit of the resource.

standard cost sheet
Form providing standard quantities of inputs used to produce a unit of output and the standard prices for the inputs.

See Exhibit 16.8 for the basic data for the analysis of Peak's production cost variances in the standard cost sheet. This **standard cost sheet** provides the quantities of each input required to produce a unit of output along with the budgeted unit prices for each input. Notice that overhead "quantity" is expressed in terms of direct labor-hours because

Input	(1) Standard Quantity of Input per Unit of Output	(2) Standard Input Price or Rate per Unit of Input	(3) Standard Cost per Unit of Output (Case)
Direct material	4 pounds	$ 0.55 per pound	$2.20
Direct labor.	0.05 hour	20.00 per hour	1.00
Variable overhead.	0.05 hour	12.00 per hour	0.60
Total variable manufacturing costs. . .			$3.80

Exhibit 16.8

Standard Cost Sheet, Variable Manufacturing Costs, August—Peak Division

that is what is being used to apply the overhead. Thus, the standard cost per unit of input for overhead is really the standard labor-based burden rate.

Direct Materials
Peak determines the standard price of the materials it uses to make the drink as follows. For simplicity we assume that a single material (powder) is used and each unit of drink requires 4 pounds of this powder. Peak's purchasing manager estimates that the cost of powder with the correct specifications and quality should be $0.55 per pound. The $0.55 is the standard price for a unit of input, not output. The standard materials cost for a unit of output, a case of the drink, is $2.20 (= 4 pounds × $0.55 per pound).

Direct Labor
Direct labor standards are based on a standard labor rate for the work performed and the standard number of labor-hours required. The standard labor rate includes wages earned as well as fringe benefits, such as medical insurance and pension plan contributions, and employer-paid taxes (for example, unemployment taxes and the employer's share of an employee's Social Security taxes). Most companies develop one standard for each labor category.

We assume that Peak Division has only one category of labor. The standard labor cost for each good unit of the drink completed is $1 (= 0.05 hour × $20 per hour).

Variable Production Overhead
We discussed in Chapters 6 and 7 the way that companies determine an activity measure to apply production overhead. Peak uses a simple variable overhead basis, direct labor-hours, to determine its variable overhead standards. Management reviewed prior-period activities and costs, estimated how costs will change in the future, and performed a regression analysis in which overhead cost was the dependent variable and labor-hours the independent variable. After analyzing these estimates, the accountants determined that the best estimate was $12 per standard labor-hour as the variable production overhead rate. The standard variable overhead cost for each good unit of drink completed is $0.60 (= 0.05 hour × $12 per hour).

Variable Cost Variance Analysis

Standard costs are used to evaluate a company's performance. Comparing the budget (prepared using standard costs) to actual results identifies production cost variances. We now review production cost variances in detail.

LO 16-5
Compute and use variable cost variances.

General Model

The conceptual **cost variance analysis** model compares actual input quantities and prices with standard input quantities and prices. *Both the actual and standard input quantities*

cost variance analysis
Comparison of actual input amounts and prices with standard input amounts and prices.

Exhibit 16.9
General Model for
Variable Cost Variance
Analysis

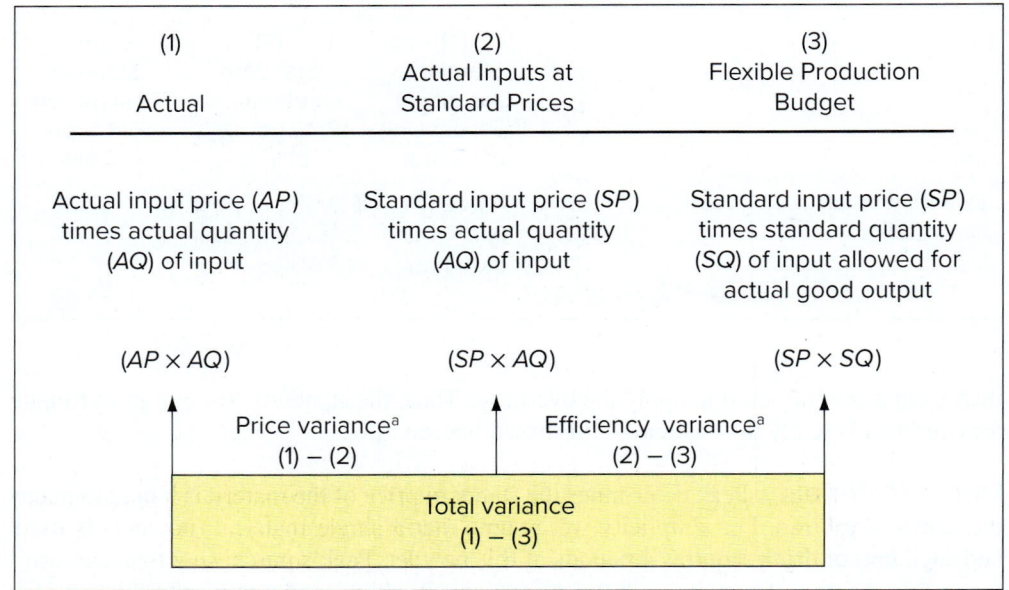

(1)	(2)	(3)
Actual	Actual Inputs at Standard Prices	Flexible Production Budget
Actual input price (*AP*) times actual quantity (*AQ*) of input	Standard input price (*SP*) times actual quantity (*AQ*) of input	Standard input price (*SP*) times standard quantity (*SQ*) of input allowed for actual good output
($AP \times AQ$)	($SP \times AQ$)	($SP \times SQ$)

Price variance[a]
(1) − (2)

Efficiency variance[a]
(2) − (3)

Total variance
(1) − (3)

[a] The terms *price* and *efficiency variances* are general categories. Terminology varies from company to company, but the following specific variance titles are frequently used:

Input	Price Variance Category	Efficiency Category
Direct materials	Price (or purchase price) variance	Usage or quantity variance
Direct labor	Rate variance	Efficiency variance
Variable overhead	Spending variance	Efficiency variance

We shall avoid unnecessary complications by simply referring to these variances as either a *price* or *efficiency* variance.

price variance
Difference between actual costs and budgeted costs arising from changes in the cost of inputs to a production process or other activity.

efficiency variance
Difference between budgeted and actual results arising from differences between the inputs that were budgeted per unit of output and the inputs actually used.

total cost variance
Difference between budgeted and actual results (equal to the sum of the price and efficiency variances).

are for the actual output attained. A **price variance** and an **efficiency variance** can be computed for each variable manufacturing input (see Exhibit 16.9). The actual costs incurred—Column (1)—for the time period are compared with the standard allowed per unit times the number of good units of output produced—Column (3). This comparison provides the **total cost variance** for the cost or input.

Some companies compute only the total variance. Others make a more detailed breakdown into price and efficiency variances. Managers who are responsible for price variances would not be held responsible for efficiency variances and vice versa. For example, purchasing department managers are usually held responsible for direct materials price variances, and manufacturing department managers are usually held responsible for using the direct materials efficiently.

This breakdown of the total variance into price and efficiency components is facilitated by the middle term, Column (2), in Exhibit 16.9. In going from Column (1) to Column (2), we go from *actual price* (*AP*) times *actual quantity* (*AQ*) of input to *standard price* (*SP*) times *actual quantity* (*AQ*) of input. Thus, the variance is calculated as

$$\text{Price variance} = (AP \times AQ) - (SP \times AQ)$$
$$= (AP - SP) \times AQ$$

The efficiency variance is derived by comparing Column (2), standard price (*SP*) multiplied by actual quantity of input (*AQ*), with Column (3), standard price (*SP*) multiplied by standard quantity of input allowed for actual good output produced (*SQ*). Thus, the efficiency variance is calculated as

$$\text{Efficiency variance} = (SP \times AQ) - (SP \times SQ)$$
$$= SP \times (AQ - SQ)$$

This general model could seem rather abstract at this point, but as we work examples, it will become more concrete and intuitive to you.

As the general model outlined in Exhibit 16.9 is applied to each variable cost incurred, a more comprehensive cost variance analysis results. The general model of the comprehensive cost variance analysis will be applied to Peak Division's variable production costs. The comprehensive cost variance analysis will ultimately explain, in detail, the unfavorable variable production variance of $25,680 that we calculated in Column (2) of Exhibit 16.5.

As we proceed through the variance analysis for each production cost input—direct materials, direct labor, and variable production overhead—you will notice some minor modifications to the general model presented in Exhibit 16.9. It is important to recognize that these are modifications to one general approach rather than a number of independent approaches to variance analysis. In variance analysis, a few basic methods can be applied with minor modifications to numerous business and nonbusiness situations.

Direct Materials

Information about Peak Division's use of direct materials for August follows:

Standard costs
  4 pounds per case @ $0.55 per pound . . . .   = $2.20 per case
Cases produced in August . . . .   = 80,000
Actual materials purchased and used
  328,000 pounds @ $0.60 per pound . . . .   = $196,800

These relationships are shown graphically as follows:

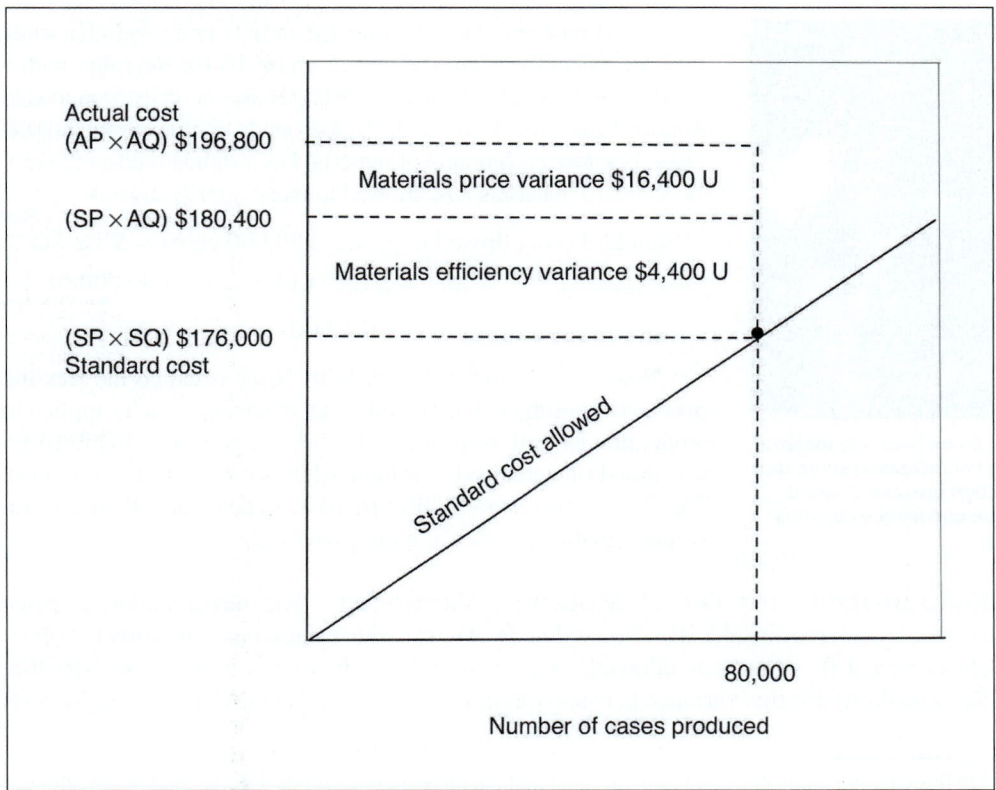

Actual cost
(AP × AQ) $196,800

Materials price variance $16,400 U

(SP × AQ) $180,400

Materials efficiency variance $4,400 U

(SP × SQ) $176,000
Standard cost

Standard cost allowed

80,000

Number of cases produced

An alternative way to view these variances graphically follows. Material quantities are shown on the horizontal axis and the prices for the materials are shown on the vertical axis. The area of the outside box is $196,800 (= $0.60 × 328,000 pounds), the actual price multiplied by the actual quantity of material.

The area of the box on the lower left-hand side is the standard or budgeted cost of the materials for the actual quantity of output produced, $176,000 (= $0.55 × 320,000 pounds). The areas of the other two boxes are the price and efficiency variances.

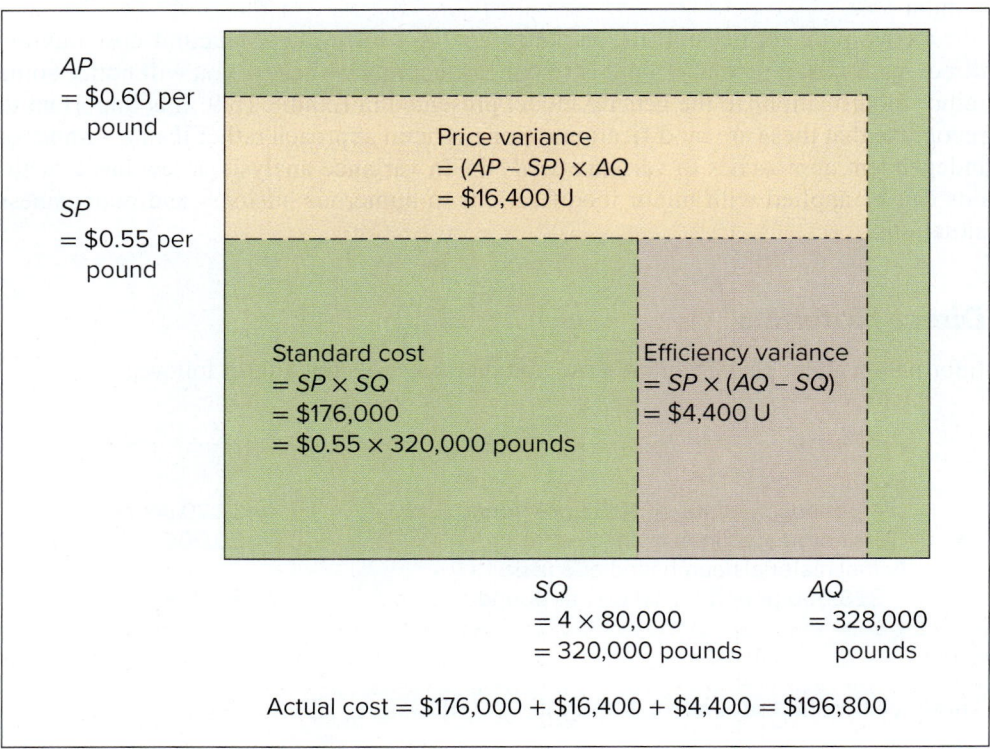

AP
= $0.60 per pound

SP
= $0.55 per pound

Price variance
$= (AP - SP) \times AQ$
= $16,400 U

Standard cost
$= SP \times SQ$
= $176,000
= $0.55 × 320,000 pounds

Efficiency variance
$= SP \times (AQ - SQ)$
= $4,400 U

SQ
= 4 × 80,000
= 320,000 pounds

AQ
= 328,000 pounds

Actual cost = $176,000 + $16,400 + $4,400 = $196,800

For a maker of wooden products, an unfavorable material efficiency variance can be a signal of increased scrap that results from an inefficient production process. A wood cutting station with saws that have dull blades could be the cause. James Hardy/PhotoAlto

flexible production budget
Standard input price times standard quantity of input allowed for actual good output.

Based on these data, the direct materials price and efficiency variance calculations are shown in Exhibit 16.10. Note that with a standard of 4 pounds per case and 80,000 cases actually produced in August, Peak expects to use 320,000 pounds to produce the 80,000 cases. Because each pound of material has a standard cost of $0.55, the standard materials cost allowed to make 80,000 cases is

$$\text{Standard cost allowed to produce 80,000 cases} = SP \times SQ$$
$$= \$0.55 \times (4 \text{ pounds} \times 80,000 \text{ cases})$$
$$= \$176,000$$

Note that Column (3) of Exhibit 16.10 is called the **flexible production budget.** The flexible budget concept can be applied to production as well as to sales. The flexible budget in Exhibit 16.5 was based on actual sales volume (that is, number of cases *sold*). The flexible budget in Exhibit 16.10 is based on actual production volume (that is, number of cases *produced*).[1]

Responsibility for Direct Materials Variances   The direct materials price variance (see Exhibit 16.10) shows that in August, the prices paid for direct materials exceeded the standards allowed, thus creating an unfavorable variance of $16,400. Responsibility for this variance is usually assigned to the purchasing department. Reports

---

[1] In this case, the number of units sold is equal to the number of units produced. We discuss situations in which production and sales differ in Chapter 17.

Exhibit 16.10 Direct Materials Variances, August (80,000 Cases)—Peak Division

(1)	(2)	(3)
Actual	Actual Inputs at Standard Price	Flexible Production Budget
Actual materials price $(AP = \$0.60)$ × Actual quantity $(AQ = 328{,}000 \text{ pounds})$ of direct materials	Standard materials price $(SP = \$0.55)$ × Actual quantity $(AQ = 328{,}000 \text{ pounds})$ of direct materials	Standard materials price $(SP = \$0.55)$ × Standard quantity $(SQ = 320{,}000 \text{ pounds})$ of direct materials allowed for actual output
$(AP \times AQ)$	$(SP \times AQ)$	$(SP \times SQ)$
$\$0.60 \times 328{,}000$ $= \$196{,}800$	$\$0.55 \times 328{,}000$ $= \$180{,}400$	$\$0.55 \times 320{,}000$ $= \$176{,}000$

Price variance[a]
$196,800 - $180,400
= $16,400 U

Efficiency variance[a]
$180,400 - $176,000
= $4,400 U

[a] Shortcut formulas:

$(AP \times AQ) - (SP \times AQ)$
$= (AP - SP) \times AQ$
$= (\$.60 - \$.55) \times 328{,}000$
$= \$16{,}400 \text{ U}$

$(SP \times AQ) - (SP \times SQ)$
$= SP \times (AQ - SQ)$
$= \$.55 \times (328{,}000 - 320{,}000)$
$= \$4{,}400 \text{ U}$

Total variance
$= \$20{,}800 \text{ U}$

to management include an explanation of the variance, for example, failure to take purchase discounts, higher transportation costs than expected, different grade of direct materials purchased, or changes in the market price of direct materials.

The explanation for Peak's variance was the closure of a nearby vendor's plant, which required a change in suppliers and increased transportation costs that caused the price of materials to be higher than expected. The long-term effect on prices is uncertain, so management has begun market research to determine whether Peak should attempt to increase sales prices for its drink.

Direct materials efficiency variances are typically the responsibility of production departments. In setting standards, an allowance is usually made for defects in direct materials, inexperienced workers, poor supervision, and the like. If actual materials usage is less than these standards, a favorable variance occurs. If usage exceeds standards, an unfavorable variance occurs.

At Peak, the unfavorable materials efficiency variance was attributed to an increase in the amount of scrap that results from the blending process. One of the new employees hired in August required some time to learn to work efficiently with the powder. The production supervisor claimed that this was a one-time occurrence and anticipated no similar problems in the future.

Direct Labor

To illustrate the computations of direct labor variances, assume the following for Peak Division:

Standard costs: 0.05 hour per case @ $20 per hour = ...	$1 per case
Number of cases produced in August.	80,000
Actual direct labor costs	
Actual hours worked	4,400
Total actual labor cost	$79,200
Average cost per hour (= $79,200 ÷ 4,400 hours)	$18

Exhibit 16.11   Direct Labor Variances, August (80,000 Cases)—Peak Division

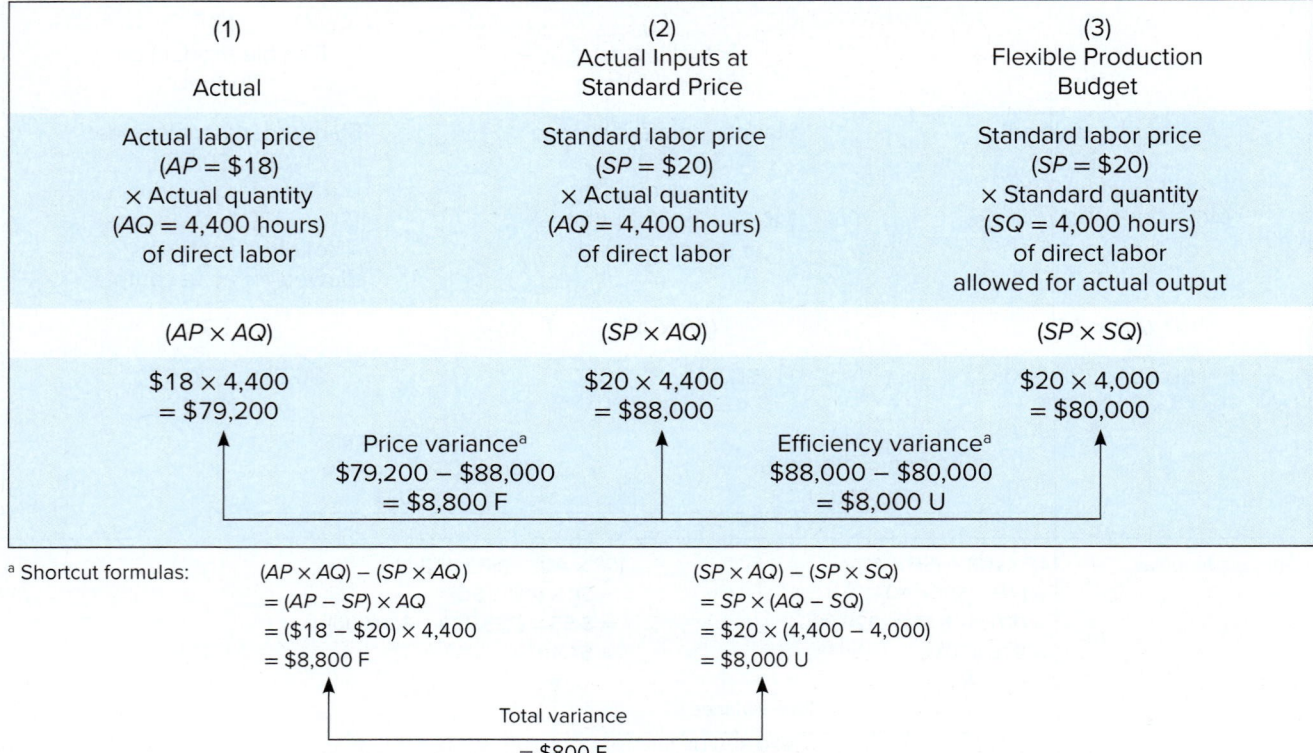

ᵃ Shortcut formulas:

$(AP \times AQ) - (SP \times AQ)$
$= (AP - SP) \times AQ$
$= (\$18 - \$20) \times 4,400$
$= \$8,800$ F

$(SP \times AQ) - (SP \times SQ)$
$= SP \times (AQ - SQ)$
$= \$20 \times (4,400 - 4,000)$
$= \$8,000$ U

Total variance
$= \$800$ F

See Exhibit 16.11 for the computation of the direct labor price and efficiency variances.

Direct Labor Price Variance   The direct labor price variance is caused by the difference between actual and standard labor costs per hour. Peak Division's direct labor costs were less than the standard allowed, creating a favorable labor price variance of $8,800. The explanation given for this favorable labor price variance is that Peak hired less-experienced employees in August; they were paid a lower-than-standard wage, thus reducing the *average* wage rate for all workers to $18.

Wage rates for many companies are set by union contract. If the wage rates used in setting standards are the same as those in the union contract, labor price variances will not occur.

Labor Efficiency Variance   The labor efficiency variance is a measure of labor productivity. It is one of the most closely watched variances because production managers usually can control it. Unfavorable labor efficiency variances have many causes, including the employees themselves. Poorly motivated or poorly trained workers are less productive; highly motivated and well-trained employees are more likely to generate favorable efficiency variances. Sometimes poor materials or faulty equipment can cause productivity problems. Poor supervision and scheduling can lead to unnecessary idle time.

Production department managers are usually responsible for direct labor efficiency variances. Scheduling problems can stem from other production departments that have delayed production. The personnel department could be responsible if the variance occurs because it provided the wrong type of worker. The $8,000 unfavorable direct labor efficiency variance at Peak Division (see Exhibit 16.11) was attributed to the inexperienced worker previously mentioned. Note that one event, such as hiring inexperienced employees, can affect more than one variance.

Variable Production Overhead

To illustrate the computation of variable production overhead variances, assume the following for Peak:

Standard costs: 0.05 hour per case @ $12 per hour = ...	$0.60 per case
($12 is the variable production overhead rate)	
Number of cases produced in August	80,000
Actual variable overhead cost in August	$53,680

See Exhibit 16.12 for the computation of the variable production overhead price and efficiency variances.

Variable Production Overhead Price Variances The variable overhead standard rate was derived from a two-step estimation of

1. Costs at various levels of activity.
2. The relationship between those estimated costs and the basis, which is direct labor-hours at Peak Division.

The variable overhead price variance actually contains some efficiency items as well as price items. For example, suppose that utilities costs are higher than expected. The reason for this could be that utility rates are higher than expected or that kilowatt-hours (kwh) per labor-hour are higher than expected (for example, if workers do not turn off power switches when machines are not being used). Both are part of the price variance because together they cause utility costs to be higher than expected. Some companies separate these components of the variable overhead price variance; this is done for energy costs in heavy manufacturing companies, for example.

At Peak Division, the $880 unfavorable price variance for August (see Exhibit 16.12) was attributed to waste in using supplies and recent price increases for petroleum products used to maintain the machines.

Exhibit 16.12 Variable Overhead Variances, August (80,000 Cases)—Peak Division

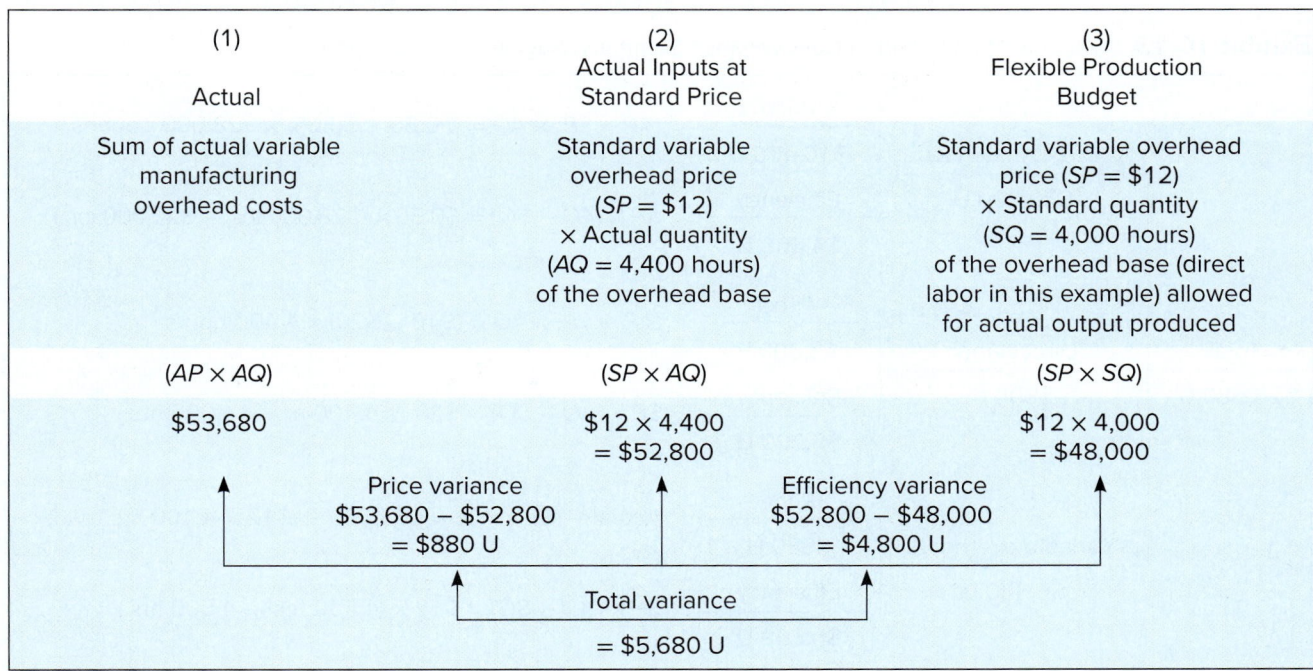

(1)	(2)	(3)
	Actual Inputs at	Flexible Production
Actual	Standard Price	Budget
Sum of actual variable manufacturing overhead costs	Standard variable overhead price (SP = $12) × Actual quantity (AQ = 4,400 hours) of the overhead base	Standard variable overhead price (SP = $12) × Standard quantity (SQ = 4,000 hours) of the overhead base (direct labor in this example) allowed for actual output produced
(AP × AQ)	(SP × AQ)	(SP × SQ)
$53,680	$12 × 4,400 = $52,800	$12 × 4,000 = $48,000

Price variance
$53,680 − $52,800
= $880 U

Efficiency variance
$52,800 − $48,000
= $4,800 U

Total variance
= $5,680 U

Variable Overhead Efficiency Variance

The variable overhead efficiency variance must be interpreted carefully. It is *not* related to the use (or efficiency) of variable overhead. It is related to efficiency in using the base on which variable overhead is applied. For example, Peak applies variable overhead on the basis of direct labor-hours. Thus, if there is an unfavorable direct labor efficiency variance because actual direct labor-hours were higher than the standard allowed, there will be a corresponding unfavorable variable overhead efficiency variance. Peak used 400 direct labor-hours more than the standard allowed, resulting in the following direct labor and variable overhead efficiency variances:

Direct labor efficiency (Exhibit 16.11)	
$20 × 400 hours =	$ 8,000 U
Variable overhead efficiency (Exhibit 16.12)	
$12 × 400 hours =.	4,800 U
Total direct labor and variable overhead efficiency variances	
$32 × 400 hours =.	$12,800 U

Variable overhead is assumed to vary directly with direct labor-hours, which is the base on which variable overhead is applied. Thus, inefficiency in using the base (for example, direct labor-hours, machine-hours, units of output) is assumed to cause an increase in variable overhead. This emphasizes the importance of selecting the proper base for applying variable overhead. Managers who are responsible for controlling the base will probably be held responsible for the variable overhead efficiency variance as well. Whoever is responsible for the $8,000 unfavorable direct labor efficiency variance at Peak should be held responsible for the unfavorable variable overhead efficiency variance.

Variable Cost Variances Summarized in Graphic Form

See Exhibit 16.13 for a summary of the variable production cost variances. Note that the total unfavorable variable production cost variance of $25,680 is the same as that derived in Exhibit 16.5. The cost variance analysis just completed is a more detailed analysis of the variable production cost variance derived in Exhibit 16.5.

Exhibit 16.13   Variable Manufacturing Cost Variance Summary, August—Peak Division

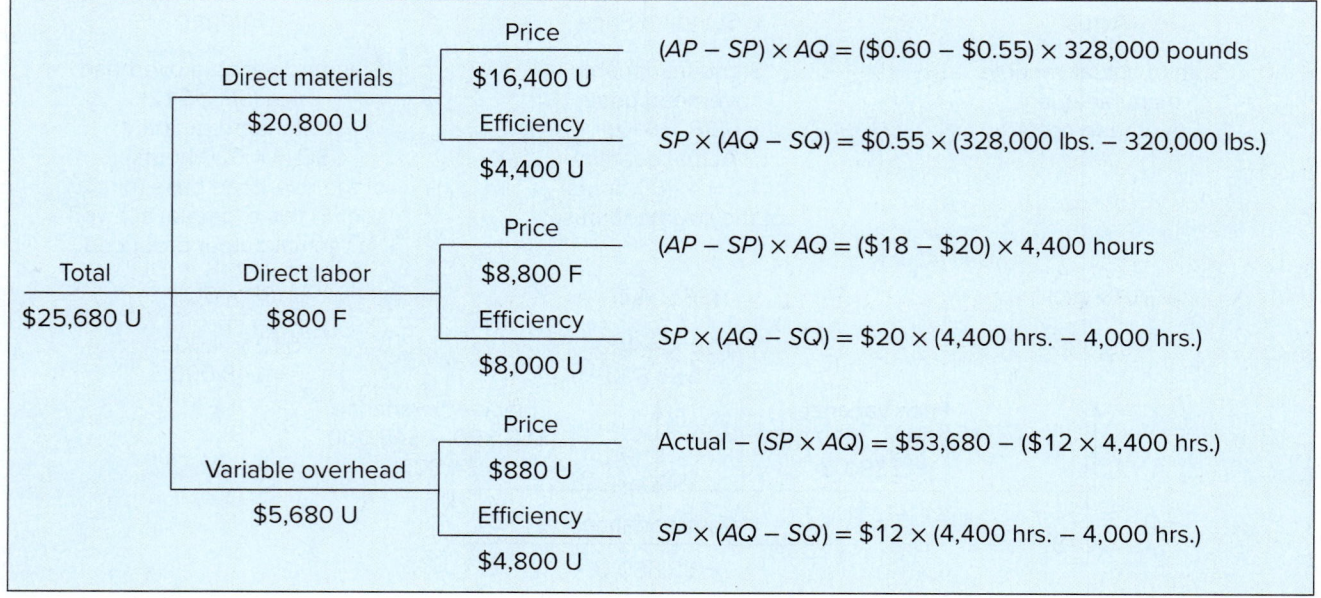

A summary of this nature is useful for reporting variances to high-level managers. It provides both an overview of variances and their sources. When used for reporting, the computations at the right of Exhibit 16.13 usually are replaced with a brief explanation of the cause of the variance.

Management might want more detailed information about some of the variances. Extending each variance branch in Exhibit 16.13 to show variances by product line, department, or other categories can provide this additional detail.

Self-Study Question

2. Last month, the following events took place at Superior Supplies:
    - Produced 100,000 "leatherlike" digital music player cases.
    - Had standard variable costs per unit (that is, per case):

Direct materials: 3 pounds at $1.50............	$ 4.50
Direct labor: 0.20 labor-hour at $22.50.........	4.50
Variable production overhead:	
.20 labor-hour at $10.00	2.00
Total per case...............................	$11.00

- Incurred actual production costs:

Direct materials purchased and used:	
325,000 pounds at $1.40	$455,000
Direct labor: 19,000 labor-hours at $25	475,000
Variable overhead	209,000

    Compute the direct materials, labor, and variable production overhead price and efficiency variances.

    The solution to this question is at the end of the chapter.

Fixed Cost Variances

Variance analysis treats fixed production costs and variable production costs differently. Because fixed costs are unchanged when volume changes (at least within the relevant range), the amount budgeted for fixed overhead is the same in both the master and flexible budgets. This is consistent with the variable costing method of product costing in which fixed production overhead is treated as a period cost.

LO 16-6
Compute and use fixed cost variances.

Fixed Cost Variances with Variable Costing

The income statements in Exhibit 16.5 were prepared using variable costing. Therefore, there is no absorption of the fixed costs by units of production. All the fixed manufacturing overhead is charged to income in the period incurred. Fixed overhead has no input–output relationships and, thus, no efficiency variance. The difference between the flexible budget and the actual fixed overhead is entirely due to changes in the costs that make up fixed overhead (for example, insurance premiums on the factory are higher than expected). Hence, the variance falls under the category of a price variance (also called a **spending or budget variance**).

The fixed manufacturing overhead in both the flexible and master budgets in Exhibit 16.5 was $200,000. The actual cost was $195,500. See Exhibit 16.14 for the variance analysis. Note that it has no calculation of the efficiency with which inputs are used.

spending (or budget) variance
Price variance for fixed overhead

Exhibit 16.14

Fixed Overhead
Variances, August—Peak
Division

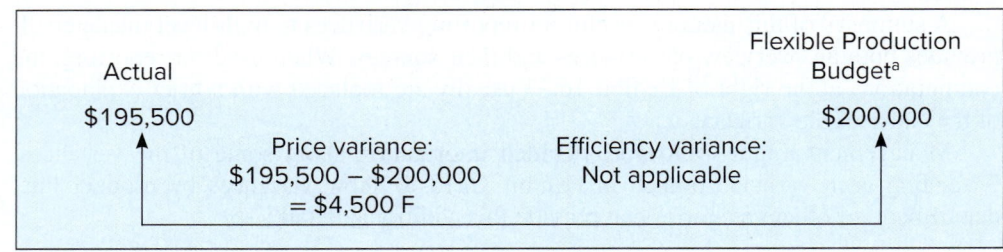

ᵃ For fixed costs, there is no difference between the flexible and master (or static) budget within the relevant range.

Visualizing Cost Variances

Exhibit 16.15 graphically summarizes the production cost variances by resource type. As Exhibit 16.15 shows, the largest variance is related to materials. By comparison, both labor (with a favorable variance) and overhead (with an unfavorable variance) are much smaller.

Exhibit 16.16 provides a more detailed breakdown of these cost variances. Although the summary information in Exhibit 16.15 is useful to identify potential areas for study, the results in Exhibit 16.16 show that summarizing variances may lead managers to overlook potential areas of improvement. In Exhibit 16.16, for example, we see that materials are certainly a possible area for further analysis, but the detailed results in Exhibit 16.16 show that labor costs might also provide an important area for operation improvements. Although the overall labor variance is relatively small, the individual components show that result to be the combination of larger, but offsetting, price and efficiency variances.

Absorption Costing: The Production Volume Variance

So far, we have assumed that fixed manufacturing costs are treated as period costs, which is consistent with variable costing. If fixed manufacturing costs are unitized and treated as product costs, another variance is computed. *This occurs when companies use full absorption, standard costing.*

Exhibit 16.15   Cost Variances by Manufacturing Resource

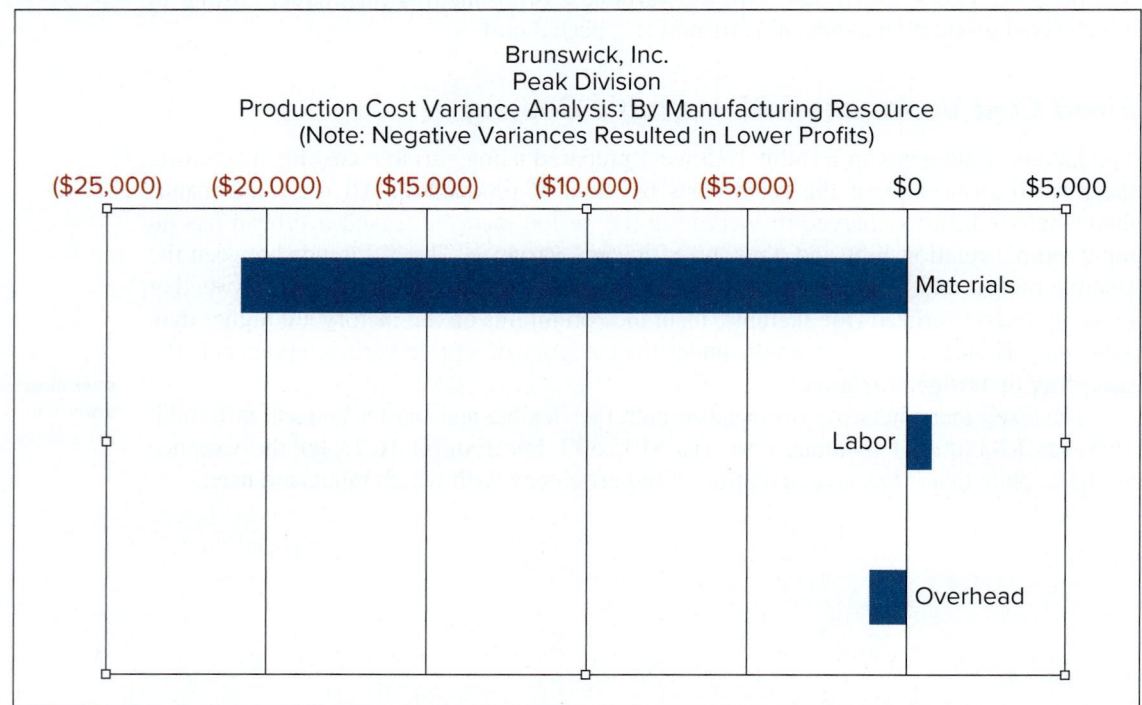

Exhibit 16.16   Cost Variances by Manufacturing Resource: Details

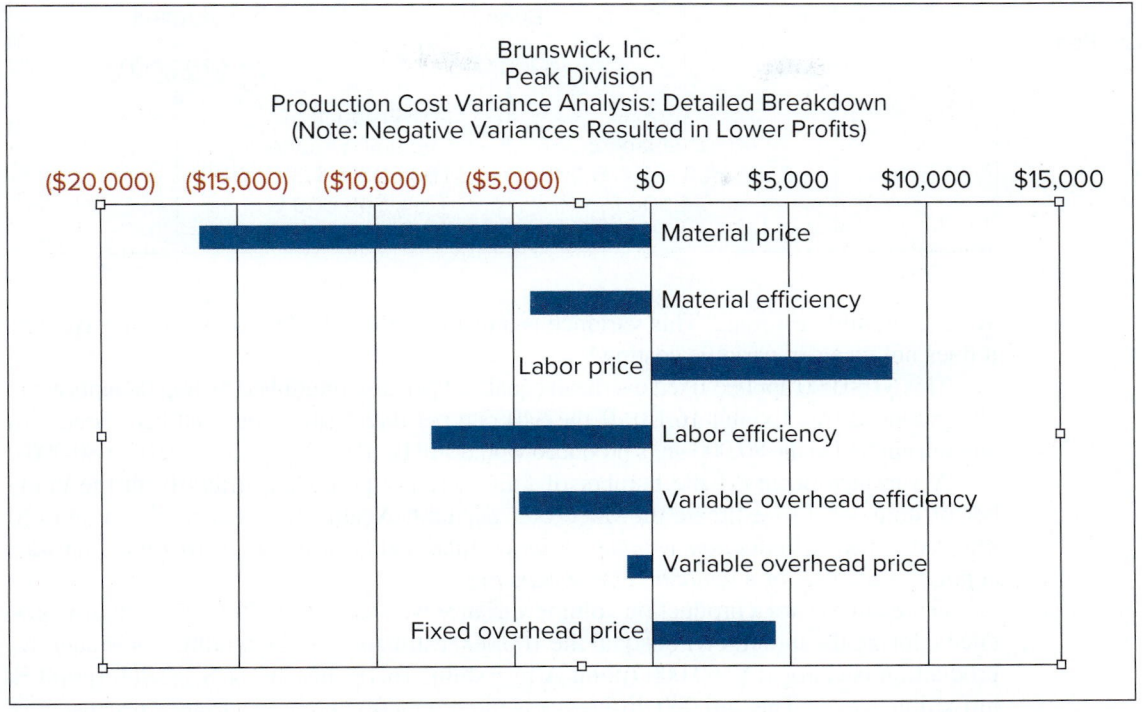

Brunswick, Inc.
Peak Division
Production Cost Variance Analysis: Detailed Breakdown
(Note: Negative Variances Resulted in Lower Profits)

Developing the Standard Unit Cost for Fixed Production Costs   Like
other standard costs, the fixed manufacturing standard cost is determined before the start
of the production period. Unlike standard variable manufacturing costs, fixed costs are
period costs by nature. To convert them to product costs requires estimating both the
period cost and the production volume for the period. From Chapter 7, we know that

$$\frac{\text{Standard (or predetermined)}}{\text{fixed production overhead cost}} = \frac{\text{Budgeted fixed manufacturing cost}}{\text{Budgeted activity level}}$$

The estimated annual fixed manufacturing overhead at Peak was $2,400,000, and the
annual production volume was estimated to be 1,200,000 cases, or 60,000 direct labor-
hours at .05 hour per case. Thus, Peak determines its standard fixed manufacturing cost
per case as follows:

$$\frac{\text{Standard cost}}{\text{per case}} = \frac{\$2,400,000 \text{ budgeted fixed manufacturing cost}}{1,200,000 \text{ cases (budgeted activity level)}} = \underline{\underline{\$2.00 \text{ per case}}}$$

The rate could be computed per direct labor-hour, as follows:

$$\frac{\text{Standard cost}}{\text{per case}} = \frac{\$2,400,000 \text{ budgeted fixed manufacturing cost}}{60,000 \text{ hours (budgeted activity level)}} = \underline{\underline{\$40.00 \text{ per hour}}}$$

Each case is expected to require .05 direct labor-hour (= 60,000 hours ÷ 1,200,000
cases), so the standard cost per case is still $2 (= $40 per hour × .05 hour per case).

If 80,000 units are actually produced during the month, $160,000 (= $2 per case ×
80,000 cases) of fixed overhead costs is applied to these units produced. The **production
volume variance** is the difference between the $160,000 applied fixed overhead and the
$200,000 (= $2,400,000 ÷ 12 months) budgeted fixed overhead as in Exhibit 16.17. In
this situation, a $40,000 unfavorable production volume variance exists. It is unfavorable
because less overhead was applied than was budgeted; production was lower than the

production volume variance
Variance that arises because
the volume used to apply
fixed overhead differs from
the estimated volume used to
estimate fixed costs per unit.

Exhibit 16.17

Fixed Overhead
Variances, August—Peak
Division

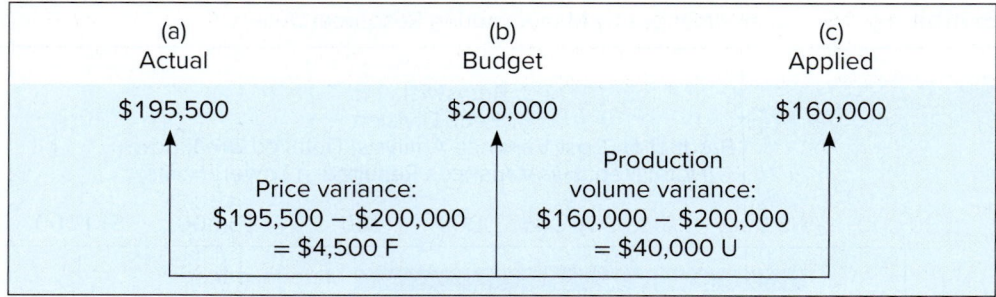

(a) Actual	(b) Budget	(c) Applied
$195,500	$200,000	$160,000

Price variance:
$195,500 − $200,000
= $4,500 F

Production
volume variance:
$160,000 − $200,000
= $40,000 U

average monthly estimate. This variance is a result of the full absorption costing system; it does not occur in variable costing.

This $160,000 applied fixed overhead equals $2 per case multiplied by 80,000 units actually produced (see Exhibit 16.18). If the $40 rate per direct labor-hour had been used, the amount applied to the 80,000 units produced would still be $160,000 (= $40 × 0.05 × 80,000).

A variance occurs if the number of units actually produced differs from the number of units used to estimate the fixed cost per unit. Again, this variance is commonly referred to as a *production volume variance* (also called a *capacity variance,* an *idle capacity variance,* or a *denominator variance*).

Our example has a production volume variance because the 80,000 cases actually produced during the month do not equal the 100,000 estimated for the month. Consequently, production is charged $160,000 (point A in Exhibit 16.18) instead of $200,000 (point B in Exhibit 16.18). The $40,000 difference is the production volume variance because it is caused by a deviation in production volume level (number of cases produced) from that estimated to arrive at the standard cost.

If Peak had estimated 80,000 cases per month instead of 100,000 cases, the standard cost would have been $2.50 per case (= $200,000 ÷ 80,000 cases). Thus, $200,000 (= $2.50 × 80,000 cases) would have been applied to units produced, and there would have been no production volume variance.

Exhibit 16.18   Fixed Overhead Variances, Graphic Presentation—Peak Division

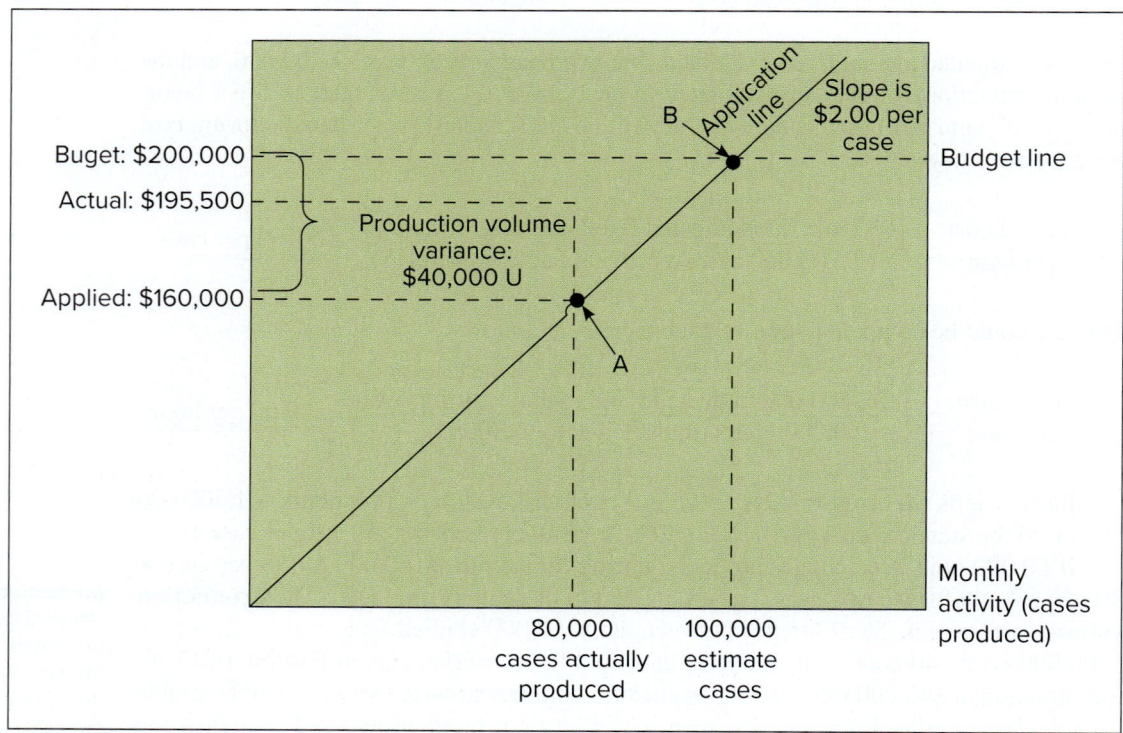

The production volume variance applies only to fixed costs; it occurs because we are allocating a fixed period cost to units on a predetermined basis. It does not represent resources spent or saved. This is unique to full absorption costing. The benefits of calculating the variance for control purposes are questionable. Although the production volume variance signals a difference between expected and actual production levels, so does a simple production report of actual versus expected production quantities.

Compare with the Fixed Production Cost Price Variance   The fixed production cost price variance is the difference between actual and budgeted fixed production costs. Unlike the production volume variance, the price variance commonly is used for control purposes because it is a measure of differences between actual and budgeted period costs.

Exhibits 16.17 and 16.18 summarize the computation of the fixed production price (spending) and production volume variances. Reviewing them will help you see the relationship between actual, budgeted, and applied fixed production costs.

Summary of Overhead Variances

The method of computing overhead variances described in this chapter is known as the *four-way analysis of overhead variances* because it computes the following four variances: price and efficiency for variable overhead, and price and production volume for fixed overhead. See Exhibit 16.19 for a summary of the four-way analysis of variable and fixed overhead variances based on facts given in the chapter.

Exhibit 16.19   Summary of Overhead Variances, Four-Way Analysis, August—Peak Division

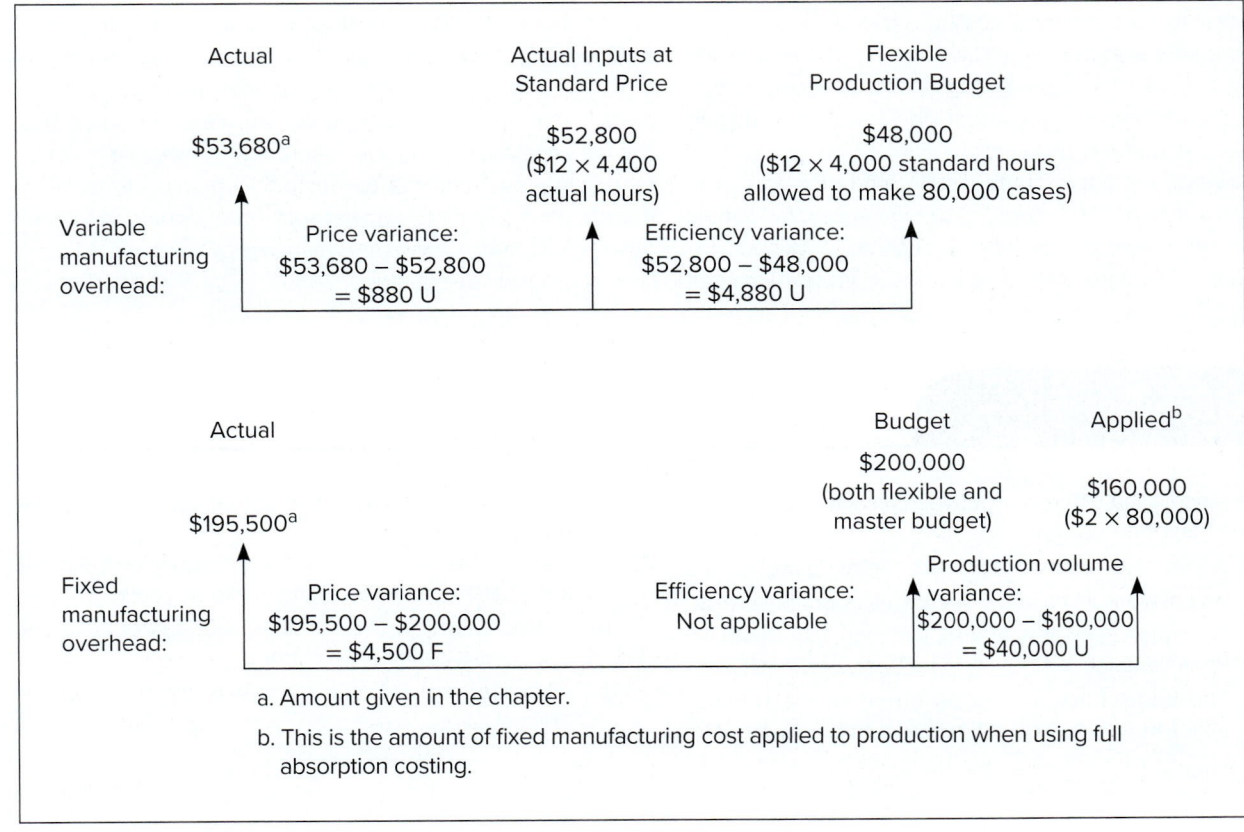

a. Amount given in the chapter.

b. This is the amount of fixed manufacturing cost applied to production when using full absorption costing.

Self-Study Question

3. This question follows up Self-Study Question 2. Assume that the fixed production cost budget for the month was $320,000, and actual fixed production overhead costs were $332,000. The estimated monthly production was 80,000 cases (or 16,000 standard labor-hours).

Compute the fixed production overhead price variance and the fixed production overhead production volume variance.

The solution to this question is at the end of the chapter.

Key Points

Several points regarding overhead variances are important:

- The variable overhead efficiency variance measures the efficiency in using the allocation base (for example, direct labor-hours).
- The production volume variance occurs only when fixed production cost is unitized (for example, when using full absorption costing). Furthermore, the budgeted fixed overhead might not equal the amount applied to units produced.
- There is no efficiency variance for fixed production costs. Do not confuse production volume variance with an efficiency variance.

Business Application   Does Standard Costing Lead to Overproduction?

Standard costing systems base the reported product costs on standards, such as those in Exhibit 16.6. Analysts and others have long criticized standard costing as motivating behavior that does not increase company value. For some observers, the problem is that standard costing systems lead managers and workers to increase production, even if it only builds inventory, because the focus is on unit costs. In addition, standard costing appears to be an additional system, requiring resources to develop and maintain.

As always, it is important to distinguish between a concept and a practice. The concept of standard costing is simply that firms can create benchmarks against which to evaluate performance. Standard costing, as usually practiced, includes

the development of standard costs for fixed overhead and consequently for production volume variances. Managers evaluated by variances that include production volume variances do have an incentive to overproduce. This is the reason that performance evaluation systems, including standard costing, should be applied with an understanding of the undesirable incentives they provide managers. In the case of production volume variances, we have noted that the variance represents the difference between the actual production level and the production level used to develop the standard cost for fixed overhead. Rarely would this difference reflect managerial performance that a firm would want to encourage or discourage.

Key Takeaways

1. A variance is the difference between an actual and a budgeted number:
   a. A favorable variance increases operating profits.
   b. An unfavorable variance decreases operating profits.
   c. A simple example is a profit variance, calculated as Profit variance = Actual profit − Budgeted profit.
   d. The budget may be based on either the original (master) budget or a flexible budget. A flexible budget is adjusted for actual sales or actual output.

2. Greater insights can be gained by decomposing the profit variance based on the items that make up profit:
   a. Sales activity = (Actual sales − Budgeted sales) × Budgeted contribution margin.
   b. Sales price = (Actual price − Budgeted price) × Actual sales.

(Continued)

(Continued)

c. Variable manufacturing cost = (Actual variable cost – Budgeted variable cost) × Budgeted sales.

d. Fixed manufacturing cost = (Actual fixed cost – Budgeted fixed cost).

e. Selling and administrative (SG&A) = (Actual SG&A – Budgeted SG&A).

3. Production cost variances can be decomposed by resource and by price or usage (efficiency):

a. Price variance = (Actual price – Budgeted price) × Actual quantity used.

b. Efficiency variance = (Actual quantity used – Budgeted quantity) × Budgeted price.

c. Fixed cost variances depend on whether the firm is using contribution-margin (variable) costing or absorption costing:

- Contribution margin costing:
  - Fixed overhead price = (Actual fixed cost – Budgeted fixed cost)

- Absorption costing:
  - Fixed overhead price = (Actual fixed cost – Budgeted fixed cost)
  - Production volume variance = (Actual production – Budgeted production) × Budgeted fixed overhead rate.

SUMMARY

This chapter discusses the computation and analysis of variances. A *variance* is the difference between a budget, or standard, and an actual result.

The following summarizes the key ideas tied to the chapter's learning objectives:

LO 16-1 Use budgets for performance evaluation. *Budgets* provide a view of anticipated operations and enable management to measure the performance of employees in various areas of the production and sales processes.

LO 16-2 Develop and use flexible budgets. The *master budget* is typically static; that is, it is developed in detail for one level of activity. A *flexible budget* recognizes that variable costs and revenues are expected to differ from the budget if the actual activity (for example, actual sales volume) differs from what was budgeted. A flexible budget can be thought of as the costs and revenues that would have been budgeted if the activity level had been correctly estimated in the master budget. The general relationship between the actual results, the flexible budget, and the master budget follows:

Actual	Flexible Budget	Master Budget
Actual costs and revenues based on actual activity	Costs and revenues that would have been budgeted if actual activity had been budgeted	Budgeted costs and revenues based on budgeted activity

LO 16-3 Compute and interpret the sales activity variance. The sales activity variance is the difference between the operating profit in the master budget and the flexible budget. This difference (or variance) occurs because the actual number of units sold is different from the number budgeted in the master budget.

LO 16-4 Prepare and use a profit variance analysis. The *profit variance analysis* outlines the causes of differences between budgeted profits and the actual profits earned. Variances are separated into four categories: production, marketing and administrative, sales price, and sales activity.

LO 16-5 Compute and use variable cost variances. The model used for calculating variable production cost variances is based on the following diagram, which divides the total variance between actual and standard into *price* and *efficiency* components.

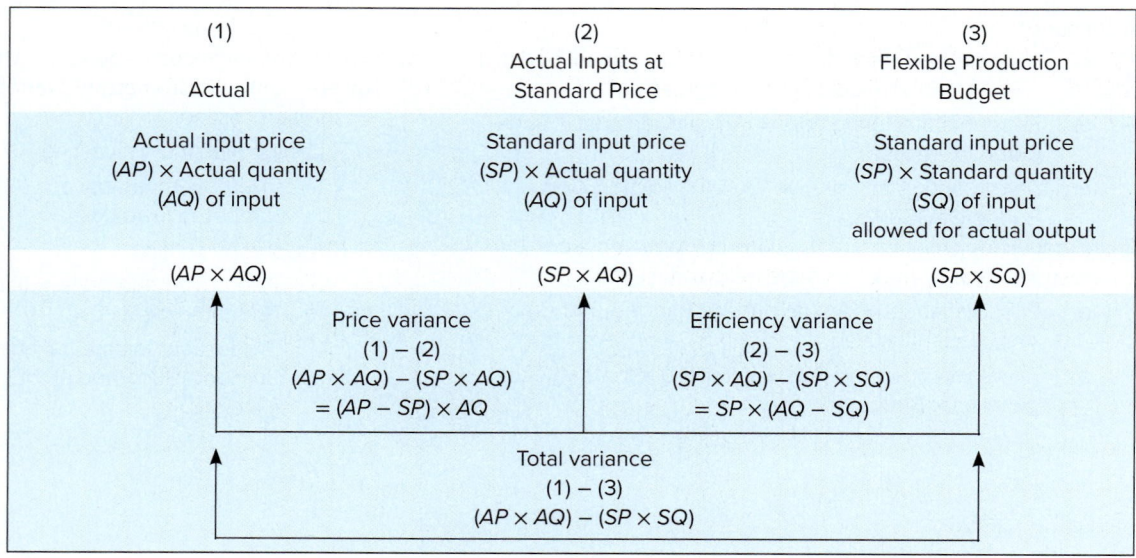

(1)	(2)	(3)
Actual	**Actual Inputs at Standard Price**	**Flexible Production Budget**
Actual input price (*AP*) × Actual quantity (*AQ*) of input	Standard input price (*SP*) × Actual quantity (*AQ*) of input	Standard input price (*SP*) × Standard quantity (*SQ*) of input allowed for actual output
(*AP* × *AQ*)	(*SP* × *AQ*)	(*SP* × *SQ*)

Price variance
(1) − (2)
(*AP* × *AQ*) − (*SP* × *AQ*)
= (*AP* − *SP*) × *AQ*

Efficiency variance
(2) − (3)
(*SP* × *AQ*) − (*SP* × *SQ*)
= *SP* × (*AQ* − *SQ*)

Total variance
(1) − (3)
(*AP* × *AQ*) − (*SP* × *SQ*)

LO 16-6 Compute and use fixed cost variances. Fixed production costs have no efficiency variance. The price variance is the difference between actual fixed costs and the fixed costs in the flexible budget. If fixed costs are unitized and assigned to units produced, a production volume variance also can arise. The production volume variance is the difference between the budgeted fixed costs and the amount applied to production.

LO 16-7 (Appendix) Understand how to record costs in a standard costing system. In a standard costing system, work in process is recorded at standard costs, and variance accounts collect the difference between actual and standard costs. Variances are closed to cost of goods sold (because we assume that production equals sales in this chapter).

KEY TERMS

cost variance analysis, *741*
efficiency variance, *742*
favorable variance, *732*
financial budgets, *731*
flexible budget, *734*
flexible budget line, *734*
flexible production budget, *744*
operating budgets, *731*
price variance, *742*
production volume variance, *751*

profit variance analysis, *737*
sales activity variance, *735*
sales price variance, *737*
spending (or budget) variance, *749*
standard cost sheet, *740*
standard costing, *756*
static budget, *734*
total cost variance, *742*
unfavorable variance, *732*
variance, *731*

APPENDIX: RECORDING COSTS IN A STANDARD COST SYSTEM

LO 16-7
(Appendix) Understand how to record costs in a standard costing system.

standard costing
Accounting method that assigns costs to cost objects at predetermined amounts.

When using **standard costing**, costs are transferred through the production process at their standard costs. This means that the entry debiting Work-in-Process Inventory at standard cost could be made before actual costs are known. In process costing, units transferred between departments are valued at standard cost; in job costing, standard costs are used to charge the job for its components. Actual costs are accumulated in accounts such as Accounts Payable and Wages Payable and are compared with the standard costs allowed for the output produced. The difference between the actual costs assigned to a department and the standard cost of the work done is the *variance* for the department.

The following sections discuss the flow of costs in a standard cost system, compare the actual and standard costs of work, and demonstrate how the variances are isolated in the accounting system. The variances are based on the calculations introduced in the chapter. Standard cost systems vary somewhat from company to company, so in reality, the method presented here might be modified to meet a company's particular needs.

The example in this appendix continues the Peak Division example in this chapter. All variances were computed earlier in this chapter.

Direct Materials

In the example in this chapter, we assume that materials are purchased as they are used so that there are no material inventories. In Chapter 17, we discuss the case where the firm purchases and stores materials prior to use. In August, Peak purchased and used 328,000 pounds of materials and paid $0.60 per pound. The standard for materials is four pounds of material per case at a standard cost of $0.55 per pound. The information for this entry comes from Exhibit 16.10.

Work-in-Process Inventory	176,000	
Materials Price Variance	16,400	
Materials Efficiency Variance	4,400	
Accounts Payable		196,800

To record the purchase and use of 328,000 pounds of material at an actual cost of $0.60 per pound and the transfer to work in process at a standard use of 4 pounds of material allowed per case and a standard cost of $0.55 per pound.

Direct Labor

Direct labor is credited to payroll liability accounts, such as Accrued Payroll or Payroll Payable, for the actual cost (including accruals for fringe benefits and payroll taxes) and charged to Work-in-Process Inventory at standard. The following entry is based on the facts about the standard costs allowed for Peak Division as described in the chapter and in Exhibit 16.11.

Work-in-Process Inventory	80,000	
Direct Labor Efficiency Variance	8,000	
Direct Labor Price Variance		8,800
Wages Payable		79,200

To record the purchase and use of 4,400 hours of direct labor at an actual wage rate of $18 per hour and the transfer to work in process at a standard use of 0.05 hour of labor allowed per case and a standard cost of $20 per hour.

Variable Manufacturing Overhead

Standard overhead costs are charged to production based on standard direct labor-hours per unit of output produced at Peak. Overhead costs often are charged to production before the actual costs are known. This is demonstrated by the following sequence of entries:

1. Standard overhead costs are charged to production during the period. The credit entry is to an overhead applied account.
2. Actual costs are recorded in various accounts and transferred to an overhead summary account. This accounting procedure is completed after the end of the period.
3. Variances are computed as the difference between the standard costs charged to production (overhead applied) and the actual costs.

This approach is similar to that used to charge overhead to production using predetermined rates in normal costing, which we described in Chapter 7.

Based on the data from the chapter and Exhibit 16.12, variable overhead is charged to production as follows:

```
1. Work-in-Process Inventory .........................     48,000
       Variable Overhead (Applied) ......................              48,000
```

Note that overhead is applied to Work-in-Process Inventory on the basis of standard labor-hours allowed. As we shall see shortly, over- or underapplied overhead represents a combination of the variable overhead price and efficiency variances.

Actual variable overhead costs are recorded in various accounts and transferred to each department's variable manufacturing overhead account as follows:

```
2. Variable Overhead (Actual)............................     53,680
       Miscellaneous Payables and Inventory Accounts..........              53,680
```

Variable overhead variances were computed in the chapter (see Exhibit 16.12): price, $880 U, and efficiency, $4,800 U. These variable overhead variances are recorded by closing the applied and actual accounts as follows:

```
3. Variable Overhead (Applied) ......................     48,000
   Variable Overhead Price Variance..................        880
   Variable Overhead Efficiency Variance .............      4,800
       Variable Overhead (Actual).......................              53,680
```

Fixed Manufacturing Overhead

For the purposes of this example, we assume that Peak uses full absorption costing as we did in the chapter. As with variable overhead, Peak applies fixed overhead based on standard labor-hours allowed. For Peak, the standard fixed overhead rate is $40 per hour. First, we record the application of fixed overhead to production:

```
1. Work-in-Process Inventory ...........................    160,000
       Fixed Overhead (Applied)...........................             160,000
```

Next, Peak records the acquisition or use of actual fixed overhead:

```
2. Fixed Overhead (Actual) .............................    195,500
       Miscellaneous Payables and Inventory Accounts.......             195,500
```

Finally, Peak records the fixed overhead variances and closes the actual and applied fixed overhead accounts:

```
3. Fixed Overhead (Applied)........................    160,000
   Fixed Overhead Production Volume Variance .......     40,000
       Fixed Overhead Price Variance..................               4,500
       Fixed Overhead (Actual) ......................             195,500
```

Transfer to Finished Goods Inventory and to Cost of Goods Sold

When all production work has been completed, units are transferred to Finished Goods Inventory and to Cost of Goods Sold at standard cost.

Finished Goods Inventory   This month, 80,000 cases were finished and transferred to Finished Goods Inventory. The standard unit cost of a case is $5.80 (= $3.80 variable cost + $2 applied fixed overhead). After they have been finished and inspected, the cases are transferred to a finished goods storage area and recorded by the following entry:

Finished Goods Inventory	464,000	
Work-in-Process Inventory		464,000

To record the transfer of 80,000 cases to finished goods inventory at a standard cost of $5.80 per case.

Cost of Goods Sold   For this example, assume that the company sold all 80,000 of the cases it produced for $10 per case. This was recorded by the following entries:

Accounts Receivable.	800,000	
Sales Revenue		800,000
Cost of Goods Sold	464,000	
Finished Goods Inventory		464,000

To record the sale of 80,000 cases at a price of $10 per case and a standard unit cost of $5.80 per case.

Close Out Variance Accounts to Cost of Goods Sold

In the chapter, sales were assumed to equal production, so there were no ending inventories. (We explicitly consider in more detail the case of production not equaling sales in Chapter 17.) In this example, we assume that the company closes all variance accounts to Cost of Goods Sold. In many firms, this will occur at the end of the year, but we assume, for illustrative purposes, that Peak Division closes all variance accounts at the end of the month. The following entries accomplish this:

Cost of Goods Sold	61,180	
Direct Labor Price Variance	8,800	
Fixed Overhead Price Variance.	4,500	
Materials Price Variance		16,400
Materials Efficiency Variance		4,400
Direct Labor Efficiency Variance		8,000
Variable Overhead Price Variance		880
Variable Overhead Efficiency Variance		4,800
Fixed Overhead Production Volume Variance		40,000

To close the variance accounts to Cost of Goods Sold.

Thus, the total Cost of Goods Sold is $525,180, which is equal to $464,000 in standard costs plus the net production cost variances of $61,180.

REVIEW QUESTIONS

16-1. What are the advantages of the contribution margin format based on variable costing compared to the traditional format based on full absorption costing?

16-2. How can a budget be used for performance evaluation?

16-3. "The flexible budget for costs is computed by multiplying average total cost at the master budget activity level by the activity at some other level." Is this true or false? Explain.

16-4. A flexible budget is

    a. Appropriate for control of factory overhead but not for control of direct materials and direct labor.

    b. Appropriate for control of direct materials and direct labor but not for control of factory overhead.

    c. Not appropriate when costs and expenses are affected by fluctuations in volume.

    d. Appropriate for any level of activity.

                                            (CPA adapted)

16-5. What is the standard cost sheet?

16-6. What is the basic difference between a master budget and a flexible budget?

    a. A flexible budget considers only variable costs; a master budget considers all costs.

    b. A master budget is based on a predicted level of activity; a flexible budget is based on the actual level of activity.

    c. A master budget is for an entire production facility; a flexible budget is applicable only to individual departments.

    d. A flexible budget allows management latitude in meeting goals; a master budget is based on a fixed standard.

                                            (CPA adapted)

16-7. Standards and budgets are the same thing. True or false?

16-8. Actual direct materials costs differ from the master budget amount. What are the three primary reasons for the difference?

16-9. Fixed cost variances are computed differently from the variances for variable costs. Why?

16-10. How are actual direct labor costs used in a standard cost system? Does this differ from their use in a normal costing system? If so, how? If not, why not?

CRITICAL ANALYSIS AND DISCUSSION QUESTIONS

16-11. What is the advantage of preparing the flexible budget? The period is over and the actual results are known. Is this just extra work for the staff?

16-12. What is the link between flexible budgeting and management control?

16-13. "Actual revenues are greater than budgeted for December, so our revenue variance is favorable." Give an example of when this would be "good" news and when it could be "bad" news.

16-14. Pick an organization you know, such as a school, a local firm, a business, an entertainment business, a sports team, and so on. Identify an example of when a favorable cost variance (actual cost relative to a budget) is not good news for the performance of the organization.

16-15. Give two reasons why dividing production cost variances into price and efficiency variances is useful for management control.

16-16. A rush order for a major customer has led to considerable overtime and an unfavorable variance for production costs. Is this variance the responsibility of the marketing manager, the production manager, both, neither, or someone else?

16-17. "My firm has a wage contract with the union. Therefore, we do not need to compute a labor price variance; it will always be zero." Comment.

16-18. The production volume variance indicates whether a company has spent more or less than called for in the budget. True or false?

16-19. The production volume variance should be charged to the production manager. Do you agree? Why or why not?

16-20. A CEO tells you, "Division A always reports large, favorable variances. This saves us a lot of time because we do not have to spend time reviewing their results." Comment.

16-21. "Production cost variances are not useful in my company. There is substantial learning that takes place, so we are more efficient, the more we produce. A standard cost sheet doesn't reflect that." Do you agree?

16-22. Reviewing the variance report for one of the manufacturing plants in your company, you see a large unfavorable fixed cost price variance and large favorable production volume variance. You contact the plant controller, who says that there is no problem: "The two variances together are almost zero." How would you respond?

All applicable Exercises are included in Connect.      **EXERCISES**

16-23. Flexible Budgeting   (LO 16-2)

The master budget at Monroe Manufacturing last period called for sales of 42,000 units at $42 each. The costs were estimated to be $26 variable per unit and $524,000 fixed. During the period, actual production and actual sales were 45,000 units. The selling price was $41 per unit. Variable costs were $28 per unit. Actual fixed costs were $515,000.

Required
Prepare a flexible budget for Monroe Manufacturing.

16-24. Sales Activity Variance   (LO 16-3)

Refer to the data in Exercise 16-23.

Required
Prepare a sales activity variance analysis like the one in Exhibit 16.4.

16-25. Profit Variance Analysis   (LO 16-4)

Refer to the data in Exercises 16-23 and 16-24.

Required
Prepare a profit variance analysis like the one in Exhibit 16.5.

16-26. Flexible Budgeting   (LO 16-2)

The master budget at Cherrylawn Corporation at the beginning of the year was based on sales of 275,000 units with revenues of $3,300,000. Total variable costs were budgeted at $1,925,000 and fixed costs at $950,000. During the period, actual production and actual sales were 255,000 units. The actual revenues were $3,442,500. Actual variable costs were $6.50 per unit. Actual fixed costs were $980,000.

Required
Prepare a flexible budget for Cherrylawn Corporation.

16-27. Sales Activity Variance   (LO 16-3)

Refer to the data in Exercise 16-26.

Required
Prepare a sales activity variance analysis like the one in Exhibit 16.4.

16-28. Profit Variance Analysis   (LO 16-4)

Refer to the data in Exercises 16-26 and 16-27.

Required
Prepare a profit variance analysis like the one in Exhibit 16.5.

16-29. Flexible Budget   (LO 16-2)

The Main Street plant controller at Nowak Enterprises sends you the following graph to explain the plant's costs.

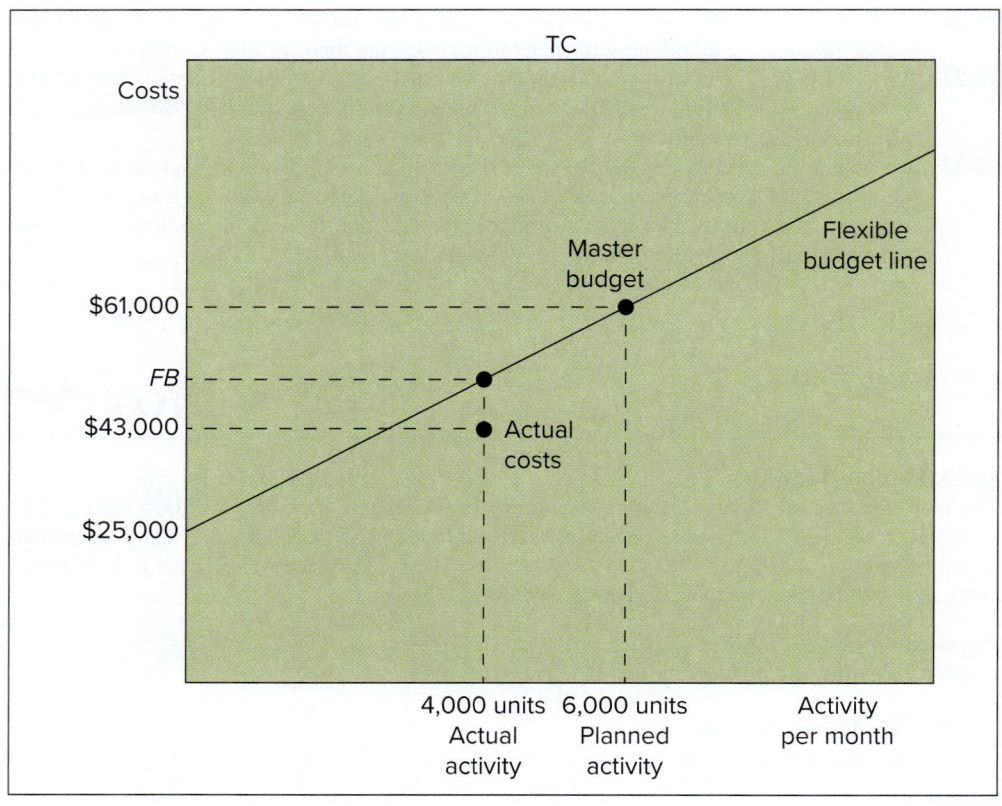

Required

Given the data shown in the graph, determine the following:

a.   Budgeted fixed cost per period.

b.   Budgeted variable cost per unit.

c.   Value of *FB* (that is, the flexible budget for an activity level of 4,000 units).

d.   Flexible budget cost amount if the actual activity had been 12,000 units.

(LO 16-2)   **16-30. Fill in Amounts on Flexible Budget Graph**

The following graph is from Welton Associates.

Required

Find the missing amounts for (a) and (b).

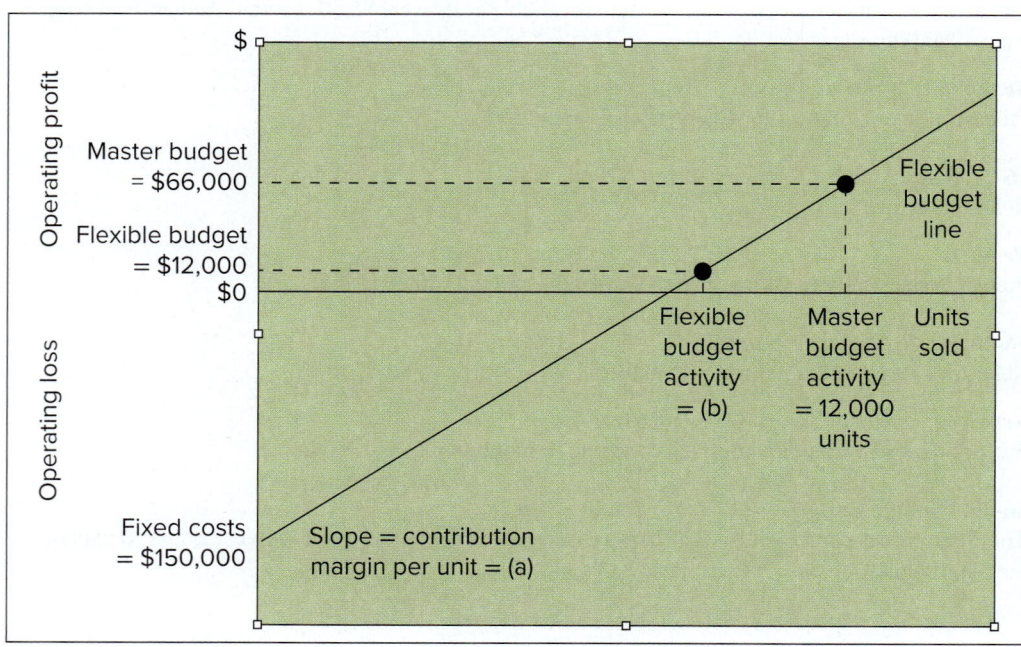

16-31. Flexible Budget   (LO 16-2)

The following graph is from Floyd & Company.

Required

Label (a) and (b) in the graph and give the number of units sold for each.

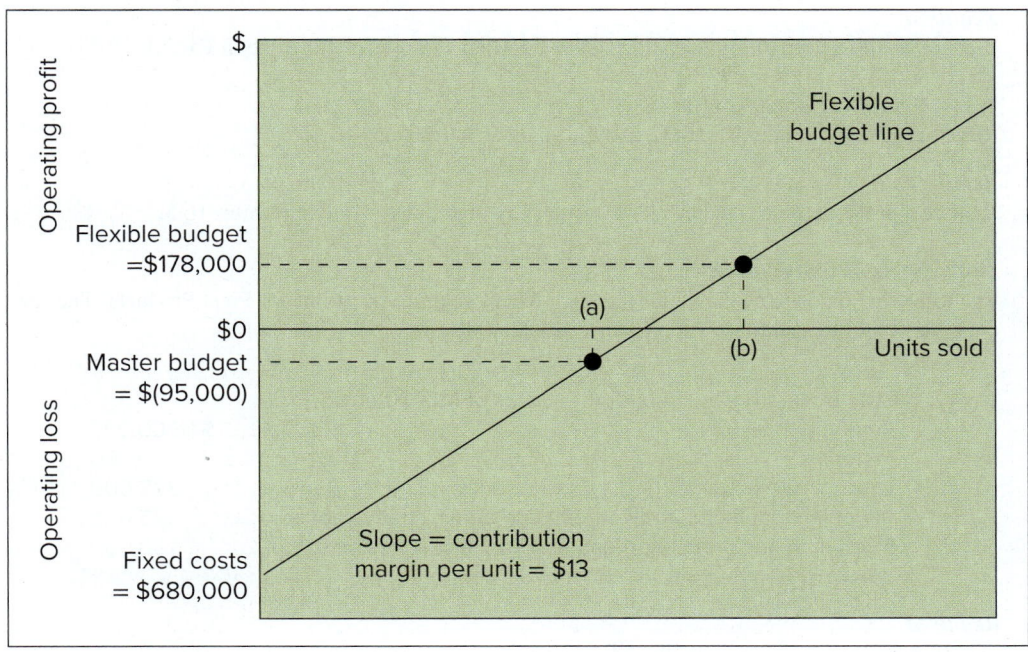

16-32. Prepare Flexible Budget   (LO 16-2)

Fournier Fixtures produces a variety of manufactured items for the home and building industry. The company produces only when it receives orders and, therefore, has no inventories. The following information is available for the current month:

	Actual (based on actual orders for 392,000 units)	Master Budget (based on budgeted orders for 350,000 units)
Sales revenue.	$7,448,000	$7,000,000
Less		
Variable costs		
Materials	2,600,000	2,310,000
Direct labor	230,000	210,000
Variable overhead	1,180,000	1,050,000
Variable marketing and		
administrative	860,000	770,000
Total variable costs	$4,870,000	$4,340,000
Contribution margin.	$2,578,000	$2,660,000
Less		
Fixed costs		
Manufacturing overhead	1,560,000	1,580,000
Marketing	475,000	460,000
Administrative.	300,000	325,000
Total fixed costs	$2,335,000	$2,365,000
Operating profits	$ 243,000	$ 295,000

Required
Prepare a flexible budget for Fournier Fixtures.

(LO 16-3)   **16-33. Sales Activity Variance**
Refer to the data in Exercise 16-32.

Required
Prepare a sales activity variance analysis for Fournier Fixtures like the one in Exhibit 16.4.

(LO 16-4)   **16-34. Profit Variance Analysis**
Refer to the data in Exercise 16-32 and the analysis in Exercise 16-33.

Required
Prepare a profit variance analysis for Fournier Fixtures like the one in Exhibit 16.5.

(LO 16-3)   **16-35. Sales Activity Variance**
The following data are available for the most recent year of operations for Prest Products. The revenue portion of the sales activity variance is $225,000 U.

Master budget based on budgeted sales of 45,000 units:	
Revenue	$1,500,000
Materials	510,000
Labor	375,000
Variable manufacturing overhead and administrative costs	75,000
Fixed manufacturing overhead and administrative costs	180,000

Required
a. How many units were actually sold in the most recent period?
b. Prepare a sales activity variance for the most recent year for Prest Products.

(LO 16-3)   **16-36. Sales Activity Variance**
Selected data for March for Irvington, Inc. follow. The variable material sales activity variance is $21,600 U.

Flexible budget based on actual sales of 9,750 units:	
Revenue	$280,540
Materials	93,600
Labor	73,840
Variable overhead	46,800
Fixed costs (manufacturing and administrative)	40,800

Required
a. How many units were budgeted for March in the master budget?
b. Recreate the master budget for March.

(LO 16-1)   **16-37. Assigning Responsibility**
Engleside Components produces testing equipment for medical devices. Recently, one of the company's usual suppliers was unable to fill an order, so the purchasing manager chose a supplier who had been approved. The price was significantly higher than the original supplier and the variance in manufacturing costs was charged to the purchasing department. Working with the new part turned out to be much easier than with the initial part and the labor required was significantly lower. The production department was credited with the favorable variance on labor costs.

   The purchasing manager argues that the purchasing department should receive some or most of the credit for the labor savings because it was their choice of vendor that resulted in using the new part. The production manager responds that the system is consistent with how variances have been assigned in the past.

Required
Write a short memo to the plant manager explaining how you would assign responsibility.

16-38. Flexible Budget   (LO 16-2)

Golden Food Products produces special-formula pet food. The company carries no inventories. The master budget calls for the company to manufacture and sell 120,000 cases at a budgeted price of $60 per case this year. The standard direct cost sheet for one case of pet food follows:

Direct materials	(3 pounds @ $2)	$6
Direct labor	(0.25 hour @ $32)	8

Variable overhead is applied based on direct labor-hours. The variable overhead rate is $16 per direct labor-hour. The fixed overhead rate (at the master budget level of activity) is $12 per unit. All nonmanufacturing costs are fixed and are budgeted at $2.2 million for the coming year.

At the end of the year, the costs analyst reported that the sales activity variance for the year was $336,000 favorable.

Required

Prepare a flexible budget for Golden Food Products for the year.

16-39. Profit Variance Analysis   (LO 16-4)

Refer to the information in Exercise 16-38. The following is the actual income statement (in thousands of dollars) for the year for Golden Food Products:

Sales revenue.	$7,800
Less variable costs	
Direct materials	800
Direct labor	992
Variable overhead	515
Total variable costs	$2,307
Contribution margin.	$5,493
Less fixed costs	
Fixed manufacturing overhead	1,480
Nonmanufacturing costs.	2,125
Total fixed costs	$3,605
Operating profit	$1,888

Required

Prepare a profit variance analysis like the one in Exhibit 16.5.

16-40. Variable Cost Variances   (LO 16-5)

Refer to the information in Exercises 16-38 and 16-39. During the year, the company purchased 320,000 pounds of material and employed 32,500 hours of direct labor.

Required

a.   Compute the direct materials price and efficiency variances.

b.   Compute the direct labor price and efficiency variances.

c.   Compute the variable overhead price and efficiency variances.

16-41. Variable Cost Variances   (LO 16-5)

The standard direct material cost per unit for Willis Group was $124 (= $31 per gallon × 4 gallons per unit). During the period, actual direct materials costs amounted to $1,635,480, materials used totaled 55,440 gallons, and 13,200 units were produced.

Required

Compute the direct materials price and efficiency variances for the period. (Refer to Exhibit 16.10 for the format to use.)

(LO 16-5)   **16-42. Variable Cost Variances**

Records at the Farnsworth Corporation contained the following data for the most recent period of activity:

Actual total direct labor cost	$468,100
Actual direct labor-hours worked	15,100
Standard direct labor-hours allowed for actual output (flexible budget)	14,200
Direct labor price variance.	$45,300F
Actual variable overhead	$347,300
Standard variable overhead rate per standard direct labor-hour	$22

Variable overhead is applied based on standard direct labor-hours allowed.

Required

Compute the labor and variable overhead price and efficiency variances.

(LO 16-5)   **16-43. Variable Cost Variances**

The records of Heritage Home Supplies show the following for July:

Standard direct labor-hours allowed per unit of output	4
Standard variable overhead rate per standard direct labor-hour	$24
Good units produced	3,400
Actual direct labor-hours worked	13,175
Actual total direct labor cost	$483,200
Direct labor efficiency variance.	$15,810F
Actual variable overhead	$316,200

Required

Compute the direct labor and variable overhead price and efficiency variances.

(LO 16-5, 7)   **16-44. (Appendix used in requirement [b]) Variable Cost Variances**

Rankin Fabrication reports the following information with respect to its direct materials:

Actual quantities of direct materials used	33,600 gallons
Actual costs of direct materials used	$186,480
Standard price per unit of direct materials	$5.60
Flexible budget for direct materials	$196,000

Rankin Fabrication holds no materials inventories.

Required

a. Prepare a short report for Rankin's management showing direct materials price and efficiency variances.

b. (Appendix) Prepare the journal entries to record the purchase and use of the direct materials using standard costing.

(LO 16-5, 7)   **16-45. (Appendix used in requirement [b]) Variable Cost Variances**

Information on Chicago Crafters direct materials costs follows:

Quantities of alloy purchased and used	77,200 pounds
Actual cost of alloy used	$3,782,800
Standard price per pound of alloy	$47.00
Standard quantity of alloy allowed	80,000 pounds

Chicago Crafters carries no materials inventories.

Required

a.   What were Chicago Crafters' direct materials price and efficiency variances?

b.   (Appendix) Prepare the journal entries to record the purchase and use of alloy using standard costing.

16-46. Fixed Cost Variances   (LO 16-6)

Information on Grixdale Partner's fixed overhead costs follows:

Overhead applied..............	$1,225,000
Actual overhead	1,149,000
Budgeted overhead	1,200,000

Required

What are the fixed overhead price and production volume variances? (Refer to Exhibit 16.17 for the format to use.)

16-47. Graphical Presentation   (LO 16-6)

Refer to the data in Exercise 16-46. Management would like to see results reported graphically.

Required

Prepare a graph like that shown in Exhibit 16.18.

16-48. Fixed Cost Variances   (LO 16-6)

Coe Parts applies fixed overhead at the rate of $6.80 per unit. Budgeted fixed overhead was $197,200. This month 28,120 units were produced, and actual fixed overhead was $192,100.

Required

a.   What are the fixed overhead price and production volume variances for Coe Parts?

b.   What was budgeted production for the month?

16-49. Fixed Cost Variances   (LO 16-6)

Annland Components applies fixed overhead at the rate of $5.10 per unit. For October, budgeted fixed overhead was $513,825. The production volume variance amounted to $3,825 favorable, and the price variance was $12,750 unfavorable.

Required

a.   What was the budgeted volume in units for October?

b.   What was the actual volume of units produced in October?

c.   What was the actual fixed overhead incurred for October?

16-50. Fixed Cost Variances   (LO 16-6)

Refer to the information in Exercises 16-38 and 16-39.

Required

What are the fixed overhead price and production volume variances for Golden Food Products?

16-51. Overhead Variances   (LO 16-5, 6)

The (partial) cost sheet for the single product manufactured at Briarcliff Corporation follows:

Direct labor	(2 hours @ $30)	$60
Variable overhead	(2 hours @ $9)	18
Fixed overhead.....................	(2 hours @ $11)	22

The master budget level of production is 45,000 direct labor-hours, which is also the production volume used to compute the fixed overhead application rate. Other information available for operations over the past accounting period include the following:

Actual variable overhead incurred	$ 411,000
Actual fixed overhead incurred.	463,000
Direct labor efficiency variance.	63,000 F
Variable overhead price variance.	6,000 U

Required

a.   What was the variable overhead efficiency variance?

b.   What was the fixed overhead price variance?

c.   What was the fixed overhead production volume variance?

(LO 16-5, 6, 7)   **16-52. (Appendix used in requirement [c]) Comprehensive Cost Variance Analysis**
The River Plant of Carlisle, Inc. produces a particular metal fixture used in aerospace and maritime industries. The following information is available for the last operating month:

- The plant produced and sold 27,600 fixtures for $72 each. Budgeted production was 30,000 fixtures.
- Standard variable costs per fixture follow:

Direct materials: 4 pounds at $4	$ 16.00
Direct labor: 0.1 hour at $40.	4.00
Variable production overhead: 0.4 machine-hour at $20 per hour	8.00
Total variable costs	$28.00

- Fixed production overhead costs:

Monthly budget	$810,000

- Fixed overhead is applied at the rate of $30 per fixture.
- Actual production costs:

Direct materials purchased and used: 105,000 pounds at $4.20	$441,000
Direct labor: 2,730 hours at $40.50.	110,565
Variable overhead: 12,000 machine-hours at $19.40 per hour	232,800
Fixed overhead.	817,000

Required

a.   Prepare a cost variance analysis for each variable cost for the River Plant.

b.   Prepare a fixed overhead cost variance analysis.

c.   (Appendix) Prepare the journal entries to record the activity for the last period using standard costing. Assume that all variances are closed to Cost of Goods Sold at the end of the operating period.

(LO 16-5, 6)   **16-53. Comprehensive Cost Variance Analysis**
Wetherbee Tech Services (WTS) is a chain of computer maintenance technicians for households and small businesses. The following data are available for last year's services:

- WTS recorded 120,000 tech calls last year. It had budgeted 125,000 calls, averaging 90 minutes each.
- Standard variable labor and support costs per tech call were as follows:

Direct IT specialist services: 90 minutes at $54 per hour	$81
Variable support staff, supplies, and overhead: 30 minutes at $24 per hour	12

- Fixed overhead costs:

> Annual budget. $4,140,000

- Fixed overhead is applied at the rate of $36 per call.
- Actual tech service call costs:

> Direct IT specialist services: 120,000 calls averaging
>   84 minutes at $56.00 per hour. $9,408,000
> Variable support staff, supplies, and overhead: averaging
>   40 minutes per call at $22.50 per hour × 120,000 calls   1,800,000
> Fixed overhead   4,378,000

Required

a. Prepare a cost variance analysis for each variable cost for last year.

b. Prepare a fixed overhead cost variance analysis like the one in Exhibit 16.17.

16-54. Overhead Variances   (LO 16-5, 6)

The Faraday Plant of Hindle, Inc. shows the following overhead information for the current period:

> Actual overhead incurred. . . . . $630,000 ($165,600 fixed and $464,400 variable)
> Budgeted fixed overhead . . . . $168,480 (8,640 direct labor-hours budgeted)
> Standard variable overhead
>   rate per direct labor-hour. $45
> Standard hours allowed
>   for actual production. . . . .   10,080 hours
> Actual labor-hours used . . . .   10,440 hours

Required

What are the variable overhead price and efficiency variances and the fixed overhead price variance?

All applicable Exercises are included in Connect.      **PROBLEMS**

16-55. Solve for Master Budget Given Actual Results   (LO 16-2, 4)

The following are the actual results for Bentler Associates for the most recent period:

> Sales volume . . . .   63,360 units
> Sales revenue $823,680
> Variable costs
>   Manufacturing   190,080
>   Marketing and administrative   38,550
> Contribution margin $595,050
> Fixed costs
>   Manufacturing   371,500
>   Marketing and administrative   103,450
> Operating profit. $120,100

The company planned to produce and sell 72,000 units for $12.50 each. At that volume, the contribution margin would have been $648,000. Variable marketing and administrative costs are budgeted at 5 percent of sales revenue. Manufacturing fixed costs are estimated at $5 per unit at the budgeted volume of 72,000 units. Management notes, "We budget an operating profit of $2.50 per unit at the budgeted volume."

Required

a. Construct the master budget for the period.

b. Prepare a profit variance analysis like the one in Exhibit 16.5.

(LO 16-4)   **16-56. Find Missing Data for Profit Variance Analysis**

The following, partially complete profit variance analysis is from October for La Salle Manufacturing:

	Reported Income Statement (18,000 units)	Manufacturing Variance	Marketing and Administrative Variance	Sales Price Variance	Flexible Budget ([a] units)	Sales Activity Variance	Master Budget (19,200 units)
Sales revenue	$468,000			(b)	$486,000	(c)	(d)
Variable manufacturing costs . .	(e)	$14,400 F			(f)	$9,120 F	(g)
Variable marketing and administrative costs	(h)		(i)		(j)	(k)	$57,600
Contribution margin	$297,600	(l)	(m)	(n)	(o)	(p)	(q)

Required

Find the values of the missing items (a) through (q). Assume that the actual sales volume equals actual production volume. (There are no inventory level changes.)

(LO 16-4)   **16-57. Find Data for Profit Variance Analysis**

McCoy Industries has prepared the following, partially complete profit variance analysis:

	Reported Income Statement (based on actual sales volume)	Manufacturing Variance	Marketing and Administrative Variance	Sales Price Variance	Flexible Budget (based on actual sales volume)	Sales Activity Variance	Master Budget (based on budgeted sales volume)
Units	(a)				(b)	10,000 F	50,000
Sales revenue	(g)			$16,200 F	(h)	(i)	$135,000
Less							
Variable manufacturing costs	(n)	(o)			$86,400	(j)	$72,000
Variable marketing and administrative costs	$19,440		(p)		$21,600	$3,600 U	(c)
Contribution margin	(q)	$8,100 U	(s)	(x)	$54,000	(k)	$45,000
Fixed manufacturing costs	(r)	1,800 F					(d)
Fixed marketing and administrative costs	16,200		(v)		$13,500		(e)
Operating profit.	(t)	(u)	(w)	$16,200 F	$18,000	(l)	(f)

Required

Find the values of the missing items (a) through (x). Assume that actual sales volume equals actual production volume. (There are no inventory level changes.)

(LO 16-2)   **16-58. Prepare Flexible Budget**

Nottingham Forest Products reports the following information concerning operations for the most recent month:

	Actual (based on actual sales of 4,800 units)	Master Budget (based on budgeted sales of 4,000 units)
Sales revenue	$228,700	$188,000
Less		
Manufacturing costs		
Direct labor.	50,302	39,000
Materials.	31,520	27,200
Variable overhead.	16,608	13,100
Marketing	7,805	6,200
Administrative	7,215	6,500
Total variable costs.	$113,450	$92,000
Contribution margin	$115,250	$96,000
Fixed costs		
Manufacturing	38,930	37,400
Marketing	14,860	12,200
Administrative	9,510	10,400
Total fixed costs.	$63,300	$60,000
Operating profits.	$51,950	$36,000

There are no inventories.

Required

Prepare a flexible budget for Nottingham Forest Products.

16-59. Sales Activity Variance   (LO 16-3)

Refer to the data in Problem 16-58.

Required

Prepare a sales activity variance analysis for Nottingham Forest Products like the one in Exhibit 16.4.

16-60. Profit Variance Analysis   (LO 16-4)

Refer to the data in Problem 16-58.

Required

Use the information for Nottingham Forest Products in Problem 16-58 to prepare a profit variance analysis like the one in Exhibit 16.5.

16-61. Prepare Flexible Budget   (LO 16-2)

The results for March for Savery Parts follow:

	Actual (based on actual sales of 14,700 units)	Master Budget (based on budgeted sales of 17,500 units)
Sales revenues	$263,865	$318,500
Less		
Variable costs		
Direct material.	51,520	63,100
Direct labor.	44,102	52,300
Variable overhead.	34,103	41,200
Marketing	12,204	13,100
Administration	18,191	21,400
Total variable costs.	$160,120	$191,100
Contribution margin	$103,745	$127,400
Less		
Fixed costs		
Manufacturing	36,460	33,000
Marketing	16,802	15,000
Administration	24,506	27,000
Total fixed costs.	$ 77,768	$ 75,000
Operating profits.	$ 25,977	$ 52,400

Required
Prepare a flexible budget for Savery Parts for March.

(LO 16-3)   **16-62. Sales Activity Variance**
Refer to the data in Problem 16-61.

Required
Prepare a sales activity variance analysis for Savery Parts for March like the one in Exhibit 16.4.

(LO 16-4)   **16-63. Profit Variance Analysis**
Refer to the data in Problem 16-61.

Required
Prepare a profit variance analysis for Savery Parts for March like the one in Exhibit 16.5.

(LO 16-5)   **16-64. Direct Materials**
Information about direct materials cost follows for Jennings Chemicals:

Standard price per gallon	$56
Actual quantity used............................	4,370 gallons
Standard quantity allowed for production	4,400 gallons
Price variance	$17,043 U

Required
What was the actual purchase price per gallon?

(LO 16-5)   **16-65. Solve for Direct Labor-Hours**
Parkdale Courier Service employs several delivery specialists. The following reports the information for these specialists for April:

Standard rate	$18.20 per hour
Actual rate paid	$19.30 per hour
Standard hours allowed for actual deliveries	16,400 hours
Labor efficiency variance......................	$14,560 U

Required
Based on these data, what was the number of actual hours worked and what was the labor price variance?

(LO 16-5, 6)   **16-66. Overhead Variances**
Monitor Devices shows the following overhead information for the current period.

Budgeted fixed overhead.........................	$460,000
Standard variable overhead rate per machine-hour.............................	$52
Standard machine-hours allowed for actual production	5,320 hours
Actual overhead incurred	$730,800, 60% of which is fixed
Actual machine-hours used	5,435 hours

Required
What are the variable overhead price and efficiency variances and fixed overhead price variance?

(LO 16-5)   **16-67. Manufacturing Variances**
Wisner Fabrication prepares its budgets on the basis of standard costs. Variances are analyzed and reported monthly. There are no materials inventories.

The following information relates to the current period:

Standard costs (per unit of output)
Direct materials, 5 pounds @ $12.00 per pound $60
Direct labor, 1.5 hours @ $30 per hour.   45
Factory overhead
Variable (30% of material cost)   18
Total standard cost per unit. $123

Actual costs and activities for the month follow:

Materials used . . . .   26,300 pounds at $12.40 per pound
Output . . . .   5,500 units
Actual labor costs . . . .   8,940 hours at $32 per hour
Actual variable overhead $95,790

Required
Prepare a cost variance analysis for the variable costs.

16-68. Overhead Cost and Variance Relationships   (LO 16-5, 6)
The following partial information is contained in the variance analysis received from the Western
Plant of Eastlawn Company. All plants at Eastlawn apply overhead on the basis of direct labor-hours.

Flexible budget for variable overhead based
on 3,500 direct labor-hours $98,000
Actual total overhead incurred $489,300
Actual direct labor-hours worked   3,562
Direct labor-hours used to determined the fixed
overhead application rate   3,250
Price variance for variable overhead . . . . $6,450 F
Price variance for fixed overhead . . . . $12,514 U

Required
a.   Prepare a variable overhead analysis like the one in Exhibit 16.12.
b.   Prepare a fixed overhead analysis like the one in Exhibit 16.17.

16-69. Analysis of Cost Reports   (LO 16-1, 4)
The following is a typical monthly report used to evaluate managers at the six manufacturing
plants of Missouri Foundries:

{PLANT NAME}
Cost Report
For the Month of {MONTH}

	Master Budget	Actual Cost	Excess Cost
Raw material.	$540,000	$552,600	$12,600
Direct labor.	228,000	225,200	(2,800)
Overhead	180,000	197,280	17,280
Total.	$948,000	$975,080	$27,080

Required
Identify and explain at least three changes to the report that would make the cost information more
meaningful and less threatening to the production managers.

(CMA adapted)

(LO 16-1)   **16-70. Change of Policy to Improve Productivity**

Hart Business Solutions operates call centers for multiple clients. Hart has suffered declining profits and is looking at ways to improve its performance. Because of competition in the industry, Hart managers do not believe they can raise prices without worsening the problem. It must either cut costs or improve productivity.

The company uses a standard cost system to evaluate the performance of the call center staff, specifically the operators who handle 95 percent of all calls. It investigates all unfavorable variances at the end of the month. The average time taken for a call rarely is less than the standard, resulting (in the managers' opinions) unnecessarily in extra staff (and higher costs). In most months, the variance is small, but generally unfavorable. The solutions that Hart managers decide to adopt is to lower the standard time allowed for a call. The center supervisor has informed the operators that they are expected to meet these new standards, just as they came close to the older standards.

Required

Will the lowering of the standard costs (by reducing the standard time of a call) result in improved profit margins and increased productivity? Explain.

(CMA adapted)

(LO 16-5, 6)   **16-71. Comprehensive Variance Problem**

The Valley Plant of Patton Supply manufactures a single product. The standard cost sheet for the product follows:

Direct materials, 2 pounds at $10.00 per pound..............	$20
Direct labor, 0.8 hour at $31.25 per hour....................	25
Factory overhead applied at 120% of direct labor	
(variable costs = $18; fixed costs = $12)....................	30
Variable selling and administrative cost	10
Fixed selling and administrative cost........................	12
Total unit costs...	$97

Standards have been computed based on a master budget activity level of 20,000 direct labor-hours per month. Actual activity for the past month was as follows:

Materials used	46,500 pounds at $9.90 per pound
Direct labor...............	17,800 hours at $32 per hour
Total factory overhead	$657,000
Production	22,500 units

Required

a.   Prepare variance analyses for the variable and fixed costs. Indicate which variances cannot be computed. Materials are purchased as they are used.

b.   Complete the following table with the total variance for a resource. Be sure to indicate whether the variance is favorable or unfavorable. If the total cannot be determined, enter a "?".

Resource	Amount U/F
Direct materials	
Direct labor	
Overhead	

(CPA adapted)

(LO 16-7)   **16-72. (Appendix) Recording Costs in a Standard Costing System**

Refer to the information in Problem 16-71. Assume there are no beginning inventories or ending inventories. All production was sold on account for $2,500,000. Selling and administrative costs were incurred as budgeted. Selling and administrative costs were paid in cash.

Required

Prepare the journal entries to record the activity for the last month using standard costing. Assume that all variances are closed to Cost of Goods Sold at the end of the month.

16-73. Find Actual and Budget Amounts from Variances   (LO 16-5, 6)

Copland Components manufactures an electronic device for vehicle manufacturing. The current standard cost sheet for a device follows:

Direct materials, ? ounces at $2.80 per ounce	$? per device
Direct labor, 0.4 hour at ? per hour	? per device
Overhead, 0.4 hour at ? per hour.	? per device
Total costs.	$30 per device

Assume that the following data appeared in Copland's records at the end of the past month:

Actual production	96,000	units
Actual sales	90,000	units
Materials costs (505,000 ounces)	$?	
Materials price variance.	63,000	U
Materials efficiency variance.	70,000	U
Direct labor price variance	18,750	F
Direct labor (37,500 hours).	918,750	
Overapplied overhead (total)	25,200	

There are no materials inventories.

Required

a. Prepare a variance analysis for direct materials and direct labor.
b. Assume that all production overhead is fixed and that the $27,000 underapplied is the only overhead variance that can be computed. What are the actual and applied overhead amounts?
c. Complete the standard cost sheet.

(CPA adapted)

16-74. Variance Computations with Missing Data   (LO 16-5, 6)

Anthon Corporation has provided the following information regarding last month's activities.

Units produced (actual).	10,500
Master production budget	
Direct materials	$237,600
Direct labor	201,600
Overhead	267,000
Standard costs per unit	
Direct materials	$3.96 per liter × 5 liters per unit of output
Direct labor	$33.60 per hour × 0.5 hour per unit
Variable overhead	$28.50 per direct labor-hour
Actual costs	
Direct materials purchased and used. . .	$207,480 (53,200 liters)
Direct labor	176,472 (5,160 hours)
Overhead	272,000 (58% is variable)

Variable overhead is applied on the basis of direct labor-hours.

Required

Prepare a report that shows all variable production cost price and efficiency variances and fixed production cost price and production volume variances.

(LO 16-5, 6) **16-75. Comprehensive Variance Problem**

Robinwood Fixtures manufactures two products, K4 and X7. The company prepares its master budget on the basis of standard costs. The following data are for September:

	K4	X7
Standards		
Direct materials	0.75 pound at $6.00 per pound	1 pound at $6.60 per pound
Direct labor	1.25 hours at $24 per hour	1.5 hours at $30 per hour
Variable overhead (per direct labor-hour)	$19.20	$21.00
Fixed overhead (per month).	$402,408	$477,360
Expected activity (direct labor-hours).	17,250	23,400
Actual results		
Direct materials (purchased and used).	9,300 pounds at $5.40 per pound	14,100 pounds at $6.90 per pound
Direct labor	14,700 hours at $24.30 per hour	22,200 hours at $30.60 per hour
Variable overhead	$291,060	$454,212
Fixed overhead	$376,740	$475,200
Units produced (actual).	12,000 units	14,400 units

Required

a. Prepare a variance analysis for each variable cost for each product.

b. Prepare a fixed overhead variance analysis for each product like the one in Exhibit 16.17.

(LO 16-7) **16-76. (Appendix) Recording Costs in a Standard Costing System**

Refer to the information in Problem 16-75. Assume that the company carries no beginning or ending inventories. Sales in March totaled $3,800,000 for both products combined.

Required

Prepare the journal entries to record the activity for the last month using standard costing. Assume that all variances are closed to Cost of Goods Sold at the end of the month.

(LO 16-5, 6) **16-77. Variance Analysis with Missing Data**

The following information concerning actual results is available from Hamburg, Inc.:

Sales volume	72,000 units
Sales revenue	$756,850
Variable costs:	
Manufacturing	198,520
Marketing and administrative	127,900
Fixed costs:	
Manufacturing	202,750
Marketing and administrative	62,440
Operating profit.	$165,240

The company planned to sell 64,800 units at a price of $11 each. Variable marketing and administrative costs are budgeted at 15 percent of revenue. You have discovered that the manufacturing fixed costs are budgeted to be $3 per unit at the budgeted volume. You know that the company policy is to budget for an operating profit of $2.55 per unit. Finally, you recall that the master budget for fixed marketing and administrative costs is $64,800. Hamburg does not carry any inventories.

Required

Prepare a report explaining the differences between the actual results, flexible budget, and the master budget.

16-78. Profit Variance Analysis (LO 16-2, 3, 4)

Harlow Parts produces a single product at its Superior Plant. The master budget for July follows:

	A	B
1	**Harlow Parts**	
2	**Superior Plant**	
3	**Master Budget**	
4	**(For July)**	
5		
6	Quantity	8,000
7		
8	Revenue	$ 1,520,000
9	Variable manufacturing cost	576,000
10	Variable SG&A cost	96,000
11	Contribution margin	$ 848,000
12	Fixed manufacturing cost	192,000
13	Fixed SG&A cost	350,000
14	Operating profit	$ 306,000
15		

The following operating income statement shows the actual results for July:

	A	B
1	**Harlow Parts**	
2	**Superior Plant**	
3	**Operating Results**	
4	**(For July)**	
5		
6	Quantity (units)	9,400
7		
8	Revenue	$ 1,710,800
9	Variable manufacturing cost	700,394
10	Variable SG&A cost	109,040
11	Contribution margin	$ 901,366
12	Fixed manufacturing cost	203,040
13	Fixed SG&A cost	360,000
14	Operating profit	$ 338,326
15		

Required

Prepare a profit variance analysis for the Superior Plant for July such as the one in Exhibit 16.5.

16-79. Production Cost Variance Analysis (LO 16-5, 6)

Refer to the information in Problem 16-78. Variable overhead is applied on the basis of machine-hours. The standard cost sheet follows:

Standard production costs				
Direct materials	5.00 kg.	@	$6.00	$ 30.00
Direct labor	0.50 dlh*	@	30.00	15.00
Variable overhead	0.75 mh**	@	36.00	27.00
Fixed overhead	0.50 dlh	@	48.00	24.00
Total unit cost				$ 96.00
*Direct labor-hours				
** Machine-hours				

The actual resource usage for July per unit of output follows:

Actual production costs					
Direct materials	5.25	kg.	@	$5.80	$ 30.45
Direct labor	0.48	dlh*	@	32.00	15.36
Variable overhead	0.70	mh**	@	41.00	28.70
Fixed overhead	0.48	dlh	@	45.00	21.60
Total unit cost					$ 96.11
*Direct labor-hours					
** Machine-hours					

Required

Prepare a manufacturing cost variance analysis for the Superior Plant for July such as those in Exhibits 16.10, 11, 12, and 17.

(LO 16-2, 3, 4)   16-80. Profit Variances—Analysis and Visualization

Refer to the information and analysis of Problem 16-78.

Required

Help the managers at Harlow understand the implications from the profit variance analysis by writing a short summary of your analysis. Include visualizations to highlight your conclusions.

(LO 16-5, 6)   16-81. Production Cost Variances—Analysis and Visualization

Refer to the information and analysis of Problem 16-79.

Required

Help the managers at Harlow understand the implications from the production cost variance analysis by writing a short summary of your analysis. Include visualizations to highlight your conclusions.

INTEGRATIVE CASES

(LO 16-2)   16-82. Ethics and Efficiencies

Keewee Company manufactures a single product for the military. Keewee Company had steady work, but it only had a return on investment of 6 percent.

The CEO of Keewee Company did a test flight of Keewee's product and subsequently had a heart attack and died. The board of directors hired a new CEO of the company. The board of directors had been disappointed for many years at the meager 6 percent rate of return. The board of directors offered the new CEO a substantial bonus if he raised the return on investment to 10 percent.

The new CEO went about his task of raising the return on investment. It turned out to be easier than he ever imagined. By installing a new standard cost system, he substantially improved efficiencies in the operations of the company. He made remarkable progress in turning the company around. In fact, the new CEO anticipated a return on investment of 15 percent for the year.

This created a dilemma for the new CEO. The board had promised a bonus if he reached the 10 percent threshold, but no additional bonus if he exceeded the 10 percent threshold. He discovered that if he deferred some revenue until next year, and prepaid some of next year's expenses, he would achieve a return on investment of 11 percent. (The company should have debited a prepaid expenses account, but they debited expenses instead.) He justified this action by saying he was "saving for a rainy day."

Before the end of the year, he renegotiated his contract with the board of directors, which specified additional bonuses if he exceeded the 10 percent percent return on investment.

Required

Why would the new CEO want to defer some revenue and prepay some expenses? Is this ethical?

(CMA Adapted)

16-83. agm-online: Performance Measurement and Variances

I thought the Internet would be an ideal way to distribute our products. We've had a lot of success with our direct sales, but now we can reach a much larger audience. The baskets we make and sell appeal to people everywhere. I thought about opening stores in other towns or maybe even franchising, but the web offers me a way to expand without losing control.

That's why the results for the first quarter of our web-based unit are so disappointing. We expected a small loss because of marketing and other start-up expenses, but I was not prepared for the beating we took.

Maya McCrum, President and CEO, AGM Enterprises

Organization

AGM Enterprises is a small, family-owned and -managed company that produces and sells wooden baskets. The company was founded in 1947 in California by Autumn McCrum as a way of supplementing the family income. The business remained small until 1990, when Maya McCrum took it over from her mother. Until that time, all orders were taken by the senior Ms. McCrum and all baskets were handmade by her. Ten years ago, Maya moved to a model of having "dealers" take orders and opened a small workshop where part-time labor produced the baskets. The dealers were also looking to supplement their incomes and, supplied with a small display inventory, displayed the baskets at home or at parties, and took orders. Order fulfillment was handled directly by AGM Enterprises personnel, who shipped finished baskets directly to customers. Little production inventory was kept.

Last year, Maya McCrum evaluated the costs and benefits of two alternative distribution channels in an attempt to expand the business beyond the West Coast. One alternative was to franchise the business. Maya was concerned that she and the managers of AGM would lose control, especially control over quality, which she felt distinguished AGM baskets. The other alternative was to begin taking orders over the Internet. Maya chose the Internet option. The company added a new managerial position, chief technology officer (CTO), and established a subsidiary, agm-online, to handle the new business. In an unusual move for the company, Maya went outside the small circle of family and friends and hired as the CTO Mary Brown, who had experience on both the technical and management sides of a local Internet start-up. Mary was looking for something new where she could be in charge of an entire operation and was excited that she could combine this with her interest in basket weaving. It was agreed that if she could meet or exceed her budget for the first year of operation, she would be given a substantial piece of agm-online.

The executives of AGM Enterprises considered the initial foray into the Internet to be an experiment to see if the "anonymous" approach would be effective in selling baskets. Until this time, AGM considered its network of dealers to be crucial in the growth it had experienced in the last several years. To this end, a separate workshop (factory) was established in Pennsylvania. One of the reasons for selecting Pennsylvania was the availability of part-time labor at lower costs than in California. Another was to attempt to penetrate the East Coast market by locating a workshop there, taking advantage of more immediate access to local market tastes and trends. It was decided that the Pennsylvania operation would produce exclusively for agm-online business and the California workshop would continue to handle the orders from dealers.

Most of the staff functions for agm-online were provided and controlled by AGM Enterprises. Mary Brown and Donna Cunha, the senior vice president of marketing for the parent company, jointly decided the marketing budget. While the budget was decided jointly, media decisions and advertising campaigns were run directly from the parent organization. Personnel and financial services were also centralized.

Mary contracted with a major telecommunications company to provide web hosting services for the operation. She wanted to go with a telecommunications company rather than a local Internet service provider (ISP) for reasons of reliability. The back office operations (billing, payroll, etc.) would be maintained on personal computers at the agm-online office.

The Initial Plan

AGM Enterprises (and agm-online) have a July 1 fiscal year, and the launch of agm-online was designed to coincide with the beginning of fiscal year 1. Maya and Mary decided that agm-online would initially offer only one of the company's many baskets for sale. Company managers believed this would simplify production scheduling and help maintain quality control for the workforce. The basket to be offered was the round basket, one of the company's most popular. The standard cost sheet for the basket is shown in Exhibit 16.20.

Exhibit 16.20

Standard Cost
Sheet—agm-online

Selling price			$25.00
Materials			
Reed (pounds per unit).	0.4 pound @ $5	$2.00	
Handle.		4.10	$6.10
Direct labor.	0.5 hour @ $12		6.00
Variable overhead.	0.5 hour @ $1		0.50
Fixed overhead			2.00
Total standard cost			14.60
Standard gross profit per unit			$10.40

The cost accounting system at AGM Enterprises and the one adopted for agm-online is a full absorption, standard cost system. Overhead is assigned to products (at standard cost) and not recognized in income until the product is sold. Variable overhead is allocated on the basis of direct labor-hours and fixed overhead on the number of units. The fixed overhead rate is based on an estimated production level for the quarter. All variances from standard are recognized in the period recorded.

Because of the uncertainty surrounding the demand for baskets using this new channel, the first-quarter budget was designed to be "easy" to meet. In addition, relatively large marketing expenses were budgeted for promoting the new channel at related websites and in craft publications. This was especially important in some of the East Coast publications because AGM had a small share in these markets. The first-quarter operating budget is shown in Exhibit 16.21. The marketing and administration budget included the costs incurred by the parent for providing these services, as well as the cost of the small staff assisting Mary Brown and Jeff Lancaster, the production manager at agm-online.

First-Quarter Results

At first, things went well for agm-online. Sales in July were sufficiently strong that managers thought the initial sales forecast might have been too limiting. Beginning in mid-August, however, events turned against the new operation. Workers at the telecommunications company went on strike. At first, there was little impact. On August 9, however, a phone line leading to the server was damaged. Because of the strike, the site went off the air. It was one week before supervisors were able to get the site back up. Although difficult to estimate, Mary suggested in a message to AGM Enterprises that the company lost about 5 percent in unit sales (i.e., about 400 baskets). She based this estimate on the fact that lines were down 7 days of the quarter (about 7.7 percent) but that some of the customers that were not able to connect would return when service was restored. Others would simply click on the next site their search engine identified.

In order to try and counteract some of the negative publicity that had occurred, agm-online offered some concessions to customers. One concession was free shipping on all orders over $100. (Initially, shipping was billed to the customer at cost.) This added $13,000 to the Marketing and Administration expenses for the quarter. Also, at Mary's request, additional marketing campaigns costing $32,000 were launched in craft magazines and on cable television. These efforts helped make up for the lost sales.

Exhibit 16.21

Operating Budget, First
Quarter—agm-online

Budgeted sales and production.		8,000 baskets
Revenue		$200,000
Variable costs		
Materials	$48,800	
Labor	48,000	
Variable overhead.	4,000	100,800
Budgeted contribution margin		$ 99,200
Fixed overhead		16,000
Budgeted gross profit.		$ 83,200
Marketing and administration		90,000
Operating profit (loss).		$ (6,800)

As sales were falling, the company was also hit by the booming economy in the state when the basket makers were finding better part-time employment in the local industries. As a result, agm-online had to increase the wage rate simply to maintain production.

Not all the news was bad, however. Mary had immediately identified a modification in the production process at the Pennsylvania workshop that reduced the scrap on each basket by 20 percent. This modification was used on all baskets produced in the quarter. (In the original process, scrap occurred in the initial cutting of the material and, therefore, no labor was lost because of the scrap.) In addition, she maintained the level of quality, so the company received no returns and many comments about future purchases. Still, she was concerned that this poor first-quarter showing was going to be difficult to make up.

> I came here because I wanted to work at a company that, first, I had a significant ownership stake in and, second, would allow me to pursue my interest in the craft of basket weaving full time. I'm afraid that, because of the strike, I won't meet the first-year budget and will lose my bonus shares. I think Maya is a fair person, but she has to answer to the other owners. They might not be so willing to assume that these results are because of events out of my control.

Exhibit 16.22 shows the actual results for the quarter. The actual direct (materials and labor) production inputs are shown in Exhibit 16.23. Actual total variable overhead for the quarter was $5,760 and actual fixed overhead was $16,000.

Next Steps

As Maya contemplates the future of the new distribution channel, she is concerned as well about the effect of the first quarter on her agreement with Mary.

> I would really like the answer to just one question: Should we rewrite our agreement? From what I have seen, Mary is really dedicated to the business. On the other hand, an agreement is an agreement. If we revise it now, what kind of problems will we have in the future?

Required

a. What were the factors that caused actual quarterly income to be less than budgeted? Quantify the effect of each of these factors. Be as specific as possible.

b. For which of these factors, if any, should Mary be held responsible?

c. Should Maya rewrite the agreement with Mary?

(Copyright © William N. Lanen, 2023)

Actual sales and production	8,000
Revenue	$176,000
Standard cost of goods sold	116,800
Gross profit	$ 59,200
Production cost variances	12,960
Marketing and administration	135,000
Operating profit (loss).	$ (88,760)

Exhibit 16.22

Actual Results, First Quarter—agm-online

Input	Quantity	Total Actual Cost
Materialsᵃ		
Reed	2,400 pounds	$11,520
Handle.	8,000 handles	31,200
Direct labor	4,800 hours	65,280

ᵃ All materials used in production. There are no materials or work-in-process inventories.

Exhibit 16.23

Actual Direct Production Quantities and Costs—agm-online

SOLUTIONS TO SELF-STUDY QUESTIONS

1.

	Flexible Budget[a] (based on actual activity of 110,000 units)	Sales Activity Variance (based on variance in sales volume)	Master Budget (based on planned activity of 100,000 units)
Sales units.	110,000	10,000 F	100,000
Sales.	$1,100,000	$100,000 F	$1,000,000
Less costs			
Variable costs			
Variable manufacturing costs (at $3.80 per unit).	418,000	38,000 U	380,000
Variable selling and administrative (at $0.90 per unit)	99,000	9,000 U	90,000
Total variable costs	$ 517,000	$ 47,000 U	$ 470,000
Contribution margin.	$ 583,000	$ 53,000 F	$ 530,000
Fixed costs			
Fixed manufacturing overhead	200,000	0	200,000
Fixed selling and administrative costs	140,000	0	140,000
Total fixed costs	$ 340,000	0	$ 340,000
Profit	$ 243,000	$ 53,000 F	$ 190,000

[a] Calculations for flexible budget:
$1,100,000 = (110,000 ÷ 100,000) × $1,000,000
$418,000 = (110,000 ÷ 100,000) × $380,000
$99,000 = (110,000 ÷ 100,000) × $90,000
U = Unfavorable variance
F = Favorable variance

2.

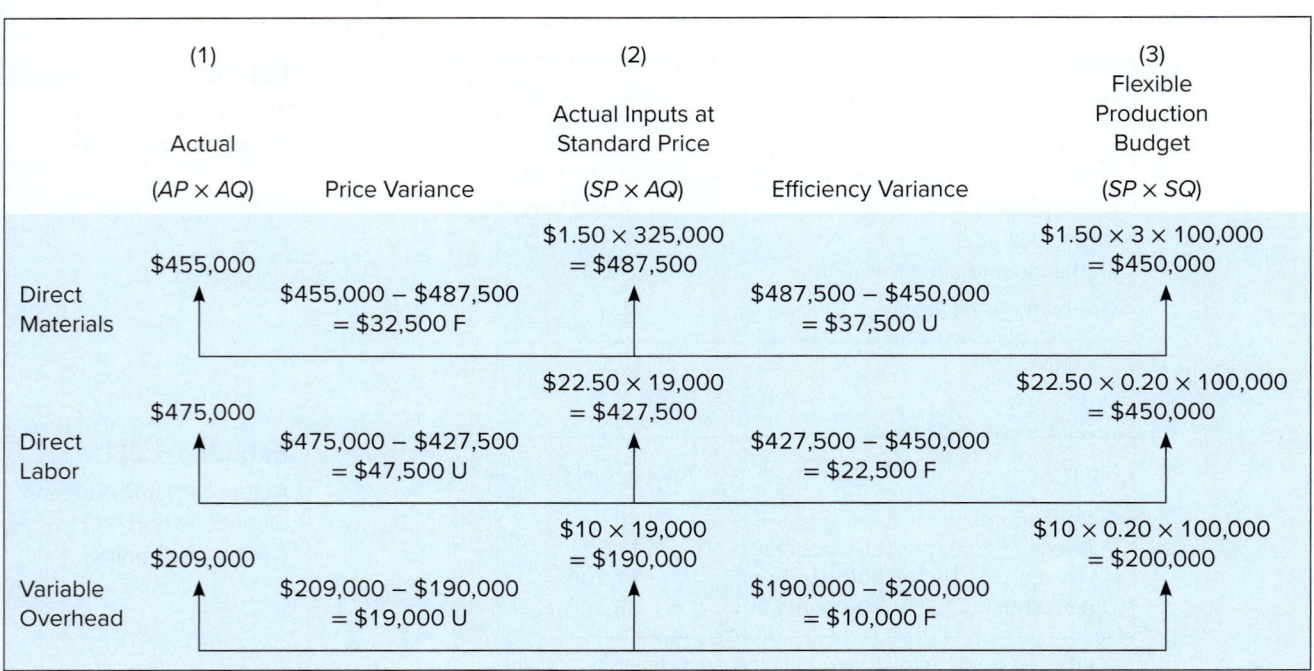

3.   The fixed overhead rate is $4 per unit (= $320,000 ÷ 80,000 cases).

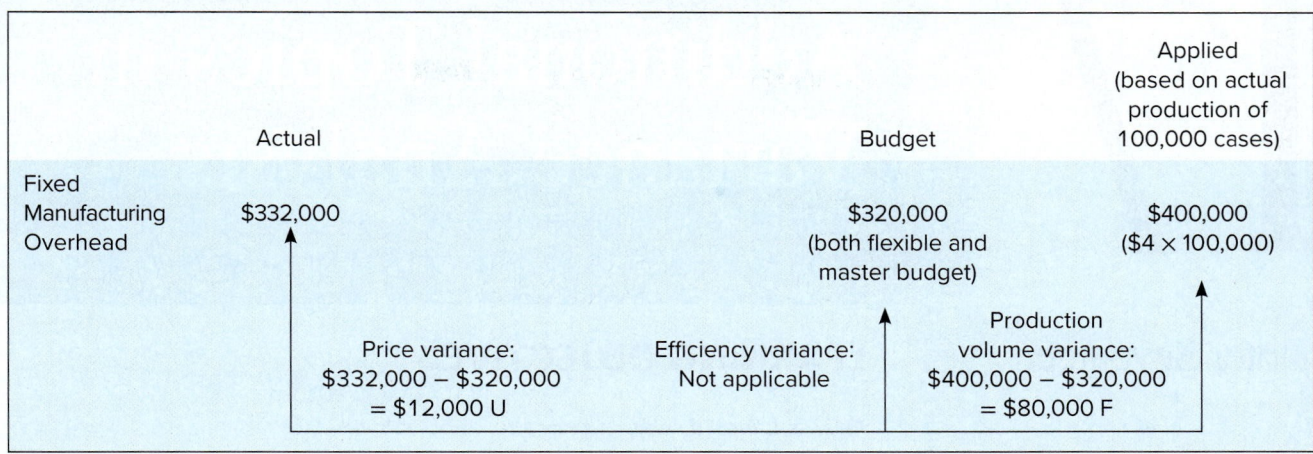

	Actual		Budget	Applied (based on actual production of 100,000 cases)
Fixed Manufacturing Overhead	$332,000		$320,000 (both flexible and master budget)	$400,000 ($4 × 100,000)
		Price variance: $332,000 − $320,000 = $12,000 U	Efficiency variance: Not applicable	Production volume variance: $400,000 − $320,000 = $80,000 F

17

Chapter Seventeen

Additional Topics in Variance Analysis

LEARNING OBJECTIVES

After reading this chapter, you should be able to:

LO 17-1 Explain how to prorate variances to inventories and cost of goods sold.

LO 17-2 Compute direct materials purchase variances when the amount used is not equal to the amount purchased.

LO 17-3 Use market share variances to evaluate marketing performance.

LO 17-4 Use sales mix and quantity variances to evaluate marketing performance.

LO 17-5 Evaluate production performance using production mix and yield variances.

LO 17-6 Apply the variance analysis model to nonmanufacturing costs.

LO 17-7 Determine which variances to investigate.

Ariel Skelley/Blend Images LLC

❝We learned a great deal by studying the variances in the Peak Division [see Chapter 16]. Now we are ready to extend that analysis to understand the results in more detail. Some of the questions we have include whether our revenue shortfall was due to general industry trends or a loss in our share of the market. Interestingly, we learned so much by applying variance analysis to manufacturing that some of our corporate staff managers want to apply it to their operations.❞

Keith Hunter, the CFO of Brunswick, Inc., talked about the results of the initial application of variance analysis at the Peak Division and the next steps he and the division are planning. Hunter is particularly interested in deciding how to address the shortfall in revenues in Peak and wants to know more about the relative effect of industry and company factors on the month's results. He is also planning to introduce other divisions at Brunswick, Inc., to variance analysis.

In this chapter, we discuss additional topics in using variance analysis to evaluate and control operations of the organization. We draw on the intuition developed in Chapter 16, so the basic ideas of variance analysis remain the same. Here, in Chapter 17, these ideas are used to illustrate their use in a variety of common situations that face many firms. We start by understanding how the presence of inventory affects our earlier analysis of variances. We then develop variances that arise when firms are interested in understanding better their sales activity variance. Specifically, we evaluate how unexpected changes in the following factors affect sales:

- Market share.
- Industry growth rates.
- The mix of products that customers purchase (for firms that sell a range of related products at different prices).

After looking more closely at sales variances, we turn to production and cost variances, where we analyze the input efficiency variances by considering the mix of inputs that can substitute for one another. We conclude by applying our analyses to service firms and developing a method to monitor variances and take corrective steps as warranted.

Profit Variance Analysis When Units Produced Do Not Equal Units Sold

Recall that in Chapter 16, Peak Division was projected to produce and sell 100,000 units but, in fact, only produced and sold 80,000. Suppose instead that Peak had produced 90,000 units but still only sold 80,000. How would this affect our prior analysis, and what new information is useful for managers to consider as they evaluate operations? Note that the assumption that production was greater than sales has no effect on the sales activity variance because the master budget and flexible budget are based on *sales volume*. Thus, Columns (5), (6), and (7) of Exhibit 16.5 remain unchanged. In addition, the sales price variance is based on units sold, so Column (4) remains the same. Generally, marketing and administrative costs are not affected by *producing* 90,000 instead of 80,000 units, so we assume that they do not change. This allows us to focus on Columns (1) and (2), which do change.

We assume that actual variable production manufacturing costs are $4.121 *per unit* (based on $329,680 ÷ 80,000 units as in Chapter 16) and actual fixed production costs are $195,500 *for the period*. This leaves the fixed production cost variance of $4,500 F unchanged. In addition to the $4,500 favorable fixed overhead price variance, there is now a $20,000 unfavorable production volume variance caused by producing 90,000 units when the budget called for production of 100,000 units [$20,000 = (90,000 − 100,000) × $2.00].

The variable production cost variance changes. In the month that units are produced, the following variable production cost variances are computed:

Units produced × (Actual variable cost − Standard variable cost) = Variance

> **LO 17-1**
> Explain how to prorate variances to inventories and cost of goods sold.

The example in Chapter 16 for *80,000 units produced* (Exhibit 16.5) is computed:

$$80,000 \times (\$4.121 - \$3.80) = \$25,680 \text{ U}$$

The example in this chapter for *90,000 units produced* (Exhibit 17.1) is computed:

$$90,000 \times (\$4.121 - \$3.80) = \$28,890 \text{ U}$$

The entire variable production cost variance for units *produced* in August is $28,890 U. This amount can be treated as a period cost and expensed in August, or it can be prorated to units sold and units still in inventory. If prorated, 8/9 (80,000 units ÷ 90,000 units), or $25,680, is charged to units sold in this case because 10,000 of the 90,000 units produced in August are still in inventory at the end of August. Most companies would write off the $28,890 variance due to August's production as a period expense. The $28,890 appears as a variance (Exhibit 17.1).

Note that the actual variable production costs of $332,890 in Exhibit 17.1 are really a hybrid: $304,000 in flexible budget costs (based on 80,000 units sold this period multiplied by $3.80 estimated variable cost per unit) plus the $28,890 variable production cost variance from the 90,000 units produced this period.

If the variances are not prorated, the following journal entry is made to close out the production cost variances (note that there is no production volume variance because with variable costing all fixed costs are expensed):

Cost of Goods Sold	24,390	
Fixed Overhead Price Variance	4,500	
Variable Production Cost Variances		28,890
To close production cost variances to Cost of Goods Sold.		

If the company prorates the variances between inventory and cost of goods sold, the entry is as follows:

Cost of Goods Sold	21,680	
Fixed Overhead Price Variance	4,500	
Finished Goods Inventory	2,710	
Variable Production Cost Variances		28,890
To close production cost variances to Finished Goods and Cost of Goods Sold: $21,680 (8/9 of the variances) is closed to Cost of Goods Sold and $2,710 (1/9 of the variances) is closed to Finished Goods Inventory.		

Reconciling Variable Costing Budgets and Full Absorption Income Statements

Assume that Peak Division produced 90,000 units and sold 80,000 of them in August. There was no beginning inventory on August 1, so the ending inventory on August 31 was 10,000 units. Using variable costing, the entire *fixed production cost* of $195,500 is expensed as shown in Exhibits 16.1 through 16.5 and Exhibit 17.1. This would not be the case, however, when standard, full absorption costing is used and production and sales volume are not the same.

Assume that an allocation base of 100,000 units is used for fixed production costs. Then, under standard, full absorption costing, each case of product is allocated $2 (= $200,000

Exhibit 17.1 Profit Variance Analysis When Units Produced Do Not Equal Units Sold, August—Peak Division

	(1) Actual (based on 80,000 units sold)	(2) Manufacturing Variances (based on 90,000 units produced)	(3) Marketing and Administrative Variances	(4) Sales Price Variance	(5) Flexible Budget (based on 80,000 units sold)	(6) Sales Activity Variance	(7) Master Budget (based on 100,000 units budgeted)
Sales revenue	$840,000			$40,000 F	$800,000	$200,000 U	$1,000,000
Less costs							
Variable costs							
Variable manufacturing costs	332,890	$28,890 U			304,000	76,000 F	380,000
Variable marketing and administrative costs	68,000		$ 4,000 F		72,000	18,000 F	90,000
Contribution margin	$439,110	$28,890 U	$ 4,000 F	$40,000 F	$424,000	$106,000 U	$ 530,000
Fixed costs							
Fixed manufacturing costs (net)	195,500	4,500 F			200,000	0	200,000
Fixed marketing and administrative costs	132,320		7,680 F		140,000	0	140,000
Profit	$111,290	$24,390 U	$11,680 F	$40,000 F	$ 84,000	$106,000 U	$ 190,000

Total variance from flexible budget
= $27,290 F

Total variance from master budget
= $78,710 U

Exhibit 17.2

Reconciling Income Using Standard, Full Absorption Costing and Standard, Variable Costing—Peak Division

	A	B	C	D
1		**(1a)**	**(1b)**	**(1c)**
2		**Actual (using standard, full absorption costing)**	**Fixed Costs Assigned to Inventory Using Standard, Full Absorption Costing (inventory adjustment)**	**Actual (using standard, variable costing)**
3	Sales revenue	$ 840,000		$ 840,000
4	Less			
5	Variable manufacturing costs (at standard)	304,000		304,000
6	Variable manufacturing costs variances (net)	28,890		28,890
7	Variable selling & administrative costs	68,000		68,000
8	Less			
9	Fixed manufacturing costs	160,000	$ (40,000)	200,000
10	Fixed manufacturing price variance	(4,500)		(4,500)
11	Fixed manufacturing production volume variance	20,000	20,000	
12	Fixed selling and administrative costs	132,320		132,320
13	Operating profit (loss)	$ 131,290	$ (20,000)	$ 111,290
14				

fixed manufacturing costs divided by an allocation base of 100,000 cases). A portion of the fixed production costs is allocated to the 10,000 units in ending inventory:

$$10,000 \text{ units } \times \$2 = \$20,000$$

or

$$(10,000 \text{ units } \div 100,000 \text{ units}) \times \$200,000 = \$20,000$$

If actual absorption cost were used, the ending inventory would include $21,722 [= (10,000 units ÷ 90,000 units) × $195,500].

Thus, only $175,500 (= $195,500 − $20,000) of the actual fixed production costs are expensed in August using standard, full absorption costing. This includes $160,000 of fixed manufacturing costs in standard cost of goods sold (= 80,000 units × $2 per unit), an unfavorable production volume variance of $20,000 (= 10,000 units × $2 per unit), and a favorable budget variance of $4,500. In this case, full absorption operating profit would be $131,290 in August, or $20,000 higher than variable costing operating profit.[1] This $20,000 difference in profits is due to the accounting system, not to managerial efficiencies. Care should be taken to identify the cause of such profit differences so those due to accounting methods are not misinterpreted as being caused by operating activities.

See Exhibit 17.2 for the reconciliation of the reported income statement under full absorption with that under variable costing. The comparison of budgeted to actual results presented in Exhibit 17.1 is still used; however, columns (1a) and (1b) are shown to reconcile actual results using variable costing to those using full absorption costing.

Materials Purchases Do Not Equal Materials Used

LO 17-2

Compute direct materials purchase price variances when the amount used is not equal to the amount purchased.

So far we have assumed that the amount of materials used equals the amount of materials purchased. Now we show how to calculate variances when the quantities purchased and used are not the same.

---

[1] Similarly, if the number of units sold exceeds the number of units produced, the reverse will be true; that is, full absorption operating profit will be lower than variable costing operating profit.

Recall the following facts from the Peak Division example:

Standard costs:	
4 pounds per case @ $0.55 per pound	= $2.20 per case
Cases produced in August:	80,000
Actual materials purchased and used:	
328,000 pounds @ $0.60 per pound	= $196,800

Now let's assume instead that 350,000 pounds were purchased in August at $0.60 per pound, 328,000 pounds were used, and there was no beginning materials inventory on August 1.

See Exhibit 17.3 for the variance calculations. Note that the **purchase price variance** differs from the example in Chapter 16 because it is based on the materials purchased. The efficiency variance is the same as in the previous example because it is based on materials used, which has not changed.

purchase price variance Price variance based on the quantity of materials purchased.

One advantage of using a standard costing system is that managers receive information that is useful in making decisions to improve performance. The sooner the information is received, the sooner it can be used. If materials are stored, recording the purchase at standard cost provides information on price variances earlier than if the company waits until the materials are used. Therefore, the following journal entry is used to record the purchase of materials at Peak Division in August:

Materials Inventory.	192,500	
Material Price Variance	17,500	
Accounts Payable		210,000

To record the purchase of 350,000 pounds of material with an actual price of $0.60 per pound and a standard price of $0.55 per pound.

Exhibit 17.3   Direct Materials Variance Computations When Materials Purchased Do Not Equal Materials Used—Peak Division

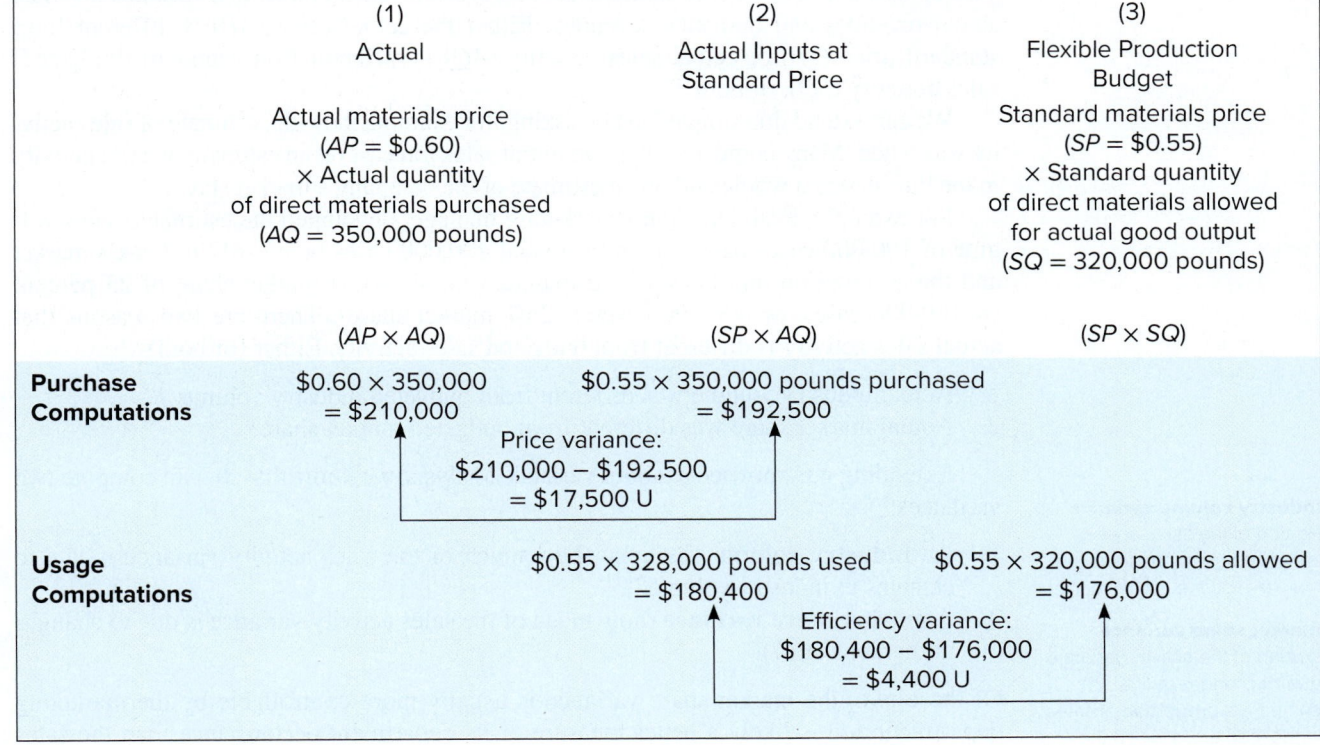

Once the material is in the materials inventory, all units have the same cost. When Peak used the material in August, it made the following entry:

Work-in-Process Inventory	176,000	
Materials Efficiency Variance	4,400	
Materials Inventory		180,400

To record the use of 328,000 pounds of material with a standard price of $0.55 per pound. Standard use is 320,000 pounds.

Self-Study Question

1. Turlock Tube, Inc., manufactures metal tubing. The standard materials usage for each unit is 0.5 pound. The standard cost of metal is $4 per pound. Actual results for September follow:

Production.	100,000 units
Materials used.	52,000 pounds
Materials purchased (67,000 pounds) . . .	$261,300

Compute the materials purchase price variance and the materials efficiency variance for September.

The solution to this question is at the end of the chapter.

Market Share Variance and Industry Volume Variance

LO 17-3

Use market share variances to evaluate marketing performance.

The general approach in variance analysis is to separate the variance into components based on a budgeting formula. For example, budget revenues can be expressed as

$$\text{Budget revenues} = SP \times SQ$$

where SP is the standard price of output and SQ is the master budget quantity (sales activity). Two components are used to estimate revenues, so two factors lead to a variance between actual revenues and budgeted revenues: Either the actual price (AP) is different from standard price (SP) or actual sales quantity (AQ) is different from standard (budgeted) sales quantity (SQ), or both.

We can extend this simple idea by asking, for example, how the estimate of sales activity was made. Many companies base an initial sales forecast on an estimate of sales activity in the industry as a whole and on an estimate of the company's market share.

For example, Peak Division's marketing manager developed the estimated sales volume of 100,000 cases based on an estimated 400,000 cases being sold in Peak's market and the assumption that Peak would maintain its historical market share of 25 percent (= 100,000 cases, or 400,000 cases × 25% market share). There are two reasons that actual sales activity is different from budgeted sales activity. Either (or both)

1. Actual industry volume was different from budgeted industry volume.
2. Actual market share was different from budgeted market share.

Extending our knowledge about variance analysis, we know that we can compute two variances:

industry volume variance
Portion of the sales activity variance due to changes in industry volume.

1. An **industry volume variance** (how much of the sales activity variance is due to changes in industry volume?).

market share variance
Portion of the activity variance due to changes in the company's proportion of sales in the markets in which the company operates.

2. A **market share variance** (how much of the sales activity variance is due to changes in market share?).

Of these two, the market share variance is usually more controllable by the marketing department and is likely a better measure of its department performance than the sales activity variance in total.

Exhibit 17.4 Industry Volume and Market Share Activity Variances—Peak Division

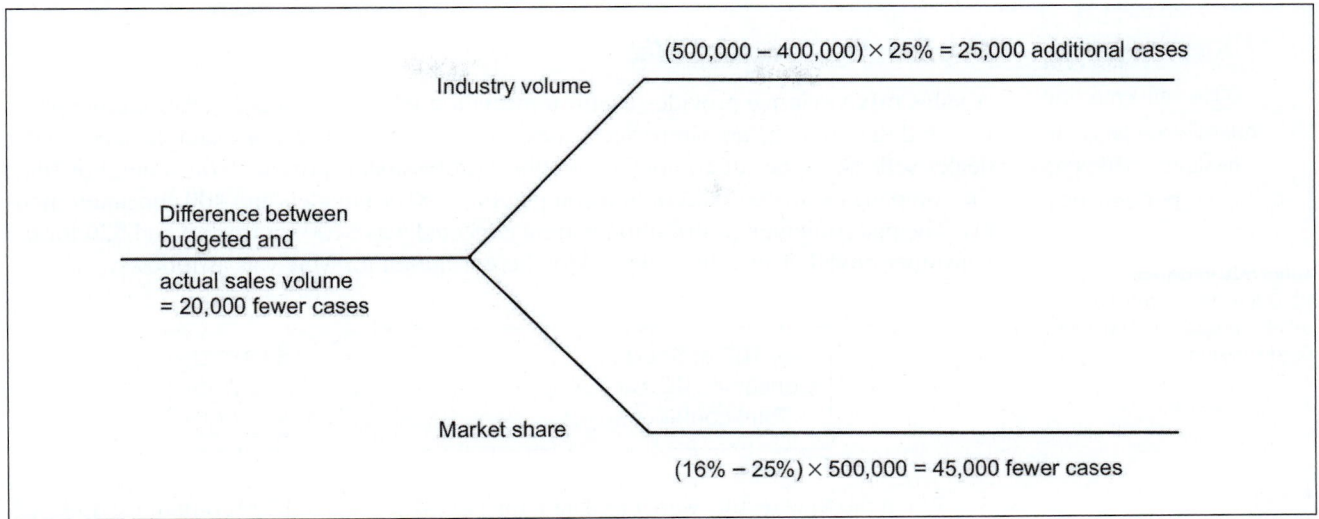

The volume in the industry increased from 400,000 units to 500,000 because a change in tastes led to increased consumption of energy drinks; Peak's market share, however, fell dramatically from 25 percent to 16 percent (= 80,000 cases ÷ 500,000 cases) as customers sought newer brands. Hence, the 20,000-unit unfavorable activity variance (the difference between the 80,000-unit actual sales and the 100,000-unit budgeted sales) can be broken down into an industry effect and a market share effect (see Exhibit 17.4).

The 20,000-unit decrease can be split as follows. Due to industry volume, Peak would have sold 25,000 additional cases, which is 25 percent of the actual increase in industry volume. However, Peak lost sales of 45,000 units as its market share fell from 25 percent to 16 percent.

Multiplying each figure by the standard contribution margin gives the impact of these variances on operating profits.

Industry volume variance	($10.00 − $4.70) × 25,000 F	=	$132,500 F
Market share variance.	($10.00 − $4.70) × 45,000 U	=	238,500 U
Sales activity variance.	($10.00 − $4.70) × 20,000 U	=	$106,000 U

The sales activity variance of $106,000 is exactly the same sales activity variance we computed in Exhibit 16.4. By decomposing it into an industry volume and a market share variance, we have additional information that can be used to make operational improvements next period.

The use of the industry volume and market share variances enables management to separate that portion of the activity variance that coincides with changes in the overall industry from that which is specific to the company. Favorable market share variances indicate that the company is achieving better-than-industry-average volume changes. This can be important information for marketing managers, who are constantly concerned about their products' market share.

Self-Study Question

2. Suppose that actual volume in Peak Division's industry was 250,000 cases and its actual sales volume was 80,000 cases (as before).

   a. Compute the industry volume and market share variances.

   b. Is your assessment of Peak management's performance different from the situation in the text in which actual industry volume was 500,000 cases? Why?

   The solution to this question is at the end of the chapter.

Sales Activity Variances with Multiple Products

LO 17-4

Use sales mix and quantity variances to evaluate marketing performance.

sales mix variance
Variance arising from the relative proportion of different products sold.

Evaluating Product Mix

A **sales mix variance** provides useful information when a company sells multiple products and the products are (imperfect) substitutes for each other. For example, a computer dealer sells two types of computers, graphics professional (pro) and consumer. For May, the company estimated sales of 500 computers—100 pro models and 400 consumer models. The per-computer contribution margin expected was $100 for the pro and $20 for the consumer model. Thus, the budgeted total contribution for May was as follows:

Pro: 100 at $100	$10,000
Consumer: 400 at $20	8,000
Total contribution	$18,000

When the May results were tabulated, the company had sold 500 computers, and each model had provided the predicted contribution margin per unit. The total contribution was a disappointing $14,000, however, because instead of the predicted 20 percent pro to 80 percent consumer mix sold, the actual mix sold was 10 percent pro and 90 percent consumer, with the following results:

Pro: 50 at $100	$ 5,000
Consumer: 450 at $20	9,000
Total contribution	$14,000

Companies that sell many related products budget sales by assuming a sales mix. Computing a sales mix variance gives managers information on whether the budgeted mix was achieved.
Marcello Bortolino/E+/Getty Images

The $4,000 decrease from the budgeted contribution margin is the sales mix variance. In this case, it occurred because 50 fewer pro models were sold (for a loss of 50 × $100 = $5,000) while 50 more consumer models were sold (for a gain of 50 × $20 = $1,000). The net effect is a loss of $80 (= $100 – $20) in contribution margin for each consumer model that was sold instead of a pro model. (This emphasizes the importance of assuming the products are substitutes. If a store sells, among other things, jewelry and garden tractors, the mix variance is probably not as useful as when comparing two products that are substitutes.)

Evaluating Sales Mix and Sales Quantity

Assume that Custom Electronics makes and sells two models of electrical switches, industrial and standard. Data on the two models for February are on the following page.

Although there are several approaches to calculating a sales mix variance, our computation allows us to break down the sales activity variance into two components:

sales quantity variance
Variance occurring in multiproduct companies from the change in volume of sales, independent of any change in mix.

1. Sales mix variance (which measures the effect of substitution of one product model for another).
2. **Sales quantity variance** (which measures the effect of changes in sales quantity, holding the sales mix constant).

See Exhibit 17.5 for calculations applying this to the Custom Electronics example. The sales price variance is unaffected by our analysis. The sales activity variance is broken down into mix and quantity variances. In this case, it appears that the industrial model has been substituted for the standard model.

A		B	C	D	E	F	G	H
	1	**Industrial**		**Standard**		**Total**		
2	Standard selling price	$ 15.00		$ 5.00				
3	Standard variable costs	8.00		2.00				
4	Standard contribution margin per unit	$ 7.00		$ 3.00				
5								
6	Budgeted sales quantity	10,000		40,000		50,000		
7	Budgeted sales mix	20%		80%				
8	Budgeted contribution margin	$ 70,000		$120,000		$ 190,000		
9								
10	Actual sales mix	23%		77%				
11	Actual sales quantity	9,200		30,800		40,000		
12	Budgeted contribution margin at actual quantities	$ 64,400	(a)	$ 92,400	(a)	$ 156,800		
13	Sales activity variance					$ 33,200	U	(b)
14								
15								
16	(a) $ 64,400 = $ 7 per unit × 9,200 units; $ 92,400 = $ 3 per unit × 30,800 units							
17	(b) $ 33,200 U = $ 156,800 − $ 190,000							
18								

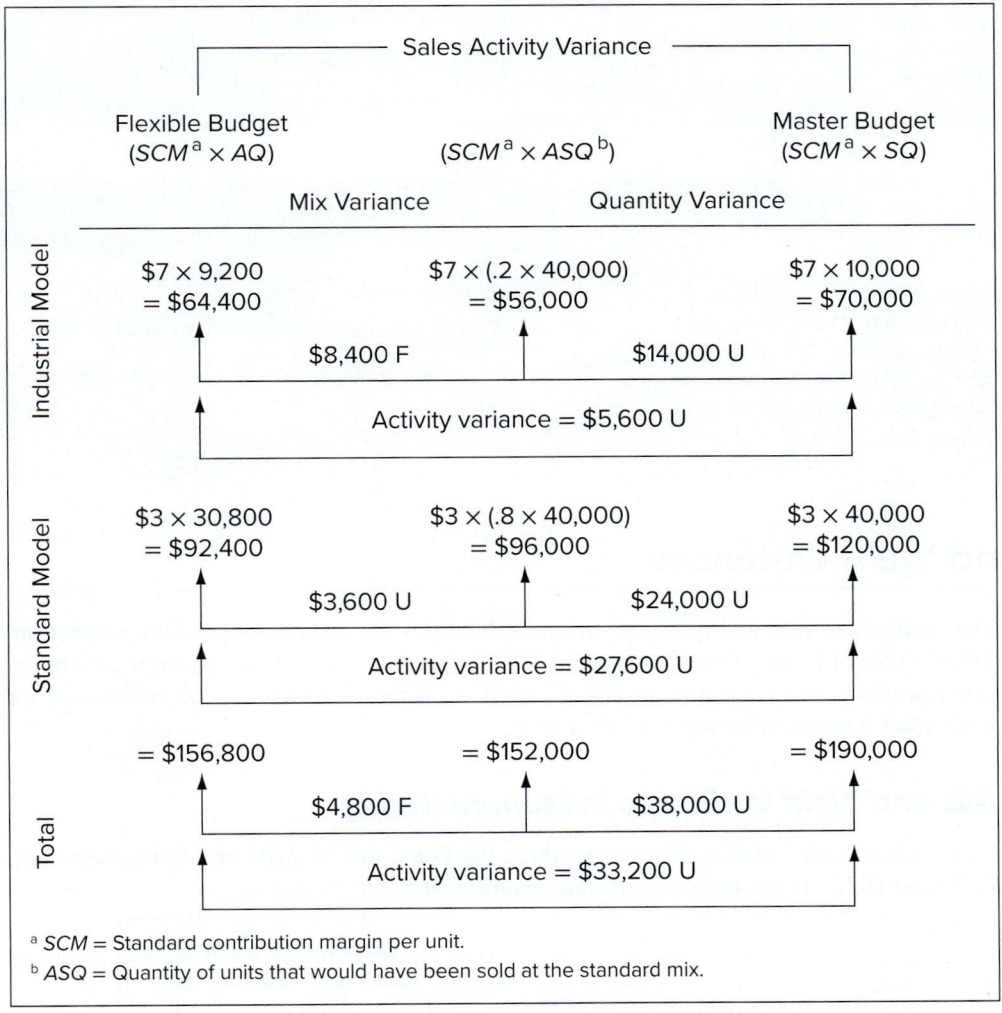

Exhibit 17.5

Sales Mix and Sales Quantity Variances, February—Custom Electronics

By separating the activity variance into its mix and quantity components, we have isolated the pure mix effect by holding constant the quantity effects, and we have isolated the pure quantity effect by holding constant the mix effect.

Source of the Sales Mix Variance

Although we have calculated the mix variance of each product sold to show the exact source, the total mix variance ($4,800 F) is most frequently used. In this example, the favorable mix variance results from the substitution of the higher-contribution industrial model for the lower-contribution standard model.

Business Application — Sales Mix and Financial Reporting

Firms often explain financial results in terms of variances between current and last period's operations. For a beverage maker, preparing a budget requires assumptions about, among other things, the mix in packaging. Boston Beer Company, Inc., maker of several beverages including Sam Adams beers and ales, delivers its products in kegs and in cans and bottles. Actual sales mix for the two packaging methods can affect both revenue and costs.

In its Form 10-K (Annual Report) for the year ended 2019, the company noted:

Significant changes in the package mix could have a material effect on net revenue. The Company primarily packages its products in kegs, bottles and cans. Assuming the same level of production, a shift in the mix from kegs to

bottles and cans would effectively increase revenue per barrel, as the price per equivalent barrel is lower for kegs than for bottles and cans. The percentage of bottles and cans to total shipments increased by 4.3% to 89.4% of total shipments for the year ended December 28, 2019 as compared to the year ended December 29, 2018.

In 2020, when the COVID-19 pandemic closed bars and restaurants, a great deal of beer consumption shifted to consumers' homes. Because the pandemic was unexpected at the time of budget preparation, we would expect an even more dramatic mix variance as customers rapidly shifted from kegs to bottles and individually packaged beverages.

Source: Boston Beer Co., Inc., Form 10-K, For the Fiscal Year Ended December 28, 2019, p. 32.

Self-Study Question

3. Assume that the master budget has sales of 2,400 units of alpha and 1,600 units of beta. Actual sales volumes were 2,640 of alpha and 1,560 of beta. The expected contribution per unit of alpha was $2 ($8 price – $6 standard variable cost), and the expected contribution of beta was $7 ($13 price – $6 standard variable cost).

Compute the sales activity variances and further break them down into sales mix and quantity components.

The solution to this question is at the end of the chapter.

Production Mix and Yield Variances

Our analysis of mix and quantity variances for sales also can be applied to production. Often a mix of inputs is used in production. Chemicals, steel, fabrics, plastics, and many other products require a mix of direct materials, some of which can be substituted for each other without affecting product quality.

Mix and Yield Variances in Manufacturing

Jersey Chemicals makes a cleaning product, EZ-Foam that is made up of two chemicals, C-30 and D-12. The standard costs and quantities follow:

Direct Materials	Standard Price per Gallon	Standard Number of Gallons of Chemical per Gallon of Finished Product
C-30......	$ 5	0.6
D-12......	15	0.4
		1.0

The standard cost per unit of finished product is

C-30: 0.6 gallon @ $5	$3
D-12: 0.4 gallon @ $15	6
	$9

During September, Jersey Chemicals had the following results:

Units produced	100,000 gallons of finished product
Materials purchased and used	
C-30	55,000 gallons @ $5.20
D-12	49,000 gallons @ $14.00
	104,000 gallons

Our computation of the materials efficiency variance breaks down the direct materials efficiency variance into two components:

1. The **production mix variance** measures the impact of input substitution.
2. The **production yield variance** measures the input–output relationship holding the standard mix inputs constant.

The mix variance for costs is conceptually the same as the mix variance for sales, and the yield variance is conceptually the same as the sales quantity variance. In this example, material D-12 appears to have been substituted for material C-30. This should be reflected in the production mix variance. In addition, standards called for 100,000 gallons of materials to produce 100,000 gallons of output. However, 104,000 gallons of input were actually used. The overuse of 4,000 gallons is a physical measure of the production yield variance and will be reflected in that measure.

To derive mix and yield variances, we use the term *ASQ,* which is the actual amount of input used at the standard mix. Calculations for the three variances (price, mix, yield) for Jersey Chemicals are shown in Exhibit 17.6. Note that the sum of the mix and yield variances equals the materials efficiency variance, which was discussed in Chapter 16. In examining these calculations, recall that the standard proportions (mix) of direct materials are C-30, 60 percent, and D-12, 40 percent; 104,000 gallons were used in total. Thus, *ASQ* for each material is as follows:

C-30:	0.6 × 104,000	= 62,400 gallons
D-12:	0.4 × 104,000	= 41,600 gallons
		104,000 gallons

By separating the efficiency variance into its mix and yield components, we have isolated the pure mix effect by holding constant the yield effect, and we have isolated the pure yield effect by holding constant the mix effect.

We have calculated the mix variance for each direct material to demonstrate its exact source. However, it is the total mix variance ($74,000 U) that is used most commonly. In this example, the unfavorable mix is caused by a substitution of the more expensive direct material D-12 for the less expensive direct material C-30. To be precise, the substitutions are as follows:

Decrease in C-30: (55,000 − 62,400) =	7,400 gallons @ $ 5	=	$ 37,000 decrease
Increase in D-12: (49,000 − 41,600) =	7,400 gallons @ $15	=	$111,000 increase
Net effect in gallons	–0–		
Net effect in dollars			$ 74,000 increase

production mix variance
Variance that arises from a change in the relative proportion of inputs (a materials or labor mix variance).

production yield variance
Difference between expected output from a given level of inputs and the actual output obtained from those inputs.

Exhibit 17.6   Production Mix and Yield Variances—Jersey Chemicals

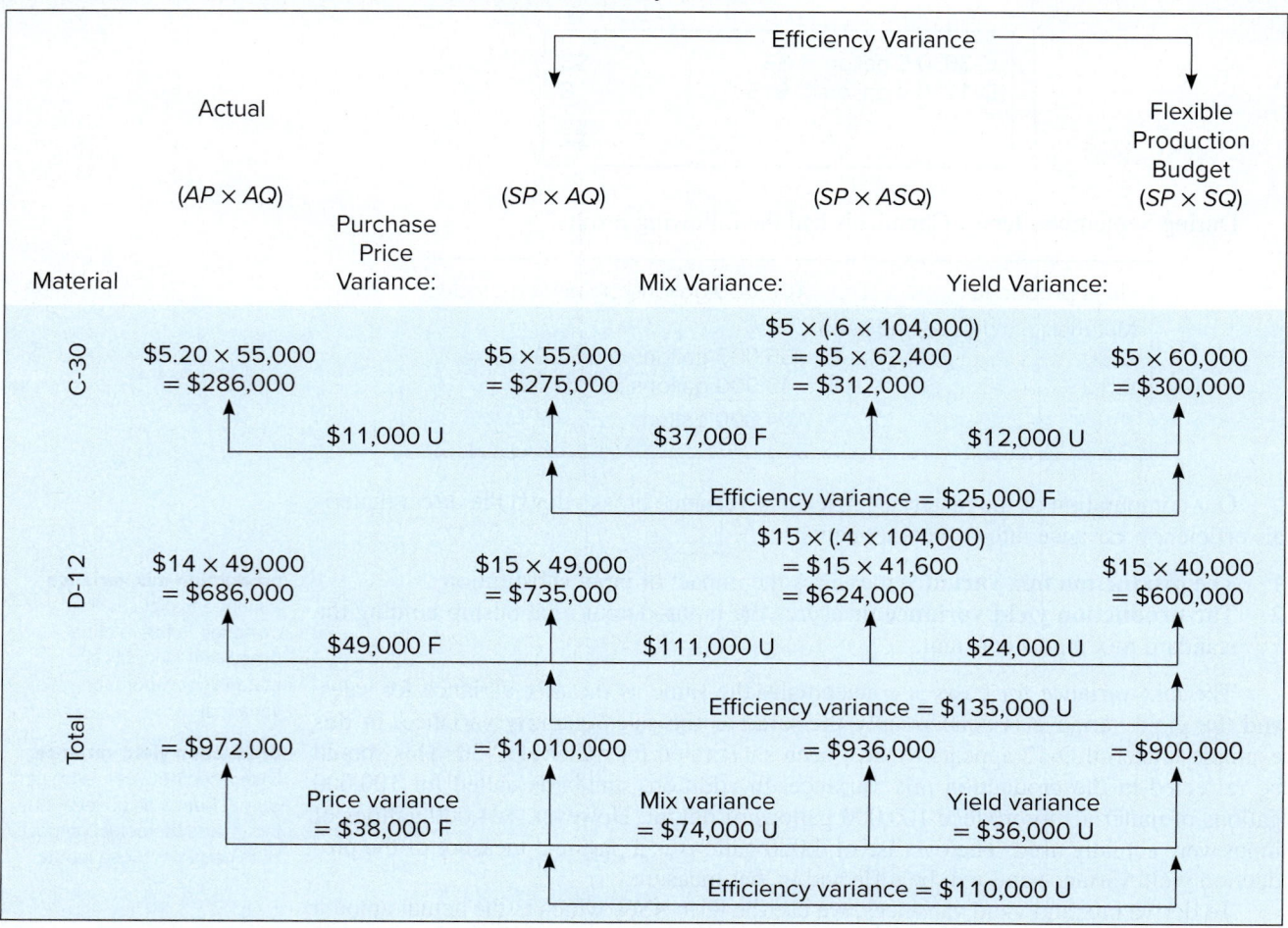

As previously indicated, the yield variance results from the overuse of 4,000 gallons, or more precisely:

Material C-30:	(62,400 − 60,000)	=	2,400 gallons @ $ 5	=	$12,000 U
Material D-12:	(41,600 − 40,000)	=	1,600 gallons @ $15	=	24,000 U
Total					$36,000 U

The journal entry to record the purchase and use of materials at Jersey Chemicals follows:

Work-in-Process Inventory	900,000	
Materials Price Variance—C-30	11,000	
Materials Yield Variance—C-30	12,000	
Materials Mix Variance—D-12	111,000	
Materials Yield Variance—D-12	24,000	
Materials Price Variance—D-12		49,000
Materials Mix Variance—C-30		37,000
Accounts Payable		972,000

To record the purchase and use of 55,000 gallons of C-30, with an actual price of $5.20 per gallon and a standard price of $5.00 per gallon, and 49,000 gallons of D-12, with an actual price of $14 per gallon and a standard price of $15 per gallon. Standard usage to produce 100,000 gallons of EZ-Foam is 60,000 gallons of C-30 and 40,000 gallons of D-12.

4. Duluth Castings Company makes a product, X-Tol, from two materials, Ticon and VF. The standard prices and quantities are as follows:

	Ticon	VF
Price per pound	$12	$18
Pounds per unit of X-Tol	6 pounds	3 pounds

In May, Duluth produced 35,000 units of X-Tol using the following actual prices and quantities of materials.

	Ticon	VF
Price per pound	$11.40	$16.80
Pounds purchased and used.	216,000	114,000

a. Compute materials price and efficiency variances.

b. Compute materials mix and yield variances.

The solution to this question is at the end of the chapter.

Variance Analysis in Nonmanufacturing Settings

Using the Profit Variance Analysis in Service and Merchandise Organizations

The comparison of the master budget, the flexible budget, and actual results also can be used in service and merchandising organizations. The basic framework in Chapter 16 is retained. *Output* is usually defined as sales units in merchandising, but service organizations use other measures, such as the following:

LO 17-6

Apply the variance analysis model to nonmanufacturing costs.

Organization	Units of Activity in Number of
Public accounting, legal, and consulting firms	Professional staff hours
Hotel.	Room-nights, guests
Airline.	Seat-miles, revenue-miles
Hospital	Patient-days

Merchandising and service organizations focus on marketing and administrative costs to measure efficiency and control costs. The key items to control are labor costs, particularly for service organizations, and occupancy costs per sales-dollar, particularly for merchandising organizations.

Efficiency Measures

The need for analysis of price and efficiency variances in nonmanufacturing settings is increasing. Banks, fast-food outlets, hospitals, consulting firms, retail stores, and many other organizations apply the variance analysis techniques discussed in both Chapter 16 and this chapter to their labor and overhead costs. In some cases, an efficiency variance can be used to analyze variable nonmanufacturing costs; its computation requires a reliable measure of output activity. Ideally, this requires some quantitative input that can be linked to output.

For example, personnel in the purchasing department of Peak Division are expected to process 10 transactions per day. The standard labor cost is $175 per day including benefits. During August, personnel worked 120 staff-days

Many service functions consist of routine transactions. Variance analysis provides a manager with information on employees' efficiency. Aaron Roeth Photography

Exhibit 17.7

Nonmanufacturing
Variance Analysis,
Purchasing Department—
Peak Division

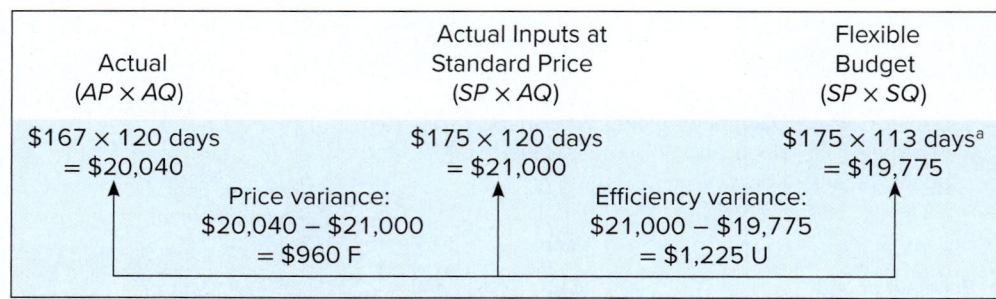

	Actual $(AP \times AQ)$	Actual Inputs at Standard Price $(SP \times AQ)$	Flexible Budget $(SP \times SQ)$
	167×120 days $= \$20,040$	175×120 days $= \$21,000$	175×113 days[a] $= \$19,775$
		Price variance: $\$20,040 - \$21,000$ $= \$960$ F	Efficiency variance: $\$21,000 - \$19,775$ $= \$1,225$ U

[a] 113 staff-days = 1,130 transactions ÷ 10 transactions per staff-day

and processed 1,130 transactions. The actual labor cost was $20,040. For 1,130 transactions, the number of standard staff-days allowed is 113 (= 1,130 transactions ÷ 10 transactions per day). Favorable price and unfavorable efficiency variances were computed (Exhibit 17.7). The calculations in the exhibit are similar to the ones used for labor variances in manufacturing.

Computing nonmanufacturing efficiency variances requires some assumed relationship between input and output activity. Examples include the following:

Department	Input in Number of	Output in Number of
Mailing	Labor-hours worked	Pieces handled
Personnel.	Labor-hours worked	Requests processed
Food service	Labor-hours worked	Meals served
Consulting	Billable hours worked	Customer revenues
Nursing.	Labor-hours worked	Patient-days
Check processing	Computer-hours worked	Checks processed

In general, jobs with routine tasks lend themselves to efficiency measures, and jobs with nonroutine tasks, such as most administrative positions, do not.

Mix and Yield Variances in Service Organizations

Companies also substitute different types of labor. Deloitte might substitute partner time for staff time on a particular audit job, for example. Suppose the Cleveland office has bid a job for 3,000 hours: 900 hours of partner time at a cost of $300 per hour and 2,100 hours of staff time at a cost of $100 per hour. Due to scheduling problems, both the partner and the staff member spend 1,500 hours on the job. If the actual costs are $300 and $100 for partner and staff time, respectively, there is no labor price variance. But even though the 3,000 hours required were exactly what was bid, the job cost is $120,000 over budget.

$$\begin{aligned} \text{Actual cost} &= (1{,}500 \text{ hours} \times \$300) + (1{,}500 \text{ hours} \times \$100) \\ &= \$450{,}000 + \$150{,}000 \\ &= \underline{\$600{,}000} \end{aligned}$$

$$\begin{aligned} \text{Budgeted cost} &= (900 \text{ hours} \times \$300) + (2{,}100 \text{ hours} \times \$100) \\ &= \$270{,}000 + \$210{,}000 \\ &= \underline{\$480{,}000} \end{aligned}$$

The $120,000 variance results from the substitution of 600 hours of partner time at $300 per hour for 600 hours of staff time at $100 per hour. The production mix variance is the difference in labor costs per hour ($300 − $100 = $200) times the number of hours substituted (600): $200 × 600 hours = $120,000.

Two factors are important when considering mix variances. First, there is an assumed *substitutability of inputs,* just as there was an assumed substitutability of sales products to make the sales mix variance meaningful. Although partner time may have been substitutable for staff time, the reverse may not have been true. Second, the input costs must be different for a mix variance to exist. If the hourly costs of both partners and staff were the same, the substitution of hours would have no effect on the total cost of the job.

Changes in Bank Distribution Channels—a Mix Variance Interpretation

Business Application

Our discussion of sales and production mix variances has focused on specific product features, whether different models for sale or different input mixes in production. However, the intuition and thought process you have developed in Chapter 16 and applied in this chapter can be used to think about how the variance analysis structure can be used to analyze other sources of profit and cost deviations from budget.

Consider one prominent service industry—banking—and how the service is delivered. For simplicity, we can identify two distribution channels for bank services: online and branch visits. Many banking services can be handled through either channel, but the two channels have different costs and profit impacts (for both the bank and the customer). Although banks have for some time been encouraging customers to use online channels for many services, the change has not been immediate. Therefore, banks need to budget for both channels.

However, in early 2020, due to the COVID-19 pandemic,

Branch traffic fell more than 30% in April and the first three weeks of May compared with the same period last year. . . .

If it is true that the online channel is less costly, this will be one cause of a favorable profit (cost) variance. Although measuring this variance may not be as straightforward as the sales or production mix variances discussed in the chapter, we know that we can measure what we might call the "channel-mix variance" as follows:

$$\text{Variance} = \begin{array}{c}\text{Flexible budget at actual volume}\\\text{at actual channel mix}\end{array}$$
$$-$$
$$\begin{array}{c}\text{Flexible budget at actual volume}\\\text{at standard channel mix}\end{array}$$

Although this is consistent with our previous variance definitions, the calculation is not as straightforward. One reason is that the two channels require not only different costs, but different resources. Instead of substituting one type of labor for another, the bank is substituting technology, often a substantial investment and a fixed cost, for the variable costs of teller services.

But the increased reliance on digital channels also poses a challenge for banks: making sure their platforms can handle more users and more transactions.

The trade-off between labor and technology is not unique to banks. It was an issue for virtually all service industries during COVID-19 as businesses struggled to hire workers and to modify work for safety.

More generally, this example illustrates that variance analysis is a tool to be used by managers to control the operations of their organizations in a variety of circumstances. Rather than just apply the most common variances, with ready-made formulas, the variances collected and analyzed should be designed for the questions and decisions these managers face.

Source: McCaffrey, Orla, "People Aren't Visiting Branches. Banks Are Wondering How Many They Actually Need," *The Wall Street Journal,* June 7, 2020.

Keeping an Eye on Variances and Standards

How Many Variances to Calculate

LO 17-7
Determine which variances to investigate.

We noted at the beginning of Chapter 16 that every organization has its own approach to variance analysis, although virtually all are based on the fundamental model presented here. The variances that will be important for a particular company will depend on the strategic imperatives for the company. What are the essential things that the company must do well to succeed? Once managers are clear on this, they can work with accountants and cost analysts to determine whether the costs of providing specific analyses are sufficiently beneficial to warrant the time and effort necessary to complete the calculations. Because of the unique circumstances in each organization, we cannot generalize very much about which variances should be calculated. Managers and accountants in each organization should perform their own cost–benefit analysis to ascertain which calculations are justified.

In deciding how many variances to calculate, it is important to note the **impact** and **controllability** of each variance. When considering *impact,* we ask, Does this variance matter? Is it so small that the best efforts to improve efficiency or control costs would have very little impact even if the efforts were successful? If so, it's probably not worth the trouble to calculate and analyze. Hence, detailed variance calculations for small overhead items might not be worthwhile.

When considering the *controllability* of a variance, we ask, Can we do something about it? No matter how great its impact, if nothing can be done about the variance, justifying spending resources to compute and analyze it is difficult. For example, materials purchase price variances are often high-impact items. They are difficult to control, however, because materials prices fluctuate because of market conditions that are outside the control of managers.

In general, high-impact, highly controllable variances should get the most attention, and low-impact, uncontrollable variances should get the least attention. Labor and materials efficiency variances often are highly controllable. With sufficient attention to scheduling, quality of employees, motivation, and incentives, these variances often can be dealt with effectively. An example of a high-impact but difficult-to-control item for many companies has been the cost of energy. Many organizations, from airlines to taxicab companies to steel mills, have been able to do little about rising energy costs in the short run. Over time, of course, they can take actions to reduce energy usage by acquiring energy-efficient equipment. In general, the longer the time interval considered, the greater the ability to control an item.

When to Investigate Variances

After computing variances, managers and accountants must decide which ones to investigate. Because their time is a scarce resource, managers must set some priorities. This can be done by using cost–benefit analysis. Only the variances for which the benefits of correction exceed the costs of follow-up should be pursued. In general, this is consistent with the **management by exception** philosophy, which says, in effect, "Don't worry about what is going according to plan; worry about the exceptions."

This is easier said than done, however. It can be almost impossible to predict either the costs or benefits of investigating variances. So, although the principle is straightforward, the application is difficult. In this section, we identify some characteristics that are important in determining which variances to investigate.

Some problems are easily corrected as soon as they are discovered. When a machine is improperly set or a worker needs minor instruction, the investigation cost is low and the benefits are very likely to exceed the costs. This is often true for a usage or efficiency variance, which is reported frequently, often daily, so that immediate corrective action can be taken.

Some variances are not controllable in the short run. Labor price variances that are due to changes in union contracts and overhead spending variances resulting from unplanned utility and property tax rate changes might require little or no follow-up in the short run. Such variances sometimes prompt long-run action, such as moving a plant to a locale with lower wage rates and lower utility and property tax rates. In such cases, the short-run benefits of variance investigation are low, but the long-run benefits could be higher.

Many variances occur because of errors in recording, bookkeeping adjustments, or timing problems. A variance reporting system (and the accounting department) can lose credibility if it makes bookkeeping errors and adjustments. For this reason, the accounting staff must carefully check variance reports before sending them to operating managers.

impact
Likely monetary effect from an activity (such as a variance).

controllability
Extent to which an item can be managed.

management by exception
Approach to management requiring that reports emphasize the deviation from an accepted base point, such as a standard, a budget, an industry average, or a prior-period experience.

Updating Standards

Standards are estimates. As such, they might not reflect conditions that actually occur, especially when standards are not updated and revised to reflect current conditions. If prices and operating methods are changed frequently, standards could be constantly out of date.

Many companies revise standards once a year. Thus, variances occur because conditions change during the year but the standards do not. When conditions change but are known to be temporary, some companies develop a **planned variance**. For example, we discussed in Chapter 10 the problems caused by using expected production to allocate fixed overhead using expected activity when a firm has excess capacity. For this reason, some firms use a long-run "normal" volume to allocate fixed production costs. In a year when expected activity will be below normal volume, the company expects, or plans for, an unfavorable volume variance.

planned variance
Variance that is expected to occur if certain conditions affect operations.

Using a planned variance, the company sends managers the right signal about product costs, but, because they planned for the unfavorable production volume variance, it does not affect the performance evaluation and control activity.

Monitoring Variances with Charts

One approach to helping managers decide when to investigate variances is based on the concept of process control charts. Long associated with the quality control approach to operations management, **process control charts** provide a graphical approach to highlight performance and signal when a process is "out of control." The idea is based on monitoring the variation in a process. Process outcomes vary for two general reasons. First, there are normal operating fluctuations caused by random, uncontrollable events (weather, special events, and so on). These are considered to be "noise" that cannot be corrected and is a normal part of the environment.

process control chart
A graph or other visualization that plots or reflects process outcomes over time.

Other fluctuations are caused by something systematic in the process, such as the introduction of less (or more) skilled labor, machine deterioration, or other factors. The fluctuations, as reflected in the process outcome, are a "signal" that something has changed and is causing the process measure to vary from its expected value. The purpose of a process control chart is to ignore the normal fluctuations due to noise and investigate when the fluctuation is signaling a systematic problem. The problem is separating the signal from the noise.

To do this, process control charts plot process outcomes over time on a chart that is centered around the mean outcome and with lower and upper limits set based on the estimated variation of the process. Typically, these lower and upper limits are set at ± 3 standard deviations. However, keep in mind that for accounting variances, the reliability of the statistical estimates is lower because they are typically based on relatively few observations. Over time, as variances are reported, managers may choose not to investigate a variance as long as it remains "in process," that is, as long as any fluctuation is less than three standard deviations from the mean. If the process outcome (a variance) rises above or falls below one of the control limits, it is an indication to managers to investigate the causes of the variance.

We illustrate this idea with information from another division at Brunswick, Inc. (the parent company of Peak Division). The Supplements Division at Brunswick manufactures various nutrition supplements. Data on the materials efficiency variance for the previous 24 months at the Supplements Plant is shown in Exhibit 17.8.

As indicated in Exhibit 17.8, the materials efficiency variances reflect a fair amount of variation over time. The variances are both favorable and unfavorable. Is there any reason to investigate these variances, or are they merely reflecting "noise" in the production process?

To help answer this question, managers at the Supplement Division estimated the mean and standard deviation of this variance based on information from the production of a related product. They estimated a mean variance of $0 and a standard deviation of $3,300. With this information, they prepared the process control chart shown in Exhibit 17.9.

Exhibit 17.8

Monthly Materials Efficiency Variance at Supplements Division: Unfavorable Variances Shown as Negative Numbers (in parentheses)

	A	B
	Month	**Variance**
1	1	$ 181.6
2	2	11,602.8
3	3	6,685.1
4	4	(706.1)
5	5	7,318.3
6	6	(1,048.0)
7	7	(2,762.0)
8	8	1,866.0
9	9	(1,591.0)
10	10	4,262.8
11	11	(5,035.5)
12	12	(1,213.7)
13	13	8,296.9
14	14	(10,627.7)
15	15	9,194.4
16	16	569.4
17	17	5,129.1
18	18	(6,588.5)
19	19	(1,011.1)
20	20	(2,113.9)
21	21	(1,029.9)
22	22	6,527.7
23	23	1,406.4
24	24	9,110.3

Exhibit 17.9 Process Control Chart for Materials Efficiency Variance—Supplements Division

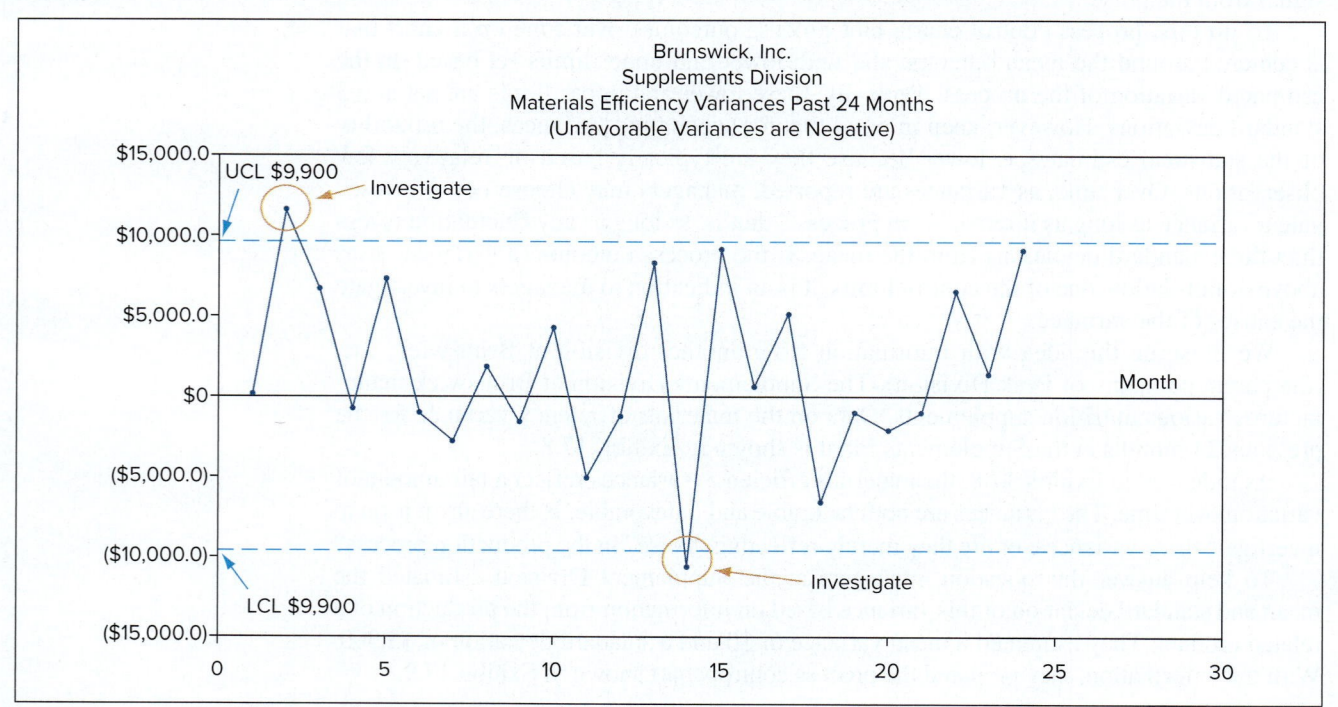

The process control chart in Exhibit 17.9 graphs the materials efficiency variance over time. The two dashed lines represent the upper and lower control limits, which are three standard deviations from the mean. Managers monitoring this chart will consider most months' variation to be "within limits." However, the variances in month 2 ($11,602.8 F) and month 14 ($10,627.7 U) are outside the control limits. The managers will investigate these variances to determine if something needs to be corrected or if one or both represent an unusual event.

One major challenge to applying the concept of process control charts to accounting variances is that it is often not feasible to obtain reliable statistical measures of the process. This is partly because many processes do not remain the same long enough to generate a reasonable base of observations to estimate the statistics. This does not mean that the concept of control charts is not useful for monitoring variances, however. The charts provide a useful visual report of what is occurring. Consider, for example, the 24 months of data on materials efficiency variance from the Supplements Plant. Suppose the data had been as shown in Exhibit 17.10. The monthly variances are the same, but the pattern is different.

The managers at the Supplements Division do not believe that they have reliable estimates of the standard deviation, so they ask for the process control chart with no control limits included. The resulting chart is shown in Exhibit 17.11.

Although there are no control limits, the chart in Exhibit 17.11 is still useful for managers trying to decide whether to investigate the variances. There appears to be a definite trend with the six most recent months having unfavorable variances. It should be noted that the large number of favorable variances in the months 9–16 would also warrant investigation.

Process control charts are a useful tool for managing variances. Remember that they are a managerial, not scientific, tool. Managers have scarce resources, so it is important

	A	B
1	**Month**	**Variance**
2	1	$ 181.6
3	2	(706.1)
4	3	1,866.0
5	4	569.4
6	5	6,527.7
7	6	11,602.8
8	7	6,685.1
9	8	(1,591.0)
10	9	7,318.3
11	10	4,262.8
12	11	8,296.9
13	12	(1,213.7)
14	13	9,194.4
15	14	(1,011.1)
16	15	5,129.1
17	16	9,110.3
18	17	1,406.4
19	18	(2,762.0)
20	19	(5,035.5)
21	20	(2,113.9)
22	21	(1,029.9)
23	22	(10,627.7)
24	23	(1,048.0)
25	24	(6,588.5)
26		

Exhibit 17.10
Monthly Materials Efficiency Variance at Supplements Division: Unfavorable Variances Shown as Negative Numbers—A Different Pattern

Exhibit 17.11   Process Control Chart for Materials Efficiency Variance—Supplements Division

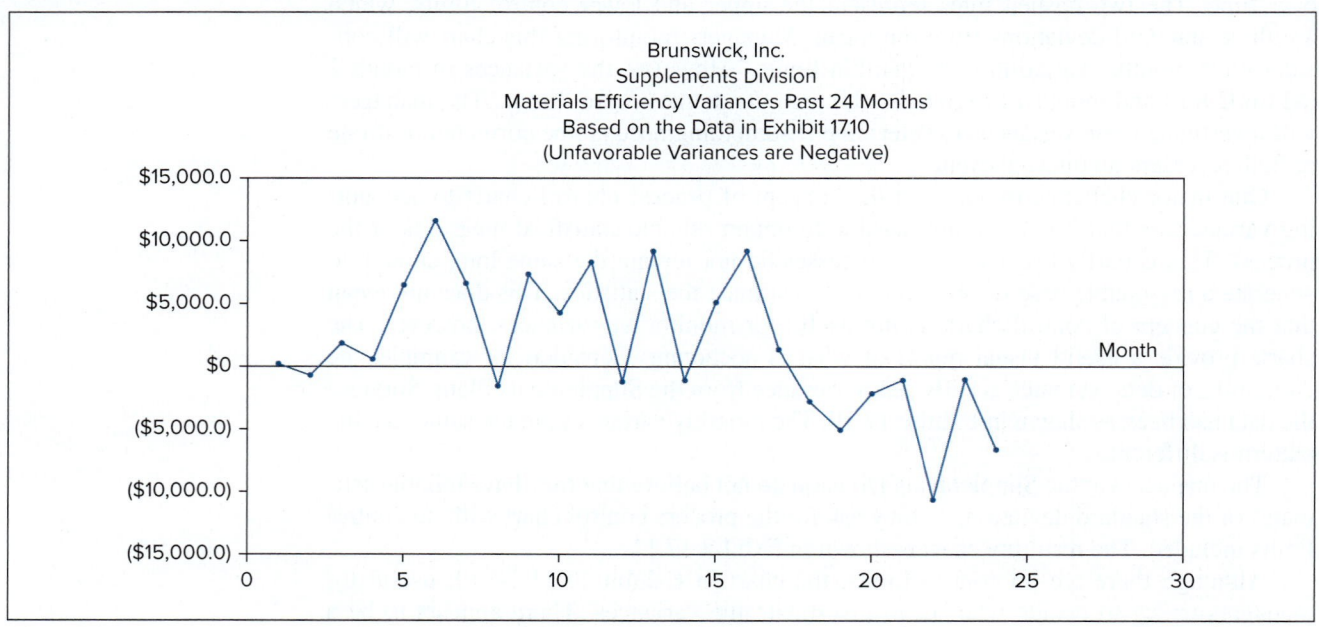

that they focus on the variances that are important and controllable. The process control chart can help in this allocation of resources, but it should be applied based on the experience of the manager and the circumstances of the organization.

One approach for doing this is to apply "rules of thumb" that incorporate managers' experience about variance causes and controllability. That is, for some variances, the control limits might be set at some multiple of the spending on the resource. For example, investigation occurs if the purchase price variance is 20 percent greater or less than the budgeted cost of direct materials. This is analogous to the idea of materiality, where you want to capture those variances most likely to affect decisions made by managers.

Key Takeaways

1. The sales activity variance can be decomposed in terms of either industry activity or product mix:

   a. Industry Activity:

      - Industry volume variance: (Actual industry volume − Budgeted industry volume) × Budgeted market share

      - Market share variance: (Actual market share − Budgeted market share) × Actual industry volume

   b. Product Mix:

      - Sales quantity variance: (Actual sales quantity − Budgeted sales quantity) × Standard contribution margin per unit at standard mix

      - Sales mix variance: (Actual sales mix − Standard sales mix) × Standard contribution margin at actual sales quantity

2. The materials efficiency variance can be decomposed in terms of input quantities required and the mix of inputs:

   a. Yield variance: (Actual inputs − Standard inputs) × Standard prices at standard input mix

   b. Mix variance: (Actual inputs − Actual quantity of inputs at standard mix) × Standard prices

3. Variances should be monitored and investigated based on two factors

   a. Importance: Do the variances represent a significant part of cost or profitability?

   b. Controllability: Is it likely that the cause of the variance, once determined, is something that managers can correct?

   c. A useful managerial tool for monitoring variance is a process control chart.

SUMMARY

This chapter discusses extensions to variance analysis. Variances can be calculated to help managers understand the effect of industry trends, sales mix, and production mix and yield. Variances can be used in service industries and manufacturing. If significant, variances should be analyzed and investigated to determine their cause.

The following summarizes key ideas tied to the chapter's learning objectives:

LO 17-1 Explain how to prorate variances to inventories and cost of goods sold. Manufacturing cost variances for a period are sometimes prorated among Inventories and Cost of Goods Sold. This has the effect of restating cost of goods sold and ending inventories to actual cost

LO 17-2 Compute direct materials purchase price variances when the amount used is not equal to the amount purchased. Materials might be purchased before use and placed in inventory. In order to have timely information on variances, firms often compute the materials price variance based on the materials quantity purchased rather than the materials quantity used.

LO 17-3 Use market share variances to evaluate marketing performance. The market share variance tells how much of the sales activity variance is due to changes in market share (rather than general market conditions).

LO 17-4 Use sales mix and quantity variances to evaluate marketing performance. The sales mix variance measures the impact of substitution (customers substituting one product for another). The sales quantity variance measures the impact of selling more or less, holding sales mix constant.

LO 17-5 Evaluate production performance using production mix and yield variances. The production mix variance measures the change in the relative proportion of inputs (materials or labor). The production yield variance measures the difference between expected output from a given level of inputs and the actual output obtained from those inputs.

LO 17-6 Apply the variance analysis model to nonmanufacturing costs. An efficiency variance can be used to analyze variable nonmanufacturing costs. This efficiency computation requires a reliable measure of output activity. Ideally, this requires some quantitative input that can be linked to output. In general, jobs with routine tasks lend themselves to efficiency measures, and jobs with nonroutine tasks, such as most administrative positions, do not.

LO 17-7 Determine which variances to investigate. Setting priorities for investigating variances requires performing a cost–benefit analysis. Only the variances for which the benefits of correction exceed the costs of follow-up should be pursued.

KEY TERMS

controllability, *800*

impact, *800*

industry volume variance, *790*

management by exception, *800*

market share variance, *790*

planned variance, *801*

process control chart, *801*

production mix variance, *795*

production yield variance, *795*

purchase price variance, *789*

sales mix variance, *792*

sales quantity variance, *792*

REVIEW QUESTIONS

17-1. What complication arises in variance analysis when the number of units produced is not the same as the number of units sold?

17-2. "Variance analysis can be useful in a manufacturing environment where you know the standards, but it wouldn't be useful in a service environment." True or false?

17-3. How would you recommend accounting for variances at the end of the year? Why?

17-4. What does a manager learn by computing an industry volume variance?

17-5. Why is there no efficiency variance for revenues?

17-6. For what decisions would a manager want to know market share variance?

17-7. If the sales activity or materials efficiency variance is zero, there is no reason to compute a mix and quantity or yield variance. True or false?

17-8. What are several examples of companies that probably use materials mix and yield variances?

17-9. What is "management by exception"?

CRITICAL ANALYSIS AND DISCUSSION QUESTIONS

17-10. What is the advantage of recognizing materials price variances at the time of purchase rather than at the time of use?

17-11. How could a professional sports firm use the mix variance to analyze its total stadium revenues?

17-12. A computer company always sells the processing unit and monitor together as a bundled package. Is there any benefit to computing a sales mix variance under these circumstances?

17-13. How could a hospital firm use the mix variance to analyze its revenues?

17-14. How could a hospital firm use the mix variances to analyze salary costs regarding emergency room services?

17-15. "There is no reason to investigate favorable variances; only unfavorable variances indicate problems." Do you agree?

17-16. A business school dean asks you for help in understanding the school's inability to meet its budget. What are some of the variances you think might be important to consider? Why?

17-17. Consider a firm in the "sharing economy," such as Uber, Lyft, or Airbnb. Do you think they would benefit by computing and evaluating (1) market share and industry volume variances; (2) sales mix and sales quantity variances; and (3) production mix and yield variances?

17-18. Consider the Business Application "Changes in Bank Distribution Channels—a Mix Variance Interpretation." In what ways would the mix variance described there be similar to the sales mix and production mix variances described in the chapter? In what ways would the variance be different?

17-19. "A process control chart will tell managers when to investigate variances." Do you agree?

EXERCISES      All applicable Exercises are included in Connect.

(LO 17-1)   **17-20. Prorating Variable Overhead Cost Variances**

Volte Corporation produces small electric appliances. The following information is available for the most recent period of operations:

Standard variable overhead rate......................	$2.50 per direct labor-hour
Actual output......................................	25,000 units
Actual direct labor-hours used........................	34,500
Standard direct labor-hours	1.5 per unit
Actual direct labor cost incurred	$819,000
Standard direct labor-hour rate	$22
Actual variable overhead incurred	$92,500
Actual units sold....................................	20,000 units

Volte never has any work-in-process inventories and began the year with no finished goods inventory.

Required

a. What was the variable overhead price variance for the period?

b. What was the variable overhead efficiency variance for the period?

c. Assume that Volte writes off all variances to Cost of Goods Sold. Prepare the entries Volte would make to record and close out the variances computed in requirements (*a*) and (*b*).

d. Assume that Volte prorates all variances to appropriate accounts. Prepare the entries Volte would make to record and close out the variances computed in requirements (*a*) and (*b*).

17-21. Prorating Direct Labor Cost Variances   (LO 17-1)

Post Parts manufactures components used in audio and video systems. The year just ended was Post's first year of operations and it is preparing financial statements. The immediate issue facing Post is the treatment of the direct labor costs. Post set a standard at the beginning of the year that allowed 0.25 hour of direct labor for each unit of output. The standard rate for direct labor is $42 per hour. During the year, the company produced 250,000 units. A count of the ending finished goods inventory showed 15,000 units remaining in the warehouse. There are never any work-in-process inventories at Post. Post used 59,500 hours of labor. Total direct labor costs for the year amounted to $2,647,750.

Required

a. What was the direct labor price variance for the year?

b. What was the direct labor efficiency variance for the year?

c. Assume Post writes off all variances to Cost of Goods Sold. Prepare the entries Post would make to record and close out the variances.

d. Assume Post prorates all variances to the appropriate accounts. Prepare the entries Post would make to record and close out the variances.

17-22. Variable Cost Variances: Materials Purchased and Materials Used Are Not Equal   (LO 17-2)

Fischer Fabrication reported the following information concerning its direct materials:

Direct materials purchased (actual).	$365,000
Standard cost of materials purchased	$352,000
Standard price times actual amount of materials used	$324,000
Actual production.	55,000 units
Standard direct materials costs per unit produced	$6

Required

Compute the direct materials cost variances. Prepare an analysis for management like the one in Exhibit 17.3.

17-23. Prorating Direct Materials Cost Variances   (LO 17-1)

Refer to the information in Exercise 17-22. Assume that Fischer Fabrication had no beginning finished goods inventory and only produced one product. A count of inventory showed that 4,400 units remained in the warehouse.

Required

a. Assume Fischer writes off all variances to Cost of Goods Sold. Prepare the entries Fischer would make to record and close out the variances.

b. Assume Fischer prorates all variances to the appropriate accounts. Prepare the entries Fischer would make to record and close out the variances.

17-24. Variable Cost Variances: Materials Purchased and Materials Used Are Not Equal   (LO 17-2)

The cost analyst for Sheffer Systems collected the following data concerning direct materials:

Actual production.	36,000 units
Direct materials purchased (actual).	$716,300
Standard cost of materials purchased	720,000
Standard direct materials costs per unit produced	17
Standard price times actual amount of materials used	626,200

Required

Compute the direct materials cost variances. Prepare an analysis for management like the one in Exhibit 17.3.

(LO 17-1)   **17-25. Prorating Direct Materials Cost Variances**

Refer to the information in Exercise 17-24. Assume that Sheffer Systems had no beginning finished goods or direct materials inventory and only produced one product. Sheffer sold 27,720 units during the period.

Required

a.   Assume Sheffer writes off all variances to Cost of Goods Sold. Prepare the entries Sheffer would make to record and close out the variances.

b.   Assume Sheffer prorates all variances to the appropriate accounts. Prepare the entries Sheffer would make to record and close out the variances.

(LO 17-3)   **17-26. Industry Volume and Market Share Variances**

Appoline Juices budgeted sales of 87,000 units of Grape, assuming that the company would have 30 percent of 290,000 units sold in a particular market. The actual results were 78,000 units sold by Appoline, which represented a 26 percent share of the total market. The budgeted contribution margin is $11 per unit.

Required

Compute the sales activity variance, and break it down into market share variance and the industry volume variance.

(LO 17-3)   **17-27. Industry Volume and Market Share Variances**

Logan Passport Services budgeted sales of 8,000 units of its Basic Visa Service (BVS). This was based on its estimated 5 percent share of this service in the relevant regional market. Actual sales of the BVS for Logan totaled 11,200 units on total industry volume of 140,000 unit for this service. The budgeted contribution margin for BVS is $85 per unit. The actual contribution margin for BVS was $92.

Required

Compute the sales activity variance, and break it down into market share variance and the industry volume variance.

(LO 17-3)   **17-28. Industry Volume and Market Share Variances**

Piper Products sold 406,000 units during the last period when industry volume totaled 2.8 million units. The company originally expected to sell 442,500 based on a budgeted market share of 15 percent. The budgeted selling price was $13 per unit. Budgeted variable costs were $5 per unit. Budget fixed costs were $1,770,000 and applied based on units produced.

Required

Compute the sales activity variance, and break it down into market share variance and the industry volume variance.

(LO 17-3)   **17-29. Industry Volume and Market Share Variances**

Gerisch Consolidated sold 21,150 units of its only product last period. It had budgeted sales of 24,300 units based on an expected market share of 25 percent. The sales activity variance for the period is $340,200 U. The industry volume variance was $194,400 U.

Required

a.   What is the budgeted contribution margin per unit for the product?

b.   What is the actual industry volume?

c.   What was the actual market share for Gerisch?

d.   What is the market share variance?

(LO 17-4)   **17-30. Sales Mix and Quantity Variances**

Olivet Devices sells two models of fitness devices. The budgeted price per unit for the wireless model is $38 and the budgeted price per unit for the wireless and cellular model is $83. The master budget called for sales of 40,000 wireless models and 10,000 wireless and cellular models during the current year. Actual results showed sales of 31,000 wireless models, with a price of $35 per unit, and 12,000 wireless and cellular models, with a price of $80 per unit. The standard variable cost per unit is $25 for a wireless model and $60 for a wireless and cellular model.

Required

a. Compute the sales activity variance for these data.

b. Break down the sales activity variance into mix and quantity parts.

17-31. Sales Mix and Quantity Variances   (LO 17-4)

Allonby Foods processes frozen meals for sale in grocery and other retail outlets. Two versions are produced: The FlavorPak version has a budgeted price of $16 per case and a standard variable cost of $9 per case. The Gourmet version has a budgeted price of $29 per case and a standard variable cost of $18 per case. At the beginning of the year, the Marketing Group at Allonby estimated that the company would sell 60,000 cases of the FlavorPak version and 36,000 cases of the Gourmet version. The actual results for the year showed that 56,700 cases of the FlavorPak version and 37,800 cases of the Gourmet version were sold. Total revenues generated by sales of both versions amounted to $1,993,950, with $1,058,400 coming from the Gourmet version sales.

Required

a. Compute the sales activity variance for the year.

b. Compute the mix and quantity variances for the year.

17-32. Sales Mix and Quantity Variances   (LO 17-4)

Beatrice Math Tutors offers two tutoring models: individual and group. The individual model provides one-on-one tutoring, while the group model consists of groups of no more than four students. The individual model has a budgeted average price of $275. The group model has a budgeted average price of $75. The manager of the tutoring center believes that 65 percent of the customers will choose the group model. The individual model averages $185 and the group model averages $45 in budgeted variable cost. The manager estimates that about 160 people will purchase tutoring services in any month.

For October, the tutoring center served a total of 170 customers, including 110 that chose the group option.

Required

a. Compute the sales activity variance for the tutoring center for October.

b. Compute the mix and quantity variances for October.

17-33. Sales Mix and Quantity Variances   (LO 17-4)

Lee Lighting produces two models of floor lamps: Standard and Smart. The two differ primarily in the quality of the materials and the additional electronics required for the Smart lamp. At budget, Standard sells for $18 per unit and has a variable cost to produce of $12. The Smart lamp sells for a budgeted $64 per lamp and has a budgeted variable cost to produce of $46. Lee expects to sell 40 percent Smart lamps, and budgeted sales at a total of 98,000 lamps of both models for May. Lee actually sold 94,000 lamps, of which 39,500 were Smart lamps. Smart lamp actual revenues represented 40 percent of May total actual revenue.

Required

a. Compute the sales activity variance for Lee for May.

b. Compute the sales mix and sales quantity variances for May.

17-34. Materials Mix and Yield Variances   (LO 17-5)

Proctor Cleaning Products manufactures a product using a process that allows for substitution between two materials, X-1 and Y-7. The company has the following direct materials data for its product:

Standard costs for one unit of output
X-1 ....   68 units of input at $1.00
Y-7 ....   12 units of input at $4.60

The following results were reported for January:

Units of output produced...................	18,000 units
Materials purchased	
X-1.....................................	1,200,000 units at $1.02
Y-7.....................................	220,000 units at $4.55

Proctor has a policy of holding no inventories of any kind.

Required

a. Compute materials price and efficiency variances.

b. Compute materials mix and yield variances.

(LO 17-5) **17-35. Materials Mix and Yield Variances**

Windward Chemicals produces a product using a process that allows for substitution between two materials, Sol-1 and Sol-2. The company has the following direct materials data for its product:

Standard costs for one unit of output	
Sol-1.....................................	60 units of input at $3.00
Sol-2.....................................	120 units of input at $4.50

The company had the following results in June:

Units of output produced....................	1,900 units
Materials purchased and used	
Sol-1.....................................	132,000 units at $2.70
Sol-2.....................................	228,000 units at $4.80

Required

a. Compute materials price and efficiency variances.

b. Compute materials mix and yield variances.

(LO 17-5) **17-36. Materials Mix and Yield Variances**

Casino Pest Control (CPC) provides services to residential households by an application of a special chemical mix that varies somewhat in proportion based on environmental factors. CPC mixes two chemicals, Red-10 and Blue-12, in proportions depending on the climate and the particular pest problems of the neighborhood. A standard mix calls for a tank of the mixture to combine 60 percent Red-10 and 40 percent Blue-12. That is, a quart of the standard mixture contains .6 quart of Red-10 and .4 quart of Blue-12. Red-10 has a standard cost of $7 per quart and Blue-12 has a standard cost of $17.50 per quart. Each quart can treat 100 square yards. CPC expected to treat 500,000 square yards in May.

CPC actually treated 510,000 square yards in May. The company used 2,920 quarts of Red-10 and 2,120 quarts of Blue-12. The actual total cost of Red-10 purchased in May was $22,192 and $34,980 for the Blue-12. CPC does not hold any materials inventory.

Required

a. Compute the materials price and efficiency variances for the season.

b. Compute the materials mix and yield variances for the season.

(LO 17-5) **17-37. Labor Mix and Yield Variances**

Pembridge Burritos has two categories of direct labor: unskilled, which costs $16 per hour, and skilled, which costs $30 per hour. Management has established standards per "meal," which has been defined as a typical meal consisting of a burrito and a drink. Standards have been set as follows:

Skilled labor.....................	2.5 minutes per equivalent meal
Unskilled labor..................	10.0 minutes per equivalent meal

For the year, Pembridge sold 75,000 equivalent meals and incurred the following labor costs:

Skilled labor.......................	3,050 hours	$ 88,450
Unskilled labor.....................	13,100 hours	212,875

Required

a. Compute labor price and efficiency variances.
b. Compute labor mix and yield variances.

17-38. Flexible Budgeting, Service Organization

(LO 17-6)

Kentford Associates is a small professional services firm. Last month, Kentford billed more hours than expected, and profits reflected this.

	Reported Income Statement	Master Budget
Billable hours[a]..	5,805	5,400
Revenue..	$1,124,000	$1,080,000
Professional salaries (all variable)......................	524,000	500,000
Other variable costs (e.g., supplies, computer services)....	156,000	140,000
Fixed costs	260,000	275,000
Profit..	$ 184,000	$ 165,000

[a] These are hours billed to clients. They are fewer than the number of hours worked because there is non-billable time (e.g., slack periods, time in training sessions) and because some time worked for clients is not charged to them.

Required

Prepare a flexible budget for Kentford. Use billable hours as the measure of output (that is, units produced).

17-39. Sales Activity Variance, Service Organization

(LO 17-6)

Refer to the data in Exercise 17-38.

Required

Prepare a sales activity variance analysis like the one in Exhibit 16.4 of the previous chapter.

17-40. Profit Variance Analysis, Service Organization

(LO 17-6)

Refer to the data in Exercise 17-38.

Required

Prepare a profit variance analysis for Kentford Associates like the one in Exhibit 16.5 of the previous chapter.

17-41. Sales Price and Activity Variances

(LO 17-5)

Oakman Accounting Partners is a small tax and accounting services firm. Each billable hour of partner time has a $960 budgeted price and $450 budgeted variable cost. Each billable hour of staff time has a budgeted price of $250 and a budgeted variable cost of $150. For the most recent year, the partnership budget called for 7,500 billable partner-hours and 30,000 staff-hours. Actual results were as follows:

Partner revenue	$7,675,000	7,800 hours
Staff revenue	$8,120,000	33,000 hours

Required

Compute the sales price and activity variances for these data. Also compute the mix and quantity variances.

(LO 17-7)   **17-42. Investigating Variances**

Refer to the information in Exercise 17-41.

Required

Write a memo to the senior manager of Oakman Accounting Partners recommending which variances from the past year the firm should investigate along with your reasons.

(LO 17-6)   **17-43. Variable Cost Variances**

The standard direct labor cost per call for Crescent Call Centers (CCC) is $5.25 (= $21 per labor-hour ÷ 4 calls per hour). Actual direct labor costs during the period totaled $82,810. Also during the period, 4,180 labor-hours were worked, and 14,800 calls were handled.

Required

Compute the direct labor price and efficiency variances for the period. (Refer to Exhibit 17.7 for the format to use.)

(LO 17-7)   **17-44. Investigating Variances**

Refer to the information in Exercise 17-43.

Required

Write a memo to the managers at Crescent Call Centers recommending which variances they should investigate this period along with your reasons.

PROBLEMS    All applicable Problems are included in Connect.

(LO 17-1)   **17-45. Prorating Overhead Costs**

Gateshead Indistries manufactures a single product and started the year with no inventories. Selected information about results for the period just ended include the following:

Actual fixed manufacturing overhead	$224,400
Actual variable manufacturing overhead	306,000
Applied fixed manufacturing overhead	214,000
Applied variable manufacturing overhead	314,000
Budgeted fixed overhead	207,400
Variable overhead efficiency variance	6,500 U

Thirty percent of this period's production has not been sold. There are never any work-in-process inventories.

Required

a. Assume Gateshead writes off all variances to Cost of Goods Sold. Prepare the entries the company would make to record and close out the variances.

b. Assume Gateshead prorates all variances to the appropriate accounts. Prepare the entries the company would make to record and close out the variances.

17-46. Variable Cost Variances: Materials Purchased and Used Are Not Equal

(LO 17-2, 7)

Larned Company makes a storage box using metal. The company uses a standard costing system. Variable overhead is allocated on the basis of direct materials usage (pounds). Overhead is allocated to units based on expected production of 13,500 units. Larned maintains a materials inventory, so the amount of material used is not necessarily the same as the amount of material purchased in any one month.

The standard cost sheet for a single box follows:

Direct material	0.5 pound @ $8	$ 4.00
Direct labor.	0.2 hour @ $30	6.00
Variable overhead.	0.5 pound @ $4	2.00
Fixed overhead		3.00
		$15.00

March financial results show that the average purchase price of metal was $8.20 per pound. The purchase price variance was $1,540. The variable overhead efficiency variance was $1,200 favorable. Good output produced totaled 12,000 units.

Required

a. How many pounds of metal were purchased in March?

b. What was the direct materials efficiency variance in March?

c. How many pounds of metal were used in March?

d. Which, if either, of the direct materials variances (price or efficiency) would you recommend Larned management investigate? Why?

17-47. Industry Volume and Market Share Variances: Missing Data

(LO 17-3)

Pasadena Industries has prepared the following graph similar to the one presented in Exhibit 17.4:

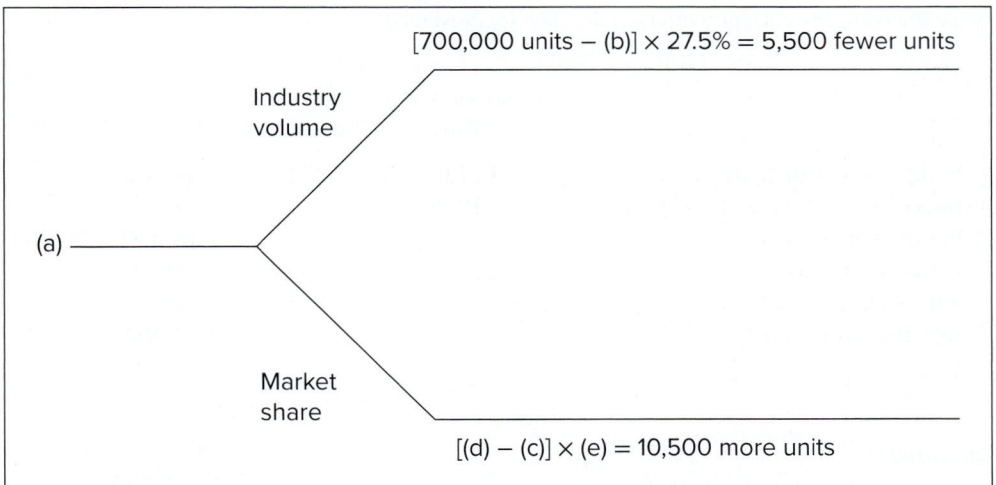

Required

a. The difference between actual and budgeted sales volume.

b. Budgeted industry volume.

c. Budgeted market share percent.

d. Actual market share percent.

e. Actual industry volume.

(LO 17-3)   **17-48. Industry Volume and Market Share: Missing Data**
The following graph is similar to that in Exhibit 17.4. It has been prepared for Longacre Parts.

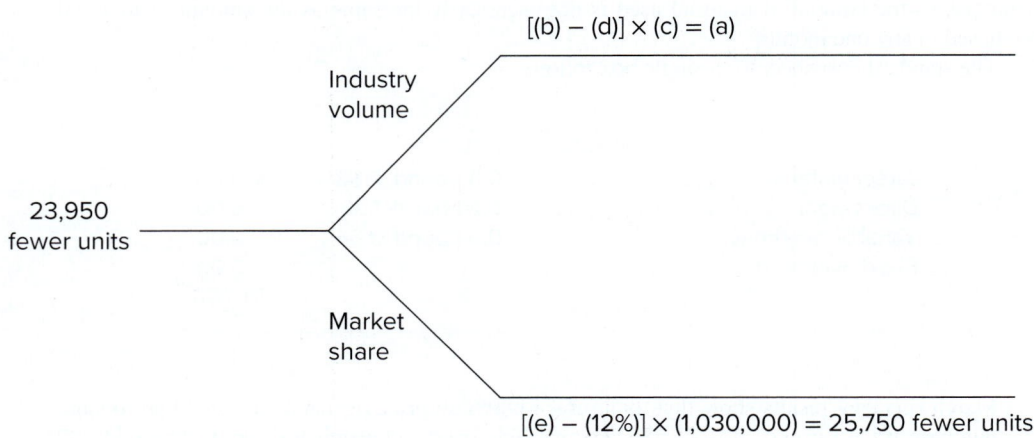

$$[(b) - (d)] \times (c) = (a)$$

Industry volume

23,950 fewer units

Market share

$$[(e) - (12\%)] \times (1,030,000) = 25,750 \text{ fewer units}$$

Required

a.   Industry volume variance.
b.   Actual industry volume.
c.   Budgeted market share.
d.   Budgeted industry volume.
e.   Actual market share.

(LO 17-4)   **17-49. Sales Mix and Quantity Variances**
Wilde Vintners produces and sells wine. The following data concern the three varietals of white wine the company currently offers. Sales data for November are given as follows:

	Sauvignon Blanc	Chardonnay	Riesling	Total
Budgeted selling price...............	$21.00	$25.00	$15.00	
Budgeted variable cost	$9.00	$11.00	$6.00	
Budgeted selling quantity	30,000	45,000	15,000	90,000
Actual selling price	$21.50	$23.90	$16.40	
Actual variable cost..................	$8.15	$12.50	$5.60	
Actual selling quantity	32,000	41,500	14,200	87,700

Required

a.   Compute the sales price variance for all three wines.
b.   Compute the sales activity variance for Wilde Vintners for November.
c.   Compute the mix and quantity variances for Wilde Vintners for November.

(LO 17-6)   **17-50. Analyze Performance for a Restaurant**
Lothrop Consulting Group is a small firm that offers services to two business segments: not-for-profits (NFPs) and corporate clients. Lothrop's business model is to rely to a great extent on non-employee consultants (called "advisors") who are paid on an hourly basis. Lothrop is planning to expand operations into international markets and is concerned that its reporting system might need improvement. The master budget income statement for the company's latest quarter follows (in thousands).

	NFP	Corporate	Total
Sales revenue	$1,500	$2,500	$4,000
Costs			
Advisor compensation	$ 600	$1,000	$1,600
Miscellaneous expenses	50	75	125
Travel.	130	475	605
Equipment rental.	100	200	300
Advertising	30	80	110
Depreciation	50	76	126
Lease cost	80	150	230
Salaries.	120	200	320
Total costs.	$1,160	$2,256	$3,416
Operating profit.	$ 340	$ 244	$ 584

The company uses the following performance report for management evaluation:

LOTHROP CONSULTING GROUP
Net Income for the Quarter
($000)

	Actual Results				Over- or
	NFP	Corporate	Total	Budget	(Under-) Budget[a]
Sales revenue.	$1,800	$2,000	$3,800	$4,000	$(200)
Costs					
Advisor compensation[b]	$ 780	$ 950	$1,730	$1,600	$ 130
Miscellaneous expenses[b]	55	55	110	125	(15)
Travel[b]	136	500	636	605	31
Equipment rental[b]	110	180	290	300	(10)
Advertising	42	75	117	110	7
Depreciation	50	76	126	126	
Lease cost.	94	160	254	230	24
Salaries	125	190	315	320	(5)
Total costs	$1,392	$2,186	$3,578	$3,416	$ 162
Operating profit	$ 408	$ (186)	$ 222	$ 584	$(362)

[a] There is no sales price variance.
[b] Variable costs; costs not identified as variable are fixed.

Required
Prepare a profit variance analysis for the *Corporate* Business of Lothrop. (*Hint:* Use sales revenue as your measure of volume.)

(CMA adapted)

17-51. Nonmanufacturing Cost Variances   (LO 17-6)
Leverette Mortgage Lenders (LML) is a financial institution that originates mortgage loans. The company charges a service fee for processing loan applications. This fee is set twice a year based on the cost of processing a loan application. For the first half of this year, LML estimated that it would process 300 loans. Correspondence, credit reports, supplies, and other materials that vary with each

loan are estimated to cost $180 per loan. The company hires a loan processor at an estimated cost of $155,000 per year and an assistant at an estimated cost of $110,000 per year. The cost to lease office space and pay utilities and other related costs is estimated to be $320,000 per year.

During the first six months of this year, LML processed 280 loans. Cost of materials, credit reports, and other items related to loan processing were 3 percent higher than expected for the volume of loans processed.

The loan processor and assistant cost $129,850 for the six months. Leasing and related office costs were $153,000 for the six months.

Required

Prepare an analysis of the variances for LML. (*Hint:* Loans are the output.)

(LO 17-6)   **17-52. Performance Evaluation in Service Industries**

Graves Bank & Trust (GB&T) estimates that its overhead costs for policy administration should be $55 for each new account opened and $0.60 per year for each $1,000 of deposits. The company set a budget of opening 35,000 new accounts during the coming period. In addition, it estimated that the total deposits for the period would average $67,200,000.

During the period, actual costs related to new accounts amounted to $1,840,500. The bank opened a total of 34,300 new accounts.

The cost of maintaining existing accounts was $45,950. Had these costs been incurred at the same prices as were in effect when the budget was prepared, the costs would have been $46,700; however, some costs changed. Also, deposits averaged $71,300,000 during the period.

Required

Prepare a schedule to show the differences between master budget and actual costs.

(LO 17-7)   **17-53. Investigating Variances**

Refer to the information in Problem 17-52.

Required

Write a memo to the managers at Graves Bank & Trust recommending which variances they should investigate this period, along with your reasons.

(LO 17-4)   **17-54. Revenue Analysis Using Industry Data and Multiple Product Lines**

Earle Soup Company makes three varieties of soups: Bean, Tomato, and Vegetable. Sales volume for the annual budget is determined by estimating the total market volume for soups and then applying the company's prior-year market share, adjusted for planned changes due to company programs for the coming year. Volume is apportioned among the three varieties of soup based on the prior year's product mix, again adjusted for planned changes for the coming year.

The following are the company budget and the results of operations for the most recent quarter.

Budget (all units and costs in thousands)				
	Bean	Tomato	Vegetable	Total
Sales—units	30 cases	30 cases	60 cases	120 cases
Sales—dollars.	$1,200	$2,400	$3,600	$7,200
Variable costs.	840	1,920	2,760	5,520
Contribution margin	$ 360	$ 480	$ 840	$1,680
Manufacturing fixed cost	240	240	360	840
Product margin	$ 120	$ 240	$ 480	$ 840
Marketing and administrative costs (all fixed)............				300
Operating profit.............				$ 540

(Continued)

Actual (all units and costs in thousands)

	Bean	Tomato	Vegetable	Total
Sales—units	24 cases	30 cases	63 cases	117 cases
Sales—dollars.	$ 972	$2,400	$3,600	$6,972
Variable costs.	672	1,932	2,784	5,388
Contribution margin	$ 300	$ 468	$ 816	$1,584
Manufacturing fixed cost	252	264	378	894
Product margin	$ 48	$ 204	$ 438	$ 690
Marketing and administrative costs (all fixed)............				330
Operating profit.............				$ 360

Industry volume for the quarter was estimated at 1.2 million cases for budgeting purposes. Actual industry volume for the quarter was 1,140,000 cases.

Required

a. Prepare an analysis to show the effects of the sales price and sales activity variances.
b. Break down the sales activity variance into the parts caused by industry volume and market share.

(CMA adapted)

17-55. Sales Mix and Quantity Variances   (LO 17-4)
Refer to the data for the Earle Soup Company (Problem 17-54).

Required
Break down the total activity variance into sales mix and quantity parts.

17-56. Materials Mix and Yield Variances   (LO 17-5)
McKinney Solvents produces a wide variety of products for the manufacturing industry. The standard mix for producing a single batch of 100 gallons of its biggest-selling product is as follows:

Input Chemical	Quantity (in gallons)	Cost (per gallon)	Total Cost
X-1	22.5	$50	$1,125
X-2	40.0	25	1,000
X-3	62.5	16	1,000
	125.0		$3,125

There is a standard 20 percent loss in liquid volume during processing due to evaporation. The finished liquid is put into 10-gallon containers for sale. Thus, the standard materials cost for a 10-gallon container is $312.50 [= ($3,125 ÷ 100 gallons) × 10 gallons per container].

The actual quantities of direct materials and the cost of the materials placed in production during March were as follows (materials are purchased and used at the same time):

Input Chemical	Quantity (in gallons)	Total Cost
X-1......................	12,200	$ 597,800
X-2......................	19,400	494,700
X-3......................	29,900	484,000
	61,500	$1,576,500

A total of 5,000 containers (50,000 gallons) were produced during March.

Required

Calculate the total direct materials variance for the liquid product for the month of March and then further analyze the total variance into:

a. Materials price and efficiency variances.

b. Materials mix and yield variances.

(LO 17-5) **17-57. Materials Mix and Yield Variances**

Stearn & Company makes a lubricating oil using two grades of petroleum (Alpha and Beta). Within certain limits, the two grades can substitute for one another, so the actual mix of inputs often differs from the standard mix. Stearn holds no materials inventories. The standard cost of a unit of output follows.

Input Grade	Quantity	Cost per Unit of Input	
Alpha......................	0.5 unit	$14	$ 7
Beta.......................	1.0 unit	8	8
Cost per unit of output			$15

A total of 60,000 units were produced during February. The actual inputs purchased and used during February were as follows:

Input Grade	Total Quantity	Cost per Unit of Input
Alpha	31,800 units	$13.85
Beta	56,700 units	8.10

Required

Prepare a complete materials variance analysis showing the materials price variance, the materials efficiency variance, the materials mix variance, and the materials yield variance.

(LO 17-5) **17-58. Labor Mix and Yield Variances**

Pease Contractors is a local home remodeling company. In analyzing financial performance, the accountant compares actual results with a flexible budget. The standard direct labor rates used in the flexible budget are established each year at the time the annual plan is formulated and held constant for the entire year.

The standard direct labor rates in effect for the current fiscal year and the standard hours allowed for the actual output of work for August are shown in the following schedule.

Worker Classification	Standard Direct Labor Rate per Hour	Standard Direct Labor-Hours Allowed for Output
Supervisor	$50	1,800
Skilled	30	2,250
General.....................	20	4,950

The actual direct labor-hours worked and the actual direct labor rates per hour experienced for the month of August were as follows.

Worker Classification	Actual Direct Labor Rate per Hour	Actual Direct Labor-Hours
Supervisor	$54	2,112
Skilled	32	2,112
General	18	5,376

Required

Calculate the dollar amount of the total direct labor variance for August for Pease Contractors. Break down the total variance into the following components:

a. Direct labor price and efficiency variances.

b. Direct labor mix and yield variances.

(CMA adapted)

17-59. Investigating Variances   (LO 17-7)

Refer to the information in Problem 17-58.

Required

Write a memo to the managers at Pease Contractors recommending which variances they should investigate this period, along with your reasons.

17-60. Derive Amounts for Profit Variance Analysis   (LO 17-6)

The Berry Bowl sells fresh fruit cups from a cart. The owner want to compare this quarter's results with those for last quarter. The owner believes that the last quarter's operations were "what we expected given the number of cups we sold." Assume that the following information is provided:

	Last Quarter	This Quarter
Number of cups.	7,000	7,450
Revenues	$28,420	$29,055
Variable costs.	10,780	12,410
Contribution margin	$17,640	$16,645

Required

Compute the flexible budget and sales activity variance and prepare a profit variance analysis (like the one in Exhibit 16.5 of the previous chapter) in as much detail as possible. What impact did the changes in number of cups sold and average revenues (i.e., sales price) have on The Berry Bowl's contribution margin?

17-61. Flexible Budget   (LO 17-6)

You are a county supervisor for Firwood County and are preparing for the monthly supervisor meeting where the operations of various units are reviewed. One of the units that the county government operates is a motor pool with 50 vehicles. The motor pool furnishes gasoline, oil, and other supplies for the cars and hires two mechanics who do routine maintenance and minor repairs. Major repairs are done at a nearby commercial garage. A department manager oversees the operations.

Each year, the manager of the motor pool prepares a master budget for the motor pool. Depreciation on the automobiles is recorded in the budget to determine the costs per mile. One factor in the performance evaluation of the motor pool manager is actual expenses compared to budgeted expenses.

The following schedule presents the master budget for the year and for the month of September. It also includes the actual September results along with the variances relative to the master budget:

FIRWOOD COUNTY
Motor Pool Budget Report for September

	Annual Master Budget	One-Month Master Budget	September Actual	Over- or (Under-) Budget
Gasoline..............	$ 226,800	$18,900	$18,600	($300)
Oil, minor repairs, parts, and supplies........	20,160	1,680	1,690	10
Outside repairs...........	15,120	1,260	1,270	10
Insurance...............	33,600	2,800	2,814	14
Salaries and benefits......	168,000	14,000	13,800	(200)
Depreciation	147,840	12,320	12,100	(220)
Total cost.............	$ 611,520	$50,960	$50,274	($686)
Total miles	1,176,000	98,000	88,200	
Cost per mile............	$0.52	$0.52	$0.57	
Number of vehicles	50	50	48	

You are aware that the motor pool manager's annual evaluation and prospects for promotion will be discussed at the meeting and that supporters will point to the fact that the September results indicate good performance. You have not formed an opinion of the motor pool manager's performance, but you would like to be prepared for the discussion you know will take place.

Required
Based on the Motor Pool Budget Report for September provided above, prepare an analysis of the manager's performance that you believe provides a reasonable assessment.

(CMA adapted)

(LO 17-3, 7)   **17-62. Industry Volume and Market Share Variances—Variance Investigation**
La Salle Outfitters organizes wilderness tours. For the most recent touring season, the industry volume variance showed La Salle sold 336 more tours than expected, but the market share variance resulted in 96 fewer tours than expected. The standard contribution margin from a single tour is $640. The industry trade group reported that the number of tours sold during the season was 1,400 greater than expected. La Salle's revenues total $1,200,000 for a typical season.

Required
a. What budgeted market share does La Salle use in planning its budget? If it is not possible to calculate this based on the information given, what additional information is required?
b. What was the actual market share La Salle captured during the season? If it is not possible to calculate this based on the information given, what additional information is required?
c. Would you recommend that La Salle investigate the industry volume variance, the market share variance, or neither one? (They do not want to spend the resources investigating both.)

(LO 17-6, 7)   **17-63. Variances and Variance Investigation: Data Analysis and Visualization**
McKinley City Tours offers small group guided walks. The following information for July provides the original budget:

	Master Budget
Number of tours	1,200
Revenue	$114,000
Variable costs....................	57,600
Contribution margin	$ 56,400
Fixed costs......................	30,000
Operating profit..................	$ 26,400

McKinley actually sold 1,440 tours in July. The price variance was $2,880 unfavorable, the variable cost variance was $5,760 unfavorable, and the fixed cost variance was $1,500 unfavorable.

Required

a. Prepare the operating income statement for the actual July results for McKinley.

b. The following table provides the previous 24 months of price variances for McKinley City Tours.

	A	B	C
1	**Month**	**Variance**	
2	1	$ (146.4)	
3	2	(312.5)	
4	3	(1,943.2)	
5	4	866.9	
6	5	242.8	
7	6	421.6	
8	7	385.6	
9	8	1,542.9	
10	9	946.3	
11	10	122.3	
12	11	(2,065.8)	
13	12	(1,847.6)	
14	13	490.2	
15	14	(455.2)	
16	15	(726.6)	
17	16	(1,488.1)	
18	17	2,840.9	
19	18	1,211.4	
20	19	(1,368.5)	
21	20	(2,760.3)	
22	21	(1,066.0)	
23	22	(1,336.9)	
24	23	(1,131.5)	
25	24	(150.9)	
26			
27	**Note: Unfavorable variances in parentheses.**		
28			

The controller at McKinley tells you that the financial analysis team believes that these variances come from a process with a zero mean and a standard deviation of $950. Prepare a short memo with your recommendation on whether the July price variance should be investigated. Include any visual support for your recommendation.

17-64. Variances and Variance Investigation: Data Analysis and Visualization   (LO 17-6, 7)

Goodwin Advisors offers financial advice on an hourly basis. The following information for the second quarter is the flexible budget based on the actual volume of 3,500 hours:

	Flexible Budget
Number of advising hours	3,500
Revenue	$1,120,000
Variable costs.	595,000
Contribution margin	$ 525,000
Fixed costs	150,000
Operating profit.	$ 375,000

The master budget for the second quarter was based on selling 4,000 advising hours. The price variance was $52,500 favorable, the variable cost variance was $70,000 unfavorable, and the fixed cost variance was $5,000 favorable.

Required

a.   Recreate the master budget for the second quarter for Goodwin.

b.   Prepare the operating income statement for the second quarter for Goodwin.

c.   The following table provides the previous 24 quarters of variable cost variances for Goodwin Advisors:

	A	B	C
1	**Month**	**Variance**	
2	1	74,156.5	
3	2	21,978.5	
4	3	38,921.4	
5	4	34,607.0	
6	5	44,177.6	
7	6	34,493.8	
8	7	24,771.1	
9	8	(7,373.8)	
10	9	19,819.0	
11	10	13,150.2	
12	11	12,210.2	
13	12	(1,732.9)	
14	13	4,293.4	
15	14	928.0	
16	15	(24,708.0)	
17	16	34,529.3	
18	17	(7,429.7)	
19	18	(17,836.4)	
20	19	(17,918.0)	
21	20	4,432.8	
22	21	(29,220.1)	
23	22	(30,004.0)	
24	23	(69,958.9)	
25	24	(42,142.4)	
26			
27	Note: Unfavorable variances in parentheses.		

The report from the financial analysis team at Goodwin states that these variances come from a process with a zero mean and a standard deviation of $25,000. Prepare a short memo with your recommendation on whether the second quarter variable cost variance should be investigated. Include any visual support for your recommendation.

INTEGRATIVE CASE

(LO 17-7)   **17-65. Racketeer, Inc. (Comprehensive Overview of Budgets and Variance)**
"I just don't understand these financial statements at all!" exclaimed Mr. Elmo Knapp. Mr. Knapp explained that he had turned over management of Racketeer, Inc., a division of American Recreation Equipment, Inc., to his son, Otto, the previous month. Racketeer, Inc., manufactures tennis rackets.

   "I was really proud of Otto," he beamed. "He was showing us all the tricks he learned in business school, and if I do say so myself, I think he was doing a rather good job for us. For example, he put together this budget for Racketeer, which makes it very easy to see how much profit we'll make at any sales volume (Exhibit 17.12). As best as I can figure it, in March we expected to have a volume of 8,000 units and a profit of $14,500 on our rackets. But we did much better than that! We sold 10,000 rackets, so we should have made almost $21,000 on them."

"Another one of Otto's innovations is this standard cost system," said Mr. Knapp proudly. "He sat down with our production people and came up with a standard production cost per unit (see Exhibit 17.13). He tells me this will let us know how well our production people are performing. Also, he claims it will cut down on our clerical work."

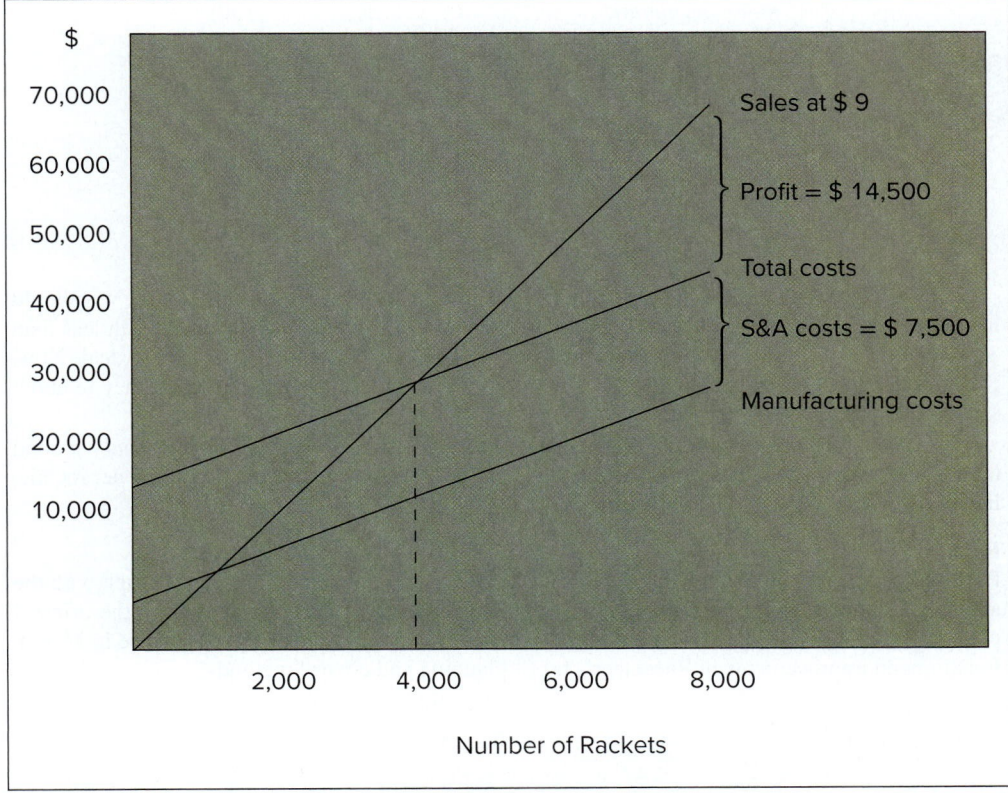

Exhibit 17.12
Profit Graph—
Racketeer, Inc.

	Per Racket
Raw material	
Frame (one frame per racket).............	$3.15
Stringing materials: 20 feet at 3¢	
per foot.............................	0.60
Direct labor	
Skilled: 1/8 hour at $9.60 per hour.......	1.20
Unskilled: 1/8 hour at $5.60 per hour	0.70
Plant overhead	
Indirect labor..........................	0.10
Power.................................	0.03
Supervision	0.12[b]
Depreciation	0.20[b]
Other.................................	0.15[b]
Total standard cost per frame.............	$6.25

Exhibit 17.13
Standard Costs[a]—
Racketeer, Inc.

[a]Standard costs are calculated for an estimated production volume of 8,000 units each month.

[b]Fixed costs.

Exhibit 17.14

Income Statement,
March—Racketeer, Inc.

> **RACKETEER, INC.**
> **Income Statement**
> **For the Month of March—Actual**
>
> | | |
> |---|---:|
> | Sales revenue | |
> | 10,000 rackets at $9 | $90,000 |
> | Standard cost of goods sold | |
> | 10,000 rackets at $6.25 | 62,500 |
> | Gross profit after standard costs | $27,500 |
> | Variances | |
> | Materials variance | (490) |
> | Labor variance | (392) |
> | Overhead variance | (660) |
> | Gross profit | $25,958 |
> | Selling and administrative expenses | 7,200 |
> | Operating profit | $ 18,758 |

Mr. Knapp continued, "But one thing puzzles me. My calculations show that we should have earned profit of nearly $21,000 in March. However, our accountants came up with less than $19,000 in the monthly income statement (Exhibit 17.14). This bothers me a great deal. Now, I'm sure our accountants are doing their job properly. But still, it appears to me that they're about $2,200 short."

"As you can probably guess," Mr. Knapp concluded, "we are one big happy family around here. I just wish I knew what those accountants were up to . . . coming in with a low net income like that."

Required

Prepare a report for Mr. Elmo Knapp and Mr. Otto Knapp that reconciles the profit graph with the actual results for March (see Exhibit 17.15). Show the source of each variance from the original plan (8,000 rackets) in as much detail as you can and evaluate Racketeer's performance in March. Recommend improvements in Racketeer's profit planning and control methods.

Exhibit 17.15

Actual Production Data
for March—Racketeer, Inc.

Direct materials purchased and used	
Stringing materials	175,000 feet at 2.5¢ per foot
Frames (some frames were ruined during production)	7,100 at $3.15 per frame
Labor	
Skilled ($9.80 per hour)	900 hours
Unskilled ($5.80 per hour)	840 hours
Overhead	
Indirect labor	$800
Power	$250
Depreciation	$1,600
Supervision	$960
Other	$1,250
Production	7,000 rackets

(Copyright © Michael W. Maher, 2012)

SOLUTIONS TO SELF-STUDY QUESTIONS

1.

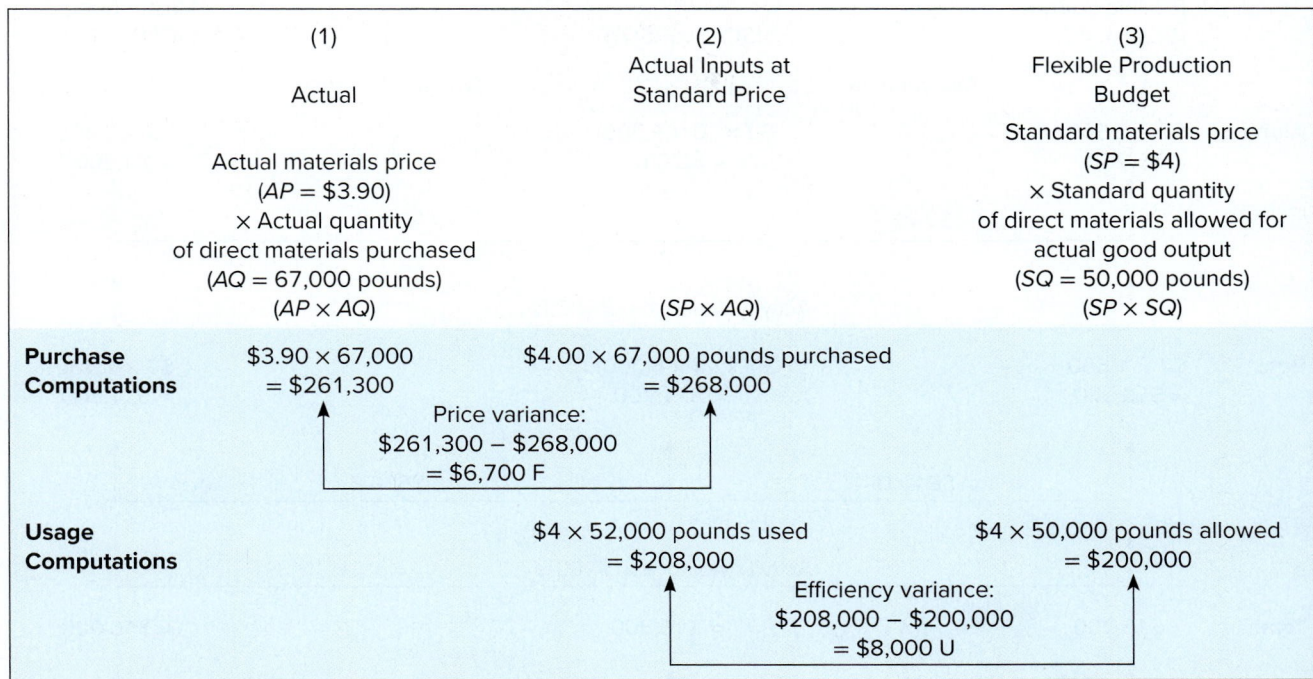

	(1) Actual	(2) Actual Inputs at Standard Price	(3) Flexible Production Budget
	Actual materials price $(AP = \$3.90)$ $\times$ Actual quantity of direct materials purchased $(AQ = 67{,}000 \text{ pounds})$ $(AP \times AQ)$	$(SP \times AQ)$	Standard materials price $(SP = \$4)$ $\times$ Standard quantity of direct materials allowed for actual good output $(SQ = 50{,}000 \text{ pounds})$ $(SP \times SQ)$
Purchase Computations	$\$3.90 \times 67{,}000$ $= \$261{,}300$	$\$4.00 \times 67{,}000$ pounds purchased $= \$268{,}000$	

Price variance:
$\$261{,}300 - \$268{,}000$
$= \$6{,}700$ F

| **Usage Computations** | | $\$4 \times 52{,}000$ pounds used
$= \$208{,}000$ | $\$4 \times 50{,}000$ pounds allowed
$= \$200{,}000$ |

Efficiency variance:
$\$208{,}000 - \$200{,}000$
$= \$8{,}000$ U

2.   *a.*

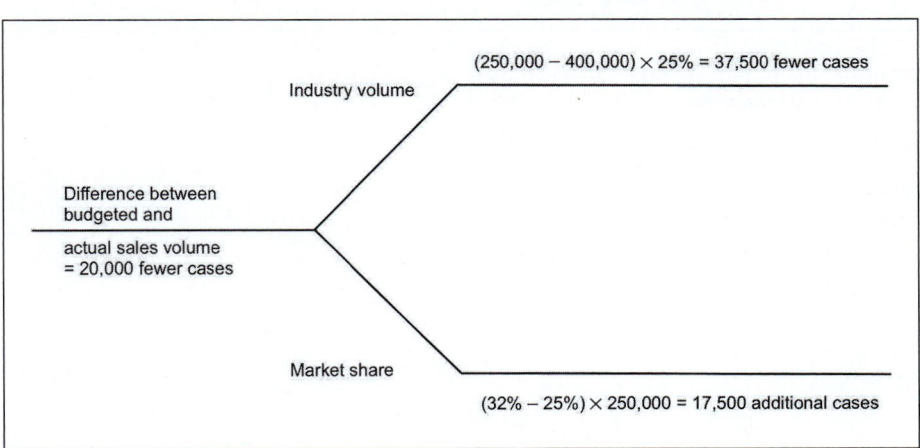

Industry volume
$(250{,}000 - 400{,}000) \times 25\% = 37{,}500$ fewer cases

Difference between
budgeted and

actual sales volume
$= 20{,}000$ fewer cases

Market share
$(32\% - 25\%) \times 250{,}000 = 17{,}500$ additional cases

Industry volume variance	$(\$10.00 - \$4.70) \times 37{,}500$ U	$\$198{,}750$ U
Market share variance	$(\$10.00 - \$4.70) \times 17{,}500$ F	$\underline{92{,}750}$ F
Sales activity variance	$(\$10.00 - \$4.70) \times 20{,}000$ U	$\underline{\$106{,}000}$ U

b.   Because Peak management most likely has more control over the market share variance, our evaluation of its performance in this case is going to be more favorable than it was given the original facts in the text.

3.

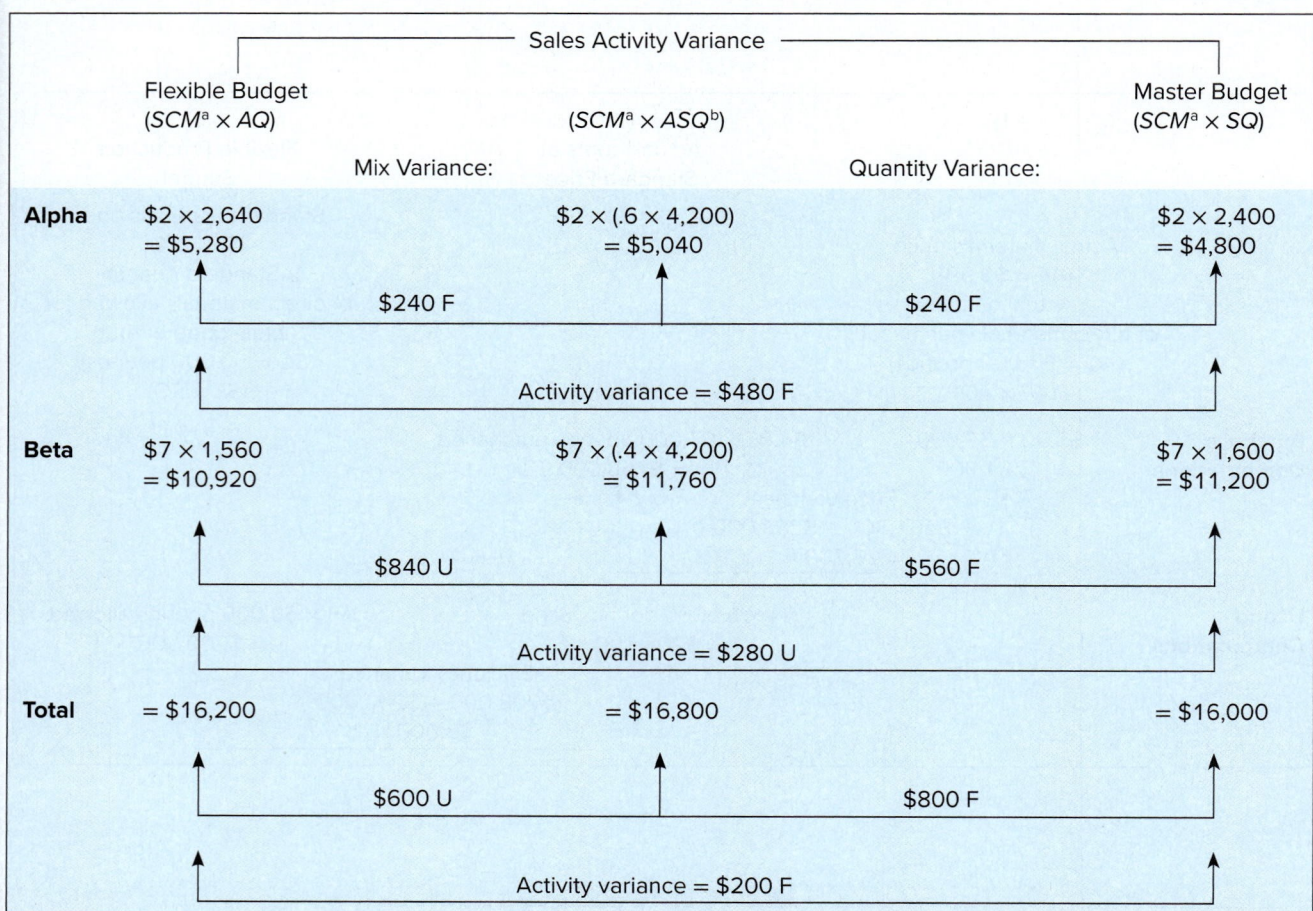

^a *SCM* = Standard contribution margin per unit.

^b *ASQ* = Quantity of units that would be sold at the standard mix:

Total units sold = 2,640 + 1,560 = 4,200

Standard mix:

Alpha . . . .   0.6 × 4,200 = 2,520

Beta . . . .   0.4 × 4,200 = 1,680

4.

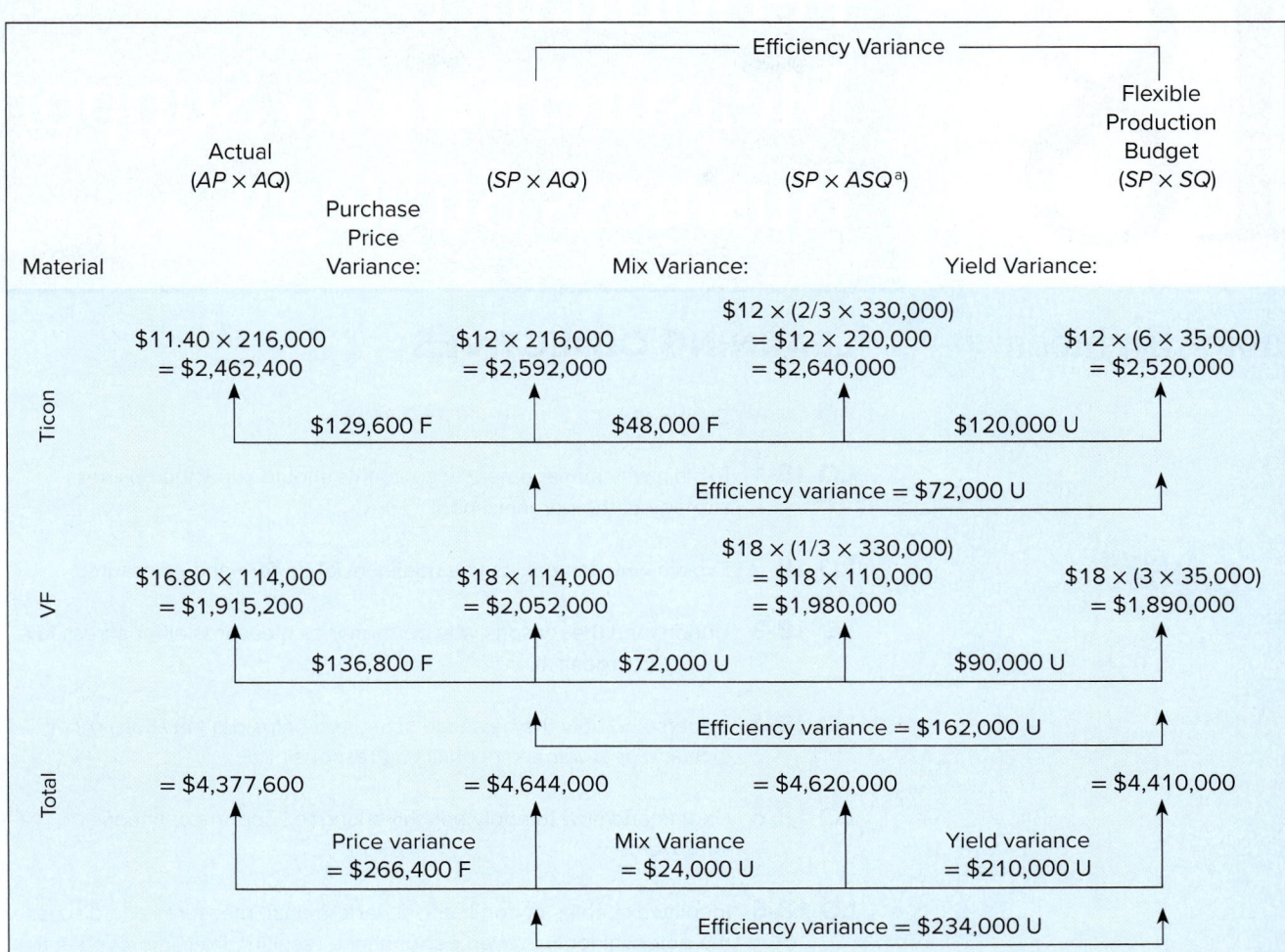

a Calculation of *ASQ:*
  Total pounds used   216,000 + 114,000 = 330,000 pounds
  Standard mix:
    Ticon . . . .   2/3 × 330,000 = 220,000 pounds
    VF . . . .   1/3 = 330,000 = 110,000 pounds

18

Chapter Eighteen

Performance Measurement to Support Business Strategy

LEARNING OBJECTIVES

After reading this chapter, you should be able to:

LO 18-1 Explain why management accountants should know the business strategy of their organization.

LO 18-2 Explain why companies use nonfinancial performance measures.

LO 18-3 Understand the reasons why performance measures differ across levels of the organization.

LO 18-4 Understand how the balanced scorecard helps organizations recognize and deal with their conflicting responsibilities.

LO 18-5 Understand how to apply benchmarking to support continuous improvement.

LO 18-6 Identify examples of nonfinancial performance measures and discuss the potential for improved performance resulting from improved activity management.

LO 18-7 Explain why employee involvement is important for an effective performance measurement system.

> **The business is really starting to take off. The good news is that I've been able to hire some good people to manage many of the day-to-day activities, so I can think about our long-term strategy. One of the problems I am wrestling with now is how to measure the performance at both the corporate headquarters and the individual stores. I've thought about putting a general profit-sharing plan in place. After all, if we all do our jobs, our profits ought to increase and we all benefit. The problem is that I'm not sure a general plan that applies the same performance measure to everyone will give employees the right incentives.**

Megan Okoye, president and founder of Silo Coffee and Tea (SCT), was talking about the problems of developing a performance measurement system for her midsize chain of coffee shops operating in the plains states. SCT has experienced rapid growth, even in the turbulent crowded market of coffee shops, and the company is ready for a more structured performance measurement and compensation system. The problem is that the usual metrics of ROI and EVA do not seem to provide the feedback some of the managers are seeking.

Strategy and Performance

As we noted at the beginning of Chapter 1, the goal of cost accounting is to help managers maximize value creation in organizations. Cost accountants provide managers with information and analysis about the efficiency and effectiveness of activities.

In this chapter, we introduce methods and measures that link performance measures to business strategy. This approach is part of a company's management control system. First, we must decide what performance to measure. Imagine you are on a hiking expedition. You measure the performance of your trip by how many miles you cover. That sounds fine, but what if your purpose in taking the trip was to catch fish? There is a mismatch between your performance measure and the purpose of your hiking trip.

In the same way, companies might incorrectly develop performance measures that don't tie back to the purpose of the company. In short, they measure the wrong things. To avoid measuring the wrong things, we need to make sure we understand a company's strategy.

Does this discussion seem out of place to you in a book on cost accounting? It's not because the performance measures that accountants develop must tie directly to concepts in strategy and organizational behavior. To start, we have to know what kind of performance adds value to the company. As one example, keeping costs down usually adds value. However, if reducing costs means reducing product quality, the activity may actually *undercut* the company's value. In this case, cost reduction is unlikely to be the most important performance measure.

To understand what the right type of performance is, we need to know the company's strategy for success. We define **business strategy** as a company's specific approach for deploying the organizational assets and capabilities required to meet its customers' needs competitively, while delivering the desired returns to stakeholders. The *business strategy* is another high-level component of the *strategic plan* defined in Chapter 13. **Stakeholders** are groups or individuals who have an interest in what the organization does. They exist within and beyond the boundaries of the company. Stakeholders include employees, customers, suppliers, shareholders, and debt holders. More broadly, the community in which the company does business and even society as a whole are also stakeholders.

A successful business strategy provides all stakeholders a competitive return on their involvement with the firm. If a firm is not offering its employees a wage that gives them a satisfactory return on their time and energy, they'll find employment elsewhere. If customers do not feel they are getting value for their money, they will buy elsewhere. And so on.

The business strategy identifies the firm's *value proposition*. A **value proposition** states how the organization will create value for all stakeholders. This statement may also imply the firm's *mission*. Its **mission** consists of its purpose and goals. A *mission statement* helps make sure that all employees understand the firm's mission and value proposition.

LO 18-1
Explain why management accountants should know the business strategy of their organization.

business strategy
A company's specific approach for deploying the organizational assets and capabilities required to meet its customers' needs competitively, while delivering the desired returns to shareholders.

stakeholders
Groups or individuals, such as employees, suppliers, customers, shareholders, and communities, who have an interest in what the organization does.

value proposition
How the organization will create value for all stakeholders.

mission
Why an organization exists; its purpose and goals.

A **mission statement** describes an organization's values, defines its responsibilities to stakeholders, and identifies the major business strategies that it will use to meet its commitments.

For example, here is the mission statement of Silo Coffee and Tea (SCT), introduced at the start of the chapter:

> Silo Coffee and Tea provides a wide range of espresso drinks made from organic beans, sourced in an ethical manner, to customers in a welcoming environment.

Here is its business strategy:

> Silo Coffee and Tea will provide a competitive return to its shareholders by offering customers the best coffees, at a reasonable price, in stores that emphasize personal, but efficient, service.

Just two statements tell us a great deal about SCT. The firm consists of stores offering upscale coffees in a premium physical environment. SCT is not competing with restaurants or fast-food chains. Customers should expect knowledgeable employees, who might offer suggestions about new drinks or coffees. Customers expect personalized service, efficiently delivered.

The Foundation of a Successful Business Strategy

Managers start forming strategy by identifying the company's core resources and capabilities. Core resources and capabilities are those things that, if used well, can make the company successful. These could be the motivations and intelligence of the company's people, which we find in many high-tech companies. These could be legal patents (in pharmaceutical companies, for example) or trademarks. They could be secret recipes, as in Coca-Cola and Kentucky Fried Chicken. Core resources and capabilities create the opportunity to earn significant profits.

Having identified the company's core resources and capabilities, managers consider various methods of achieving success. Of many frameworks for thinking about strategy, we present one of the most popular, by a scholar named Michael E. Porter, in *Competitive Strategy: Techniques for Analyzing Industries and Competitors* (New York: Free Press, 1998). As you read the next section, apply the framework to companies that you already know. For example, how do Walmart, Southwest Airlines, the *The Wall Street Journal*, a local coffee shop, or McDonald's fit this framework? As you pursue your careers, whether you are employed by one company or work with multiple clients, you will find opportunities to use this framework to add value.

Porter Framework

Porter identified three types of companies that are successful. They are

1. Cost leaders.
2. Product differentiators.
3. Focused competitors.

Cost Leaders   Cost leaders, such as Walmart, Fidelity Investments, and Southwest Airlines, have a high-volume production of an undifferentiated product, called a commodity. The product that they sell is identical or nearly identical to their competitors' products. How do they become successful? They are the low-cost providers in their industry. They get profits by relentlessly searching for efficiency. You probably know that at Southwest Airlines, everyone pitches in to clean the airplane while it is at the gate. This practice shortens the turnaround between arrivals and departures to 20 or 30 minutes—a much shorter time than many competitors. Cost leaders price aggressively and sell a high volume of product.

Cost leaders are heavy users of the methods discussed in this book. They use sophisticated cost methods, inventory management, and efficiency variances.

Product Differentiators   In contrast, the product differentiator earns a premium price for a product with unique features. While there may be fewer customers who value these features, those who do are willing to pay more for them and are not easily tempted to buy a cheaper product. Companies that use this strategy obtain profits by earning large margins. (Because margins are determined by both price and cost, differentiators must also manage costs, of course.) Makers of premium brand pharmaceuticals like Novartis, luxury luggage brands like Louis Vuitton or Hartmann, and luxury cars like BMW and Lexus follow a product differentiation strategy.

Product differentiators must develop products that customers value. To do so, they use measures of marketing performance and the balanced scorecard, discussed later in this chapter. At the same time, they use methods such as target costing as discussed in Chapter 4 to help maintain profitability.

Focused Competitors Finally, the focus strategy (also called a *niche strategy* or *segmentation strategy*) requires a company to select a narrow segment of customers or products and apply a combination of the cost leader and product differentiation strategies. Many local companies in small towns and in neighborhoods of cities follow this strategy. Grocery chain H.E.B. successfully matches store offerings to the demands of customers who enjoy Hispanic foods. Sprouts Farmers Markets and Trader Joe's have a similar niche in the organic foods, high-service niche.

Focused competitors use a combination of sophisticated marketing and cost methods (including customer profitability analysis discussed in Chapter 10). In addition, they use efficiency measures and measures of marketing performance to ensure the targeted segment is profitable.

A firm's choice of strategy may change, of course. A change might be motivated by new leadership, a change in competitive environment, or some other disruption that leads to a reassessment of "business as usual." Such a change is described in the Business Application "A New Strategy for an Old Business."

A New Strategy for an Old Business *Business Application*

When events disrupt the competitive environment, a previously successful strategy may not work. The disruption can come from external forces, such as wars, natural disasters, or other calamities, or from innovation and new technologies that render previous ways of doing business obsolete. One such innovation was the internet and the associated capabilities of people to interact online.

Among the industries seriously affected by the growth of the internet and associated technologies was the business of news, especially the print media. Old-line newspapers, such as the *The Wall Street Journal,* the *Washington Post,* and many local newspapers found that their main source of revenues, advertising, was drying up as companies found value in targeted ads for their desired demographic groups. At the same time, readership of the print media fell from a high of about 62.8 million in 1987 to an estimated 28.5 million in 2018.

Many newspapers responded to this threat by developing digital versions of the print paper that could be sold to subscribers who would read the news on their smartphone or tablet. This was the path followed by *The New York Times* (*Times*), one of the highest circulation newspapers in the U.S. At first, this strategy appeared to work. This was due in part to the reputation of the *Times* and the confidence that companies had in it as a place to advertise. However, in the early 2010s, the growth in the digital platform was slowing, if not declining.

Mark Thompson began his role as CEO of the *Times* in 2012, and since that time, digital consumers of the *Times* have increased over tenfold. He believed that a different strategy was required in the new environment:

> The psychology . . . was that all you had to do was get a bigger audience and transfer the . . . economics of print advertising to digital. I didn't buy that. . . . The question . . . is fundamentally about willingness to pay. And the bet was that news is like entertainment. . . . The better stuff users will pay for.

In other words, the new CEO found the organization trying to build and exploit economies of scale in the new digital platform but believed that would not be sustainable. Instead, it would lead to underinvestment in news content, and, in any case, advertising was falling off. Rather than following what was essentially a "cost leader" strategy, the company moved to a "product differentiation" strategy built around features customers would be willing to pay for. Examples of these products include a cooking (recipe) site, a daily crossword, podcasts, and product reviews.

The result of the new strategy was an increase in digital revenue as a percentage of total subscription revenue from 14 percent in 2012 to 87 percent in early 2020.

Sources: https://www.journalism.org/fact-sheet/newspapers; Thompson, Mark, Yael Taqqu, and Raju Narisetti, "Building a Digital *New York Times:* CEO Mark Thompson," McKinsey & Company, August 2020, https://www.mckinsey.com/industries/technology-media-and-telecommunications/our-insights/building-a-digital-new-york-times-ceo-mark-thompson.

Self-Study Question

1. Based on what you know about Silo Coffee and Tea, how would you classify the organization according to the Porter framework?

   The solution to this question is at the end of the chapter.

Beyond the Accounting Numbers

LO 18-2

Explain why companies use nonfinancial performance measures.

Financial performance measures, especially those that come from the company's accounting systems, are commonly used to evaluate employee performance. They are easily quantifiable and can motivate employees to improve the company's accounting profits. Many shareholders focus on financial measures, such as accounting profit, which the business press reports as they are announced. Therefore, financial measures are very good at getting managers' attention.

Unfortunately, financial measures suffer from several flaws. First, they are not useful in identifying operational problems. Suppose you play a sport or game (say golf, bowling, pool, softball, or even a video game) and your only feedback is the score that you get at the end of the game. Let's say you are disappointed in your score. How do you improve? The final score does not tell you what you did wrong. That score is like a set of financial performance measures: It tells you how you performed but not how you can improve.

Second, financial measures are typically reported on a monthly, quarterly, or annual basis. They do not tell you how you are doing in real time.

Third, many people in the organization do not see how their work translates into financial results. Many management gurus claim that receptionists, people who answer the phones, and people who respond to general contacts for a company are critical to customer development and customer satisfaction. Customer development and satisfaction lead to increased revenues, which should lead to higher earnings. But using earnings or return on investment to measure the performance of receptionists, people who answer the phones, and people who respond to general contacts makes little sense.

These flaws reduce the value of financial performance measures as an operational control device.

In recent years, more and more companies have begun using nonfinancial metrics such as customer satisfaction and product quality measures. A primary reason for this is that nonfinancial performance measures direct employees' attention to those things that they can control. In addition, they are often reported more frequently, providing more timely feedback to employees about their performance.

For example, consider the case of a desk clerk at a hotel, who can have an important effect on customer satisfaction and, as a result, repeat business. Measuring the clerk's performance in terms of customer satisfaction would be meaningful. (Many hotel chains such as Hilton or Holiday Inn have customer satisfaction/survey forms in the rooms.) On the other hand, it would be difficult to measure the effect of the clerk's performance on the hotel's profits because profits are affected by many factors outside the clerk's control. Furthermore, the clerk might not even understand how profits are earned or calculated. Therefore, it makes sense to reward the clerk directly for creating customer satisfaction rather than for any effect on profits.

This chapter discusses ways to evaluate performance "beyond the numbers." Performance evaluation starts by understanding the organization's objectives and strategy. For example, does the firm want to be a low-cost producer or an innovator? In what markets will it compete? The organization evaluates performance by first defining what it wants to accomplish. Then it develops criteria that help it evaluate its performance in achieving those accomplishments.

Recall from Chapter 12 that in management control systems, performance measurement must be consistent with the way in which subordinates are authorized to make decisions. The assignment of decision authority, in turn, depends on the subordinate's local knowledge. We will use this framework throughout the chapter to ensure that the performance measures we develop are consistent with the rest of the management control system.

Responsibilities According to Level of Organization

Effective performance measurement is based on two factors. First, it leads all organization members to focus on the organization's objectives and reflects how individuals or units contribute to those objectives. Second, it is designed to reflect the decision authority delegated to local managers. Understanding the manager's decision authority is important because decision authority determines what the manager controls.

LO 18-3
Understand the reasons why performance measures differ across levels of the organization.

Effective systems use performance measures that emphasize different things at different levels of the organization. At the lower levels, such as a teller window at a Bank of America branch or a packaging line at Dell Inc., nonfinancial performance measures focus on factors such as customer satisfaction and product quality; these measures reflect what these employees control. Measures that emphasize customer satisfaction are used, for example, for employees who deal directly with customers, at Verizon retail stores, Taco Bell, and Delta Air Lines. The performance measures for employees in production, such as those at Dell or Motorola Mobility, emphasize product quality.

At middle levels in organizations, nonfinancial performance measurement often focuses on how well the operating systems work together and how effective these systems are in comparison with those of competitors. At this organizational level, coordination and improvement of ongoing activities take place in addition to redesigning products and processes. For example, at Delta Air Lines, poor customer service caused by poorly trained gate agents is the responsibility of middle managers. The following are some of the nonfinancial performance measures that organizations use to evaluate middle managers' performance:

- Amount of unwanted employee turnover.
- Frequency of meeting customer delivery requirements.
- Employee development performance, such as quality and amount of training.
- Success in dealing with business partners, such as quality of supplier relations and frequency with which orders are miscommunicated to suppliers.

At the top levels of an organization, performance measurement focuses on determining whether the organization is meeting its responsibilities from the perspective of its stakeholders. An organization's stakeholders are groups or individuals who have an interest in what the organization does. Stakeholders include shareholders, customers, employees, the community in which the organization does business, and, in some cases, society as a whole. For example, employees depend on an organization for their employment. Shareholders depend on an organization to generate a return on their investment. Performance measurement at this top level requires delicately balancing trade-offs.

People at different levels in the organization have different responsibilities. Consequently, the performance measurement system measures different things at different levels in the organization. In general, performance measures should relate to what people at different levels control.

Business Model

We can use the statement of strategy and the description of the responsibilities at different levels of the organization to develop a framework for designing appropriate performance measures at Silo Coffee and Tea (SCT). One useful framework is a **business model** that links the roles of various employees and levels in the organization and illustrates how the successful completion of these roles will result in achievement of the firm's goals.

For a given strategy and environment, many business models could be appropriate. See Exhibit 18.1 for the business model for SCT. It describes how a profitable store

business model
Description of how different levels and employees in the organization must perform for the organization to achieve its goals.

Exhibit 18.1   Example Business Model—Silo Coffee and Tea

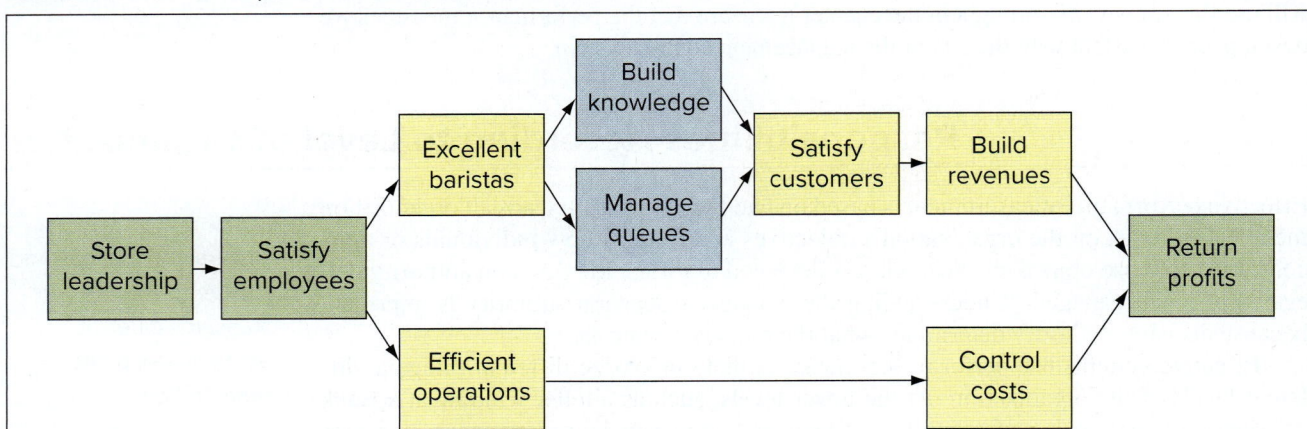

operates in the restaurant business. The store manager exercises leadership to motivate and satisfy employees. A store has two general types of employees: baristas and operating personnel (these might be the same people). If operating personnel are effective, the store will operate efficiently and control costs. There are two aspects to the barista's role. First, they must be knowledgeable and must constantly develop their knowledge about the origins and the characteristics of various coffees. Second, they must perform the balancing act of providing personalized service (fixing the drink to the customers' wishes) while keeping the line of customers moving. If they achieve these goals, the store will satisfy the customers. Satisfied customers will return to the store, building revenues. Combined with effective cost control, the store will return profits to the company.

The business model in Exhibit 18.1 is only one that we could design to illustrate how an individual store at SCT achieves the company's strategy. Failure to perform certain functions, for example, to have knowledgeable baristas, is likely to result in a failure to achieve the firm's strategy of providing a competitive return by offering outstanding customer service. We will return to our business model when we discuss balanced scorecards and strategy maps.

Self-Study Question

2. How might the business model in Exhibit 18.1 differ, if at all, if SCT's strategy were to offer low-cost (undifferentiated) coffee experience to customers who are not particularly interested in specialty coffees?

The solution to this question is at the end of the chapter.

Multiple Measures or a Single Measure of Performance?

LO 18-4

Understand how the balanced scorecard helps organizations recognize and deal with their conflicting responsibilities.

What performance measurement plan makes sense for Silo Coffee and Tea (SCT) when it considers its store managers? The model in Exhibit 18.1 suggests two alternatives:

1. SCT can use store profits to evaluate store managers.
2. SCT can use multiple measures that reflect performance based on the factors in the business model.

The advantage of the using store profits only is that it is relatively simple and reflects the organization's ultimate goal—profitability. The advantage of the second alternative is that Megan Okoye, SCT's president, can influence store managers' decisions by changing the components of the performance measurement system to reflect changes in the firm's strategy. By including (or excluding) measures such as customer satisfaction, employee satisfaction, store costs, and so on, in the store managers' evaluations, she will give managers incentives to make decisions that will improve those areas. At the same time, she will communicate to the same managers those areas that SCT views as important for achieving success. Finally, by using multiple measures, SCT can evaluate the store manager not only on the result (profit), but also on how the profit was earned.

The choice between a single measure and multiple measures depends on who has better knowledge about operating a profitable store. With a single measure, store profitability, store managers could operate their stores differently because they have different beliefs about the business model that links their actions to the store's financial results. Some managers will concentrate on operational efficiency, and others will emphasize providing good customer service. If the store managers are more knowledgeable than the corporate staff about local conditions and what local clients value, a single measure might be preferable.

If the corporate office has better knowledge of what it requires to operate a profitable store, using multiple measures provides a way to communicate this knowledge and achieve common store operations. In the case of SCT, Megan Okoye decides that multiple measures will provide better control and evaluation of store operations by linking a store manager's evaluation to specific actions. She now needs to decide how to implement this plan.

Balanced Scorecard

One structured approach to implementing a system with multiple measures is the **balanced scorecard,** which is a set of performance targets and results that shows how well an organization has performed in meeting its objectives relating to its stakeholders. It is a management tool that recognizes organizational responsibility to different stakeholder groups, such as employees, suppliers, customers, business partners, the community, and shareholders. Often different stakeholders have different needs or desires that the managers of the organization must balance. The purpose of a balanced scorecard is to measure how well the organization is doing in view of those competing stakeholder concerns.

The balanced scorecard is more than just a set of multiple performance measures. See Exhibit 18.2. The focus of the balanced scorecard is to balance the efforts of the organization in meeting its financial, customer, process, and innovation responsibilities.

The distinctive feature of the balanced scorecard is that the measures are derived from identifying what drives an organization's success as viewed from the perspectives of different stakeholders in the organization. As presented in Exhibit 18.2, the balanced scorecard has four views or *perspectives:*

1. Financial.
2. Customer.
3. Internal business process.
4. Learning and growth.

Traditionally, business organizations have focused on financial results, which mainly have reflected the shareholders' interests (financial perspective). In recent years, organizations have shifted attention to customer service issues (customer perspective), to quality and process improvement (internal business process), and to employees and their development (learning and growth). A balanced scorecard for any particular organization could be based on other perspectives if they are important for the organization's success. For example, a community perspective might be important.

Within each perspective, the scorecard identifies the goals, or objectives, for the organization. These goals and objectives are often determined in part by the competitive environment. For example, a financial goal could be growth in earnings per share. For the internal business process perspective, it could be reduction in *cycle time,* the time taken to produce a unit.

balanced scorecard
Performance measurement system relying on multiple financial and nonfinancial measures of performance.

Exhibit 18.2 Balanced Scorecard

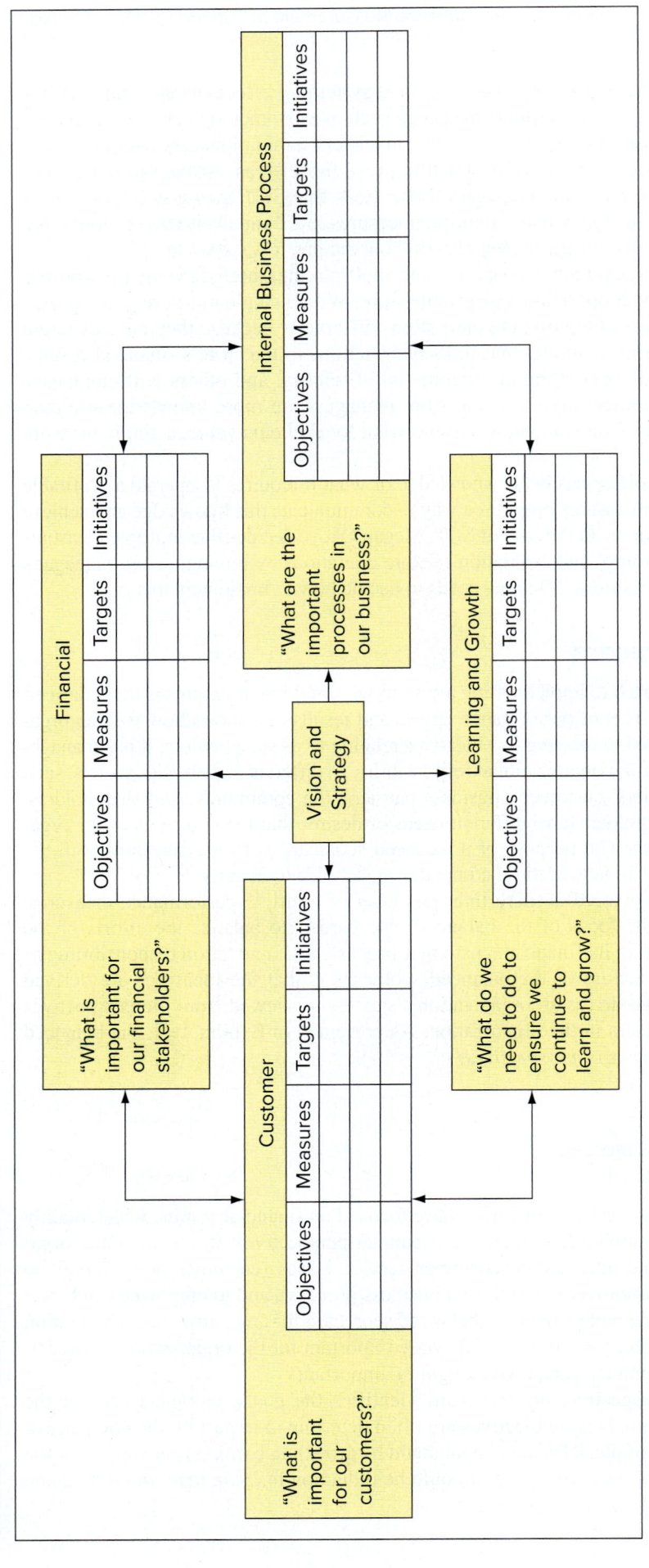

Source: Kaplan, R. S., and Norton, D. P., "Using the Balanced Scorecard as a Strategic Management System," *Harvard Business Review*, vol. 74, no. 1, p. 75.

Once the organization has specified the goals, it next identifies the measures that will be used to evaluate its progress in meeting the goals. For some goals—earnings per share growth or cycle time reduction, for example—the measure is relatively clear. For others—increased customer satisfaction, for example—it is less clear how to specify the measure. This step is important. Managers will work to improve the measure because that is the indicator of progress toward the goal. If the measure is incorrectly specified, it is possible for the managers to be successful in improving the measure but for the organization to fail to meet its goals.

Next, the organization sets targets for each of the measures. Example targets include 10 percent growth in earnings per share, five-minute reduction in cycle time, or 10 percent improvement in on-time arrivals. With the measures and the targets, managers now identify the initiatives, or plans, they have for achieving these targets.

Looking at a scorecard, such as the one in Exhibit 18.2, the managers have a better understanding of the links among the perspectives. This means it is less likely that initiatives will be developed that are inconsistent among the perspectives.

Many companies have developed and used the balanced scorecard. Exhibit 18.3 lists some of these organizations, although there are many more, including several in the health care, education, and government sectors. Each organization has its own scorecard, of course, but many, if not most, include the four perspectives listed here.

The balanced scorecard has been used primarily at the top management level to support the organization's development of strategies. For example, Kaplan and Norton describe the development of the balanced scorecard at an insurance company as follows:[1]

Step 1.   Ten of the company's top executives formed a team to clarify the company's strategy and objectives to meet responsibilities.

Exhibit 18.3   Selected List of Organizations Using the Balanced Scorecard

Ann Taylor Stores	Media General
Blue Cross/Blue Shield of Minnesota	NCR Corp.
BMW Financial Services	Northern States Power Company
Boston Lyric Opera	Northwestern Mutual
British Telecommunications Worldwide	Nova Scotia Power, Inc.
Caterpillar, Inc.	Pfizer Inc.
Cigna Property & Casualty	Philips Electronics
Crown Castle International Corp.	Reuters America, Inc.
Defense Logistics Agency	Ricoh Corp.
DuPont	Royal Canadian Mounted Police
Equifax, Inc.	Saatchi & Saatchi Worldwide
ExxonMobil Corp.	Sears Roebuck & Company
Fannie Mae	Siemens AG
Ford Motor Company	T. Rowe Price Investment Technologies, Inc.
General Electric Company	U.K. Ministry of Defence
Hilton Hotels Corp.	UPS
Honeywell	U.S. Army Medical Command
IBM	Verizon Communications Inc.
Ingersoll-Rand	Volvofinans (Sweden)
KeyCorp	Walt Disney World Company
Lloyds TSB Bank	Wells Fargo Bank

Source: Balanced Scorecard Institute, Washington, D.C.

---

[1] R. S. Kaplan and D. P. Norton, "Using the Balanced Scorecard as a Strategic Management System," *Harvard Business Review* 74 (no. 1): 75.

Step 2. The top three layers of the company's management (100 people) were brought together to discuss the new strategy and to develop performance measures for each part of the company. These performance measures became the scorecards for each part of the business and reflected the company's desired balance in satisfying different stakeholders.

Step 3. Managers began eliminating programs that were not contributing to the company's objectives.

Step 4. Top management reviewed the scorecards for each part of the organization.

Step 5. Based on its reviews in step 4, top management went back to step 1 to refine and further clarify the company's strategy and objectives.

Organizations using the balanced scorecard generally have found it to be helpful for top and middle management to shape and clarify organization goals and strategy in the face of competing stakeholder wants.

Exhibit 18.4 illustrates the balanced scorecard for SCT, which was developed after several meetings with managers and employees. The new scorecard was helpful for collecting information and identifying goals and objectives, but Megan Okoye wanted to do more. She wanted a way to communicate how the company's strategy, illustrated in the business model shown in Exhibit 18.1, was linked to the balanced scorecard. The business model was helpful in developing the performance measures included in the scorecard, but Megan was not sure that it was the most effective way to describe the firm's strategy. As a result, she decided to use what is known as a **strategy map** to communicate the strategy to SCT's managers and employees.[2] The strategy map for SCT is shown in Exhibit 18.5.

Although the strategy map might appear complicated, it is not. It links the objectives or goals in each of the perspectives. By drawing a strategy map, a company can determine if it is missing measures in any of the perspectives or if it has goals that do not seem to be linked to other parts of the map. Notice that in Exhibit 18.5 each of the goals has at least one arrow starting or ending at the goal. Further, in the Learning and Growth, Internal Business, and Customer perspectives sections, each of the goals has an arrow leaving, indicating that these goals are not the ultimate objectives of the organization, but goals that need to be achieved if the organization's ultimate objectives are to be met.

With the scorecard and strategy map complete, Megan Okoye can now turn her attention to the operational performance of SCT.

strategy map
A visual device to communicate an organization's strategy.

continuous improvement
Continuous reevaluation and improvement of the efficiency of activities.

benchmarking
Continuous process of measuring a company's own products, services, or activities against competitors' performance.

LO 18-5
Understand how to apply benchmarking to support continuous improvement.

Continuous Improvement and Benchmarking

Continuous improvement is a philosophy that many organizations are utilizing to meet their responsibilities and evaluate performance. It means continuously reevaluating and improving the efficiency of the organization's activities. Continuous improvement is the search to (1) improve the activities in which the organization engages through documentation and understanding, (2) eliminate activities that are nonvalue-added, and (3) improve the efficiency of activities that are value-added.

Benchmarking involves the search for and implementation of the best way to do something as practiced in other organizations or in other parts of one's own organization. Using benchmarking, managers identify an activity that needs to be improved, find who is the most efficient in performing that activity (sometimes in one's own organization), carefully study the process of the one who is most efficient, and then adopt (and adapt) that efficient process to their own organization. Two companies often used in benchmarking are Amazon, the online retailer, and Walmart. They are considered very good at supplier management and logistics, respectively.

Benchmarking organizations that are "best in class" identifies areas to improve and provides ideas on how to change by adopting efficient processes. Echo/Juice Images/Getty Images

---

[2] R. S. Kaplan and D. P. Norton, *Strategy Maps: Converting Intangible Assets into Tangible Outcomes* (Boston: Harvard Business School Press, 2004).

Exhibit 18.4 Balanced Scorecard—Silo Coffee and Tea

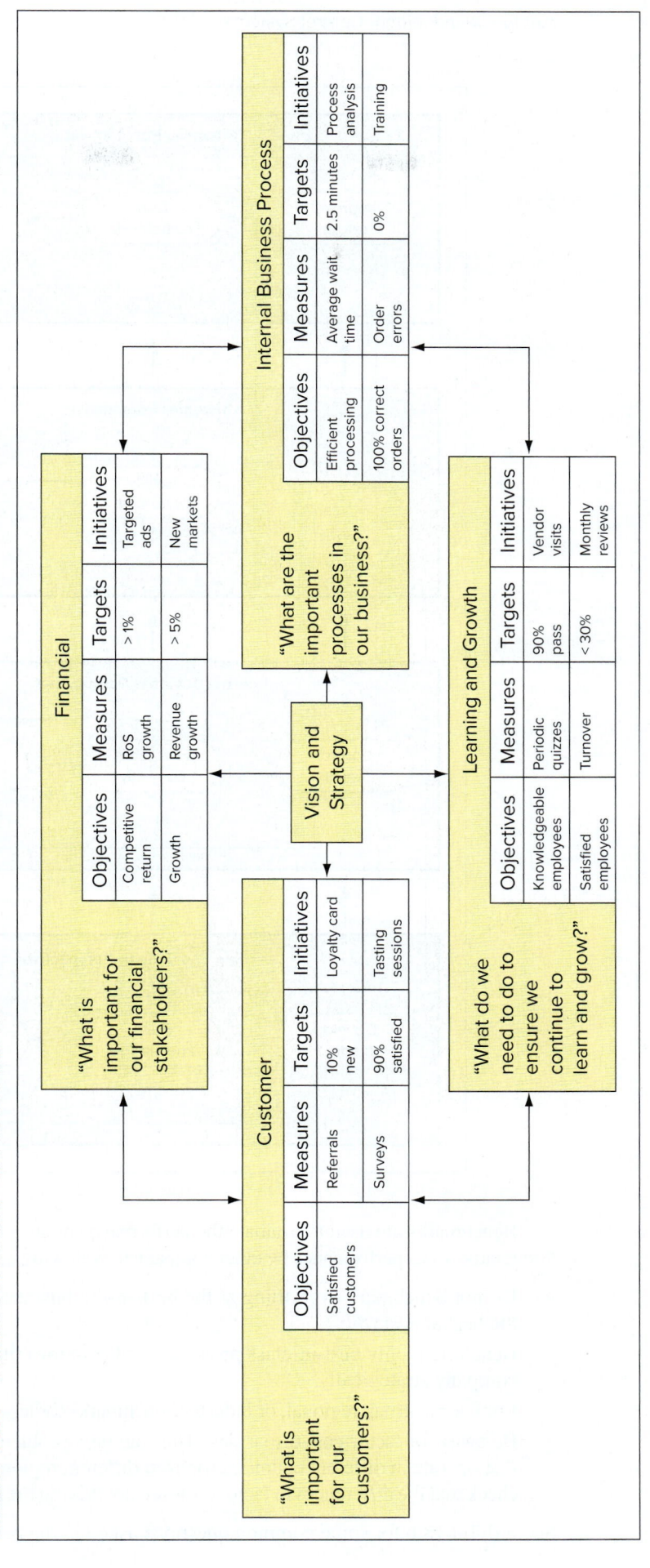

Exhibit 18.5
Strategy Map for Silo
Coffee and Tea

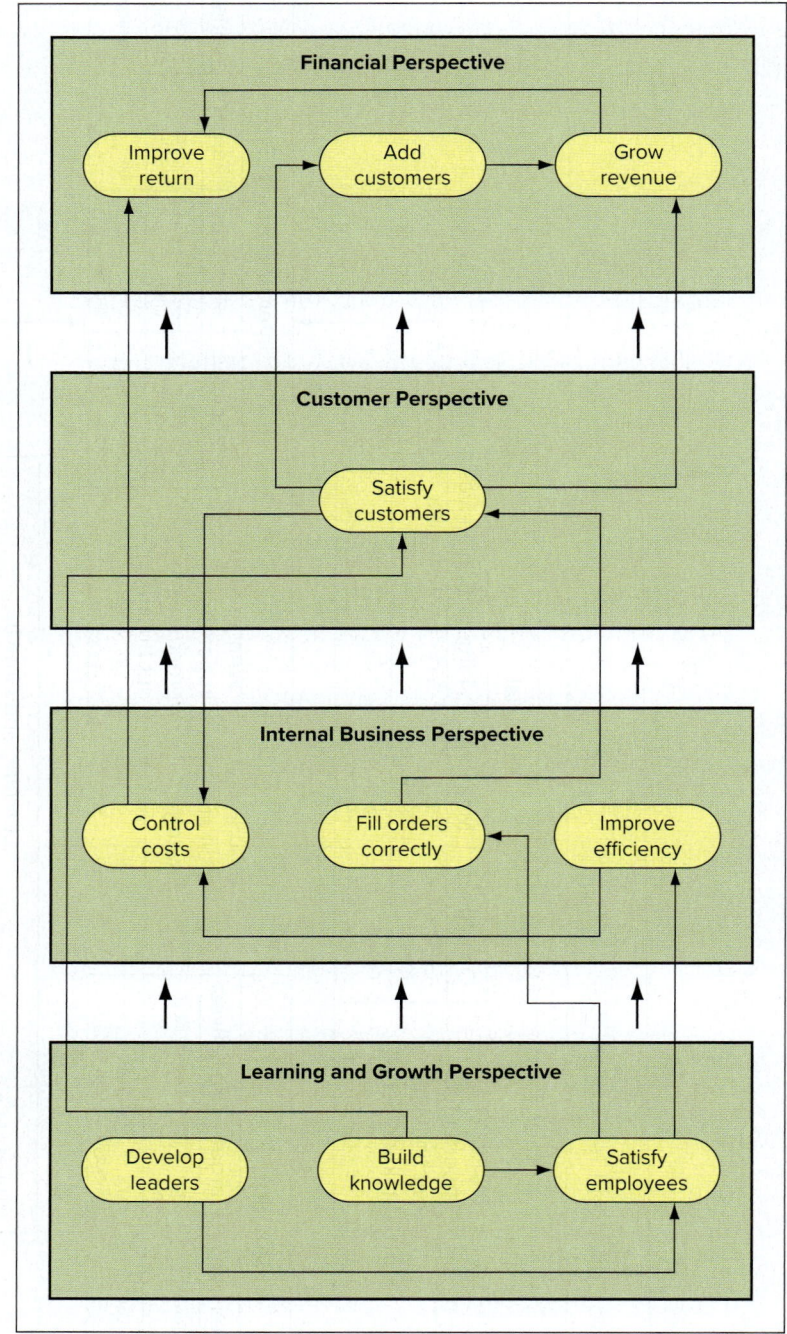

Benchmarks are used to evaluate the performance of an activity, operation, or organization relative to its performance by other companies. Following are some important guidelines:

- Do not benchmark everything at the best-in-the-business level. No company can be the best at *everything*.
- Benchmark only best-in-class processes and activities that are most important to the company strategically.
- Look for internal, regional, or industry benchmarks for less important support activities.
- Be aware of factor cost disparities. This can be a problem when benchmarking firms that operate in different countries (or even different regions of the same country). Also check that the differences in factor costs are not driving the use of different technologies.

See Exhibit 18.6 for some common questions asked in the benchmarking process.

Product Performance
- How well do our products perform compared to those of our competitors? (Many U.S. automobile, steel, camera, and television companies found that, much to their dismay, they were not performing well in the 1980s and 1990s compared to their Japanese competitors.)

Employee Performance
- How well do our employees perform compared to our competitors' employees? Are our employees as efficient as our competitors' employees? Are our employees as well trained as our competitors' employees?

New Product/Service Development
- Are we as innovative as our competitors in developing new products and services?

Cost Performance
- Are our costs as low as those of our competitors?

Exhibit 18.6
Common Benchmarking Questions

Using the Balanced Scorecard to Monitor Performance   Just over 15 months after Megan Okoye adopted the balanced scorecard, she is ready to share some results. Because there are eight different measures, she has decided to share results for four "representative" stores as well as the corporate (SCT) results. The dashboard, prepared using Tableau, is shown in Exhibit 18.7.

Exhibit 18.7   SCT Balanced Scorecard: Selected Stores and Corporate—Quarter 1, Year 2

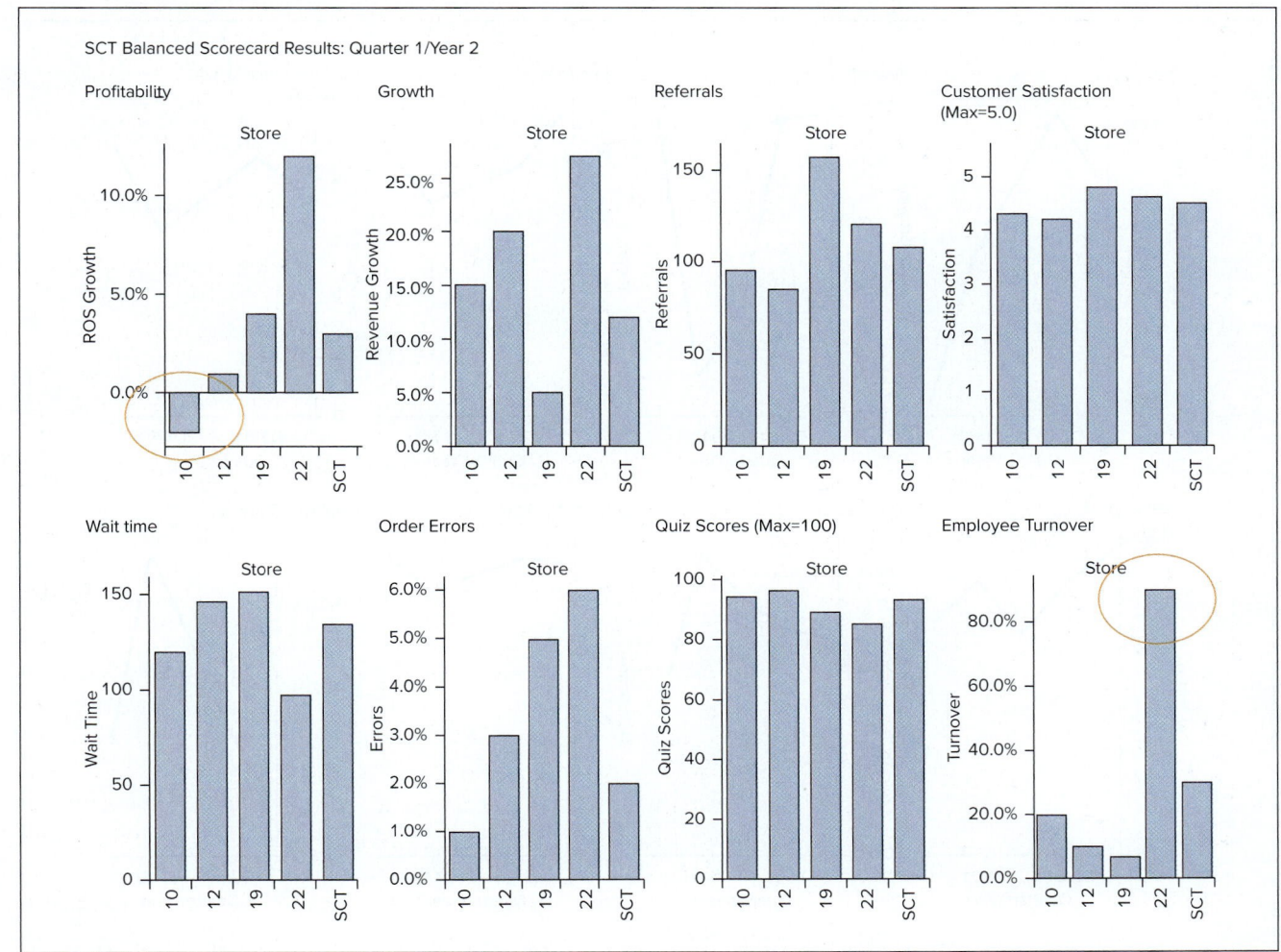

Megan identifies two concerns (circled) that she has after reviewing these results. First, looking at the employee turnover in Store 22, she is unsure why it is so high this year. She is surprised, in part, because the financial results are so strong. However, she also notices that the errors in Store 22 are also high. She plans on looking more closely at this.

The more concerning result is the lower return on sales results for Store 10. Megan is surprised because she replaced the store manager a year ago and thought the new manager was doing a better job. The other perspectives showed Store 10 to be reasonably close to the store average, except for the errors in orders, which was much lower than other stores. She wants to understand better what may be behind these results.

One of the advantages of many dashboard visualization tools is that they provide a way to drill down on results. Specifically, Exhibit 18.8 provides a look at the Scorecard results for Store 10 alone over the last five years.

Looking at the dashboard, we can identify at least two trends. First, prior to Quarter 4, all measures were worsening (remember, higher employee turnover, at least above a certain level, is undesirable). This view makes clear why Megan replaced the previous manager. It also suggests a reason for the declining profitability in Quarter 5 (which continued a trend from Quarter 2). Improving many of the other measures, such as customer satisfaction, error rates, and so on, requires investing in staff training and customer experiences. Although these expenditures are not guaranteed to result in higher profitability in the future, Megan believes they are necessary to make Store 10 a success. She will, however, continue to monitor Store 10 using the dashboard.

Exhibit 18.8   SCT Balanced Scorecard Results, Last Five Quarters—Store 10

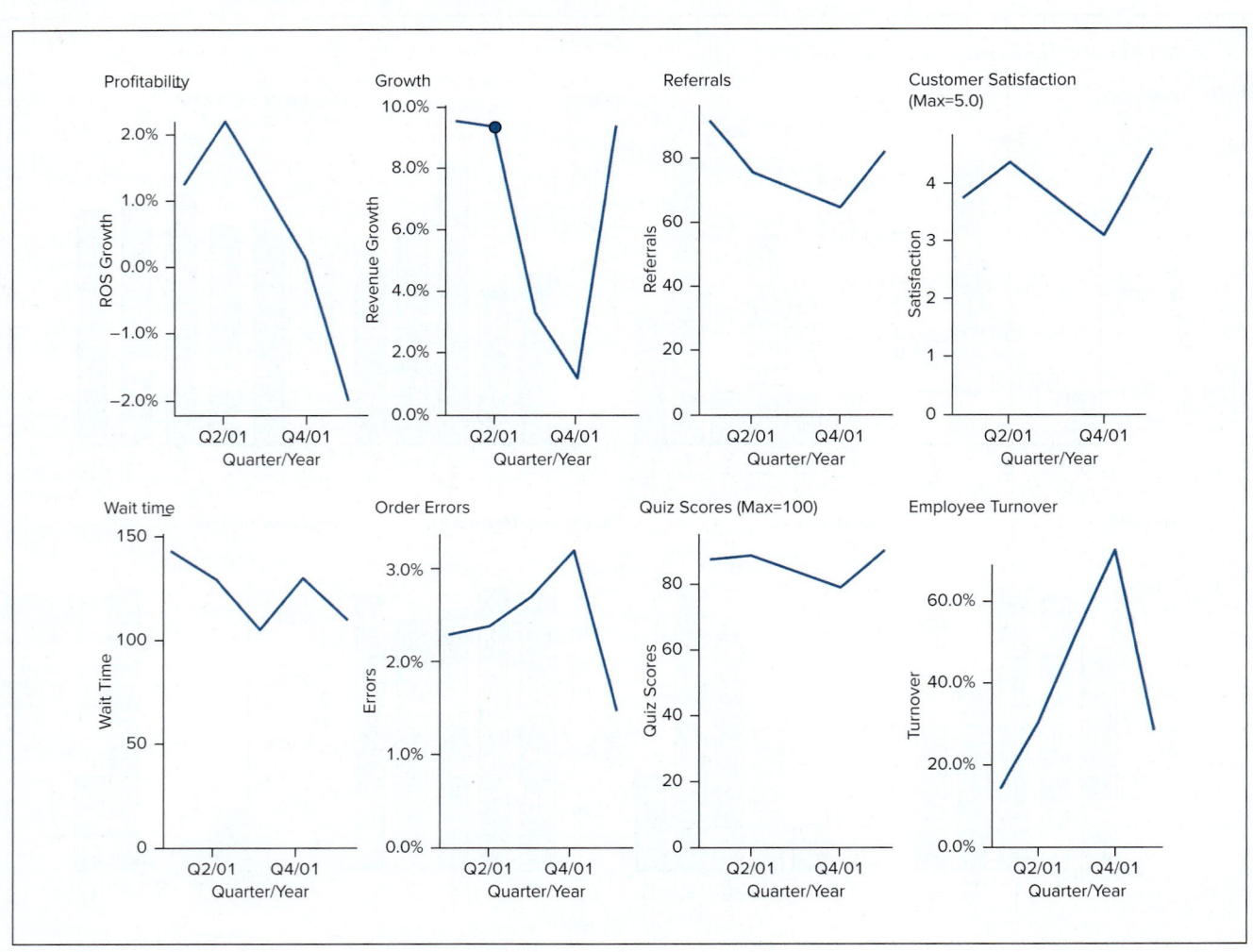

3. Silo Coffee and Tea selected six performance measures. *The solution to this question is at the end of the chapter.* Link the six measures to the four perspectives of the balanced scorecard by filling in the following blanks.

Perspective	Performance Measure	Linked to Perspective Number?
1. Financial	Employee satisfaction	_____
2. Customer	Store costs	_____
3. Learning and growth	Store profitability	_____
4. Internal business processes	Employee learning	_____
	Queue length	_____
	Customer satisfaction	_____

Performance Measurement for Control

Silo Coffee and Tea (SCT) developed multiple performance measures as a way to evaluate the achievement of its store managers. These measures also provide a way to improve performance by making changes to (controlling) operations. In other words, establishing measures to assess performance is useful not only for evaluation but also for control. In Chapters 16 and 17, we discussed how to use financial measures for control by computing variances to determine where improvements could be made.

At the beginning of this chapter, we noted that although financial measures are useful for getting managers' attention, they are less useful for identifying problems. In the remainder of this chapter, we consider nonfinancial measures and how they can be used to improve performance.

Some Common Nonfinancial Performance Measures

Performance measures must be based on the organization's responsibilities, goals, and strategies, which are likely to be different for each organization. The following are examples of performance measures that you are likely to use, or see used, in organizations. We organize our discussion around the balanced scorecard perspectives. For example, we give examples of customer satisfaction measures, which are clearly important to the success of any organization, and of functional measures of how well the organization's internal processes are functioning. Our objective is to give you a sense of the types of nonfinancial measures that organizations use, not a comprehensive cookbook of the measures available.

LO 18-6
Identify examples of nonfinancial performance measures and discuss the potential for improved performance resulting from improved activity management.

Customer Satisfaction Performance Measures

Customer satisfaction measures reflect the organization's performance on several internal factors, including quality control, delivery performance, bookings and purchase orders, and market share.

Quality Control The objective of quality control is to increase customer satisfaction with the product, reduce the costs of dealing with customer complaints, and reduce the costs of repairing products or providing a new service. Measures may include number of customer complaints, number of service calls, and number of returns.

Delivery Performance The objective of delivery performance is to deliver goods and services when promised. Measures may include the percentage of on-time deliveries and percentage of deliveries damaged.

Bookings and Purchase Orders   Bookings and purchase orders are a lead indicator of revenues. Companies have to measure bookings and purchase orders "off the books" because they are not recorded as sales. In some companies, such as Boeing, announcements of purchase orders have an effect on the companies' stock prices. Clearly, investors view purchase orders as important signals of a company's future success. A decrease in bookings and purchase orders sends a signal to management to devote more marketing effort to generate sales.

Market Share   Measuring a company's share of the market for each product is like grading on the curve. A company's sales might be increasing. However, if the market is growing faster than the company's sales, the company is, in effect, experiencing a decline in sales.

Of course, customer satisfaction measures are important, not as an end, but because the organization believes there is a link between satisfied customers and firm profitability. Recall that in Chapter 10 we discussed how to measure customer profitability. An organization needs to ensure that it is measuring the satisfaction of customers that drive profitability.

Functional Performance Measures

As well as monitoring its performance in serving external customers, an organization must evaluate its internal functional process performance. Many activities are performed throughout the product life cycle. The level of efficiency of processing activities affects the organization's overall performance in meeting its responsibilities to other stakeholders, such as stockholders and employees. See Exhibit 18.9 for several internal functional performance measures used by organizations.

Exhibit 18.9

Functional Measures of Performance

Accounting Quality
- Percentage of late reports
- Percentage of errors in reports
- Percentage of errors in budget predictions
- Degree of manager satisfaction with accounting reports

Clerical Quality
- Number of errors per document page
- Number of times messages are not delivered
- Quality of product/development engineering
- Percentage of errors in cost estimates
- Degree to which product meets customer expectations

Forecasting Quality
- Percentage of errors in sales forecasts
- Number of forecasting assumption errors
- Decision-maker satisfaction with forecasts

Procurement/Purchasing Quality
- Percentage of supplies delivered on schedule
- Average time to fill emergency orders

Production Control Quality
- Time required to incorporate engineering changes
- Time that assembly line is down due to materials shortage

Quality Assurance Quality
- Wait time on customer inquiries
- Wait time on customer support calls
- Time to answer customer complaints

Sources: Most of these measures are drawn from much longer lists in Fellers, G., *The Deming Vision: SPC/TQM for Administrators,* ASQC Quality Press, 1992; and Talley, D., *Total Quality Management,* ASQC Quality Press, 1991. Some of these measures were developed by the authors.

As you can see, many internal performance measures also relate to the organization's performance with respect to its customers. For instance, quality assurance relates *directly* to customer service performance, while production control and product development relate *indirectly* to customer satisfaction.

Manufacturing Cycle Time

The total time it takes to produce a good or service is called **manufacturing cycle time.** It includes processing, moving, storing, and inspecting. It is commonly believed that a product's service, quality, and cost are all related to cycle time. As cycle time increases, so do the costs of processing, inspecting, moving, and storing while service and quality go down.

manufacturing cycle time
Time involved in processing, moving, storing, and inspecting products and materials.

Manufacturing Cycle Efficiency

Manufacturing cycle efficiency measures the efficiency of the total manufacturing cycle. Manufacturing cycle efficiency for one unit is calculated as follows:

$$\text{Manufacturing cycle efficiency} = \frac{\text{Processing time}}{\underset{\text{time}}{\text{Processing}} + \underset{\text{time}}{\text{Moving}} + \underset{\text{time}}{\text{Storing}} + \underset{\text{time}}{\text{Inspection}}}$$

manufacturing cycle efficiency
Measure of the efficiency of the total manufacturing cycle; equals processing time divided by the manufacturing cycle time.

This formula calculates a percentage representing the time actually spent processing the unit. The higher the percentage, the less the time (and cost) that needs to be spent on nonvalue-added activities such as moving and storing. Higher-quality control of the process and inputs results in spending less time on inspections.

Productivity

Manufacturing cycle efficiency focuses on the effective use of time. **Productivity** focuses on the efficient conversion of inputs into outputs. Productivity measures may be developed for individual key inputs and simply expressed as a ratio of the two values. For example, in the automotive industry it is common to report the labor-hours per vehicle produced, in passenger air travel companies report labor costs per seat-mile (the product of the number of seats on the plane and the miles flown on a route), and in retail it is common to report the sales per square foot of retail space. These measures are termed **partial productivity** measures because each measure considers output or output value (for example, autos, seat-miles flown, or retail sales) in relation to only one input (for example, labor-hours or retail store space). Partial productivity measures are typically measured as[3]

productivity
A measure that expresses the conversion of inputs into output.

partial productivity
Measure that expresses the relation between output and a single input.

$$\frac{\text{Output (quantity or value)}}{\text{Single input such as labor (Quantity or value)}}$$

Partial productivity measures are closely related to the manufacturing efficiency variances that we studied in Chapter 16. The efficiency variance is the difference between the actual quantity of input per unit of output (partial productivity) and the quantity of input per unit of output that was forecast or budgeted, valued at the standard price of the input. The efficiency variance is a good basis for assessing how a manufacturing plant is doing as compared to engineering standards of performance. If these standards do not change over time, they are also a basis for assessing whether the plant is improving. However, if a firm's manufacturing processes are not operating at competitive levels, this may not be revealed by an efficiency variance because the plant may be attaining the engineering standard that is set at an uncompetitive level.

---

[3] Productivity measures are generally measured as output divided by input. Thus, larger numbers imply greater productivity. Some common efficiency (or productivity) measures in certain industries might be expressed as inputs divided by outputs. For example, in the automotive industry, the measure of labor-hours to vehicles produced is a common measure. As a result, lower numbers imply greater efficiency. In this chapter, we express all productivity measures as outputs produced divided by inputs.

The partial productivity measure is an absolute measure of the efficient conversion of input to output that can be used to compare different business units and, when publicly available data permit it, to allow benchmarking against competitors. In the world auto industry, it has become common to compare manufacturers on the basis of assembly labor-hours per vehicle. During the 1980s, it was large differences between labor-hours of Japanese manufacturers and U.S. and German manufacturers that led manufacturers worldwide to embrace the lean manufacturing methods that were pioneered by Toyota Motor Company.

In general, using less input to achieve a given level of output implies a more efficient production or service process. Companies that operate many similar business units (i.e., manufacturing plants or retail stores) may use measures of productivity to compare business units' performance and to identify the best practices that will result in improvement and learning throughout the company. However, an important assumption when comparing, for example, the sales per square foot of a retail establishment is that the stores are indeed comparable.

Suppose one store is located in a large shopping mall with high rental charges and another is located in a small rural town where rent is much lower. Because the rental rates are high, the mall store is smaller and maintains less inventory in stock but replenishes inventory frequently from warehouses located in the same town. Because the rental rates are low and it costs more to replenish inventory from warehouses that are located in a distant city, the rural store is larger, keeps more inventory, and is restocked weekly. In this case, it would be misleading to use the sales per square foot of retail space as a way to compare productivity because the key input, retail space, isn't comparable.

One way to make the ratios more comparable is to compare the *value* of the retail square footage to the value of sales produced. In this manner, the differing rental rates offset differences in the quantity of retail space for the two stores. It is possible then that both stores are equally productive; that is, that they both produce the same sales per unit cost of their retail space. An important contemporary example of this trade-off can be found in firms' outsourcing decisions. Often, the outsourcing decision involves moving production offshore to an international location where labor costs are markedly lower than in the firm's home country. However, in many cases, lower labor wages (cost per hour) are offset by even lower labor productivity (that is, more labor-hours per unit of output) because the workforce is less educated or skilled. Only when the firm compares the total value of labor input per unit of output is it possible to compare the two manufacturing locations and determine where partial labor productivity will be highest.

Comparing stores in urban shopping malls to rural stores can be misleading because the urban stores are often smaller and require more frequent inventory replenishment. Andrew Resek/McGraw Hill

While comparing input value to output value solves some problems of comparability, it can still be misleading to compare stores that have very different operating strategies, particularly if the operating strategies call for a different mix of inputs. For example, key features of the mall store's strategy of using limited space are low inventory levels and rapid inventory replenishment, and a key feature of the rural store's strategy is holding more inventory to guard against stockouts that might occur when inventory replenishment only occurs weekly. Similarly, in the outsourcing example, the international location with lower labor costs may also use more manual production processes. In contrast, the firm's local operations may employ more automated, technologically sophisticated machinery. The two production facilities use a different mix of labor and capital, so any partial productivity measure that compares only units of output to units of labor or units of capital will reveal stark differences. However, these differences are rooted in different operations strategies and do not necessarily indicate differences in productivity.

One approach for comparing the productivity of business units that use a different mix of inputs (or even different inputs) is to calculate **total factor productivity.** Total factor productivity is a ratio of the value of output to the value of all key inputs. So in the example of the two stores, we might identify labor, inventory, and retail space as the essential business inputs. Then a total factor productivity measure can be constructed as a ratio of the value of sales to the sum of the value of labor, retail space, and inventory carrying costs. By combining inputs, business units that use a different mix of inputs (for example, high value of retail space and low value of inventory as compared to low value of retail space and high value of inventory) can be compared. Evidence of the importance of total factor productivity is found in the passenger airline business, where financial analysts regularly cite the cost per seat-mile as an influential factor in their buy and sell recommendations for airline stocks. In a competitive pricing environment, those airlines that can deliver service at lowest cost are in a better position to profit and grow.

total factor productivity
Ratio of the value of output to the value of all key inputs.

An Illustration of Various Productivity Measures

We illustrate the computation of the various productivity measures using Desert Metals Fabricators (DMF), a small metal fabrication firm located in a medium-sized southwestern city. Exhibit 18.10 provides selected operating data for the past two years for DMF as well as government data on operations of all firms in the country in the same industry as DMF. The production process combines metal (usually steel), direct labor, and overhead (plant, machines, etc.) and produces fabricated parts. Physical output is measured in tons as well as in the value of the output sold.

The managers at DMF are interested in the performance of DMF both over time and in comparison to its competition. The company had recently undertaken many efficiency improvement initiatives, and the managers were hoping to see improvements in productivity.

We can compute two partial productivity measures. These correspond to the use of material input and labor input and are computed as follows:

$$\text{Material productivity} = \text{Tons output} \div \text{Tons input}$$

and

$$\text{Labor productivity} = \text{Tons output} \div \text{Labor-hours input}$$

Exhibit 18.11 provides the results.

Reviewing the results in Exhibit 18.11, the managers at DMF noted that both material and labor partial productivity had improved, with the biggest improvement in labor productivity. They were happy to see that they had improved to industry-average material productivity. However, they also saw that the company still lagged the industry in labor productivity, so their work was not finished.

The partial productivity measures make it difficult to assess the performance of the company relative to the industry or to the firm over time because different measures

Exhibit 18.10   Comparative Operating Data—Desert Metal Fabricators (DMF)

	DMF		Industry[a]	
	Year 2	Year 1	Year 2	Year 1
Tons of metal input.	20,000	15,000	4,000	3,500
Labor-hours.	50,000	48,000	8,000	7,500
Material cost (per ton of input).	$300	$270	$290	$260
Average direct labor rate (per hour)	$18	$15	$22	$20
Overhead cost	$3,100,000	$2,100,000	$700,000	$680,000
Output (tons).	18,000	12,000	3,600	3,100
Output (value) per ton	$600	$580	$625	$610

[a] Industry physical amounts are in thousands of tons and thousands of hours. Industry overhead cost is in thousands of dollars.

Exhibit 18.11
Partial Productivity
Measures—Desert Metal
Fabricators (DMF)

	DMF		Industry[a]	
	Year 2	Year 1	Year 2	Year 1
Tons of metal input.	20,000	15,000	4,000	3,500
Output (tons)	18,000	12,000	3,600	3,100
Material partial productivity	0.900	0.800	0.900	0.886
Labor-hours.	50,000	48,000	8,000	7,500
Output (tons)	18,000	12,000	3,600	3,100
Direct labor partial productivity	0.360	0.250	0.450	0.413

[a] Industry amounts are in thousands (tons or hours).

indicate conflicting results. To resolve this, managers at DMF decided to look at total factor productivity, including input materials, labor, and overhead. They computed this by dividing the value of the output produced by the value of the three inputs. The results of their analysis are shown in Exhibit 18.12.

The results in Exhibit 18.12 indicate that DMF has improved company productivity, but it still lags behind the industry. However, the managers at DMF were pleased that the improvement in total factor productivity at the company showed a greater relative improvement (from 1.013 to 1.080) than the overall industry productivity. They believed that if they continued their improvement efforts, the company had a chance to meet the average industry productivity in year 3.

Nonfinancial Performance and Activity-Based Management

Many experts argue that organizations should manage by using activity data rather than cost data. Knowing the amount of time it takes to produce and deliver a product (e.g., to handle materials and to rework defects) can lead to improvement. The activity data could be used to identify problems, suggest an approach to solve problems, and prioritize improvement efforts.

Organizations also can find value in knowing the amount of time it takes to complete a sequence of activities. As cycle time goes up, it is thought that cost goes up and service and quality go down. So, as the efficiency of value-added activities is improved or as nonvalue-added activities are eliminated, the process cycle time and cost will fall. Many believe a product's service, quality, and cost are related to cycle time and that by eliminating long cycle times, companies can reduce the costs of nonproduction personnel, equipment, and supplies. Customers also value a prompt response and a short order-processing time.

The use of nonfinancial performance measures is increasing as companies recognize the benefits these measures provide. However, not all companies see a performance improvement.

Exhibit 18.12
Total Productivity
Measures—Desert Metal
Fabricators (DMF)

	DMF[a]		Industry[b]	
	Year 2	Year 1	Year 2	Year 1
Value of metal input[c]	$ 6,000	$4,050	$1,160	$ 910
Value of labor input	900	720	176	150
Overhead.	3,100	2,100	700	680
Total value of inputs.	$10,000	$6,870	$2,036	$1,740
Value of output.	$10,800	$6,960	$2,250	$1,891
Total factor productivity.	1.080	1.013	1.105	1.087

[a] DMF amounts are in thousands of dollars.
[b] Industry amounts are in millions of dollars.
[c] $6,000,000 = 20,000 tons of input × $300 per ton, and so on.

Frequently, this occurs because they fail to link the measures to the firm's goals. Firms often make four mistakes when trying to measure nonfinancial performance:[4]

1. Not linking measures to strategy.
2. Not validating the links.
3. Not setting the right performance targets.
4. Measuring incorrectly (using invalid measures).

Using a business model that identifies the connections between the measures and the firm's goals helps avoid these problems.

Objective and Subjective Performance Measures

The measures we have been describing to this point are generally objective. That is, different people can look at them and agree that the method used to calculate the measure was correct. For example, the number of defective units is an objective measure of quality performance because we can all agree that the number is calculated correctly (assuming we all agree on what a defective unit is). We might, however, still disagree as to whether defective units is an appropriate measure of quality.

Many other performance measures are subjective, however. That is, two managers can view the same set of facts and come to different conclusions. Subjective measures can include a supervisor's assessment, perhaps on a scale of 1 to 5, of an employee's performance. Subjective measures allow managers to consider many factors, including those outside the employee's control, which could distort an objective measure.

Suppose, for example, that Sara Johnson, the Great Bend store manager at SCT, is evaluated based on store profitability. Suppose that the discovery of a tainted food at the firm's Hillsboro store caused customers to avoid the Great Bend store. If the objective measure of profitability alone was used to evaluate Sara's performance, it is likely that she would receive a negative report because of the drop in business. If a subjective measure were included, her supervisor could consider the reason for the drop in profitability, which is beyond Sara's control.

The Risks of Focusing on Efficiency   *Business Application*

As health care is one of the largest industries in the United States, the efficiency of the healthcare system is critical in providing affordable, effective care. The management of hospital systems, both private and not-for-profit, has been focused on efficiency and is encouraged to do so by both investors and government agencies. As a result, successful systems, such as Banner Health, a not-for-profit system operating in the western United States, had, prior to 2020, reduced staff and increased outpatient care relative to hospital stays.

In 2020, however,

> . . . when the pandemic hit, the strategies that had helped it become a model for other hospital systems suddenly became weaknesses. . . . Banner's hospitals filled with very sick patients needing one-on-one help from critical care nurses. There weren't enough.

Banner managed to cope, but in doing so, it "overtaxed" existing staff, trained other staff "on the fly," and hired many temporary staff, driving up the pay to levels that poorer hospitals could not afford.

We saw earlier how the pandemic affected supply chains, causing serious problems for companies that had been following a lean strategy. But the pandemic also

> . . . exposed weaknesses in the "just-in-time inventory" of nursing staff in the same way it did for personal protective equipment. . . .

Pursuing efficiency, Banner Health may have become fixated on improving what is easily measurable. One author argues that "not everything that is important is measurable, and much that is measurable is unimportant."

(Continued)

---

[4] C. Ittner and D. Larcker, "Coming Up Short on Nonfinancial Performance Measurement," *Harvard Business Review* 81 (no. 11): 88.

(*Continued*)

This is not to say that performance measures should not be used, but that they should be used with an understanding of both the results they are designed to encourage along with an understanding of any "perverse" incentives the measures create. It is important to not let a focus on "objective" measures overshadow the need for managerial judgment when evaluating performance.

Sources: Gold, Russell, and Melanie Evans, "Why Did Covid Overwhelm Hospitals? A Yearslong Drive for Efficiency," *The Wall Street Journal*, September 17, 2020; Muller, Jerry, "A Cure for Our Fixation on Metrics," *The Wall Street Journal*, January 12, 2018.

Self-Study Question

4. Four activities at Cinderella Slipper Company require the following average time (in hours):

Transporting product.	3.0
Manufacturing product	7.2
Inspecting product.	1.0
Storing inventory	4.8

Calculate the manufacturing cycle efficiency.

The solution to this question is at the end of the chapter.

Employee Involvement

LO 18-7

Explain why employee involvement is important for an effective performance measurement system.

One advantage of nonfinancial measures is that employees directly involved in operations are more likely to understand them. The measures used to evaluate performance reflect each unit's understanding of its contribution to the organization. By computing and reporting these nonfinancial measures, the company benefits by encouraging line employees to participate in performance improvement activities. Many organizations involve workers in creating ideas for improving performance on critical success factors. Suggestion boxes are only one example of this involvement. Worker circles and team meetings provide a forum for workers to suggest ideas for improvements. Successful managers know that workers have good ideas for improving companies' operations. After all, the workers are much closer to those operations than managers.

Worker involvement is important for three reasons:

1. Many managers believe that when workers take on real decision-making authority, their commitment to the organization and its objectives increases.
2. When decision-making responsibility lies with workers closer to the customer, workers are more responsive to customer concerns and can make informed decisions.
3. Giving decision-making responsibility to workers uses their skills and knowledge and motivates them to further develop those skills and knowledge in an effort to improve the organization's performance.

How do companies evaluate their own performance in involving workers and increasing their commitment to the company? See Exhibit 18.13 for a list of performance measures that organizations can use to assess how well they are doing in terms of worker involvement and commitment. Increasing the percentages on these measures demonstrates the organization's attempt to increase worker involvement and commitment to it. For example, managers may attempt to increase worker commitment by providing mentors for them. (See top item in Exhibit 18.13.) A worker's involvement in mentor programs is likely to increase their commitment to the organization.

Effective worker involvement presents three challenges for management. First, management must create a system that conveys the organization's objectives and critical success factors to all members. Information and training sessions and the performance

• Worker development	Percentage of workers in mentor programs	
• Worker empowerment	Percentage of workers authorized to issue credit	
• Worker recognition	Percentage of workers recognized by awards	
• Worker recruitment	Percentage of employment offers accepted	
• Worker promotion	Percentage of positions filled from within the company	
• Worker succession planning	Percentage of eligible positions filled through succession planning	

Exhibit 18.13
Worker Involvement and Commitment Measures

indicators themselves determine the extent to which employees understand what behavior is desired of them.

Second, the measures the organization uses to evaluate individual performance determine the system's success in promoting goal congruence. Management must analyze the performance measures chosen by each organizational unit to make sure that they (1) promote the desired behavior, (2) are comprehensive, (3) support the achievement of organization objectives, and (4) reflect the unit's role in the organization. Finally, management must ensure that the performance measures are applied consistently and accurately.

Difficulties in Implementing Nonfinancial Performance Measurement Systems

Companies benefit from using nonfinancial performance measures, but their implementation is not free of difficulties.

Fixation on Financial Measures

Most top managers have a good understanding of financial performance measures. They have an intuition that says (in general) that a divisional return on investment (ROI) of 20 percent is good and a divisional ROI of 4 percent is bad. They usually do not have such an intuitive understanding of nonfinancial performance measures. Further, financial analysts demand to know management's estimates and the company's actual financial results. Likewise, shareholders and boards of directors want to see financial results. These are strong influences that steer management toward financial performance measures.

Reliability of Nonfinancial Measures

However much accounting data are criticized, they have an element of objectivity that rarely applies to nonfinancial performance measures. For example, accounting data are subject to scrutiny from external auditors and tax authorities. Accounting conventions and tax rules provide an element of external review that nonfinancial measures do not receive.

Lack of Correlation between Nonfinancial Measures and Financial Results

Finding a cause-and-effect relationship between nonfinancial measures and financial results is difficult. There are at least two reasons for this problem. First, the nonfinancial measures may be flawed. There may be a causal link between good customer relations and profits, but measuring "good customer relations" is difficult. Second, there may not be a real economic link between the activity and profits. Using the example of good customer relations again, it might be so costly to develop good customer relations that the costs exceed the benefits. Third, it is difficult to measure the financial performance that results from the activity. For example, the positive results of employee training and product development may not appear in stock returns or financial reports for many years.

Key Takeaways

1. Business strategy is an organization's approach for using assets to meet stakeholders' demands.
   a. Stakeholders include investors, customers, employees, and others with an interest in the organization
   b. The business strategy defines the value proposition, which describes how the organization will create value for its stakeholders.
   c. One classification of business strategies that can be successful is the Porter framework, which includes
      - Cost leaders
      - Product differentiators
      - Focused competitors
2. Effective performance measurement achieves two goals:
   a. It leads management and other employees to focus on the organization's interests.
   b. It reflects the decision authority delegated to local managers.
3. An effective performance measurement system consists of both financial and nonfinancial measures
   a. Financial measures such as profit or stock price do a good job of reporting performance but are too aggregated and not timely enough to direct managers toward areas for improvement.
   b. Nonfinancial measurements are more useful for identifying areas for improvement and can be used to focus on specific objectives:
      I. Common nonfinancial measures include customer satisfaction, quality, and efficiency measures such as cycle time and productivity.
      II. Nonfinancial performance measures encourage employee involvement in the operation of the organization.
   c. The balanced scorecard combines financial and nonfinancial measurements to provide managers with a view of several perspectives, such as
      - Financial
      - Customer
      - Internal business processes
      - Learning and growth
   d. The balanced scorecard can be used with a strategy map that summarizes and communicates the organization's strategy.

SUMMARY

This chapter discusses innovative ways to evaluate performance "beyond the financial numbers." The following summarizes key ideas tied to the chapter's learning objectives:

LO 18-1 Explain why management accountants should know the business strategy of their organization. In order to develop performance measures that lead to higher value, management accountants need to know how value is created in the organization.

LO 18-2 Explain why companies use nonfinancial performance measures. Nonfinancial measures of performance are more timely and more understandable, especially for operating employees.

LO 18-3 Understand the reasons why performance measures differ across levels of the organization. At lower levels in the organization, control and performance measurement focus on how people carry out the daily activities that create the organization's products. At the middle level, performance measurement focuses on the organization's ability to meet its responsibilities to various stakeholder groups, how well the operating systems work together to meet these needs, and how effective these systems are compared to those of competitors. At the upper level of the organization, performance measurement focuses on whether the organization is meeting its responsibilities and performing well from the stakeholders' perspective.

LO 18-4 Understand how the balanced scorecard helps organizations recognize and deal with their conflicting responsibilities. The balanced scorecard concept recognizes that organizations are responsible to different stakeholder groups and must perform well on several dimensions for success. The balanced scorecard is a set of performance targets and results that shows how well the organization has met its objectives relating to financial, customer, process, and innovation factors.

LO 18-5 Understand how to apply benchmarking to support continuous improvement. Continuous improvement is the search to eliminate nonvalue-added activities and improve the efficiency of activities that add value. Continuous improvement uses a tool called *benchmarking,* which is the search for and implementation of the best methods as practiced in other organizations.

LO 18-6 Identify examples of nonfinancial performance measures and discuss the potential for improved performance resulting from improved activity management. Customer satisfaction measures are directed at evaluating service, quality, and cost. The efficiency of just-in-time production is measured by manufacturing cycle time and manufacturing cycle efficiency, the goal being a manufacturing efficiency of 1.

LO 18-7 Explain why employee involvement is important for an effective performance measurement system. Worker involvement is important for three reasons: (1) It increases commitment to the organization and its goals, (2) it leads to more responsive and informed decision making, and (3) it utilizes worker skills and knowledge. Management must create a system that conveys the organization's goals and critical success factors to the workers.

KEY TERMS

balanced scorecard, *835*
benchmarking, *838*
business model, *833*
business strategy, *829*
continuous improvement, *838*
manufacturing cycle efficiency, *845*
manufacturing cycle time, *845*
mission, *829*

mission statement, *830*
partial productivity, *845*
productivity, *845*
stakeholders, *829*
strategy map, *838*
total factor productivity, *847*
value proposition, *829*

REVIEW QUESTIONS

18-1. Why is it important for management accountants to understand business strategy?

18-2. A balanced scorecard is a set of two or more performance measures. Do you agree? Why or why not?

18-3. What is a business model?

18-4. What are the advantages of financial measures of performance? What are the advantages of nonfinancial measures of performance?

18-5. What is a critical success factor?

18-6. Why do effective performance evaluation systems measure different things at different levels in the organization?

18-7. What is benchmarking?

18-8. How is benchmarking used?

18-9. What is the difference among a firm's value proposition, its mission, and its mission statement?

18-10. What is the difference between an organization's mission and its strategy?

18-11. What performance factors do measures related to customer satisfaction attempt to evaluate?

18-12. Why is manufacturing cycle efficiency important to most organizations?

18-13. Why measure delivery performance?

18-14. Why is worker involvement important to an organization's success?

18-15. How do companies evaluate their own performance in getting workers involved and committed?

CRITICAL ANALYSIS AND DISCUSSION QUESTIONS

18-16. Consider a locally owned coffee shop, a Starbucks store, and a retail gas station that offers fresh coffee in its convenience stores. Characterize these stores according to the Porter strategy framework.

18-17. Consider your campus bookstore. Who do you think are the stakeholders? What do you think are its critical success factors? How would they differ from those of a retail bookstore in a city without a college?

18-18. Consider the Business Application "A New Strategy for an Old Business." Prior to the internet, the *The New York Times* (and other papers) offered news, a crossword puzzle, recipes, and so on. The are also offered in the newer digital model of the paper. What makes the digital version a different strategy?

18-19. Consider a class you are taking (perhaps cost accounting) or have taken in the past. Was your evaluation based on a single measure of performance (a final exam, for example) or did the instructor use multiple measures of performance (perhaps a quiz, midterm exam, class participation, an essay, etc.). Why do you think your instructor used multiple measures (if they did)? Which would you prefer? Why?

18-20. Again, consider a class you are taking (or have taken). Did the instructor use solely objective measures (scores on numerical exams, for example) or did they use a mix of objective and subjective (short-essay questions, for example). Why do you think both objective and subjective measures were used (if they were). Which do you prefer? Why?

18-21. If customers are satisfied, they will buy your products and profits will increase. Therefore, you only need to measure profit. Comment.

18-22. Consider the number of customer complaints as a measure of customer satisfaction. How does this measure customer satisfaction? How does it fail to measure customer satisfaction?

18-23. "I know how to satisfy customers—give the product away." How does a system with multiple measures of performance address this concern with evaluating managers in part on customer satisfaction?

18-24. "My company is unique. We can't use benchmarking." How would you respond?

18-25. A friend tells you that the Business Application "The Risks of Focusing on Efficiency" demonstrates "that trying to achieve efficient operations is not a good idea." Do you agree? Explain.

EXERCISES      All applicable Exercises are included in Connect.

(LO 18-1)   **18-26. Strategy and Management Accounting Systems**

Kipling's Taco Shop was the only establishment serving tacos and other quick bites in a small college town for more than 20 years. Service was limited to the walk-up window, with no delivery and no inside seating. The owner of Kipling's focused on well-made and generously filled tacos and burritos at price that was competitive with local fast-food burger chains. However, as the college and the surrounding town grew, national competitors such as Taco Bell and regional competitors such as Del Taco entered the market. Both chains have taken a noticeable slice of business from the company, so Kipling's management has decided to abandon the current low-price strategy and instead move up-market. It has decided to partner with a local brewpub and open a store that serves specialty Mexican and other Latin American food using fresh ingredients sourced locally to pair with specialty in-house beers as well as soft drinks from Latin America.

Required

a. How will the changes in business strategy of Kipling's affect the business model and the performance measures that will be important for running the business?

b. How will the core assets and capabilities of Kipling's need to change as it changes the eatery's business strategy?

(LO 18-1)   **18-27. Business Strategy Classification**

Consider the following large organizations. Would you classify them as primarily cost leaders, product differentiators, or focused competitors according to the Porter strategy framework? Why?

Organization	Primary Product/Service	Dominant Porter Strategy
Bahama Breeze	A restaurant chain focusing on seafood with a Caribbean style	
Costco, Inc.	Retail consumer and household goods and groceries	
Dell Technologies	Computers, networking devices, and cloud services	
Kate Spade	Designer handbags, shoes, and so on	
Tesla	Manufacturer of electric vehicles	

18-28. Nonfinancial Performance Measures   (LO 18-2)

Consider the following jobs. Identify a nonfinancial performance measure that you would recommend.

a.   Flight attendant
b.   Hotel parking valet
c.   Sports venue ticket-taker
d.   Bank teller
e.   Restaurant wait-staff

18-29. Performance Measures and the Balanced Scorecard   (LO 18-3, 4)

Walden Tire Store is a chain of tire and auto accessory retail stores.

Required

Walden discloses that it uses a balanced scorecard with seven performance measures. Link the measures to the perspectives of the balanced scorecard by labelling each performance measure with the appropriate perspective number.

Performance Measure	Perspective
a. Revenue growth _____	1. Financial
b. Installation errors _____	2. Customer
c. Training hours _____	3. Learning and growth
d. Complaints _____	4. Internal business processes
e. Ratings on social media _____	
f. Store profit _____	
g. Turnaround time on tire replacements _____	

18-30. Performance Measures and the Balanced Scorecard   (LO 18-3, 4)

Crawford County Park is a historical center and recreation area located in a rural county. It is a not-for-profit organization that relies on ticket sales, memberships, and donations for financial support.

Required

Crawford Park management discloses that it uses a balanced scorecard with eight performance measures. Link the measures to the perspectives of the balanced scorecard by filling in the following table:

Performance Measure	Perspective
a. Online course credits completed by staff _____	1. Financial
b. Ratings on a local social media page _____	2. Customer
c. Average wait time for tickets _____	3. Learning and growth
d. Member retention (renewal) _____	4. Internal business processes
e. Operating surplus (revenues less expenses) _____	
f. New memberships _____	
g. Staff-to-visitor ratio _____	
h. Concession revenue _____	

18-31. Different Performance Measures across the Organization   (LO 18-3)

At one time, a well-known communications firm measured all managers at all levels on return on net assets (RONA). Write a report to the firm's CFO indicating why you believe that the use of a single performance measure for managers at all levels will not be effective.

18-32. Balanced Scorecards and Strategy Maps   (LO 18-4)

Romeyn Food Markets has decided to adopt a balanced scorecard to monitor performance. The company's strategy is to be a provider of premium foods, sourced from local farms and nationally known organic suppliers. The initial scorecard recommended by a consultant includes the following measures in each of the perspectives:

Perspective	Objectives	Perspective	Objectives
Financial	Reduced cost per square foot for operating costs Increased return-on-sales	Internal	Minimize inventory levels Minimize employee-to-customer ratio
Customer	Complaints	Learning and growth	Maintain wage levels at local chain average or below

Required
Comment on the scorecard and make recommendations about adding or deleting measures to align the scorecard with the company's strategy.

(LO 18-4)   **18-33. Balanced Scorecards and Strategy Maps**
Gordon Industries has the following mission statement:

> To be the low-cost leader in package delivery services.

Gordon's CEO tells you that the financial staff has developed the following initial balanced scorecard:

Perspective	Objectives	Perspective	Objectives
Financial	• Increased profit margin • Increased share of time-sensitive packages	Internal	• Delivery time
Customer	• Repeat orders • Customer referrals	Learning and growth	• Employee satisfaction • Employee retention

Required
Comment on the scorecard and make recommendations about adding or deleting measures to align the scorecard with the company's strategy as defined by its mission statement.

(LO 18-5)   **18-34. Benchmarks**
Match each of the following specific measurements to its benchmark category:

a. Number of product recalls	1. Employee performance
b. Percentage of orders with errors	2. Product performance
c. Staff turnover rate	3. Supplier performance
d. Time to approve purchase contracts	4. Support performance

(LO 18-5)   **18-35. Benchmarks**
Match each of the following specific measurements with its benchmark category:

a. Raw materials quality	1. Employee performance
b. Time card errors	2. Product performance
c. Unexpected scrap	3. Supplier performance
d. Warranty claims	4. Support performance

(LO 18-6)   **18-36. Performance Measures**
Observe the operations of a fitness center and identify an important nonfinancial performance measure for it.

18-37. Manufacturing Cycle Time and Efficiency   (LO 18-6)

Steger & Company has the following average times (in minutes):

Inspecting product....................	1.00
Manufacturing product	3.00
Storing inventory.......................	2.50
Transporting product..................	5.50

Required

Calculate the manufacturing cycle efficiency.

18-38. Manufacturing Cycle Time and Efficiency   (LO 18-6)

Canfield Components produces machine parts. The average times for its largest volume product (in hours) follow:

Inspecting product................	1.02
Manufacturing product	7.41
Storing inventory.................	1.70
Transporting product..............	2.22

Required

Calculate the manufacturing cycle efficiency.

18-39. Functional Measures   (LO 18-6)

For each category of functional measures listed in Exhibit 18.9, add one additional specific measurement that is not already listed.

18-40. Partial Productivity Measures   (LO 18-6)

RST Airlines operates call centers for customer service in four locations: Minneapolis, Phoenix, Boise, and Singapore. Although all four call centers can handle any inquiries, calls from elite customers are generally routed to the Boise center, and international calls as well as domestic calls between midnight and 6 a.m. (Central U.S. Time) are routed to Singapore.

The following information provides the call center representative-hours worked and the number of calls handled for the most recent period:

	Minneapolis	Phoenix	Boise	Singapore
Representative-hours.........	8,430	10,200	7,220	14,300
Calls handled................	60,696	61,710	30,324	73,216

Required

a.   Compute the partial productivity measures for representatives for the four locations.

b.   Comment on the results. Are there factors other than efficiency that might affect the results?

18-41. Partial Productivity Measures   (LO 18-6)

Top management at Reisener Corporation are looking to improve productivity in corporate staff functions. One area targeted for the initiative is the Human Resources (HR) department. The following data were collected for three relatively routine actions for the most recent period: hiring, separations, and transfers (within Reisner facilities).

	Hiring	Separations	Transfers
Staff-hours	1,600	800	2,000
Personnel actions completed...........	72	24	72

Required

a.   Compute the partial productivity measures for labor for the three actions.

b.   Comment on the results. Are there factors other than efficiency that might affect the results?

(LO 18-6) **18-42. Partial Productivity Measures**

The controller's staff at McNichols Lubricants is responsible for preparing quarterly performance reports. One report evaluates quarter-to-quarter improvement in partial productivity of the two main inputs in the production process: base chemical and labor. Management at McNichols is particularly interested in the results because there have been numerous efficiency improvement programs instituted at the company recently.

Data for the last two quarters follow:

	Quarter 2	Quarter 1
Barrels input...............	13,500	9,000
Labor-hours	2,700	2,250
Barrels of output............	10,044	8,190

Required

a. Compute the partial productivity measures for labor for quarter 1 and quarter 2.

b. Compute the partial productivity measures for material for quarter 1 and quarter 2.

c. Comment on the results. Have the efficiency improvement programs resulted in greater productivity?

(LO 18-6) **18-43. Partial Productivity Measures**

Canfield Transition Centers is a not-for-profit organization to teach new technical skills to individuals looking to change careers. Canfield operates four campuses (Construction, Electrical, Plumbing, and Carpentry). Because the programs require all-day (eight-hour) attendance, each campus operates a cafeteria, which is funded by various business and civic organizations. The CFO of Canfield is committed to ensuring that the centers operate as efficiently as possible and monitors the productivity of all functions, including support functions. Data on meals served and staff-hours for the cafeterias at the four campuses for the most recent reporting period follow:

	Construction	Electrical	Plumbing	Carpentry
Meals served..........	4,592	3,762	5,727	3,114
Staff hours	410	380	460	360

Required

a. Compute the partial productivity measures for cafeteria staff for each of the four campuses.

b. Comment on the results. Which campus appears to be most productive? What issues are there in making a comparison across campuses?

(LO 18-6) **18-44. Partial Productivity Measures**

Cahalan is a network of clinics performing laser surgery for vision correction. Each clinic tracks the number of patients treated and the number of professional-hours spent on the laser patient procedure. Consultations, follow-up visits, and so on are tracked separately. The following data are from three clinics for the most recent reporting period:

	East	South	North
Procedures completed	330	1,260	714
Professional hours	550	1,680	1,020

Required

a. Compute the partial productivity measures for professional staff for each of the three clinics.

b. Comment on the results. Which clinic appears to be most productive? What issues are there in making a comparison across clinics

(LO 18-6) **18-45. Total Factor Productivity**

Ternes Manufacturing produces metal products primarily used in the construction industry. The three main inputs in production are materials (metal), labor, and overhead. Data for the previous three reporting periods follow:

	Period 3	Period 2	Period 1
Materials cost	$ 49,000	$ 63,500	$ 58,750
Labor cost.	28,150	37,820	34,200
Overhead	41,050	46,600	44,850
Value of product produced.	135,930	177,504	162,604

Required

a. Compute the total factor productivity for the previous three reporting periods.

b. Briefly evaluate the efficiency of the operation at Ternes.

18-46. Total Factor Productivity
(LO 18-6)

Trombly Fabrication has three production facilities located in the state, each producing the same basic mix of products. Facility 1 was the original plant and the only one for several years. Facilities 2 and 3 were added recently to handle the increased volume. Data for the three facilities on output and the three primary inputs for the most recent period follow:

	Facility 1	Facility 2	Facility 3
Value of product produced.	$532,698	$270,108	$229,432
Materials cost	210,000	125,400	110,700
Labor cost.	79,820	27,100	23,200
Overhead	87,980	68,900	58,900

Required

a. Compute the total factor productivity for the three production facilities.

b. Briefly evaluate the comparative efficiency of the three production facilities.

18-47. Specifying Nonfinancial Measures
(LO 18-2)

Write a memo to Megan Okoye outlining how you would recommend measuring "correct orders" for Silo Coffee and Tea. Be sure to discuss the advantages and disadvantages of your proposed measure.

18-48. Employee Involvement
(LO 18-7)

In many manufacturing plants, employees on the manufacturing lines are empowered to stop the line (halt production on a particular assembly line) if they see something they believe is "not right." For example, if they begin to see units that appear outside specification, they can stop the production line.

Required

Write a brief memo commenting on the advantages and disadvantages of this policy.

All applicable Problems are included in Connect.    **PROBLEMS**

18-49. Core Assets and Capabilities
(LO 18-1)

Consider the following well-known companies and their key products and services:

Company	Primary Product/Service	Core Asset or Capability	Noncore Asset or Capability
Dr Pepper	Soft drink		
McDonald's	Fast-food franchiser		
The Metropolitan Museum of Art (New York City)	Art museum		
Peloton	Exercise equipment		
Tesla	Electric vehicles		
Walmart	Retailer		

Required

Identify one thing that is a core capability for each. Also identify one capability that companies have that is not core.

(LO 18-2) **18-50. Financial versus Nonfinancial Performance Measures**

A company is considering using sales revenue (selling price multiplied by sales quantity) as a performance measure for its marketing manager. The newly hired compensation analyst suggests that it might be better to just use the sales quantity (a nonfinancial measure) instead.

Required

Write a memo discussing the advantages of each potential measure. Be sure to include factors that would lead you to prefer one measure over the other.

(LO 18-4) **18-51. Balanced Scorecards and Strategy Maps**

Brace Parts manufactures components for the audiovideo equipment industry. At a recent corporate retreat, the management of Brace reviewed the company strategy and decided that Brace had a strategic advantage in being able to differentiate several of its major products. The managers then set about to develop a strategy map part of the development of a balanced scorecard to help communicate the strategy to other management and line employees of the firm. The following is a draft of a map that was the initial basis for discussion.

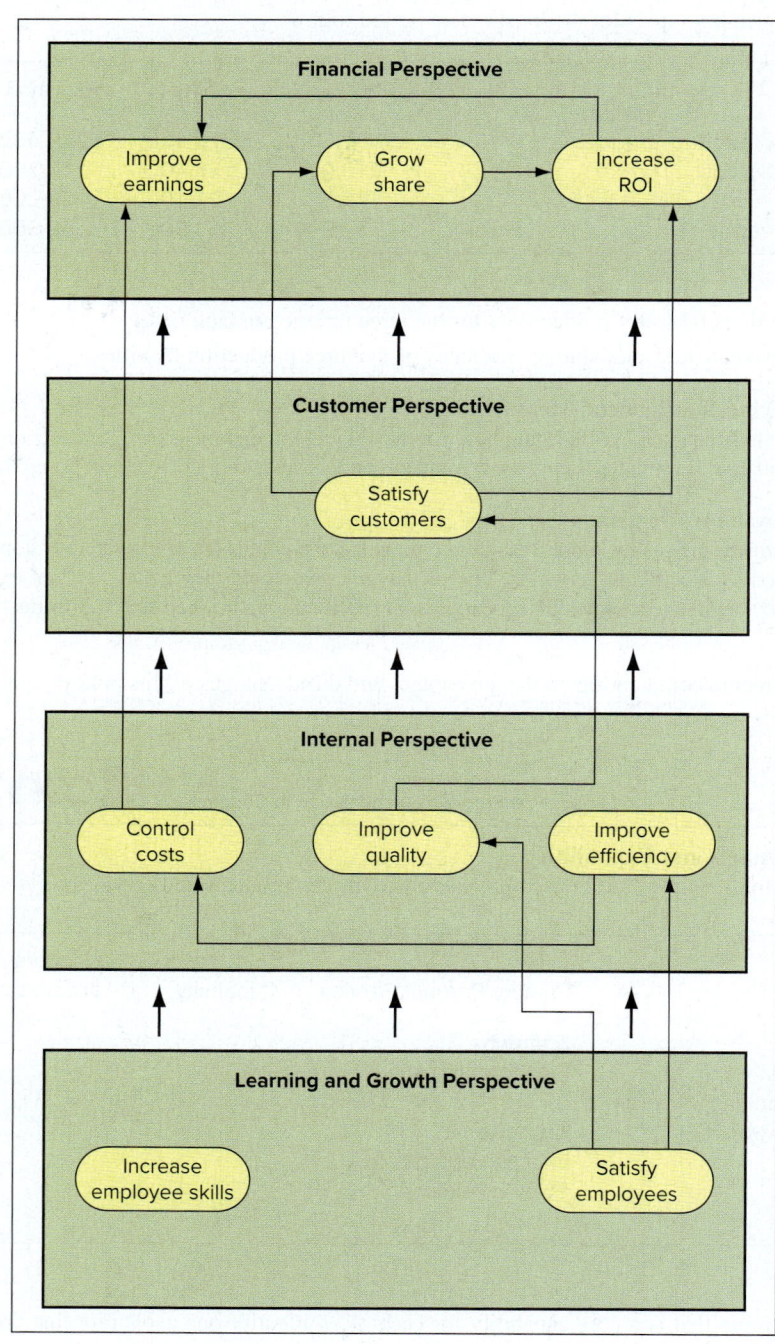

Required

a.   Using the strategy map, comment on the performance measures used for each of the four per-
     spectives of the scorecard. Would you recommend any changes to the measures? If so, what
     changes would you make? Why?

b.   What are the strengths and weaknesses of the draft strategy map as developed by Brace?

c.   Recommend changes to the map that will better communicate the strategy for Brace personnel
     and incorporate your recommendations from requirement (*a*).

18-52. Balanced Scorecards and Strategy Maps   (LO 18-4)

Stansbury Stores is a general grocery and convenience items retailer. The business is quite competitive and margins are thin. The company recently reviewed its performance measurement system
and decided to adopt a balanced scorecard. As a part of that review, the management of Stansbury
used the following map to communicate its strategy to its department managers and selected other
employees.

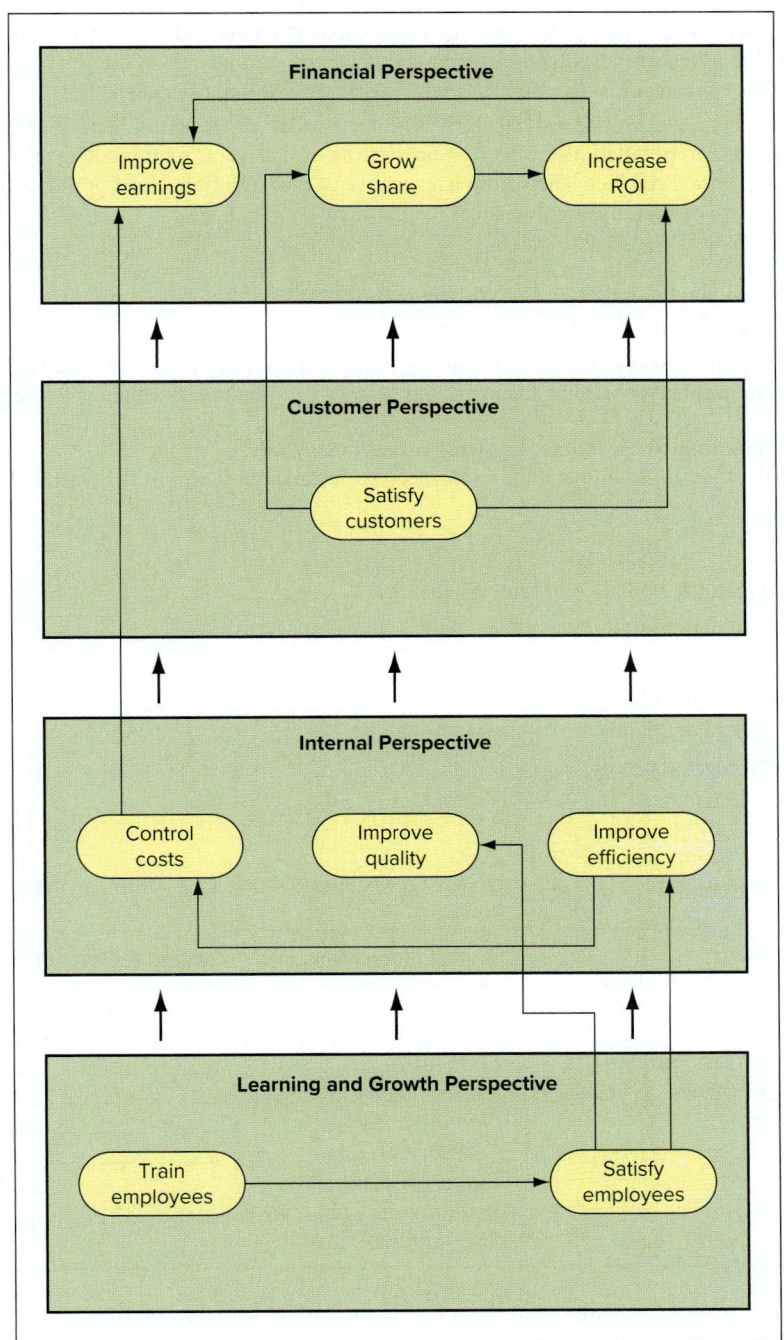

Required

a.   Using the strategy map, comment on the performance measures used for each of the four perspectives of the scorecard. Would you recommend any changes to the measures? If so, what changes would you make? Why?

b.   What are the strengths and weaknesses of the strategy map as developed by Stanbury?

c.   Recommend changes to the map that will better communicate the strategy for Stanbury Stores and incorporate your recommendations from requirement (*a*).

(LO 18-5)   **18-53. Benchmarks**

Write a report to the CEO of Acer Incorporated (a manufacturer of laptops) recommending specific benchmark measures. Include specific competitors against which to measure.

(LO 18-1, 5)   **18-54. Mission Statement and Benchmarks**

Mission statements can be difficult to write, especially for not-for-profit organizations engaged in charitable work. Consider the following two statements from relief organizations:

·   American Red Cross: "The American Red Cross prevents and alleviates human suffering in the face of emergencies by mobilizing the power of volunteers and the generosity of donors." (https://www.redcross.org/about-us/who-we-are/mission-and-values.xhtml).

·   Médecins Sans Frontières (Doctors Without Borders): Médecins Sans Frontières provides assistance to populations in distress, to victims of natural or man-made disasters and to victims of armed conflict. They do so irrespective of race, religion, creed or political convictions. (https://www.msf.org/who-we-are)

Required

a.   What do you think these mission statements do well?

b.   What, if anything, would you change?

c.   Identify the mission statement for your organization (school, company, or other) or for a company or organization you admire. Compare and contrast that mission statement with the two here.

(LO 18-3, 4)   **18-55. Performance Measures, Drawing a Business Model**

A regional airline discloses that it uses a balanced scorecard with the following performance measures:

·   Profit
·   Gate agent assessments
·   Load factor (percentage of seats filled)
·   Pilot simulation training hours
·   On-time arrivals
·   Cancellation rate
·   Customer complaints
·   Revenue per seat-mile
·   Lost luggage rate

Required

a.   Link the measures to the perspectives of the balanced scorecard by filling in the following table:

Perspective	Performance Measure	Linked to Perspective Number?
1. Financial	Profit	_____
2. Customer	Gate agent assessments	_____
3. Learning and growth	Load factor	_____
4. Internal business processes	Pilot simulation hours	_____
	On-time arrivals	_____
	Cancellation rate	_____
	Customer complaints	_____
	Revenue per seat-mile	_____
	Lost luggage rate	_____

b.   Present a business model as in Exhibit 18.1 that would lead the company to choose this set of measures.

18-56. Performance Measures, Drawing a Business Model   (LO 18-3, 4)

The owner-manager of Molena Restaurant describes the balanced scorecard measures used to assess performance by listing the following performance measures:

- Beverage and wine revenue
- Customer complaints
- Kitchen staff training
- Order errors
- Profit
- Reviews on social media
- Table turnover
- Wait-staff assessments
- Wine training for wait staff

Required

a.   Link the measures to the perspectives of the balanced scorecard by filling in the following table:

Perspective	Performance Measure	Linked to Perspective Number?
1. Financial	Beverage and wine revenue	_____
2. Customer	Customer complaints	_____
3. Learning and growth	Kitchen staff training	_____
4. Internal business	Order errors	_____
processes	Profit	_____
	Reviews on social media	_____
	Table turnover	
	Wait-staff assessments	_____
	Wine training for wait staff	_____

b.   Present a business model as in Exhibit 18.1 that would lead the company to choose this set of measures.

18-57. Productivity Measures   (LO 18-6)

Terrell Industries produces a single product at its Roosevelt facility. The product has two main inputs, metal and labor, with additional costs being included in manufacturing overhead. The plant carries neither work-in-process nor finished goods inventories. Information from the previous four quarters of production follows:

	Q1	Q2	Q3	Q4
Metal input (pounds).	194,000	210,000	240,000	230,000
Labor input (hours)	9,700	10,560	12,500	11,500
Sales (pounds)	164,900	184,800	204,000	190,900
Average price of metal per pound	$ 0.62	$ 0.66	$ 0.70	$ 0.65
Average wage rate per hour	32.00	34.00	28.00	30.00
Average sales price per pound.	6.20	5.95	6.10	6.00
Manufacturing overhead (total).	387,224	418,660	397,000	421,820

Required

a.   Compute the partial productivity measures for metal for the four quarters.
b.   Compute the partial productivity measures for labor for the four quarters.
c.   Compute the total factor productivity for the four quarters.

18-58. Performance Measures   (LO 18-6)

Prevost Chemicals manufactures an industrial solvent at its only processing plant. A liquid chemical and labor are the two primary inputs. All other resources are included in manufacturing overhead. The plant never has any work-in-process or finished goods inventories. Information from the previous four periods of production follow:

	Period 1	Period 2	Period 3	Period 4
Chemical input (gallons).............	125,000	129,280	128,000	120,000
Labor input (hours)	12,500	11,200	15,000	10,100
Solvent sales (gallons)	110,000	113,120	120,000	103,020
Average price of chemical per gallon........................	$ 2.00	$ 2.10	$ 1.95	$ 2.25
Average wage rate per hour........	28.00	26.00	31.00	34.00
Average sales price per gallon......	10.26	10.00	9.80	10.60
Manufacturing overhead (total)......	236,000	245,312	245,400	243,080

Required

a.   Compute the partial productivity measures for chemical for the four periods.

b.   Compute the partial productivity measures for labor for the four periods.

c.   Compute the total factor productivity for the four periods.

(LO 18-6)   **18-59. Operational Performance Measures—Visualization**

Henderson Parts manufactures parts for turbines. The company is in the process of adopting lean manufacturing techniques to remain competitive. Part of the effort is to eliminate as much of the nonvalue-added time in production as possible. The plant controller prepares a weekly production efficiency report and sends it to corporate headquarters. The data compiled in these reports for a recent eight-week period follow:

Performance Measure (%)	Week							
	1	2	3	4	5	6	7	8
Manufacturing cycle efficiency	65%	68%	62%	75%	77%	81%	82%	85%
Order errors............	5	4	4	7	9	12	14	18
Customer returns	2	1	0	4	6	7	6	12

Required

a.   Write a memo to the company president evaluating the plant's performance. Use data visualizations as appropriate.

b.   If you identify any areas of concern in your memo, indicate your recommended action for management to take. Indicate any additional information you would like to have to make your evaluation.

(LO 18-6)   **18-60. Operational Performance Measures—Visualization**

Boleyn Cycles produces several models of high-end bicycles and related products. The company collects various operational performance measurements monthly and reviews them as part of its continuous improvement program. The company has recently been evaluating its inventory policies as a possible source of improvement. As a part of the effort, the plant reports the ratio of beginning-of-month inventory to monthly sales (in units) and the percentage of orders that cannot be filled because of stockouts. The data compiled in these reports for the latest eight months follow:

Performance Measure (%)	Month							
	Jan.	Feb.	Mar.	Apr.	May	Jun.	Jul.	Aug.
Manufacturing cycle efficiency.........	52%	56%	61%	54%	60%	64%	52%	58%
Inventory/sales ratio (units)	3	5	10	7	3	9	7	11
Stockouts (% of orders)...............	4	3	1	2	5	4	3	1

Required

a.   Write a memo to the company's vice president for operations evaluating the plant's performance. Use data visualizations as appropriate.

b.   If you identify any areas of concern in your memo, indicate your recommended action for management to take. Indicate any additional information you would like to have to make your evaluation.

18-61. Productivity Measures   (LO 18-6)

Refer to the data in Exercise 18-42 (McNichols Lubricants). From the accounting records, you also gather the following information for the two years.

	Quarter 2	Quarter 1
Cost of inputs (per gallon).................	$ 14.00	$ 16.50
Wage rate (per hour)	37.00	35.00
Total manufacturing overhead..............	343,500.00	310,014.00
Selling price of output (per gallon)	85.00	82.00

Required

a.   Compute the total factor productivity measures for quarter 1 and quarter 2 based on the three inputs (materials, labor, and overhead).

b.   Comment on the results.

c.   Describe briefly the advantages and disadvantages of the total factor productivity relative to the partial measures computed in Exercise 18-42. Would it be useful to report both?

18-62. Productivity Measures—Working Backwards   (LO 18-6)

Venice Textiles produces cloth. The inputs are fabric, labor, and overhead. Fragmentary productivity records from plant files for the last period show the following:

Fabric price (per bolt)	$30.00
Sales price (per bolt).................	$120.00
Sales revenue	$2,160,000
Manufacturing overhead	$510,000
Total factor productivity	1.60
Total labor costs	$120,000

Required

Determine the partial fabric (materials) productivity.

18-63. Objective and Subjective Performance Measures   (LO 18-6)

A common method of measuring performance in many college and university courses is to combine objective measures (test scores, for example) with subjective measures (class participation measures, for example). These scores are weighted and combined to determine a final grade.

Required

a. Write a memo that discusses the advantages and disadvantages of using multiple measures of performance, including some that are objective and some that are subjective.

b. Can you identify a situation in which you would prefer to be evaluated using a purely objective measure (exam scores)? A purely subjective measure (class participation)?

(LO 18-7) **18-64. Employee Involvement**

The interaction between customers and line employees is often more direct in service industries than in manufacturing firms. At the same time, we often observe that employees in many service firms (for example, in hotels and airlines) are given authority to respond to customer concerns without having to seek approval from their supervisors. Desk clerks in hotels or gate agents for airlines, for example, are often allowed to offer upgrades, early check-ins, late check-outs, special seats, and so on, as a way to apologize for or remedy problems. It is also a way to proactively build customer satisfaction.

Required

a. How can policies that allow employees to make these decisions help the organization? How might they harm the organization?

b. You observe these policies less frequently in other service organizations such as banks and other financial institutions. Why might this be the case?

(LO 18-7) **18-65. Employee Involvement**

Many firms in the service industry have empowered their customer-facing employees to handle service complaints on the spot rather than having the customer contact a corporate customer service center. For example, some airline and hotel companies authorize flight attendants and desk clerks to issue frequent-flyer miles or hotel loyalty points for minor service failures.

Required

a. What nonfinancial benefits might these companies expect from this form of employee empowerment?

b. What are some issues that may arise that create other negative impacts on the firm?

c. In addition to any indirect financial benefits that may result from the program through increased customer and employee satisfaction, can you think of any financial benefits of this initiative for these companies?

(LO 18-4, 6) **18-66. Balanced Scorecard—Data Analysis and Visualization**

Tarnow Manufacturing produces metal components and is organized in four geographic divisions (North, South, East, and West). The company adopted a balanced scorecard approach to performance measurement several years ago. Although there were some initial modifications to the measures used, the current scorecard has remained the same for over two years. The scorecard has four perspectives with two measures in each perspective (the words in parentheses are the short titles used for the measures).

Financial	Customer
• Market share (Share)	• Customer satisfaction (Cust. Sat.)
• Gross margin % (Margin)	• Delayed deliveries (Delays)
Learning & Growth	**Internal**
• Course modules completed % (Modules)	• Manufacturing efficiency (Efficiency)
• New product sales % (New Prod.)	• Defect rate (Defects)

Some of the measures, such as market share and gross margin percentage, are common, but some of the others require explanation. Customer satisfaction is measured on a scale of 0–100 percent based on periodic surveys. The percentage modules completed measures the training course modules available to employees and which they are "strongly" encouraged to complete. The company believes this is one of the keys to their strategy to become known for new and innovative products. In addition to the training measure, they also measure the percentage of sales made up of new products (that is, products introduced in the last year). This is measured as a percentage of total revenue.

Scorecard results for the most recent quarter for the four divisions and for the company as a whole follow:

TARNOW MANUFACTURING
Balanced Scorecard Results
Fourth Quarter Year 01
(All Results Are Percentages)

Measure	Corporation	North Div.	South Div.	East Div.	West Div.
Share	11.0%	10.0%	13.0%	4.0%	18.0%
Margin	42.0	39.0	28.0	51.0	22.0
Cust. Sat.	88.0	92.0	82.0	73.0	94.0
Delays	3.2	3.0	4.2	6.5	12.0
Modules	87.0	91.0	85.0	72.0	64.0
New Prod.	10.0	8.0	12.0	16.0	4.0
Efficiency	57.0	54.0	49.0	67.0	60.0
Defects	6.0	8.0	3.0	12.0	4.0

Required

a. Prepare a strategy map that would support the choice of the measures in this scorecard.

b. Evaluate the fourth-quarter performance of the four divisions. Use visualizations as appropriate to illustrate your analysis.

c. The CFO would like an analysis of the performance of the East Division for the past year. You are provided with the following information. (Again, use visualizations as appropriate in your analysis.)

TARNOW MANUFACTURING
East Division
Balanced Scorecard Results
Quarters 1–4, Year 01
(All Results Are Percentages)

Measure	Quarter 1	Quarter 2	Quarter 3	Quarter 4
Share	7.0%	8.0%	6.0%	4.0%
Margin	37.0	39.0	45.0	51.0
Cust. Sat.	84.0	87.0	81.0	73.0
Delays	2.8	3.1	7.0	6.5
Modules	94.0	90.0	81.0	72.0
New Prod.	8.0	11.0	18.0	16.0
Efficiency	54.0	56.0	68.0	67.0
Defects	4.0	5.0	9.6	12.0

18-67. Balanced Scorecard—Data Analysis and Visualization   (LO 18-4, 6)

Norfolk Advisors operates a network of offices that provide business and financial advice to small businesses. Each office is managed by an office director. The office director is given relatively wide latitude in running the office, although any products sold, especially financial products, are determined by the corporate office. The company adopted a balanced scorecard approach to performance measurement several years ago. Until that time, office profit relative to the budget was the primary (and some directors would say only) measure that counted. Although there were some initial modifications to the measures used, the current scorecard has remained the same for the past five quarters. The scorecard has four perspectives with two measures in each perspective (the words in parentheses are the short titles used for the measures).

Financial
- Profit as a percentage of budget (Profit)
- Revenue growth (Rev-Gro)

Learning & Growth
- Employee satisfaction (Empl. Sat.)
- Certificate exams passed (Certs Passed)

Customer
- Customer satisfaction (Cust. Sat.)
- Customer growth (Cust-Gro)

Internal
- Trading errors (Trade Errors)
- Regulatory actions (Reg Actions)

Some of the measures, such as profit as a percentage of budget and revenue growth, are common, but some of the others require explanation. Customer satisfaction is measured on a scale of 0–100 percent based on periodic surveys. Employee satisfaction is based on a survey of office employees and is taken quarterly. The survey is administered by the Corporate Human Resources Department. Certificate exams passed are passed on industry-based training modules, which grant certificates based on examination results. All employees are expected to be continuously updating their skills. Regulatory actions are based on issues identified with the operation of an office identified by federal or state regulators.

The management of Norfolk Advisors believes that rewarding directors based on multiple dimensions rather than profit alone will result in long-term benefits. They have told managers that all four perspectives of the scorecard are equally important and their compensation will be set to ensure that the message is received.

Scorecard results for the most recent quarter for a sample of five offices follow:

NORFOLK ADVISORS
Balanced Scorecard Results
Fourth Quarter Year 01
Selected Offices Only

Measure	Office				
	N-01	N-02	N-03	N-04	N-05
Profit	102%	97%	95%	112%	106%
Rev-Gro.................	1.5%	6.0%	13.0%	15.0%	8.2%
Cust. Sat................	91%	84%	94%	76%	81%
Cust-Gro	1.1%	(2.0)%	0.4%	7.9%	5.3%
Empl. Sat.	90%	83%	88%	68%	74%
Certs Passed	89%	95%	97%	98%	91%
Trade Errors	3.2%	2.6%	1.5%	2.3%	4.1%
Reg-Actions	2	3	1	2	4

Required

a. Prepare the strategy map that would support the choice of the measures in this scorecard.

b. Evaluate the fourth-quarter performance of the five selected offices. Use visualizations as appropriate to illustrate your analysis.

c. The president of Norfolk Advisors would like an analysis of the performance of the office N-04 for the past year. The director of that office was routinely the best performer prior to the introduction of the scorecard. You are provided with the following information. (Again, use visualizations as appropriate in your analysis.)

NORFOLK ADVISORS
Office N-04
Balanced Scorecard Results
Quarters 1–4, Year 01

Measure	Quarter 1	Quarter 2	Quarter 3	Quarter 4
Profit	115%	108%	113%	112%
Rev-Gro	18.0%	16.0%	14.0%	15.0%
Cust. Sat.	78%	68%	72%	76%
Cust-Gro	4.3%	9.1%	5.6%	7.9%
Empl. Sat.	76%	81%	75%	68%
Certs Passed	92%	94%	89%	98%
Trade Errors	2.9%	3.2%	2.1%	2.3%
Reg-Actions	1	0	3	2

INTEGRATIVE CASE

18-68. Balanced Scorecards and Strategy Maps   (LO 18-4)

Following several years of tight budgets, administrators at the University of California, Davis, looked for ways "to do more with less." Janet Hamilton, vice chancellor of administration, researched books and articles, met with consultants, and talked to her counterparts at universities across the United States to find new management methods that could change the university from a bureaucratic organization to one that is customer-oriented. She learned about reengineering, total quality, and a variety of other management techniques. None of the management techniques appealed to her, until she came across articles about the balanced scorecard. She believed that the balanced scorecard was the right tool for the Davis campus, and she set about implementing it.

At first, Hamilton did not call her approach a "balanced scorecard" because she feared that employees would think of this as just another management fad to endure until the administration went on to something new. Instead, she pilot-tested the balanced scorecard ideas in one service department, environmental health and safety (EHS), until it worked. With the success of EHS behind her, she moved to implement the balanced scorecard in other service departments, such as police, fire, and printing services.

Each department developed its own particular performance measures to achieve the following objectives (we have shortened the list to save space):

Organizational Learning and Growth

- Create a workplace that fosters teamwork, pride, and integrity.
- Attract and retain a highly skilled workforce.
- Encourage and reward enterprising behaviors.

Business and Production Process Efficiency

- Develop clear policies, simple procedures, and efficient work processes.
- Anticipate the future, and design programs and services to ensure future success.

Customer Value

- Consistently satisfy customers.

Financial Performance

- Ensure financial integrity for capital and financial assets throughout the campus.
- Deliver services in a cost-effective manner.

Required

a. Was the vice chancellor overly cautious in not calling her approach a "balanced scorecard"?

b. Comment on the wisdom of beginning a balanced scorecard with a pilot project. Would it be possible to extrapolate the experience of a service department, such as environmental health and safety, to an academic unit, such as a college of business?

c. What opportunities and difficulties do you see in applying a balanced scorecard to a university setting?

Source: Adapted from interviews with university administrative staff.

SOLUTIONS TO SELF-STUDY QUESTIONS

1. SCT fits well with the focused competitor strategy. It is neither a cost leader, such as Dunkin' or McDonald's McCafes, nor a product differentiator such as Starbucks or Peet's. SCT will build a brand reputation within a niche of customers interested in specialty coffees and stores with a bit more personalized service. It will not compete on cost with the cost leaders in the industry, but it will manage costs so it can price at or below the product differentiators and still be profitable.

2. The business model for a low-cost (undifferentiated) coffee shop would place more emphasis on the bottom half of the flowchart linking efficient operations to costs. For example, it would include steps on filling an order, transaction time, and so on, while having less emphasis on the top half. In the case of a low-cost coffee shop, the "barista" is primarily an order taker who is not required to have as much knowledge about various coffees.

3.

Perspective	Performance Measure	Linked to Perspective Number?
1. Financial	Employee satisfaction	3
2. Customer	Branch costs	4 (or possibly 1)
3. Learning and growth	Branch profitability	1
4. Internal business processes	Employee learning	3
	Queue length	4
	Customer satisfaction	2

4.

$$\text{Manufacturing cycle efficiency} = \frac{\text{Processing time}}{\underset{\text{time}}{\text{Processing}} + \underset{\text{time}}{\text{Moving}} + \underset{\text{time}}{\text{Storing}} + \underset{\text{time}}{\text{Inspection}}}$$

$$\text{Manufacturing cycle efficiency} = \frac{7.2}{7.2 + 3.0 + 4.8 + 1.0} = 45\%$$

Capital Investment Decisions: An Overview

Appendix

Introduction

Capital investment decisions are the responsibility of managers of investment centers (see Chapter 12). The analysis of capital investment decisions is a major topic in corporate finance courses, so we do not discuss these issues and methods here in any detail. However, because cost accountants and cost analysts are involved in the development of performance measurement techniques for investment center managers, we provide an outline of the issues and methods of capital budgeting in this appendix.

Capital investments often involve large sums of money and considerable risk. Specific investments over a certain dollar amount, often in the $100,000 to $500,000 range (or less for small companies), require approval by the board of directors in many companies. Although the final decision about asset acquisition is management's responsibility, accountants, economists, and other financial experts have developed capital investment models to help managers make those decisions. Accountants and analysts have the particularly important role of estimating the amount and timing of the cash flows used in capital investment decision models.

Analyzing Cash Flows for Present Value Analysis

Capital investment models are based on the future cash flows expected from a particular asset investment opportunity. The amount and timing of the cash flows from a capital investment project determine its economic value. The timing of those flows is important because cash received earlier in time has greater economic value than cash received later. As soon as cash is received, it can be reinvested in an alternative profit-making opportunity. Thus, any particular investment project has an opportunity cost for cash committed to it. Because the horizon of capital investment decisions extends over many years, the **time value of money** is often a significant decision factor for managers making these decisions.

To recognize the time value of money, the future cash flows associated with a project are adjusted to their present value using a predetermined discount rate. Summing the discounted values of the future cash flows and subtracting the initial investment yields a

time value of money
Concept that cash received earlier is worth more than cash received later.

A-1

net present value (NPV)
Economic value of a project at a point in time.

project's **net present value (NPV),** which represents the economic value of the project to the company at a given point in time.

The decision models used for capital investments attempt to optimize the economic value to the firm by maximizing the net present value of future cash flows. If the net present value of a project is positive, the project will earn a rate of return higher than its **discount rate,** which is the rate used to compute net present value.

discount rate
Interest rate used to compute net present values.

Distinguishing between Revenues, Costs, and Cash Flows

A *timing difference* often exists between revenue recognition and cash inflow on the one hand and the incurrence of a cost and the related cash outflow on the other hand. When this occurs, it is important to *distinguish cash flows from revenues and expenses.* Note that capital investment analysis uses *cash flows, not revenues and expenses.* For example, revenue from a sale often is recognized on one date but not collected until later. In such cases, the cash is not available for other investment or consumption purposes until it is collected.

Net Present Value

present value
Amounts of future cash flows discounted to their equivalent worth today.

The **present value** of cash flows is the amount of future cash flows discounted to their equivalent worth today. The *net present value* of a project can be computed by using the equation

$$NPV = \sum_{n=0}^{N} C_n \times (1 + d)^{-n}$$

where
C_n = Cash to be received or disbursed at the end of time period n
d = Appropriate discount rate for the future cash flows
n = Time period when the cash flow occurs
N = Life of the investment, in years

The term $(1 + d)^{-n}$ is called a *present value factor.* A financial calculator or computer spreadsheet is the most efficient way to compute present value factors and net present values. Tables of present value factors are at the end of this appendix in Exhibit A.8.

An *annuity* is a constant (equal) payment over a period of time. The present value of an annuity can be computed by calculating the present value of the individual payments and summing them over the annuity period. Alternatively, they can be computed by multiplying the annuity payment by the sum of the present value factors. The present value factors for an annuity are shown in Exhibit A.9 at the end of this Appendix.

If you use the table in Exhibit A.8, look up the factor by referring to the appropriate year and discount rate. For a discount rate of 8 percent and a cash flow of $1 at the end of two years, the present value factor in Exhibit A.8 is .857. For a discount rate of 8 percent and a cash flow of $1 at the end of *each* year for two years (an annuity), the present value factor in Exhibit A.9 is 1.783 (= 0.926 + 0.857, from Exhibit A.8).

Applying Present Value Analysis

Consider two projects. Each requires an immediate cash outlay of $10,000. Project 1 will return $12,000 at the end of two years; Project 2 will return $6,000 each year at the end of years 1 and 2. If the appropriate discount rate is 12 percent, the net present value of each project can be computed as follows:

Project 1		
Cash inflow	$12,000 \times (1 + .12)^{-2}$	
	$= \$12,000 \times .797$	$ \$ 9,564
Cash outflow.		(10,000)
Net present value.		$ \$ (436)
Project 2		
Cash inflow	$\$6,000 \times (1 + .12)^{-1} + \$6,000 \times (1 + .12)^{-2}$	
	$= \$6,000 \times .893 + \$6,000 \times .797$	$10,140
Cash outflow.		(10,000)
Net present value.		$ \$ 140

The starting time for capital investment projects is assumed to be time 0. Therefore, any cash outlays required at the start of the project are not discounted. We enter them at their full amount.

At a discount rate of 12 percent, Project 2 is acceptable, but Project 1 is not. Project 2 will earn more than the required 12 percent return, while Project 1 will earn less. The reason is that, although both projects returned a total of $12,000, Project 2 returned half of it one year earlier.

You should check for yourself to see that, at a 15 percent discount rate, the present value of both projects is negative. Therefore, if the required rate were 15 percent, neither project would meet the investment criterion. Alternatively, at 8 percent, both projects have positive net present values and would be acceptable.

Capital Investment Analysis: An Example

We present the following numerical example to illustrate the basics of capital investment analysis. The owners of Woodson Stores are considering an expansion of one of the company's distribution centers, which will require some additional equipment. Basic data for the investment are shown in Exhibit A.1.

An important factor in capital investment analysis is the impact of taxes on the cash flows the investment will require and the benefits it earns. The relevant tax laws change frequently as a response to economic conditions, policy choices, lobbying efforts, and so on. The purpose in this appendix is not to identify the correct tax treatment, but to illustrate how selected tax policies can be incorporated into the analysis. Therefore, while the choices Woodson makes might be appropriate and available in some time periods, they might not be in others. Always consult with a tax expert before assuming that an investment being considered will offer the same tax choices that Woodson selects here.

For this example, we assume that Woodson chooses to use straight-line depreciation for tax purposes and ignore the possibility that Woodson might have chosen a more accelerated method. We also assume that Woodson is not eligible to expense any portion of this investment for tax purposes as might be allowable at certain times and in certain circumstances.

Equipment cost.	$6,000,000
Economic and tax life	5 years
Disposal value	$600,000
Additional annual cash revenue	$2,100,000
Additional annual cash operating expenses	$350,000
Increase in working capital required.	$800,000
Tax rate	20%
Discount rate.	12%

Exhibit A.1
Selected Expansion Data—Woodson Stores

Problem A-19 examines the effect of changing this assumption and what happens to the analysis if Woodson is allowed to expense the investment for tax purposes in its first year.

Categories of Project Cash Flows

This section outlines a method for estimating cash flows for investment projects, which we illustrate using the expansion project of Woodson Stores. We start by setting four major categories of cash flows for a project:

1. Investment cash flows.
2. Periodic operating cash flows.
3. Cash flows from the depreciation tax shield.
4. Disinvestment cash flows.

Each category of cash flows requires a separate treatment.

Investment Cash Flows

There are three types of investment cash flows:

1. Asset acquisition, which includes
    a. New equipment costs, including installation (outflow).
    b. Proceeds of existing assets sold, net of taxes (inflow).
    c. Tax effects arising from a loss or gain (inflow or outflow).
2. Working capital commitments.
3. Investment tax credit, if any.

asset acquisition
Costs involved in purchasing and installing an asset that can involve the disposal of old assets, resulting in a gain or a loss.

Asset Acquisition   **Asset acquisition** involves both the cost of purchasing and installing new assets and the cash inflows that can result from the proceeds, net of taxes, of selling replaced equipment. Additionally, there could be a loss or gain from the difference between the sale proceeds and the tax basis of the equipment being replaced.

The primary outflow for most capital investments is the acquisition cost of the asset. Acquisition costs can be incurred in time 0 and in later years. In some cases, they are incurred over periods of 10 to 20 years. All acquisition costs are listed as cash outflows in the years in which they occur. Installation costs are also considered a cash outflow.

If the depreciation tax basis of the replaced equipment does not equal the proceeds received from the sale of the replaced equipment, a gain or loss will occur and will affect the tax payment. The tax effect will be considered a cash inflow (for a loss) or a cash outflow (for a gain).

The calculation of this category for Woodson is straightforward because it is not disposing of another asset. The initial outflow is the $6,000,000 purchase price of the equipment.

working capital
Cash, accounts receivable, and other short-term assets required to maintain an activity.

Working Capital Commitments   In addition to the cash required for the purchase of long-term assets, many projects require additional funds for **working capital** needs; for example, a retail establishment needs to have cash available in a bank account because future cash payments often precede cash receipts. The working capital committed to the project normally remains constant over the life of the project, although it is sometimes increased because of inflation. Woodson plans to commit an additional $800,000 in working capital at time 0 to maintain a cash balance in a bank account to cover future cash transactions.

investment tax credit (ITC)
Reduction in federal income taxes arising from the purchase of certain assets.

Investment Tax Credit   An **investment tax credit (ITC)** allows a credit against the federal income tax liability based on the cost of an acquired asset. This credit effectively reduces the cost of making investments by giving companies a credit against their corporate income taxes equal to, for example, 10 percent of the purchase price. The investment tax credit has been in effect at various times since the early 1960s and often is targeted at

only certain types of investments (solar energy–related investments, for example). Currently, there is no investment tax credit for which Woodson qualifies.

Periodic Operating Cash Flows

The primary reason for acquiring long-term assets is usually to generate positive *periodic operating cash flows*. These positive flows can result from *revenue-generating* activities, such as new products, and from *cost-saving* programs. In either case, actual cash inflows and outflows from operating the asset are usually estimable in a straightforward manner. The most important task is to identify and measure the cash flows that will differ because of the investment. *If the revenues and costs are differential cash items, they are relevant for the capital investment decision.*

Periodic operating flows include the following:

- Period cash inflows (+) and outflows (−) before taxes.
- Income tax effects of inflows (−) and outflows (+).

Costs that do not involve cash (depreciation, depletion, and amortization) are excluded. If cash costs in other departments change as a result of the project, the costs of the other department(s) should be included in the differential cash flow schedule. Woodson forecasts annual increases in cash revenues of $2,100,000 and increased cash operating expenses of $350,000. After tax, these will result in net cash flows of $1,400,000 [= ($2,100,000 − $350,000) × (1 − 20%)].

Financing costs such as interest costs on loans, principal repayments, and so on are excluded under the assumption that the financing decision is separate from the asset-acquisition decision. Under this assumption, the decision to acquire the asset is made first. If the asset-acquisition decision is favorable, a decision will be made to select the best financing. For analysis purposes, asset acquisitions typically are recorded in the full amount when the cash purchase payments are made, regardless of how that cash was acquired. The cost of financing is included in the discount rate.

Tax Effects of Periodic Cash Flows   The income tax effects of the periodic cash flows from the project are also computed and considered in the present value analysis. Note that for purposes of calculating the net present value, only the tax effects related to differential project cash flows are considered.

The steps to compute the net operating cash flows for the project are repeated for each year of the project's life. In some cases, the computations can be simplified by using an annuity factor if the project is expected to yield identical cash flows for more than one year.

Cash Flows from the Depreciation Tax Shield

To measure the income of an organization or one of its subunits, depreciation is used to allocate the cost of long-term assets over their useful lives. These depreciation charges are not cash costs and thus do not directly affect the net present values of capital investments. However, tax regulations permit depreciation write-offs that reduce the required tax payment. The reduction in the tax payment is referred to as a **tax shield.** *The depreciation deduction computed for this tax shield is not necessarily the same amount as the depreciation computed for financial reporting purposes.* The predominant depreciation method for financial reporting has been the *straight-line method.* With this method, the cost of the asset, less any salvage value, is allocated equally to each year of the expected life of the asset. Income tax regulations allow depreciation write-offs to be made faster.

tax shield
Reduction in tax payment because of depreciation deducted for tax purposes.

The tax allowance for depreciation is one of the primary incentives used by tax policymakers to promote investment in long-term assets. The faster an asset's cost can be written off for tax purposes, the sooner the tax reductions are realized and, hence, the higher the net present value of the tax shield. In recent years, tax depreciation has been accelerated to allow write-offs over very short time periods regardless of an asset's expected life. To maximize present value, it is usually best to claim depreciation as rapidly as possible.

The depreciation tax shield affects the net present value analysis in two ways:

1. Depreciation tax shield on acquired assets.
2. Forgone depreciation tax shield on disposed assets.

Consider the tax depreciation schedule of the new equipment that Woodson Stores is evaluating. It has a depreciation tax basis of $5,400,000 over five years. This is computed as the outlay cost of the equipment ($6,000,000) less the estimated disposal or salvage value of $600,000. The equipment is assumed to have a five-year life for tax purposes, so using straight-line depreciation, annual depreciation on the equipment is $1,080,000 (= $5,400,000 ÷ 5 years). (All amounts given in this text are for illustrative purposes only. They do not necessarily reflect the amount of depreciation allowed by the tax regulations, which varies by type of asset and often changes as Congress passes new "tax reforms.") As a result of depreciation expense, Woodson's tax payment will be lower by $216,000 (= $1,080,000 × 20% tax rate) every year. It is important to note that the depreciation expense itself is not included in the analysis. It is not a cash expense. (More important, we have already included the cost of the equipment in the initial outlay. To include the depreciation expense would be to double-count the equipment cost.)

Disinvestment Cash Flows

disinvestment flows
Cash flows that take place at the termination of a capital project.

Cash flows at the end of the life of the project are called **disinvestment flows.** The end of a project's life usually results in some or all of the following cash flows:

- Cash freed from working capital commitments (now treated as a cash inflow).
- Salvage of the long-term assets (usually a cash inflow unless there are disposal costs).
- Tax consequences for differences between salvage proceeds and the remaining depreciation tax basis of the asset.
- Other cash flows, such as employee severance payments and restoration costs.

Return of Working Capital
When a project ends, some inventory, cash, and other working capital items that were used to support operations are usually left over. These working capital items are then freed for use elsewhere or are liquidated for cash. Therefore, at the end of a project's life, the return of these working capital items is shown as a cash inflow. In the example of Woodson Stores, it will have $800,000 in working capital available for other uses, which is the money it put in the bank to facilitate cash transactions.

It is important not to double-count these items. Suppose that cash collected from a customer was already recorded as a cash inflow to the company, but it was left in the project's bank account until the end of the project's life. It should not be counted again as a cash inflow at the project's end.

The return of working capital is recorded as an inflow when it is freed for use in other organizational activities. If that does not occur until the end of the project's life, the cash inflow is included as part of disinvestment flows.

Salvage of Long-Term Assets
Ending a project often includes the disposal of its assets. These are often sold in secondhand markets or to salvage companies. In some cases, more money can be spent disassembling the assets and disposing of them than their sale gains. Any net outflows from the disposal of a project's assets become tax deductions in the year of disposal. The *net salvage value* (sometimes negative) of an asset is listed as a cash inflow or outflow at the time it is expected to be realized (or incurred), regardless of its book value or **tax basis**. The difference between the book value (tax basis) and the net salvage value can result in a taxable gain or loss.

tax basis
Remaining tax-depreciable "book value" of an asset for tax purposes.

For an asset replacement decision, the forgone salvage value (and related tax effects) from the old asset must also be considered. For example, assume that "asset new" replaced "asset old" for the next five years. Asset old could be sold for $2,000 at the end of five years; asset new could be sold for $10,000 at the end of five years. If asset new replaces asset old, the $8,000 incremental salvage value should be the disinvestment cash flow for the analysis. Any additional taxes paid (or tax payments reduced) because we are salvaging asset new instead of asset old should be included in the analysis.

Tax Consequences of Disposal

Any difference between the tax basis of a project's assets (generally, the undepreciated balance) and the amount realized from project disposal results in a tax gain or loss. Therefore, a company's tax liability is affected in the year of disposal. Tax laws on asset dispositions are complex, so tax advice should be sought well in advance of the proposed disposal date. Here, we assume that any gains or losses on disposal are treated as ordinary taxable income or losses.

Suppose that an asset is carried in the financial accounting records at a net book value of $80,000 and is salvaged for $30,000 cash. The tax basis of the asset is $10,000, and the tax rate is 20 percent. What are the cash flows from disposal of this asset?

First, the company receives the $30,000 as a cash inflow. Second, it reports a $20,000 taxable gain, which is the difference between the $30,000 cash inflow and the $10,000 tax basis. This $20,000 gain is taxed at 20 percent, resulting in a $4,000 cash outflow. The net-of-tax cash inflow on disposal is $26,000, the net of the $30,000 inflow and the $4,000 cash outflow, as follows:

Cash inflow..	$30,000
Tax payment	
($30,000 cash inflow − $10,000 tax basis) × 20% tax rate	(4,000)
Net-of-tax cash inflow..	$26,000

Woodson Stores plans to dispose of the equipment for $600,000, the disposal value in Exhibit A.1. Because this is the amount included when computing depreciation, there is no loss or gain on the disposition and, therefore, no tax effect.

Other Disinvestment Flows

The end of project operations can result in a number of costs not directly related to the sale of assets. It could be necessary to make severance payments to employees. Sometimes payments are required to restore the project area to its original condition. Some projects incur regulatory costs when they are closed. A cost analyst must inquire about the consequences of disposal to determine the costs that should be included in the disinvestment flows for a project.

Preparing the Net Present Value Analysis

As soon as the cash flow data have been gathered, they are assembled into a schedule that shows the cash flows for each year of the project's life. These flows can be classified into the four categories just discussed:

1. Investment cash flows.
2. Periodic operating cash flows.
3. Cash flows from the depreciation tax shield.
4. Disinvestment cash flows.

Exhibit A.2   Cash Flow Schedule with Present Value Computations—Woodson Stores

		0	1	2	3	4	5
8				Year			
9		0	1	2	3	4	5
10	Annual cash flows						
11	Operating cash flows		$ 1,400,000	$ 1,400,000	$ 1,400,000	$ 1,400,000	$ 1,400,000
12	Depreciation tax shield		216,000	216,000	216,000	216,000	216,000
13							
14	Disinvestment flows						
15	Return of working capital						800,000
16	Proceeds on disposal		-	-	-	-	600,000
17	Total cash flows	$ (6,800,000)	$ 1,616,000	$ 1,616,000	$ 1,616,000	$ 1,616,000	$ 3,016,000
18	Present value factor	1.000	0.893	0.797	0.712	0.636	0.567
19							
20	Discount rate	12%					
21							
22	Present value of inflows	$6,619,480	$1,443,088	$1,287,952	$1,150,592	$1,027,776	$1,710,072
23	Less investment	$ (6,800,000)					
24	Net present value	$ (180,520)					
25							

A summary schedule that shows the total of the annual cash flows and the net present value of the project is prepared. This summary can be supported by as much detail as management deems necessary for making the investment decision.

Exhibit A.2 contains the analysis for the investment decision for Woodson Stores. The project is expected to earn less than the 12 percent used to discount the cash flows because the net present value of the project is less than zero. (If the net present value of the project had been greater than zero, the project would have been expected to earn more than the 12 percent used to discount the cash flows.)

The negative net present value of the project, ($180,520), is computed as the sum of the present values of each year's cash flows.

Using Microsoft Excel to Prepare the Net Present Value Analysis

The computations shown in Exhibit A.2 illustrate how to compute net present values using the present value factors in Exhibit A.8. However, these calculations are built-in functions in Excel, so there is no reason to compute (or enter) individual present value factors. We illustrate in the series of exhibits that follow how to complete this calculation using Excel directly.

Before we illustrate the process, we modify the spreadsheet slightly to remove the present value factors and set up the Excel calculation. The basic spreadsheet is shown in Exhibit A.3. In addition to removing the rows with the present value factors, we have introduced some new cells: one with the discount rate; one for the computation of the present value of the cash inflows; one with the initial investment amount; and one for the computation of the net present value.

The first step is to select the cell (B19) where the present value of the cash inflows for periods one through five will be computed. (Because the Excel function we use assumes that all cash flows occur at the end of the period, we have to compute the present value of the cash inflows and then subtract the initial cash investment.)

After selecting cell B19, select the net present value function. This is a built-in function in Excel that you can access as follows. On the main menu, select the Formulas tab. Depending on the version of Excel you are using, this will reveal a set of "books" containing different types of formulas in the "library." Click on the "Financial" book. This will show a drop-down list of formulas. Scroll down and select "NPV," as shown in Exhibit A.4.

Exhibit A.3   Spreadsheet for Calculation of Net Present Value Using Microsoft Excel

	A	B	C	D	E	F	G	H
1					Year			
2		0	1	2	3	4	5	
3	Investment flows							
4	New equipment	$ (6,000,000)						
5	Working capital	$ (800,000)						
6								
7	Annual cash flows							
8	Operating cash flows		$1,400,000	$1,400,000	$1,400,000	$1,400,000	$1,400,000	
9	Depreciation tax shield		216,000	216,000	216,000	216,000	216,000	
10								
11	Disinvestment flows							
12	Return of working capital						800,000	
13	Proceeds on disposal		-	-	-	-	600,000	
14	Total cash flows	$ (6,800,000)	$1,616,000	$1,616,000	$1,616,000	$1,616,000	$3,016,000	
15								
16	Discount rate	12%						
17								
18								
19	Present value of inflows							
20	Less investment	$ (6,800,000)						
21	Net present value							

Exhibit A.4

Insert-Function Dialog Box

A new dialog box will open, as shown in Exhibit A.5. This dialog box will ask for two types of inputs. First, enter (or point to the cell with) the discount rate. Click on the box labeled "Rate" and either enter the rate (12%) or point to the cell with the rate (B16). Notice how choosing cell B16 results in the rate (12%) being displayed to the right of the box. Next, point to the input box labeled "Value1" and enter or point to the range with the cash inflows (C14:G14). (To enter the range, select C14 and then, holding down the left mouse button, drag the cursor across the range, stopping at cell G14.)

Exhibit A.5

Enter the Data for the
Calculation

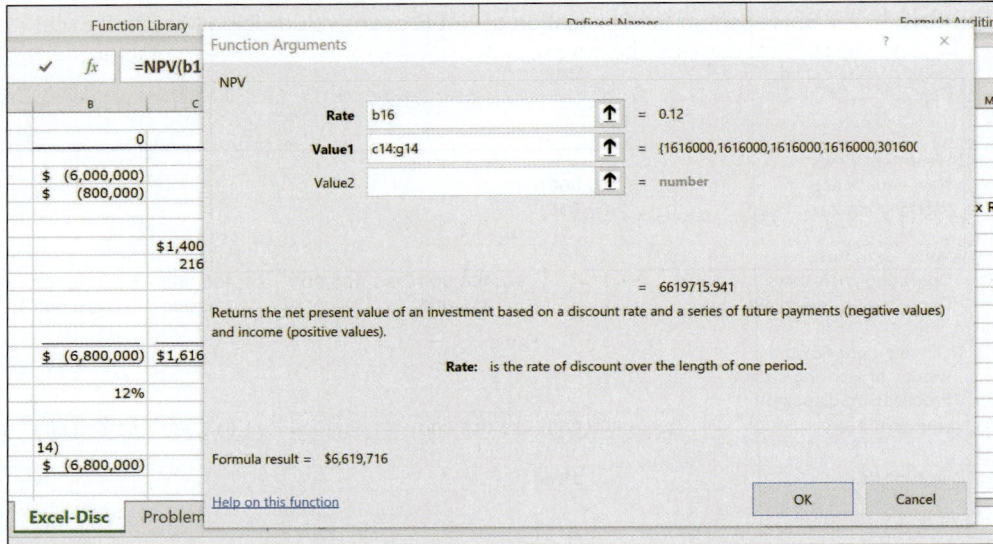

Once the two boxes are complete, select "OK." The present value of the cash flows will appear in the cell. This is shown in Exhibit A.6. Note two things:

1. The format of the cell might not match the formatting of the other cells (for example, the present value might be displayed with two decimal places).
2. There might be an error indicator that appears. In this case, it is likely that an adjacent cell was not used (and should not have been used). It is possible to turn this off, but as it is the default operation, you may see it.

Finally, we subtract the initial investment (add the negative initial cash flow) to obtain the net present value. This is shown in Exhibit A.7. (Note that we have formatted the cell to be consistent with the rest of the spreadsheet.) The resulting net present value

Exhibit A.6   Results of the Present Value Calculation

B19   fx   =NPV(B16,C14:G14)

	A	B	C	D	E	F	G	H
1					Year			
2		0	1	2	3	4	5	
3	Investment flows							
4	New equipment	$ (6,000,000)						
5	Working capital	$ (800,000)						
6								
7	Annual cash flows							
8	Operating cash flows		$1,400,000	$1,400,000	$1,400,000	$1,400,000	$1,400,000	
9	Depreciation tax shield		216,000	216,000	216,000	216,000	216,000	
10								
11	Disinvestment flows							
12	Return of working capital						800,000	
13	Proceeds on disposal		-	-	-	-	600,000	
14	Total cash flows	$ (6,800,000)	$1,616,000	$1,616,000	$1,616,000	$1,616,000	$3,016,000	
15								
16	Discount rate	12%						
17								
18								
19	Present value of inflows	$6,619,716						
20	Less investment	$ (6,800,000)						
21	Net present value							

of a negative $180,520 differs from what we calculated using the net present value factors (a negative $180,284) because the net present value factors used in Exhibit A.2 have been rounded to three decimal places.

Exhibit A.7   The Net Present Value of the Investment

L24		⋮	✕	✓	*fx*			

	A	B	C	D	E	F	G
1				Year			
2		0	1	2	3	4	5
3	Investment flows						
4	New equipment	$ (6,000,000)					
5	Working capital	$ (800,000)					
6							
7	Annual cash flows						
8	Operating cash flows		$1,400,000	$1,400,000	$1,400,000	$1,400,000	$1,400,000
9	Depreciation tax shield		216,000	216,000	216,000	216,000	216,000
10							
11	Disinvestment flows						
12	Return of working capital						800,000
13	Proceeds on disposal		-	-	-	-	600,000
14	Total cash flows	$ (6,800,000)	$1,616,000	$1,616,000	$1,616,000	$1,616,000	$3,016,000
15							
16	Discount rate	12%					
17							
18							
19	Present value of inflows	$6,619,716					
20	Less investment	$ (6,800,000)					
21	Net present value	$ (180,284)					

Self-Study Question

1. Nu-Concepts, Inc., a southeastern advertising agency, is considering the purchase of new computer equipment and software to enhance its graphics capabilities. Management has been considering several alternative systems, and a local vendor has submitted a quote to the company of $15,000 for the equipment plus $30,000 for software. Assume that the equipment can be depreciated for tax purposes over three years as follows: year 1, $5,000; year 2, $5,000; year 3, $5,000. The software can be written off immediately for tax purposes. The company expects to use the new machine for four years and to use straight-line depreciation for financial reporting purposes. The market for used computer systems is such that Nu-Concepts could sell the equipment for $2,000 at the end of four years. The software would have no salvage value at that time.

    Nu-Concepts management believes that the introduction of the computer system will enable the company to dispose of its existing equipment, which is fully depreciated for tax purposes. It can be sold for an estimated $200 but would have no salvage value in four years. If Nu-Concepts does not buy the new equipment, it would continue to use the old graphics system for four more years.

    Management believes that it will realize improvements in operations and benefits from the computer system worth $16,000 per year before taxes.

    Nu-Concepts uses a 10 percent discount rate for this investment and has a marginal income tax rate of 20 percent after considering both state and federal taxes.

    a.   Prepare a schedule showing the relevant cash flows for the project.

    b.   Indicate whether the project has a positive or negative net present value.

    The solution to this question is at the end of the Appendix.

Exhibit A.8   Present Value of $1

Year	½%	1%	2%	4%	5%	6%	8%	10%	12%	14%
1	0.995	0.990	0.980	0.962	0.952	0.943	0.926	0.909	0.893	0.877
2	0.990	0.980	0.961	0.925	0.907	0.890	0.857	0.826	0.797	0.769
3	0.985	0.971	0.942	0.889	0.864	0.840	0.794	0.751	0.712	0.675
4	0.980	0.961	0.924	0.855	0.823	0.792	0.735	0.683	0.636	0.592
5	0.975	0.951	0.906	0.822	0.784	0.747	0.681	0.621	0.567	0.519
6	0.971	0.942	0.888	0.790	0.746	0.705	0.630	0.564	0.507	0.456
7	0.966	0.933	0.871	0.760	0.711	0.665	0.583	0.513	0.452	0.400
8	0.961	0.923	0.853	0.731	0.677	0.627	0.540	0.467	0.404	0.351
9	0.956	0.914	0.837	0.703	0.645	0.592	0.500	0.424	0.361	0.308
10	0.951	0.905	0.820	0.676	0.614	0.558	0.463	0.386	0.322	0.270
11	0.947	0.896	0.804	0.650	0.585	0.527	0.429	0.350	0.287	0.237
12	0.942	0.887	0.788	0.625	0.557	0.497	0.397	0.319	0.257	0.208
13	0.937	0.879	0.773	0.601	0.530	0.469	0.368	0.290	0.229	0.182
14	0.933	0.870	0.758	0.577	0.505	0.442	0.340	0.263	0.205	0.160
15	0.928	0.861	0.743	0.555	0.481	0.417	0.315	0.239	0.183	0.140

Year	15%	16%	18%	20%	22%	24%	25%	30%	35%	40%
1	0.870	0.862	0.847	0.833	0.820	0.806	0.800	0.769	0.741	0.714
2	0.756	0.743	0.718	0.694	0.672	0.650	0.640	0.592	0.549	0.510
3	0.658	0.641	0.609	0.579	0.551	0.524	0.512	0.455	0.406	0.364
4	0.572	0.552	0.516	0.482	0.451	0.423	0.410	0.350	0.301	0.260
5	0.497	0.476	0.437	0.402	0.370	0.341	0.328	0.269	0.223	0.186
6	0.432	0.410	0.370	0.335	0.303	0.275	0.262	0.207	0.165	0.133
7	0.376	0.354	0.314	0.279	0.249	0.222	0.210	0.159	0.122	0.095
8	0.327	0.305	0.266	0.233	0.204	0.179	0.168	0.123	0.091	0.068
9	0.284	0.263	0.225	0.194	0.167	0.144	0.134	0.094	0.067	0.048
10	0.247	0.227	0.191	0.162	0.137	0.116	0.107	0.073	0.050	0.035
11	0.215	0.195	0.162	0.135	0.112	0.094	0.086	0.056	0.037	0.025
12	0.187	0.168	0.137	0.112	0.092	0.076	0.069	0.043	0.027	0.018
13	0.163	0.145	0.116	0.093	0.075	0.061	0.055	0.033	0.020	0.013
14	0.141	0.125	0.099	0.078	0.062	0.049	0.044	0.025	0.015	0.009
15	0.123	0.108	0.084	0.065	0.051	0.040	0.035	0.020	0.011	0.006

Exhibit A.9   Present Value of an Annuity of $1

Year	½%	1%	2%	4%	5%	6%	8%	10%	12%	14%
1	0.995	0.990	0.980	0.962	0.952	0.943	0.926	0.909	0.893	0.877
2	1.985	1.970	1.942	1.886	1.859	1.833	1.783	1.736	1.690	1.647
3	2.970	2.941	2.884	2.775	2.723	2.673	2.577	2.487	2.402	2.322
4	3.950	3.902	3.808	3.630	3.546	3.465	3.312	3.170	3.037	2.914
5	4.926	4.853	4.713	4.452	4.329	4.212	3.993	3.791	3.605	3.433
6	5.896	5.795	5.601	5.242	5.076	4.917	4.623	4.355	4.111	3.889
7	6.862	6.728	6.472	6.002	5.786	5.582	5.206	4.868	4.564	4.288
8	7.823	7.652	7.325	6.733	6.463	6.210	5.747	5.335	4.968	4.639
9	8.779	8.566	8.162	7.435	7.108	6.802	6.247	5.759	5.328	4.946
10	9.730	9.471	8.983	8.111	7.722	7.360	6.710	6.145	5.650	5.216
11	10.677	10.368	9.787	8.760	8.306	7.887	7.139	6.495	5.938	5.453
12	11.619	11.255	10.575	9.385	8.863	8.384	7.536	6.814	6.194	5.660
13	12.556	12.134	11.348	9.986	9.394	8.853	7.904	7.103	6.424	5.842
14	13.489	13.004	12.106	10.563	9.899	9.295	8.244	7.367	6.628	6.002
15	14.417	13.865	12.849	11.118	10.380	9.712	8.559	7.606	6.811	6.142

Year	15%	16%	18%	20%	22%	24%	25%	30%	35%	40%
1	0.870	0.862	0.847	0.833	0.820	0.806	0.800	0.769	0.741	0.714
2	1.626	1.605	1.566	1.528	1.492	1.457	1.440	1.361	1.289	1.224
3	2.283	2.246	2.174	2.106	2.042	1.981	1.952	1.816	1.696	1.589
4	2.855	2.798	2.690	2.589	2.494	2.404	2.362	2.166	1.997	1.849
5	3.352	3.274	3.127	2.991	2.864	2.745	2.689	2.436	2.220	2.035
6	3.784	3.685	3.498	3.326	3.167	3.020	2.951	2.643	2.385	2.168
7	4.160	4.039	3.812	3.605	3.416	3.242	3.161	2.802	2.508	2.263
8	4.487	4.344	4.078	3.837	3.619	3.421	3.329	2.925	2.598	2.331
9	4.772	4.607	4.303	4.031	3.786	3.566	3.463	3.019	2.665	2.379
10	5.019	4.833	4.494	4.192	3.923	3.682	3.571	3.092	2.715	2.414
11	5.234	5.029	4.656	4.327	4.035	3.776	3.656	3.147	2.752	2.438
12	5.421	5.197	4.793	4.439	4.127	3.851	3.725	3.190	2.779	2.456
13	5.583	5.342	4.910	4.533	4.203	3.912	3.780	3.223	2.799	2.469
14	5.724	5.468	5.008	4.611	4.265	3.962	3.824	3.249	2.814	2.478
15	5.847	5.575	5.092	4.675	4.315	4.001	3.859	3.268	2.825	2.484

KEY TERMS

asset acquisition, *A-4*
discount rate, *A-2*
disinvestment flows, *A-6*
investment tax credit (ITC), *A-4*
net present value (NPV), *A-2*

present value, *A-2*
tax basis, *A-6*
tax shield, *A-5*
time value of money, *A-1*
working capital, *A-4*

REVIEW QUESTIONS

A-1. What are the two most important factors an accountant must estimate in the capital invest-ment decision?
A-2. What does the *time value of money* mean?
A-3. What is the difference between revenues and cash inflows?
A-4. What is the difference between expenses and cash outflows?
A-5. What is the difference between depreciation and the tax shield on depreciation?
A-6. The present value factor for an annuity to be paid over ten years with a discount rate of *r* is the product of the present value factors for a single payment received at the end of each year, for years 1 through 10. True or false?
A-7. What are the four types of cash flows related to a capital investment project, and why do we consider them separately?

CRITICAL ANALYSIS AND DISCUSSION QUESTIONS

A-8. Given two projects with equal cash flows but different timing, how can we determine which (if either) project should be selected for investment?
A-9. If the net present value of a project is positive, we should invest in it. If it is negative, we should not. Do you agree?
A-10. Is depreciation included in the computation of net present value? Explain.
A-11. "The total tax deduction for depreciation is the same over the life of the project regardless of depreciation method. Why then would one be concerned about the depreciation method for capital investment analysis?" Comment.
A-12. "Working capital is just the temporary use of money during the life of the project. What is ini-tially contributed is returned at the end, so it can be ignored in evaluating a project." Comment.
A-13. In Chapter 14, we discussed performance measurement in investment centers, where the managers have decision authority over asset usage (for example, adding new plants). The financial performance measures discussed in Chapter 14 (ROI, residual income, and EVA) were based on accounting income, which measures plant cost by depreciation. Why is it possible that a project to build a new plant can have a negative residual income in the first year, but have a positive net present value?
A-14. Consider the situation in question A-13. If a manager is instructed to choose projects based on net present value and that they will be evaluated on residual income, what managerial control issue might arise?

EXERCISES  All applicable Exercises are included in Connect.

A-15. Present Value of Cash Flows
Ironwood Charities is considering an investment in one of its buildings that is expected to return the following cash flows:

Year	Net Cash Flow
1	$12,000
2	24,000
3	40,000
4	55,000
5	45,000

This schedule includes all cash inflows from the project, which will also require an immediate $140,000 cash outlay. The organization is tax-exempt; therefore, taxes need not be considered.

Required

a.   What is the net present value of the project if the appropriate discount rate is 8 percent?

b.   What is the net present value of the project if the appropriate discount rate is 4 percent?

A-16. Present Value of Cash Flows

Grove Media plans to acquire production equipment for $800,000 that will be depreciated for tax purposes as follows: year 1, $320,000; year 2, $180,000; and in each of years 3 through 5, $100,000 per year. A 10 percent discount rate is appropriate for this asset, and the company's tax rate is 20 percent.

Required

a.   Compute the present value of the tax shield resulting from depreciation.

b.   Compute the present value of the tax shield from depreciation assuming straight-line depreciation ($160,000 per year).

A-17. Present Value Analysis in Nonprofit Organizations

The Minock Group, a nonprofit organization that does not pay taxes, is considering buying laboratory equipment with an estimated life of seven years so it will not have to use outsiders' laboratories for certain types of work. The following are all of the cash flows affected by the decision:

Investment (outflow at time 0)	$5,000,000
Periodic operating cash flows:	
Annual cash savings because outside laboratories are not used	950,000
Additional cash outflow for people and supplies to operate the	
equipment.	150,000
Salvage value after seven years, which is the estimated life of this	
project	280,000
Discount rate.	6%

Required

Calculate the net present value of this decision. (Refer to Exhibit A.2 in formatting your answer.) Should The Minock Group buy the equipment?

A-18. Investment Decision with Unknown Economic Life

Mitchell Company is considering an investment in a new machine. Managers at the company are uncertain about the economic life of the machine because of the speed of innovation in the technology. The machine requires an investment of $1.56 million. After-tax cash flows are estimated to be $650,000 each year the machine is operating (and not obsolete). The company uses a 14 percent discount rate in evaluating capital investments.

Required

What is the minimum economic life of the machine (in whole years) that would be required for it to have a positive net present value? Ignore tax effects.

All applicable Problems are included in Connect.   **Mc Graw Hill** connect   **PROBLEMS**

A-19. Compute Net Present Value; Expense Investment for Taxes

Consider the example of Woodson Stores in the text. Suppose that Woodson qualifies for and decides to take advantage of a tax law that provides "bonus" depreciation on the investment. Assume that this allows Woodson to deduct the cost of the investment, net of salvage value, in the first year of the investment. As a result, of course, no more depreciation is taken in years 2 through 5. Assume all other facts as in the text.

Required

a.   What is the net present value of the investment assuming full expensing in the first year?

b.   Will Woodson choose to invest in this case?

A-20. Compute Net Present Value; Compare to Accounting Income

St. James Cleaners is considering investing in a new machine. The machine costs $20,000 and has an economic life of five years. The machine will generate cash flows of $5,000 (cash revenues less cash expenses) each year. All cash flows, except for the initial investment, are realized at the end of the year. The investment in the machine will be made at the beginning of the project. St. James Cleaners is not subject to any taxes and, for financial accounting purposes, will depreciate the machine using straight-line depreciation over five years. The company uses a 16 percent cost of capital when evaluating investments.

Required

a.   Suppose St. James Cleaners acquires the machine. By how much will annual accounting income increase or decrease in each of the five years? Is the sum over the five years positive?

b.   Does the machine acquisition have a positive net present value?

c.   Comment on the results in requirements (a) and (b).

A-21. Sensitivity Analysis in Capital Investment Decisions

Green & Company is considering investing in a robotics manufacturing line. Installation of the line will cost an estimated $15 million. This amount must be paid immediately even though construction will take three years to complete (years 0, 1, and 2). Year 3 will be spent testing the production line and, hence, it will not yield any positive cash flows. If the operation is very successful, the company can expect after-tax cash savings of $10 million per year in each of years 4 through 7. After reviewing the use of these systems with the management of other companies, Green's controller has concluded that the operation will most probably result in annual savings of $7.2 million per year for each of years 4 through 7. However, it is entirely possible that the savings could be as low as $3.0 million per year for each of years 4 through 7. The company uses a 12 percent discount rate.

Required

Compute the NPV under the three scenarios.

A-22. Compute Net Present Value

Lodi Fabrication is evaluating a proposal to purchase a new turbine to replace a less efficient machine presently in use. The cost of the new equipment at time 0, including delivery and installation, is $450,000. If it is purchased, Lodi will incur costs of $25,000 to remove the present equipment and revamp its facilities. This $25,000 is tax deductible at time 0.

Depreciation on the new machine for tax purposes will be allowed as follows: year 1, $90,000; year 2, $157,500; and in each of years 3 through 5, $67,500 per year. The existing equipment has a book and tax value of $250,000 and a remaining useful life of 10 years. However, the existing equipment can be sold for only $100,000 and is being depreciated for book and tax purposes using the straight-line method over its actual life.

Management has provided you with the following comparative manufacturing cost data.

	Present Equipment	New Equipment
Annual capacity (units)	900,000	900,000
Annual costs:		
Labor	$ 67,500	$ 56,000
Depreciation	22,500	31,000
Other (all cash)	108,000	45,000
Total annual costs	$198,000	$132,000

The existing equipment is expected to have a salvage value equal to its removal costs at the end of 10 years. The new equipment is expected to have a salvage value of $135,000 at the end of 10 years, which will be taxable, and no removal costs. No changes in working capital are required with the purchase of the new equipment. The sales force does not expect any changes in the volume of sales over the next 10 years. The company's cost of capital is 18 percent, and its tax rate is 20 percent.

Required

a. Calculate the removal costs of the existing equipment net of tax effects.
b. Compute the depreciation tax shield.
c. Compute the annual forgone tax benefits of the old equipment.
d. Calculate the cash inflow, net of taxes, from the sale of the new equipment in year 10.
e. Calculate the tax benefit arising from the loss on the old equipment.
f. Compute the annual differential cash flows arising from the investment in years 1 through 10.
g. Compute the net present value of the project.

INTEGRATIVE CASE

A-23. Residual Income, Performance Evaluation, and Investment Decisions

Concord Media is a midsize advertising and public relations firm with several divisions. Division presidents at Concord are evaluated and compensated using residual income. Residual income is based on beginning-of-the-year net asset values and using the corporate cost of capital.

Presidents are allowed to authorize capital expenditures up to $500,000 but are expected to follow the guidelines of the Corporate Finance Group, which require completing a net present value analysis of the investment along with identifying any nonfinancial factors that were considered. The corporate cost of capital to be used for all new investments is 16 percent.

The president of the Pacific Division is looking over a proposal that the operating manager in the division has put together. The president has promised to get back to the manager "within a day or two" with a decision on whether to proceed with the project. The president had been reviewing some forecasts of business activity, which suggests next year (when the project will first be operational) will be a tough one financially.

Selected information on the project follows:

Investment required	$330,000
Economic (and tax) life of investment	6 years
Salvage value.	$0
Increase in annual cash flows before tax.	$115,000
Working capital requirements.	$0

Because tax policies are determined at the corporate level, the guidelines of the Corporate Finance Group state that the NPV analysis should assume straight-line depreciation for both tax and accounting income determination based on the economic life of the investment less the salvage value to be returned at the end of the investment. The tax rate to be assumed is 22 percent.

Required

a. Prepare the net present value analysis for the proposed project.
b. Calculate the residual income for each year of the life of the project.
c. What recommendation will the divisional president make with respect to the project?

SOLUTION TO SELF-STUDY QUESTION

1.   *a.* and *b.*

	Year				
	0	1	2	3	4
Investment flows					
New equipment	$(15,000)				
Software ($30,000 × 80%)[a]	(24,000)				
Old equipment ($200 × 80%)	160				
Annual cash flows ($16,000 × 80%).		$12,800	$12,800	$ 12,800	$ 12,800
Depreciation tax shield ($5,000 × 20%)		1,000	1,000	1,000	
Disinvestment flows ($2,000 × 80%)					1,600
Total cash flows	$(38,840)	$13,800	$13,800	$13,800	$14,400
Present value factor at 10%.	1.000	0.909	0.826	0.751	0.683
Present values[b].	$(38,840)	$12,544	$11,399	$10,364	$9,835
Net present value.	$ 5,302				

[a] 80% = 1 − 20% tax rate, which converts before-tax flows to after-tax flows.
[b] Present value factor shown is rounded to three places. Present value factors are shown in Exhibit A.8.

Glossary

account analysis   Cost estimation method that calls for a review of each account making up the total cost being analyzed.

activity-based cost management   Approach that uses activity-based costing data to evaluate the cost of value-chain activities and to identify opportunities for improvement.

activity-based costing (ABC)   Costing method that first assigns costs to activities and then assigns them to products based on the products' consumption of activities.

actual activity   Actual volume for the period.

actual cost   Cost of job determined by actual direct material and labor cost plus overhead applied using an actual overhead rate and an actual allocation base.

adjusted *R*-squared (R^2)   Correlation coefficient squared and adjusted for the number of independent variables used to make the estimate.

administrative costs   Costs required to manage the organization and provide staff support, including executive salaries, costs of data processing, and legal costs.

appraisal costs (also called *detection costs*)   Costs incurred to detect individual units of products that do not conform to specifications.

artificial intelligence (AI)   The simulation of human intelligence and behavior by computers.

asset acquisition   Costs involved in purchasing and installing an asset that can involve the disposal of old assets, resulting in a gain or a loss.

balanced scorecard   Performance measurement system relying on multiple financial and nonfinancial measures of performance.

behavioral congruence   Alignment of individual behavior with the best interests of the organization regardless of the individual's own goals.

benchmarking   Continuous process of measuring a company's own products, services, or activities against competitors' performance.

big data   The volume and speed with which information is generated and made available.

bottleneck   Operation where the work required limits production.

break-even point   Volume level at which profits equal zero.

budget   Financial plan of the revenues and resources needed to carry out activities and meet financial goals.

budgeted balance sheets   Statements of budgeted financial position.

business model   Description of how different levels and employees in the organization must perform for the organization to achieve its goals.

business strategy   A company's specific approach for deploying the organizational assets and capabilities required to meet its customers' needs competitively, while delivering the desired returns to shareholders.

by-products   Outputs of joint production processes that are relatively minor in quantity or value.

cash budget   Statement of cash on hand at the start of the budget period, expected cash receipts, expected cash disbursements, and the resulting cash balance at the end of the budget period.

centralized   Describes those organizations in which decisions are made by a relatively few individuals in the high ranks of the organization.

coefficient of determination   Square of the correlation coefficient, interpreted as the proportion of the variation in the dependent variable explained by the independent variable(s).

compensation and reward system   System that specifies how the subordinate will be compensated for his or her performance based on a stated measure of performance.

conformance to specification   Degree to which a good or service meets specifications.

constraints   Activities, resources, or policies that limit or bound the attainment of an objective.

contingent compensation   Compensation that is based on measured performance.

continuous flow processing   System that generally mass-produces a single, homogeneous output in a continuing process.

continuous improvement   Continuous reevaluation and improvement of the efficiency of activities.

contribution margin   Sales price – Variable costs per unit.

contribution margin per unit of scarce resource   Contribution margin per unit of a particular input with limited availability.

contribution margin ratio   Contribution margin as a percentage of sales revenue.

control account   Account in the general ledger that summarizes a set of subsidiary ledger accounts.

controllability   Extent to which an item can be managed.

controllability concept   Idea that managers should be held responsible for costs or profits over which they have decision-making authority.

conversion costs   Sum of direct labor and manufacturing overhead.

correlation coefficient   Measure of the linear relation between two or more variables, such as cost and some measure of activity.

cost   Sacrifice of resources.

cost accounting   Field of accounting that measures, records, and reports information about costs.

cost allocation   Process of assigning indirect costs to products, services, people, business units, etc.

cost allocation rule   Method used to assign costs in the cost pool to the cost objects.

cost center   Organization subunit responsible only for costs.

cost drivers   Factors that cause, or "drive," costs.

cost flow diagram   Diagram or flowchart illustrating the cost allocation process.

cost hierarchy   Classification of cost drivers into general levels of activity, volume, batch, product, and so on.

cost management system   System to provide information about the costs of process, products, and services used and produced by an organization.

cost object   Any end to which a cost is assigned; examples include a product, a department, or a product line.

cost of capital   Opportunity cost of the resources (equity and debt) invested in the business.

cost of goods sold   Expense assigned to products sold during a period.

cost of invested capital   Cost of capital multiplied by the assets invested.

cost of quality system   A system that reflects the tension between incurring costs to ensure quality and the costs incurred with quality failures.

cost pool   Collection of costs to be assigned to the cost objects.

cost structure   Proportion of fixed and variable costs to total costs of an organization.

cost variance analysis   Comparison of actual input amounts and prices with standard input amounts and prices.

cost-benefit analysis   Process of comparing benefits (often measured in savings or increased profits) with costs associated with a proposed change within an organization.

cost-plus transfer pricing   Transfer pricing policy based on a measure of cost (full or variable costing, actual or standard cost) plus an allowance for profit.

cost–volume–profit (CVP) analysis   Study of the relationships among revenues, costs, and volume and their effect on profit.

critical success factors   Strengths of a company that enable it to outperform competitors.

critical thinking   A systematic process used to analyze a business issue or decision.

current cost   Cost to replace or rebuild an existing asset.

customer expectations of quality   Customer's anticipated level of product or service (including tangible and intangible features).

data analytics   Systematic evaluation of information to address a decision problem.

data visualization   How the results of the data analysis are summarized and presented.

death spiral   Process that begins by attempting to increase price to meet reported product costs, losing market, reporting still higher costs, and so on, until the firm is out of business.

decentralization   Delegation of decision-making authority to a subordinate.

decentralized   Describes those organizations in which decisions are spread among relatively many divisional and departmental managers.

delegated decision authority   Specification of the authority to make decisions in the organization's name.

Delphi technique   Forecasting method in which individual forecasts of group members are submitted anonymously and evaluated by the group as a whole.

department allocation method   Allocation method that has a separate cost pool for each department, which has its own overhead allocation rate or set of rates.

dependent variable   *Y* term or the left-hand side of a regression equation.

differential analysis   Process of estimating revenues and costs of alternative actions available to decision makers and of comparing these estimates to the status quo.

differential costs   With two or more alternatives, costs that differ among or between alternatives.

differential revenues   Revenues that change in response to a particular course of action.

direct cost   Any cost that can be directly (unambiguously) related to a cost object at reasonable cost.

direct labor   Labor that can be identified directly with the product at reasonable cost.

direct manufacturing costs   Product costs that can be feasibly identified with units of production.

direct materials   Materials that can be identified directly with the product at reasonable cost.

direct method   Cost allocation method that charges costs of service departments to user departments without making allocations between or among service departments.

discount rate   Interest rate used to compute net present values.

discretionary cost center   Organization subunit whose managers are held responsible for costs where the relationship between costs and outputs is not well established.

disinvestment flows   Cash flows that take place at the termination of a capital project.

distribution chain   Set of firms and individuals that buys and distributes goods and services from the firm.

divisional income   Divisional revenues minus divisional costs.

dual transfer pricing   Transfer pricing system that charges the buying division with costs only and credits the selling division with cost plus some profit allowance.

dual-rate method   Cost allocation method that separates a common cost into fixed and variable components and then allocates each component using a different allocation base.

dumping   Exporting a product to another country at a price below domestic price.

dysfunctional decision making   Decisions made in the interests of local managers that are not in the interests of the organization.

econometric models Statistical methods of forecasting economic data using regression models.

economic value added (EVA) Annual after-tax (adjusted) divisional income minus the total annual cost of (adjusted) capital.

efficiency variance Difference between budgeted and actual results arising from differences between the inputs that were budgeted per unit of output and the inputs actually used.

engineering estimate Cost estimate based on measurement and pricing of the work involved in a task.

enterprise resource planning (ERP) Information technology that links the various systems of the enterprise into a single comprehensive information system.

equivalent units Number of complete physical units to which units in inventories are equal in terms of work done to date.

estimated net realizable value Sales price of a final product minus additional processing costs necessary to prepare a product for sale.

expense Cost that is charged against revenue in an accounting period.

external failure costs Costs incurred when nonconforming products and services are detected after being delivered to customers.

favorable variance Variance that, taken alone, results in an addition to operating profit.

final cost center Cost center, such as a production or marketing department, whose costs are not allocated to another cost center.

financial accounting Field of accounting that reports financial position and income according to accounting rules.

financial budgets Budgets of financial resources—for example, the cash budget and the budgeted balance sheet.

finished goods Product fully completed, but not yet sold.

first-in, first-out (FIFO) process costing Inventory method whereby the first goods received are the first ones charged out when sold or transferred.

fixed compensation Compensation that is not directly linked to measured performance.

fixed costs Costs that are unchanged as volume changes within the relevant range of activity.

flexible budget Budget that indicates revenues, costs, and profits for different levels of activity.

flexible budget line Expected monthly costs at different output levels.

flexible production budget Standard input price times standard quantity of input allowed for actual good output.

full absorption cost All variable and fixed manufacturing costs; used to compute a product's inventory value under GAAP.

full cost Sum of all costs of manufacturing and selling a unit or product (includes both fixed and variable costs).

generally accepted accounting principles (GAAP) Rules, standards, and conventions that guide the preparation of financial accounting statements for firms registered in the United States.

goal congruence Agreement by all members of a group on a common set of objectives.

gross margin Revenue – Cost of goods sold on income statements. Per unit, the gross margin equals Sales price – Full absorption cost per unit.

gross margin ratio Gross margin divided by sales.

high–low cost estimation Method to estimate costs based on two cost observations, usually at the highest and lowest activity levels.

historical cost Original cost to purchase or build an asset.

impact Likely monetary effect from an activity (such as a variance).

independent variable *X* term, or predictor, on the right-hand side of a regression equation.

indirect cost Any cost that *cannot* be directly related to a cost object.

indirect manufacturing costs All product costs except direct costs.

industry volume variance Portion of the sales activity variance due to changes in industry volume.

intermediate cost center Cost center whose costs are charged to other departments in the organization.

internal control A process designed to provide reasonable assurance that an organization will achieve its objectives.

internal failure costs Costs incurred when nonconforming products and services are detected before being delivered to customers.

international financial reporting standards (IFRS) Rules, standards, and conventions that guide the preparation of the financial accounting statements in many other countries.

inventoriable costs Costs added to inventory accounts.

investment center Organization subunit responsible for profits and investment in assets.

investment tax credit (ITC) Reduction in federal income taxes arising from the purchase of certain assets.

job Unit of a product that is easily distinguishable from other units.

job cost sheet Record of the cost of the job kept in the accounting system.

job costing Accounting system that traces costs to individual units or to specific jobs, contracts, or batches of goods.

job shop Firm that produces jobs.

joint cost Cost of a manufacturing process with two or more outputs.

joint products Outputs from a common input and common production process.

lean accounting Cost accounting system that provides measures at the work cell or process level and minimizes wasteful or unnecessary transaction processes.

lean manufacturing   Approach to production that looks to significantly reduce production costs using solutions such as just-in-time inventory and production, elimination of waste, and tighter quality control.

learning phenomenon   Systematic relationship between the amount of experience in performing a task and the time required to perform it.

local knowledge   Information about local conditions, markets, regulations, and so on.

make-or-buy decision   Decision concerning whether to make needed goods internally or purchase them from outside sources.

management by exception   Approach to management requiring that reports emphasize the deviation from an accepted base point, such as a standard, a budget, an industry average, or a prior period experience.

management control system   System to influence subordinates to act in the organization's interests.

manufacturing cycle efficiency   Measure of the efficiency of the total manufacturing cycle; equals processing time divided by the manufacturing cycle time.

manufacturing cycle time   Time involved in processing, moving, storing, and inspecting products and materials.

manufacturing overhead   All production costs except direct labor and direct materials.

margin of safety   The excess of projected or actual sales over the break-even volume.

margin of safety percentage   The excess of projected or actual sales over the break-even volume expressed as a percentage of the actual volume.

market price–based transfer pricing   Transfer pricing policy that sets the transfer price at the market price or at a small discount from the market price.

market share variance   Portion of the activity variance due to changes in the company's proportion of sales in the markets in which the company operates.

marketing costs   Costs required to obtain customer orders and provide customers with finished products, including advertising, sales commissions, and shipping costs.

master budget   Financial plan of an organization for the coming year or other planning period.

mission   Why an organization exists; its purpose and goals.

mission statement   Description of an organization's values, definition of its responsibilities to stakeholders, and identification of its major strategies.

negotiated transfer pricing   System that arrives at transfer prices through negotiation between managers of buying and selling divisions.

net present value (NPV)   Economic value of a project at a point in time.

net realizable value method   Joint cost allocation based on the proportional values of the joint products at the split-off point.

nonvalue-added activities   Activities that do not add value to the good or service.

normal activity   Long-run expected volume.

normal cost   Cost of job determined by actual direct material and labor cost plus overhead applied using a predetermined rate and an actual allocation base.

operating budgets   Budgeted income statement, production budget, budgeted cost of goods sold, and supporting budgets.

operating leverage   Extent to which an organization's cost structure is made up of fixed costs. It is calculated as contribution margin divided by operating profit.

operating margin ratio   Operating income divided by sales.

operating profit   Excess of operating revenues over the operating costs necessary to generate those revenues.

operation   Standardized method or technique that is repeatedly performed in making a product.

operations costing   Hybrid costing system used in manufacturing goods that have some common characteristics and some individual characteristics.

opportunity cost   Forgone benefit from the best (forgone) alternative course of action.

optimal transfer price   The transfer price that leads both division managers to make decisions that are in the firm's best interests.

organization goals   Company's broad objectives established by management that employees work to achieve.

outlay cost   Past, present, or future cash outflow.

overapplied overhead   Excess of applied overhead costs over actual overhead incurred during a period.

partial productivity   Measure that expresses the relation between output and a single input.

participative budgeting   Use of input from lower- and middle-management employees; also called *grass roots budgeting*.

peak-load pricing   Practice of setting prices highest when the quantity demanded for the product approaches capacity.

performance evaluation system   System and specification of how the subordinate will be evaluated.

period costs   Costs recognized for financial reporting when incurred.

physical quantities method   Joint cost allocation based on measurement of the volume, weight, or other physical measure of the joint products at the split-off point.

planned variance   Variance that is expected to occur if certain conditions affect operations.

plantwide allocation method   Allocation method using one cost pool for the entire plant. It uses one overhead allocation rate, or one set of rates, for all of a plant's departments.

practical capacity   Amount of production possible assuming only the expected downtime for scheduled maintenance and normal breaks and vacations.

predatory pricing   Practice of setting price below cost with the intent to drive competitors out of business.

predetermined overhead rate   Cost per unit of the allocation base used to charge overhead to products.

present value   Amounts of future cash flows discounted to their equivalent worth today.

prevention costs   Costs incurred to prevent defects in the products or services being produced.

price discrimination   Practice of selling identical goods to different customers at different prices.

price variance   Difference between actual costs and budgeted costs arising from changes in the cost of inputs to a production process or other activity.

price-fixing   Agreement among business competitors to set prices at a particular level.

prime costs   Sum of direct materials and direct labor.

principal–agent relationship   Relationship between a superior, referred to as the *principal,* and a subordinate, called the *agent.*

prior department costs   Manufacturing costs incurred in some other department and transferred to a subsequent department in the manufacturing process.

process control chart   A graph or other visualization that plots or reflects process outcomes over time.

process costing   Accounting system used when identical units are produced through a series of uniform production steps.

process reengineering   Changing operational processes to improve performance, often after examining activity-based costing data to determine opportunities for improvement.

product costs   Costs assigned to the manufacture of products and recognized for financial reporting when sold.

product life cycle   Time from initial research and development to the time that support to the customer ends.

production budget   Production plan of resources needed to meet current sales demand and ensure that inventory levels are sufficient for future sales.

production cost report   Report that summarizes production and cost results for a period; generally used by managers to monitor production and cost flows.

production mix variance   Variance that arises from a change in the relative proportion of inputs (a materials or labor mix variance).

production volume variance   Variance that arises because the volume used to apply fixed overhead differs from the estimated volume used to estimate fixed costs per unit.

production yield variance   Difference between expected output from a given level of inputs and the actual output obtained from those inputs.

productivity   A measure that expresses the conversion of inputs into output.

profit center   Organization subunit responsible for profits and thus revenues, costs, production, and sales volumes.

profit equation   Operating profit equals total revenue less total costs.

profit margin ratio   After-tax income divided by sales.

profit plan   Income statement portion of the master budget.

profit variance analysis   Analysis of the causes of differences between budgeted profits and the actual profits earned.

profit–volume analysis   Version of cost–volume–profit analysis using a single profit line.

project   Complex job that often takes months or years to complete and requires the work of many different departments, divisions, or subcontractors.

purchase price variance   Price variance based on the quantity of materials purchased.

reciprocal method   Method to allocate service department costs that recognizes all services provided by any service department, including services provided to other service departments.

regression   Statistical procedure to determine the relation between variables.

relative performance evaluation (RPE)   Managerial evaluation method that compares divisional performance with that of peer group divisions (i.e., divisions operating in similar product markets).

relevant range   Activity levels within which a given total fixed cost or unit variable cost will be unchanged.

residual income (RI)   Excess of actual profit over the cost of capital invested in the unit.

resources supplied   Expenditures or the amounts spent on a specific activity.

resources used   Cost driver rate multiplied by the cost driver volume.

responsibility accounting   System of reporting tailored to an organizational structure so that costs and revenues are reported at the level within the organization having the related responsibility.

responsibility center   Specific unit of an organization assigned to a manager who is held accountable for its operations and resources.

return on investment (ROI)   Ratio of profits to investment in the asset that generates those profits.

revenue center   Organization subunit responsible for revenues and, typically, marketing costs.

sales activity variance   Difference between operating profit in the master budget and operating profit in the flexible budget that arises because the actual number of units sold is different from the budgeted number; also known as *sales volume variance.*

sales mix variance   Variance arising from the relative proportion of different products sold.

sales price variance   Difference between actual revenue and actual units sold multiplied by budgeted selling price.

sales quantity variance   Variance occurring in multiproduct companies from the change in volume of sales, independent of any change in mix.

scattergraph   Graph that plots costs against activity levels.

semivariable cost   Cost that has both fixed and variable components; also called *mixed cost.*

separation of duties   No one person has control over an entire transaction.

service department   Department that provides services to other subunits in the organization.

short run Period of time over which capacity will be unchanged, usually one year.

special order Order that will not affect other sales and is usually a short-run occurrence.

spending (or budget) variance Price variance for fixed overhead.

split-off point Stage of processing that separates two or more products.

stakeholders Groups or individuals, such as employees, suppliers, customers, shareholders, and communities, who have an interest in what the organization does.

standard cost Cost of job determined by standard (budgeted) direct materials and labor cost plus overhead applied using a predetermined overhead rate and a standard (budgeted) allocation base.

standard cost center Organization subunit whose managers are held responsible for costs and in which the relationship between costs and output is well defined.

standard cost sheet Form providing standard quantities of inputs used to produce a unit of output and the standard prices for the inputs.

standard costing Accounting method that assigns costs to cost objects at predetermined amounts.

static budget Budget for a single activity level; usually the master budget.

step cost Cost that increases with volume in steps; also called *semifixed cost.*

step method Method of service department cost allocation that allocates some service department costs to other service departments.

strategic long-range plan Statement detailing steps to take to achieve a company's organization goals.

strategy map A visual device to communicate an organization's strategy.

subsidiary ledger account Account that records financial transactions for a specific customer, vendor, or job.

sunk cost Cost incurred in the past that cannot be changed by present or future decisions.

supply chain Set of firms and individuals that sells goods and services to the firm.

target cost Equals the target price minus desired profit margin.

target price Price based on customers' perceived value for the product and the price that competitors charge.

tax basis Remaining tax-depreciable "book value" of an asset for tax purposes.

tax shield Reduction in tax payment because of depreciation deducted for tax purposes.

theoretical capacity Amount of production possible under ideal conditions with no time for maintenance, breakdowns, or absenteeism.

theory of constraints (TOC) Focuses on revenue and cost management when faced with bottlenecks.

throughput contribution Sales dollars minus direct materials costs and variables such as energy and piecework labor.

time equations Time equations allow managers to adjust the times for orders with different characteristics.

time value of money Concept that cash received earlier is worth more than cash received later.

total contribution margin Difference between revenues and total variable costs.

total cost variance Difference between budgeted and actual results (equal to the sum of the price and efficiency variances).

total factor productivity Ratio of the value of output to the value of all key inputs.

transfer price Value assigned to the goods or services sold or rented (transferred) from one unit of an organization to another.

trend analysis Forecasting method that ranges from a simple visual extrapolation of points on a graph to a highly sophisticated computerized time series analysis.

t-**statistic** *t* is the value of the estimated coefficient, *b*, divided by its standard error.

two-stage cost allocation Process of first allocating costs to intermediate cost pools and then to the individual cost objects using different allocation bases.

underapplied overhead Excess of actual overhead costs incurred over applied overhead costs.

unfavorable variance Variance that, taken alone, reduces operating profit.

unit contribution margin Difference between revenues per unit (price) and variable costs per unit.

unused resource capacity Difference between resources used and resources supplied.

user department Department that uses the functions of service departments.

value chain Set of activities that transforms raw resources into the goods and services that end users purchase and consume.

value proposition How the organization will create value for all stakeholders.

value-added activities Those activities that customers perceive as adding utility to the goods or services they purchase.

variable costs Costs that change in direct proportion with a change in volume within the relevant range of activity.

variance Difference between planned result and actual outcome.

weighted-average process costing Inventory method that for product costing purposes combines costs and equivalent units of a period with the costs and the equivalent units in beginning inventory.

work in process Product in the production process but not yet complete.

working capital Cash, accounts receivable, and other short-term assets required to maintain an activity.

Index

Note: Page numbers in **boldface** refer to key terms; page numbers followed by e refer to exhibits; page numbers followed by n refer to notes.

A

ABC. *See* activity-based costing
ABCM. *See* activity-based cost management
account analysis, **193**, 193–194, 194e
accounting income (divisional income)
  adjusting with EVA, 655–660, 656e, 659e, 660e
  defined, **646**
  as performance measure, 646–648, 647e, 650
accounting systems
  assessment framework for, 9–11
  cost vs. financial, 6, 7e
  customers (users) of, 7–8
  rules and standards for, 7
activities
  activity analysis, 448–449
  actual activity, **461**
  efficiency and continuous improvement, 838, **838**
  identifying in ABC, 395–396
  nonvalue-added, **10**
  value-added, **4**, 4–5
activity-based costing (ABC)
  in administration, 404–405, 405e
  allocation bases in, 403–404
  cost flow diagram, 396e
  cost flows through accounts, 402e
  cost hierarchy, 397, 397e
  customer costs application, 452–456, 453e, 454e, 455e
  defined, **394**
  examples of, 255–256, 257e, 397–399, 398e, 399e
  in health care, 404
  hospital costs, 408
  key points about, 401
  vs. plantwide and departmental, 399–401, 400e
  steps in, 394–396
  time-driven, 406–408
  vs. traditional two-stage cost allocation, 396–397
  users of, 405–406, 405e
activity-based cost management (ABCM)
  activity analysis in, 395, 448–449
  benefits of, 449
  capacity cost management, 458–464, 460e, 461e, 463e
  capturing cost savings, 457
  costs hierarchy in, 451
  customer costs in, 452–456, 453e, 454e, 455e
  defined, **447**
  lean manufacturing and, 449–450

quality cost management, 465–470, 467e, 468e
  in service organizations, 449, 449e
  supplier costs in, 456–457, 457e
activity levels
  cost behavior and, 191–192
  flexible budgets and, 734, 735e
  relevant range, 195
actual activity, **461**
actual cost
  defined, **295**
  as transfer price basis, 703
adding or dropping products
  differential analysis of, 150–152, 151e
  reported product costs and, 385–387, 386e
adjusted R-squared (R^2), **201**
administrative costs. *See* marketing and administrative costs
administrative duplication, 550
AICPA (American Institute of Certified Public Accountants), 21
Airbus, 141
Albertsons, 104
allocation bases
  in activity-based costing, 403–404
  capacity as, 461
  choosing multiple, 255–256
  choosing single, 254
  cost flow diagram, 251e
  in job costing example, 296
  for predetermined overhead rate, 253, 254e
  service department example, 497, 497e
Amazon, 5, 150, 838
American Airlines, 14, 405e
American Institute of Certified Public Accountants (AICPA), 21
antitrust law, 142, 142n
Apple Inc., 548e, 691
appraisal costs (detection costs), **467**
Areeda, P.E., 142n
artificial intelligence, **597**
assets
  on budgeted balance sheet, 607, 608e
  intangible, 650
asset turnover ratio, 650

B

balanced scorecard
  companies that use, 837, 838e
  defined, **835**
  development process, 837–838
  example of, 839e
  perspectives in, 835–838, 836e
balance sheets
  budgeted, **607**, 608e
  divisional, 649, 649e

Banner Health, 849
Bank of America, 833
behavioral congruence, **555**
behavioral issues. *See also* ethics
  bonus plans and, 560, 565, 596
  performance measures and, 565, 610–611
  transfer pricing and, 700–701, 703–704
benchmarks
  continuous improvement and, 838–842
  defined, **838**
  development of, 840, 841e
big data, **17**
billable hours, 47
BMW, 831
Boeing Aircraft, 141, 257, 844
bonus plans, and behavior, 560, 565, 596
bookings, as performance measure, 844
Booz Allen Hamilton, 53
Boston Beer Company, Inc., 794
bottleneck(s), **156**
break-even point, **100**
break-even volume, 100–101, 101e
budget, **14**, **591**
budgeted balance sheets, **607**, 608e
budget plan. *See* master budget
budgets and budgeting. *See also* master budget
  vs. actual costs, 13–15, 14e
  budget (spending) variance, **749**
  defined, **14**, **591**
  ethical problems in, 610–611
  financial budgets, **731**
  flexible, **734**, 734, 735e
  flexible production budget, **744**
  fraud link, 565
  in governmental organizations, 611
  human element in, 594–595
  marketing and administrative, 602–603, 603e
  operating budgets, **731**
  for performance evaluation, 731–732
  in retail and wholesale companies, 609–610
  in service organizations, 610
  static, **734**
  under uncertainty, 611–614, 612e
  zero-based budgeting, 615–619, 618e
burden (manufacturing overhead), 50
business decisions, cost accounting trends in, 15–20
business model, **833**, 833–834, 834e
business strategy, **829**, 829–831
business units (investment centers). *See also* divisional performance measures
  defined, **554**
  performance measures of, 557, 645

by-products
  accounting for, 516–517, 517e
  defined, **516**

C

capacity management
  allocation bases, 461
  assigning cost of unused, 462
  computing cost of unused, 460–462, 461e
  resource use and, 458–460, 459e, 460e
  seasonality and cost of unused, 462–464, 463e, 464e
capacity variance, 752
cash budget
  defined, **605**
  example of, 605e
  multiperiod cash flows and, 605–607, 606e, 607e
cash flow, multiperiod, 605–607, 606e, 607e
centralized, **548**
centralized organizations, 548–549
CEO (chief executive officer), 22, 585
CFO (chief financial officer), 8e, 22
Cheesecake Factory, The, 142
Coca-Cola Company, 655, 707, 830
coefficient of determination, **199**
compensation and reward system, **552**
compensation systems, 559
competitiveness, 591
Competitive Strategy (Porter), 830–831
complexity, as resource-consuming activity, 403–404
conformance to specification, **466**
constraints
  defined, **153**
  theory of, 156–157
Continental Airlines, 136
contingent compensation, **559**
continuous flow processing
  defined, **257**
  job costing and, 257–258
continuous improvement, **838**, 838
contribution margin, **63**, 64e
contribution margin income statements, 65–66, 65e
contribution margin per unit of scarce resource, **153**
contribution margin ratio, **100**, 100–101
control account, **282**
controllability, **800**
controllability concept, **558**
controller, 8e
conversion costs, **51**
Cooper, Cynthia, 567
coronavirus, 733. *See also* COVID pandemic
corporate costs, allocation, 561
corporate culture
  effect of, 135–136, **145**
  outsourcing of, 135–136, **145**
correlation coefficient, **199**
cost, **46**
cost accountant, 8e
cost accounting
  in decision making, 11–15, 12e
  defined, **6**
  ethics in (*See* ethics)
  vs. financial, 6, 7e
  rules and standards for, 7
  terminology in, 45–46, 67, 68e
  trends in, 15–20

users and uses of, 7–11
Cost Accounting Standards Board, 299
cost allocation. *See also* allocation bases; service department cost allocation
  in cost management systems, 247
  defined, **52**
  department vs. plantwide, 392–393
  dual-rate method, **562**, 562–564
  government contracts and, 299
  joint costs, **510**, 510–515, 510e, 512e, 513e, 514e
  in management control systems, 562–564
  misrepresentation of, 299–300
  process of, 52–54
  two-stage, 255–256, 255e, 256e, 388–393, 390e, 391e, 392e, 396–397
cost allocation rule, **52**
cost analysis. *See also* differential analysis
  life-cycle costing, 141
  target costing, 142
cost behavior
  estimating (*See* cost estimation)
  fixed vs. variable, 58–59
  patterns of, 59–60, 59e, 191–192
cost-benefit analysis, **10**
cost centers
  defined, **553**
  delegated decision authority, 553–554
  performance measures of, 740–741
  responsibility accounting, 553–554
cost data
  for decision making, 11–15, 12e
  managerial purposes—budgeting, 27
  for performance evaluations, 10–11
  for price quotation, 60e
cost drivers
  in activity-based costing, 395
  cost hierarchy of, 396–397
  defined, **11**, **394**
  examples of, 395e
  in TDABC, 408
  in two-stage cost allocation, 390–392
cost estimation
  account analysis method, 193–194, 194e
  common assumptions, 207
  data problems in, 207
  effect of method differences in, 208, 208e
  engineering method, 192–193
  formula for, 192
  learning phenomenon effects on, 204–206, 205e
  managing operations and forecasting revenue, 191
  reasons for, 191
  regression analysis, 198–200, 199e
  statistical analysis, 195–200, 197e, 199e
cost flow diagrams
  activity-based costing, 396e
  allocation bases, 251e
  customer costs, 454e
  defined, **52**, 53e
  direct method, 499e
  product costing, 247–248, 247e, 250e
  reciprocal method, 505e
  step method, 502e
  two-stage cost allocation, 256e, 389e, 391e
cost hierarchy
  in ABCM, 451
  defined, **397**, 397e
cost leaders, 830
cost management systems. *See also* activity-based cost management

cost allocation in, 247, 255–256
  defined, **245**
  design of, 248
  in multiple-product, discrete process industry, 250–255, 251e, 252e, 253e, 254e
  production processes and, 256–268, 258e
  reasons for, 245–246
  in single-product, continuous process industry, 248–250, 250e
cost object, **52**
cost of capital, **653**
cost of goods manufactured and sold, 56
cost of goods manufactured and sold statement, 57, 55e
cost of goods sold
  budgeted (production costs), 599–600, 599e, 601e
  defined, **49**
  in master budget, 601e, 602
  prorating variances to, 785–788, 787e
  in retail and wholesale, 47–49, 48e
  in standard cost system, 759
cost of invested capital, **653**
cost of quality system, **466**
cost-plus pricing, 140
cost-plus transfer pricing, **703**
cost pool, **52**
costs
  appraisal (detection), **467**
  for control and evaluation, 12–14, 13e
  conversion, **51**
  current, **661**
  defined, **46**, 67, 68e
  direct, **53**
  direct manufacturing, **50**
  vs. expenses, 46
  in financial statements, 47–52, 47e, 48e, 51e
  full, **60**
  full absorption, **60**
  historical, **661**
  indirect, **53**
  indirect manufacturing, **50**
  inventoriable, **54**
  of lean production, 450
  in manufacturing, 50, 51e, 60–64, 61e
  marketing, **51**
  normal, **295**
  opportunity, **46**
  outlay, **46**
  period, **50**
  in predatory pricing, 142
  prime, **51**
  prior department, **349**
  product , 50, 51e, 60–64, 61e
  semivariable (mixed), **59**
  sunk, **136**
  small business failures and, 3
  step (semifixed), **59**
  target, **142**
  types of, 46
  variable, **58**
cost structures
  CVP analysis of, 104–105, 110
  defined, **104**
cost systems. *See* cost management systems
cost variance analysis, **741**. *See also* variance analysis
cost-volume-profit (CVP) analysis
  alternative cost structures in, 109–110
  assumptions and limitations of, 110
  break-even analysis, 97

break-even and target volumes, 100–101, 101e
for cost structure analysis, 104–105, 110
defined, **97**
example of, 99–101
graphic presentation of, 102–103, 102e
income taxes in, 107–108
margin of safety, 105
multiproduct analysis, 108–109
profit equation in, 98–99
profit-volume analysis, 103, 103e
using spreadsheets, 106–107, 106e
COVID pandemic
break-even analysis, 97
channel-mix variance, 799
cost savings by outsourcing service centers, 509
drop in resources, 448
excess capacity resources, 464
financial result, 794
fixed-costs crisis, 388
gross margin, importance, 64
health insurance industry, 733
insourcing, 150
lean production, 450
not-for-profit, 849
portfolio for profit, 456
cradle-to-grave costing, 141
critical success factors, **591**
critical thinking
data analytics and, 17–18
defined, **17**
CRM (customer relationship management), 16e
cross-functional teams, 9
Crown Castle International Corp, 837e
cumulative average-time learning model, 205n
current cost, **661**, 661–663, 662e
customer expectations of quality, **466**
customer profitability, 452, 469
customer relationship management (CRM), 16e
customers
cost determination, 452–455, 453e, 454e, 455e
cost flow diagram, 454e
cost management and, 455–456
profitability of, 452, 456
customer satisfaction performance measures, 843–844
customer service, 16e
CVP analysis. *See* cost-volume-profit (CVP) analysis

D

data analytics
critical thinking and, 16–18
CVP analysis, 110
defined, **17**
for managing operations and forecasting revenue, 191
data visualization, **18**
death spiral, **387**
decentralization
advantages of, 549
cost-cutting approach, 550
defined, **548**
disadvantages of, 549–550
transfer pricing and, 689–690
decentralized, **548**
decentralized organizations, 548–550
decision making
cost data for, 11, 12e
decentralized vs. centralized, 548, 549

dysfunctional, 549
learning phenomenon in, 206
make-or-buy decision, 144–149, 146e, 147e, 148e, 149e
manager functions in, 9–11
outsourcing decision, 507–509, 846
product choice decisions, 152–156, 153e, 154e, 155e
reciprocal method and, 507–509
reported product costs and, 385–388, 386e
sell-or-process-further decision, 515, 515e
suboptimal, 650–651, 654, 655, 664
delegated decision authority, **552**
delivery performance, 844
Dell Inc., 142, 833
Delphi technique, **596**
Delta Air Lines, 104, 833
denominator variance, 752
department allocation method
defined, **393**
vs. plantwide and activity-based, 399–401, 400e
in two-stage cost allocation, 389e
departments (term), 12
dependent variable, **198**
detection costs (appraisal costs), **467**
Diageo, 655
Diego Pharmaceuticals, 705–706
differential analysis
adding or dropping products, 150–152, 151e
closing business unit, 150–152
defined, **136**
full-cost pricing fallacy, 137–138
make-or-buy decisions, **144**, 145–148, 146e, 147e, 148e
product choice decisions, 152–156, 153e, 154e, 155e
sell-or-process-further decisions, 515, 515e
short- vs. long-run pricing, 138–141
special order pricing, 138–140, 138e, 139e
total vs. differential format, 137
of transfer pricing, 692
differential costs
in decision making, 11, 12e
defined, **11**, **136**
vs. total costs, 137
differential format, 137
differential revenues, **11**, 12e
direct costs
in cost allocation, 53–54
defined, **53**
in job costing example, 283–284, 283e, 284e
direct labor, **50**. *See also* labor costs
direct manufacturing costs, **50**
direct materials
in cost of goods manufactured and sold, 56
defined, **50**
in master budget, 599–600, 599e
in standard cost system, 757
in variable cost variance analysis, 743–745, 745e
as variable production cost, 741
variances with unequal quantities purchased and used, 788–790, 789e
direct method
cost flow diagram, 499e
defined, **498**
examples of, 498–500, 498e, 500e
limitations of, 500
discrete production process
vs. continuous, 256
job costing and, 250–254, 256–257

discretionary cost center, **554**
distribution chain, **5**
divisional performance measures
companies use, 646
divisional income, **646**, 646–647, 647e
divisions (units) described, 556–557
economic value added, **655**, 655–660
investment base measures and, 660–663, 661e, 662e
questions to consider, 645
residual income, **653**, 653–655, 654e
return on investment, **648**, 648–653
suboptimization and, 651–653, 664
use of, 646
divisions (term), 12, 645, 691. *See also* investment centers
DoorDash, food delivery, 105
dropping products
differential analysis of, 150–153, 151e
reported product costs and, 385–388, 386e
dual-rate method
defined, **562**
example of, 562–564
dual transfer pricing, **703**
dumping, **143**
dysfunctional decision making, **549**

E

econometric models, **597**
economic value added (EVA)
defined, **655**
example of, 656, 656e
limitations of, 657–660
performance measure, 657
efficiency
continuous improvement and, 838, **838**
in cost leaders, 830
efficiency variance, **742**, 797–798
employee involvement, 850–851, 851e
engineering analysis and the construction of healthcare projects, 193
engineering estimates, **192**, 192–193
enhance sales predications, using AI, 597
Enron, 566
enterprise resource planning (ERP), **15**, 15–16
environment, and management control system, 551
Epson, 141
equivalent units
computing costs per unit, 340–341, 340e, 346–347
computing units of production, 337–339, 338e, 344–346
concept of, 335–336, 336e
defined, **336**
overstating to commit fraud, 338
ERP (enterprise resource planning), **15**, 15–16
estimated net realizable value
defined, **511**
example of, 512–513, 512e, 513e
ethics
budgeting and, 610–611
codes of, 21–22
ethical dilemmas, 21
fraudulent acts, 338, 564–565
importance of, 21
in job costing, 298–300
Sarbanes-Oxley Act of 2002, 22–23, 566
EVA. *See* economic value added

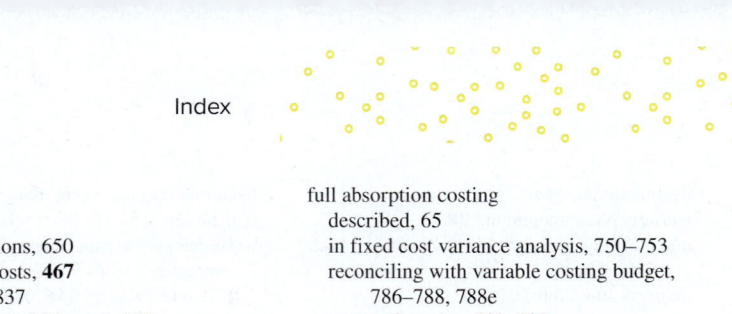

expenses
    defined, **46**
    in ROI limitations, 650
external failure costs, **467**
ExxonMobil, 4, 837
EY (formerly Ernst & Young), 257

F

Facebook, 452, 691
factory burden, 50
factory expense, 50
factory overhead, 50
failure costs, 467
failure rates, in small business, 3
FASB (Financial Accounting Standards
    Board), 707
favorable variance, **732**, 733
FedEx, 16, 105, 138, 456
Fidelity Investments, 830
FIFO process costing. *See* first-in, first-out
    process costing
final cost center, **496**
financial accounting, **6**, 7e
Financial Accounting Standards Board
    (FASB), 707
financial budgets, **731**
financial ratios
    for comparing divisional income, 647, 647e
    in evaluating ROI, 649
financial statements, costs in, 47–52, 47e, 48e,
    51e. *See also* income statements
finished goods
    in cost of goods manufactured and sold,
        57–58
    defined, **54**
    in standard cost system, 759
first-in, first-out (FIFO) process costing
    defined, **340**
    example of
        cost flows in T-accounts, 341, 341e
        five-step process, 343–347, 345e
        production cost report, 345e
        vs. weighted average, 340–341, 341e, 346,
            348, 348e
first-stage allocation. *See* two-stage cost
    allocation
fixed compensation, **559**
fixed costs
    defined, **58**
    as differential costs, 136
    production cost variances, 737, 749–753,
        750e, 751e, 752e
    scattergraph estimate, 197e
    unit fixed costs, 61–62
    vs. variable costs, 58–60
fixed product mix, 108
flexible budget
    defined, **734**
    vs. master budget, 734–736
    sales activity variance, **735**, 735–736, 736e
flexible budget line, **734**, 735e
flexible production budget, **744**
focus strategy, 831
Foreign Corrupt Practices Act of 1977, 566
four-way overhead variance analysis, 754, 753e
fraud. *See also* ethics
    overstating equivalent units, 338
    performance evaluations and, 564–565
full absorption cost, **60**

full absorption costing
    described, 65
    in fixed cost variance analysis, 750–753
    reconciling with variable costing budget,
        786–788, 788e
    as transfer price, 702–703
full cost, **60**, **137**, 140
functional performance measures, 844–845, 844e

G

GAAP (generally accepted accounting
    principles), **7**
General Electric, 557, 655n, 837e
generally accepted accounting principles
    (GAAP), **7**
General Motors, 152, 385, 549, 619
goal congruence, **555**
goals, organizational
    in balanced scorecard, 835
    defined, **592**
    linking to performance measures, 848–849
Goldman Sachs, 555, 555n, 567
Google, 691
governmental organizations, 611
government contracts, and cost allocation, 299
grass roots budgeting, 594
gross book value, 661, 661e, 662e
gross margin
    in cost of goods sold, 49
    defined, **62**, 63e
    importance of, 64–65
gross margin income statement, 65–66, 65e
gross margin ratio, **648**
Grubhub, food delivery, 105

H

Haier, 141
Harrah's Entertainment, 16e
Hartmann, 831
H.E.B., 831
Herman Miller, 655
high-low cost estimation, **196**
Hilton, R., 205n
Hilton hotels, 832
historical cost, **661**, 661–663, 662e
Holiday Inn, 832
Home Depot, 58, 554
Honda, 135–136
Honeywell International Inc., 258
hospital costs, 408
Hovenkamp, H., 142n
HP (Hewlett Packard), 405
Hyundai Motors, 16e

I

idle capacity variance, 752
IFRS (international financial reporting
    standards), **7**
IKEA, 16e, 142
IIA (Institute of Internal Auditors), 21
IMA (Institute of Management Accountants),
    21–22, 156n
impact, defined, **800**
incentives (rewards)
    effects on behavior, 560, 611
    link to fraud, 564–565
    sales forecasting and, 595–597

income statements
    activity-based, 460e
    budgeted, 603, 604e
    contribution margin, 65–66, 65e
    in CVP example, 99, 99e
    divisional, 646, 647e
    generic, 47, 47e
    gross margin vs. contribution margin,
        65–66, 65e
    manufacturing companies, 55, 55e
    projected, 12e
    retail and wholesale, 47–49, 48e
    service organizations, 47, 48e
    traditional, 62, 65
income taxes, 107–108, 705–706
incremental unit-time learning model, 205n
independent variable, **198**
indirect costs
    in cost allocation, 53–54
    defined, **53**
    predetermined rate formula, 395
indirect manufacturing costs, **50**
industry volume variance, **790**, 790–791, 791e
information services, 508
input. *See* output and input
insourcing, 150
Institute of Internal Auditors (IIA), 21
Institute of Management Accountants (IMA),
    21–22, 156n
intangible assets, 650
intellectual property (IP), 691
intermediate cost center, **496**
intermediate market, 692–694
    imperfect, 699
internal auditors, 8e, 567
internal control, 22, **566**, 566–567
internal control system, fails, 567
internal failure costs, **467**
Internal Revenue Service (IRS), 691
international financial reporting standards
    (IFRS), **7**
inventoriable costs, **54**
inventories
    basic inventory formula, 598
    prorating variances to, 785–788, 787e
    values of (*See* product costing)
investment base measures
    beginning, ending, or average balance, 663
    gross vs. net book, 661, 661e, 662e
    historical vs. current costs, 661–663, 662e
investment centers. *See also* divisional
        performance measures
    defined, **554**
    performance measures of, 557, 646

J

JetBlue Airways, 104
JIT (just-in-time) methods, 16e
job
    defined, **256**, **281**
    vs. projects, 301
job costing
    defined, **257**
    ethical issues in, 298–300
    example of
        assigning costs, 282–285, 283e, 284e, 285e
        cost flows through T-accounts, 288e
        cost summary, 287e
        job cost sheet, 288, 289e

over-, underapplied overhead, 289
    overhead application, 286–287, 286e, 289
vs. operation costing, 353, 355–356
vs. process costing, 256–258, 335, 336e, 352
of projects, 301
in service organizations, 296–298, 298e
summary of steps, 296
two-stage approach, 296
job cost sheet
    defined, **282**
    in job costing example, 288, 289e
job order costing system. *See* job costing
job shops
    accounting records in, 282
    defined, **281**
    in product costing comparison, 258e
Johnson & Johnson, 21, 549
joint cost, **510**, 510e
joint cost allocation
    with by-products, 516–517, 517e
    methods of
        evaluation of, 514–515
        net realizable value method, **511**,
            511–512, 512e
        physical quantities method, **514**, 514e
    product demand and, 516
    reasons for, 510–511
joint products, **510**
just-in-time inventory methods, 54
just-in-time (JIT) methods, 16e

K

Kentucky Fried Chicken, 830
Kim, Joseph, 192

L

labor costs
    in activity-based costing, 403
    direct vs. indirect labor, 48
    in job costing example, 284, 284e
    in master budgets, 600, 600e, 610
    in standard cost system, 756
    in variable cost variance analysis, 745–746,
        746e
    as variable production cost, 740–741
    variance analysis of, 797–799, 798e
lean accounting, 16e, **450**
lean manufacturing
    ABCM and, 449–450
    defined, **449**
learning phenomenon
    in decision making, 206
    defined, **204**
    effects on cost, 204–206, 205e
    learning curves, 204, 215–216, 216e
    in performance evaluation, 206
left-hand side (LHS), of regression equation, 198
legal issues, in pricing decisions, 142–144
Lexus, 831
liabilities, on budgeted balance sheet, 607, 608e
life-cycle costing, 141
Lisbon Furniture, 292–295
local knowledge, **549**
long-range plan. *See* strategic long-range plans
long run
    pricing decisions, 136, 137–138
    vs. short run, 136
Louis Vuitton, 831

M

Maher, M., 205n
make-or-buy decision
    defined, **144**
    differential fixed costs and, 144–148, 146e,
        147e, 148e
    opportunity costs of making, 148–149,
        149e
management by exception, **800**
management control systems
    compensation systems, 559–560
    cost allocation in, 560–564
    decentralization and, 548–550
    defined, **551**
    elements of, 552
    evaluation framework, 551
    fraudulent acts link, 564–565
    performance evaluations in, 558–560
    performance measures in, 555–557, 843
    purposes of, 547, 548
    responsibility accounting and, 553–555,
        554e
managerial costing, 65
managers
    alignment with organization, 547–548
    as decision makers, 9–10
    evaluation of, 10–11 (*See also*
        performance evaluation; performance
        measures)
    goal and behavioral congruence in, 555
    key financial players, 8–9, 8e
manufacturing companies
    costs in, 50–52, 51e
    income statements for, 50, 55, 55e
    production cost flows, 54–55, 54e
manufacturing cycle efficiency, **845**, 845
manufacturing cycle time, **845**, 845
manufacturing overhead
    defined, **50**
    fixed overhead variances, 749–753, 750e,
        751e, 752e
    four-way variance analysis, 753, 753e
    in job costing example, 284–285, 284e,
        285e,
    in master budget, 600–601, 601e
    misrepresentation of, 299–300
    overapplied, underapplied, 289
    overhead application, 286–287, 287e,
        289–292
    predetermined overhead rate, 252, 286
    in reported product costs, 385–387, 386e
    in standard cost system, 757–758
    in variable cost variance analysis, 747–748,
        747e
    as variable production cost, 741
margin of safety, **105**, 105–106
margin of safety percentage, **106**
marketing, cost accounting in, 16e
marketing and administrative costs
    activity-based costing of, 404–405
    budget for, 602–603, 603e
    defined, **51**
    in financial statements, 47, 49
    variances in, 737–739
marketing costs, **51**
market price–based transfer pricing, **701**
market researchers, 596
market share, as performance measure, 844
market share variance, **790**, 790–791, 791e

master budget
    budgeted balance sheets, **607**, 608e
    budgeted income statement, 603, 604e
    budgeting process, 595
    cash flows in, 605–607, 605e, 606e, 607e
    components of, 592–593
    defined, **592**
    example of
        cost of goods sold in, 601, 601e
        overhead in, 600, 601e
        production cost forecasts in, 599–600,
            599e
        production forecasts in, 598–599, 599e
    vs. flexible budget, 734, 735e
    marketing and administrative costs in,
        602–603, 603e
    organizational and individual interactions in,
        594e
    revisions to, 602
    sales activity variance, 735–736, 736e
    sales cycle and, 604–605
    sales forecasts for, 595–597
materials
    direct vs. indirect labor, 50
    in job costing example, 283, 283e
materials waste, 67
McDonald's, 142
McDonald's Corporation, 549, 646
McKinsey & Company, 593
Memorial Sloan-Kettering Cancer Center,
    257
Mercedes Benz, 142
merchandising organizations. *See* retail and
        wholesale companies
Merck, 141
Microsoft Corporation, 592, 592e
Microsoft Excel® uses
    cost-volume-profit analysis, 106–107, 106e
    make-or-buy analysis, 147–148, 147e,
        148e
    product choice analysis, 153–156, 154e,
        155e
    reciprocal method, 519–521, 520e
    regression analysis, 198, 199e, 210–215,
        211e, 212e, 213e, 214e, 215e
minimizing investments, 157
minimizing other operating costs, 157
mission, **829**
mission statement, **830**
mixed (semivariable) cost, **59**
Motorola, 751
multiperiod cash flows, 605–607, 606e
multiple regression, 200–201
multiproduct CVP analysis, 108–109
myopia, as ROI limitation, 650

N

negotiated transfer pricing, **704**
netback (workback) method, 511
net book value, 661, 661e, 662e
net income, vs. operating profit, 47
net realizable value method
    defined, **511**
    estimation of, 512–513, 512e, 513e
    example of, 511–512, 512e
new strategy, for an old business, 831
niche strategy, 831
Nikon, 388
Nissan, 258

nonfinancial performance measures. *See also* performance measures
  customer satisfaction, 843–844
  functional performance, 844–845, 844e
  implementation difficulties, 851
  for middle managers, 833
  mistakes in using, 849
  objective vs. subjective, 849
  productivity, **845**, 845–848, 845n, 847e, 848e
  reasons for using, 832
nonlinear relations, in regression analysis, 202, 202e
nonmanufacturing (period) costs, **51**, 51–52
nonvalue-added activities
  defined, **10**
  identification of, 448–449
Norfolk Southern Corporation, 191
normal activity, **461**
normal cost, **295**
normal costing, **295**
not-for-profit organizations, 3, 598, 629
Novartis, 831

O

oil industry, 97
OLS (ordinary least squares regression), 200
1MDB scandal, 555
OPEC (Organization for Petroleum Exporting Countries), 144
operating budgets, **731**
operating leverage, **104**, 104e
operating margin ratio, **648**
operating profit, **47**
operation, defined, **258**, **353**
operation costing
  defined, **258**, **352**
  examples of, 258–259, 258e, 259e, 352–355, 354e, 355e
  vs. job and process costing, 353, 355–356
opportunity costs
  defined, **46**, 46, 46n
  of making, 148–149, 149e
  in transfer pricing, 698–699
optimal transfer price, **690**
ordinary least squares (OLS) regression, 200
organizational units
  decentralized types, 553–555, 554e
  managerial responsibility and, 12–13, 13e
  performance measures of, 556–557
Organization for Petroleum Exporting Countries (OPEC), 144
organization goals, **592**
outlay cost, defined, **46**
outliers, in regression analysis, 202, 203e
output and input
  in efficiency measures, 797–798
  in nonmanufacturing organizations, 797
  in productivity measures, 845
outsourcing
  corporate culture effect of, 135–136
  reciprocal method and, 507–509
  risks, 509
  in supply chain, 5
  in value chain, 16e
overapplied overhead
  defined, **290**
  in job costing, 289–296
overhead. *See* manufacturing overhead

P

Pacific Gas & Electric Company (PG&E), 246
partial productivity, 845, 848e
participative budgeting, **594**
peak-load pricing, **143**
performance evaluation. *See also* incentives (rewards)
  budgets used for, 731–732
  controllability concept, **558**
  cost data for, 10–11, 12–14, 12e, 13e
  goal and behavioral congruence and, 555
  learning phenomenon in, 206
  prior department costs and, 350–352
  questions to consider, 556
  relative performance evaluation, **559**
  responsibility accounting for, 553
performance evaluation system, **552**
performance measures. *See also* divisional performance measures
  balanced scorecard, 835–838, 836e, 837e
  benchmarks, 16e, **838**, 840, 841e
  business model and, **833**, 834e
  business strategy and, **829**, 829–830
  cost variance, 740–741, 741e
  effects on behavior, 560, 610–611
  employee involvement in, 850–851, 851e
  financial measure flaws, 832–833
  fraud link, 564–565
  in management control systems, 555–557, 843
  multiple vs. single, 834–835
  nonfinancial measures
    customer satisfaction, 843–844
    functional performance, 844–845, 844e
    implementation difficulties, 851
    for middle managers, 833
    mistakes in using, 849
    objective vs. subjective, 849
    productivity, **845**, 845–848, 845n, 847e, 848e
    reasons for using, 832
  profit variance, 732–734, 732e, 733e
  relative vs. absolute standards in, 558
  responsibility level and, 833
  risks of focusing on efficiency, 849
  of suppliers, 16e
  at Walmart, 653
period (nonmanufacturing) costs, 50, 51–52
Pfizer, 141
physical quantities method, **514**, 514e
physical resources, in process costing, 337, 338e, 344
planned variance, **801**
planning. *See* master budget; strategic long-range plans
planning budget. *See* master budget
planning and budgeting, during great uncertainty, 593
plantwide allocation method
  vs. activity-based, 399–400, 400e
  defined, **392**
  vs. departmental-specific rates, 392–393
Porter, Michael E., 830
practical capacity, **461**
predatory pricing, **142**, 142
predetermined overhead rate
  allocation base for, 253, 254e
  defined, **252**
  in job costing, 286
predictors (independent variables), 198

prevention costs, **466**
price discrimination, **143**, 143
price-fixing, **144**
price takers, 693
price variance, **742**
pricing decisions. *See also* transfer pricing
  cost-plus approach, 140
  differential analysis in, 137–138
  legal issues, 142–144
  life-cycle costing in, 141–142
  long-run, 140
  short- vs. long-run, 138, 141
  special orders, 138–140, 138e, 139e
  target costing in, 142
prime costs, **51**
principal–agent relationship, **548**
prior department costs
  costing methods and, 350, 351e
  defined, **349**
  vs. prior period costs, 349–350
  responsibility for, 350–352
prior period costs, 349–350
process control chart, **801**, 801–804, 802e, 803e, 804e
process costing
  cost flows in T-accounts
    FIFO costing, 347, 347e
    weighted-average costing, 341, 341e
  defined, **257**
  FIFO vs. weighted average, 348, 348e
  five-step process
    FIFO costing, 343–347
    summary of steps, 349e
    weighted-average costing, 337–341, 337e, 338e, 339e, 340e, 341e
  vs. job costing, 256–258, 335, 336e, 352
  vs. operation costing, 353, 355–356
  production cost report
    FIFO costing, 345e
    weighted-average costing, 341–343, 342e
process reengineering, **449**
product costing. *See also* activity-based costing; job costing; process costing
  cost allocation in, 247, 255–256
  cost flow diagram for, 247–248, 247e, 250e
  job vs. process, 257–258, 335, 336e, 352
  multiple product industry, 250–254, 251e, 252e, 253e, 254e
  production processes and, 256–258, 258e
  reasons for, 245–246
  responsible for, 246
  single product industry, 248–250, 250e
  work-in-process inventories, 249–250, 250e
product costs
  components of, 51e, 60–62, 61e
  defined, **50**
  in process costing, 339–340
product differentiators, 830–831
production budget, **598**, 599e
production cost report
  defined, **341**
  example and explanation, 341–343, 342e
production costs
  forecasts of, 599–600, 599e
  variable, 737, 740–741
production decisions
  adding or dropping products
    differential analysis of, 150–152, 151e
    reported product costs and, 385–387, 386e
  closing business unit, 152
  make-or-buy, 145–148, 146e, 147e, 148e

product choice, 152–156, 153e, 154e, 155e
take-back laws and, 141
typical questions, 144
production forecasts, for master budget, 595, 598–599, 599e
production mix variance
defined, **795**
in manufacturing, 794–796, **795**, 796e
in service organizations, 798–799
production processes
continuous vs. discrete, 256
product costing and, 257, 258e
production volume variance, 750–753, **751**
production yield variance
defined, **795**
in manufacturing, 794–796, **795**, 796e
in service organizations, 798–799
productivity, as performance measure, **845**, 845–848, 847e, 848e, 848n
product life cycle, **141**
profitability
customer, 452, 469
fraudulent reporting of project completion, 301
multinational tech companies, 691
profit centers
defined, **554**
performance measures of, 557
profit equation, **98**, 98–99
profit margin ratio, **648**, 650
profit plan, **593**
profit variance, 732–734, 732e, 733e
profit variance analysis
components of, 737–740
defined, **737**
example of, 738
in nonmanufacturing settings, 797–799, 798e
prorating variances from, 785–788, 787e
profit-volume analysis, **103**, 103e
projects
costing issues, 301, 302e
defined, **301**
Public Service of New Mexico, 104
purchase orders, 844
purchase price variance, **789**
purchasing, budgets for, 609–610, 610e

Q

quality control, 843
quality cost management
cost of quality systems, 466–467, 468e, 469
defining quality, 466
TQM and, 465
trade-offs in, 467–470, 468e

R

rate of throughput contribution, 157
raw materials, 50
reciprocal method
cost flow diagram, 505e
decision making and, 507–509
defined, **503**
example of, 503–505, 504e, 505e, 506e
using computer spreadsheets for, 519–521, 520e
recycling, costs of, 141
regression analysis
assumptions in, 203
cautions, 204
common problems with, 201–203

for cost estimation, 196–198, 197e
defined, **198**
multiple regression, 200–201
using Microsoft Excel®, 198, 210–215, 211e, 212e, 213e, 214e, 215e
relative performance evaluation (RPE), **559**
relevant range, **59**, **195**
reported product costs, and decision making, 385–387, 386e
residual income (RI), **653**, 653–655, 654e
resources
in activity-based costing, 394–395, 403–404
complexity and, 403–404
physical, in process costing, 337, 338e, 344
responding to a sudden drop in, 448
used and supplied, 458–460, 459e, 460e
resources supplied, **459**
resources used, **458**
responsibility accounting
defined, **553**
organization unit classifications, 553–555
responsibility centers, **12**, 13e
restaurants, 448
retail and wholesale companies
budgets in, 609–610, 610e
cost of goods sold in, 47–49, 48e
income statement for, 47–49, 48e
variance analysis in, 797–799, 798e
return on investment (ROI)
defined, **648**
divisional balance sheets for, 649, 649e
investment base measure and, 660–663, 661e, 662e
limitations of, 650–653, 652e
role in control, 649
revenue centers
defined, **554**
performance measures of, 557
reworked products, 67
RI (residual income), **653**, 653–655, 654e
right-hand side (RHS), of regression equation, 198
ROI. *See* return on investment
RPE (relative performance evaluation), **559**
Rynco Scientific Corporation, 338

S

Safeway, 104
Sainsbury, 16e
sales activity variance
budgeted vs. actual, 735–736, 736e
defined, **735**
with multiple products, 792–794, 793e
sales cycle, 604–605
sales forecasts, for master budget, 595–597
sales mix variance, **792**, 792–794, 793e
sales price variance, **737**
sales quantity variance, **792**, 792–794, 793e
sales volume (sales activity) variance, 735–736, 736e
Sarbanes-Oxley Act of 2002, 22–23, 566
scattergraphs, **196**, 196, 197e, 198e
segmentation strategy, 831
segment reporting, 707–708
segments (term), 12
sell-or-process-further decisions, 515, 515e
Selto, F., 206n
semifixed (step) cost, **59**
semivariable (mixed) cost, **59**

sensitivity analysis, 611–614, 612e
separation of duties, **566**
service costing. *See* product costing
service department, defined, **495**, 496e
service department cost allocation
allocation base example, 497, 497e
comparison of direct, step, and reciprocal methods, 506–507, 506e
concept of, 495–497
direct method, 498–500, 498e, 499e, 500e
methods compared, 506–507, 507e
reciprocal method
decision making and, 507–509
explained, **503**, 503–506, 505e, 507e
using computer spreadsheets for, 519–521, 520e
step method, 500–503, 502e
service organizations
ABCM in, 449, 449e
budgets in, 610
income statement for, 47, 48e
job costing in, 296–298, 298e
variance analysis in, 797–799, 798e
short run
defined, **136**
pricing decisions, 138–141, 138e, 139e
simultaneous solution method. *See* reciprocal method
small business failure rates, 3
Solomons, David, 655n
Southern California Edison, 104
Southwest Airlines, 104, 548, 830
special orders
defined, **137**
pricing decisions, 138–140, 138e, 139e
spending (or budget) variance, **749**
split-off point, **510**
spreadsheets. *See also* Microsoft Excel® uses
CVP analysis, 106–107, 106e, 107e
for sensitivity analysis, 612, 612e
Sprouts Farmers Markets, 831
spurious relations, in regression analysis, 202–203
stakeholders, **829**
standard cost, **295**
standard cost center, **554**
standard costing
defined, **756**
overproduction and, 754
recording costs in, 756–759
standard cost sheet, **740**, 741e
standards, updating, 801
statements of financial position, 607, 608e
static budget, **734**. *See also* master budget
statistical analysis
activity relevant range, 195
high-low cost estimation, 196–198
number of observations in, 196
regression analysis, 198–200, 199e
scattergraphs, 196, 197e, 199e
step (semifixed) cost, **59**
step method
cost flow diagram, 502e
defined, **500**
examples of, 500–503, 502e
limitations of, 501–502
strategic long-range plans
business strategy, **829**, 829–831
competitiveness and, 591
defined, **592**
as master budget component, 592–593

strategic opportunities, 10
strategy, and management control system, 551
strategy map, **838**, 840e
suboptimization, 651–653, 654–655, 664
subsidiaries (term), 12
subsidiary ledger account, **282**
sunk costs, **136**, 651
suppliers
    cost determination, 456–457, 457e
    performance measures of, 16e
supply chain, **5**

T

Taco Bell, 833
tactical short-range profit plan, 592–594
take-back laws, 141
target costs, **142**
target price, **142**
target volumes, 101, 101e
TDABC (time-driven activity-based costing), 406–409
Tesco, 23
Tesla, 204
theoretical capacity, **461**
theory of constraints, **156–157**, 156n
third-party costs, 706
throughput contribution, **157**
time-driven activity-based costing (TDABC), 406–409
time equations, **408**
total contribution margin, **98**
total costs, vs. differential, 137
total cost variance, **742**
total factor productivity, **847**, 848e
total format, 137
total quality management (TQM), 16e, 465
Toyota Motor Company, 142, 145, 447, 846
Trader Joe's, 831
transfer pricing
    behavioral issues in, 700–701, 703–704
    cost-based, 601–603
    defined, **689**
    global practices, 705, 705e
    importance of, 689
    management intervention and oversight, 700–701, 704
    market price–based, **701**
    multinational, 705–706
    negotiated, **704**
    optimal price determination, 691–698, 692e
        no intermediate market, 694–698, 696e, 697e
        perfect intermediate market, 693–694
    price-setting principle, 698–699, 702e
    in segment reporting, 707–708
    tax issues in, 705–707
    at Weyerhaeuser, 708
transferred-in costs, 349–350
Treadway Commission report, 564, 565
treasurers, 8e
trend analysis, **596**
t-statistic, **200**
two-stage cost allocation
    activity-based costing as, 394, 396–397
    allocation bases in, 255–256
    basic steps in, 255, 388–389
    cost driver choice, 390–392
    cost flow diagrams, 256e, 389e, 391e
    defined, **255**

department allocation method
    first-stage allocation, 389e
    vs. plantwide allocation, 392–393

U

underapplied overhead
    defined, **290**
    in job costing, 289–296
unfavorable variance, **732**
unit contribution margin, **98**
United Airlines, 12, 104
UnitedHealth Group, 733
United Parcel Service, Inc. (UPS), 456
United States Postal Service (USPS), 58
unit fixed costs, 61–62
Universal Studios, 257
University of Utah Health Care System, 16e
University of Utah Hospital, 408
unused resource capacity, **459**
UPMC, 404
UPS (United Parcel Service), 16e
user department, **495**, 496e
U.S. Postal Service, 58
USPS (U.S. Postal Service), 58

V

value, in productivity measures, 846
value-added activities, **4**, 4–5
value chain
    accounting and, 6
    components of, 4e
    cost accounting methods, 15, 16e
    defined, **4**
value creation
    accounting data for, 3–6
    activity-based cost management for, 447–451
value income statement, 65–67, 66e
value proposition, **829**
variable costing, 65
variable costs
    defined, **58**
    as differential costs, 136
    vs. fixed, 58–60
    production costs, 737, 740–741
    scattergraph estimate, 197e
variable cost variance analysis
    cost variance summary, 748–749, 748e
    direct labor, 745–746, 746e
    direct materials, 743–745, 745e
    general model, 741–743, 742e
    production overhead, 747–748, 747e
variance
    defined, **731**
    favorable vs. unfavorable, **732**, 732–733
variance analysis
    determining which to investigate, 800
    direct labor price variance, 746
    direct materials, 788–790, 789e
    fixed costs, 749–753, 750e, 752e
    fixed overhead variances, 752e
    industry volume variance, **790**, 790–791, 791e
    labor efficiency variance, 746
    market share variance, **790**, 790–791, 791e
    in nonmanufacturing settings, 797–799, 798e
    planned variance, **801**
    process control charts, 801–804, 802e, 803e, 804e

production mix variance, 794–796, **795**, 796e, 798–799
production yield variance, 794–796, **795**, 796e, 798–799
profit variance, 732–734, 732e, 733e, **737**, 737–739, 738e, 785–788, 787e
purchase price variance, **789**
purposes of, 733
sales activity, **735**, 735–736, 736e
sales mix variance, 792–794, 793e
sales quantity variance, 792–794, 793e
summary of overhead variances, 753, 753e
variable costs, 741–749, 742e, 745e, 746e, 747e, 748e
variable overhead efficiency variance, 747e, 748
variable production overhead price variances, 747, 747e
variance interpretation, 799
Verizon, 833
visualizing cost variances, 750, 750e
visualizing profit variances, 739–740, 739e, 740e
volume-based allocation, 403–404

W

Walmart, 591, 653, 830, 838
weighted-average contribution margin, 108–109, 343–344
weighted-average process costing
    defined, **339**
    example of
        cost flows in T-accounts, 341, 341e
        five-step process, 337–341, 338e, 339e, 340e, 341e
        production cost report, 341–343, 342e
    vs. FIFO, 339–340, 340e, 348, 348e
weighted-average revenue, 108–109
Wells Fargo Bank, 690
Weyerhaeuser, 708
what-if thinking (sensitivity analysis), 611–612, 612e
Whirlpool, 141
wholesale companies. *See* retail and wholesale companies
workback (netback) method, 511
work in process
    in budgets, 601n
    in cost of goods manufactured and sold, 56–57
    defined, **54**
    equivalent units concept, 335–336, 336e
    product costing and, 249–250, 250e
WorldCom, 566, 567

X

X term, 198

Y

YouTube, 452
Y term, 198

Z

zero-based budgeting, current experiences, 619